A. Australoid
B. Bushmen
C. Caucasoid
M. Mongoloid
N. Negroid
P. Pygmy

Fig. 1. (*Front Endpaper*)

Brown: Oceans (diminished) and Inland seas (enlarged)
White, with crinkled brown border: Ice sheets
Green: Occupied areas expanding
White: Unoccupied area
Star: North Pole
Bow: Origin of bow

THE EVOLUTION OF MAN AND SOCIETY

by Professor C. D. Darlington, F.R.S.

CHROMOSOMES AND PLANT BREEDING
Macmillan, 1932

RECENT ADVANCES IN CYTOLOGY
Churchill, 1932

THE EVOLUTION OF GENETIC SYSTEMS
Cambridge University Press, 1939
Oliver and Boyd, 1958

THE FACTS OF LIFE
George Allen and Unwin, 1953

CHROMOSOME BOTANY AND THE ORIGINS OF CULTIVATED PLANTS
George Allen and Unwin, 1963

GENETICS AND MAN
George Allen and Unwin, 1964

CYTOLOGY (3RD ED.)
Churchill, 1965

THE CONFLICT OF SCIENCE AND SOCIETY
Watts, 1948

DARWIN'S PLACE IN HISTORY
Blackwell, 1959

with L. F. La Cour, M.B.E.
THE HANDLING OF CHROMOSOMES (5TH ED.)
George Allen and Unwin, 1969

with K. Mather, C.B.E., F.R.S.
THE ELEMENTS OF GENETICS
George Allen and Unwin, 1961

GENES, PLANTS AND PEOPLE
George Allen and Unwin, 1959

with E. K. Janaki-Ammal
CHROMOSOME ATLAS OF CULTIVATED PLANTS
George Allen and Unwin, 1945

with A. P. Wylie
CHROMOSOME ATLAS OF FLOWERING PLANTS
George Allen and Unwin, 1956

with A. D. Bradshaw (edited)
TEACHING GENETICS
Oliver and Boyd, 1963, 1966

The Evolution of MAN AND SOCIETY

C. D. DARLINGTON

London
GEORGE ALLEN AND UNWIN LTD
RUSKIN HOUSE · MUSEUM STREET

FIRST PUBLISHED IN 1969

SBN 04 575011 4

PRINTED IN GREAT BRITAIN
in 10 on 11pt Times type
BY UNWIN BROTHERS LIMITED
WOKING AND LONDON

QUOTATION

. . . it is not Truth but Opinion that can travel the World without a Pass-port. For were it otherwise, and were there not as many internal forms of the mind as there are external figures of men, there were then some possibility to perswade by the mouth of one Advocate—even Equity alone . . . there being nothing wherein nature so much triumpheth as in dissimilitude. From whence it cometh, that there is found so great diversity of Opinions; so strong a contrariety of inclinations; so many natural and unnatural, wise and foolish, manly and childish, affections and passions in mortal men.

Sir Walter Ralegh, *History of the World* (preface) 1614 (eds. 1677, 1820)

PREFACE

Forty years ago I had the opportunity of travelling among the peoples of what we now call the Ancient East. I was struck by the differences between their societies and those I already knew. They raised questions in my mind which, it seemed, ought to be answerable in terms of historical or in terms of biological principles, or perhaps of both. But, as I gradually discovered, neither the history nor the biology was yet at our command.

During the years that have passed however the situation has changed. Both in history and in biology conjecture has been giving place to prediction, verification, and connectedness; even between history and biology themselves connections have begun to appear and to take shape. So much so that during the last ten years it has become possible to put these connections into words and to illustrate the words with tables, maps, and diagrams. At last the temptation to do so became irresistible. The result is what I have tried to do in the present book.

The attempt, it will be seen, could have no point unless the same principles could be shown at work all the way through man's evolution and history. This was my starting point and it proved also to be my conclusion. There is in the whole account a continuity and a unity. It is a continuity which leaves almost nothing irrelevant; and it is a unity which underlies the unity of mankind.

The result will mostly, I believe, make sense for the general reader; perhaps more sense than history has generally pretended to make. It will however be an unaccustomed sense which the reader will want to judge or verify for himself. To do this he will, I admit, need some specialized knowledge, some acquaintance with my own evolutionary views, some knowledge of how men and women live in different parts of the world. Moreover if, as I say, almost nothing is irrelevant, the appropriate evidence cannot all be laid out within the convenient space of one book. What I have written therefore is merely a sketch which raises more questions than it settles; it is a sketch of what later hands will no doubt be able to do much better.

C. D. DARLINGTON

Botany School and Magdalen College, Oxford
September 1968

ACKNOWLEDGEMENTS

To many colleagues quoted in the text I am indebted for help and guidance. In addition I should like to record my thanks for their kindness to particular friends:

The late N. I. Vavilov and his colleagues who helped and encouraged me in Russia and Transcaucasia in 1929 and 1934. Also Mr B. J. Gilliat-Smith, the Romany scholar, who befriended me at those times as H.B.M. Consul General in Tabriz and in Leningrad.

Professor H. Kihara and Dr F. A. Lilienfeld who introduced me to Japan in 1933.

Dr E. K. Janaki Ammal who guided my steps in India (in Travancore and in Orissa) in 1933 and 1937.

My father, the late W. H. R. Darlington, who introduced me to the problems of dialect and place names and the work of the poet Lucretius.

The late Harold Peake who, between 1936 and 1940, taught me some of the rudiments of archaeology.

Professor Raymond Dart who helped me in Johannesburg, Dr L. S. B. Leakey in Nairobi and Dr Michael Gwynne in Kenya generally, in 1963; and Professor J. D. Hofmeyr who guided me in South and South West Africa.

Dr Eileen Erlanson, Dr James Gregor, Dr Travis Osborne and Dr H. S. Whittaker who introduced me to many American problems between 1932 and 1967.

Professors G. R. Driver and O. R. Gurney, Mr Colin Hardie and the late Mr K. B. McFarlane who, at Magdalen College since 1953, explained to me many Semitic, Hellenic and mediaeval problems.

Dr Philip Tyler and Dr Paul Harvey who helped me with wide-ranging historical discussions.

Mr R. W. Hamilton and Mr Bernard Fagg and their colleagues who gave me the facilities of the Ashmolean and the Pitt-Rivers Museums in Oxford.

I must repeat my acknowledgements here to my correspondents who went to so much trouble to help me on the subject of cousin marriage, especially Lord Henley, Dr R. S. Lucas, Miss Petronella Göring and Mr Peter Calvocoressi.

Finally I should like to thank Sir Cyril Burt, Professor J. H. Hutton, the late Dr Isaac Burkill, Professor W. G. Hoskins, Dr I. Morgan Watkin, Mr C. C. Marshak (of Samoa), Dr Conway Zirkle, and M. Philippe Périer, for advice in correspondence which I found invaluable.

CONTENTS

TEXT FIGURES: MAPS and DIAGRAMS*

DRAWN BY JOHN STUART SHAW

TABLES (INCLUDING TIME CHARTS)

PEDIGREES

ABBREVIATIONS USED IN PEDIGREES

Ab	Archbishop
B	Bishop
b–s	brother–sister marriage
C	Count
(c)	marriages with first cousins
ca	circa
(c–1)	first cousin once removed
ch.	children
cos.	consul
D	Duke
d, with date	died
dep.	deposed
E	Emperor
(E)	eunuch
Ea.	Earl
g.d.	granddaughter
g.g.d.	great granddaughter
g.g.g.s.	great, great grandson
g.g.s.	great grandson
g.m.	grandmother
g.s.	grandson
hrs. pres.	heiress presumptive
K	King
k	killed
L	Lord
M	murdered, assassinated or executed
o	of
out	outbreeding
♀	unnamed woman
P.M.	*Pontifiex Maximus*
P.S.	*Princeps Senatus*
r	reigned
s, d	son, daughter
Q	Queen
u–n	uncle–niece marriage
w	wife
x	mating or marriage
(x)	political marriage probably unconsummated
wavy descents:	bastardy
wavy underlines:	Emperors

CAPITALS = royal
Capital Initials and Small Letters = non-royal
Roman type = male
Italic = female

Part I

The Foundations

In the evolution of animals and plants change often proceeds in one direction for a long time. It was in the brain that change followed this course in certain apes and consequently took the lead in their evolution. By its changed character it came to govern the whole development of that group of species which included man's ancestors. Its predominance in turn demanded a number of other radical changes in sexual and social behaviour. These determined the character of modern human societies and prepared for the upheaval which brought the paleolithic world to an end.

1

ORIGIN OF MAN

I. MONKEYS AND MEN

MAN'S ANIMAL ORIGINS were first seriously discussed in 1699. In that year a certain Edward Tyson dissected a chimpanzee which had been brought to London from Africa and discovered its close resemblance to man. For Africans the kinship had always been obvious. But for Europeans it was not until Darwin assembled the general evidence for evolution and introduced the explanatory principle of natural selection that a belief in the separate origin of man could be superseded. For his argument in the *Origin of Species* Darwin mobilized the whole of the available knowledge of the past and present behaviour of plants and animals. Only then could civilized men, or some of them, be persuaded to make the deeply repugnant assumption of an hereditary continuity with the rest of the living world.

Darwin's methods are still those we have to use today. But our materials are more abundant—some would say too abundant—and our methods are highly diversified. When we find that human haemoglobin in its commonest form differs at only three points from that of the gorilla we know that this counts as evidence of kinship. When we find that man has almost the same chromosome number as the apes we take this also as evidence of common descent.

But all this is not our main interest today. What we are concerned with is not to show where man came from. That we no longer doubt. But to show how he came; to show the processes by which some ape-like animals became men; processes of breeding, of variation and of selection which can be explained to us in terms of what we can see and, if need be, test by experiment. To help us here we have two new instruments out of Darwin's reach but arising from his work: the science of genetics and the fossil record of our ancestors.

To begin with, we must look again comparatively at the monkey family.

Le Gros Clark and others have pointed out the immense range of structure in monkeys. Related living families show a succession of types which might represent a fossil series, an evolutionary succession, arrested at different stages. For example, the reduction of the snout and of the sense of smell, the development of two-eyed stereoscopic sight and of prehensile hands and feet, the adoption of a two-footed gait, and the flattening of the incisors and of the claws, the expansion of the fore-brain and the increased convolution of the cerebral hemispheres, the lengthening of the life cycle and of the life span, the reduction of fertility: all these have been happening independently in different groups of monkeys.

The order of these remarkable changes would not be so clear if they had not occurred in parallel in different groups, notably in the Old and New World monkeys which have been separated since soon after the unrecorded origin of the whole group in the Eocene period. For example the method of movement by what Keith called 'brachiation', swinging by immensely long arms, has been independently discovered by the Old World apes and by the New World spider monkeys. Again these parallel changes would not be so obviously adaptations to, or exploitations of, a tree-living habit if we could not see them sometimes reversed in ground-living monkeys like the dog-snouted baboons of Africa.

At this point we have to ask ourselves what parallel change means and what evidence may exist of it elsewhere in life. Clearly parallel change implies a long-continued process, working in one direction and not like most evolution in many directions. It implies also a deterministic process such as we have in the evolution of the horse's foot or the giraffe's neck or the elephant's trunk. Such processes are well known under various names such as Henry Fairfield Osborn's orthogenesis and Rensch's directed evolution. What do they mean? They mean that change, established by natural selection, usually reduces the advantage of further change in the same direction. But in certain exceptional conditions it has the reverse effect: it actually enhances the advantage of such further change. Instead of the response showing, as they say, the negative feed-back usual with natural selection, orthogenesis shows positive feed-back. It may then speed it up, perhaps by increasing the size of the population subject to selection. These principles, as we shall see, have dominated human evolution but in a way that has come to be recognized only recently, and long after the discoveries of the earliest fossil remains of man.[1]

II. APE-MEN

Man's ancestors may have separated from the apes in the Miocene about 20 million years ago and somewhere in the three Old World continents. But the first remains of them that we know are grouped in a more recent time and a more confined space. They have been found on the eastern side of

1 Recently also this principle has been found to apply in an utterly remote evolutionary field, that is in the development of hybrid species with chromosome interchanges in plants (Darlington 1963a).

Africa and restricted to a time between 2 million and half a million years ago. They were first discovered and correctly interpreted by Raymond Dart at Johannesburg in 1923 and our knowledge of them has been expanded first by Broom and Robinson and later by Leakey in East Africa.

These ape-men, the first of which Dart named *Australopithecus*, had four astonishing—or as most experts of the time thought, incredible—properties:

(i) They made tools from horn, bone and later stone.
(ii) They had reduced canines and indeed almost human teeth.
(iii) They had more upright and human stance than any ape.
(iv) But their brain cavities were well within the range of size of the apes, i.e. mostly from 450 to 550 c.c. as compared with a maximum for an ape of 750 c.c.

Furthermore the types of fossils described by Robinson, Leakey and others were highly variable. They seemed to represent several divergent and non-interbreeding forms; they were presumably competing species which were living side by side in the same kind of open country. Again these strains seemed to evolve over a long period in parallel. Some of them gave place to more human descendants while others, perhaps the pure vegetarians, continued with less change for some time and eventually died out.

Thus the earliest men had abandoned the forest; they were omnivorous; they were walkers not climbers; and they were able to make their living and defend themselves with the help of their own handiwork. Dart assumed that free hands had given man his ability to make weapons and tools which in turn had freed him from the need to tear with his teeth. So it was that he had opened out a new way of life for himself. But he had reached this point before the great development of his brain; that is the characteristic human brain with its elaborate cerebral cortex co-ordinating movement and perception, hand and eye.

These early men in giving rise to, and also giving place to, modern men then went on to enlarge their brains and improve their two-footed gait and posture by processes which have continued down to the present day. That is for half a million years or, to speak in terms of human breeding, 20,000 generations. Having acquired in the course of these changes adaptability to a great range of new habitats, and being perhaps also impelled by widespread desiccation in Africa and Asia, fluctuating with successive ice ages, they spread over most of the habitable Old World. They passed from Africa into Southern Europe and Southern Asia generating new, dissimilar races adapted, we must suppose, to widely different climates between Western Europe, China, Java and South Africa. The remains found in Java have been named *Pithecanthropus* and we may refer to this stage in human evolution by this name. Or we may call it middle paleolithic.[1]

[1] The names of genera for stages in human evolution are permissible; the names of species hardly so. For species are defined by their intersterility and of that buried bones can tell us nothing. The apparent discontinuity between them is merely due to the wiping out of most of the record. With few enough bones each can be given a new name. So far as such names pretend to refer to the direct

III. THE FIRST EXPANSION

Over their vast new area the new men kept at first a fairly uniform structure and a uniform habit of making of tools. Both uniformities are an indication of slow evolutionary change. Nevertheless it is change, as Le Gros Clark points out, already speeded up in relation to the stable forms of the apes. It is because the apes have changed so little and so slowly that we can speak roughly of man's being descended from something like apes. The two branches, men and apes, had separated 20 million years ago and neither branch had made much change in the first nine-tenths of that time. Now man was to change faster and faster.

The reason for man's increased rate of change was still within him. He was standing more upright. His brain had increased in size and he was using it to make better tools. His weapons included his first missiles which were sling stones and for prey he could now count on larger animals whose bones he had learnt to cook with fire. The fire, which he kept though he could not make it, opened up a new and varied diet of grain and roots as well as meat. All these changes in turn altered the conditions of survival and favoured in turn the selection of other changes, always connected with changes in the brain, which expanded in its size and in its aptitudes.

At this time the signs of insertion of tongue muscles in the jaw bones may indicate the beginnings of speech. And increase in numbers of milk teeth in infants of the type found near Pekin may indicate the increasing period of dependence of the child on its mother. As the brain of the adult man came to be larger (in modern man it is more than twice as large in proportion to the body as in the ape) so the time needed for its growth grew longer. Woman's pelvis grew no larger and pregnancy remained of the same length at about 38 weeks. But childhood dependence extended from 11 years to nearly 20 years. To accommodate the dependence, to allow parents to bring up a whole family the life span also had to be doubled, and no doubt was gradually doubled, to give us our three score years or more.[1]

IV. DIVERGENT AND PARALLEL EVOLUTION

Such is our basic knowledge of the evolution of early man.

Two questions now force themselves on us together. First, *Pithecanthropus* is the middle stage in an immensely long change in one direction, that of enlargement and improvement in man's brain. How has this change occurred in man, and indeed to different extents in all men? Secondly, what has happened to those first geographical races of man which arose half a million years ago? They are represented by remains in East Africa, in Java, near Pekin and in parts of Western Europe. Are they in some sense the forerunners of the great modern races of man? This was the suggestion made by Weidenreich from the study of the latest of these discoveries, the Pekin man.

ancestry of man they are bogus names. For how can there have been any discontinuity in our ancestry greater than that between the parents and children whose continuous succession makes up that ancestry?

[1] Koenigswald (1960).

It has been supported by Coon from a detailed comparison of the fossil remains. Particularly the evidence points to a continuity of the differences in tooth structure between European and Chinese remains down to the present day.

These two questions are bound up together. For it is clear that the human brain has undergone directed change in the last half million years. In the mere matter of size the case of man is analogous with that of the horse, the giraffe or the elephant. There is a limit to an increase in brain size. But in another respect, that of organization, it is doubtful whether there could be a limit; and in some instances we shall see the organization of the brain superseding the increase in volume. What was it, however, that made the brain the site of directed improvement in man? Once he was provided with hands that could make tools which were of supreme value to his survival, improvement of his brain became advantageous. Every improvement in the brain that guided the work of the hands in making the tools, in using the tools, and in foreseeing new uses and new makes, was bound to be advantageous—almost without limit—to the individuals so improved. We can see that this is so since even today the limit of these advantages has not been reached. Differences in these improvements are still today subject to selective survival; they are still matters of success and failure, and even of life and death.

How did these advantages express themselves? Clearly one invention led to another. Each development in the association of hand and eye by the brain opened a new field of activity which made further associations of hand and eye more useful. And indeed more necessary; for with each advance man's intelligence displaced his former methods of defence by tooth and claw and made him more dependent on his intelligence. Thus a process of directed evolution of the brain was set in motion. Which means that isolated races were bound to change in the same direction in parallel with one another. This evolutionary process was, in a surprising sense, a continuation of the improvements which had benefited monkeys when they began to live in trees. But it actually resulted from the reverse movement out of trees. It was what had happened to the baboons. With them it had led to the origin of many new species. With man it led to the origin ultimately of only one species, but a species such as had never existed before, a species with a monstrously capacious brain.

It is not difficult to see that improvement of the brain in man has had a self-exaggerating effect with a positive feed-back. It is also not difficult to see in general terms how it has had this effect. But we must also ask a third question about it. What part has natural selection played in this far-reaching operation? We shall later be considering particular instances, but here we may notice one principle at the root of man's social and mental evolution. It is that every improvement in the brain by its nature leads to new ideas and new inventions. Each invention propagates its own inventors and leads to their multiplication, and expansion. And these in turn lead to their hybridization with other stocks and the production of yet more genetic combinations with similarly enhanced capacities. The cyclical effect may be

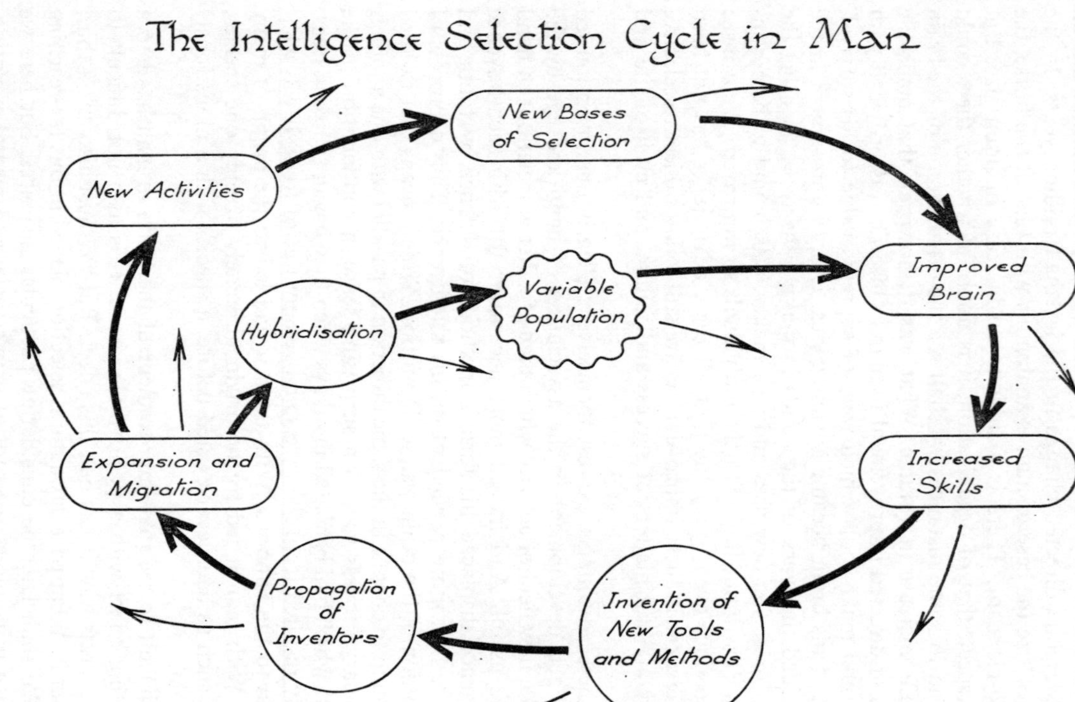

Fig. 2. Diagram showing some of the cyclical and self-exaggerating effects of natural selection on variation in the human brain leading to orthogenesis in paleolithic times: to be contrasted with the neolithic effect where invention often led to disruptive selection.

witnessed today. It is therefore worth while to represent it diagrammatically (Fig. 2).

Given this situation of directed evolution an important corollary follows. The brain had acquired a dominant position in man's relationship with his environment. Geographical adaptation, of course, was always bound to be important; but the use of the brain and the improvement of its use was bound to become relatively and in the long term more important. Which means that, on the one hand, man's external habitat was the agent of the diversified change which controlled the evolution of his races. But, on the other hand, man's internal character was the agent of the directed change which controlled the evolution of his species. The races and the species were evolving by different methods.

In its simplest terms this is the situation of divided and contrasted control that leads us to expect the resultant history as Coon interprets it. That is a history of parallel evolution in the great geographical and small local races of man over a period of half a million years until the coming of the last ice age.

V. THE LAST ICE AGE

The whole of the last million years, the important period for us, we know geologically as the Pleistocene. It has been interrupted by a succession of ice ages, five major spells broken by four warmer ages and themselves varying by smaller oscillations. Of these, the critical one for man was the last which endured 100,000 years and reached three peaks. These are estimated to have been about 115, 72 and 24 thousand years ago. The last glaciation locked so much water up in great ice caps in the Antarctic, North America, Greenland, Scandinavia, Siberia and Tibet that the level of the sea fell nearly 200 metres. Islands such as Britain and Japan were joined on to the continental mainlands. The islands between Australia and Asia formed an almost continuous bridge and America and Asia were actually joined. Asiatic bats could fly across to Australia and deer could make their way into America.

Great movements of men as well as animals became possible with this climatic vicissitude. They also became necessary. People had to move out of the frozen north following the animals and plants they needed. It was therefore a period of enforced migration through passes and across or between channels, obstacles which themselves fluctuated.

From these movements there arose great changes in the distribution of the major races of men. Branches of the Mongolian peoples in successive waves crossed the Bering Straits and spread during a period of about 8000 years all over America. The last of these movements was that of the Eskimo which reached Alaska perhaps only 2000 years ago, and Greenland only in A.D. 1300.[1] Other branches pressed southwards into South-East Asia apparently pushing the Australoid peoples before them into New Guinea whence, taking with them their domesticated dog, the dingo, they passed

[1] F. Semenov (1964).

over into Australia. Similarly, Capoid or Bushman-like people from North Africa expanded into South Africa. In Europe there had been a type of Caucasian, taking his name from the Neanderthal skull, with a brain as large as our own but with a low overhanging brow and receding chin, of a kind still represented among the Australoid peoples. He was displaced by new types resembling modern peoples and named after the Cro-Magnon skull found a hundred years ago in the valley of the Dordogne.

The Neanderthal people were remarkable for their sharp physical divergence from their successors. They dominated Europe and South-West Asia for thirty thousand years, making characteristic implements called Mousterian. They buried their dead with care, piously removing their heads and eating their brains, a ceremony which foreshadows the religious feelings of later peoples.[1] The new men may have hybridized with the Neanderthalers, giving intermediate and variable people in Palestine. A gap of thousands of years between the occupations of one cave (at Shanidar in Kurdistan) indicates that the replacement may have been due to competition rather than direct conflict. But for us the Neanderthal man is important in showing that parallel developments may lead to failure as well as to success, to dead ends as well as new openings. And the pace of change was now faster than it had been although still not so fast as it is today.

This period of movement was bound to be a period of great hybridization between migrating tribes. Such hybridization might be at different levels. Some crossing would be between related tribes. But would there also be crossing between the main sub-divisions of mankind? The existence of an outlier of the Caucasian race, the hairy Ainu, in the north of Japan; the surviving remnants of somewhat Mongoloid people, related to the Bushmen, to be found in the Transvaal, in Tanganyika, and even in the Fezzan; the small groups of Mongoloids intruding and surviving on the eastern side of the Deccan; the traces of Australoids left intact in Malaya; all these are evidence that certain small isolated human groups can resist hybridization and keep their racial integrity over great periods of time.

The difference in character among close neighbours in Formosa, in Assam and the Chota Nagpur Hills in India have been described and illustrated by Coon with these points in mind. The wealth of relic peoples in New Guinea as well as in Indonesia is still little known. Evidently groups of peoples diverging in the main regions of Europe, Asia and North Africa during the period from 30,000 to 10,000 B.C. must have broken away from their nearest relatives and penetrated into other regions. It was probably during this immense period of wandering that fair-haired peoples found their way into Japan, China and North Africa. And small groups with other European characteristics found their way into southern India and Ceylon. Those that happened to discover highly distinct mountain habitats remote from the disturbances of the future were able to preserve their character so that we find them unchanged at the present day. Extreme differences of climate and vegetation between neighbouring districts have required as great

1 And also the practice of a modern tribe in New Guinea which, in this way, propagates a fatal virus disease (kuru). (Gajdusek 1964, *ref.* ch. 3.)

differences between the peoples who were to inhabit and develop them as between those in different continents.

In many animal species similar processes of differentiation have occurred in the course of a great explosion of population. But as a rule they have been accompanied by the growth of barriers to hybridization over which the animals themselves had no control. With man such barriers undoubtedly developed in the form of preferences for mating within the group. But these barriers were conditional and subject to intelligent modification. It was during this great period we may suppose that an ability to hybridize often proved to be selectively advantageous. Thus, the Bushmen, whose colour and countenance show their mongolian affinity, have evidently hybridized with their neighbours all over South and East, and perhaps even North, Africa. Other hybridizations are less certainly assignable to an early period merely because so much has happened since then. But it need not be doubted that hybridization did occur: genes flowed from one great group to another contributing to their variations and their prospects of evolution.

VI. THE PALEOLITHIC CLIMAX

The greatest achievements of paleolithic man are shown us by his tools, his art, and the evidence of his prowess in hunting. These have been discovered chiefly in Europe and their discovery has been well described by Bibby. They are paralleled but not equalled by what we can still see of the surviving paleolithic peoples, the Eskimo, the Bushman, the Ainu of Japan and the Australian Aborigines. For these are all peripheral people and peripheral people are usually backward. Just as the Fuegians were the most backward of Amerindians so were the Tasmanians the most backward inhabitants of Australia.

The peripheral peoples of mankind would seem to have lagged behind the central peoples in invention as well as in physical development. It would also seem that people who have depended on collecting have lagged behind the hunters, fishers, fowlers and trappers, in these respects. Notably the collecting and carrion-eating tribes of Kerala in southern India are culturally the most backward and mentally the least intelligent although close neighbours of civilized peoples for some 3000 years.

There must have been a wide range of capacities among the paleolithic peoples of the world at the end of the last ice age. And the peoples most advanced by hybridization and recombination were inevitably those living where the greatest movements occurred in the central parts of the great land masses.

If however we compare the paleolithic peoples not with one another but with their successors we notice another important principle. The Bushmen and other hunters have certain special properties. Their extraordinary perceptual faculties were noticed by early anthropologists. They can now be described most exactly in terms of the genetics of colour blindness.[1] These faculties put them in a class reached only by rare individuals among civilized

[1] R. H. Post (1962).

peoples today. The hunter knows his game animals: he understands their breeding, respects their close seasons and has some idea of conserving them. These gifts have not only been selected by his practice of hunting and are not only expressed by his capacity for drawing animals. They are shown by his immense and accurate knowledge of the plants of his country and of their uses for food, for drugs and for poisons. Fifty such species are known to the Bushmen in the Kalahari desert. Mangelsdorf reminds us that it was paleolithic man who had discovered the chief plant sources of caffeine and related stimulants in all parts of the world. It was also he who learnt how to extract the toxic principle from manioc, purifying a food and preparing a poison in one operation.

The superiority of the hunter-collector over the civilized man in what concerns his own survival is therefore unquestionable. It is a genetic superiority for which no training can compensate. But equally he is inferior in certain respects necessary for civilized life. He finds counting difficult, whether it is counting people or seeds or days. He can remember a thousand faces but he cannot number five heads. He also finds regular manual work tedious. And long-term prudent calculation is beyond his reach. In consequence he finds the cultivation of the soil irksome. No training or persuasion will cause him to change his opinion.[1]

The paleolithic hunter, like the gipsy in Europe, is a wanderer. He has always lived by wandering and all his instincts are adjusted to the needs of wandering, adjusted to resist settlement. Nothing but hybridization will change him. His instincts reappear in some classes, professions and peoples of advanced societies and are altogether excluded from others. His feckless-ness, his interest in killing game, his yearning for movement are found at the top and at the bottom of society for reasons we shall later have to examine.

The collector is a little more open to the possibilities of cultivation than the hunter. In Kerala, collecting tribes (unlike the Australian aboriginal hunters) can readily be persuaded, as Burkill has pointed out, to cultivate the yam. And having done so will propagate themselves as quickly as their supply of food. But this is because the cultivation of these roots requires little labour and less care. It is not a serious step from their own habit of collecting.

Many paleolithic peoples of our time avoid contact with their neighbours. Others maintain a prudent restraint. But others again, like the fishers and hunters of New Guinea and the Trobriands described by Malinowski and others, barter their produce with one another to their mutual advantage.[2] The same is true of the pygmy hunters and Negro cultivators in the Congo. It is a short step from this intercourse to the procuring or producing of

[1] These characteristics have been described by Galton in the Damara who in this respect are entirely paleolithic. And van der Post has discovered in the Bushman a wit and humour of his own. The Bushman notes that ostriches lay one egg away from the rest of the clutch. Why? Because, says he, the hen ostrich is forgetful and needs the odd egg to remind her of what she is doing.

[2] See also Daisy Bates (1938, *ref.* ch. 3).

goods with a view to barter. And this seems indeed to have been what happened with regard to the mining of flints and making of weapons in the last stage of paleolithic life in Britain, as has been demonstrated by Grahame Clark. With the panning of salt, here is perhaps, since it still continues, the oldest marketing trade in the world. And the beginning of marketing was one of the significant steps in the evolution of human societies.

2

THE EXPANDING SPECIES

I. EXPANSION AND INTERACTION

THAT MAN HAS EVOLVED from less distinguished ancestors is indisputable. Our next problem is more difficult. It is to enquire into the causes and the consequences of this evolution, and particularly of its last and most accessible stages. A main part of the causes seems to lie in the abilities and achievements of the new men, their tools, their art, their speech. Also a main part of the consequences seems to consist in his immense diversification, the production of innumerable different kinds of men. If the reverse is argued, namely that the achievement is a consequence and the diversification is a cause, let us agree. For, as we have already hinted, these processes were interacting. In evolution we are dealing all the time with interactions which in man, as we shall see, merely become more complicated than in other animals.

II. THE IMPLEMENTS OF EXPANSION

a. Tools and Boats

What carried the new men of Europe and Asia to the ends of the earth was their ability to invent new kinds of tools and use them in new ways, in general terms, to master their environment, to change and diversify the conditions of their lives. These new inventions are the product of the last 20,000 years, the last stage of the paleolithic, frequently known as the mesolithic, in which man's main expansion was taking place.

The first of these inventions were improved stone implements made with a combination of skill and forethought which had not been seen before. They included the machine tools designed for making other implements. New forms of mineral such as obsidian were discovered and exploited. Flint chisels could be used for finer work with horn, ivory, bone, and wood.

Fabrics could be woven from rushes, withies, and bark. Baskets could be made for storing grain. Gourds could be collected for storing water and in due course for making wine. Needles could be made and used for sewing hides and making clothes. Vegetable drugs could be extracted for healing and comfort, vegetable poisons for hunting and fishing.[1]

Man was thus in a fair way to mobilizing the animal, vegetable, and mineral resources of the earth for his own use. He knew where to find them, how to recognize them and name them, and what to do with them.

Most important of these inventions were the ones which increased his efficiency as a hunter, a fisher, a collector and a traveller. His abilities as a builder can only be surmised. As a hunter and a fisher, however, primitive peoples today prove his prowess. Harpoons and spears and other missiles extended the range of game he could kill; the skill with which the northward advancing ice-age hunters in Europe used them to catch mammoths and whales has been described by Bibby.

A different kind of knowledge is brought to us by the study of the spread, not of peoples as such, but of the inventions themselves. Raglan has shown how the bow and arrow were invented probably in Central Asia some 15,000 years ago. They spread from this centre all over the northern hemisphere. Evidently the success of the bowman in hunting enabled him to multiply. It was he himself who spread his own invention from Asia into America and westwards into Europe and Africa.

The successes of the hunting man were however too great: he over-killed his prey. As Martin has shown, these successes came wherever a new invention appeared in a new field. In Africa 100,000 years ago men with Acheulian flint weapons exterminated many genera of great mammals which they killed for food. In North America a worse catastrophe befell when man first appeared in the continent with even better weapons 15,000 years ago. And in Madagascar a small repetition was enacted when men arrived 1800 years ago in that great island. Thus there came about a series of those irreversible disasters which, unnoticed by the inventors, have since paleolithic times followed in succession each new invention with its ensuing access of human prosperity. They were sudden disasters in relation to the evolutionary time scale. But none of these disasters was sudden enough, in relation to the individual life, to be noticed by those who did the damage.

For us the most significant, and for man the most harmless, of his inventions were those he used to carry him over the water. They not only increased his power and his means of subsistence. They also spread his populations over rivers and oceans. The ice age carried men into the continents of America and Australia. But it did not carry them into the islands of the Pacific, the Atlantic and the Indian Oceans. To reach them men had to make boats.

The simplest forms of watercraft have arisen independently in many places with the use of local materials. Great trees were used for dug-out

[1] These processes have been admirably described by Coon, Clark, Derry and Williams and also in specialized works such as those of Mangelsdorf and B. S. Dodge.

canoes in Africa and Australia and also in India. Rafts were made from bamboo in China, balsa in Peru, and rushes in Easter Island. They were floated with blown-up skins on the Ganges or with calabashes (*Crescentia cujeta*) in Central America. And they were fitted with sails in many places. Baskets, round or oval, were made into coracles, curraghs, kuffas and kayaks by coating with bitumen or covering with skins. Bark canoes were developed independently in America, China, Africa and Australia.[1]

These inventions have survived with little change to the present day. Both the dug-out canoe and the coracle have only just died out in Europe.[2] In their long existence they have themselves accomplished great things. On the one hand they have given rise by a long pedigree of invention to the modern forms of boat, the sampan and junk of the Chinese, and the keeled boat of the west, carvel built in the Mediterranean, clinker built in the north. On the other hand they have demonstrated most directly the principle by which the expansion of peoples has been limited or promoted. Each invention of a new kind of boat has reacted on the inventor. It has opened a new territory, a new environment, first to the inventor, then to his family, and then to his tribe. In this way it happened that the Eskimo created the kayak; the kayak also created the Eskimo. And the Eskimo then proceeded to create something more, the freighter canoe, the umiak, which took him even further.

Later we shall see with even more emphasis what the invention of the outrigger canoes did to expand the habitat of the islanders of Indonesia and what their long boats did for the Vikings, while on a smaller scale the Caribs were occupying the islands of the West Indies. Each of these inventions promoted the breeding and multiplication of the people who were a little more skilful or intelligent, persevering or enterprising, than their neighbours. It took a step forward in the long selective process of the mental improvement of mankind.

b. Art and Magic

As the ice was beginning to recede, perhaps about 12,000 B.C., man began to reveal his human character to us. It happened perhaps first in the south-west corner of Europe where men from Africa met men from Asia near the Pyrenees. Neanderthal man had already begun to bury his dead; to think of the past and the future; to identify himself with nature. But now, first solid figures, then graphic art, sprang from the hands of the new Cro-Magnon people, people who were known by their implements as Magdalenians; and it spread through the paleolithic world. It was an art connected with magic, with myth, and with religion. As the Abbé Breuil showed us, it has fixed for ever the record of the hunters' knowledge of the moving animal world. It was a knowledge based on the superb perceptions of people who, like the Bushmen and the Australian Aborigines, depend on hunting for their survival.

Near its centre it was smothered by alien civilization. Further afield it was

1 See Hornell (1946), Armstrong (1967).

2 The Rogers family of Ironbridge on the Severn, the home of modern iron-smelting, has made paddled coracles, formerly skin-covered, certainly for ten, but perhaps for several hundred, generations (Jenkins 1959).

embedded in the earliest neolithic culture of Chatal Hüyük in Anatolia. It contributed to the art of Egypt. It was scattered in the rock paintings of all Africa continuing as long as the paleo-peoples survived. It died out with the Bakafula in Somaliland about 1800 and with the Bushmen in Basutoland at the same time. Born independently with other hunters, it survives still in Australia.

All these forms of art and the religious beliefs that went, and still go, with them are in a sense contemporary. They belong to the period of man's second world-wide expansion, they express the joy of discovery of his prodigious new powers as a hunter. But beneath this joy there flourished, as they do to this day, witchcraft and cannibalism, the darker or less creative elements of his social, intellectual or spiritual life.

Whether paleolithic art and magic was or was not the work of special castes moving and breeding independently of the tribes among whom, or for whom, they worked is however an open question. The caste situation exists today among witch doctors in Africa but it has not been recorded among paleolithic tribes strictly preserved from contamination by more advanced societies.

c. Speech

At the same time that these great inventions were appearing speech must have been growing in importance. It was bound to be a slow process. The organs of biting, chewing, swallowing and breathing had to be transformed into the means of articulation. Not only must the larynx, palate and tongue, the teeth and the lips be structurally adapted to this novel function but the muscular and nervous control of all the organs and the corresponding structures in the brain must be organized in the same connection.

The process of inventing language, that is the ability to communicate by speech, must indeed have occupied a large part of human evolution. It must have begun at the beginning of man, for it was closely connected with changes in the posture of the head, the relations of the throat and larynx, and the arrangement and use of his teeth. These processes together have taken much more than a thousand generations. And they have proceeded, as studies of language and of comparative anatomy equally show, independently and with different effects in the great human races.

The common principles of human speech no doubt have certain common origins. But they have for long developed in parallel in the great human races. This common mental achievement is combined with a wide variation in articulating apparatus. It is owing to this variation that when we look at the races of man today we find them speaking ten thousand different and mutually unintelligible languages. The utmost skill of linguists in arranging these languages has failed to reduce the number of their kindred or related groups to less than a hundred families. Language families are unrelated in respect of the sounds used for similar things yet in view of the great number of families the people speaking them must often be of recent common origin.

We may express this paradox by saying that while the evolution of speech is ancient and slow, the evolution of language is recent and rapid. And this is due to the fact that on this occasion mind developed in advance of flesh and bone. The evolution of the nervous structure underlying speech was established and relatively stable when the evolution of the mouth was still rapidly proceeding. Hence the extreme variability of its structure and capacity for sound production among the living races of man. This indeed is what we observe from the comparison of different races and peoples whether in the anatomy of their lips, tongues and teeth or in the phonetic character of their languages, where we find quite a different importance attached to vowels and consonants and clicks, quite different complements of consonants, some rich, some poor, quite different uses made of intonation, whether for the meaning of the word as in Chinese, or the purpose of the sentence as in most European languages.

There is one interesting consequence of these two contrasted processes of evolution which we can use as a means of demonstrating them. It is that they sometimes come into conflict.

They do so whenever one group of people adopts or takes over the language of another, a process which has been occurring with increasing frequency in recent times, the adoption being always imperfect. It modifies both grammar and sound. But above all sound. It does so because every people has a genetically different sound-producing apparatus from every other. And all people *prefer* to use the sounds and the combinations of sound that come most easily to them.

From these principles certain consequences ensue. Every standard form of speech represents an attempt by individuals to conform to the habits of the community of which they wish to form a part. Languages therefore change and evolve phonetically with the people who speak them. They split into dialects as peoples split into breeding communities. Of these effects on the later history of man we shall be noticing repeated tests and verifications.[1]

[1] This approach rests on three main types of evidence which have so far been overlooked by linguists:

(i) The fossil evidence of the foundations of speech in early man are naturally confined to the teeth whose individual racial and evolutionary differences have been discussed by Tratman (1956), Hunt (1959) and Coon (1963). The contemporary evidence of genetic differences as between races has been surveyed in teeth by Lasker and Lee (1957) and linguistically in relation to clicking and sucking noises by Stein (1949) and Du Brul (1958). The specific test of one-egg twins has been applied to teeth by Gabriel (1948), to speech defects by Luchsinger (1961).

(ii) The experimental evidence from the total mouth-and-face behaviour in man has been examined in relation to speech by Ballard and Bond (1960, 1961, 1962).

They conclude that genetic variations occur between individuals, families and races in the structure of the mouth and face; these variations affect the ease of articulating particular sounds and lead different individuals to make the same sound by different movements. For example S is produced (but not pronounced) in two different ways by Londoners. Further, different designs of artificial teeth are required to give the best results in speaking different languages.

(iii) The historic evidence for genetical control of sound production and its relation to phonetic evolution in language I have summarized (Darlington 1947,

The development of language was bound to interact with every other evolutionary development. For each genetic improvement in the speech apparatus would favour the family in which it occurred and those around them: their own speaking group and their own breeding group—which are in effect the same group. Great expansions of human population were therefore likely to be expansions of people who had new abilities and new ideas and who could express them and understand them in speech; in other words, to use a practical definition of a modern term, more 'intelligent' people. It must have been a selective process based on an earlier development of the mind and culminating in the great expansion of populations at the end of the paleolithic age.

Selection however was not the only process mediated by speech. There was also differentiation. Peoples resembling one another in mental and physical structure spoke the same language: they spoke together and bred together. But peoples diverging in mental and physical structure inevitably diverged in speech. And those speaking different languages were inevitably discouraged from speaking and from breeding together. The consequences of this divergence we must now consider.

III. THE RESULTS OF EXPANSION

a. The Origin of Races

The second great paleolithic expansion of man which has been going on for nearly a thousand generations has been followed, as we shall see, by other smaller expansions. During the last 10,000 years these have partly overlaid its results and, as we may say, partly scrambled them. Nevertheless we can still see its rough outlines.

The outstanding character of the world distribution is the wide variation between different groups of people living in different regions. This is variation between large groups occupying large areas as well as between smaller groups in smaller areas. It comprises differences in appearance and in behaviour. Darwin, observing these differences and weighing them from the point of view of evolution by natural selection, came to the conclusion that these differences had a largely genetic basis. There were indeed geographical races and sub-races of man like those found in other widely distributed species of animals. But, whereas the differences between animal races usually adapted them in an obvious way to the different climates and conditions under which they lived, in man this was only partly true. The adaptation was imperfect in a capricious way which Darwin regretted not being able to explain.

In order to see our way through this problem we have to think in terms

1949, 1964). Brosnahan (1961, 1962) has explained the linguistic principles concerned with mapped examples from European languages. Simplified maps of the language families of the world are given by Lundmann (1961).

Problems of the Bushman clicks, Chinese tonality and the Polynesian musical register will be discussed later.

of small ecological differences as well as large climatic ones. We have to examine our new knowledge of disease and of blood groups. And we have to put all these things into the framework of the human movements of which the great expansion consisted.

b. Polymorphism and Hybridity

Blood Groups: Human races, as they were separated 10,000 years ago, may well have differed absolutely in certain genetic respects: colour of hair and skin, shape of nose, mouth and eyelid, structure of palate and teeth, and in innumerable local adaptations to climate and way of life. These differences have become blurred by the mixture of races in some regions especially in the New World. As a result we have communities and even families in which the primary genetic differences which used to distinguish human races are now being recombined. Some differences, however, which recombine within the human communities and families today are not derived from race mixture and we now have to find out what they do, what they show, and where they come from.

About half the people in the world have blood which, if mixed with the blood of the other half, will clot it. This is not a question of differences between races or between nations or even between villages or between families: the differences exist within the family, within most families. The reason for this astonishing situation was discovered in 1900. The blood fluid or plasma of a portion of the population contains certain active proteins which react specifically to coagulate the red blood corpuscles of individuals not having these substances. The production of these proteins is controlled by particular genes of which there are three kinds: A, B and O. Each individual having chromosomes and genes from two parents has two of these alternatives or alleles. All human beings are therefore of one of six kinds: AA, AB, AO, BB, BO, OO. And every population of human beings is permanently mixed in respect of these genes and is characterized by the proportions of the four which are distinguishable: AB, AA and AO, BB and BO, and OO.

Today many millions of human beings in all parts of the world have had their blood recorded for its character in this respect. Many of them indeed in a dozen other similar respects. The results, which have been described by Mourant, have given us a picture of human variation and a clue to its evolutionary and migratory and racial origins which is in some ways historically decisive.

The important principles are the following:

(i) All human populations down to the family level are mixed or hybrid in respect of a dozen or more such gene-differences. They are hybrid but without hybridization beyond that provided by the customary practice of outbreeding.

(ii) Every one of the genes responsible is not only hereditary but highly stable. Several indeed are recognizably connected with corresponding genes in the apes and monkeys.

(iii) The mixture of genes in each population is maintained not by its neutral effect, for many of them are highly active, but by the advantage that the hybrid such as AB has over the pure type such as AA or BB. And perhaps also by the advantage that all populations have from being variable. The variation or polymorphism is thus what is described by Ford as a stable or balanced polymorphism.

(iv) The proportions of these genes differ characteristically in populations of different geographical areas much as we might expect them to do on the archaeological and fossil evidence of human movement.

(v) In addition some genes have undergone secondary changes giving a number of alternatives for one gene and some of these are characteristic of particular races such as the African Negro. Thus in ABO, Rhesus, and MN systems Negroes have unique properties distinct from Europeans, derived perhaps from hybridization with Bushman ancestors.

(iv) In the regions where the paleolithic expansion brought man into previously uninhabited territories, we should expect the most rapid movement and multiplication of small advancing groups and hence a chance loss of some gene alternatives left behind in spite of the hybrid advantage. That is what we find in Australia where in large areas the B allele in the ABO system, and in America the A as well, had been lost during the paleolithic expansion. The B allele in the same way seems to have been lost among the eastern Polynesians. Conversely a new gene known as Diego which arose in Eastern Asia has been swept all over America where it reaches its highest frequency.

The blood group genes thus already provide us with genetic pedigrees helping us in our general study of human movements. A second group of genes responsible for variations in the respiratory pigments produced in the red blood corpuscles gives us information different in kind but equal in value for the tracing of human history.

Haemoglobins: In our common ancestors of late paleolithic times the respiratory pigment of the blood existed in one specific chemical form. A trace of a variant was found in foetal blood. Recently however, new chemical types of haemoglobin began to appear in the races which developed in different parts of the Old World.

These defective variants number several dozen. Each is due to a specific gene mutation and many, perhaps most, cause serious anaemia and are fatal in the pure state. In the hybrid state, however, combined with the normal gene, they produce a mixed haemoglobin, or a reduced amount of it, which does not kill its possessor.

These mutant genes, as Allison first showed, are confined to the Old World tropics. In this area, about three thousand years ago, *Falciparum* malaria, perhaps contracted from apes either in West Africa or in South-East Asia, began to spread among the new human populations.[1] Hybrid

[1] Bray (1965), Berry (1967, ch. 28); see Darlington (1964) and ch. 24.

people with mixed blood pigment in respect of these genes were able to survive an attack of malaria. The parasite finds the abnormal blood pigment indigestible and fails to establish itself. The mutant genes therefore spread as a selective response of man coming to live in dense populations in contact with malaria and therefore suffering severely from the infection. With one-third abnormal genes in the population about one-ninth will die of the defect. But nearly one-third, although of reduced vigour, will be immune to the disease.

In its origin each of these blood defects was characteristic of a certain race and for long remained so. For example Hb_S, responsible for sickle-cell anaemia, like certain blood groups, is characteristic of the African negro. He took it across the Atlantic in frequencies that have only slightly and slowly diminished with the reduction of malaria in America. Competing with, and apparently excluding Hb_S from South-East Asia, is a milder variant Hb_E which proves to be capable of co-existence with a third great complex of genetic anaemias. These cause mere deficiency in quantity and, arising from many genetic causes, they stretch from Spain to China.

Thus the evolution of human haemoglobin has recently been greatly accelerated. Owing to the wide dispersal, large numbers, and dense populations exposed to disease there are many variations of the haemoglobin molecule among the present races of man while only three have arisen to distinguish man as a whole from the gorilla. The last three thousand years have produced more evolution than the previous twenty million.[1] Even so the mutation that has occurred has not been fast enough to allow different peoples to acquire the best type of blood pigment for disease. The fact that different genes have been used in different regions shows that mutation has usually occurred only once in each race or each region and little exchange has so far occurred between different races.

The evolution or history of the human blood shows that the condition underlying polymorphism is one of balanced or permanent hybridity. It is this condition which is so powerful in helping a population or a species to meet an external emergency, especially the emergency of a new disease. For if the population is hybrid, only a part may be destroyed by any one epidemic of the disease. With each succeeding epidemic it will have a new chance of increasing its genetic resistance by selection and ultimately surviving.

c. Disease

As man expanded over the world he met new enemies in each region, new insects, lice or ticks, new worms and flukes, new microbes both, bacteria and viruses. And often these were combined; the mosquito carried the malarial parasite; the rat carried the flea that carried the plague bacillus.

The new sources of disease grew in proportion to the density of man and hence to the success and prosperity of man; or rather they grew out of proportion, for the small parasites were favoured by the increase in the intermediate parasite as well as in man himself. The bearings of this principle we shall see at a later stage.

[1] Zuckerkandl and Schroeder (1961), *Nature 192:* 984.

At the same time a second principle operated: man diversified and his diseases diversified. We have seen how in different regions his blood was able to respond in different ways to the same parasite. But of course in other regions without the parasite he did not respond at all. The occupation of new continents, especially America, made possible the largest test of the principles of evolution of disease. For in the Old World and in the New both the human races and their diseases evolved in complete isolation from one another. The Americans had left behind certain Old World diseases along with certain Old World genes. When the two groups were, in the end, brought together it seems the larger parasites may have been less dangerous to the new people than to their accustomed victims.[1] But the smaller parasites, protozoa, bacteria and viruses, were more dangerous to new people. Measles and smallpox destroyed the pure unhybridized populations of America and Polynesia; syphilis damaged the populations of the Old World. The smaller or peripheral group, the native American, as noted by Archdall Reid, never has created any native quarter, any unhybridized population, in a city. The larger or central group suffered less than the smaller because it had more diseases, more resistance to them, and in general more variability.

Within the Old World populations, however, differences in disease resistance were sufficiently acute to be noticed when Europeans visited the white man's grave in West Africa. It was indeed the observation of these differences which led W. C. Wells in 1813 to state for the first time the great principle of natural selection as a basis of the differentiation of races. The extent of this ecological variation in human races has however never been exactly surveyed.[2] All that we can say is that all such differentiation must powerfully reinforce the barriers to human movement and human mixture. It seems likely that the fear of disease has (for example in India) underlain the fear of mixture especially since such a fear could have saved many peoples from extinction.[3]

d. Ecology

During his prolonged period of expansion, man differentiated, by processes which Coon has described, into local communities having many divergent means of livelihood by hunting, fishing and collecting. He also became locally or ecologically adapted to a wide range of conditions, forest and desert, mountain and seashore. Some of the peoples arising in this way illustrate in their descendants today the rules known from the study of other mammals.

One of these rules is that cold favours a large or squat build, heat a small

[1] The evidence is indirect: e.g. the rejection of Europeans by Hawaiian lice quoted by Darwin; and the specific distinction between *Cimex lectularius* of Europeans and *C. rotundatus* of the Negro.

[2] For example the Russian expansion into Persia was limited by unknown diseases (ch. 24).

[3] The Maoris in New Zealand escaped extinction but only it would seem by hybridization: those who survive are not pure Maori.

or lanky build. Dwarf or pygmy peoples, mostly hunters, in fact appeared independently in many tropical countries. Some were forest dwellers as in the East Indies, Malaya and the African rain forest. Others were desert dwellers like the Bushmen of South Africa. And others again were islanders, and collectors and fishers, like the Andaman people. Several peoples, equally in the Australian desert and in the Arctic, developed the cold-limb adaptation which withdraws blood from the limbs and conserves heat in the naked body when asleep in the open on cold nights. On the high plateaux of the Andes and in the Himalayas a great development of the heart and lungs and probably of the haemoglobin content of the blood made work possible in a rarefied atmosphere. This adaptation, as Coon suggests, has preserved the Andean plateau peoples from the hybridization with Europeans which has destroyed most of the exposed lowland native peoples of America.

Resistance to heat under conditions of an assured food supply is a simple problem. It has been accomplished by the Nilotic peoples of the Sudan who have given rise to the Dinkas and the Watutsi, the two tallest and slimmest peoples in the world. The problem of the Bushman is more difficult. He has to endure extremes of heat and cold and also of glut and want. The Bushman has probably developed his small size in adaptation to desert conditions to which he has recently escaped from larger pursuers. The Bushman's experience is revealed by his early wrinkled skin so different from that of the regularly fed forest pygmy. His women have met this difficulty by acquiring a capacity to lay down their varying store of fat on the buttocks. As with the hump of the camel, another desert animal, localization allows an easier loss of heat than an even distribution over the body.[1]

The most striking differences are seen today between adjoining peoples separated by a sharp difference in altitudes. The precipitous boundaries between Sikkim and Bengal, between Persia and Iraq, between Abyssinia and the Sudan, and even on a lesser scale and of a more recent origin, between the Alps and Italy, are accompanied by differences in physique and temperament, racial differences in the human populations which correspond with the differences in the accompanying flora and fauna in being ecologically adaptive.

These sharp differences are all the more remarkable for what Coon has called the 'bellows' effect of successive ice ages, unparalleled in the previous history of the earth, which have sucked and blown human populations up and down, north and south, on the earth by their alternations during the formative period of man's history.

They lead us to expect that certain races in certain regions will move more freely back and forth while other races in other regions will be ecologically anchored; they will form immovable islands in a fluid world. The boundaries of such islands indeed appear to be the great escarpments which separate

[1] This steatopygy is found sporadically on the east side of Africa amongst all the people who have, as we shall see, hybridized with the Bushmen. Probably however Darwin was right when, relying on Galton's measurements and Burton's observations, he supposed that sexual selection had carried on with the improvement of the buttocks where ecological adaptation left off (see ch. 28).

plain and plateau peoples, where, as Coon says, successive peoples follow one another up the mountainside like layers in a cake.[1]

e. Climate, Colour and Mutation

Among the present races of man there is a wide range of pigmentation of the skin between white and black. Pigment reduces the synthesis of vitamin D by the skin so useful in the higher latitudes; but nearer the equator it helps to keep the body cooler and it also protects the skin from damage by sunlight. For example skin cancers arise most frequently among pale people in sunny climates. It is therefore evidence of adaptation by natural selection that darker peoples live nearest to the tropics and there is a gradient of skin colour correlated with latitude.[2]

Closer study shows however that this correlation is highly erratic. Adaptation is clear although obviously not rigorous. In Eastern Asia apart from Ainu and other small Caucasoid intrusions we find only yellow people, a coherent mass differing from those in any other part of the world except for a resemblance with the Bushmen of South Africa. They are the Mongolian race in its original home and are more homogeneous in all respects than the western peoples. Above all they show very little colour gradient. Adaptation to sunlight over a range of 40° of latitude is almost absent. Why? It would seem that their isolation from stocks carrying black pigment has given no scope for selective change and adaptation.

The same principle is carried over to the aboriginal peoples of America. As we saw, they reached America by way of the Bering Straits towards the end of the last ice age. Like the Mongolians of the Old World the American or Amerindian peoples reaching the tropics show no serious adaptive variation in colour. Darwin was the first to be struck by the extraordinary lack of physical differentiation in colour as well as feature between the Botacudos of Brazil and the people of Tierra del Fuego.

These two situations, the contrast between Caucasians and Mongolians, provide us with a test, a natural experiment of great significance. Where colour variation is present it is selected and distributed adaptively. But where it is not present it does not easily arise. In 20,000 years not one gene has mutated. There was therefore no response to the change of environment when the Amerindian peoples moved into the tropics in the New World. Even in the Old World, where Mongoloid people had to expel their darker-skinned Australoid predecessors, natural selection in favour of pigment failed to keep them out: it failed to counter-balance their other genetic advantages.

[1] Many rare ecological types at a paleolithic level have no doubt been extinguished in the last century by epidemics of European origin, *e.g.* the slightly web-footed Duck-people or Aigu-ambu of New Guinea who lived by fishing and fowling in the water; their survivors were discovered by Monckton (1920).

[2] The demand for darker skins is so great that certain peoples in tropical regions of the New World and the Old, in the Gulf of Venezuela and in the Hadhramaut, darken their fair skins as a protection against the sun (ch. 24 and Bisch 1963). For a detailed consideration see G. A. Harrison (1961).

The evidence even carries us further. There are in Malaya, in Indonesia, and in the Philippines, black Australoid people, pygmies or Negritos with peppercorn hair. These people in the 10,000 years or so that they have co-existed with Mongoloids have interbred with them little if at all. The barrier to outbreeding (or racial prejudice) has largely kept the two groups apart except in Melanesia. And it has prevented the establishment in Eastern Asia of a colour gradient like that in Europe.

It was long ago supposed by John Hunter, and recently by Keith, that black was the original colour of man and that lighter colours therefore must have arisen by mutation. Now that we know of the existence of light brown or yellow-skinned people in almost all parts of the world, and notably in the Mongoloid and Capoid races, it would be easier to suppose that this was the original type and that mutations had independently occurred to white in Europe to give the Caucasoids, to dark brown or black in Southern Asia to give the Australoids, and to black in Africa to give the Negroids.

In these terms the time scale of human colour evolution becomes clear. The differentiation of white, yellow and black races took place over a period of half a million years by mutation. Then Negro and Australoid races probably developed their pigmentation independently just as they have their haemoglobin mutants and with no greater frequency. The failure to develop darker pigmentation in Mongoloid and Amerindian peoples living in the tropics for some 10,000 years, and especially the uniformity of the Amerindian races, is in keeping with these assumptions.[1]

Certain other inferences may be drawn from this evidence. Brown men must have made their way into Australia and yellow men into South Africa before the black mutation had spread out of its original stocks. Further, the southern Indian black peoples must have filled their country before any paler invaders appeared. The African negro peoples arrived or arose in Africa last of all for it was only they who could successfully occupy the tropical steppes and complete the southward colonization of Africa which they were still in process of doing when the white man arrived.

Another example of failure of human races to adapt to climatic change is shown by the folded eyelid of the Mongolian peoples of Eastern Asia. This property has been supposed to be an adaptation to extreme cold, fittingly found therefore in the Eskimo, and fittingly lost or undeveloped in the Amerindian peoples. It is not lost, however, in the people of southern China. And it is well developed in the remote sub-tropical Bushmen. Thus, either mutation and hybridization have failed to provide the variation, the choice of types, on which selection could work and adaptation prevail, or the folded eyelid is no disadvantage anywhere.

[1] Recessive pure albinos occur in about one in 10,000 of most Bantu peoples. They are not reversals to European pigmentation but are totally without pigment and pink-eyed. They seem to represent a balanced polymorphism, one per cent of albino genes floating in equilibrium in the population. They are not therefore the direct result of mutation. This situation occurs with further complications in New Guinea, the Trobriands and Panama. In some other countries albino babies are killed.

IV. NEW PRINCIPLES

At this stage it is worth asking how far human evolution has resembled and how far has it differed from that of other animals.

Variation by recombination in outbreeding communities followed by natural selection is clearly the common principle. But clearly the circumstances in which natural selection is operating are being changed in a new way. The fluctuations in outbreeding, the modes of selection, are being made and changed by man himself. Or rather perhaps (although individuals have not yet come into focus) by individual men. Evolution is in this way being speeded up. Hence distribution is suddenly extended. In all previous evolution mutation must have been very important. It must have kept pace. But now it does not keep pace. Its slowness, as with colour in the New World, was a limiting factor at the end of the paleolithic period. This is no longer true today since migration and hybridization have broken through the limitation. They have often successfully done in one generation what had failed in several thousand; or undone in one generation what had been built up in several thousand.

Consideration of colour gives us some useful hints about the evolution of modern man. One is that the genetic diversity of this new species allowed him to expand from small beginnings over almost all the dry land of the world in three main steps in the course of half a million years. Another is that this variability was not great enough to provide in this short time, that is with these few generations, equally good adaptation in the remoter parts of all the curiously disposed land masses of the world. The groups of exploring or invading hunters were small and were not able by their diversity to fill all the ecological niches offered to them in vast new empty lands. This was partly due to the great distances and to the sea and mountain barriers to movement and mixture. But it was also partly due to genetic isolation, to the fear of one race for another. This fear is most noticeable today among pygmies. It was probably much stronger among the dispersed hunting peoples of former times whose appearance, speech and smell were all at least as strange and distasteful as among the denser and more sophisticated populations of today.

Finally the greatest diversity and also the best adaptation to environment was for these reasons to be found at the end of the paleolithic period and at the centre of the largest land mass which was to be the region of most startling development, that is between Europe, Asia and Africa.

At an earlier stage of our history it seemed that the development of the brain, the increase of mental capacity, was the driving force in human evolution. Does this account of the paleolithic expansion bear out the same view? It seems to do so. In the first place, directed evolution of the brain in the whole of mankind has favoured the parallel evolution of the great races of man. In the second place, the imperfect physical adaptation of all human races suggests that their mental capacity has been the dominant factor in their survival; physical disadvantages, some of them incurred by the growth of the brain, had to take second place.

Always in the past it has been necessary to use our knowledge of evolution in plants and animals to help us in explaining man. Now we actually find our knowledge of man in advance of that in other organisms. With the giraffe's neck we might think that directed evolution was evidence of the inheritance of an acquired character, or at least of a mysterious direction imposed on evolution by something external to the organism. Here in the development of man we can see how his different organs, hands, feet, brain, jaw, did not improve harmoniously side by side towards their goal. Rather we see how one condition, internal or external, forced a change on one organ which in turn forced a change on another organ. In each instance the change can be seen in terms of natural selection as an advantage for the organism but a dislocation for the separate organs.

It is for these reasons that we see the fossil lines which have run parallel to man's own line repeatedly dying out, whether they are Australopithicines a million years ago or Neanderthal man only 40,000 years ago. Sometimes the dominant forms, having become intersterile with rarer obscure parallel types, may have lost the ability to produce successful genetic recombinations and have accordingly disappeared.

Further, chemical changes are more precise in demonstrating natural selection than are structural changes. Mutations affecting haemoglobin and skin colour are evidently exceedingly rare. For this reason different mutations have affected haemoglobin in different races of men geographically isolated from one another. These races have therefore never been able to exchange the genes concerned and test their merits one against the other. Man has therefore been suffering from the painful results of his over-hasty success. They are results which we shall continue to observe at all later stages.

3

BREEDING SYSTEMS

I. BREEDING HABITS AND SEX DETERMINATION

THE IDEA that new kinds of animals or men may differ in form or habit by heredity from older kinds is easy to apprehend. The idea that they may be favoured by natural selection and so displace older kinds is also easily grasped. So many examples of artificial selection producing the same results were expounded by Darwin that we can have no difficulty in understanding what happens. Moreover the chromosome mechanism and the Mendelian experiment show us just how the new arises from the old, how it separates from its alternative or allele and how it maintains its new character. There is, however, another field for natural selection which is at least as important, which Darwin found puzzling and anyone today may still need to weigh carefully. It is the selection of changes in the processes of breeding and in the mechanism of heredity itself. Such changes concern reproduction and fertility, the ratio of the two sexes, of their differentiation, of their habits of mating. Indeed they concern everything that happens in the passage of their chromosomes and their genes from one generation to another.

Darwin was puzzled by these problems because he could not see how natural selection could favour one kind of individual over another on the grounds of a difference which affected, not itself, but only later generations of unborn descendants. The answer is that properties of breeding such as the time of mating, or the length of gestation, or the number of chromosomes and the way they exchange genes, are all hereditary; they are all racial.[1] We know this from experiments and evolutionary studies with animals and plants and we now have to ask ourselves how far these conclusions are supported when we apply the evidence to man. Let us therefore take a quick look at what we may

[1] Or, to use precise terms, there is such a high genetic component in their manifestation that when the individual is selected the race is also favoured. For a general discussion see Darlington (1958).

call man's genetic system. Let us compare this genetic system with what we know of the apes and see what indication it gives us of the evolution that has taken place.

Man has twenty-three pairs of chromosomes, one pair less than the gorilla and the chimpanzee, one more than his other closest relatives the gibbons. Other monkeys have as few as eighteen or as many as thirty pairs. In twenty million years the numbers of chromosomes of men and apes have thus changed very little. But their content and structure have of course changed, particularly that of their sex chromosomes. Sex is determined by the difference between two chromosomes known as X and Y, the Y being like an X but shorter. Women have XX and men XY so that the equality in the numbers that are born of the two sexes is due to the equality in numbers of sperm with X and with Y chromosomes produced by males.

The two sex chromosomes in man, as in all other animals, are less stable than the other chromosomes. They are under special selective stress. But all the chromosomes are concerned with the differentiation of the two sexes. Not only is this true of the primary sexual characters but also of the general differences between the sexes in respect of physique, intelligence and temperament. In other words the whole hereditary resources of a race or species are available for developing the mutual adjustment of the sexes.

We have, of course, only scanty information about the adjustment of the sexes in the evolution of man but what we have is indispensable for understanding the process.

In the first place two different forms of sexual life are found among the apes. In chimpanzees and gorillas the female mates only in periods of sexual heat or oestrus which occur at ovulation once a month. In gibbons the female will mate at any time. This difference in physiological character is believed to have decided (or more correctly to have interacted with) the different modes of life of the two kinds of ape. Chimpanzees and gorillas, described by Carpenter, Goodall and Schaller, like the baboons, described by Zuckerman and others, live in groups of females with their offspring often dominated by one male who, when his powers fail, is displaced by a younger rival. Gibbons on the other hand live in single monogamous families, father, mother and young ones.

From this account it is clear that at some stage of the evolution of man, probably an early stage, man's habit of living became like the gibbon's. Modern man has inherited a continuous sexual life with almost continuous matability which in turn has favoured, and been favoured by, continuous family life and parental care. Perhaps, as Coon suggests, monogamy was further favoured amongst those races of men whose hunting and other enterprises took them far afield. From what we see today, however, sexual habits have varied with domestic needs. Races of men have evidently often changed their habits by genetic adaptation in response to these changing needs.

How has this versatility come about? In apes and indeed in mammals generally the existence of the sexual heat not only restricts mating to one or two days in the month; it restricts it to one or two unions for each pregnancy. One copulation may, and usually does, secure a whole litter of offspring. But without restriction, as in man, ten or a hundred matings may take place with only a single offspring. Indeed in the extreme case a whole lifetime of mating may lead to no offspring at all. Thus in man the continuous sexual life is secured at the expense of about a hundred times as much production of sperm by the male and a hundred times as much sexual activity as is needed for the reproduction of a species with a cyclical mating activity. Sperm-redundancy, as specialists describe it, increases from 10^8 to 10^{10} or more. Thus in man, unlike other animals, sexual intercourse has ceased to be just a means of reproduction. But it has not become just an end in itself. Rather it is something between the two, an activity devoted equally to maintaining the continuity of the family and the structure of society.[1]

Man's family life was however always adaptable or versatile. His continuous sexual activity, to be sure, established monogamy as his basic, standard, or normal habit. But it also opened the way to a number of deviations that were only slightly foreshadowed by the behaviour of monkeys; notably to polygyny, to polyandry, and to what we may call the phasic homosexuality of the younger age-grades of males. This is a necessary counterpart of polygyny among the older males. In primitive tribes of man, Coon with collecting tribes, and Murdock with food producers, both estimated that three-quarters had such polygyny as the climax of male development. How these systems developed and diversified, we shall see later. Certain changes peculiar to man, however, have proved overwhelmingly and irreversibly successful. Man's continuous sexual life was the first great innovation in his breeding system. It was followed by a breeding crisis which led to a series of other innovations.

II. THE BREEDING CRISIS

a. Evidence of Primitive Man

In order to find out how the earliest of modern men, say 30,000 years ago, managed their breeding we have to look at the most primitive kinds of men who survive today. Anthropologists have searched out these people. They have described their habits with great accuracy and their evidence has given us a picture which shows most significant agreement; significant that is of the behaviour of our common ancestors.

The evidence comes from people who are living in a not very advanced stone age. They include the Aborigines of Australia, the Negritos of the Andaman Islands, the pygmies of the Congo forest, and the Bushmen of the Kalahari desert.

To these we may add the newly extinct Tasmanians and Fuegians and many less-known groups in New Guinea and South America.

All these people breed within tribes of a few hundred families. This rule of breeding within their group is one they inherited from all their animal ancestors without noticeable change until a very late stage. But the tribe of

[1] Theologians and moral philosophers have discussed this question at great length with diverse conclusions which, as we shall see later, have had short-term effects of importance for the history of man.

course may verge on extinction; and it may expand to the point at which it splits. The common characteristic of these primitive communities is that they have no social differentiation by abilities or profession, by habits or beliefs. There is a genetically somewhat homogeneous group differentiated only by sex and by age. And this differentiation by sex and age always refers to occupation: men and women, old and young, always turn their hands to different activities although the type and degree of divergence is variable.

The first important consequence of this condition is that the tribe has no chief. Its oldest men may guide it but they have no authority as others understand it. The people, says the headman, if there is one, will not take orders. Sometimes also several age groups may be separated in their work and place of living but we may doubt whether this habit, occurring in East and West Africa, is genuinely primitive or paleolithic.

How then, it may be asked, does the primitive tribe hold together. What gives it unity? The answer is through its breeding system. And this has two aspects. First, there is the coherence which is due to all breeding being within the group, which is thus said to be *endogamous*. The second aspect of the breeding system is that all marriage must be outside the family which is thus said to be *exogamous*. The combination of these two principles means that the whole group has common ancestors; and ostensibly nothing but common ancestors.

This breeding system favours inbreeding relative to what is usual in larger and more advanced societies. It is calculated, as we may say, to produce the greatest genetic uniformity in any breeding group. It thus provides the genetic basis of harmony and coherence. This coherence is further emphasized by the expressed belief in having common ancestors who are named or symbolized. The instinctive uniformity is reinforced by something that is, or pretends to be, rational. The two can be shown to support one another, for tribes can adopt strangers, and strangers can adopt ancestors. The practice of genetic assimilation and the principle of moral support, as we shall see, run together through the evolution of all societies.

Primitive people therefore usually take a keen interest in their genetic relationships. They have an obsession with kinship which is maintained among civilized people only in their aristocracies. They notice their descent in groups from common ancestors. They often carry their recognition back for many generations but it is then necessarily confined to one kind of line, the male or the female.

In the extreme example found in the Australian Aborigine the whole tribe is divided into two moieties. All marriage must take place between moieties; none within them. The moieties are thus said to be exogamous. Each moiety is derived, or supposed to be derived, from a common ancestor or ancestress. Or, as described by Jolly and Rose, there may be four or six or eight such sections. Elsewhere in Africa, Asia or America, the tribe is composed of many 'extended' families with common descent reckoned only for five or ten generations, quite enough however to provide materials for historical and political discussion with, of course, a mythical ancestor or ancestors in the background. The ancestors are associated with a species of animal or plant known as a totem which is the badge of the group. Again this is an idea with a strong genetic or instinctive component favoured obviously by selection and widely represented among civilized peoples today.

The extended family was first described by the American anthropologist Lewis Morgan in 1871 among American Indians. These were people not primitive in other respects, but retaining a primitive breeding system. Morgan pointed out that within these families all members of the same generation knew one another as brothers and sisters while the parental generation were seen as mothers and fathers. This kind of classificatory system, or treatment by classes as opposed to individuals, corresponds to a feeling of unity within lineages which is characteristic of relatively inbred societies at all stages of evolution. It has the great selective advantage in the hazardous life of a primitive community that it makes the care of children a corporate rather than an individual responsibility. It is a form of life insurance and it has much of the character of a welfare state.

The classificatory system, like the unity within families which it implies, is conceivable only in homogeneous groups which are relatively and uniformly inbred: in which individuality and privacy are disregarded and in which the spouse's relatives are always acceptable. It is inconceivable in the outbred groups typical of advanced societies where cousins could rarely be mistaken for sibs and would frequently resent any such mistake.

Elsewhere the avoidance of inbreeding may be achieved by considering individual relationships. For example the Ashanti tribesman must marry into another household. Since his descent is matrilinear he may marry his father's brother's daughter. But he may not marry his mother's sister's daughter. And where descent is patrilinear the reverse is the case. But by any system of descent he is forbidden to marry under his own roof: his mother, his sisters and his daughters are taboo.

The taboo against incest may be reinforced by a prohibition of eating together of successive generations. For example, according to Meyer Fortes, the Nyakyusa in Central Africa do not allow fathers and children to live in the same villages. This type of prohibition, concerned to prevent *in*breeding, comes to be exploited at a later stage of evolution to prevent *out*breeding.

The rule of exogamy in one form or another applies to all known human societies. Kinship by descent is always recognized and mating with one's own kin is always held to be wrong, one's own kin being those who are classified as kindred under one's own social system. This rule we can ascribe with certainty to our common ancestors at the beginning of modern man.

At a later stage in evolution, when property became recognized, matrilinear inheritance of property arose in matrilinear families. The property, although it belongs to men, is then inherited by their sisters' sons, not their own. And it is their sisters' sons, not their own, whose affairs they manage. It also generally goes with a matrilocal habit, children staying with their mother's household rather than with their father's. The royal family of Travancore in this respect followed the same rules as the neighbouring paleolithic hill tribesmen.

Such a system went with a kind of matriarchy, ownership and management by women. Yet matriarchy is too strong a word for any living system. All we can say is that in matrilinear societies (as in Malabar) women's influence reaches its highest, and in patrilinear societies (as in Arabia) it reaches its lowest, level.

Formerly it was also supposed that, since the function of the father is less obvious than that of the mother in reproduction, the matrilinear habit preceded the patrilinear in evolution and was superseded by it only through the influence of stockbreeders. In Europe and India the evidence of religion and mythology, as we shall see, supports this view. But it has been thought to make little sense elsewhere, particularly in Africa, where there is a matrilinear belt running across the south of the continent. Rather it seems, as we shall also see, that the two systems arise from varying compromises in predominance between the two sexes arising from the genetic nature of their differentiation in different races, in adaptation to different and changing modes of life.[1]

b. The Incest Taboo

The rejection of inbreeding, the incest taboo, may well have been the one nearly stable component of the human breeding system and its evolution since the common origins of man half a million years ago. At the beginning we must suppose that man did not reject incest any more than does an ape or a dog or a fly. All other animals disregard genetic relationships because of course they do not know them; they do not recognize their kindred. Why did man at some stage of his development adopt a rule without precedent among animals? Why did he make it a sacred principle, a moral law, as it has remained through all the later vicissitudes of his history?

To understand this clear innovation in behaviour, the first of his sexual revolutions, we must turn for a moment to the plant world. Darwin took up the study of plant breeding in order to solve this very problem. Flowering plants are largely hermaphrodites. They bear germ cells of both kinds, male and female, on the same individual. Yet in nature the pollen rarely fertilizes the seed of the same plant. The plant has an incest taboo as effective as man's. The mechanism is a chemical one which prevents the pollen growing on a style of the same or even of related plants. Man's mechanism, man's behaviour, is thought to be the result of custom and religious or civil law. It is however much older than any of these. It arises from instinct. It has developed by natural selection. In man as in plants the origin of the mechanism is evolutionary and genetic. Let us see how this comes about.

Any kind of organism, so far as we know, can be closely inbred and never-

[1] The region of the world in which female government (by queens or prime ministers) seems to be most developed is round the Indian Ocean: Madagascar, Transvaal, ancient Sheba, Malabar and Ceylon, with a Melanesian outlier in Tonga. There were the Muslim Queen of the Maldive Islands who received a visit from Ibn Battutah about A.D. 1300 and the Queen of Tahiti visited by Melville. As Darwin pointed out, the degree of sexual dimorphism in size is racially variable and genetically controlled. This is true mentally as well as physically and may be demonstrated as between different geographical races in India. At a later stage it is connected with the varying roles played by the two sexes in cultivation and in herding.

theless enjoy lasting success in a stable world. The result is to produce a uniform and predictable race as fertile as may be wished and entirely suitable to the world it lives in. This success of inbred races, as we shall see, has often been achieved with man and it is known in all the chief races of animals and plants that he has bred. In a stable world it allows, it even guarantees, success. But in a changing world it brings disaster. For the inbred race in plants, animals or men is uniform and predictable like a variety of potato. And like a variety of potato it is also unchanging. Faced with new situations, new environments, it is quickly displaced in competition with the adaptable out-breeding races or species.

What happened when man, unlike any of his ancestors, developed his family life, extended his perceptions, enlarged his memory, and began to recognize his kindred, to give names to mother and son, to remember individuals and to think of them in terms of personal sentiment? Clearly he had come to a parting of the ways, a crisis in his history. His instincts might lead him towards inbreeding, towards incest; or they might lead him away from it. Breeding evidence in human societies where cousin marriage is permitted indicates that there is a hereditary genetic or instinctive component in such behaviour. Some races of animals prefer to mate with their likes; others with unlikes. In these circumstances human stocks which varied towards the rejection of incest would have, not at once but after a few hundred generations, an advantage over those who favoured or allowed incest. For they alone would be variable and adaptable. They alone would do new things and think in new ways. The future would be with them. And, as with every new genetic type of human being, they would displace their alternatives or rivals and people the world with their kind.

So it must have been that new races of men arose who were adapted to different parts of the world and widely different from one another. Such may indeed have been the basis of the first paleolithic expansion. So it must have been also that tribes of men came to be deeply interested in ancestry and kinship. They began to rationalize their instinctive habits. They used their interest and knowledge to develop elaborate and diverse types of structure reckoned by kinship and having the effect of preventing incest. It has been suggested that the value of kinship structures lay in their giving a coherence to a chiefless tribe. It has also been thought that without such a structure disaster would be inevitable. Families would be unstable, as Coon puts it; or larger human groups would be endlessly fissiparous, as Levi-Strauss argues. But such a structure, such habits and beliefs, can arise only by genetic adaptation. And with strict inbreeding no genetic adaptation can occur. No disaster can be avoided. The fundamental crisis must therefore have been over the whole evolution of the species rather than over the organization of the family or the tribe. And the effect of its resolution meant nothing less than to fix the shape of human societies for ever.

c. Outbreeding at Work

The means by which man's instinctive rejection of inbreeding has been applied or enforced have been enormously diversified. It has been applied, in the first instance, against the background of man's imperfect and variable recognition of kinship. And later it has been enforced against the background of all the elaborations of advanced society. The fact that some tribes will recognize two, others four or eight, intermarrying lineages; that some will accept ancestry in the male line, others in the female line; that some will allow marriage of father and daughter, others of mother and son; give a wonderful haphazardness to the rules of mating in primitive communities. They seem to make little sense and much nonsense. And civilized societies can carry absurdity to even greater lengths.[1]

It is worth considering the experimental evidence of what happens in animals with different systems.[2] A rule of mating only with the most distantly related individuals within the tribe is compatible with the greatest uniformity in the character of the progeny and therefore the greatest stability in the tribe. It will however favour instability when the tribe varies in size. If, owing to a change of the climate or of the food supply or of the competition of neighbours, or an attack of disease or a new invention, the numbers expand or contract, aberrant types appear. Some of these will be good, some bad, all will be new. What more could one want than this? If evolution could be planned it would seem there could be no better plan than this. And it is precisely this plan which many primitive peoples seem to approach. In so far as others are less regular in their behaviour they will be more variable in their results: their instability will not have to wait on external change.

Erratic processes of breeding therefore, strange though it may seem, are not at all out of keeping with what we know of evolution before man. What is needed above all is to favour stability but to avoid stagnation; to keep the genes and chromosomes stirred up. If they can be kept moving the society is safe. Its future is unlimited. If they settle, if they solidify, then the society is in jeopardy. It has limited prospects. We shall see at a later stage examples of how this can happen despite obedience to the incest taboo and the most respectable conformity with the moral laws which were derived from it.

Flexible breeding regulations have not only general, but also certain special, advantages. If the rules of breeding are exactly prescribed what freedom has the man or woman in choosing a mate? In fact certain systems allow them no freedom of choice and this is in itself an obstacle to two kinds of process, indispensable for all the later evolution of man, physical, mental, and social. The first of these is Darwin's *sexual selection*. The second, which we shall consider later, is *assortative mating*.

III. MATING POSTURE AND SEXUAL SELECTION

A second change in man's sexual evolution developed perhaps over the same period as the incest taboo and like it proved to be irreversible. As he became more upright, he found it possible to change his mode of copulation. He gave up the general mammalian type, back-to-front, and took to the characteristi-

[1] For example in Persian law marrying the relative of a homosexual lover is forbidden (R. Levy, 1957).

[2] See Darlington and Mather (1949, 1950) and E. B. Ford (1964).

cally human type, face-to-face. Or rather, no doubt certain individuals changed, their families multiplied and the habit spread. His method today, however, is wonderfully variable and in advanced societies, for reasons we shall see, it is always versatile.[1]

If this change took place midway in the evolution of modern man it may have occurred independently in the main races of men. The selective tensions it induced are still unreleased and the further anatomical changes it favoured are still incomplete. These tensions and changes would appear to be of two main kinds according to whether their direct effects are structural, psychological or social.

The directly structural effects are seen in the great anatomical variation of genitalia between human races and individuals today.[2] Only in one direction has adaptation reached its limit. The development of pubic hair in both sexes, unknown in any of our ancestors, became necessary to avoid damage from friction in coitus. It is now universal; so also is the useless but developmentally correlated axillary hair.

The directly psychological and social effects of face-to-face mating have initiated evolutionary sequences which will no doubt continue as long as man exists. The female orgasm may have been one selective response according to Ford and Beach. Susceptibility to rape was evidently another. Intensified sexual selection was certainly a third. Concentrating attention on the face and breasts of woman, the reversal of position has, to use Haldane's words, tended to change man's idea of beauty from the steatopygous Hottentot to the modern European, from the Venus of Brassempouy to the Venus of Milo. Sexual selection, acting more slowly than Haldane supposed, has favoured the appearance of forms of beauty, first in woman and secondarily in man. These, not being found in the apes or even in some of the more primitive men and women today, are, we may suppose, recent improvements.

The idea of sexual selection is Darwin's particular contribution to evolutionary theory and he introduced it to meet the problem of human evolution. The greater part of his *Descent of Man* is devoted to explaining the action of sexual selection in animals. The theory is that, in all species of sexually differentiated animals, individuals of both sexes vary genetically in their attractiveness to the opposite sex. Those which are more attractive or more aggressive are likely to leave more progeny. Each sex will then evolve in the direction of enhanced sexual success. This process will modify, or assist, or conflict with, what we should expect from plain natural selection. Indeed, since Darwin at this time had misgivings about the effectiveness of natural selection, sexual selection would, he thought, predominate in directing the evolution and divergence of human races.

[1] As revealed by the reliefs of the Black Temple of Puri in Orissa and, a thousand years later, by the Honeymoon cartoons for which Utamaru in Japan sacrificed his career. The first evidence of such experimental practices may be seen in the face-to-face mating of gorillas in captivity (Schaller, 1965).

[2] The extreme example is the Bushman, she with a pubic apron or 'tablier egyptien', he with a horizontal penis which gives him the tribal name of Up-Cock or Quae-Quae (Trevor, 1950, *Chambers's Enc.*, L. van der Post, 1958).

Today we do not need to share Darwin's misgivings about natural selection in order to see the point of sexual selection. In the evolution of man the development of the beard is no doubt due to sexual rather than natural selection. In the evolution of woman the hairlessness of the body is manifestly due to sexual selection. At the same time the theory throws a new light on the most ancient of human prejudices. We know how Adam complained of Eve's enticing and deceptive arts. Yet it is now clear that these arts are themselves the effect of man's continually more discriminating preference over the last thousand generations for those women who enticed and deceived him most successfully.

On the other hand the property of the man's being always taller and stronger than the woman is one which probably arises from natural combined with sexual selection. So also does the fact that the difference in height is greater in one race than in another: 60 mm. in Europe or Australia, 200 mm. in Java according to Darwin.

The question is bound to be asked: how is it that selection can alter one sex without altering the other? The answer could be given in Darwin's time only in general terms. Now we can say the chromosome mechanism which leads to the two sexes being begotten and born in nearly equal numbers also makes the two sexes genetically as different as two species; sometimes two very remote species. They have different chromosome sets and they can evolve, in part, independently. How does this happen?

In what is primary and crucial for sexual fertility, on the one hand, the two sexes usually evolve independently. When the independence breaks down, when the chromosome mechanism gets mixed up, which frequently happens in heterogeneous outbred communities, individuals are produced who are intersexual, homosexual, neuter or sterile in any one of a hundred different ways. In what is secondary, on the other hand, like hairlessness, the two sexes evolve only in part independently. Thus the male, in selecting for hairlessness in women, has also been selecting for hairlessness in men. In selecting for good looks in women he has also been selecting in the same direction less effectively in men.

Darwin thought of sexual selection as having improved the physical beauty of mankind. It is only since his time that its specific effect on the evolution of courtship in animals has been understood. In man too we cannot doubt that all the social graces have been advanced by the increasing part that courtship played in the sexual success at which it has aimed; and indeed in social life as a whole on which sexual life is based. It would not be too much to say that, while dancing flourished among monkeys and apes, love, laughter and song came into the world during the emergence of modern man. And they were an indispensable part of the process.

IV. TRIBAL ENDOGAMY

In the sparse populations of hunting and collecting peoples of the middle paleolithic the working unit, that is the group adjusted in size to the practical convenience of making a living, was presumably also the breeding unit. In the absence of violent change all mating would be within this unit. But when the population was denser in the late paleolithic expansion the different units or tribes would begin to confront one another. In these circumstances the arrangements for outbreeding *within* the tribe (that is, ensuring exogamy) were bound to be connected with those for avoiding outbreeding *between* tribes (that is, ensuring endogamy).

What is this problem? It is that throughout the animal world there is a general preference for living and working within the group in which one is born and hence for mating and breeding within that group. But there is never an exclusion of mating outside the group; this is even true when the result is to produce a sterile mule. In man, as in animals, genetic differences in smell are no doubt a basis of repugnance for wide crosses, for example between Chinese and European or between Negro and pygmy.[1] But for closer crosses more delicate discriminations arise based on behaviour and habit. In man, more than in animals, his social instincts as well as his individual needs tend to turn the preferences of the majority into the customs and the laws of the whole society. It is not surprising therefore that human societies generally devise methods of separating groups—which we may call tribes—and of giving them a formal character and a binding unity.

The results of this process we see widely amongst primitive and not-so-primitive peoples today. In the first place men, following the same rules as birds, have ceremonial and seasonal gatherings. Such gatherings have a ritualized character which they have developed, as Huxley has shown, under the influence of natural selection. They are part of the breeding system and have their effects on every aspect of reproduction. They serve, not only to bring together different exogamous clans of a tribe, but also to mark it off from other tribes. They define socially what is to be permissible sexually.

The best known of these customs is perhaps the Australian corroboree. Other kinds of custom, directed specifically to maintaining the individuality of the tribe and of the breeding group, are developed in the denser populations of tropical countries, especially India and South-East Asia.

One of these special solutions is a practice found widely in central India and Assam and as far afield as parts of Melanesia and Polynesia. It is the dormitory system described by Majumdar by which boys and girls of the tribe are brought together between the ages of 14 and 20. They are boys of one clan-village and girls of another according to the rules of exogamy. Experimentally and with agreeable rituals they form the sexual attachments which are most likely to be permanent; and most likely therefore to preserve the combined exogamous and endogamous rules, and hence the genetic unity, of the tribe.

A third body of customs maintaining tribal endogamy is connected with the adornments and mutilations with which many tribes characterize either the men or the women. They are practised at the time of the ceremonies of initiation at sexual maturity which themselves emphasize the unity of the

[1] Genetic specificities in smell are the basis of attraction between mates both in mammals and insects. But in man with the decay of oestrus and the decay in the sense of smell this is not to be expected and is not known to occur.

breeding group. No general account has ever been given of the evolution and distribution and classification of this highly significant body of behaviour which includes amongst its thousands of variations every form of clothing and ornament or lack of it, tattooing, scarring, hairdressing, plucking, depilation, tooth-filing and tooth extraction, tongue- and cheek-holing, lip-studding and, most effective of all because it is directly sexual, circumcision of the foreskin.

Every one of these proceedings, we are bound to notice, tends to stabilize the unity of the tribe and the practice of endogamy. Yet in the beginning (which goes back to animal life) those who invented such practices were always unconscious of the effect and they still usually remain so today. They are instinctive in origin although they appear to be rational in effect.

A fourth body of behaviour holding communities together, and the most important of all, is speech. Every breeding group or tribe of human beings differs from every other in the words and sounds it uses in its speech: it has its dialect. Its difference has genetic causes because the average character of the vocal apparatus differs in every tribe from every other. But the difference also has genetic consequences in keeping groups apart. How important a barrier speech might be between primitive peoples is indicated in the precise racial distinctions between the mating songs of birds. But as societies have advanced speech has evidently become a superb instrument of racial discrimination and assortative mating.

Tribal distinctions thus become the means of maintaining and deepening the genetic separation from which they arise. Crude as they are, we are bound to see in them the forerunners of the more delicate divisions of speech and manners, dress and ceremonial which arise in the process of civilization and have the same genetic effects in advanced societies. The same instincts, the same fears and desires, the same respect for ancestors and companions, the same reverence, tradition and need for conformity, the same ceremonial exhibitionism, have held together all later groups of kindred souls.

The unity of the human tribe is evidently sustained by all the barriers which separate it from other tribes. They are barriers all of which have instinctive and, in a modest sense, intellectual components. The mental evolution of man has therefore carried with it a growth of tribal feeling which is one of the properties that sets him apart from his animal ancestors. One particular aspect of this tribal feeling was the attachment for territory. Many other animals have an attachment to territory but with man it set him on a course which was to touch the whole of his later development.[1]

All the four kinds of barrier between tribes are together effective enough under stable conditions. But they are not proof against conflicts, when men are killed and women are captured. Nor are they proof against changing conditions when tribes contract and fuse to form double tribes, as is supposed to have happened in the history of the Australian peoples. The tribal organization provides for the continuance of prosperity. In a dangerous emergency it has to be reconstructed: inbreeding gives place to outbreeding; stability gives place to evolution and a new start is made.

[1] Washburn and De Vore (1961).

V. POPULATION CONTROL

The idea of natural selection arose from two sources both suggesting an extravagant elimination of the unfit. There was the artificial selection of plant and animal breeders discussed by Darwin; and there was the 'struggle for existence' discussed by Malthus. Both stared the observer in the face. Everyday observation of plant and animal life bore out the assumption of a vast wastage of life. Nature, as Tennyson put it, seemed to be 'red in tooth and claw'. Today however the study of man himself, especially early man and primitive man, the comparison of human behaviour with that of birds and mammals generally, and the understanding of the breeding system, its integration and adaptation, all these have put a different complexion on things; they have given the genetic history of man and of animals a thriftier and also a kindlier aspect.

The first step in the new argument was taken by Carr Saunders[1], who by a massive and memorable survey (in 1922) showed that man in primitive societies has always controlled his own reproduction by custom. His customs in primitive, and to a less extent in advanced, societies have been suited to prevent undue or sudden increases in population. They have always tended to produce not a maximum increase but an optimum density. Abortion, infanticide, restricted intercourse and various contraceptive devices[2] are the means employed to limit the numbers of offspring. Control of initiation in primitive tribes delays marriage and reduces the birth rate. Those who are prevented from marrying or mating by warrior grading or postponed initiation, or even polyandry, are forced into homosexuality which then becomes a major agent of family limitation. The old are generally left to die. And in extreme crisis the infants are eaten.[3]

In practice the whole ceremonial and social control by the tribe of its breeding habits, whether concerned with exogamy, endogamy or the limitation of numbers, is evidently part of the genetic system of the tribe. It holds together as a body of practices based on instinct, determined by heredity, perfected by selection and adapted to secure the prosperity and the peaceful multiplication of the tribe.

A second step has been taken by Wynne Edwardes who has shown us that the territorial instincts of birds and mammals, their defence of territories, their courtship procedures, the ritual gatherings of their social communities which are also sexual communities, all these are related to corresponding procedures in man and serve the same functions as those described by Carr Saunders. They are adaptive parts of the genetic system. They replace expansion by balance. And in doing so they replace conflict by compromise and negotiation.

[1] Carr Saunders acknowledges Bacon to have forestalled him in the essay *Of Vicissitude of Things*. He was also foreshadowed by Galton, Karl Pearson, Kropotkin and Wilfred Trotter (see Darlington, 1964). His importance lay in his unconscious or implicit approach to the idea of the genetic system which had not then been formulated.

[2] Finch and Green (1966).

[3] Daisy Bates (1938); *cf.* Gajdusek (1964) and Benedict (1966).

With all these processes sexual selection is also wrapped up, but on this view plays a secondary role to the control of population; it is decorative rather than fundamental in its effects on animal and human evolution.

A third step has been taken by Christian and other American investigators in the physiological study of fertility. Their experiments and observations in nature with a number of species of mammals, notably rodents, have shown that overcrowding depresses reproduction. A degree of crowding that is not likely to endanger food supply and of which the individuals concerned are unconscious nevertheless reacts on the production of hormones controlling their sexual activity and fertility. Moreover the introduction of strangers into the territory of a community may have the same effect.

It might be thought that these changes, being mediated by the central nervous system, are under the control of the will and the reason. For the territorial instincts of a bird and a man are clearly not unrelated. But we now learn that under crowded or unfriendly conditions, in some species, the testes of the males shrink. Now it is hard to believe that anything analogous to the action of the human will is responsible for such an abdication of virility. On the contrary it becomes clear that social organization, the physiological responses and the genetic character of the group have to be suited to one another. And none of them can be softened by argument or subjected to reason: they are instinctive and irrational.[1]

The comparison of population control in men and animals has another far-reaching consequence. The preservation of a stable population with an optimum density not only avoids war, famine, and pestilence: it preserves the whole habitat. Cattle need not destroy their pastures. Predators need not destroy the cattle. A balance can be preserved in nature by adjusted instincts of species which are, as we realize, mutually necessary. It is a similar principle to that applied rationally by the contemporary hunter of hares or hedgehogs who respects the breeding season of his game animals. But in his recent evolution man's instincts and reason have been thrown into disarray by the rapidity of his own inventions. This disarray first affected, as we have seen, his killing of game. Later it affected, as we shall see, his own breeding.

Our immediate problem however is that of competition between one people and another. We have always thought of it in terms of physical strength, disease resistance and sudden death. Now we see that a physiological mechanism can anticipate the dangers of conflict. Competition between parents and offspring can be avoided by an automatic control, an adaptive feed-back mechanism. But what happens when two races meet, one having a strong population-restricting mechanism and the other having partly lost such a mechanism? Clearly a decisive advantage may be gained by the second group. Modern man, by means we shall see, has lost some of the primitive population-controlling devices that we suppose his ancestors to have had. Hence we have had those unrestrained increases in population supposedly

[1] Possibly reactions of this kind, genetically and physiologically controlled, rather than infectious diseases, are responsible for the diminution of certain paleolithic hunter populations, such as those described by Cowell in the Mato Grosso, in the neighbourhood of civilized people.

leading to war, famine and pestilence which severally or together tend to restore equilibrium. This assumption by itself was the basis of the classical argument of Malthus. The further assumption that they work selectively and so lead to evolutionary change is Darwin's rider to Malthus.

We now have to put an intermediate term into this sequence of cause and effect. We have seen that evolutionary selection can itself control and adjust the parts of the breeding system and with them the processes of heredity and the degree of fertility. A large part of the science of genetics is concerned with studying how these things happen. The individual, it now seems, may be made genetically either susceptible or not susceptible to the density of the population. We are therefore led to suspect that fertility is controlled with even greater adaptive subtlety than was imagined.

These considerations help us to understand what happened at certain stages in human evolution. On the one hand there is the disappearance of Neanderthal man; on the other hand the exercise of population control which, combined with increased and diversified skills, allowed the rapid expansion of his successors without much conflict to the ends of the earth. Probably man has increased his genetic tolerance of high population density as he has increased his skill in exploiting his territory. The tolerance was therefore controlled and the expansion was not just an explosion.[1]

The tolerance of dense populations was one condition of the vast multiplication of our human species which has in a million years increased perhaps 20,000 fold; to a greater size than any other mammalian species even including our own parasite, the brown rat. Man has spread over the world, forming different races but never splitting, as other mammals have always done, into different intersterile species.

Why? The answer lies in the fact that big changes in the number and structure of human chromosomes are blocked at several stages. First, hybrids in respect of such changes are blocked by their high rate of abortion and consequent infertility. Secondly, pure forms derived from these hybrids are blocked by the action of the incest taboo. And, thirdly, adaptability continually favours the large old breeding group at the expense of small new groups. The incest taboo, however, has been the decisive agent in holding together not only each human tribe but also the whole human species.

VI. CONNECTEDNESS AND ADAPTATION

Previous students of these problems have often recognized their connectedness and have seen that this connectedness is a biological one. But they have had to study them piecemeal since it is only now that the experimental evidence can be assessed and used to bring the different parts together.

The connection lies in the fact that the control of the breeding system, whether operating merely physiologically as in plants or physiologically and socially as in animals, is always in its basis genetic: it is always a part of heredity. It has manifestly therefore been developed under natural selection

[1] As suggested by Schwidetzky (1950) and Coon (1962); *cf.* A. F. C. Wallace (1961).

which has favoured an economical utilization of the reproductive resources of the species. Such an advantage must have been operating in the course of human evolution and we have to find out how far the advantage or the control may have lapsed or changed in character or effect. For example, if man has all the parts of the animal breeding system represented in his own make-up adaptively co-ordinated and genetically controlled, we have to find out how far these processes are still instinctively controlled and how far rational processes now enter into their management. This is the question that arises in all human behaviour as to the extent to which the development of the cerebral cortex has superseded the earlier instinctive direction of our activities.

The first answer to this question seems to be that the change-over is still in progress. It differs very much between different individuals and different races. But probably it does not differ as much as people used to suppose. Above all, the rules for endogamy and exogamy to which teachers and thinkers, priests and lawyers, have wished to give a rational explanation have almost entirely an instinctive basis. They have long-range effects beyond rational prediction. Abortion and infanticide, on the other hand, with immediate short-range effects, no doubt have a largely rational basis. Indeed it is the prevention of abortion and infanticide on the part of others that has the instinctive forces behind it. Between these two extremes we shall have to form our own opinions on the basis of the evidence to come.

In order to see the position as a whole we may represent the connectedness, the adaptive connectedness, of the parts of the human breeding system in a diagram (Fig. 3). It will be seen at once that the system as a whole is crucial for the survival of human societies. Each type of behaviour must therefore be subject to selection, adaptation and co-ordination. This is true whether it is under instinctive or rational control. As we proceed to examine the evidence of history we shall be able to form an opinion as to how the instinctive and rational elements are opposed or balanced or combined and how they contribute to success or disaster. We shall see how far the working of a genetic system in which all the processes of heredity and reproduction are mutually adapted and interdependent, the system inferred in plants and animals, applies to man.

VII. REASON, INSTINCT AND MORALS

The customs and morals of paleolithic man now begin to take shape. They depend on, and vary with, the character of each breeding group of people. Groups vary in their respect for human life, particularly in their respect for the new-born infant and the aged. None can afford to keep the defective infant although many will care for the aged and infirm. Most will admit the right of retaliation. All probably have a sense of territory. None have acquired a sense of other kinds of property and it is in this respect that they come into grievous conflict with more advanced peoples. But far and away the most important parts of their behaviour and morals are concerned with their breeding systems and it is here that we can see their profoundly instinctive basis.

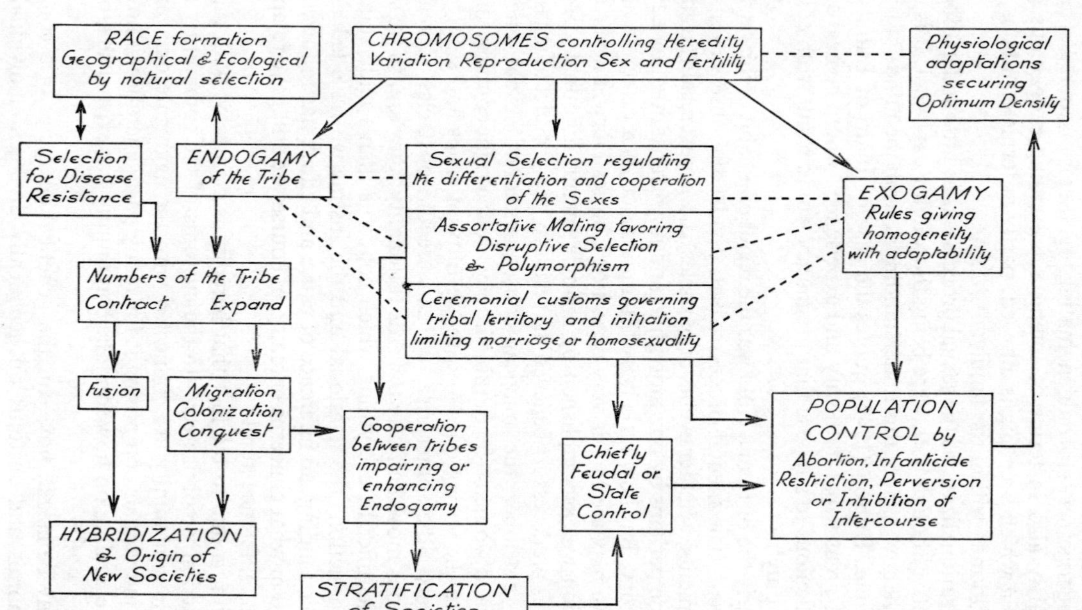

Fig. 3. Diagram showing the connections between the variable factors shaping the breeding system in man on the assumption that all human behaviour has genetic effects which are subject to natural selection.

The development of the breeding system in man, its restrictions of inbreeding and outbreeding, rested on instinctive attractions and repulsions—a hierarchy of impulses based on and canalizing the indispensable sexual appetite. These instincts were rationalized; partly in magical terms related to eating, for when eating together is forbidden, mating together is discouraged and later forbidden; partly also in terms of totems representing exogamous groups, groups between which breeding is allowed, partly in terms of taboos against intimacy of all kinds within the family.

In all these rationalizations the sexual process was as little understood as the laws of heredity although both were being thoroughly exploited. It is difficult for us to realize how remote this understanding is from the minds of primitive or simple people. Hutton (1946) quotes the case of Inato of Lumitsami, 'a Sema chief of great tribal authority and experience', whom he heard 'affirm that it was ridiculous to suppose that pregnancy would result from coition on one occasion only'.

To him clearly the birth of a child was the result of a habit of life rather than of a single event. The mental process which divides the observations of life into single elements, whether events or particles, is, we must recall, an advanced discovery made perhaps by one individual and now transmitted by education to all and sundry. But how little it is still understood as a principle of causal explanation we may see in this very case. For Charles Darwin never realized that fertilization was accomplished by a single sperm. Like Inato of Lumitsami, he and his predecessors believed the result to be a product of mass action.

When we remember the magical consequences of sexual intercourse between men and women—favourable if they are the right couples, unfavourable if they are the wrong ones—on the fertility of crops and stock and the success of every other enterprise, we can see the obstacles to reasoning. Modern religions move half way towards rationality: they are, as we shall see later, semi-scientific. In everything which concerns man's understanding of his own reproduction, the irrational and the instinctive have led the way. Rational understanding, an inference of cause and effect, has followed a long way after. And in what concerns heredity, of course, we still have to apologize for making any inference at all.

This situation is due to the fact that heredity is connected with reproduction; reproduction is connected with the customs of the community and the customs of the community are connected with the aggregate or average instincts of the individuals composing it for many past generations: how many generations depending on how long the community has existed as a breeding unit.

Now, it may be asked, how can the genetical character of a community enforce its morals and customs on genetically divergent individuals? The answer is that it does not always succeed in doing so. Pioneers, rebels or scapegraces occur in every genetically heterogeneous community and, unwilling to conform, they are forced to quit: they reject and are rejected by the establishment; they become outlaws; they move out and try to join another group if they can find one to take them. Such situations have been recorded in all stages of the evolution of society. They usually appear as a conflict between old and young. Again where divergences agree, they succeed in changing the standards of morals or customs. But this does not happen in inbred groups which are homogeneous and stable.

The principle by which the average and traditional character of the community determines morals and enforces conformity with them may be understood by an analogy with another process in human evolution, that by which the average character determines the standard of correct speech in every community. Divergent individuals find it difficult to conform. The impediments to normal speech fail to disappear at four, at eight, or even at twelve years of age. Efforts are made by the parents and by the child to achieve conformity since, as with morals, conformity is more comfortable and more secure. But where the genetic divergence is sufficient the efforts fail. On the other hand if divergences agree they may change the standard of speech and evolution takes place.

There is therefore an exact analogy between speech and morals in their genetic basis. Both rest on the genetic character of the group. Both evolve with the group. But both are subject to lagging from the inertia of the group. Both show evidence of deference. And when deference is insufficient both demonstrate a conflict between different ages within the group. The two can therefore be used to help one another in the study of human groups and their evolution.

Part II

Provident Societies

The discovery of cultivation in the Ancient East meant that the cultivator now knew how to think for the future. He had acquired the mental faculty of providing for his crops and stock and also for himself, his habitation and his community. Time and space, society and religion, of necessity began to have new meanings for him. He evolved more quickly and diversified into agricultural and pastoral, settled and shifting tribes equipped with different technical abilities. The new peoples spread at different rates from their original Nuclear Zone. Moving into the richest valley soils they discovered in the course of several millennia how different kinds of people might live in mixed societies, helping one another, protecting and subjecting one another, but without breeding with one another. They had invented the stratified society of social classes and with it they proceeded to develop the city and create the nation.

4

THE COMING OF AGRICULTURE

I. TIME, PLACE AND MOVEMENT: OLD AND NEW WORLD

MAN'S HISTORY IS SPLIT into two by the division between the old and the new stone ages to which Lord Avebury gave the names of paleolithic and neolithic. These ages of course we no longer think of as two stages in the world's history but rather as two stages in man's development which he separated when he began at different times in different places to make his living by the tillage of the soil and the growing of crops.

To this transformation Gordon Childe gave the name of the *neolithic revolution*. The excavations of archaeologists, checked by radioactive dating and the microscopic study of plant and animal remains, enable us to scale this transformation in time and to map it in place. Not only this: the first plants and animals that man took into his keeping, we can now compare with both their wild relatives and their cultivated or domesticated descendants.

These new methods allow us to say, not only when and where agriculture began, but also what kinds of things then happened. They even enable us to consider what these things have meant for the succeeding stages of human history.

Excavation shows that the first signs of human settlement with remains outside caves can be connected with agriculture. They are found in two regions. The first is in the arc of country described by Breasted as the Fertile Crescent which surrounds the basins of the Euphrates and the Tigris and lies between Palestine, Syria, Kurdistan and Luristan. It is a region we may call Nuclear Asia. The second is in the region which runs from New Mexico to Guatemala and Ecuador which we may describe as Nuclear America.

The probability is that in both regions settlement had begun with the cultivation of crops.[1] Wheat and barley were followed by peas, lentils and flax in the Old World; beans and squash were followed by maize in the New World. The probability also is that, in both Old and New World, what have been found and dated at about 7000 B.C. are not the earliest settlements. The beginnings may well have been two thousand years earlier.

The first steps in cultivation were not in the bottoms of valleys but on well-watered hillsides. With them went continual improvements in stone and wooden implements; in hoes for tilling the soil, flint sickles for reaping and stone querns for grinding the grain. Soon they had spread from their first centres far into Persia, into Palestine and into the Balkans.

In the nuclear area new village communities depending more and more on agriculture were establishing themselves by 6000 B.C. and the new arts of making pottery and wooden vessels were beginning to appear, displacing the older baskets as a means of storing grain. The same inventions did not lead to this transformation until about 2000 B.C. in Mexico and perhaps a thousand years later in Peru.

How do we account for the time and place of these developments and for the resemblances and differences between the Old World and the New?

At once we see that the two developments taking place at the same time on opposite sides of the world show them to have been independent. Then why did they take place at that time? The reasons are evident and connected. Man had reached at this moment the limits of mental and physical evolution, of tribal organization, and above all of genetic and consequent cultural diversity, which were attainable under conditions of hunting and collecting. His achievements at this time included his uses of all mineral, animal and vegetable materials that were available to him in the world; uses for the manufacture of the tools and weapons, shelters and clothing, boats and containers. All the most important drugs and poisons of later ages he knew how to find, to extract and how to exploit. He had discovered the secrets of weaving if not of spinning, of wine-making if not of brewing and distilling, of grinding grain if not of baking bread or pottery, of mining of gold and copper and precious stones if not of smelting ore. The derivative arts of painting and perhaps music he had already superbly cultivated.

All these wonderful skills were tribally dispersed and disconnected. It was the times that brought them into fruitful connection. The change of the climate at the end of the last ice age between 10,000 and 8000 B.C. had the most drastic effect on man of any change in his history. For the first time his movements all over the world were affected. Never before can there have been so much hybridization yielding so many new kinds of people and so many new ideas. And the greatest effect was inevitably at the cross-roads of movement, in the fertile corners of South-West Asia and of Central America. Now men learnt not merely to dig for roots but to plant them; not merely to collect seed but to save it and to sow it; and finally to wait for the crop and again keep the seeds of their crops for sowing again. They intelligently learnt

[1] Described by Mellaart and Helbaek for Chatal Hüyük; by Braidwood, Helbaek and Reed for Jarmo in Kurdistan, and by Willey for Tamanlipas in Mexico. See also Graham Clarke and Stuart Piggott (General).

this lesson in two similar regions with crops which could sustain most of the needs of life if eked out with their earlier practices of hunting and collecting.

So much for the resemblances; what about the differences between the Old World and the New? The crops of Nuclear Asia were more diverse than those of Mexico and Peru. And the peoples likewise. The whole geographical situation, the variety of communications and the choice of climates with mountains, rivers, deserts and seas in easy proximity, was responsible for the greater diversity of both plants and peoples in the Old World centre. They therefore increased and diversified more quickly.

There was another important factor: the presence of a great number of species of wild animals valued for meat as well as bones and hides in the regions adjoining the Nuclear Area. At an early stage, although probably not at the very beginning, remains of goats and sheep, pigs and oxen began to appear in the agricultural settlements in addition to the dogs which were already there. These animals were little different from the wild types. They had evidently found shelter and security and had multiplied in the new settlements. Domestication had begun. In Mexico there was nothing but the turkey. In Peru, nothing but the wild ancestors from which the llama and the alpaca were bred.

Now we might expect that the domesticated animals and crops would begin from an early stage to feed and help one another as well as to feed and help the people who looked after them, multiplying the opportunities of life. It is not surprising therefore that the New World, having begun agriculture at almost the same time as the Old, with its poorer animal resources advanced in parallel but more slowly during the eight thousand years that were to pass before the two worlds came into contact.

II. THE PROCESS OF DOMESTICATION

a. Crops

The first crops that men sowed and reaped were wheat and barley. Or, rather, we ought to say wheats and barleys, for each was of several kinds. It was a natural mixture which included two-rowed barley and two kinds of wheat, einkorn and emmer, whose ancestors still grow wild in Anatolia and between the desert and the hills from Kurdistan to Palestine. Gradually, as their remains show, and as the crops of today show, these plants were changed under the conditions of cultivation. In the wild species the main stalk of the ear shatters so that the ripe grain is shed from the ear still enclosed in and protected by its chaff. Each husk of the chaff has a roughened bristle or awn which gives the ear its bearded appearance and has the property of catching in the fur of any passing animal. These were, all of them, characteristics common in wild grasses, developed under natural selection and adapted to protect the grain, to distribute it widely and to help it in boring into the earth where it would later germinate. These were the characteristics gradually lost in the process of domestication. How did it happen?

In the first place we notice a change in the appearance of the grains. Six-rowed barley replaced two-rowed. And in Anatolia and Persia a new wheat, which we know as bread wheat, began to displace the older kinds. Bread wheat had 21 pairs of chromosomes instead of 7 and 14 pairs like the wild species. It was a new hybrid high-yielding type which had arisen in cultivation.

Beneath the obvious changes another more significant transformation was taking place. When man began to harvest and sow the grain of the wheat the devices by which it had been protected, scattered and buried in nature ceased to have a value for the survival of his new crop plant. Quite the reverse. The shattering of the ear meant a loss of his crop: it meant less harvest and more work in gleaning. The closed husk meant more work in thrashing. The awn meant a loss in scattering. One by one these aids to natural propagation disappeared until the farmer had the modern wheats whose grain falls out of the beardless husks leaving behind the whole ear unshattered. The new bread wheat never appeared in the fully shattering wild form and all the other grains followed suit. The same change overtook in some degree every seed crop which man brought into cultivation: barley, oats, rye, various millets and rice. In maize, to be sure, the result is somewhat different for the grain is not loosely shed but the whole ear is protected by gigantic husks. Also in botanically very remote plants such as buckwheat, hemp and poppies the structures concerned are different but the principle the same.

The evidence for these changes was discovered by the Russian agriculturist Nikolai Vavilov (1887–1943) who proposed an explanation for them which we now find explains even more than he imagined. His suggestion was that the principal changes arising in cultivation were not due to any intentional artificial selection by the cultivator but were inherent in the method of cultivation itself. They were due to what Darwin had described as *unconscious selection* or, as we might say, to operational selection. Later with a wealth of evidence Vavilov was able to show how they were due partly to the removal of the pressure of natural selection from the plant when it began to be cultivated and partly to the new pressures of selection by sowing, tillage and harvesting.[1]

As Darwin had suggested, and as we can agree, unconscious selection merged with, and at a later stage in the development of agriculture it was partly displaced by, conscious selection. But unconscious selection was what gave agriculture its start. How this happened was first recognized by a plant geographer, Engelbrecht. This German investigator suggested that after the first crops were established the processes of plant cultivation and improvement were thrust upon primitive man by an inevitable sequence of events to which he had contributed little conscious control and little invention.

After wheat the first crops according to Engelbrecht were of two kinds. There were those plants like gourds and tomatoes which grew on his own dunghills from the seeds of fruits man had eaten. These he described as *habitation weeds*. And there were other plants which grew with the crops he cultivated imposing themselves on him very often by displacing the crop that he imagined he was growing. These he described as *crop weeds*. Barley in this way might mix itself with wheat and come to dominate the crop where the conditions favoured it.

Testing this hypothesis in central Asia, Vavilov was able to show that rye,

[1] For a detailed account and references see Darlington (1963).

appearing as a weed of wheat at low levels, slowly displaced wheat as the crop was taken high up the mountains or further northwards. Similarly wild buckwheat, which is a weed of cultivated buckwheat in Germany, takes its place on the slopes of the Himalayas at 15,000 feet.[1] It has become, as we may say, a secondary crop.

The most striking examples of such secondary crops are the millets. Grains are called by this name because thousands of seeds seem to be borne by one ear; and all of them were too small to attract the first cultivators. Four important and distinct species of millets were brought into cultivation, at dates which are still uncertain, by farmers moving into poorer and drier lands in Asia and Africa:

(i) Indian millet (*Panicum miliaceum*) Indus valley 2500 B.C.
(ii) Chinese millet (*Setaria italica*) Turkestan to China 2500 B.C.
(iii) Finger millet (*Eleusine coracana*) Abyssinia 2000 B.C.
(iv) Great millet (*Sorghum vulgare*) Central Africa 1500 B.C.

The last of these was taken to India in post-Vedic but pre-Persian times, probably about 900 B.C. Thence it was taken east to China and west to Babylonia, reaching Egypt in Byzantine times.[2] The rest, according to the *Flora Italica*, seem to have been brought back by traders into the Mediterranean in Roman times and are today known also throughout the tropical world.

Today yet another field for unconscious selection has revealed itself in our crop plants. These plants, like man himself, have their breeding systems. Most have invisible devices which secure cross-fertilization and hence regular outbreeding. These adaptations are superfluous and even disadvantageous in a crop plant. They have accordingly been surrendered. The ancestors of barleys, wheats, peas, and the many kinds of beans were and are regularly cross-fertilized. Their descendants are regularly self-fertilized. They are therefore absolutely true-breeding. Here is an evolutionary change which man has resisted in his own species but has quite unconsciously established in his crop plants by the process of cropping itself.

Today therefore we have no doubt that unconscious selection played a dominant part in the development of cultivated plants. It not only altered the character of each domesticated crop. It also continually introduced new crops into domestication as the cultivators spread from their original fields into new areas with new soils, new climates and new weeds. As the cultivators from their hills descended into the river valleys, the richer soils made it possible for stronger, richer and more abundant crops to prosper. And of these new crops some were of the same species and others of new species.

Conscious selection began to play its part when men realized that the flax grown for fibre on the hillsides and brought down to the valley bottoms produced larger seeds. These could be pressed for oil and they were grown therefore as linseed. The same sequence reappeared much later with hemp,

[1] As an Arab peasant in Palestine harvesting a weed-crop of the scabious, *Cephalaria syriaca*, for forage replied to a botanist's enquiries: 'Who sowed this crop? The Devil sowed it.' This same crop is sown for its oil seeds in Anatolia (M. Zohary, 1962).

[2] Doggett (1965, *ref.* ch. 28).

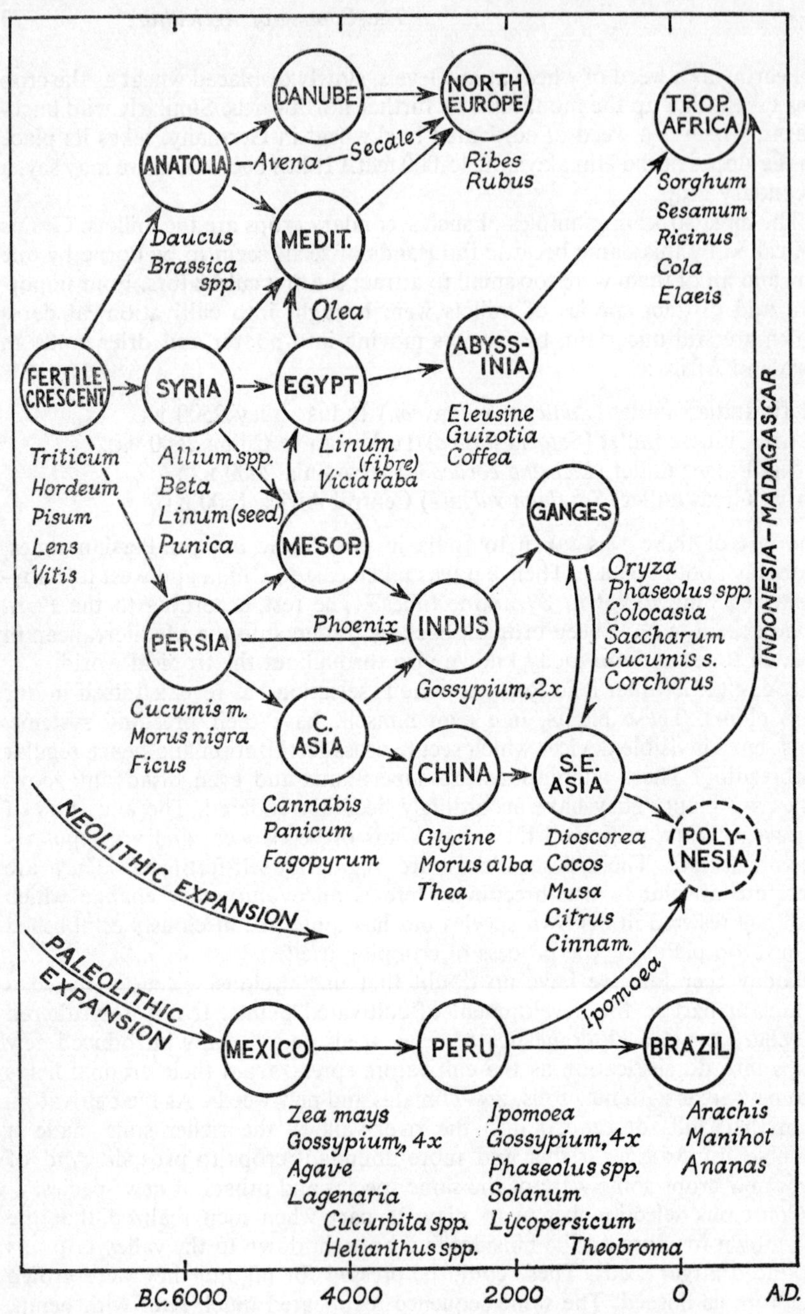

Fig. 4. The Expansion of Agriculture Dated by Crops
Diagram to show the divergence of cultivators from their original centres in the Old and New Worlds and their meeting in Polynesia.
From Darlington (1963)

the additional use as a drug being discovered from sniffing the soothing smoke by the campfire as, Vavilov tells us, still happens today in Turkestan. In this way many crops came to have different uses and to be selected for them so as to meet quite different needs in the diversifying economy of the farming community.

The wild ancestors of many crop plants have been lost. The field bean, the date and the olive have disappeared probably because all the lands they once occupied have now been brought under cultivation. Some however have been transformed and become new species of plant altogether. Such, as we have seen, is the bread wheat. Such also is maize which is utterly transfigured from the wild teosinte of Mexico from which it has undoubtedly arisen.[1]

Otherwise, in spite of tremendous migrations and hybridizations, we can without much hesitation trace the origins of our modern cultivated plants back to their paleolithic ancestors of ten thousand years ago. But whether the ancestors of the new crops had disappeared or not, their situation had now been transformed. They had been changed into new plants no longer capable of surviving in nature but fitted only to survive under conditions which man had learnt to create for them. They were dependent on the cultivator. And the cultivator, of course, was dependent on them.

b. Stock

The animals that men brought under their care before 6000 B.C. were the sheep and the goat from the highlands of Persia and Anatolia. Later the ox from the lowlands of Mesopotamia, and the pig probably from the forests of the Zagros and Taurus mountains came under his control. Most of these were soon derived from various races of each species which hybridized in domestication. Indeed the domestic cow was often mated to a wild bull as the husky bitch is mated to a wolf. Only when he had reached central Asia 3000 years later and southern Arabia nearly 4000 years later did man tame the horse and the camel. (Table 1.)

The domestication of animals seems to have had the same beginnings and followed the same directions as that of plants. That is to say the wild cattle forced themselves on man's attention and proffered their services. Doubtless in time of drought and famine they poached on his preserves, preserves fenced off to serve his needs as a cultivator. Sooner or later therefore they found themselves rounded up in his corrals, protected from predators, and provided with grazing. And in due season they were slaughtered by him for their flesh. There was thus, as Galton first suggested, an unconscious element at the beginning of stock-raising.[2]

[1] Undoubtedly, but contrary to the expert opinion of Mangelsdorf; for the chromosomes of teosinte and maize are almost identical and their hybrids as fertile as either parent. They are classified by botanists as species of different genera *Euchlaena mexicana* and *Zea mays* and therefore represent the most striking instance of the evolution of a new species under the control of man.

[2] Zeuner's conclusions from the study of animals seem however to have been quite independent of the similar conclusions which had been reached forty years earlier with plants.

Table 1. *Domesticated Mammals of the Old World* After Zeuner (1963), Cockrill (1967) and others

Paleolithic (O.W.& N.W.)	*wild distribution*	*sites and dates of domestication*	*geographical expansion*	*main uses and aims of selection*	*hybridization*
1. DOG (Scott & Fuller 1965)	N. temp. many races (wolf)	many independent 15000 B.C. (?)	universal including paleolithic. Australia (dingo)	1. hunting 2. hauling 3. herding (in domestication of ruminants) 4. guarding 5. meat	still crosses with wolf (same chromosome no.)
2. REINDEER[1]	subarctic forest and tundra races (E)	N. Eurasia 10000 B.C. (?)	panarctic	free ranging, migrating and breeding	nil
Neolithic (O.W.)					
3. GOAT[1] (R)	C. Asia and S.E. Europe	Persia, Anatolia 7000 B.C.	followed both agricultural and pastoral expansions; often displaced by sheep	1. meat 2. milk 3. skin and hair	all wild races crossed
4. SHEEP[1] (R)	as above	Caspian steppes 6500 B.C.	main agent of pastoral expansion throughout O.W.	1. meat 2. milk 3. wool	all wild races crossed
5. CATTLE[1] (R)	Persia, S. Europe, India (E)	1. Anatolia 6000 B.C. 2. Indus valley 2500 B.C. (independent)	agricultural and pastoral	1. meat (except in India) 2. milk (except in China) 3. haulage, everywhere 4. thrashing corn	Eur.-Indian hybrids colonized Africa and S.E Asia
6. WATER BUFFALO (R)	India (E) S. China (E)	Indus 2000 B.C. China 1000 B.C.	to Indonesia, Europe and Brazil with agriculture	as above	F_1 cross with cattle is sterile in both sexes
7. YAK (R)	Tibet to Mongolia (E)	Nepal *c.* 1000 B.C.	confined to arctic climate (over 2000 m.)	meat, milk, haulage and carriage (raised for milk in Tibet and Mongolia)	female mule with cattle fertile
8. PIG[1]	Europe to China (wild boar)	Anatolia 6000 B.C. China (?) 2000 B.C.	originally woodland later near universal	meat and skin (and collecting truffles)	all races have been crossed

		Egypt … B.C.	with pastoralism (Babylonia 2000 B.C.)	1. carriage 2. riding 3. milk	mule with horse bred since *c.* 1500 B.C.
10. ONAGER	S.W. Asian steppes	Sumeria 3000 B.C.	(E) displaced by horse 1500 B.C.	haulage	as above but not always distinguished from feral asses
11. HORSE[1]	Eurasian steppes, tundra and forest	Caspian 2250 B.C.	with pastoralism to Egypt 1600 B.C. to China 1500 B.C.	1. meat 2. haulage 3. riding esp. in war 4. milk	races probably crossed while under selection
12. CAMEL (R)					
a. Dromedary (one-hump)	Arabia (E)	1200 B.C.[3]	N.W. Africa to India (southern)	1. carriage 2. riding 3. milk	Mules raised where the species overlap in Anatolia
b. Bactrian (two-hump)	C. Asia	500 B.C.	Anatolia to Mongolia (northern)	as above	
13. ELEPHANT					
a. Indian	Syria, India, China	Indus: 2500 B.C.	S. Asia	1. jungle haulage 2. battle	captured more often than bred in captivity
b. N. African (Carrington 1958)	N. Africa (E)	Egypt: 280 B.C.	Italy: Hannibal	battle only (E)	

[1] Existing originally in many wild races, ecological and geographical.

[2] The 'wild ass' or kiang of the Himalayan region is reckoned to be a species of horse.

[3] Reference in Genesis quoted by Zeuner is imaginative ante-dating Professor G. R. Driver tells me.

Notes: (i) All these species except the ass, the onager and the elephant have dominated the racial evolution of some of their most important domesticators (see Raglan 1939, 1962).

(ii) Dogs, cattle, pigs and camels have been independently domesticated at more than one site.

(iii) All the mules mentioned are F_1 hybrids which follow Haldane's Law, i.e. sterile in the male but partly fertile in the female, the homozygous sex.

(iv) Asses in Syria, pigs in Polynesia, Soay sheep in St Kilda, horses in New Mexico (mustangs) have gone wild or become 'feral'. In Australia most recently domesticated animals have generated feral populations, e.g. ass, water buffalo, camel, goat, pig, fox, rabbit, cat; and the Aboriginals' dog gave the feral dingo. (Grzimek 1967.)

(v) Nos. 2, 10 and 13 may be described in different senses as semi-domesticated. Only Nos. 9 and 13b are found in Africa.

R: Ruminant. E: Extinct as wild or as domesticated animals.

Beyond all these things domesticated animals also found themselves the object of selective breeding. Now the breeding of animals was more easily understood and more easily controlled than that of plants. It was indeed obviously understood by paleolithic man although the result, from keeping the best instead of killing the best, naturally reversed the effect of the hunter's selection from an early stage. It must therefore have been less unconscious and more purposeful. When he found cows and ewes that would release their milk to his handling, and other cattle that were docile enough to be harnessed to a plough and sheep that did not moult their incipient wool and could therefore be sheared rather than pulled, he would undoubtedly prefer them to the wild type and prefer to breed from them. And both his children and his cattle would multiply more quickly than the children and the cattle of his neighbour who had less skill or less sense. For in all this we must not fail to insert the proviso that this man, and his children, would have their advantage provided that they were sharp enough to see what had happened, to see the profit it could bring them and to know what action to take.

There was therefore in stockbreeding a scope of alertness and enterprise likely to create different opportunities from those which would arise in the course of the cultivation of crops. And they proved to be opportunities indeed, not only immediate opportunities for individuals but also self-exaggerating opportunities which carried forward whole families, tribes and peoples, the pastoral peoples.

III. THE NEW PEOPLE: FARMERS AND HERDSMEN

As the crops and the stock of the new farmers slowly multiplied, diversified and became adapted to their new uses so also did the farmers themselves. Like their crops and stock they were subject to selection. The vagaries of the climate, the difficulties of experimenting with new sites and new soils, the problems of dealing with their paleolithic neighbours, all these were tests of aptitude or, as we may say, of intelligence. But it was, above all, the utterly new problem of managing their new plant and animal resources which was bound to impose the severest selective stress on the new farmers. How did they react?

In the first place it is clear that after 4000 years of farming two new kinds of people emerged from this selective process. First, there were peasants, such as we see today in Kurdistan, who lived on permanent sites and depended on cultivation but also bred livestock. And, secondly, there were herdsmen who depended entirely on breeding livestock and shifted their pasturages with the season as they still do, moving into the moister and cooler mountains in the summer.

These two kinds of people were already beginning to show the characteristics that we know in them today, characteristics portrayed in the Biblical legend of the conflict of Cain the cultivator with his younger brother, Abel the stockbreeder. Both of these radically departed from the character of the contemporary paleolithic hunter, Enkidu, the man represented in the epic of Gilgamesh who had however disappeared from the scene in the later

Hebrew account of the evolution of mankind. The cultivator had learnt a patience and industry unknown to the hunter. He had acquired prudence, foresight and even avarice. He had learnt to know his land and to love what he knew. For he moved slowly and each little community of a couple of hundred people would constitute a durable breeding group.[1] But the fact that obsidian could be brought from mountains 200 miles to the north and shells from the distant gulf shows us that hunters had now become traders. Social relations were bound to give rise to breeding relations and the long process of hybridization between the neolithic and the paleolithic peoples which was to enrich both of them had begun.

Looking back on this momentous experience of the early farmers with our remote and somewhat unprejudiced eyes, we can see that what happened was that, just as the crops became adapted to the men (their men), so the men became adapted to the crops (their crops). The whole concern became one system. It became, like the genetic system of a species, fused into one evolutionary unit or entity whose parts are mutually dependent and come to be mutually adapted. Man-and-crop became one evolutionary system (Fig. 4).

This idea of the integration of the man with his environment can of course be expressed in mystical terms and the first person to do was the farmer himself who left the records of his beliefs in the religions of all his descendants. The notion of the Sky as the Father God and the Earth as the Mother Goddess spread with the expansion of the cultivators and their crops from the Nuclear Region.

For the farming peoples however the relations of the two sexes both in heaven and on earth underwent a dramatic change as the processes of farming themselves developed. In Chatal Hüyük at first we are shown a society in which women are the masters. They even have larger beds. But later, with the invention about the fourth millennium of a wooden plough drawn by the domesticated ox, and manageable only in the hands of a ploughman, the relative positions of the sexes, divine and human, are reversed. New peoples appear in which man is the master as he already was becoming among the herdsmen. The balance of the gods continually shifts like the fortunes of battle in the *Iliad*. And power rather than fertility begins to predominate.

Formerly it was taken for granted that the first stage in the advance of society was the domestication of animals. The transition, it was thought, from the hunter to the herdsman was so trifling. The evidence that this could not be so we owe directly to the archaeologists who showed the beginnings of agriculture. But it was the anthropologist, Lord Raglan, who pointed out (in 1962) the utter contrast between the hunter and the herdsman: the hunter with his bursts of furious activity interrupted by idleness and dissipation and the herdsman who devotes his youth and manhood to his cattle with devotion that he never spares and labours that never cease, morning, noon or night. That is why the care of cattle arose from the care of crops: it demands an even higher devotion. That is also why pure tribes which are not genetically herdsmen, whether they are paleolithic or neolithic in habit, cannot be

[1] There were indeed, according to Braidwood, twenty-four houses and twelve successive levels at Jarmo.

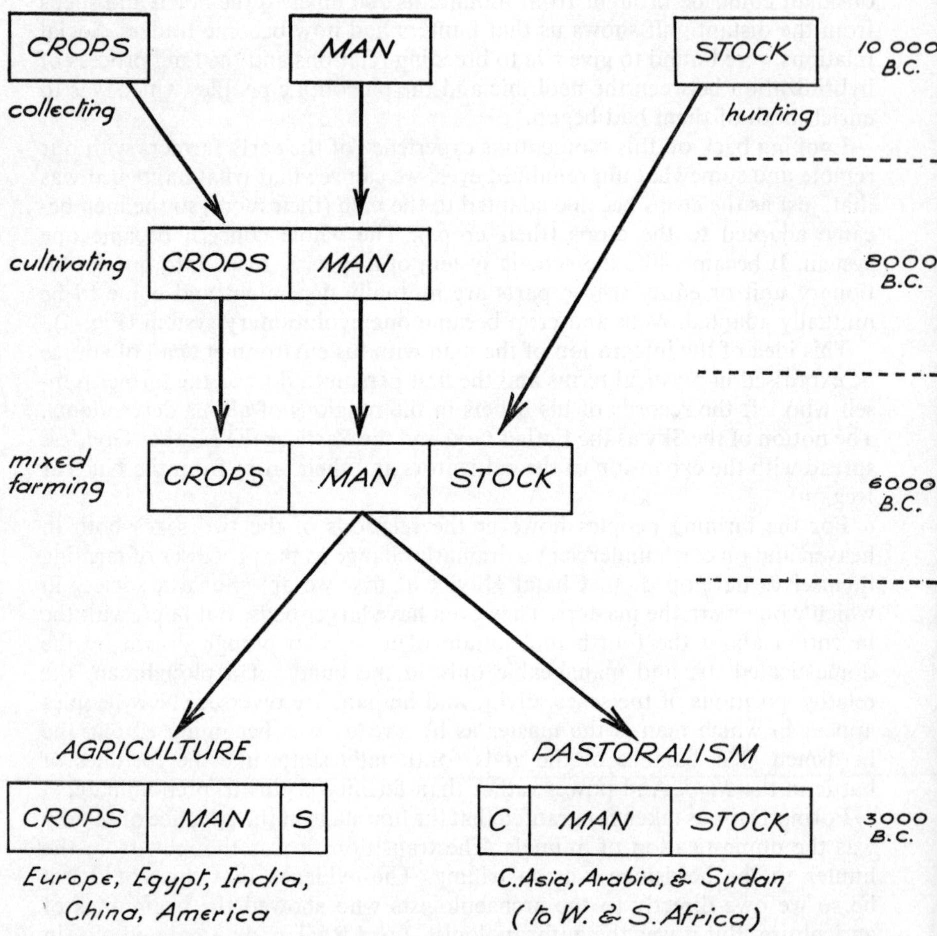

Fig. 5. Diagram showing the mutual selection of crops and man and of stock and man, giving, first, integrated farming and, later, specialized forms of farming with different rates of movements with consequent different distributions in space of agricultural and pastoral peoples arising over the period 10,000 to 3000 B.C.

persuaded to take up the labours and responsibilities of the pastoral life. Nor, conversely, can the pastoralist be persuaded to turn his hand to the heavier service of the soil.

Thus as with the crop and the cultivator in the domestication of cattle both parties to the transaction, both the animal and the herdsman, are transformed.

The two are by steps mutually selected and mutually adapted. But, if the process of domestication is always reciprocal, it is not always equal. The reindeer may be regarded as semi-domesticated since its migrations, its feeding and its breeding are almost uncontrolled. The Lapp who follows these migrations is, however, fully dependent on them and may therefore be said to be more fully domesticated than his own herd. On the other hand the Bedouin (described by Thesiger), who sew up the anus of the refractory camel to make her let down her milk, suggest to us that neither the camel nor they themselves are entirely domesticated.

The extreme attachment of the herdsman to his animals has often led to extreme specialization in his choice of stock. The Lapps with their reindeer, the Bedouin with their camels, the Masai with their cattle, not for meat but for milk and blood, the Scythians, Huns and Mongols, often with a sole attachment to the horse, all these have a character related to their animals. To this highly successful adaptation, man, as we might expect, has contributed even more than the animal. The extraordinary success of later conquerors relying on the horse or the camel is clearly one of the results.

The different kinds of herdsmen diverged from one another as well as from the cultivator who later came to use animals in his cultivation for ploughing and carting. The herdsmen developed the character, the instincts and the intelligence, as Galton and Raglan observed, necessary for success in the different undertakings on which their livelihood depended.

As the domestication of each species proceeded the herdsmen migrated and were led into new habitats. The aims of their selection and consequent mode of evolution were again bound to change and diverge.

In moving through Asia and Europe both the herdsman and the herd encountered and hybridized with undomesticated or wild races of their species. In Africa however the hybridization was slight. As we shall see later, the Hamitic races pushed to the south and west of the continent, hybridizing little with native peoples. Both for their cattle and for themselves hybridization occurred only later when the humped cattle and their herdsmen entered from India, the Yemen and Abyssinia.

The introduction of new races of animals by hybridization of the cultivated and the wild was analogous with the same processes in plants. But there was obviously nothing analogous to the unconscious displacement of a crop by its weeds. On the contrary new animals must have been picked up and deliberately domesticated. This happened both to the camel and to the horse in the hands of herdsmen. But it was cultivators who, having lost their original cattle, domesticated the native cattle of India and Burma, the humped zebu, the gaur, the banteng and, above all, the water buffalo. Thereafter herdsmen carried the zebu into Africa and the rest into Indonesia and China.

IV. THE NEOLITHIC EXPANSION

The neolithic peoples of the Nuclear Region expanding after the sixth millennium in all directions encountered varied new conditions. Climate, soil and vegetation gave them opportunities of occupying river valley or steppe, woodland or forest, and forced on to them new crops which they had unknowingly acquired. Paleolithic neighbours and wild animals, all alike changed and confronted them with new dangers and new choices. It was from this diversity of situations that the great variety of types of modern farming have arisen by means and with consequences which are plainly to be seen today. They are all means and consequences in which evolution is concerned that is to say genetic change in men, in crops and in stock. It is evolution on a scale and with a speed unprecedented in human history.

The results that we see are the creation of communities of five main types. First, there is the early mixed kind of community in which grain and other crops are grown and are used in part to feed animals which also help in the cultivation. Secondly, there is the even earlier type of community of the pure grain farmer with little or no livestock. Among these there is a sharp divergence between the people who slash and burn, exhaust the soil and move on; and those who drain and irrigate, conserve the soil and settle on it. It is a divergence between the short-sighted who become more so and the prudent who also become more so.

And thirdly there is the pure stock farmer, the herdsman or pastoralist raising few or no crops. He in turn exists in all degrees of specialization. He may raise many kinds of stock. Or he may specialize, as we saw, on one kind.

Thus out of the first communities of farmers and after some four or five thousand years of selective development and evolution, combined with local hybridization, there emerged new kinds of people scattered over Nuclear Asia who cultivated a wide range of crops, bred a range of livestock and made their living in the mountains and the plains, on the edge of the forest and of the desert. The new communities depended sometimes purely on breeding one or several kinds of livestock, sometimes on mixed farming, sometimes perhaps purely on cultivation. They also traded in minerals and other special products with tribes which were now attaching themselves to the profits of this new mode of existence. In other words there were new incipient races of men which had come to differ from the earlier paleolithic races in the course of over a hundred generations of selection. The size of the communities, the density of the populations and the speed of evolution had all increased.

In these circumstances it is remarkable that the new types of man did not expand and move out of the narrow Nuclear Area more quickly than they did. The apparently silent millennia had however been occupied with a number of difficult technical adjustments of need and invention. First among these we may place the establishment of new grain-based industries. Their connections in time and space and with the different kinds of grain are still conjectural but they must be noted if we are to measure either their causes or their effects.[1]

The following are the most significant series:

(i) Bread wheat was connected with grinding and baking and therefore with the use of hot stones and later of ovens and also of yeast for leavening the bread.

[1] The subject has been introduced by Braidwood and others (1960).

(ii) Barley was connected with malting and the brewing of beer which led to the production of the yeast needed for baking.
(iii) Oats, rice and millet were connected with boiling which required pottery whose invention (like that of metal-smelting) was naturally connected with the use of ovens.
(iv) Fruit-growing was connected with fermentation by yeast and the making of wine, for which gourds rather than pottery could be used (Oppenheim, 1960).

These and many other connections were established during the little known ages. Their consequences are to be seen from the fact that pottery was invented on the same northern side of the Nuclear Zone where bread wheat, as opposed to emmer, was first grown. And pottery, having been invented, spread in advance of wheat and even of agriculture: it was separated by its later uses from the conditions which had favoured its origin.

The long delay of the silent millennia was also a measure of the varied genetic and evolutionary changes that had to be brought about before agriculture could spread to new climates. It was a measure of the severity of the selection that had to be applied to the new races of farmers and also to the races of crops and stock on which their farming depended. It was only then that the new peoples could break out of their accustomed climates and latitudes. It was only in the fifth and fourth millennia B.C. that they were prepared to invade Egypt, India and Northern Europe.

The dates of the earliest settlements in the new countries can only be surmised. We can be certain however that the valley of the Indus, the mountains of Abyssinia, and the island of Britain were all reached before 3000 B.C. They were all reached by farmers, spearheads of the neolithic advance, who had adapted themselves to new climates by hybridizing with hunting and collecting peoples. These were the endemic geographical races of paleolithic men that the new people had met in friendly, sociable and sexual encounter on their path of colonization. For this was the first time in history that tribes or races of people who met one another were of necessity complementary and helpful to one another.[1]

In consequence of this mixture of peoples there were altogether new types of tribe coming into existence everywhere along the advancing frontier of colonization. The method of shifting agriculture by slashing and burning the forest was practised by some. It damaged the soil as far afield as Britain.[2] Pastoralism with seasonal movement of cattle was practised by others. The transfer of women by capture from agricultural to fishing and collecting tribes, that is from the neolithic to the paleolithic, led to the production of peoples who had learnt their trades and also inherited their skills from both stocks. Their hereditary character, their talents and limitations, enabled them to carry over a part of their ancestral cultures from both sides. Thus the

[1] This encounter is reflected in the legend of the Tower of Babel and the confusion of tongues which survived in both Nuclear Areas and were handed down both to the Hebrews and the Aztecs (L. E. M.). It was first discussed archaeologically by Sir Thomas Kendrick in 1925 and Bibby has given an illuminating account of the evidence.

[2] Dimbleby (1962).

midden folk of Jutland in the third millennium were able to make crude pottery although they could not polish flints. Similarly, as we shall see, in both Africa and China pastoralism as well as the making of pottery could run ahead of agriculture.

These products of neo-paleo hybridization are significant for the development of culture since they show the universal dependence of the exchange and transmission of ideas and aptitudes on the exchange and transmission of genes. Now, unless the conditions of propagation of small populations are extremely favourable some of the components of their culture are always lost.[1]

On the advancing frontier conditions were, of course, far from favourable. Many remarkable new devices were invented to preserve the immigrants, like the lake-dwellings which, as we shall see, occupied sites all over central Europe. The first neolithic invaders of Britain, like the lake-dwellers, are believed to have come, not from the advance up the Danube basin, but from Africa by way of France. They had thus already been selected twice for their ability in building and in navigating boats across the open sea, a problem that the Danubian peoples had so far avoided. The paleolithic people found already in Britain and Ireland must in part have arrived before the sea broke through although others perhaps had crossed the sea.

Everywhere the geographical races of paleolithic people made the essential local contribution to the character of peoples which has persisted in Europe, Asia and North Africa down to the present day. This is shown by the characteristic distribution of blood group frequencies which persist to the present day.[2] Indeed, in a limited sense, the spread of agricultural peoples crystallized the paleolithic peoples in the mould into which they had cast themselves in the movements of the receding ice age.

V. THE HABITAT

Paleolithic man, as we suppose, was adjusted genetically and instinctively to his habitat. It was a habitat which changed slowly through the alterations of the climate. And apart from the animals he killed it hardly changed at all through his own evolution or his own exertions. He took care in the ways we have seen to keep the numbers of his descendants stable. As a rule, although not always, he also took care not to destroy the animals and plants on which these descendants would rely for their subsistence.

Neolithic man was faced with a new kind of situation in several ways. In the first place the climate was changing unusually fast. The storm belt which had watered the steppe lands of both Arabia and North Africa, of Sindh, the Tarim Basin and the future Gobi desert, was moving northwards. Vast regions which were open to the pasturage of the earliest herdsmen were therefore drying up. Throughout the Mediterranean the rainfall had declined.

[1] The basic study of the loss of culture in primitive communities we owe to Lord Raglan (1939): see ch. 27.

[2] For example with the central B maximum and the peripheral O maximum described in his world survey of blood groups by Mourant (1962).

Under these conditions, which repeated the events at the ends of earlier ice ages, the forests around the Nuclear Area would have provided a vast reservoir of water. For it has been estimated that forests feed the rainfall by their evaporation about as copiously as the same areas of ocean. And the roots of the trees protect the hillside soil from being washed away. But with the coming of agriculture all this was changed.

The pioneer cultivator, needing more land, felled the trees that bordered his fields. Often he prudently saved the specimens he valued. So it was that the vine and the olive, the fig and the walnut, the almond and the cherry, came into cultivation. It still happens so today in Anatolia. But sometimes, as we have seen, with less foresight he felled the whole forest. He even burnt the forest; he still does that also. Moreover, when he needed timber for houses, for boats and for fuel, fuel for heating, cooking, baking pottery and later smelting, he again felled trees. We see the problem and the policy which solved it expressed in the second millennium B.C. in its simplest terms. It was Joshua who said to the children of Joseph, 'If Mount Ephraim be too narrow for thee (and if thou be a great people) get thee up to the wood country and cut down for thyself there' (Joshua 17: 15). In this way the forest lands of the Mediterranean have been reduced in 6000 years from nearly a million square miles to a tenth of their former range. The buffer against climatic change has been steadily and unremittingly removed.

The consequences of tree felling were diverse. Hot and dry countries were dried up more quickly and quite irremediably. Hilly countries had the soil washed off the hillsides. Wet and cold countries, notably Britain, were ruined by lack of drainage. What had been forest became ploughed land; and in Ireland the ploughed land, no longer drained, became peat bog in which scores of monuments of the second millennium B.C. now lie buried.[1]

Later cultivators on the frontier made matters worse for themselves by reckless slash-and-burn methods. But in the Nuclear Region the slow early development seems to have been more prudent. Or, perhaps we should say, the imprudent cultivators were the ones who did not survive. The prudent ones were those intelligent enough to hoe and later to plough *en corniche*, along the contours.

The first steps in irrigation must be looked for in the early processes of hoe-tillage which gave rise to contour hoeing and ploughing and hence inevitably to terraces. These often demanded the support of stone walls. They also often provided for channels carrying water to the crops of the kinds still commonly seen in the Ancient East.

The terracing of hillside cultivation for the preservation of both the soil and the water that fell on it must have come very early. The evidence of its antiquity is provided by its linguistic connections.[2] The earliest Semites connected the planting of vines with the piling up of terraces. This probably happened in the sixth millennium B.C. and preceded the movement of cultivators into the valley bottoms.

[1] See Evans' and also Glacken's summaries in Thomas (1956). Also Jacks and Whyte (1939), Lowdermilk (1946), Glesinger (1960), and Dimbleby (1967).

[2] See Pfeiffer in Thomas (General) p. 251; also note ch. 9.3.

Terrace cultivation spread wherever the advancing cultivators tried to work on steep hillsides. The same system which we find on the hillsides of the Rhine valley and in the strip lynchets of Britain was independently established in Peru long before the time of the Incas. With it went channelling and control of water and the development of irrigation first in the valley bottoms of Mesopotamia and Egypt. Later, with the discovery of rice in the Ganges delta, came the wonderful organization of the wet paddy fields in terraces which spread into South East Asia. This system reached its climax in the Philippine island of Luzon. Beginning about 700 B.C. stone terraces were built on a vast scale. The stone walls making soil-and-water dams up to eighteen feet high are still repaired and maintained today with soil carried uphill in baskets by the Ifaguo tribe. These enterprises parallel the massive dyke building achievements of the Netherlands which possibly began at the same time and certainly have the same ancestry in the Nuclear Region of Asia.

Rice cultivation in the wet paddy fields has always been able to maintain itself against interference. This is partly because the cultivator has been protected by his walls and his water from the disturbances of war. The same is true of irrigation in Egypt.[1] But in Mesopotamia the situation has been less favourable and more exposed. Invaders have destroyed the canals often with the industrious people who maintained them. The irrigating waters have silted up the dykes. And their evaporation has salted up the lands for reasons that the early cultivators could not well have foreseen. In these ways some of the richest lands in the world have been first impoverished and then forsaken.

The effects of cultivation on the land have thus been diverse: beneficial or destructive subject to the diverse actions of different climates, crops, soils, peoples and their complex interactions. The same cannot be said of the effects of pastoralism.

The herdsman, in early times, was expanding his range and expanding it with greater freedom and greater speed than the settled cultivator. Sometimes he occupied the land that had been ruined by cultivation; but more often he ruined it himself. Moving between the desert and the sown, his goats and later his camels could destroy the dwindling vegetation and prepare for the advance of the blown sand. The expansion of the Sahara over most of the last 4000 years is to be attributed to this terrible process of attrition and its continuance may be witnessed today in South and East as well as in North Africa.

The herdsman has not been content to allow his stock to destroy the herbage. Since before the time of Diodorus Siculus the goatherds in Italy have burnt the forest to extend their grazing. And in the highlands of Scotland Fraser Darling has shown how the sheep have been brought to do in the north what in the south was the work of the goat and the camel.

These processes, some creative and some destructive, have arisen from the invention of agriculture and stockbreeding and the rapid increase in the human

[1] It is also true of the lakeside *chinampas* of the central valley of Mexico which were established at the end of the first millennium B.C. Here skilful nursery techniques have preserved the land from salting. They provided the technical and material basis for the rulers of the Aztec Empire and still today furnish seven crops in a year (Coe, 1964, *ref* ch. 25).

population which ensued. In all his previous evolution, since it did not destroy him, we must suppose that the destructive consequences of man's inventions—his progress, as we usually describe it—must have been kept within measure by the kinds of genetic change involving population control, which we have examined. These genetic changes operated through instinctive and physiological processes. Now however rational processes had taken the lead in giving man suddenly an unprecedented control, for good or ill, over his environment.

The prodigious step forward that had been taken had suddenly released the cultivators from a large part of the pressure of natural selection which had previously maintained the instinctive standards of behaviour to be expected in a wild animal. New standards based on reason and foresight had not been established. How could they have been? The peasant and the herdsman could now look ahead a whole year. Later extraordinarily gifted men would appear (according to the Biblical legend of Joseph) who could look ahead seven years. Astronomically they would soon be able to foretell the lunar cycles of eighteen years. But to look ahead agriculturally for several human generations was too much to expect of the newly developed rational faculties. Indeed we cannot confidently expect it today.

The period which began with the great expansion of agriculture, a period which has lasted 9000 years, has been a period fraught with peril owing to the difficulties inherent in replacing instinctive by rational processes. This replacement has been going on, we may suppose, for a million years. But it is only during the last stage that it has threatened us with disaster. We shall soon see how this pattern of conflict between reason and instinct repeats itself.

5

BABYLONIA

I. THE COLONIZATION OF MESOPOTAMIA

By THE MIDDLE OF THE SEVENTH MILLENNIUM B.C. the earliest cultivators with their grain, pulse, and other improved crops had spread in all directions except north. They had moved westwards to Thessaly and Macedonia and across the sea to Cyprus; southwards through Syria and along the Jordan valley and in a small outlier they had reached the Faiyum oasis in Egypt; and eastwards they had gone deep into the Persian tableland. They had begun to form settlements in all these areas. Their hoes, sickles, querns and storage pits show the success of their cultivation. And the bones of goats, sheep and cattle show the value of their domesticated animals for food. During the next millennium and a half (6500 B.C. to 5000 B.C.) the great advance, the great inventions, were made on which civilization was going to be built. What were they?

First, there was the spinning of textiles, first wool and then flax, in Anatolia. With the spinning went the weaving already foreshadowed by the basket work of paleolithic man. Secondly, there was the invention of pottery probably in southern Anatolia. Thirdly, there was the working of stone and baking of brick for the building of houses.

These inventions spread over the whole of our agricultural heartland. They spread slowly. Pottery spread less than 1000 miles in more than a thousand years. The reason for this slowness was probably that the new inventions depended on the activities of the bulk of an undifferentiated people. They moved only by the movement of a whole people, that is to say of a tribe of cultivators. There were however products or side-lines of these activities which moved quickly. When copper came to be smelted, perhaps in the highlands of Anatolia, in the sixth millennium it quickly appeared over the whole area. Cyprus quickly came to be valued for the ore which it has yielded ever since. And when someone discovered how to paint pottery at about the same place and the same time the new art was spread within a few hundred years over the whole heartland. The painter was later to become a writer and his varying designs projected the use of symbols from a magical past into a practical and literate future.

Such rapid movements were a sign that paleolithic tribes like those which had made their living by trading in flint and obsidian were now making their living by new specialized activities. These mobile people were making themselves useful to the sedentary neolithic communities whose growing stability and prosperity were thus beginning to communicate themselves to a variety of racial groups which were economically dependent but socially independent.

Now in the period from 5000 B.C. to 3500 B.C. there was no great expansion of our heartland. Nor was there any great development in the size or character of the settlements (Table 2). What was the reason for this pause? There was

Table 2. *The Sizes of Ancient Settlements and Cities*
After Mumford (1961) and others

Site	*District*	*Area (acres)*	*Population (estd.)*	*Date*	*Author*
JARMO	Kurdistan	3·5	150	7000 B.C.	Braidwood
CHATAL HÜYÜK	Cappadocia	32	2000	6000 B.C.	Mellaart
JERICHO	Palestine	8	2000	6000 B.C.	Kenyon
KHIROKITIA	Cyprus	15	1500	5500 B.C.	Mellaart
OLD UR	Sumeria	220	34,000	2800 B.C.	Woolley
URUK	Sumeria	1100	50,000	3000 B.C.	R. M. Adams
GREATER UR	Sumeria	1300	250,000	2200 B.C.	Woolley
MOHENJO-DARU	Indus	600		2000 B.C.	Piggott
MEGIDDO	Palestine	3·5		1600 B.C.	
GURNIA	Crete	6·5		1400 B.C.	
MYCENAE (CITADEL)	Greece	12		1200 B.C.	Schliemann
KARKEMISH	Syria	140		1200 B.C.	
NINEVEH	Assyria	1800	120,000[1]	600 B.C.	Layard
BABYLON	Babylonia	1060	200,000	500 B.C.	Saggs 1965

[1] Plausibly estimated by Jonah 4: 11 (O.T.).

one main reason. The early agricultural people had expanded to the limits of the region to which they and the crops and stock on which they lived were ecologically and climatically adapted. Fortification at Jericho in the sixth millennium and at Mersin in Anatolia in 4500 B.C. indicates the stress of expanding populations which were unable to burst out of a confined area. It also means fighting and after each conflict the mixing and hybridization of peoples, victors and vanquished.

It was not until they could control the water of the great rivers for irrigation that they were able to occupy the richer lands of the valleys and support settlements of more than a couple of thousand people. The custom of contour ploughing had led, as we saw, before the origins of the Semitic peoples, to the building up of walled terraces for cultivation which in turn led to the building of dams and sluices and works of irrigation which were designed to save both the soil and the water.

Control of water was probably connected with several other discoveries, the use of the ox for ploughing and later the ass for carrying the earth, the alloying of bronze and its use in tools, and the use of writing, discoveries which were stretching, testing and subjecting to natural selection new technical and intellectual potentialities of the mind in the new peoples. These developments occupied the fifth and fourth millennia.

Meanwhile from the purely biological side there was another series of limitations which had to be overcome. Men had never before lived in large groups. As we have seen, neither their fertility nor their freedom from disease could be guaranteed under crowded conditions. Settled agricultural people are generally cleaner than hunters or herdsmen. This is the result of new habits of avoiding pollution of water and new degrees of cleanliness, themselves a symptom of instinctive habits favoured by natural selection during those early testing times. They were habits which were later to be systematically taught and religiously inculcated. Side by side with these new practices, genetic resistance to new parasites and new diseases were no doubt also being acquired by natural selection.

These difficulties were first faced and partly met as the hill people moved into the growing delta of the Tigris and Euphrates rivers. During the fifth millennium B.C. they occupied larger and larger sites as they improved both their methods of engineering and their crops and stock. In the middle of the fourth millennium they began to settle and to build the first cities in the flat marshy plain which later became known as Sumer. Here they found a complex of natural canals, an immense field for ploughing by oxen, vast supplies of reeds for building and of fish, and above all the date palm to be transplanted for food to new and drier lands.[1]

There was, however, one other great process that they invented, and indeed had to invent, in the course of this movement. This was the process of creating a new and more complex society, a stratified society. For the evidence of how they did it we have to draw on our whole knowledge, both earlier and later, of man and society.

II. ORIGIN AND EXPANSION OF SUMERIA

The cities of Sumer occupy a dozen well-known sites in the delta where the Euphrates and the Tigris used to meet the Persian Gulf before they met one another. During the fourth millennium, owing no doubt to the skill of the people in watering and tilling the soil, these cities increased and surpassed in size and wealth all earlier settlements. Their development occurred in a series of stages which have been named after the places where they were first brought to light.

First, there was the stage of Ubaid in which flint implements and hand-made pottery dominate the scene. Secondly, there was the stage of Uruk (Erech of

[1] Wilfred Thesiger has described the place and the people as they are today; Woolley and Mallowan have described the excavations.

Genesis, Warka of today) when a wave of peaceful colonizers brought in the fast-spinning potter's wheel and natural alloys of bronze.

These two invasions evidently came from the mountains by different routes and fused together to make a single people under a priestly government. They were a people who must have spoken a language which we know as Sumerian, a language which, since it was the first to be written, has no known antecedents; and, as a whole, also no descendants.

A third wave of invaders were again strangers. By later analogy they were probably pastoral people, for they came as conquerors who subdued the native peoples; and by subduing united them as subjects or sometimes as rebels. Legend gives them a southern origin and fathers upon them the invention of all the arts. By the time they were overthrown, about 3000 B.C., the whole country had been transformed. In place of priestly governments there were now warlike kings sharing ceremonial authority and material wealth with the gods with whom they had compromised and partly displaced. Writing was now established and dynastic history was beginning to be written.

The cities of Sumer were dominated by temples, the towering *ziggurats* which came over a period of 2000 years to be superimposed on the same site in each city. It is a habit which has always been followed by religious foundations. In them the picture-writing developed showing such things and numbers as had first been seen in 3500 B.C. Soon there appeared sculptures, figurines, and seal reliefs representing gods, priests, kings, soldiers, captives and wild and domesticated animals. These designs illustrated religious, military and civil ceremonies which were conducted either in the open with chariots drawn by onagers or in temples and houses. Such buildings were first made of mud bricks, later of burnt bricks; over a thousand years they came to be more and more elaborately furnished.

These works, both large and small, demonstrate the great business of organization going on in the new cities. This was obvious from their very size and sustained existence. The main part in this work of social organization, involving administration and education as well as religion, was centred in the priesthood and conducted by the priests, that is by a particular social group, a literate and intellectual class. For the first time the written documents show us the stratification of society although no doubt such stratification had already existed for a couple of millennia or more in earlier cities without writing.

This priesthood recognized the superior authority throughout Sumer of a single centre, the holy city of Nippur. Thus the whole group of cities were bound together by religion in spite of the wars which later separated them, wars conducted by their divided military rulers, their royal dynasties. Later the priesthood of Nippur must have sponsored or supported the rule of one Sumerian city over all the rest. The priests must have come to terms with the warriors as the gods had come to terms with the kings in establishing a principle of imperial government. This situation has repeated itself again and again in later history owing to the mutual usefulness of opposed classes with religious and with military authority.

The growth of war and of the 'great men' who led in war changed the character of city life. Now we see fortifications. We also see the activities of soldiers in victory and defeat. We see captives brought in procession to the king. What happened to them? At first no doubt they were slaughtered. But later somebody discovered that defeated enemies could be more useful to the victor if they were kept alive than if they were killed. A new social class was created, a class of slaves. It was a class that could be further expanded by capture when the paleolithic and pastoral mountain tribes were raided for both men and women slaves. The dynastic texts show that the sales of slaves became more numerous after 3000 B.C.

This discovery or invention of slavery was one of the critical steps in the development of society. Its beginning was favoured by the existence of agriculture. But its growth must have been favoured by the existence of city societies with a wide range of employments. Of these the most important were the socially organized works of long-term value such as the building of temples and of canals; to these later were to be added the mining of metal ores, the rowing of galleys, and the building of roads.

Through the writings of the priests we learn of the other classes in Sumerian city society.[1] There were traders and artisans connected with the supply and working of the timber, metal ores, and other minerals which came down the slow and safe Euphrates (or copper river) from Anatolia in exchange for grain. When cities sprang up near the Mediterranean bend of the Euphrates they showed the influence of the craftsmen of Sumer.[2] The business of making cities thus spread from Sumer. It spread up the river, and more slowly into the Persian highlands. And it spread, not like agriculture or pottery, as a slow mass movement but, like the finer arts, as a trade or class movement. Now clearly the sections of society were separable. The cultivators were relatively fixed; the city people were relatively mobile. To the paleolithic and neolithic expansions a new kind of movement, a class or caste expansion, had succeeded.

The Sumerian expansion is the prototype of all later class expansions. It is almost invisible as compared with the mass expansions which followed as well as preceded it. The numbers of people concerned were very few. But they were the ancestors of very many, and if we look at them carefully we see their significant and far-reaching effects. The men who took socketed axes from Sumer to the west of Anatolia, probably Troy, prepared the way for vast

[1] A temple archive in a Sumerian parish of 1200 workers classifies them as follows:

25 scribes
20 craftsmen { carpenters and smiths; potters, leather and stone workers; mat and basket weavers }
80 soldiers and labourers
90 herdsmen
100 fishermen
250–300 slaves

(R. M. Adams (1960); see also Mallowan, Derry and Williams.)

[2] Woolley (1961) and Mallowan (1961).

movements a few hundred years later in the Danube basin. They also prepared the way for the cutting of masonry and the sailing of ships which would soon be seen in Egypt and in Cretan waters, as well as in the Persian Gulf and on the great River Indus. The men who first studied astronomy and practised writing in Sumer propagated the calendar makers and scribes who instructed the priests of Egypt and the merchants of Ugarit and Byblos. The earliest pictograms of Sumer were 2000 in number in about 3200 B.C. By 2900 B.C. they had been reduced to 500 syllabic characters which were now cuneiform or wedge-cut figures made in clay. The hieroglyphics in the Egyptian King Narmer's palette of 3100 B.C. are therefore probably still sacred symbols. They had been adapted, varied, and carried across from Sumeria by a priestly group.

Similarly groups of craftsmen must have taken the fast-spinning potter's wheel to India and west to Egypt and later to Greece. Other groups took the other larger wheel that was derived from it. This was not an expansion of rulers who imposed a language or established an empire. It was an expansion of technicians, scribes and mathematicians, usually at that time attached to the society of priests and the management of temples. But their descendants proved to be the differentiated classes of artisans and of intellectuals of the western world.

III. GILGAMESH

The archaeological evidence of the origin of civilization in Sumer may be compared with the poetic record. The epic of the priest-king Gilgamesh was recited and elaborated perhaps for a thousand years before it was set down in many versions, Sumerian and Babylonian, which survive today. It tells the story of the conflict between the city peoples and the wild men of mountain and desert. It also tells of the conflicts between men and gods who were the gods served in common by the priests and peoples of all Mesopotamia. And it tells of conflicts between men and the forces of nature, above all the flood, a disaster of which friendly gods warn the favoured ones who were to survive it.

This and other Sumerian myths are obviously close to the common origins of legends handed down to and by the Hebrews and the Greeks. They contain the same moral lessons of pride and punishment and they also represent the painful seductions, the intermittent catastrophes which marked the growth of the earliest societies from savagery to civil life. Note especially how the Sumerian Noah takes craftsmen on to his boat knowing, as the earliest Hebrews did not, that the skilled worker was indispensable for the maintenance of civilized, that is city, life.

Some have suggested and others denied that the Sumerians have understood the processes of the evolution of society better than their more sophisticated successors. But the evidence was much more clearly presented to them. The steps they had to retrace were fewer and more recent and less mysterious. The wild man whom they bring on the stage to re-enact history was still present in the hills and the desert around them unspoilt by their civilization and still worshipping gods not very distant from their own. Indeed more than this: he and his womenfolk were continually being captured and enslaved by the men of the cities who could even in part understand his speech.

The problem of what myth has to do with history will return to us again and again. As we move away from this point of earliest contact however we may reflect on the deep simplicity of the words in which these men recorded their wonder at the world they were beginning to explore:

'This too was the work of Gilgamesh, the king, who knew the countries of the world. He was wise; he saw mysteries and knew secret things; he brought us a tale of the days before the flood. He went a long journey, was weary, worn out with labour, and returning engraved on a stone the whole story.'

(*trans. N. K. Sanders*, 1960)

IV. THE MOVEMENT OF CIVILIZATION

In the two thousand years following the establishment of the Royal Dynasties in Ur and the first flowering of Sumerian civilization we see a series of transformations in the government of Mesopotamia. They are at first sight bewildering. They show three aspects. First, there is the movement of the centres of civilization and empire northwards. Secondly, there is the replacement of Sumerian as the language of government by Semitic forms of speech spoken by the peoples of the desert or steppe. Thirdly, there is the unification of larger, more powerfully organized regions as the empires of successive military rulers.

Side by side with these transformations there was a stability of beliefs, of techniques, of linguistic forms and of the organization of society often paralleled later in Asia although never in Europe. How did this come about?

Take first the northward movement.[1] After a thousand years of irrigation the lands of Sumer began to suffer from the accumulation of salt. At first the deterioration was met by the substitution of the poor crop of barley for the more valuable crop of wheat. Later the centre of wealth inevitably moved north to fresher lands in Babylonia and beyond. At the same time the development of the mineral wealth of Anatolia, Armenia and Persia led to an increasing use of metals in peace and war. It was reflected in the strengthening of the hill peoples, first to the north in Assyria, and later in Elam, whose capital Susa was to become the first capital of the Persian Empire.

The basic discoveries which followed from the invention of pottery depended on the use of the furnace in smelting metal ores, first copper, then bronze, then iron hardened by carburation. All of these inevitably were the inventions of men living where the ores were found in the mountains of Armenia and Persia. Their results reached Mesopotamia in succession about 3000, 2600 and 1300 B.C.[2]

[1] Refer for the agricultural evidence to Jacobson and Adams (1959); for the economic consequences to Mallowan (1961); for the political and commercial history to Saggs (1965).

[2] These same metal workers it was, no doubt, who descended into Sumeria and made a parallel invention, that of glass-making, which appeared about 2500 B.C., whence it was taken to Egypt a thousand years later in the days of the New Kingdom.

The remote origin of iron led to its scarcity in Mesopotamia which is revealed by the relative values of metals in 1760 B.C. at Mari on the mid-Euphrates (according to Saggs):

IRON = 120; GOLD = 60; SILVER = 15; LEAD = 1

The metallurgy of the mountains thus gave an advantage to the people in the north. It was their hardened steel which, a thousand years later, is supposed to have given its strength to the Assyrian cohorts and laid the foundations of their Empire. But it was this steel also from which the ploughshares of their peasants were forged and new and more difficult soils in the hills were brought under cultivation.

The improvement of cutting tools also led no doubt to the shearing of wool. Another cutting operation which probably developed at this time could however have been accomplished just as well with flint implements or with the teeth. This was the castration of ram lambs, which led only too soon to the castration of boys and men, indebted, captive or otherwise enslaved. This practice, as we shall see, was to influence the evolution of societies down to our own time.

What happened in Mesopotamia in general was a refinement and elaboration and combination of techniques invented elsewhere. But throughout the history of Mesopotamia technical invention continued to retain the respect of a society to whom abstract thought was still without verbal connotation. Priests and kings were equally close to the technical problems of agriculture, war and trade until the end of the Babylonian Empire. Sennacherib the Assyrian boasted of his reforms directed to improving mining, metalwork and irrigation. He was perhaps the last great monarch to claim the priority of his scientific inventions.

Thus the failure of the soil and the remoteness from metal sources impoverished the south of Mesopotamia and moved the centres of wealth and power into the north. To bring this about it was not necessary for peasant populations to move. All that was necessary was for them to multiply in the north and to fail to multiply in the south. The people who moved were the same classes who had been moving in the Sumerian expansion: the craftsmen, the priests, the administrators and the rulers. Talent, in the shape of people with superior gifts, always flies from an impoverished country to a new and potentially richer country. And that is why the centre of civilization moved slowly away from its Sumerian origin: as it has indeed been moving almost ever since.

V. THE POLITICAL SUCCESSION

From the beginning the Sumerian cities were subject to attack from the west by shepherd tribes; their flocks shifting from summer to winter, as they still do, grazed the steppe land which has now become the near-desert of Arabia. These tribes, whose descendants are the Bedouin of today, were the original speakers of the Semitic languages. To them Mesopotamia, the land between the two rivers, was Iraq, the border of the desert. The bow, with its stone-headed arrow, was their weapon and like all pastoral people they controlled their numbers and their wealth by fighting: by raiding one another's flocks. In the war between the tribesmen and the city people the tribesmen wanted and took food, goods and treasure; the city people took prisoners of whom they made slaves: slaves who sometimes became masters. The city society was thus continually enriched by new stocks of value especially in fighting. Ultimately, not in Sumer, but on the northern frontier, the intruding people, the intruding language, and a particular intruding ruler, took control.

The ruler was Sharrum-kin or Sargon the Great as we call him. He set up his capital at Akkad, an unknown site near Babylon, on the northern border of Sumer and in the narrow neck of Mesopotamia. Sargon's revolution gives us the first exact date in our record: 2371 B.C. It was the foundation of an Akkadian Empire.

The new King of Akkad persuaded by his merchants, according to Albright, invaded Anatolia in the north and conquered Sumer in the south. He then claimed to have mastered the whole land 'from the Upper Sea to the Lower Sea'; that is from the Mediterranean to the Persian Gulf. For the first time in history a great territory was governed from one centre in one city. A new governing class of fighting men speaking the Semitic language of the pastoral peoples was after many vicissitudes imposed on the whole of Mesopotamia.

The government of Sargon's family was overthrown 130 years later by the attacks of other barbarous pastoral peoples. Semitic-speaking desert tribes, known to their enemies as Amorites, occupied Akkadia and Elamite mountaineers conquered the revived cities of Sumeria. But Sargon's empire had introduced new possibilities of movement and exchange, co-operation and government which have never since been extinguished. The possibilities were realized and exploited by the rulers of a new capital, Babylon (the Gate or Meeting Place of the Gods). Their dynasty lasted for 300 years (Table 3) and is known to us chiefly through its greatest king, Hammurabi (1792–1750). This man was great, not so much in the extent of his conquests which were moderate, or of his kingdom, which was only one of many federal fragments of Sargon's empire, but in its exact, responsible and consequently prosperous, organization.

The first Babylonian Empire (although not the city itself) was repeatedly submerged under new invasions. The attacks came now, not from the Semitic desert shepherds, but from the mountaineers. These people were equipped with new weapons: first with horses and chariots and secondly with iron weapons, and last of all with the larger riding horses bred by the Persians even further east. It was from the fusion of these invaders that the Assyrian rulers rose gradually to supremacy in the ninth century B.C. occupying by conquest not only all Mesopotamia but also Syria, Palestine and temporarily Egypt as well. The Assyrians were Semitic-speaking but they began as northern invaders mastering the south with their chariots and their armour. They were the third and last of the combinations of races to build empires in Mesopotamia.

What this Assyrian Empire depended on was the vast flat area of Mesopotamia. It was an area in which the government maintained good communi-

Table 3. *Time Chart of Mesopotamia*

After Moscati (1960); Mallowan (1961); Saggs (1965).

City sites begin to appear from Nineveh to Ur.	4000 B.C.
First symbols on pottery: Kish. Writing in Sumeria.	3500–3100 B.C.
Bronze and potters' wheel: Uruk. Seals in Assyria.	
SUMERIAN SUPREMACY	2900–2400 B.C.
Dynasties I and II in Ur. (16 Royal Tombs)	
Semitic invasions begin (shepherds): 2600 B.C.	
AKKADIAN EMPIRE (Sargon I)	2371–1900 B.C.
KINGS of SUMER and AKKAD	2230–1900 B.C.
Dynasty III in Ur, *Gudea* in Lagash	
Isin-Larsa Dynasties (Elamite)	
1st BABYLONIAN EMPIRE	1894–1595 B.C.
Hammurabi: 1792–1750. Code 1751	
Aryan and other northern invasions begin (horsemen): 1600 B.C.	
2nd BABYLONIAN EMPIRE (Cassite)	1595–1100 B.C.
Rise of Assyria: 1350–1200:	
Movements of Sea Peoples Crisis: 1200 B.C.	
Babylonian Revival: 1160–1103 B.C.	
ASSYRIAN SUPREMACY	850–612 B.C.
Shalmaneser V deports Israel: 722 B.C.	
Sennacherib sacks Babylon: 689 B.C.	
Esarhaddon occupies Lower Egypt: 673–670 B.C.	
3rd BABYLONIAN EMPIRE	612–539 B.C.
Nebuchadnezzar II: 605–562, marries Median princess; deports Judah 586 B.C.	
PERSIAN SUPREMACY	525–331 B.C.
Cyrus conquers Anatolia 547; Babylon 539; Egypt 525	

cations kept open by mule or horse traffic and provided with an efficient news service. By this means it established an administrative hierarchy of indirect rule. The Empire was protected by a multiracial army, composed of levies and mercenaries, engineers and siege train, transport and commissariat. And the government was morally supported by an ancient priesthood of common origins and devoted to the service of the king.

VI. THE PRIEST AND THE SCRIBE

a. Origins

Primitive peoples today show us by their beliefs and behaviour what the pre-scientific superstitious beliefs of the founders of neolithic society must have been. Paleolithic peoples had, and still have, a variable but often profound interest in the explanation of the universal problems of creation, birth, death and fertility and also of the special problems of strange events, the averting and curing of ills, the expulsion of the demons they suppose to be responsible for such ills, and the foretelling of the future by divination as well as the twisting of it in a favourable direction by the placation of gods or devils. All these powerful interests are known to have been canalized, codified and elaborated by shamans, sorcerers and witch doctors. Such people exploit their greater knowledge of nature, their incipient science, by guiding or misguiding those with less knowledge. Thereby they create a profession which is the beginning of an hereditary priesthood.

This professionally organized belief is superimposed on the beliefs of primitive people in gods, beliefs which require no interpreter. But they are different gods with different names, features and functions in different tribes and they have different places in the mythical history of the tribe. When new cities came to be built in Mesopotamia by the coming together of different kinds of people there was the possibility of either combination or conflict between their different beliefs. Only where there was combination and agreement however could any city expect to survive.

In this work of combination the incipient priesthood with their supply of magical technique and power evidently played the chief part. Mythologies were fused; the regional gods and goddesses of warring ancestral tribes were united in relatively harmonious families whose pedigreed members had the diverse and specialized duties and professions which the ancestral peoples had contributed to the new complex society. Rituals were elaborated suitable to the needs of contrasted classes. Divination by the use of omens and the observation of stars was expanded to meet the exigencies of civilized life. From the explanation of what had happened in the past it aspired to the foretelling of what would happen in the future.

All these ancient services naturally cohered in the growth of a unified priesthood. To them, however, the pressing technical needs of the new societies had to be added. Someone had to regulate the calendar adjusting the supernumerary eleven days of the solar year to meet the prior claims of the twelve lunar months: the seven-day week was to come later. Someone had to survey land, to control and design wells, to engineer canals, and to plan fortifications. Someone had to calculate numbers of people, amounts of materials, expectations of requirements and, when all was done, to recite or record the achievements of kings.

b. The Basis of Class

To meet these novel demands, as it slowly grew from Jericho to Babylon, the city was adapted by the variety, the genuine diversity, of the people that it brought together. But when it had brought them together the plan of the city shows that it did not mix them up as freely moving individuals. They cohered in groups corresponding to their different origins.

Three main groups are shown by the plan of Babylon before all the other great cities of later times. There were the priests attached to their temples; there were the warriors and administrators attached to the palace or citadel; and there was a mercantile group of unattached traders and artisans who were free to move from one city to another and were in consequence often strangers. They were grouped in streets according to their several trades. So they have been, more or less, in all cities until today. It was an arrangement whose beginnings can still be seen where distinct and complementary tribes will settle themselves down next to one another for purposes of barter; for example in Arabia as described by Doughty and in the characteristic Indian village. The same situation has been shown archaeologically in neolithic Palestine.

It is easy enough to see how this separation of trades and professions should exist at the beginning of a city. But how was such a separation preserved? The answer is twofold. In the first place people marry within the trade. The trade is the basis of social relations and sexual relations follow from social relations. This is true whether the parents or the children make the choice of partners. The result may be described as a process of assortative mating, the simple principle underlying all social structure.

The second part of the principle on which the preservation of professions and all the later conservation of society rested, was a rule discovered by this most conservative of professions, the priesthood. According to them the Storm God, ENLIL, had laid down the law that a son should follow the calling of his father. This of course had been the rule from the beginning of the process of combination. But the fact that the god re-stated the law shows that traditional practice was beginning to be endangered by the continual flow of immigrants into the growing cities of Sumeria and the hybridization and genetic recombination which were bound to follow.

This rule was to reappear in the Theodosian Code over 2000 years later, and it has of course attained its climax in the development of Indian society. It is a rule which we shall see re-stated whenever a society is threatened with disintegration. It is the basis of stability in the stratified city society just as it was when we described it as endogamy in treating of the paleolithic tribe.

c. *The Effect of Writing*

At a certain stage in the development of Sumeria, writing came to be taught. Schools were set up in which all the arts and sciences derived from writing, soon including the art of speaking, were passed on to the children of those who wanted or needed this instruction. Thus an educated class was created and a barrier was set up which has persisted ever since between the educated and the uneducated divisions of society.

The governing classes, kings and priests, administrators and engineers, military, medical, and commercial scribes, were those who learnt to write with varying success. Each new race of conquerors began, we may be sure, by being illiterate. But after a few generations following some intermarriage with their predecessors, they began to boast of their knowledge of the divine art of civilized men.

The invention of writing had, it was seen, brought power to the writer. It brought coherence to the whole body of writers as well as to the whole body of learning which could be written. It had led to the formation of a scribal class with their own scribal god, NABU. It was this Nabu whose name appears in those of the later kings of Babylon. By that time he had, by a process familiar among gods, displaced his own father, MARDUK, as the supreme Lord of Heaven. It was Nabu also whose power was grasped by the Assyrian kings when they claimed to be able to read and write. This claim was well supported for Ashurbanipal, Esarhaddon's successor, undertook to establish the library of Nineveh which is the foundation of modern Assyriology.

The priests were the people who must have led the way in the development of writing and profited most by it. Their superiority in writing and in the applications of writing evidently gave them their predominance at the beginning of Sumerian history. Immediately afterwards, however, the simplification of writing by their efforts must have helped to break down the barriers between them and the rest of society; an effect which they could hardly have foreseen. In Egypt by contrast no such displacement of language occurred, there was no reform of the script and no barriers were broken down.

d. The Language and the Alphabet

When Sumer came under the dominion of Akkad, the Semitic speech of the new rulers became the official language of their Empire. But this new Empire needed the art of writing which was the possession of the priests and scribes of Sumeria: it was the vehicle of their religion and the instrument of their government and their commerce. The priesthood of Sumeria had not been conquered: it was rather they who conquered Akkad and the succeeding empires of Mesopotamia.

The evidence of this cross-conquest, an operation which was so often to be repeated, lies in the history of the language. The Sumerian written language continued as the vehicle of Akkadian religion; and the Sumerian characters continued to be used for all writing. These characters the Sumerian scribes were forced to transform to suit the needs of a Semitic language not tonal but inflected.[1] From picture-writing it had to be put into the syllabic symbols of the cuneiform script. This process of accommodating an old script to a new language also was repeated again and again. The next stage was the alphabetic script used by the Phoenician merchants of Ugarit and Byblos. So it was that clumsy adaptations set the process of writing on the road towards the phonetic and alphabetic system which gave us the pattern of modern writing (Table 4).

A few Sumerian words passed over into the less sophisticated speech of the Semites and some seem to have survived both in the Arabic and in the Aryan languages of today.[2] Their continuity demonstrates the genetic maintenance and far-ranging movement of the classes of people who made these things, used these words and ideas, and handed them on to newer societies.

e. The Sedentary Priesthood

The cities of Babylonia with their great temple remains bear witness to the strength of the priesthood. The historical texts confirm this impression. In Babylon there were two great temple areas. There were also (according to Saggs) nearly 400 smaller altars and nearly a thousand shrines. The temples

[1] The history of the decipherment is related by Saggs (1965).

[2] For example, in Aryan speech, *ox*, the socketed *axe*, and the *copper* it was forged from and in Arabic, *najjar*, a carpenter, show what made the deepest impressions on barbarous and on civilized peoples at this time (Piggott, 1952; Mallowan, 1962).

Table 4. *A Genealogy of Alphabets and hence of Professional Scribes*
After Derry and Williams (1959); Woolley (1961).

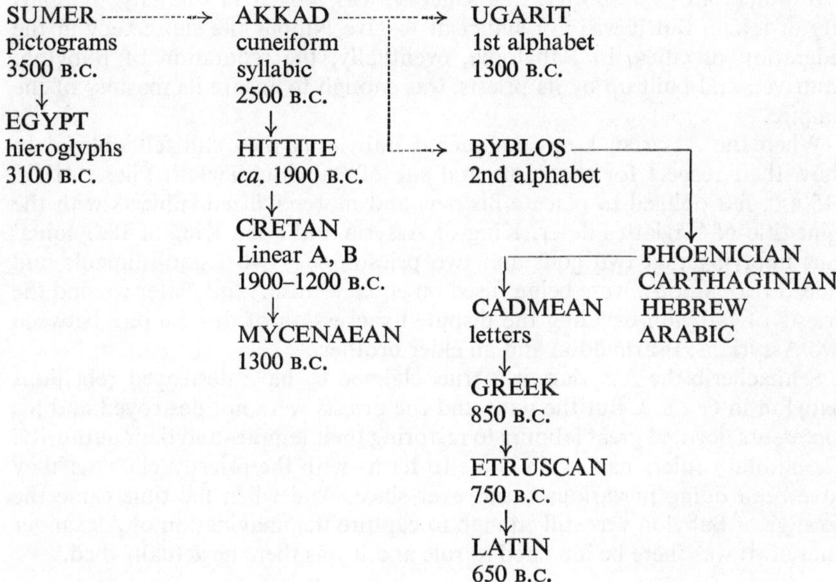

Note:

Side by side with the evolution of letters is a more trivial and more haphazard evolution of their arrangement in lines; up-and-down, right-to-left, or reversed or alternate i.e. *boustrophedon*, as in ploughing by ox. This last appears, sometimes in isolation (in Hittite hieroglyphic and Siculan), sometimes as a transition in reversing direction (in Cretan pictographic, in most of the early alphabetic scripts and in a Brahmi inscription of Asoka, 280 B.C.). The Easter Island and Panama (Cuna Indian) scripts, undeciphered, significantly agree in having boustrophedon with alternate lines inverted (Heyerdahl and Ferdon). The also undeciphered Phaistos disc from Crete (*a.* 1800 B.C.) has a spiral arrangement of characters.

owned, and were supported by, vast estates and employed their own establishments of slaves. Between their activities and those of the private trader there must have been some of the contrast we see today between public and private enterprise.

The priests were thus, what they were often to be later, a state within a state. They were an hereditary hierarchy existing side by side with the military and commercial hierarchies. But there was one overpowering difference between the priesthood and the rest. In Sumeria cities fluctuated in their hegemony. In Babylonia dynasty followed dynasty. Different races invaded and successively conquered the great centres of power establishing themselves as military governing classes.

But what made these places as centres of power was the continuous and fixed authority of the priests: continuous by virtue of the continuity of the people's devotion; and fixed by virtue of its own control of the sedentary means of food production; a control which it owed to its own education and skill in administration and engineering.

In Sumeria this authority, this sanctity, was lodged in one city, Nippur, city of ENLIL. But it was not sufficient to give Nippur the supremacy in the federation of cities. In Babylonia, eventually, the reputation of Babylon, contrived and built up by its priests, was enough to ensure its mastery of the Empire.

When the Assyrian kings conquered Babylonia they still felt obliged to show their respect for the name and site of Babylon. Tiglath Pileser III in 745 B.C. felt obliged to placate his new and more civilized subjects with the joint title of 'Tiglath Pileser, King of Assyria and Pulu, King of Babylonia' thus implying that two gods and two priesthoods, two Establishments and indeed two nations, were being fused on equal terms. A little later we find the priests of Babylon deciding the disputed succession of this Empire between two Assyrians, Esarhaddon and an elder brother.

Sennacherib the Assyrian, it is true, claimed to have destroyed rebellious Babylon in 689 B.C. But the gods and the priests were not destroyed and his successors devoted great labours to restoring their temples and their authority. The military rulers had again come to terms with the priestly class, as they have been doing in various forms ever since. And when the time came the prestige of Babylon was still enough to capture the imagination of Alexander himself. It was there he intended to rule and it was there he actually died.

f. The Mobile Priesthood

The priesthood owed their permanence to their attachment to sacred shrines which grew in sacredness and in wealth as the objects of pilgrimage. But they were also capable of movement, of expansion, of following the opportunities of growing wealth in new cities by setting up new cults. The development of Babylonian religion from its foundations in Sumeria is a symptom of this migration in a general sense. In a particular sense so is the spread of the myth of Tammuz. As the memory of the dying Sumerian king acquired divinity and attracted worship, priests attached themselves to his cult and spread the appropriate rites which were their means of subsistence.

As the Empire based on Babylonia grew, the priests added the gods of one city to those of another, extending the national pantheon. In doing so they would insist that corresponding gods were in fact the same god. And by ancestral origins they were no doubt often right, the priests themselves expanding from Sumer had carried their gods with them.

The inventions and the gifts which the priests carried with them included the scientific as well as the supernatural. The most important of these was mathematics. We recognize today a certain polarity or opposition between the understanding of words, which is very ancient, and the understanding of numbers, of which we have no evidence among paleolithic people, no evidence indeed before civilization. Yet in the beginning, in Sumeria, writing words and writing numbers both arose together from the work of artists and craftsmen. It was when they came to Babylon that they first diverged. For when the verbal script had to be rearranged the language of numbers seems to have been translated unchanged. So it came to be used as the basis of Babylonian technology and administration to be passed over later by capable men through the kingdoms of Anatolia to the Ionian Greeks.

Thus priests, more slowly than traders but quickly enough, travelled and migrated following the opportunities of their calling. The continuity of priestly traditions and myths, the common ancestry and kinship of their innumerable gods and above all the common Sumerian speech and writing of the priests, all show the effects of the permanence of the priestly class and no less of its mobility and diffusion.

g. *The Harmony of Gods and Peoples*

But there was another aspect of this community of priests. It also represented to men a community of the gods whose power they propitiated and whose actions they explained to their worshippers.

Explained is, to be sure, too crude a word for the transcendental relations of the god and the priest, the temple and the worshipper. For over the three millennia of Mesopotamian civilization the larger part of the work of explanation was transferred by the priests to their servants the artists whose splendid works have been so well preserved for us. These works later teachers were to denounce as graven images. But they still convey to us, as André Parrot puts it, the identification of man and god. The harmony of the gods was thus indeed the harmony of the priests and of the people. It was this harmony which in war perhaps mitigated the horrors of conquest and in peace certainly introduced the practice of tolerance to the widening community of races within widening empires. It was thus the continuing work of the priesthood and the framework of their religion which made possible the achievement of a multi-racial stratified society.

Take one practical instance of this co-operation. In introducing his code and in concluding it with curses against faithless successors Hammurabi invokes by name:

Merodach or *Marduk* (of Babylon) and *Ea*, *Anu* and *Bel*, *Sin* and *Shamash*, *Ishtar* (or *Astarte*), *Mama* and *Zamama*, *Amunit* and *Adad* (of the Amorites), *Damgal-nunna* and *Dagan*, *Nergal* and *Ninazu*, *Beltis* and *Zarbanit*, *Nintu* and *Nin-Karrasha*, and, last and least, the still unnamed god of the city of Assur which was later to give its name to Assyria.

So they stand, twenty gods and goddesses in the descending order of the age and sanctity of their protected cities in Sumeria and Babylonia. And to crown his list Hammurabi ends with *Anunnaki*, the great Assembly of all the Gods whose friendship as the Shepherd of Salvation (or Defender of the Faith) he claims to enjoy.

In the sequel this notion of harmony was taken by the Persian Empire of Cyrus and it was translated into Greek as the *homonoia* of Alexander. It was the great virtue of Mesopotamian religion. But in it there was also an inherent vice. The principle of tolerance and the practice of assimilation meant that moral standards could never be raised. They were always subservient to a political end: the great end of tolerating heterogeneity, of welcoming universal collaboration. To preserve this collaboration, this conformity, new intellectual advances, new scientific discoveries, astronomical or genetic, hygienic or medical, had to be concealed rather than developed. The priests must continue to exorcize the supernatural causes of eclipses even when the natural causes were already known to them. They had to pretend to be charlatans even when they were not. The rule was bound to apply to them, as it did later to the Roman priests, that one augur could not look at another without smiling.

For this reason when the great moral issues of social and sexual behaviour became prominent in city life the priests seem to have preferred to leave the ungrateful task of expounding them to the lay ruler. These matters were left to the lawgiver. They were later given practical expression in the Code of Hammurabi and later still in the hymns (quoted by Saggs) to the Sun God Shamash.

Thus Mesopotamian religion played its great role in the formation of cities in the third millennium. But the wealth and power it then gave to its priesthoods made them resist change. The change was bound to come in small and mobile, poor and primitive societies. It was also bound to come later when the impact of the magic and science of the new metal workers could lead to diverse, eclectic, and, as we may say, the experimental effects. This we shall see when the Jews come into our history.

VII. THE CODE OF HAMMURABI

A black diorite column inscribed with the 282 articles of his code was set up in Babylon in the last year of the reign of Hammurabi (1751 B.C.). It stood there perhaps for 800 years before it was stolen by a king of Elam, taken to his capital at Susa and partly defaced. If Hammurabi's laws did not last for ever, as he had intended, at least the code stood as the basis of the criminal and civil law throughout the history of Babylonia. No doubt also it was one of the things that brought fame to the city, its priests and its kings, throughout that time.

This code of laws, as we have seen, claimed the support of the several and assembled gods of the land. Yet it was not the work of the several or assembled priesthoods of the land. There were many gods but there could be only one law. This law was the revision of earlier codes, undertaken with prolonged labour, of which the texts give evidence, by this great king: a product himself, if we may judge from the recorded marriages of Babylonian kings, of the fusion of many races. (Table 5.)

The first characteristic we notice in the code is that its main concern is not with property but rather with human social and sexual relations. It condemns incest; it protects children; it punishes injury on the principle of an eye for an eye. It thus covers what we regard as the field of morals, of the behaviour which is determined among primitive peoples by the aggregate instinctive character of the tribe. Thus the Babylonian priesthood had left these supremely biological problems to the secular authority. And these were the very problems which were to be taken up so thoroughly by the Hebrew priesthood when they wrote Leviticus a thousand years later.

The reasons, we may take it, are twofold. On the one hand there is no point

Table 5. *Overlapping Classification of the Code of Hammurabi by Numbers of Sections*

After Edwards (1934); Saggs (1965).

1.	*Family and Sexual Relations:* marriage, inheritance, adultery, incest, concubinage, divorce, desertion and adoption	68
2.	*Land or Territory:* management, irrigation and rents	50
3.	*Trade, Barter, Usury and Debts*	38
4.	*Cattle, Agriculture, and Gardening*	27
5.	*Hire, Wages and Salaries*	26
6.	*Theft and Assault:* claims and punishments	40
7.	*Slave Duties and Ownership*, permanent (32), debtor (4)	36
8.	*Feudal Soldiers*, serving or captured	19
9.	*Physicians and Surgeons:* rights and penalties	10
10.	*Priestesses:* marriage and inheritance	7
11.	*Judicial Procedure:* evidence, ordeal, sorcery, etc.	5

in making laws which no one expects to be broken. The earliest societies were derived directly enough from paleolithic tribes to maintain the universal instinctive rules with very little transgression. It was only when the heterogeneous multiracial city societies arose that aberrations, genetic departures from traditional standards began to appear and that transgression called for interference, denunciation and punishment.

On the other hand it was only in homogeneous and fairly primitive societies that uniformly acceptable rules could be made for dealing with these transgressions. Those conditions were the ones which arose among the pastoral Hebrews when they encountered city peoples, wicked peoples who had different standards from themselves.

The Babylonians evidently never made up their minds to condemn sexual aberrations apart from incest. Monogamy was usual; polygamy took the form of concubinage, probably of slaves. Prostitution, including sacred prostitution of females and males, presumably eunuchs, was evidently accepted and homosexual relations were therefore not condemned. Human life was valued in relative terms according to age and social rank, for which indeed much of the definition comes from the code. But abortion, infanticide and sexual perversion were probably the accepted means of population control directly inherited from paleolithic times.

Superimposed on these genetic rules of largely paleolithic origin were other primitive rules. For example trial by ordeal was prescribed where, as in dealing with sorcery, written and verbal evidence seemed insufficient. Next came the rules for stabilizing the complex economic structure of agricultural and urban origin. Prices were fixed for rents and wages, for injury and theft. Above all the damage to people had to be valued according to their social rank, damage to a slave being reckoned as damage to his owner.

Here we get the precise rules for the status of slaves, rules which were to be closely followed by Hebrew Law. Permanent slaves who could be sold as chattels were probably always of foreign origin. Either they or their forebears had been captured in war. Between warring states there was continual loss of prisoners who were not as a rule returned or exchanged. They constituted slave populations which were breeding populations and potential recruits for different social classes. But the fate of individual slaves depended on their character. They were treated selectively. The men could acquire property. Both men and women could be emancipated; they could marry free spouses and bear free children. Thus the foreign bondsman had no rights but he or she often had opportunities. And these opportunities were one of the chief means both of social stratification and racial hybridization in the ancient world.

The native freeman could be enslaved for crime. And he could sell his wife or his children to pay his debts. Or in the last resort he could sell himself. But none of the transactions could lead to permanent enslavement of the native. All could work their way to freedom. This distinction between the native and the foreigner is characteristic of slavery throughout the world and throughout history. The native was virtually serving a period of detention or imprisonment which did not change either his social or his national status. The foreign slave changed both.

The most complex articles of the law as stated by Hammurabi are those which lay down the rules for payments in marriage, divorce and inheritance, payments measured in weights of silver. Here evidently the different arrangements, derived from the agricultural, pastoral and urban societies whose fusion gave rise to Babylonia, have themselves fused. The dowry bride-price and the marriage settlement can hardly all be consistent with one another. But in Hammurabi's code they all tolerantly co-exist following no doubt the customs of different races which had become different social classes.

VIII. SOCIAL STRUCTURE

The historical and legal texts of Babylonia and Assyria give us some notion of the structure of society. Naturally it was a changing structure and no exact analogies can be made with other societies. It is clear however that there are two kinds of division, a vertical cleavage and a horizontal stratification (Table 6).

Take first the vertical cleavage. There is a rough division into what we may call military, priestly, and civil, secular or mercantile. It was a division which probably allowed a good deal of exchange and intermarriage between the highest ranks of all three. There is an enormous diversification of duties in the priesthood corresponding with the complex origins and functions of the priests. The degree of connection between the free temple servants and other free artisans is not clear. Probably between the two grades of free artisans, those with and without slaves, transitions would be possible as the prosperity of families rose or fell. Slaves would also be transferable by sale between temple and mercantile service but we do not know how common this would be.

The independent character of the mercantile section of city society is indicated by the status of an official to whom the modern title of mayor has been given. Already at Mari in the time of Hammurabi such an official could be elected by the citizens and his name proposed to the king for approval. Such a principle shows the compromise and negotiation, the checks and

Table 6. *Diagram of the Structure of Society in Babylonia*

As indicated by historical and legal records and archaeological evidence (using names of classes from Saggs 1965).

Military	*Priestly*	*Civil or Secular*
Royal Families connections: early: priestly later: international	*High priestly Families* Administrative Ritual Priests and Priestesses	—
Feudal Landowners and Farmers Officials and Officers	Diviners, Exorcists, Scribes, Bankers (Usurers), Teachers, Artists, Male and Female Prostitutes	AMELU or Full Citizens Mercantile Administrative (Mayors)
Tribal or Feudal Levies and	Temple Servants and Artisans	MUSHKENU[1] Plebeians (with slaves)
Mercenaries (from outside)		MAR UMMIA Artisans and Pedlars (not having labourers and slaves)
	PERMANENT SLAVES (WARDU) (by descent from outside)	

[1] Cognate with the French: *mesquin.*

balances, between the different elements which have always been needed for the healthy development of a complex society.

The most notable property of Babylonian society is the close similarity of its civil or secular section with all other ancient societies and many modern ones. Its horizontal stratification shows the distinction between three great classes:

First there is the full citizen, the patrician of the Romans.

Secondly, there is the permitted resident or client or stranger, the plebeian of the Romans, the *ger* of the Hebrews.

Thirdly, there are the slaves of various grades according to their local or foreign origins.

These class divisions are all connected with supposed racial and geographical origins. Foreignness is always a class disadvantage except in the military field where its value is reversed; the foreign soldier is more likely than the native to found a dynasty and an empire.

IX. THE SKILL OF THE RULER

In the transformations of Mesopotamia it is easy to see that new lands were richer than old, new cities better sited than their predecessors. It is easy to see that new techniques were more efficient than old, the bow of the desert was bound to overcome the lance of the city and the horse and chariot were bound to sweep away the unarmoured foot soldier. But these triumphs in themselves were momentary. What made them—or some of them—into permanent advances in human history was the political skill with which the conqueror made use of the cultural skills, the genetic gifts, of the people he had conquered.

The first example of this political achievement we see in the victory of Sargon and the incorporation of Sumerian arts in Babylonia. A second example is the achievement of Hammurabi in exploiting religion in the service of the law and in the mitigation of the condition of slaves. A third example is in the principle of deportation.

The idea of deportation had been learnt by shrewd Mesopotamian rulers probably at an early stage. They were close enough to the earth to have observed the diverse skills practised by travelling craftsmen. As conquerors they saw the lesson driven home. The conquered people could do things that they could not. They assumed correctly that the different small professional groups in the Ancient East, whether they were scribes or musicians, lawyers or blacksmiths, had different innate capacities selected over numerous still remembered generations. They wanted to see these skills made available in their own capitals. And in one stroke of deportation they did what is carried out more slowly in the modern world by the spontaneous migration of individuals. But, however it happens, society is given a diversified character and a stratified structure which together enrich its total activities. For the newly imported people preserve their separate characters as a breeding group so long as this separate character continues to be economically valuable to them; or even, with the help of religion, a little longer.[1]

With the Assyrians the practice of deportation assumes the character of a control by the government of the general movement and structure of society. The Assyrian kings wanted not only to organize their supplies of labour most effectively. They also wanted to break up dissident groups or resistance movements among their subject nations. Thus when Esarhaddon of Assyria occupied Egypt in 671 B.C. we find him importing Negro slaves (or 'Ethiopian' labourers) to Nineveh. But at the same time he is exporting skilled (Aramaic speaking) Syrians as administrators to Egypt.

A century later Nebuchadnezzar II was deporting the Jewish urban and educated class to Babylon partly to pacify Jerusalem and partly to enrich the society of his own capital with new technical and cultural resources. It was these people to whom Jeremiah recommended a policy of social accommodation. This policy was so successful that when the opportunity to return came a large part of the exiles preferred to stay in their new home. This again is a situation which has often repeated itself.

By the end of its time Babylonian society had silently assumed the greatest

[1] The process of deliberate mixture has been continued by great rulers, Greek and Roman, Christian and Muslim, and in Turkey down to the present century. It is only since 1915 that religious and racial persecution has systematically set about reversing the process.

complexity known in the ancient world. It was a genetic complexity and it was a religious, a technical and a cultural complexity. It was the integrated whole, the combination of the parts, that made the character of the civilization.

In the end the integrated whole broke down. The state died. But many of the parts with their capacity of self-propagation separately survived. Thus when we say that Babylonia was finally reduced to a province of the Persian and Hellenistic Empires we mean that the latest conquerors, the newest governing class, refused to submit to the domination of the Babylonian priests and their religion. They brought their own priests and their own gods. And they had their own ideas. But the technical and intellectual castes of Babylonia remained as the creative material of succeeding empires. The structure had been shattered; its human no less than its linguistic elements had been anonymously dispersed; but pieces of them were re-assembled, some on a more easterly, most on a more westerly, site; and what has proved itself of most value has always been somewhere preserved.

6

EGYPT

I. WHERE THE EGYPTIANS CAME FROM

THE PIONEERS OF THE NEOLITHIC EXPANSION have left no trace of their entrance into Africa. The silt of the Nile delta has long submerged the relics of that momentous step in human history alongwith, or rather below, much else that came later. We cannot be far wrong, however, in saying that they came during the sixth millennium B.C.; and they came from Palestine along the Mediterranean coastal strip. They may also have been already differentiated into Hamitic-speaking pastoralists and cultivators speaking languages which, like Sumerian, have disappeared.

The incoming peoples found a Nile flowing through savannah country supporting a rich animal life. On its marshy banks, and in those forested oases which have slowly dwindled over the ages to leave only the frugal tamarisk, they were able to hunt or to tame wild cattle and wild asses, lions, hippopotami, and ostriches. Spreading out over this country the pastoral peoples divided into two groups. Some went west to populate North Africa. They were the ancestors of the Berbers. Some went south. They were the ancestors of the Hottentots and also of the Nilotic and many other cattle-rearing peoples. And some remained, where they still are, in the eastern desert, the Bedja people.

The earliest traces of the invaders that we find are from the period of the following millennium. They are at various sites along the Nile. These traces include, first, unpainted wares, then, when the new technique came in from Anatolia in 3600 B.C., also painted pottery and many other refinements of taste.

These traces include also wheat and barley, evidence of baking, fragments of hoes and sickles, remains of sheep, goats and pigs, and the metal copper. The invaders were concentrated, although not confined, near the Nile whose

September flood they were learning to utilize for their crops. The tribes of cultivators were scattered from the delta to near the First Cataract by Aswan 600 miles further south. Communication over this great distance at first was difficult and the marshy Nile only served to separate the east and the west. However, the use of sailing boats was favoured by the current from the south all the year and by the wind from the north in the winter; soon they joined together the north and the south as well as the east and the west.

Already during this undocumented period the cultivators were being guided by a priesthood and centred at the site of On, the temple of the Sun which the Greeks knew as Heliopolis. Clearly by interpreting the mystery of the Nile flood in terms of heavenly bodies and in due course replacing a lunar with a solar calendar these people would make themselves, their guidance, and their beliefs indispensable to the cultivator. They would have taken a step in establishing mutual respect and mutual support in the developing society. Such people may have accompanied incoming cultivators from the valley of the Euphrates; or they may have come later.

In the latter half of the fourth millennium this peaceful scene was disturbed by the intrusion of armed invaders. These people have left records in writing as well as evidence in physical works from which we can put together an account of their origins, their character and their achievements. The invasion happened perhaps in more than one wave and by more than one route. One way would be along the coastal strip; the other by boat down the Gulf of Akaba, across the head of the Red Sea up the trade route along the Wadi-el Hammamat which would be watered at that time. So they would come to Coptos on the Nile, the nominal place of origin of the Copts, the Egyptians. Certainly two separate governments were established by the invaders, one in the delta at Buto, the other in Upper Egypt at Hierakonpolis (to use the Greek name).

The new governing class were shown by their bones to have been bigger men of a distinct race from the subjugated predecessors. They remained distinct in their behaviour and no doubt in their language for a number of generations. In language they may have contributed the Semitic elements to Egyptian or Coptic, the language which was to remain stable until it took in a little Greek after Alexander; that is for 3000 years.

The new dynastic race and civilized aristocracy, as Emery describes them, evidently brought order and prosperity into the country. They seem to have established a feudal society with a national labour service. By occupying the peasants during the idle season this service provided the great works needed for the management of the Nile flood. This *corvée* was obviously later applied to the building of the great tombs which have recorded and preserved the history of Egypt. Indeed it was still there (as Kees points out) supplied by the descendants of these same peasants, when other peoples came to build the Suez Canal in the nineteenth century.[1]

The kings of the northern and southern lands, Lower and Upper Egypt, are recognized in inscriptions by their red and white crowns. But about 3200 B.C.

[1] The irrigation system also continued unchanged until it had to be adapted to the needs of cotton cultivation in the 1820s (*cf.* Darlington, 1963).

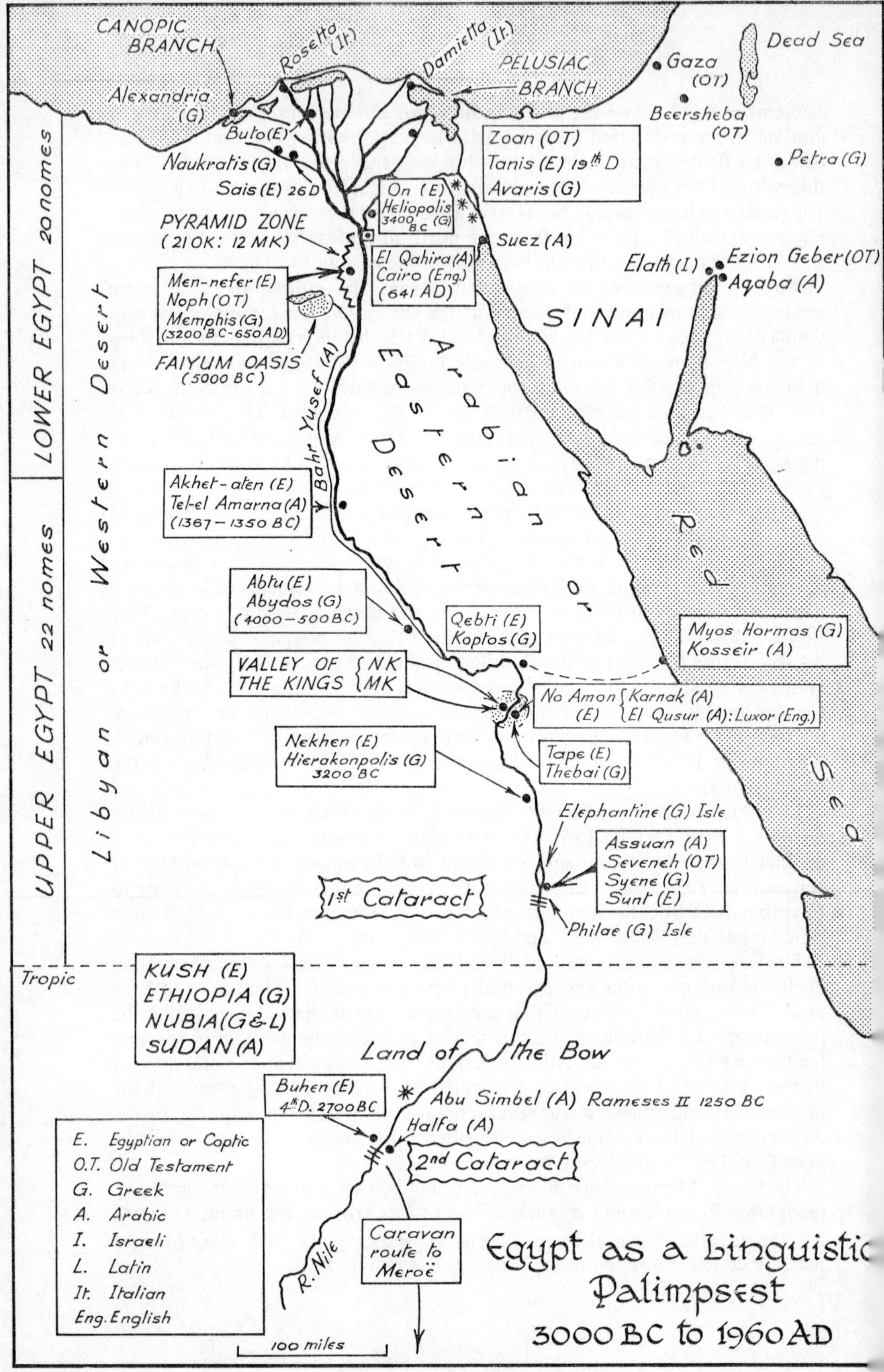
CANOPIC BRANCH
Rosetta (It)
Damietta (It)
PELUSIAC BRANCH
Dead Sea
Gaza (OT)
Beersheba (OT)
Petra (G)
Alexandria (G)
Buto (E)
Naukratis (G)
Sais (E) 26D
Zoan (OT)
Tanis (E) 19th D
Avaris (G)
On (E)
Heliopolis
3400 BC (G)
PYRAMID ZONE
(210K: 12 MK)
Suez (A)
Elath (I)
Ezion Geber (OT)
Aqaba (A)
El Qahira (A)
Cairo (Eng.)
(641 AD)
Men-nefer (E)
Noph (OT)
Memphis (G)
(3200 BC-650 AD)
FAIYUM OASIS
(5000 BC)
SINAI
LOWER EGYPT 20 nomes
UPPER EGYPT 22 nomes
Libyan or Western Desert
Arabian or Eastern Desert
Bahr Yusef (A)
Akhet-aten (E)
Tel-el Amarna (A)
(1367 – 1350 BC)
Red Sea
Abtu (E)
Abydos (G)
(4000 – 500 BC)
Qebti (E)
Koptos (G)
Myos Hormos (G)
Kosseir (A)
VALLEY OF THE KINGS {NK MK
No Amon (E) {Karnak (A) El Qusur (A): Luxor (Eng.)
Tape (E)
Thebai (G)
Nekhen (E)
Hierakonpolis (G)
3200 BC
Elephantine (G) Isle
Assuan (A)
Seveneh (OT)
Syene (G)
Sunt (E)
1st Cataract
Philae (G) Isle
Tropic
KUSH (E)
ETHIOPIA (G)
NUBIA (G&L)
SUDAN (A)
Land of the Bow
Buhen (E)
4th D. 2700 BC
Abu Simbel (A) Rameses II 1250 BC
Halfa (A)
2nd Cataract
E. Egyptian or Coptic
O.T. Old Testament
G. Greek
A. Arabic
I. Israeli
L. Latin
It. Italian
Eng. English
R. Nile
Caravan route to Meroë
100 miles
Egypt as a Linguistic Palimpsest
3000 BC to 1960 AD

the southern King Narmer brought the north under his rule.[1] Having done so he stabilized his position in a manner which has been repeated throughout recorded history by marrying a princess, Nithotep, of the northern house.

Not until 400 years later, however, when the last King of the Second Dynasty again married a princess of the northern house, were dispute and conflict between the governing classes of the two lands brought to an end. Later still the union was symbolically sealed by the invention of a joint red-and-white crown which foreshadows the various heraldic devices of other and later nations and dynasties (Emery, Fig. 68). The son of this dynastic union took a site between the two former capitals, although nearer to the northern one, to build Memphis. This city was to be the capital of Egypt, off and on, for 2000 years.

A more serious conflict than that between rival governors was that between the governors and the governed. It came to a head in the middle of the Second Dynasty. The dynastic race described themselves as the 'Followers of Horus' whereas the native people worshipped the god Set. Again the conclusion of the conflict was sealed by representing the king under two symbols, one (the falcon) in the name of Horus, the other in the name of Set.[2]

Homogeneous beliefs were not however to be established in this stratified society merely by such artful devices. Thus while the governing classes became settled in their view that Horus was Good and Set was Bad, the peasantry at least in the south preferred to think that Set was everything and Horus nothing. This view, according to Emery, persisted as long as the native gods continued in Egypt: the racial division in becoming a class division remained a religious division.

What happened under these first two dynasties in Egypt was one of the most decisive, and thanks to the body of excavation culminating in the recent work of Emery, one of the most demonstrative processes in human history. For during these formative generations a complex society was created from the fusion of two simpler ones born, by two groups of people distinct in their racial origins, one based on a native peasantry, the other based on an incoming war-like group. Who were the incoming people?

[1] I am assuming that the Narmer celebrated from his palette was the same person as the first Pharaoh described by the Ptolemaic chronicler Manetho as Menes. The evidence is discussed by Emery, Gardiner and Aldred.

[2] Emery, Figs. 59 and 68.

Fig. 7. OK, MK, NK: Old, Middle and New Kingdoms.

Notes:

i. Silting by the Nile since Roman times has filled up 40 miles at the head of the Gulf of Suez and also the old canal of the Pharaohs shown here. This connected the basin of the present canal with the eastern or Pelusiac branch of the Nile and is marked by the stelae of Darius, shown by asterisks.

ii. Heliopolis was the site of the Sun Cult priesthood who replaced the lunar by the solar calendar under the Third Dynasty.

Based on the Baedeker Guide Maps, the Hand List of Egyptian Names, and Margaret Murray.

It was Henry Frankfort who first suggested that they were connected with Sumer. The later evidence has established this conclusion. The rulers themselves may have come from Syria or the borders of Anatolia. But the builders, craftsmen and artists who came before them, between 3400 and 3200 B.C., evidently came from Sumer. As Gardiner puts it, they infiltrated; and they repeated in Egypt the heroes grappling with rampant lions, the prowed boats, the long-necked entwined and composite animals, not least the cylinder seals, all of them Sumerian designs.

These Sumerian characteristics are found at sites all the way from Memphis to Hierakonpolis. In a few generations they dwindled and died out leaving only the imprint of the Egyptian character, a new character that was to endure a long time. There was never, we may note, a reverse movement from Egypt to Sumer but this seems to be connected with the fact that, for reasons we shall explore, the Egyptian population never expanded. Egyptian artists of their own free will never emigrated and never colonized. They went abroad only when exiled or deported. The main part in their own external trade they even left to Phoenicians and Greeks. To them evidently, as to many later peoples, their own land seemed the best beyond compare.

The Egyptians revealed their new character and capacity in a thousand tombs which displayed the real life of the people while attempting to depict an imaginary after-life. They owed style and technique to Sumer. They owed administrative ability to the Asiatic conquerors. They owed industry and tenacity to the earlier incoming peasantry also from Asia. But to the African paleolithic foundation, on which everything else had been built during two millennia of settlement, they owed their genuinely Egyptian properties: a cheerfulness which is more sympathetic to us than the mood of any other ancient people, a cheerfulness recovered by the Minoans and the later Greeks; a personal naïveté and delicate solicitude which provided privies in the tombs for the awakening dead; and above all those wonderful perceptions of the paleolithic hunter-artists who have scattered their memorials from the Atlas mountains to the Kalahari desert, men who were inevitably drawn into employment by the prosperity and discrimination of the Egyptian rulers.

It was on this racially complex society gradually integrated by cross-breeding and adjusted to the stable opportunities of the Nile valley that the prodigious flowering of the Egyptian Old Kingdom took place under the Third and Fourth Dynasties, those kings to whom we owe the great pyramids.

II. THE RULERS

The Third Royal Dynasty of Egypt, beginning about 2800 B.C., twelve generations after the unification of Narmer, introduced a second transformation. Its visible sign was a new religion, or rather a new domain within the multifarious world of Egyptian religions. In place of the earliest cult of the Dying God of Osiris, of the aboriginal god Set, and of the royal Horus, a new god began to make himself felt. He was Rê, the Sun God, the symbol and the instrument of the priesthood of Heliopolis. But he was adopted and worshipped especially by the king, by Pharaoh himself, and hence by the governing class. With their god the sun Priests brought in the practice of preserving the body as a mummy and housing the mummy in a tomb. Above all they wanted to house the mummies of kings whose lives would continue to strengthen and protect their people for ever. So they began the building of pyramids.

These new practices have dominated all later knowledge of Egypt. But it is also clear that they dominated Egypt itself. It seems that they came into Egypt like all other innovations with a group of immigrant people from Asia, in this case the immigrant priests of the sun cult.

These people had used their knowledge of the sun and the heavens to calculate a calendar, to predict the flood of the Nile recurring every September, and to control the waters of the flood in irrigation. The new religion they established was thus the means of converting a knowledge of mathematics, astronomy and engineering into an instrument of political power. It developed with the changing circumstances of power during the following millennia. Its central feature was the idea that each succeeding Pharaoh, while he continued in his person to worship God as Rê the Sun, the god of his family and his class, was himself worshipped by his people as the incarnation of a god, at first as Horus and later as Osiris.

This religion was clearly a work of collaboration between one family or class of military rulers and another family or class of priests with their satellite scholars and technicians. It was a collaboration whose vicissitudes we can follow throughout the life of ancient Egypt. Indeed, in a modified sense and in disguised forms we may say the collaboration, disguised or diminished, still survives in civilized societies today.

The first fruits of this collaboration, or at least the fruits most obvious today, were, as we have seen, the pyramids. These pyramids spread for sixty miles along the rising land on the sunset side of the Nile valley, and they spread over a period of a thousand years from the Third to the Twelfth Dynasties. Others there were, including those of the Eleventh Dynasty near Thebes, in Upper Egypt, which have been stripped and destroyed. Surely we must look upon them as monuments of pride, superstition and servitude. But is this all? The men who had harnessed the Nile in the Old Kingdom, and reclaimed the Faiyum oasis and probably much more in the Middle Kingdom, evidently felt the need to exercise and display their skill in engineering and their power in government to their subjects and their successors. Nor did they fail in their intention. The man who designed and organized the building of the step pyramid at Saqqara for Pharaoh Djoser is known to us by the name of Imhotep. He is a man revered as the father of astronomy and deified as the father of medicine. Further, the man who built the second and greater pyramid for Cheops a century later is known to us not only by name, as Hemon, but as a cousin of the Pharaoh. The features of both of these men are impressed on us by their portrait busts.

Thus for the first time in history we begin to see the individual men who directed and developed the life of a growing people and civilization connected with their names, their faces, their achievements and their personal reputations. We see them as selected members of a governing class, men with a sense of history as well as a sense of their own place in it. Men whose belief in their immortality has proved not to be a mere superstition but has been confirmed by events. But let us note that the great Egyptians had only half our historical sense and that the more primitive half: they were interested in their connection with their descendants rather than with their ancestors. They had the character of a *rising* governing class.

III. ROYAL DYNASTIES

Our arrangement of Egyptian kings we owe to the Egyptian priest Manetho who introduced the Greek notion of dynasties (Table 7). It is unalterable but it is also arbitrary. Probably the breaks between dynasties correspond to breaks in succession in the male line. But successive dynasties are often joined, as in later ages, by marriage of the upstart ruler with a daughter of his dead or ousted predecessor. These breaks occur also within Manetho's dynasties; but the female line is held in little less respect than the male.

Some of Manetho's dynasties he obviously separated because no family connection was known. After the Hyksos interruption the new line of the Eighteenth Dynasty was known to have derived from a feudal ruler of Thebes. Later dynasties sprang from invading Libyan and Ethiopian princes who were themselves connected by intermarriage with the Egyptian governing class. And they no doubt reinforced this connection as a means of establishing themselves.

Table 7. *Time Chart of Manetho's Egyptian Dynasties*

After Murray (1949); B.M. Guide to Collections (1964) and Cottrell (1950).

	Dynastic Nos.	*Period: Total* (B.C.)	*Average*[1]	
Archaic	2D (1–2)	3200–2800	(200 yrs)	Unification
OLD KINGDOM	4D (3–6)	2800–2300	(125 yrs)	1st Pyramid
1st Interregnum	4D (7–10)	2300–2100	(50 yrs)	Civil War
MIDDLE KINGDOM	3D (11–13)	2100–1700	(130 yrs)	1st Empire
2nd Interregnum	4D (14–17)	1700–1550	(40 yrs)	Hyksos invasion
NEW KINGDOM	7D (18–24)	1550–712	(120 yrs)	2nd Empire
Late Period	2D (25–26)	712–525	(95 yrs)	Decline[2]
PERSIAN RULE[3]	4D (27–30)	525–332	(50 yrs)	—
Alexander and the Ptolemies	1D (31)	332–30	(300 yrs)	—

[1] Note: the steady average lengths of Manetho's main dynasties indicates that he chopped up the Old, Middle and New Kingdoms for the benefit of Ptolemy Philadelphus into somewhat arbitrary units as near to 125 years as possible.

[2] Assyrian ascendancy: invasions of Egypt by Esarhaddon (680–669) and by Ashurbanipal (668–630) who sacked Thebes.

[3] Persian rule but Aramaic administrators.

Are we then to suppose that an unbroken line of descent connects the first Pharaohs with the last? In the sense of conventional legitimacy no such descent can be claimed. But in the sense of a genetic continuity within a governing class, which was able to assimilate and marry with its royal neighbours of Libya and Nubia and its own high-priestly nobility, we cannot doubt that a connection persisted, a powerful and effective connection which was not completely broken even by the Ptolemies. Cleopatra, we may suppose, was not only descended from the Pharaohs of the First Dynasty; she was most likely to be descended from them along a thousand lines of ancestors.

Precise relationships are naturally often hard to determine but it is worth while noting the best available evidence for the character and marriage system. This we find in the Eighteenth Dynasty for here we have the longest succession and the one which includes the greatest and best known of all the Pharaohs (Pedigree 1).

The history of the dynasty is however dominated by two extraordinary individuals, one, a minor but successful figure, the other a major but unsuccessful figure. The first was Queen Hatshepsut. This formidable and probably sterile woman was not the only Egyptian queen to assume the office of Pharaoh. But she lasted longest. In life she wore the royal beard and in death she was buried in the Valley of the Kings. She reigned conjointly and in succession with her father, her husband and her stepson. In the third of these reigns[1] she succeeded in keeping this stepson out of power for a period of twenty years. Only after that was he able to take command and, in the following years, to conquer Nubia, Palestine and Syria.

The second dominating figure in the history of the dynasty was the reformer Amenophis IV. His unconventional opinions were inherited from his father and particularly from his father's action, which he repeated with Nefertiti, in marrying outside the royal family: he married into what appears to have been (according to Desroches-Noblecourt) the priestly governing class of Nubia. The king thus had unusual and unrelated parents and was himself an unusual hybrid.

The reform which Amenophis IV undertook was to destroy the political and social power and the theological monopoly of the priests of Amon at Thebes. His intention was to displace the worship of Amon by that of the Globe of the Sun, *Aten*, a Sun which shone not only on priests but on all men equally. To do this he built a new capital which he named Akhet-aten. At the same time he re-named himself Akhen-aten and in his children's names he gave the same honour to his god.

The conflict which ensued was not only the most important in Egyptian history. It foreshadowed the greatest conflicts of the future by involving at the same time, and thus connecting, the problems of social policy and religious belief. The king was defeated. His party, for he was evidently the leader of the progressive elements in Egyptian society, was submerged. His son who succeeded him changed his name back from Tutankh-aten to Tutankh-amen. And his own name and his works were erased, so far as possible, from the record of history.

[1] During which in 1495 B.C. she organized the great botanical expedition to Somaliland, the Land of Punt, in search of the sources of frankincense and myrrh.

What was the cause of Akhenaten's failure? An important factor, perhaps the decisive factor, was the disastrous results of his marriages. His incestuous marriages gave only daughters;[1] his other marriages gave sons who died young. It was in these circumstances that a military adventurer Horemhab was able to put an end to the dynasty, to seize the throne and to restore the old order of the priests of Amon.

Politically and indeed genetically the obsessive incest of Akhenaten seems to have destroyed the Eighteenth Dynasty. The history of the dynasty thus shows us certain properties that we have to watch in the study of all royal and governing families. The political privileges which they enjoy, no less than the political pressures to which they are subject, lead them to flout the breeding rules that are popularly acceptable. By doing so they sometimes produce disastrous, and at other times splendid, results in ways that we shall try to understand. These results at the same time demonstrate the role of the individual and the family in history. For we can now see that, before the inevitable subjection of Egypt by the Aryan empires equipped with horses and steel some 600 years later, the imperial enterprise and administrative skill of men of the Eighteenth Dynasty were responsible for bringing the influence of Egypt to bear for a few generations on the whole of the Ancient East: probably from the Pillars of Hercules to the valley of the Indus.

There is one respect in which this influence, reflecting the character of Akhenaten himself, stretches across the seas and across the ages. The life and death of the king have been held to make him the prototype of Oedipus. The detailed comparison of Velikovsky shows us, first, the Sphinx-oracle of Amon predicting his early death, secondly, his youth spent in hiding, thirdly, his swollen legs, due to a genetic abnormality, progressive lipodystrophy, fourthly, the sphinx destroyed, fifthly, the returned prince erasing his father's name and taking his mother as his Great Wife, sixthly, his deposition by his son

[1] This preponderant survival of daughters from incestuous marriages agrees with Galton's account of the Ptolemy family which followed a similar breeding pattern. Genetically it is not perhaps unexpected since the survival of males suffers with both extreme outbreeding and extreme inbreeding, through their being the XY sex (Darlington, 1964; but see Kirby *et al.* Lancet 1967 (2): 139). Politically, however, the absence of sons threatened the survival of a dynasty: an heiress was naturally exposed, as Akhenaten's daughters were, to seizure by any aggressive usurper.

---

1. Military autocrat, non-royal, first to be buried in the Valley of the Kings.
2. Also married daughters of the Kings of Babylon, Assyria and Mitanni.
3. The Oedipus situation (Velikovsky 1960).
4. Ankhsenpa-aten may have written to Shubbuliliuma, King of the Hittites, asking for his son in marriage to avoid marrying her grandfather AYI (Cottrell 1950).
5. The sister of Nefretiti was probably taken by Horemhab, nominally the last Pharaoh of the dynasty but a usurper (1348–1320), to secure his position in the absence of any surviving royal daughter.

I–V: Five marriages of Akhen-aten.
(i)–(iii): Three daughters of Nefretiti.
(*a*)–(*c*): Three marriages of Ankhsenpa-aten.

Pedigree 1. The Rise and Fall of the Eighteenth Dynasty (1570–1320 B.C.): a Tentative Genealogy

After M. Murray (1949); A. Gardiner (1961); Desroches-Noblecourt (1963), with supposed dates of reigns from British Museum Guide to Collections (1964)

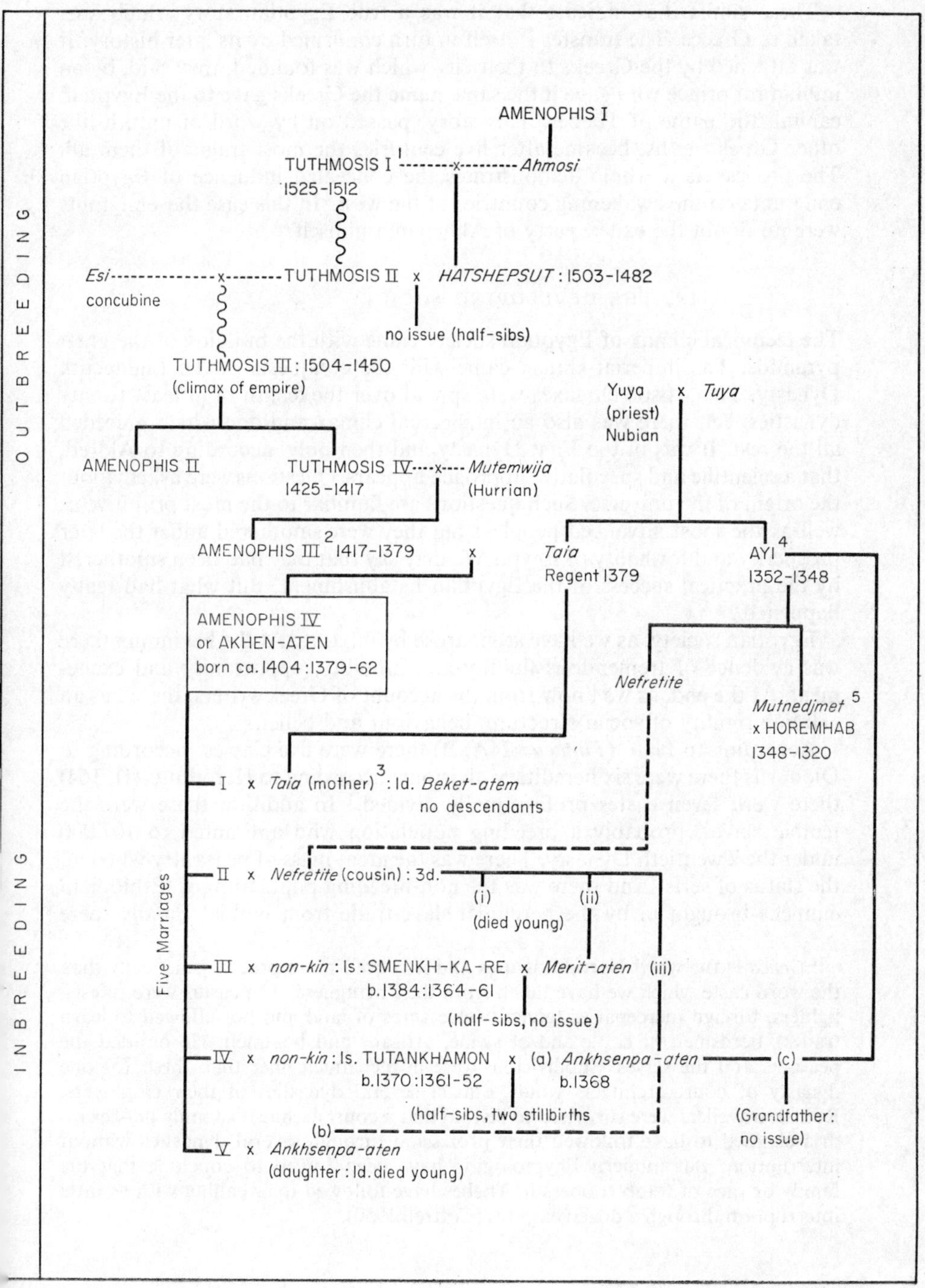

(Smenkh-Ka-Re), the burial of this son without honour, his brother (Tutankhamen) supplanting him, dying, and being buried in splendour.

These similarities indicate that it was a true Egyptian story which was taken to Greece. The transfer is itself in turn confirmed by its later history. It was attached by the Greeks to their city which was founded, they said, by an immigrant prince who gave it the same name the Greeks gave to the Egyptian capital, the name of Thebes. This story, passed on by word of mouth like other Greek myths, became after five centuries the most tragic of them all. The process as a whole demonstrates the concealed influence of Egyptian emigrants on the awakening countries of the west. In this case the emigrants were no doubt the exiled party of Akhenaten himself.

IV. THE DEVELOPING SOCIETY

The technical climax of Egyptian society came with the building of the great pyramids. The imperial climax came with the conquests of the Eighteenth Dynasty. The artistic climaxes were spread over the length of at least twenty dynasties. But there was also an intellectual climax and one which preceded all the rest. It was in the First Dynasty and then only, according to Aldred, that a scientific and speculative approach appears. Questions were asked about the origin of the universe. Such questions are familiar to the most primitive as well as the most advanced peoples; but they were smothered under the later prosperity and formality of Egypt. We may say that they had been smothered by the practical success of the Egyptian Establishment. But what had really happened?

Egyptian society, as we have seen, arose by mixture. At the beginning there was evidence of tremendous fluidity and mobility, opportunity and excitement. At the end, as we know from the account of Greek writers, there was an extreme rigidity of social structure, behaviour and belief.

According to Plato (*Timaeus* 24A, B) there were five classes; according to Diodorus there were six hereditary divisions; according to Herodotus (II, 164) there were seven castes professionally divided.[1] In addition there were the temple slaves, probably a breeding population who amounted to 107,000 under the Twentieth Dynasty. There was the great mass of peasantry who had the status of serfs. And there was the non-breeding population of 'Ethiopian' eunuchs brought in by the perennial slave-trade from Nubia. Finally there

[1] *Genea* is the word Herodotus uses and it is even more precise genetically than the word caste which we have taken from the Portuguese. The castes were priests, fighters, foreign mercenaries (given twelve acres of land and not allowed to learn trades), herdsmen of cattle and of swine, artisans and boatmen. He omitted the peasants and the slaves. Subdivisions were in fact much finer than these, for one dynasty of court architects would outlast several dynasties of their employers. Roman travellers were surprised to be told that a court architect's family in Alexandria claimed to have followed their profession through several dynasties without interruption. But modern Egyptologists have been forced to conclude that the family or race of tomb robbers in Thebes have followed their calling with as little interruption through a dozen empires (Cottrell 1950).

were foreign colonies of Greek merchants at Naukratis, Jewish mercenaries at Elephantine, and probably Anatolian copper miners in Sinai.

The processes by which the rigid system crystallized out from the fluid system would be a matter of surmise if they had not been repeated so often in the course of history. The Egyptian evolution seems to have followed the usual lines. That is to say an original fluidity in the choice of occupation is changed by assortative mating into an hereditary system which, in the absence of disturbance, in the absence of technical innovation or political upheaval, leads to the formation of professional castes. Such castes favour, and are therefore favoured by, a stable administration.

The usual conditions for this kind of development existed in Egypt. The mass of the people show a strong aversion for foreigners. In the Middle Kingdom strict rules were made to prevent the immigration of Negroes otherwise than as slaves from Nubia.[1]

A later Pharaoh makes use of the popular feeling when he arouses his people to expel the Asiatic intruders. So Kamose, describing his achievements in expelling the Hyksos peoples about the year 1600 B.C., writes:[2]

'One prince rules in Avaris, another in Ethiopia and here I am, associated with an Asiatic and a Negro.' However, later: 'I pounced on the foe like a falcon. . . . I broke down his walls, I slew his people, I captured his women. My soldiers were as lions with the spoils of the enemy: slaves, flocks, fat and honey.'

Note the different fates of men, women and slaves. These attitudes rested on a foundation of strong popular prejudice. In the New Kingdom shepherds (that is Hebrew shepherds) are an abomination to the Egyptians; the Egyptians eat apart from these Hebrews (Genesis 43: 32 and 46: 34).

The royal and noble families however evolve on very different lines from the masses. Under the New Kingdom they indulge themselves with foreign wives. These wives are of the princely class who seem to have created a royal caste of international scope in the middle of the second millennium. Nor was this all. When Amenophis III took a Mitanni princess (Gilukhipa) as his fourth wife, 317 unmarried ladies were brought with her, according to Gardiner. The racial character of the Theban Establishment can scarcely have failed to alter in later generations with such a powerful and selected infusion from an unrelated stock.

All nations as they develop discover a need for the co-operation of people of other countries having aptitudes that they lack. And if they flourish they have no difficulty in attracting such people. This was above all the position in Egypt. She turned for soldiers to pastoral peoples, the Bedja of her own hinterland, of Libya, of Sardinia and of Palestine. She turned for boat-builders and sailors where everyone else turned, to Phoenicia. Where she turned for miners we are not so certain but it is surmised that those Kenites mentioned in Exo-

[1] A fort was constructed at Buhen to repel Nubians in Old Kingdom times. The growing power of Nubia therefore may have been due to the establishment of an Egyptian governing class as well as to immigration from the south favoured by the increasing Egyptian trade in slaves, gold and ivory (Kees 1961).

[2] Edited by J. B. Pritchard, 1955.

dus, came from the northern countries where the metal ores themselves were first found. Last of all she turned for merchants to Greece and in their track came the travellers, Herodotus and Plato.

In this influx of foreigners Egypt was no different from the countries of Mesopotamia, Persia and Anatolia. But she was quite different in what she did with them. The other countries absorbed and assimilated foreigners. The Egyptians were more aloof. Their long isolation and superiority of civilization, which for long daunted even the Greeks, made them less willing to accept foreign immigrants, and the gods of their immigrants, on a footing of equality. It also seems to have prevented them from colonizing and assimilating their own dependencies. It prevented the Egyptian Empire becoming a reality in the sense of the empires that were to follow it and in the end destroy it.

V. THE PROFESSIONS

a. Priests

The priestly and temple communities of Egypt had a life of parallel complexity with the lay administration. The great temple centres which slowly grew up out of their scattered and improvised beginnings had a priesthood which became hereditary. It became subdivided into professional classes. On the male side there were readers and scribes, purifiers and sacrificers, prophets and musicians; and on the female side there were musicians, singers and concubines of the god. The whole organization was bound to collaborate with the lay government but it was also bound to compete with it for authority. As has happened in all other societies the sovereign endeavoured to use the priesthood for his own purposes and vice versa. The sovereign tried to play off the priests of Amon against those of Rê, moving his capital in order to escape from one or exploit the other. The most notable example of this shift was the establishment of the Aten capital by Akhenaten when the accumulated wealth of the priests of Amon at Thebes had made their ruling families too overbearing; too apt, that is, to make unfavourable prophecies through their Oracle.

In these uncertain conditions often interrupted by rebellion it is important to define the social and genetic relations of the priesthood and the nobility as the two sides of the establishment. We know that they intermarried. We know that a priest marrying Pharaoh's daughter might succeed to the throne (as Ayi did). We know also that in the last stage of Egyptian society, with the decline of the secular power after Rameses II in the Nineteenth Dynasty, the office of High Priest of Amon in Thebes became hereditary.[1] At this time they married into the Royal Family; their wives enjoyed high rank and title as 'Chief Concubines of the King of Gods'. When therefore Libyan warrior princes (or mercenary leaders) took over the government in the north, as the Twenty-first Dynasty, with their capital at Tanis, the High Priests of Amon were able (so Gardiner supposes) to govern the south as viziers and commanders-in-chief and in effect as sovereigns and dynasts.

[1] We may accept one-tenth of what the priest told Herodotus: not 345 but perhaps thirty-four or thirty-five High Priests may have succeeded one another from father to son.

Thus the subdivision and fixity of castes in the lower ranks of society seems to have left a governing class, until far into the New Kingdom, which was varied and versatile, broad and adaptable.

b. Craftsmen

The archaeologists to whom we owe almost all we know of ancient civilizations largely depend for their interpretation on the works of craftsmen. Yet it so happens that the Egyptian craftsman was in a different position from the rest of the society in which he lived. He was, like the peasantry, much protected and isolated from contact with the outside world. He was confident of the superiority of Egypt to all other countries in race and culture, climate, wealth and religion. The continuity of his traditions was maintained over an immense period. But in addition to all these advantages he enjoyed a freedom and safety of movement which was not to be surpassed until the Persian Empire was established. This was due to the protection of the deserts, the navigation of the Nile, and the peaceful authority of a government which scarcely needed to fortify its cities against internal or even external enemies.

It is as a result of these conditions that, as Gardiner points out, already under the First Dynasty there is a complete 'identity' of every vessel, tool or seal in Egypt between Memphis and Abydos. It was a freedom of movement among the technical classes which gave, Coon argues, uniformity to the culture. It also gave a coherence and strength to the government since it meant that there was a single freely mixing breeding group responsible for governing the whole of Egypt.

These conditions were a source of strength to Egypt for 2000 years. The system was badly shaken by the invasion of the Hyksos with their horses and chariots and their bronze in the eighteenth century B.C. Shaken but also fortified; for the Hyksos not only left their horses and chariots and their bronze behind them, they also must have left some or all of the men who bred the horses, built the chariots, and forged the bronze. But evidence shows, according to Kees, an even more profound change introduced by the Hyksos. For in the Old Kingdom pigs were freely tolerated and were to be found in the delta even in the temples of Osiris. But in the New Kingdom pork was forbidden to the aristocracy. Such a change could hardly have taken place without hybridization at this social level, that is between the aristocracies of the native and the invading peoples. The race of Hyksos had left its mark.

The perfect continuity and stability of Egypt survived until the new peoples of the north came across the desert. Egypt had no iron ore and no iron workers. She fell before the steel weapons of the Assyrians, the Persians and the Greeks. Ever afterwards she was to be trodden underfoot by foreign conquerors. Living for 2500 years under foreign governors who spoke Aramaic, Greek, Latin, Arabic, Turkish, French, English, and Arabic again, the Egyptians lost most of what was native to them. But still today they possess the relics of their language, their religion and their art.

c. Scribes

The business, the profession, one might say the industry, of writing was crucial for the maintenance of Egyptian society. No society that went before it had depended on writing to this extent. Every society that has followed has succeeded in proportion to its dependence on writing. Now Egyptian writing developed through the bringing together of two chief inventions presumably by the inventors. They were the invention of the symbols used in writing to convey information and the invention of the materials on which to impress these symbols. The inventors had created a secure and remunerative position, a privileged position, for themselves in Egyptian society to which they were soon able to add the business of teaching. But we can hardly doubt that the first persons they taught were their own children who would be the obvious inheritors of the parental privileges as priestly scribes.

The original writing was derived as we suppose, in common with the Sumerian, from pictures engraved on pots. To these pictures additional syllabic and alphabetic signs were added to indicate relations between words. The whole system made what we call *hieroglyphic* writing which was changed or improved, as the priestly scribes would say, from generation to generation. It was changed quickly enough to make the earliest writing unintelligible to the latest scribes who had (as happened also in China) failed to keep the key to their own history: their interest, as we noticed, was always directed to the future rather than the past.

Now equally in the invention of the symbols and of materials for writing, the Egyptians played an important part. The paper reed was abundantly used for food and clothing as well as for boat and sail making. Already under the First Dynasty it was used to make the first kind of paper. This material, to which we give the name of *papyrus*, remained the main source of writing materials for three thousand years, preserving for us not only the records of the Egyptians but also the imaginative writings of the Jews and the Greeks.[1]

The cheapness and convenience of papyrus as compared with brick and stone must have given a great evolutionary advantage in every activity depending on writing to the Egyptians, to the script they used and to the people they employed to use it. One visible consequence of these advantages was the development of many derivative forms of script; first of all there was a cursive *hieratic* script derived from the hieroglyphic and used in Egypt for writing on papyrus already under the First Dynasty; secondly, over the whole millennium from the time of the Hyksos invasions, there began to be other scripts used by satellite and subject peoples, notably the people of Ugarit and Byblos who were the midwives of modern alphabetic writing.

The Egyptians themselves never developed alphabetic writing and only went so far as to produce a syllabic script, known as *demotic* to the Greeks, under the Twenty-second Dynasty. This script designed for base and commercial uses slowly disappeared in competition with the Greek and Hebrew alphabets under the Ptolemies even for writing Egyptian. The hieroglyphic writing, sustained by the Egyptian religion and priesthood, survived with them to the end of the fourth century A.D. This stability of Egyptian writing must have favoured the stability of Egyptian thinking. But what did it derive from? It derived partly from the stability of the materials used for writing.

[1] It was killed in the end by an unrestricted exploitation in Egypt, where the plant is now extinct, coupled with the development of modern paper-making (see ch. 15).

But to an even greater extent it derived from the character of the people who did the writing.

The history of Egyptian writing becomes intelligible when we remember that the profession of scribe had become hereditary. The three different kinds of script were themselves latterly the work of three different groups within the profession employed by the priests, the administrators and the traders. It is a history of conservatism reflecting genetic stability within each genetic subdivision.

VI. WHAT BECAME OF THE EGYPTIANS

Our exact knowledge of the history of Egyptian communities in relation to language and religion enables us also to discriminate between the genetic history of their urban and their rural populations. It enables us to say something about what happened to them. The peasantry were rapidly converted to Islam and to the use of the Arab language by the Arab conquerors in the seventh century. But, like other conquerors, the Arabs did not change the peasant race who continue to show both the superstitions[1] and the physical characteristics of the ancient cultivators. Their faces still marvellously recall the features of the Pharaohs whose tombs they are employed to excavate.[2]

The ancestors of the Egyptian peasant boldly entered Egypt 7000 years ago as free men, masters as they thought of their own destiny and their own world. But their descendants for the last 5000 years have been at the bottom of the nation. They have made the unchanging servile foundation of the shifting and floating structure of Egyptian society.

The urban population on the other hand were new races. The Christian Copts kept their speech but they had hybridized with Greeks and Jews both Christian and pre-Christian during the ten centuries before Islam. The urban Muslims had also hybridized with Arabs. Neither community therefore corresponds to the urban population of ancient Egypt whose rulers and priests, artists and craftsmen, were largely dispersed to new centres under the Persian, Greek and Roman Empires. For them, as for the Jews, this was a phase of *diaspora* to whose separate episodes we shall later refer.

Owing to a misreading of the evidence, Flinders Petrie believed that the First Egyptian Dynasty began one Sothic cycle of 1460 years earlier than we now assume. This mistake made it possible, or even necessary, to suppose that all other civilizations had arisen by diffusion from the first inventors in Egypt. Now we know that the earliest diffusion was into Egypt not out of it. We also know that the diffusion consisted not just in a movement of ideas but in a movement of the people who had the ideas and knew how to use them.

Now we must ask what movements of people and of ideas there were out of

[1] For example odd tenacious villages have remained Christian and, according to Margaret Murray, celebrate the New Year feast of Osiris on the night of the High Nile in mid-September. Also, in Thebes the feast of Amon is still celebrated with a boat procession thrice yearly in honour, however, of a Muslim saint, Abu'l Heggag.

[2] *Daily Telegraph*, October 26, 1960. For reasons of prestige the Egyptian peasant has exaggerated his Arab ancestry, accepted by Lane (1836).

Egypt. We notice at once that there was no obvious and large-scale imperial colonization by Egyptians in the satellite and dependent countries. No doubt Egyptians did play a part in establishing governing classes in Nubia and Libya. But they have left few surviving Egyptian traces. The same is true of Syria and Palestine. The Phoenicians who traded and navigated for the Egyptians for 2000 years, providing ships and timber, show little decisive influence apart from the possible practice of early writing.

Acknowledged influence of Egypt is therefore generally lacking. There was no sweeping expansion of an Egyptian governing class carrying with it the Egyptian language. Why? There are two probable reasons whose relative importance we cannot assess. One is that no native military caste was ever established in Egypt. The Egyptians, as Kees points out, relied first on the pastoral tribes of the surrounding desert. Then from the Sixth Dynasty the Bedja herdsmen of Nubia were recruited. Later under Rameses II we find Kushite and Sardinian guards. Then came Libyans, Ionians and Carians. Finally the leaders of these mercenaries took over the government, in the tenth century as Libyan, and in the eighth century as Nubian kings.

All these people were attracted to Egypt and kept in Egypt, as the natives had been, by the country's wealth, by the crops of native wheat and Nubian gold. But we still have to ask ourselves why the immigrant fighters themselves did not expand. The answer may be that the Egyptians had a method of population control adjusted to prevent expansion. Strabo (quoted by Gibbon, ch. 21) tells us that the Egyptians were the only people he knew who did not practise infanticide. This perhaps merely means that they practised perversion or contraception or abortion to an extent which made other forms of population control unnecessary.

The expansion or diffusion of Egyptian influence has a character strangely contrasted with the glory it produced in Egypt itself. When the Egyptians fell under the rule of the literate Persian Empire naturally we can trace their movements from historical documents. Darius is able to boast of what Egyptian craftsmen were doing to embellish his capital. But when they moved into the barbarian world unaccompanied by scribes their activities became anonymous. It became an independent migration of individuals and of families. Refugees of civil wars, exiled noblemen and generals, sought land and power in Aegean lands. Egyptian priests and artists made their way to Crete and later passed into Greece and Italy. Egyptian craftsmen and especially metal workers bringing the smelting of, first copper, then bronze, and last of all Assyrian iron, made their way up the Nile on the ancient caravan route from Buhen to Meroë whence these crafts, as we shall see, were to spread all over Africa.

But are we not to suppose that other Egyptians struck out for themselves into the illiterate world of the barbarians in Europe as well as in Africa? Can we not see the influence of Egyptian priests and masons in the megalithic tombs and temples which sprang up after the construction of the pyramids wherever Phoenician sailors might have carried them, to Mycenae, to Malta and to the western shores of Europe and of India? These are questions we may keep in mind as we move into this outer and darker world.

Part III

Expanding Peoples

The tribal expansion of cultivators into new lands was followed by a class expansion of miners and metal workers, merchants and priests, of navigators and warriors. All these penetrated into the vast territories of the paleolithic world. Here and there they hybridized slightly with the new neighbours they encountered and created successful new races or classes which spread from their places of origin. The vast expansions of the Aryan and Semitic families of languages record for us the special gifts of the warrior classes who first spoke them. So also do the later and more specific achievements of the Jews and the Greeks who discovered how to write history and wrote it to such purpose that they changed the course of history.

7

THE MAKING OF EUROPE

I. THE DISCOVERY OF METALS

We must now go back to look at something much more modest than the flowering of great civilizations, something obscured by their greatness.

The new order of life, the new degree of prosperity, beginning in the agriculture of the river valleys during the fourth millennium, reacted on the poorer peoples outside. These were largely still paleolithic people, though slightly hybridized with neolithic contacts, living in the backward parts of Asia, Africa and Europe. The new demand for supplies of hard stone, flint and obsidian, and of precious stones, had created and supported new activities in the mountainous regions where these materials were found. Axe factories, of which four have been located in Britain, worked for a national market. Mining for flints, of which we see good examples in the chalky regions of Western Europe, had become an industry.[1]

It was the special activity of mining communities with an understanding of what rocks could yield and how they could be handled. Native copper, alluvial gold and meteoric iron had been discovered, melted, hammered, and cast for use or ornament. Trade routes had been established carrying the products of mining to the distant centres of demand and carrying back manufactured goods in exchange.[2]

[1] This was a paleolithic activity which expanded in contact with a neolithic market and also by limited interbreeding with neolithic peoples. On the 34 acres of pits at Grimes Graves, in Norfolk, mining had begun several millennia before the farmers arrived. It continued until the iron age invasions of the sixth century B.C. But its greatest prosperity was in the third millennium when the population suddenly increased by immigration and the immigrants brought with them new techniques: lamps, ladders and antler-picks enabled them to dig shafts thirty feet deep (see Ministry of Works guide).

[2] The human side of these advances has been admirably set out by Coon (1955), the technical side by Derry and Williams (1960).

Meanwhile in advanced agricultural settlements the requirements of baking bread had changed the open hearth into the charcoal oven and had led inventive minds to the idea of firing pottery in kilns.

With a forced draught higher temperatures gave harder pottery. They also made possible the extraction of copper from malachite, of lead and silver from galena, and of tin from cassiterite. The charcoal used for firing offered itself as the agent for reducing ore to metal. Soon the possibilities of hardening copper by hammering and alloying it began to be realized. The fact that tin was relatively rare and usually remote from copper added zest to the search for its ores. Their deliberate mixture seems to have happened first in Europe, probably in Bohemia, early in the third millennium.

The problems that had to be solved in the smelting of iron and later in the hardening of steel by hammering and by tempering were even more abstruse than those solved by the coppersmiths. The knowledge of the one must surely have contributed to the development of the other. The higher melting point of iron, 1535° instead of 1083°C, was the first difficulty. After smelting, one step was of the highest significance. This was the discovery of cementation by hammering which was made in the middle of the second millennium probably by an iron-working tribe in the Taurus mountains in Anatolia, Biblically connected with Tubal Cain in Genesis and with the Kenites in Exodus. The discovery is established by the gift of a steel dagger to Hattusilis III, King of the Hittites, to a friendly monarch about 1260 B.C. The dagger deposited in Tutankh-amen's tomb a century earlier was perhaps a similar gift. Other discoveries followed. But with all these advances steel remained scarcer and more precious than bronze.

The processes of bronze and steel manufacture are thus derived from a long succession of discoveries; each of them is now obvious but it was original and momentous when it was first made; and it led to a combined understanding in the hands and heads of the miners and smiths who worked the ore and the metal. The results were the culmination of a thousand-year programme of research, teaching and application.

It was not only a prolonged programme; it was a vast integrated, coherent, and ultimately world-wide programme. How was such a programme organized? We can tell from looking at the end of its evolution.

What we find is that in all primitive societies where metal working is carried on the people concerned exist as separate tribes, castes, or communities. They exist alongside the other craftsmen but without interbreeding. In ancient Ugarit of about 1500 B.C., which was perhaps his and their home town, stood the figure of the patron deity of the guild of metal workers wearing an ingot torque of copper. When they travelled among the tribal societies of Central Europe they evidently lived apart from the barbarians for, as Gordon Childe points out, they were buried apart. Today this caste organization is best known in India, in Arabia where it was described by Doughty, and generally in Africa from Morocco to Natal. Very widely the metal workers are wandering groups who trade while they work. In Europe the relic form is seen to be still ecologically distinct and viable in the wandering tinkers and gipsies.

Two aspects of the ancient blacksmiths' work were each recognized. One was the aspect of skill and intelligence stressed in the myths of Tubal Cain and of the Kenites who are connected with the origin of the Hebrew priesthood. The other was the aspect of hereditary magic seen in the smiths stressed in the rituals of the Bavenda and the Zulus in South Africa. But the initiation of Shakar and the forging of his spear, and the myths of the sword of Aryan heroes, all have the same meaning. These magical and fraudulent devices are all a reflection of the separation between people who understood the tricks of the trade and those who did not; between people inside and people outside a mystery; between therefore a privileged caste and the unprivileged stranger or slave. This distinction of course survives in advanced societies in freemasonry and it is the essence of priesthood.

It will now be clear what happened with the development of discoveries in metallurgy. They were kept within families for two combined reasons: on account of their enormous economic value; and because the family provided in its heredity and its environment the best conditions for training or apprenticeship. Those families should have multiplied and spread in proportion to their success and their prosperity. But it seems that they did not always spread. Why?

The iron workers of Anatolia remained for centuries in one place. They were stabilized perhaps, as Gurney suggests, as a peasant people smelting iron in the winter months. Continuing to exploit their invention they were preserved by their close co-operation with the King of the Hittites. But when disaster befell the Hittite Empire about 1200 B.C. the iron workers carrying their skill with them were dispersed; they were scattered, we shall see, to the ends of the earth. They were soon providing the steel for the brief conquests of the Assyrians; later the Anatolian iron workers reached central Europe and there, in Carinthia and about 500 B.C., they discovered certain ores from which steel might be made directly. In doing so they laid one of the foundations of the Etruscan and the Roman Empires. It must have been one of their eastward moving fractions which shortly afterwards brought the iron industry to China. And it was certainly they who, carried south by the Assyrians, established it in Nubia in the fifth century B.C. Indeed Nubia which had been a satellite of Egypt as a gold-producing country attracted enough warriors as an iron-producing country to become an independent kingdom for 800 years with its capital at Meroë. In turn, when Meroë was sacked, the iron-working castes were scattered west and south bringing the iron age at last to the rest of Africa, an Africa which had no bronze age at all.

Ever since, or even before, Christian Thomsen in 1836 used the expressions stone age, bronze age and iron age, the inventions of metal-working have been known to have been critical for the development of civilization. But their effects are now seen to be more intricate than these simple names imply.

The displacement of stone by copper and of copper by harder metals as we now see had proceeded slowly by expansion from the sites of invention of each new improvement. Many new inventions have failed to reach the remote periphery of mankind. Many expansions have been blocked, as we shall see, by seas and mountains, deserts and diseases. And each improvement has been applied with differential zeal to different activities and professions. For example men have seized on bronze and steel for swords and ploughshares leaving the softer copper for women's employment. Copper has only now disappeared from the industrialized kitchen and it is still the dominant metal in the ancient bazaars from Meshed to Marrakesh.

Nevertheless each new invention had a sudden and dramatic effect. The new metals transformed the tools and the weapons that men used. Their search for metals created trade and movement all over the accessible earth and sea. The felling of timber for fuel led to the destruction of forests for which the axes and the ploughs were now being made available. But beyond all these effects the development of metals meant something quite different: the creation of new kinds of men.

It does not matter whether we call these people new tribes, which they were at first, or new castes, which they soon became, or new races, which they also were in a very special sense. What matters is that the new men who made new metals, new tools and new weapons in turn created the conditions and the opportunities for yet other kinds of new men who could use the new weapons and tools, and master the new and richer societies that these things made possible. They were all warriors who struggled into power in the bronze and the iron age. They thought themselves heroes and others soon thought them gods. At first, far away from the Ancient East, these barbarous people spent two thousand years in combining with the ancient races and in assimilating the ancient centres of civilization. We must now see how this happened.

II. THE COLONIZATION OF EUROPE

a. Agriculture by Land

Already in the seventh millennium agricultural settlements were appearing on the European shores of the Aegean but over 2000 years passed before the eastern farmers penetrated deep into the colder and wetter regions to the north. This long pause perhaps allowed for some improvement in the climate. It certainly allowed for great improvement in technical resources, especially in the working of timber, the making of pottery, and the production of strains of crops and stock able to withstand the winters of Central Europe. The use of oxen for ploughing, we may suppose, was one of the thresholds to be crossed.

There was also another problem no more and no less important than that of acclimatizing and accustoming the new races of farmers to the severity of European conditions. This difficulty however was more easily overcome. For the neolithic people being not only farmers but hunters and collectors in their spare time naturally hybridized with their paleolithic neighbours. They captured women; and sometimes they exchanged them in the course of other trade, and in fluctuating conditions of famine and plenty among both kinds of community.

So it was that neolithic colonization of Europe began an advance over the ridge into the Danube basin and up the other Black Sea rivers. By the end of the fourth millennium the cultivators had reached the shores of the North Sea and the Baltic. By this time however the longer but milder route by the coasts of North Africa and Spain through France had brought other colonists into Central Europe and also northwards and across the Channel into the new island of Britain.

These long lines of neolithic expansion were being paralleled at the same time in Africa and Asia, but it is only in Europe, where they were shorter, that the detailed interactions which accompanied them have been open to study. In the first place the advancing farmers were diversified as they moved forward. In some respects their culture became thinner. For example if, as sometimes happened, they lost the means of growing flax in the course of moving north they might also lose the art of weaving and turn to the use of skins for clothing instead. They thus lost some of their refinements but they also gained others. For example the Lake Dwellers who established villages on over 300 sites all over Central Europe acquired those new special skills which preserved them undisturbed from 3000 to 1500 B.C.[1] But, above all, the migrating farmers formed splinter groups of largely pastoral peoples who were free to advance more quickly and in fact reached Northern Europe before the more heavily equipped and less mobile agriculturists.

These new types of colonists (as we have already seen) had often benefited by hybridization with the local populations of natives. Moreover the effect was reciprocal as is clear from the fact that paleolithic people such as the Midden Folk in Denmark sometimes began to adopt the neolithic crafts, which they found easiest, cattle-rearing and pottery-making, without undertaking the staple business of cultivation.

When neolithic and paleolithic peoples meet we indeed regularly find new habits of life appearing in which two main groups have been distinguished:

(i) *Secondary neolithic*, by Stuart Piggott, referring to neolithic peoples who, after arriving in a country, have borrowed customs from purely paleolithic inhabitants (such as putting basket patterns on pottery or the use of antlers) without abandoning agriculture.

(ii) *Sub-neolithic*, by Grahame Clark, referring to paleolithic peoples who have borrowed customs other than agriculture (such as pottery-making) from neolithic peoples.[2]

The distinction between these two groups seems to be genuine and to be based on two opposed methods of hybridization followed, as Atkinson points out, by natural selection favouring certain economically viable combinations. The secondary neolithics are neolithic groups which have incorporated small numbers of paleolithic people, usually women. The sub-neolithics are paleolithic groups which have similarly incorporated neolithic elements. What is significant about this distinction is that it implies the absence of equal or symmetrical fusion. It is a principle that equal fusion of unequal races, genetically and ecologically contrasted races, never occurs. It seems to be psychologically excluded and practically unworkable at all stages of human evolution. What happens when unequal races combine is stratification.

[1] For an account of their archaeological discovery, see Bibby (1957).

[2] This situation, resulting from the capture of women, may be seen today among the nearly paleolithic people in the Mato Grosso (Cowell) and north of the Amazon (Guppy).

On this view we might expect that when two peoples meet, as we shall see the bronze traders met the secondary neolithic herdsmen in Britain, we should find not merely hybrid types of burial like the 'circle barrows' of Wiltshire but also a momentary difference in the mode of disposal of bodies between the two sexes, the men being buried, the women cremated. This, according to Atkinson, is just what is found. But in addition there is the wonderful display of diversity that we should expect in later generations from hybridization. Individual differences expressed themselves in new ways of doing things, in the creation of new cultures, in what we call originality.

In consequence of these genetic changes the population of Europe developed a diversity aptly matched by the ecological diversity of the most diversified of all continents. Different tribes, hunting, collecting and fishing, agricultural and pastoral, were distributed in different suitable situations in which they did not greatly disturb one another. They were penetrated by migrant traders, miners, metal-workers and other craftsmen. And the whole complex maintained itself in peaceful relations fostered by the mutual usefulness and co-operation of the different groups each of which had all it could do to maintain itself at a low density without fighting with its neighbours. Gold was for long the commonest of metals and it was indeed what later tradition was to remember as a Golden Age.

b. Religion by Sea

It was at this pregnant agricultural stage in the middle of the third millennium B.C. that a new kind of movement made itself felt in Western Europe, a movement whose archaeological remains are out of all proportion to the numbers of people involved. People began to spread into the western Mediterranean islands who observed customs of collective burial in stone tombs. These people left their mark in Malta, in Sicily, in Apulia. In Sardinia they continued building castles, known as *nuraghi*, over a period of about 1500 years (2500 to 1000 B.C.). Thence they moved further west diverging along various routes. By way of the south of Spain and Portugal they reached Ireland, Scotland, the Orkneys and Denmark. By way of Aragon, Navarre and Brittany they reached the west of England. By way of France they reached the North Sea coast and the south of Sweden (Fig. 8).

These people adapted themselves everywhere to the local modes of life. They contributed nothing obvious to the material welfare of the people to whom they introduced themselves. What they did was to offer them a radically new idea of government and of the relations of the individual to society. It was an idea concerned with the practice of burial and of the magic or the sanctity of places associated with the dead by the building of tombs. In addition they were able to offer the technical means of putting these ideas into practice by the shaping and handling of large stones, hence the relations of the living and the dead.

Who were these *megalithic* people and where did they come from? We have to realize that they were not simple communities of one tribe or race or even nation. They are better described as expeditions composed of several kinds of people. First, there were the priests organized to spread by teaching their own

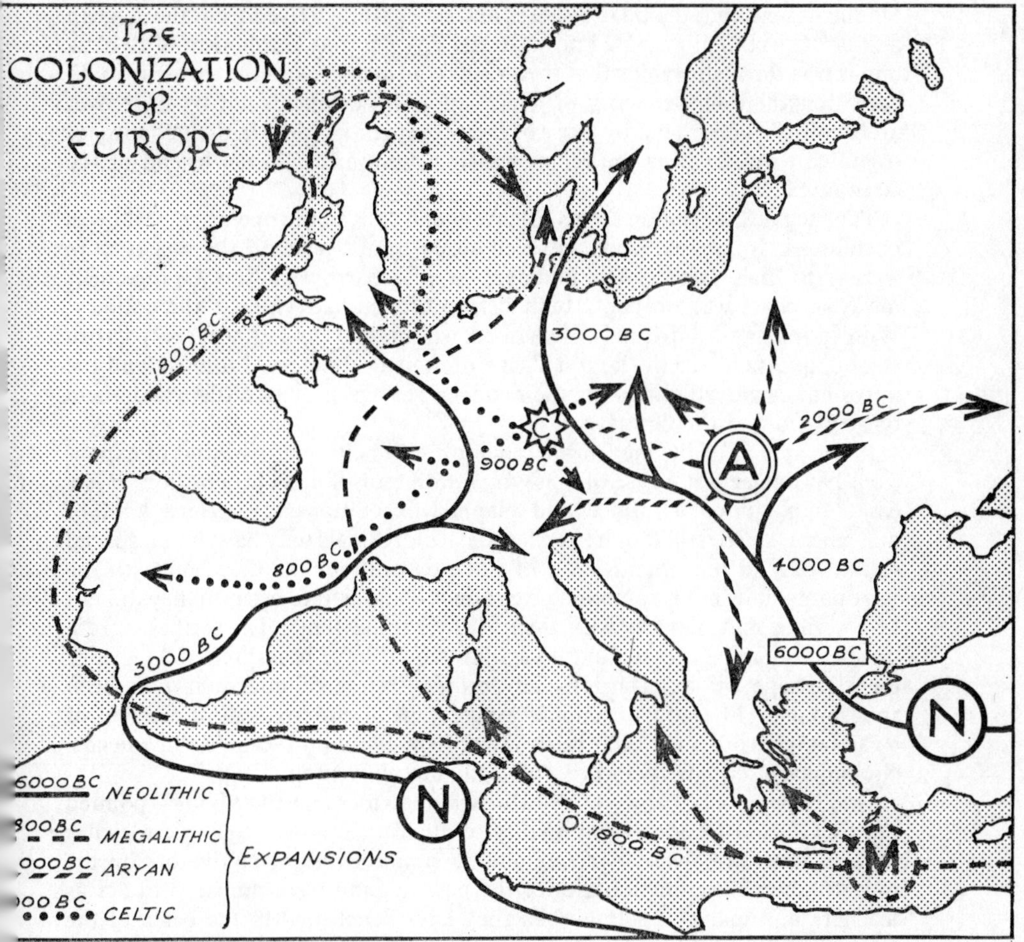

Fig. 8. Successive expansions over Europe superimposed from 6000–800 B.C.

N. Neolithic from 6000–3000 B.C.
M. Megalithic about 1800 B.C., mainly by sea.
A. Aryan primarily from 2000 B.C.
C. Aryan secondary (Celtic ironage, partly by sea) from 900 B.C.

Simplified diagram after Bibby (1956); Stuart Piggott (1965)

spiritual ideas and ceremonial practices and no doubt thereby to establish their own social influence. Secondly, there were craftsmen, both masons and engineers. Thirdly, there were boatbuilders and navigators. All these people came from the Ancient East bringing the ideas and techniques of their countries with them. On the one hand, the priests, the masons and the engineers evidently derived not very remotely from Egypt where the erection of the first pyramid in 2750 B.C. is not very far from the time of origin of the movement.

On the other hand, the boat-builders and navigators derived from the Aegean and Phoenicia. Sailors were known to the Egyptians as Gabli, men of Byblos, and it was through Byblos that the priests, the masons and the seamen would come together. The memory of these sailors is sustained, not by their own archaeological relics, but by those of their companions. And in their country of origin can we not hear the echo of their achievements in the legend of the Argonauts?

The megalithic religion seems to have taken root in Europe wherever it was introduced. Impressive earth-covered stone tombs near all the coasts bore witness to their success. The immense circular barrow of New Grange near the Irish coast was probably built before bronze had entered the country. With its passages intricately decorated within and its surface coated with shining quartz it was the largest shrine of a great cemetery. From Ireland the missionaries moved on, taking their converts as agricultural settlers with them to Scotland and the Orkneys.

In the spread of the megalithic religion we thus have a new kind of expansion. No longer is it a case of mass migration, nor of class penetration; it is a case of integrated, stratified and planned expeditions. This third kind of movement we are still familiar with today. Individuals may have had a special role to play in the organization of these expeditions (as they had with the Argonauts) but that is something we cannot demonstrate because they did not take scribes and papyrus with them. Why should they? The scribes were a distinct and affluent caste and no scribes would have been prepared to work their passage on a hazardous adventure. Unless of course it had been sponsored by Pharaoh with some expectation of employment at the end of it, as happened nearly 2000 years later when Pharaoh Necho's Phoenicians circumnavigated Africa and recorded the fact in writing.

One happy consequence of the absence of scribes and their books, pointed out by Gordon Childe, was a fluidity of doctrine among megalithic socieites both in time and space. Arriving among simple tribes of cultivators on the western shores the missionaries of the new religion were prepared to act as teachers and magicians. But when they later penetrated to the basin of the Seine they found themselves preaching to people to whom war had brought conquest and conquest had brought chiefs, military leaders and a hierarchy of authority. The priests found themselves in a privileged position and in a richer society.

The new synthesis arising in this way was so successful that it seems to have expanded in all directions. The ideas of the megalithic priests had four aspects, social and technical, religious and magical.[1] Their combination had the same effect of expanding a population as had the breeding of wheat, the building of boats or the casting of bronze. And, like all these others, they were preserved by a professional and hereditary caste. For how many generations? This question we can now answer.

[1] The awe in which great stones, high places, mighty chiefs and the forging of metals were held is happily combined in the name of the tomb standing by the bronze age Ridgeway in Berkshire, recently reconstructed by Professor Stuart Piggott, and known as *Wayland's Smithy*.

c. The Great Temples

Nearly a thousand years after the advent of the megalithic priests great new building works began to appear in the countries they had colonized. These were the open stone temples of Britain and France of which the most famous are Avebury, Stonehenge and Carnac. The temples and the tombs were built next door to one another. Both were erected under the supervision of priests. Both were built of stone. And the temples constituted an even greater engineering achievement than the tombs. The cartage and erection at Carnac of a stone 60 feet high and weighing 350 tons is a feat unsurpassed in antiquity. So also is the transport of the eighty blue stones each of four tons overseas from the Prescelly mountains in Pembroke to Wiltshire. Evidently therefore the organization of these groups of people had kept intact over the thirty generations, the millennium, which is covered by the two achievements.

The society for which the temples were built was however quite different from the one for which the earlier tombs and barrows had been constructed. The new people were no longer concerned merely with revering the dead. They now assembled to worship the sun. The holes dug for the earth gods were filled in. The wooden roofs were replaced by circles open to the sky. The alignment of the great stone avenues as much as the minute ornaments in the contemporary graves of the chiefs showed the sun as the focus of their religion. Whether again there was any connection with Egyptian religion does not greatly matter. But the technical connection with Egypt is shown since the shaping of the stones at Stonehenge uses the same technique as that of the Egyptian obelisks. And when the whole monument had been built the shape of a dagger was inscribed on one of the sarsens of a trilithon as though to inform us that Mycenae was the country of origin of the master mason.

The understanding of Stonehenge was for centuries a matter of romantic curiosity. It has only been in the hands of recent investigators that the full harvest of devoted study has been reaped. We owe it to Atkinson that the succession of events in the years between 1900 and 1400 B.C. can be exactly traced. It is a succession of events of great moment for the genesis of the European peoples in revealing the twin principles of continuity and amalgamation.

The critical discovery is that the stone lintels of the great trilithons are copies of wooden lintels with the mortice and tenon joints used in the earlier wooden neolithic temples—or so we presume since they are still used today.[1] Further the stone circle is a feature of the worship of certain Beaker people known in other countries who on the trade journeys passed close by the Prescelly mountains where they had found the bluestones for their altar. The whole arrangement thus suggests a fusion of religions like that of which the hybrid barrows were a more modest and more local symptom. But here it is designed as a stroke of policy to cement the union of a multiracial society. And it was an arrangement demanding the authority of a great king and the skill and organization of a complex community—or, shall we say, nation?—for which it was designed.

[1] Best illustrated by Atkinson (1956).

A later discovery of the properties of the great temples and also of the 300 smaller stone circles in Britain shows us most clearly where the megalithic priests came from and what gave them their power. Hoyle has argued that Stonehenge could be and probably was used to predict eclipses. Thom has shown that the stone circles were set to an accuracy of 1 : 1000 to predict not only the calendar for the year but the clock for the day and the night. They could also be used to observe the 18-year cycle of revolution of lunar nodes.

These demonstrations of astronomical and mathematical skill leave no doubt that the people responsible were derived as stable castes from the Ancient East, probably from Egypt. They also leave no doubt that the great practical value of their work gave them a natural as well as a supernatural authority over the agriculturists they served and ruled. It was a union of science and religion whose power only began to be dissolved by the Greeks in Ionia a millennium later.

The great temples are the show pieces of bronze age achievement carried from civilization into the outer world of barbarism and illiteracy. But there are many lesser markers of what ambitious navigators were doing. Their rock carvings for example range from Bohuslan in Sweden to the Canary Islands. They show the ships in which they rowed on their great voyages, ships which provided the means of discovery and conquest for their descendants the Vikings. They explain the origins of northern boatbuilding as well as of so much of northern invention and enterprise. We need not suppose, with Brøgger, that these bold sailors discovered America and took bronze with them. But we must suppose that they settled in the northern countries at the places which they marked with megaliths. And that, having settled, they bred and propagated their race. For these places can still be recognized today by the different blood group frequencies of the populations descended from them.[1]

The establishment of the Mediterranean people on the Atlantic coasts of Europe led to these fixed settlements and to a life which existed and developed and differentiated independently of its Mediterranean origins. It gave rise to new forms of building, of travelling, and of social structure.

But it also led to a continuity in the practices of commerce and communication. The Phoenicians who were still visiting Britain 2000 years after the original settlements were merchants at the dying end of a long period of civilized intercourse. It was dying on account, it has been supposed, of the rise of iron and decline of tin. It was dying also on account of the strength and coherence of new empires. And today the remains of that intercourse may be seen in the appearance of the people in the regions they visited and in such ancient customs as the use of the long Mediterranean spade and the making of clotted cream still common to Syria and Cornwall and found nowhere else in the world.

The vast fluidity of the bronze age was temporary. It was due, as has often been pointed out, to the search for the metals needed to make bronze, and to the availability of ships to carry the searchers. But it also depended on the vast empty spaces that cried out for colonization and on the religious enthusiasm that drove the colonists forward on their inspired mission to which the people they settled amongst, and also their present descendants, owe so much.

[1] E. S. Brown (1965).

d. Beakers and Battle-axes

At the turn of the millennium, about 2000 B.C., new movements began in various parts of Europe which were the result of the awakening interest in metals and especially the knowledge of where copper and tin ores could be found. This interest had led to the use of rivers like the Elbe and passes like the Brenner for the development of a network of trade routes carrying amber and gold and connecting fixed agricultural settlements. In a barbarian fashion Europe had been mapped.

It was soon after this time that a race of bronzesmiths or tinkers appeared. They had been attracted to the south of Spain by the presence together of copper and tin. They radiated from the south of Spain with their bronze all over Western Europe. They even moved against the general flow of craftsmen eastwards to Sicily. These are the people Harold Peake named Beaker Folk from the bell-shaped pottery cups they made. Perhaps, as Bibby suggests, they bartered beer in their beakers. Certainly they must have traded in much more than bronze, which was too great a luxury for them to use, for example, in making their own arrowheads. During the centuries of their existence the Beaker Folk brought the remote parts of Europe for the first time into a cultural connection. They did so of course only by virtue of their maintaining themselves genetically independent. They may have interbred with the natives but they did not interbreed freely enough to lose their identity.

At the same time as the Beaker people were bringing one kind of unity to Europe by trading, another kind of unity was being forced on it by fighting. The people responsible are recognized by their polished stone battle-axes. These weapons were unique in history for they were modelled on the antler axes of the paleolithic hunters, but in detail they were copied from the softer copper axes cast by the contemporary smiths of Anatolia. The battle-axe people were pastoralists as the most successful fighters always have been. When they were first seen in the south of Russia about 2500 B.C. they depended on cattle. Later they picked up horses from their eastern neighbours and indeed it was probably through them that the horse, drawing its wheeled cart or chariot, was spread over Central Europe. It was certainly through this chariot in turn that they were spread into Anatolia and Persia. There they are given the names known to literature as the Hittites and the Mitanni. And they spoke languages of the family known as Aryan.[1] It is these languages which we must now use to trace the next steps in the history of man in Europe.

III. THE ARYAN EXPANSION

a. Origins

In the third millennium B.C. the European peoples spoke, as they do today, many different languages. But at that time these languages were more diverse in their stock of words, in their modes of handling words and sentences and in the sounds they used to express words. That is to say in etymology, in

[1] The Hyksos, following Josephus, have usually been thought of as Semites. But at the time they entered Egypt with chariots (in 1800 B.C.) they must have had recent Aryan connections in their leadership.

grammar and in phonetics they were less closely related than they are today. They probably belonged to what we should now call several extinct language families, those of the still unassimilated aboriginal paleolithic peoples.

We have many grounds for believing that this is so, historical and archaeological, biological and linguistic. But most neatly of all perhaps on the ground of place names. They reveal, as Wilhelm von Humboldt first showed, that in naming places earlier languages were used which have now disappeared from ordinary speech. For example in Britain we can easily recognize English, Danish and Norman, Latin and two kinds of Celtic names. We can also less easily recognize a residuum from earlier languages which belong to none of these, such as Thames, Albion and Britain itself.[1]

How many families of languages may have been submerged in Europe we do not know. We can see them spoken by the Lapps and by the peoples of the Caucasus. One of them, Basque, has been in process of slow submergence from a prime in the third millennium B.C. when it may have stretched as the speech of a shepherd people from Liguria to Lisbon.[2]

Already in the expansion of the desert peoples, we have seen the means by which Hamitic and Semitic languages displaced the earlier forms of speech in Mesopotamia and Egypt and spread over Africa. We have also seen that they did not spread by the extermination of the earlier people but by hybridization as well as by incorporation in a new social structure with stratified classes. Sometimes the conquered peoples with the lost languages found themselves at the bottom of the new society. But sometimes they found themselves, like the Sumerian priests, somewhere near the top; they were then capable not only of surviving but even of penetrating far into other lands in later ages.

The fact that Sanskrit and the modern languages of northern India are related to Latin and Greek and the modern languages of Europe was first noticed by that versatile and enquiring scholar, Sir William Jones, during the ten years (1784–1794), when he was brought into the service of the East India Company at Calcutta by Warren Hastings. We now think of these languages as the Aryan family. Although they are stretched across two continents we attribute to them a common ancestry and a common origin, somewhere between the Danube and the Don and at some time before the end of the third millennium B.C.

We can now apply our knowledge to the two interlocked problems of the origin of these languages and of the evolution of the peoples that speak them.

Historically these languages come into our picture when Aryan-speaking people invaded the lands occupied by literate and civilized societies. This happened when the Hittites appeared in Anatolia about 1900 B.C. Early in the second millennium, however, conquering Scythians (according to Mongait) must have stretched from the Carpathians to the Caucasus. Soon afterwards, but long before we can recognize them, related peoples, the Mitanni, Hurrians

[1] Humboldt's theory of the historical and ethnic stratification of place names was generalized and expanded by Isaac Taylor in the seven editions of *Words and Places* between 1864 and 1908, as well as in the *The Origin of the Aryans* (1889). For a modern discussion see Dauzat (1963) and the diffuse reports of 'toponymic' congresses.

[2] Hubschmidt (1951).

and others, had entered Iran. Yet other Aryans are believed to have invaded the Indus valley in the middle of the second millennium.

The Greeks reached Mycenae about 1700 B.C. and made themselves known in Crete by their inscriptions in the Linear B script of about 1500 B.C. The Latins, by inference, arrived in Italy many centuries later. All this we may describe as the civilized and literate impact of the Aryans.

Speakers of other groups of Aryan languages have quite a different history and our knowledge of them arises in quite a different way. What they did was concealed from us until recently since it was by impact on barbarian and illiterate peoples. It was also much slower in generating its results. The Celts arose in Germany in the eighth century B.C. The Teutons and the Slavs made themselves known even later, while of the movements of the Illyrians in the south and the Lithuanians in the north we know nothing.

This recital however already shows us that there was an expansion of the Aryan languages. But its character was that, not of steady expansion, but rather of a series of fire-cracker explosions each of which shifted the focus of activity and of propagation; each of which in doing so created new centres with their own potentialities of expansion and diversification.

We now have to ask ourselves two questions. First, what caused each of these explosions? Secondly, what effect did the resulting movements have on the peoples and the languages they spoke?

In the first beginning of the Aryans it seems likely that the invention of the battle-axe played a part. A pastoral tribe with great fighting qualities and speaking the original Aryan speech probably over a few generations imposed its rule, establishing and multiplying itself as a governing class, over a wide area. It was an area remote from the sea (since the word for sea did not enter its vocabulary).[1]

It must have been at the beginning of their development that the Aryans encountered and assimilated people hailing from Mesopotamia and bringing with them also some of the arts and the materials of civilization. For they had brought with them bronze and cattle, and knew them, as Piggott tells us, by their Sumerian names. In a few more generations these people met the purveyors of horses in the east; and in the west they probably encountered the purveyors of megalithic religion, art and technology.

Where and when these meetings occurred there must have been hybridization of peoples. In this way new combinations of techniques and ideas must have come about. From these in turn the new expansions we know might be expected to follow.

There is no point, at the moment, in asking just where and when these new combinations took place. But from what emerged we can see that new Aryan people moved and conquered over a wide area, covering the territory between Western Europe and India almost within the second millennium. Evidently therefore they were small ruling groups of great mobility; evidently they used horses; hence they moved east across the steppes more quickly than they moved west through the forest. And evidently the people they ruled were often peasant cultivators, settled people of mixed paleolithic and neolithic extrac-

[1] Paul Thieme (1958).

tion, who did not wholly move with them. Interbreeding was bound to occur but the different ruling castes did not at all quickly diverge. They retained for over a thousand years a remarkable similarity of character. Whether we think of the Homeric heroes in Greece, the heroic kings in Ireland or in India, or the early patricians in Rome, there appears the same pattern of warlike masculine gods, military prowess and patriarchal government.

We now have to look at what happened when these peoples moved in different directions. We have to distinguish between their civilized and their barbarian impact.

b. Civilized Impact: the Hittites

The first evidence of the Aryan character and capacity and pattern of development is given us by the Hittites. Here we have an invading tribe breaking into the mountain-bordered centre of Anatolia and creating on the northern fringes of the Babylonian world a confederation and an Empire and its successor states which, as described by Gurney, lasted over a thousand years (Table 8).

Table 8. *Simplified Classification of Languages Used in Writing Within the Hittite Empire*

After Gurney (1961).

Origin	*Lay*	*Clerical*	*Gods*
Paleolithic (indigenous)	HURRIAN (Urartu)	HATTIAN[1] (priests to several gods)	mainly Female Deities (agricultural
Neolithic (immigrant)	——	SUMERIAN (for scribes)	origin)
Aryan (invading from the north and east)	HITTITE LUWIAN (dialects) MITANNIAN[2]	PALAIC (priests of one god) TABALIC[3] (for scribes)	mainly Male Deities
Semitic (penetrating from the south)	——	AKKADIAN (diplomatic and commercial)	(pastoral origin)

[1] A dead language by 1800 B.C.
[2] Ruling class, breeding horses and having proto-Indian gods (Indra, Varuna *et al.*).
[3] A Luwian dialect in Cilicia also known as Hieroglyphic Hittite.

This Empire was itself the seat of the oldest agricultural settlements in the world and had long been penetrated by Mesopotamian craftsmen and traders. Within it developed quickly a new complex society joining all these elements together. How did this happen?

At the bottom of society, and its foundation, were of course the native cultivators; as in Mesopotamia and Egypt, they were serfs bound to the soil. There was also a class of slaves protected, as under the Code of Hammurabi, by the law and by the king. Above them was an urban society of merchants and craftsmen continually recruited from abroad; especially from Mesopotamia, for Babylonian and Assyrian merchants made themselves responsible for trade in the Hittite dominions.[1] In this way there developed a class structure at once professionally and racially stratified. Other specialists there were too who played a part of their own in strengthening the state. There were men from the east who brought in horses, and bred and managed them for purposes of war. And perhaps above all, in the estimation of the king, were the native tribe of miners, smelters and smiths who provided the ironwork for the military forces.

What held all these people together would seem to have been the military strength derived from the combination of warriors and weapons. Side by side with these however was the priesthood, a hierarchy diversified by region, by language and by race and itself dedicated to a pantheon of a thousand gods. This was indeed a confederate pantheon whose union undoubtedly, as in Babylonia, was the means of uniting the nation. What a problem they faced and solved is shown by the languages preserved in the written records. For, apart from illiterate and forgotten dialects, nine languages were in literate use; almost all of them were invading languages which were in process of suppressing the native forms of speech; and all of them in turn were to be suppressed by later invaders.

The sorting out of these languages and of the multilingual society which used them illuminates some of the processes of the Aryan expansion. What had happened was that five different warlike tribes, speaking different languages of the Aryan family, had won their way into Anatolia and established themselves as governing classes. One of them, speaking the true Hittite, had made itself the master of the others. Another had succeeded in controlling and organizing the priestly ceremonial of an Aryan god. The other three were in command in different regions; and one of them, Tabalic, had picked up from the conquered peoples with whom it had hybridized its own hieroglyphic form together with the ox-plough or *boustrophedon* style of writing.

If the subject peasant peoples are represented in the written, records it is by the priestly language, Hattian, and the local language nearest to Mesopotamia, Hurrian, for these are both unrelated to either the Aryan or the Semitic families. The Semitic Akkadian, already the *lingua franca* of Mesopotamia, is indispensable for diplomatic and also for commercial use among the merchant colonies. Last of all, Sumerian survives but it is written now in Akkadian cuneiform and used only by the professional scribes.

Within this great melting-pot the Aryan language of the Hittites was incorporating the roots of indigenous languages and modifying its sounds to fit the tongues of the nation they were creating. Tabernas, the title of all later kings, they produced by garbling the name of their first king *Labernas*. This monarch was himself the head of a governing class, created we must suppose by the combination of the chiefs of the five confederate states. The royal kinsmen

[1] Ozguç (1963).

constituted the Great Family. It was they who held the highest offices in the Empire. And it was they who, in due course, married into other royal families and, in the time of the Egyptian Eighteenth Dynasty, laid the foundations of an international royal caste.

The relics of this great civilization are known to us because its early chieftains, invading Anatolia, encountered men who could cut stone and build with it. These men built the fortresses which we see in the Hittite capital of Hattusas or Boghazköy, just as the Greeks built a citadel at Mycenae, or later in the Acropolis of Athens. This is a pattern which was to be repeated wherever the Aryans found themselves on the frontier of their expansion. We see the same effect much later in their conflicts with one another, in the Castle at Dublin or in the Kremlin at Moscow. For, as they assimilated subject peoples, their own character and language diversified and they everywhere created nations which struggled for power.

The military citadel was the regular and recurring focus of assimilation. In it were the warriors and administrators. Around it collected the dependent and settled craftsmen. Around them in turn were the merchants and travellers. And in the countryside beyond were the peasants, guaranteed in the possession of the land they loved by the rendering of services and produce to the rulers who protected them. From the citadel the use of the governing Aryan language, whether Hittite or Greek, passed out into the dependent community. It was a community subjected and protected in varying degrees according to the varying opportunities of race relations which, with the development of a common language and common religion, became the class relations of a new nation.

These are the kinds of process we can infer from putting together what we know of modern societies, what archaeology tells of the ancient city, and what literature tells us (for example in the interpretation of Fustel de Coulanges) of the structure and developing law and religion of ancient Aryan society.

c. Barbarian Impact: the Celts

In the general respect that it synthesized a multiracial society the Hittite Empire provides a model of the effects, the successful and lasting effects, of the Aryan expansion. It is however clear that the time, place and action of this synthesis, its causes and its consequences, had a specific character for each of the expanding groups. The tribes invading India met a racial situation with extreme contrasts which we shall need to consider on its own. Those moving north into the Baltic, on the other hand, found themselves in an almost empty paleolithic world and avoiding both hybridization and evolution maintained the greatest purity and stability in their Aryan speech. The Slavs, who developed later, after their language was more changed, then advanced also into an almost empty world to the east. A very flat world it was with good communications. For these reasons they preserved a great uniformity among languages covering a wider area than any others of the Aryan family.

The most wide-ranging of all Aryan migrations and conquests, however, on the evidence of living languages, were carried out by the Celts. They completed their movement on the western fringe of Europe but they went east as well as west. The Celts have left their place names in the rivers Danube, Dee and Don (in Russia as well as England), in the provinces of Gaul, Galatia and Galicia (in Poland and in Spain), in the Italian Appenines as well as the Welsh mountains. Yet this appearance is racially the most deceptive of all.

In Central Europe, remote from the new inventions, we get our first glimpse of the Celtic warrior in the thousand graves of Hallstatt dating from the beginning of the first millennium B.C. At this time close to the sources of iron and of the salt which gives its name to Salzburg as well as to Hallstatt, and not far from the communications of the Danube basin, a rich community established itself. Rich enough, that is, to import for its ornaments, not only bronze, but also the works of Etruscan artists. Strong enough to have wide authority since its weapons were iron in advance of the more northern peoples. These were the Celts who were later to develop the type of art known as La Tène which they spread, along with their language, over most of Europe.[1]

What was the real origin of the Celts? What was the spark which fired the explosion of Celtic-speaking tribes in the region of Hallstatt? There cannot be much doubt that traffic up the Danube had brought traders, craftsmen and miners from Anatolia into this part of Central Europe. Here they found iron ore. The men who forged the iron and the warriors who wielded the weapons came together. In the fifth century they made a new invention, the iron horse-shoe. Soon they discovered its far-reaching possibilities. Mounted on horses, the Celtic tribes proved for a little while invincible. They nearly submerged their civilized southern neighbours. So it was, according to Heichelheim, that they were able to occupy Rome in 387 B.C. and to defeat the Macedonian king a hundred years later, establishing themselves in Anatolia in the province named Galatia.

The Celts owe their lasting fame to what they did in their settled life in the west. They owe it to their military and agricultural, religious and artistic activities. And, in addition, to their languages and literature which still survive. These activities did not arise, however, from the moment of origin of the Celts. They arose rather from the combinations of the castes and tribes of different origins brought under the control of Celtic chieftains. The kinds of people who created these results have been coming to light from the study of their work at the time and the traces it has left behind.[2] What appears most clearly is that they were diverse. As the Celtic domination spread over Western Europe, the system of Celtic life evolved by the establishment of common languages, common customs and common religious practices and mythological beliefs.

In this development it was natural that the smiths played a prominent part. Their work was the foundation of the whole conquest. How they combined their magic with that of the earlier paleolithic, neolithic and bronze age peoples, we do not know. But we can see that the chemistry of the smiths was

[1] Bibby has described the meaning of the discoveries of Hallstatt and La Tène and of the contemporary Slavs of Biskupin.

[2] For place-name evidence see Bosch-Gimpera (1951); for the rest see Anne Ross (1967).

now more effective than the spectacular astronomy and engineering of earlier ages.

The Aryans, as a whole, differentiated in spreading and changed most where they had moved furthest. The same was bound to be true of the Celts. To the west they brought the iron age. There they arrived latest and there alone the Celtic languages now survive. But the people who speak these languages are inevitably less like the original Celts than many peoples who have been robbed of the speech of their ancestors by Latins and Germans. Like the names of many other races and languages, the name of Celt has been used to give a spurious stability to swiftly evolving situations.

The people who speak Celtic languages must owe their special character rather to the earlier people who existed in the western countries, people who arose as we have seen from the fusion of neolithic, megalithic and beaker peoples, people too with the largest paleolithic content in Europe. Their governing classes, to be sure, will have had a Celtic component and we shall see later what happened to them.

d. Speech and Society

What effects arose from the Aryan conquests? Clearly the movement of peoples was bound to lead to a mixture of ideas and of heredity, to recombination both cultural and genetic, to an enhanced stratification of societies which were cemented by their Aryan rulers. It also led to the expansion of languages which themselves reached a new level of discernment and so favoured the cultural development of the peoples who spoke them.

From the succession of all these reactions arose a profound evolutionary, and in consequence social and mental, transformation of the peoples affected. As Gordon Childe puts it, the Aryans 'appear everywhere as promoters of true progress and in Europe their expansion marks the moment when the prehistory of our continent begins to diverge from that of Africa or the Pacific'.[1]

e. Community and Dialect

The diversification of the language spoken by different Aryan communities requires of course more dimensions than can be represented on the kind of family tree popularly used for demonstrating their history. It was accompanied, and in a sense determined, by the integration of language within each community. Now the primitive community, that is the unstratified paleolithic community, as we saw, is relatively homogeneous and relatively stable. It has no abiding cleavages or discontinuities within it. Moreover its breeding system is adapted to avoid sudden genetic changes. As a rule therefore its language is stable and every individual is relatively well adjusted by his structure to speak it perfectly.

But when a new stratified society comes into being, as with the Hittites, their constituent members, having spoken dissimilar languages, now learn to

[1] We cannot however leave unamended Childe's suggestion (1926) that a higher language 'generates' a higher mentality. The primary process is when men improve language. It is a secondary and derived process when language improves men. Here the biologist has to be explicit and even dogmatic.

speak the same language. This is a new situation. The new common language is bound to be under stress. Historical examples show that it becomes garbled. It moves towards a common phonetic and grammatical character for the new nation. But the racial differences survive as local differences and class differences within the nation. These are represented in the character, behaviour, and speech of communities and classes. In consequence every social or mating group in a nation continues to be represented by a dialect in speech.

The slow synthesis of each of the new stratified communities produced a new language incorporating new roots, eroding or simplifying the old grammar but especially shifting its phonetic character, accommodating the old speech to the new and different teeth and tongues of other races. It is on this account that we find the loss of certain sounds as well as the reduction of the complex inflexions of the original speech in modern Aryan languages. It is a process that can be studied very easily on the map of Europe. There, the movements of races in the course of the Aryan expansion have left a contour map of the distribution of blood groups which is a reflection of the changes which have shifted the phonetic complement of speech. The result of these changes is that the descent of languages as assessed by etymology has no connection with their classification by phonetics.[1]

The language of an advanced society which is protected from alien intrusion settles down to a uniformity and stability which is proportionate to the absence of movement within it. Only in Lithuanian, the language of an isolated forest people, does the continent of Europe allow us to see this situation.[2]

The phonetic evolution and differentiation of the Aryan languages is a history of instability: the master language being forced on, or taken up by, subject peoples. For, having been taken up, it was changed by an infinite number of individual concessions. These are acts of accommodation. The individual accommodates himself to the average practice of society since this is the best way to make himself understood. Indeed, we may say, in the long run, speech being as indispensable as it is, accommodation is the only means of survival.

These biological principles are necessary for the understanding of society as well as of speech. They are therefore worth stating in strict terms. The properties of all organisms arise, we say, from the interaction of their heredity with their environment. In speech the environment of the individual is the speech of the community; that is something derived from its collective genetic character. In primitive society the individual is genetically indistinguishable from the community. In a stratified or multiracial society the individual may diverge very far from the average of the community. He adapts himself with an effort,

[1] For example the dental fricative TH overrides the distinction between Celtic, Teutonic and Latin tongues and even between the Aryan and Basque families (Darlington, 1947; Brosnahan, 1961).

[2] After a thousand years of near isolation the greatest stability has however been maintained in Iceland. In Polynesia, after the same passage of time similarly undisturbed, phonetic differences distinguish the remote island groups; but they are not of the order arising in the same time with greater racial heterogeneity within the small space of England.

different individuals achieving conformity (as we saw earlier from the work of Ballard) in different ways. When the effort is too great for particular *groups* the common speech splits into local dialects with class differences. These correspond with the tribal differences in primitive speech. But, when the effort is too great for particular *individuals*, they develop what we hear as defects of speech in respect of the standard of the group.

The evidence of the genetic control of the evolution of language is perhaps easier to understand in its social and biological relations if we notice that it is somewhat closely paralleled by the genetic control in the evolution of morals. Here also the standards of behaviour derive from the average opinion of the community, an opinion felt, expressed and accumulated over many generations. The individual whose character comes closest to the average of the community finds least difficulty in conforming with its beliefs and behaviour. But for some individuals a great effort is required and for others the effort is too great, social delinquency corresponding to speech defect. Classes and communities may diverge openly or covertly. And practices and beliefs evolve owing to genetic changes in society.[1]

IV. WHY EUROPE WAS DIFFERENT

We asked, at an earlier stage, why it was that agriculture began in South West Asia. Similarly at this stage, five millennia later, we may ask why it was that the greatest movements and activities were going on in the heart of Europe. The answer is that they were promoted by the existence of a territory rich in forests and minerals, diverse in soils, free from the diseases most dangerous to man and, after the retreat of the ice, accessible to colonization by sea and river, colonization moreover from the growing centres of civilization which were near at hand.

It was the impact of the civilized peoples on the paleolithic peoples by migration, by mixture, by hybridization, and by the consequent creation of new races which generated new societies with new languages. These new societies were capable themselves of technical advances of the kinds that we recognize in the barbarian world.

These were the primary effects. The secondary effects were the assaults of the new barbarian peoples on the civilized states to whose peoples they owed a significant part of their own ancestry. Europe was to be for 3000 years the short-term victim, and long-term beneficiary, of these repeated assaults, this continued disturbance without which, as other continents show, the develop-

[1] Note that the principles of economy of effort and of the adaptation of the child to the community are discussed by Jesperson (1922) who was, of course, writing before any genetic theory of dialect and language. Note also that the environment may be changed at other levels in both linguistic and moral connections. Thus in a community technical advances alter the practical effects and hence the moral significance of sexual relations. Similarly mouth mutilations will alter the sound complement that will be preferred in any language. Further, as we shall see, in slave societies, both ancient and modern, slave and free interact but in different ways in respect of language and of morals. *Cf.* Darlington (1961).

ment of its civilization would have been slowed down or brought to a standstill.

We now have to examine the development and the consequences of the long intercourse between the civilized and the barbarian peoples. It was an intercourse in which documentary history shows us what happened in war, while archaeology indicates more clearly what happened in peace.

8

THE GREEKS

I. THE RISE OF CRETE

THE FIRST FARMERS arrived in Greece and settled in the plain of Thessaly as early as the seventh millennium B.C. It is not known whether they made their way round the Thracian shores from Anatolia or crossed the Aegean on rafts or coracles. The crossing can be made without losing sight of land. The first settlers no doubt soon appeared in eastern Crete and penetrated to the centre at Knossos. There the mud-brick houses must have been built and re-built for an immense period for they raised a mound thirty feet deep below the foundations of the first palace of Minos of about 2000 B.C.

The early colonists in Crete have connections with Anatolia from which they had obviously brought their crops, their stock and their goddess-figurines. They also show their connections with Palestine to which they owed some of their pottery. But throughout the neolithic age they changed very little. Their traffic with the mainland must have been irregular and uncertain.

What mattered, of course, was the improved sailing ships which with the coming of bronze could be built by Phoenicians notably from Ugarit on the coast of Lebanon. It was these ships that decided the destiny of Crete by bringing new people to its shores. The first people they brought would certainly have been shipbuilders attracted by the forests of cypress and cedar and other useful timber that clothed its mountains. The second arrivals would no less certainly have been sailors attracted by the safe havens on both the northern and southern shores.

These new colonists established the regular connection of Crete with ports in Europe, Asia and Africa. Gradually they made Knossos into the metropolis of the Mediterranean. Its trade, above all with Egypt, made it possible for Sir Arthur Evans in excavating Knossos to date its remains by their Egyptian content in three main zones: Early, Middle and Late Minoan corresponding with Old, Middle and New Kingdoms in Egypt. Each of the continents, each of the countries, with which the Cretans came into contact made their own contribution to its life, its culture and inevitably its population. The Carians of the Aegean islands served to man the ships. The people of Byblos sent not only carpenters but evidently scribes. The people of Libya may well have offered warriors as they did to Egypt. We see their African influence in the bare breasts of the women, in the Libyan sheaths or codpieces of the men. We also see it in their art with its gay sensuality which was not to emerge again in Europe until the time of the Baroque.

What of the royal and priestly castes who established their centres of government at Knossos and elsewhere? All the three great neighbouring regions and civilizations contributed to them. One dynasty may have been refugees from civil war in Egypt bringing with them not only, as Herodotus says, the names of gods who later found a home in Greece, but also those practices of ritual and divination which were to dominate the later classical world.

Other dynasties, according to the legendary evidence adduced by G. L. Huxley, suggest Phoenician and Anatolian connections (Pedigree 2).

Pedigree 2. Phoenician Connections

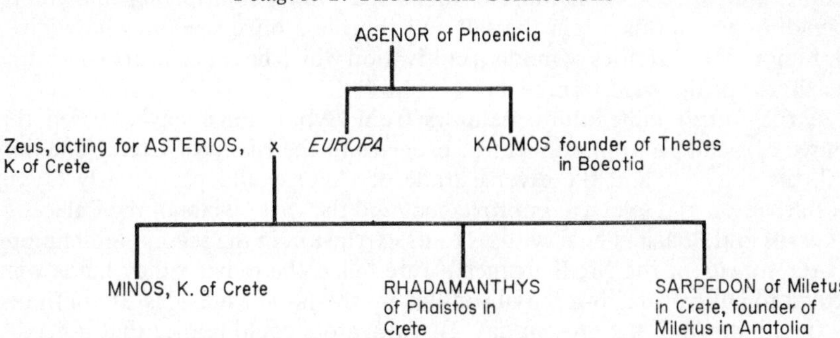

Thus Herodotus offers us an international family tree. Here an exciting love affair must not distract us from linguistic connections of which the historian could not be aware: for both Rhadamanthys and Sarpedon are Luwian names from Anatolia. Again the Luwian language contributed to the Greek in Linear B the notable word *Labyrinthos*, cognate with *Labrus*, the double axe, symbol of rule, and the Hittite *Labarnas* which we have already met. Thus one of the Minoan dynasties must have had Luwian as well as Phoenician ancestors. These Luwians, in helping to establish the mercantile rule of Crete about 1900 B.C., were bound to have brought with them Babylonian traders such as were at that time established in Anatolia.

At the bottom of this society there remained as always the original colonizing peasants and herdsmen, the Eteo-Cretans of the *Odyssey*, the *perioikoi* (or *perioeci*) of Aristotle (*Politics:* 1271b. 30). These people kept their name as a separate race probably because they had kept their separate language. The languages spoken in Crete might remain different for a great period in the different social classes as they did in the Hittite Empire.

The achievements of the Minoan society of the early second millennium not only transformed Crete, they transformed the Mediterranean. And, as we have seen, they probably reached out into the Atlantic, to the Canaries in the south and to Britain in the north. In doing so the Minoans enriched themselves but they also exposed themselves. They had turned the sea, which had been a barrier to communication, into a means of communication. It became the easiest and quickest means for the movement of peoples. The sea was no longer a protection against invaders; it carried them to their victims.

II. CULTIVATION AND THE OLIVE

At this point we must consider the history of the olive which was to play a silent but, to us, impressive part in the development of the Mediterranean.[1] The wild olive is a straggly and thorny bush which grew wild near the coasts of Syria and Anatolia in the sixth millennium B.C. Here the expanding neolithic farmers first met it. Soon an observant gatherer of its fruits noticed an unusual tree with larger and oilier fruit. He also discovered that he could propagate it easily from cuttings. When he did so the improved variety and the tribe of people who discovered it must have started jointly multiplying and jointly spreading. From this origin the tall and thornless olive seedlings have given the hundreds of varieties of modern cultivation which have been carried around the shores of the Mediterranean.

In the fourth millennium seafarers from Byblos must have carried this source of wealth and instrument of progress to the island of Crete. The limy soil, the salty air and the diverse trade of Crete would particularly favour its cultivation and selective improvement and the vast oil jars of the Palaces of Knossos and Phaistos bear witness to its expansion in the second millennium. As the forests of the Mediterranean were felled the richer valley lands were turned to cultivation; but the olive filled up the poorer hillsides. It continued its spread down to the present day. Its cultivators could rejoice that it needed little moisture. But the olive, which expanding seemed to have been the gift of the gods, was on a longer view the seed of ruin.

Thus for a long time, indeed for the 1000 years between 2500 and 1500 B.C., the development of Crete, apart from occasional earthquakes, seemed prosperous. Two balanced processes were represented by the export of timber and oil to Egypt: forest trees were being felled and olive trees were being planted. As the olive provided the lustral oil with which successive dynasties of priest-kings were being anointed the deep green landscape turned first grey and then white; the soil accumulated in a million years was being washed from its hillsides in a few centuries. The natural wealth of the country was being stripped away with the soil. The population was perhaps as numerous as ever in the middle of the second millennium but it was a population which now depended on its trade in African slaves, in Cypriot copper and in Nubian gold. The small island now depended on the profits of trade and on food imported over the hitherto peaceful seas.

The same transformation, following in the wake of the axe, the plough, and

[1] Morettini (1950).

the olive in their westward progress, was to overtake in turn all the civilized states of the Mediterranean, reaching next the adjoining mainland of Greece.[1]

Crete may even in its last stage have been short of native timber. In these circumstances, when foreign invaders came, they were free first to subject the island, and then to loot and to destroy it. From the destruction that eventually came there was no recovery. The princes departed and pirates took their place. The natives, the lower orders, the Eteo-Cretans, ultimately came into their own to wait for the next conquerors. The impoverished centre of a peaceful world had no place in the warlike times that lay ahead. But with Crete as with Sumer we know that the priests, the artists and the seafarers found other places where they could make a living and a home. Their descendants, weak in number but strong in action, we shall meet in other parts of the Mediterranean sometimes speaking Greek and sometimes other languages.

III. THE MYCENAEAN WORLD

Part of the Aryan tribes moving southward at the beginning of the second millennium entered Anatolia founding the Hittite, Luwian, and other kingdoms. A part of the Luwians seem to have turned aside from Anatolia and penetrated through the plain of Thessaly into the centre of Greece to leave as their record the famous names of Corinth and Parnassus (from the Hittite, *Parna*, a house). Other tribes, perhaps later, settled regions which tradition assigns precisely, Attica to the Ionians, the Peloponnese to the Arcadians and the neck of Greece to the Aeolians. We need not suppose however that these tribal distinctions had much to do with regional differences in later classical Greece. During the intervening thousand years the invaders had formed separate states and separate nations. They had done so in stratified societies of different kinds. Each made its own combination with the peasant population it found in its own regions and also, as we shall see, with later immigrants from the east and the south. It was from these non-Greek differences that was to arise the later opposition between Athens and Sparta.

At this point we have to notice the transformation in the historians' view of Greece during the ninety years which have followed Schliemann's discovery of the graves and tombs of Mycenae.[2] Excavation of the prehistoric remains of the Greeks has steadily re-asserted the truth of the legendary foundations, or we may say the oral tradition of history, preserved by Homer and Hesiod and affirmed or enlarged by Herodotus, Thucydides and Pausanias. Subject of course to the reservations we make from comparison with the economic, social and genetic evidence from other societies.[3]

We are therefore justified in accepting the tradition, reported by Hesiod, which tells us that in the course of these invasions other bodies of invaders or colonists arrived in Greece. They came by sea and they came from the opposite direction, from the Ancient East. One was the party of Cadmus which

[1] Plato (*Kritias*), and also Baulier and Langham (1955).

[2] Described by Cottrell.

[3] Hammond and Burn have recently surveyed the evidence and explained the reservations.

founded the city of Boeotian Thebes, the place to which, as we have seen, the legend or history of Oedipus came to be attached. Another Phoenician party, bringing Phoenician names for its heroes and its gods, was concerned in the foundation of Corinth where a neolithic settlement had been established more than a thousand years earlier. Yet another party, perhaps the first, entered the hospitable Gulf of Nauplia, founded the first city of Greece and named it after the plain which was known as Argos to its Greek inhabitants. Here it was that the citadels of Mycenae and Tyrinthos later arose to command the valley and win the hegemony of Greece for their kings.

The colonists of the Argos district, the Argolid, called themselves Danaoi. They claimed to come from Egypt and they might well have been Hyksos refugees expelled from the Nile delta by the liberation of Amenophis, founder of the Eighteenth Dynasty about 1570. This, as Huxley suggests, would 'account for the swift rise of true civilization in the Argolid in the sixteenth century B.C.' More precisely it would account for the introduction of administrators and scribes, merchants and builders into the province of mainland Greece most accessible to ships coming from the Egyptian ports. It was a province already provided with settled peasants and northern warriors. And looking at the great walls of Agamemnon's citadel and tomb we can see how well those builders must have completed the human fabric of the new society. A century or two later the Minoan rulers of Crete and of the Aegean were displaced by invaders from these new Mycenaean kingdoms who brought the Aryan speech of the Greeks into the island. This uniform governing class language combined with a new script to give the Linear B tablets of accounts which were used in common by the Palaces of Knossos in Crete, of Pylos in the Peloponnese, and of Thebes in Boeotia. It was the same kind of uniformity that was later to be demonstrated by the caste of bards and preserved in Homer. The two are separate prototypes of the two bases of uniformity underlying all later literary languages.

The evidence of the growth of Mycenaean civilization that we learn from Greece and Crete is neatly paralleled by that from the ruins of Ugarit. It is worth pondering what Woolley (in 1958, pp. 113–114) says of this great port on the coast of Syria:

'After 1400 B.C., by which time the Mycenaeans had overrun Crete and wiped out the dynasty of Minos, Ugarit becomes almost a Mycenaean colony. The city proper is girt with cyclopean stone walls pierced by vaulted sally-ports—walls exactly like those of Tiryns in the Greek Peloponnese; and in the harbour town attached to it the wealthy merchants lie buried beneath the floors of their houses in vaulted stone tombs that recall earlier tombs in Crete, Cyprus and Mycenae, and the objects deposited with the dead are mainly Mycenaean. Obviously there was in the town a colony of Mycenaean Greeks who were among the leaders of the local society, the chief merchants in what was a very prosperous commercial community and, we may be sure, the prime movers in the Phoenician expansion which was to spread over the Mediterranean that hybrid civilization in which the arts of Egypt, Mesopotamia, Anatolia and the Aegean all played a part.' And Woolley very properly adds:

'This is not merely a matter of professional interest to the archaeologist; it is a vital fact for the historian who would trace the development of the modern world from its roots in antiquity.'

What indeed was that *hybrid* civilization? It was something created and maintained by a stratified society, a society built up by the working together of many peoples, Minoan merchants, Mycenaean scribes, Egyptian masons and artists, Aegean sailors, Phoenician boatbuilders and also priests, each caste except the slaves preserving its own genetic independence, and hence its own separate traditions, while learning, some readily, some reluctantly, to speak the common Semitic language on which the society depended for its well-being.

The Mycenaean governing class who followed the Danaoi on the mainland had a multiracial origin less pronounced than that of the Minoans whom they displaced in the island. In both, nobles, merchants and artisans had infiltrated from the Ancient East into a peasant community which had itself come much earlier from another part of the Ancient East. The difference lay in the new warrior element from the waves of expanding Aryans which successively struck Greece in the first nine centuries of the second millennium.

IV. THE DORIAN INVASION

In the period of two generations between 1250 and a culminating attack on Egypt in 1191 came the second great thrust of the expanding Aryan peoples into the Ancient East. Invaders from the northern Balkans burst into the Mediterranean world. They penetrated Anatolia; they destroyed the Hittite Establishment setting up their own kingdom which we know as Phrygia. Later under the name of Dorians they invaded the centre and south of Greece. We are then told that, in the guise of the 'Peoples of the Sea', the same invaders attacked the Egyptians who threw them back. But they were able as Philistines to settle in and give their name to Palestine; and to set up colonies in Crete, Libya, Sicily and Italy. These maritime achievements could not, however, have been the work of inland Aryans who knew nothing of the sea. Rather they represent the fragments of the Anatolian and Balkan peoples already subjugated by the Aryan invaders. A very notable later fragment was the one we call Etruscan which established a new federation of states in the north of Italy. Homer's Trojan war, wherever his Troy may have also been, was, as Seton Lloyd puts it, an incident in the succeeding tumult.

The character of these movements both on land and on sea, and of the people who made them, becomes much clearer when we look at the people who invaded Greece. The name of Dorians is given to the warrior tribes who settled in most of the Peloponnese occupying Corinth and founding Sparta. Destroying Mycenae, they then crossed the sea to conquer Crete and Rhodes. But these great events were spread over two centuries. Many of the dispossessed people of all classes fled into Attica and, sooner or later, overseas. But some of their leaders, whose families were of Mycenaean, Minoan and ultimately Phoenician extraction, were adopted by the invading warriors.

Nor was this their only assimilation. Even before they had passed the isthmus of Corinth the invaders had adopted the priests of Apollo at Delphi as their guides and sponsors.

The Dorians were thus transformed in their class structure and enriched in their social resources by their own victorious invasion. To this transformation they owed their later progress. For their first advance they were perhaps indebted to better arms and better training for wars. For their later advance they were certainly indebted to new kings who were hybrids and new priests who claimed, and rightly claimed, to have come from the most ancient lands.

The Dorians had recognized three hereditary and professional groups within their society which, according to Hammond, were described as 'tribes' on account of their racially distinct origin. But as the Dorians advanced these tribes were converted into what we understand as castes. To these three they added a fourth, the royal caste from which, as we shall see, they were to derive their own kings.

The new Dorian society thus began by being conscious of its class structure and their conquests made them no less so. The peasants whom they subdued in the rich plain of Laconia they inserfed as *helots* (from Helos on the Laconian shore). They were of two kinds, family serfs and state serfs. The shepherds in the hills as well as strangers in the towns they laid under tribute as *perioikoi* (a name and an idea not unlike the Hebrew 'stranger'). Last of all they had their private chattel slaves.

V. THE EXPANSION

a. Anatolian Dispersal (1100–900)

The Dorian invasion led to the occupation of most of central Greece by the invaders. It led at the same time to the flight of a part of the defeated and dispossessed peoples. Some took refuge in the mountains and others overseas. But at such a time of crisis we naturally have to distinguish between what happened to the rulers and the ruled. Some of the Mycenaean leaders seem to have come to terms with the Dorians. The native Heracleidae for example established themselves as kings among the new settlers in Sparta. Codrus and his family from Pylos on the other hand led some of his own people into Attica where he was able to join forces with the Athenians in repelling the invaders. Others of the aristocracy took a leading part in organizing emigration across the Aegean. This movement proved to be of great importance for the survival of the Greeks and the future of civilization.

The first emigrations came probably from the first invaded country to the south of Thessaly. They were given the mythical name of Aeolian.[1] Their voyages began in 1130 and their destinations are uncertain. They wandered into Thrace and thence into the northern islands and the Troad coast. They founded the cities of Mitylene and Kyme. The second group of emigrations began after the Athenians under Codrus had repulsed the invaders. They were organized by the Athenians and were known as *Ionian*. But according to

[1] Hesiod names Aeolus, Ion and Doris as the mythical progenitors of the three Hellenic tribes.

Herodotus they were a mixed population of Boeotian and other refugees. They founded twelve cities including Ephesus, Miletus and Phocaea.[1]

Yet a third emigration is that of the Dorians themselves. They settled, as we saw, in Crete, Rhodes, Cos and also in the city of Halicarnassus. But the Dorians were not sailors and had no ships. Some of their colonies were admitted to be joint enterprises and were founded several generations after the invasion. We must therefore suppose that they had quickly begun a profitable co-operation with the sea-going communities amongst whom they had settled.

These three movements, springing from the Aryan expansion, reversed the direction of migration across the Aegean during the previous three millennia. They profited by the disintegration of the earlier military organization and authority both Hittite and Mycenaean. They took the form of invasion and occupation of islands and coastal territory that was already (according to Boardman) sparsely occupied by Greek and pre-Greek peoples. Mycenaeans and Phoenicians, Carians and Lydians were there already. In establishing themselves it seems therefore that the colonists had to rely on co-operation and probably leadership from Mycenaean nobles, and also on good new weapons and tools, probably the iron sword, the iron adze and the iron ploughshare.

Each of the twenty or more cities that were founded in this way thus arose from both conflict and co-operation. Each city arose from the fusion of several racial stocks speaking their own dialects and worshipping their own gods. Each city was led by a founder whose descendants presided over the local games and, when the city prospered, enjoyed the titles of kings or priests of the favoured cult. These families continued in their honours and offices sometimes for twenty or thirty generations, piously recorded in parallel with the hereditary priesthood they brought with them to maintain the shrines and the oracles on which depended the emotional unity and coherence of each little state.

Who were the ancestors from whom the colonial governing class were descended? Herodotus gives us the answer to this question. Coming to Athens as an alien writer from Dorian-Carian Halicarnassus he was not too well disposed to the Ionian aristocracy. 'Those who consider themselves the noblest of the Ionians', he tells us, 'brought no women with them but married Carians whose parents they had killed.' To them would naturally be assimilated the kings they elected who were also of diverse and mixed origin. The posterity of this governing class would assert their claim to Athenian descent. They would celebrate their Athenian caste festivals all the more vigorously for the condescension with which the resident Athenians affected to regard them.

In spite of this apparently unplanned hybridization the early migrations constituted the first planned processes of social construction of which we know. The colonies they founded were also the first specifically Greek invention. For they combined the Phoenician and Mycenaean trading post

[1] On hybrid sites, however, for *Miletus* was perhaps *Millawanda* of the Hittites and *Milwatos* of the Mycenaeans (Huxley 1966).

with an internal agricultural market which made the colony self-supporting. Each successful colony could in a couple of generations bud off its own colonies in turn. And each in turn was selected for increased enterprise and restlessness, in a word, for colonizing capacity. The capacity thus proved to be self-propagating.

Beneath these great migrations there must always have been a peasant section of the population which remained sedentary and immobile. This is obviously true of the helots of the Laconia and of the inland peoples behind the coastal cities of the Aegean colonies, Aeolian, Ionian and Dorian. This peasant substrate who had changed their rulers helped to give uniformity and coherence to the new groupings. For example the Aegean islands now peopled anew from all parts of the mainland were now able to re-assert their unity of earlier, pre-Greek, times in the joint annual festival of Apollo which they celebrated at Delos.

Table 9. *Approximate Dating of the Dark Age in the Greek-speaking World:* 1225–700 B.C.

After Hammond (1959); Boardman (1964) and others.

BREAKDOWN		
Sea People's raids	on CYPRUS	1225
	on EGYPT	1221
	defeated by Rameses III	1191
INVASION		
Phrygians invade Anatolia; Fall of Troy		1200
Dorians	invade Laconia	1120
	repulsed by Athenians (led by Codrus, King of Pylos)	1050
	migrate to Crete, Rhodes and Cos	1050–950
FLIGHT		
Aeolians cross to Lesbos and the Troad		1130–1000
Mycenaeans received in Attica		1000–900
Ionians migrate to Chios, Samos, Ephesus		
REVIVAL		
Phoenician alphabet introduced		840–760
Ionian League formed		
Olympic games inaugurated		776
Colonization begins again: Miletus founds Sinope		770
Midas of Phrygia marries daughter of Agamemnon of Kyme and sends throne to Delphi		750
Iliad and *Odyssey* composed by Homeridae in Chios		740–680
First coinage: Lydia-Aegina		680–660

b. Mediterraenean Colonies

By the middle of the eighth century peace had brought prosperity to the Greek cities of the mainland, of the islands, and of the new eastern colonies. The basis of this prosperity was however dangerously shifting. The felling of forests on the hillsides was beginning to have the same effects as in Crete. Enterprise was undiminished but, in the absence of war, overpopulation was obvious. People had to be sent abroad. Some went willingly; others were chosen by lot.

Piracy was one of the opportunities which the sea offered to the seafarer and, as we saw, it was the one which tempted the Cretans most. But commerce and colonization are what have left the conspicuous and successful record in history.[1] Commerce gave rise to the *emporion* and was chiefly developed in the ports of the ancient states, in Anatolia and Phoenicia and also, after much negotiation, in Egypt. The *emporia* were largely the Greek quarters of ancient cities and they came to constitute a network over a large part of the Ancient East. It was a network through which Greek artists and artisans mixed with the artists and artisans of Phoenicia, Egypt, Babylonia and Persia. They mixed, they exchanged ideas and to a certain extent they interbred. To a certain extent also the eastern artisans emigrated to the Greek cities of the west. The flow was in both directions. What to the Greeks was the process of 'orientalization' discussed by Boardman, must have meant a process of occidentalization of the technical classes of the more ancient east.

In addition, what the Greeks were receiving from the east, they were also passing on further west. This they did by their second type of movement, that of colonization, the formation of new homes, *apoikia*, which were new self-governing cities. They were all ports on the coasts of the undeveloped countries of the western Mediterranean. It was a movement of pure occidentalization. The settlers were usually people of highly differentiated character representing stratified societies capable of carrying all the components of their new civilization. The site chosen was often one visited earlier by Mycenaeans or Phoenicians and in country still sparsely peopled by tribal cultivators. It was usually chosen, as we shall see, on the advice of the Oracle of Delphi. The colonists themselves were also chosen on experienced advice. They were led by noble adventurers with their warlike followers. They included seamen and navigators, traders, farmers and artisans in the proportions that the site demanded. And later, administrators, lawyers and artists followed. They followed if success came to the colony; or equally if disaster came at home, as happened when in the sixth century the Persians reached the Aegean.

The future of a colony was bound to depend on the breeding relations established between the Greeks and the natives. These depended on two factors: the character of the Greeks and the character of the natives. Certain of the Dorian colonies seem to have been of the pure warrior caste as in Sparta. Having no peasant helots or herdsmen *perioikoi* with them, they expected to reduce the local peasants or herdsmen to this status. This they usually succeeded in doing. The Libyan herdsmen became the *perioikoi* of Cyrene. The Sicilian peasants became the helots of Syracuse.

What Herodotus tells us of the colonization of Cyrene by the Dorians in 640 B.C., reinforced by the evidence of Boardman, provides the most significant account of Greek colony formation. In the first place it arose through the crowding out of the small Dorian island of Thera. In the second place it was led by a Mycenaean king directed by the Oracle of Delphi. The priests claimed to know that there was an opportunity for Greek farmers in this province and

[1] See Boardman (1964).

their claim was vindicated. The neolithic expansion had carried agriculture across North Africa to the mountainous west where the Berber peoples maintained it. But it had quickly destroyed the forests and exhausted the diminishing water supplies of Libya leaving subsistence only for sheep.

The Libyans welcomed colonists who fortunately had no sheep with them. Rightly so, in the first instance, for the Greeks brought an understanding of engineering and of water control; they brought new and improved crops; and especially they brought the olive. At first, the colonists married some native wives, so generating a diverse and adaptable population. In due course the Dorian colonists treated the herdsmen as they did in Greece itself, as *perioikoi*, inferior castes. And in due course also a princess of the royal house married the Egyptian Pharaoh Amasis of the Twenty-sixth Dynasty. Long after the Persian conquest in 515 the Greek province continued to prosper.

Several of the Greek cities in Cyrene still survive today in spite of the dwindling resources of the country. But on the north side of the Mediterranean and on the Black Sea many hundreds of colonies were founded of which nearly half still exist and a few like Naples and Constantinople are as populous today as ever before. Some of these were modest sites like little *Kerasoun* from which we get and name the cherry. Others grew in splendour. The most striking of these arose from the most remote enterprise, the founding of Massalia (or Marseilles) in the far north-west in 600 B.C. The founding city was Phocaea, itself an Aeolian colony on the coast north of Smyrna whose destruction by the Persians in 531 may be said to have brought the Greek colonizing movement to a standstill. Massalia became the centre of a group of coastal colonies but its influence, as Boardman shows, spread far inland. It not only brought the vine and the olive to Gaul; it produced a new civilization which has never been entirely interrupted to this day. It was a civilization in which the barbarian arts of Hallstatt and La Tène were fused with those of the civilized world. It was the second of the five great steps which created the French people.

We need not believe the story that one of the leaders of the Massalian expedition was chosen for her husband by the daughter of the Celtic king on the very day of his landing. But it is certain that here as elsewhere intermarriage occurred, class by class, between the Greeks and the local inhabitants. Thus, while the predominantly Greek character of each colony was maintained, the basis of friendly intercourse with the neighbouring populations was also established and extended. The genetic differentiation of town and country, of course, still persists in these places today. So also does the genetic community of all the ports around the Mediterranean coasts which arose from the foundation of these colonies: the sea and their ships bound them together genetically as it did culturally.

VI. THE MOVEMENT OF SOCIETY

a. The Meeting of Peoples

The origins of the Greeks show us for the first time certain principles which throughout history govern the combination of societies. When two stratified societies meet whether through trade or conquest, the different classes of

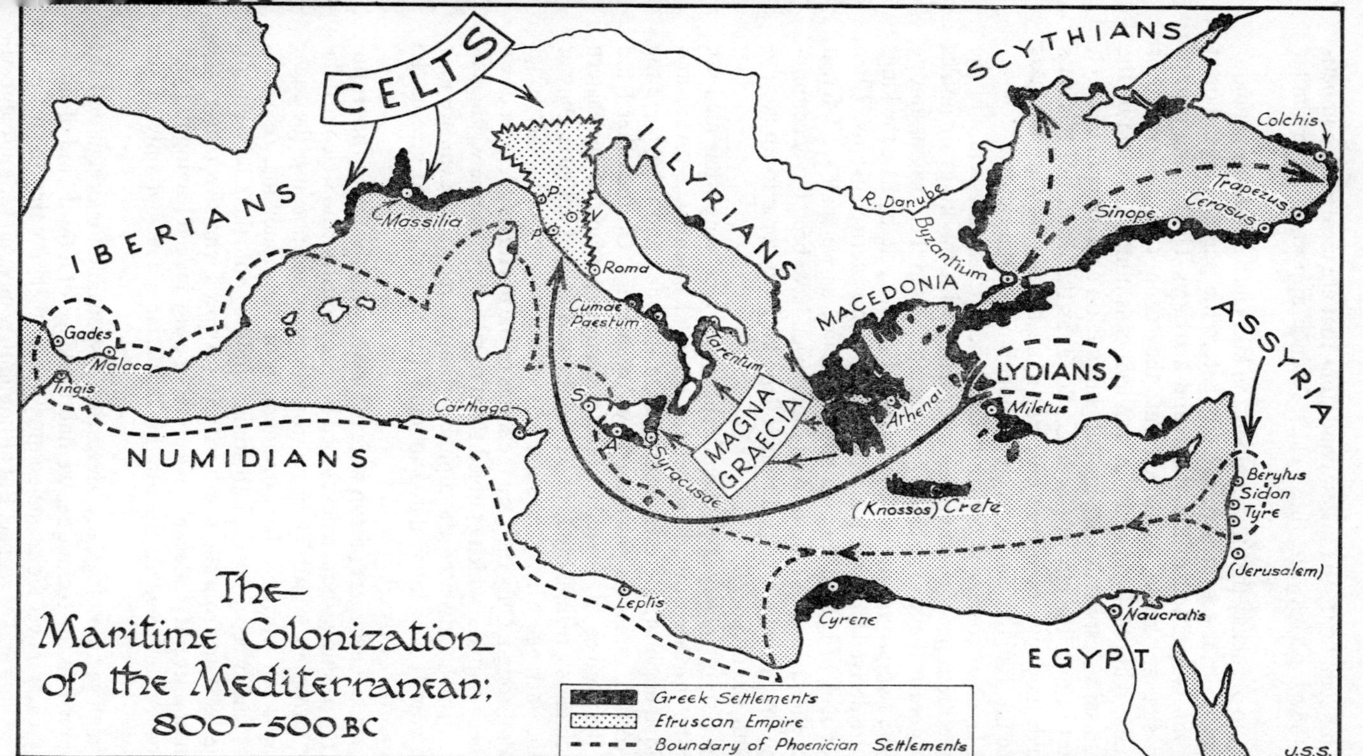

Fig. 9. The Maritime Colonization of the Mediterranean from 800–500 B.C. by Phoenicians, Greeks and Etruscans The connection between the Phoenician base and the western colonies was broken when the mother country was annexed by the Assyrians (580 B.C. ?).

Note: The Greeks were closely bound to the cultivation of the olive; the Phoenicians less so; the Etruscans not at all.

After F. Van Der Meer, map 1,

society react independently to the new conditions that are created. A competition at once develops between those classes which appear to serve similar purposes.

It is at the top of society that this competition takes its fiercest form and our ancestors' genetic transaction here actually enters the pages of legend or of history. For this is a matter of life, death and marriage. The leading men of the defeated side are killed, or driven out; they cannot be enslaved. For example, Baalu, King of Tyre, or Belus as Virgil calls him, is expelled by the Assyrians and sails westwards with his daughters Dido and Anna in 666 B.C., to rule if not to found the city of Carthage. So far as the women of this class are concerned, they may be driven out. But more usually they are taken as wives or, like the Trojan women, as slave concubines of the victors.

A second layer of society is constituted by the priests, the seers and the oracles. Later these people sometimes intermarry with the kings or nobles with whose interests they are so closely connected. And in their origins among the Greeks the two groups are equally mixed. For the priests, like the kings and nobles, are derived from the fusion of Aryan with eastern elem ents. When the Oracle of Delphi helped the incoming Dorians, as we shall see later, it was a part of the process of fusion. And it may well have been the accommodation of the oracles which helped some of the kings to come to an accommodation with the invaders.

A third section of society is that concerned with recording what men do. Here when the northern invaders met the civilized orientals a severe and perhaps unique clash of interests occurred. On the one hand there were the bards of Mycenae, minstrels patronized by Aryan kings. On the other hand there were the scribes of Crete, eastern craftsmen patronized by eastern officials. Each class presumably kept within its own field of activity. Only at the end of the dark age when migration was scrambling the old society does writing break through. Only then are the songs of the northern poets set down on the southern papyrus which enabled them to survive when the writings of the Phoenicians who invented the alphabet disappeared; set down, we may notice, with vowels now intercalated to show the metre, and to give us the script of the Greeks as we know it.

Similarly when the forgers of iron were dispersed with the fall of the Hittite Empire it is the people without a developed bronze industry who welcomed the blacksmiths into their midst. The new iron weapons are put into the eager hands of barbarian warriors. It is invaders from the mountains, Assyrians and Persians, who sweep away the Babylonians holding onto their old weapons. And it is the Dorians from the north with iron swords who sweep away the rich and conservative Mycenaeans. Sweep them away indeed leaving in Pylos and Knossos written records not of the barbarian poets but only of the civilized clerks.

With a fourth section of society, the artists responsible for design and the artisans responsible for technique, we find evidence of a third kind of interaction. They carry ideas from one country to another, notably from Egypt to Phoenicia, Crete and Mycenae. But although they meet no serious competitors in the relatively undeveloped countries to which they emigrate they naturally depend for their livelihood on their new masters and they express only the ideas which these usually less civilized masters respect. Migration of artists, even without hybridization, therefore involves change and sometimes deterioration in their art.

The loosening of society following the great invasions meant a freedom of movement, described by Finley, for all these men of skill, the men described in the *Odyssey* (XVIII, 382) as *demio-ergoi* or workers for the community. It was these people who moved into the Greek-speaking world at the end of the dark age and constituted the genetic basis of its intelligentsia and made the genetic break with the Mycenaean world. They did so on account of the temporary freedom of expression and diversity of social structure which scores of Greek cities developed during the eighth and seventh centuries as they threw off monarchical government and developed their arrangements and devices for government by discussion.

The Homeric society, as Finley has pointed out, was *ruled* by kings who were *advised* by nobles (or men with ancestors) and *applauded* by ordinary freemen. This limitation of arbitrary government by custom was derived from the racial character and social structure of the Aryan invaders of Greece. It distinguished them from most of the ancient peoples who however provided the genetic elements of the *demio-ergoi.* The combination of the two contained the seeds of all the systems that the Greeks developed.

Their freedom and their diversity proved to be temporary. Internal competition and external pressure, political and constitutional stabilization and the growth of writing, the restriction on movement and hence on intermarriage, all tended to crystallize the *polies*, their social structure, their religious doctrines and their intellectual invention. All these things happened together and their connection is established, as we shall see, by the difference in rate of evolution, and the contrasted results of evolution, in Athens and Sparta.

b. Sparta

From about 820 to the end of the Peloponnesian war the Spartan state developed a fixed constitution which in the end, in 404, triumphed over the whole of Greece. The constitution, attributed to Lycurgus, a lawgiver, and discussed by Aristotle in his *Politics*, was believed by the Spartans to be derived from principles laid down by the Minoans in Crete. In the two hundred years of Dorian invasion it is indeed evident that they had incorporated people and ideas from the conquered country. The system that they established brought to an end the ceaseless warfare that had preceded it. It was based on the exclusive power of the warrior caste. This power was exercised however, not through separate families, but through an organized State authority responsible for purging all ranks of society. The warriors and their women, as we have so often been told, were selected rigorously from birth for physical capacity and later for social character. The serfs were subject to regular political inspection and annual culling.

In this system the authority of the State was exercised by two kings, priestly and fighting rulers but without other authority; by a Council originally of twenty-seven heads of families but later elected by all the old men; and by an Assembly of all the full citizens. Who were these full citizens? They were as Herodotus and Aristotle have described them, males of the warrior class who had graduated from military service and, at the age of thirty, become eligible to set up house and consummate marriage. Here therefore is a society organized to maintain itself by dividing the reproductive life of its men into two customary or statutory periods: one period homosexual and devoted to training and fighting; and the other period heterosexual and devoted to government, breeding and domestic life. It is a system known in primitive societies in many parts of the world.

The ruthless dedication or obedience of the Spartan warriors to war and to the State is well illustrated by one instance of their treatment of their own women and children, described by Boardman. During twenty years the whole army was away fighting to reduce the neighbouring valley of Messenia to serfdom. Unwilling to return before the victory but wishing to console their womenfolk and maintain the population, they sent home a party of younger men who begot a whole generation of bastard children. The State, however, following its rules with characteristic rigour, refused the rights of citizens to these Partheniai. Instead it despatched them in the year 706 to found a colony, the only colony founded by Sparta. The harbour was well chosen, and around it, under the name of Tarentum, grew the greatest Greek city in Italy.

The Spartans may be best described as having discovered during the ninth and eighth centuries the principles of success in iron age warfare and as having decided to govern their state on the basis of these principles. A similar answer was given to this problem on a larger scale during the following centuries by the Assyrians and by the Romans. The Spartan principles they owed to their sage Lycurgus, or to the Delphic Oracle, who in the ninth century directed them to fuse their five tribes living in five villages to make a single state. The power which they gave this state, a power so beneficent in establishing law and order and in suppressing the feuds which distracted every other Greek community, was the very power which in the end enslaved them.

The obedience to military discipline was extended to the whole of civil government, agricultural production and domestic life. The only question was how to distribute authority among the warrior caste. The conclusion reached was to separate the function of the hereditary kings as leaders in war from that of elective Ephors who were leaders in peace; and to leave the Assembly as a merely consultative body.

At the beginning it seems that the Spartan aristocracy was as flexible as any other. Indeed during the seventh century all the Dorian states prospered in the arts of peace as well as of war. But several factors reacted with one another in conducing to tighten its rules. One was military success against its neighbours. Another was the suppression of all criticism and the extermination of all critics both inside and outside the aristocracy. Yet another was the rejection of commercial activity in favour of a stabilized communist equality, whence it happened that the artistic and commercial classes were discouraged and no longer wanted to be promoted into the aristocracy. They probably migrated to the Dorian states, to Corinth, Megara or Rhodes. And selective migration[1] proved, as it so often does, to be an irremediable genetic loss.

The result of these developments was to make the Spartan aristocracy a pure race.[2] They were genetically almost as homogeneous as any isolated primitive tribe. And they were accordingly as little disposed to political in-subordination as they were capable of artistic invention. There was however this difference. The Spartan aristocracy at the height of its success was a large tribe. It counted on 5000 warriors to meet the army of Xerxes at the battle of Plataea in 479. That was in addition to 5000 *perioikoi* and 35,000 helots. Four generations later, following the war with Athens, their numbers had shrunk to less than a quarter. At this size they must have become a very pure race indeed. And the symptoms of their purity had become emphatic and disastrous.

c. *Athens*

During the Dorian invasions the kings, both Mycenaean and invading, were necessary leaders in war. The families of the Heracleidae, the Penthelidae and the Codridae held together (as Hammond puts it) diverse racial groups in military units. But, when new cities were settled and boundaries fixed even in the new colonies, the status of the kings dwindled. In Sparta the Heracleid King, inherited from the Mycenaean régime, retained the title of *basileus* but he was reduced to the rank of a magistrate in peace, controlled by the Council of Elders, that is by the eldest warriors, nobles or patricians. The same was true in Athens and Corinth. In Ephesus and Miletus he was reduced to the title of priest. The land-owning, horse-riding aristocracy of each small state was soon bound together in a close-knit group of kindred who could rely on one another as a group better than they could rely on a single family. Only in commercial Corinth did a single family of the Heracleidae prevail.

The solution was the result of the size of the city state. But it was also the means of perpetuating the city state for it prevented the formation of a royal caste which could have united all the city states.

The aristocratic system was of course also unstable; for without Spartan communism wealth became unequal and families decayed or died out. After half a dozen generations the governing body was narrowed to an oligarchy or to the government of a single family sometimes represented by a single tyrant. Later the growth of commerce and wealth often allowed tyrants from outside to break through the charmed but inbred circle of the aristocracy, bringing sometimes liberation and sometimes oppression, sometimes prosperity and sometimes disaster. Out of these sudden vicissitudes the growing commercial cities from time to time took the opportunity to widen the scope of control by the classes responsible for trade, art and invention.

Thus the military success of Sparta in the eighth century was due to the fitness and suitability of the Spartan social system for the purposes of a military

[1] Or, in the current phrase, brain drain.

[2] We are often told by popular writers that there are no examples of pure races of men. We shall be noting many examples and observing the predictable similarity in their history.

power. So the Spartans believed and so we also must agree. The commercial success of Athens on the other hand was due, not to the fitness of its social and political system, but rather to its incapacity and repeated breakdown.

Power in Athens was concentrated in the heads of chiefly houses in whom the land of the settled tribes or clans was vested. It was concentrated in them by family loyalty, priestly duty and ancient tradition. And, of course, also by the military and diplomatic skill for which ancient as well as recent aristocracies have usually been selected through the opportunities and dangers to which wealth and power expose them.

But the new prosperity of Athens was the work of a new class of racially different origins. The city had begun by welcoming the refugees of the Dorian invasions and it continued for long to be a city hospitable to strangers. Until the first Persian invasion it remained a city without walls. The growth of trade, the primacy in the pottery business wrested from Corinth, the development of silver-mining at Laurium and of sea fishing, all these arose from the efforts of artisans and specialists largely attracted to Athens from older countries and also from other states of Greece. In their privileges these people were the *perioikoi* of Athens. They had no rights to office in government or even to voting in elections. They had no legal protection for their property or their persons. Yet the future of the State depended on them.

A conflict thus developed, not so much between the two classes, for the aristocratic families had no regular policy except the squabbling for power. It was rather a conflict between aristocrats concerned with their own class and those concerned with the interests of the nation as a whole. The solution was reached by the application alternately of two contrasted methods. First came the legal reforms of one aristocrat, Solon, in 594–591. Secondly came the exercise of absolute power by a second aristocrat and mining magnate, Peisistratus, and his family (546–510). This period of tyranny was an interruption of the laws of Solon. It established the rights of immigrants in Athens against the privileges of the natives. Thus it made Athens the natural capital of all the Greeks. Thirdly, came another step in legal reform by a third aristocrat, Cleisthenes, in 510. The two steps in legal reform established the basic rights of all taxpayers. They meant that the urban trading and artisan communities were able to vote, to sit on juries, and to hold office. Naturally the system was still tilted—as in all later democracies—in favour of the man of wealth and leisure who could devote his time to politics, to attending meetings of the public Assembly, and generally manipulating the machinery of government.

To the Attic peasant, and to some extent to the Athenian townsman, these tremendous struggles between tribes and between classes in the seventh century were not just struggles about their own rights. They were also struggles about heroes, shrines and gods. This was not true of the aristocracy and the priesthood. They had kindred interests and were kindred by origin. They knew what they were doing. It is therefore all the more remarkable that the reforms of Solon and Cleisthenes gave the artisan protection and opportunity; and consequently they increased still further the attraction of Athens for craftsmen and traders from all over the Greek world and outside it. They even allowed a stream of selected talent to flow into Athenian society by liberation from the large community of slaves in the population.

When, by the reforms of Cleisthenes, peasants in their clans and craftsmen in their guilds, often of foreign or slave origin, were united in a common register, the overpowering influence of the old chiefly families was brought to an end. The positions of the gods had been preserved but their functions had shifted in favour of the city and the nation.

The system created by the new Athenian constitution was still factious and unstable. It was interrupted by dictatorship as well as by the panic of the ever-superstitious mob. But the decisive switch it gave to the structure of Athenian society resulted, after the two or three generations which the possibilities of breeding lead us to expect, in the golden age of Athenian achievement in the Persian war and in the peace which followed. For the victory of Marathon came a hundred years after the reform of Solon.

VII. THE UNITY OF THE GREEKS

a. The Poets

The unity of the Greeks, which they came to recognize at the end of the dark age, rested on the use of a common language which distinguished them from barbarians. It was a language differentiated like all others into dialects but its several strands were reunited in the literary form adopted by the great poets.

It is strange that the poets associated with the Aryan rulers have had their name written large on the page of history by virtue of the fact that they disdained to write themselves. These bards collected, embellished and recited songs in praise of their royal masters, the race of heroes whom we today know from their own words composed over a period of 3000 years. They despised writing since they had been bred in an age and country which knew no writing and they had achieved their social rank and function as the prizes of verbal invention and verbal memory.

This great gift was concentrated in certain groups of men whose activities were specialized in different ways in different societies as poets and minstrels, chroniclers and priests. The evidences of their work retained by feats of memory were preserved in literature as soon as writing was permitted to intrude into the heroic world. We may see it reflected not only in the work of bards but also in the verbal prodigies of the Druids in Britain which Julius Caesar noted with respect. We may see its traces scattered today equally in the verbal memory of the Brahmin and in the literary genius of the Irish people to which we shall later return. We may also suppose that the wandering poets, whom we connect with Aryan heroes, were no less welcome in the courts of Semitic kings and contributed to what became the sacred Hebrew scriptures.[1]

The significance of the guilds or professional castes of the bards was that, being illiterate and having a gift by heredity and training which enabled them

[1] See also R. Graves (1947). The shouters of praises who have been heard in the kraals of Bantu kings should probably however be thought of as an independent development favoured by the parallel conditions of a warlike caste in an illiterate but music-loving society.

to dispense with writing, a gift that was even more conservative than writing itself, they naturally opposed the use of writing and the spread into the barbarian world of the scribe who had established himself so well in Mesopotamia and Egypt. They defended, and for five thousand years have continued to defend, the retreating frontiers of the unwritten word.

So it was that the Sanskrit Vedas, the Homeric poems and the Icelandic Sagas were not written down until the age they recorded was dead. The founders of our literature, by a paradox, were not only illiterate: they were anti-literate. There was a conflict of professions which was resolved in Israel only by the Babylonian captivity and in the Greek world only by the coming of literacy from Ionia to Athens. This conflict is represented by the further paradox that side by side in the Mycenaean and Late Minoan world there existed the unwritten Homeric masterpieces created by barbarians and the written kitchen records of Pylos and Knossos compiled by civilized clerks of Phoenician ancestry.[1]

The Trojan war had happened in the middle of the thirteenth century. The supposed account of it handed down to us in the *Iliad* and the *Odyssey* describes the world of that heroic Mycenaean age exalted and magnified for the ears of its Dorian inheritors of the following centuries. The question as to whether Homer was one man or many is not in these circumstances the crucial one. The question is as to whether he was one family or several families and one generation or several generations. In view of the cohesion of each poem, the integration of Ionic, Attic and Aeolic dialects, and the differences between the two long poems, discussed by Finley, the most likely answer is perhaps one wandering family expanding and dispersing over the Aegean islands in the course of half a dozen generations between 1000 and 700 B.C.

After the language itself, the common inheritance of Greek poetry beginning with and dominated by Homer gave the second prop to the unity of the Greek people. In a sense we ought to say also that Homer sprang from the unity of the Greeks since the bardic tradition which he put together was created by them as well as by him. It stood for the union of great deeds and great words, a union of the travelling poet with the now sedentary people. This union was expressed not only in their speech but in their attitude to nature or, as they thought of it, their attitude to the gods.

b. Gods, Priests and Oracles

Their gods the Greeks had received in variety from the Ancient East. Seers, oracles and priests had brought them to Greece, coming along with those rulers who first founded cities in Crete, in the Argolid and in Boeotia. These gods came equipped with a personal history or mythology which they had brought from the older lands.[2] During the dark age, we may say, the gods, the people and the priests first got to know one another. On the larger scale of the relations between tribes, between classes, and between cities, the

[1] And preserved for us in the tablets of Linear B, deciphered by Ventris and Chadwick (see Alsop, 1965).

[2] As revealed in one way by Herodotus for Egypt and in another way, as we shall see, for Israel.

accommodation came later. And in the process of accommodation the character of the Greeks in their family and tribal life became defined.

The ideas used in this accommodation and the people who carried these ideas probably came from Anatolia as well as from Phoenicia, Crete and Egypt. The main focus of their development seems to have been the shrine of Apollo at Delphi. For it was at Delphi that an Oracle of the Egyptian pattern first appeared.

When all the available resources are used to reconstruct the sequence of development of Delphi we learn more about the Oracle than he, or she, or it could ever have known. We also learn something about the processes serving to unite Greek society. There is a wild spot on the northern wooded slopes above the Gulf of Corinth where volcanic fumes burst out of the hillside. Before the Greeks, other peoples had named the mountain *Parnassus* and had made this spot into the home of their gods. Poseidon of the sea came to terms with the Serpent of the earth as he did with Athena in Athens. The place was called Pytho from its Oracle, and the priestess became the Pythoness.

In due course a body of priests from Crete bearing the image of Apollo in the shape of a dolphin took refuge here; probably they had been chased out by the Mycenaeans. After a not entirely fictitious contest the two priesthoods joined forces; the shrine of the Oracle became the home of the Pythian Apollo, and the place became Delphi.

After the Dorian invasion yet another body of priests bearing their god, the Dorian Hercules, sought out the sanctuary at Delphi. They and their god were accepted. Now the hereditary prophetic establishment entered its golden age. Twelve neighbouring tribes found it in their common interests to bear the burdens and share the advantages of association with the Oracle of Delphi. These tribes soon found themselves forming a Council of Neighbours or *amphictyones* to administer the shrine. One, as with the Semites, would no doubt serve the Oracle for a month in each year. And on the advice of the Oracle they also found themselves organizing Pythian games. These meetings recurred at first every eight years but later, after 590 B.C., every four years. They gave rise to the athletic contests and musical festivals of Olympia, and later of Delos; and they united all the Greek peoples with a new kind of religious and social bond.

The business of the Oracle was to advise all those who came from far and near and were able to pay for the advice. It gradually made Delphi the best centre of information in Greece and beyond, information which was itself turned to account by the Oracle. It directed internal reform when it advised Solon in Athens. It organized external relations when it advised Midas of Phrygia or Amasis of Egypt. And it controlled foreign and colonial policy for the several Greek states. As its reputation grew, religion and literature, politics and commerce all came within the scope of the Oracle. The ritual mechanism of giving advice bears little relation to the modern practices of diplomacy. But its method of obtaining intelligence by secret enquiry or espionage was entirely modern. And its advantages were thoroughly understood from the seat of the Persian Empire in the east to the little Roman Republic in the west: indeed throughout the western world.

All this power sprang from the racial, linguistic and cultural unity of the Greeks. And naturally it was in general used to serve that unity. But the obstacles to genuine unity, for reasons that are now evident, it never succeeded in overcoming.

VIII. THE DIVISION OF THE GREEKS

The Greek-speaking peoples had inherited from their Aegean and Carian, Minoan and Phoenician ancestors an understanding of ships and a love of the sea and of the olive. All these things kept them near the shores of their sea-bound lands. In the whole world there are no lands more split up by mountains and by water. Yet in the early stage they were united by kings, Minoan and Mycenaean. These were all kinsmen and could hold together the sparse populations of peasants and herdsmen in a feudal hierarchy by ties of personal loyalty. At a later stage the communities of townsmen, enterprising and individual people, rejected the rule of kings and chose in various ways to govern themselves. Then the natural barriers between their valleys and their islands were reinforced by the growing differences of character between the peoples.

Each people developed its own mode of governing, its own constitution slowly giving greater authority to the body of citizens and less to the kings and landowners. Each people developed its own kind of trade, its own colonies, and its own arts; it favoured its own shrines, celebrated its own festivals; and, despite the efforts of the Delphic Oracle, it followed its own calendar. Protecting themselves against the intrusion of strangers, they reserved the rights of citizenship to the sons of citizens and to those immigrants whom they most valued. Herodotus, born in Halicarnassus, as we saw, was treated as an alien in Athens. They were slow to allow naturalization. More than this, they scrutinized the claim to *epigamia* or the right to marry the citizens of other city states: every citizen community therefore moved toward an inbred homogeneity.

There was another factor in the disunity of the Greeks: their fierce individuality of which Homer gives us his own picture. The subdivision of the island of Samos into five separate states reflects equally its mountainous contours and this proud and parochial individuality in the people. Homer to be sure became a main force in creating the unity of the Greeks. But how did he do it? By portraying the character and foreshadowing the actions that were destroying that unity! The quarrelsome pride of Achilles was to cost them much when they confronted the Persian king; and it was to ruin them utterly when Athens and Sparta confronted one another. For with the Greeks, as with other nations, it was the class of heroes which took charge in time of war and for whose follies the people suffered.

The differences in behaviour and achievement of the different Greek cities have often been discussed in terms of their inherited differences of racial character. Now we can see these differences growing within each from its own evolution, from the selective changes resulting from divergent social systems and an always selective migration. One of these we ought to notice since it underlies the origins of the scientific method we are attempting to use at this very moment. It concerns the origins of Greek science and Greek philosophy.

The new colonies across the Aegean were most distinguished in their intellectual contribution to the Greek-speaking world. It is not surprising that they introduced the problems and ideas of the Ancient East to Europe and that in doing so they laid the foundations of the European discussion of science and philosophy. But it is surprising that what they offered was something that the later Greeks, or more particularly the Athenians, so largely rejected. The evolution of Anaximander and Empedocles, the determinism of Leucippus, the atomism of Democritus culminated in the view of nature attributed to Epicurus and recorded for us by Lucretius. It was a view opposed to the superstitions of the day. Politically it proved to be inopportune and the scientific apparatus which it was fitted to set in movement still lay far in the future (Table 10).

Table 10. *Ionian Origins of Early Greek Philosophers*

After Burnet (1930).

Thales[1] (640–546)	b. Miletus
Anaximander (610–547)	b. Miletus
Anaximenes *fl.* 545	b. Miletus
Pythagoras *fl.* 532	b. Samos, migrated to Italy
Heraclitus *fl.* 501	b. Ephesus
Parmenides *fl.* 470	b. Elea (Velia), colony of Phocaea
Empedocles[2] *fl.* 440	b. Akragas (Agrigentum), colony of Rhodes
Anaxagoras[3] 500–428	b. Clazomenae
Leucippus *fl.* 450	b. Miletus, migrated to Elea
Democritus *fl.* 420	b. Abdera, colony of Clazomenae

[1] Travelled in Egypt and Babylonia.
[2] Apparently the only non-Ionian.
[3] First philosopher to reside in Athens.

The cheapness and abundance of slave labour, it is often said, inhibited the development of modern science in the ancient world; or in the Muslim world. But the free labour of modern Europe was no less cheap and abundant. And the invention of the microscope and the telescope, the compass and the chronometer, crucial for modern science, had little to do with the supply of manual labour. What the ancients lacked was the freedom of movement of people of all classes; the free exchange and unlimited storage of ideas provided by printing and paper; and of course the immense genetic and environmental range of the peoples of modern Europe by whom those ideas were to be produced.

In the genetical and geographical circumstances of Greece, conflict and war were inevitable. The states united for a moment against the Persian king. He was, as it happens, the man who knew more about how to solve their problem, the means of unifying peoples, than anyone else in the world. But it was the one principle they failed to learn from him. And having failed they destroyed themselves as city states in the final conflict between Athens and Sparta. They continued thereafter merely as a people waiting for others to rule them.

What the Greeks had done however in the critical four centuries of their city life they owed to both their unity and their disunity. It was that they collected, combined, and were later able to pass on, within their inbreeding community, a large part of the human materials necessary for western civilization. Where the other part of those materials came from we must now enquire.

9

SEMITES AND JEWS

I. THE ORIGIN OF THE SEMITES

DURING THE FOURTH MILLENNIUM, while agriculturists were colonizing the valley of the Euphrates, pastoralists, depending at first entirely on the sheep and the goat, were spreading out over the drier steppe land to the south. One group of these shepherds, speaking an ancestral Hamitic language, migrated into Africa; they spread in the course of three thousand years over the length and breadth of the continent. Another group, speaking an ancestral Semitic language, spread during the third millennium all over Arabia and began to break into the cultivated fields on their borders. On the east, as we have seen, they raided and eventually conquered the rich peoples and cities of Sumer and Babylonia. On the west they attacked the even older peoples and cities on the poorer lands of Syria and Palestine. Later they reached the south. Here they had no civilization to attack. On the contrary the bearers of civilization from Syria and Egypt reached them during the second millennium along the incense routes of the Hejjaz through Arabia Felix of the Romans, Sheba of the Jews, the Yemen and Hadhramaut of the Arabs.

During these movements, which we may name the first Semitic expansion, the simple shepherd tribes were themselves undergoing great changes. They encountered metal workers, bronzesmiths and other craftsmen during the third millennium. A settlement at Beersheba of about 3000 B.C. illustrates the way in which craftsmen and pastoralists were co-operating in adjoining groups of dwellings a few hundred yards apart while keeping their separate character and not intermarrying. It is a habit described by travellers in Arabia such as Doughty to this day, and paralleled in Europe by the gipsies.

Later these people received the horse from Central Asia (in 1600 B.C.); and they discovered and domesticated the camel in Arabia (about 1200 B.C.). They retained for a long time a homogeneous paleolithic social structure.

Slowly however the enslavement of captives diversified the tribes. Their elected chiefs or sheiks began to establish themselves as hereditary kings, members of an inter-tribal royal caste. And other groups of craftsmen, musicians and priests began to appear among them.

In the middle of the second millennium all the steps in this evolution were to be found among different Semitic-speaking tribes. The people known as Habiru (or Hebrews as we call them) existed, some of them as small nomadic tribes. But their kinsmen, like the people of Moab, Ammon and Edom, were already fused with cultivators to form settled nations with their kings and nobles, freemen and bondsmen, priests, and strangers or Gerîm.

Others again were now living in cities, in Babylonia and Canaan. What happened, as we have seen, was that the Semitic language, originally a mark of race, a pastoral race, had been imposed on non-Semitic peoples, first agricultural and then urban, who now had semi-Semitic governing classes. They were, as we may say, assimilated Semites.[1]

The greatest confusion arose with the advent of horsemen. The people who called themselves Hyksos or Kings of Shepherds could hardly themselves be Hebrews.[2] Rather they were pastoral people who had brought horses from the Caspian region into Armenia and had there equipped themselves with chariots and other weapons with which their children had swept through Syria. After three or four steps in hybridization on their long journey they had made themselves or their children kings of the Canaanites and Hebrews. Their new subjects no doubt they used in subduing Egypt.

This was the most spectacular of the early onslaughts of pastoral peoples on peasant and urban populations. It was the forerunner of innumerable victorious assaults which were to break, and also to make, the history of one country after another down to the present day in Africa. The freedom of movement of the pastoral peoples, their aggressive, adventurous and adaptable frame of mind, meant that they were the first to see the uses in war of the techniques that were continually being invented by their settled neighbours for purposes of peace.[3] We may not be certain which party to this unintended collaboration was the more intelligent but we can be quite certain that they differed in the kind of intelligence they showed. We may also not be certain of which party was the more successful. The pastoral people always conquered on the first impact. But we find that they did

[1] The Semitic languages had, of course, to be wrenched into new shape to fit the needs of settled life. Thus, Professor Driver tells me, the verb *Karāmen* which means 'to heap up', as of bricks, in Babylonia, becomes *Kerem*, a terraced 'vineyard' in Hebrew and hence *Kerm* a 'vine' in Ethiopic. This development indicates the importance of terraced cultivation among the assimilated Semites of the third millennium B.C. When *Karmâ* in Syriac comes to mean an 'abacus', the stage of urban civilization has been reached; Mount *Carmel* retains the original meaning.

[2] The suggestion comes from Manetho, and later from Josephus (see Shotwell, 1939).

[3] As Yadin points out (1964) each tribe of Israel had its own special means of warfare. Judah had shield and spear. Benjamin prided itself on using bows and slings and being ambidextrous with both (I Chronicles 12). These differences must have had racial origins and selective effects.

not produce a governing class unmixed with the priests and artificers or even the peasants they had apparently conquered.

South-West Asia, as we saw earlier, enjoyed a special advantage at the end of the ice age as the cross-roads of three continents. Now, with the bronze age five thousand years later, we find a second climax of movement affecting the narrowest strip in this crucial region. For the corridor of the Levantine coast was the very isthmus through which all traffic between the two great river valley civilizations was bound to pass. And the movement now was not merely one of slow-moving self-sufficient tribes but also of pastoral warriors and of mobile specialized groups, caravans of traders and craftsmen. Again, the Levantine corridor was country remote enough and broken up enough to be difficult to subdue, even more difficult to control, and especially prone to break up into small self-contained inbreeding units.

Bearing these conditions in mind we need not be surprised to find that the influence of Egypt and Babylon was concentrated on this narrow neck of land, though their control could usually be repulsed. Or that the kinds of development that arose were strikingly and adaptively divergent.

The divergence arose between the two provinces of Canaan: the one to which we may give the Homeric name of Phoenicia; and the other to which we may give the Hebrew name of Israel. How did this happen?

II. THE PHOENICIANS

The narrow strip of cultivable land between the Levantine coast and the mountainous hinterland was what supported the first population of Phoenicia. But what made the character of Phoenicia after the beginning of the third millennium were three priceless assets: its position between the two civilizations of Mesopotamia and Egypt; its possession of a unique series of harbours; and the availability of timber denied to its neighbours. The occupation and development of the harbours seems to have begun near the northern end of the coast, at Ugarit, and to have proceeded southwards to Aradua (Ruad), Byblos, Berytus (Beirut), Tyre and Sidon.[1]

The Phoenician harbours were not only naturally protected from the sea; they were situated on islands or headlands which were also naturally protected from the land behind them. This meant that the Phoenicians, like the Minoans at the same time, were freed from preoccupation with the attacks of warlike neighbours. It is as though their success with their first harbour had led them to search for another like it; each success thus multiplying the maritime community that had selected it.

A second foundation for this success lay in the mountains that stood behind these harbours. For the mountains were themselves an additional protection and they offered the materials, unlimited as they seemed, for commerce. From their timber, ships could be built, ships to carry more timber to the adjoining rich and almost timberless land of Egypt. The cedars of Lebanon

[1] The geography of Phoenicia and its meaning have been described and illustrated by Harden (1962). See also Woolley (1960), Culican (1960), Grollenberg (1959) and *I.L.N.* (Sept. 21, 1963).

which have now all but vanished met in succession the needs of Pharaoh and Solomon, of Sargon and Darius.

On this view it is not surprising that the population and the prosperity of Phoenicia were built up on a scale of compound interest; or exponentially as we may say. Slowly at first, more urgently later the Phoenicians collected their resources of human talent: merchants and navigators, boat-builders and craftsmen, dyers and weavers, administrators and scribes, multiplied in their cities. Probably a great new impetus to this growth came, as Harden has suggested, with the collapse of the Minoan and Mycenaean Empires which were connected and almost entangled with the commerce of Phoenicia. Clearly a contribution would then be made to the diverse racial capacity of the Phoenician cities by Minoan exiles seeking refuge in them.

Certain it is that only after the movements of the Sea Peoples did the city of Tyre begin to plant colonies along the coasts of the Mediterranean. Utica and Carthage in Tunis, Motya in Sicily, Valetta in Malta, Cadiz in Spain, Mogador in Morocco, followed one another in westward succession. They were colonies sited precisely on the model of the mother city and they retained an attachment to the Phoenician homeland over the two thousand miles of intervening sea.

For nearly a thousand years the Phoenicians and their colonies remained the leading navigators and merchants in the world. When Pharaoh Necho in 600 B.C. wanted to circumnavigate Africa it was (as Herodotus relates) a Phoenician fleet that he hired to do the job. And when Alexander the Great three hundred years later occupied Phoenicia and besieged Tyre it was not just the buildings and walls of the cities that he wanted in his power; it was the navy, the shipyards, the craftsmen and the sailors. It was, as Arrian explains, Phoenicia as the basis of sea power that gave him the control of the Mediterranean. So long as Phoenicia remained free she kept in close union with her colonies. And after the subjection of the homeland by the Assyrians and Persians, her colonies, unlike the Greek colonies, continued united and ruled by their own capital Carthage. Clearly with them, in contrast to the Greeks, commerce took precedence over every other activity; and for commerce a connectedness of government was the prime need.

The source of this achievement lies in the immense diversity of the people of Ugarit. In no city of its time, the middle of the second millennium, were there probably more languages spoken than in Ugarit. The progress of trade continually increased their number and six of them survive in inscribed tablets.

Ezekiel's Lamentation for Tyre (ch. 27) gives us a geographical picture of the range of Phoenician trade and of the diversity of the people whose skill contributed to the success of the Phoenician kingdoms.

For their ships, he tells us they had:	For their men they had:
shipboards from firs of *Senir*	calkers from *Gebal* (Byblos)
masts from cedars of *Lebanon*	mariners from *Sidon* and *Arrad*
oars from oaks of *Bashan*	pilots from *Tyre*
sails from linen of *Egypt*	soldiers from *Persia*, *Lud* and *Phut* (Libya)

For their trade they had:

- all metals from *Tarshish* (Spain)
- wheat, honey, oil and balm from *Israel*
- wine, wool from *Damascus*
- iron, cassia, calamus from *Dan* and *Javan*
- spices, gold, precious stones from *Sheba* (Yemen)
- sheep, goats from *Arabia* and *Kedar*

All this looks like a confusion of peoples. So it would have been if they had not been stratified in their own racial and professional groups. But if there was not a confusion of peoples there was certainly a confusion of tongues. And it was this no doubt which in turn pointed to the need for an alphabet and the means for its invention. The first known alphabetic inscription is on a stone coffin of Ahiram, King of Byblos *c.* 950 B.C. (see Table 4). This invention preserved for us both Homer and Moses. And it must have stimulated every other technical invention that followed it.

What was the source of the diversity of Phoenician peoples? It lay in the attraction that the prosperity of Phoenicia held for people all over the ancient world who were fitted to profit by trade and seamanship. People were drawn there by the expectation of commercial success. The character that the people developed was what we might foresee. Their ideas were largely second-hand. Their art was largely second-rate, more valued, as Harden puts it, for the price than the possession. Their literature has failed to survive and this is not just that papyrus is perishable but that no one, or rather no literary class, was concerned to preserve it: it failed to make history.

It is however in the matter of religion that the Phoenicians, or Canaanites as they called themselves, are so significantly contrasted with their neighbours and their linguistic kindred, the Jews. Here they seem to have contributed only what the Jews held to be the worst abominations. They worshipped the same gods and paid the same priests as in Babylon. They paid for the same things: the temple prostitutes, women and boys. And in addition they developed infanticide into a religious rite. Everywhere else in the ancient world, except in Egypt, according to Herodotus, infanticide was practised. But everywhere else it was selective and eugenic. Only in Phoenicia, it seems, was the burning of live infants an undiscriminating sacrifice, a religious orgy.

Thus the Phoenicians had their own character which arose from their own maritime success and contributed to its development operating selectively on a richly diverse population. This success made them secondarily into a human channel through which many of the talents and of the techniques of the ancient world passed westwards over the waters of the Mediterranean. It was they who took what archaeologists note as 'orientalizing influence' into the art of Greece and Italy. It was their scribes more specifically who took their letters to the Greeks and Etruscans. It was their craftsmen who in the eighth century decorated Etruscan tombs, for example, at Praeneste. It was their sailors and goldsmiths who carried the figure of Samson (or was it Herakles?) battling with a lion to Aliseda far up the valley of the Tagus in Spain.

Buried works of art betray the movements of Phoenicians all over the Mediterranean. But the documentary records show that they went further than their artistic traces reveal. They opened up the mineral wealth of the south of Spain, the Tarshish of Ezekiel, presumably by taking in their ships miners of Anatolian origin: the Tibarenoi, the Chalybes, the Kenites, to give them the non-Canaanite names under which we shall hear of them elsewhere. Later they took further colonies of these miners to Cornwall whence their descendants spread the mining industry into other continents.[1]

These far-reaching connections disclosed by archaeology and literature put us in a different frame of mind when we look at the disputed mythology which uses names alternately Phoenician and Canaanite, or Greek and Latin. According to Harden, the Dido who fled to Carthage and whose love for Aeneas of Troy was connected by Virgil with the foundation of Rome, was the same person as Elissa, the sister of Pygmalion King of Tyre; she was also a great-niece of the Jezebel who married King Ahab and introduced the abominations of the Canaanites to the people of Israel.

These were real individuals, people whose actual movements carried the diverse ideas and abilities of the Ancient East into the western world. These people did what they did because they were international travellers and international marriers and breeders. They belonged to a noble caste which did not respect the divisions of language and religion that meant so much to the ordinary citizens of new nations descended from them many generations later.

From them were indeed descended oppositions between Israel and Canaan, between Carthage and Rome. How these classical oppositions came about we are now able to see.

III. THE ORIGINS OF THE JEWS

We know much more of the origins of the Jews, and from more various sources, than of any other of the Semitic-speaking peoples for one very simple reason. They attached to themselves at an early stage a class or caste of priests who used history for their purpose. This was no other than that of ensuring the survival of the race or group of tribes to whom they were attached. Religion they held to be the prime means of this survival since religion was the business of binding people together. And they came to regard the history of the people and of the religion as the chief instrument to be used in this grand design.

The records embodied in the first sixteen books of the Bible, Jewish or Christian, for they are the same, provide us with the chief evidence of the origin and early history of the Jews. It is evidence which has to be collated with the documentary, archaeological and linguistic evidence from the contemporary neighbours of the children of Israel. And it has to be interpreted in the light of the joint social, political and religious purpose with which these books were put together.

[1] To Cornwall, as we saw, they perhaps took other arts.

Such interpretation has produced a wide agreement on the main issues that concern us. The Israelite people who occupied Palestine at their most coherent moment and in their most central epoch, at the time of David and Solomon, were of highly diverse and largely recognizable origins. One of these origins lay in the nomadic shepherd tribes moving over great areas in the northern Arabian desert. They were probably contained within the group of *Habiru* and kinsmen of Edom and Moab. One or more of the tribes (associated with the name of Joseph) had dwelt in Egypt. They seem to have entered at the time of the Hyksos domination and to have been allowed to stay there on payment of tribute under the Eighteenth Dynasty. But they came into conflict with a new Pharaoh and had to leave. When they left they were guided by a priestly leader named Moses.

In their journey through the deserts of Sinai, Edom and Moab, they entered into alliance with related tribes with whom in several waves they attacked the cities and occupied part of the countryside of Canaan. Their priests had led them to expect a land flowing with milk and honey (for the shepherds), where bread should never be scarce (for the peasant) and whose stones are of iron or of brass (for the miners and smiths, Deuteronomy 8: 9). Under warrior leaders, to one of whom, Joshua, the chroniclers give an heroic stature, they established a foothold in Palestine.

What they found in Palestine and what they did there we can also reconstruct, following Albright. They found Canaanite cities, interspersed with Hebrew agricultural settlements and some deserted bronze age villages.[1] They also found infiltrations of pastoral tribes, their own kinsmen. Faced with this complex situation the leaders of the invasion offered a graduated solution. How they proposed to deal with the inhabitants of the Promised Land is set out in Deuteronomy 20: 10–18. The three ways of dealing with conquered peoples (as opposed to captive individuals) known to the ancient world of the iron age are expressed here in classical and precise form:

(1) 'Of the cities of the Promised Land (namely of the Hittites, the Amorites, the Canaanites etc.) . . . thou shalt save alive nothing that breatheth.'

(2) 'Of the cities far off: (*a*) if it make the answer of peace . . . then all the people found therein shall be tributaries unto thee, and shall serve thee;' (*b*) 'if it will make no peace with thee, then thou shalt besiege it.'

'And when the Lord hath delivered it into thine hands, thou shalt smite every male thereof with the edge of the sword: but the women and the little ones and the cattle . . . shalt thou take unto thyself.'

Proceedings of this character were no doubt taking place over several generations, during which there were many setbacks: Judah 'drave out the inhabitants of the mountain; but could not drive out the inhabitants of the valley, because they had chariots of iron' (Judges 1: 19).

In addition to tribal bondsmen there were also individual captives who were

[1] They also had to fell forests to get more land for agriculture (Joshua 17: 15–18; Deuteronomy 20: 19–20), a process which has continued ever since to devastate Palestine (Lowdermilk, 1946).

enslaved under the conditions that are laid down in Leviticus. Being foreigners they could be bought and sold. Women taken as wives had to be freed: they were assimilated with the invaders. Thus a new society was constructed. In this society the military and priestly leaders of the invaders, who now described themselves as the Bani-Israel or the Children of Israel, became in some sense a governing class.

From Chronicles to Nehemiah (as de Vaux points out) we have the first evidence after Mesopotamia of specialization and localization of trades, family and usually hereditary, which had been the basis of industry ever since the beginning of cities. In one village the Benjamites work wood and metal. Weaving and dyeing flourish in another. At Jerusalem there is a bakers' street. A fullers' field, a gate of shards, a jewellers' quarter show other trades clustering in groups and of course breeding in groups. The trades formed guilds which were called 'families' with 'fathers' as heads, having their own shrines and later their own synagogues.

The merchants who provided for the Jewish markets were at first always foreigners—especially, of course, Phoenicians. So much so that 'Canaanite' came to mean tradesman. It is clear that races of traders were incorporated late in the Jewish people. And they came from the tradesmen and caravaners who settled down outside Jerusalem. The transformation was completed in Babylonia and Hellenistic Egypt when (as in the Christian Renaissance) commercial profit became legitimate.

The new nation however had uncertain loyalties and correspondingly uncertain boundaries. It depended for its unity on the rites and teachings of a common religion. This at first meant the common shrine that had been set up in a tent at Shiloh. This shrine, which with other peoples would have been an idol or Palladium, with them was a box. They called it the Ark of the Covenant (Joshua 24). But gradually it came to mean more. It came to mean the presence of God, their unique God. It came also to mean the common history and the common law of the people. Both of these were given to the people by the spokesmen of their God, that is by the class of priests who claimed to take their origin among the kindred of Moses. Who were these priests.

IV. THE KINDRED OF MOSES

The origin of Moses is not so much obscure as complex, complex in a plausible way. His name is Egyptian. The legend links him with the family of Pharaoh. It also tells us that, after an Ethiopian woman, he married Zipporah, one of the seven daughters of Jethro the priest of Midian. And he takes pains to explain to his father-in-law how he has instructed and organized the Children of Israel according to certain rules for which he asks Jethro's approval (Exodus 18).

Now the Midianites were the people living athwart the spice and incense trade route into southern Arabia. They were the first to bring camels into touch with the Israelites. A section of them were smiths who were known as Kenites; such people might be expected to join forces with migrating warlike herdsmen. Being iron workers they claimed descent from Tubal Cain the traditional inventor of iron-smelting and forging.[1]

It was from Moses' brother Aaron that the body of the Jewish priesthood, the Levites, claimed to be descended. They gave the name Leviticus to one of the books of their priestly writings and they claimed to have sprung from Levi one of the sons of Jacob. But Egyptian names cropping up in the priestly families of Israel (for Example, Hophni and Phinehas, the scapegrace sons of Eli) make it clear that they had foreign connections with the priesthoods and the governing classes of other peoples which they wished to conceal. It is clear also that iron workers with their technical sophistication and their known use of magic throughout the ancient world had something very important to offer to the founders of a priestly society. Do the contrasted brothers, Moses and Aaron, thus represent a hybrid ancestry for the priesthood? It seems so.

The genealogies of the Children of Israel like those of all primitive—and some less primitive—peoples were largely invented. They were skilfully fitted together for a purpose which was at once social, religious, and political. Common descent meant kinship. And kinship meant unity because kindred were united by a bond or contract with one another. It was just this bond which in due course became a covenant with their invisible God, the God present, together with the Book of the Law, in the Ark of the Covenant (Deuteronomy 31: 26).

During the seven or eight generations which followed the invasion of Palestine the Levite priesthood developed the ideas which, in the absence of a monarchy, could bind the invading tribes together. One of these ideas was the fiction of common descent from a patriarch ancestor, Jacob or Israel, who had a covenant with his god which could now be extended not only to his pure and patrician descendants but to all their servants and to the strangers, the *gerîm*, within the gates of their cities. These were the people whose name the Jews significantly translated into Greek by the word *proselyte*.[2]

For the purpose of conversion and assimilation—which were the same process—the tribes of Israel had to be twelve, as with any such religious federation, to serve in monthly rotation the national shrine. And they were attributed to the twelve sons of Jacob. There was some difficulty about this owing to the shifting character of the tribes. The unsettled pastoralists of Reuben probably disappeared into the desert while Simeon and part of Levi were assimilated with other tribes. Also we cannot fail to notice that the Children of Israel applied to their priests the Canaanite name of *Kōhēn* which survives to this day. But the story served its purpose and has convinced many later generations.

The second great task of the priests was to codify the common rules and

[1] The origin is clear, Professor Driver tells me, since Cain is cognate with *Qain*, meaning smith in Arabic, while *Tabiru* means smith in Assyrian and is derived from the *Tibarenoi*, the name of a tribe connected with the *Chalybes*, the reputed inventors of iron-working in the classical world.

[2] In terms of their origin as outsiders the other Greek word, *perioikoi*, more correctly describes them. For the Spartans, however, the outsiders were people who stayed out while for the Jews translating the Pentateuch they were people who came in: they were proselytes.

customs of the tribes and so to develop laws of behaviour which should unite, preserve and strengthen their people. These laws they attributed to the mediation of Moses. Evidently, however, they developed over many oral generations before their basis took even a provisional form in writing in the first five books of the Bible. They were generations devoted to the most successful study of social behaviour and of its biological causes and consequences.

Let us consider what these laws were.

V. THE EVOLUTION OF THE LAW

a. The Moral Law

The earliest ideas of the Israelite priesthood developed over a period of six hundred years before they were embodied in the form in which we see them in Leviticus and Deuteronomy. During this time the priesthood had itself evolved by incorporation of new elements into the Israelite community and by repeated selection of new leading families. Aaron's family displaced the descendants of Moses; Zadok anointing David supplanted lesser Levites; David having taken Jerusalem, its priests became supreme over the servants of provincial shrines. And when the tribes of Judah alone survived in captivity it becomes fitting for us to speak of the Jews instead of the Hebrews or Israelites out of whom they had selectively developed.

The direction of change in the priesthood and in the community as a whole was however established by the original ideas of Moses and his kindred which set the whole movement going. These original ideas represented a departure from the practices of all ancient peoples, a break with the past. For every other people there was a priesthood with its appointed rituals and its central and local shrines dedicated to different visible gods. But for the Israelites in place of an assembly of images and a variety of competing cults and rituals there was a single invisible God whose rites and laws the whole people and their whole community of priests were bound by covenant to maintain.

These Mosaic rites and laws came to be written during and after the period of the Captivity. They came at the same time to be corroborated by the single coherent history and literature of the Hebrews which we find in the Old Testament. It is this total apparatus which shows us that the Jews were in process of becoming a people different from all others. How they were different, how they had changed, depended on the character of the laws.

In their moral character, the Mosaic laws, like the myths that accompanied them, could have been, and probably were, largely taken from Babylonia and Egypt by the ancestors of the priests who carried them over into primitive society. The laws of marriage and divorce, polygamy, prostitution and slavery are all there. But there is also something new. There is an assertion of equality between rich and poor in the face of the law. There is a protection for the stranger and the slave. There is a right of admission to Jewish society, subject to obedience to the law and to the lapse of a number of generations. All these things constitute another break with the past in the method of constructing a society.

A third break with the past appears in the strict rejection of the practices of magic. All superstitious ceremonies designed to alter the course of nature otherwise than through the priests are prohibited. Sorcerers, enchanters, witches, wizards, necromancers, exorcists, diviners, astrologers, soothsayers, interpreters of dreams, fortune-tellers, and casters of nativities, whether proposing to heal or to hurt, all these are forbidden on pain of death.

The prohibition of the black arts as the work of false devils was, to be sure, inherent in the principle of rejecting all supernumerary powers or divinities. It was a rule consolidating the law as subject to one god and one priesthood. As such it was a step in professional strategy. Nevertheless it profoundly changed the moral climate: it slowly created an environment which for the first time favoured moral and intellectual integrity at the expense of superstition; it favoured the mature and adult at the expense of the primitive and infantile mind.

The Mosaic rules therefore demanded an improvement on both the ferocity and the superstition of primitive society as generally witnessed in Genesis and Exodus; they were for this reason resisted. Indeed their slow enforcement is the subject of dramatic episodes which run through the whole of the Jewish chronicles.

As Cruden points out, all the denunciations of witches did not prevent Saul from using the Witch of En-dor to conjure up the spirit of Samuel. And Joseph was still recorded as making his fortune from interpreting dreams. What the Mosaic law did was to initiate a programme of reform. It is one which has still not wholly won its cause among any civilized or uncivilized people three thousand years later.

b. The Breeding Programme

The moral programme of the laws is accompanied by a ritual programme which seems to have no rational connection with it and to stand on an entirely different footing. The two are connected merely by their historical effects. The ritual programme is based on circumcision. Circumcision among the Semites may have begun as a substitute for the blood sacrifice from which Isaac was to have suffered. Or it may have begun with its use as a caste mark among the governing class of the Egyptians. However that may be, as a means of establishing a breeding barrier between tribes or between classes it is an advance on the use of the disfigurements more generally practised in Africa.[1]

Now, however, circumcision was to be a means, not of separating social classes but, even when they were of obviously different racial origin, of uniting them. Thus God commands Abraham that every male child 'born in the house or bought with money' shall be circumcised (Genesis 17: 10). But, conversely, all intermarriage with those who had not been circumcised, and who had not been brought up in the house, or 'within the congregation', was absolutely excluded (Deuteronomy 7: 2).

At first, the rite of circumcision was the mark of the tribe. But as the tribe became identified with its God and the teaching of its priests, it became the

[1] Although as a pagan survival practised in Arabia it can be, apart from cannibalism, the most barbarous of all religious rites surviving today. (Thesiger 1959, see ch. 16.)

mark of religion and the witness of the law. Instead of God being marked by the figure of an idol, he was marked on the figure of his worshipper.

The invisible God and the marked worshipper, the hereditary priesthood and the fixed shrine, the written law and the connected chronicle, were a powerful combination. They proved to be, indeed, not irresistible, for many resisted them, and many more escaped from them. But they proved as a combination to be indestructible. Burning the shrines, dispersing the priests, dispersing, enslaving or massacring the people, all these misfortunes were survived. The combination was thus one of the great successful steps made in the evolution of society.

Like other steps in the evolution of society, as we have seen in Sparta, its effects were not fully foreseen. They depended on allowing the Jews to mix with other peoples and to work with other peoples, and for other peoples, without breeding with them. They stood apart from other peoples because their God stood apart from other gods. He could not be joined in a hierarchy or pantheon of gods as among all the neighbouring nations. Even the kings of the Jews were transformed by this novel apartness. Alive or dead they were powerless to clothe themselves in that divine quality which descended on other eastern kings. And their ancestry although largely fictitious remained entirely human.

After the notion of an invisible God came his instrument, the law, at first equally invisible but later written. We can all see the importance of the law as a moral code subordinating the instinctive activities of the individual to the needs of society, a society which was slowly becoming more complicated. This moral code with its humane and equalitarian compassion was something which all the derived religions have pretended to take over. It was a system which was already struggling to mitigate the horrors of the developing iron age society. And it has contributed to the survival of all the communities which have inherited it. But there were other aspects of the law which assisted the survival and the multiplication of the Jews for quite different reasons.

The Jewish law, as we can read in Leviticus, has a second element. It makes rules about health, clothing and food, and the care and killing of animals for food. In their origin these rules were a compounding and codifying of the ancient or recent beliefs of the ancestral peoples, Hebrews, Canaanites, Midianites and others. Sometimes they rested on sound inferences; sometimes they were what we call superstitions; sometimes they contained a symbolical suggestion. But the rules for food all had one grand consequence. It was to keep those who followed the rules eating apart from those who did not follow them.[1]

Now eating apart means living apart; and living apart means in effect breeding apart: it means what we call genetic isolation; it is the basis of race formation. Those who propounded the Jewish law were, we may suppose, not unaware of this principle; for the circumstances were well known. Their own account shows the Egyptians refusing to keep company with Hebrew shepherds (Genesis 46:34), and we shall find that other religious teachers have made the same discovery and applied it for the same purpose. The development of all

[1] See Simoons (1961).

the ritual and other restrictions on feeding thus strengthened the genetic unification of the Jewish people and its genetic separation from other peoples.[1]

A third element in the Jewish law was not concerned with genetic isolation but with selective propagation; that is with strengthening and multiplying the people who had been separated, the seed of Abraham or the Children of Israel. This element aimed at enhancing the fertility of parents and the survival of their offspring. At this stage science predominates over superstition.

One part of these rules is based on the common instinctive inheritance of mankind: the rejection of incest and, in addition, any circumstances which might conduce to incest, such as indecent exposure. Only slowly did this rule become precise enough to have excluded marriage with a half-sister. For example Abraham's marriage with Sarah is taken for granted. And when Amnon, son of David, rapes his half-sister Tamar, it is a matter for revenge by her full brother rather than for rebuke by the priest (II Samuel 13). The prejudices of patriarchal society, it seems, prevented at this stage any curtailment of masculine privileges provided that no loss of fertility or other damage could be shown.[2]

Another part of the breeding rules goes clean against the practice of the other nations of the Ancient East. It makes yet another break with the past in giving a new direction to the evolution of society. All other ancient peoples maintained practices of paleolithic origin which tended to limit the population. The Mosaic law, on the other hand, prohibits sodomy, bestiality and masturbation; it condemns infanticide and the prostitution of Jewish women; it reproves transvestism. Above all it denounces the customary association of religious shrines with these practices.[3]

The connection between these prohibitions is shown to be one of encouraging fertility from the detailed care with which the law specifies other means to the same end. Thus the law frees the newly married man from military service for one year to allow him to ensure begetting offspring. It prescribes the severe mutilation of a woman who unfairly tries to help her husband in a fight by seizing his opponent's testicles (Deuteronomy 25: 11). It requires segregation for 'uncleanness of issues' as a defence against venereal disease (Leviticus 15). And of course (in Ruth) it advocates the levirate, the practice by which a man takes his dead brother's wife as his own wife, in order to 'raise up the name of the dead upon his inheritance'.

In its total effects the Mosaic law favours the survival of the people who obey it. Further the effects of its specifically genetic articles favour not the

[1] It was the law in this sense which therefore became the crux of dispute at the beginning of the Christian era.

[2] The basis of the rejection of incest was, no doubt, a universal instinctive revulsion. Whether there was at this stage the modern rationalization in terms of supposed loss of fertility is unknown. A semi-rationalization in terms of indecency is suggested by the words used in condemning incest: 'to uncover the nakedness' of one's kindred is what the law prohibits.

[3] The frieze of the Bulls at Tarquinia is unique in appearing to condemn sodomy as a means of population control. It is dated about 500 B.C. and may therefore be derived from earlier Hebrew origins (see Hus 1961 and ch. 13).

individual but the multiplication of the individual: they favour the race. All these effects are selective. They discriminate against the heathen nations, the gentiles who worship other gods.

This powerful selective advantage is based on hereditary intellectual qualities in the first place of the priests and in the second place of those who obey the priests. And it has ensured the survival of the Jews and through them of the intellectual qualities which their mode of life selectively favoured. It ensured their survival through captivity, dispersal and persecution. But all these vicissitudes did not befall a people that was either homogeneous or stable. On the contrary it was heterogeneous and continually evolving. How this was so we must now consider.

Table 11. *Time Chart of Jewish Evolution: 1720-50 B.C.*

After E. S. Bates (1939); Moscati (1959, 1960); Albright (1957); de Vaux (1958); Grollenberg (1959); Orlinsky (1960); H. G. May (1962); Yadin (1964); Kenyon (1965).

HYKSOS in EGYPT	1720–1550
Incursion of Habiru or Hebrews (Joseph)	*c.* 1600
Hebrew EXODUS from Egypt (MOSES)	1300
Appearance of Kenites or Midianites	
Israelites invade Palestine (Joshua)	1250
Shiloh becomes sanctuary of the Ark	
Sea Peoples invade Palestine (Philistines)	1200
Rise of the Monarchy (Samuel-Saul)	1100–1005
KINGDOM of DAVID and SOLOMON	1005
Jerusalem as Sanctuary; earliest sacred writings	–925
ISRAEL and JUDAH divided: dynastic marriages; Assyrian threat	925–722
Amos, Hoseah, Micah, Isaiah I	
Capture of Samaria: Israel deported to Nineveh (Sargon II)	722
Josiah and Jeremiah in Jerusalem: Deuteronomy rediscovered	621
Capture of Jerusalem: Judah deported to Babylon (Nebuchadnezzar)	586
BABYLONIAN CAPTIVITY	586–453
Ezekiel and Isaiah II	
Jews released by Cyrus the Persian:	
Partial return to Jerusalem: rebuilding of the Temple	539
Ezra the Priest and Scribe in Jerusalem	
Composition of Leviticus; Rule of High Priests	
Jewish Colonies throughout Persian Empire	450
Foundation of Alexandria with guarantee of Jewish privileges	*c.* 330
Translation of Books of Moses (Pentateuch) into Greek	280
Final Writing of Psalms, Ecclesiastes, Daniel, Ecclesiasticus	*c.* 150
Wisdom of Solomon (Alexandria)	*c.* 50

VI. THE POLITICAL CHRONICLE

Four political events stand out in the iron age history of Palestine. The first is the establishment of a united monarchy by David with its capital at Jerusalem. The second is the division of this monarchy between the two tribes of Judah and the ten tribes of Israel with their capital at Samaria.

The third is the deportation of Israel to Nineveh and of Judah to Babylon. The fourth is the return of the Jews of Babylon from exile and captivity.

David seems to have begun his career as a captain of Philistine mercenaries trained in the use of foreign weapons.[1] What his own ancestry was we cannot be certain. But he obtained the military support of the tribes and the blessings of the Levites in a whole programme of political and military operations. He turned against the Philistine overlords and then drove them out. He captured the sacred shrine of the Jebusites at Jerusalem. He installed a new family of priests of the House of Zadok in his new capital. He strengthened his position by marrying the daughters of many small kings. Thus he united almost the whole of Palestine under his rule.

His son Solomon enlarged the kingdom into an empire. It stretched from the River Orontes to the Gulf of Akaba and the copper mines of Ezion-geber. He entered into treaties with the greatest kings, marrying their daughters and establishing trade on a scale never before known in Palestine.

These achievements were probably the result of a combination of Philistine armour with Jewish manpower and priestly diplomacy. However that may be, the results were much out of keeping with the religious tradition of the people. Dynastic marriages, the importation of foreign gods, the use of foreign mercenaries, all had disastrous effects on the practice of the law, the purity of belief and the domination of the priests. The religious chronicles illuminate the conflict between priests and kings. They play down the material advances and the technical organization of the new kingdom since these were all due to foreign artisans inimical to the native priest. David appears as a hero and a bard with Homeric attributes and sinful practices, which have to be excused (I Kings 9:21). Solomon shines not only as a skilful administrator but also as a legendary wise man whose wealth accrues from his wisdom. Each is accredited with some of the supreme literary productions of the Jewish people. Both are guilty of a sustained disregard of priestly teaching. Each gives the obnoxious name of Baal to one of his sons.

No wonder that religion dissolves and the empire with it. The southern kingdom retains in its capital the sacred shrine which is now housed in a splendid temple built by Canaanite artisans to an Egyptian design. The northern kingdom is more deeply corrupted by contact with Phoenician queens and the priests of Baal; and from its position it succumbs first to the northern invaders. It is in the divided kingdoms that the scene is set for ten generations of conflict between religious teaching and foreign civilization, a conflict which is only cut short by the exile and the captivity.

The deportation had a whole series of decisive effects on the people of Israel and Judah. Nebuchadnezzar took away most of the royal family from Jerusalem, the best fighting men and craftsmen. Quisling kings were appointed. It is added that 'none remained save the poorest of the land'. Some however had escaped to Egypt and elsewhere. On the return from exile, therefore, a few 'nobles of Judah' were found to have been reinstated.

It is clear that the deportation like other migrations, voluntary or forced,

[1] The Philistine overlords allowed no smith to work for the Hebrews (I Samuel 13: 19) 'lest the Hebrews make them swords or spears'.

was selective. The tribes of Israel, the 27,290 prisoners from Samaria, were lost. This means that they lost their religion which they had already shown themselves ready to lose;[1] and they were therefore absorbed in the other peoples and other religions of the Assyrian Empire. The tribes of Judah, or rather their governing and urban classes, kept their priests and their religion and therefore maintained themselves as a community and as a race. The return from exile however again divided them. Some stayed in Babylon; some returned to Jerusalem; and some were dispersed to various parts of the Persian Empire forming colonies of merchants which persisted, or of soldiers (as at Elephantine in Egypt) who perhaps disappeared. Later they were ready, as in Egypt, to welcome the coming of Alexander and the beginning of a new age.[2]

The Jews who moved into the western parts of the Persian Empire were among the significant survivors. They were the only deported people of antiquity whom we can trace: because, as we saw, their religion proved in their hands, or in the hands of their teachers, to be fixed and indestructible. They were however a highly selected remnant. And they held a unique position in the societies in which they lived. For they were no longer a nation. Nor were they a class. They were a group of skilled and partly intellectual classes differing from all other such classes in two vital respects. First, they were largely cut off from intermarriage with the other classes of the societies in which they lived. And, secondly, they were entirely liberated from the control of their own former military governing class.

The Jewish intellectuals were thus free. What did they do with their freedom? On the one hand, in the service of their own people, they were free to re-write their history and use it to modernize their laws. One far-reaching step in this undertaking was the regularizing of the seven-day week, a reform for which Ezra the Scribe was finally responsible about the year 445 B.C. It was one of the great landmarks in the history of society. What Ezra seems to have done was to take the name of the Babylonian *shabbatu*, the day of the full moon, which was also a day of rejoicing, to combine it with various days of ill-omen, and to turn them into the Hebrew *shabbat*. This was to be a day of rest and prayer, regularly recurring without regard to the phases of the moon. He then established his work by touching up the Creation story in Genesis and the Mosaic commandment in Exodus. After this there was no turning back. Ezra's reform after 130,000 weeks has stretched to the ends of the earth and is unlikely to be superseded.[3]

On the other hand in the service of the Persian Empire the Jewish intellectuals were quickly picked out to play a special part. It was, as the Books of Esther and Daniel show us, a part valued by the kings and envied by their servants of other races.

To succeed in this way required a re-orientation of Jewish attitudes. For survival demanded a rejection of foreign religions. But it also demanded an acceptance of foreign peoples. In achieving this remarkable accommodation

[1] Their priests were 'the lowest of the people which were not of the sons of Levi' (I Kings 12: 31).

[2] See Josephus on Alexandrian Jews (*ref.* ch. 14).

[3] Martin Nilsson (1920) *cf.* H. and J. Lewy (1943).

the writings of the prophets were largely responsible; notably the writings of the priestly prophet Ezekiel.

VII. THE PROPHETS AND THE EXILE

The preservation of sanctuaries, the recording of the laws, and the editing of the chronicles had been the work of the Levites, or of those groups continually re-selected from the Levites who were established as priests. After the setting up of the monarchy they became privileged, endowed and largely committed to the monarch. In a word they became an establishment. Hence when Jeroboam seceded he had to establish new shrines and a new priesthood in his own kingdom. At this point the character of the Jewish people began to assert itself in a new way. Men appeared from all ranks of society to protest against the errors of the government and the betrayal of the nation's inheritance or covenant.

These men were what the people called prophets. They were the men who by their individual genetic character utterly rejected the environment they lived in and by doing so created a new environment. Who were they?

It was among the pastoral fringes of Israel that the most passionate fundamentalism was upheld. For example the Rechabites were an hereditary sect of shepherds who denounced living in houses, tilling fields or drinking wine. In this attitude they foreshadowed Mohammed and many later teachers. (II Kings 10; Jeremiah 35: 6–10). No doubt this practice has suggested to Graves and Patai that the prophets, or some of them, were members of a guild who dressed as shepherds in honour of a pastoral god. The social evidence however suggests something more surprising: the prophets seem to have been men from every walk of life. Elisha was a rich farmer, Micah a poor villager, Amos a shepherd; Jeremiah and Ezekiel were Levites and Isaiah was a rich citizen of Jerusalem. These men were imbued with a belief in their own people and in the ideas that had made that people what it was.

The result was a situation unique in ancient times. The prophets spoke and wrote against the establishment. Their writings were preserved by their followers for several reasons. Obviously they were admired as literature by a people deeply sensitive to the poetic style, the social insight, and the historic meaning of their utterances. Obviously also there was a profound division, as in other societies at all times, between the governing class and the people. The conflict was often one between political strength and religious unity: Elijah broke the alliance of Israel with Phoenicia and lost both nations their independence. Jeremiah was imprisoned for predicting the inevitable disaster. Many other prophets were put to death.

In captivity, however, the importance of the prophets was further enhanced. Here were these men, who could have been produced only by the Jewish people, translated into the midst of an entirely alien civilization, the most advanced civilization in the world. Moreover they were now liberated from their own governing class. Their horizon was suddenly enlarged. It was in these circumstances that Ezekiel and the second Isaiah produced their works and brought a new depth into Jewish thought, making explicit what had hitherto been implied in Jewish history.

What the prophets of the old kingdoms had been asserting with their splendid phrases was the dramatic polarity and opposition between the transient interests of the political state and the durable interests of individual belief and integrity. What the prophets of the Exile were asserting no less splendidly was that their religion, their rituals, laws and chronicles would preserve the Jewish people more effectively than the power of Babylon could preserve the greatness of its Empire. This was a practical policy as well as a spiritual doctrine. And it succeeded. It proved to be true. For in fact Babylon fell and the Jews survived. The prophets preserved the Jewish people. And the Jewish people were thus able to preserve the prophets.

VIII. THE THEORY OF WINNOWING

From the legends of many races the Hebrew bards and chroniclers had put together a common line of descent from Adam. All these races, Sumerians, Babylonians, Hittites and others, had no doubt contributed to the ancestry of the Jews. But the Hebrew myth condenses the history of some 7000 years into half that time. In doing so it neatly condenses a record of racial conflicts into a succession of disputes between brothers or kinsmen: Cain and Abel, Abraham and Lot, Isaac and Ishmael, the twins Jacob and Esau, and finally Joseph and his brethren. Similarly there was the selection of Noah from among his kinsmen: and the sorting out of the three sons of Noah (Shem, Ham and Japhet) and the sons of Shem (Asshur, Elam and Aram), who gave their names to peoples; they are names which are still used as arguments for persecution or slavery to this day.

Each of these symbolizes the genetic differences between brethren, and between the tribes that sprang from them, differences connected with their habit of life. Each represents the genetic principle of recombination to which, as we have seen, the most significant families owe their origin. Each represents in its way the revolutionary steps which marked the origin of the Jews from the Hebrews and the Israelites as settled life struggled with wandering life and tillage with herding.

Each of the later conflicts was followed by the selection and differential multiplication of one line or stock or tribe at the expense of the other. In the language of the prophets this was a process of *winnowing*, a process they and their people very well understood. To the priesthood this process of discrimination was evident in the decay of the line of Moses and the elevation of the line of Aaron to office and authority. It was a discrimination which was to be repeated often. Ezekiel himself was instrumental in establishing, at the expense of ordinary Levites, the line of Zadok, which in due course gave rise to the Sadducees who were displaced in their turn.

It was Isaiah first, and then Ezekiel, who gave precision to this doctrine of the 'survival of the remnants'. It is a doctrine which has been rightly compared with the biological principle of the 'survival of the fittest'.[1] The

[1]Isaiah 6: 13, 10: 22; Ezekiel 14: 22—see *E.B.* 1929: Judaism.

disappearance of Israel and the survival of Judah were bound to offer an object lesson. It was a lesson which was repeated when Nehemiah returned and the foreign wives that the erring inhabitants of Jerusalem had married were expelled from the Jewish community (Nehemiah 10: 28; Ezra 9).

The important rules which governed the behaviour of the Jews in captivity illustrate the process of winnowing. The first rule was the maintenance of their laws which they owed to the priesthood. These ensured their integrity as a breeding group existing as a racial caste in the empires in which they were swallowed up. It is a caste which still exists today as those who visit the tomb of Ezra in Hamadan (the former capital, Ecbatana) may see for themselves.

The second rule followed from the injunction given them by Jeremiah in his letter. They must 'seek the peace of the city' to which they had been carried away. In other words they must submit to existence in a multi-racial society. It was a new ordeal for the Jews, to which however they accommodated themselves, learning to contribute more and more to the prosperity of alien communities with a succession of alien governing classes.

The success of the Jews in this new life was however a success for one part of the nation which preferred collaboration as opposed to another part which preferred to return and to rebuild Jerusalem. It was itself an example of winnowing by selective migration, a choice between environments by individuals, the environments being those established by a home community and by a foreign community.

The Jewish people continued as in the past not only to lose old elements but also to incorporate new elements. Both processes were selective. Their social structure also was continually changing. The priesthood was purged from time to time, the Levites giving place to the Sadducees. Under the Persians these became the official administrators of Jerusalem and a social and economic distinction arose among them between high-priestly and ordinary families. And when, under the influence of Greek philosophers, sophisticated argument began to displace primitive ritual, the transformation was achieved by the Pharisees (or Rabbis, as they became) displacing the Sadducees who disappeared with the destruction of the centre of their activities, the Temple, by the Romans in A.D. 70.

IX. THE DRIVING FORCE

The triumphs of the Jewish people in their Babylonian and Persian exile were a product of evolution whose genetic steps we can thus partly trace. When we read the account of Joshua's invasion of the Promised Land we find nothing to distinguish it from the ruthless conquests of any other late bronze age people in which the enemy is offered the alternatives of slavery or destruction.

But when we examine the Code of Deuteronomy and study the rules for the treatment of slaves we see the compassionate principles of the earlier Babylonians reappearing. The Code of Hammurabi is improved upon. The foreign bondsmaid can be taken as a concubine and her progeny can be admitted into the Jewish community. The Jewish breeding group could, with discrimination, be enlarged. Hybridization was possible and evolution was to be expected. It was evolution, after Ezra, partly controlled by conformity with public opinion, that is by submission to the Torah, to the law and the light. Those, like the ten tribes, who did not conform often disappeared from Jewish history which means that they disappeared from history altogether. But there was also the possibility of revolution with consequences which we shall see later.

The experience of the Exile had awakened the Jews to the practical importance of their religious teaching. When Ezra brought back the books of the law to Jerusalem in the middle of the fifth century they were read with other scriptures in special meeting places or *synagogues* built for the purpose. A new level of instruction, of literacy, and hence of discrimination, was thus established, and indeed a new intellectual approach to religion. Instead of the ritual sacrifices of the priests of a shrine or temple there was a learned teacher who could converse with the congregation. For the first time a whole people were brought together by a teaching of their own, a teaching of history, religion and the rules of good behaviour.

It was these practices and the men who carried them out at this time that were the middle step in the creation of the Jewish people. It is at this time that 'the significance which Israel attributes to its own history becomes the driving force of that history itself'.[1]

The climax of this driving might be seen by some as the Book of Job, written probably after Alexander's conquest. Others might see it in the mission of Jesus or the writings of Paul. Of the totality of literary achievement however there can be no doubt. It was one of the high points of human achievement. It covered in its range every aspect of great literature and of human expression save one: that of humour, or wit or fun. That is a side of human nature and literature that appeared in the contemporaries of Job in Greece. It came from Europe and Africa. And it appeared among the later Jews after they had incorporated other racial elements from Europe and Africa; that is after another racial assimilation.

[1] Moscati (1960).

Part IV

The Process of Empire

Language and religion united the peoples of ancient states and gave them the interbreeding from which a national character sprang. But the power of horsed warriors with steel weapons, the growth of writing and technology and the use of coined money made possible the conquest and control of large territories. Cyrus and Alexander grappled with the revolutionary problems, military, political and social, arising from the subjection of many peoples to one ruler. But the long-term problem of perpetuating a dynasty defeated them. It was only the slow experimental growth of the Roman oligarchy which showed how a governing class could maintain an empire by continually renewing itself. In doing so it assimilated to the name 'Roman' the whole of the social structure of western civilization.

10

PERSIA

I. MEDES AND PERSIANS

THE GREAT TABLELAND east and north of Mesopotamia had harboured some of the earliest agricultural settlements. Throughout the fourth millennium its sparse populations had been exchanging craftsmen and traders with the richer people of Mesopotamia. Scribes from Sumer must have given them their earliest notions of writing since early in the third millennium pictorial figures began to be replaced by linear and cuneiform scripts.[1] Foremost in this advance was inevitably the country in the south, nearest to Sumer, and it may have been in Elam at this time that the potter's furnace and the potter's wheel were invented.

The second millennium with its bronze weapons brought war in place of trade as the chief means of the mixing of people, of genes and of ideas. War in the first place was mainly between Babylon and Elam: later it spread northwards. Ruling dynasties in the mountains and the plain alternately displaced one another by war and married one another to establish peace.[2]

At the same time came the great Aryan movements southward from east of the Caspian, movements which were to give the name of Iran to the whole country. These movements, as in Europe, covered over a thousand years and many tribes and people took part. Western tribes established the kingdom of the Mitanni; eastern tribes invaded India; and a great array made their way into Iran. The earliest invaders were often peaceful in their penetration. Later came massive and warlike groups of Medes and Persians. And in the eighth century lighter and swifter bands of Scythians and Cimmerians swept through the whole region to the frontier of Egypt.

[1] Recently deciphered by Hinz (1964).

[2] The great treasure of Sakiz, near the salt lake of Urmiah, is supposed by Ghirshman to have been a gift celebrating the marriage of an Assyrian princess to a Scythian, that is Aryan, king.

The later invaders owed their great success to their use of stronger horses to mount their bowmen. They indeed created cavalry and by their success compelled first the Assyrians, then the Greeks, and finally the Romans to adopt cavalry (still without stirrups) as the decisive arm in war. They also converted the ancient villages of the cultivators into the fortified camps (as at Siyalk) which established the new Aryan governing class equipped to subject and to defend the country.

The issue of the 'hybrid', as Ghirshman puts it, between the Aryan pastoral invaders and the native agricultural and hunting peoples showed 'astonishing vitality' both economic and military. And, we may add, artistic for in the eighth century the Luristan bronzes show the originality we might expect from a combination of the Assyrian artisan and the Scythian patron.

The victory of Sargon of Assyria in the eighth century over the northern kingdom of the Medes was the last success of the Mesopotamian empires against the gathering strength of the newcomers. For after a century of subjection the Medes had learnt enough and taken enough from their conquerors, including no doubt some women, to turn the tables on them. In 612 B.C. they joined with Babylon in throwing over the rule of Nineveh. Soon their kings had brought the adjoining provinces of Armenia and Persia under their control. Their capital however was still at Ecbatana, the Hamadan of today. This was the 'place of assembly' of the Medes 6000 feet above sea level, sited and fortified to resist the expected invasion of their Assyrian enemies. It stood remote from the great trade and military routes which were becoming more and more necessary as the areas of government grew greater.

The kingdom of the Medes therefore proved to be merely the prologue to the Empire of the Persians which followed sixty years later. How the Persians won this Empire and how they kept it are parts of the same problem.

II. CYRUS AND DARIUS

It was about the year 700 that a chieftain, ruling a tribe in a remote valley known to them as Parsumash, in what we now call Luristan, established the name of his people as Persians and left his own name to his descendants as Achaemenes.[1] But it was Ariaramnes, the grandson of this man, who left us the family's first written record. He declares himself in the first of all inscriptions in the Persian language as King of Persia, 'a land of fine horses and good men'. This statement was soon to be confirmed. But at the time what mattered most about it was that it was written in an alphabetic cuneiform script which was new to Persia. Evidently the Persian ruler had met a Babylonian scribe: at one stroke the king had adopted the idea of writing his own language and of using the most modern script to do so. Thus he showed (as Ghirshman says) the enterprising character which in a few generations was to make his family great.

The next step in the advance of the Achaemenid family was taken in the

[1] All Persian names have been first made known to us by the Greeks in a Greek form which the English usually Latinize. Darius gives a name for his family in the inscription on Behistun which we transliterate as HAKHIMANI.

fourth generation when a nephew of Ariaramnes, Cambyses I, married a daughter of his suzerain, the King of Media. This union of two royal lines had many fabulous sequels related by Herodotus. It might have been designed to achieve either hybrid vigour or dynastic security. It in fact achieved one at the expense of the other for the young heir, Cyrus (Kurosh in his own tongue, Kyros in Greek), six years after inheriting his principality, formed a federation of seven princes, rebelled against his grandfather and dethroned him.

This unusual proceeding was violent enough but it was not followed by the usual violent consequences. Instead of destroying Ecbatana, murdering the king and massacring the inhabitants, Cyrus treated his opponents as his friends, employed them as his servants, and made their city his own capital. Indeed he established a dual monarchy as king of two equal peoples, the Medes and the Persians.

This first victory was followed by a succession of greater triumphs. He defeated and captured Croesus, King of Lydia, and in due course he liberated, as he wished it to be understood, the whole of the Babylonian Empire and made a new capital of Babylon. To protect his eastern frontier he had already subdued Parthia, marched against the tribes of Bactria and penetrated as far as Samarkand. To his two capitals he now added a third. This was Susa, the ancient capital of Elam lying thirty miles south-west of modern Dizful, where the mountains meet the plain and four rivers lead down into the Persian Gulf. What had been for 3000 years the gateway where armies, merchandise and ideas had been entering Persia now became the centre of gravity of a great federation of peoples united under one ruler.

The success of Cyrus was due to his diplomatic as well as his military skill. Neither the Lydian lancers nor the Greek hoplites were a match for the mobile archers or the camel corps of the Persian king. But as one victory led to others, the victor adjusted his methods to exploit the expanding resources at his command. The Greek colonies of Anatolia were taken by assault or bribery, by the corruption of the Delphic Oracle or by the mere acknowledgement of their merchants of the advantages of belonging to what was now the largest free trade area in the world.

When Cyrus died fighting on his eastern frontier, the vast extent of his dominions was inevitably a source of danger to his successors. The framework of government was supported by the slenderest possible establishment. His heir Cambyses was the product of a cousin marriage. He was compelled like nearly every ruler in this dynasty to begin by murdering a brother. He was then able to annex Egypt. Having done so, he followed Egyptian custom and married his sister.

The two steps of murdering a brother and marrying a sister were both a tribute to the principle of legitimacy. But together they effectively terminated Cyrus' branch of the Achaemenid family. When Cambyses died he was followed by a brother[1] who was murdered and displaced by a cousin who was also a great-grandson of Ariaramnes. This was Darius the Great.

[1] Olmstead considers this was a real brother not an imposter (Gaumata the Magian) as his successor pretended.

Darius proved to be a ruler as constructive and also as experimental as the founder of the dynasty. He was perhaps the most enterprising administrator of all time. Our opinion of him, to be sure, is partly based on his own accounts, notably the famous trilingual inscription at Bisitun. Standing athwart the main road from Ecbatana to Babylon (and also we may say, from China to the Mediterranean) this great monument proclaims in Babylonian, Elamite and Persian the achievements of the King of Kings—a title still used by his heirs today. The story tells of how he brought his apparently disintegrating Empire back under control, defeating eight kings in twice as many battles. This story is borne out by all the other evidence.

What made Darius not merely a great king but the pioneer of a new age was his willingness to use the abilities of others; to exploit the skill or inventiveness of people of every kind that his Empire, the Empire made by Cyrus, had for the first time put at the disposal of one man. His first problem was that of governing a state two thousand miles long from capitals which were remote from its strategic and commercial centres. His solution, which was to be imitated with varying success by the rulers of all later empires, was threefold: decentralization, communication and toleration.

Take first decentralization. He already had three capitals for his own personal government. To these he added a fourth, Persepolis, for ceremonial grandeur. He divided the Empire into twenty provinces under Persian governors known as satraps (a word cognate with the Hindustani *Khshatriya* or warrior). Supported by their Persian military colonies, with their Persian officers in every city in the Empire, these men were able to make use of the administrators of previous kingdoms. They were able to utilize the Phoenician (alphabetic) writing, the Aramaic and Greek languages, the Babylonian law, the Lydian coinage, the Greek mercenary soldiers, and all the other modern techniques and technicians that were available to the imperial government. And it was to their adaptability in making use of these diverse men, methods and ideas that the Persians, according to the Greek Herodotus, owed so much of their success.

Within the great satrapies Darius set up a wide range of subordinate administrations. These were the civilized provinces, the tribal communities, the personal domains (*monarchoi*), the royal domains (*paradeisoi* or parks for hunting). And finally there were the city states (*poleis*) which were all in the west, for in the east there were still only villages. These city states to be sure were not governed on the principles ostensibly favoured by Greek cities during their democratic interludes. Rather they were ruled by the tyrants who were equally familiar to the cities but who were now nominated to guarantee a policy subservient to the needs of the Great King.

Between the new administrative regions the basis of communication was the roads, notably the great road from Susa to Sardis which was later continued to Ephesus on the Aegean. A great mobilization of labour and talent was necessary for this work and Darius' own account of his building of his new palace at Susa gives us a striking picture of his methods.

Darius in his inscriptions gives us with pride a list of the works and the workmen he used, as follows:

(i) *Timber:* Cedar was brought down from Lebanon in Phoenicia by Assyrians, Carians and Ionians. Yaka wood was brought from Gandara and Carmania. Both were worked by Sardians and Egyptians.
(ii) *Stone:* the columns from Elam; the cutters were Ionians and Sardians.
(iii) *Brick:* baked by Babylonians; walls decorated by Medes and Egyptians.
(iv) *Gold:* from Sardis and Bactria; the goldsmiths were Medes and Egyptians.
(v) *Precious stones:* from Sogdiana and Chorasmia.
(vi) *Ivory:* from Ethiopia, Sind and Arachosia.[1]

The king was sharply aware that his power and glory were reflected as much in the diversity of the people who obeyed him as in the splendour of the work they performed.

Such a great concourse of craftsmen, it might seem, would lead to a promiscuous mixture of races. Some mixture without doubt always occurs in these circumstances. But the natural tendency of racial groups to keep apart was also maintained by the administrative convenience of separating trades and languages. The royal monopoly in all building operations[2] meant keeping each trade in one street where it constituted a caste, a breeding community, sometimes continuing to the present day.

How enterprising the Persians were in their adoption of foreign people and ideas may be shown by a contrast. The Hittites took their ideas of sculpture from the Babylonians and Egyptians. But they were not willing to take the sculptors. They thought they could do it themselves. The results, as Seton Lloyd points out, were inept. It is a mistake that people have been making ever since. But the Persians took the best people from everywhere and gave them suitable jobs to do. Darius and Xerxes probably paid the wage for the job if we judge by the results they got in Susa and Persepolis.

The crown on the achievement of the Persian kings was however the practice of toleration which ran through their government. Instead of slaughtering kings, like Croesus, as the Assyrians had done and the Romans would do, they protected them. Having forgiven their defeated enemies they then employed them. So also they tolerated—and employed—other gods than their own. Within the Empire were a vast range of races and religions. Each religion had its own racial origin. They themselves worshipped no idols but, as Herodotus puts it, 'sun, moon, earth, fire and water'. But to each sect of idol-worshippers Cyrus and Darius gave its own freedom of worship and its own civil jurisdiction. The Jews, who were specially favoured and respected, were allowed to return to Jerusalem to rebuild their Temple. In Egypt the school of medicine of the Temple of Saïs was likewise restored.

The small numbers of the governing military class made this degree of cultural freedom necessary. Their undisputed control also made it possible. But, during the two centuries that it survived, the new principle was already

[1] See Moscati (1960).
[2] As Woolley (1961) points out for the Assyrian kings' relief-makers.

Pedigree 3. The Achaemenid Family with years of reigns
After Sykes (1921); Olmstead (1948); Girshman (1964) and C.A.H. (Vol. 4)

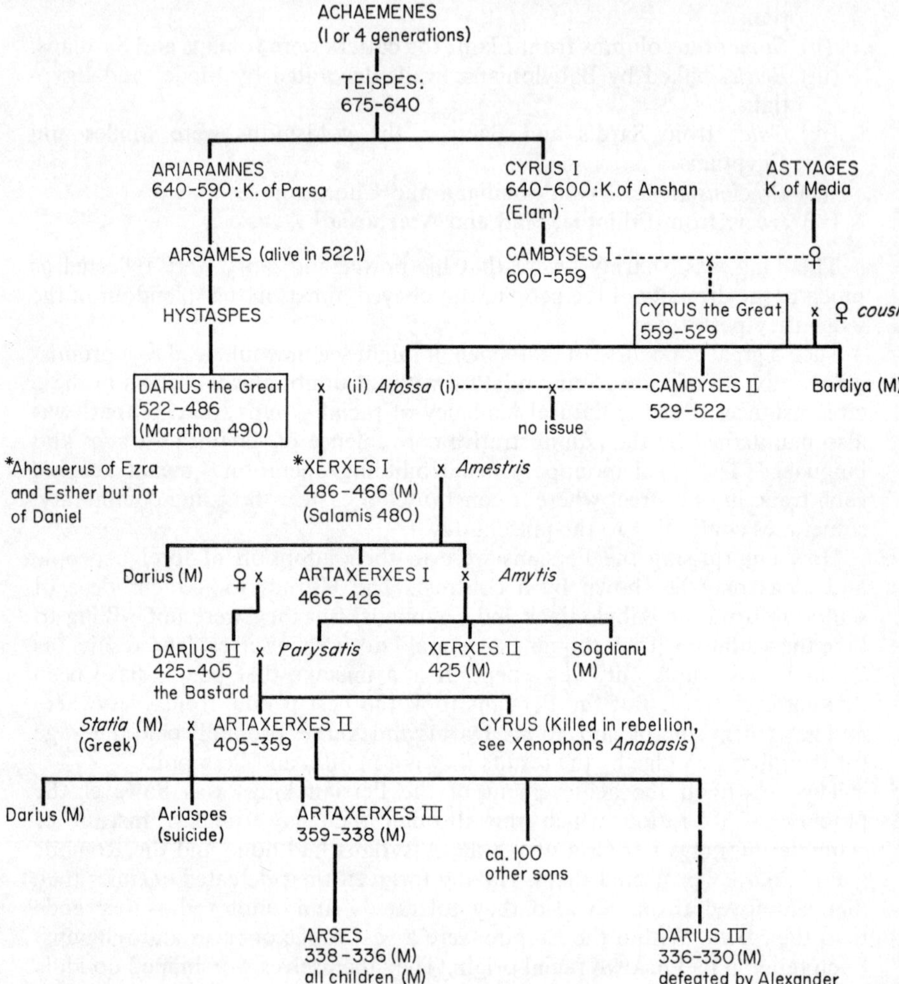

able to work a revolution in the religious thinking and the social processes which were bound up together in the whole body of subject peoples.

III. THE DECLINE OF THE ACHAEMENIDS

The problems bequeathed to their successors by Cyrus and Darius were unprecedented and might have been thought overwhelming. But they also bequeathed a devoted body of public servants and an almost divine authority attaching to their names, an authority which went unchallenged for two centuries. It seems to have been this extraordinary prestige and the need for protecting it from contamination or conspiracy which led Darius and all his successors to marry within their family. As with the Eighteenth Dynasty in Egypt, this inbreeding led straight to those political consequences they hoped to avoid. It also led to the most extravagant defects of character in regard to which the successors were sharply contrasted with the founders of the family.

The two great kings Cyrus and Darius were the results of outbreeding between different ruling families. Cyrus himself however changed the system. He married a cousin who bore him his successor. This was Cambyses who murdered his brother, married his sister Atossa and, when he committed suicide leaving no heir, had extinguished his branch of the family in the male line. This sister married the successor, Darius, who was her third cousin. Unfortunately the children of Darius by earlier non-royal wives were excluded. That is to say the succession was confined to inbreeding, breeding within the Achaemenid family. The Empire therefore passed to Xerxes, the offspring, like Cambyses, of a cousin marriage. Xerxes was irritated, like his father, by the conspiracies between his subject Ionian Greeks and the free Greeks of the peninsula. Being a man of few ideas he repeated his father's mistake. He repeated the assault on the city states. His father's hopes had been set back in the land battle at Marathon. Xerxes' hopes were destroyed ten years later, by sea at Salamis, and by land as well at Plataea.

Xerxes' ideas were confined to domestic adventures which in their failure however paralleled his military exploits. For Xerxes was prepared to sacrifice the peace of the world to the aim of seducing the wife and daughter of a loyal brother whom he murdered. He was then himself murdered by his chief minister who put his successor on the throne. It is an unhappy picture in which Herodotus and the Book of Esther concur.

The successor of Xerxes however is said to have murdered all his brothers and married a sister. Three of his sons succeeded by murdering their predecessors. The survivor called himself Darius but was nicknamed the Bastard. Thus at this stage again the legitimate line had extinguished itself by murder. The wife of this Darius, Parysatis, probably his half-sister, bore him two sons. The heir was Artaxerxes II. His brother was the Cyrus whose abortive rebellion is the subject of Xenophon's *Anabasis*. Artaxerxes had many wives including one daughter Atossa and, when his son Artaxerxes III came to the throne, he found it necessary to murder a total of several dozen brothers and sisters. Now the steepest decline of the dynasty and the Empire had occurred. The satraps had begun to rule as independent hereditary monarchs. And the figure of Mithras had appeared as a rival to Ahuramazda.

The end of the dynasty was also a climax of murder. The year 338 was a year of critical importance on Persia's western frontier. But it was then that the chief minister, a eunuch named Bagoas, chose to poison the king and all his sons except one whom he set up as a puppet. This last son in turn he poisoned three years later, leaving no heir to the great family except a cousin who took the now traditional name of Darius. This man began to reign by promptly poisoning the poisoner. It was he who had to meet the last dreadful crisis of the Empire.

Such is the story. It seems a tedious story until we notice its social and genetic implications characteristically intertwined. The founders of the Achaemenid family knew how to conquer an empire and how to govern it. But they were baffled as many had been before by the problem of breeding a dynasty, a dynasty isolated from the whole world by its unprecedented power. They imagined that by close inbreeding, including incest, they would preserve at once the isolation and the authority of the royal line. They supposed that polygamy would insure against destruction. They assumed that the murder of rival claimants, that is the nearest kinsmen, would protect the person of the king. They hoped that the service of eunuchs, who would be without ambition, would guarantee their own safety. And all these expectations were defeated.

Nine generations showed that selection in favour of assassination could more than keep pace with selection in favour of fertility. And probably, as we shall see later, ambitious families discovered how to produce eunuchs who were interested in power for its own sake. Later dynasties have, some of them, followed the same fatal course. Others have learnt means of avoiding certain of the pitfalls. What we have to accommodate ourselves to is a paradox which seems to insult the intelligence of man. It is that the paltry predicaments of kings and queens may have as much consequence as the migrations of millions of their people; and that the greatest events in history may be bound up with the smallest as well as the largest actions of momentarily and accidentally leading figures. This is one of the lessons we may learn from the narrative of the inquisitive Herodotus.

IV. THE PERSIAN REVOLUTION

a. Free Movement

If the people of the Persian Empire had behaved like their rulers the two centuries of their rule would indeed have taken the world back into a darker age. But it did nothing of the kind. For the great masses it was an age of peace and progress such as their ancestors had never known. While the political structure was disintegrating the economic and cultural life of the ancient world was being strengthened by the free movement of people concerned in the exchange of goods and ideas; and, of course, women.

Goods and ideas are connected in practice and the evidence for their movements reaches us often by connected channels. The fowl, the peacock and the sugar-cane were brought by Darius to the Mediterranean from India, which received in exchange the Aramaic alphabet. And it was by the explicit instructions of Darius that the Persians brought sesame to Egypt and rice to Mesopotamia. The great barriers, which since the neolithic expansion, and all through the bronze age, had separated the development of agriculture in its European, its Indian and its Chinese branches, were thereby first broken down. It is a process which has been continued by sudden steps down to the present days, each step diversifying and enriching the resources of the natural regions of the earth.

The movements of livestock had a more immediate and decisive effect. The

Persians brought the improved strong riding-horses of the Medes into use all over their Empire and beyond it, into Europe in the west, into India and China in the east, into Arabia in the south. Soon afterwards their own alfalfa, which we know as the Greeks did by the name of Medish grass (*Medicago*), followed the horse providing it with fodder. The riding-horses brought military power into inaccessible mountains. And to the people of one region, Thrace and Macedonia, they gave a military power that was to change the art of war and bring down the Empire of the Persians themselves.

The horse not only gave power to the peoples who mastered it. It gave power to the class which could afford to keep it. By its expense it separated the rich equestrian from the poorer foot soldier. It was a step in the long process of consolidating and extending the authority of governing classes, classes which since the bronze age had everywhere been increasingly derived from the Semitic and Aryan pastoral animal-loving tribes.

It was Cyrus who at an early stage had astonished and defeated the cavalry of Croesus by bringing the camel, presumably the Bactrian camel, into battle. Cambyses in turn took the Arabian camel, domesticated six centuries earlier by the people on the spice route from the Yemen to Midian. But of course the camel-drivers were Midianites and we cannot doubt that both the herds and the herdsmen multiplied as they passed along the north coast of Africa into the country of the Berbers. There the Greek word for Numidia gave us our term for all wandering herdsmen, the nomads. There too the camels and the camel-drivers, crossing the Sahara, created the trade in Negro slaves and also created a new race of people, the veiled Tuareg, who lived by this trade.

Soon the camel was spreading from Arabia into Abyssinia and Somaliland and wherever it went, often followed by the horse and the goat, it grazed and over-grazed the meagre pastures on the edge of the desert where it alone could live. For the next two thousand years the regiments of new livestock were to eat their way through the declining vegetation left by the ice age climate and to extend the boundaries of the desert, extend them irremediably at the cost of later generations of men.

b. Free Belief

Freedom of religion, when it sprang into being in the Persian Empire, meant something very different from what it means in our world today.[1] It meant the transformation at once of the priests, the people, and the religions themselves. It meant that, in great cities throughout the Empire, priesthoods were brought face to face with people who could choose what to believe, what cults to follow, what priests to support. Languages themselves were competing and beliefs expressed in language were subject to a double source of instability and innovation.

In this new world the priests themselves competed for individual adherents. Conversion became practical politics. It was a new kind of politics in a new kind of society and one which affected the structure of society itself. To be sure it was only momentarily that religion was de-tribalized; and only momentarily were the barriers to hybridization lowered. Permanently, however, a new

[1] See Edmund Meyer, *E.B.* (1929).

principle was brought into action. Now the success of a religion was bound to depend on two independent and often opposed factors.

The first factor was the original basis of long-term success as measured by the survival and reproduction of the community. This kind of success is based on the primary function of all religion in binding together the whole community united, or supposed to be united, by kinship through common ancestors. It is also based on the institution of rules governing food and health,[1] marriage and sexual fertility,[2] religious tolerance and social co-operation. The second factor was the new one of short-term success in winning proselytes by its appeal to individuals; that is in gaining converts, the most numerous in quantity and the most useful in quality and social influence.

The interaction of these factors has influenced and perhaps dominated the evolution of society in the western world ever since the time of Cyrus and Darius.

It was not entirely a coincidence that several remarkable developments appeared along with the religious toleration of the Persian government. An immense variety of mixed societies were brought into being by the new Empire. These were societies in which Armenians, Greeks, Phoenicians, Egyptians and Jews were following their own cults, living their own lives, maintaining their own inbred communities while profiting from the immense social and economic convenience of co-operation. These religio-racial communities have provided the social pattern of all great empires down to the present day. They are, as we may say, still endemic in the region where they began, the Persian Empire.

Leading up to this stability of pattern, this crystallization, was a period of fluidity. New cults evolved and increased by conversion more rapidly than ever before in the more fluid or mobile elements of society, namely the administration, civil and military, of the Persian Empire itself. Notable among these was the development of the Zoroastrian religion.

Zoroastrianism, like its contemporary Buddhism in India, was derived racially not from the Aryan invaders but rather from the native sources reacting against the brutality of these invaders. This is shown notably by their common rejection of blood sacrifices and their common appeal to the brotherhood of man. It is also indicated by two traditionally accepted circumstances. First, that Zoroaster's teaching arose in the country of the Medes at the same time that they were being attacked and subdued by the Assyrians. And, secondly, that Zoroaster was himself expelled from his homeland to take refuge in the east. Zoroastrianism, however, as Ghirshman points out, was from an early period sustained by the Achaemenian rulers. This may have contributed both to its downfall and to theirs. For after five generations the dynasty and the priesthood began to compromise with the cult of idols.

What happened was that Zoroaster's teaching came to be split between two movements. It was purified by one party and popularized by the other. The purification is known to us only in its modern survival, as the religion of a professional and intellectual emigrant minority, the Parsees in India.

[1] Simoons (1961). [2] Darlington (1960).

The popularization, for which the priestly tribe of the Magi seem to have been responsible, is best known in the form of the worship of idols. Of these the most important, already appearing under Artaxerxes II, was Mithras, the messenger of God who became God himself. It was an evolution found also in the Mandaean derivative of Christianity, and indeed in Christianity itself.

One of the ideas of Zoroastrianism proved to have the remarkable capacity of infecting, as we may say, all other religions under the conditions of the Persian Empire. We may regret that it had so little influence on the reigning family. It was the idea of an opposition between good and evil. This idea may be seen in its earliest form in the sacred *Avesta* of the Parsees. Much later it spread westwards under the name of Manichaeism. This opposition, polarity or dualism, whichever we like to call it, was carried over into an after-life, into the world of eschatology. There it suggested a division amongst a hitherto undisciplined array of gods and people, into those who are good and those who are evil. One could imagine opposed squadrons of spirits; there could be hierarchies of angels culminating in a Supreme Being on the one side, and of devils culminating in Satan on the other. Following the same line of thought one could also imagine, indeed one almost had to assume, a polarity of residence: heaven to reward the good, hell to punish the rest. Ever since the Persian Empire all western religions, first Judaism, then Christianity, and lastly Islam, have benefited or suffered from the influence of these ideas or impersonations of ideas by which the most abstract and also gratuitous generalizations were endowed with the most concrete properties.

The enormous scope allowed to the fancy by the problem of re-allocating divine and diabolical functions may be illustrated by the example of the Yezidi, a Zoroastrian sect. This minute and pure-bred community, reversing the polarity envisaged by their founder, devoted themselves to the worship of the devil in the gorgeous shape of a peacock. They are still said to maintain their cult in the gloomy fastnesses of Kurdistan where they are able to keep their practices, apart from the celebration of the sabbath on a Wednesday, secret even from Freya Stark.

The genetic causes of these differences of beliefs are perhaps trivial. And the problem of their ancestral classification as between Zoroastrian and Jewish or Christian and Muslim is certainly trivial. But their genetic consequences are momentous. From their diversity arose the separation of what Omar Khayyam counted as the sixty-nine warring sects. For these sects are inbred and hence hereditary in their descent, specialized and hence professional in their activity. They depend for their survival, therefore, less on the names they give to gods and devils, than on the viability of the different kinds of work which each contributes to a multiracial and multi-religious society.

It was under these novel conditions that the foundations were laid for those diverse religio-racial communities which have maintained themselves throughout the lives of the successive empires inheriting, over a period of 2500 years, the peoples of the Persian Empire. Each community has maintained itself by its own professional and specialized contributions to the complex society in which it has lived. One of the communities which prospered beyond all others was the Jewish community. Owing to its stricter rules directed to health and fertility, its controlled body of hereditary teachers, and the keener intelligence of the people needed to understand and obey these rules, it multiplied and spread not only in Judaea but all over the Persian Empire. For this reason, between the reign of Cyrus and the birth of Christ the Jewish community increased in numbers from perhaps a hundred thousand to nearly fifty times that number, an estimated four and a half million.

Another community which spread was that of the Greeks. Again a common language and literature, common teaching, a native intelligence and a racial pride equal to that of the Jews and the Persians, advanced the Greek communities and they spread wherever the Persian peace protected them. The imperial road brought Greek artists, prostitutes and slaves to Persepolis. Greek mercenaries fought in Egypt for Cambyses as well as against him. Indeed they fought on both sides in all the Persian wars. And Greek traders and explorers went as far afield as the Indus and the Oxus.

c. Decay

At the same time that the Persians were opening the way for other peoples the foundations of their own greatness were decaying. The reason we can now see lay precisely in their tolerance. They kept their Aryan religion, the worship of Ahuramazda, the one creator, as the cult of their own military caste. But they paid their respect to all other cults and used all other priesthoods. They did not adopt the tribal Magian priesthood as the instrument of their imperial power, as their Sassanian successors in Persia were to do. Nor did they tie the Zoroastrian teaching to their official establishment. On the contrary they allowed it to disperse and diversify producing the largely homosexual cult of Mithraism as a purely military and professional convenience. Xerxes felt compelled to pull down the Temple of Marduk in Babylon, but it was too late. The toleration which was to do so much for the future undid, as it was bound to undo, those who had created it.

For their administration, also, the Persians were unable to establish a uniform and homogeneous class of scribes writing a uniform language. In the west they used the Babylonian administrators' Aramaic characters. In the Greek provinces they used Greek. And in their own country, in the poor highlands of Persia, they probably used a hybrid educated class who imposed the foreign Aramaic script on their own language.

In their heterogeneity the religion, language and literature of the Persian Empire merely reflected the absence of any coherent middle class, professional, technical or artistic. The unity of the Empire was the creation of a few men in a family of genius who operated through a military caste. These were men who, under their great kings, could conquer and could govern. But they could not provide the moral framework, the intellectual cement, or even the verbal formulae to hold together a great society.

The magnitude of the Persian achievement in knitting together the many races of their Empire hastened its own breakdown. But it prepared the way for a successor who should add one more ingredient, and one more race, bearing one more culture, to the stratified complex of the central ancient society.

11

MACEDON

I. THE ECLIPSE OF THE CITIES

THE REPULSE OF THE PERSIAN INVASIONS was followed by the proud expansion of the victorious Greek cities. Foremost now was Athens. Quickly she made herself mistress of a league of maritime states which in turn she transformed into an empire. This was the Athens of a glorious half-century whose wealth built the Parthenon; whose hospitality continued to attract, if it did not always welcome, immigrants from Greek colonies and from the Ancient East;[1] the city whose teeming population applauded the plays of Aeschylus, Sophocles and Euripides and whose fleet had the audacity to attack the Persians at Memphis, nearly driving them out of Egypt.

But at the end of this half-century followed disaster; the conflict with Sparta, the Peloponnesian war, brought eclipse to both the contending states. How did this come about?

During the sixth century the two communities, as we have seen, had continually diverged. In the beginning their divergence had been racial. It arose from a racial difference between the governing classes. The contrast in their position, the one shut into its territory, the other open to the sea, to trade and to foreigners, immigrants from the Ancient East, had enhanced this initial difference. While the military needs of Sparta had promoted military discipline and the exclusiveness of a military caste, the maritime needs of Athens had promoted movement and, as we have seen, had weakened the barriers between classes. But it had also led to an intermittent conflict between conservatives and reformers in Athens. Both sides were represented in the aristocracy and the victory of one party had led to the emigration of the

[1] As Thucydides puts it: 'the most powerful victims of war or faction from the rest of Greece took refuge with the Athenians as a safe retreat and at an early period became naturalized'.

other. When the conservatives were defeated and exiled they could rely on the hospitality of Sparta. When the reformers were expelled they might seek refuge in Persia, in Macedonia or in Italy.

The liberalization of Athens was reluctant and incomplete; and in the end it was reversed. The suspicion between social classes made them prefer a police force of slaves and Scythian archers rather than of their own less privileged citizens. And the fear of increasing the numbers of the unprivileged by immigration was never out of mind. Themistocles, who led the Athenians to victory at Salamis, would have been out of politics and out of command but for the reforms of Cleisthenes twenty years earlier which allowed *epigamia.* For his mother was not an Athenian; perhaps, Burn suggests, not a Greek. And Herodotus the historian, although admitted to Athens, was not admitted to its citizenship: only if he had been rich enough to equip a warship for the state would an alien Greek have secured naturalization.

Only thirty years later the reaction set in. It was sponsored by the leading Athenian aristocrat, Pericles, a grandson of Cleisthenes. In 451 the reform of Cleisthenes was reversed. Athenian parentage on both sides was again required for citizenship. Thus immigration was again restricted. It was at the same time that Athenian documents began to replace 'Athens and her Allies' by plain Athens, the mistress of an Empire whose dependencies were paying her tribute first in ships then in money. The racial distinction between citizen and non-citizen, which was in danger of lapsing, was thus legislatively restored. One exception proves the rule: the son of Pericles by his mistress Aspasia, who hailed from the colony of Miletus, was allowed by act of the Assembly without payment to give up his mother's nationality and become a full Athenian citizen.

The struggle for equality of opportunity continued as long as Athens lasted. Seventy years later just before his death in 348, when that aristocratic bachelor Plato was revising his *Republic*, he was still inveighing against the encroachments of immigrants who claimed equality with citizens, and of slaves who abused the freedom their masters allowed them; of the young who argued with their elders, and of women whose licence was unspeakable.

For all these ups and downs of policy, hybridization between the governing classes of Athens and Sparta never occurred. The divergence of race, of culture and of interests between the two cities therefore never diminished. Between them there was perpetual bickering. Submerged only with difficulty in the emergency of the Persian wars, it sprang up again as soon as the enemy was driven out. And the Persians, both the Great King and the Satrap of Lydia, soon learnt that if they could not defeat the Greeks in battle they could pay them to fight one another.

The culmination came with one long war, the Peloponnesian war which divided most of the Greeks between Athens and Sparta. It was the equality of the contest that made it so disastrous to the contestants. The struggle began in 431 and lasted on and off for twenty-seven years. We are fortunate in being able to follow its course from the accounts of an Athenian commander, Thucydides, who was a writer with a new kind of sophistication. For he actually describes the tragic events of the conflict without any reference to the gods or the omens which played so large a part in the popular and public view of the conduct of war in his time.

In the development of the conflict the Athenians were faced one after another by problems which they had never had to face during the Persian invasions. While the Athenian blockade protected the Spartans from the danger of infection Athens, now full of refugees, was struck by an Egyptian plague in three years out of four. The Athenian slaves, twenty thousand of them, who worked their mines on Mount Laurion on whose product their silver currency was based, escaped to the Spartan enemy only forty miles away. The Spartans, with Persian subsidies and Sicilian ships, disputed the command of the sea. An Athenian expeditionary force despatched to capture Sicily was destroyed, both army and navy, at Syracuse. Slowly Athens was reduced from power to prostration.

There had not been many massacres. Destruction had been ruthless but orderly. Their prisoners and their defectors, when they were not ranking Spartiates or rich Athenians, both sides preferred to kill in cold blood. The people of Mytilene and Melos were denied the privilege of equality with Athenians. But they were punished as traitors if they rejected the obligations of subjects. The men were killed; the women and children were enslaved, which meant that both males and females could be sold into prostitution. We notice the harshening under pressure of war of the ancient rules which limited the enslavement of fellow countrymen. And when the naval war ended with the capture of an Athenian fleet, the 4000 prisoners were slaughtered by the order of the Spartan general Lysander. At this point we may say that the iron age was reaching the limits of ferocity.

Peace came with surrender in 404. But the victory of Sparta was no victory for Greece. It brought harmony neither between nor within societies. The notion of compromise had not taken root anywhere in the rocky soil of the peninsula. Aristophanes' anti-war play, *Lysistrata*, had been tolerated in Athens six years before the peace. The necessity of war seemed still incontestable. But five years after the peace Socrates was to be found guilty of blasphemy, by a vote of 281 to 220, and condemned to death. An attack on the gods was an attack on the highly vulnerable social order, a criticism of the hierarchy of nations as well as of social classes.

The eclipse of Sparta was an example of what has always happened to the society with an exclusive and therefore inbred governing class. The habit of fighting with her neighbours was ineradicable because the habit of inbreeding was itself ineradicable. This was true, not only of the inbred, homogeneous and conservative aristocracy, but also of the equally inbred, homogeneous and conservative *perioikoi* and helots who, for twenty generations, had lived and worked and fought alongside them. It is indeed wrong to dwell on the antagonism of the social classes in Sparta as the cause of its trouble. It was rather the result, the accidental result, of the fierce austerity of a social code in which the supposed needs of the governing class had been the absolute guide to conduct. For it has been suggested that, in the beginning, it was the *perioikoi* who had rejected the severity of the Spartan code. It was only later that the ruling class came to reject the *perioikoi*.

Whatever the earlier steps in the evolution of Sparta may have been, the last stages are well documented. The increasing scale of war, fed by Persian money and by mercenary armies, led to losses too great for the fertility of the ruling class to replace. Outbreeding was excluded. So was immigration. By the time of the last Spartan attack, the whole of their power, apart from subject peoples and helots, was reduced (on Hammond's estimate) to 1200 men. And when 400 men had fallen at the battle of Leuctra in 371, the Spartans were never again able to put an army of their own into the field. At Leuctra the Spartans had been defeated by the novel tactics of a Theban general, Epaminondas. Nine years later, at the battle of Mantineia, the new power of the Thebans fought the older warring states of Greece to a standstill.

The fearful strife of the cities would seem to be enough ground for their decay. But decay works in ways that its victims cannot altogether apprehend. War meant the neglect of agriculture, the hastening of erosion and deforestation, the breakdown of drainage. All these were the likely opportunities for the spread of a disease which was in the next millennium to fill the cultivated lowlands of the Mediterranean, the disease of malaria. Outside the thickly populated city regions men were still safe from this plague. Outside the city states were the colonies continually recruited by exiles who would restore and enlarge and distribute the inheritance of Greece. And these exiles knew that the future of the Greek world now lay, not in the old cities of the peninsula, but in the new lands around it.

II. THE NATURAL HISTORY OF AGGRESSION

The conquerors who became governing classes, Aryan in Persia and Greece, Semitic in Babylonia, and mixed in Assyria, had prospered and multiplied in proportion to their success in aggression. For a long time this meant in proportion to their increasing lack of restraint in aggression. For a long time selection was favouring those who attacked first and killed most. They were leaving most progeny. But in the end they destroyed themselves.

We must ask however: who were 'themselves'? What were the units of conflict and the units of destruction? Always of course the individual or the family may appear as units. Both in Persia and in Greece, traitors and tyrants operated as individuals and succeeded or failed as families. But there is a striking contrast between Persia and Greece in the dominant mode of conflict.

In Persia the ferocity of conflict reached its peak in the royal family. Men and women were slaughtered by their own brothers in the struggle for the throne. Evidently also a large number of men of the governing class were castrated as a means of advancement in the struggle for power. The eunuch Bagoas seems to have been an abler governor than the two kings he poisoned or the third king who poisoned him. This practice, and the inbred family character of suspicion and ruthlessness in the Achaemenids, favoured their survival at first; but in the end it ensured their ruin.

The same principle applied at a different level with the governing classes of the Greek cities. Ruthless aggression favoured their survival up to the point at which they ruined one another. To a large extent, owing to the unity of each small city state, whatever its constitution, the state was the unit of suspicion, of aggression and even of survival. Athens destroyed the Mytileneans, loyal and rebel alike; and we shall see the same rule applied to Thebes. The climax of aggression was therefore reached in Greece with the destruction of the city state.

The conclusion of conflict in Persia was the destruction of a family or a clan. In Greece it was the destruction of a system of government, the system of cities which strove to stand apart, and of cities which contrived by various means to give a say in government to their free citizens. Much has been said of the contrast between this freedom of government in the Greek cities and its restraint by Persian kings. But we must not overlook the significance of the contrast between freedom of movement, geographical movement and social movement, in Persia and its restraint in Greece. At this stage in the evolution of society the two contrasted systems, each with its own freedoms and its own restraints, were evidently incompatible with one another.

III. WHO WERE THE MACEDONIANS?

On the northern border of the closely knit city states of peninsular Greece lay the colder countries and looser, poorer and more backward societies of Epirus, Illyria, Macedonia, Paeonia and Thrace. These lands had been colonized or rather penetrated in the seventh and sixth millennia by the first cultivators entering Europe from Anatolia. Three thousand years later they had been entered by successive southward waves of the Aryan expansion. The tribes which settled in the north spoke Greek and Illyrian dialects which were ancestral to modern Macedonian and Albanian. But during the first millennium a reverse movement began to set in from the south to produce a new mixture and new stratification in society.

The migrants moving northwards were in part the Greek colonists who, as we have seen, were founding cities on the coasts of the Aegean. But in addition there were others who were neither conquering tribes nor colonizing citizens. They were individuals or groups or even classes of people filtering out of cities and filtering into countries without cities, bringing by their migration the arts and practices of cities into the villages of the barbarians. These movements were of course continuing the expansion of civilization that had been proceeding for three millennia. And they were always selective since they depended on the choice of the individual guided by his talents and aptitudes both in his movements and in their direction.

The most obvious of the northward migrants were the people coming in the eighth and seventh centuries from the Ionian and other cities. But from all the shores and islands of the Aegean they moved into the less densely populated hinterland. They were chiefly traders in timber and metals. But they also included prospectors and miners, administrators and adventurers. Less obvious were the refugees from wars and revolutions. Whenever and wherever disturbances occurred in the civilized Mediterranean world, exiles and their followers from the overthrown government would fly overseas to find a refuge or found a colony. These people, whose prototypes were Cadmus, Dido and

Aeneas, by force or stratagem or marriage, made themselves into the little kings of the barbarous frontier peoples. And it was their descendants polygamously propagated who made an increasingly numerous and increasingly civilized nobility (or 'dominant clan' in the phrase of Hogarth) in the border countries of Epirus, Macedonia and Thrace. These people maintained the monarchical type of state which their ancestors had brought with them. So they claimed, and the claim is not likely to be very wide of the mark. For they spoke Greek, as distinct from the local dialect of their people; and they knew enough of Homer and of their own pedigree to trace their descents from the kings of Argos or Mycenae, from Herakles or from Achilles. Alexander I of Macedon, who later gave his sister in marriage to a Persian satrap, when a young man, was thus able, according to Herodotus, to enforce his claim to compete as a Greek in the Olympic games. But we need not doubt that Minoan, Phoenician and Egyptian ancestors were the remote but genetically significant founders of their dynasties and their castes.

The Macedonian rulers in the time of Darius were too poor to own slaves; the queen, as Herodotus puts it, would do her own cooking. Nor could they employ mercenaries; their armies were composed of their own peasantry; and they were commanded by their own nobles, their own peers, companions, or *hetairoi* as they called them. But these rulers were in the most favoured position for trade, for mining, and for receiving the immigrants from Greece whom their opportunities invited. They encouraged gold and silver mining; they struck their own coins; they built roads; they exported timber; they entertained promising strangers; they strengthened their position by marriage into the families of the most aggressive neighbouring rulers in Europe and Asia; they negotiated submission or alliance with the Persian king invading Greece or the Athenian Republic struggling with Sparta. They grew in strength and in influence.

In the conflicts of the fifth century, peninsular Greece had suffered a loss of wealth and men which might have been reparable. But it had also suffered damage to the soil which was irreparable. The vegetation which, according to Plato's description in *Kritias*, had already been damaged by the erosion of the previous five centuries, was now permanently impoverished. Now Athenian ships had to be built with Macedonian timber. Meanwhile Macedonia had suffered not at all. It was a new unspoilt country. Politically and socially the people had advanced. They had gained by being brought into closer contact with their more advanced neighbours. The great Persian armies invading Greece, so dangerous for wealthy and resisting cities, must have brought great benefits to a poor and collaborating province, a temporary satrapy of the Empire.

IV. KING PHILIP

The decisive moment came in 359 when, after years of turmoil, Philip, son of Amyntas, became ruler of Macedon.

The throne of Macedon, as of Saxon England, was secured by election. The nobles made their choice among the heirs. A royal mother answered for legitimate descent; seniority and reputation were advantages; and they might be assisted by violence. The kings were polygamous with royal and non-royal, Greek and non-Greek wives and concubines. A young king was therefore surrounded by half-brothers, half-cousins, half-uncles and stepmothers who were willing to assist or hinder the operations of government. As a half-uncle of the nominal king, Philip began his reign as the regent. But the abilities he then displayed led without violence to his election as king.

Here let us note that the election of a monarch by his chief subjects or nobles is not an empty or idle word. In the short term it introduces a balance into the structure of society and the processes of its government. In the long term *election* in the language of politics must be translated as *selection* in the language of biology. And events were to prove that the selective process was here operating with far-reaching effects to be favourably contrasted with what happened in Persia.

Early in life Philip had had good opportunities of training which he had exploited remarkably well. In the year 367, as a boy of fifteen, he had been put by an earlier regent, his brother-in-law Ptolemy of Alorus, as a hostage in the hands of Epaminondas the Theban commander. He stayed in Thebes three years. Here he devoted himself to a serious study of the arts of war, taking his lessons from the greatest of artists, Epaminondas himself.

The Theban general had applied new ideas to the tactics of battle, the first new ideas in a field of thought long stabilized by the successes, equal successes, of the Spartans and the Athenians. Epaminondas had discovered that he could use his phalanx of infantry to attack obliquely instead of directly. He had discovered how to adapt the movements of his cavalry and infantry to one another; and how to suit both to the lie of the land and the needs of the occasion. His successes in battle, as we have seen, had made Thebes for the first time—and only for his time—predominant in Greece.

What Epaminondas had done to reform the action of an army in war inspired Philip to reform its whole structure and training in peace. When he was able to take control in Macedon he began to plan an organization for his forces which should reflect and respond to the organization of the society or federation of societies which he governed. He wanted a professional standing army with a hierarchy of rank and authority based on the hierarchy of his own people. But his conception of his own people was one in which the distinction between Macedonian and Greek as well as between Macedonian and Thracian or Illyrian was to be skilfully allowed to lapse. The Persian satrapy of Macedonia had been abandoned but Persian cosmopolitanism had left its mark.

In this new army of Philip, the heavy horses of Thrace and Thessaly were able to carry heavier men with a heavier weight of armour than the earlier Asiatic cavalry had borne. His heavy infantry he armed with long defensive pikes leaving the lighter forces with classical spears. Among his horsemen he separated his nobles, his élite *hetairoi*, recruited into his service as boys. To them the freedom of country life gave, with the opportunity of hunting, an advantage in the practice of horsemanship over the inhabitants of cities, an advantage which European aristocracies have cherished, and been selected to cherish, together with their horses and their hounds down to the present day.

At the same time he separated élite footguards. On all his diverse arms and regiments he bestowed a discriminating hierarchy of titles, marks of status which attracted a devotion that had earlier been attached to tribes. The Thessalians, Thracians, and Paeonians still retained their skills in special weapons. But soon these allies became confederates, and these confederates subjects, merging their differences in a military discipline which, they discovered, brought its own reward.

The reward and the success in battle which these innovations brought were so great that they have left their traces on the practice of war down to the present day. What we have to notice now, however, is that they show the swift and shining events of war, no less than the slow dull course of peace, reflecting the same processes by which races, classes and individuals of different genetic character co-operate and compete. It is from this blend of co-operation and competition, recognized by the greatest rulers, that there spring the power and purpose of nations.

For these reasons, ever since the time of Philip, and first of all among the successors of Philip, whether in undeveloped countries or in periods of disorder anywhere, armies have offered the organized social structure, the mutual reliability of differentiated classes, needed for a government and for an establishment. Armies have offered alternatively a threat to the civil government, or a guarantee of the continuance of government when the hierarchy of civil authority has failed.

In the work of Epaminondas and Philip, originality and initiative broke into military affairs in Greece, as we might expect, a century later than it had penetrated into the work of poets, philosophers and politicians. But since it developed so late the man in whom it developed was able to call upon all the resources of Greek civilization in order to improve his authority and bestow their gifts on the whole world. And these were just the tasks which Philip set himself to accomplish.

His experience in Thebes, we can see, had had a profound influence on his mind. It was not only Epaminondas whose career he observed and studied. Spartan exiles, Athenian playwrights and philosophers, Persian diplomats and local politicians were evidently among the people he met. The consequences of Greek disunity were clear to everyone. The means of uniting the Greeks became clear to Philip. They were means in which home administration, foreign diplomacy, and skill in war were to be equally valued and successively exploited. And beyond all these the importance of Greek tragedy, as revealed by the writers of Athens, was evidently present to his mind, guiding his attitude to the suspicious politicians of Athens who seemed to hold this supreme cultural, and therefore political, prize in their gift.

One final instrument of unity was to be won only by providing unity with a purpose. And for Philip the purpose of unity came to be the overthrow of the Persian Empire.

It took Philip twenty-two years of war and diplomacy to pacify his own country, subdue his barbarian neighbours, and reduce the city states of

Greece to submission. Following his victory over the Athenians and their allies at Chaeronea, near Thebes, in 338 came the culmination. It was Philip's election in 337 as chief autocrat or captain general of a League of Greek states based on the confederacy and council of the Amphictyonies. At once and together Philip and the League declared war on Persia.

The following year, 336, the vanguard of 10,000 had just crossed the Hellespont into Asia when the king, so successful in great affairs, was overtaken by domestic disaster. His father with two wives had had six sons. Philip, with six wives, had succeeded in begetting only two legitimate sons, both by Olympias, his royal queen. One of them was an epileptic. The other, his sole effective heir, was Alexander. Before committing both himself and Alexander to battle he was persuaded to ensure his line against the danger of extinction by marrying a seventh wife and begetting an extra heir (Pedigree 4).

This politico-matrimonial device, however, as we have seen before in such cases, incurred the very dangers it was designed to avoid. First, it embroiled him with Olympias and her son Alexander. The trouble was settled by another marriage—between Philip's daughter by Olympias and her brother the King of Epirus—when, unguarded during the ceremonial procession, Philip was killed by the stab of an obscure assassin.[1]

Utter confusion might have followed the sudden removal of the most powerful figure in Greece had it not been for the character of the heir. Alexander was a young man. He was just twenty years of age. But he was the most capable and confident young man of which history has any record. At once he set himself to restore order. Three possible rival claimants to the throne he promptly put away. Setting out to establish himself as the complete successor of Philip, within two years he had made himself master of the Balkans from the Danube to the Corinthian isthmus.

The critical event in these campaigns was the mutiny of Thebes and Athens. It was, on the part of Thebes, an armed revolt against the League and against its new captain general. Alexander stormed and took Thebes and left it to the League to pronounce the penalty of *andrapodismos*; the city was to be razed to the ground and all its free men, women and children were to be sold into slavery. Alexander executed the sentence. But, having done it, he was never forgiven by his enemies; the enemies, that is, of monarchy in the Greek states. They had been used to slaughtering one another; they were accustomed to killing all free men of an opposing army or a rebellious city. But the humiliation at the hands of a monarch was an excuse for undying hatred, even though the monarch was a Greek vowed to liberate Greeks from a foreign oppressor.

When Alexander left Greece to invade the Persian Empire he therefore

[1] The assassin seems to have been a discarded boy-friend of Philip. How far responsibility for his action should be apportioned between Persian or Athenian agents, the divorced Queen Olympias, and her son Alexander, who had quarrelled twice with his father, and as Plutarch remarks, wanted above all things that the conquest of Asia should be left for him, these questions have been disputed from that day to this.

Pedigree 4. The Family of Alexander the Great
After Hogarth (1897)

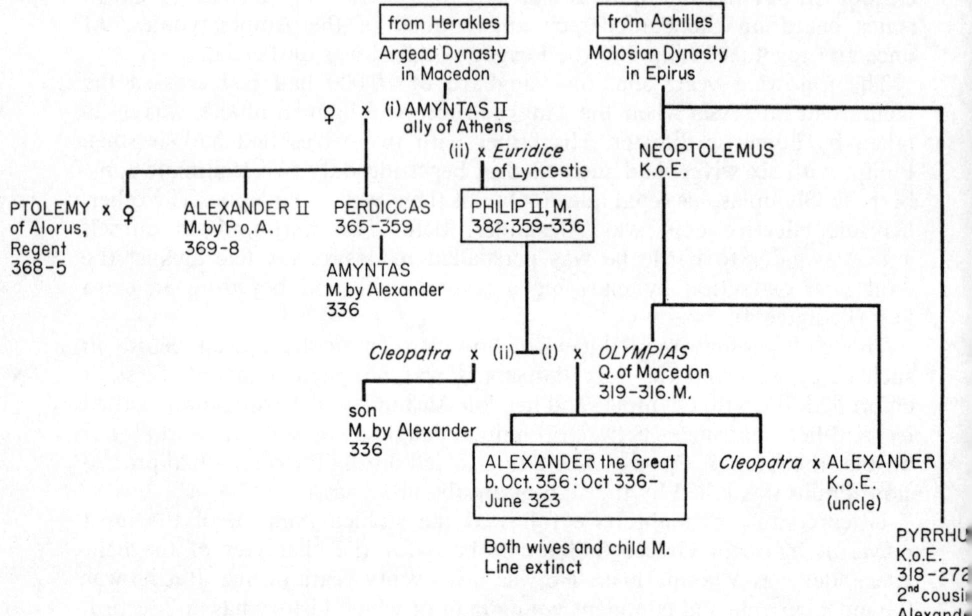

took with him only half his Macedonian forces. The other half he had to leave behind to keep a watch on his enemies in Greece, notably in Athens.

V. ALEXANDER

a. The King

In two years Alexander had established himself. He had secured his base for the attack on Persia. He now assembled his army. In the spring of 334 he set out with a force of 40,000 men and 6000 horses. His own Macedonian troops were the hard core. The Thracian and Thessalian cavalry, the Paeonian and Cretan archers and spearmen were a powerful aid. The contribution of the Greek states was conspicuous by its smallness. It was a diverse force in race, training and habits. But it was united by its use, in some form, of the Greek language, by its practice of the Greek games, and by its susceptibility to the Greek religion and hence to the Athenian drama. Compared therefore with the armies of the Persian King it was a national force. Its religious and racial unity was a weapon which Alexander, following his father's example, made it his business to strengthen.

At the outset, however, Alexander had other purposes than mere conquest, purposes to which Aristotle's tuition in history, religion and science had made its contribution. In his company travelled a well-chosen body of scholars and historians, botanists and geographers. And under his pillow at night, next to his dagger, he laid a copy of the *Iliad* edited by his tutor.

Across the Hellespont he accordingly at once took certain ceremonial steps. He turned west to the site of Troy and solemnly dedicated himself and his armour to the Homeric gods. He had begun a crusade. Then, having only a month's food supply and seventy talents of borrowed money, he lost no more time in searching out the enemy. Fifty miles to the east on the River Granicus he met the forces of the western satraps. They were equal in number to his own. The cavalry were Persian. After a fierce struggle they were routed and made good their escape. The fate of the infantry was different. They were the Greek mercenaries who, since the time of Xenophon and his ten thousand, had fought in every Persian army. Of these only a few Athenians seem to have been made prisoner. The rest, as traitors to Greece, were killed without quarter, nearly twenty thousand of them.

Alexander then occupied Sardis, the western terminal of the road to Susa. By June he had liberated Ephesus, Miletus, Halicarnassus and other Aeolian, Ionian and Dorian colonies which had been subject to Persia for over 150 years. Liberation meant then, as it does today, a reversal of the authority and wealth of classes and parties. In all the cities of Anatolia there were Greek colonies living in Greek quarters. They now became the privileged class: the traders and the craftsmen were reinforced by the soldiers and administrators. But when Alexander made this reversal he introduced what was for the Greeks a surprising idea: he condemned retribution; he demanded reconciliation. This was to be the doctrine of his Empire.

The principle of reconciliation or *homonoia* was not new to the Greeks; but its practice was a reversal of many generations of habit; and its application to foreigners was utterly strange, strange notably to Alexander's tutor, Aristotle. Alexander had not learnt it from the Greeks, or from their gods. He had learnt it from the practice of the Persians in the six generations since Cyrus the Great. And he had learnt it through his father who had pursued it as a policy steadfastly and generously in his long struggle with the politicians and the orators of Athens.

Over a year had been spent in consolidating his position in Anatolia when, the cold season approaching, Alexander moved south. Disregarding the main Persian army on his flank he made his way along the road into Phoenicia. Quickly Darius cut his communications close to where, commemorating the spot, the town of Alexandretta was later built. Alexander turned back to protect himself and the armies met at Issus. It was an overwhelming power that he faced but it was squeezed into so narrow a coastal strip that it could not be fully deployed. And it was Alexander who attacked.

Again the main strength of the Persians lay in their Greek mercenary force, thirty thousand hoplites, heavy infantry. Again the Persians fled before the battle was lost: but this time their flight was led by their King; and the Greek mercenaries also now fled without waiting for disaster to overtake them. Darius had escaped but he had left, as an additional prize in the hands of the victor, his wife, his mother and his children.

Alexander now moved south and after a fearful siege took Tyre. He destroyed the town and sold the people into slavery, 30,000 of them. Thereby he became master of the Mediterranean, for the Persian fleet had consisted of Phoenician sailors in Phoenician ships. Now, by slavery, these people were put at the disposal of the new governing class of Alexander's Empire. While besieging Tyre, however, Alexander received an offer of peace from Darius. The Great King offered him Anatolia, Syria and Egypt in exchange for a peace to be sealed by marriage with his daughter. The circumstances were recorded by Alexander's biographer, Ptolemy, and repeated by Arrian. The choice before Alexander was one of the most fateful in history. His commanders were older men than he. Many of them had wives and children at home. To them the offer seemed a good one. Why not be content with half the world, asked Parmenio. But Alexander had no wife or family at home. And he wanted the whole world. He rejected the offer.

A few months later Alexander entered Egypt, again as a liberator. He was acclaimed Pharaoh, visited the shrine, and consulted the Oracle of Ammon in the Western Desert. Now his status and his ancestry were confirmed. It was rumoured that the new king was not only a god, but the son of a god. Now also it was clear that the principle of *homonoia* was being reinforced by an identification of the gods of different people. Melkart in Tyre had become Herakles. Ammon in Egypt had become Zeus. And Marduk was waiting in Babylon to be assimilated. Only if he had visited Jerusalem (which he probably did not) he might have been rebuffed by the priests and the people.

The following summer Alexander returned into Asia. He marched into Assyria with the purpose of occupying Mesopotamia and, taking his party of royal captives with him, he crossed the Tigris. Darius had assembled an army of a quarter of a million men or more at Arbela, the modern Erbil. Now there were only 6000 Greek mercenaries left with him. But he had resorted to many ingenious innovations; to longer spears, scythed chariots and spiked cavalry traps. Advancing to the plain of Gaugamela he went so far as to level the ground in preparation for the battle. Here on the morning of October 1 331, Alexander attacked.

In all history the battle of Arbela is the most discussed in its action as well as the most momentous in its consequences. It was the climax of development both of the Macedonian army as an instrument and of Alexander as its commander. The fact that the two together were able to defeat on its own prepared ground the army of the Great King, an army five or perhaps ten times theirs in number, is evidence of their capacities. But we happen to know in great detail how the originality of Alexander combined with the discipline of his troops, and the courage and skill of both, to produce this overwhelming result.

Again at an early stage Darius read the signs of disaster; he lost his nerve, leapt from his chariot, mounted a horse and fled. The army disintegrated. Alexander might have followed the Great King and ruthlessly sought him out. But no: he left his enemy for the time being to run as far as he liked; having brushed him aside as though he were a fly he turned south to follow his own administrative programme of occupying Babylon and the old Babylonian Empire. In due course he proceeded to take Susa, to seize the treasure of Darius in Ecbatana, and, on the way, bearing in mind what Xerxes did in

Athens 150 years earlier, to burn Persepolis. Only in the following August did Alexander, passing Rhagae (Teheran), overtake the fugitive band of Darius in the Elburz mountains to find the King, the last of the Achaemenids, left for dead by his companions.

Table 12. *Time Chart of the Conquests and Explorations of Alexander the Great*
From Arrian and Hogarth (1897).

BIRTH		Oct. 356
Tuition by Aristotle		343–340
Regent of Macedon		340
Succeeds Philip as king		Sept. 336
CONQUEST OF PERSIAN EMPIRE	Crossing of Hellespont	April 334
	Battle of R. Granicus	May 334
	Battle of Issus, Capture of Tyre	333
	Seizure of Egypt	332
	Battle of Arbela or Gaugamela	Oct. 331
	Ecbatana occupied	April 330
Darius murdered Alexander *Basileus*		Aug. 330
OCCUPATION OF BACTRIA AND SOGDIANA	Kandahar and Kabul	June–Nov. 329
	Sir Darya	June 328
	Samarkand	Jan. 327
INVASION OF THE PUNJAB	Indus crossed	March 326
	Porus defeated (Hydaspes)	
RETURN	Indian Ocean reached	Aug. 325
	Nearchus' return voyage	Oct.–Dec. 325
	Marriage festival at Susa	324
Babylon		Feb. 323
DEATH		June 323

b. The Emperor

The next three years Alexander spent with his army in establishing his government in Persia and Bactria. Partly he followed his road-mappers, his *bematistae*, and partly he trod unbeaten tracks in pursuit of nomadic guerilla fighters on the Scythian frontier of the Empire. But it was in the great places of government—for example Samarkand—that during these years the effects of his conquest began to show in the person and policy of the conqueror.

For now he went beyond concord and conciliation. He adopted the manners and clothes of the Persians. He trained their nobles to be his guards and to provide him with an auxiliary or perhaps a substitute army. He began to demand from his companions not the respect that was due to a Macedonian ruler but the prostration expected (since Cambyses) by a Persian king.

The King who shook hands with his companions before the battle of Issus demanded their obeisance in Susa. At the same time the violence of his mother's temper combined with his father's addiction to wine led to the most outrageous insults. And these in turn led to conspiracies. His faithful friend Parmenio together with his son were put to death. His boon companion Cleitus was killed in a drunken quarrel. He was destroying the very men who had earlier saved his army and his life by their devotion. To his followers it seemed that the three years in Persia following the death of Darius had transformed the character of the conqueror. What Herodotus had written of Cambyses only a hundred years earlier was proving true of Alexander: that power and privilege corrupt absolutely.[1] But soon the old plan of conquest restored Alexander to the heroic mould of his character. He had meant what he said when he told Darius that he alone was to be King of Asia. His Empire was to be the whole world whose boundary was, he reasonably imagined, the surrounding ocean.

Discipline was restored when Alexander proceeded to the next step in this great plan, the conquest of India. He met the Indian King, vaguely known as Porus, on the banks of the Jhelum river. Here he had his toughest encounter. It was not the elephants but, as Plutarch says, the mercenaries that made the backbone of the Indian army. These were, as in later days, recruited from the war-like tribes of India, and as the Persian King's mercenaries had been in Europe.

After this battle and hard-won victory, the Macedonian troops refused to march further. The boundary of the inhabited world, the *oikoumene*, the mouth of the Ganges, seemed near to Alexander. But for them it was too far. The pride and the courage of the Macedonian army proved to be matched by its independence even in face of its superb commander. Reluctantly obeying he made his way down the Indus, founded a city near the mouth, and, embarking a part of his forces in a fleet under his Cretan admiral Nearchus, who returned by the Persian Gulf, he himself led his main army with terrible exertions by land back to Ecbatana.

The following year, in 324, he took his army to Susa and there he celebrated a great marriage festival. What was this extraordinary ceremony?

The marriage at Susa was a ceremony in Persian style for himself and eighty of his chief *hetairoi* with women of the Persian royal caste or clan. He and his beloved Hephaistion ('who alone' as Hogarth puts it, 'awoke a gentle emotion in the breast of the lonely conqueror') married two sisters, daughters of Darius. At this time, Arrian tells us, there were 10,000 other Macedonians in the army who had picked up women in the conquered lands. They had their unions confirmed by registration and fortified by a gift of money from their imperial commander and benefactor. And a vast pavilion was put up for the feast which celebrated the occasion.

This stroke of imagination might seem to have been just a religious ceremony or a political expedient. But Alexander intended something more permanent, a reconstruction of society. He intended to unite the governing classes and the governing peoples, Greek, Macedonian and Persian, of his

[1] An idea borrowed by, and in England usually attributed to, a later historian, Lord Acton.

new empire.[1] Indeed he intended to go further and by forced or financed transplantations to apply his genetic and social theory by extending the hybridization of his people.

Busy with these plans and others to control the great rivers, to construct new fleets in order to map the coasts of Arabia, to protect or to absorb the western Greeks, and to attack the Empire of Carthage, Alexander returned to Babylon which he was making into his capital. Here he paid the price of his violent labours. He fell sick of a fever and, after a week's illness, on June 28, 323, he died. He was nearly thirty-three years of age.

c. The God

Of all the tasks awaiting Alexander's successors the only one to be promptly and amicably accomplished was to make him into a god. During his life the priests of Zeus, Ammon, Ahuramazda and divers deities of Babylon had agreed in assuring him of his divine nature. After his death scepticism prevailed in his own country and it was only in his Roman Empire, after great racial changes had taken place, that Augustus Caesar, acting no doubt on political advice, was able to decree that Alexander was the thirteenth god on Olympus. In the east there was no such delay. Throughout the Asiatic and Egyptian provinces, his worship was quickly established and the attendant myths that gathered round his cult remain to this day fastened to most of the places where he trod. His body, a relic beyond price, had been neatly abstracted from Babylon by Ptolemy to be enshrined in Alexandria. And, though the peoples of India had forgotten him, Islam, the religion of submission, brought him back to them by conquest as an additional prophet a thousand years later.

For many centuries, in many lands, the myth of Alexander continued to exert a religious, social and literary influence which is difficult to separate from the reality. But the reality, the actual career of Alexander, has to be the great hinge and fulcrum of human history. For us it also happens to be the geometric middle of human development. To transpose a conundrum with which Alexander was familiar, as many men have lived after Alexander as had lived before him. We are thus half way on our journey. And the scene of his life still lies (as he imagined it did) in what is the middle of the inhabited world.

If we look at the map which shows us Alexander's march across the face of Asia we are first astonished by the distance he covered. But this is scarcely more wonderful than the achievements of Cyrus and Darius so long before. What is wonderful is the combination of plans and purposes which Alexander here put into effect. For this time it was not merely conquest without parallel. It was also exploration and colonization without parallel. It was in the combination of the military and political, the artistic and commercial, the technical and scientific, that Alexander surpassed his predecessors. He surpassed them by using all they had left him; and also by using all that Greece could give him.

[1] Common prisoners, who would ordinarily be enslaved, did not come into Alexander's scheme: he later slaughtered a contingent of them as a tribute to the gods on the death of Hephaistion.

How then are we to judge the character of Alexander? We may classify his actions by conventional standards. But if we do so we are met by utter inconsistency. It is an inconsistency outrageously at variance with the naïve conflict of good and evil in the religion of Persia which was to dominate so much of the future thought. Outrageously at variance too with the tastes of Alexander's biographers. For Plutarch, and recently Hogarth, have both told us that their hero was 'beyond the suspicion of sin'.

Here was a man who murdered his friends when drunk as readily as he killed his enemies when sober. And whether or not he was a party to the assassination of his father would make little difference to our opinion of his character. He bitterly repented his crimes but did not amend his habits. So deeply religious was he, but so happy to be a god. A dynast, yet modelling himself on Achilles; a pervert, and even less willing than his father to beget the offspring he needed to perpetuate his dynasty.

Utterly inconsistent, as it appears to us, when we put all the circumstances together, Alexander's character is full of meaning. He inherited his talents from his father and his temper from his mother. His father's government and his battles provided a school for the son more fitting even than the study of Homer or the guidance of Aristotle. More fitting because it was neither from Homer nor from Aristotle that he learnt the idea of reconciling the quarrelsome peoples he subdued. The father, indeed, had created an environment suitable for himself which proved to be even more suitable for his son.

Philip is the classical instance of a great innovator bred by many generations of assortative mating and selective survival, selected by the nobility of their own nation and by the process of war. Philip was a man who begot progeny capable of continuing his work in war and politics and government. In principle the cause is the same as with the smelting of iron or the writing of verse or the invention of religious laws and cults. The difference lies in the documentation. What these kings did, visibly and at once, shifted the lives of nations and the course of history. What they did had effects which were copiously and immediately recorded. The choices of their wives and mistresses and the survival of their children are equally well known. And we have to remember that, whether kings have children or have no children, the intentions and the consequences are always both political and genetic.

Those who are not (like his imitators) dazzled by Alexander's achievement are likely to be revolted by it. It may well shock us to consider that he, so near the edge of sanity, had it at his whim to turn right and conquer Persia and India or turn left and destroy Rome and Carthage. We know that this dizzy power has led so many imitators astray. Yet the original example alone happened at the right time.

It was only at this time that one man could by his own conquest compress the evolution of many centuries into a few years. How this happened we must now consider.

VI. THE SUCCESSORS

a. Three Generals

Devotion to male companions Alexander had carried even further than his father had done with even more dangerous consequences. His love of Hephaistion had led him to postpone marriage and when he married the lovely Bactrian princess Roxana she remained childless for four years, indeed until after his death.

On Alexander's death Roxana murdered his second wife Stateira, the daughter of Darius. She then gave birth to Alexander's son. Both the widow and the son were in their turn murdered by Cassander, one of the ruthless successors. So the dynasties of Cyrus and Alexander, separately and combined, were brought to an end. Thereafter the successors, the *diadochi*, ruled: it was the generals and their wives that mattered.

The struggles of these generals so tediously chronicled recall and partly reproduce the struggles of the city states. There were however several important differences. The armies that were fighting were largely mercenary and far less numerous in proportion to the people than they had been in Greece. Whole cities were no longer destroyed or enslaved. The damage was largely at the top. Marriage and murder were the chief weapons of the dynasts but they were both restricted to what became the royal caste. Formerly the people had suffered for the follies of their rulers. Now it was the rulers and their families who paid most of the price.

Three of these, after bitter conflicts, gained control of the three main parts of Alexander's Empire. They were, in order of their age:

(i) Antigonus Cyclops or the One-eyed (382–301) who established his family as the rulers of the European part, Macedonia and Greece, for a century and a half.
(ii) Ptolemy Soter (367–283) whose dynasty governed Egypt for two and a half centuries.
(iii) Seleucus Nicator (356–281) who set up his family as rulers of the Asiatic part, subject to continual loss of fragments, for two centuries.

The dynasties established by two of these generals remained of the royal Greek caste, which was of largely Macedonian and Greek ancestry, for several generations. These rulers put away their Persian wives. With the third, Seleucus, it was different.

b. The Seleucids

Seleucus had prepared himself for the government of Persia by training the Persian nobles in the new hybrid army that Alexander had recruited. Also, having married his Achaemenid princess, he kept her: she became the title to the throne he had acquired as well as the mother of his dynasty.

The marriage of Seleucus had consequences which reached far beyond Persia. For, as Megasthenes the ambassador who arranged it relates, the daughter of Seleucus married Chandragupta, the founder of the Maurya Dynasty, and himself the bastard son of a king by a low caste woman. By this

Pedigree 5. Macedonian Connections: a Tricontinental Dynastic Network

From Megasthenes et al.

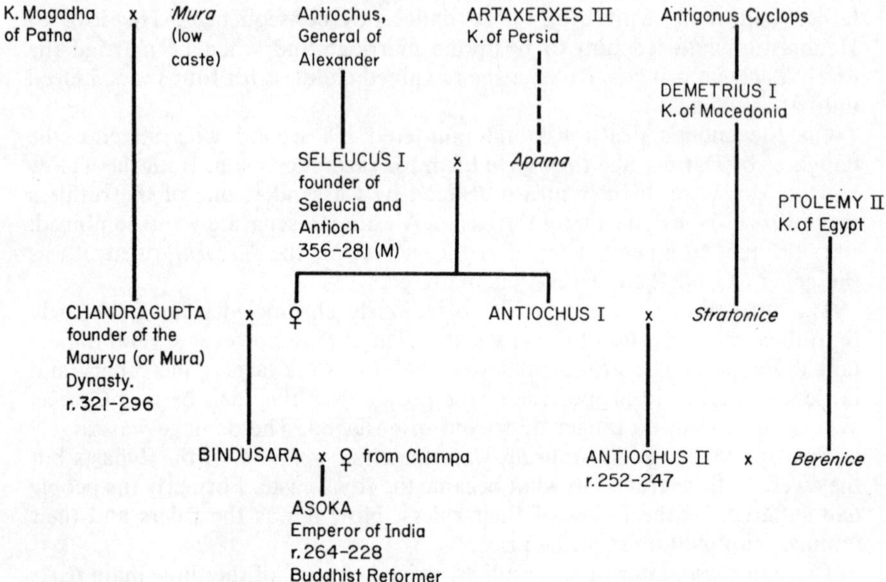

marriage the royal houses of Macedonia and Persia were united with the founder of an Indian dynasty (Pedigree 5).

This marriage is remarkable in two respects. First, it demonstrates the principle of assortative mating on the highest level, among ruling families. By it an international, or in this extreme and unparalleled case an interracial or intercontinental, royal caste came into being. Since the time of Alexander such castes have played an increasing part in organizing and stabilizing the relations of governments and hence of nations.

Secondly, this marriage demonstrates, what need not surprise us, a particular and complex genetic and cultural reaction. In the second generation it gave rise to Asoka. Now Asoka became the ruler of the greatest of all Indian empires. It was the greatest in extent and in effect because Asoka attempted to impress on Indian society a western idea that was repugnant to it. With the help of the Buddhist priesthood he attempted to break down the system of class divisions designed for their preservation by the priestly caste of Brahmins.

Asoka's revolution is always said to have failed. But we do not know what the world would have become without it. Its effect on the distribution of Buddhism in China, Japan and South-East Asia, and its effects on Indian caste structure, remain today.

The year of Alexander's invasion proved to be the first, and for a long time the last, exact date in Indian history. The written word of the Greeks failed to supersede the power of Indian or rather Brahminical verbal memory. We know that a century after Asoka the Bactrian Greek kings invaded and subdued the Ganges valley bringing a new Greek infusion into the governing classes of these rich regions. We know also that while Greek influence slowly faded from the Bactrian coinage, it remained imprinted on Indian sculpture for a thousand years—and of course may be seen today in the caves of Ajata. Thus the political effect of Alexander's invasion of India quickly disappeared. But the genetic and social effects, as we shall see later, owing to the caste system itself, have proved to be permanent.

c. The Ptolemies

The successor who left the greatest mark on history was Alexander's most literate companion, Ptolemy the son of Lagos, whose chronicle of Alexander was the only first-hand record of his life. Ptolemy wisely or cunningly seized for himself the richest province of the Empire, Egypt, a province small enough and defensible enough to be governed well and governed separately. He was also far-sighted enough, as we saw, to seize the body of Alexander for his new capital of Alexandria. But his supreme act of foresight lay in his understanding of Greek learning. What he evidently understood was that by preserving the men and the materials of Greek literature he could enhance his own reputation and power; he could indeed make them the chief prop of his kingdom and his dynasty.

Alexandria became the capital of a country despotically governed by a Macedonian ruler and his army. They were assisted by a native Egyptian administration and by a priesthood who learned to become proficient in Greek and therefore to absorb Greek ideas of commerce, engineering, and technology. In a world distracted by war Alexandria became a haven of peace.

The Library and the Museum which Ptolemy and his successors established in Alexandria had the effect of attracting the scholars, playwrights and philosophers from all parts of the Empire, but above all from Athens. Soon the new city became the intellectual capital of the world. It was maintained in this position by the intelligent support of five generations of the dynasty combined with the wealth and stability of the country they governed.

To understand the powerful continuity of Greek influence in Egypt we have to remember the underlying continuity of their governing class and of the Ptolemaic Dynasty itself. The Ptolemies soon combined in their breeding programme all the habits of incest, promiscuity, polygamy and pederasty to be found in the royal families of Greece, Persia and Egypt. These hazardous practices they protected by an organization of eunuchs both in the harem and in the council chamber. The royal line however has certain properties (see Pedigree 6) which may now be defined as follows:

First, all recognized marriages with legitimate offspring were within the royal Greco-Macedonian families of Cyrene, the Seleucids, and the Ptolemies themselves. They were fertile dynastic marriages.

Secondly, there were in addition many dynastic marriages which were infertile probably because they were never consummated: the marriage alone was the political end.

Pedigree 6. Pedigree of the Ptolemies

Simplified after E. R. Bevan, E.B. (1929) and personal communication. See Tarn (1933)

The late E. R. Bevan in answer to my question (letter of June 23, 1943) considered that: 'In the case of the Ptolemies there is no reason to suppose that the issue of brother-and-sister marriages were not really the children of the royal pairs.' He adds: 'But it is quite uncertain who Cleopatra's mother was.' Her father's marriage with his sister was probably political like her own marriages with her two boy brothers.

In order to make the correct interpretation of fertility and viability I have distinguished natural from violent deaths and, tentatively, consummated from non-consummated marriages.

Galton in his *Hereditary Genius* made the first attempt at a genetic understanding of the Ptolemies. Three corrections are here made to this pedigree:

(i) Ptolemy I wished to be regarded as the bastard son of Philip of Macedon on dynastic grounds in order to be on a level with Seleucus but Tarn (1933) has discredited the claim.

(ii) Ptolemy II was not the true uncle of his wife Arsinoë I.

(iii) Ptolemy IV begot his heir by his full sister.

The climax of the dynasty came with Ptolemy VII who lived with his sister, murdered her son, and married her daughter.

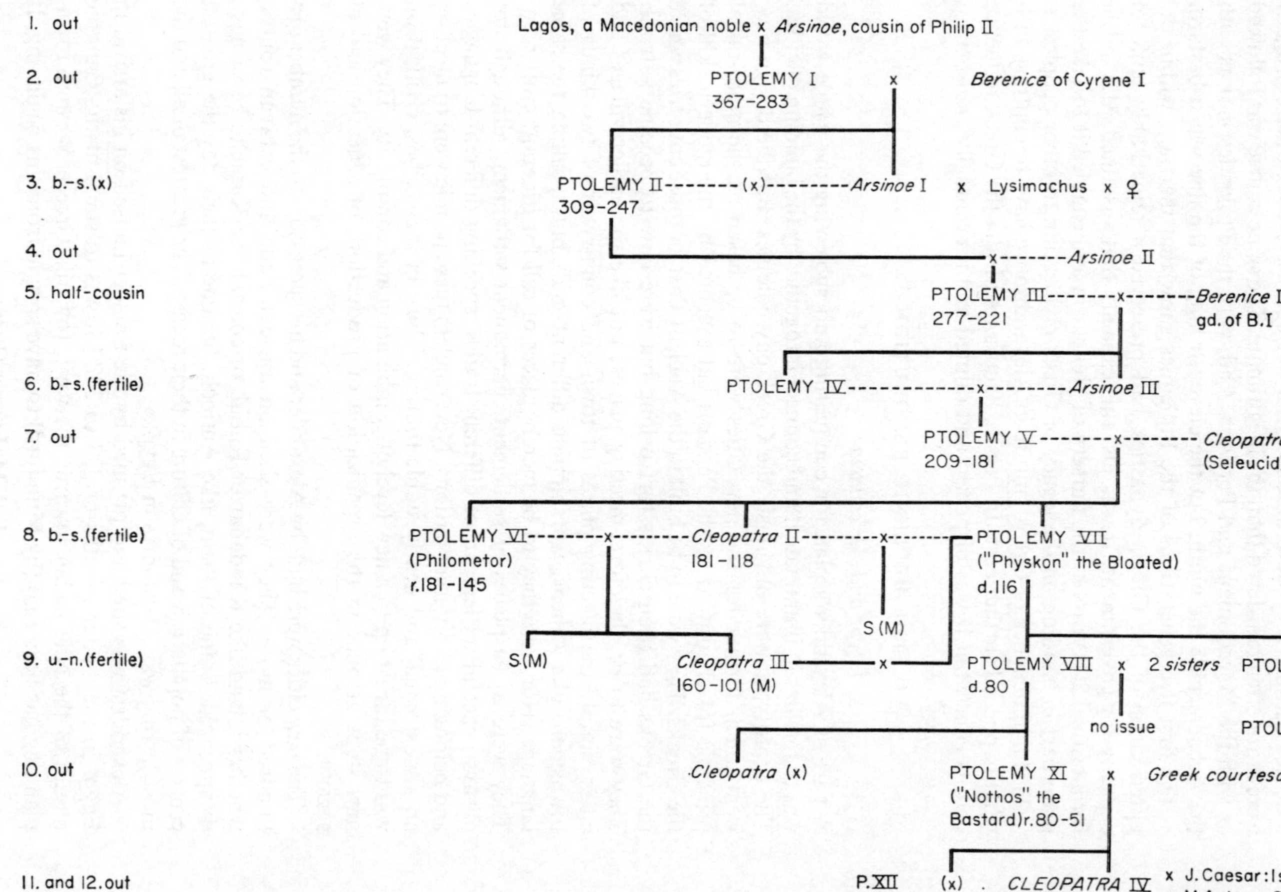

GENERATIONS
1. out
2. out
3. b.-s.(x)
4. out
5. half-cousin
6. b.-s.(fertile)
7. out
8. b.-s.(fertile)
9. u.-n.(fertile)
10. out
11. and 12. out
Lagos, a Macedonian noble x Arsinoe, cousin of Philip II
PTOLEMY I 367-283
x
Berenice of Cyrene I
PTOLEMY II 309-247
(x)
Arsinoe I
x Lysimachus x ♀
x Arsinoe II
PTOLEMY III 277-221
x
Berenice II gd. of B.I
PTOLEMY IV
x
Arsinoe III
PTOLEMY V 209-181
x
Cleopatra I (Seleucid)
PTOLEMY VI (Philometor) r.181-145
x
Cleopatra II 181-118
x
PTOLEMY VII ("Physkon" the Bloated) d.116
S (M)
S(M)
Cleopatra III 160-101 (M)
x
PTOLEMY VIII d.80
x 2 sisters
no issue
PTOLEMY IX
PTOLEMY X (M)
Cleopatra (x)
PTOLEMY XI ("Nothos" the Bastard) r.80-51
x Greek courtesans et aliae
P.XII 61-47
(x)
CLEOPATRA IV 69-30
x J. Caesar: 1s.
x M. Antony: 2s, 1d.

Thirdly, following a fruitful uncle-niece marriage there were equally fruitful brother-sister marriages. These resulted in the extinction of the legitimate line, not because they were unsuccessful, but because the legitimate progeny were more often murdered than the illegitimate. The same course was followed as with the Macedonians and Persians. And, with the Ptolemies, not as with the Achaemenids the ninth, but the eleventh king of the line was a bastard.

The first five generations of the Ptolemies show that marriage within the gifted circle of the Greek dynasties had preserved a remarkably uniform capacity for government. It was just this capacity that sustained Alexandria for a critical 200 years as the nursery of Hellenism and enabled it to take the main part in handing on the legacy of Greek civilization to other peoples.

This maintenance of Greek culture in Alexandria we have to contrast with what happened further east. In Persia, Bactria and India the Greek influence had its effect, but it was dispersed and diluted and it eventually vanished.

VII. THE HELLENIC REVOLUTION

a. Egypt and Alexandria

A part of Alexander's plan for conquering and subjecting the whole world was to fertilize it, illuminate it and connect it together by the building of cities. The prototypes were obviously the Greek city colonies. But the design now went much further for the new cities were to be based on the multi-racial principle foreshadowed by the Persians but executed by the modern skill of the Greeks. They were to be built in the Ancient East, in those countries where the Greeks had been clients for so long but were now to become patrons. They were to be, therefore, meeting places; not like the earlier villages and cities, simply the meeting places of town and country or of two kinds of townsmen, like Athens, worshipping different gods but speaking the same language. Nor were they to be merely places of call for itinerant craftsmen. They were to be places of settlement, permanent settlement, although not always peaceful settlement, of different trades, speaking different languages, and belonging to different nations. Nevertheless these people were to meet on an almost equal and nearly stable footing. Thus, in these cities, civilization was to be thrust on to a new level of combination and complexity. They were new steps at once in the organization of production, of education and of society.

The new cities were built by Alexander and his successors to the number of a hundred or more. They were sited on ancient trade and caravan routes, whether inland like Kandahar or Kabul, or coastal like Karachi. Most have disappeared. Some of them, like Antioch, became in their day the greatest centres of population and of culture in their region. The greatest of all and the most lasting was Alexandria in Egypt.

Alexandria was sited and planned by the founder himself on his arrival in Egypt in the winter months of 333 to 332.[1] It was to stand at the Canopic mouth of the Nile facing towards the west, towards Greece. Western town-planning has been said (by Mumford) to have sprung from this beginning. It

[1] E. M. Forster (1938).

was to consist of three quarters. First, there was the Greek or Royal quarter. It had to accommodate palaces for rulers, temples for priests, civil buildings and a market place in Greek style for Greek residents and traders and their slaves, slaves that were to increase in numbers with each battle won and each city stormed. Here also was the great Library and Museum or university.

In this Library the Ptolemies collected about half a million items, the written legacy of Greek culture. The extent to which its treasures were destroyed in Caesar's siege (48 B.C.), or replenished by Antony from Pergamon (35 B.C.), or further looted by Christians in the reign of Theodosius and by Arabs after their conquest (A.D. 640) are all disputed.[1] But it is beyond dispute that this Library together with its successors collected by the other Hellenistic kings in Pergamon and in Macedonia were the main stimulus for the cultivation of literature in the ancient world and for the later growth of deference for literary scholarship in Christendom and Islam.

Secondly, there was the Jewish quarter. The Jews having welcomed Alexander, he gave them great privileges. He went so far (according to Josephus) as to allow them to call themselves Macedonians. Hence they were able to preserve their customs and their community intact. Hence also there soon arose in Alexandria the largest Jewish population in the world. It was a population, however, which now spoke and read and wrote the language of the Greeks.

Thirdly, there was the Egyptian quarter which seems to have been the poorest of the three in its inheritance both of wealth and culture. The exclusive habits of the Egyptian governing class, associated with their esoteric priestly speech and writing (as Goad has explained) already before Alexander had forced them to surrender most of their cultural initiative to the Jews. They may well have done so by the conversion of the most enterprising Egyptians to Judaism. Now it further cut them off from the Greek governing colony. But they were still strong enough to foment revolt when the dynasty fell into trouble under Ptolemy Physkon. And strong enough to keep their language alive so that in the end the last Greek ruler of Egypt, Cleopatra, could actually (according to Burn) speak Egyptian. Afterwards pagan Egyptians, reinforced by Jews and converted to Christianity, preserved the ancient Egyptian community and its speech as the Coptic people and language.

b. Hellenization

The spread of Greek culture following the conquests of Alexander provides us with the most significant of all tests of the processes operating in history. Here we have a demonstrable assemblage of people having certain accomplishments. These accomplishments concern language and literature, art and science, history and philosophy, religion and the techniques of government and war. As accomplishments they are differential and separable with respect to individuals, social classes and even geographical races. How far were they maintained, disseminated or dispersed; how far were they encouraged, enlarged or destroyed, by the tremendous upheavals which began with Alexander's conquest?

[1] See Bury's notes on Gibbon.

At first sight the turmoil of the Hellenistic world, which was the active centre of the civilized world after Alexander, may seem baffling beyond hope. The vicissitudes of war and politics, the movements of people and ideas, the transformation of religion, the confusion of tongues and the revolutions of races and classes beggar our description. Do they also beggar our understanding? In fact if we remember to connect all the elements which we know to be connected the connections themselves become significant.

Alexander had given an administration to his Empire which at the beginning and at the top was Macedonian or Greek. What we have seen of the royal families shows that it remained wholly Greek in the west, including Egypt, for several generations. It was this predominantly Greek governing class which maintained the Greek educated and skilled classes, and which in turn maintained Greek culture, ideas and techniques, principles of administration and law, methods of colonization and commerce, all those things which the Greeks had developed on the foundations they maintained until they could be handed over to their successors, that is to other societies which followed them.

Beneath this expansion or dispersal of governors and also of philosophers and artists was a vast expansion of the population of the Greek cities. The erosion of the soil of Greece had long been driving its population overseas in all directions. They had gone westwards as teachers and masters, eastwards as pupils and servants. Now their chief movement was into the rich eastern lands where their social position was happily reversed. Here also now they came as teachers and masters. Alexander's triumph and his brief example were enough to establish some degree of racial and religious toleration. They were also enough to give a social advantage to Greek names, Greek speech and consequently Greek art, literature and religion, an advantage they did not lose for a thousand years. The western cities displayed a massive conversion to the practice or the show of being Greek, to Hellenism. This conversion was similar in its cause and its consequences to the religious conversions of later times. Its causes were desire for social and cultural advancement. Its consequences were intermarriage of the favoured classes. From Greek marrying non-Greek there thus arose new peoples blending the cultural and genetic inheritance of the Greeks and their more ancient neighbours, in Babylonia, Assyria and Egypt.

For seven centuries, the Greek peninsula had been the nursery where Aryan invaders hybridized with eastern immigrants and by inbreeding produced their unique race and their unique culture. Now this people, carrying their culture with them, were dispersed over a world which was prepared, by colonization and conquest, to receive, to propagate and to elaborate it.

In this propagation and new hybridization an important factor was the attachment of foreign slaves, both artisans and intellectuals, to Greek owners established in the new Greek cities. Every battle won and every city stormed threw a new population of slaves to be distributed through the markets to cities, the places where they were thought most useful. The most obvious of these transfers was the removal of the 30,000 enslaved Tyrians. Where did they go? Undoubtedly to other sea-ports but especially to the Greek quarter of Alexandria. These people it has been assumed were the foundation of the maritime success of the new Egyptian capital. Their leading men by their merits were slowly liberated. Speaking Greek and reading Greek literature, they would now count as 'new Greeks'; they would intermarry with 'old Greeks' and create a hybrid population. It was from this hybrid population that there sprang a new Alexandrian race and the achievements of Alexandrian science. What had happened earlier in Sicily and southern Italy now happened not only in Alexandria but also in Antioch and Tarsus, in Cyprus, in Syria and Palestine.

Between the Zagros mountains and the Mediterranean Sea educated 'Greeks' were now speaking a uniform educated language, the *koiné*. The old Greek trading and artisan communities and garrison towns were now reinforced by the Macedonian hegemony and the Greek invasion which followed it. In the cities everybody wanted to speak Greek, to have a Greek name, even if he was a Jew. And, unless he was a Jew, he wanted to worship Greek gods or gods with Greek names.

The Jews found themselves in this world of mixture subjected to new pressures on their traditional habits and beliefs. A portion of them became what the Acts of the Apostles were to describe as 'Grecians'. This was a cleavage foreshadowing the divisions of a later day. And in Alexandria, these Greek-speaking Jews, having forgotten Hebrew and not having learnt Aramaic, found it necessary to translate their ancient books into Greek. So it was that the seventy-two learned but progressive Jews came to write out the Septuagint and to introduce their sacred writings to the inquisitive eyes, first of Ptolemy II, and then of the Greeks in general. In doing so they prepared for the spread not only of Judaism but also, unwittingly, of its Christian successor.[1] Soon the reverse process occurred. Greek words began to appear in the Hebrew Talmud. Between Greeks and Jews communication had been established. It proceeded in full flood for three centuries and was perhaps the greatest achievement of Hellenism.

Hellenization was a consequence of urban movements, movements of Greeks into cities outside Greece. Where the movement was strongest, into Anatolia, the native languages disappeared from the written record within three centuries. But doubtless the peasants and herdsmen through this great area were as little hybridized with immigrant people as they were stimulated by immigrant ideas. It was probably their masters and governors who carried the idea of the three-course rotation from Euboea over the Hellenic world.[2] Greek, Jewish and later, as Burn points out, Christian culture made little progress in the countryside. But each new race or religion, and the two were bound to converge, contributed a new class to the creation in the cities of the most highly stratified and most highly civilized societies in the world.

c. *Race and Language*

The Greek language forged by thirty generations of increasingly civilized usage was, as has often been suggested, not only the vehicle of Hellenism

[1] The task, beginning with the law and continuing with the prophets, seems to have occupied not seventy-two days, as once supposed, but nearly three centuries.

[2] Invented in the fourth century according to Heichelheim.

but the means of creating it. Its capacity for abstract expression, in which it is so markedly contrasted with the ancient Semitic languages, liberated the ideas, to use their word, of the Greeks. In the Hellenistic world it also liberated the ideas of the other peoples who learnt Greek. On the other hand, its concrete character, which compelled the Hebrew, having no word for 'male', to say 'they that piss against the wall', is what gives much of its poetic character and lucid strength to Hebrew literature and hence to the Christian Bible.

Often before in history people had changed their forms of speech. But now for the first time, two peoples of highly contrasted character, speaking the most sophisticated languages, were brought on a large scale within speaking distance of one another. This is a situation to which we have long been accustomed. So long that we think of it generically. This is a mistake. Each time it happens the impact of new people on an old language has its own specific intellectual consequences. These, like the phonetic consequences, may be superficial or profound.

Consider what this situation means. A language is the creation of its own community, its own breeding group of common ancestry or at least kinship. It is not merely the vehicle of culture, it is a part of the culture. It is a product of the heredity of the group. But it also provides the world in which the individual lives, a world to which individuals in evolution become adapted. Or to put it another way: it is through human language that the heredity of the race becomes the environment of the individual.

Now a foreign language is a product of a different race with a different way of speaking phonetically and a different way of thinking grammatically and idiomatically. It seems likely therefore that the use of Greek by strangers was one of the stimuli which advanced the civilization of the Hellenic world just as the use of Hebrew (in translation) was to advance the civilization of later peoples. It was a stimulus superimposed on populations in which hybridization, recombination and selective migration were already transforming society.

d. Hellenism

The first aspect of the Greek expansion was the creation of a hybrid intellectual community capable of understanding and using the whole of the culture of the ancient world. The second aspect was the elaboration by this community of something new which we may call Hellenism. This new culture or civilization embraces some of the highest achievements of ancient science and art. It is the philosophy and religion however that concern us most here for it is in them that we find the seeds of the future transformations of society.

Before Alexander the great intellectual centre of attraction in the Greek world had been Athens. Aristotle (384–322) came from Stagira on the edge of Macedonia and although he returned to live in Philip's capital as Alexander's tutor (342–335) it was to Athens that he came in his prime to hear Plato. Diogenes the Cynic (413–323) came from far Sinope to Athens where he exchanged words with Alexander. Epicurus (341–270) came to Athens from Ionian Samos. And he brought with him not only the materialism of Democritus but also his own atomic theory of heredity whose rediscovery underlies our interpretation of human society in these pages.

After Alexander philosophers still made their way to Athens for many generations. Zeno (*c.* 350–264) who came to Athens to teach in 314 propounded a view of life which dominated the ancient world for several centuries and came to be known as Stoicism. It owed much to the Cynics and also to the Atomists. But this Zeno claimed to be of Phoenician descent and three of his chief disciples were men of Tarsus, a city with a Jewish colony which later became famous.

Here we see men elaborating Greek ideas in the Greek language but men undoubtedly deriving from the more ancient and more eastern communities. We also see men moving to the centres most suitable for the propagation of their own ideas: seeking out the best market for their intellectual goods. The best market for philosophy was that created by Socrates, Plato and Aristotle in Athens. But for science and technology it was that created by the Ptolemies and their Museum in Alexandria.

The contrast between the moral and philosophic attitude which prevailed in conservative Athens and the experimental and scientific enterprise which was possible for Greeks in Alexandria may be shown by the example of Aristarchus of Samos, cited by Farrington. This astronomer, as we should expect, of Ionian origin, was the first to suppose that the earth revolved round a fixed sun. His writings are lost. But we know of them because he was denounced for his impiety by the chief of the Stoics in Athens. His hypothesis was thereupon buried without further reference—to be rediscovered and redenounced nearly 2000 years later.

These people were, by their movements, indications of the process of Hellenization and they were at the same time the agents of the creation of Hellenism. Never before were nations so swiftly transformed in race and culture as during this age. The readiness of the transformation was due to the insertion of a middle class into the society of the Greek cities. It was a class essentially of Greek origin but not predominantly a Greek race. Through its Greek speech and culture it cemented societies together and made them thenceforth much more difficult to transform. It also raised problems of the relations of classes, the justification of slavery and war and the nature of religion which had not been a source of anxiety before.

Town and country, educated and uneducated classes, can scarcely have diverged any more by the growth of Hellenic civilization since the genetic basis of their divergence was hardly disturbed. But the divergence became more explicit especially in the matter of religious beliefs. For religion at an earlier stage had been a means, indeed the proper means, of binding people together. Now ancient religion was no longer able to cope with the tremendous strains imposed by the heterogeneity of the new societies. There were strains between those who loved war and those who hated it; between those who worshipped idols and placated their gods with blood sacrifices and those (like the Stoics) who rejected these things; between those who loved slavery and those who deplored it. Under an enlightened monarch, like Antigonus Gonatas, brotherhood had in some measure been achieved between different races. But it had not been achieved between the different classes into which different races had been converted.

The movements of Hellenization created these problems. They also created the people capable of thinking about them. None did so more effectively within their proper moral field than the Stoics and their views profoundly concern our present study of society.

The Stoic view, the view of Zeno's *Republic*, that justice is natural and not conventional is as close as it could be to the present-day biological view that morals represent the instincts of the community (or at least of the majority) and are not externally imposed. So also is the Stoic view that freedom and obedience are both consistent with the subordination of the individual to the needs and claims of society. Indeed it is the thesis of the present writer that the distinction between co-operation and subordination is continually being smoothed by adaptive change, change continually favoured by natural selection.

Where we may differ is in supposing that genetic differences between races and classes, between slave and free, between men and women, will themselves be smoothed out in this process to give an indisputable brotherhood of man. But this was a view very suitable to the processes of accommodation within the Hellenic societies. It was a doctrine of Stoics, coming from Tarsus. These ideas were not apparent in the fierce wars of Alexander's successors since they were the ideas of an intellectual class, and not of a governing class. But they were undoubtedly conveyed back to Tarsus where they may be said to have germinated three centuries later.

The view of the Epicureans that the gods took no part in human affairs, and the doctrine of the Stoics that prayers and sacrifices to idols and shrines were ineffective, gradually came to be accepted by the intellectual classes of the Hellenic world. It was in this world that the Jews existed as an influence continually at work against all kinds of pagan superstitions and that their teaching continually spread by conversion both at the intellectual and at the popular level. Many movements thus combined to introduce a basis of discussion, if not of unity, between the educated people of all races within the Hellenic world. But at the same time they introduced a cleavage between this class and the uneducated masses who continued to adore images and to crave for the more primitive and bloody rituals.

The ancient world, indeed we may say from his beginnings, ancient man had always been deeply impressed by the inequality and diversity of human beings in their physical and mental character. In the Hellenistic world thinking men, Greeks and Jews, had come to be impressed by the need to tolerate diversity and to smooth the edges of inequality. Christianity was soon to assert the claims of the individual as against those of society by assuming the moral equality of individuals. The soil in which this idea germinated was the soil of Hellenism.

12

ROME

I. THE COLONIZATION OF ITALY

ITALY, LIKE ALL OTHER EUROPEAN COUNTRIES, was colonized by successive waves of peoples derived from the expansion of agriculture, of metal-working, of commerce and of city-building, expansions from their Asiatic and later their Greek sources. In this process of Italian colonization for the first time we see the historic and literate succeeding and overlapping with the prehistoric and legendary; the process thus begins to appear (Table 13) in a more defined complexity.

Table 13. *Colonization of Italy:* 3000–300 B.C.
See Maps in *Italia Storica* (1961).

PRE-LITERATE		
1. PALEOLITHIC:	from Africa and Europe:	up to 3000 B.C.
2. NEOLITHIC:	agricultural and pastoral:	3000–2000 B.C.
3. MEGALITHIC:	Apulia and the islands:	2500–2000 B.C.
4. BRONZE AGE:	(ARYAN): successive waves of military conquerors from Central Europe:	1800 B.C. onwards
5. IRON AGE:	(i) trading groups of smiths crossing the Adriatic from the Balkans:	*c.* 800 B.C.
	(ii) Celtic-speaking tribes from Central Europe: Gauls	*c.* 400 B.C.
LITERATE		
6. GREEK-SPEAKING, from coastal cities in Greece and Anatolia founding and spreading from coastal cities of the south:		800–320 B.C.
7. ETRUSCAN-SPEAKING, from inland Lydia with diverse followers: inland and coastal colonists, founding and spreading from cities in Tuscany:		*c.* 750 B.C.

During the third and second millennia B.C. neolithic and bronze age peoples had brought agriculture into Italy mostly by land from the north. They had sparsely populated the most fertile unwooded parts of the peninsula. They were both herdsmen and cultivators. The neolithic immigrants spoke languages which, apart perhaps from Basque, have now disappeared. The bronze age invaders represented early waves of the Aryan expansion owing their mobility and aggressiveness to their pastoral occupation. The only colonists who had direct connections with the civilized east were the megalithic people whose kinsmen raised Stonehenge in Britain. These settled only in the islands and in the Gulf of Tarentum. Great tombs in Malta, towered *nuraghi* in Sardinia, and modest dolmens in Apulia are their remains. They made little impact on Italy.

In the eighth century direct eastern colonization of Italy began. At the same time as the Phoenicians were founding ports on the African and Spanish coasts, the other maritime peoples, those on the shores of the Aegean, both mainland and island, began to settle on the southern and western coasts of Italy. The migration was thus selective: it indicated the climatic preference we should expect from geographical races. The Aegean or Greek colonies are easily recognized by documentary records in the Greek language. In this way we know that Cumae (on the coast near Naples) was founded in 757 B.C. by the parent Ionian city of Cyme on the coast of Lydia. The unmixed connection of the colony with the parent is thus precisely recorded at its beginning. It is also confirmed by later history which shows such Greek colonies largely retaining their Greek character and their limited intention of establishing sea-ports, racially apart from their barbarian hinterland.

At the same time there were colonies formed further north which were predominantly Aegean but not predominantly Greek-speaking. They were established on the coast by people who, unlike the Greeks, were willing to push inland and found inland cities. These were the people who in the course of a couple of centuries mastered the country and partly settled the land between the Tiber and the Arno. Since there has been so much dispute about them we may as well make sure what they were called: for us they are Etruscans after the Latin names *Etrusci* or *Tusci*. Among themselves they were *Rasenna*; to the Greeks they were *Tyrsenoi* or *Tyrrhenioi*, whence the Italian name for the Tyrrhenian Sea; and it has been suggested that connections of theirs were known to the Egyptians of the thirteenth century B.C. as *Tursa*.[1]

II. THE ETRUSCANS

It is not surprising that when Greek and Roman historians long afterwards came to write about the origins of the Etruscans whose language they did not usually understand they gave us contradictory accounts. Herodotus 300 years after the event represented an overflow of Lydian population as setting sail from Smyrna to make colonies in Italy under the king's son Tyrrhenus. But after another 500 years Dionysius of Halicarnassus was quite sure that since the language they spoke was recognizable neither as Lydian nor as an Aryan

[1] See Hus (1961); Bloch (1962); Richardson (1966).

language (as we should call it) they must have grown up where they were found, must be indeed the utterly original or aboriginal pre-Aryan inhabitants of Tuscany.

The Lydian theory of Herodotus found most favour with the Romans; Virgil, Horace and Ovid all refer to the Tiber as the Lydian river. But we have now another ground for supporting the same view. The Etruscans brought a Grecian alphabet with them which has allowed their language to be partly deciphered. And inscriptions in their alphabet found on the Island of Lemnos (and prior to the Athenian occupation of 510 B.C.) are held to be in a language akin to Etruscan. These indications however tell only a part of the story.

The total character of Etruscan development agrees with the view that they began as a warrior group from inland Anatolia. But it also demands that they must have brought with them miners and smiths attracted to their colony by the prospect of iron in Elba and copper on the mainland. For very soon it was the working of these metals that supplied the strength to their cities. They must have had a stout company of seamen and shipbuilders, probably Phoenician as well as Aegean, since they were soon in command of a fleet strong enough to attack the Greeks of Massilia and to colonize Corsica as well as Elba; and since it was with the Phoenicians of Carthage that they allied themselves in these advances. They must also have come equipped with stone masons and builders since from Mycenaean beginnings they soon surpassed the Greeks in their arches and vaults, aqueducts and drains, inventions which their successors were in the course of time to spread into many lands. Finally, they must have brought priests with them who established oriental gods, and specifically Babylonian practices of divination, on Italian soil.

Other aspects of Etruscan history are fortunately and brilliantly preserved for us by the tombs which are still revealing their secrets. They devoted more care to the disposal of the dead, that is the wealthy dead, than any other people except the Egyptians. The tombs associated with the twelve main cities, even the small proportion surviving, show us the progress of their invasion and the development of their governing class from the eighth to the second century B.C. Their first settlement was near the coast at Tarquinia. Here, finding an easily fortified site, they built their city, quelled the local tribesmen and established their state under a priestly prince, the *lucumo*. Here therefore we meet not the diplomatic and commercial approach which was usual and probably necessary for the later Greek colonists. Rather we find a military invasion penetrating inland.

Moving slowly northwards as their strength and numbers grew, and keeping to hilly defensible country (Fiesole not Florence is their foundation), they set up twelve *lucumonies* or city states which were federated and united by their celebration of an annual religious festival. This meeting, known as the *Fanum Voltumnae*, recalls the eastern practice of Arabs, Israelites, and Greeks (and later to be followed by the Latins). It was held in a sanctuary near the modern Orvieto, a place perhaps earlier sanctified by the neolithic or paleolithic populations who were being absorbed.

As they moved north the character and habits of the colonists changed. They gave up burial and took to cremation. They also lost the distinctive and oriental character of their art as they began to exploit different methods and materials in each new city they founded. This character was primarily due to the invading and foreign governing class but that class evidently mixed with the aristocracy of the tribes which they brought under their control, a process Roman history was later to repeat.

The highly local character which each city retained reminds us of the Greek city state. It also reminds us of the people of Tuscany today and for a good reason. Broken country was clearly favoured, perhaps for its defensibility as well as for its resemblance to their homeland. This broken country meant poor communications which in turn meant separate breeding communities even for the governing classes.

The political consequence of this genetic particularism was lack of national unity. Its artistic consequence was extreme local stability. This is well illustrated by Alain Hus. 'The Lion at Vulci', he says, 'seems to disown his immediate models and go back to his Hittite ancestors, almost 1000 years older, whom he has never known.' The genetic continuity overrides the cultural discontinuity. It picks up again the thread where it had been left and forgotten.[1]

In the sixth and fifth centuries the varied eastern origins, the advanced technology, and the strong leadership of Etruscan society kept it at the head of development in Italy. In this they were supported by close relations with Greece. They maintained their own temple—their own embassy one might say—at Delphi. They imported Attic pottery in vast amounts. More Attic vases have been found, Bloch remarks, in Etruria than in Attica. Greek sculpture inspired them as theirs, for example the she-wolf of the Capitol, made in Veii, later inspired the Romans. At the same time Greek theatre must have played its part in Etruria since we derive from Etruscan roots such basic theatrical names as *histrio*, *persona* and *scoena*.

It was in these centuries with the Etruscan door wide open to the east that Etruscan culture blossomed and the Etruscan Empire spread. They moved south to occupy Rome and to found Capua in the sixth century. And having been rebuffed from Cumae and ousted from Rome they successfully moved north in the fifth century to colonize the Po valley and to found the cities now known as Bologna, Mantua and Modena.

While Etruria and Latium had been developing under the influence of maritime colonists, other migrants from Anatolia had been travelling overland following the routes of the neolithic expansion, taking with them the new techniques of prospecting for iron, smelting the ore and forging the iron. They had encountered Aryan tribes in the upper Danube basin, tribes which had moved west, kinsmen of those who had earlier moved east. These people, profiting by the discovery of new ores in Austria (the Roman Noricum) and even tougher iron to make tools and weapons, multiplied their numbers and expanded their territories. They created, as we have seen, the Hallstatt (or

[1] Hus also points out the marvellous continuity between Etruscan art and what appeared 2000 years later in the Tuscan Renaissance. When we compare the terra cotta head called Malavolta from Chiusi with Donatello's St George we are faced with the genetic repetition after sixty generations of both the sculptor and his model.

Salzburg) and La Tène cultures of the archaeologists, and the Celtic peoples of the linguists and historians or rather the governing classes of the Celtic peoples. They invaded the country to which they gave the name of Gaul in the west and the provinces to which they gave the names of Galicia in Spain and in Poland and later (after Alexander) the province of Galatia in Anatolia.

These people had not failed to benefit by the improved breeds of horses introduced into Europe by the Persians. They had also benefited by the movement and settlement of craftsmen from the civilized world, including, as their remains show, the Etruscans themselves. The combination no doubt gave them several valuable inventions. It is not surprising therefore that iron shoes for their horses, which in turn made their chariots more formidable, should have upset the balance of power in Europe.

The Gauls invaded Italy at the end of the fifth century. They poured over the Alps looting the rich cities of northern Italy and holding Rome up to ransom.[1] By dislocating Etruscan society this invasion may well have caused a southward migration out of Etruria into Latium. Certainly it took away the last impulse from the Etruscan cities and gave a new impulse to Rome.

For the failure of Etruscan society a number of deeper causes were at work before the coming of the Gauls. First, there was their attitude to religion. They relied with more than Babylonian faith on the *disciplina Etrusca* (as the Romans called it), the art of divining the future by inspecting the liver of birds. Now many other peoples, and later peoples, have suffered from this and related superstitions. But Ionian and Attic philosophy was a symptom of a scientific intelligence and scepticism which were going to infect the minds of statesmen and generals in the ancient world and to remove this influence from the control of policy and strategy. It seems likely that the Etruscan priesthood were strong enough to preserve the stultifying formulae on which their privileges and perquisites undoubtedly rested.

Another quite different circumstance worked to preserve the interests of priests or magicians and to defeat the development of Etruscan society. That was isolation. The hills and mountains of Tuscany which fostered so prosperous a society in its beginnings, and made it and others regard it as a great nation, later shut it off from the trade routes by sea and land; shut it off also from the new ideas and new people of the fifth century. These hills even cut up their own people into fragments, into quarrelling cities as incapable of combining as those of Greece. And even less capable of resolving the conflicts between their social classes, between patricians and plebs and slaves.

These ideas and people might have accompanied the imaginative literature of the Greeks and Jews in opening a world which was never opened to the Etruscans. But their language, and again their priesthood, were additional barriers to their development. We can see this most clearly in the fate of the Etruscan language itself in Rome. After many centuries of existence it slowly disappeared. It faded away because it had no intellectual class to advance it as Greek and Latin were later to be advanced. In much of this history the Etruscan cities resembled Carthage. And like Carthage they succumbed

[1] In the words attributed to Brennus the Gaul, '*Te tero Roma manu nuda, date tela, latete*'.

to Rome, a city which in the end had absorbed enough of their people and their skills to erase, very nearly, the memory of the nation which had created them.

III. THE ORIGINS OF ROME

The origins of Rome seem to be shadowy enough. But in fact Rome is the first city whose mode of origin we can trace from excavation and from documents as well as from the evidence of religion and literature.

The region south of the Tiber had been avoided by Etruscan and Greek invaders, perhaps owing to its having too few minerals or too much volcanic action. It became thinly occupied by Latin-speaking peoples however about the ninth century. There were farmers in the plain and shepherds in the hills living in villages under patriarchal systems of clan government. The villages were connected as tribes, which again celebrated joint religious festivals at sacred sites.

The dangers of attack from Etruscan cities and the opportunities of trade arising from the presence of Etruscan colonists who knew how to build such cities, led villages to coalesce, to build walls, to elect military leaders, to regulate joint festivals, joint trade and in short to make the beginnings of cities themselves.

One of these embryonic cities which arose in the eighth century was Rome and its position from the beginning was the key to its life. For though it was built on hills, first one hill then another, and at first partly shielded by marshes, the cultivated lands which sustained it were remarkably exposed. Only twelve miles to the north lay the Etruscan city of Veii which defied Rome until Camillus took it in 396 B.C. In the hills to the north-east lay Sabine settlements. And in the hills to the south-east were warlike Volscian cities. Only from the sea was Rome, like some of the Etruscan cities, protected by distance.

The power of the Roman aristocracy, as of any other military governing class, depended on the part they had to play in defending the city and attacking its neighbours. Now the Romans, with a city built at the meeting place of Latins and Etruscans, on very modest hills in a very flat plain, as even the Gauls were able to show, stood on the most exposed site in the world. It was a miracle that they survived at all as an independent state. At each crisis of survival the aristocracy might be strengthened or weakened. There was an agonizing readjustment of rights and obligations, a shifting compromise between the governors and the governed which was reflected in the development of the constitution and the law.

Rome's lack of protection was made good by the advantage of movement and meeting and a perpetual military activity and alertness. The city lay at the meeting of two trade routes: the road joining Etruria to the Greek colonies in the south and the road taking salt from the mouth of the Tiber to the peoples of the hills. The city was also itself composed by the meeting of several peoples, first Latin and Sabine, later Etruscan. Corresponding to these were three villages of ten wards each. The clan names also, as Münzer shows, fell into several regional groups:

Latin: *Aemilii, Cornelii, Manlii*
Sabine: *Claudii, Valerii*, and perhaps *Fabii*
Alba Longa (later): *Julii, Servilii*
Etruscan: *Licinii* (Lecne)

The rulers elected by the federated clans were, as we might expect, successively from different groups, described as Latin, Sabine and Etruscan. And when King Tarquin was expelled Consul Tarquin temporarily succeeded him. Within the city for long after this expulsion there remained the Etruscan quarter where the Etruscan language was spoken.

To enjoy the protection of the new city, and particularly of the patrician leaders of each clan in the city, came groups of wandering people in great variety. Some were traders, others craftsmen; others were slaves captured from older centres, Etruscan and Greek. These provided the working and professional classes, the plebs. They were the clients who supported their patrons, took their names, obeyed their orders and their laws, paid their taxes, learnt to speak their language, and in the end were permitted to worship their gods.

In addition to patricians and plebs there were slaves whose numbers were increased with time, partly by capture in war and partly by breeding as a class. At first debtors seem to have been imprisoned rather than enslaved and war captives were often released at the end of a war. Enterprising slaves were apt to run away when the small Roman state was in difficulties. It is in 430 B.C. that we first hear of Volscian prisoners of war, presumably plebeians, being sold as slaves. Later when Roman sway extended it became possible to keep under control a large slave population.

Then the Romans began to adopt and to improve on eastern systems of slave markets, slave schools for gladiators, the exploitation of slave labour in mines, galleys and fields, and the brutal punishment of fugitives. Then, too, their captives, Thracian and Gaulish, showed them in a series of rebellions the limitations of slavery.

IV. ROME AND THE ETRUSCANS

We have to separate two kinds of relationship of Rome with the Etruscans: their political relations with Etruscan rulers and their social relations with the Etruscan people at all levels. The first lasted perhaps for a hundred years, the second lasted for over a thousand years—if indeed they have ever ceased. Both were bound to leave their genetic traces in Roman life.

Rome illustrates the rule that the first cities of the west were always founded and built by men from the Ancient East. Etruscan colonists must have helped in the beginnings. Etruscan kings turned those beginnings into a city, drained, paved and walled like their own. It was Tarquinius Superbus who constructed the great social works: the *circus maximus*, the tripartite temple of Jupiter, Juno and Minerva on the Capitol, the joint shrine of Romans, Sabines and Etruscans. It was he also who built the main drain and sewer, the *cloaca maxima*. For this great work, if we take Livy's word for it, he gathered engineers from all over Etruria. It was his predecessor Servius Tullius who organized the legion and the order of battle with knights and light and heavy infantry suitably disposed. It was he too who introduced the census of property and population for purposes of taxation and military service. He divided them into five classes by the weapons their wealth allowed them to afford. He also devised the graded system of voting by 'centuries' (*comitia centuriata*), the two wealthier and less numerous classes having a majority of centuries.

The Etruscan census tells us that the Roman territory of about 500 square miles, by drainage and improved implements which it also owed to the Etruscans, provided for a population of a few hundred thousand and an army of 20,000 men.

These kings who were probably, as Livy says, of Greek as well as Italian origin, intermarried with the Roman patrician clans, introducing the Etruscan family names, and the distinction of race might in a few more generations have ceased to matter. The conflict between the Etruscans and the Romans (as Roman historians put it) was really less of a racial conflict than one between kings and patricians, kings who did not respect the fighting patricians because they found the working plebeians often more useful to them. The effect of the conflict was the expulsion of the kings, which meant a loss of territory, of commerce and of civilization. It also meant the establishment of a patrician oligarchy, narrowly nationalistic, and exclusively military, a class of people bent on preserving their powers against the intrusion or encroachment of outsiders, above them or below them.

The new Roman Republic continued however to wear all the social trappings of Etruscan civilization. The *fasces* of the lictor, emblems of law and punishment; the *toga* of the senator, emblem of authority; the triumphs of the victors glorifying war; the divination of the augurs; the Mediterranean goddesses enshrined with Aryan Jupiter, their names slightly transformed; as well as the language of religion and the theatre; all these remained to show the Etruscan debt.

The combats of paired gladiators which became a permanent feature of Roman life were also inherited from the Etruscans.[1] In the history of human culture they recall the rites of human sacrifice practised by Sumerians and Scythians at royal burials; but for the Romans they came to be a sporting ritual regularly repeated to entertain the people much like the public executions and the bull fights of later days. Prisoners of war, too bold to enslave and too wild to liberate, were the natural recruits for the profession of gladiators. It was a practice which in the course of centuries, as we shall see, contributed to the downfall of Rome.

If we turn from patricians to craftsmen we find evidences of a different kind of fusion. In the four centuries following the foundation of Rome, Hus

[1] The first Roman instance was a match between three pairs of gladiators at the funeral games of Marcus Brutus in 264 B.C. Fifty years later Hannibal perhaps picked up the idea from them since he arranged combats among prisoners before the battle of Ticinus to warm up his men for the fight (Livy XXI). See also Grant (1967).

describes a Latin city such as Praeneste (the modern Palestrina) with works of art in Etruscan style displaying Greek myths, decorated with imitation Egyptian hieroglyphs and marked with the names of Phoenician owners. Such was the world of Mediterranean craftsmen and traders at this stage.

Meanwhile the Latin language was beginning to digest both the concrete and abstract terms of Greek culture: the *olive* and the *machine* appeared on Latin soil and in Latin writing. The migrating craftsmen crossed the barriers between warring states and maintained an international continuity between Italy and the east throughout the early development of Rome.

It was in the hereditary priesthood that the fusion of Etruscan and Roman ideas arising from the intermarriage of their patrician clans showed most clearly. The forebears of the Etruscans must have acknowledged a priestly caste with independent authority. In the Uruk of Gilgamesh, palace and temple were close together; in Egypt, Pharaoh was God. But priests and military were divided effectively and usually into two castes. So also was it in Israel.

But the Aryan idea held the patricians to be the source of religious as well as military power. This idea was less impaired in Rome than in Greece. On the national scale the Roman patricians appointed priests and priestesses from their own caste and all religious authority rested in them before the nation as well as within the family. In Rome the political and religious powers were vested in one governing class. This gave a unity of purpose and ruthlessness of policy to the development of Rome. It also governed the evolution of the governing class itself and of its moral and legal code.

The supreme authority of war, the supreme virtue of courage in the soldier, of obedience in the wife, the son, and the slave, all these were perhaps necessary for a people who should in their circumstances survive; certainly they were necessary for a people that should win an empire by conquest. This novel unity of priest and ruler was a source of power and of continuity during its rise to the Roman governing class. But it exposed the State to dangers from which only a religious revolution could, in the end, extricate it. It was the absence of any balance of power or any court of appeal in the Roman State, between or within the classes or the families, that was to make Juvenal's question ultimately so fitting: '*Quis custodiet ipsos custodes?*'

Taking it all in all it was the genetic infusion of Etruscans, Greeks and other aliens into the patricians and the plebs which slowly transformed Roman society and gave it the new direction it was to take in the fifth century, the aggressive and ambitious direction which led through class conflict and national conflict to world dominion.

V. THE EVOLUTION OF GOVERNMENT

a. The Constitution

The development of government in Rome gives us some of the best evidence of the racial origins and social development of the people. The legend is that at the beginning Romulus chose a hundred heads of the pastoral families who constituted the governing class to form a senate, an advisory council of elders.

It no doubt derived from the common Aryan origin discussed by Fustel de Coulanges and thus corresponded with the Gerousia of Sparta and the Areopagus of Athens. This senate was still convened by the Etruscan kings who summoned heads of the greater and lesser, that is the older and newer families, of the three tribes, Roman, Sabine and Etruscan, to the number of 300.

The expulsion of the kings, as we have seen, arose from their conflict with the patrician families. With this conflict would be bound up the interests of the kings in the urban community of Rome, the interests of the patricians as land and serf owners and as military leaders. Hence, when the kings departed, the prosperity of the cities decayed and the influence of the urban classes declined.

The victorious patricians were confronted with grave problems of government. The first problem was to control the diverse subject classes of Greeks, Etruscans and hybrids, merchants and craftsmen who depended on them for protection. They solved it by continuing to exclude these classes, the *plebs*, from the executive and legislative offices of government. So divided, inevitably custom deepened the distinction between the governors and the governed. At the beginning it was a distinction of racial origin connected with differences in mode of living and confirmed by religious ceremonies and beliefs. The distinction was maintained and indeed enhanced by the segregation of the two classes in marriage and the prohibition of interbreeding. Stability was further secured by the overwhelming authority of the *pater familias* with power of life and death over his family and the absolute rule that no son could hold public office while his father lived.

The second problem was to safeguard themselves against the dangers of any one of them gaining control and restoring a monarchy or a tyranny, examples of which were becoming familiar to them in the Greek cities. Two main principles guided the senate here. One was to make all offices at least paired. Under this principle of 'collegiality' every officer must have a colleague. Originally many offices were connected with the tribes whose union had made Rome; they were connected above all in a military sense since the tribes were also military formations. The oldest of these offices was that of *praetor*, or judge. There were several praetors. But after the expulsion of the kings two of them became known as *consuls*. These were the chief magistrates. They were paired rulers and they were limited to one year only, taking office on the Ides of March each year. They were elected by majority votes of *comitia* of the free citizens assembled for the purpose and voting in military groups, the centuries. The candidates however were nominated by the senate from the ranks of the patricians, that is heads of families. In turn the members of the senate came to be nominated or summoned by the consuls from the members of the ex-magistrates, all patrician.

The voting was controlled by special officers elected for the purpose. Their business was to make the quinquennial census of citizens and their property. In doing so they followed the system attributed to the King, Servius Tullius, but doubtless improved in the Republic, of dividing the citizens into *classes* (the original use of the term) according to their qualifications of property and skill: *equites* or horsemen (including patricians), *fabri* or craftsmen, and heavily and lightly armed foot soldiers. These classes voted in the assemblies of the people chiefly through *comitia* of centuries which were, as we saw, weighted in favour of, not just the patricians, but the upper classes in general. Thus the division of the people for use in military service and taxation became also the means of regulating their voice in electing magistrates and legislators, administrators and priests.

This organization allowed the people opportunities for criticism but no opportunity for government or reform. The patricians were in control. Rebellion in some form was the only remedy. What happened? The armed plebs would walk out to the Aventine or Janiculan hill with or without fighting. Five such 'secessions' are recorded: 494, 449, 445, 342, 287 B.C. Each time they won their point. The patricians gave way. They made some legal or constitutional concession which appeared to give some advantage to the plebs.

b. The Advance of the Plebs

A record of the concessions and of their timing is illuminating. The office of consul was nominally opened to plebeians in 367, that of praetor in 337. But the candidates were nominated by the senate and it was not till 172 that both consuls were plebeian. The office of *censor* was established in 443. In 312 the censors were given the custody of the senate rolls and the duty of summoning senators. In 351 their office had been opened to plebeians: after 339 one of the two had to be plebeian; but not until 131 were there two plebeian censors.

The minor office of *quaestor* was originally judicial but later financial. Quaestors had been nominated by consuls but after 449 they were elected by the people in tribes. The office was opened to plebeians in 421, the number being raised from two to four. It remained throughout the Republic a step, the lowest step in the *cursus honorum*, the political career which led to the higher offices.

On the other side of the picture are the more modest offices created by and for the plebs. The office of *tribune* of the people was established about 490, probably from military origins and analogies. The tribunes were plebeians elected by the plebeians to protect their lives and properties. In 449 their number was increased to ten. But they could not be re-elected and it was only if they were unanimous that they had the right to veto the acts of the patrician magistrates. They also summoned assemblies of the people to vote resolutions. These *plebiscites* after 200 years, in 287, gained the force of law on a par with decrees ratified by the senate, but it was not till a century later that the tribunes became eligible for membership of the senate. Without the insignia of magistrates they had thus at last put themselves on an effective level with the great patrician officers. They had acquired a positive and constructive role in the government of the city and the republic. But in doing so (owing to the strength of the senate) they began to find themselves not the spokesmen of the people in the senate so much as the spokesmen of the senate to the people.

The last and smallest office of the State arose from the religious rites of the plebs. The common temple of the plebs on the Aventine Hill was dedicated to the fertility of the earth, to the goddess *Ceres*. This cult accorded with the origins of part of the plebeians as cultivators. It came, however, not with cultivation, but by a short cut through the Greeks. And it came in 493, just after the expulsion of the Etruscans. The custody of this house was committed to the *aediles* who later took over the care of buildings, archives, streets and public games. Having thus made themselves indispensable, they found that in the reform of 367 two patrician aediles, elected annually like themselves, had been added to the number. This office had thus become a step in a political career conferring in due course senatorial dignity.

By the third century the senate, recruited as it was from ex-magistrates, had come to represent about equally the patricians and those propertied plebeians who were now interested less in trade than in the traditional business of the patricians, that is in civil government and in military command.

The priesthood, like the magistracy, developed as a shrewd compromise between traditional forms and evolutionary needs. But it was a different kind of compromise. Through the five centuries of the Republic the priestly officials were elected by popular vote. They also, at first, were taken only from patrician families. But the chief appointments of magistrates were of paired officers, consuls, praetors, quaestors and so on, and for a limited period, usually of one year. Their authority was thus checked to avoid the suggestion of monarchy. The chief appointments in the priesthood on the other hand were entirely unrestricted; they were single; they were appointed for life; and they bore monarchical titles.[1]

The great priestly offices were moreover attached to almost royal families with almost royal names and they were almost hereditary. Thus the *rex sacrorum* who exercised the priestly functions of a king was at first chosen from a *gens* of royal antecedents, the *Marcii*, to whom the heroic name of *Coriolanus* is attached. Again, the office of *princeps senatus*, which had a princely status, was long held by the *Fabii*, the most noble of the *gentes* after the Tarquins. Before the first Punic war it passed from father to son in this Sabine family for three generations and at the crisis of the second Punic war it returned to them in the person of the dictator, *Q. Fabius Cunctator*.

These considerations have suggested to Münzer that the difference between monarchy and republic should be considered as a conflict between families, which was tempered so as to permit every gradation in practice between the principles of monarchism and collegiality; or, as we might say, oligarchy.

VI. THE EVOLUTION OF CLASSES

a. Within Rome

At an early stage the plebs might well be grateful to live on sufferance and in security. The land belonged to the patricians; the law and the language were theirs. The gods, the city's gods and the family's gods, were theirs. And they alone by taking the auspices could discover what the gods had decided for the city or the family. The plebs were of many foreign races, people without ancestors, laws or gods worthy of respect.

[1] Münzer (1920).

This view had one kind of justification in origins. It came to have another kind of justification after Roman society had existed for five or ten generations. During this time marriage had existed only within the patrician class. This class had formed after five or ten generations not a pure race but a noticeably homogeneous community. It had been engaged in waging war with Rome's neighbours without interruption. The temple of Janus had been closed to celebrate peace only once in a century. Or was it twice? Military prowess was the only serious test of virtue. Exposure beginning in infancy continued throughout life. Like the Spartans the Roman aristocracy had been rigorously selected for the character of a governing military class, a character which is quite different from that needed to do the menial work in town and country on which society in a baser sense depended. We may see the classical example of the behaviour of this group in the adventure of the *Fabii* when the clan by itself conducted its war with Veii and left only one boy alive to carry on its line. Yet this ruthless selection did not reach the tragic climax of Spartan history for a reason which we can now consider: their relations with the plebs.

Like all governing classes, the Roman patricians despised the plebeian multitude. Their attitude, as Fustel de Coulanges first pointed out, was like that of the governing castes in Athenian and also in Hindu society. But as time went on the character of the plebs was also changing, and changing in a different way. For the plebs were not restricted to inbreeding. They made their own marriages according to their own rules. Consequently they were, as a population, more richly diversified than the patricians. Undoubtedly from an early stage they included elements from distant shores. Undoubtedly also they included artificers of many origins. Builders and engineers came to Rome, as we saw, from all over Etruria. Soothsayers who were employed by the State were always Etruscans except during wars with Etruscan cities when Rome had recourse to the Delphic Oracle.

As the life of Rome grew more elaborate, it was because the plebs were themselves becoming more diverse and in part more capable and more enterprising. As Rome became richer it was largely because the plebs were creating and also enjoying more wealth. The plebs, or rather their political leaders, naturally became aware of this changing position.

Nor is it hard to see where their leaders might come from. Patricians were not allowed to marry plebeians. But they frequently and notoriously, sometimes by rape, had offspring by plebeian women. The plebs were enriched by this crossbreeding while the patrician class remained closed to it by the chastity of their women. Hence in Rome, as in all other societies with this class division and this breeding system, the plebs with a share of patrician ancestry came to demand a share of the patrician privileges. First, they asked for protection from their protectors. The office of tribunes was set up. Next they demanded the right of intermarriage. There were prolonged struggles and arguments, largely flavoured by religion. How could a hybrid race or class diagnose the will of the gods, the patricians' gods? But in the end the right was conceded. Thirdly, they demanded the right to be consuls. New executive offices were then created to which they could be elected. But they were not in fact elected. Why? Because the plebeians for a long time, by a principle of deference which has continued through the ages, preferred to vote for patrician candidates.[1] Lastly, the plebeians demanded the right to own the land they had been fighting for. And even this right they slowly won for themselves. In the end, we may ask, what distinction remained between patrician and plebeian? The rank was transmitted as in later aristocracies solely in the male line. It therefore became meaningless in its direct genetic effect. But it remained meaningful as an object of spurious deference and a source of certain real privileges. Or lack of privileges; for patricians would sometimes seek to be adopted by plebeians in order to take the posts that were now reserved for plebeians. In general therefore the distinction was effective simply as a means of setting up a social gradient favouring the marriage of families that were poor and old with families that were rich and new. But, as we shall see, this proved to have a decisive effect in the last days of the Republic.[2] (Pedigrees 8 to 11.)

It was a slow process of struggle by which the plebs won a higher position in Roman society. Slow by virtue of the resistance of the propertied—materially, spiritually and racially propertied—class to invasion of their privileges and contamination of their race. But slower still by virtue of the developing strength of the Roman administrative system which, as we saw, labelled every man by his rank, property and military duties. The efficiency of the Roman legion was related to the accuracy of the census which in turn reacted on their class for purposes of marriage and helped to stabilize the social system.[3]

Slowly a class structure arose which allowed social diffusion and promotion and hence adaptability as understood in modern stratified societies. At the same time in twenty generations of such diffusion a genetic coherence grew up by limited interbreeding. What Livy describes as a sense of national unity (*consociare* is the word he uses, Book II) slowly emerged. A consciousness indeed of a national character and national unity which slowly spread from Rome to her allies. It did not spread quickly enough to preserve the nation from the dreadful struggles of the social and civil wars. But it did save Rome from destruction in the crisis of foreign attack. And the world still recognizes the character of its unity by giving it the name Roman.

b. Within Italy

Parallel with the changes taking place inside Roman territory were changes in the relations of Rome and her neighbours, the surrounding peoples whom she reduced by war to alliance or subjection. These relations were on two levels. On one level the craftsmen and traders of the whole Mediterranean world visited Rome and must have enriched her population since they left their traces

[1] Deference is Bagehot's term for the situation where a few patricians believe that merit should replace birth though far more plebeians believe that birth itself is merit.

[2] Its parallel effects in the evolution of modern aristocracies are enhanced by primogeniture. There also we find recently, and for the same reason, the renunciation of nobility.

[3] As in Britain and with caste in British India in the nineteenth century.

archaeologically. On another level it is through laws and literature that we find out what happened.

In the matter of laws Rome's relations were always ambiguous, never more than in Italy in the third century. Was Rome subjecting her neighbours or protecting them? It is much the same question that we ask of the social classes inside Rome. And the answer to both changed with the passage of time: subjection became protection; obligations evaded became privileges pursued and demanded. Cities which had fought for their independence would later fight for an association which meant dependence.

It was at the end of the Latin war in 330 that the right of *conubium* was established between Rome and her allied neighbours, Latin as well as Etruscan, Campanian and Samnite. It was a selective right. Each ally was allowed to interbreed with Rome but they were not allowed to interbreed with one another. Rome thus made herself the axis round which her subject peoples were compelled to rotate. She was applying a new principle in the political and at the same time in the genetic development of society: *connube et impera.*

We have seen this principle operating in the form of dynastic marriage since the beginning of the early kingdom in Egypt. But now we see it operating at all levels of society at the same time. Take first the governing level where Münzer has been able to explore its effects through the study of names.

Foreign names appear in Roman society: *Plautii* from Praeneste, *Manilii* and *Fulvii* from Tusculum; unknown names *Junii* and *Livii* marry into the patrician *Aemilii*; *Atilii* from Cales, *Otacilii* from Beneventum, *Ogulnii* from Etruria, are taken under the wing of the *Fabii*; *Pompeii* from Picenum interbreed with *Cornelii*; and *Calavii* from Capua exchange daughters with the *Claudii* and *Livii* (as Livy himself reports, XXIII and XXVI).

These marriages served immediate political purposes on the two levels of the families concerned and of the governing classes of the various cities. Equally also their genetic consequences were felt on two levels. For the leading men of the Roman Republic were derived from this fruitful hybridization. But, at the same time, a social gradient was established between Rome and her allies or subjects. What Rome gained the others lost. The capital began to drain the abilities out of the Italian provinces. When it had done so the noble Roman families, now world-rulers, had acquired a status which led them to despise the provincials and often to decline intermarriage with them. In the early and growing Republic however this fragmentation and segregation were still in the future.

Taking the business of marriage control within the expanding Republic as a whole, we see that what began as a political device, with perhaps a sentimental reminiscence of the rape of the Sabine women, became the basic process of evolution assimilating the Roman with the Italian social structure. It was a process of regulated *epigamia* whose repression had blocked the evolution of the Greeks in Greece. And this contrast in turn arose from the geographical contrast between communications and trade in Italy and Greece.

The genetic supervision of development turned Roman society, first into

Italian society and then into something wider. It could not have been maintained had it not been supported continually by the Roman impetus, by the growth of the Roman people and of the Roman military, economic and political power. And this meant also the growth of geographical extent and redistribution of racial content. The social and genetic cohesion of the Roman domain was continually assisted by the planting of veterans in farming colonies favoured by privileges like those awarded by treaty to the Latin cities.

Cohesion was further reinforced at the level of the commercial classes. The roads which Roman governments built to connect the city with her outposts were built for the passage of armies. But in due course they served for the passage of goods. And that meant the passage of traders and artisans. All this directed communication meant the extension of the feeling of community from Rome to her possessions. Hence it meant the extension of intermarriage between them, within professions, within castes. It created a common stratification of society throughout the Roman world. So the central position of Rome, the roads running to Rome and the trading and breeding position of her people all tended to establish her unique opportunity for expansion which no other city (such as Carthage or Capua) could have challenged.

We are now able to see the position of Rome in Italy in the third century. The warlike mountain tribes that stood behind it had been a continual handicap to the development of Rome. But during the fourth century its position had been transformed. Their subjection to Roman society, and integration with it, made them, their men, their crops, timber and minerals, a source of strength in peace and war.

Rome's connection with Italy was still most imperfect. There were defections in war as well as contributions. Such defections had been foreshadowed in the Empires of Darius and Alexander. But unlike their systems the Roman connection had grown up over many generations. The result was an organic, genetic, racial continuum. It held at all levels of society. But above all it concentrated in the capital a governing class which was being steadily recruited from the most capable and most aggressive governing families of almost the whole of Italy.

VII. THE STRUGGLE WITH CARTHAGE

a. Carthaginian Society

The establishment of Rome as the leader of a league of Italian city states led her into a third kind of conflict, a national and racial conflict with another expanding power across the Mediterranean. Close to where Tunis now stands stood the port and city which we know as Carthage. The Greeks knew it as the Phoenician colony of Karchedon but it knew itself as the Canaanite colony of Kart-Hadasht founded by Dido in 814 B.C. In common with its eastern parents this city failed to produce a creative or historical literature. It failed to support the class of people who produce and maintain such a literature. In this respect it resembled the Rome of its own day: in literature it had been little Hellenized and it had been Judaized not at all. This failure left their Latin enemies in a position to describe and explain their downfall in Latin terms and to give the Carthaginians themselves the names by which we know them.[1]

When Tyre fell under the control of the Babylonians about 573 the duty of leading and of protecting the Phoenician colonies naturally fell to Carthage. The western city prospered on this opportunity. It became the first city to create and control an empire, a far-flung maritime state of many peoples. The population of the city itself grew in the third century perhaps to half a million. Its strength rested on three chief races and classes of people engaged in three kinds of work.

First and foremost were the aristocracy, the commercial people of the city itself and their kindred in the other colonies, people of partly Phoenician (or, in Latin, Punic) descent but interbred first with Greeks and Egyptians and later with the chiefly class of Libyans, Berbers and Iberians.

Secondly, there was the rich farming community in the province occupying half of modern Tunisia. These must have been people of eastern Mediterranean origin hybridized with the local pastoralists. They were slowly expanding westwards along the Moorish coast introducing agricultural and urban settlements. They spoke a civilized Phoenician dialect which lived on until the third century A.D. Contemporaries usually seem to have meant these people by the term 'Libyphoenician' and according to Livy they were despised as half-breeds by the Carthaginian aristocracy.

Thirdly, there were the Numidian and Moorish pastoralists speaking their own Berber languages. They were fighting tribes, skilful horsemen, valuable but uncertain allies whose ruling families married with one another and also with the Carthaginians; the notable instance being Syphax and Sophonisba (Pedigree 7).

Among all these people crucial importance attaches to the Punic governing class. The Carthaginians like the Roman nobles had displaced their kings; Magonids were reduced when Tarquins were expelled. But in Carthage the wealth came from commerce, and there was more of it, and they used it differently. For they had to pay foreigners or subjects to serve as mercenary troops. And through their maritime character the Carthaginians probably had much wider opportunities for outbreeding; indeed too wide for there was no dynastic organization such as we see in Republican Rome. If Hannibal married a Greco-Spanish wife, as we believe, he was doing what the older Roman aristocracy did not attempt to do for another two or three centuries.

The Carthaginian nobles thus might seem to have had an advantage over the Romans at this period by virtue of their knowledge of the world. But they had reacted to the growth of Hellenic power as the Romans had to the growth of Etruscan power: by an attempt to reject the culture. The development of Punic art (according to Warmington) indicates a check in the immigration of Greeks into Punic society. At the same time the language and the priesthood

[1] Six recent accounts have surveyed the evidence from excavation and documents: Warmington (1960) and Picard (1963) on Carthage; Harden (1962) on the Phoenicians, with Dido's pedigree, p. 53; Cottrell (1960) on Hannibal; Handford's introduction to Sallust (1963) and Radice's introduction to Livy (1965); Toynbee's discourse (1965) on the Punic wars.

must have hindered both Greek and Hebrew influence on the development of literature or the life of the people.

An example will show how the religious barrier worked and came to constitute a racial barrier.

The legends of Isaac, of Jephthah's daughter, and of Iphigenia, show that the sacrifice of children to appease a jealous god had existed among the Jews and Greeks. But it had been replaced by animal sacrifice with the growth of cities. The Greeks and Romans practised infant exposure but as a means of population control and eugenic selection rather than as a religious rite. Among the Phoenicians however the dedication of infants to burning in moments of crisis became a cult, pursued to be sure without enthusiasm by the educated nobility but with positive frenzy by the people.[1]

When therefore after a defeat in Sicily in 310 B.C. the priests discovered that nobles had substituted bought children for their own they corrected the abuse and demanded the offering of 500 infants of registered noble birth (Diodorus Siculus). The priests were thus encouraging the vulgar and primitive superstition as a means of supporting their own authority against the interests, the policy and the good sense of the aristocracy. In its genetic effects this was the most dangerous policy that had ever been recorded in any society. The Greeks had no tender feelings about the slaughter of prisoners for convenience. And after the defeat at Cannae the Romans, instructed by the sacred books, were willing to appease the gods (as Livy blushes to record) by burying alive under the forum two couples (male and female), Greek and Gaulish. But among the Greeks and Romans, whose priests were nobles, the sacrifice of noble children and the division of interests it implied could never arise. It aroused in them a deep revulsion of feeling. And the practice gave evidence of divergence of class structure and hence of instinctive behaviour between the Roman and Punic societies which would inevitably be aggravated by the barrier to interbreeding which it created.

The racial structure and means of subsistence of its territory enabled and required Carthage to develop in quite a different way from its parent people in Asia. Carthage was able to enrich herself with trade, not only by sea, but also across the Sahara. The camel, newly spreading, and exploited by the precursors of the Tuareg (the *Gaetuli*) was the basis of a trade in gold and ivory and Negro slaves that has continued to this day. The produce of this trade, by sea and land, enabled Carthage to engage mercenary armies first from Numidia, later from the Balearics and Spain and later still from Gaul and Italy. These armies were a protection when they were paid. But they could be a danger when funds ran short.

There was a second source of danger in the Carthaginian armament. The Phoenician fleets had been built with their own timber, growing, as it were, in their own back garden. The coasts of North Africa were already, if we again refer to Sallust, showing the effects of over-grazing: they were treeless. The connection with Phoenicia had been broken once more and for ever by the conquests of Alexander. In the fourth century Sicily had repaired this loss.

[1] Its reality has recently been confirmed by the discovery of the cremated bones of infants (Harden 1960).

The loss of Sicily in the first Punic war was in turn repaired by the occupation of southern Spain. But this land, so valuable for metals, could scarcely make good the loss of supplies of timber and ships. Shipwrights and sailors from Sicilian and Italian, Greek and Etruscan ports were now able to create naval power for Rome. Moreover, in the second Punic war Greek ports like Massilia lent their fleets to Rome.

The over-felling of timber for shipbuilding in war was indeed, like the over-grazing by cattle in peace, a self-aggravating disaster; and cattle now included camels in Africa. The soil erosion which followed prevented the restoration of forests and pastures. It created undrained swamps and, in the third century, it seems likely that these began to harbour mosquitoes which African armies invading Europe infected with malaria. So it was that, following Crete and Greece, North Africa and Sicily took the pathway to desolation at a pace accelerated by war. It was a pathway that Italy was to follow later.

In these circumstances the rulers of Carthage were in a precarious state. Their danger was interpreted differently, it would seem, by maritime and military interests as well as by aristocratic and plebeian parties. For, like the Romans, the Carthaginians were engaged in dispute between the old families in the senate and the new people in the popular Assembly. But in addition the army, being a professional and mercenary body, was inevitably difficult to control. Certainly they allowed it to be a third limb of the State, electing its own generalissimo who was also in effect a civil proconsul and a diplomatic plenipotentiary. It was the mutinous Carthaginian mercenaries in 337 who handed over the island of Sardinia to Rome. On the other hand the Carthaginian officers seem to have been able to elect Hannibal as their own commander, as they had on a previous occasion elected his father, Hamilcar. And it was to his gifted family that Carthage owed her capacity to attack in the second Punic war.

b. The War with Hannibal

In the year 221, Hasdrubal, Governor of Carthaginian Spain, was assassinated. The army elected Hannibal, his brother-in-law and Hamilcar's son, as his successor and the senate acquiesced. They knew that it meant a victory for the army party and a decision for war with Rome. Hannibal was twenty-six years old.[1] He was committed by his father's will and his own character to making war on Rome (Pedigree 7). In the first war with Rome, Carthage had lost the islands of Sicily, Sardinia and Corsica. It was Hannibal's object to take them back and to destroy the rival power.

To Hannibal Rome may well have seemed a poor city, half the size of Carthage, hampered by a system of electing new consuls and tribunes, new commanders for its army, every year; an army which was not professional but merely a militia newly conscripted every year; hampered moreover by its own and its allies' racial inferiority and cultural backwardness.

Hannibal could hardly be expected to understand that he was faced by a

[1] Hannibal is said to have been born in 247 in Majorca, an island which curiously enough after many vicissitudes similarly harboured the pre-Corsican Bonapartes.

people slower but more homogeneous than his own; and a people naturally devoted to war. He knew the Greeks; he understood their language, their history and their military methods. He knew how Alexander had humbled and subdued the city states. And he noticed his own likeness to Alexander without recognizing the likeness of the Romans to the Macedonians, in having, to return to Livy's words, a sense of community which was something new in the world.

So, just as Alexander took over Philip's plan, Hannibal took over his father's plan for attacking the enemy of his people. And, just as Alexander, lacking sea power, marched round the shores of the Mediterranean to find his enemy, so also did Hannibal. The opportunities of the first Punic war had turned the Romans into a sea power and had deprived the Carthaginians of the control of the sea routes. Hannibal therefore in the year 218 advanced along the coasts of Spain and Gaul. The diversity of his African, Spanish, and Balearic army could have been a source of weakness. But trained by Punic officers and commanded by Hannibal, it was a source of strength. It was moreover supported by his own newly domesticated North African elephants, a race now extinct.[1] Picking up an army of recruits on the way, he crossed the Alps and invaded the Italian peninsula.

In a succession of battles over a period of twelve years all over Italy Hannibal destroyed one Roman army after another. But always a new army appeared dogging his footsteps from one beleaguered city to the next. He lacked the forces needed to assault Rome, and two armies sent to help him and commanded by his brothers were successively defeated on the way. Sicily which had been won over to Carthage was won back to Rome. Spain likewise. The Carthaginian senate, faithful too long, found itself confronted by a Roman army in Africa and recalled Hannibal. But it recalled him only to defeat. Peace was made and Carthage surrendered her colonies, her fleet, her elephants, and her right to make war, even in self-defence.

c. *The Crisis in Religion*

In Rome the crises of the war were accompanied by crises of faith. From Livy's description we can divine the struggle that must have been raging beneath the surface between belief and unbelief, superstition and scepticism. We can see that it always had a class and race connection.

During the dark days of 212 with Spain lost, and Sicily, Capua and Tarentum unrecovered, people in Rome noticed that unfamiliar rites were being practised by foreigners. Underground religions of immigrant classes were creeping out into the open. Compromise was inevitable. After the Latin Festival on April 26 the Sybilline books were consulted and the senate voted to acknowledge officially the Greek rites of Apollo with a public sacrifice and a public collection.

Eight years later there was another crisis. Mago, Hannibal's brother, was in Etruria. The population of Rome had been gravely depleted by the war and the censors arranged for the erection on the Palatine of a shrine to the Great Mother, the eastern fertility goddess. These were concessions of the

[1] Carrington (1955).

governing class to secure the loyalty of the new foreign populations which had entered Rome from the east. The movement would continue for five centuries and the resulting concessions likewise. The struggle between religion and heresy, between native tradition and foreign innovation, thus makes a secondary plot in the background of the Punic wars.

There was one rebel, the radical and plebeian Gaius Flaminius. This consul owed his election for the year 217 to his policy of curbing the commercial activities of senators. So impatient was this man of upper-class superstitions that he hurried away to take command of his legions at Ariminum on the Ides of March. He would not wait to attend his formal investiture in Rome, to proclaim the Latin Festival, to celebrate the annual sacrifice to Latin Jove on the Alban Mount, to offer prayers in the Capitol, and finally to take the auspices. Many unnatural events had followed these affronts to the gods. The senate attempted to expiate them by a present to Jupiter of a golden thunderbolt weighing fifty pounds. The officers like the senate were disturbed by their commander's independence. The troops, on the other hand, admired it. When a month later, however, Livy records that they were all destroyed in the battle of Lake Trasimene, he finds Hannibal's generalship a sufficient explanation.

It was in this extremity that a dictator was appointed, Quintus Fabius Maximus Cunctator, who recommended the two steps of consulting the Sybilline books and at the same time avoiding battle.

d. Leaders and Peoples

What has made the second Punic war so impressive to all later generations is the matching of the prowess, skill, wealth and genius, both collective and individual, between the two greatest powers in the western world at that time.

Hannibal's invasion of Italy at the beginning promised to be just a military struggle between two powers. Gradually however it took on a more diverse and elaborate character. The people involved were all the civilized and barbarous communities on the shores of the western Mediterranean. Spain and Italy were the two main theatres of war, but the King of Macedonia saw his chance of engaging Hannibal in his own struggle with the cities of Greece. The control of the sea was used by Rome to capture his envoys. The cities of Italy were everywhere divided between senatorial and popular parties which strove to take advantage of the ebb and flow of the rival powers. In Rome itself and in Carthage rival factions plotted for or against rival policies and commanders. Prisoners were exchanged or ransomed. Slaves were enlisted to fight for their freedom and Roman slaves captured by the Carthaginians would sometimes escape and return with useful messages for the Romans. The Oracle of Delphi was consulted by Rome. An offer of citizenship to the Latin allies was proposed but silenced in the Roman senate. Popular politicians were elected consuls only to lose their armies and their lives at Trasimene and Cannae. Thus the struggle took on the character of a world war, a war which deepened some cleavages in every society and healed others, and in doing so became a test of the structure and character of each.

It also became a test of the genius of the great leaders on the two sides. The

Pedigree 7. Pedigree of the Barca family: leaders of the Carthaginian military or plebeian party

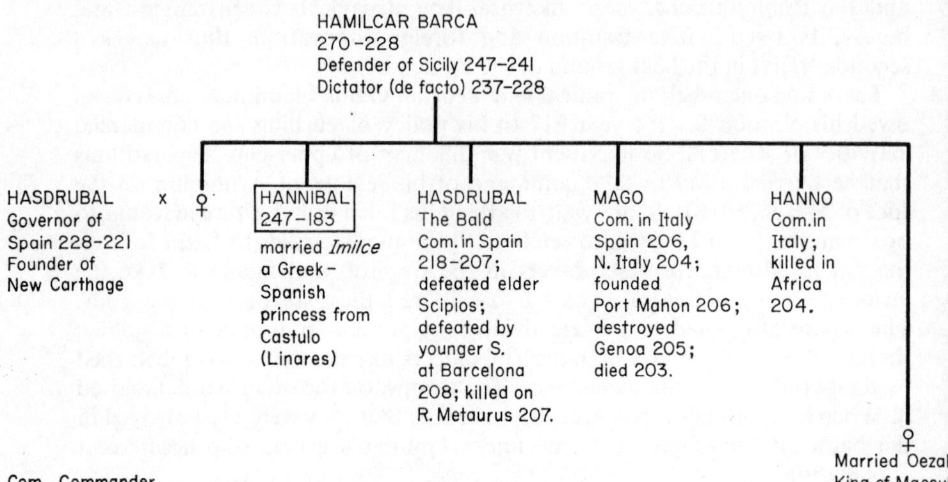

Com., Commander

Notes:

The Carthaginians like the Romans had too few names to distinguish people. Hence there are the following additional contemporary homonyms:

HASDRUBAL: i. Son of Gisgo, Commander in Spain 209–206 and in Africa 206–202. His famous daughter Sophonisba married Syphax, King of Numidia.
ii. A commander in Italy.
iii. 'The Kid', member of Senate, anti-war, peace delegate 202.

MAGO: Three other commanders, one at Gades, one at New Carthage, one in Italy.

HANNO: One in Senate (opponent of Hannibal), two in army (one killed in Spain 218, the other in Africa 204).

Carthaginian leadership depended entirely on the family of Hamilcar Barca amongst whom Hannibal was supreme (Pedigree 7). Hannibal owed something to the continuity of his authority and the prestige which his early victories gave him. For over twelve years his enemies in Carthage failed to prevent him acting as viceroy and plenipotentiary.

On the Roman side no single person had the power of Hannibal and can therefore be fully compared with him. Nevertheless we have the opinion of one of the best critics,[1] that in Scipio he met a pupil who became his master. Scipio's ultimate victory was the climax of nine years of training in organization, politics and administration as well as in battle.

What were in fact the origins of these two leaders? The story of the Punic wars owes much to their dramatic contrast.

The Carthaginian governing class did not base its power on its own military achievement. The city and the rural population were alike (as Livy puts it) unwarlike and the State was consequently opposed to the second Punic war, the war of revenge. It depended on its ability to hire soldiers to fight for it. The rank and file were their own plebeians of diverse and hybrid origins

[1] Liddell Hart (1927).

assisted by Greek infantry and Numidian horsemen. But for commanders they usually relied on men who professed to be Carthaginians.[1] Some of these like Hasdrubal Gisgo seem to have owed their command to wealth and birth. Their great commanders however were all of one family, a new family, that of Hamilcar Barca (the Thunderer). He sprang into fame at the end of the first Punic war and nothing is known of his birth. It may well be that he was of plebeian and hybrid origin. This possibility is supported by Hannibal's record. The Carthaginian commander is supposed to have married a Spanish woman of Greek extraction. He is known to have been familiar with the Greek language. His policy in Carthage when he was elected consul six years after his defeat was vigorously popular. He introduced the Greek idea of annual elections of magistrates. After his exile from Carthage in 195 B.C. he took refuge with the King of Pergamon. And he was alone among the Carthaginians in his reputation for wit and learning.

On this view the continuance of the Punic war against Rome was the work of a military party in Carthage, partly perhaps of foreign origin, opposed to the commercial aristocracy. In Rome on the other hand the war was maintained by the aristocracy, particularly the party of the Scipios, supported, with variable enthusiasm, by the plebeian and immigrant classes. The new men were perhaps more successful as commanders however with the new weapon, the fleet; the aristocracy were undoubtedly more successful with the old weapon, the army. The lack of plebeian enthusiasm is most clearly shown by the defection of the twelve nearest colonies of Rome at the worst moment of crisis. Similarly, when Hannibal was negotiating with Italian cities, he often found the plebeian party more friendly to Carthage: the patricians by the right of *conubium* were often (as in Capua) already connected with Roman patrician families.

In confronting Hannibal the Roman commanders were at a multiple disadvantage. They were usually pairs of consuls elected by the people's Assembly for one year. They often shared the command or they had their field action decided by the drawing of lots. And when defeated they usually thought it their duty to die in battle. Thus nine Roman commanders died in the war. All of them were consuls or former consuls: two Scipios, Flaminius, Paullus, Gracchus, Postumius Albinus, Marcus Marcellus, Quinctus Crispinus and Gnaeus Fulvius. Hence Roman commanders could never learn by experience. The only great commanders who survived were those who avoided meeting Hannibal until they had had experience, namely Q. Fabius Maximus and the younger Scipio who went to Spain as commander. The same principle applied to the Carthaginians. Hasdrubal the Bald may have lost the war by throwing away his own life. On the other hand the man who avoided death with the greatest skill and success was the wily Numidian prince, Masinissa. Defeated three times in battle by his rival Syphax he always escaped; and in the end he won.

The younger Scipio's solution of the problem decided the result of the war

[1] In the previous war Carthage had, however, engaged a Spartan general, Xanthippus, for one year with excellent results. He reorganized the Carthaginian army and destroyed the invading Roman force.

and the destiny of Rome. Here was a man descended from several generations of notable commanders. He had seen his father defeated by Hannibal. But he responded not by himself confronting Hannibal in Italy but by undertaking, at the age of twenty-six, the command of the expeditionary force to Spain where his father had been killed. There he developed his own art of war, learning from Hannibal and eventually surpassing him both in strategy and in diplomacy. In public relations and stage management, and in the use of oaths and omens, he seems to have learnt from Alexander as well as from Hannibal. For, if he did not invent the story, an aristocratic story, that he had been begotten on his mother by a python, it certainly served him well.

Again we may note that the family and kindred of the Scipios, as of Hannibal, stood apart from their countrymen in their intellectual, artistic and literary interests. The Romans were introduced to the great works of

Table 14. *Time Chart of the Second Punic War*
See Radice (1965).

ASSAULT ON ROME	1. Hannibal's siege and capture of SAGUNTUM		219–218 B.C.
	2. Invasion of Italy: Gaul and Alps	July–Oct.	218
	Battles of Ticinus and Trebbia	Nov.–Dec.	218
	Battle of Trasimene	April	217
	Battle of Cannae	May ?	216
	3. Gauls, central and southern tribes, Greek colonies (except Tarentum, Metapontum, Croton and Locri), southern allies including CAPUA, desert to Carthage		216
GREECE	4. King Philip of MACEDON allied to Carthage		215
	4a. Greek and Pergamon coalition against Macedon		211
SICILY	5. Death of King Hiero: Syracuse joins Carthage		214
	5a. Syracuse recovered by Rome		212
SPAIN	6. Scipio brothers attempting to conquer Spain		217–211
	defeated and killed		212–211
ITALY	7. Capua besieged and recovered by Romans; Hannibal marches to Rome—and back again		211
	8. Tarentum (except citadel) and other Greek colonies taken by Hannibal		212
	recovered by Fabius		209
	9. Stalemate in Italy: Hannibal confined to south		210–203
	9a. Twelve Roman colonies refuse aid		209
	9b. Hasdrubal crosses Pyrenees and Alps defeated and killed on R. Metaurus (Ancona)		207
ASSAULT ON CARTHAGE	10. Scipio the Younger reconquers Spain		210–206
	captures New Carthage 209, Battle of Ilipa (Seville)		206
	10a. Assembles forces in Sicily		205
	10b. Invades Africa, joins Masinissa		204
	defeats Hasdrubal Gisgo		203
	11. Scipio makes armistice; Hannibal recalled to Africa		203
	12. Hannibal defeated by Scipio and Masinissa at battle of Zama		202

Greek art when the treasures of Syracuse were brought to them by Marcellus after its capture in 212. But it was by the patronage and enterprise of the Scipios that the Romans later won from the Greeks both their literature and its practitioners (Table 14). It was indeed the Scipios who were responsible both for Rome's conquest of Greece and for the Greek conquest of Rome which followed it over the succeeding centuries (Pedigree 8).

e. The End of Carthage

Fifty years after her defeat Carthage had paid off her indemnity in yearly tribute to find herself once more the object of fear and hatred among the Roman veterans of the great war. They saw that she could manage her business almost as well without the power she had forfeited. Having lost the war she seemed to be winning the peace. In Cato's eyes there was not room for both Rome and Carthage.

Cato may have been right. But we cannot help admiring the opposite opinion of Publius Scipio Nasica. This extraordinarily liberal-minded man maintained that competition with Carthage was necessary for the sound development of Rome. He was overruled. After three years' siege Carthage was taken and destroyed and the surviving remnant of her people enslaved. The whole province of 'Africa' became a Roman colony with adjoining Numidia a protected and allied kingdom. The die had been cast. The overseas Empire was to grow. Rome was to expand to the limits of her military power. Given the character that had been bred into it, how could the Roman governing class do otherwise?

Did nothing survive of Carthage? The city and the State were certainly extinguished. The governing class disappeared. But fragments of its people survived and expanded in its colonies from Leptis Magna to Mauretania and from Cadiz to Carthagena. They preserved in these places their language and religion which in turn preserved their race and their character. Men of varied abilities, men for whom, as we shall see, Rome was later to receive the credit, writers and emperors, senators and saints[1] were undoubtedly descended from the Carthaginians who brought civilization from the ancient east to the western Mediterranean and with it had first penetrated into both Africa and the Atlantic.

VIII. THE BREAKDOWN OF THE REPUBLIC

The Romans, according to Livy, conquered the world against their own will. This was the view of a patriotic historian. But the Romans after the war with Hannibal were as ever a deeply divided people. Moreover, they were divided by the interests of social classes whose social functions and constitutional rights were rapidly changing, and with them their genetic structure also.

Take first the governing class. In them the capacity for military and civil government had been united and constantly selected since the foundation of the Republic. Their courage, skill and versatility had carried them through the war with Hannibal. It had also swept them on to attack and destroy all the

[1] Not only Augustine of Hippo but, as Warmington points out, the author of the Christian schism, Donatus, who is named in literal translation as *Muttumbaal.*

competing powers and to conquer all the barbarian countries in the Mediterranean basin. Successively Africa and Spain, Greece and Anatolia, fell to them. Diplomacy and chicanery had been added to their armament in the process. They were changing. They were now adapted to new and more splendid achievements than those demanded of the small city state. How did this happen?

After the Licinian Laws, as we saw, the plebeians had gradually become eligible for office and government and intermarriage with the patrician class. But the senate retained the right to name candidates for election. And the senate consisted of former officers. The consequence of such a system could be predicted. Instead of the patrilinear family division between patrician and plebs there grew up a new and practical distinction between those whom senators did and did not see fit to recruit into their own body and their own class: between the *novus homo* like Cicero who succeeded and others who did not.

The senate thus became a self-nominating, self-recruiting and self-propagating body: a closely intermarried group recognized as the senatorial class. They were also described as the *gnobiles* or *nobiles*: that is the people who were known by the names of their families owing to members of these 'families' having served in office and hence in the senate. This class however was internally stratified. There were some families, usually bearing patrician names, who were more successful in reaching the consulship. One able man could secure the consulship for only one year. But if he had a large, presentable and ambitious series of brothers he could keep his family in the consulship year after year. In successive generations different families thus established consular dynasties often maintaining some consistent policy, liberal or imperial, conservative or progressive.

The leading consular families built up their political position and also developed their genetic character by dynastic marriages based on political aims or property interests, as their offices show (Table 15). At the same time impoverished patrician families were marrying outside the senatorial class, sometimes into prosperous provincial families of no political account but as we shall see with important genetical results of quite another kind.

The governing class like any other nobility was thus greatly influenced in its development by the principle of deference, the respect due not only to a man's proved abilities but also to those remembered in his ancestors. In the Roman case there were new absurdities, some of which still persist today. In the first place female lines of ancestry were ignored: a male patrician was thus worth more than a female. In the second place, names could be changed by adoption (Pedigree 8). Both these irrational practices loosened the breeding system and favourably influenced the development of the Republic and the Empire.

The senatorial class, however, was not able or willing to recruit itself freely from the ablest of Roman citizens. The strict division of both aptitudes and privileges between them and the people outside led to a deep cleavage. Who were the people outside? The general body of Roman citizens were, with the growth of the Empire, irreparably dispersed. No officer, no system, could now ascertain the wishes of the whole citizen body scattered over

Table 15. *The Roman Religious Office of* Pontifex maximus *in Connection with the Holding of Political Offices:* 253 B.C.–A.D. 14.

After Münzer (1920).

D., Dictator. P.S., *Princeps senatus.* M.E., *Magister equitum* (or Deputy Dictator).

Accession Year	*Name*	*Consul*	*M.E.*	*D.*	*Censor*	*P.S.*
253	Ti. Corancanius[1]	280	246	—	—	—
243	L. Caecilius Metellus[1]	251, 247	249	224	—	—
221	L. Cornelius Lentulus	237	—	—	236	220
213	P. Licinius Crassus[1]	205	210	—	210	—
183	C. Servilius Geminus[1, 2]	203	208	202	—	—
180	M. Aemilius Lepidus	187, 175	—	—	179	179
152	P. Cornelius Scipio Nasica Co.	162, 155	—	—	159	147
End of third Punic war	. . . . .					
141	P. Cornelius Scipio Nasica Se.	138	—	—	—	—
132	P. Licinius Crassus Mucianus[1]	131	—	—	—	—
130	P. Mucius Scaevola[1]	133	—	—	—	—
115	L. Caecilius Metellus[1]	119	—	—	115	—
103	Cn. Domitius Ahenobarbus[1]	96	—	—	92	—
89	Q. Mucius Scaevola[1]	95	—	—	—	—
82	Q. Caecilius Metellus Pius[1]	80	—	—	—	—
63	C. Julius Caesar	59, 48, 46	—	48–44	—	—
44	M. Aemilius Lepidus	46, 42	45, 33	—	—	—
12	C. Julius Caesar Augustus	43	—	—	—	—

Repeats: 3 Mucii (one adopted by a Licinius precedes his brother), 3 Caecilii, 3 Cornelii, 2 Aemilii, 2 Julii.

[1] Of plebeian family. [2] A renounced patrician.

Notes:

The pontifices like all the State priesthoods were confined to the patricians until 300 B.C. after which half the college were elected from plebeians. Unlike the magistracies the *Pontifex maximus* was a lifelong and undivided, and hence in a sense monarchical, office like that of *Princeps Senatus.* His election was made by 17 (chosen by lot) of the 35 tribes into which the Roman citizens were divided after 241 B.C. Nevertheless the choice was even more restricted than that of the political heads, never going outside them. And the 17 names in this list come from only nine gentes. From Augustus the situation changed: the emperors up to Gratian (A.D. 375) took the office without exception.

Thus the choice under the Republic was always influenced by religious respect for family (even if it was only an adopted name). This respect was justified by experience so long as conditions remained stable since it also controlled marriage prospects and thus indicated a breeding group.

Pedigree 8. Family connections of *Publius Scipio Africanus* showing the effects of kinship, marriage and adoption on the political, military and intellectual development of Roman society (after F. Münzer 1920 and *O.C.D.* 1949)

Notes:

i. The middle name is that of the patrilinear gens, patrician or plebeian, which in its feminine form is given to all daughters. Adopted sons commonly take the three names of their adoptive father to which their own gentile name is added adjectivally. Patricians could revoke their status. There were thus plebeian branches of many of the patrician gentes, older and younger. Moreover plebeians could acquire patrician status both in early Rome and after the dictatorship of Caesar.

ii. Most marriages here are within 'consular' families, whose ancestors have been consuls and therefore military commanders for one or more generations. They involve cousin marriages of political allies as well as paired kindred marriages establishing political parties. They disregard the ancestral and largely religious distinction between patrician and plebeian.

iii. For the military history of *P. Scipio* see Liddell Hart (1927).

iv. *M. Livius Salinator* had married a daughter of Pacuvius of Capua who in 216 defected to Hannibal (Münzer 1920). His adoption of a patrician was unprecedented.

v. *L. Aemilius Paullus* gave two of his three sons to be adopted leaving the third to preserve his name and fortune so mimicking modern primogeniture. The third son however died prematurely and the name was extinguished.

vi. This table illustrates the practice that, in arranging all Roman noble marriages, the antiquity of the name, the wealth of the family, and the reputation of the kindred on both male and female sides, were considered together with political interest (Münzer 1920).

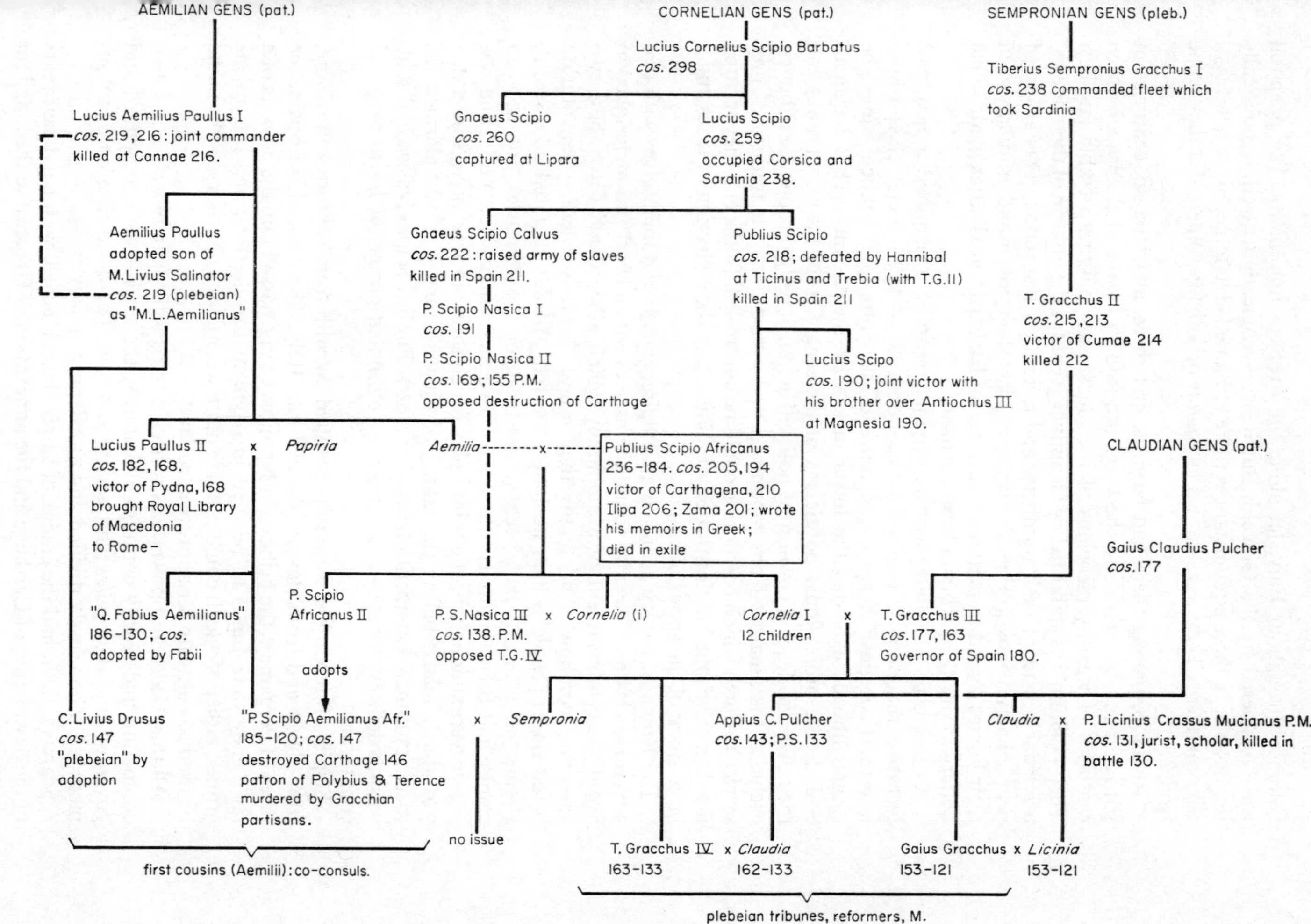

AEMILIAN GENS (pat.)
CORNELIAN GENS (pat.)
SEMPRONIAN GENS (pleb.)
Lucius Cornelius Scipio Barbatus cos. 298
Tiberius Sempronius Gracchus I cos. 238 commanded fleet which took Sardinia
Lucius Aemilius Paullus I cos. 219, 216: joint commander killed at Cannae 216.
Gnaeus Scipio cos. 260 captured at Lipara
Lucius Scipio cos. 259 occupied Corsica and Sardinia 238.
Aemilius Paullus adopted son of M. Livius Salinator cos. 219 (plebeian) as "M.L. Aemilianus"
Gnaeus Scipio Calvus cos. 222: raised army of slaves killed in Spain 211.
Publius Scipio cos. 218; defeated by Hannibal at Ticinus and Trebia (with T.G.II) killed in Spain 211
T. Gracchus II cos. 215, 213 victor of Cumae 214 killed 212
P. Scipio Nasica I cos. 191
P. Scipio Nasica II cos. 169; 155 P.M. opposed destruction of Carthage
Lucius Scipo cos. 190; joint victor with his brother over Antiochus III at Magnesia 190.
CLAUDIAN GENS (pat.)
Lucius Paullus II cos. 182, 168. victor of Pydna, 168 brought Royal Library of Macedonia to Rome –
x Papiria
Aemilia x
Publius Scipio Africanus 236–184. cos. 205, 194 victor of Carthagena, 210 Ilipa 206; Zama 201; wrote his memoirs in Greek; died in exile
Gaius Claudius Pulcher cos. 177
P. Scipio Africanus II
adopts
"Q. Fabius Aemilianus" 186–130; cos. adopted by Fabii
P. S. Nasica III cos. 138. P.M. opposed T.G. IV
x Cornelia (i)
Cornelia I 12 children
x
T. Gracchus III cos. 177, 163 Governor of Spain 180.
C. Livius Drusus cos. 147 "plebeian" by adoption
"P. Scipio Aemilianus Afr." 185–120; cos. 147 destroyed Carthage 146 patron of Polybius & Terence murdered by Gracchian partisans.
x Sempronia
no issue
Appius C. Pulcher cos. 143; P.S. 133
Claudia x P. Licinius Crassus Mucianus P.M. cos. 131, jurist, scholar, killed in battle 130.
first cousins (Aemilii): co-consuls.
T. Gracchus IV 163–133 x Claudia 162–133
Gaius Gracchus 153–121 x Licinia 153–121
plebeian tribunes, reformers, M.

colonies throughout Italy, let alone the overseas dominions. The proposal was considered by the Gracchi. But it was technically as well as politically impossible. In these circumstances there remained certain people, a new class, who mattered. They were known as *equites* or knights. Where did they come from?

At the beginning there had been, at first three, and later six centuries of patrician cavalry. To these the kings are said to have added another dozen centuries of wealthy plebeians of the oldest and most respectable families. Their position was stabilized by an annual grant for the upkeep of their horses, a regular census of their numbers, and a military inspection. This group of people had no constitutional organ to express their power and gradually even their horses ceased to matter in warfare, for barbarian auxiliaries made much better cavalry than Roman business men.

As this class of *equites* lost its original meaning it acquired a new and lucrative function. It became an economically defined social class whose intermarriage gave it some coherence of structure and political aim. The *equites* already excluded the lower orders by their wealth. They began to exclude the professional politicians of the senate from their own ranks and their own privileges. They now by political action, largely through the tribunes, excluded the senators from commerce, and even from their traditional jury service through which corruption could be controlled. In the end they secured for themselves the administration of finance and the collection of taxes and a large share of the spoils of empire.

The Romans, having acquired an empire, thus found themselves with two governing classes. They also found themselves with a constitution designed to avoid the establishment of a monarchy which alone could force these two classes to combine. And finally they found themselves with a constitution based on a 'people' which no longer existed. All this required adjustment. Former adjustments had been successful over the centuries but now an empire had been acquired in the space of two generations. New wealth and new power were suddenly brought into play which threw society into disorder in a way that already, before the taking of Carthage and Corinth, alarmed the wiser statesmen. Competition between states, Publius Scipio Nasica had said, was needed. He foresaw the dangers of unlimited power for his ill-prepared countrymen.

Scipio's forebodings were fully justified. Wealth from capture and tribute, from slaves and from slavery, flooded into Italy. The minerals of Spain, the taxes of Pergamon, the bribes of a Numidian king, passed into the pockets of a few. They were funds to be used in payment for elections and for private armies, either of which could provide more wealth, or to buy slaves who could be used to cultivate misappropriated lands.

All this wealth and power was collected to pass through two channels, two competing and legally contrasted channels, the *nobiles* who conquered and governed, and the *equites* who bought and sold. There was thus no establishment but a hopelessly divided and unbalanced society.

Scarcely, then, had the climax of empire been reached, within a dozen years of the destruction of Carthage and the annexation of Greece and the kingdom

Table 16. *Time Chart of the Expansion of Rome*
After Grant (1960).

TRADITIONAL and ARCHAEOLOGICAL	
Foundation by Romulus	753 B.C.
Occupation by Etruscans	575–509
Defeat of Greeks of Massilia by Etruscans and Carthage	535
Defeat of Etruscan fleet at Cumae	474
1. THE STRUGGLE FOR ITALY 509–265 B.C.	
Rome subdues	
(*a*) with Latin allies, the mountain tribes	
(i) Sabines and Sabellians	500–300
(ii) Samnites	340–290
(*b*) Latin League itself	380–340
Rome captured by Gauls and ransomed	390
Rome subdues or assimilates	
(i) Etruscan cities	396–280
(ii) Capuan province (from Samnites)	341
Veii 396; Tarquinia 308; Volsinii, Perugia, Arezzo 294	
2. THE FIRST SOCIAL STRUGGLE 490–287 B.C.	
Establishment of tribunes to protect plebeians	*c.* 490
Twelve Tables: Written Code of Law	450
Licinian Laws: Plebeian right to intermarry, and to consulship	367
Plebeian Assembly acquires law-making powers	287
3. THE STRUGGLE FOR EMPIRE 264–30 B.C.	
With Carthage:	
1st Punic war: 75,000 slaves, Sicily annexed	264–241
Corsica and Sardinia annexed	239
2nd Punic war: (Hannibal) Spanish province annexed	218–201
3rd Punic war: Carthage destroyed; Africa annexed	149–146
With Hellenic Powers:	
Defeat of Seleucids at Magnesia	189
Pergamon annexed	133
Macedonia and Greece annexed	148–146
The Completion:	
Pompey annexes Syria, Palestine and Armenia	64–62
Julius Caesar conquers Gaul	58–52
Octavius annexes Egypt	30
4. SECOND SOCIAL STRUGGLE 135–30 B.C.	
Slave revolts in Sicily	135–131 104–100
Abortive social and agrarian reforms of T. and G. Gracchus	131–121
Italian civil wars and dictatorships	95–30

of Pergamon, than civil tumult began to break out. A slave revolt in Sicily, a violent demand for redistribution of land and for restrictions of the power of the senate, the massacre of the reformers in the streets of Rome by the organized forces of the aristocratic party in the senate, all these heralded the onset of civil strife.

The conflict came to a head through the action of two plebeian tribunes, sons of a marriage between a Scipio and a Gracchus. The senate had been willing to exclude itself from commerce in order to exclude the *equites* from politics. Tiberius Gracchus admitted the *equites* to political and administrative duties. He and his brother in effect attempted to redistribute the authority of the senatorial and popular classes; at the same time they attempted to redistribute the ownership of the cultivated land in Italy. They failed in these attempts. But they established the cleavage of the nobility into two parties: the conservative majority, the *optimates*, and the reforming minority, the *populares*. The conflict of these parties occupied the Roman world for a century.

Between the two parties in the senate, the *optimates* and the *populares*, there were two issues. One was a constitutional issue. It concerned the rules of government, the relative rights of the senate and the Assemblies of the people, the Roman citizens who now for the most part lived too far away to vote in any case. The other was the economic issue, the management of the land of Italy; and the division of the spoils of empire, the whole surplus wealth and accumulated treasure of the western world.

Political party however is too gentle a word to apply to this situation. The habit of ruthless aggression in which they have never been surpassed was aggravated by the flow of wealth into Italy—and in their possession. The machinery of government intended for a small city state was hopelessly distorted by the new powers attached to it. The nicely adjusted checks and balances by which the separate orders in Rome had regulated their interests dissolved under its influence. It was then that Juvenal's bread and circuses acquired their meaning and that the hired assassin began to play his part. And the heroism of soldiers was entirely at the beck and call of one after another of the most vindictive and unscrupulous politicians of the time.

So it was that Marius, Cinna and Sulla, Pompey and Caesar, Antony and Octavian contended for power. Whether their aims were directed to maintaining or displacing the governing class or particular allies or rivals, the result of victory was always a massacre of the defeated party, and the confiscation of their estates, a process dignified under the legal name of proscription.[1]

The struggles of the civil wars devastated the cultivated land of central Italy and depleted the stock of people who had cultivated and also defended its soil. From neither of these disasters did the heart of the Empire ever fully recover. But out of them came a constitution which was capable of governing that Empire and a class of people which was capable of working the constitution.

It happened in this way. In the decade 90 to 80 B.C. the unprivileged Italian allies or subjects of Rome, peoples whose loyalty and strength had saved

[1] If you will not tell us whom you are going to kill, Sulla was asked in the senate, will you not tell us whom you intend to spare? So Plutarch puts it.

Rome during the war with Hannibal, attempted to throw off her yoke. The confederate rebels profiting by the disunion of their rulers nearly succeeded in making themselves the masters of the city and hence of the Empire. The upper classes of Etruria and Umbria with their property interests and marriage connections saved the situation in the first instance (according to Syme). But two lasting remedies were discovered. On the political side, the extension of the franchise to the Italian peoples south of the Po reduced the rebellion of the cities. And on the military side, the destruction of their leaders, the transfer of their lands to the ownership of Roman citizens, and the planting of 100,000 Roman veterans on the conquered territories, all these steps broke the resistance of the mountain tribes to Rome.

Table 17. *Time Chart of the Dictators*

Massacre of Gaius Gracchus and his partisans		121 B.C.
War on Jugurtha, King of Numidia		112–105
MARIUS, the victor, as consul, reforms the army		105–100
Italian cities and tribes form *Conjuratio Italiae*		95–90
Roman citizenship for all south of Po		89
{ Unconstitutional rule of CINNA in Rome		87–83
{ SULLA reconquers Greece from Mithridates		85
Samnite and Civil War; Sulla dictator; proscription; constitution restored		83–79
Rise of POMPEY and CRASSUS		76–60
slave rebellion of Spartacus		73–71
Pompey given power to clear the seas		67
—annexes Syria and Judaea		65, 63
CAESAR joins in Triumvirate		60–53
commander in north: conquers Gaul		59–49
Pompey sole consul		52
Caesar crosses the Rubicon: dictator		49
defeats Pompey at Pharsalus		48
reconquers Anatolia, Africa and Spain		47–45
assassinated by 'republicans'		44
Second Triumvirate: republicans defeated at Philippi by ANTONY and OCTAVIUS		42
Empire divided		42–31
Antony's fleet scattered at Actium; Egypt occupied		31
Octavius' curriculum of promotion:—		
Caesar instructs senate to create him a patrician	45	
adopted as son in Caesar's will	44	
declares himself *imperator*	38	
elected consul	31–23	
elected *princeps senatus*	28	
takes the name or title of *Augustus*	27	
assumes *tribunicia protestas* and (jointly with Agrippa) *imperium proconsulare*	23	

Note:

The decisive three battles in 48, 42 and 31 were all fought in the Greek area: Thessaly, Macedonia and Epirus.

These changes were designed to meet the urgent needs of war; but they completed a long transformation in the character of Italian society. A uniform governing class was established throughout Italy, speaking a uniform Latin language with a cultivated accent, and looking to Rome as the focus of their national pride. And of course calling themselves Roman. At the same time Rome had become the seat of a government which appeared more and more to represent this Italian governing class. The senate depleted by proscriptions was enlarged first by Sulla to 500 and then by Caesar perhaps to 900. The enlargement was based no longer merely on ancient Roman ancestry and even local Roman interests, but rather on loyalty to the dictator. Thus the genetic basis of the governing class was rapidly broadening with immediate effect. At each new crisis the executive powers in the state were passing into the hands of the man who was most effective as military commander and civil administrator. Such a man sometimes happened to be a statesman.

Indeed the period of the civil wars which brought the old landowning senatorial class to ruin was marked by the emergence of a number of individuals of rare and varied genius. These men were all of them of obscure or mixed origin, outside the close-knit consular families of the last century. Two, Sulla and Caesar, bore famous patrilinear names. Marius who reformed the army, and Cicero who reformed the speech and thought of Rome, were new men from Arpinum. Pompey who cleared the seas and conquered the east came from Picenum. Was he of Etruscan or Illyrian extraction? It no longer mattered. Caesar's nephew and adopted son Octavius was the product of a union of impoverished patricians and enterprising provincials, the first of a new hybrid race. It is his ancestry and posterity, his character and work, that must now be considered together.

13

AUGUSTUS AND THE EMPIRE

I. THE RISE TO POWER

THE YOUNG MAN OCTAVIUS was wintering in Appollonia, an old Corinthian colony on the opposite side of the Adriatic, when he heard of Caesar's assassination, and realized that he was now Octavianus and Caesar's adopted son. He, and probably no one else at that moment, caught a glimpse of the past and the future in their perspective. For, like Alexander, and at the same age, he was the contested successor of a great ruler. But the ruler this time was greater and the succession was to be more greatly contested: indeed throughout the same passage of time, the thirteen years that had been allowed to Alexander to conquer and rule his Empire. For Octavian had to begin almost where Caesar had begun, almost at the beginning.

Not quite at the beginning however. Caesar had mastered the Empire by force of arms and Rome itself by force of character. Rome had not seen much of him since he went to Gaul fifteen years before his death. Caesar's conquest of Gaul he had publicly intended to give Rome a frontier safe against the barbarian attacks which had repeatedly endangered the Republic. He succeeded in this aim and the frontier he won, and the nation he made within it, became in a sense the bulwark of Roman civilization for two thousand years. But Caesar had also a personal and private aim. He wanted to provide himself with the means of taking over Rome itself: that means was a large army of veterans and a large fortune from the sale of captives as slaves. In this aim he also succeeded. The first achievement dazzled the people, the second scared the senate. The two together meant that the name of Caesar had come to be a title of honour and power in itself. It needed no *Magnus* to make it seem great.

Octavian of course bore that name: *Julius Caesar Octavianus*, and he used it to unite the party opposed to the assassins, to establish his partnership with Antony, to divide the Empire with him, and finally to overthrow him. He was a consul at twenty and at thirty-three he had succeeded as ruler of the Empire.

But while Octavian was using Caesar's name to reach Caesar's goal—the government of the Empire by one man—he did so by avoiding the warfare which had made Caesar's name; and by avoiding also the titles of dictator or king, which had seemed the fitting recognition of Caesar's conquests.

In all this Octavian was helped by the disasters as well as the glory inherent in Caesar's career. More than a million men (on Pliny's estimate) had died in Caesar's fifty pitched battles; half of them would be Italians. To this fearful price were soon to be added the list of men proscribed by Antony and Octavian. Three hundred senators and 2000 knights were named and half perhaps were butchered. They included Cicero whom Octavian had called father. The chiefs were eliminated in order to get control of Italy; their followers in order to pay the armies with the confiscated estates.

The loss of life among the warlike leaders of Roman society had at last reached the point where the survivors preferred a peaceful policy and where the political and unwarlike gifts of Octavian began to be valued as a virtue, a virtue never acknowledged in Rome before, and acknowledged now only because the pure Roman Republican nobility had ceased to exist.

This was a transformation that we can understand because Europe has seen it many times repeated. We can also understand why, the capacity for civil war having failed, a capacity for foreign conquest also faltered. Great armies and great generals (though no longer of the old patrician families) were to keep Rome's frontiers in the coming centuries. But it had become an effort. And in the policy of the Empire it became clear that a great expansion into Central Europe had now become too heavy a commitment. The limited engagement to invade Britain was thought to be a sufficiently arduous and glorious substitute for the too ambitious conquest of Germany. There would not have been this retrenchment, still less a retreat, if the old foundations of Roman war-making, patrician and peasant, had not been destroyed, uprooted or dispersed, in the last wars of the Republic.

Octavian thus found himself at the head of a State whose people were ready to live, for the first time in their history, without war. But it was a people still unwilling to change its forms of life in other respects. Educated and uneducated, rich and poor alike, they still wanted to keep the forms of the Republic under which they had grown great.

Fig. 10

The growth of Roman power from the first Punic war (264 B.C.) to the reign of Antoninus Pius (A.D. 142). The dates are those of acquisition arbitrarily assessed since the Romans in general *annexed* barbarians but *liberated* or confederated Italians and Greeks, each process advancing by expedient steps. Notable instances are the destruction of Carthage (149 B.C.), the fall of Numantia in Spain and the bequest of Pergamum (both in 133 B.C.), the seizure of Egypt on the death of Cleopatra, the campaigns of Agrippa and Tiberius in the north. Further, three territories shown by double dates were relinquished and also north Britain whose date is uncertain: Germany by Augustus (A.D. 9), Armenia and Mesopotamia by Hadrian (A.D. 117) and Dacia when invaded by the Goths (A.D. 250).

The important fortified *limes* marked are in Britain, Germany (built by Domitian, A.D. 88) and Dacia (after Trajan). The line from Africa to the mouth of the Danube separates Greek and Latin speech in the third century.

After Grundy (1925); F. Van Der Meer (1954); L'Italia Storica (1961)

THE ROMAN EXPANSION
SCANDIA
Antoninus 142 AD
Hadrianus 122 AD
44 AD
GERMANIA
7 BC–9 AD
88 AD
SARMATIA
MARE CASPIUM
GALLIA
50 BC
RHÆTIA
NORICUM
15 BC
PANNONIA
9 BC
DACIA
105–250 AD
PONTUS EUXINUS
PARTHIA
ARMENIA
114–117 AD
GALLÆCIA
Lugdunum
G. CISALPINA
121 BC
NARBONENSIA
45 BC
133 BC
HISPANIA
206 BC
DALMATIA
167 BC
MŒSIA
29 BC
THRACIA
46 AD
BITHYNIA
GALATIA
25 BC
CAPPADOCIA
17 AD
MACEDONIA
168 BC
Pergamum
133 BC
Ephesus
CILICIA
MESOPOTAMIA
Antiochia
SYRIA
Seleucia
Capua
Tarentum
Saguntum
Car. Nova
Gades
Carthago
Syracusae
MELITE
CRETA
CYPRUS
65 BC
JUDÆA
Petra
A. PETRÆA
112 AD
ARABIA DESERTA
42 AD
MAURETANIA
NUMIDIA
105 BC
Leptis
Alexandria
CYRENAICA
LIBYA
31 BC
ÆGYPTUS
ARABIA FELIX
LATIN
GREEK
Roman Federation 268 BC
Lost 216; recovered 202 BC
Gained 239 BC
Gained 206–133 BC
Annexed 149 BC
Temporary frontiers
Limes
Permanent frontiers of Empire
J.S.S.

The titles of its officers and the temples of its gods, people of all ranks wished to preserve. Both through sentiment and policy Octavian was entirely of the same opinion provided that the power remained in his own hands. If new consuls were needed every year he was prepared to nominate them. If the senate's authority was needed for legislation he was prepared to divide it by lot into advisory committees. If a *princeps senatus* and a *pontifex maximus* were required to preserve law and religion he might even be persuaded to do honour to these offices by taking them himself. He might also be willing to assume an ancient religious title such as, we have seen, concealed a monarchical character existing so very long ago. *Augustus* was the title courteously offered and decently accepted.

The real power however was a different matter. That went with the soldiers and with having the money to pay them. It also went with propaganda, with religion, with the smooth unassuming title *princeps*, a title which had no definition but the one it would acquire by use. The status of the ruler, defined by the skilfully permitted growth of usage, reflected what it would have been dangerous for the traditional precision of the Latin language to reveal, namely the racial and social diversification of the people he ruled. To his intimates and admirers Augustus was perhaps known by various uncomplimentary names. To the wider body of senators whose rank and movements he controlled (for they might not leave Italy without his indirect permission) he was known as a human and fallible *princeps*. To the Roman army he was seen in person as *imperator*. To the Roman people who worshipped his genius at the altars provided for his cult he was *divi filius*, the son of a god, as well as being *pater patriae*, the father of his people. But to the subject kings and peoples he was himself divine. *Omne ignotum pro magnifico*. In Egypt (as Syme puts it) he was the direct and proper successor to the Pharaohs and Ptolemies, the supreme king and god who allowed of no living competitor, no political or proconsular rival. And for us today: does not mankind of all races and persuasions still submit at long range to imperial propaganda by flattering Julius and Augustus with the ridiculous inconvenience of putting two long months together?

The political and religious status of ruler and ruled bound them together in a complex union or network. For military force, economic interest, family sentiment, religious superstition and historical experience all played their part in creating power and authority.

In organizing this power and authority Augustus showed a combination of two hitherto incompatible ancestral gifts, patrician pride and plebeian modesty. For he allowed himself to delegate authority to others who knew better and to do so on a scale which had never been known in government, least of all in Roman government, before. In following this practice to an extreme he created something new. In place of the tightly knit oligarchy of nobles or the lonely figure of Caesar the world was now governed by a large and newly co-ordinated group, an incipient establishment.

The first characteristic of this establishment was its contradictory composition. Its chief members had been chosen to make good the shortcomings of the *princeps*. Augustus was no great general. His greatest victories were won by avoiding battle. But he found an utterly reliable commander in Agrippa, the builder of the original Pantheon and the great aqueduct of Nemausus or Nîmes. This austere plebeian of unknown origin whose youthful abilities, like his own, had perhaps been picked out by Caesar, was willing to do the work while he handed the honours to his master. Again Augustus was no great connoisseur of the arts. His taste in theory and practice was plebeian. But he found in the Etruscan Maecenas an aristocrat who was able to organize learning and literature in the service of the State, and provide by the way an office of diplomacy and propaganda. Virgil, Horace and Livy could between them convince the world that the rule of Augustus was required by the laws of historical development and of religious prophecy.

These men were closest to the ruler. Others whose advice he could take were members of his privy council, men from outside the senate. They likewise had the diverse origins and talents needed and selected chiefly to assist Agrippa in managing taxation and coinage, developing mining, building roads, aqueducts and ports, and to assist Augustus in supervising the priesthood and reforming the calendar and the law.[1]

Table 18. *Origins of Latin Writers and Others in Order of Birth*

See *O.C.D.*, Grant and Pottinger (1960).

LIVIUS ANDRONICUS	284–204 B.C.	Tarentum (Greek)
PLAUTUS	*c.* 240–184	Sarsina, Adriatic port
ENNIUS	239–169	Rudiae (Calabrian)
TERENCE	*c.* 195–159	Carthage, slave
VARRO	116–27	Reate (Sabine)
CICERO	106–43	Arpinum (Volscian)
CAESAR	102–44	Rome, patrician
LUCRETIUS	*c.* 94–55	unknown
SALLUST	86–35	Amiternum (Sabine)
CATULLUS	84–54	Verona (Etruscan)
VIRGIL	70–19	Mantua (Etruscan)
MAECENAS	*c.* 69–8	Arretium (Etruscan)
HORACE	65–8	Venusia (Samnium), son of a slave
LIVY	59–A.D. 17	Padua (Etruscan)
TIBULLUS	54–19	Praeneste, equestrian
PROPERTIUS	*c.* 50–*c.* 10	Assisi (Umbrian)
OVID	43–A.D. 17	Sulmona (Samnite)
SENECA	5 B.C.–A.D. 65	Corduba, Spain
COLUMELLA	A.D. 10?–*c.* 70	Gades (Cadiz), Spain
PLINY THE ELDER	23–79	Verona (Etruscan)
LUCAN	39–65	Corduba, Spain
MARTIAL	*c.* 40–104	Bilbilis, N.E. Spain
JUVENAL	*c.* 50–*c.* 130	Aquinum, Latium
TACITUS	*c.* 55–*c.* 120	N. Italy?
SUETONIUS	*c.* 69–*c.* 140	Rome?
APULEIUS	*c.* 123	Madauros, African

[1] See Suetonius and Syme.

The chief of these servants of the new state Augustus had found everywhere except in Rome itself. So far as writers are concerned we know their origins very well (Table 18). But for the body of his civil service he very largely had to turn to the population of men who had been brought to Rome as slaves, the prisoners of war from the Greek-speaking east. Of the million inhabitants of Rome nearly half were slaves.[1] These men by heredity and training were able to provide him with the administrative and scientific techniques of the Hellenistic kingdoms. They laid the foundations of a new society. Notwithstanding its abuses, which were appalling at this particular stage of development, the Roman management of slavery must be given credit for the astonishingly rapid success of the new organization.

II. THE NEW DEAL

Under the Republic the man with senatorial ambitions was a man with senatorial connections. He had his permitted career with the ages fixed at which he might be elected to each office. This *cursus honorum* disintegrated during the civil wars. Under Augustus it reappeared in a new shape. All men might hope to achieve promotion but the promotion was now variably regulated for individuals and within their families. The numbers of slaves an owner might free were restricted. The freedman might enter the police; or through the civil service he might become an *eques* who might in turn command a legion, become a tribune and hence, after a further generation, his descendants might be senators. But through the army, not freedmen but only their sons, might rise through the rank of centurion to be *equites*. Under Tiberius and Claudius these rules were tightened and five generations of Roman citizenship had to elapse before the posterity of a slave could find himself wearing the red shoes of an order of society which had in the meantime been losing the reality of power.

Augustus thus promoted, and also restricted promotion, for servile and foreign elements which were a new governing class, a provisional establishment. At the same time he obviously recognized the conflict between his long-range genetic ideas and his practical and short-range policy. He, and perhaps his wife Livia even more, wanted to preserve the blood of the ancient Roman aristocracy from disastrous dilution. The surviving remnant must be encouraged to propagate. He did not know that the despised and dispersed Jews had solved this eugenic problem. Still less did he enquire how they had done so. On the contrary he tackled his problem in the accepted Roman and patrician way. He attempted the moral regeneration of the upper classes by statute law.

How did he proceed? In two *Leges Juliae* of 18 B.C., and again in the *Lex Papia Poppaea* twenty-seven years later, he legislated for the future of his race. These laws on the one hand prescribed taxes on bachelors and fines for adulterers of senatorial and equestrian rank. And, on the other hand, they promised promotion and gratuities for citizens who had legitimate children: ten gold pieces per head, Suetonius records. Further he restricted and

[1] Far too many, as Seneca pointed out later, to risk giving them a recognizable mark or costume (see Cowell and also Finley).

graduated the stages in the liberation of slaves and in the rights acquired by men and women who had been liberated: particularly no more marriage of freed women slaves to senators!

To make his point clear Augustus addressed the senate quoting the speech *de prole augenda* of Q. Caecilius Metellus Macedonicus. Here the consul of 143 B.C. discussed the desirability of increasing the birth rate and the possibility of making marriage compulsory with this end in view.[1]

These were policies both morally and racially conscious. They had begun probably long before the foundation of the city and they were to be continued as long as the Empire and its religion lasted. They were based on assumptions of heredity and selection readily understood in the ancient world where the principles of cattle-breeding were generally thought to be a sound guide for the management of human propagation.

Now on a modern genetic view at least in one respect these principles never had a better chance of success: the immense heterogeneity of Roman society gave selection the freest possible play. They failed however because they made certain assumptions, big and little, which to us are obviously fallacious.

What were their fallacies? The first was that the Roman governing class was well fitted to deal with conditions in the world which they had partly made themselves. But, as we can see, the conditions they were fitted to deal with were those they had already destroyed. Military expansion had been replaced by peaceful maintenance. A small state had been replaced by a vast federation. Racial unity and moral coherence had been replaced by an utter diversity of character and aims only momentarily concealed by a peace of exhaustion. The Roman governing class, having achieved its aim, had nothing else to do. It had lost its conscious purpose, the basis of its assortative mating and hence its social coherence. As a class therefore it disappeared. How and where it went we shall have to enquire.

The second fallacy was due to failure to see the paradox of Rome's position. For Roman and Italian society, while culturally and politically dominating the Empire, was physically and biologically only a small and dependent part of the Empire. And the dominance was to give way to the dependence, for reasons we shall examine, after only a few generations.

But before looking at the Empire we must glance at what was happening in Rome itself. Already in his time the government of Augustus proved incapable of regulating the flow of wealth into the city. In spite of his apparent power and glory the ruler's policy to his capital continued to be governed by fear. He had his praetorian guard composed of nine cohorts of true-born Italians in Italy. He also had his personal bodyguard composed of equally

[1] One of the ways in which the laws of Augustus acted to change the rate of propagation differentially among classes was in discouraging infanticide by exposure (*expositio*) among citizens. The exposure of their male children was already forbidden by law. Now the exposure of females may have been reduced. Among slaves on the other hand the issue was primarily commercial between killing of females and castrating of males. The sex-ratio of nearly two-to-one in tomb inscriptions suggests that more female than male infants were killed (Tenney Frank, 1916; see also Buchan, 1937; *C.A.H.* 10, ch. 14).

true-born Germans in Rome. The two together did not enable him to dispense with the practice of keeping the citizens quiet by offering them bribes; by the policy of giving them *panem et circenses*. The phrases of Juvenal seem to be a commentary on the reforms of the *princeps*: those reforms were drowned in the wealth of the great city.

Hardly less serious was the inability of Augustus to control the behaviour of his own family. To understand this we must look more clearly at the character of the man himself and see what kind of family his political and dynastic ambitions had burdened him with.

III. THE MAN AND THE DYNASTY

The private character and the public actions of Augustus have to be understood in the light of his ancestry and his marriages.

Two opposed interpretations there may be of his gifts. Either he was a man of genius and his work was the product of far-seeing statesmanship dedicated to the creation of a society and a system of government which should endure—as indeed it has endured, in some senses, to the present day. Or he was a man exactly fitted to the needs and opportunities of his situation by a frigid temperament, a slow intelligence, a snobbish deference to antique social status, and a willingness to follow advisers shrewder and more imaginative than himself.

Between these two views of Augustus our knowledge of his ancestry enables us to steer a middle course. He was the first ruler of Rome with an ancestry fitting him to see both sides of the question in the long conflict between nobility and people. While his puritanism and his superstition were merely old-fashioned Roman, surely some of his necessary conviction in his governing role, and his happiness in exercising it, must have come from the Julian family. Surely also his understanding of the common people, his patient application to business, his thrifty finance, his snobbery or deference to high birth and his lack of chivalry must have come from his middle class ancestors.

All of these characteristics combined to meet the needs of the time. And not only of this time for they met the needs of a whole age. Many of those who followed him, probably all of those who were later to succeed in the office he had created, had the same new and double origin which hereditary succession in the Roman Empire, for reasons we shall see, managed to stabilize.

So much for the man. Now let us look at his marriages and his relations with women (Pedigree 10).

He began as Octavian, the consul, aged twenty, with a betrothal of marriage to *Servilia*. It was unconsummated. Next, to please his troops and placate his ally or rival, he married Antony's stepdaughter *Claudia*. The marriage was again unconsummated (Antony, to square accounts, married his sister Octavia but he begot several children). Thirdly, Octavian married, as the third husband, *Scribonia*. No one, certainly not Octavian, liked Scribonia and on the day she gave birth to his child Julia—the only child he

Pedigree 9. Family of Caesar: Stage I, Dictatorship

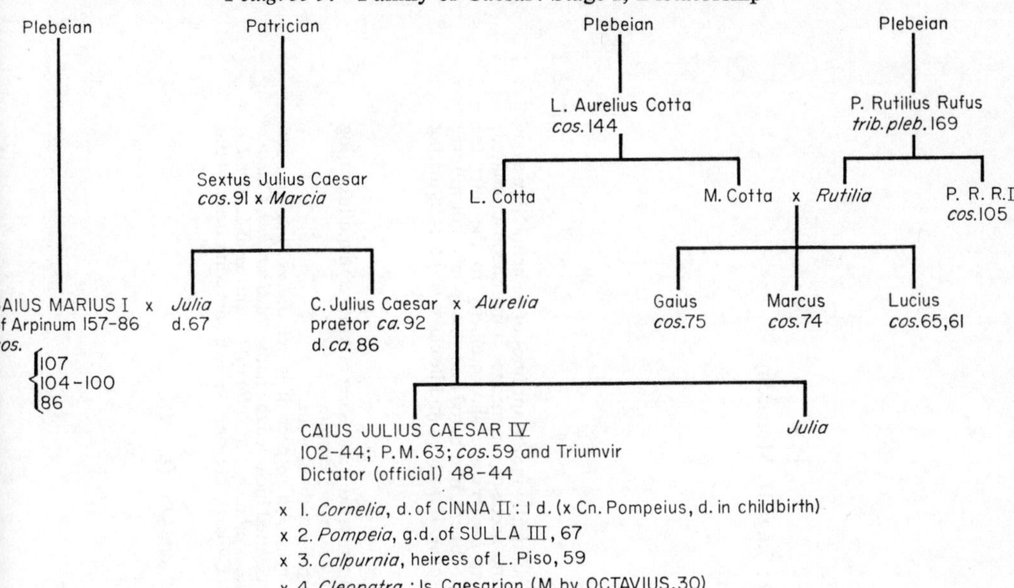

Notes:

i. This branch of the *Caesar* family has no close connection with the consular family of the same name. Julia's father and brother attain office after, and on account of, her marriage to *Marius*.

ii. The interrupted line of effective dictators is shown in capitals, numbered: I–IV. Marius, Cinna, Sulla and Julius.

claimed or acknowledged—he divorced her to marry again. His fourth wife, *Livia Drusilla*, was at her marriage six months pregnant by her previous husband whom she had first to divorce. Her two sons, Octavian's stepsons, by this husband were Drusus and Tiberius.

Octavian had now reached the prime of manhood. He was twenty-four. He lived with Livia for the remaining fifty-three years of his life and reign. But he had no children by her. Politically and socially, however, the marriage was a success. They were of the same hybrid origin. And, though her mother's family was as modest as his father's, her father's family were Claudians even more exalted than the Julians: according to Syme they turned the political scales in his favour.

The evidence so far suggests that Augustus' marriages, his infidelity to the first three and his fidelity to Livia, were all equally political. Livia was less a wife than a political partner. Like the sybaritic Maecenas and the puritanical Agrippa, she was his guide, philosopher and friend. His emotional and physical character, sexless and heartless, thus deprived Augustus of the possibility of establishing a dynasty by producing sons. But in his political dealings it was a source of strength. Take Cleopatra. Caesar and Antony had gone to Egypt partly for Cleopatra and had begotten her sons. Not so, young Octavian. He went there for her kingdom and her money; and he killed her

Pedigree 10. Family of Caesar: Stage II, Monarchy

The family of Augustus to show the social origins of the politically important lines of descent. Numerous kindred, mostly murdered (as in other pagan dynasties) and accessory marriages some unconsummated, mostly without surviving issue, are omitted. The consular *insiders* are shown chiefly to the left; the provincial and commercial *outsiders* are shown to the right. Rulers, numbered and in capitals, fall in three groups: (i) Generals: I and III outbred patricians; (ii) Statesmen: II outbred middle class; (iii) Misfits arising from inbreeding following outbreeding: IV, V, and VI.

Notes:

i. Cleopatra by Antony had two sons and a daughter who married Juba, King of Mauretania, illustrating the illegitimate genetic dispersal of the Roman nobility over the Empire.

ii. *Agripinilla* ignoring the incest laws also married her uncle without issue.

iii. *Julia* (i) was banished for treasonable sexual irregularities in respect of which *Jullus Antonius*, son of *Antony* and *Fulvia*, was executed, while the nobles relegated included the names of *Gracchus*, *Claudius Pulcher*, *Cornelius Scipio* and *Quinctius Crispinius*. In the similar case of *Julia* (ii) her husband *L. Aemilius Paullus* was executed. Her daughter's daughter *Junia Calvina*, her only known surviving descendant, was relegated for incest (Syme).

After Münzer 1920, Syme 1939, and O.C.D. 1949.

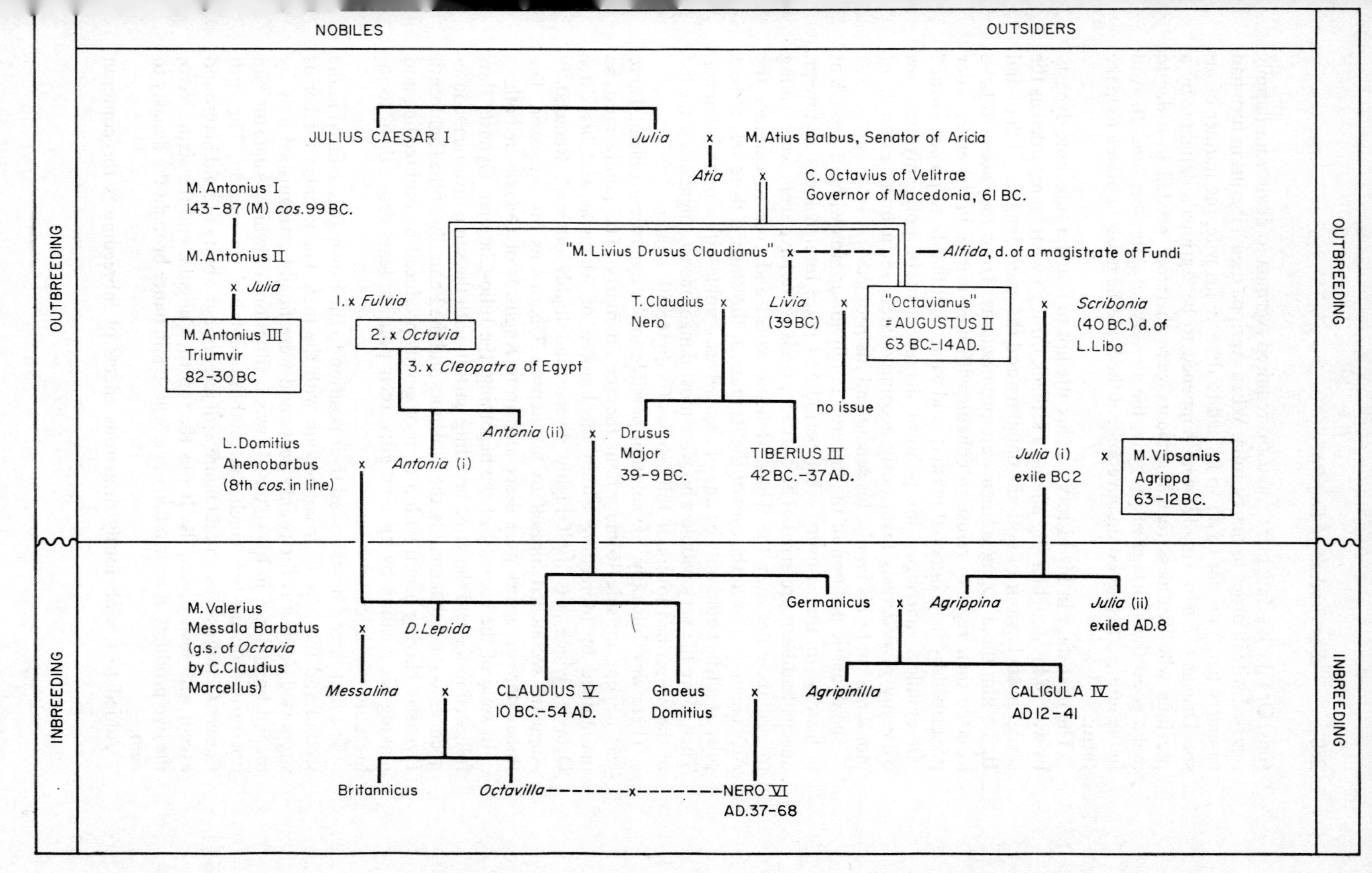

NOBILES
OUTSIDERS
OUTBREEDING
INBREEDING
JULIUS CAESAR I
Julia
x M. Atius Balbus, Senator of Aricia
Atia
x C. Octavius of Velitrae
Governor of Macedonia, 61 BC.
M. Antonius I
143–87 (M) cos. 99 BC.
M. Antonius II
x Julia
M. Antonius III
Triumvir
82–30 BC
1. x Fulvia
2. x Octavia
3. x Cleopatra of Egypt
"M. Livius Drusus Claudianus" x
Alfida, d. of a magistrate of Fundi
T. Claudius
Nero
Livia
(39 BC)
"Octavianus"
= AUGUSTUS II
63 BC.–14 AD.
Scribonia
(40 BC.) d. of
L. Libo
no issue
L. Domitius
Ahenobarbus
(8th cos. in line)
Antonia (i)
Antonia (ii)
Drusus
Major
39–9 BC.
TIBERIUS III
42 BC.–37 AD.
Julia (i)
exile BC 2
M. Vipsanius
Agrippa
63–12 BC.
M. Valerius
Messala Barbatus
(g.s. of Octavia
by C. Claudius
Marcellus)
D. Lepida
Germanicus
Agrippina
Julia (ii)
exiled AD. 8
Messalina
CLAUDIUS V
10 BC.–54 AD.
Gnaeus
Domitius
Agripinilla
CALIGULA IV
AD 12–41
Britannicus
Octavilla
NERO VI
AD. 37–68

sons. Or take his daughter: Augustus required Agrippa to divorce his happily married wife in order to marry Julia. When Agrippa died Tiberius in turn had to marry her. In order to do so he had to divorce his wife, the mother of his son Drusus (32 B.C.–A.D. 13) who happened to be Agrippa's daughter by a previous wife. Ruthless rearrangements were therefore needed in order to make good the shortage of progeny, the sterility, of Augustus himself. And in the interests, as he would have said, of the State, he never hesitated to make them.

The next stage in his history was his attempt to found a substitute dynasty by way of his daughter. It suffered a setback through what he regarded as the sexual misbehaviour of both the daughter and the granddaughter, Julia I and II. To him these young women were promiscuous. To us they seem to have asserted their right to refuse to cohabit with men merely in the exact order prescribed by their imperial master. And what right had he to preach virtue? His childless marriages, his political management of polygamy, and his company of pederasts luxuriously accommodated, set a queer example of moral reform to his family, his senate and his people.

The dynastic position of the imperial family group was without precedent in history. In almost every other period and place foreign kings or foreign queens had been preferred. The Macedonians, as we have seen, were willing to cast their net over the whole Hellenic world and even to embrace the Achaemenids. But in the eyes of the Romans at this stage, if there was to be a ruler at all, he could only be one of themselves, a noble with a patrician name. These were the very people who were most dangerous to Augustus as the list of the proscribed lovers of Julia shows (Pedigree 10, notes).

There was thus only one solution possible to the dynastic problem. There was no one outside Rome whom they could marry. The family must be maintained by inbreeding within the kindred of Augustus and his sister Octavia, which was itself highly diverse and highly outbred. Reluctantly Augustus reconciled himself to his stepson Tiberius as his successor. The three later successors were descended from Augustus or Octavia or both.

In spite of the contrast at the beginning, the Julio-Claudian Dynasty thus followed in the end the same breeding pattern with the same historical consequences as the Achaemenids, the Ptolemies and the Pharaohs of the Eighteenth Dynasty. Having begun with a man of genius produced by outbreeding and making his position by his own gifts, their political fears drove them to inbreeding which led to failure.

The first three Caesars owed their position to their own gifts assisted in the second and third by their connection with the first. The talents of Tiberius supported Augustus for twenty years and were finally extinguished only by mental breakdown in his sixties. It was a situation for which Augustus had not provided and for which the establishment had no remedy. The fifth Caesar, Claudius, was an odd figure with just enough ability to hold his ground except with his womenfolk. It was the fourth, Caligula, and the sixth, Nero, the two products of cousin marriage, whose unbalance brought the dynasty to ruin.

Added to the obviously disastrous effects of inbreeding is the common disease of polygamous dynasties for which the Achaemenids and the Ptolemies again provide a model. It is that each heir attempted to kill all his possible rivals as soon as he inherited the power to do so. Augustus killed Caesar's and Antony's sons. Tiberius killed Julia's son by Agrippa and the toll of murder grew until, with the death of Nero, no male descendant of Augustus survived. The only surviving line was that of Julia I—Julia II—Aemilia—and the Julia Calvina referred to by Suetonius. By four generations of female descent the divine blood was thought to be watered to an innocuous dilution. They were no longer murdered; they merely dissolved in Roman or cosmopolitan society.

IV. THE SUCCESSION OF CAESARS

As the basis of government was broadened, first under Caesar and then under Augustus, the official interest in the diminishing ancient ancestry was itself continually increasing. In claiming descent from kings and from gods, the Julian line was pandering to the deepest longings of the new society. So long as it was a Roman line the ruler, the *princeps*, was the object of religious awe by virtue of his lineage. With the extinction of the line the first step was taken in dissolving the special relation of the ruler to the capital and of the capital to the Empire.

After Nero every ruler took the title of Caesar, adopting himself as it were into the extinct ruling family. But there was no longer a connection by descent. The Flavians, a Sabine family, probably like Augustus of mixed origin, acquired their power through the command in the army of the first two and were extinguished by the failure of the third. Following Domitian came a series of emperors who were strong enough to nominate their successors and wise enough to nominate capable successors. That is, until Marcus Aurelius, having married his first cousin, nominated the product of their marriage, the lamentable Commodus who was, none too soon, assassinated.

The four men, Trajan, Hadrian, Antoninus Pius and Marcus Aurelius, were all derived from Romans who, as we shall see, commonly migrated to the Spanish and Gallic provinces and married into the native governing class. They begot the ablest of rulers after Augustus; they were also the first rulers to see the Roman Empire from outside Italy; to see it therefore in some sense as we see it today.

After Marcus Aurelius, however, the evolution of the Empire had carried it beyond the position at which a continuous centralized authority could make itself felt. The army, as Septimius Severus discovered, was the sole continuous source of power. And the army was ceasing to be one army but a number of armies attached to different provinces and different generals who continually in the third century disputed the succession in civil war.

In the absence of a governing class based on hereditary proprietorship or priesthood, an hereditary military caste had taken over control. This is the characteristic solution at all times in states which suddenly expand beyond the traditional means of control. The size of the Roman Empire, the appearance of regional cleavages within it, the impoverishment of its Italian centre, the intermittent pestilences and the weight of barbarian attack all made the break up inevitable. Only the originality and resources of Diocletian and Constantine delayed and partly averted the catastrophe.

V. THE EVOLUTION OF THE EMPIRE

a. Races and Languages

The Empire of Augustus was inhabited by about 60 million people. They increased perhaps to 100 million by the time of the first plague in A.D. 168 and thereafter diminished. These people were divided in their racial and geographical origins, in their occupational and social classes, in their religious customs and beliefs and in their speech. In forms of speech or dialect they were divided into two groups about equal in number at this time. The first were those destined to be preserved and to increase through their connection with literate and civilized languages; the second were those destined to decline or to disappear with their tribal organization (Table 19).[1]

Table 19. *Chief Languages of the Empire in Order of Numerical Importance*
After Goad (1958).

LITERATE (and civilized)	ILLITERATE (and tribal)
Greek*	Gaulish†
Latin†	German*
Egyptian*	Celt-Iberian and Basque*
Aramaic (and Hebrew*)	Illyrian*
Punic	Berber*
	Anatolian (various)
	Nubian

* directly surviving † indirectly surviving.

Under Roman administration, civil, religious and military, Latin extinguished all the illiterate dialects in the cities of the west during the first three centuries of Roman rule. And during the following centuries the Christian religion seems to have extended this domination to the agricultural country although it never captured the pastoral peoples, the Britons, Basques or Berbers. Meanwhile in the east Greek spread at the expense of the illiterate dialects of Anatolia as well as of Aramaic. Egyptian, on the other hand, held its own in town and country alike in the form we know as Coptic.

The Jewish population we are able to trace owing to its exact religious documentation. Jews had multiplied twentyfold since their exile and dispersal in the hands of the Babylonians. They now numbered, in addition to a couple of millions in Persia, Babylonia, Arabia and Abyssinia, between four and six millions in the Empire. Three-quarters already were Greek-speaking in Egypt and Anatolia. Perhaps one-quarter spoke Aramaic in Palestine and Syria.

[1] Between the two we might put the defeated and expiring Etruscan. Its speakers however were destined to take their revenge on the Latins through their descendants, since in Tuscany they moulded the form of modern Italian.

In the crushing of the Jewish revolts by Titus and Hadrian, this last fraction were largely destroyed, enslaved, or dispersed, and the survivors passed largely to the Greek- and Latin-speaking world. There they were subject to intermittent persecution and expulsion. A first colony had been driven out of Rome already in 139 B.C. and a second group were ordered to leave Italy by Tiberius. Some moved further west to Sardinia, Majorca and Spain.[1] Others founded the original Jewish colony in Cologne which persisted to give rise to the Jews of Germany and the Yiddish language.[2] But some managed to stay for good in Italy. In all these movements they carried with them and propagated their craftsmanship and commerce, their religion and learning. And to judge from the inscriptions in their Roman catacombs they continued till the third century to speak Greek. For majority populations, however, there was an administrative line separating Latin in the west from Greek in the east (Fig. 10).

b. Selective Migration

The most striking effect of the peace of Augustus lay in the opportunity it gave for the movement of people. This movement governed their re-settlement in new combinations and new societies. The possibility of free movement already existing in the peninsula of Italy had in two centuries been expanded to an area twelve times as large within the Empire. At the same time Romans were able to trade across Asia bringing silk from China; across the Indian Ocean bringing cinnamon from India by the monsoon; newly discovered by Hippalus; across Africa bringing ivory from the Niger; and across Europe bringing amber from the Baltic.

This trade was made easier when the roads built by Roman armies connected the capital with all the frontiers. It was also made safer by the elimination of the slave-trading pirates of Crete and Cilicia who had been enjoying a free run of the Mediterranean since the extinction of Tyre and Carthage and the chaos of the civil wars.

Meanwhile the armies themselves constituted peoples in movement. At the beginning Tiberius had seen the need to move the legions away from the newly occupied provinces in which they had been raised. This policy however met with difficulties in transport and slowly lost its effectiveness. Armies were recruited mainly from peasantry and they often had to be reinforced locally. As time went on they were concerned with defending their homelands from barbarian, that is foreign, invasion. Thus armies racially mixed in origin became professional and national military castes. Racial specialists, the Balearic slingers, Cretan archers and Numidian horsemen inherited from Hannibal and the Punic wars, disappeared. All equally were equipped with the Spanish sword introduced by Scipio. And when they were settled as veterans in *coloniae* they must have been further mixed, first, by their choice of new lands for farming and, secondly, by the fact that they took barbarian wives—legally so after Hadrian.

In this process of forming *coloniae*, new techniques of drainage and irrigation were provided by engineers largely of Italian or Punic origin. New

[1] See M. Grant. [2] Parkes (1963).

varieties of crops and new breeds of livestock also were taken from the Mediterranean into the northern countries to meet the needs of troops from the south. Notably the vine was planted in northern Gaul and the Rhineland.[1] At the same time the western Mediterranean was benefiting from the imported fruits of the Ancient East, the olive from Greece, the walnut and the cherry which Lucullus had brought from Kerasos in Anatolia. It was also benefiting from the new technique of grafting which allowed the cultivator to propagate improved fruits from single trees on wild stocks so that one variety could be spread in a few years over the whole Empire.

Who distributed these new crops and stocks and new techniques in the new lands of the west? Clearly Roman occupiers were chiefly responsible. Of these there were several kinds. After the battle of Pydna in 168 B.C., the lands of the conquered and undeveloped countries were open to purchase and protected occupation by the conquerors. Except to replace such destroyed cities as Carthage and Corinth, colonies with ready-made stratified classes in the old-fashioned Greek or Punic sense were no longer needed. Following the building of military centres, merchants infiltrated the tribal capitals. Wealthy men began to set up their villas in the country, recruiting local labour for agricultural and industrial development. And schemes were worked out for veteran colonization in regions, notably in the Danube and Rhine valleys, where drainage and deforestation made agriculture feasible.

The new societies that developed in these ways were always hybrid societies. It was not often that a settlement was established as at Carteia (near Gibraltar) specifically for the sons of mixed marriages. But that is what all Roman provincial settlements must have been. Modest members were the *considentes* or traders who settled in frontier posts. But at the top there were administrators of Roman origin intermarried with families of native chiefly or priestly origin who were now members of 'provincial councils'. From these were soon to arise men whose abilities took them back to the centre of imperial government in Rome, governors, commanders and writers.

The first of these were the writers from Spain. Next came the emperors from Spain and Narbonensian Gaul. All these probably owed something of their character to Punic and Greek admixture. Later the Punic and the Illyrian provinces in turn became important (Table 20).

Another indication of this reverse movement of talent to the centre is to be seen in the structure of the Roman senate whose members were nominated by the emperors in order to maintain a conservative and traditional bias. The members of the senate ceased to be chiefly Italian during the third century. The first strangers were again men from Spain and Narbonensian Gaul. Later, with the growth in their relative wealth and power, Asia and Africa increased in their contribution and began to outweigh the rest. Who were these men? The Spaniards and the Gauls must have been, like the emperors from these parts, the result of interbreeding between the Roman governing class and the leading citizens among the people they were governing. Senators from Africa and Asia could be genuinely local in origin but they also would often be the products of Roman dispersal and the creation of the

[1] See Marrison, 1957.

Table 20. *The Succession and Kinship of the Roman Emperors*

Illustrating the dispersal of authority and development of morals. See Clinton, *Fasti Romani* (1850); *O.C.D.* and Grant (1960).

X.E., Christian Expansion. X.P., Christian Persecution.

1. JULIO-CLAUDIAN DYNASTY: 27 B.C.–A.D. 68 (see Pedigree 10)		
27 B.C.–A.D. 14	*Augustus:*	adopted son of Julius Caesar
A.D. 14–37	*Tiberius:*	stepson of A.
37–41	*Caligula:*	g.g.s. and g.g. nephew of A. (assd.)
41–54	*Claudius:*	g.nephew of A., g.s. of Mark Antony (poisoned) X.E.1
54–68	*Nero:*	nephew of Caligula (suicide) X.P.1
	DISORDER	
2. FLAVIAN FAMILY: (Sabine family, commercial) 69–96		
69–79	*Vespasian:*	1st Jewish war, 66–70
79–81	*Titus:*	Colosseum built
81–96	*Domitian:*	X.P.2 (assd.)
3. ADOPTIVE SUCCESSION (Hispano-Gallic) 96–193		
96–97	*Nerva:*	senate now nominated, from east and west
97–117	*Trajan:*	R-Spanish family. X.E.2 begins
117–138	*Hadrian:*	1st c. once removed. 2nd Jewish war, 135. Married T's g. niece
138–161	*Antonius Pius:*	R-Gallic family
161–180	*Marcus Aurelius:*	nephew-in-law and son-in-law X.P.3. First plague: 165
180–193	*Commodus:*	son by cousin marriage, with Faustina (assd.)
	DISORDER	
4. MILITARY GOVERNMENT AND SUCCESSION: 193–283		
193–211	*Septimius Severus:*	Punic (b. Leptis Magna) internationalizes Praetorian Guard 202: X.P.4 in Africa and Syria
211–217	*Caracalla:*	son; titular citizenship for freemen in all provinces to increase taxes (assd.)
	DISORDER	
218–222	*Elagabalus:*	Syrian. X.E.3 begins
222–235	*Alexander Severus:*	churches allowed; bishops used as advisers
235–238	*Maximinus:*	Thracian-barbarian, rises from the ranks. X.P.5
238–249	DISORDER:	six tyrants. 1st period of invasions: Germanic 235–284
249–251	*Decius:*	Pannonian; killed on frontier Goths begin settlement within Empire X.P.5 (official) Cyprian martyred
251–254	DISORDER:	secession of Gaul and Syria Franks over-run Gaul and reach Spain Berber rising. Plague

4. MILITARY GOVERNMENT AND SUCCESSION: 193–283 (*continued*)

254–260	*Valerian:*	captured by Sassanids
260–268	*Galienus:* son	X.E.4 (assd.) 40 churches in Rome: Christian governors of provinces
268–283	Five Emperors:	Germans in Placentia, Vandals in Pannonia, Goths harass Greece and Anatolia by sea
268–270	*Claudius II*	
270–275	*Aurelian:*	Dacia lost; Rome and other cities walled

5. DIVIDED AND COLLEGIAL EMPIRE: 284–476
(see Hodgkin 1880)

284–304	West	East	
	Maximian	*Diocletian*	senior 'Augustus'
	Constantius I ×♀ g.n. of Claudius II	*Galerius*[1] ×♀	junior 'Caesar' 293

[1] Thracian, others Illyrian

Final X.P. (West 303–305, East 303–311)

306–324	Civil Wars
306/324–337	*Constantine the Great* son of C.I. divorced *Minervina* to marry *Fausta* d. of *Maximian*; executes *Crispus* his son by M. on ground of adultery; adopts Christianity 313–337; founds Constantinople 327–330
337–371	*Constantius* (assd.) *Constans* (assd.) *Constantine*, sons by Fausta
361–363	*Julian the Apostate*, half-nephew and son-in-law of Constantine; killed in Persian war

new governing class whose activities are described in the younger Pliny's letters.

The great reverse movement into Rome was however the movement of slaves. Usually the new slave market of Delos is spoken of as the great entrepôt of the slave-trade. But Rome itself (and its port of Ostia) was a second and crucial stage in their selection and distribution. Here one selected fraction were by manumission raised to the rank of freemen and clients of their former owners and in due course filled the trades and professions of the Empire. These were especially the Greek-speaking people who carried the diverse skills and culture of the east, Babylonian and Jewish, Persian and Phoenician. It was however free groups of craftsmen mainly passing through Alexandria who brought glass-blowing from Sidon to Campania and later to Gaul; and who established the wool industry in Lombardy which would later spread to Flanders where it may be said in twenty generations to have created a new race of people, the Flemings.

Another selected fraction, largely from the European frontiers, were destined for the gladiatorial schools and were sacrificed in appalling numbers to satisfy the perverted tastes of the Italian city populations. This practice was to continue in the west throughout the life of the pagan Empire and contribute greatly to its ruin. A third selected fraction was destined to agriculture in Italy and elsewhere. And since the supply of slaves greatly diminished after the wars of expansion ceased, this last fraction ceased to be expendable. Instead of suffering exposure or castration the slaves became a breeding community. These were slowly converted into a community of serfs attached to the land and owned by the landed proprietor.

All these movements were selective. The abilities and the inclinations of the migrant populations, slave or free, could never be without influence on their destination. That is why the great division between urban and rural populations persisted. Four-fifths of the Empire was based on agriculture. Most of this fraction stayed fixed at all times and what moved largely stayed in agriculture. One-fifth was in cities and it was this fraction whose migration from east to west altered the character of the western cities in the way that shocked well-bred Romans like Juvenal and Tacitus.

These people were continuing the movement from the Ancient East that had in the first instance established the Greek and Etruscan cities in Italy. They brought with them a culture which had now advanced another 700 years. They were no longer organized in contingents of fighting men but of slaves and traders. They were no longer men of the warrior class but of the trading, professional and intellectual classes. So far from being able to attack they were not prepared even to defend themselves. And coming in much larger numbers they brought with them their own well-organized imaginative religious rites of Greek, Egyptian, Persian and Jewish origin, the rites of the mystery religions.[1]

The orientalizing of the west was thus a process repeating in form but not in quality what had happened in Greece 700 and also 1700 years earlier. It profoundly changed the character and the destiny of the Roman Empire. It altered the military potential especially of the people of Italy. And it also altered their social theory. Here was a land situated in the middle of the Mediterranean whose people had conquered the Mediterranean and had been dispersed all over the Mediterranean. But it was now occupied by different people who no longer wished to conquer but were becoming, through their immigrants, more and more concerned with civilization.

It was a land at the centre of an Empire in which selective migration had completed its task of creating stratified societies of balanced character and multiracial origins, societies which fitted each region and each district to support itself with less and less trade, and less and less movement. The austere fighting Republic, the base for attack on all its neighbours, had become the most opulent and most vulnerable land in the western world.

[1] As Tenney Frank puts it: 'the mystery cults permeated' the west only to such an extent as the west was 'permeated by the stock that had created those religions'.

c. Sorting Out

The original movement might seem to have turned the whole Empire into a melting-pot in which all discrimination of race and class would disappear. To be sure people were mixed up geographically on an unprecedented scale. But the mixing was always selective: it was in direction of movement, in choice of occupation and association and breeding partners; and, of course, in the survival of offspring. All these processes continued with changing effect as the economic structure of the Empire crystallized in a new form.[1] The growth of local self-sufficiency and the reduction of trade—including the slave-trade—brought with them local inbreeding from which in the course of ten generations local differentiation of character began to appear; or rather to reappear, for the main agricultural basis of the population had not geographically shifted.

With the development of cities however a new kind of crisis had appeared. The original and persisting distinction of racial character and consequent opposition of behaviour and belief between town and country had grown into a political problem. This is difficult for us to understand in modern Europe since we are accustomed to the infiltration of countrymen into the neighbouring towns which has been gradually moulding their relationships over the centuries. But in the Roman Empire the great cities were all of eastern foundation. The early ones were Phoenician, Greek and Etruscan; the later ones were nominally Greek, planted by Alexander; and the Roman cities were derived from these early ones or from Roman garrisons with their eastern traders. These cities evolved the sophisticated character which we associate with Greek civilization and which was due to the specifically Greek principle of synoecism whereby different castes of society, soldiers, administrators, merchants and craftsmen learnt to live together. Meanwhile in the country quite a different kind of society was developing which was to underlie feudalism, the self-supporting estate, with no trade, no intellectual life, no literacy.

The local rural populations proved to be so stable that they did not quickly or easily migrate into the cities. The original opposition between city and country therefore failed to mellow. Doubtless it was fortified by extreme differences of culture and of language. It was also fortified by differences of religion which were hardly to be diminished by the conversion of townsmen to a new religion and their description of the countrymen as *pagani*.

The racial opposition between town and country, according to Rostovtzeff, found its focus and reached its climax in the anarchy of the third century. During this time the greatest cities of Gaul and of the east were looted. The people of Autun and Lyons, Antioch, Alexandria and Byzantium were massacred by insurgent peasant armies.

The process of local crystallization was also reflected in the development of the army and its use in the development of agriculture.

From the time of Severus the citizen-legionaries began to be recruited in the region they were garrisoning; they were given land on completion of their

[1] Discussed by Heichelheim, Westermann and others.

service. Then, in 212, all free-born provincials became citizens. The distinction between the legions and the auxiliaries recruited from the adjoining tribal peoples ceased. The holding of land became hereditary and carried with it the equally hereditary obligation of military service. Thus the whole organization, still known by its grand old names, was now split up into the foreshadowing of territorial and feudal fragments which moreover were increasingly, although not ostensibly, based on kinship. They presented a foreshadowing of a territorial or feudal society. The structure of the Empire, from a maximum of unity arising from fluidity at the beginning, had by its end achieved a maximum of disunity. This disunity arose from a degree of genetic sorting-out which it had never known before and was not to know again for another thousand years.

The consequence of inbreeding and genetic differentiation was thus the growth of local particularism which legislation could only accept and exploit. This had never been lost in the east where the populations even of the cities still traced their ancestry to the nations which had existed before Cyrus and Alexander. Egypt was the first to re-assert its individuality with the revival of the Coptic language. But in the west, dialects derived from Latin displaced the mother tongue. Each was forced into its own path of phonetic evolution through the racial differences between the people of Italy, Gaul and Spain and between the armies raised in these countries. In turn this differentiation must have helped to enhance the local differences in politics and religion and the cleavage of societies within the Empire.

It was thus the interaction of genetic, economic and administrative conditions which broke the Empire into the fragments whose reality was recognized by Diocletian in 288. After the tremendous impact of five centuries the two halves came apart. Each in Horace's phrase[1] had won a victory. But neither was subdued. They remained themselves still fundamentally, racially, genetically different. Thereafter east and west continually diverged. The basis of their divergence seemed to be the supreme cleavage between the Greek and Latin languages and the culture they carried; but rather this was the expression of the difference. Underneath was the genetic cleavage between the nations so differently constructed despite the fusions, the migrations and the interactions of the past three millennia.

[1] Horace's epigram: '*Graecia capta ferum victorem cepit, et artes intulit agresti Latio*' (when Greece was conquered, she subdued her savage conqueror and introduced the arts to rustic Latium) reminds us that the poet, as the son of a slave, knew more about the Greek racial origins of Latin culture than he would be likely to declare (Table 18).

Part V

World Religions

The expansion of Rome opened Europe to the immigration of the eastern peoples who had created the arts and the ideas of civilization. Although their earlier origins were in Anatolia and Mesopotamia, Syria and Egypt they now spoke Greek or Latin. In their religious ideas what mattered was the contrast between the Jewish and the pagan. It was these people and these ideas which converted the literate Roman citizens, and later the illiterate barbarian kings, to the new religions demanding a respect for human life, admitting the unity of mankind, and questioning the virtues of war and slavery. Jewish ideas came to be reformed or distorted to accommodate these developments under the opposed forms of Christianity and Islam: opposed because they maintained their class structure in different ways. Meanwhile in India, a world of its own, the genetic separation of social classes itself became the means of unity and the chief end of religion.

14
CHRISTIANITY

I. THE SOCIAL PROBLEM

THE GROWTH OR ACTIVITY of the Christian religion was of no obvious public importance until the latter part of what was to be known as the third century of the Christian era. At that point the leaders of this religion, taking a new and longer view of the future of society, began to take part in a struggle for the control of the Roman Empire. The forces at work in transforming society were in this way themselves transformed.

In order to understand this delayed impact, the slow as well as the sudden processes of this revolution which affected thought and behaviour and social structure, we have to go back to its origin among the Jewish people in Palestine. Then we shall be able to follow the movements of these people, and the ideas, beliefs and practices they carried with them, westwards into Europe as well as westwards and southwards into Africa.

II. THE JEWISH REFORMATION

The people, and in consequence the beliefs, of the Jews passed the last centuries before the Christian era in a state of upheaval. The assaults of the decaying Hellenistic monarchies and their pretensions to religious authority had led to the successful rebellion of the Maccabees. A Jewish state had been established which, in turn decaying, was put by the Roman suzerains under the administration of Herod the Great. At the same time the Jewish religion—and people, for the two can never be properly distinguished—had expanded so that it now had over four million adherents scattered as a more or less irritating minority over the pagan world of three continents.

How had this expansion come about? Partly, we may be sure, it was due to the character and the practices of the Jews: their religious and genetic coherence, their cleanliness, their devotion to the family, their obedience to

Torah, the Law and the theory of the Law, and the bookish and bigoted understanding that they implied. These diverse properties and habits added up, as had been intended, to make for biological or racial success.

Beyond all this however the Jews had succeeded by conversion and conquest. Sometimes the two were synonymous. The Maccabee prince Hyrcanus I (134–104 B.C.) conquered Samaria in the north and Idumaea in the south and where he conquered he also circumcised. Polygamy also enabled the Jews to assimilate and improve[1] subject populations, multiplying both the people and the faith.

All this propagation meant hybridization and, as usual, the process can be best illustrated from the ruling families. The Maccabees burst on the Hellenic world as fanatical Jewish fundamentalists named Matthias, Judas and Simon. But in two generations they had become, by outbreeding, the Hellenic Hasmoneans now named Hyrcanus and Aristobulus, men far removed from the zeal of their Hebrew grandparents. Their successor, Herod the Great, half Nabataean Arab and half Idumaean, in the way of all usurpers, married the last heiress of the Hasmonean family: he raised and also destroyed the hybrid brood which ended monarchy in Israel.

Racial heterogeneity reached a peak in these turbulent times among the people as well as among their rulers. With it came unprecedented diversity of belief within the Jewish fold. It was a diversity which expressed itself in a rich flow of religious, social and political ideas, some shallow and crazy, others profound and creative. Jewish practice since the return from the Captivity had favoured just this flow of ideas. In place of the ritual sacrifice conducted by priests there had developed, as Parkes has explained, the habit of reading the scriptures in the synagogue or meeting place. It was a habit which had led to the people thinking for themselves. They had been thinking in a country open to the ideas of all the great ancient civilized people around them, people who were dominated, under Hellenism, not by the military castes who had made the ancient empires but by the professional, learned, administrative classes who had prospered and developed their own humanity beneath the glittering surface of the new states.

We understand very well from what has happened in later and quite recent times how reformation, and the rejection of priesthood, can arise when heterogeneous peoples begin to think for themselves. What follows is always a splitting into sects, some more primitive, some more advanced, than the orthodox practice; but all of them self-propagating and even self-supporting breeding groups; all of them angrily disputing. So it was with the Jews. There were the Sadducees, representing the exploiting class attached to the families of the High Priests claiming descent from Zadok. And opposed to them were the learned and liberal Pharisees softening the bloody, ruthless and primitive law in modern, humane and practical terms. But beyond these divisions of urbane society were zealous groups fired with a passion for prompt and radical solutions. Some of these owed their ancestry to the puritanical Rechabites (of II Kings 10: 15 and Jeremiah 15). Others like the Ebionites, perhaps the same as the Nazarenes, were led from the struggle with the powers of darkness

[1] Grading-up is the corresponding stockbreeders' phrase.

to develop notions such as that of an opposition in an after-life between heaven and hell. Others again like the Mandaeans who continue with us today, had an obsession of washing and a cult of baptism for the removal of sins. And in the background were the mystery cults of Anatolia and the derivatives of Persian Zoroastrianism; people with beliefs (like those described by Frazer) in a God whose death and resurrection are needed to revive nature in the spring of the year.

Five centuries of torment and anguish had followed the return of the Jewish teachers to Judaea, centuries passed under foreign oppressors, Greek and Roman, and marked by conflict between kings and priests who belonged to their own race or, like Herod, had been converted to their own religion. Need we wonder that in these circumstances Babylonian and Persian ideas made a deep impression on this suffering and imaginative people? Or that new sects flourished in proportion to the hope they offered of an escape from the miseries of material life into a world where, following Isaiah (11: 7), the wolf really would dwell with the lamb? To such causes we may attribute the appearance in Palestine and in Egypt of writings in Hebrew, Aramaic, or Greek which fall under the heading of *apocalyptic*.

The most notable of these writings date from the two centuries before and the first century after the Christian era. There was, for example, the Book of Enoch, part of which was indited in the little northern province of Galilee. For us their interest is twofold. They foretell the coming of an 'anointed one', a *messiah* who will save mankind, or those who deserve to be saved, from present suffering. Sometimes the reward on earth is immediately gratifying as where the righteous (among the males) will have the opportunity of begetting 1000 children before they die. Sometimes the bliss is to be that of a spiritual life in another world. And this other world is peopled with angels and devils of Persian origin who filled the gap left in simpler minds by the Jewish rejection of alien gods. Here we meet the seven heavens. Here also the four messengers of God, the archangels, Michael and Gabriel, Uriel and Suriel (or Raphael), appear. For a long time these names have lost their power as sources of moral guidance to mankind. But for many centuries they have had the illusion of reality for many ordinary people, an illusion which poets, painters and priests have been pleased to indulge.

Standing apart from such superstitions was the profound and austere teaching of the Essenes. This sect, known first from the writing of Josephus, has now been more fully revealed to us in its historic meaning by the discovery of the Qumran scrolls.[1]

The Essenes derived their teachings from the strict and uncorrupted Jewish scriptures. They regarded themselves as the one and only faithful remnant, the elect of the elect, the subject of a New Covenant with the Lord such as had been promised by Jeremiah. They were destined, if perfect, to be saved at the expected coming in the last days of the Messiah, the anointed messenger of the Lord. But they were open to admit converts both Jewish and Gentile. Admission, apparently by baptism in water, followed examination by strict rules and was subject to dangers of penance and expulsion. The community,

[1] Translated by Vermes (1965).

constantly engaged in the struggle between good and evil, was governed by the two hereditary orders of the Jews, the infallible priests, the true or pretended 'Sons of Zadok', and their assistants the Levites. Among the priests a leader, the anonymous Teacher of Righteousness, was celebrated, a man who laid down the rules of the community and who, following Pslams 50 and 51, preached good works in preference to devotion by the gift of animal sacrifices. This teacher, we are told, was persecuted and exiled, although probably not killed, by the kings or high priests of the time.

Among the Essenes there was a community, perhaps the one responsible for the scrolls of Qumran, practising monastic celibacy. The main body however was a breeding group whose rules embodied principles with revolutionary genetic consequences. What were these rules? In the first place, the Essene Rules forbade polygamy and uncle-niece marriage, two traditional breeding practices which were characteristic of the Jewish upper classes. In this reform was inevitably implied a new respect for women that had been excluded by the warrior codes of the pastoral peoples both Semitic and Aryan.

In the second place, the Essene Rules established the duties of the community to the poor, the stranger and 'the maid for whom no man cares'. In the third place, the rules united the faithful as a community by ritual ablutions, common property, common meals and the exclusion of eating (and hence of marrying) outside the group. All of these rules would be assisted by the keeping of their own calendar of feast days for these set them apart from the rest of the Jewish population; and indeed from the rest of mankind.

How novel, how revolutionary, were these rules? To be sure the notion that words of prayer and praise were more acceptable to God than blood sacrifices went back to the second Isaiah and reflected the advanced ideas of Jews and Greeks alike. But dogmatically asserted it meant a break with the theory and practice of both the priestly and warrior castes of the ancient world. And it led to the substitution of a milder symbolism of two kinds. First were the sacraments, common meals and other ceremonies whose words and gestures were designed to unite the community with God and with one another. And second was the giving of alms to the poor, of necessity their own poor, whose benefit represented a service to God. So eating, drinking, and social service were thriftily turned to serve the spiritual, social and material needs of the Essene community.

III. THE BIRTH OF CHRISTIANITY

The body of Christian beliefs had at its beginning a documentary basis in a number of books purporting to record the life of the founder of the Christian community. This founder was a Jewish teacher known by the name of *Jesus* and given the title of *the Christ* which are taken to be Hellenized forms of the Hebrew phrase: Joshua the Messiah. The events described in the books occurred about A.D. 30 among Aramaic-speaking Jews in Judaea and Galilee.

These books were, we believe, first compiled in Greek over forty years later in the decades following the siege of Jerusalem and the destruction of its

Temple in A.D. 70. The most convincing of them were the four gospels (or god-spels in Old English) which were later selected from a number of works of similar character. The 'apocryphal' gospels, some of which we still have, were then rejected.

Misgivings about the documentary basis of Christianity have given rise to such obvious questions as:

Was there one original person to be identified as Jesus?
If so, how far were the gospels a true record of his activities?
Again, if so, was his teaching original or unique?

Conflicting answers have been given to all these questions and always will be. But the last century's accumulated enquiries allow us to decide all the issues that matter to us. What we now know of the origin and spread of Christianity agrees so well with what we know of similar events in later times that our fundamental questions are answered.

In the first place, we may assume, indeed we have to assume, that Jesus lived, taught and died at the times and places required by the notable names given in the gospels, those of Herod the King, Pontius Pilate the Procurator of Judaea, and Caiaphas the High Priest.

In the second place, however, we have to admit that the miraculous elements in the stories were inserted by his reporters and editors. Swept away by the enthusiasm and the feeling of certainty that we always find in new converts, they introduced items in which they had complete faith; they hoped to arouse that same faith in others who heard or read the message.

At the beginning the miraculous items in the story brought conviction to many and doubts to few. Today the situation is reversed. It has been reversed by the growth of science and the spread of knowledge. But, even at the beginning, the gospels of different missionaries were addressed to the persuasion of different audiences. They stressed different kinds of improbable phenomena. Mark, the scribe of Peter, tells to the Jewish traders in Rome, a very plain and practical class of people, the plainest and least embroidered tale. For the Greeks, Luke adorns his narrative with Hebrew poetry, unfamiliar and sublime. For the later Hellenic people of Ephesus, John produces a remote and mystical interpretation. But all of them record the miracles of healing and feeding which experience has shown to be indispensable for the conversion of disease-ridden and famine-stricken people. In an over-populated country they were what the plagues had been for Joseph and the manna for Moses.[1]

It was Matthew's invention, however, that really made history. For the more sophisticated Jews in Judaea, Matthew introduces the details that are needed for the history of a Jewish Messiah: the resurrection and the ascension, the descent through a father of the House of David as well as the conception by a virgin without the help of such a terrestrial father: Isaiah 14: 7

[1] As Tyler has recently shown, the claim to have healed the bodies of the living rather than the promise to save the souls of the dead is what convinces and converts primitive people. That is in peace: in war the experience of victory conveys the message to the serving soldier.

becomes Matthew 1: 23. The contradiction could be overlooked for conception by a virgin mother was the attribute of any hero; if miracles were to follow the birth of an Alexander, a Scipio, or a Jesus, they must also precede it.

When we add to these elements of invention the fact that the teaching was not in its details original we might conclude that Christianity had a discreditable beginning, owing as much to what was false in it as to what was true. But it is the fact that we can now separate the false from the true in the gospels that enables us to see the strength, the unity and the boldness of the whole scheme. If the miraculous provided a lesson for the multitude, it was the ethical and social teaching and its mystical framework that mattered for apostles who were to teach more sophisticated people. Thus, though the separate elements were already known, the totality of them was something new. They put together the liberal opinions of the Jewish sects of the day in a practical and also in a poetic form with all the power of Jewish prophetic literature. It was not history; but as a whole, through being believed, it became history.

Reinforcing this coherence were the dramatic circumstances of the trial and crucifixion, foreseen by their victim as the fulfilment of the prophecies of Isaiah and Jeremiah and leading perfectly to the Christian doctrine of atonement. When it was added to the Jewish scriptures, this became a supreme doctrine. It supremely satisfied those who read and believed those scriptures in promising that one death would atone for all time for the sins of all believers. It demanded, to be sure, that those scriptures should be attached to the Christian gospels. But there they were, at once available throughout the Roman Empire, in the vernacular Greek of the Septuagint.

The founder of Christianity may have believed that the end of the world and the Day of Judgment were at hand. The apostle Paul, however, acted on the assumption that time remained for him to convert not only the Jews but the Gentiles as well. He was the first to see, perhaps in a blinding flash, that the mission of Jesus made it possible to pass over to the Gentiles the teaching, not only of Jesus, but of the whole Jewish scriptures as well. This is what the Jewish priestly kings had been trying to do within the scope of the Aramaic language and of the narrow lands in which it was spoken. But to a Jew like Paul speaking Greek, armed with the Septuagint, and the teachings of Jesus, and protected by the peace of the Roman Empire, suddenly the dizzy possibility became clear of uniting mankind in one belief. He could by dropping the pedantries of the law and by adopting the notion of redemption by a Saviour, to use Gibbon's words, convert a religion of defence into one of attack. He could unite the ideas of Greeks, Jews and Persians, bridge the gap between the prophets and the Stoics, and lead all peoples into one fold. It was an apocalyptic vision.

IV. SCHISM IN THE JEWS

So long as the Jewish city continued the Christian bishops of Jerusalem continued to be known as Jews: they were bishops who had been circumcised and also baptized. Thereafter the schism instituted by Paul split the Jewish community in two throughout the Roman world. Already in the time of Claudius, as Suetonius implies, the difference was causing public tumult in Rome. Soon in every city there were two sects disputing the loyalty of the Jews, two sects competing in numbers by conversion and by propagation.

Both sides were quickly aware of this competition and its effects showed in adjustment on the Christian side. The Christians were more flexible, not only because their doctrines were less established and still unwritten, but also because they were the more hybrid group, continually incorporating new Gentile converts of the most diverse origins. For they could convert by baptism on a scale with which orthodox Jews, painfully demanding circumcision and exact restrictions on food, competed at a disadvantage.

The contrast in genetic situation between the Christians and Jews was to become even sharper with the passage of time. For the mixed or multiracial urban Hellenistic community, which had assimilated nearly everything that mattered genetically in ancient civilization, now admitted under the name of Christian converts the one element it had earlier excluded, the Jews. To this new fertilizing process (or gene-flow, as we may call it) we may probably trace the intellectual leaders of the Christians of all later times. At the same time the faithful unconverted Jews continued to compete with the challenge of Christianity. Judaism in Anatolia continued to derive distinguished scholars from its Hellenistic converts.

Reflecting the struggle for the soul of the Jewish people was a long struggle over the texts. The Christian story of the Virgin Birth had been inserted by or in Matthew in order to appear to confirm the prophecy of Isaiah. Much earnest study culminating in the sixfold collation of Origen, the *Hexapla*, had been devoted to clarifying, comparing and completing the Septuagint and the Greek translations of the Hebrew scriptures. Naturally out of this assortment the Christians and the Jews (both of them often Greeks of Gentile origin) each chose the readings that suited their own interpretations and rejected the distortions of the other. In the first three centuries of the Christian era the two religions consequently diverged at just those points of scripture needed to sustain their doctrinal differences.

V. THE CHRISTIAN THEORY OF POPULATION

The doctrinal steps taken by the Christian teachers in these early years of competition with the Jews affected the future of Christians and Jews alike, that is as breeding populations. Indeed, as it turned out, they affected the whole future of Europe. There were several main issues: cleanliness, marriage and propagation; all of these were linked with the preservation of human life; all of them were vital for the control of the numbers and character, the quantity and quality of the population.

Christian ideas on cleanliness must be counted a step back from those of civilized people either pagan or Jewish. When Jerome came to Rome as an Illyrian immigrant he found a city with 900 public baths. But he felt that these resorts of profane pleasure would be better converted to sacred baptisteries. The man who had bathed in Christ, in his opinion, needed no second bath.[1]

The Christian rejection of washing and tolerance of filth was to continue down to our own day. It was to devastate Christian cities with plague, generation after generation. Milder epidemics began in Rome with Marcus Aurelius but became more serious with Justinian in Constantinople.[2] They continued, one disease replacing another, up to the last century in Europe. The damage was selectively disadvantageous to Christians in relation to Jews in the same cities; and also in relation to non-Christian cities, notably, as we shall see later, in Islam.

The consequences have been far-reaching. Until recently rules of hygiene have always depended on religion for their enforcement in multiracial and stratified societies. The right rules have therefore been indispensable for any religion that was to expand into warm countries with dense populations. Christendom had thus been permanently deflected away from southern countries by its neglect of cleanliness, its opposition to nudity and washing.

The second great issue was that of marriage as a social institution. When the Church began to take an interest in marriage it did so in order to control it in the interests of both society and itself. These two aspects of its own interests we can separate although the Church itself did not do so. It made marriage a sacrament, that is a rite controlled by priests. And it began to lay down the rules limiting its permission, its ceremonial, its social intentions and obligations, and its annulment.

In most of these steps the bishops found the Old Testament a better guide than the New. But in two vital respects they turned to the New: in widening the forbidden degrees of inbreeding and in narrowing the possibilities of polygamy. In the first instance, both of these innovations were no doubt favoured by the Church because they increased its power to interfere in what had hitherto been private concerns. Both of them had far-reaching consequences because they in fact restored a control of the breeding system by society, a control which had been loosened or lost in the course of the rapid numerical growth of pagan societies. They therefore had beneficial effects from which the Church itself gained power.

The third great issue was that of propagation. The early Christian Fathers and their contending sects were deeply divided in the course they should pursue in order to reconcile the Christian demand for chastity with the human need for love. In this conflict society's need for marriage and the Church's need for Christians won the day; if it had not done so the story would have ended there. Paul's recommendation that it was better to marry than to burn was the correct one and when the learned Alexandrian Origen rejected it, having himself castrated about the year 205, the Church rightly

[1] Other factors helping in the decline of washing were perhaps the decay of the Roman aqueducts and the Christian idea that nudity and mixed bathing led to sexual promiscuity (whence the transference of the word *bagnio* in Italian to mean brothel).

[2] This plague, according to Clinton, began in Egypt in 541, spread over Syria in 542 and culminated in Italy and Persia in 543.

rejected him: he never became a saint. His contemporary Tertullian foreshadowed the solution that was to be reached in succeeding centuries, namely to exclude all sexual relations outside a marriage celebrated under the auspices, according to the rules, and with the purposes laid down by the Church.

From the Church's control of marriage its interest spread to the whole breeding system of Christian society. It was an interest that was favoured by the biological principle, understood by Jewish lawgivers, that the propagation of the faithful was a necessary and prior condition for the propagation of the faith.[1]

If the Church was to permit propagation, monogamy was bound to be the prescribed sexual relationship within the Christian community. This step, which opposed it at once to Jewish tradition, again fitted it well for expansion in Europe where monogamy was already established. The kings of recently converted dynasties, like Charlemagne, naturally did not expect to obey such rules but they could be enforced on his subjects. The effects of Christian monogamy were short-term and social as well as long-term and genetic. Socially, so far as it was effective, it stabilized the upper classes whom it restricted and set apart from the population as a whole. Genetically, it established a formal distinction between legitimate offspring from mating within classes and illegitimate offspring from mating between classes. The consequence of this distinction (which we shall later have to explore) was to create the special dynastic character of European government.

A further social consequence of Christian monogamy was of quite another kind. It brought back a regulation of married life like that of early Republican Rome. But it combined with this regulation a respect for women which we know only from earlier peoples. The frescoes of Thebes, Knossos and Tarquinia all glow with a feeling for women which had been overcast ever since the triumphs of the iron age warriors, those Aryan and Semitic pastoralists, in the course of the first millennium B.C. The conquered peoples, suppressed into the lower orders of society, were thus being raised in social status and their ancient attitudes were being resurrected by the new Christian teaching.

This change of attitude had diverse, far-reaching and in the end revolutionary effects. It reacted in turn on the cult of the mother goddess, on the importance of women rulers (Pedigree 11), on the authority of the Christian Church, on the celibacy of its clergy, and on the habits of European Jews. To all of these we shall return later.

Out of these debates on marriage came a novel toleration for two parallel ways of life. Like the Essenes, the early Christians were torn between the short-term benefits of chastity and the long-term benefits of children. And like the Essenes, they came to admit a cleavage in society between those

[1] A modern object lesson in this principle is provided by the contrast between the success of the colonizing Mormons or the Mennonites and the failure of the Sandemanians. The first exalted propagation and conversion and multiplied; the second rejected conversion and disappeared. Brigham Young (1801–77) was survived by 17 wives and 47 children, all Mormons. A Mennonite in Minnesota who lived to 94 was survived in 1950 by 300 descendants, all Mennonites; see Darlington (1961).

who wish to breed and those who do not. They came to see the value of monasticism. This practice owes its origin to the breakdown of caste in India following Asoka's advancement of Buddhism. He is believed to have sent monastic missionaries to Ptolemaic Egypt where, long afterwards, their practices were passed to both Christians and Muslims.

The practice of monasticism has no authority in Jewish scripture. There was no reason why it should. The demand for monasticism arises only where class crossing in stratified societies leads to increased outbreeding and produces a proportion, usually up to one-tenth, of men and women who are averse from marriage or incapable of breeding. While the vast majority of the population continued to breed, the newly outbred Christian communities thus provided a steady supply of men endowed with what is called a 'gift of continence' suited to a celibate or monastic life.[1]

A priestly or monastic dedication to celibacy thus for the first time protects and unites in a potentially useful life people who had hitherto been disregarded in the universal post-neolithic pursuit of fertility. Meanwhile the rest of the community wishing to breed is protected by marriage. And the Virgin Mary, in whose person chastity and fecundity are miraculously united, may be properly adored by both.

The religious recognition of celibacy in the earliest Christian society was perfectly matched by its exclusion, not only of incest, but of inbreeding in a more extended sense. The forbidden degrees of kindred exactly prescribed the high degree of outbreeding which conduced to sporadic infertile recombination. Thus the development of monasteries under the rule of Benedict was most favoured at the time of the breakdown of the Roman Empire. And when imperial control and protection broke down, these monasteries, each of them economically and intellectually self-sufficient, proved to be the means of preserving the seeds of the ancient Mediterranean civilization over the whole Christian world from Ireland to Ethiopia.

Outside the field of religious seclusion, on the other hand, the Christians followed with undiminished enthusiasm the opposite and older doctrine that men and women were intended for marriage, and that marriage was intended for sexual propagation. Moreover, they were taught that every new life produced was sacred since it was dedicated in baptism to Jesus. On this side, the encouragement of propagation and the preservation of life, the full Jewish doctrine could be applied with all its formidable prohibitions. No onanism, no sodomy, and no incest; no castration, not even, as Origen discovered, self-castration; no abortion, no exposure, and no infanticide; no suicide and no homicide. And in addition to all these: no polygamy.

At this rate there was very little the Christians could do except legitimately multiply: all the pagan or rather paleolithic devices for population control, prudent and traditional, they condemned and abandoned. Other things being equal therefore, like the Jews the Christians were bound to increase relative to their pagan neighbours. Conversely, those cults like Mithraism which relied on homosexual ecstacies, were bound to decay in biological competition

[1] The detailed evidence and genetic explanation of this far-reaching principle I have described elsewhere (1960, 1961).

with Christianity. So indeed it happened: the Christians in the end triumphed in the cities of the Eastern Empire, less clean, to be sure, and more subject to plague, but also more crowded and more populous than had ever been known before in the western world.

VI. THE HUMANIZATION OF PAGAN SOCIETY

While the religious ferment was being spread westwards by Christianity through the middle-class professional strata of the Roman world, the same westward movement of eastern peoples was leading to a reform of ideas and manners in pagan society at an apparently different social and intellectual level. The evidence of this movement has been comprehensively set out by Lecky who showed that its liberalizing tendency was parallel with that of Christianity. Yet the men who expressed it were opposed to Christianity and indeed to the religious outlook as a whole. These were the pagan philosophers whose changing opinions were reflected in the laws enacted by pagan emperors.

On the side of the philosophers and the intellectuals this liberalizing movemen was continuous from the time of Aristotle and Alexander in the fourth century B.C. to the time of Constantine and Augustine in the fourth century A.D. The phrase '*nihil humanum a me alienum puto*' which expressed the central idea of humanism passed from the Greek Menander by way of the Carthaginian Terence to the Roman Cicero and his following of Stoics to find itself in the end just where the Christians in each of these countries had arrived from their Jewish origins.

The political and social expression of these ideas naturally suffered a setback from the Roman imperial expansion. It might be possible to speak like Cicero (*De Finibus*) of the '*caritas generis humani*'. But it was not possible to put the principle into effect in laws and manners while the Roman patricians were butchering one another at Pharsalus and Philippi or taking their most heroic enemies, Jugurtha and Vercingetorix, to be strangled in the dungeons of the Mamertine gaol. Nor could compassion make headway against Seneca's traditional eugenics: 'We drown the weakling and the monstrosity: it is not passion but reason to separate the fit from the unclean' (*De Ira* 1: 18).

The liberal philosophical doctrines came from the east, notably from Cyprus, the meeting place of Jews and Greeks. They came from the teachings of Zeno who asserted that 'all men are by nature equal and virtue alone makes the difference between them' (*Diogenes Laertius*). This principle found its way through Cicero into Roman law which began to assume that men were born free until the contrary was proved. It expressed itself also in the extension of citizenship now required to raise taxes but so repugnant in earlier times to the Roman oligarchy. But above all it expressed itself in the gradual restriction in the powers of the owner over his slaves, of the father over his sons, and of the husband over his wife. So Hadrian revoked, not perhaps effectively, the power of owners to kill slaves; Alexander Severus revoked the already obsolete right of fathers to kill their grown-up sons; and Diocletian, the persecutor of Christians, tried to stop fathers selling their children as slaves.

The humanity of the philosophers and even of the rulers meant nothing to the masses who demanded their ferocious gladiatorial entertainments with ever-growing appetite. The combats were supposed to arouse the military spirit of the people. But it was in fact when the military spirit had largely evaporated that Titus built his Colosseum. There 80,000 spectators who would never fight themselves were able to witness the slaughter of his Jewish prisoners. And there thirty years later, with the Vestal Virgins in the seats of honour, Trajan was able to celebrate his triumph with the destruction of 5000 pairs of gladiators. It has been said that it was the only Roman practice that that conservative Roman, Juvenal, failed to denounce. More men must have died in these games than in all Caesar's battles. These men fought to amuse Rome. Their descendants might have fought to defend it. In this respect the contrast between the western and the eastern peoples is illuminating. In Greece, indeed in the Hellenic and Judaic world generally, the craze for blood never established itself. The part of the Empire which survived never indulged itself in this wanton sacrifice.

There was thus no attempt in the pagan world to reconcile the practices of the people with the precepts of philosophers. Cicero and Caesar were content to be the officers of a religion which they privately regarded with contempt. They exploited the auguries to control the people and to encourage the troops. As Gibbon puts it: 'The various modes of worship which prevailed in the Roman world were all considered by the people as equally true; by the philosopher as equally false; and by the magistrate as equally useful. And thus toleration produced not only mutual indulgence but even religious concord.'

But the Christians, adopting the intolerant fervour of the Jews, wanted everybody else to believe and to behave, as they did, with humanity. They undertook to organize their community with the morality of their founder, which was also that of the philosophers. In achieving this object they were powerfully assisted by possessing the breeding system of the Jews; by applying to their own uses the efficient administration of the Romans, adapted by the skill of Tertullian and others; and by a ceremonial life which grew out of the sacred writings of their own heterogeneous community, handed down and enriched through successive generations.

They knew, as the Essenes had known, that excommunication and the fear of hell were the basis of a fiercer discipline than the imperial government with all its tortures could devise. They sometimes tried to use them as weapons for conversion and then they brought persecution down on themselves. But within the community they established a stern uniformity of conduct, a deference to their own rules. Now, although such public deference must always engender private hypocrisy, it is in practice the only weapon invented by man for raising the conduct of a heterogeneous society above the average genetic and instinctive level. By contrast when we consider the gladiatorial games in Rome we can see how such a society with a different basis of deference may be brought down to the lowest instinctive level.

The combination of deference, hypocrisy and improvement we have seen in the development of Christian marriage. Its ideals have never been maintained in practice nor could there be any social advantage in maintaining them. But the public appearance of maintaining them has enabled Christian societies to benefit from the institution of marriage in a way that has largely contributed, as we shall see, not only to the early survival of Christianity but also to the later development of European civilization.

During the third century, however, the opinions of the educated classes of the pagan Empire began to come within reach of the Christian teaching. It was then that the great crisis of persecution arose.

VII. EXPANSION AND PERSECUTION

It used to be said that Christianity spread through its compassionate appeal to the underdog. But can this have been so? Two-thirds of the population of the Empire are supposed to have been slaves or serfs at the beginning of the Christian era and three centuries later when the Emperor himself was converted only about one in twenty were Christians. The conditions and processes of conversion were evidently very diverse. What sometimes disturbed the imperial government was that well-to-do people who should offer rich sacrifices in the temples, through conversion, were failing in their duty. From them the 'contagion', to use Pliny's word, could spread into the countryside. But for a very long time it failed to do so.

In their early life in Rome the Christians, for whom meeting and reading and discussion were indispensable, had taken advantage of the Roman respect for tombs to organize themselves legally as burial societies. Their catacombs had consequently been respected by the authorities through all the early persecutions. The growth of the Christian communities led to a growing confidence and hence to waves of persecution. But it was not until the third century and the great persecution of Decius that their catacombs were for the first time invaded and desecrated.

The emperors saw the Christians in many different lights. All objected to their rejection of sacrifices to the emperor. At first they were no worse in this respect than the Jews. But their belief in the devil was offensive to the pagans of all classes. Moreover it assisted their fervent proselytism and increased both their numbers and the dangers of disloyalty to the basic political principle of the Empire.

In addition, particular emperors had their personal reasons for liking or disliking Christians. Some, like Alexander Severus and Gallienus, found Christian bishops, the leaders of congregations, useful as advisers and administrators. Most disliked their foreign or unfamiliar superstitions. A few like Marcus Aurelius even disliked superstition as such. So policy shifted from one ruler to another. But the larger trends ceased to be within the power of the government to control. A wave of expansion would give the Christians confidence—even insolent confidence—which led to alternate waves of alarm and persecution. The last two of these approached a state of civil war. It was a civil war in which pagan authorities appeared to win every battle. Yet, as Tertullian had foreseen, persecution merely strengthened the faith: the blood of the martyrs proved to be the seed of the Church.

But what Church? In Europe Christianity had spread effectively only among the partly educated classes of the cities. There it had made its way in close contact with an orthodox and centralized priesthood. And, assisted by educated women, to whom for the first time the new religion gave status and consideration, it had made its way into the precincts of the palace. But in the provinces of Asia and Africa, suffering more and more from delegated management and harsh taxation, Christianity had shown itself capable of adjusting its appeal to quite different conditions. The scriptures, both in the Old and the New Testaments, had shown compassion for the tribulations of the Jews. They now seemed to be the voice of redemption in a new sense, indeed the voice of rebellion against a merely ceremonial pagan priesthood subservient to a foreign establishment, remote from the people as well as devoid of social or intellectual content.[1]

The breaking up of the Roman Empire into separate inbred racial societies thus offered the developing Christian teaching, full of social and political implications, the golden opportunity of meeting local needs by local beliefs. The Church fell into schisms which represented the ancient character of the Syrians, the Egyptians and the Carthaginians; sects which spoke in the ancient languages of these people, Aramaic, Coptic and even Punic; and heresies which fiercely asserted their own views in opposition to the authority of the churches in Rome; and also in opposition to one another.

The Christian teaching introduced a number of incredible beliefs which allowed for unlimited diversity of interpretation. In the differences between the views that were held on the question of whether Christ was God or Man, or both or neither, there may have been some differences in racial predisposition, some genetic component. But these differences were inexpugnably connected with diverging national interests. And it is certain that these had both a genetic basis and long-term political effects.

VIII. DIOCLETIAN'S PROBLEM: CONSTANTINE'S SOLUTION

The Empire had been beset by external enemies and internal divisions for a hundred years before an Emperor was elected who understood the revolutionary, and perhaps reactionary, steps that were needed to deal with the threat to its existence. This Emperor was Diocletian, like several before him and many after him, a general of Illyrian origin.

Diocletian examined the value of Rome as a capital. He saw that however strong it had been for attack it was weak for defence. He saw that the fighting men were no longer in Italy but in the provinces on the frontier. He also saw that in its social character, senatorial and proletarian, Rome merely hampered any military government. He decided therefore to desert Rome and to establish several military capitals each with its own commander or emperor facing the barbarian attackers on the northern frontier. Milan and Trier in the west, Sirmium in the centre, and Nicomedia in the more protected east were the citadels he chose. Thus there were two senior emperors named

[1] In the view of Jones (1964) and of Frend (1965).

Augustus and two juniors named Caesar. By this means for three generations the invaders were kept at bay.

Freed from the domination of an unserviceable past Diocletian was able to create an absolute monarchy. But it was a monarchy shared with partners, the other emperors, on the ancient Roman principle of collegiality. And it was based on administrative and military classes whose authority, consolidated by intermarriage, looked as though it might be passed down by nomination or heredity or both.

In its absolute authority the new system followed an oriental model. To sustain it further Diocletian considered a corresponding religious reformation. He examined the merits of various oriental religions which he evidently compared with the judicious eye of a magistrate. Evidently also he thought first of his mixed conscript armies. It was natural enough therefore that he should bolster the Persian cult of Mithras the Redeemer, bloodthirsty, homosexual and military. And natural too that he should reject the pacifism of the Christians, bookish and even effeminate as it may have seemed. It was natural but it was also mistaken. For the military cults, so appealing to the soldiery, were no help at all in binding together the civil population which was still the body of the Empire itself.

This last decision, chiefly due to his younger colleague, Galerius, had led to the final, and once again ineffective, persecution of the Christians. It was at this moment that the young Constantine, aged eighteen, was called to the deathbed of his father at York and to the acclamation of the troops as the new Augustus. That was in the year 306. But the division of the Empire into four, which preserved peace under Diocletian, now merely defined the powers which should engage in war. And there were many campaigns of civil war between that first acknowledgement of success and its completion with absolute power for Constantine, with all colleagues defeated and slain eighteen years later.

This was a civil war of unexampled character. At an early stage, especially through his Edict of Toleration at Milan in 313, Constantine had made it clear that he intended to support the God of the Christians who had victoriously supported him. There might have been a conversion; but there was certainly going to be an alliance between the new ruler and the new religion. This decision of Constantine's was to change the course of history. Gibbon describes these events by telling us that Constantine used the Church to help him in climbing the steps of the throne. But why did he choose this unlikely approach?

It is clear that the Christian Emperor, like his pagan predecessors, expected to find in the new religion a servant and not a master. Instructed, so he said, by a vision of a sign in the sky, he adopted the heraldic emblem of Christ as his banner, his *labarum.* When he did so, he expected that the Christian Church, and if possible the Christian God, would fight on his side. His expectations were confirmed by military success. But this did not mean that his own divine cult should be abandoned to the dismay of his pagan worshippers. Nor that pagan symbols should vanish from his coinage. Nor again that Christian sweetness should temper the stern justice of the converted sovereign. He did not hesitate to put to death Crispus, his eldest son, Fausta, the mother of his five younger children or Maximian her father. Nor did his Christian children in their turn hesitate to murder one another. The relationship of Christian rulers to the Christian God has usually been one of alliance rather than submission. The stronger the ruler the less the submission. So it was with Constantine. He was guided by his understanding of what the leaders of the Christian community, through the principles they taught, the scriptures they relied on, the ceremonies they had devised, and the administration they had created, could do for the government of the Empire.

The men and the methods of the new religion were what were wanted at that time because they were capable of creating a bond between a wider range of classes and races of people than did all the unscriptured pagan religions of the past. This was the vision he saw, not the sign in the sky, and it was this vision that made him great not only in the eyes of the Church. Men have found it strange that a man so impulsive and often so weak as Constantine should have had the insight to see such a vision. But why not? Imagination does not usually inspire a correct and repetitive routine. And with imagination Constantine continued to display his gifts.

Once he held all the reins of military power in his hands Constantine, now sole and single Emperor, began to lay plans for the founding of a new single capital city, a new Rome. It must be central for trade and government; it must be a citadel impregnable against attack; it must be a holy city dedicated to the saints and the ceremonies of the Christian religion. He chose the obscure thousand-year-old Greek colony of Byzantium. It was a momentous decision. The site was admirable. It stood at the meeting place of continents and of seas but above all at the meeting place of races. The Greeks, after moving west for a thousand years, were now to move east again. Here now Greeks, Romans, and (through their Christian converts) Jews also, came together for the first time. They were genetically mixed by the Christian religion just as they were politically combined by Constantine. The union of these peoples created a new civilization which was to last in its full unity for another thousand years.

Before he could tackle this task however Constantine had another more urgent and more intractable problem to deal with. He had to see that the Church he was in process of adopting had the unity and authority that he needed to support his Empire.

IX. THE COUNCIL OF NICAEA

When Constantine, as a reigning monarch, proposed partly to forgo his own divinity in order to augment or embrace the divinity of Christ he had one example to guide him. In the year 312 a Cappadocian bishop had sent to Armenia a certain Gregory. This man, who became known as 'the Illuminator', had baptized Tiradates, a youthful friend of Constantine, as the first Christian king. The missionary and the king, attempting to convert the whole nation, found that the native hereditary priesthood objected. They feared losing their reserved portions of the pagan animal sacrifices. They were assured by the bishop, and probably by the king, that the love-feasts or sacramental

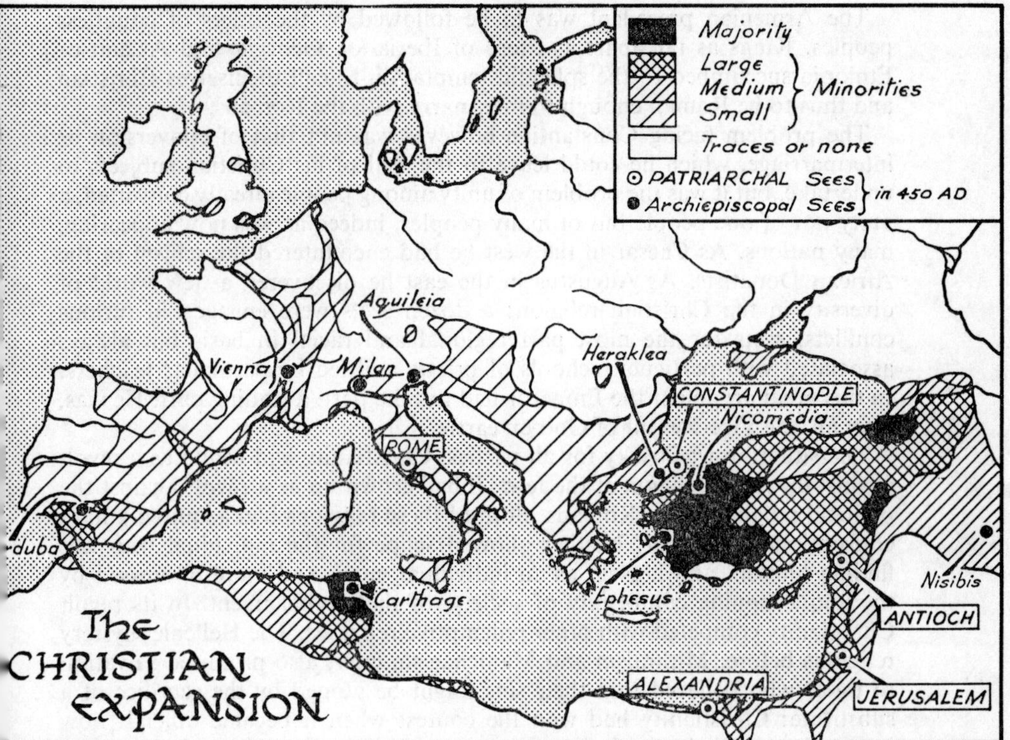

Fig. 11. The distribution of Christians in the Roman Empire at the time of the conversion of Constantine (Edict of Milan, 313) from documentary and archaeological evidence.

After 'L'Italia Storica' (1961, fig. 57)

The eight archiepiscopal sees are as follows:
East: Nisibis, Ephesus, Heraklea.
West: Carthage, Corduba, Vienna (on Rhône), Milan and Aquileia.

meals of the Christians would be held; meat sacrifices would be continued and their portions would be religiously reserved. On these Levitical conditions the priesthood became Christian, with Gregory as their hereditary primate; and the whole kingdom was converted.

Within a few years an Armenian alphabet had been invented and an Armenian Bible appeared in the newly written and the permanently preserved language. Thus was established an Armenian Church which was soon found to be divided in beliefs and segregated in council from its parent. In turn this Church has survived. It has sustained an Armenian people, the first of many such Christian communities, whose doctrinal unity has required inbreeding and has thus maintained its racial character through countless vicissitudes and a dispersal all over the world down to the present day.[1]

[1] *E.B.* (1929); Armenian Church, and Jones (1948).

The Armenian precedent was to be followed by the rulers of countless peoples. Kings as far apart as those of Iberia or Georgia and Aksum or Ethiopia succumbed to the splendid temptation to call themselves Christian and thus to be Roman enough to intermarry with the Romans.

The problem facing Constantine however was not that of conversion or intermarriage, which he could leave to the zeal of his Christian subjects to undertake, but it was the problem of unity among people already converted, a unity not of one people but of many peoples, indeed as was now appearing, many nations. As Caesar in the west he had encountered the schism of the African Donatists. As Augustus in the east he discovered a new world of diversity in the Christian religion: a dozen sects were engaged in furious conflicts, sects for the most part regional and racial in basis but always associated with particular schools of priests and led by particular teachers. In this great argument the Emperor had to take part, a leading part. He was, after all, the Vice-Regent of God on earth.

The situation was tricky for all parties. Christianity had begun as a revolt against the racial religion of the Jews. It had grown up as a revolt against the political religion of the Romans. Both of these religions had acquired a hard conventional character. Neither allowed scope for the individual who was finding himself, and herself, as an individual, more and more oppressed by the unquestioning conformity of society, of the establishment. In its revolt Christianity competed with other redemptive religions. The Hellenic mystery religions before, Mithraism and Manichaeism later, also promised salvation to those who believed that their sins might be atoned by the sacrifice of a substitute: Christianity had won the contest when it became official: now its problems were internal.

Now Christianity had to be made into a political religion. One aspect of such a transformation had to be a versatility and ambiguity and even hypocrisy of belief. The doctrine of redemption had the feud with Judaism could be maintained. The primitive and revolutionary fervour could be diverted to the missionary frontier. But within the Empire the revolt against the State had to be abandoned for an alliance with the State. To control, or to contain, this revolt, organization and administration were needed. Fortunately the leaders of the Church were thoroughly prepared for this development.

When Constantine intervened in Church affairs he in fact found a political organization ready-made. The Church was regionally governed by bishops. Although the opinion and choice of the congregation must at first have been considered these bishops claimed to have been appointed in personal succession from the original apostles. They were accustomed to hold councils to discuss knotty points of doctrine and discipline. Such councils were devoted to maintaining unity based on scriptural and legal coherence. They were organized to resist the erosion and fragmentation of localized mystical and magical beliefs and inspirations, for example those claiming Christian origins and described as Gnosticism. Nothing could therefore be better, it seemed, both for the Empire and the Church than to hold a single Universal Council or Ecumenical Synod (Latin and Greek alternatives) to establish such a unity of the Church and the Empire. It was reasonable for the Emperor to issue his own invitations to the three hundred bishops, to pay their travelling expenses, to preside at their meetings, to write out the agenda, and to promise that if suitable decisions were reached they would be ratified and enforced by imperial decree. It was no less reasonable to assume that those decisions would conform with the needs of the Emperor himself. No less so since Constantine's baptism, still in the future, was bound to depend on a harmonious arrangement of policy.

The matter was urgent. A local Council of Bishops at Antioch had already in 324 taken the law into their own hands. They had condemned the metaphysical opinions on the nature of Christ expressed by Arius a priest of Alexandria. The Emperor therefore acted without delay. He convened his Universal Council hoping to settle the disputes of the Church once and for all. It met at Nicaea in 325. There the struggle began. It was a struggle that has never ended: 'was the Son created by, with or from the Father or not created at all?' Only four or five bishops had come from the west but one of them was the Emperor's special friend. This was Hosius of Corduba. Through the mouth of Constantine he offered a formula which caught the angry factions unprepared. Why not agree, he asked, to the *homoousion* or consubstantiality of the Father and Son? This phrase stopped the argument. A few obstinate objectors were excommunicated, that is to say thrown out. The rest agreed.

The unity was deceptive. It never really stretched beyond the national limits of Greek-speaking society and their barbarian converts. The Church so far from uniting the Empire defined and deepened its national divisions. Indeed it came to provide a verbal excuse for racial and class hatred. But for a brief moment the cracks of schism and heresy were plastered over. The Emperor could appear as the head of a Church which he had united. As the Vice-Regent of God he could return to his job of political administration.

What was this job? Obviously it was to distribute punishments for dissension and rewards for obedience. For the punishments he began by confiscating heretical churches at the same time as he dismantled pagan temples. With the treasures that he could now legally commandeer he was then able to build and endow the orthodox Christian churches, and also the palaces, with which he intended to furnish his new capital. For the rewards he was able to amend the law so as to give wealth and power to the Church itself. Bequests to churches and monasteries became legally secured endowments. So began the accumulation of wealth by pious benefaction which has continued, despite occasional interruptions, to the present day. At the same time the status of bishops was strengthened by giving them jurisdiction in cases of appeal from the civil courts. This gain of power was long contested but has rarely been altogether lost. Finally, Constantine began, indeed he had already begun, to reconstruct the law and administration in accordance with Christian social and genetic teaching as he understood it.

Thus, already in 320, the Christian Emperor had abolished Augustus' taxes on celibates. In due course, forgetting his own family history, he checked divorce and penalized bastardy; he stopped gladiatorial games, and gave grants to the poor with a view to discouraging the exposure of infants. Most significantly, he prohibited conversion by the Jews. The Jewish practice of conversion by the circumcising of slaves became punishable by death. For the next 1500 years the Jews of Christian Europe thus became subject to loss by conversion following intermittent persecution. But they were never allowed to gain by recruitment. Which meant that they were now fixed as a racially self-contained minority.

In all these changes save the last, Constantine and his successor Theodosius the Great, who completed the official conversion of the Empire, were continuing the processes of humanization of Roman conduct and law which had been at work in the previous three centuries. But the structure of Roman society continued to rest on the basis established by hereditary slavery. To be sure the manumission of slaves now became, like marriage, a Christian ceremony. And the provision of rest days for slaves became a Christian obligation.[1] But the trade in slaves, male and female, child and eunuch, did not cease. The marriage of slave and free was still forbidden, and the intercourse of a slave with a woman owner was now a crime for both and equally punished by death.

Christian influence indeed did almost as little to hasten the decay of slavery as the decay of warfare. But it undoubtedly undertook, partly through the development of monasteries, to organize the first large-scale alleviation of the pauperism which resulted from the decay of slavery: whence the especially Christian use of the word 'charity'. Thus Christianity came to terms with society. It *condemned* murder, abortion, polygamy, incest and sodomy. But it *condoned* warfare, slavery, castration, concubinage and prostitution.

One respect we must now notice in which social structure at this time was being restored to a state earlier than that of either the Roman Empire or the Christian religion. Government remained in the hands of the rich; and it was managed in the interests of the rich. Taxation had never been adjusted to differentiate the rich from the poor in their ability to pay. The reason for this, as we shall see later, was that no ruling or royal caste, not even the oligarchy that could produce the Gracchi, was now in existence to recognize the interests of the whole society and protect them against those of a privileged section. The artisans in the cities and the peasants on the land had been made to bear the burden of the Empire from which they were benefiting less and less. In consequence they were discovering the means of escape by migration. Laws were therefore made (and collated by Theodosius and Justinian) attempting to fix men in their hereditary professions. In the interests of landlords and employers, peasants were tied to their land and craftsmen to their guilds. Although these laws may have largely failed at the time, we can recognize their remote effects on the populations of Europe long after the Empire itself had dissolved. For the relations of protection and subjection that had been created in the Empire were taken over by the barbarian invaders in the unsettled centuries to come.

[1] The Christian Church everywhere numbered the days of the week from the Lord's Day (*Kyriake* in Modern Greek). In the east the State was able to impose this numbering on the lay public. In the west, even in Italy, the Church had to leave the public to name five of its days after pagan gods, Roman and Germanic.

X. THE CHRISTIAN EMPIRE: EPHESUS

If we return to the Empire a hundred years after Nicaea we find the west overwhelmed by barbarians, Goths and Vandals, who are happily converted to Christianity and celebrating the Christian feast of Easter but, less happily, converted to the sect of the Arians, followers of Arius who was condemned at Nicaea. The Eastern Empire is in danger but still intact. Constantinople is now a great city sanctified by many churches and tombs, adorned in mosaics with the features of a Christ who is no longer the youthful beardless Alexandrian or Mithraic hero of persecution but rather the mature, benevolent, reflective, and official sage of future ages.[1] Within the Empire, however, conversion is by no means complete. Large populations in the country, even in Bythinia, are still pagan. And even in the capital small groups secretly assemble to honour the ancient gods.[2]

A much graver problem affects the life and safety of the State. It is the public conflict between schisms and sects within the established Church and between its great officials. A new Council is therefore summoned to decide what now seems to be the greatest dispute of all. The issue lies between the Patriarch Cyril of Alexandria and his rival Nestorius of Constantinople. The one asserts, the other denies, that the Virgin Mary may be described as the Mother of God or *Theotokos*. The meeting has been appropriately assigned to Ephesus, a city in which the cult of Mary has now displaced that of the virgin Diana. The Emperor, Theodosius II, being a man of piety, is deeply concerned. This we cannot doubt, for he took the course, unexampled in the antiquity of the western world, of rejecting the death penalty during his reign. He was however a timid man who was accustomed to defer to the opinions of his wife and sister. He decided not to attend the Council but to appoint or allow a deputy to preside.

With this emergency the Patriarch of Alexandria was well prepared to deal. East and west, the Empire was beset by enemies and distracted by schisms and jealousies. It was also financially bankrupt. But the Patriarch disposed of the wealth of the Church in Egypt, which was by no means bankrupt. He no longer depended on the Emperor for his travelling expenses. On the contrary his accounts show that he disbursed about a ton of gold[3] to the most influential eunuchs[4] and other officers of the court.

In these circumstances it is not surprising that the Patriarch of Egypt was

[1] Kitzinger and Senior (1941).

[2] A century later, in 542, John of Ephesus, looking into the matter for Justinian, reported the shocking discovery that the Prefect of Constantinople was an unbaptized pagan (Jones 1948).

[3] Gold only is mentioned by Gibbon and Jones but desirable consumer goods were also listed in the surviving inventory.

[4] Monarchs of dynasties, rendered uncertain by polygamy and the lack of legitimate marriage under Church auspices, made eunuchs the indispensable holders of the great offices of State. This applied first to the Persians, then the Romans, then the Muslim rulers in the west, and in the east to the emperors of China. Castration of boys was illegal in the Christian Empire. Eunuchs were therefore ostensibly imported from Persia and the Caucasus.

able to take the chair and arrange the agenda at the Council of Ephesus. But, as the discussions proceeded, public tumult broke out. The cathedral was besieged but the troops intervened and ultimately the Patriarch's views prevailed. The truth was proclaimed. Heresy was condemned; the heretic was deposed, excommunicated and banished. Peace and unity were thus restored.

The ex-Patriarch Nestorius thus found himself consigned to the furthest deserts of the Empire. His teaching was forbidden and his disciples were dispersed. From Antioch they fled beyond the frontiers. There, however, they succeeded in propagating themselves and their opinions. Still today therefore, in Persia, in China, and in India, we find Christians of the Nestorian or Assyrian communion. They are a minority, maintained as a separate breeding group by their special subdivision of Christian belief, always racially, usually professionally, and sometimes linguistically, distinguishable.

The teaching and the sufferings of Nestorius were not without profit to his followers. But for us they bring two lessons of the highest value. Their first lesson is to show that, when differences of racial character and political interest cannot be openly expressed by treason, they can be innocently but effectively disguised in terms of differences in religious doctrine. Christianity at Nicaea or Ephesus showed for the first time its capacity for exploring and exposing such differences, a capacity which the passage of centuries has shown to be inexhaustible. Later history has been concerned with illustrating the conflict between those who (like Constantine) wished to exert authority or impose uniformity and those who (like Arius and Nestorius) wished to resist both.

The second lesson is to show that this kind of dispute, now taken out of the Jewish backwater and thrust into the mainstream of world events, was based on a supreme gift for intolerance.

The religious intolerance which the Christians had inherited (in a strict biological sense) from their Jewish forebears was now being dispersed through the Christian world with the most formidable consequences. The debates of Councils and the persecutions that followed them reproduced at higher and higher magnifications the original patterns of Nicaea and Ephesus. But they never succeeded in producing a uniformity of belief. What they did produce was a temporary and conventional uniformity of expression which was subordinated to the needs of each politically and linguistically uniform society.

In modern times we are accustomed to esteem religious toleration as a virtue. But at this stage, like personal freedom, its suppression was often a constructive element in social evolution. The separate and diverging enthusiasms of the schismatic communities of the Empire created their civilization and sustained their existence. Gaulish and other languages disappeared precisely because their speakers did not embrace a heresy and receive a Bible. The peoples of Armenia, Syria and Egypt (with its offshoot in Axum) were helped by their heresies and their Bibles to retain their own languages and their own genetic coherence and character. Religion, language and breeding were for them, as for so many later peoples, mutually enhancing bases of nationality. They all went their own ways and shook themselves free of the Eastern Emperor as soon as the opportunity came.

Between Rome and Constantinople the same differences of race and language were at work in causing cleavage. There was however another difference, secondary but in itself decisive. For the bishops of Rome found themselves at the heart of the disintegrating Western Empire, with their Church more lasting than any state to which it could be attached. They discovered, and with fluctuating success developed, an authority of their own. It was an authority derived from their own racial and intellectual character and from the deference paid to the name of the city by the flood of Goths and Vandals which appeared to overwhelm them. They naturally attempted to maintain their independence. And after seven hundred years they succeeded in reversing the subordination to the State which was being fixed on the Eastern Church.

Augustine (the Carthaginian), witnessing the capture of Rome by the Goths, expected that the Church of Rome would succeed to the power of the Empire. It did not happen directly. But what did happen was made possible by several concurrent processes all of them assisted by Augustine's extraordinary insight. These included the disengagement of the professional talents of the Church from the service of the Empire; the conversion of the barbarian invaders; and the evolution of a new kind of society, of joint Roman and Germanic derivation.

Augustine had no doubt already noticed the metamorphoses that the Roman Establishment had already undergone. He had already seen the *nobiles* of the Republic replaced by a Hellenistic administration, which in turn had given way to the officer caste of provincial armies. He had seen the cleavage of the Establishment by the separation of military and civil government under Diocletian. Now he foresaw the growth of a third limb of the State, the Church with its own connections and loyalties, its own talents, and its own standards of conduct. It was this new system, genetically differentiated and politically balanced, which has been the foundation of all later systems of government in Western Europe.

XI. THE BARBARIAN INVASIONS

a. The Invaders

The barbarians who first attacked the defences of the Roman Empire were of two kinds in the matter of their speech, the Celts and the Germans. They had evidently spread over Europe in two successive explosions of population arising from a region to the west of the original Aryan centre.

The expansion of the Celts flooded Spain and Italy, Greece and Anatolia in the fourth and third centuries B.C. It had been finally checked by Caesar's conquests in Gaul and Spain, by the occupation of Britain and the building of Hadrian's wall. A joint assault of Celtic and German tribes[1] was crushed by Marius in 113–110 B.C. Later attacks were held at bay for a while by Trajan's occupation of Dacia and by Hadrian's building of a palisade, the *limes*, between the Main and the Danube. But a century later their advance was resumed. Aurelian in 272 abandoned Dacia and began to build walls

[1] As we must assume from the names Plutarch gives them: Cimbri, Teutones and Ambrones.

round Rome and other great cities. These walls were soon to be besieged, assaulted and sometimes overthrown.

What caused these great movements? They have usually been ascribed to famine. But what we have now seen of the neolithic, Semitic and Aryan expansions has suggested the opposite: they are due, not to a loss, but to a gain in food production. They are due not to a worsening of the climate but to a bettering of crops, stock and tools. Both the Celtic and the Germanic peoples must indeed have owed their spread in the pre-Aryan world of barbarians around them to their means of production in these times. For they had supplies of iron from which they made iron axes to fell trees for fuel and timber. And they had heavier iron ploughs with which they tilled the land they had cleared. The origin of the Germanic peoples seems to have lain peculiarly in the process of clearing the northern European forests so well depicted in their folklore; and it is a process which has been continued without interruption to the present day by both German and Slavonic peoples: most thoroughly of course in England.

Whether the climate had changed little or much to the advantage or to the disadvantage of Northern Europe, therefore, the peoples must have increased. The balance of numbers must have shifted. The Mediterranean was now exploited, denuded and eroded while the barbarian north was still well-timbered and unspoilt. Destitute of cities, free from plague and malaria, the north was furnished with a thriving rural industry based on land now yielding corn and cattle as well as furs, metals and fuel. But at the same time that the Germans were clearing the ground for their cultivation they were also clearing a way through Central Europe for the third great group of invaders, the horse-riding bowmen who in the fourth century rode in from the steppes. These people belonged to a third linguistic group, the Asiatic Huns and Alans, who were to be followed by their kinsmen the Tartars, Mongols, Turks and Kazaks. It was the pressure of these fighting tribes behind them which in part kept the Germans moving westwards for five hundred years.

How should we try to classify these barbarian peoples? Tacitus and later writers have given them the names that they used to describe themselves or one another. But in the course of centuries the character of these tribes was continually changing. And it was changing at several levels. By conquest or capture in war the chief of one tribe became the king of many and the warriors of one tribe or their womenfolk became the slaves of another. This led to sudden expansions of a barbarian kingdom or movements of a barbarian ruler and his fighting men. Alaric, who was elected king of the Visigoths, had been born on the Black Sea coast and died in Sicily; his brother-in-law, Ataulph, who married Galla Placidia, daughter, sister and mother of emperors, founded a kingdom in Aquitaine.

Apart from their own recombinations by intermarriage the European barbarians had been (ever since the megalithic expansion) exposed to the infiltration of craftsmen and traders, Greek and Punic, Etruscan and Roman, many of whom must have been assimilated among the northern peoples introducing the arts of civilization and some of its social stratification. Further, they had continually been exchanging captives, mercenaries and adventurers with the Roman Empire. This exchange the Romans had often used for sport, the barbarians always for profit. The later Roman commanders were often of barbarian extraction but it is also likely that the later barbarian commanders were often of Roman extraction. The exchange was, as we shall see, freest at the highest levels.

One consequence of this hybridization was an improvement in the opportunities for barbarian levies. These had been raised at first as common soldiers under Marcus Aurelius. But later they came to produce officers and finally notable commanders, like Stilicho and Rufinus, for the Roman armies.

Another consequence of hybridization was that names are no more constant in their meaning among barbarians than we have seen them to be among Romans. In a time of wide movement there was also enhanced genetic recombination; fighting men shifted their allegiance rapidly and the rapid expansions of one kingdom, Gothic or Frankish, at the expense of another, were partly due to these shifts. We think of the Gauls and Belgae as Celtic, the Vandals and Goths, Alemanni, Franks and Lombards as German, the Huns and Alans as Asiatic. But the names which are true for the language and for the mode of life of the bulk of the tribe are not true for the origins of their chieftains or their slaves. For example German tribes of the fifth century in Belgium often had chiefs with Celtic names (ending in *rix*). So had the West Saxon chiefs like Cerdic or Cedric who invaded Britain a century later.

The whole system of breeding, whatever it may have been before an invasion, was of course transformed as soon as an invasion succeeded. The barbarian chief marries the emperor's sister. Hengist marries Vortigern's daughter, and so on all down the line. Quickly the invading race hybridizes with the previous governing class. But the process varies with the social structure and racial character on both sides.

The tribal forces under the chieftains were of various sizes from the smallest groups to great armies of 20,000 fighting men or more. The chief objects were land, loot, and wives or slaves. Alaric the Goth demanded a million pounds worth of gold, silk and pepper as the ransom of Rome. He intended to colonize just as Genseric the Vandal did in Africa. But they also intended to take the women of the country and what they did in this respect differed according to class and country and was bound to determine their future.

Thus the Vandals in Africa, 80,000 of them by Genseric's count, disappeared after three generations and we may suppose that this was due to indiscriminate mating. The chieftains of all the main groups in Europe, however, married into the ruling class of Roman provincial society which itself had been derived from intermarriage of Roman and provincial ruling classes. The most ambitious and powerful, like Stilicho, Ataulph, and Genseric, married into the Imperial family itself (Pedigree 11).

Such intermarriage is what we should expect from all our earlier historical precedents. But there are reasons why we should notice its incidence. In the first place it indicates how the balance of political advantage and social status changed between barbarian and Roman and between Rome and Constantinople during the critical centuries. The respect in which the emperor at Constantinople was held obviously advanced as the Western Empire declined.

Pedigree 11

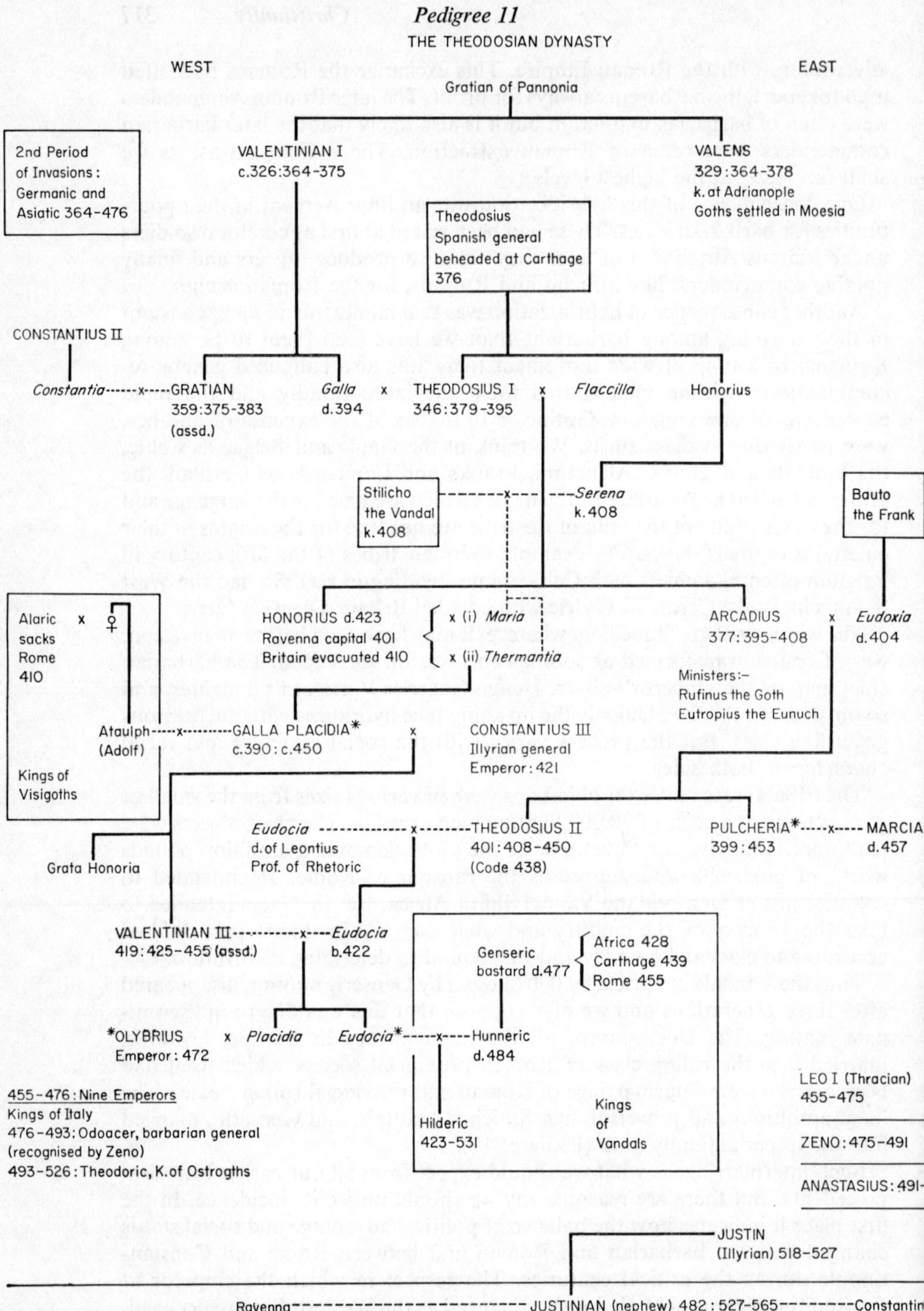

THE THEODOSIAN DYNASTY
WEST
EAST
Gratian of Pannonia
2nd Period of Invasions: Germanic and Asiatic 364-476
VALENTINIAN I c.326:364-375
VALENS 329:364-378 k. at Adrianople Goths settled in Moesia
Theodosius Spanish general beheaded at Carthage 376
CONSTANTIUS II
Constantia x GRATIAN 359:375-383 (assd.)
Galla d.394
x
THEODOSIUS I 346:379-395
x
Flaccilla
Honorius
Stilicho the Vandal k.408
x
Serena k.408
Bauto the Frank
Alaric x ♀ sacks Rome 410
HONORIUS d.423 Ravenna capital 401 Britain evacuated 410
x (i) Maria
x (ii) Thermantia
ARCADIUS 377:395-408
x
Eudoxia d.404
Ministers:– Rufinus the Goth Eutropius the Eunuch
Ataulph x GALLA PLACIDIA* c.390:c.450
(Adolf)
x
CONSTANTIUS III Illyrian general Emperor: 421
Kings of Visigoths
Eudocia d. of Leontius Prof. of Rhetoric
x
THEODOSIUS II 401:408-450 (Code 438)
PULCHERIA* 399:453
x
MARCIAN d.457
Grata Honoria
VALENTINIAN III 419:425-455 (assd.)
x
Eudocia b.422
Genseric bastard d.477
Africa 428 Carthage 439 Rome 455
*OLYBRIUS Emperor: 472
x
Placidia
Eudocia*
x
Hunneric d.484
455-476: Nine Emperors
Kings of Italy
476-493: Odoacer, barbarian general (recognised by Zeno)
493-526: Theodoric, K. of Ostrogths
Hilderic 423-531
Kings of Vandals
LEO I (Thracian) 455-475
ZENO: 475-491
ANASTASIUS: 491-
JUSTIN (Illyrian) 518-527
Ravenna
JUSTINIAN (nephew) 482: 527-565
Constantin
& THEODORA* d.547

* Co-regents (Galla Placidia and Pulcheria; Olybrius and Eudocia, Justinian and Theodora).

For a while it even seemed that he was looked upon as the head of the Christian Church to which Goths and Vandals, although not Franks, chose to belong. In the second place this intermarriage affected the development of Europe in a new way which we must now examine.

b. Their Conversion

How did the barbarians come to be converted? The experience of the Goths and the Lombards shows us the negative side of the story. They had been converted to the Arian form of Christianity before they invaded the Empire. For this reason they failed to combine easily with the Catholic nobility or people. A Catholic Bavarian princess, Theodelinda, never succeeded in converting the Lombards, even her own husband, to the Catholic and Roman faith. In due course these Lombards were driven out by the Franks whose history shows us the alternative course of development.

These more northern invaders, Franks and also Saxons, had not been converted to Christianity before the Roman Church developed its political power at the end of the fifth century. Their kings were then conveniently introduced to the political meaning of the Christian religion, of orthodoxy and heresy, by their Catholic wives. For at this time there was a wave of marriage which moved away from Rome and civilization filtering into the barbarian world. How did it operate?

The wave was of course initiated by the Christian clergy organized from Rome. The most notable steps were the mission of Augustine sent by Gregory the Great to England and the mission of the English Boniface or Wynfrith to arrest the progress of Irish and Frankish schismatics in Germany and to convert the Germans. But necessary instruments in this great expansion of the Roman Church were the women who also moved outwards with their chaplains and with the Church. Thus in 496 the Catholic Clotilda of Burgundy went north to marry and to convert the heathen Clovis, King of the Franks. And a hundred years later their great-granddaughter, the Catholic Bertha, went north to marry and convert the heathen Ethelbert, King of Kent. Later still we find a Kentish princess moving north to marry in Northumbria.

The importance of these women is not a romantic illusion. It was practical politics for their husbands and it had genetic consequences for their peoples. It was sometimes the woman who brought in the priests and sometimes the priests who brought in the woman. It was, we must assume, the prospect of marrying the sister of the Emperor Basil II of Constantinople which led Prince Vladimir of Kiev, four hundred years after Ethelbert, to adopt Christianity as a religion for himself and for his whole people.[1]

The results of the marriage-plus-conversion of princes and nobles were to direct the development of European society. The rulers of Europe were brought into a breeding community, a genetic network, which became the ruling caste of Europe and developed selectively although not exclusively for a thousand years. The relationship of this caste with Rome and Constantinople was in one sense ambiguous. It fluctuated, like so many social and political relationships, between subjection and protection; between competi-

[1] And which led him, no doubt, to put away his 800 concubines.

tion and co-operation. But in another sense the relationship was quite unambiguous. The king who relinquished his old heathen ancestors for Christian kinsmen exchanged gods who were dead or dying for kings who were alive and historically connected with the wealth, the power, the majesty of the Imperial Capital, either Old Rome or New Rome. Not only this; at their baptisms their Christian names were ritually recorded by the clergy; their marriages were sealed and blessed by popes; at their coronations they were anointed in ancient, sacred, and Hebrew ceremonies by bishops. The ceremonies could impress a people; the documents could establish a dynasty.

In return for so much service the ruler in turn had to pay regard to the advice or injunctions of the Church. Who should be married? Who should be crowned? These were questions which the Church of Rome, when it had gathered its strength, felt prepared to answer. But if it could lay down the law about the marriages and inheritance of other people it was bound also to attend to the problem of its own. Before it could develop its own potential power it had to look to its own structure, that is its genetic structure.

XII. BREEDING SYSTEMS

a. The Clergy: Prohibition of Marriage

The polarity within Christian communities between the holy state of matrimony and the even holier state of celibacy was one which developed slowly and in relation to diverging social and political conditions in east and west.

The control of sexual relations by Christian doctrine meant that the priesthood were given an authority, at first by their congregations and later by their bishops, to enforce the new prohibitions by correcting the sins which they enumerated and defined. Penance and punishment were soon in the hands of the priests. Then they discovered the power they had acquired in interpreting or administering the divine law, a power which never ceased to grow for a thousand years. This was power over the community as well as over individuals. It was a power derived from their moral intolerance, exact and exacting, a characteristic the early Christians had derived and inherited from their Jewish forebears. It was part of the racial Judaization which was sharply reversing the social character of pagan Europe. It was indispensable for the development of the Christian priesthood and for its authority over the masses, previously undisciplined in a Christian sense.

Now this authority was proportionate to the number of sins and hence to the number of rules which could be broken. The mechanism of control was therefore itself adjustable and controllable by the Church. Salvation, as Sismondi put it, had come first from belief; later it came from prayer, and finally from payment. The authority of the Church thus came to be partly translated into the visible form of revenue, into churches and monasteries, palaces and public works. But it had an invisible form which was even more significant for the evolution of society.

This was above all the Church's control of marriage. The mere fact that the rules of Christian marriage were unenforceable enhanced the power of the priests whose duty it was to attempt their enforcement. What a wonderful thing it is, argues Tertullian in effect (*Ad Uxorem*), that an act of obscenity, a condition of sin, and a reproach to mankind can be transfigured by the consent of a priest into a blessed state, an ordained sacrament, and a witness of the union of Christ with his Church. It is hard for a simple layman to question the premises which lead to such a triumphant conclusion.

At an early stage of their evolution the celibacy of monastic orders put the priesthood outside them in an anomalous position. At the time of Ephesus even bishops could keep their wives. They were enjoying the power and revenues of holiness without even appearing to sacrifice the pleasures of a sexual life. Moreover, as the Christian community acquired wealth and built churches, it became obvious that the privileges and perquisites were frequently inherited. The bishops, who no longer administered one church but an incipient diocese, were becoming a governing class as well as an intellectual aristocracy.

For the future of civilization it was most important that the early leaders of the Christian Church should multiply as they spread religion and culture over Europe. In fact they did not fail to do so. The offspring of popes were not always pillars of the Church, but if Pope Felix IV had not begotten children the Church would never have had Gregory the Great at its head and the history of Christian Europe would have followed a somewhat different course.

The possibilities were obvious enough to the ancient world and the Council of Nicaea no doubt had them in mind when it discussed imposing continence or celibacy on priests. It rejected the proposal. But a long battle had begun which reached different conclusions in east and west. There were several respects in which the celibacy of the clergy was favoured.

Only a priest without wife or children could be expected to devote himself whole-heartedly to the service of the Church. Only such a man could be trusted to forget his family in disposing of the rich property of the Church. Therefore unmarried priests (or monks) were bound to be favoured in competing for promotion. For this reason, celibacy soon became the rule for bishops and for those who hoped to become bishops. For this reason also, except in the poor, primitive and dynastic Celtic Church, ordained priests were soon forbidden to marry. But married men could still be ordained and they need not desert their wives on becoming priests.

From these rules certain consequences ensued. In the first place, it seems that many important men in the history of the Church put off being ordained until after a long and successful married life. For example Theodore of Tarsus was ordained perhaps at the age of sixty-two only in order to become Archbishop of Canterbury. In the second place, priests denied matrimony did not fail to multiply. Lecky quotes, among outstanding examples, the Bishop of Liège who was deposed in 1274 when sixty-five bastards were cited against him.[1] Conversely, throughout the middle ages the most capable royal bastards became bishops.

These examples are both socially and genetically significant. They mean

[1] Similarly in Iceland, Professor Askell Löve tells me, the last Catholic Bishop, who was killed by the Danes in 1551, left more than ten children. From him the whole modern population of Iceland is many times over descended.

that the missionaries of Christianity moving out of the ancient world into the heathen and barbarous north for a thousand years took with them not only the ancient culture but also the genetic foundations of that culture. They also mean that celibacy was largely concerned with legal inheritance. In the east the emperor could and did decide for the Church. He required no special celibate establishment since his high offices were regularly and officially manned by eunuchs.[1] But by the time of Hildebrand the Roman Church had to decide whether it was going to become an hereditary caste having the same character as the secular nobility, and competing with it, or a celibate order representing, however imperfectly, the ideals of the Christian religion. On this tremendous question feelings ran high. Great economic as well as political and spiritual issues were at stake. When Hildebrand (in 1077) demanded celibacy the married priests of Cambrai showed their opinion by an expressive gesture: they burnt their unmarried brother.

In the end the Roman Church followed the rule of Hildebrand. It established the celibacy of its clergy. But its celibacy proved to be the rejection of marriage and the denunciation of concubinage and adultery. It did not mean the rejection of breeding. As Chaucer tells us, the sons of priests continued to profit from their fathers' patronage. And, as the churches and palaces of Rome show us, the popes of the Renaissance were impartially devoted to enriching the Church and their own families. But the formation of an hereditary caste, fertile and legitimate, had been avoided.

By this renunciation the Roman Church expected to increase its wealth, its authority and its power. A celibate society would be more coherent and more obedient than a married society of comparable genetic diversity. And it might unite in opposition to an hereditary married caste whether noble or royal. These expectations were, over many centuries, amply fulfilled.

Now, we have to ask ourselves, what is the difference, social or genetic, between the Roman clergy and an hereditary caste of the ordinary kind from which for over a thousand years it has been so anxious to distinguish itself?

Experience has shown that the celibate Roman clergy who have played such a large part in the history of Western Europe, the part foretold by Augustine, have been distinguished from the lay population (so far as they are distinguished at all) by their devotion to the Church on the one hand and by their impotence, homosexuality, or promiscuity on the other.[2] All these properties have a genetic component which gives them a kind of genetic affinity or coherence. All of them are, as we have seen, genetic aberrations such as regularly arise through exceptional outbreeding or exceptional inbreeding in heterogeneous stratified societies. All of them appear equally in all such societies and in all classes of each society.

For these reasons there has never been any difficulty in recruiting the Roman clergy to secure that they represent a social cross-section of the whole society from which they have arisen. In regard to quality the high levels of the clergy who manage the Church are derived from the high levels of the laity.

[1] Runciman (1933).

[2] Or in the crude phrase of the Council of Constance (1418): *spadones aut sodomitae appellantur* (Lecky), translated as 'they are called impotents or sodomites'.

The Beauforts spring from the Plantagenets. The popes have usually sprung from, and frequently contributed to, the Italian aristocracy. Moreover in the mediaeval Church at least there were rare opportunities for the promotion of rare talents. A man like Wolsey would scarcely have risen without the Church to help him.

In regard to quantity the Church has had, of course, to devise methods for ensuring its recruitment. These have naturally arisen from the Church's interest in preserving life and in providing a welfare state. It was the first care of Christians to preserve the foundlings, the illegitimate children, whom the pagan world had removed by exposure, slavery or prostitution. Such foundlings provide the natural recruits for the institutions which protect them. But they are institutions whose members in turn can beget only illegitimate offspring. Thus in its most advanced stage this system allows celibacy and illegitimacy to provide a self-sustaining cycle of propagation parallel to that of marriage and legitimacy. Both of these systems are within the charitable arms of a forgiving Church. But the second does not recommend itself as a sound biological basis for the evolution of society.

A celibate clergy must, however, in part be genuinely sterile. So far as its sterility is the basis of its way of life the situation has its analogy among insects with neuter castes dependent on special nutrition. But here in man we have a neuter caste which, like all other social distinctions, is genetically determined although inherently not transmissible to the next generation. The paradox for us is that in the long silent early gestation of Christianity this genetic property should have been seized upon by the Church as the basis of what was, in its time and in spite of its abuses and absurdities, one of the main forces in moulding a balanced European society.

b. The Laity: Prohibition of Incest

As for all other 'unlawful lusts' the Christian Church took over the prohibition of incest from the Jewish Law (Leviticus 18: 20). But the situation was now different. The concern of the Church was not so much with sexual relations in general, that is what man may 'lie with' what woman; it was specifically with those monogamous marriages which it was willing to authorize. The Institutions of Justinian (3: 6, 9) accordingly laid down a list of kindred, assisted in the Vatican manuscript by a diagrammatic *Schema Cognationum*,[1] within which marriage was not permitted. It extended to the fifth degree of kinship, i.e. the fifth cousin or great-great-great-grandparent; similarly for uncles and aunts and third cousins twice removed.

In the passing centuries these rules have been the subject of an immense amount of discussion and negotiation interrupted only by violence and war. When (according to Bede) Pope Gregory instructed Augustine on his mission to England he merely excluded first cousin marriage. And he gave the reason, an ostensibly biological reason, that such marriages were childless.[2]

[1] I am indebted to Professor Antonio Moroni of Modena for a copy of this document of genetic history.

[2] An opinion based on Roman folklore rather than on Hebrew scripture.

As time went on the Canon Law grew and these prohibitions were extended. William the Conqueror had broken the Church's rule by marrying his possible fifth cousin Matilda of Flanders and Henry I was forbidden to allow his bastard daughter to marry her sixth cousin the Earl of Surrey. Gregory had also prohibited marrying one's stepmother, an act with a social but no biological meaning.

It was on the same social principle that Henry VIII realized he could not lawfully have married Anne Boleyn who was, he claimed, a sister of a former mistress. In this way, by a manipulation of Canon Law, the Princess Elizabeth could have been declared a bastard and excluded from the throne.[1]

What began as a simple domestic rule thus became in the course of centuries an instrument of power, both political and economic. On the one hand the pope could grant dispensations allowing the faithful to marry within the degrees he had forbidden, in return for such considerations as he decided. Now in the long struggle for authority between Church and State a king like Theodoric, in 498, might decide the choice between two rival popes; or a papal secretary, like Hildebrand, might almost decide the choice between two pretenders to a crown, like Harold and William. Evidently therefore no prudent prince would fail to secure his marriage and the legitimacy of his children by attending to the papal, or at a lower level the episcopal, prohibitions.

These consequences of papal policy were well understood by those who developed its theory and managed its practice. But there were, as always happens with genetic rules, other unforeseen effects. As the ruling families of Western Europe became more settled during the tenth century it became increasingly difficult for kings to find their children mates who were not closer than sixth cousins. In order to do so they had to look further and further afield, to the limits of Christendom and even to peep into the regions of infidelity. It was in this way that a net of royal marriages came to spread over the whole of Europe from Ireland to Constantinople and Jerusalem, from Castille to Novgorod, catching up in its invisible connections Arab and Tartar chieftains and Doges of Venice (Pedigree 15).

These recruits to the royal caste were in their origins a group of people highly selected for their abilities in war and government, abilities they continued to display. The descendants of Charlemagne are spread all over Europe and over most of its history. By contrast with the Achaemenids, the Ptolemies, the Caesars, the Theodosians, all of whom were extinguished by inbreeding and murder, the European dynasties continued in vigour and fertility and variety. The only analogy is in the Roman noble families who by Roman custom rejected inbreeding and maintained themselves as an outbred caste, an oligarchy genetically comparable with the later royal families of the whole continent.

Another novel advantage of the European dynasties was that they avoided legal polygamy. Their accessory unions gave bastard progeny who had no claim to the throne. Kings therefore on coming to the throne no longer felt obliged to secure the State by murdering all their brothers. Succession could

[1] See Howell Smith (1950).

therefore pass to a brother. This remarkable improvement in domestic and dynastic relations was again largely due to the documentary control of marriage by the legally trained clergy.

These innovations continued to preserve royal families so long as the Church preserved its independent power and enforced its rules against inbreeding. And this was until nearly a thousand years after Gregory had sent his mission to England.

Table 21. *Time Chart of the Christian Expansion.*

From Bede (725); *E.B.* 'Church History' (1929); E. S. Bates (1936); Bettenson (1943); Cheney (1948); Williamson (1959); H. G. May (1962); Parkes (1964); Vermes (1965).

A. SECULAR	
Judaea seized from Ptolemy V by Antiochus the Great	197 B.C.
Rising of the Maccabees	166 B.C.
Maccabean (Hasmonean) Dynasty of priest kings	140–37 B.C.
Annexation of Judaea by Pompey	63 B.C.
Essene deposits of scrolls at Qumran	175 B.C.–A.D. 68
Herod the Great, King of Judaea (Idumaean-Arab married to Hasmonean princess)	37–4 B.C.
First Jewish War: destruction of Temple by Titus (described by Josephus, A.D. 37–100)	A.D. 66–70
Fall of Masada: end of Essene community	A.D. 73
Second Jewish war: rebellion of Simon bar Kochba destruction of Jerusalem, fourth and last dispersal of orthodox Palestinian Jews (but not of Christian Jews)	A.D. 135
B. RELIGIOUS	
Translation of Bible into Greek in Alexandria (Septuagint)	270–50 B.C.
Last Old Testament Book in Catholic Canon	50 B.C.
Assumed birth of Jesus Christ (*Iesous Christos* in Greek)	4 B.C.
Mission of Jesus in Judaea	A.D. 27–30
Mission of Paul in Anatolia, Greece, Rome	A.D. 50–65
First Christian persecution in Rome	A.D. 66–68
Definitive writing of the gospels: Mark (Rome) *c.* 70; Matthew (Antioch) *c.* 80; Luke, *c.* 90; John (Ephesus) *c.* 120	
Gospels in Syriac *c.* 200	
Bible in Coptic *c.* 270, Ethiopic[1] *c.* 350, Armenian[1] *c.* 440 } Monophysite Churches	
Gothic[1] (Wulfila) *c.* 350	
N.T. in Latin at Carthage *c.* 180	
Bible in Latin (Vulgate) by Jerome, N.T.	*c.* 388
O.T. (with Apocrypha) from Hebrew with Jewish scholars	404
Tertullian, founder of Latin Christianity (born at Carthage)	*c.* 155–*c.* 222
Augustine on Church Supremacy (*De Civitate Dei*) (born in Numidia, 354)	413–426
Dionysius Exiguus, a Scythian monk in Rome, calculates Easter in terms of a Christian era (*annus domini*)	525

[1] First manuscripts in the language

C. CONFLICT	
Great Christian persecutions: Decius–Valerian:	250–260
Diocletian–Galerius:	303–311
Constantine decrees toleration: Edict of Milan	313
enforces Sunday as a holiday: 321	
dedicates Constantinople to the Virgin: 330	
Council of Nicaea: condemns Arians	325 (*et seq.*)
Council of Ephesus: condemns Nestorians	431
Julian the Apostate: reopens pagan temples	361–3
Theodosius the Great (Emperor 378–395)	
defines the faith, bans heresy and pagans, tolerates Jews	380
confiscates temples, ends Olympic games	394
founds 120 bishoprics in Gaul and Macedonia	
{ *Arcadius* (in Constantinople) dismisses the Patriarch, John Chrysostom	404
{ *Valentinian III* (in Ravenna) recognizes primacy of the Pope, Leo I	445
Justinian (Emperor 527–565)	
expels philosophers from schools in Athens	529
codifies the Romano-Christian laws	527–534
expels Arian Goths and Vandals from Italy and North Africa	533–552
D. CONSOLIDATION	
Benedict founds Subiaco *c.* 510 and Monte Cassino 529; lays down his rule for the conduct of monasteries	*c.* 540
Columba (521–597) founds monastery of Iona	565
Gregory the Great, Pope (g.g.s. of Pope Felix IV, *cf.* Bede)	590–604
ENGLAND	
Augustine's mission to Canterbury	597–604
Theodore of Tarsus (602–690) organizer of the Church in England reconciles Roman and Celtic Bishops at Hertford	673
Bede, historian of the Church in England	633–735
Bishop Boniface converts the Germans and Franks	716–754
FRANCE	
Charles Martel defeats Arabs at Poitiers	732
Boniface anoints Pippin King of the Franks, in Paris	752
Pepin recognizes the possessions of the Pope	754
Charlemagne (g.s. of Pippin)	742–814
{ crowned *Imperator* in Rome by Leo III	800
{ saluted as *Basileus* by the eastern envoys in Aachen	812
ROME	
Papacy in Rome subject to local lay powers	867–1048
Reforms of Hildebrand (Gregory VII) } Quarrel of Eastern and Western Churches ends in rupture: Latin Churches closed in Constantinople	1054
College of Cardinals formed	1059
RUSSIA	
Vladimir, Prince of Kiev (956–1015), adopts Christianity and marries the sister of Emperor Basil II	988

15

ISLAM

I. THE SETTLEMENT OF ARABIA

MOHAMMEDAN WRITERS refer to the ages before the coming of the Prophet as the Times of Ignorance, meaning ignorance of Islam. But they are also the times of our ignorance of what went before Islam. Even in the towns on the great caravan routes writing on the leaves of date palms had not effectively displaced verbal memory and recitation as a means of preserving the records of the past. Nevertheless we can discover enough of Arabian life to understand what led up to Mohammed's revolution. Our sources are fourfold: archaeology, language, the literature of the adjoining Roman or Byzantine Empire, and, strange to say, our knowledge of Arabia at the present day. For, while the Arabs who have left Arabia have transformed so many of the peoples of Asia, Africa and Europe, those who have stayed in Arabia, for reasons we shall see, have failed to transform themselves and have for the most part survived the revolutions of 1300 years as little changed as any people on earth.

This almost immovable quiescence (interrupted by Mohammed) is all the more significant since Arabia lies next to the nucleus of agricultural life and since invading pastoral Hamites and Semites from the Arabian desert were the main instruments in turning this agriculture into the basis of the first civilizations of the river valleys. The general course of events in the intervening five millennia is both clear and instructive. Agriculturists in the fourth and third millennia were able to make their way into fertile valleys in the south, that is into *Arabia Felix* or *el Yemen*. But at the same time pastoralists were grazing and over-grazing the tenuous herbage on the edge of an expanding desert. Under these threatening conditions the people of the Yemen and the Hadhramaut were able for long to hold their own. They did so by their industry, their skill in the conservation both of water and earth, and their enterprise in exploiting the spice crops and the trade in spices. But for the last two thousand years their cultivation has been forced slowly to retreat. At the same time their connection with the world from which they came has been cut off by warlike and unfriendly pastoral peoples who have continually attacked and damaged them and all their works.

We know very well how the poor and predatory herdsmen of the desert attacked and eventually overcame the cities of Mesopotamia. At the same time they must have invaded the south and with similar effects. They created a fighting governing class; they introduced Semitic priests with Semitic gods; and they imposed a Semitic language which they carried over into Axum and Abyssinia and which later came to be inscribed on their monuments in characters derived from the Phoenician alphabet.

These conflicts and upheavals led to the growth of the Arabic peoples and civilization. It was a slow process in which the crucial step was the domestication of the Arabian camel, the dromedary or 'runner', whose wild ancestors have long disappeared. This animal was first recorded in the keeping of the Midianites (Judges 6) in 1100 B.C. It contributed on the debit side to the erosion of Arabia, the expansion of the desert and the decay of the Hadhramaut basin with its capital at Marib.

But on the credit side it made possible the caravans which, treading their paths through the desert they had partly created, established the characteristic remotely dispersed Arabian settlements, the Arabian mode of warfare, and indeed the whole Arabian economy. But above all, given the desert which sparsely sustains them both, the camel created the race of Bedouin, the nomadic people whose ancestors discovered it: for they live with it, by it and for it.[1]

Serving the Bedouin, and served by them, are many specialized tribes nomadic and settled, living in associations which may be described at any stage of our history since they extend all over Arabia and North Africa as well and have left their traces over a period of five thousand years. One of these tribes is the Solubba, described by Doughty in Arabia; another is the Tomal of Somaliland today; both perhaps are of gypsy origin. Occasionally, attracted by their prosperity, such tribes attach themselves to fixed and stratified societies.

The processes of this association have been most significantly described for one specialized group, the Madan or Marsh Arabs of the Euphrates delta, by Maxwell. On the edge of the marshes occur settlements which may include two tribes speaking distinct dialects but both depending on the milk and dung of the water buffalo and on spear fishing and fowling. These people have no prayers or other religious observances, merely the customary food and sex taboos. But in their midst more advanced groups have intruded to constitute additional genetic castes. Some of these are socially inferior, the weavers, pedlars, gardeners, and net fishers. Others are superior, the Mandaean craftsmen and holy men of privileged ancestry, hereditary governing sheiks who may keep and breed black slaves. Finally to allow for the population to

[1] As described by so many accomplished European travellers and writers, e.g. Charles Doughty, T. E. Lawrence, Freya Stark, Wilfred Thesiger, Gavin Maxwell and Glubb Pasha.

be kept stable, on Carr Saunders' principle, there is a caste of dancers whose boys before marriage act as male prostitutes.

These conditions, although existing today, are so old that they show us how the earliest hunting, herding and cultivating people in Arabia actually met and began to establish the stratified societies from which a more complex life developed.

The camel-herding Bedouin tribes, like all other pastoral peoples, undoubtedly sprang from the fusion of agricultural and hunting tribes. Some of them have filtered into the stratified society of the urban settlements. But it is important to notice that an unchanged population has kept its primitive simplicity and independence. They have retained their paleolithic breeding system. Their environment has compelled them to do so. They have no class differentiation. And, subject to the outbreeding rules of the tribe, they are strictly inbred. The only outbreeding arises from the expulsion of outlaws. It is in consequence of this strictness that every tribe, as Doughty describes it, has its own intellectual and moral character, fixed and closed to enterprise and invention. Each tribe therefore naturally and genetically acts as a unit and hates most other tribes.

Socially and historically what was important about the Bedouin tribes in the time of Mohammed was that their activities and beliefs were tribal in the paleolithic sense. They had tribal gods worshipped as idols, tribal sanctuaries of immemorial age, and tribal wars arising from blood-feuds resting on the principle of revenge for killing whether intended or not intended. In general no one was or is given the benefit of the doubt.[1]

The whole system was precisely regulated by custom and ritual. After battle the dead were counted and the family which had lost the greater number received blood-money from the one which had lost less. The victor might not enter the tents of the vanquished. And the times of sowing and reaping were close seasons for fighting. The excess of women arising from the slaughter of men was compensated by female infanticide. If it was over-compensated, male homosexuality was in the past, we may suppose, no less common than it is now.

Such a system both in the numbers and in the practices of the population was indefinitely stable, so long as no foreign intrusion disturbed the balance of ideas or of genetic character. But these tribes have from time to time attacked and enslaved their agricultural and commercial neighbours. And it is then that they mixed and hybridized and created new things; this is what had happened in both the north and the south of Arabia.

The great desert centre of Arabia however had not been penetrated effectively by agriculture and commerce until the beginning of the Christian era. Then new people and new ideas were brought in, not by the armies of the great empires—for these had not yet succeeded in penetrating Arabia—but by the unarmed bearers of new religions largely fleeing from persecution. First, there were Jews escaping from the Babylonians, and later from the Roman destruction of Jerusalem by Titus and Hadrian. They came (as Torrey says) chiefly as craftsmen, goldsmiths and swordsmiths, but also no doubt as

[1] Hardy (1963).

traders, all living in towns. They prospered, bought slaves, converted and bred with them. Thus by hybridization in a few generations, they had multiplied, acquired land and developed oases. They had also changed their character, their colour and their language. They had sunk to a lower tribal level in their social and religious thinking. Their scriptures and their religion were now orally transmitted and in Arabic dialects.[1]

As in Europe, so also in Arabia, it was no doubt through the Jews that the Christians began to spread their religion. They came, not as craftsmen, but as monastic missionaries, chiefly of sects that were later suppressed in Arabia, heretical Nestorians, Coptic Monophysites and others spreading their religion. And also, according to Margoliouth, spreading the Arabic script. These Christians found allies in their co-religionists across the Red Sea under the Negus of Abyssinia. The struggle to gain control of the spice trade of the Yemen thus took the form of a religious war between Jews and Christians in the sixth century. Indeed it culminated in an Abyssinian raid on Mecca, perhaps in the year when Mohammed was born.

Table 22. *Time Chart of Arabia before Islam*

4th millenium B.C.	Migrants from Syria begin to cultivate wheat, barley and other crops along the coastal rim of Arabia
3rd	They develop terrace cultivation and irrigation in the fertile south with native spices and dates from the Persian Gulf, sesame and perennial cotton from Africa. Coastwise trade, perhaps Sumerian, with the Indus valley as well as with Africa.
2nd	Expanding pastoral Semites invade the south, later crossing into Africa. Their sheep, goats and later horses and camels cause deforestation and soil erosion. They impose their Amharic-type language and establish stratified societies with kings, nobles, priests, foreign traders and craftsmen and an enserfed peasantry
1st	Wars between Sabaean and other kingdoms for the control of the whole of the south and of the native and Indian spice trade with Egypt. Marib (700 feet above the sea) east of the dividing range and at the head of the Hadhramaut basin becomes the capital of the Yemen*; a great dam is built to support cultivation and resist the expansion of the desert (*c.* 700 B.C.). Phoenician alphabet introduced. Stone temples built

* Arabic for 'prosperous' land, i.e. *Arabia Felix* in contrast to *Arabia Deserta*, the barren land to the north.

II. MECCA AND MOHAMMED

At a point half-way between the Yemen and Syria the trade route between them is crossed by the track taken by the Bedouin from the winter grazing of

[1] A thousand years after their translation into Greek the Jewish scriptures were first put into written Arabic, with far-reaching consequences, by a Jew living in Muslim Egypt, Sa'adia ben Joseph al-Fayyumi (892–942). The translation was intended for the use of Jews in Palestine who had abandoned Aramaic for Arabic.

Jeddah on the coast to the summer grazing of Tayif in the highlands. At this inhospitable spot, with nothing but a well to recommend it, a black stone had been set up in ancient times to mark the place where tribes could meet and trade and have games without fighting, the same practice as that more fully recorded of the Jews and the Greeks. In the third or fourth century A.D. some enterprising people put up a tent over the stone, called it the Ka'abah and organized the sanctuary. Their settlement became known as Mecca.

Who were these people? They called themselves the Koreish and claimed to be Nabataeans who had made their way from the borders of Mesopotamia, or as we must now say, in Arabic, Iraq. They were pastoral people, patrilinear and perhaps recalling an ancestor Abraham who had first worshipped their tribal god Allah.

However they may have begun, the success of their venture changed the character and beliefs of the Koreish. The profits from the tolls, from the trade with the spice caravans and from the sale of water and idols to the Bedouin attending the annual fairs had enriched the tribe. They had acquired dependants, both clients and slaves. These might be Jews or Christians, Yemenites or Negroes. By polygamous concubinage the tribe multiplied in numbers and divided into clans. In all this mixing of races and classes there was some mixing of custom, of religion and even of inheritance, patrilinear or matrilinear. But there was of course no danger of any confusion in social status. The thirty-six clans diverged in wealth and power and in their achievements in war, trade and politics. They were accordingly graded in rank and reputation. The nobler, stronger and richer clans lived in the centre, the poorer and weaker clans on the outskirts of the growing city.

The similarity in site, in movement and in activity had thus given Mecca a social structure not unlike that to be seen in Athens or Rome a thousand years earlier. But it differed in the absence of written laws, appointed magistrates or hereditary rulers. The rights of men still depended on the issues of tribal and family feuds and the opinions of sorcerers and sybils.

What was altogether special about Mecca was its position. It was central in Arabia. Its population was a microcosm of Arabia. And it was a place of pilgrimage for all Arabia. By the sixth century the Ka'abah was a great stone cube; since the pagan Arabs were no craftsmen it had probably been built for them by Christian workmen. It contained all the tribal idols whose presence might attract the devotion of pilgrims, including, we may believe—and it is a reflection on both parties—the figure of the Virgin Mary. For the leaders of the Koreish, for the heads of the clans, therefore, polytheism, the worship of everybody's gods, had become more than a religion; it was now a rich and expanding industry.

Within the city, however, there was a gradation between the simple and superstitious people believing in their tribal gods and the relatively sophisticated, some of whom made a living out of that belief. When the sixth century saw the great movements of armies in South Arabia, with invasions of Persians and Abyssinians reaching even to Mecca (and supported by a Byzantine fleet), we may be sure that there were also others who were aware of the great

Pedigree 12. The clan and kindred of Mohammed and the Origins of Islamic Dynasties, Orders and Castes from within the Koreish Tribe of Mecca

After Lane (1860); Lane-Poole (1894); Margoliouth (1905); Hogarth (1922); Watt (1952), Glubb (1963)

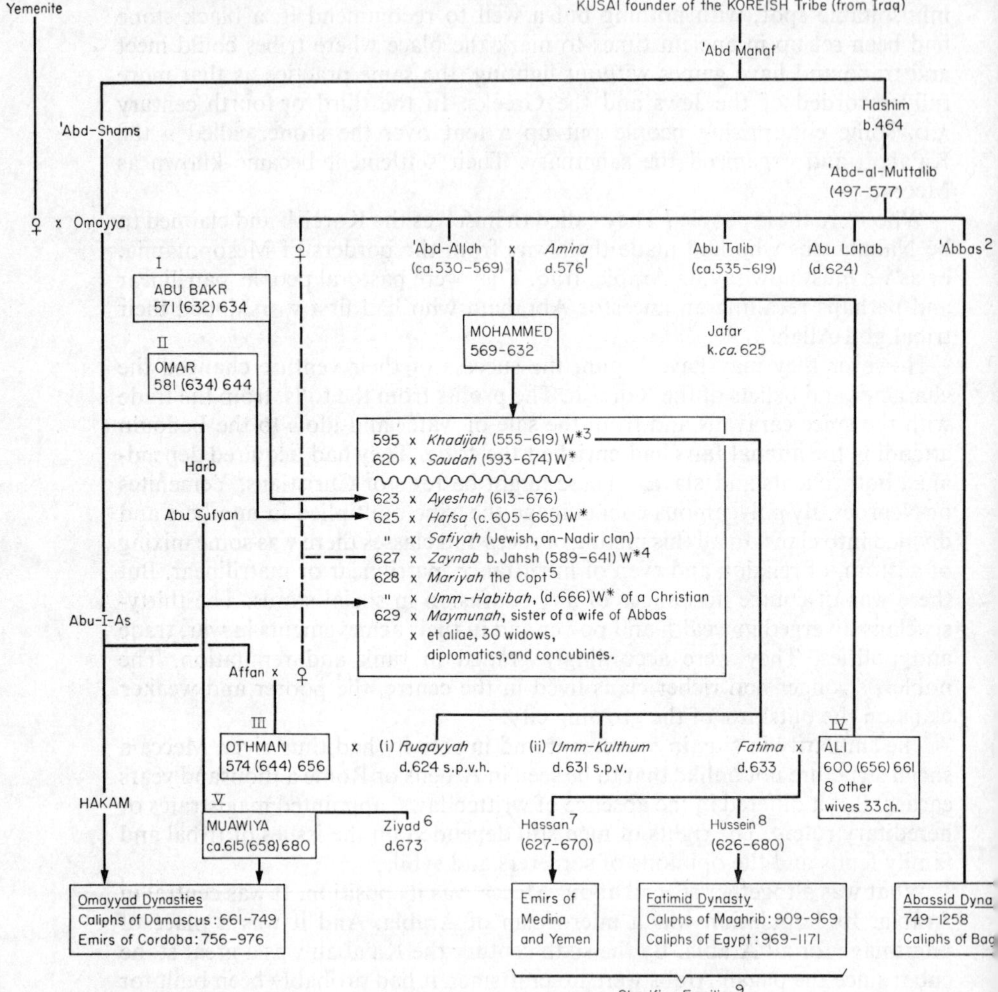

I–V. Caliphs, date of accession in brackets. Abu Bakr and Omar were of the Koreish tribe but no of the Hashim or Omayyad families. Othman's father was Omayyad, his mother Hashimite.
W*. Widows (usually of Mohammed's friends killed in battle).
1. Perhaps daughter of a Galla slave (Margoliouth, 1905).
2. With a matrilinear wife, hence the significance of M.'s marrying her sister.
3. Had a Christian cousin, Waragah.
4. Widow of M.'s adopted son Zayd, technically incest; also M.'s father's sister's daughter, a presen from the Orthodox Greek Governor of Egypt; unlike Safiyah not converted, hence a concubine
5. She bore a son Ibrahim (630–632).
6. Governor of Iraq, organizer of the eastern conquests.
7. Died in retirement at Medina.
8. Killed in revolt at the Battle of Kerbela; the descent of the Fatimids from Hussein was successfull if not authentically claimed.
9. Also the whole later European royal caste.

unifying religions and even aware of what such religions with a social code and a written history could do for the betterment of society.

Mohammed was one of the people who saw that Arabian society might be reformed. But he also saw that if it was to be reformed the attempt must be made at Mecca where the tribes met one another; and also met and hybridized with civilized people; where indeed Jews and Christians were present but not too abundant. At first, having reached the mature age of forty, he seems to have tried to persuade the elders of Mecca to accept a policy of reform. But he failed. The vested interests of the older men and of the richer clans were too strong for him. It was then that he turned to the method of inspired revelation as a means of social change.

The magnitude of the task was appalling. He set himself to convert a tribal society torn by war into a national or universal society united by law. This was what had been achieved by the creation of the Roman Empire and its conversion to Christianity over several centuries. Mohammed set out to accomplish this transformation by his own efforts and in his own lifetime. To do it he had to make war without any training in war. He had to take command in a clan of modest social status and as an orphan protected only by uncles. And he had to establish a written religion and law without, if possible, giving any evidence that he could read or write himself.

Mohammed achieved this miracle—the only one in which we may confidently believe—in the space of twenty years. First, he had to create a society by convincing himself and a few devoted friends, that he was inspired by God. Secondly, he had to govern this society so well that his enemies would come to believe the same. The first stage of this great exercise was in Mecca, the second in Medina.

Mohammed was born in Mecca perhaps, as we saw, in the year that Abyssinian raiders reached the city. Like so many people in Mecca, he was probably of mixed origin; his mother's father was (says Margoliouth) perhaps a freed Abyssinian slave; that is to say a prisoner of war. When he had married at the age of twenty-six a well-to-do widow much older than himself he had been able to begin trading. Over fifteen years his travels had taken him to all corners of Arabia if not also to Egypt and Abyssinia. During this time he had learnt by long premeditated enquiry how other societies worked. When he settled down in Mecca, about 610, it was on this basis that he began his great argument.

III. THE MISSION AND THE METHOD

Mohammed's first revelation dealt with the Day of Judgment; the Christian or Zoroastrian alternatives of salvation and damnation were explained. His second revelation showed his listeners how to be saved; the solution was Abraham's: put away the idols of your father's people and worship one god. Whence followed Paul's prescription that meat offered to idols must not be eaten. Whence in turn it followed that the believer could not eat with the idolater. The basic barrier in establishing all new societies was set up. The believers became outcasts in their own land.

These revelations were passed on to the faithful brethren by a faithful friend, Abu Bakr. They were passed on in secret so that a secret brotherhood was created. Slaves were freed when they joined this brotherhood but for this reason they could not join unless their owners joined. Abu Bakr who was well-to-do consumed his estate by loss of trade and by buying slaves.

To the orthodox idolater and the pagan Establishment the new sect was treason and, like Christians in Rome, its members were traitors. They became known accordingly as *Muslimin.*[1] Nor was their situation improved when eighty-three Muslim families escaped or absconded to the Christian Negus in his capital of Axum. During ten years the persecution of their enemies, and the courage and resource with which Mohammed met it, strengthened the infant community, breaking down within it all the ingrained tribal superstitions of kinship and idolatry. Further revelations now defined the rituals of prayer, fasting and washing, the obligations of marriage, the limits of polygamy (soon to be exceeded by the Prophet himself), the rules of inheritance, the prohibitions of incest, polyandry, and infanticide, and of the enslavement of Muslims.

Only in one respect had Mohammed hesitated to restrain Arab practice. Homosexuality he dare not condemn. The life of the desert has never allowed the suppression of sodomy. But in all other respects the Jewish rules favouring fertility and securing responsible propagation had been taken over. The immemorial system of population control derived from paleolithic societies had been not only abandoned but actively reversed.[2] By their obedience to their own new and more rigorous law the faithful established themselves as a viable community, a self-contained and self-perpetuating breeding group, a society hated and somewhat feared in Mecca, but known and somewhat respected elsewhere.

Now a non-tribal breeding group was, even within the Christian and Jewish sects, something new in Arabia Deserta. It was consequently given a new name. It was an *ummah*; a kind of Kingdom of God on earth. For nearly ten years the Muslims, the Ummah, were saved from outlawry by Mohammed's only protector, his uncle Abu-Talib. But when this loyal and far-sighted man died the situation changed. Life in Mecca soon became impossible for the community. Thoughts were clearly turning towards assassination. Mohammed with his faithful band took refuge in flight. They escaped 200 miles to the north to a rival commercial settlement high up on the mountain ridge. It was a

[1] Hogarth has discussed the origin and transformation of this term of abuse.

[2] Certain connections of precept and policy of the kind discussed by Carr Saunders must of course be doubtful. For example, according to Levy, it is possible that prohibitions of homosexual relations, and also of abortion, were removed in a later revision of the Koran under the Abbassids. I am influenced in my interpretation by the fact that, although executions for pederasty occur in some parts of Arabia (Thesiger, 1959), in other parts—and nowhere else in the world today—the marriage of two men is legally enforceable (see John Bottrill, B.B.C., August 10, 1965). Again R. A. Fisher (1930, p. 201) has argued that the Arabic expansion was the effect but not the purpose of the prohibition of infanticide. See also R. Burton (1886).

place called Yathrib which became known to the Muslims as 'the city', *el-Medina.*

In Medina Mohammed was faced with entirely different problems from those he knew in Mecca. Here was a settlement colonized if not founded by Jews, refugees from the destruction, first of Jerusalem, and then of Marib in the Yemen. The people were a mixture of Arab, Jewish and hybrid clans with a rich cultured governing class using the Hebrew alphabet for a Yiddish kind of language. To these people the Prophet's revelations seemed to be wholly primitive and partly second-hand.

They seemed borrowed and not well borrowed. It was necessary to impress them. Mohammed did so. He decided on a show of force against the people of Mecca. He sent out a body of 300 men, his own companions and 'helpers' from Medina, to waylay the Meccan caravans from the north. The attack was at Badr close to the coast. It succeeded. The Meccans were humbled. And at the same time Mohammed's position within Medina was secured. He had killed two birds with one stone.

Now the clans of Medina, unlike those of Mecca, both Arab and Jewish, were deeply divided. They had neither a single law nor a single ruler to govern them. They therefore appealed to Mohammed as a holy man to settle their quarrels. He did so. His success, which was now the success of a statesman, converted chiefs with their whole tribes to the new teaching. By degrees he became a governor and a lawgiver. As governor he appointed chiefs, dismissed lesser soothsayers and built a place of worship, a mosque. As lawgiver he issued his revelations, an oracular news-letter whose contents were later to be embodied in the Koran.

Mohammed's political success no less than his supernatural claim meant that the Messenger of God was expected to lay down the law on everything. He had to pronounce without undue delay on problems of science and art as well as on questions of politics, law and religion. He could not hesitate and he often made mistakes. Sometimes his judgments had to be revised or even reversed. And sometimes they ought to have been reversed but were maintained. But the grand lines of his policy were too overwhelmingly right to suffer from little or local setbacks.[1]

[1] The worst mistakes Mohammed made were in fields of natural science, one large and one small:

(i) By adopting a lunar year he threw the fasts and feasts of Islam out of season. This ruined the Mecca trade fairs for ever. It also gravely impeded the northward spread of Islam: the day-long fast of Ramadhan could have been kept in high latitudes only if it had always fallen in winter, that is by the use of a solar calendar.

(ii) By forbidding the men of Medina to pollinate their female date palms he ruined the Medina harvest. But the ruin was only for one year.

Both these steps, the astronomical and the botanical, were taken in ignorance or defiance of the wisdom of former ages.

IV. PROPHET AND COMMANDER—WAR ON TWO FRONTS

His one great setback was Mohammed's discovery that he could not expect to convert the Jews. At Mecca he had done everything, as he thought, to accommodate them. He had claimed Abraham as an ancestor. He had admitted Moses as a prophet. And he had accepted the Mosaic commandments. He had directed his prayers to Jerusalem. He had adopted the seven-day week of the Jews and he had boldly instituted Friday, in preparation for the Jewish sabbath, as his own day of worship. He had even celebrated the Jewish Day of Atonement with a fast. Circumcision which he did not mention was no barrier for his followers had probably already inherited the practice. And from the Jews wine could still be freely purchased.

But in spite of all this the Jews rejected him. So he reversed his policy and rejected the Jews. A Mandaean month of Ramadhan[1] took the place of the

Table 23. *Time Chart of Islam.*

After W. Montgomery Watt (1961); Glubb (1963); Gabrieli (1968).

(i) *The Foundation*

c. 150 B.C.	Himyarites from the east conquer the Sabaeans and govern the Yemen
c. A.D. 100	Jews dispersed by Titus begin to colonize towns on trade routes of Arabia
c. 200	Christian conversions in urban and nomadic communities
300–500	Struggle between Jewish Himyarites and Christian Abyssinians for control of the Yemen
c. 300	Permanent settlement established at the sanctuary of Mecca by the Koreish tribe organizing caravans between Syria and the Yemen
c. 400	Marib dam bursts and Himyarite capital moved to Sanaa
c. 500	Jews massacre Christians in Nejran (N. Yemen)
522	Abyssinians assisted by Byzantine fleet invade and occupy the Yemen
569	Abyssinians raid Mecca
574–597	Persians liberate Yemen: appoint viceroy
569	Mohammed born in Mecca
610–613	He converts Abu Bakr and begins his preaching as preserved in the Koran
617	Mohammed's followers take refuge in Christian Abyssinia
622	Migration (*hijrah*) of Mohammed and his companions to Yathrib (Medina)
623–630	The struggle with Mecca

[1] The Mandaeans were a baptismal sect (hence the Arabic Subba) probably of Babylonian origin and strongly influenced by antagonism to Christianity. They were recognized by Mohammed as the third of the 'peoples of the Book' on account of their scriptures in deviant Aramaic. Like all small minority religious groups they have come to be a caste of professional specialists. As silversmiths they still survive and may be seen in the bazaars of Iraq. They have also been described by Maxwell, as we saw, among the Marsh Arabs of the lower Euphrates.

(i) *The Foundation* (continued)

624	Meccan caravans broken at Badr. Mohammed established at Medina. Mohammed directs his followers, *Muslims*, to turn towards Mecca and not Jerusalem in prayer
627	Abortive siege of Medina by Meccans
628	Mohammed lays Jews of Khaibar under tribute, sparing their lives He summons Emperors Heraclius and Khosru and the Negus of Abyssinia to repent
630	Submission of Mecca to Mohammed
632	Death and burial of Mohammed at Medina

(ii) *The Caliphs and the Expansion*

616	Persian conquest of Syria and Egypt under Khosru
626–629	Byzantine reconquest by Heraclius

ABU BAKR: 632–634

OMAR: 634–644. The great organizer of Islam; ruling in Medina he appoints generals and governors, directs the administration, compiles the Koran, orders the expulsion of Christians from the Yemen and of Jews from Khaibar; assassinated by a Persian slave.

632–638	Muslim conquest of Syria; 639: Muawiya, Governor in Damascus
637–639	Conquest of Iraq: Kufa founded
640–641	Conquest of Egypt: Cairo founded
641	Capture of Babylon and Persepolis (Istakhr)
642	End of the Sassanids

OTHMAN: 644–656 (assassinated by son of Abu Bakr)

649	Cyprus annexed

ALI: 656–658 Capital at Kufa; assassinated

657–692	Civil wars between leaders of rival families attached to rival peoples, sects and caliphs in Hejjaz, Syria and Iraq

MOAWIYA: 658–680 establishes Omayyad Dynasty at Damascus

669, 674	M. repulsed from Constantinople
670	Cairouan founded
673	Muslims reach Oxus and Indus

ABDALMALIK: 685–705

693	Arabic coinage and Arabic language made official in place of Greek and Persian throughout Empire

WALID: 705–715

710–712	Spain invaded and overwhelmed by Muslim (Berber) army
732	Muslims repulsed at Poitiers by Charles Martel; they hold Narbonne

Jewish Day of Fasting. Instead of Jerusalem, Mecca was to be the *Kiblah* to which prayer mats would be directed. And instead of friendship a new policy of truculence made itself felt. If the Muslims could not convert the Jews might they not destroy them? And confiscate their wealth? The Muslims needed all they could get to finance their new state and their struggle with Mecca.

The new policy occupied a period of five years. One by one Mohammed picked quarrels with the three richest Jewish clans. All of them had the choice of conversion; all of them with individual exceptions rejected it following the ancient rules of Deuteronomy. The first two he expropriated and drove out into the desert. The third he destroyed on the spot. The men were beheaded; the women and children enslaved and sold.

This was the first terrifying act of Muslim aggression. Its wide implications must have been quickly apparent to those who took part in it. Mohammed's policy of Arab unity had brought strength; strength had brought wealth and slaves. One other consequence, however, they could not have foreseen. The possession of women of another people, people of the Book, with quite different talents from their own, meant a new era in the history of their race, an era of hybridization with people more civilized than themselves, hybridization moreover with a gain rather than a loss of social status.

Hardly had this policy been revealed when it underwent a far-reaching transformation. Mohammed took the war out of its narrow orbit. He attacked the Jewish settlement of Khaibar, 150 miles to the north of Medina, to which earlier refugees had made their way. The Jews surrendered but Mohammed now made up his mind that these people were too valuable to destroy. He allowed them to survive on condition of the payment of tribute. This situation had also been defined in Deuteronomy. But the rule now established by Mohammed was to govern the development of his Empire. And it was a new one.

People of the Book, Jews, Christians and Mandaeans, to whom later were to be added Zoroastrians, were not to be butchered or enslaved on conquest, even though rejecting Islam. They were to be tolerated provided they paid taxes from which Muslims were exempt. They did not know at the time that the length of the permission and the scale of the taxation would be at the will or whim of increasingly arrogant Muslim rulers. But they were safe for a time.

Thus a principle was adopted in contrast with the Christian practice of uniformity and intolerance, orthodoxy and persecution. Christianity had spread from sophisticated and stratified societies into unsophisticated and unstratified societies. Islam was attempting the reverse. It was a more difficult task requiring devious courses and purposes postponed. The simple phrases of the Koran: 'Let him believe who will: let him disbelieve who will' meant that Mohammed was recognizing the value of religious and racial minorities such as hardly existed in Christian Europe: they would be indispensable for the maintenance of his society in the Ancient East for the next thousand years.[1]

The Islamic Empire thus had by its own laws to establish the basis of racial and social stratification on which it had to rest. It did so by the practical methods derived from Mohammed's ruling at Khaibar. Taxation and conversion became the two principal parameters governing the structure of society. For clearly conversion had quickly to be discouraged or forbidden if the basis of taxation was not to be upset. Such social promotion, as Levy points out, could be reserved for favoured servants of the state. Notice then a paradox: Christian people were acceptable as subjects; Christian rulers were not acceptable at all.

At the same time that Mohammed was subduing the Jewish clans he was

[1] Later in the Ottoman Empire, as we shall see, it led to ruin.

engaging in a long struggle with the Meccans, countering their spies, intercepting their caravans and repelling their expeditions. Success and failure alternated. But the sacred pagan months were violated; the sacred pagan rules of kinship and tribal feud were broken; the pagan disunity of command and of purpose was exposed. By an extraordinary turn of policy Mohammed was able to negotiate the right for Muslims to make a pilgrimage to Mecca. There he appeared in March 629 with his wives, now a large and multi-tribal company, and 2000 Muslim warriors, demonstrating their own strength and at the same time acknowledging the supreme sanctity of the city of Mecca.

The following year Mecca submitted to her exiled prophet. He re-entered his city as its governor. The idols of the Ka'abah were thrown down and defiled and proved powerless to reply; the keys were restored to their hereditary keepers; the place was resanctified as the central shrine of Islam, a place of pilgrimage; it was a place to which no idolators and no infidels were henceforward to be admitted. The tables had been turned on the idolators. Mecca and Islam, economic interest, political and racial unity and religious doctrine were reconciled in one unparalleled revolutionary climax.

With this new supremacy Mohammed returned to Medina. There he devoted the two remaining years of his life to organizing the submission of all Arabia. Financially this meant that the converted paid modest 'alms', the unconverted a heavier annual tax, to the new ruler. But socially it meant that peace was brought to the whole of the peoples of Arabia. Their minds which had hitherto been turned backwards in time were now turned forwards. Their swords which had been turned inwards on themselves were now willing to be turned outwards. Blood-feuds were, for the moment, pacified. The terrible power which had consumed the population of the peninsula in petty strife was suddenly collected in one hand ready to attack, eager to attack, the rich neighbours who had for two thousand years despised the weakness and barbarism of the desert peoples.

This was the position which Mohammed left to his successors when he died.

V. THE MUSLIM EMPIRE

In the three generations following the death of the Prophet, precisely a hundred years, his Muslim armies had conquered their Empire. They had split the dissident and heretical southern provinces off the Roman Empire; they had invaded and mastered Morocco and Spain; they had dissolved or absorbed the Persian dominions; they had established a continuous government from the shores of the Atlantic to the borders of China. It was a government to which Arabia itself was now an almost empty appendage. But it was a government by people who considered themselves Arab because they spoke the Arabic tongue, obeyed the laws and followed the rites laid down in the sacred Arabic verses of his Koran by their own Prophet (Fig. 12).

From the military and political points of view what had happened surpassed the achievement of Alexander. It did so because it had the character of those great linguistic and racial expansions which we have previously surmised, confidently surmised, but without documentary or even archaeo-

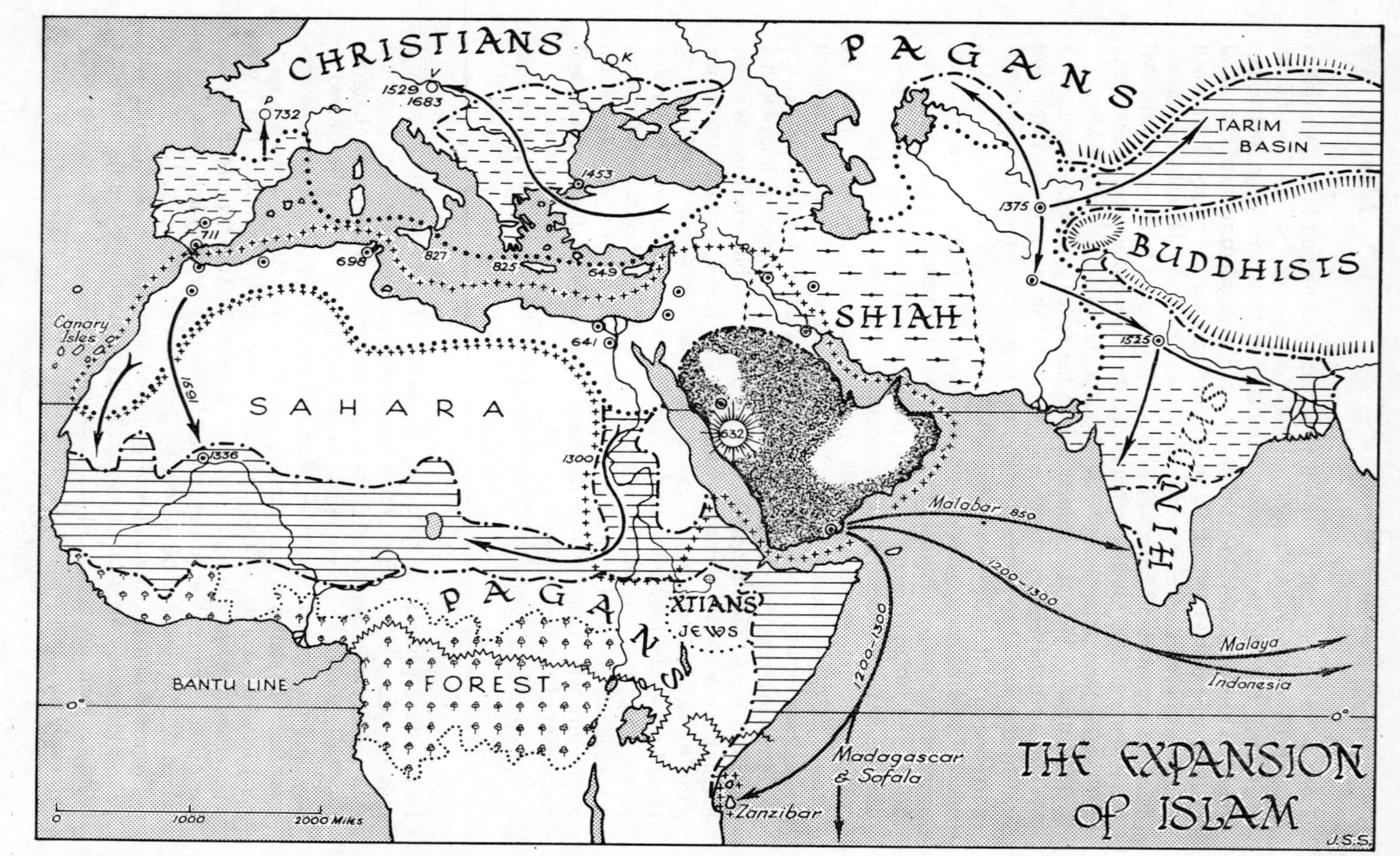
THE EXPANSION of ISLAM
CHRISTIANS
PAGANS
BUDDHISTS
TARIM BASIN
SHIAH
HINDUS
SAHARA
PAGANS
FOREST
XTIANS
JEWS
BANTU LINE
Canary Isles
P
732
V
1529
1683
K
1453
711
698
827
825
649
641
632
1375
1525
1300
1336
1691
Malabar 850
1200–1300
1200–1300
Malaya
Indonesia
Madagascar & Sofala
Zanzibar
0°
0°
0
1000
2000 Miles
J.S.S.

logical evidence. It was a Semitic expansion corresponding to the Aryan expansion inasmuch as it depended on the spread and multiplication of a governing class which was able slowly to impose its language on the peoples, or most of the peoples, it subdued. Yet the expansion and the imposition together had a pace that has never been paralleled. How did it happen? It was because three instruments of victory were brought together by the Arabs in one operation.

The first instrument of victory was the exclusive use of horsemanship by a pastoral people genetically adapted and culturally trained for fighting. In this they were like all pastoral people. But they surpassed their predecessors in the rapidity of their movements carried out in a vast desert under conditions of appalling rigour. For fifty generations the horse and the camel, added to their other weapons, had given the Bedouin the means of aggression by fighting. Inevitably they had been selected as tribes, as individuals, and especially as chieftains, for success in this fighting. The Muslim expansion was led by commanders of the Koreish tribe. They were men whose commanding position at Mecca, at the centre of the great Arabian caravan industry, guaranteed that they would be supremely accomplished in controlling the force of 30,000 Bedouin and bandits whom they mobilized for their first attack. It was these circumstances and attributes that brought success to the piratical tactics described by Glubb. It was a success that was to be repeated from a Central Asiatic base by the Turks, the Tartars, the Mongols and the Moguls.

The second instrument of Arab victory was their religion. The realization of unity and equality within their race, the exaltation of the strength, and the certainty of victory and of salvation it gave them, enabled the Arabs to sweep

---

Fig. 12. The Expansion of Islam and of its three Pastoral Peoples (Arabs, Turks and Mongols)

1. The Arabian Base in A.D. 632: stippled area.
2. Conquests up to 750: dotted line ......
3. Conquests after 750 including the limits of the Ottoman Turkish Empire (1560–1683): dot and dash boundary —•—•
4. Limit of Arabic speech as maintained today by governing classes does not depart more than 12° from the latitude of Mecca: boundary marked by crosses.
5. The boundary of the Shiah Schism is set by former Persian domination: -•-
6. Regions later lost by Islam: broken lines.
7. Arrows show directions of conquest.
8. Chief Islamic and non-Islamic cities are shown with dates of conquest, repulse, or foundation.

Notes:

i. Arab trade and exploitation in the Indian Ocean led to domination of Indonesia (in 1476), of Malaya and of East Africa (from 1200 to 1498). Contrast the failure to reach the Canary Isles.
ii. The tropical rain forest excludes pastoralists and hence Muslims.
iii. The intrusion into the Bantu language line in East Africa is due to the Nilo-Hamitic Masai: pastoral but pagan people.
iv. There are Muslim minorities today in Bosnia and Albania as well as in India.
v. The southern limits of the Mogul Empire (between 1560 and 1707) approximate to those of Aryan languages in India.
vi. Non-Muslim (Christian and Jewish) Arab speakers are still found in Palestine and the Lebanon.

away their enemies and to ride over the storms of their own family schisms which split them during thirty years in the very middle of their conquests. Here it was that the third instrument and condition of their success appeared. That they should produce many notable commanders was to be expected. That they should produce the great Omar, a man who compared as administrator and statesman with Mohammed, that was a stroke of fortune on which the Prophet had lived to congratulate himself. That they should produce a second who proved even greater, namely Moawiya, was a second stroke of fortune. For, of these two men, the one assured the conquest and the other preserved it.

But, of course, these were not just strokes of fortune. They were proofs that the proud race of the Koreish at that time had indeed something to be proud of, a capacity for government.

A last instrument of Muslim success was the nature of the Islamic society which it created and the processes of change and development which this society set in motion. These processes, so well described by Hogarth and Reuben Levy, we must now consider, taking at the same time another look at Arabia itself.

VI. ISLAMIC SOCIETY

a. The Governing Class

The Muslim programme of conquest and conversion led to a diverse treatment of the conquered populations with correspondingly diverse reactions on the conquerors. These may be examined in relation to class, race and religion. If we speak primarily in terms of class we have to distinguish governing class, peasants, craftsmen and intellectuals.

Take first the governing class. They were derived at the beginning without exception from the commanders of the conquering armies, men of the Koreish tribe. They had killed in battle or driven into exile the rulers and commanders of the defeated states. The widows and daughters of these enemies they generously took into their harems. If they were converted they took them as wives, if unconverted as concubines. In this way they created in one generation a new governing class, undoubtedly Muslim, assertedly Arab, and unmistakably both able and diverse in their abilities. They also became exceedingly numerous. The original armies issuing forth from Arabia in the seventh century may have numbered no more than a hundred thousand men. The survivors of war, including civil war, must have been fewer. But their descendants in two or three generations numbered millions: they populated the Muslim world. How are we to describe their origins in genetic terms?

At once we can see that polygamous conquerors must always be selected for a high rate of propagation. They had not so much time to spare for this work of propagation as the Sherifian Sultan of Morocco, Mulay Ismail. A thousand years after the first conquest, outdoing Rameses II of Egypt, he begot 700 sons. But certainly the genetic effect of the Arabs was enough to influence the whole Islamic world. It was also enough to beget in a few generations, at each successive expansion, a vast hybrid population. They were the people who both created and filled new cities around the camps of Kufa and

Cairo, the mosques of Cairouan and Fez, the converted church of Cordoba, and the palace of Baghdad.

Thus the grand hybridization plan of Alexander, frustrated at the highest levels by his caste-forming successors was now, under different circumstances, carried to a fruitful issue. A consequence of this hybridization was the spread of the Arabic language in which converts had to affirm their Muslim faith. Today their scattered descendants still speak it, a little distorted, but written in Arabic characters and following the rules of Arabic grammar and refreshed (or embalmed, according to our point of view) by contact with sacred scriptures in the schools devoted to their teaching. This continuity of language and religion, reinforcing the continuity of race, created the triple-bound network in space and time for the lack of which military empires have promptly fallen to pieces.

b. Peasants

So much for the rulers. The fate of the peasants was altogether different. Nearly everywhere and without hybridization they were simply converted. Being converted, they kept the land they loved. And having changed their proprietors, they paid no more and no less rent, tribute or service to a Muslim lord than they had earlier paid to a Christian or a pagan. They remained where they had always been, at the bottom of society. The Egyptian serf submitted to the Sultan in Cairo as he had to Pharaoh and Cambyses in Memphis or to Ptolemy and Caesar in Alexandria. So also in Syria, Iraq and Persia.

This was not however the whole story. Time proved that although he was now a Muslim, the peasant could and soon did declare what kind of Muslim he intended to be. It was the peasant above all who, being fixed to the land, decided that Islam should take a different colour in lands of different race; that it should indeed, like Christendom, split into sects of different racial character and regional location. This regional effect, in which ecology and genetics are united, we see most clearly in one place, namely in Persia and in the land of Iraq which had for a thousand years been dominated by Persia and infused with Persian immigrants. It was here, as we shall see, that the Shiah sect broke away from the main body of Islam.

c. Craftsmen

The third group, the skilled artisans, behaved, as we might expect from their diverse characters and opportunities, in many different ways. One trade had a particularly remarkable destiny. These were the seamen. They were by origin Phoenician and Greek and by ancestry much hybridized. After the capture of Tyre, they had surrendered the key of the eastern Mediterranean to Alexander. To Islam they seem to have yielded it without a battle. Loathing the Church in Constantinople, with most of their Syrian and part of their Alexandrian brethren, they must have been willingly converted. Moreover their adherence to the Muslim cause was quickly and mutually rewarding. For so we must understand the fall of Cyprus already in 649 to be followed by Sicily and Sardinia, Crete and Malta.

Another Muslim advance in the Mediterranean was delayed until the fifteenth century. Then the annexation of Greece was followed by the incorporation and conversion, subject to many makeshifts, of the Greek and Dalmatian as well as the Syrian and Egyptian sea-faring populations, in the Ottoman Empire. After their failure to take Malta in 1565, over a period of four hundred years the balance of sea power in the Mediterranean shifted slowly against the Muslims. Technical advance and maritime discovery in the Christian west led to desertion or emigration and conversion of the leading men. The Saracens (as we call them) gave up their islands and withdrew to their mainland bases. They declined, like the Cretans of earlier times, to their smaller achievements as corsairs or pirates.

Altogether different was the fate of the captive craftsman, the sedentary and unwarlike artisan. In the various conquered countries they dwelt in the new camps and settlements as well as in the old cities and towns. They worked in their ancient trade guilds leading their segregated lives in the new covered *suq* as they had in the old open street.[1]

They continued to follow their hereditary trades and professions. They continued also to follow their equally hereditary religions. There were Jews, Samaritans and Mandaeans. And there were the diverse Christian sects, Greek or Maronite, Coptic, Assyrian or Armenian. These different faiths continued in the cities of Islam. They maintained themselves by their rejection, not only of interbreeding with Muslims, following conversion, but also of interbreeding with one another.

Each one maintained, by generation after generation of inbreeding, the exact religion, the unquestionable beliefs in their scriptures, the habits and culture, the skills and trades of its forefathers. Each one, through being numerically small, became racially pure. It became true-breeding by the genetic isolation of the urban minority just as peasant communities become true-breeding by ecological isolation. It became a caste by virtue of its rejection of all others: those others on which, to be sure, each, being different in character from all the rest, was entirely dependent.

Thus beneath the sparkling changes on the surface of Islam lay the solid stable world of the peasant and the craftsman, partly excluded from the privileges of Muslims. They were both crystallized by their inbreeding. Both were utterly conservative; they created nothing new but they lost nothing old. They preserved everything so that we see them today working their fields or their anvils as they worked them a thousand years ago.

To be sure disasters sometimes befell them. When the Sultan, Selim the Grim, decided to establish fifty new manual crafts in the depleted society of Istanbul, he transported the whole of the guilds concerned from Cairo. Thereby he left the arts of that city, as it was claimed, irreparably damaged. He could not know that he had secured the supremacy of his capital by continuing a natural movement which had been in progress for three thousand years. The professional caste societies of the ancient world, disturbed but again stabilized by Islam, were highly successful so long as their environments

[1] As Jeremiah (37: 21) or Edward Lane described them, and as we may still see them.

were also stable. Moreover their internal stability excluded the inventions which would have changed their environments. The inventions that were eventually to undermine them came, as they were bound to come, from outside.

The various infidel sects were differentially taxed from the beginning. But in proportion as the Muslim rulers became more secure their infidel subjects were more oppressively mulcted and humiliated. They must pray in private and walk on foot; at law their evidence was void against the word of a believer; there was explicitly one law for the rich and another for the poor. And if they hoped by conversion to escape from their disabilities they might find that the door had now been closed against them. The treasury of the Sultan had come to depend on the contributions of the unbeliever.

Movement however was not denied to the dissenter. The minute and scattered congregations of the Samaritans show that they could communicate. And with the extension of Islam, repeated under successive races of conquerors, the artisans of Damascus, Muslim or infidel, might be found in later generations practising their skills in Toledo or in Samarkand and contributing to the uniform spread of what was now known as Islamic civilization.

Finally, if the limit of endurance was passed, exile did not put a term to prosperity. Out of reach of Islam, colonies of Zoroastrians, those gifted people now known as Parsees, made their way into western India; colonies of Jews crossed the seas to Cochin and into tropical Africa; groups of Nestorian missionaries carried their message to Mongolia and made themselves useful to Tartar princes in China; and Armenians eventually have taken their features, their talents and their religion to the ends of the earth.

d. Intellectuals

While the peasants of Egypt, the shepherds of the Maghrib, and the minor artisans of the cities escaped hybridization and resisted change, each new conquest or revolution threw urban society into some disorder. The breaking down of barriers was most evident with the coming of the Abbassids to Baghdad. At once birth and family came to be despised. Only merit mattered, the merits of the individual. This temper lasted, as it always does, a few generations. Then differences of achievement led to assortative mating and a new order of inequality among families, a new social stratification, crystallized out. And from this process of recombination something new emerged.

The outward sign of this transformation was the disappearance of so much that was distinctively Greek, Persian and Jewish into the body of Islamic life. In the first two generations after the conquest it had been obvious that the builders of mosques were Greek-speaking Christians. The language of administration in Syria had been Greek. Soon the builders and the administrators were speaking Arabic. But they continued the style and inherited the mathematics, and the ability to use it, of their Greek or, we may say (since Babylon, after all, is only sixty miles from Baghdad), of their Babylonian ancestors. The Persians, who resisted hybridization, preserved their language. The Jews who already existed as a persecuted minority in all parts of the Empire were valued at once for their medical skill and general literacy. The modes of action of the three peoples and their cultures on the development of Islam were, for these reasons, deeply contrasted. For, while the Greeks and the Persians operated largely through conversion, the Jews were able to exert their influence largely without conversion.

The converging effects of these manifold influences we may now consider.

e. The Persians

The extreme climate as well as the endemic diseases of the Persian tableland have from Babylonian times to the present day repelled or enfeebled invaders. The swift horsemen from Central Asia as well as from Arabia could get across. But the Russians who tried to stay were compelled to withdraw in 1720. For this reason the Persian caste structure established under the Achaemenids has never disintegrated. The Hellenistic revolution failed to shift it and the Roman expansion and the Christian conversion hardly touched it. The nation had thus been largely isolated, and its character and religion stabilized, by the time of the Muslim conquest.

The first adjustment to conquest was however sufficient to lead to a second when the Abbassids seized the caliphate and removed the capital to Baghdad, a city founded in the region of Iraq long held by the Persians.

For half a dozen generations (the characteristic period of Islamic flowering) the dynasty, the government and the army became half-Persian. The caliphs married slaves but they must have been largely captive Persians. The Prime Minister was now a *vizir* and the Persian title has been handed down throughout Islam. The Persian language had been infiltrated with Arabic terms and its script had been Arabized but the racial character of the Persians had maintained the integrity of their culture. As Hogarth puts it, the Greco-Roman situation repeated itself. The subtle intelligence of the defeated Persians overwhelmed the political strength of their Arab conquerors and gave a new twist to their artistic invention and also their religious enthusiasm.

The intelligence of the Persians expressed itself in the coming centuries in the characteristic art of the country. But it also expressed itself in their attitude to religion. It was in Persia that the Sufi sect developed. There it gave rise to the greatest of Persian poets and the most splendid part of Islamic literature; but inevitably also it gave rise to heresies which Muslim sultans found treasonable somewhat earlier than their Christian counterparts.[1]

This is what happened at the top of society, the level of the gentry, cultivated and debonair. These people had been swept away several times in history and would be swept away again. But still the national character of Persia remained. It arose, as we should expect it to arise, deep down below from the

[1] Dante describes and excuses the horrible punishment of Mohammed as the '*seminator di scandalo e di schisma*' (*Inferno*, 28: 31). But Augustine's estimate of Christian schisms was about the same as Omar Khayyam's of Muslim sects after the same interval of four centuries of faith. Each was a measure of the racial diversity incorporated which, equally in the two systems, political authority attempted but failed to extinguish. Heretics were crucified by sultans before they were burnt by popes; the first Sufi to die was Al-Hallaj in Baghdad in A.D. 922; and 500 years later there was Badr el-Din in 1420 in Konya (*cf.* Kritzeck).

mass of the people, from the craftsman and the peasant. It was from the people that a national religion asserted itself once more under the new dispensation. It was the indigenous population of Persia and Iraq which seized upon the schism of the Shiahs and made it their own. It was they who soon compelled the Arabs in Kufa to worship apart in an Arab mosque; and in Khorasan to shelter in their Arab guilds and corporations. And it is they still today who worship Ali and Hussein, the martyred seed of the Prophet, beating themselves with bloody chains, as they re-enact every year on the tenth day of Muharram the dreadful battle of Karbala.

f. The Paper Revolution

The whole of the intellectual processes involved in the expansion of Islam are brought into focus when we look at one apparently trivial event, the discovery of the means of making paper. In A.D. 751 the Arab governors of Samarkand captured some visiting Chinese experts in paper manufacture. The Chinese had probably been using bamboo fibres for this purpose invented in A.D. 97 by an official whose success was acknowledged by an imperial title.[1] The Arabs then learnt to make a tougher linen paper from the flax of Khorasan and soon began to use it extensively for writing.

This marvellous invention spread rapidly in Islam. It was not merely that it replaced costly papyrus and parchment and inferior palm leaves. It was demanded by writers for the production of books. Within a century Greek scholars were able to translate the Greek classics into Arabic and to transcribe and multiply them. A contrast, hardly to be foreseen, then began to develop between Christendom and Islam. On the one hand, the Christians were confined to the Hebrew Bible and the tedious texts of their early Fathers because their Churches objected to the competition of pagan writings. But, on the other hand, the Muslims, unable to appropriate the Hebrew and Christian writings, and having to confine themselves in scripture to the paltry learning of the Koran and its interpretations, could not afford any such prejudice against pagan wisdom. They were able to enjoy Greek philosophy, mathematics and astronomy; and they were eager to profit from Hebrew medicine.

Hence the contrast between the speed of exploitation of paper in different countries. Only 300 years later with the Crusaders did the art pass into the hands of Christians in Greece, Italy and Spain. And only after a further delay of 300 years did it become the condition for the development of printing in Germany. But it was not until a thousand years later (in 1728) that the resistance of a new religious obscurantism was overcome and paper manufacture re-introduced into Ottoman Turkey.[2]

So there came about that astonishing divergence between a Christendom darkened in ignorance and an Islam kindled with the light of learning. So it happened that, when the Arabian caliphs were dead, and in the lands outside Arabia, Muslim sultans and vizirs began to concern themselves with the sciences, with literature, and even with the idolatrous art of painting. It was these rulers and administrators who began to encourage not only the travel of

[1] Needham (1965); *ref.* ch. 26.

[2] See Derry and Williams (1959); Lewis (1965).

scholars but also the translation of Greek texts into the language of Islam. It was they who, with the taxes levied on Christians and Jews, began to endow universities from Bokhara to Cordoba which should propagate ancient learning among Muslim people. Their purpose was to maintain and advance knowledge within their dominions. But their achievement was to attract men of the learned class, and of Greek, Persian and Jewish ancestry, into the common fold of Islam.

g. Class, Caste and Slavery

The new Muslim populations were hybrid, and consequently both heterogeneous and adaptable, at the top. They provided the human materials for meeting rapidly changing conditions. Every kind of activity throughout the Empire was bound to be examined with critical eyes from a new point of view. The evidence shows us that the conquerors changed not everything but a great deal. It also shows us that the conquerors themselves were changed.

The conquerors were changed above all in their views of social structure. When they set forth, 'Equality' was inscribed on their banners. Segregation and discrimination were abandoned. Muslims never could be slaves and Islam was to forget the foolish genealogies recited in pagan times. But as soon as new countries had to be governed (as Levy shows) new opinions began to be heard. It was found that the tribe of the Koreish had to be given the highest offices; that Arabs were more suitable than Syrians; that the order of conversion among Arabs was an order of priority and a basis of rank. Soon the succession was disputed between those weaklings descended from the Prophet and the stronger Omayyads less closely connected. At the same time the seeds of strife were sown when Arabs and foreign Muslims worshipped in separate mosques.

Mohammed's revolution, like all others, was aimed at removing old and unjustifiable hereditary privileges. But, again like all others, it had had the effect of creating new ones, based on race as well as family. To establish themselves the Abbassids, in their turn, had to abolish these new inequalities. Indeed they found it necessary to rewrite history, even recent history, and to revise the Koran itself. But, having established themselves, they allowed the new fashion to fade. The caste of Seyyids who owed their privileges to descent from the Prophet have never failed to enjoy the deference due to nobility. Being numerous they can usually be honoured only for their piety and they are most successful as beggars. Yet it was their claim of descent from the Prophet which enabled the Fatimids to rule in Egypt and the Sherifian Dynasties to assert themselves in the Hejjaz and in Morocco.

At the other end of the scale, in their attitude to slavery, the Muslims proved to be no less versatile. There is nothing better, the Prophet says, than to free slaves. But it was the Abbassids themselves who first discovered that it was unprofitable and unnecessary to release the converted slave from the ties of bondage; that is unless he was an Arab by lineage. Moreover amongst slaves the Muslims followed ancient practice in distinguishing between different races and especially between black and white. We can see the consequences of this distinction best in the development of the peculiarly Muslim institution of military slavery.

The name *mameluke* which signified 'owned' in Arabic was applied from an early stage (from A.D. 820) to the Turkoman captives employed by the Abbassids as their bodyguards. These people were proud of their title of slave since it soon became evident that they were, with varying degrees of legality, the rulers of the country. This development happened independently in Baghdad in the twelfth century, in Delhi with the Ghaznawid Dynasty and in Cairo with the mamelukes, both in the thirteenth century; and last of all it happened in Istanbul with the janissaries of the Ottoman sultans in the sixteenth century.

The origin and character of the mamelukes have been described by Ayalon. The slaves, who were always of infidel birth, were brought to Cairo by foreign merchants as young boys. They were sold to the Sultan, immediately circumcised, testifying to their new faith in the Arabic phrase, and put in a military and religious school under the care of eunuchs. They were 'freed' on finishing their schooling and thereafter promoted in the Sultan's service by merit. In their highest 'Circassian' period they had to be from the tribes of the Qiptchaq steppe or of the Caucasus. They must never be African, Negro or Muslim.

This caste, usually celibate and homosexual, was continually recruited afresh from its equalitarian foundations in the slave market. Like that of other celibate groups, its character, warlike or priestly or both, was maintained by the breeding of the tribes or classes from which it was extracted.[1] And its character was proved by its success in defending Islam from the assaults of the Christian Crusaders over a period of two hundred years. During this time all high offices came to be filled by mamelukes and the mameluke leaders themselves became sultans. But if, profiting from their success, they married and bred, having no women of their own warlike race, they begot worthless progeny who, if they survived, became worthless sultans.

The slaves in the Muslim slave markets[2] were classified by nation and by colour, and the fate of the Negro slaves was different from that of the mamelukes. They were not embodied in the white Muslim community. Over the period of thirteen centuries since the Muslim conquests, rulers of Arab or Berber descent established themselves over most of northern Africa. In some places, as in the Sudan, they have hybridized freely with their Negro subjects. In other places, as in Zanzibar, or partly among the Tuareg, they have kept themselves apart with white wives and Negro concubines. In all countries of Muslim Africa the contact of Arab and Negro has generated class structure.

This is one side of the picture. On the other side we see millions of Negro slaves have been carried off from tropical Africa to Arabia, Egypt, Turkey,

[1] We are bound to notice the contrast between the mamelukes and janissaries and their antagonists, the equally celibate and supposedly homosexual Knights Templars and Knights of St John. For these also were equalitarian but in the sense that their origins must be proved noble in all lines for four generations. Their achievement culminating in the siege of Malta was equally remarkable (Bradford, 1964).

[2] Which continued in Istanbul until 1908.

Persia and the Maghrib. But they have left very little trace among living people.[1] What is the reason? Certainly Negro slaves have bred on a small scale and the effects of hybridization may be seen in the villages of Arabia and North Africa.[2] But in general it is clear that the Negro slave has been sterilized. Castration in meeting the demand for black eunuchs has been one factor. Infanticide, abortion, perversion, both homosexual and heterosexual, are other factors. Their relative importance may only be roughly estimated by those who study the works of Burton and other Arabian travellers.

An important question now arises. How could a caste structure be created and maintained in a polygamous society? There are several answers which we have already partly seen. In the first place, the polygamy of the conquering Muslim warriors could be genetically effective only when their conquests gave them large numbers of female slaves. At other times only a small section of society could indulge in a harem. And as a rule the propagation that resulted was compensated for by a high death rate either from war or murder. Further, in all Muslim societies, as we have seen, the precepts of the Koran were soon abandoned by the governing class. Mutilation was immediately adopted for Negro slaves who became in various ways the ministers of pleasure. Female infanticide certainly came back into use. And homosexual and other perversions, never forbidden, became the fashionable cult of all the governing warrior castes.

Finally, in marriage, the traditions of the urban and professional society of the ancient world found their expression in Muslim law. Lawyers insisted that if equality was excluded in society as a whole at least it should exist within marriage. The legal sponsor of marriage, the *wali*, should see that spouses were equal in social rank, that is in race, lineage, degree of liberty and occupation. It thus became difficult or impossible for a man to marry outside his own professional group, a situation which has continued to this day. Thus society, shaken by the impact of successive Muslim conquests and revolutions, quietly discovered that its convenient and stable hereditary sub-divisions had now been given a religious sanction.

Consequently, when we look today at a modern Muslim society we find the racial groups derived from successive invasions and upheavals maintained as social layers in a stratified society. In contact with Hinduism, in Pakistan, the layers appear as castes related to the Hindu castes which conquest and conversion have displaced. In contact with the west, dogma and ritual are the basis of division. In Tunis and Algeria we find the masses converted in the eighth century following the Malikite rule. Above them are the class belonging to the Hanefite sect derived from the Ottoman rulers of the sixteenth century. Among them are pockets of fundamentalist intruders of the eleventh century, Arabian Wahabites in Djerba and M'zab. But everywhere, east and west, there is the Seyyid caste of hereditarily holy men, parasitic on the body of society.[3]

[1] The contrast with the corresponding numbers of Negro slaves who over a later and shorter period have populated great regions of America we shall discuss later.

[2] Jørgen Bisch (1962).

[3] See Alport (1954); Brierley (1965).

h. The Golden Ages of Islam

The rapid expansion and recurring brilliance of Islam is sharply contrasted with the slow growth and painful uniformity of Christian development. The difference is of course connected with the fact that the one advanced by violence and aggression, the other by migration, persuasion and marriage. But while war accounts for the expansion of Islam it does not account for the sparkling creation of culture which followed the expansion. This creation, we may notice, happened only where there was something valuable before the coming of Islam. And the sparkle in each instance lasted only half a dozen generations. It lasted evidently as long as the conquest of each ancient society brought about the recombination of valuable racial components.

So it was that successively in Damascus and Baghdad, in Cordoba and Marrakesh, in Isfahan and Delhi, we see the characteristic flame of the new hybrid Islamic civilizations always based on a precarious balance between conversion and non-conversion, hybridization and non-hybridization, a balance which Muslim violence was not fitted to sustain. When the conquest ceased, with the expulsion of the Almoravids from Granada, with the retreat of the Turks from Vienna, with the collapse of the Moguls in Delhi, the intellectual and artistic as well as the political life of Islam came to a standstill.

In the end the expansions themselves ceased to be possible since Islam itself was limited by the written word which had been its strong foundation. The austere prohibitions so suitable for a poor pastoral people could not attract or convert the sophisticated, the civilized and the settled people already possessing unimagined luxuries. The prohibition of wine limited expansion into Europe with the richest vineyards in the world. The prohibition of the pig barred the way into China where pork is a necessity of life. The prohibition of dancing could never find favour with the Negro peoples of Africa to whom, by racial character, dancing is the natural bond of society.

When the limits of conquest had been reached, when Islam had been rejected by the older centres of civilization and new hybridization was excluded, decay set in, slow but everywhere irremediable. But, first of all it set in at the heart of the Empire.

VII. THE EMPTINESS OF ARABIA

Through Mohammed the Arabs created many new nations. But they may be said to have ruined their own. By the very conquests which enriched Islam and the world the heartland of Islam was drained of its most capable and enterprising people. Such a misfortune might perhaps have been made good. But unfortunately its human effects were reinforced by political and natural processes which can now be recognized.

In the first place, immediately after the great exodus, the population of the Hejjaz was still further impoverished. The Caliph Omar decreed that the presence in Khaibar and in Najran of Jews and Christians was an insult to the memory of the Prophet. They should no longer pollute the earth of Arabia. He rejected the example of the Prophet and re-established the habit and policy of Arabian intolerance: he drove out the strangers.

There remained the sea-ports on the south and east coasts from which men sailed all around the Indian Ocean. They traded and colonized, as they still do, in eastern Africa and western India and the shores of Malaya and Indonesia. But these belonged to a world outside Arabia. Within Arabia nothing was then left on that sacred earth save good Muslims, people protected from all mixing or leavening with foreigners except the pilgrims to Mecca. And these came, as it turned out, merely to be plundered or to leave their bones in the desert.

All this would no doubt have been otherwise if nature itself had taken another course. But the long decay of the Ancient East, of its climate and its soil, was continually persuading people to move out of Arabia; and indeed out of the Ancient East. Except in Egypt, the drying of the climate, the grazing of the cattle, the destruction of foreign and civil war and general misgovernment were everywhere preventing new peoples from coming in to refresh the population by mixing and by hybridization. Thus Arabia, by one stroke of the Caliph, was cleaned and closed and for ever set apart. And in due course with the further devastations of non-cultivating pastoral peoples, Turks and Mongols, the emptiness of Arabia spread to all the dry countries around it.

Inbreeding in Arabia did not lead to unity. With the sparse population, the dispersed tribes were bound to return to their own tribal unity, to the breeding system which has made them, as Thesiger puts it, the purest races on earth. They returned also to the blood-feuds which Mohammed and his teaching had momentarily stemmed. To be sure, from time to time the demand arose, often inspired from Persia, to return to the true words of the Prophet. The Karmathians in the ninth century, and their successors the Wahabis in the eighteenth, preached this fundamentalism. But while it united the tribes in larger groups it united them also in the interests of war. In this way many wars enlarged and enflamed with religious issues burnt through the peninsula. One army of fanatics in the tenth century could carry off the black stone from Mecca, suspending all pilgrimages to the Holy City. Another army of Bedouin Wahabis, suborned by the Fatimid Caliph in Cairo, could be used to devastate the Maghrib in the eleventh century, destroying its rebellious cities and turning its hard-won soil and its precious irrigation into the Sahara.

Even these people, although they did terrible damage, hybridizing with their victims, gave rise to valuable new breeds of men whose traces we can still discover from their exactly preserved religious doctrines.[1]

But the people who remained in Arabia showed no such innovations of character. They fell back into a state of stagnation as deep and no less barbarous than in the Times of Ignorance. Later and devoted teachers (such as Glubb Pasha) have attempted to break the Arab habit. But without any lasting success, for it is only by systematic and permanent interbreeding that the tribal system and tribal war can be brought to an end. Since the fall of Mecca in 692 nothing new has gone into the great dry land of Arabia and nothing new has come out: it has been the quiet centre of Islam.

[1] Notably the puritanical and utterly homogeneous and homozygous tribe living in the Saharan oasis of M'zab who provide the indispensable professional caste of grocery store-keepers in Algeria today (Alport, 1954).

Table 24. *Glossary of Inherited Islamic Titles*

After Lane (1860).

Sherif (or *Ashraf*)*:* a noble, hence a descendant of the prophet through Fatima and by a male or female line; entitled to wear a green turban; also applied to the Governor of Mecca, the Sultan of Morocco and other great men

Sayid (or *Seyyid*)*:* lord or master; title given to a man of Sherifian family of Hussein's line

Sheikh: elder; title of respect especially for the head of a family or tribe or village; entitled to wear a white turban

Hajji: non-inherited title of a man or woman who has made the prescribed pilgrimage to the Ka'abah at Mecca[1]

Caliph (or *Khalifah*)*:* an acknowledged and hereditary successor of Mohammed as civil and religious ruler; often claiming descent from the first two caliphs but not through the daughters who married the prophet

Imam: a priestly leader; according to the Sunnites elected by men and fallible; according to the Shiites appointed by God and infallible; hence a title applied to a caliph, a learned man, or a mere prayer leader for whom the imamate is a secondary and non-hereditary profession

[1] Not, as the *Oxford English Dictionary* states, to Mohammed's tomb at Mecca.

16

HINDUISM

I. THE INVESTIGATORS

HINDUISM, IT WILL BE SAID, is not a world religion. Nor is it in the sense of Christianity and Islam. Rather, like Judaism, it is a religion which has created a world of its own; but it is a world which has a meaning for the rest of mankind because in it religion and society have become explicitly aspects of one common evolution. To understand that world we have to go back to its beginnings about five thousand years ago. We have to penetrate what until recently seemed impenetrable obscurity. Now, however, by the combination and mutual correction of several means of enquiry we can form a picture of just what is significant in the origins and development and indeed the nature of Indian society.

On one side of these enquiries are the profound studies of Indian caste made during the last hundred years by Wilson, Thurston and Risley, Hodson and Hutton, studies many of them linked with the anthropological and linguistic surveys of the Indian census from which the special studies of Majumdar and others have arisen. On another side is the account of Indian pre-history arising from the excavations of the Indus civilization by Sir Mortimer Wheeler, an account admirably related to our knowledge of the Mesopotamian origins of civilization by Stuart Piggott. A third side is presented to us by our present knowledge of the means by which agricultural and pastoral peoples spread. Their movements and interactions as they came, first from South-West Asia and later by new peripheral migrations in Asia, Europe, Arabia and Africa, are now severally recognizable; and are datable from the cultivated plants and domesticated animals with which and by which they lived, bred and developed.

These give us the new understanding we need.

II. THE INDUS VALLEY

Any idea we may have of India during the fourth millennium B.C. is bound to be conjectural. But of certain essentials we can be sure. The country was still untouched by the agricultural revolution. In it dwelt paleolithic tribes of hunters and collectors. They were probably some of the densest populations of such people in the world. In some respects they are not unfairly represented by surviving hill tribes. Especially is this true of their extreme differences in means of feeding, and consequently of preferences in choice of food, from the vegetarian to the carrion eater. These differences had created that fear of pollution which is still today the great barrier to intercourse in India.[1] But they must then have been far more diverse than they are today in form, in behaviour and above all in speech. The main body were black, speaking Dravidian and other languages. But there were also intruding tribes of white peoples from the north-west and, on a larger scale, of Mongolian peoples, with their own languages, still surviving today, from the north-east.

Into this paleolithic province came, during the fourth millennium, tribes of cultivators slowly expanding from the west. Between the Khyber Pass and the coast they found several routes into the Indus valley. They are routes which, owing to the damage they have done, would no longer be passable for cultivators today. But once established in India, by hybridization with the native peoples, they must have lost their own languages and produced new races of cultivators. These people carried wheat-[2] and barley-growing into the Indus valley and they domesticated the wild humped zebu cattle which they found there. They must also have produced other races of specialized pastoralists who, spreading in advance of agriculture, began to colonize the Deccan.

All this must have happened before the turn of the millennium. Meanwhile coastwise explorers and colonists making their way from Sumeria, step by step, century by century, along the northern shores of Arabia, must have at last appeared near the mouths of the Indus. These people had something in common with the megalithic people who were later to explore the coasts of Europe. Perhaps they were led by merchants as well as navigators. But they brought with them the civilized arts of a priesthood: engineering and surveying, building and irrigation, law and writing, magic ritual and the worship of the bull. With these arts they endowed, and also inserfed, the cultivators of the Indus valley. The civilization of Sumeria, transposed in character, was in half a millennium of migration carried over to the banks of the Indus and its sister rivers. During this time, by the most spectacular operation in agricultural history, they brought across Arabia the first two African crops, cotton and sesame. With these they made the Indus valley into the first centre of tropical acclimatization in the world.

Mohenjo-daru, Harappa, and many other cities these people built and re-built in the thousand years of the Indus civilization which followed the

[1] See Luiz (1962): in Kerala is perhaps the only human tribe which can hunt by scent, the Kadars.

[2] Not any ordinary wheat but a bread wheat of the hexaploid series already known in the Nuclear Region.

first settlement. Whether they were destroyed in the middle of the second millennium by invaders, by floods or by earthquakes is uncertain.[1] But the internal reasons for the end of the civilization are clear and significant. A stratified society resting on cultivators, craftsmen and priests had attained an extreme degree of stability, the kind of stability later to be associated with caste in India. Throughout its existence they had been protected from invasion and even from disturbance. Trade with Sumer had continued but safe prosperity had given the Indus people the confidence to disregard the advances of civilization in a homeland which had now been transformed into the Babylonian Empire.

Meanwhile, however, the Indus people like the Sumerians had been destroying the basis of their own livelihood. The forests which had moistened their climate and restrained their floods had now been felled. Grazing had now extended the desert of Sindh and had perhaps already absorbed the seasonal flow of many disappearing rivers. The Aryan invaders, arriving in a Mesopotamia protected by a fringe of semi-civilized peoples, had been assimilated by the cities they attacked. But arriving suddenly in the isolated and unprotected Indus valley they destroyed the cities and their systems of irrigation. It was a ruin from which there was to be no recovery. For the population there was nothing to do but to take refuge to the south and east, in Gujerat and in the Ganges valley where primitive agriculture was slowly advancing.

III. THE GREAT CONFRONTATION

These conditions enable us to define the group of people whose relations mattered in India at the time of the Aryan invasions.

There were, first, the invaders bringing in their own cattle, crops, and bronze weapons. With them they had their own priests with their war gods and their own bards with their Aryan epic poetry. Secondly, there were the displaced Harappans. They had their craftsmen, archaic in style and largely unable to maintain the arts of their castes in their dispersal; they also had their priests similarly unable to maintain their caste of scribes but otherwise able to hold their own in competition with the Aryan priests by virtue of their understanding of something entirely new to the Aryans: the structure and behaviour of a highly stratified multiracial society. They knew how to manage such a society with the help of social laws and religious cults assisted by sophisticated rituals and magic.

Finally, there were the scattered pioneers of agriculture and stock-farming spreading by narrow corridors through the great mass of paleolithic forest dwellers. These people had already taken an Indian millet into cultivation and established the first fields in the Ganges delta for the cultivation of rice, the crop which later was to feed most of Eastern Asia. They had also already domesticated the water buffalo which was later to labour for most of tropical mankind.

The confrontation of these diverse and still diverging strains of men was

[1] See Rao (1961); Dales (1965).

one of the most obscure, yet even with our faint knowledge one of the most momentous, events in human history. It was even, if we can allow a human drama to extend over a thousand years, one of the most dramatic events in human evolution. Out of it came not all but most of what we have in India today. Out of it came the cult of the bull and also of vegetarianism and the rejection of killing. Out of it came the marriage of Aryan and Dravidian gods and goddesses corresponding to the mating of their peoples. Out of it came the Brahmin priestly caste with their doctrine of the transmigration of souls, their exploitation of the fear of pollution and the sacred theory of caste itself embodied in the Laws of Manu. And out of it, as we shall see, also came the rejection of the Brahmins and of caste itself by the Jains, the Buddhists, and other people outside the circle of the new priesthood.

To separate what was contributed by each of the components of the Indian people to these developments never could have been entirely possible since the developments themselves arose from mixture. They arose precisely from the greatest of all experiments in genetic recombination. It does however appear, paradoxically, that the arrangement of Indian society by caste was a notion derived from the Indian aboriginal peoples themselves since tribal segregation still appears strongly among them. On the other hand the association of caste with colour, with *varna*, probably arose among the Indus peoples when white minorities met black majorities for the first time in urban societies.

The multiplicity of castes in India today bears witness to the amount of mixture which occurred before the products of recombination could separate. The invaders, we may be sure, at the same time that they hybridized with the native peoples, would by polygamy preserve the purity of their own race, as they have done in all later history.

The sharp division and the one which perhaps has never until recently been blurred is that between the warriors and the priests. Between them there has always been a conflict of character, of interest, and of purpose. It is the same conflict, the same polarity, the same love-hate relationship which has dominated so much of the history of Europe. But in India it has inevitably concerned the nature of caste.

IV. THE LAWS OF MANU

a. Endogamy

After the Aryan invasions there came into being in India what we speak of as the Sanskrit literature. It was a 'literature' propagated for a long time, however, verbally and not by writing; for writing had been extinguished by the Aryans whose bards preferred the spoken and remembered word. Indeed it remained for Sir William Jones to persuade unfaithful Brahmins, in Calcutta about 1790, to commit the Vedas and the derivative religious instructions partly for the first time to writing. The dating of this literature is therefore less certain than that of the Hebrew Bible but its origins probably cover a similar range of time before and during the first millennium B.C. The exhortations of the Bhagavad Gita no doubt precede the Buddhist rejection of caste in the sixth century. But the explicit rules for enforcing caste, known as the Laws of Manu, no doubt followed the rejection of Buddhism in the third century. They sprang, like Buddhism, from the central Ganges valley and they were intended to clinch the argument with Buddhism about the structure of society.

Manu's code lays down rules for breeding and marriage in India much as Leviticus and Deuteronomy laid down the rules for Jews a little earlier. But their precision had never been equalled before. It determined the mode of evolution of Indian society.

For us the laws have five main articles:

(i) They forbid incest, that is marriage or sexual intercourse between near kindred.
(ii) They define all the known trades and professions and require them to be hereditary.
(iii) They thus create professional groups, which we know by the Portuguese word *caste*; these they place in order of rank.
(iv) They lay down rules for cleanliness: these require that the higher castes avoid the lower castes so that they cannot eat together.
(v) They thus require breeding within each caste and forbid breeding or marriage between castes.

Thus the first article makes a law of the universal prohibition of inbreeding; the other four articles make laws of what elsewhere had been merely a habit or inclination to avoid wide outbreeding and to follow hereditary and traditional practices.

The incest rules were an attempt to codify all the various prohibitions of inbreeding that existed in India while at the same time extending them. Marriage was excluded between couples having common ancestors on the male side within seven generations, on the female side within five. This rule meant in effect that spouses must have no recorded kinship whatever. Like the Catholic rule in Europe, it was of course unenforceable except for royalty; and it has never been enforced. Rather, as in Christendom, hundreds of primitive rules for excluding incest continue to evolve towards a simple uniformity.

The definition of occupations was more effective undoubtedly because it corresponded to the habits of the people. It stabilized an existing system with which the majority of people always had conformed. It did this by attaching ritual processes and mythical histories and meanings to each occupation. Every man's occupation, except the lowest, acquired a sacred significance as well as a romantic origin. This after all is true elsewhere by implication and by instinct. In Europe we may say '*il n'y a pas de sot métier*'. But in India, as in paleolithic societies, instinct had become law and both of them maintained and were maintained by heredity.

The basis of the caste system was the principle that society should consist of four groups or colours or *varna*, the same colours as were used 2000 years earlier in Egypt, another meeting place of races, for different racial groups, thus:

(i)	*Brahmin*	the priests and teachers (white)
(ii)	*Kshatriya*	the rulers and fighters (red)
(iii)	*Vaishya*	the common people, cultivators and traders (yellow)
(iv)	*Sudra*	the servants or slaves (black)

The upper groups were initiated with the sacred threads as 'twice-born'. Within each group people could eat together. Between them people could meet and speak together. But outside this genuine Hindu society were other people who could not come near the Hindu without polluting him. These were the Untouchables, the Pariahs or Outcastes, or in the continually changing political jargon, the Exterior or Scheduled Castes, the Depressed Classes, the Harijan. They had to live outside the village fence. Often they would, like lepers in mediaeval Europe, carry bells to warn respectable people of their approach. Some would carry spittoons to avoid fouling the road.[1] In south India a few were unseeable as well as untouchable; they would emerge from their dwellings only at twilight.

Between the *varna*, rules were laid down governing all social relations. A Brahmin might kill a Sudra for the cost of a cat. The reverse offence would entail immediate as well as eternal punishment. This is easy to compare with the rules in both tribal and feudal Europe. What was different was that the peoples of India accepted their castes and the codification of rules governing them. They tended to make them, since Manu, gradually stricter whereas European societies have again and again rejected these rules by overthrowing their rulers. Why was this?

Two main conditions operated to enforce and exaggerate the caste system. The first was the superstitious or instinctive reverence for the idea of eating together in a community and not admitting strangers which was ingrained not only in the tribal peoples of India but far beyond it. The idea of a sacred 'communion' is equally understood in the west. In India it reached a higher pitch. It may have done so on account of the selective value of keeping apart in permanent small groups. For India is a tropical country densely populated with human beings and also, in consequence, with infectious diseases. In India people would therefore survive best who mixed least. And that is most true where eating and drinking (and by derivation, mating) were concerned.

The second condition exaggerating the differentiation of castes was the attachment of mating rules to all the other bases of separation. The whole body of thought and practice, built up into a religious philosophy by the Brahmins, was consistent with the instincts of the earlier and even the paleolithic peoples. They themselves were at the top of a hierarchy. The doctrine of *Karma* by which every deed earned its reward assured the Brahmin that he owed his rank to the virtues of his soul in a former incarnation. It also assured the Sudra that, if he behaved well, his soul might in a future life rise in society to inhabit the body of a Brahmin; otherwise it might sink in the social scale. This notion no doubt came from Persia since it looks very like the Persian ideas of heaven and hell which later came west into Europe. It served a double purpose. It explained the present inequality.

[1] The Pot Koraga sub-caste of South Kanara (Hutton, 1946).

And it served to maintain that inequality by promising reward specifically to those who suffered most from it, and suffered most patiently.

b. Polygamy and Hypergamy

The evolution of the Indian caste system has manifestly been influenced by assimilation, invasion and revolution. Within it are contained groups of people following matrilinear as well as patrilinear inheritance. Within it also are some groups divided into clans Roman-fashion as well as others divided into moieties Australian-fashion.

Above all, it was thought necessary to keep higher caste women from contact with lower caste men. But in India, as everywhere else, it proved impossible to keep higher caste men from contact with lower caste women. The Laws of Manu provided for this contingency with appropriate punishments. Mating below the caste for women, known as *hypogamy*, was to be punished by death. For men the corresponding relationship, known as *hypergamy*, could be atoned by washing. Nowadays the woman is merely outcasted.

For the preservation of caste, however, two special devices have been invented in India. They are child marriage before puberty, and *purdah* or seclusion of women after marriage. They are neither Aryan nor Dravidian, and above all not matrilinear, in origin. They derive from the meeting of different races in India following the Aryan invasions especially from the north. They are part of the solution of the problem of co-existence.

As in Europe, the higher the caste the stricter are the rules for ensuring the chastity of women before marriage. The stricter also are the rules protecting marriage against both inbreeding and outbreeding. Thus, for this purpose, it is on Brahmin women that marriage before puberty and purdah after marriage are most strictly enforced. Any caste which wishes to raise its social status therefore has to lower the age of marriage to the limit, that is to infancy. At the same time remarriage must be forbidden even for infant widows.[1] So, to escape the penalties of low caste, the women of India have been sacrificed to a law of sexual oppression from which only the untouchables, who can sink no further, are fortunately free.

This rule, which allows hypergamy but punishes the reverse, has caused some perplexity among scholars. But, since it is, in effect, the same rule that we find in Europe governing both marriage and divorce, it hardly needs an esoteric explanation. Moreover, as in Europe and Africa, economic conditions promoted the polygamy of higher caste men in India and their hypergamy with lower caste women. Both among Hindus and Indian Muslims a man of a lower status or caste wins protection by giving his sister to a man of higher status or caste. She is a form of tribute such as the feudal lords of Europe were accustomed to receive in less regular and less permanent forms.

Whatever its social rationalization, the effect of polygamy was the same as

[1] The extreme method of avoiding remarriage, the burning of widows, was known as *suttee*. Its suppression was the only religious and social reform for which British rule in India was responsible (Woodruff, 1953; Spear, 1965).

everywhere else. It was that the conquering invaders who spread over India increased their genetic contribution to posterity at the expense of the conquered indigenous peoples. As for the progeny of the outbreeding entailed, they lost caste for a few generations, often recovering it again later subject to the merit or success of the particular group. For with caste it is not the individual who rises or falls in status in society but the whole group which the individual, he or she, advances or disgraces.

c. Exogamy

The Indian rules of exogamy naturally affect the evolution of society. But they also provide an additional means of tracing the ancestry and evolution of the separate peoples concerned.

Amongst Brahmins and Rajputs we find groups called *gôtra* derived from the *gôtra kara rishi* of early Vedic times. These are exogamous patri-clans each of which pretends to be derived from a common male ancestor. But among Brahmins they exist in various stages towards sub-castes with gradations of occupation and hence status. In both Rajputs and Brahmins hypergamy makes a contribution to outbreeding.

Indeed, in the Rarhi Brahmins of Bengal, the males of each subcaste marry below them so much—the choice being greater—that many girls in the top caste, the Kulins, would suffer the disgrace of remaining unmarried were it not that individual males have been known, on the payment of fees, to take supernumerary wives, up to sixty in number.

Among the Rajputs the outbreeding clans constitute geographical races forming a gradient or cline. They decline in social status from west to east owing it is believed to an eastward increase in crossing with darker tribes which took place during the first millennium A.D. Thus men have to look east, and women have to look west, when they marry.

Both these systems maintain outbreeding in units of increasing size. As a rule however such devices have failed. The increasing unit has broken down. Marriage between clans or *gôtras* has been replaced by marriage within the *gôtra*. It is limited only by prohibited degrees of kinship in the European style, the rules varying between castes as they do between Christian communities.

Among lower castes, on the other hand, there exist an infinite variety of outbreeding systems, matrilinear, patrilinear, territorial and totemistic. They fill the whole gamut from the Vedic-scholastic to the meaninglessly random. In the south, where the black complexion of the Brahmins often indicates their local and tribal origin, their breeding systems confirm this impression by following the aboriginal rules. These systems doubtless succeed or fail subject to natural selection and constitute extensive experiments in the evolution of societies.

The complex tribal systems of exogamy with their clan groupings and their rigorous patri- or matrilinear structure are now being replaced by simpler systems of prohibition which are easier to apply in urban life. Marriage is merely forbidden between couples who are known to be related. This simplification reaches its limit in Europe where Christians and Jews are allowed to marry anyone outside the immediate or nuclear family. In India, however, all the possible steps in simplification or breakdown can be seen. In the higher castes the restrictions are more severe. They may forbid marriage between pairs within seven generations of a common ancestor on the male side or five on the female. This is like the Roman rule of the eleventh century. In lower castes, memory is not so long. They are more like Protestants. Universally ortho-cousins (father's brother's or mother's sister's children) are excluded. But when patrilinear and matrilinear systems come in contact it seems that cross-cousin marriages (father's sister's and mother's brother's children) have been a favoured compromise. And since strictness of rule is always favoured in inbred societies, cross-cousin marriage has become obligatory in many castes—even when the only available girl is older than the boy.

V. CAUSES OF INSTABILITY

a. Religious Revolt

The Laws of Manu and the Brahmin supremacy sought a complete stability which was somewhat shaken by the two centuries of Moghul intrusion but much less shaken by that of the two later centuries of British intrusion. Indeed the introduction of European writing and scholarship may be said to have given a new lease of life to Brahminism while the British themselves were happy to constitute yet another caste in that all-absorbing, all-tolerating system.

Yet complete stability has never been attained in India. The people, the society, and the religion have been exposed to assault from within and without. Inside there have been the tribal communities from the hills to be absorbed. For 3000 years this process of assimilation has been going on slowly and continuously, just as it happened in China, without forming castes, over the same period. The primitive peoples assimilated have been converted from tribes into castes and we can still see every stage in the process. The *Kuli* tribe of Bombay became so famous for its manual labour that it became a caste which multiplied and gave us the name of *coolie*. We can often see where the process has been interrupted; a tribe, and the caste derived from part of it, then still bear the same name. We can also see tribes, like the Gonds and the Bhil of central India, who move slowly towards Hinduism as a body.

This assimilation of tribes has swelled the ranks of the lower castes and above all of the untouchables. By origin the untouchable has been a hanger-on to Hindu society, either the old rebel and outcaste or the uncivilized newcomer. He has remained half outside half inside society. Now he numbers—although no longer known by the name of untouchable—one-sixth of the Indian population.

The other ground for instability has been the repeated invasions of India by fighting peoples from the north. First were the successive waves of Aryans in the second millennium B.C. Later came the Persians, Greeks, Scythians and Huns. All these are thought to have contributed elements to the warrior caste. The most conspicuous group to derive from these invaders were those whose governing class were the Kshatriya and who, reinforced by Huns and Scythians, became known after the seventh century A.D. as the Rajput princes. These unruly people never had much use for the Brahmins or much respect for Hinduism. Their activities were a second destabilizing factor in Indian history.

In this they were continuing the conflict of the Buddhist age. The Buddha was of the warrior caste and his mission had been to break down the barriers which separated the social classes and condemned each to its own trade or calling. And in doing so, of course, to deprive the Brahmin of his social and economic privileges.

Buddhism triumphed in India for a few centuries. They were centuries during which its missionaries spread to establish their faith and also Indian civilization successfully in Mongolia, Tibet, China and Japan, as well as in Ceylon, Burma, Siam and Indo-China, everywhere indeed where civilization was more backward and caste less developed. In India itself, under Asoka, the principle of caste was severely eroded by intermarriage. He himself (as we saw in Pedigree 5) was the grandson of a low-caste woman. Many of the lower castes, to improve their status, embraced Buddhism. But in due course the Brahmin caste, the priestly party, recovered its position and Buddhism—that is the theories of the Buddha, not the idols—was suppressed. Buddhist castes—a contradiction in terms with which India later became familiar—were degraded. New caste ranks and values were established, many of which continue to this day.

The Buddhist rejection of caste affected most of Asia but it was merely the most momentous of a series of attempted reformations. A thousand years earlier, before the Aryan invasions, the Jains may have already registered their disapproval of Brahmin superstitions and Brahminical control. Being of a commercial profession and intellectual character which recall particular sects in Britain, they may well owe their origin to the Indus people rather than to any later barbarian invaders. Two thousand years later the Sikh community likewise broke the bonds of Hinduism. Each of these revolts however failed to sweep the system away. Each of them created a new minority segregated from the main Hindu population, a new community which by inbreeding was bound to become professionally specialized and therefore, in effect, one more caste, a self-appointed caste within the Hindu system.

When in the end the great Muslim invasions overpowered India yet again, caste was the most important issue. Many Indian princes were converted to a religion which freed them from Brahminism. Many of the lower Hindu castes also were attracted by what appeared to be a caste-free doctrine. These conversions have survived today. The split, irrational as it may seem, has been rendered permanent by the political division of the country between Muslim and Hindu. But the Hindus who were converted to Islam have found that they remain in castes little different from those religiously ordained and explained by the Brahmins. Indeed these castes may still be divided into clans as they were before the conversion; but they are clans blessed with Muslim names. They have exchanged the fees paid to the Brahmins for the alms paid to the Seyyids. Conversely, Muslims have been absorbed into Hinduism to form castes: they do not know it but they can still be recognized by their Muslim customs.[1]

b. Eccentricity and Crime

Once established and rigorously applied, any rules of breeding are bound to exaggerate their own effects and the rules of caste were bound to lead to certain extreme conditions of society, extreme homogeneity, extreme adaptation to trades and professions; extreme sub-division, even when the trades and the sub-division have ceased to be useful to society as a whole. These principles were noticed long before their genetic basis was understood. It is well therefore to recall the precise words in which a classical observer of Indian society assessed the long-term effects of the caste system: 'Amongst the various causes which contribute to the growth of a race or the making of a nation by far the most effective and persistent is the *jus connubii*—the body of rules and conventions governing intermarriage. The influence of these rules penetrates every family; it abides from generation to generation, and gathers force as time goes on. The more eccentric the system the more marked are the consequences it tends to produce.'[2]

Thus certain Indian castes are instructive for the relation they show to the trade castes which were formerly so important in Africa and Europe. Notable among these are the metal-working castes. Some specialize in copper and brass, others in iron. Some of the oldest are distinguished for their magical practices. Other castes are remarkable for following several seemingly unrelated or even incompatible trades. We are not surprised that the *Jugi* of Assam rear silkworms and also spin silk. Nor are we surprised that the dirty begging sect of *Aghoripanthi* have remained untouchable owing to their habit of eating dung and human corpses. Nor that the *Tawaïf*, whose daughters are dancers and harlots, are themselves musicians and pimps. But we are surprised that the *Baiti* burn lime, weave mats and make music. And that the *Kahar* of Upper India are not only porters and domestic servants but also follow a series of water trades as fishermen, well-sinkers, and breeders of water ants. Such combinations may sometimes have arisen by association and hybridization only to be preserved by the inbreeding that followed it.

But they may also have arisen from the process by which a tribe in becoming a caste has cut down the number of its occupations. Many Indian tribes in making this transformation have been arrested at a nomadic stage to give the kind of organization which foreshadows the gipsy communities that eventually wandered into Europe. Such tribes still betray the evidence of their paleolithic ancestry: the incapacity to settle, or to undertake the hard labour of settled life and also the lack of interest in property or understanding of ownership. For this reason many of them are regarded by settled societies as criminal tribes or castes.

The Indian census of 1941 recorded 2,268,000 members of '*Criminal Tribes*'.

[1] F. Barth (1960) and Hutton (1946).

[2] H. H. Risley (1915, p. 154).

More than half of them were in the United Provinces where thirty to forty tribes were under police control or observation.[1] These tribes generally claim Rajput descent and this is no doubt true in the sense of having had one noble ancestor. Some are Muslim converted probably in the sixteenth century. Most are hard to distinguish from gipsy tribes since they are largely vagrant and practise various auxiliary trades. They have a great variety of languages and many profit by their multilingual facility. Some profit by the promiscuity of their women and so would lose their genetic or racial character if it were not that continued loss and gain to and from the general population occur, changes which are always selective, favouring the established criminality of the tribe. Their systems of government show great flexibility. Some have hereditary leaders of great name and lineage and also gang councils. These are as stable as the Panchayats of settled caste Hindus, since they organize social welfare and even crime insurance and control and maintain religious ritual.

Not clearly distinguished from the Criminal Tribes are the *Criminal Castes* so well described by Hutton. Most of them have accessory means of support apart from the crime which is their expert profession. With these we might be inclined to classify the famous criminal gangs known as Thugs. Closer study shows, however, that the Thugs stand apart in the history of crime as well as in the history of society as a whole. For here was a kind of tribe created by the hereditary success of its founders and developed probably over a period of twenty generations by rigorously selective recruitment. The founders may have begun in Delhi in the thirteenth century. By 1830 their organization numbered about eight thousand men maintaining their family or caste character as Muslims and Brahmins, merchants and soldiers. It was therefore a multi-caste society of its own. It was also differentiated in co-operative functions demanding long apprenticeship and according promotion for individual merit. Its leaders or *jemadars* and their priests maintained also their strict religious character. They were devoted to a goddess Kali (or Fatima for Muslims). She demanded killing to keep the balance in human population. And she rewarded her devotees by giving them the spoils of the victims. The rituals and the jargon of inveigling, strangling and burying the traveller were exact; the obedience to omens and auspices was rigorous; and until 1830 the success of this way of life (and death) was mounting with the peace and prosperity of British India.

The Thug society covered at its height nearly the whole of India. It was eliminated in effect by the patient efforts of one man, Captain William Sleeman, between 1820 and 1848. About four thousand thugs were captured, interrogated, genealogically defined, and legally tried and convicted of murder, mass murder. Some were hanged, some transported, and some imprisoned and rehabilitated, having been used as informers. The genetic propagation of the leadership on which the organization rested was brought to an end. The whole process might be described as a 28-year experiment in eugenics and its success can be recorded, for the Thug community has never been reconstituted.[2]

[1] Majumdar (1958). [2] Woodruff (1953), Spear (1965), Bruce (1968).

In outbred societies the uncertainty of criminal life usually prevents assortative mating and the regular maintenance of criminal classes. Criminality then arises mainly by recombination. But inbreeding enables us to demonstrate the inheritance of criminality as of all the other unusual dispositions found in Indian castes.

VI. THE DIVIDED SOCIETY

All advanced societies, as we have seen, arise from a stratification of social classes whose genetic differences and mutual dependence are the permanent foundation of their advance. But in India we discover what happens when the separation of social classes becomes an end in itself and the main goal of life; when, as has been said, the one property which unites the whole people is the means by which it is divided.

In the study of societies this seems to be the extreme paradox. But we should note that in biology it is a well known principle. The great polymorphisms in man from the blood groups to sex itself are based on differences which hold, and are indispensable in holding, the species together. In the organization of societies, however, not one gene difference but many are concerned. Then it is only with the help of religion that stability can be maintained.

The pervasive power of the religion which has been brought into action in this way was unforgettably expressed by an English writer a century ago:[1]

Caste 'gives its directions for recognition, acceptance, consecration, and sacramental dedication, and vice versa, of a human being on his appearance in the world.

'It has for infancy, pupilage, and manhood, its ordained methods of sucking, sipping, drinking, eating, and voiding; of washing, rinsing, anointing, and smearing; of clothing, dressing, and ornamenting; of sitting, rising, and reclining; of moving, visiting, and travelling; of speaking, reading, listening, and reciting; and of meditating, singing, working, playing, and fighting.

'It has its laws for social and religious rights, privileges, and occupations; for instructing, training, and educating; for obligation, duty, and practice; for divine recognition, duty, and ceremony; for errors, sins, and transgressions; for intercommunion, avoidance, and excommunication; for defilement, ablution, and purification; for fines, chastisements, imprisonments, mutilations, banishments and capital executions.

'It unfolds the ways of committing what it calls sin, accumulating sin, and of putting away sin; and of acquiring merit, dispensing merit, and losing merit. It treats of inheritance, conveyance, possession, and dispossession; and of bargains, gain, loss, and ruin. It deals with death, burial, and burning; and with commemoration, assistance, and injury after death. It interferes, in short, with all the relations and events of life, and with what precedes and follows . . . life.'

[1] From J. Wilson (1877) quoted by J. H. Hutton (p. 79 of 1946 edition; p. 90 of 1961 edition).

All this tells us of the consequences of caste. It omits however the key to the system, the cause of its origin and preservation in the regulation of breeding. The uniformity of action, the conformity of belief, the submission to the past, the avoidance of anything new in the future, all these arise from the homogeneous society produced by many generations of inbreeding. It is an inbreeding which has not been dictated by the Brahmins but merely exaggerated, prolonged and enforced by them. All the stagnation which results from this inbreeding would be destroyed in one generation by outbreeding. Now caste has spread wherever Indian ideas have spread. And by a strange paradox this means that caste has spread along with the Buddhism which appears to contradict it, notably in South-East Asia. But in general it has been maintained only at the bottom of society where the opportunities of outbreeding are most strictly limited.

Whether in Burma or in Japan[1] it is only among the most despised trades, with whom marriage with others is inconceivable, that caste unsupported by the self-exaggerating effects of Hindu religion can be maintained.

The disabling effects of extreme caste must never be underestimated in India. Are there then no virtues in the system? We have to admit, in the first place, that the development of caste in India superseded slavery. And, inasmuch as caste imposed mutual obligations on all classes of society, which slavery does not, caste was to be preferred. Inasmuch as caste is more stable, we may argue its disadvantage when carried to an extreme.

In the second place, within Hindu society, caste has created and maintained an infinite capacity for toleration and for assimilation. To be sure, for the relative absence of social conflict, so contrasted with the history of such conflict that we shall be considering in Europe, stagnation is the price that has had to be paid. But caste has been the framework which has enabled, on the one side, the paleolithic peoples of India and, on the other side, Persians, Greeks, Scythians, Huns, Malays, Christians, Jews and Parsees, to be slowly fitted into Hindu society and made it, with the least conflict, into the most diverse community of races in the world.

It is this marvellous diversity of man in India which has made that country both a museum and a laboratory for the study of man. For this reason the most profound lessons in the study of society have come from India. For, if Europe has shown us how racial mixture with conflict may speed up evolution, India has shown us, up to the present day, how racial segregation with harmony can bring it to a standstill.

[1] See Hutton (1941), and De Vos and Wagatsuma (1966).

Part VI

The Emergence of Europe

The states succeeding the Roman Empire found themselves united as the custodians of western civilization and of Christianity. But they were assailed by Muslim armies, by Asiatic horsemen—Turks and Mongols—and by Viking sea-warriors. Each of these destroyed something and themselves underwent racial transformations. Each of them was in part assimilated in the painfully growing structure of European society. In this growth we have to trace the conflicts of a celibate Church with hereditary nobilities and royal castes; the freedom of migration from advanced to backward lands; the intermittent persecutions, conversions and dispersals of religious minorities especially of the Jews; and the genetic meaning and character of cities and nations.

17

THE SOUTHERN SUCCESSORS

IN THE MILLENNIUM following the fall of the Western Empire, Europe was assailed on all sides by enemies who appeared bent on the destruction of its inheritance. That inheritance, that continuity, was however preserved, not only by the Roman Church, but by a variety of other successors. To find out what they made of it we first have to consider three societies, Greek and Turkish in Constantinople, and a new society in Venice.

I. BYZANTIUM

a. The Problem

When the Roman Empire was bereft of its western half in the fifth century we conveniently speak of the surviving state by the name of Byzantium, the little predecessor of its capital. For the survivors, however, theirs was the new Rome and a greater one even than the old city itself. From its foundation, to be sure, it lasted as the heart of an empire, albeit a diminishing empire, over exactly the same length of time.

Throughout the eleven centuries from 327 to 1453, Constantinople, the Queen of Cities as its citizens declared it, aspired to maintain the culture it had inherited from the ancient or classical world. The Law of Rome, newly codified by Justinian, continued to be administered. Although the methods of its government followed the precedents of Rome the titles of its officers were now expressed in Greek. To preserve the language, literature and drama of Greece was now indeed an object of prestige and a means of social promotion. For these purposes schools and universities were supported by the State and employed a whole community of scholars. To them foreign rulers sent their sons. The churches that arose in all the cities of the Empire commemorate many generations of the greatest architects and craftsmen. In them the Christian religion was gracefully accommodated to its pagan antecedents. Its ritual, its costume, and more memorably its music, were enriched and diversified by a priestly caste which could marry and multiply. Everything in the life of the capital seemed to justify the pride of its inhabitants and their traditionally Greek contempt for the barbarian peoples.

Yet in the end, following a series of calamities, this community was dispersed or subjected and its achievement as a community appeared to be extinguished. It leaves us with a twofold problem. Why did the Empire die? And what parts of it, what disembodied remains, have survived?

b. The Success of the City

Constantine, in moving his capital from Rome, escaped from its parasitic population, that is to say from the whole of the plebs and from most of the patricians. The new city housed the people he wanted to attract, the people he needed for the institutions he wanted to create. These institutions were derived from the government of Rome. From the days of persecution before Constantine there continued a polarity, an opposition, between the old secular bureaucracy and the new ecclesiastical administration. In the west, after Constantine left, uneasily over the course of centuries, this polarity grew. It was, in a sense, to govern all future development. But in the east the two poles, as he hoped and as his successors attempted to ensure, were to be under the single control of an absolute priestly monarch, *pontifex* and *princeps*. The Patriarch was merely an influential subject, one whom a weak emperor could easily appoint and a strong emperor might easily dismiss.

The new capital immensely strengthened the military position of the ruler. Old Rome with its land roads was a base for attack. Constantinople with its sea-lanes was a base for defence. Its position made it at once a maritime and mercantile centre. It attracted ships, men to build ships, and men to man them. Those Greeks and Phoenicians who had created seamanship were still subjects of the Empire at peace or at war. The new capital therefore commanded the sea and on this command its defence largely depended.

The language of the emperors up to Justinian was the Latin of the military class. But they learnt Greek and the new population was naturally drawn from the Greek half of the old Empire. Its Greek, Jewish and Babylonian origins made this population the most highly literate in the world. The people capable of administering the Empire were waiting in the cities of Anatolia and Greece to establish the new bureaucracy. On them it depended to take over the Roman system of taxation as recorded for them in the Theodosian Code. In the new Empire this system was maintained and improved, taxes were levied on lands, imports, purchases, profits, inheritance, and on the ownership of serfs. These were supplemented by the profits from the national ownership of great estates and of all the minerals of the Empire.[1]

To this taxation, Syria, Egypt and Africa made at the beginning a great contribution. For once in history, even after paying for the bureaucracy, the proceeds were superabundant. They put Justinian, with the help of his general Belisarius, in a position to reconquer the Western Empire as far as the south of Spain. And they enabled his successors to establish, in addition to

[1] As described by Andréadès in Baynes and Moss.

the feudal militia, a powerful mercenary bodyguard with an élite corps of men from the border provinces, forces which in the tenth century came to include Slavs, Vikings and Anglo-Saxons. This was the Varangian Guard in which Harald Hardrada was to serve his apprenticeship.

Whether through piety or policy however Justinian determined to devote his wealth above all to the Church. He spent 300,000 pounds of gold on the building of St Sophia and endowed it with 365 properties near the capital. His mood proved to be perfectly fitted to the temper of his people. The endowment of churches, monasteries and nunneries, hospitals, infirmaries and orphanages, became a national cult.[1] More than a cult grew out of the discussion of theological principles and ritualistic practices. Following Nicaea, for centuries the Nature of Christ preoccupied and obsessed the public mind. Following the example of Islam the question of the propriety of religious images racked the city with riots and split the establishment asunder. And in the sunset days of the fourteenth century the doctrines or hallucinations of Gregory Palamas, Archbishop of Thessalonica, helped to renew a feeling of ecstasy in the people of the dying Empire.

For the future of mankind these manifestations of religion bore fruit in ways and in fields which the devout could scarcely have foreseen. Take the political field. Their opinions on belief and ritual sometimes united the Greeks. But these opinions always divided them from their resentful subjects in Syria and Egypt and from their suspicious rivals in Rome and the west. Nowhere better than in the divergent expressions of a common religion do we see the divergent expressions of different races. The Mediterranean peoples were split by their attitude to their common inheritance of the Christian scriptures in which they equally insisted on believing and on whose meaning they equally refused to agree.

Take next the artistic field. Benefactions to Byzantine churches meant the employment of artists and craftsmen in Byzantine cities. In consequence we are able to enjoy the superb structure of St Sophia, the splendid mosaics of Ravenna or the divine music of the Orthodox Easter. But this is only one side of the picture. The fame of these things was known at the time through merchants all over Europe. The Saxon king who was buried in his pagan ship at Sutton Hoo in 655 or, four centuries later, the Norman king preparing the insignia of his coronation, equally looked to Byzantine craftsmen to do their work and even fetched them for the purpose. So also with the Varangian princes in Novgorod or Pskov, the Norman kings in Palermo or Ravello, the Benedictine abbot in Monte Cassino, or the doge of Venice building his chapel of St Mark's.

The endowment of the Byzantine churches thus meant the prosperity and the propagation of the classes of people who were employed in them. Artists and craftsmen moved out to the frontiers of Christendom. Priests, teachers and merchants moved out beyond those frontiers. With the capture of Sicily by the Arabs in 827 intercourse with the west was cut and movement was diverted to the north. The merchants were in part looking for slaves.

[1] It culminated, according to Psellus, with Michael IV's experiment, the first of its kind, of a home for the reform of harlots (Sewter, 1966).

The priests and teachers were looking for converts. They made their way up the northern rivers from the Black Sea. And since they were able to marry and breed they slowly colonized Eastern Europe. They hybridized with the Slavs. How could they fail to civilize them? And encountering the Vikings and the Varangians arriving from Sweden they took shelter in the shadows of those original Kremlins of Novgorod and Pskov and laid the urban foundations of Russian culture.

So the great city became the City of the Emperors, Tsarigrad, to the Slavs, an object of admiration. To the west it remained for long (as Runciman puts it) the capital of Europe. To everybody its wealth was an object of envy and later of covetous design. In its greatest prosperity a million people dwelt within or about its walls. Among these there were provincial or foreign communities living segregated in their own quarters. There were Armenians and Macedonians jealously guarding their rights. There were Syrian and Italian colonies, the rival Venetian and Genoese merchants also living apart. In this respect Constantinople resembled all great cities at all times. Only later it might be seen that these colonies did not merge in the Greek community. As centuries passed they kept a dangerous and threatening independence.

The city in its prime in the eighth century seemed however not an artificial creation but a natural growth. It seemed, as has been said, to have created its Empire, as Rome had done, and not to have been created by it and from it. But when we think about it again we see that the contrast is a false one. For in the end all capitals come to be derived from the empires they appear to have created. In the end it is always from the peoples of their dominions that they have to be continually recruited. It may be their reward or their penalty. But with Constantinople it was not from the nature of this recruitment that the city ultimately suffered but rather from the failure of native recruitment when its provinces fell into the hands of others.

c. The Decay of the City

Throughout its millennium of sovereignty the city was attacked by enemies. Persians and Arabs, Franks and Venetians, Slavs and Turks, in turn invaded the provinces or assaulted the capital. The Arabs in 690 and 718, the Seljuks in 1090, the Ottoman Turks in 1391, 1397 and 1422 were repelled. The invention of Greek fire[1] and the desperate fear of the Christians for their Muslim assailants strengthened the defence. But the Frankish and Venetian Crusaders profiting by dynastic divisions took and held the city in 1204. And province by province the territories of the Empire had been torn from it until little was left but the shreds of coast around the straits.

The loss of territory and wealth by the state meant a loss of employment in the capital. The population dwindled and at the end it had fallen probably

[1] Greek fire consisted of porous pots filled with paraffin, ignited by fuses and exploded by gunpowder when thrown by hand. It was a secret weapon but the secret changed sides for the Greeks used it against the Muslims in the seventh and eighth centuries (Sewter, 1966). But it became the secret weapon of the Saracens against St Louis in the thirteenth century (Pernoud, 1963) and again of the Knights of St John against the Turks at Malta (Bradford, 1961).

to no more than a tenth of the numbers who had earlier flourished within it. It is not difficult to see where they had gone. Craftsmen, artists, preachers and teachers had fled abroad. For 850 years they had supplied the wants of the western Catholic countries, notably Italy, and the northern Orthodox countries for nearly as long.[1] These men stayed to pass on their culture and to propagate their race among the barbarian peoples. The balance of migration, the brain drain, throughout this time was against Byzantium. And in the end, under the Latin rule of the thirteenth century, the trend became irreversible.

The Greek State could have withstood these continuing losses if the Greeks themselves had understood the means of renovation. Stability however was built into the institutions of the government, the social and religious cults, the class structure of the capital and the cities. All these were well fitted to the needs of a large and prosperous Empire. Even when the wealth of the disaffected southern provinces was lost to the Arabs the Empire remained viable and defensible within its natural Greek frontiers. But now several internal disorders began to make themselves felt. Emperors skilfully struggled to cut the Empire's coat according to its diminished cloth. But they never entirely succeeded. The habit of endowing churches was not easily forgone. The taxation of Church properties and of rich individuals was only too easily resisted. Monastic estates grew and the powers of the Church grew with them. The landed nobility were either strong or uncooperative. The absolute monarch proved indeed to be diminishing in power. Why was this? It was on account of the dwindling of the governing class which went with the dwindling of the State.

d. The Rulers

As newer powers crowded around the Empire and threatened its throne, the titles and ceremonies of the Byzantine court grew in splendour. To the title of *Augustus* were added *Autokrator* and *Basileus*. To the voice of the senate or the generals was added the acclamation of the people of Constantinople. To an oriental prostration was added a Christian halo. To the Hebrew coronation were added the robes of the Sassanids and a Hellenistic diadem bestowed either by the predecessor or by an obsequious patriarch. In all these operations Constantinople succeeded in keeping one step ahead of Rome.

The succession of Emperors in Constantinople in the period from Justinian to the Latin conquest (518–1204) was a dozen times violently interrupted by usurpers attempting to found new dynasties and sometimes succeeding. These men sprang for the most part from the army but sometimes from the civil service. They were often wealthy and sometimes they were land-owning nobles. Sometimes they secured their positions by murdering or blinding their legitimate predecessors. Nearly always in addition they married into the imperial house either before or after seizing the throne. Consequently the claim of royal descent became latterly indispensable for the quiet possession of the throne. Whence it follows that a class, effectively within the military

[1] A great band of Greek artists accompanied the Princess Theophano when she went to Germany to marry the Emperor Otto II (Pedigrees 13, 15).

caste, came to be marked as alone worthy to be *porphyrogenitus* or born in the Purple Chamber.

These principles are not unlike those at work in western Christendom. Several peculiarities however distinguished the Byzantine imperial breeding system from that of the upstart royalties of the west. The first of these was due to the cultural pride of the Greeks. Their traditional contempt for barbarians, submerged by the Roman conquest, was effectively restored with the transfer of the Roman capital to Constantinople. It had far-reaching effects. On the one hand it nourished in high society a dangerous ignorance of foreigners whether infidels or heretics or merely savages. For example, the French crusaders came to Constantinople in 1096 in the belief that they might save it from the Turks. But Anna Comnena daughter of the Emperor Alexius I, writing about them thirty years later always refers to these saviours as 'Celts'. Naturally with this experience the French became as dangerous as the Turks themselves. On the other hand this pride led to a genetic isolation of the Greeks at all social levels. Thus it inevitably became a racial pride. It prevented them from assimilating the Armenian and Venetian trading communities which might have enriched their society instead of helping to overturn it.

The worst of all consequences of Greek pride was that it prevented them from intermarrying with foreign royal families. It made them demand a purely Greek monarchy. The Emperor could give his daughters or sisters to barbarian kings, as Basil II did (Pedigree 13). But he could not marry their women; not, that is, until six generations later at the end of the twelfth century when it was too late for this reformation. The Greek dynasties were therefore part of a national governing class not refreshed by the outbreeding of the western or barbarian royal caste. It was a breeding group diminishing in size and not protected by the Roman rules against inbreeding. A western emperor had to ask the pope's permission to marry his third cousin. An eastern emperor, such as Romanus III, was free in this as in all other matters to do as he pleased.[1]

The Emperors were absolute in power. But their modes of entrance and exit present a violent and terrifying record. They therefore tried to choose their ministers with as much prudence as the elected feudal monarchs of the west. To protect themselves they had picked up from the Persians a dangerous practice which they carried to disastrous lengths. The emperors, beginning already with Diocletian but continuing with his Christian successors, believed that it was safer to have ministers who were eunuchs.[2] For since eunuchs could not become fathers it was believed they would not use their positions to advance their families. Moreover it came to be assumed or agreed that a eunuch could not himself become emperor.

The castration of Romans and of free men was at first deemed improper.

[1] To be sure, the Patriarch would protest if an eastern empress, like Zoë, wanted to break the rules by marrying a third husband: but for royalty the rules were always waived and a priest could always be found to officiate.

[2] The Chinese emperors perhaps learnt it from the same masters, in the latter half of the Chou Dynasty, about 600 B.C. (according to Wittfogel: see ch. 25).

But when eight of the chief posts of the Empire were reserved for eunuchs prudent fathers began to see the advantage of meeting the public need or the national demand by arranging to have their own sons castrated. Or at least some of them. They might even begin by castrating their eldest sons, who would be able to open the doors for the younger brothers. Another thought struck members of the royal family who begot bastard sons: to castrate them before they might appear to be claimants to the throne. For example Michael I, who was deposed in 813, had his infant son castrated: the son Ignatius became Patriarch of Constantinople, an office he held for thirty years, outshining all his predecessors. Thus to the slaves freshly despatched from the frontiers to the slave market of Constantinople there was added a home-bred population of free eunuchs derived from families of high rank and great ability.

Table 25. *Origins of Byzantine Rulers and Dynasties*

From Gibbon (Ch. 48); Runciman (1933); H. St. L. B. Moss (1948); E. R. A. Sewter (1966).

1. JUSTINIANEAN (518–610)
   Justin I (518–527) barbarian general, elected by army

2. HERACLIAN (610–711)
   Heraclius (610–641) son of a governor of Carthage

3. ISAURIAN (717–802: Iconoclasts)
   Leo III (717–741) a commander of Syrian origin
   usurpers {
   Irene (797–802) who deposed and blinded her own son Constantine VI
   Nicephorus (802–811) treasurer of Empress Irene
   Leo V (813–820) Armenian commander }

4. PHRYGIAN or AMORIAN (820–867)
   Michael II (820–829) Phrygian, master of the Palace, married daughter of Isaurian Constantine VI

5. BASILIAN or MACEDONIAN (867–1057)
   Basil I (867–887) descended from Constantine the Great and Armenian Arsacids. Chamberlain of his predecessor Michael III whom he murdered
   Romanus I (919–944) admiral; seized the throne, marrying his daughter to the legitimate Emperor, Constantine VII
   Zoë (b. 980: E. 1042: d. 1055. Three husbands and one adopted son became emperors (1028–1055)

6. COMNENIAN (1057–1059, 1081–1185)
   Isaac I Comnenus (1057–1059) territorial noble of Italian descent. Revolution described by Psellus
   Constantine X Ducas (1059–1067) noble, friend of Comnenus

7. ANGELI (1185–1204)
   [Latins in Constantinople (1204–1261)] Epirus, Nicaea and Trebizond (1204–1461)

8. PALEOLOGI (1259–1453)

(7–8: } descendants of Alexius Comnenus and his wife Irene Ducas)

Pedigree 13. The Macedonian Dynasty in Byzantium: 867–1057

After Gibbon, Baynes and Moss (1940); Sewter (1966)

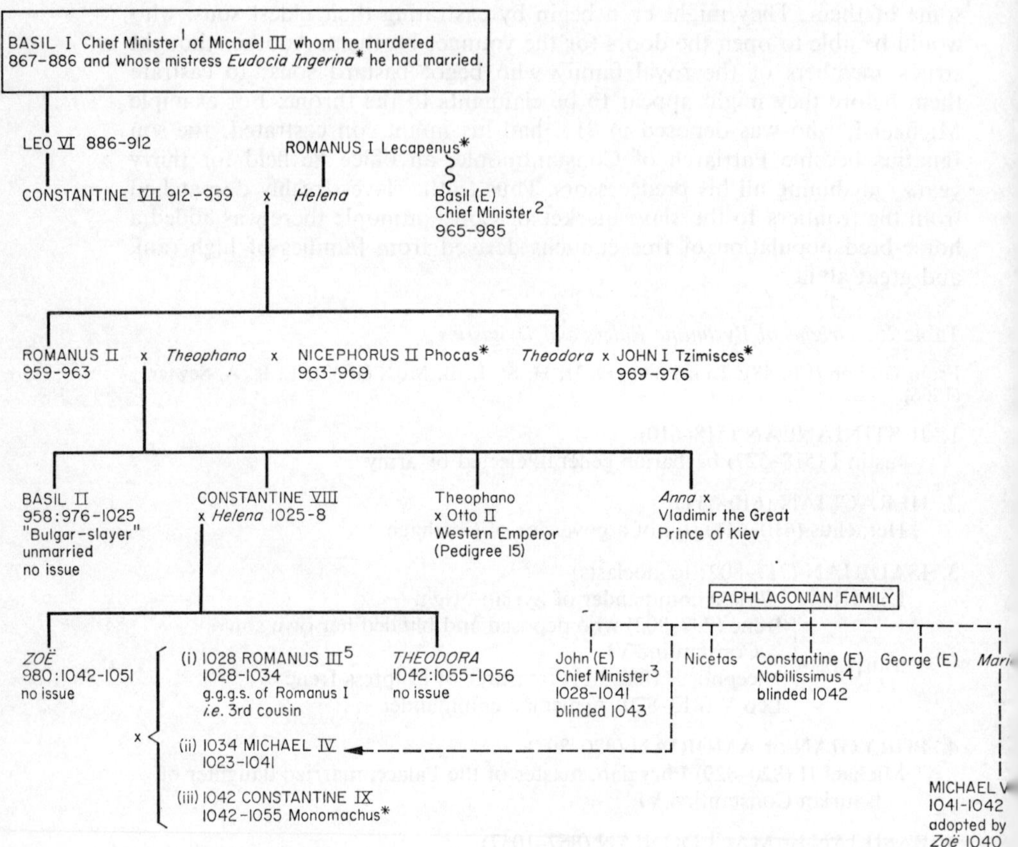

Notes:

i. Men could become emperors only by marrying Zoë or being adopted by her. As she was 48 at her first marriage the legitimate line was extinguished.

ii. The man who established the Paphlagonian family, John, the eldest son and ablest member of the family, was a eunuch.

iii. John was blinded by order of the Patriarch Cerularius in 1043. The practice of blinding fallen statesmen copied by the Normans is said to have been due to a respect for life but it took the place of imprisonment, a practice undeveloped in Byzantium.

1, 2 and 3. Chief Ministers.
1. Became Emperor. 2 and 3. Eunuchs.
1 and 2. Held office of Chamberlain *Parakoimomenus*.
3. Was *Orphanotrophus*, Guardian of the Orphans.
4. Chamberlain.
5. Poisoned by Zoë and her lover who became Michael IV.
6. Castrated all his entire adult kinsmen; had a 'Scythian' eunuch bodyguard.

* *Names of noble families.*

It has been supposed (by Runciman and others) that the eunuchs in the government were the weapon with which the Empire kept within bounds the power of the landed magnates, a power so dangerous to the feudal states in the west. There was however another unique property which preserved the Byzantine Empire. The wealth of the great cities, especially the capital, and the power exercised by its educated and intelligent administrators, these were possessions inherited from the ancient world, possessions which the west could not acquire until after a thousand years of evolution and of migration from the east, indeed partly from Byzantium itself. Only after thirty generations of growth would the educated and educable classes of western society be able to take over the government from the cruder less literate agents of feudal administration. It was the power, exercised by the cities and fluctuating with the monarch, which restrained, although it did not inhibit, the conflicts of feudal leaders with their private armies. It made the crucial difference between East and West (Fig. 15).

e. The Cult of the Eunuch

There are several social, political and evolutionary connections in which the practice of using eunuchs in the public service needs to be considered. The immediate purpose for which the eunuch was valued was for his service to the monarch himself. In this service the more important the entire man became, the more likely he was to supersede his master. But the eunuch could not do so. The more important he became therefore the more devoted he was bound to be to the master on whose favour he depended. Three of the greatest Byzantine chief ministers illustrate this contrast. The first was Basil who murdered his master, stepped into his place (that is, his bed and his throne) and founded the Macedonian Dynasty. The second and third are eunuchs; both were men of the highest ability; and both of them were faithful to their masters (see Pedigree 13).

So far so good. But there is now another question we have to ask: were their masters faithful to them? The answer is that their masters destroyed them. The eunuchs who so largely governed the Byzantine state thus proved to be dangerous to the state, not because of their inherent character as eunuchs, but because their experience showed them that they had no reason to expect fair play.

The Byzantine record has something more to tell us also on the theory of the lack of family interest of eunuchs. Look again at the case of John the Orphanotrophus. This eunuch was of modest—some said disreputable—origin in the province of Paphlagonia. By his abilities he made himself invaluable to the financial administration of the Empire. Two of his brothers had been castrated in infancy. But by his influence he was able to put two uncastrated members of his family on the throne, one as a husband, the other as an adopted son, of the aged but inexhaustible Empress Zoë.

If we now look at these two Emperors whom the Empire owed to John we find that, unlike John in his own person, they brought disaster to the nation and also to the dynasty. Family influence or nepotism was thus as powerful a motive with the eunuch as it was and is with ordinary men.

And its effects were politically just as dangerous to the sovereign and the state.

There is another theory held about eunuchs, not by their employers in former times but by popular fancy today. It is the view that they are morally or physically less courageous than ordinary men. This theory is also fallacious. In the Byzantine Empire there were eunuchs derived from all social classes whom we may compare with ordinary men in action as civil ministers, military commanders, and ecclesiastical dignitaries. We cannot know the precise numbers of the groups from whom our two samples are taken. But the evidence suggests that the eunuchs did as well as the others. We may suppose that artificial eunuchs show the same range of abilities as the natural eunuchs such as contribute to the celibate fraction of all classes in advanced societies.[1]

If we turn now from the functions of the individual eunuch to the cult of eunuchism we meet quite another problem, an evolutionary problem. Over a period of thirty generations a proportion of boys in the most gifted families in the Empire were regularly castrated. The effects of monastic celibacy were felt equally in east and west. This was an additional and artificial genetic deprivation of the educated classes. It might be argued that the proportion of men excluded from reproduction was no higher than that of men who lost their lives in those civil struggles of the west which were avoided in the east. But in those struggles of the west the issue depended on the skill, courage and judgment of mature men. In the west those struggles were competitive. They involved a threat to every incompetent ruler, a promise to every competent rebel. Both in immediate social effects and in long-term genetic effects the natural western system was salutary. It opened the door to selection, adaptation and evolution. The eastern system closed that door. It was bound to damage if not to kill the societies that adopted it.

So much for consequences. What about the causes, the conditions of development of the cult of eunuchism. The cult, it is worth noticing, could hardly have developed in face of an independent Christian priesthood. Darwinian and Christian morality might here seem to agree. It was the established subservience of the Greek priesthood to the Greek monarchy that allowed a practice, which to Christians might well appear corrupt or even abominable, to grow and ultimately to dominate the organization of government. Moreover the Roman Church had developed its own method of separating and setting in opposition hereditary and non-hereditary institutions without grossly perverting the biological foundations of society. For it was able in the end to make clerical celibacy appear almost as a natural institution.

These evolutionary arguments suggest that the cult of eunuchism contributed to the decline of Byzantium. But before we can estimate the factors at work we have to examine the systems of breeding and government by which the Byzantine Empire was assailed and eventually displaced.

[1] Taking the expression from Matthew 19: 12, and taking as an example Basil II.

II. THE TURKS

a. The Ottoman Empire

In the fifth century, the time of great movements, a vast region in Central Asia between the Sea of Aral and the Tian Shan was occupied by people we call Tartars. They were pastoral nomads, sheep-farming and carpet-making, tent-dwelling and horse-riding men who hunted and fought with the bow. They were divided by speech into two groups. To the east were those who had hybridized with the Chinese moving west into Turkestan: these we know as Mongols. To the west were those who had mixed with the Aryan tribes moving east into Persia and India: these we know as Turks or Turkomans.[1]

In the seventh century the first of these Turks were subjected and converted by the Arab conquerors to the Muslim religion, or at least to the Muslim doctrine of conquest. Having become established in the ninth century as bodyguards of the Abbassid caliphs in Baghdad they aptly improved on their masters' teaching and in the eleventh century seized the capital. Twenty years later (in 1077) they had attacked the Byzantine Empire and occupied Nicaea. They had made themselves at home in the Anatolian tableland breaking the frontier of the Taurus mountains which has remained, from Muawiya to this day, a barrier against the Arab language and the desert peoples, the boundary of Shem and Javan.

These first Turkish conquerors, the Seljuks, were gradually changed, diversified, and multiplied by hybridization with Greeks and Armenians, Persians and Arabs. They constituted the governing class of a not very stable feudal state. After two further centuries of fluctuating power the leader of a band of a few hundred horsemen in western Anatolia was able to carve out a vassal fief from their dominions. In doing so he founded the Ottoman Dynasty and Empire. While the Mongols were devouring but failing to digest the larger Empire of the Abbassids, the Ottomans were slowly nibbling away the Christian peoples of the Byzantine Empire and moving their frontier westwards.

The Turks advanced against the eastern Christians while at the same time the western Christians were advancing against the Muslims in Spain and the pagan Slavs in Germany. In all these situations the military advance was followed by the establishment of a new governing class. But, owing as much to the prestige of the Greeks as to the polygamous habits favoured by Islam, the new governing class of the Turks seems to have been more deeply transformed than that of the Christians in Spain. As the Turks advanced they converted the Christians and they also interbred with them. The conquered agricultural peoples constituted a new hybrid Turkish-speaking nation governed by hard-riding pashas also somewhat hybrid, but still highly selected for fighting on horseback and marked in rank accordingly by one, two or three horse tails.

[1] The life and character of the Turkomans were delightfully described (before he embarked on ethnology) by the comte de Gobineau in his *Nouvelles Asiatiques.* The same task has been recently attempted for the Kazaks by Lias (1955).

It was this new nation which dismembered the remains of the Christian Empire. Finally, in 1453, Mohammed the Conqueror hauled his seventy ships over the peninsula of Pera, overwhelmed the defences of Constantinople and took the city. In doing so he created the Ottoman Empire, becoming, as he put it, the Roman Emperor.

The strength and the weakness of the new Empire were visible from the start. The strength derived from its military society, in process of acquiring a standing army which was already the strongest force in Islam or Christendom. This force was based on a capital, which we may now call Istanbul, sited precisely at the meeting place of two worlds. It was a wonderful opportunity and the Conqueror did his utmost to exploit it. He did so in the first place by protecting the third great asset of his Empire which was the Greek official, commercial and learned community of his capital. The vast majority indeed stayed in Istanbul. They continued their independent life and also helped to govern the Empire for the five centuries it lasted.

The Greek Eparch continued as the Prefect of the Turkish capital and Greek scribes manned the sultan's foreign office. Above all the Greeks helped, at first, in the organization of the palace schools. These were colleges in which, for the first time in the western world, technology, industrial and military, was able to compete with law and religion. From the schools came many notable Grand Viziers; perhaps the whole dynasty of the Kuprullu family who chiefly governed the Empire during the last phase of its power.

In order to do all this, Mohammed followed the most enlightened examples of the Arab and other conquerors. This is not surprising since in his ancestry he was probably as much a Greek as a Turk, as much a scholar as a warrior. To the Greek-speaking people he gave religious freedom. While preserving and annexing their church of St Sophia as a mosque he nevertheless confirmed their appointment of a new Patriarch. And he repopulated the city with Christians from his Balkan provinces now enlarged by the annexation of Albania and Bosnia.[1] Soon he had friendly relations with the Venetians and sent for Gentile Bellini to paint his portrait.[2]

But there was a weakness which hampered the development of this society and government: it could continue to prosper only by conquest. For its civil administration it depended on captured slaves drafted into its palace schools. For its army it depended on the enrolment of captured slaves to be trained as janissaries.

Most despotic dynasties have discovered that a devoted bodyguard, which they need to protect them, is best recruited from a foreign race. The caliphs of Baghdad naturally chose the fiercest of their border peoples,

[1] The Albanians who rejected Islam partly fled abroad. They number today 100,000 in the Peloponnese and 250,000 in Calabria. These pure-breeding colonies have lived in a conservative obscurity for 500 years. The Muslim converts however stayed in Albania, hybridized with the invaders, and achieved fame in two notable figures, Mohammed Ali (1769–1849) and Mustapha Kemal Ataturk (1880–1938), as well as the Kuprullu viziers (Coles 1968). See V. and J. Newall (1963); also Norman Douglas (1915) and A. N. Burton (1965).

[2] One of the resulting works now hangs in the National Gallery in London.

the Turkomans, for this duty. The recruits specially favoured were prisoners of war. Turkomans and Circassians were thus, as we have seen, the progenitors of the mamelukes of Cairo, the band who maintained but eventually overthrew the sultans of Saladin's dynasty. Christian slaves from the European provinces on the other hand were the origin of the janissaries who at first maintained but later often threatened or controlled the government of Istanbul.

Most of the great Christian community kept apart with its own life and its own schools. Its numbers were well maintained. Gibbon records an estimate of fewer Muslims than Christians in the Istanbul of 1586. But many of its ablest men quickly removed to those Italian cities with which Byzantium had such close ties: the brain drain to the west was resumed.

The dangers of this situation were postponed by a further expansion. The Conqueror's grandson, Selim the Grim, reversing the traditional policy of the Turks attacked his Muslim neighbours, people whose prisoners, by Muslim law, could not provide slaves. He annexed the whole of the lost Byzantine provinces, Syria and Egypt. And to complete the Empire Tunis and Algeria were given to him by the Albanian corsair, Khaireddin or Barbarossa.

This vast expansion of his dominions enabled the Sultan of the Turks to take the title of Caliph of Islam. Indeed it almost persuaded him to adopt Arabic as the official language of his Empire. In addition it enabled him to restore his capital to most of its earlier splendour. It was not merely a question of the building of mosques and palaces, which he left to his successors. Selim brought the artisans from Cairo for their decoration. So thorough was his removal that, so it was said, fifty of the trades so despoiled died out in Egypt itself: an indication of the enduringly separate propagation of craftsmanship by the castes of the separate trades.

It was on this secure basis of wealth and power that his son Suleiman was able to earn the western title of Magnificent. It was on this basis too that his successor was able to reach a climax in the collaboration and conversion of Christians. It was not a question of numbers but rather of quality. Three notable Grand Viziers in turn brought his Empire to the peak of power: Ibrahim, Rustem and Sokolli and they were all born Christians.

Now, however, the Turks were brought face to face with western Christians on their home territory in Europe, people not yet equipped with the new knowledge and new inventions which would come later but with a wealth of their own. Suleiman could take Belgrade in 1521 but when he reached Vienna eight years later he was repulsed. He could drive the Knights of St John out of Rhodes in 1522 but when he tried to force them out of Malta in 1565 he was checked. Those 700 Knights of La Valette with some 8000 men brought to an end the long record of Turkish victories and prepared for the defeat of Lepanto six years later.[1]

Once checked the Ottoman Empire never recovered its forward momentum. The Empire struggled on for over three centuries against enemies who were always a little too strong. As in other Muslim empires, no one ever discovered how to organize a process of social promotion which would replace capture

[1] Bradford (1961); on the nature of the stalemate, see Coles (1968).

and conquest. On the contrary dangers mounted. The janissaries could no longer be so easily recruited. They had to be allowed to breed. And having bred they created a dangerous caste, no longer uniting the sultan to his Christian subjects but now separating him from them and hence continually threatening the throne. At the same time conquest became harder. First Persia, then Austria, Russia, and finally their own subject peoples, began to throw the Turks back. Every neighbour became more powerful while the Turks stood still.

In this melancholy process the Ottoman Dynasty, living in a strange world of its own creation, played a highly significant part.

b. The Ottoman Dynasty

The first Ottoman rulers were tribal chiefs who maintained their position and succession by the approval of their warriors, that is by victory in war. Already from Osman I the reputation of this family had secured the patrilinear succession to its members. But since the ruler was polygamous and since fertility was certainly the first requirement for a chief or monarch, he always had several sons claiming the succession at his death, if not before it. The Christian solution of legitimacy had never been entertained and was effectively excluded by Islamic law. The European solution of primogeniture was equally excluded by Turkish custom. These circumstances led to a struggle between brothers at each succession. It was a struggle governed mainly by the armed forces which meant the regular army or the janissaries. But the struggle came to be affected by changing conditions and by experience. The reigning

---

Fig. 13. The Structure and Propagation of Ottoman Society

After Lybyer (1913); Miller (1941); Merriman (1944); Ayalon (1951); Alderson (1956); Creasy (1961); Lewis (1965); Vucinich (1965)

1. Hatred of Greek Phanariote governors was responsible for Balkan Christian loyalty to the Sultan during the Greek war (1821–1832). After independence largely returned to Athens.
2. His mother rules the harem or if she is dead, his wet nurse or a stepmother.
3. No initiative but judges of legality or propriety in executions and depositions.
4. If unwanted at 25 given to Spahi (cavalry) officers but the maintained harem, active and retired, might amount to over 2000 women in the nineteenth century.
5. Princesses were confined to the capital. Their husbands (who were never of the Ulema class) were usually kept in the provinces. They and the few children born to princesses were usually killed: see Table 27.
6. Killed either by their father or their half-brother on succeeding. Suleiman himself killed his two ablest sons when they quarrelled. After Mohammed III all male heirs were allowed to live caged but their children killed until accession when contraceptive potions failed (Alderson).
7. Established at Adrianople for princes by Murad II; moved to Istanbul and switched to civil servants by Mohammed II. Here all, including princes, learnt trades.
8. The Sultan's police were sometimes the people's friends; or when independent they might degenerate to bandits: *cf.* Maxwell, 1957, on the Mafia in Sicily and Jenkins, 1961, on the Dilessi Murders.
9. Slave markets continued in Istanbul until the revolution of 1908.
10. Or *Yeni-cheri*, 'New Army': their celibacy, like that of the mameluke and unlike that of the Roman legionary, was originally life long.
11. Landed gentry like the Kuprullu family seem to have begun to establish themselves (like hereditary janissaries) only after 1595.

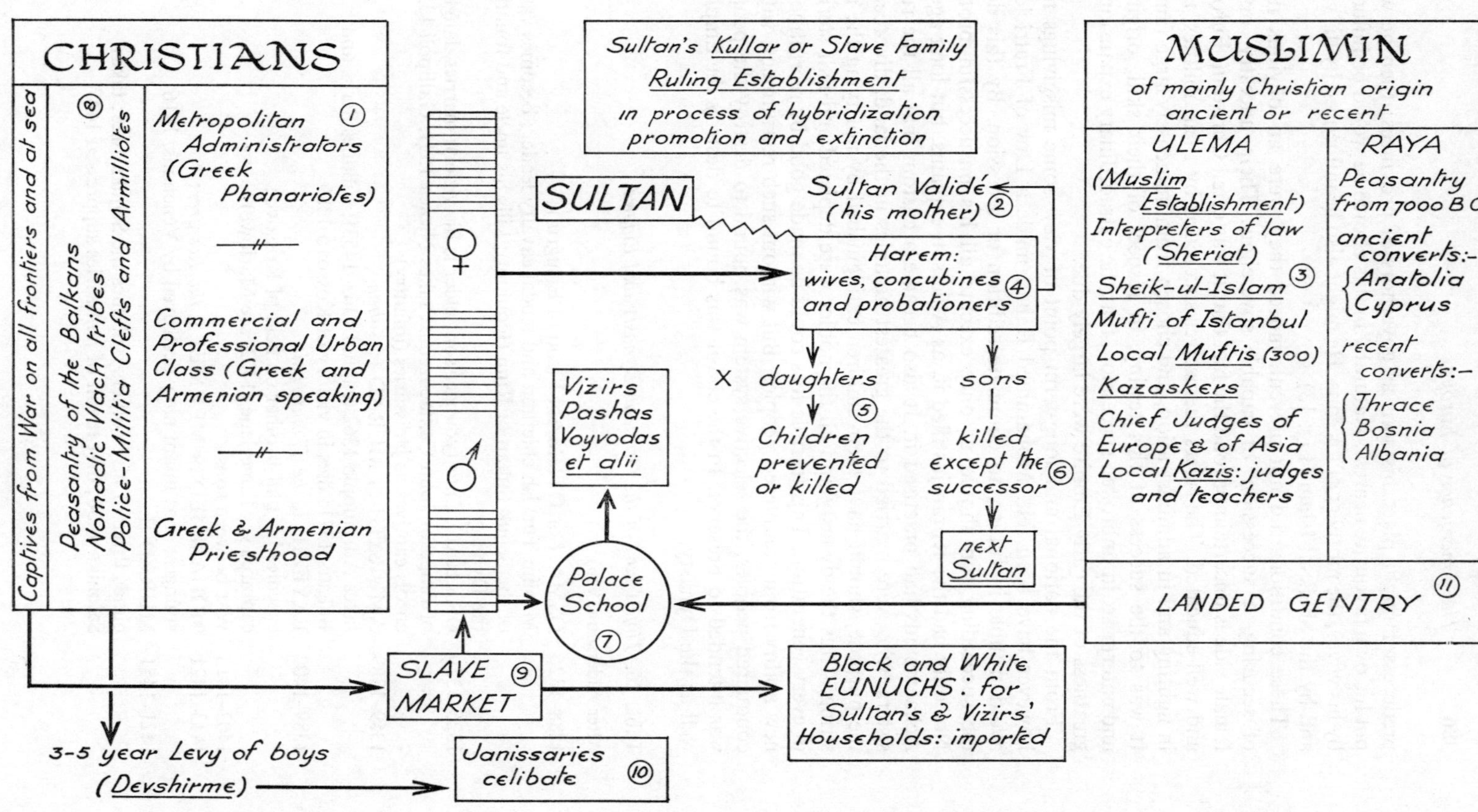

The Structure and Propagation of Ottoman Society (1453–1595)
N
CHRISTIANS
Captives from War on all frontiers and at sea
Peasantry of the Balkans
Nomadic Vlach tribes
Police-Militia Clefts and Armilliotes ⑧
Metropolitan Administrators (Greek Phanariotes) ①
Commercial and Professional Urban Class (Greek and Armenian speaking)
Greek & Armenian Priesthood
Sultan's Kullar or Slave Family
Ruling Establishment
in process of hybridization promotion and extinction
SULTAN
♀
♂
Sultan Validé (his mother) ②
Harem: wives, concubines and probationers ④
daughters ⑤
Children prevented or killed
sons
killed except the successor ⑥
next Sultan
Vizirs
Pashas
Voyvodas
et alii
Palace School ⑦
SLAVE MARKET ⑨
Black and White EUNUCHS: for Sultan's & Vizirs' Households: imported
3-5 year Levy of boys (Devshirme)
Janissaries celibate ⑩
MUSLIMIN
of mainly Christian origin ancient or recent
ULEMA
(Muslim Establishment)
Interpreters of law (Sheriat)
Sheik-ul-Islam ③
Mufti of Istanbul
Local Muftis (300)
Kazaskers
Chief Judges of Europe & of Asia
Local Kazis: judges and teachers
RAYA
Peasantry from 7000 B C
ancient converts:-
Anatolia
Cyprus
recent converts:-
Thrace
Bosnia
Albania
LANDED GENTRY ⑪

predecessor might place his sons as governors of provinces; then he would put his own favourite nearest. Naturally in this choice he would be influenced by his wives, the mothers of his sons. He might also be influenced by his viziers and by the Sheik-ul-Islam (Fig. 13).

These conditions did not prevent, indeed they were an obvious means of securing, a succession of capable sovereigns. Their ancestry on the female side is uncertain beyond the fact that it was often Christian, European and well-educated. The rulers themselves succeeded by their abilities, tested in fighting and in administration, and chosen from immensely large families. It was to the success of this testing, in respect of their skill, originality and enterprise, in unbroken succession, that the extraordinary expansion and greatness of the early Empire were largely due.

From the national and long-term point of view some misgivings might however have been felt. Mohammed II had made a Law of Fratricide to avoid trouble in future, to eliminate sedition or secession. By this decree the succeeding son should at once execute all his unsuccessful brothers. Not only had the Koran justified it, as Alderson explains, but long ago the Achaemenids had practised it. It also became a custom that all the ruler's sisters, who were married to the greatest notables in the land, divorced for the purpose, should have their children extinguished by not tying the navel string. Thus the dynasty and all the nobles were depleted and half sterilized in every generation. This terrible loss could be made good by recruitment of new ability from conquered peoples. But without such recruitment, without conquered peoples, the selective system was bound to destroy the people it was intended to preserve. In the end it was bound to destroy the Empire as well as the Dynasty.

Table 26. *Time Chart of the Ottoman Dynasty and Empire*

After Alderson (1956).

1288–1326	OSMAN or OTHMAN I (son of Ertugrul) Muslim Turkish chieftain and feudal cavalry leader; becomes vassal of the Seljuk Sultan of Rum (Iconium); kills his uncle and founds the Dynasty
1326–1359	ORKHAN, *Emir* (younger son; elder is his vizier); marries daughter of Emperor John Cantacuzenus; takes Nicaea 1331, Gallipoli 1357; enrols captives as janissaries (infantry)
1359–1389	AMURATH or MURAD I; *Sultan* takes Adrianople 1362 (capital 1362–1453); subdues Serbs and Bulgars 1371; dies in victory of Kossovo 1389
1389–1402	BAYEZID I, *the Thunderbolt* executes his half-brother on field of Kossovo; captured by Tamerlane (1402, see Marlowe)
1402–1413	War between sons
1413–1421	MOHAMMED or MEHMET I, *the Restorer*; youngest son; infant navy destroyed by Venetians, 1416
1421–1451	MURAD II blinds three of his brothers; subdues the Seljuks 1428; takes Salonika 1430; first revolt of janissaries suppressed 1447

1451–1481	MOHAMMED II, *the Conqueror*, *Kaisar-i-Rum* takes Constantinople 1453; subdues Bosnia 1464, Albania 1480, organized army, navy, landownership 1476; decrees that Sultans may always murder their brothers
1481–1512	BAYEZID II succession disputed by his half-brother; deposed by his son and the janissaries
1512–1520	SELIM I, *the Grim* executes eight Grand Viziers, annexes Kurdistan and Azerbaijan (1514), Syria and Egypt (1516–1517); takes title of Caliph (1517)[1]
1520–1566	SULEIMAN, *the Magnificent*, *the Law Giver* (*el-Kanuni*) marries Khurrem, daughter of Russian priest; takes Belgrade 1521, Rhodes 1522, Baghdad 1534; fails to take Vienna 1529, Malta 1565 Janissaries attempt deposition 1553 (aged 58)
1566–1574	SELIM II, *the Sot*, son of Khurrem Mosque of Adrianople (Edirne) built by Sinan, an ex-janissary Grand Vizier now commands in war; Lepanto 1571 Cyprus taken from Venice, 1574.
1574–1595	MURAD III murders 5 younger brothers; 103 children, 46 survive him Janissaries begin to marry; become paid hereditary Turkish caste; numbers increased: 20,000 to 48,000 (reach 130,000 in 1800)
1595–1603	MOHAMMED III murders 19 brothers on accession; Christian army auxiliaries disbanded
1603–1617	ACHMET I wife, *Khussem*, daughter of Bosnian priest, rules from 1623–1656: 3 daughters have 15 husbands, mostly viziers; fratricide replaced by caging of male heirs
1648–1687	MOHAMMED IV Mother and grandmother struggle for power; *Khussem* strangled, janissaries in control 1656 Second siege of Vienna 1683 Grand Viziers of *Kuprullu* family: *Mohammed* 1566, *Achmet* 1661, *Mustafa* 1695, *Hussein* 1700
1773–1789	ABDUL HAMID I caged 1740–1773: end of the practice of caging
1789–1807	SELIM III first reformer; attempts representative government; deposed by janissaries and killed
1808–1839	MAHMOUD II, cousin of Selim[2] janissaries abolished by massacre 1826; Greek war of independence 1821–1832; Navarino 1827
1839–1861	ABDUL-MEJID I *Tanzimat*, plan of reform
1861–1924	Six Sultans; five deposed
1924	*End of the Dynasty*

[1] But neither he nor any other Ottoman sultan made the pilgrimage to Mecca.

[2] Frequently but, according to Alderson, erroneously claimed as the son of Aimée Dubucq, cousin of Joséphine Beauharnais, captured by the Dey of Algiers.

The break in the dynasty came in two steps. The first was due to a rash and irregular act on the part of Suleiman el-Kanuni. He actually married his concubine, Roxelana, known to the Turks as Khurrem. This gave an unprecedented appearance of legitimacy to her children. The two ablest of Suleiman's sons, one of them a son of Roxelana, fell out and began a civil war in 1559. Both of them were in consequence executed together with all their young sons. If either of these men had reached the throne the expansion of the Empire might well have continued. It is obvious that Vienna might have fallen to him. As it was, the Empire came into the hands of Roxelana's favourite boy known to history as Selim the Sot. Consequently in 1566 the Ottoman Turks had what they had never had before, a worthless sultan. The failure to take Malta in 1565 was never made good. It was confirmed by the defeat at Lepanto. The first step in decline had been taken.

The second step in decline came with Selim's grandson, Mohammed III, in 1595. This man, by the Law of Fratricide, had to kill or murder nineteen brothers. To these he added on the same day fifteen concubines pregnant by his father. It seems that he, or his wives, or the public, were shaken by this experience. The Sultan decided to turn over a new leaf. In future he and his successors would not send their sons into the world. They would keep them at home. They would keep them caged in small apartments, kiosks, with their own harems, all effectively sterilized like the Sultan's daughters.

What did this mean? It meant that they would all be allowed to survive; a sultan might even have a living uncle—and be succeeded by him. But all experience and all initiative were taken from the heirs to the throne. At the same time all means of judging their ability were taken from everyone else: except, to be sure, the competing mothers and the interested eunuchs of the seraglio, those eunuchs whose influence could scarcely be more beneficial than it was in the preceding Christian Empire. Thus, for the first time, the process of selection ceased. Sultans were appointed or insinuated into their office who were demented or impotent.[1]

While the Dynasty trembled on the verge of extinction, the Empire stumbled on, ruled by the mothers and the grandmothers of its puppet princes. These women were themselves in a strange situation. For the sultans' concubines were themselves largely European. But they were trapped in an institution, the *harem*, adapted by its origins and customs to an oriental and patriarchal submission of women. They did not submit. On the contrary they often thought they could manage the state; and they usually succeeded in managing the Sultan. Some of these women chose able Grand Viziers like the four members of the Turkish noble family of Kuprullu. But others, or their sons, chose badly. The only saving feature was the devoted work of the palace school, derived from Mohammed the Conqueror, whose momentum (as Miller puts it) continued to maintain the success of the establishment until the end of the seventeenth century.

This extraordinary system was stabilized, like the earlier habit of fratricide,

[1] Alderson attributes the decay of the Dynasty to the inherited effect of imprisonment. The effects would however be indirect: a man imprisoned most of his life would never acquire discrimination in his choice of wives.

by fear. The whole complex slave family of the sultan, which had been a plaything in the hands of the great conquerors, became a source of terror and oppression to the weak men who followed them. They were afraid of their wives, of their eunuchs, of their viziers, of their janissaries, of their subject princes in Egypt and Algiers, of their subject people in Rumelia or Greece. And they were increasingly afraid of the Christian powers who increasingly insulted and threatened them.

This terrible descent from power was interrupted in 1773. In that year a Sultan came to the throne who had been caged for thirty-three years. In spite of the long rule of fear and obedience he decided to stop the appalling habit of caging. Having done so he and his successors were able, not to break, but to check the inevitable concatenation of sterilizing customs. They were able to disband and indeed to destroy the janissaries who, over a period of six generations, had transformed themselves from dedicated converted celibates into an effete hereditary caste. Beyond this, however, they were not effectively able to go. Turkish society with its equally effete governing class was crystallized in the form of a bygone age.

The Turkish army had always been commanded by foreign generals. But they were at least converts to Islam. Now they were compelled to fight under explicitly invited foreign and Christian commanders. At this stage it was only the divisions between the Christian powers that allowed the frail body of the sultan's Empire to continue. But throughout the centuries of

Table 27. *Vital Statistics of the Ottoman Dynasty*
From Alderson (1956).

Period	*Succession*	*Generations*		*Average Durations*
1288–1603: (315 years)	fratricide law only sons	13 Sultans in 13 generations	reign generation	24 years
1603–1924 (321 years)	caging rule brothers and cousins	24 Sultans	reign	13·4 years
		8 generations	generation	40·1 years

Total Numbers

SULTANS: 37 deposed: 16 { by viziers: 5; by janissaries: 5 }

WIVES[1] i.e. fruitful concubines: 410

OFFSPRING: { SONS: 401; DAUGHTERS: 451 } married: 149

bearing: { 60 sons; 55 daughters }

Wives of sultans who became mothers were of family types married in the following order:

Early: Dynastic
- (i) Turcoman ruling families, Muslim
- (ii) Greek and other ruling families, either allied and Christian or subjected and Muslim

Late: Personal
- (iii) Foreign women, Russian, Greek, Cretan, Georgian and Circassian of slave origin

[1] Of the 37 mothers of sultans 19 lived to become *Sultan Validés*.

decline the Greeks in Istanbul and Smyrna, the Jews in Salonika, and, until 1827, the Genoese in Chios, continued to sustain the commercial life of a state which had always been able to convert and assimilate fighting men but had failed to convert or assimilate or hybridize with merchants or scholars. Ottoman society lived divided and slowly died of its division.

III. VENICE

a. The Rise

The inhabitants of the Venetian plain, living in towns and villages overrun by the barbarians in the fifth century, rich and poor alike, sought safety in inaccessible places. Some took refuge with the Emperor in Ravenna. Others found homes around the great brackish lagoons sheltered by sandbanks which stretch along eighty miles of the coast. Here was a region, half 'dead' marsh and half live waterways dotted with small islands, where fishermen, fowlers and salt-panners had for ages made their living.

For centuries these people, having settled, as it was said, 'like sea-birds on mud banks', went back and forth trying out the possibilities of this unlikely habitat. But gradually they discovered, and profited by the discovery, that they had a harbour; and it was a harbour facing the rich and ancient east. It was also a harbour having the rare advantage in the Mediterranean of an ebb-and-flow, an Adriatic tide, of three feet.[1] It was enough to flush a densely inhabited lagoon.

The people of different towns (Aquileia, Concordia, Altinum and Padua) established themselves on different islands. They were guided or governed by leaders from the Greco-Roman administration. At first more difficult than Ragusa or Amalfi, less honoured but scarcely less multiracial than Salerno,[2] the Venetian islands proved in the long run to be better sited than any of these for a great business: that of connecting Europe and the north with the rich countries of the east and the south.

The connection or the confrontation was indeed just the one that Athens had made a thousand years earlier and Argos and Crete a thousand years before that. But now the place of union had moved some 800 miles further on. In these havens then it was that traders and seamen from around the Adriatic coasts began to settle. They were people often led by their priests, always followed by builders and craftsmen, and among them, as time would show, some fighting men.

Already in 466 they had set up twelve townships which were to have their separate and varied histories. Malamocco, the earliest capital, later sank in the mud. Torcello in the north built its cathedral in the seventh century but like Mazzorbo (*Major Urbs*) it was soon deserted on account of malaria. Chioggia in the south remains a city to this day.

The people in these new towns at once began to elect delegates, democrati-

[1] W. G. East (1956); Chiodi (1957).

[2] Where the university, 'ancient' in 846, is said to have been founded by a Latin, a Greek, an Arab and a Jew.

cally styled tribunes, to order their own affairs and to negotiate with Gothic kings or Byzantine generals. We find them in 697 taking the advice of the Patriarch (for here the Greek title held its own) of one of their parishes and electing a single magistrate to assert their rights. Soon in 810 this *doge* is defying Pippin the son of Charlemagne and prudently removing his headquarters to a safer site in his labyrinthine principality. This site was on the Rivo-Alto or Rialto in the middle of a tight central cluster of 180 islands. A few years later the reputed bones of the evangelist St Mark were purchased or purloined from the Christian subjects of the Muslim sultan in Alexandria. They were deposited and enshrined in a new chapel of the doge, dedicated to the saint, and designed by Byzantine architects. Then indeed the city felt secure.[1]

Now, taking the name of its tribal forefathers, the place could be known as Venice, the capital of a Venetian Republic, set up in a coign of vantage from which its rulers were able with respectful but firm diplomacy (neatly detailed by Pirenne) to claim their independence of popes and emperors, eastern or western. And when occasion offered and they happened to sell Christian slaves to Muslim dealers, who could wisely challenge them?

They claimed that they had themselves 'created' this habitation, and made it a safe abode which could be threatened only by the sea itself. Surely there never was a city where more obviously over the centuries (as Horatio Brown puts it) 'the people and the place had made one another'. For, in the long hard years of social diffusion, selective migration and survival not all who had come had chosen to stay: and not all who had chosen to stay had succeeded in surviving.

Gradually the doge grew stronger. Time and again his single guidance saved the infant community from disaster. He was evidently chosen from a capable and experienced governing class of Roman and Greek origin, and the military and political capacity of a few families in the city making up this class led to their securing the office in direct family succession. But after four hundred years, in the twelfth century, the skilful exploitation of the crusaders, whose profits Venice shared with rivals in Genoa and Pisa, had suddenly increased the wealth and the numbers of the merchant class. The Republic's fleets now mustered in her employment the most vigorous and varied community of sailors, navigators and shipbuilders in the Mediterranean. Her colonies, with their privileges established by agreement in the chief ports of the Arab and Greek Empires, assembled under her name the most enterprising traders of many races and several religions. Naturally the governing families began to quarrel for the first place.

In the struggle for leadership the doges, in the first place, recommended their sons as their deputies, and in due course nominated them as their

[1] The political and commercial value of these relics began to be fully understood about 1200. The bones of the martyred Stephen were then secured for another Venetian church. And in 1395 (according to Jusserand) pilgrims were told they might see an ear of St Paul, the staff of St Nicholas, an arm of St George, ashes of St Lawrence, three stones thrown at Stephen, a water-pot from Cana and a tooth of Goliath weighing 12 lb.

successors.[1] They next began to seek alliance with the governing families on the mainland. But when the doge married a daughter of the Marquis of Tuscany or the King of Hungary[2] he was clearly failing to distinguish between the interests of the Republic and those of his own family. Responsible citizens looked upon Venice as a state apart from all the others; so indeed it was. And to this apart-ness they now saw a great danger. They might have met the danger by the assassination of doges who aspired to become kings. But they did not. Instead they discovered a more civilized method, a new constitutional formula.

The crisis was precipitated by a political and military miscalculation. The Emperor in Constantinople had confiscated the property of the Venetian colony in his capital. A Venetian expedition of revenge had been shattered. The responsibility lay with the doge and also with the populace who had encouraged him. Both were discredited. Members of the senate, the elected legislature representing the whole class of propertied merchants, took the opportunity to improve their position. They concerted their actions. Their first task was to check the doge. They might have done this by limiting his term of office. But instead they chose first to enlarge his signorial council. Next they introduced a new obligation, a coronation oath, the *promissione ducale*, which they imposed on the incoming head of the state. Then, little by little, they strengthened the oath and weakened the office. The doge remained the ceremonial centre of Venetian life. In pageantry he soon rivalled the pope and the emperor. But in his powers he was reduced to advising his own advisers.

This revolution came about by easy steps in the century between 1171 and 1275. It was accompanied by other quite different constitutional changes which revealed and also defined the character of the developing governing class. For while checking the man above them they used the same skill in checking the men below them: they determined to disfranchise the general body of citizens. This also they did in two steps. First, in 1171, they set up a Grand Council. Unlike previous bodies this assembly was not to be elected directly by the citizens. It was to be nominated by elected delegates. Two delegates from each of the twelve parishes were to nominate forty members to the council making 480 in all. In this way all but the established and the well-known families were excluded from office.

The second step came a century later in 1297 and it completed the whole operation. The Grand Council then voted a decree (known as the *Serrata del Maggior Consiglio*) by which its membership should require no process of election. It should be continued as the inherent right of all those who had already sat in it. It should likewise be continued in their descendants in the male line for ever; each member was to take his seat at twenty-five years of age. The notables had become nobles.

b. The Summit

These constitutional reforms (as the nobles thought them) were not adopted

[1] Villehardouin describes the tearful scene when Enrico Dandolo combines this proposal with religious exhortations (see Shaw, 1963).

[2] Pedigree 15.

without much argument and some bloodshed. But when they had been adopted it could be seen that a democratic assembly had extricated itself from the people it had undertaken to represent. The members of the Grand Council had turned themselves into an hereditary governing class. Or rather it was a caste. For these chosen few had shut out the people from intermarriage with them. If there was to be marriage outside their caste it would be, as the doges had already shown, with the even older landed nobility of the mainland. Naturally therefore we find that the births, deaths and marriages of the new nobility were being recorded by an official college of heralds, the *Avvogadori*, in permanent registers. These were the *Libri d'Oro* which established the names and character of the Venetian nobility for fifteen generations.[1]

The Venetian revolution accomplished several changes without precedent and in one respect it even reversed the most obvious precedents in history. For the patricians of Athens and Rome had broadened their bases and dispersed their privileges as their cities grew in wealth and power. But the self-made patricians of Venice were creating privileges for themselves, such privileges as no one had ever enjoyed before; such privileges also as the contemporary feudal nobilities, with all their landed property, fortified castles, and bound tenants, could never expect to acquire.

Venice was an unapproachable island republic. But within this island they had made another island, a genetic island, equally unapproachable. How did the Venetian nobility come to advance themselves to this extent above all the world? It was by their success during the two centuries of the Crusades, from 1096 to 1291. It was a success in pointing the hot aggressive impulse of the northern warrior class in the direction that would suit their own cool commercial interest. The Eastern Empire crumbled at their assault. When Constantinople fell to the Crusaders in 1204 Venice inherited a quarter of the capital and the control of the Aegean. These successes had given them complete faith in their own abilities as a governing class. At the same time it had destroyed their faith in the abilities of the individuals or the masses who had from time to time unluckily interfered with them.

Nor can we deny this judgment. For the short term of ten generations the Venetian oligarchy proved to be the most successful government in the world: that is not only in its own interests, or in those of Venice, but in those of mankind at large. They knew their city and held it to be impregnable. They knew one another and held themselves to be indivisible. And, sure enough, a hundred years later with the defeat of the blockading Genoese in 1381, they had made their Republic mistress of the Mediterranean.

To make their triumph over Genoa yet more memorable, the Grand Council voted to make an enduring genetic experiment. They resolved to pick out thirty citizen families who with blood or money had helped most in the struggle and to reward them with promotion to their charmed circle,

[1] A similar book was kept by the Byzantine-Genoese merchants in the Aegean island of Chios, the community which after the massacre of 1822 re-established itself and its merchant banks in Marseilles, London and Baltimore. It has now been published in England (Argenti, 1950).

with membership of the council. The honour was accepted with gratitude. Well might it be for such an act was never to be repeated.[1]

Venice was now in process of winning an empire. Venetia and half of Lombardy, Istria and Dalmatia, Crete and Cyprus, and later Morea and the Aegean islands became her colonies. It was an empire dedicated to preserving what the Byzantine Empire had unwillingly handed on. But it was also an empire energetically advancing its powers and its services as far as they would reach.

They rejected papal control; and for a long time they also rejected religious intolerance. For them St Mark was as good as St Peter and in travelling he went as far. Venetians were no longer content to meet the northerners in the Fairs of Champagne. Within thirty years Venetian galleys, the 'Flemish Fleet', were calling at Southampton and they had set up their 'factories' in London and Bruges. In doing so they opened up the northern world not only to trade but also to Italian migration. The influx of Mediterranean people, royal, ecclesiastical and diplomatic, commercial and artistic, into the northern countries had hitherto been intermittent. Now it would never cease.

The two centuries which followed the closing of the gates might be seen as the climax of Venetian commercial and military power. There was nothing to suggest that anything had gone wrong. During this period the structure of the government might be represented in a diagram (Fig. 14). As Davis has put it, the working was not as straightforward as the diagram: 'By the sixteenth century the government which the Venetian ruling class directed had become a very complicated structure. Its complexity was partly the result of a strong Venetian attachment to tradition. Government bodies were rarely abolished, but tended to change their nature as centuries passed. As a result of this process, lines of authority between them were often hazy and responsibilities were not always clear. Some bodies absorbed a combination of executive, legislative and judicial functions. The complexity also resulted from a policy of keeping authority diffused; most responsibility was not in the hands of individuals but of committees of noblemen. . . .

'At the pinnacle was the splendid, venerable, but almost powerless doge.'

Many ancient and opulent corporations, for example the Church of Rome and the universities in England, have followed this kind of pattern. But Venice offers us the neatest of models, neatest because it is most strictly hereditary.

c. The Breeding Crisis

(1) *The Decline in Numbers*. The discovery of the new routes to India and to America in the last decade of the fifteenth century faced Venice with an economic crisis. The old trade with the east and the new trade with the west were both taken by the nations with Atlantic ports and Atlantic seamen.[2] Disaster, it has usually been supposed, was inevitable even if it had to wait for three hundred years. In fact, the impact on Venice was made irremediable

[1] Except for the families of popes, e.g. the Borghese. Note the official recognition of families whose influence the principle of celibacy was supposed to have repudiated.

[2] Who had often emigrated from Venice and Genoa (Coles 1968).

The System of the Venetian Government

(after Davis 1962)

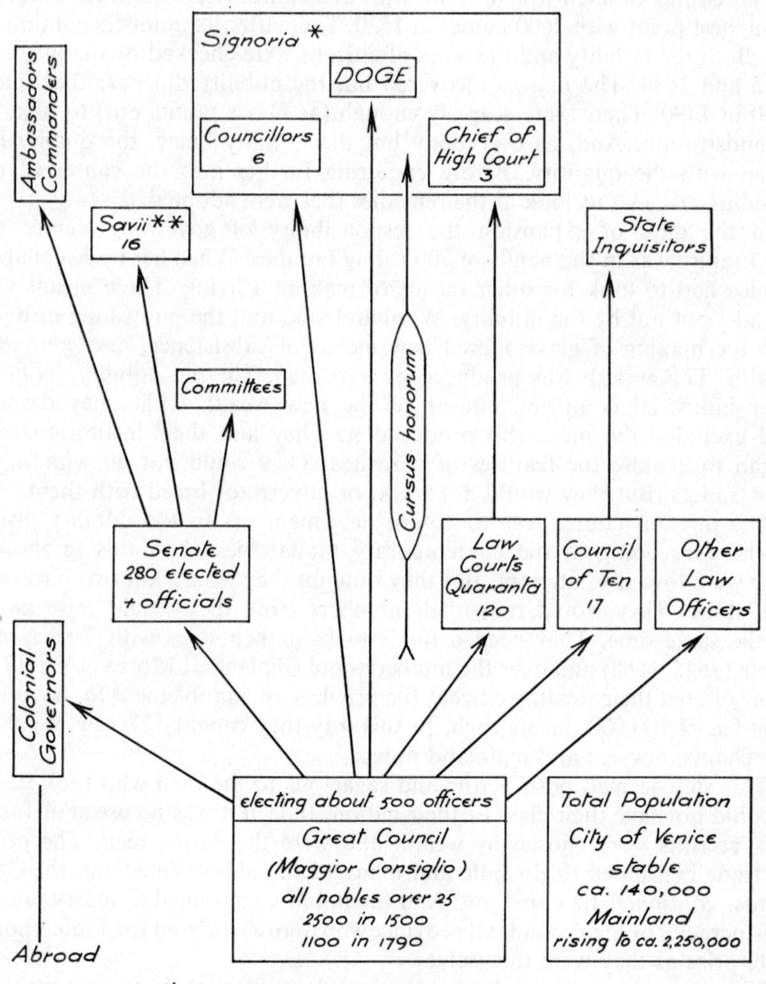

* Signoria + Savii = Pien Collegio

** Offices concentrated latterly in less than one tenth – the wealthiest – of the noble families

Fig. 14

only by the remedies that the Venetian nobles thought fit to take. They were concerned, as we might expect, to preserve their families, their caste and their state. And it was in this order of priority, as it now appears, that they approached their problems.

Publicly, therefore, the first problem to be noticed and tackled was that of a decline in numbers of the ruling class.

The Grand Council which began with 210 names inscribed in 1296 reached its highest point with 2600 names in 1520. Thereafter its numbers continually fell. Both the nobility and the mass of citizens were checked by the plague in 1575 and 1630. The masses recovered but the nobility did not: they fell to 1100 in 1790. There were scarcely enough (as Davis points out) to man the administration. And, as everybody but the nobility knew, the quality had fallen with the quantity. Before enquiring further into the causes of this breeding crisis let us look at the remedies that were adopted.

In the days of expansion the responsibility of governing Venice and her Empire was in the hands of 700 ruling families. When her trade collapsed Venice had to look for other means of making a living. These means were found—but not by the nobility. Wool and silk, and the publishing of books and the making of glass offered new means of subsistence, new sources of wealth. This wealth was produced by new men. The old nobility, as in the later industrial countries, consumed the new wealth while they despised and excluded the men who produced it. They and their institutions thus began to acquire the features of parasites. They could not do without the new traders. But they would not work, or govern, or breed with them.

The obvious course was to co-opt new members to the nobility just as rulers were doing in the contemporary monarchies. And this in the end they were forced to attempt. But they thought they would kill two birds with one stone. They would raise their numbers. And they would raise money at the same time. They needed funds to fight their wars with Turkey over Crete (1645–1668) and over the mulberry and silk land of Morea (1685–1716). They offered their wealthy citizens the privilege of ennoblement for an admission fee of 100,000 ducats each. In this way they caught 127 new members, merchants, lawyers and mainland nobles.[1]

This step seemed both heroic and sagacious to the men who took it. But it could not save their class or their nation. Indeed it was no use at all for the new recruits were chosen by wealth and were the wrong men. The profits of trade continued to dwindle and many of the ablest Venetians, the Canalettos, continued to move out. And the nobility continued to marry into the aristocracies of their mainland province who were as unfitted for contemporary enterprise as they were themselves.

This however was not the lesson they drew from their experience of advancing decay. They felt that their mistake had been in their last admission to have allowed traders to stain the purity of their breed which they seem

[1] This sale of honours was not new. It seems to have been invented by Philip the Fair of France in 1302. While the Venetians were taking over only new social territory he however was taking over new physical territory, in Flanders (see Marc Bloch, 1940, 1961).

to have conceived as wholly Roman. They therefore painfully resolved to sell another batch of patents of nobility; but this time it would be only to landed aristocrats. At this point the Council of the Republic were brought face to face with a terrible reality: only ten applications were received for forty places offered. In the world outside, the Venetian nobility had outlived their reputation.

(2) *The Restricted Family*. Look now at the causes of decline of the nobility. By its own decrees the council had tied up the future of the Republic with their own married propagation. Yet this is the connection which they never saw, the problem they never faced.

When the nobles realized that they could no longer increase their wealth they became preoccupied with the desire to preserve it. Imitating the gentry of the mainland with whom they had begun to intermarry they took the wealth out of enterprise and put it into landed property which they hoped to preserve intact for their descendants. In this first conservative step they probably succeeded. The second step was also conservative.

If the nobility were to keep land intact for their descendants they had to ask: how many descendants? The nobles of Venice were no longer adventurous warriors or explorers. They no longer bred Marco Polos and Cabots. They were not even prone to the diseases of the lower orders of society.

They had no rule of primogeniture such as, particularly in England, preserved and enlarged the largest estates. There was nothing they could do consistent with decent behaviour except to restrict the numbers of their descendants by restricting their own reproduction; or at least legitimate reproduction. This they did by a process of 'restricted marriages'. Families were able to agree that only one son should marry. The family would thus never multiply and its property would never be divided.

Only the homogeneity of inbreeding could have produced harmonious agreements by which this practice, described by Davis, established itself. Naturally the calculation often miscarried. A tenth of their numbers were lost in each of the plagues of 1575 and 1630. To celebrate the return of health the survivors might build the great church of Santa Maria delle Salute and Monteverdi might compose a great mass. But their numbers never recovered from these unforeseen punishments. Hence, just as the rulers diminished in aptitude for the duties of ruling which they had reserved for themselves, they also diminished in the numbers available to perform these duties.

Landed gentry are peculiarly susceptible to this Venetian disease. Especially in England[1] they have discovered the art of enlarging their fortunes and extinguishing their families by the single stroke of marrying heiresses. That is to say they marry women who owe their wealth to a lack of brothers and hence to a parental infertility which they inherit along with their estates.

But the complete Venetian disease was something more. It arose from the absolute power of the ruling class. Here they were caught unawares in the same predicament as the Ottoman sultans, their unhappy contemporaries. They were in the grip of a system, a code of behaviour and a standard of living fixed by their own unlimited authority. The ruling class had no monarch

[1] As Erasmus Darwin, Galton and Fisher have pointed out.

to correct its two disastrous mistakes: segregated breeding to keep itself pure and restricted marriage to keep itself rich. One of these mistakes any community, noble or peasant, might and often did survive; the two together were fatal.

Two more questions we need to ask about the restricted family.

First, what was its origin? All nobilities which fail to accept primogeniture probably restrict their families. The origin of the practice lies in the first communities to be restricted in their occupation of land, that is in the peasantry. The sub-division of peasant properties is a disaster which was already noted in France before the Revolution by Arthur Young. But it is sometimes avoided by restricted marriages. There may then be a '*pacte de famille*' like that in Venice; by such an agreement only half the family marries and only the eldest inherits the land.[1]

The custom of restricted marriages in Venice finds its parallel, however, at the top as well as at the bottom of society, and in Asia as well as in Europe. Among the Nambuthri Brahmins of Malabar, who are patrilinear, caste marriage is restricted to senior sons. The younger sons marry only Nayars, that is women of a matrilinear caste to which their children belong.[2] A number of interesting consequences ensue:

(i) the numbers, property and status of the Brahmin families are conserved but
(ii) the genes of the upper caste flow into the lower, and
(iii) the Laws of Manu are satisfied: the eldest son is enough to repay the pious debt to the souls of the ancestors; additional sons are a work of lust.

Thus a kind of restriction or primogeniture of marriage is accepted on various grounds in various societies as an alternative to a restriction or primogeniture of inheritance.

What then was the total effect of restricted marriage in the Venetian noble families on their breeding behaviour and genetic structure? The practice was in part a masculine subterfuge. Rarely it might restrict breeding on both sides. Brothers are said to have sometimes cohabited with one wife polyandrously on the Tibetan principle and with the same motive of limiting progeny. But usually it meant restriction only on the female side. Daughters were consigned to nunneries. As Casanova showed in Venice (with *La Bella Monaca*) and Diderot no less in France (with his novel, *La Religieuse*) they went most unwillingly. It was one of the corrupt practices to which monastic institutions lend themselves. The sons also might enter the Church.[3] Pre-

[1] The most detailed description is said to be that of the customs of the now extinct Melouga family in the Lavedan valley of the Pyrenees (in his work, *Organisation de la Famille*, by Frédéric Le Play, *cit.* Demolins 1898, p.13). See also Pfeifer (1956).

[2] See Thurston (1909); Hutton (1961) and *E.B.* (1929) art.: 'Henogamy.'

[3] The number of clerics increased, according to Davis, in the last century of the ruling class. And two families, no doubt assisted by their recent purchase of Venetian nobility, achieved the papacy; they gave us unmemorable names: Alexander VIII (1689–91) and Clement XIII (1758–69).

serving estates was indeed one of the uses of clerical celibacy and the most thoroughly exploited in the foundation of the crusading orders of knighthood which perfectly fitted the younger sons of the landed gentry. For the sake of the rich family a clerical son avoided the cost of legitimate offspring. At the same time his illegitimate children were class crosses of value to society as a whole.

Breeding was no doubt also genuinely restricted on the male side. Abortion, infanticide, and after the sixteenth century, contraception, were no doubt as common in Venice as elsewhere.[1] Homosexual relations, which are bound to be tolerated among sea-faring as among desert-dwelling men, not only flourished in Venice but made it a permanent centre of attraction to travellers from less tolerant societies.[2]

But with all these reservations there must have been breeding, illegitimate but fertile, between classes. There must have been a flow of genes from the nobility into the citizen and artisan classes of Venice; a flow at the expense of middle and lower class husbands. In this respect Venice would agree with the pattern of the rest of Europe. It would disagree with the pattern of the Ottoman society. For when the Ottomans demanded a restriction of heirs, they killed them: all were legitimate and all perished together.

(3) *The Lesson.* The explanation that is often given and usually believed for the decline of Venetian society is that it was due to inbreeding of the ruling class. Any number of successful societies, tribal and civilized, however have been as inbred as the Venetian ruling class. Decline in all societies is connected, not with inbreeding or outbreeding as such, but with a switch from one to the other. Now, with a switch to inbreeding, such as happened in Venice, a second condition is indispensable for disaster. It is that the competition and selection which led to earlier success must be removed. This condition is, of course, the one which the Venetian ruling class, like any other, but with unusual success took steps to secure. For when it closed its gates in 1297 rejecting future recruitment of successful outsiders it established inbreeding and it eliminated internal competition in one step and, with the two exceptions we noticed, for ever.

By the time that its economic crisis came, the Venetian nobility had become a harmonious and homogeneous population. They were utterly entangled in their net of well-constructed habits. They fitted their own families and their own society. They fitted their own life and their own laws. The privileges they had acquired and the constitution they had made for themselves, fitted them as neatly as their own lagoon. For them, whatever might be true of the ordinary citizens, nowhere in the world could possibly be as comfortable or as civilized as Venice. They were therefore entirely unfitted to explore the new modes of activity that were displacing their own. Only an outbreeding and heterogeneous society could have met the crisis with enterprise and enthusiasm. As indeed the Atlantic nations did.

[1] To judge by Montesquieu's letters from Venice to Lord Waldegrave; see also James Boswell's *London Journal.*

[2] As we may see from the visits of Byron, John Addington Symonds, and our historian, Horatio Brown. The experiences of Benvenuto Cellini in Paris throw light on the earlier Italian reputation.

When they began to restrict their families therefore they did the only thing that seemed possible. But their remedy through its genetic effects, as we have so often seen, aggravated the very dangers from which they were trying to escape. It made their caste less fitted for the task which it would allow no others to share.

d. The Achievement

The Venetian nobility destroyed themselves by processes known elsewhere but with them to be observed in the neatest experimental isolation. They destroyed themselves, yet their efforts on the way created memorials that have survived them, the most durable being the city of Venice itself. The use they and the Republic made of their and her wealth attracted men of talent from all over the western world. The churches of Venice brought architects and artificers from Byzantium and Egypt to build them; painters from near and far, Titian and El Greco, to decorate them; musicians such as Willaert, the Fleming who came in 1527 to invent a new method of spacing their choirs and to compose music for them.

The libraries of Venice, which derived from Petrarch's bequest of 1374, brought to the city the German and French printers who copied the books and made them into the greatest instrument in the revival of learning.[1] Padua being under the government of Venice after 1405, its university received all these copyright books. These in turn enabled it to attract Vesalius, Galileo, Scaliger and Tasso and led it in due course, in 1545, to found the first botanic garden in Europe.

For this enterprise we may well be indebted to the Jews who, expelled from Granada in 1492 and benefiting from the shrewd and self-interested hospitality of Venice, set up their ghetto there.[2]

At the same time Venice passed on to the world outside her talented pupils, the Cretan, El Greco, or the Chioggian whom we call John Cabot. Usually unknown when they left, like Marco Polo they became famous elsewhere.

The absence of literature and drama from the record denotes a racial character in the Venetians, a gap in their interests and their abilities. Having printed much they wrote little to be remembered and the censorship of the Committee of Ten did not encourage frivolous invention which was uncongenial to them. For in general, those who went into Venice, and those who came out, had something in them peculiar to the character of Venice, to the taste, judgment and education of that utterly selfish, frequently decadent but always discriminating race of people, the Venetian nobility.

The reason for this specific effect of Venice on the course of history is that under the fixed ruling class, there was a shifting citizen class. It was their world which acted as a channel through which people were passing

[1] Steinberg (1955).

[2] In 1492; first mentioned in 1516 (Parkes 1962). This was two centuries before the Armenians were in their turn given asylum and brought their treasures to the little island of San Lazzaro in 1717.

for the whole of the thousand years of the city's most active life. It was a stream of people, a stream moving in many directions but predominantly out of the Ancient East and the Mediterranean world into Northern and Western Europe. It was like other streams passing through other cities of Italy. The movement of these streams was one of the effective processes in the making of modern Europe and western civilization.

18

THE NEW NATIONS

I. THE BREAKDOWN OF THE WEST

WHEN THE ROMAN EMPIRE in the west crumbled in the fifth century, men everywhere found themselves confronted by unfamiliar neighbours and conditions, by uncertainties of authority and communication. Barbarian kings or generals, Roman landowners or *senatores*, Catholic clergy often of Greek, Syrian or African extraction, Mediterranean seamen and Jewish merchants slowly learnt to speak a Latin tongue, acknowledged with varying deference a Byzantine emperor, disagreed over their religious beliefs but, by and large, discovered means of making their living on a foundation of the unchanging land and the unmoving peasants who cultivated it.

It was a world in which two kinds of opposed groups continued their opposed movements. On the one hand were the fighting tribes of the north and east, led by their aggressive chieftains. Franks, Saxons and Lombards, Bulgars and other Slavs, were making their way south and west and establishing their government over territories, that is especially over rural land. On the other hand, but not in military formation, were the people of the eastern Mediterranean, moving out of the settled Eastern Empire and forming colonies in the sea-ports and cathedral cities of the west. These were the literate, civilized, Hellenized and Judaized, Christian people whose skill and intelligence, experience and education were indispensable for the administration of the western provinces. They knew how to write and they imported Egyptian papyrus for the purpose. They brought in the grain and the spices, the textiles and the weapons that the new Europeans demanded. They also brought in ideas. They created a great Latin and Christian community with a continuity of commerce. Europe, Africa and Asia were united by the Mediterranean. It was a unity reinforced by the polite harmony of the Pope and the Emperor neither of whom recognized fully the dangers or the opportunities of his position.

Meanwhile, beneath the surface of recorded history changes were taking place which were bound to alter the character of Europe. The men who helped the new rulers to govern their states were described as Romans. They were men like Boëthius and Cassiodorus who wrote Latin, and wrote with distinction. Often they retired from government and from family life to go into monasteries or into the Church. There they found another world. Theodore of Tarsus could in his old age undertake to organize the Church in England (in 675) or Boniface from England serving a Syrian pope could put the Church of Germany and France into a Latin shape (in 722).

During these great activities it is clear that the different races now brought together were forming different classes of the new society. They were confirming and also diversifying the social stratification of the northern peoples. But it is also clear that the immigrants were hybridizing with the native peoples and with one another. This was more particularly so in the cities and in the higher ranks of society and it is for this reason that we find the conflict of the opposed methods of government under the Merovingian kings in France described by Pirenne: a classical bureaucracy espoused by Ebroin (with Arnulf, as Mayor of the Palace and Archbishop) and an hereditary aristocracy by the family of Charles Martel. The three layers of authority might appear to be Roman emperor, Barbarian king, and Roman minister or barbarian noble; but in fact all of them were in a state of hybridization.

We saw how, as soon as their power was felt, the Gothic and Vandal chieftains married into the Roman imperial family. (Pedigree 11). This practice continued until the distinction between barbarian and Roman ceased to be possible. We do not know enough about the ancestry of the early barbarian kings since the most notable of them, like Charles Martel and William the Conqueror, were bastards. But we can hardly suppose that, since they were more in contact with Romans than their subjects, and were the first to learn Latin, they were the only ones not to mate or marry with civilized Roman women.

In the first seven generations of Gothic and Frankish rule in the west we must therefore suppose a great new integration of society to have taken place. The results of this integration appeared when the crisis of the Muslim invasions struck the Christian world between 632 and the coming of Charlemagne.

II. THE WORLD OF CHARLEMAGNE

The Muslim conquest of Syria and North Africa meant, as we have seen, that half the ancient sea-faring people of the Mediterranean became Muslim and were able to turn the great ports of Tyre, Alexandria and Carthage (which they quickly transformed into Tunis) into naval bases. From these bases they were able to attack the whole of the islands and the northern coasts of the sea. Everywhere they were successful except against the great city of Constantinople, the ports of Amalfi, Naples and Gaeta and, within the Adriatic, Ragusa and Venice. Inland they were beaten back by Charles Martel at

Poitiers in 732 but five years later aided by their sea power they were able to capture Avignon. And still a century later (in 838) they could attack Marseilles and in 849 they could land at Ostia and inspect the defences of Rome itself.

The assault of the Muslims meant that both the west and the east of Christendom, both the Pope and the Emperor, were faced with a crisis. They were also compelled to face it separately. To the Emperor Heraclius it was a crisis not only in defence and economy but also in religious doctrine. He was inspired to make a desperate concession to the Monophysites of Syria and Egypt. He proposed to accept One Life for Christ in exchange for Two Natures. In two steps, 638 and 648, Monothelism took the place of Monophysism. A later Emperor, Leo the Isaurian, himself a Syrian, made a second concession to Syrian and Muslim prejudices. He condemned the use of images by the Church.

The first of these revelations failed to save the southern provinces; the second failed to recover them. It was not a theological formula or a ritual device but a racial difference that severed the Greeks from the Syrians and Egyptians. At the same time both concessions alienated the Western Church. And 50,000 Greek monks or clergy banished from the east (according to Gibbon) sought the hospitality of Rome. It was the last great movement in the Hellenization of the west. It was also one of the first great examples of the principle of uniformity in Christendom.

In happier days the power of Byzantium would have prevented the pope from contradicting his imperial suzerain. But now the weakness of Byzantium invited the pope to confiscate the Greek churches in the south of Italy and to direct their income to the papal treasury. It invited him also to consider that western kings might respect him more and protect him better than the Eastern Emperor.

These were the circumstances in which the Frankish house of Pippin established a new era in European history. They rose to power in three generations. The father was Charles Martel who began as Mayor of the Palace of the Frankish King, the successor of Clovis of the Merovingian line. Between 717 and 741 he established himself by victory in war as the effective ruler of the kingdom. His son was Pippin who, inheriting his father's rank and power, asked the pope in Rome whether he or the titular king should rule. The pope agreed that Pippin should be king in 751; conversely Pippin agreed five years later that the pope should be master of his Roman territory.[1] Thus the pope and the new king, having recognized one another's authority, became mutually dependent. The grandson was Charles (or Charlemagne) who took the north of Italy from the Lombards, and drove back the Muslims in Spain and the pagan Saxons and Slavs in Central Europe. This great conqueror, having now Rome within his dominions was prepared to be crowned by the pope in Rome. Thus on Christmas day 800 he became *serenissimus Augustus, a Deo coronatus, magnus, pacificus, imperator*; in other words the successor of the Caesars, the Roman Emperor. Not quite so powerful as he seemed to be, or as his edicts made him out to be, but undoubtedly

[1] As he continued to be until September 30, 1870.

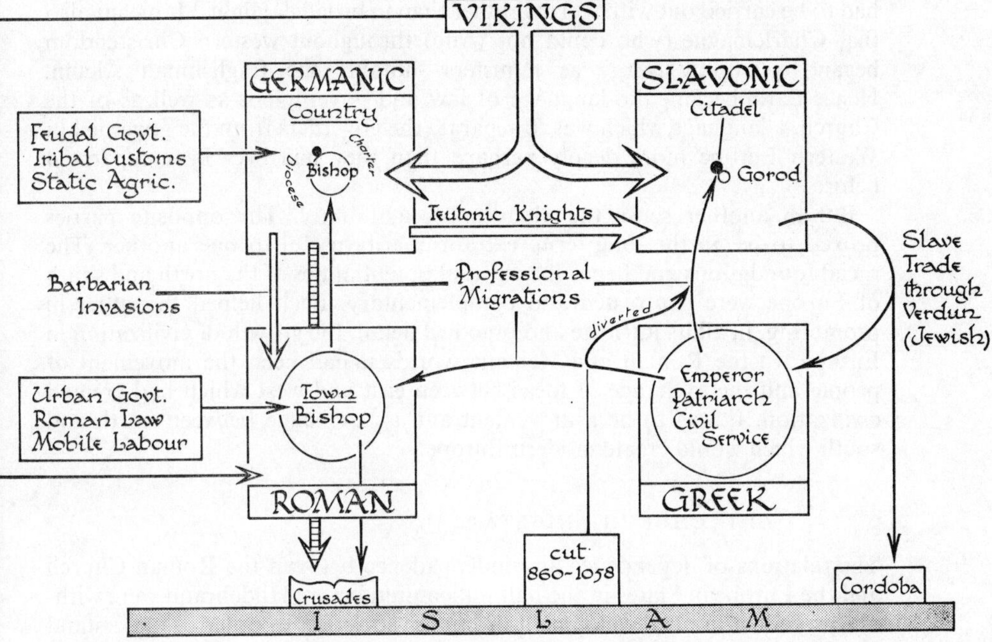

Fig. 15. Diagram to show the changing relations of authority and movement, co-operation and conflict between inhabitants and invaders, town and country, State and Church, in the four quarters of Christian Europe.

After Pirenne, Bloch, Grayler and others

the most powerful figure in Christendom. Yet still he was under an obligation to God's representative, the pope, who crowned and anointed him.

Charlemagne's chief capital was Aix-la-Chapelle or Aachen. Here he was buried. Here was the centre of his power. He had made his alliance with the head of the Church in Rome; but it faded. The Carolingian line collapsed in the tenth century; its dominions were shattered into a score of fragments. The idea of an empire had to be painfully restored by Otto the Great in Germany in 962 and from him the principle of a Holy Roman Empire was descended. Between these descendants and the Roman Church, quarrel was usually more evident than friendship. Yet concealed beneath the quarrels the basic advantage of co-operation lay. The equivocal relations between Church and State were initiated by Frankish kings, English (not Anglo-Saxon but Anglo-Celtic) missionaries (Boniface and Alcuin) and Greco-Roman administrators (like Theodore) in the seventh and eighth centuries. They were supported by this overriding advantage of co-operation between different kinds of people which governs the whole development of society. It meant co-operation between north and south, between country and city, between baron and bishop, between men of aggression and war and men of law and peace. It meant balanced power instead of absolute power. Now assassination and murder had to be carried out with secrecy rather than in broad daylight.[1] It meant also that Charlemagne (who could not write) throughout western Christendom began to employ clergy as ministers—notably the Englishman Alcuin. Hence Latin became the language of law and government as well as of the Church, a language which was to separate the governers from the governed in Western Europe more deeply perhaps than they had ever been separated before.

But in another sense the alliance brought unity. The opposite parties proved to be, in the long term, extraordinarily useful to one another. The racial foundations and hence the cultural potentialities of the north and south of Europe were contrasted and complementary. Each helped the other in promoting, in all its intricate and practical detail, the growth of civilization in Europe. In the Roman and Hellenic worlds it had been the movement of people and the exchange of ideas between east and west which had created civilization. It was to be a movement and an exchange between north and south which would create modern Europe.

III. CHURCH AND STATE

The relations of dependence and independence between the Roman Church and the European States in the half millennium before Hildebrand were without precedent in the development of human societies. In order to understand them we have to look at the genetic character and the social functions of the two opposed but co-operating groups, the clerical and secular communities.

Here was the Christian Church with its centre established in Rome. It constituted a hierarchy of authority which, depending on religious tradition, asserted the right to advise, to correct, and to interfere with governments established by force. It did so on the basis of rules of behaviour which often conflicted with the instincts, morals or interests of particular classes, notably the rulers.

The coming of this Christian Church into the Roman Empire had been, as we have seen, a revolution. And the revolution was still continuing. The Church's purpose and its meaning had been to create some kind of unity and equality. With equality it never had much success. But within the geographically restricted framework of the Western Empire, under a racially somewhat restricted governing class, and dynastic establishment, partly of its own creation, the Church did indeed create a kind of unity, a politically and culturally effective unity. It did so however by introducing a new kind of differentiation and a new basis of inequality with a value which lay in its cutting clean across the previously effective differentiations of society. It was a differentiation based on literacy, a faculty at that time largely beyond the reach of kings and princes.

The novelty of Christianity for Europe in which it was to be imitated by

[1] E.g. no one knows how Charlemagne disposed of his nephew or how Henry I of England disposed of his brothers.

Islam, lay in its reliance on a book. The principle which had distinguished the ancient priesthoods from the people was now applied on a vast scale. The use of scripture made reading and writing a decisive barrier in society, an instrument of inequality which became the means of disseminating an ostensibly equalitarian religion. Once again the illiterate had to be told what the literate said it meant. The priestly languages, Hebrew, Greek and Latin, to which Arabic soon came to be added, were the instruments of separating still further the people from the learned, the priestly, the *ulema*.

The Catholic priest found his Latin as useful in England as the Muslim lawyer found his Arabic in Spain or Indonesia in establishing the power and authority of his organization. Meaningless words became the new idols of religions which denied idolatry: scripture in part replaced sculpture.

When the specious character of the unity derived from the Latin language was discovered and the national character of the northern peoples reasserted itself, the Reformation allowed the scripture to reappear in the vernacular languages. The division between literate and illiterate was then, with immense confusion and strife, partly or momentarily dissolved. But during the thousand years of its relatively undisputed authority Rome established a social framework which, until the present century, has governed the evolution of European society. It did so by its independence. If we compare it with what happened in Constantinople, Byzantine or Ottoman, it was a partial and fluctuating but none the less significant independence of the secular government.

There was nothing new in the opposition between two opposed authorities in society. The conflict between priests and kings was new to Rome and indeed to Europe. But it was familiar in most of the older eastern societies and peoples, Egyptian, Persian and Hebrew, from which European society was partly derived. But now the priests were strengthened by two unprecedented advantages. The first was the impressive literate, legal and ceremonial apparatus accumulated by the Church from the inheritance of Jews, Greeks and Romans and it was an apparatus which it had marshalled in developing its own means of government and conversion during this second half-millennium.

The second new advantage of the priesthood was the vow of celibacy. Hildebrand, who was pope as Gregory VII from 1073–1085, recognized the establishment of celibacy to be the crucial means of completing this evolution. For him celibacy meant foregoing, not sexual relations or cohabitation, nor family life, nor even the procreation of children, but merely the procreation of legitimate children with enforceable hereditary interests, economic and social.

The original virtue of celibacy attached to the priesthood was seen when the Church was poor. It lay in the special saintliness of those who seemed to be different from ordinary men and women. For in them impotence was described as continence and a human failure became a divine gift. The second virtue lay in the necessity, when the Church became rich, of avoiding the inheritance of wealth and power; it was intended to prevent, and largely succeeded in preventing, the growth of a self-propagating caste of priests.

Popes in Rome cannot have failed to notice that emperors in Constantinople, when they confirmed so many patriarchs in their appointments, were influenced in favour of eunuchs. They were supposed, as we have seen, to be free from family ambitions. Nor can popes have failed to notice that Byzantine notables had their more promising sons castrated to improve their chances of high office—whether in Church or State. By a rule or vow of celibacy, however, the Roman priest could, and throughout the middle ages did, enjoy nearly all these political advantages without an irreversible change of state and with the very minimum of personal inconvenience. By developing marriage as a state of legal union the Church was distinguishing a third state of illegal union which was compatible with 'celibacy' and was of immense social significance in Europe. The contrast between the Ottoman and Venetian systems of family planning shows just how significant it was.

The third virtue of celibacy, unlike the others, was not apparent to the Church at the time—or even at any later time. It lay in a property of the Church, which emerged slowly and unawares after the time of Charlemagne; the property that the Church as a whole became a mirror image of these societies.

How did this happen? As we have seen, in a heterogeneous society, stratified but unstable, outbreeding will give rise to a fraction of individuals who are indifferent to marriage or prefer celibacy. This fraction amounts to about one-tenth. And it is found in all sections of society except those that are protected from outbreeding, as for example under conditions of serfdom. The celibate Church therefore came to be recruited from nearly all sections of society and hence in its social and intellectual character to represent nearly all sections of society reflecting their class diversity of character and of aptitude.

There were however several other momentous consequences of the celibacy or non-marriage of the clergy. The first was that by processes of heredity *outside* the Church a varied and stratified structure was constantly maintained *inside* it: the Church was a para-hereditary society. The second was that the Church, by its education, its interest in scholarship, its hierarchical discipline and attenuated family connections, was able to give a unity to its genetically diverse components greater than that of secular society. It was, for example, able to open the way to social promotion for the children of poor parents, and especially for the bastard children of class crosses.[1]

But more important than any individual action was the long-term principle that the Church was able and willing at every level to impose its own interest in social harmony on the class conflicts going on outside it. This principle influences and sometimes dominates the evolution of government for the thirty crucial generations of European society, that is until the Reformation.

Against these contributions of the Church to the development of European society, all made in its own interests, we must of course set its pursuit of

[1] That is to say, when dispensation was granted. It also then provided a kinder solution to the problem of pretenders to the throne. A Beaufort could be made Bishop of Winchester who otherwise might have been blinded, like Robert of Normandy, or castrated, like a Byzantine prince. Michael I (811–813) when deposed, to protect his son's life, as we saw, had him castrated (Runciman, 1933).

wealth and power, and its method of selling salvation; its propagation of idolatry and every other superstition that was also in its own interests; its enforcement of uniformity with the suppression of every kind of new independent or individual thinking and hence its persecution of Jews and heretics; its indifference to every manifestation of despotism whether by torture, or public execution of individuals or the enslavement or extermination of whole races so long as they were not against its own interests; its ultimately disastrous failure to adapt its theories of population and dogmas of sexual life to the changing needs of society.

Most of these unenlightened habits and practices have been adopted, although less successfully maintained, by the Church's reformed and politically more dependent successors. Are they perhaps inherent in the conditions under which Churches attempt to survive? To answer this question we need to consider the alternatives known to history. They may help us to take another step in measuring the role of religious belief in the development of society.

The new Europe of which we are speaking, with its balance of Church and State, arose from the Western Empire. It arose in the sixth, seventh and eighth centuries. And it arose with the character it had because that Western Empire, as Pirenne has put it, was shut off from civilizing immigration, shut off from the natural centre of its civilization in Constantinople, shut off by the Muslim conquests and the growth of Islam. Thus Islam was not only one basis of comparison with Christianity, the great control to the Christian experiment as a means of creating a universal society. It was also, in a more decisive way than Pirenne supposed, one of the factors in creating western Christendom and western Europe.

IV. THE ORIGINS OF FEUDALISM

Feudal societies arise where central authority cannot be operated from cities through lack of currency, lack of communications, lack of security, lack of literacy and of the educated mechanisms of urban society generally. A central authority has then to be supported by obligations not of payments but of service, obligations passed down from the king to the level of the peasant on whose cultivation of the soil, and on whose devotion to the soil, the whole society ultimately depends.

The powerless Romanized Merovingian line of Clovis was in the ninth century replaced as kings of the Franks by their more Germanic Mayors of the Palace (Pedigree 14). The replacement was due to several administrative advances made by Charles Martel, advances breaking with Roman tradition but tending to unite the two societies and systems in a new way. The first was that the Roman system of direct taxation, administered by appointed Roman counts, would no longer work. The state was now impoverished (on Pirenne's view, by the Muslim expansion) and without gold. On its eastern, Austrasian side, literacy, communications, and security had all deteriorated. For these various reasons the state must now depend on armed forces, not of free men paid by the king, but of bound men. How were they to be bound? By serving their local lords, with rent, labour or fighting, lords who were in

Pedigree 14. The Lineage of Charlemagne
After Eginhard, et al.

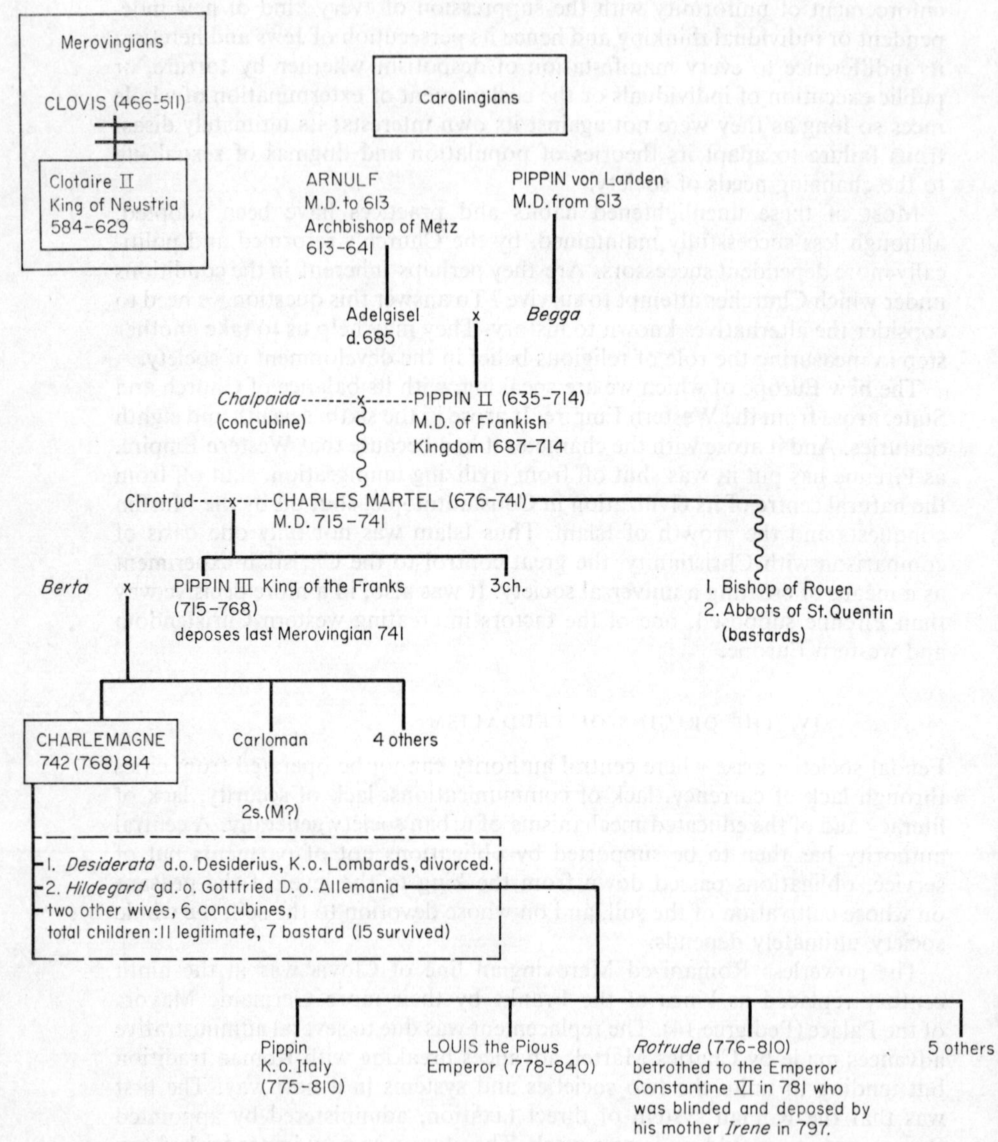

M. D. Major Domo, Hausmeier, Mayor of the Palace or Chief Minister.

turn bound to serve the king in return for holding land granted to them by the king. The foundations were in personal contract of man to man, a contract blessed by the Church.

The second discovery of Charles Martel was that the conquest of new territories would provide the gifts of land to fighting men who would bind themselves to him as vassals, bringing forces proportionate in strength to their new estates. To these could be added lands obtained by the confiscation of Church properties which, having been accumulated on a great scale by the benefactions of the pious or the sinful, were already excessively large.

These two discoveries were developed and extended by his son and his grandson. Owing to their success in conquest they were gradually able to establish the principle that kings were the owners of the land: all land must therefore be held by vassals, barons or bishops, who were bound to serve the king. No lord could be trusted—or would be trusted—who would not pay homage to the ruler. And conversely none who paid homage, even counts in the Roman reckoning, need be paid in money for their services.

Feudal society developed from the combined military success and administrative skill of Charles Martel and his son and grandson. It spread over their dominions and later over the whole of expanding western Christendom and beyond. It was never stable, never complete, but for four centuries it dominated Europe and after a thousand years its traces have not yet flickered out. Its strength depended partly on the mutual value of protection and subjection, which it shares with all government. And partly on its suitability for primitive conditions, for it provided rank and title and ultimately legal status to the military vassals of the king, who were to become the upper classes, while, for the lower classes, it guaranteed the cultivator's life and living and hence a secure place even in an insecure society. But above all its strength depended on its immense adaptability. This adaptability has to be considered at two levels. At the higher levels it concerned the character of the ruler and the vassal; at the lower levels it concerned the life of the serf.

Feudal society arose from the attempts of rulers to impose new rules on the people they ruled. The first people to feel the impact of the new ideas, the people at the centre of origin of expanding feudalism, were those living between the Loire and the Rhine. Here it was that, as Bloch puts it, 'the mingling of Romanized elements and Germanic elements—more pronounced here than elsewhere—had most completely disrupted the structure of the two societies'. In other words a hybridization of the governing classes had led to a variety of new recombinations, an enterprise in attempting new administrative devices and in exploiting the old instinctive relation of 'territorial lordship and personal dependence'.

But side by side with this mixing in the top layers of society there had also been a mixing at the bottom of communities of peasants. Cultivators appeared both in Normandy and in parts of the Danelaw in England who proved to be (and can we not still see it?) the most stubbornly independent or even insubordinate people in the world. Not even the Norman Conqueror could extract an oath of fealty from them. It was such men who offered to serve as peasant warriors by 'mutual oaths', the free owners of allodial properties uncommitted to the feudal system of service and protection.

V. FEUDAL INHERITANCE

Feudal holdings were derived from barbarian custom although they were written in terms of Roman law. When they became hereditary they naturally followed or imitated (as Maine puts it) the earlier local forms or customs, family organization and accompanying systems of land-holding. These existed in two contrasted types which weie also stages of evolution:

(i) inheritance equally among all children or all sons;
(ii) inheritance by a single heir who might be chosen amongst themselves, by the father in his lifetime or in consultation with the lord, or by the acceptance of the rule of primogeniture.

The first system was no doubt the primitive one since it is the obvious arrangement for a purely agricultural tribe where all work the land and all fight for their chieftain. Where land is limited for working, or a fixed hierarchy is needed for fighting, or a single office for government, the single heir, and especially the eldest heir, is favoured. Everybody, the tenant, the lord, or the king, may suffer, although they suffer in different ways, by division of a farm, a fief or a kingdom.

The consequences of these rules of inheritance have governed the evolution of landed aristocracies and of peasantries based as they are on agriculture. They have also influenced marriage customs and modes of population control, as we have seen, even in the mercantile society of Venice. The elder son or chieftain from having been merely the agent of a community—with obligations and rights—became the owner of an estate.

In the feudal society, as time went on a sharp divergence grew up between two extreme types of tenure. On the one hand, the menial or servile status of those who had to work the land for their living, the villeins or serfs, was described as unfree. Rightly so, because they were fixed on the land they worked. Their rights of work, movement and marriage were controlled by their lords, in the lords' courts. On the other hand those who had to serve their lord, or their king, by fighting were protected by the king in the royal courts. They were described as free and their holdings were fiefs. They needed less protection: they endured less subjection.

This divergence, which was not by any means new in history, was the basis of the oppression of the ploughing man by the fighting man in all succeeding centuries. And most of all where the peasant population was expanding without outlets by emigration, by war, or by movement into the cities. It was also the basis of a divergence in social and genetic structure. The free orders of society could move and marry over a wide territory. The unfree were compelled to marry within narrow manorial communities. Their inbreeding gave a diversification of character between localities and a uniformity within localities, a transformation reflected in the stability and homogeneity of each community, and also in the evolution of European societies and dialects.

The evolution of the peasant populations was influenced, like that of slave populations in antiquity, by the opportunities of escape. In the course of the whole 5000-year period of the agricultural colonization of Western Europe there has been a slow increase in the area brought under the plough and a slow decrease in waste and woodland. This meant a decrease in the freedom of movement and choice of activity of the working people. This continual decrease for long restricted the liberty of the peasant community and for long bound the serf more and more closely to the soil. It was a bondage to which the growth of the cities and of industry and the opening of new continents only in recent times effectively alleviated.

VI. THE ROYAL CASTE

Feudal society rules were created by the strong Carolingian kings. Their weakness became clear when the crown fell into feeble hands which it did on the death of Charlemagne. Under Louis the Pious, or Good-natured, and his sons among whom the Empire was divided, the vassals discovered that they could take charge of their own estates or territories and each fragment was a viable entity. They went on to discover that they could transmit these estates to one or more of their own sons. On the continent the custom was for the king to be able to create knights whose descendants in the male line would all inherit knightability or nobility. Hence derived a strict caste division cutting across society. In England this custom fell into disuse. The caste division across society came into being but it cut across society at a lower level. It separated a large servile class from the whole of free society. The free society was itself divided with infinite gradations by the action of primogeniture which in turn favoured a genetic diffusion between the urban society, still poor but slowly getting richer, and the landed aristocracy.

The struggle between rulers was never again the entirely free fight, *bellum omnium in omnes*, that it had been in former times. Another Empire was reconstituted under a new line of rulers by Otto the Great who justified his authority by his own achievements. Similarly in France the Capet family were able to set up a new dynasty which ran in parallel with the Carolingians for a century (888–987) and then superseded them.

In France, Germany and Poland, monarchy following the Capets became nominally elective, but always the choice was limited to one or two dynasties. Thus the feudal society allowed a competition, a struggle in which a capacity to govern succeeded in winning the power to govern. A number of ruling families established themselves governing Castile and Leon, France, Burgundy, and Hungary, who intermarried with one another and with their most powerful vassals, partly to strengthen themselves internally, partly to enlarge their territories by dowries. At the end of the tenth century this network of dynastic intermarriage spread to the outskirts of Christendom, accompanying the spread of conversion, of ceremonial, of coronation and of civilization in general. England and Scotland, Denmark, Sweden and Norway, Poland and Novgorod, came into this community of ancestry and of kinship. Unlike the Muslims, as Bloch points out, those who entered the circle were protected

Pedigree 15 The Origins of the European Royal Caste

A part of the marriage network of the European royal families of the ninth and tenth centuries to illustrate the following characteristics:

i. transfer of territories as dowries (Greek south of Italy transferred with Theophano to the Western Empire);
ii. elective principle in the Western Empire within one family connection;
iii. parallel dynasties, Carolingian and Capetian in France;
iv. placing of younger sons or bastards by the kings in bishoprics and by the Emperor in the papacy;
v. failure of some marriages and of whole lines by sterility;
vi. broadening of the genetic basis of the connection by the marrying of newly selected (barbarian and pagan) families into the first established but decaying great families.

Dates given are of birth, accession, deposition and death.
Derived chiefly from Isenburg's tables (1953) which are arranged by patrilinear houses; *also Tout 1898, George 1904, Runciman 1958, et al.*

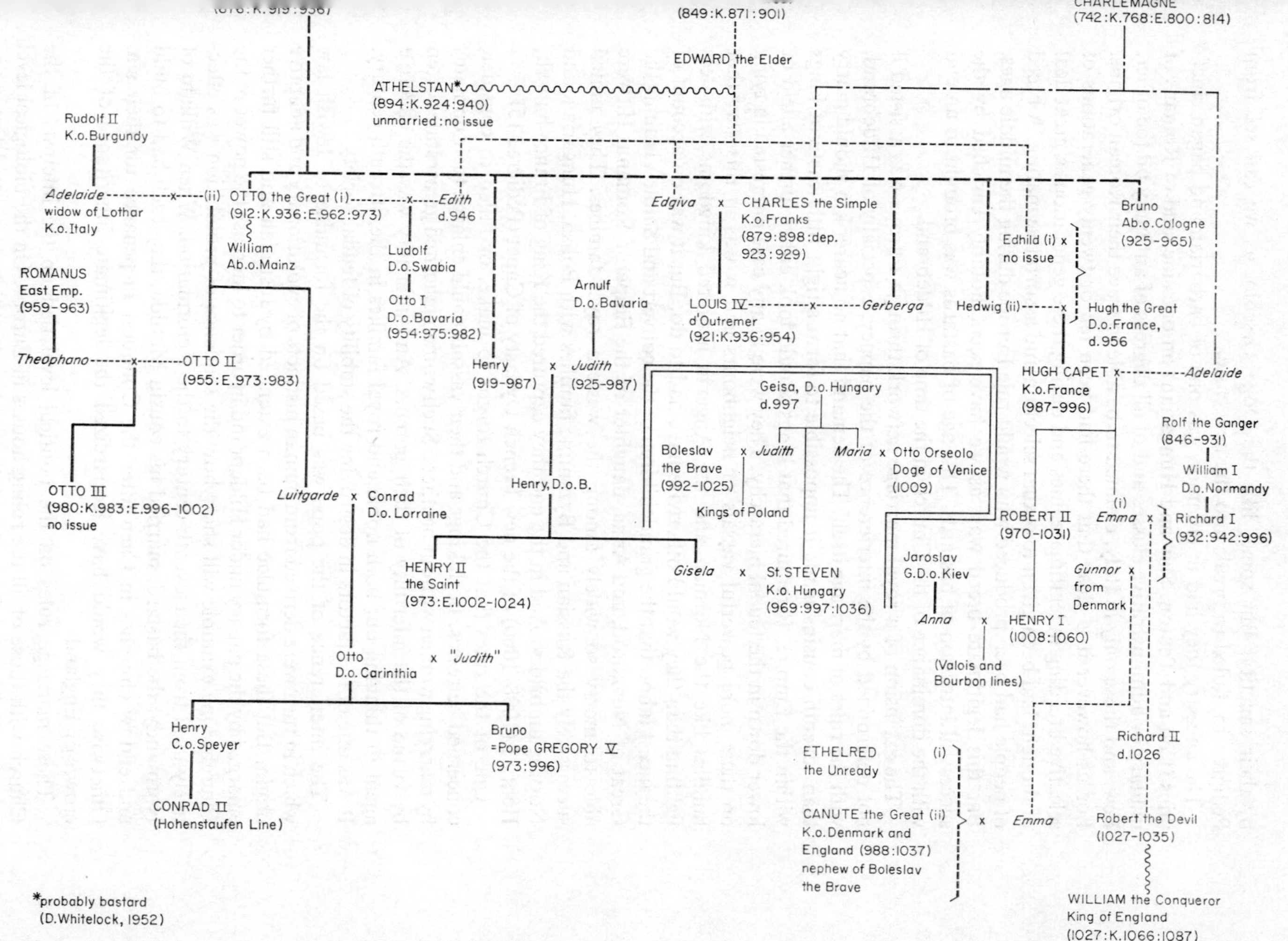

CHARLEMAGNE
(742:K.768:E.800:814)
(849:K.871:901)
EDWARD the Elder
ATHELSTAN*
(894:K.924:940)
unmarried: no issue
Rudolf II
K.o.Burgundy
Adelaide
widow of Lothar
K.o.Italy
OTTO the Great (i)
(912:K.936:E.962:973)
(ii)
Edith
d.946
William
Ab.o.Mainz
Ludolf
D.o.Swabia
Otto I
D.o.Bavaria
(954:975:982)
ROMANUS
East Emp.
(959-963)
Theophano
OTTO II
(955:E.973:983)
OTTO III
(980:K.983:E.996-1002)
no issue
Luitgarde
Conrad
D.o.Lorraine
Henry
(919-987)
Judith
(925-987)
Arnulf
D.o.Bavaria
Henry, D.o.B.
HENRY II
the Saint
(973:E.1002-1024)
Gisela
St. STEVEN
K.o.Hungary
(969:997:1036)
Edgiva
CHARLES the Simple
K.o.Franks
(879:898:dep.
923:929)
LOUIS IV
d'Outremer
(921:K.936:954)
Gerberga
Hedwig (ii)
Edhild (i)
no issue
Bruno
Ab.o.Cologne
(925-965)
Hugh the Great
D.o.France,
d.956
HUGH CAPET
K.o.France
(987-996)
Adelaide
Geisa, D.o.Hungary
d.997
Boleslav
the Brave
(992-1025)
Judith
Maria
Otto Orseolo
Doge of Venice
(1009)
Kings of Poland
ROBERT II
(970-1031)
Jaroslav
G.D.o.Kiev
Anna
HENRY I
(1008:1060)
(Valois and
Bourbon lines)
Rolf the Ganger
(846-931)
William I
D.o.Normandy
Richard I
(932:942:996)
(i)
Emma
Gunnor
from
Denmark
Otto
D.o.Carinthia
"Judith"
Henry
C.o.Speyer
CONRAD II
(Hohenstaufen Line)
Bruno
=Pope GREGORY V
(973:996)
ETHELRED
the Unready
(i)
CANUTE the Great (ii)
K.o.Denmark and
England (988:1037)
nephew of Boleslav
the Brave
Emma
Richard II
d.1026
Robert the Devil
(1027-1035)
WILLIAM the Conqueror
King of England
(1027:K.1066:1087)
*probably bastard
(D.Whitelock, 1952)

by their sanctity. But some, like the Doge Orseolo, as we can see from Pedigree 15, failed to break into the new caste.

The ancestry they had in common was one of barbarian and pagan chieftains (Celt and Teuton, Slav and Hungarian) on one side, and of Romans of military or administrative classes and of all degrees of antiquity on the other. Few, and those only in Italy, claimed to be able to trace their Roman origins. For us however it is clear that there had been ten or twenty generations of selective breeding in legitimate lines and during these generations a great deal of thought had been given to sexual selection and assortative mating. A breed of people had been produced who would rule Europe during the middle ages. But this legitimate breed was, as we have seen, notably enriched by the successful intrusion of bastards. This age of bastards was brought to an end with the dominance of the Church in the time of Hildebrand.

The extension of a royal marriage network through Europe was assisted if not determined by the interference of the papacy, especially of Hildebrand, with the rules of marriage itself. The demand that no nearer kin should marry than seventh cousins made it impossible to form a tight little caste of kings within the Empire. It required that kings should look either further afield or lower down in the feudal hierarchy. They were in any case interested in tying up their more powerful vassals or neighbours and it was in this way that families like the Norman and the Angevin acquired kingdoms with less fighting than they would otherwise have had to do. But it was on account of the incest taboo that the grandchildren of the convert and Saint, Vladimir the Great of Novgorod, and Anna, daughter of the Emperor Romanus II, were able to marry so widely among the western royal families. They united successively the Russian and Byzantine families with Polish, Hungarian, and Norwegian brides. And in the end they captured the King of France himself, Henry I (1008–1060) of the new French Dynasty of Capet (Pedigree 15).

One of the rules that the Church forgot to make, or failed to consider, concerned heiresses. Both kings and their vassals could enlarge their domains by marrying women without brothers. Such women inherited great estates often by virtue of the infertility of their parents. And infertility was the effective agent in thinning out both noble and royal families in the fifteenth century. It was one of the factors in destroying the stability of feudal society.

The interference of the pope was based on the formulae of Jewish law which in turn were derived from human instincts of evolutionary and adaptive origin. But these formulae had been extended by Justinian and still further enlarged by the papacy under Hildebrand in order to increase the power of the Church. One example will show how the sequence of prohibition was effectively used from the eleventh century to the Reformation. When William of Normandy, the bastard, married his cousin Matilda, they each had to build and endow churches in Caen after the Conquest in penance for their sin. Otherwise they would have jeopardized the legitimate inheritance of the crown of England.

These marriage rules on the political level tied up the interests of the Church with those of all the ruling houses in Europe. On the biological level they determined the character of the royal caste which dominated Europe in the middle ages. How important they were in this respect will be seen when we consider what happened after they broke down under the stress of the Reformation in the sixteenth century.

VII. THE GROWTH OF CITIES

a. Town versus Country

Civilization is the mode of activity created by cities and it is through the cities of the Roman Empire that its civilization was preserved and passed on to the present day. These cities were impoverished and depleted in population by the breakdown in communications and government of the fifth century and the consequent loss of the trade on which they depended. But their life continued at a slower pace. Barbarian kings and barons saw the value of merchandise and of the taxes that could be levied on it. And bishops, who took the place of governors, saw the value of kings and barons who could be converted to Christianity and used to establish authority over their extensive dioceses.

So, after three centuries, with the coming of Charlemagne, it could be seen that cities had survived their painful diminution. They were once more the means by which the artisans, the merchants and the clergy could settle down and also move about from one country to another as they had in Roman times.

Now however their position in the organization of the State was radically changed. The new rulers were not city bred. They were illiterate warriors. Their origin was outside the ancient Roman city structure and their government was designed to be independent of it; and even independent of the money and the written words which were the vehicles of city life. There had always been a gulf between town and country but Roman government had partly bridged that gulf. Now the bridge had been broken.

We have already seen the polarity between State and Church in the west as a whole. This polarity was also a polarity between north and south, since it was represented by the contrast in the importance of cities in the north and the south (Fig. 15). In Italy, and also in Provence, until the Albigensian Crusade destroyed them, the cities were soon able to dominate the country. Some, like Venice, Pisa and Amalfi, were still being fed by immigration from the east. The barons of Gothic or Lombard extraction even came to live in such towns; they had obviously intermarried with Roman senators' families. By hybridization they were urbanized. But the northern barons remained aloof, marrying within their own caste, incurably rustic, and with a vocation for war for which the Crusades were later to provide an opening. The reason was that the northern towns were small and poor and the barons despised them and their inhabitants. They despised their laws, their trade, their money and their menial and peaceful activities which were all utterly opposed to their own way of life.

In this attitude the northern barons stood apart, not only from the townspeople and the Church, but also from the developing royal caste with its embryonic administrative class who were continually pushing their way into it. These people were sufficiently romanized, sometimes through bastard offspring, to be more educated and more educable than their own baronage in a legal and literary, an artistic and perhaps even a technical sense (Pedigree 16).

The northern towns however grew stronger. Those of Roman origin grew under the protection of their bishops and around a cathedral. Others, like Ghent as described by Pirenne, or Oxford also of the eleventh century, grew under the protection (or subjugation, for the two are never separated) of a baronial citadel. Such cities may still be recognized, like Dublin with its Castle of the twelfth century, Moscow with its Kremlin of the fifteenth century. In these cases the military and mercantile communities lived in two adjoining communities, each with its own Church.

b. Isolation versus Assimilation

The processes of fusion or accretion by which cities have developed can be followed in Europe in long evolutionary sequences. In the Roman city of Exeter there had been a Celtic population. In Saxon Exeter they kept their own quarter whose planning, as a kind of slum or shanty town with narrow winding streets, Hoskins could still recognize in the twentieth century, notwithstanding the fact that the Celts had been expelled as troublesome by Athelstan a thousand years ago. The Celts in their frontier city had failed to be assimilated by the Saxons: they were too equal for slavery, too different for marriage.

A different situation occurred after the Norman Conquest. French merchants and artisans followed the new rulers, if indeed they did not on a small scale precede them, and set up their own communities outside Nottingham, Stamford and other Saxon towns. The communities eventually lost their separate character because the Normans accepted the language of the English majority and were merged with, that is to say hybridized with, the natives. How influential they proved to be even in London is however shown by the fact that it was their name of *mayor* which superseded the Saxon title for the head of a city government.

All such colonizations have the same genetically selective and culturally enriching effect. But the urban colonization often differs from rural colonization in its speedier effect. This is due to the fact that rural colonies are in separate villages and hybridization between adjoining villages of different race is of extremely low frequency, as low as it was perhaps in Exeter. For this reason rural colonies retain their separate character for centuries and even for millennia. Examples are Albanian colonies in Calabria and Sicily, a Lombard colony (of bargemen) on the Arno, German colonies planted by Charles V in Spain (described by George Borrow in *The Bible in Spain*), Moravian colonies planted by the English in Ireland. There are also the floating Vlach populations of the Balkans and the gipsies to whom we shall return.

There are movements of an urban character which are similar in cause to those concerned with rural industries and activities. Miners in Britain were at first no doubt all derived by descent from flint-miners in the chalk country and from tin-miners in Cornwall. Migration probably carried them in Roman times to the Forest of Dean, Derbyshire and elsewhere. And in modern times they have sunk their shafts in all continents. But Elizabeth's ministers introduced copper-miners into the Lake District. They probably came from Bohemia or Moravia and their German names still persist today.

One trade which has a particularly definable evolution is that of dyke-building, draining and water-engineering. It must have begun in Egypt and Babylonia and developed in northern Italy. But in mediaeval Europe its great exploitation and extension came in the Netherlands. There the dyke-men took on Dutch speech and a Dutch character. Over many generations they made Holland—and Holland made them so that it was as Dutchmen that they spread over Europe and over the world.[1]

Mining and draining illustrate the principle that it is only by inbreeding that crafts are maintained. For it is only where a craft prospers and a colony can be formed that inbreeding can preserve it. When the colony decays, outbreeding begins and the caste with its craft is modified or superseded.

The contrast between static and dynamic colonization is sometimes almost experimentally precise. The Flemish peasants and townsmen, planted as a block by Henry I in Pembroke, combined with earlier Viking settlers and are still recognizable by the racial character and blood groups of the people in 'Little England beyond Wales'.[2] But the Flemish weavers introduced by Edward II and Elizabeth merged in the English city population of weavers within a few generations. The difference is one of degree, probably between a rate of hybridization of less than one in a thousand in the country and more than one in a hundred in towns. Such a difference means that the rural colony by persisting fails to enrich the rural society which remains conservative and stable; the urban colony on the other hand, as it disappears by outbreeding, gradually releases new variation and keeps the society adaptable and, as we say, progressive.

A new stage was reached when new merchants, migrating beyond royal or feudal authorities, could build their own cities and make their own laws and defend them without the help of kings or barons. These cities on the frontiers of Christendom, like Hamburg and the Hansa towns, followed the Italian example. They were able to express their hatred of the baronial class and the feudal society. No knighthoods, no royal salutes for them. They elected their own magistrates. They founded their guilds which developed their own hierarchy and, after an era of mobility and promotion, they acquired an hereditary class structure. They depended, to be sure, on charters from kings. But they were charters which a powerful city was able to negotiate on equal terms.

The city thus became a political element, one of the orders of mediaeval society. London acknowledged the Conqueror and the Conqueror acknowledged London. But afterwards the capital had to consider its interests in face not only of the king, but also of the barons and, after the Black Death, of the serfs. From these groups it was always both racially distinct and politically at variance. When conflict broke out between the other orders of society, strong cities took the weaker side. London backed the English barons

[1] van Veen (1962). [2] Morgan Watkin (1965).

against King John, while Paris backed his weaker opposite number, Philip Augustus, against the French barons.[1]

The power of the cities slowly made itself felt in the administration of the law. The rational townsman detested the superstitions of the barbarian and the warrior; he rejected the trial by ordeal and the duel. He quickly overcame the one, and eventually, even for nobles, superseded the other, with theicivilized and Roman use of the evidence of witnesses. What was less fortunate was that, threatened by a mixed, mobile and overcrowded population, he abandoned the tribal custom of paying fines as punishment for crimes. He replaced them with brutal punishments, mutilations, castrations, disembowellings and hangings, practices which civilization had brought from the Ancient East and to which the Church in 1163, as we shall see, added the new feature of burning. The public execution of these sentences provided until recently the chief civic entertainment in Europe.[2]

c. Mobility of Populations

The development of the city was made possible by the freedom with which urban artisans could move from one town to another. In their dealings with Muslim states or with Byzantium, special arrangements had to be negotiated but throughout western Christendom there were opportunities for seeking new employment. Selective migration, each man looking for the place where he could best be employed, therefore governed the development of cities. And this migration was inevitably from the big cities of the south to the small cities of the north.

At the same time cities opened their gates to recruit their numbers from a variety of small unprotected communities. The merchants of Ghent invited the country weavers to come into the city where the wool imported from England could be conveniently supplied to them and the cloth conveniently collected for export.

So the city with its hospitality systematically trapped the solitary worker and induced him to settle. It also casually trapped the stray refugee from feudal society. The serf who lived in a city for over a year could often claim his freedom. *Die Stadtluft macht frei* is the proverb quoted by Pirenne. But the cities by unlocking feudal society changed themselves as well as the society. They integrated their immigrant founders with the local population and acquired a regionally racial, or as we can soon say, national character. They also extended their breeding communities by incorporating elements of the rural population, always the more enterprising elements.

This movement was, like all changes of habitation, selective; it therefore set going a brain drain on the countryside exaggerating the contrast between the alert and progressive citizen and the bucolic conservative peasant. Protected from this loss, rustic populations, like those of mountainous Wales and

[1] Pirenne (1925).

[2] My grandfather as a boy saw the last public hanging of a woman in England (at Chester Castle, 1851). The justification of this practice ostensibly was that it protected prisoners from the danger of being privately put away.

Scotland in contrast to England, still provide a reservoir of what may properly be called native intelligence.

In this development what is important is the preservation of separate racially distinct groups so that they can by very slow hybridization convert themselves into socially distinct groups, competing and co-operating throughout the long period of hybridization and conversion. Open conflict at one extreme, and rapid hybridization at the other extreme, would have destroyed both the races and the cultures that came into contact. In different parts of Britain, in England, Scotland and Ireland, as in other developing countries, all these types of development and adjustment may still be seen and their results compared.

In this selective migration the capital had a special position. Mediaeval kings appeared to follow their business around: but they were really following their food. Charlemagne and William the Conqueror, being usually at war, were seldom at home. King John, as we know, took his crown about with him. But gradually they allowed their administration and their treasure to accumulate in the capital. In London the mixed character of the capital still stands out on the map with the Tower at one end, the Palace at the other and the city, the law, the nobles (now displaced), the administration and the government neatly placed along the river between them.

London's position as a sea-port particularly favoured its international development. A continual flow of immigrants led to the formation of quarters for each national, political, social or commercial group. The resulting stratification is of immense continuity documented by both street names and historical records.[1] Nevertheless there was always pressure on the alien to disguise his origins, to change his name and his speech, and to assimilate with the native population. Of these effects we shall see more evidence later.

To this capital came men seeking their fortunes not just from the surrounding countryside but from the whole nation. The legend of the arrival of Dick Whittington who was to become Mayor of London under Henry IV is in this respect correct. Wealth and power attracted enterprise and ability. Thus the same distinction developed for Paris or London between the metropolis and the provinces as had existed for Babylon and Athens, Alexandria and Rome, a distinction at once genetic and intellectual.

The same distinction between capital and provinces arose later in Scotland and Ireland. But when their capitals ceased to be seats of government and centres of promotion they ceased to attract. Indeed they in turn began to lose by emigration to London. The same succession of movements is seen in the growth of Vienna under the increasing Empire of the Hapsburgs and later of Berlin under the Hohenzollerns: these cities began to represent the whole racial variation of the Empire from which they came to be derived.

This growth and spread of European cities is bound to be compared with other processes of development. Europe was, as Pirenne puts it, colonizing herself. In doing this she was continuing the processes by which megalithic colonists invaded the Atlantic seaboards founding their religious cults and later Greeks and Phoenicians migrating in more complex groups founded

[1] Rasmussen (1934); Ekwall (1954); Mitchell and Leys (1958).

their Mediterranean cities. But the processes of colonization were now even more complex.

They made up indeed a large part of mediaeval life. The movements were organized by kings, by cities and by guilds. They were both military and mercantile, industrial and rural. They included the vagrant and the vagabond at one end of the social scale and the lords and ladies accompanying a royal bride at the other. They have included the refugees from floods in Flanders, from the invasions of Muslims and from the persecution of Christians. They have continued with little interruption for over a thousand years.

d. Evolving Social Classes

The history of European cities is inseparable from the history of immigration into them. Its effect was inevitably to produce heterogeneity. But it has not been a mounting heterogeneity. London, to the Venerable Bede in the eighth century (730), was a city of many nations. So it still is. But throughout those twelve centuries the proportion of foreign-born citizens has rarely been as great as one-tenth. Moreover all immigrant groups have associated with and married into their own national groups. These groups have shed their foreign languages but they have kept together as professional classes, and also as religious communities or sects.[1] Hybridization therefore has been limited by an assortative mating which has been broken down only by changes in the kinds of occupation arising from changes in the means of production, education and government and by the abandonment, especially in time of war, of foreign speech and foreign names.

The most obvious changes in occupation in European societies during the last thousand years have been due to that separation of making from selling which has been discussed by Tawney. In the ancient city (as still in the modern Islamic bazaar) the artisan sold his own work and each trade lived, worked and bred in one quarter or one street to which it gave its name, the name it still often keeps. But as the mediaeval city grew, the families more skilled and more specialized in their skills in each profession separated. The miller parted from the baker and became richer than the baker. Ultimately the professional barrier between working groups and hence between breeding groups was replaced by an economic sub-division between social classes, between the different grades of skill and reward in each profession. The urban society was still stratified and even more finely stratified, but the strata and their boundaries had changed.

Summing up, we see that European life everywhere, in town and country, in capitals and provinces, developed under tension between social groups or classes differing in racial origin, professional occupation, dwelling place, habits of life and political interests. There was an opposition and also a balance between king, barons and peasants, between peasants and artisans and also between Church and State. But this opposition was also always a balance, for each depended on all the others. And this balance in turn was always changing through changes in modes of production, changes which

[1] E.g. in Norwich where such groups had their own saints and their own churches before the Reformation (Green and Young, 1964).

themselves largely arose through migration, selective migration of individuals, families and whole communities, and the slow, limited hybridization that was always to follow between the differing communities of towns.

The whole system was held together, as it still is, with remarkably little force. Henry VIII, tyrant as he was, and the hammer of a revolution, as Rasmussen points out, had a bodyguard smaller than a single one of the City of London's trained bands. Society held together because in the towns, as in the country, the same genetic groups with the same breeding and kinship relations continued as in the tribal life of neolithic and even of paleolithic times. The same instincts were operating, the same needs were being satisfied for the bulk of the population, that is for the less privileged and less articulate majority. These instincts were and still are operating above all to preserve the coherence of the small groups which, although now crowded together, have become, through selective migration, genetically even more distinct than when they were scattered in separated territories.

It was in this slowly moving system that a few people with a few new ideas and a few inventions in the fifteenth century suddenly destroyed the equilibrium of ages and released the storms in whose heat the class structure of the mediaeval world softened and partly melted, storms that we know as the Renaissance and the Reformation.

19

THE NORTHERN INTRUDERS

I. THE VIKINGS

THE CHRISTIAN POPULATIONS of Northern Europe became aware in the course of the eighth century of a terrible enemy, the heathen Vikings, who fell upon their coasts, burning their settlements and carrying off their people as slaves. The raiders sprang from an unknown and illiterate world but it was a world with a long history of its own.

Scandinavia was peopled by several kinds of paleolithic or sub-neolithic tribes. Apart from hunters and collectors there were reindeer-herding Lapps and Finnish fishermen, both from Central Asia. Among these the early neolithic cultivators had settled. Later the Goths from across the Baltic had given the country its predominant language; and megalithic explorers passing over or around Britain had brought their own religion and their monuments.

During the first millennium B.C. a new race, the Royal Scyths of Asgard, near Stalingrad, had made a connection between the Ancient East and the south of Sweden. These far-ranging people with an heroic cult of Odin were kinsmen of those whose encounter with Darius is described by Herodotus and whose carpeted tombs have been found at Pazyryk in the Altai. They had established horse caravans which, in exchange for amber, honey and furs, brought to the north the iron worked by the Chalybes of the Lake Van region of Anatolia.

This possibly quiet and certainly remote backwater of human life was abruptly disturbed by the Roman defeat of Mithridates in 64 B.C. The Scyths and the Chalybes, both deprived of their iron, seem to have joined together and moved along their familiar route to the Baltic lands. It was a movement of Odinic and Vanic peoples at first foes and later friends whose fusion, according to de Tourville and Périer, is celebrated in the *Yglynga Saga*. It was a movement covering some centuries and favoured by an improvement of the northern climate which was to reach its peak at the end of the millennium.

These migrants reaching Sweden subdued and partly fused with the Goths who themselves moved on to occupy southern Norway. The populations arising thus ranged between two contrasted types. To the west were the Gothic peasants, enterprising, independent and diverse people, living in timber houses on sheltered fiords in small matriarchal family groups. To the east on the open coast and building stone houses were patriarchal communities in which Scythian chieftains with their cult of Odin ruled over pre-Aryan tenants and thralls.

With this mixture of races and societies of Scythian pastoralists, Scandinavian sea-farers and Gothic farmers there were the conditions for hybrid enterprise and rapid evolution. During the first eight centuries of the Christian era, the Scandinavians in fact began to receive immigrants who set them further on the road to their great expansion. Firstly Roman iron and iron workers came in, chiefly through the Marcommani of Bohemia. Secondly Roman shipbuilders and seamen arrived through Gaul and the Rhine ports. Thirdly with iron axes the forests were felled and agriculture moved further into the interior of both Sweden and Norway. Finally trade developed with the Eastern Empire. Fighting men went to serve in the Byzantine forces.[1]

Returning, they brought with them not only treasures of gold and silver but also craftsmen, free or enslaved, who made tools, weapons and jewellery which would be of use to them in peace and war.[2]

It was this direct recruitment which enabled the Vikings to plan their camps in Denmark with Roman precision, using the Roman foot measure. Much more complicated no doubt was the improvement of shipbuilding. The ships of the more southerly Angles and Saxons had depended on oars alone for their various invasions, as shown by the Sutton Hoo ship of about A.D. 650. But during the seventh century the Scandinavians took the oar-propelled ships of their southern neighbours and mastered the problem of designing a boat that would sail the open seas, not in all seasons, but at least through a long summer. They learnt how to construct clinker-built ships of up to 50 tons, keeled, masted and with square sails.[3]

During the following century the Viking leaders, the chieftains of coastal settlements, discovered something else: they saw that they now had the command not only of rivers and coastal waters and the narrow seas but of a large part of the unknown ocean itself. Their new ships gave them the opening for trade, for exploration and finally for colonization. From trade also they proceeded to piracy, the capture of men and women, and the trade in slaves. The ship had given them the same mobility (as Lundman points out) that the horse had given to the contemporary Bedouin. Without much doctrinal guidance therefore the Vikings were soon able to follow the same path on the watery fringe of the Roman Empire which the Muslim Arabs were pursuing on the opposite desert fringe at the expense of the settled Christian people in between them. It was the path of enslavement, polygamy and hybridization.

[1] Pirenne notes that the first Arab coin in Scandinavia is dated 696: it could not be much earlier.

[2] See Schoenbeck (1966).

[3] See Brønsted (1960); Bibby (1957); Hornell (1946) and on Sutton Hoo (as well as Pazyryk) Woolley (1958).

We may stop at this point to ask what exactly we mean by the name Viking. The answer is that we mean certain people selected for their success as seafarers under hereditary leaders or chieftains. They were people who sailed out from the creeks, harbours or *viks* of the Scandinavian coasts; and they sailed during a limited period from the eighth to the eleventh centuries. They were mixed in origins but they all spoke Scandinavian dialects. The men who were led were partly the Scandinavian coastal peasantry but they included also men of other nations who had thrown in their lot with the Vikings. Their unity therefore consisted in their way of life and that way of life was the way of the ships. Over those twelve generations they had made their ships, and their ships had made them. That is in the sense that their survival, always selective, depended on their ability to handle their ships with success. Along with their older gods, and especially Odin the god of war, they therefore worshipped their ships and they buried their kings and queens in them.

If we ask why the great expansion of the Vikings happened in those four centuries the answer probably lies in a second condition added to their own invention of ships and seamanship: it was a peak of climatic improvement.[1] It was a peak which favoured their own propagation and opened the northern world to their settlement as it had done to the neolithic people two millennia earlier. The orderly character of the expansion, for there seems to have been less war among the Scandinavian peoples before they emigrated than afterwards, may have been due (as Lundman suggests) to the development of a rule of primogeniture among them. It was certainly this rule which influenced all their later social organization.

In the course of the four centuries during which they swept the seas the Vikings greatly changed their character. They hybridized with many peoples and founded several nations. We may now see how this came about.

II. THEIR EXPANSION

a. Colonists in Ireland

It was a rapid evolution and the mode of it varied in the four great fields of their maritime expansion. The first of these fields was the Western Isles. Beginning about the year 700 with the empty Feroes and nearly empty Shetlands and Hebrides, the Norse Vikings moved on at the end of the century to the inhabited coasts of Ireland and western Scotland. To all these places they took peasant colonists. But in Ireland they went further. By building

[1] Revealed by changes in vegetation inferred from pollen analysis: see Godwin (1960) and Turner (1965).

Fig. 16. The Viking Expansion A.D. 800–1100

Stippled. Primary Viking Homelands with Three Capitals: Trondheim (Norway); Uppsala (Sweden); Roskilde (Denmark).
Striped. Secondary Colonies: Novgorod; Berezany; Dublin; Reykjavik.
Dotted. Tertiary Kingdoms of England, Sicily, Kiev.

Europe after Dunan (1693), Oxenstierna (1967), America after Debenham (1960) and others, Russia after Hoetsch (1966)

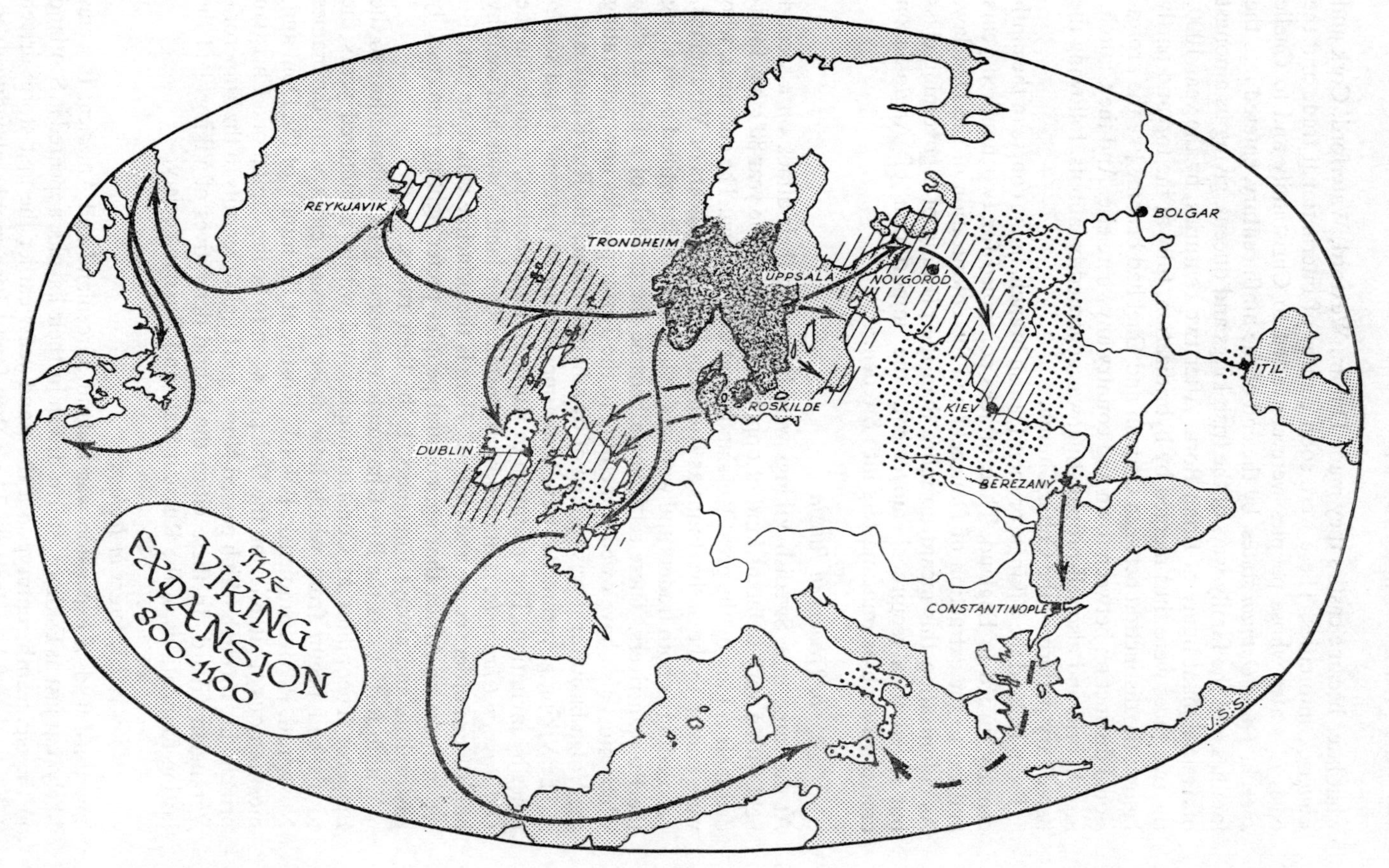
The VIKING EXPANSION 800-1100
REYKJAVIK
TRONDHEIM
UPPSALA
NOVGOROD
BOLGAR
ITIL
ROSKILDE
KIEV
DUBLIN
BEREZANY
CONSTANTINOPLE
J.S.S.

what later became castles they made Dublin, Wexford, Waterford, Cork and Limerick into cities. These were soon centres of international trade and the basis of states whose peoples were converted to Christianity and to Gaelic speech. These *Ostman* states, by the end of the ninth century, entered into the families and the family wars of the Irish kings and queens, giving us amongst others the giant figure of Brian Boru. After two centuries, by the year 1000, the two races were thus merged by hybridization, fully at the top and partly below: the distinction between Ostman and Gael had become like the professional distinction between town and country anywhere else. And the Church, also hybrid and also self-propagating, was governed by abbots, following the hereditary pattern of the Celtic Church.

From Ireland the Vikings, or their Danish branch, in the course of the ninth century turned to England. Their attacks continued for two hundred years and led to the extraction of Danegeld and the colonization of the Danelaw. As colonization this meant no more than the planting of a governing class but it led to a reciprocal movement, the importation of Anglo-Saxon craftsmen such as mint masters into Sweden.

b. Traders in Russia

At the same time Swedish Vikings were beginning their attack on a second field with a very different kind of opportunity. About the year 800 they founded their colony by the great Russian lake at Old Ladoga. The colonists, who were known to the native Finns as Ruotsi or Rus, Varaegears or Varangians, proceeding as both traders and warriors, established their fortified posts along the Russian rivers. These settlements became the citadels of a federal state which must also have owed something to the Tartar peoples now penetrating the Volga basin for it was spoken of by a hybrid name, the Rus Khaganate.

The Viking governments were sometimes set up by agreement and sometimes by invitation. The invitation to Rurik and his brothers, recorded in the *Old Russian Chronicle*, is quoted by Brønsted: 'Our land is wide and wealthy but it lacks order: come and rule us.' Here is the principle which we can also see in India or Africa that agricultural peoples prefer fighting men, usually pastoralists and always foreigners, to be their rulers.

Within forty years the Rus Khaganate was sending its ambassadors to the Emperor Theophilus at Constantinople. And within a hundred years the towns had begun from which later arose Russian cities with the names Novgorod, Pskov, Smolensk, Polotsk, Rostov at the mouth of the Don, and, most famous of all, Kiev on the Dnieper, soon to be the capital of a Christian principality through which passed Norse and English recruits to the Emperor's Varangian Guard. In these cities the hybrid derivatives of Vikings laid the lasting foundations of the Russian State and Russian society.

c. Explorers in Iceland

The third field of expansion was Iceland, Greenland and America. It seems likely that just as Eskimos, storm-driven in their kayaks, appeared in Scotland in the eighteenth century, so a thousand years earlier the first storm-driven Vikings chanced on Iceland. There they found Irish monks already settled.

These were presumably a breeding colony but later they returned home. A few years later, in 872, there arose a great Norse chieftain, Harold Haarfagre,[1] who reduced the small chieftains to submission. The defeated or outlawed party went into exile. During the next fifty years they organized expeditions which colonized Iceland and created there a new people and a new society.

The backbone of this society consisted, not of Viking chiefs, but of the 1100 sheep and grain farmers from the fiords who, together with smiths and boat-builders, fishermen and hunters, made a balanced and self-supporting community. Within a hundred years they numbered (according to Gwyn Jones) 40,000 people. With their independent traditions they established their own parliamentary assembly. This *Althing* first met in 930 and continued until, three hundred years later, the King of Norway once more brought them under his hand.

In addition to the Norse farmers there were Irish colonists, both royal and thrall, but apparently not Christian. During the first two centuries of heroic and warlike life the Irish seem to have had little effect on the course of Icelandic history. But in the year 1002 the Norwegian King Olav Triggvason, a Christian convert, sent envoys to Iceland who persuaded the *Althing* to vote on Christianity: they voted for obligatory national conversion. Owing to the unstable balance between free and slave, Norse and Irish, fighting and farming communities, and also to the unique isolation of Iceland, this conversion produced a genuine and immediate effect without parallel in any other country. It reversed the standards of behaviour and the mode of life. The next generation of Icelanders, instead of fighting and burning, turned their talents to telling stories about fighting and burning; and about their great voyages. In consequence we have the records of what happened in the critical century of Iceland's development, records which are more exactly true than any other such records in history. This revolution Iceland owed to the Irish part of the population. The gift for narration is still as clear as ever in Ireland today. And in the Icelanders no less so for they are the most literate and bookish people in the world. But it reached its first great climax in the Icelandic Sagas.

The narrative gift was probably brought to Iceland by pagan bards of the *filid* class who objected to the new literate and Christian régime in Ireland. Well they might, for their ancestry went back to the common roots of Aryan epic poetry at the beginning of the bronze age in Europe. Their poetic narratives were composed over a period of six generations. They still bring back to us the lives of the Icelandic heroes with their commonly Irish names.[2] They demonstrate the character of the Icelandic people, hardly changed over a thousand years in their institutions, their talents, and their language. They make us ask why there should be such an unparalleled conservatism. The answer is that with a deteriorating climate their population has failed to

[1] A great enough chieftain for the names of his seven wives and the total of their twenty sons to be recorded in von Isenburg's *Stammtafeln*.

[2] The most notable of these is the Irish *Niul* which became Icelandic *Njall* (of the Saga) and also Norse *Nils* and *Nilsson*. Whence Norman *Fitzneel*, modern *O'Neill*, English *Nelson*, and bogus Latin *Nigellus* or *Nigel*.

increase and failed to attract foreign immigrants: it has remained small and isolated and increasingly homogeneous.

The historic episode for which we value the Sagas most is their famous account of the discovery of Greenland and America. Another stormy voyage brought Erik the Red with fourteen out of twenty-five ships safely to Greenland. There he founded his colony in 986. And in the year 1000 his son, Leif Eriksson, after a third storm-driven escapade, lighted upon the shores of Cape Cod. A later attempt to colonize the coast as far south as Long Island failed. But trade in timber (according to Gwyn Jones) was maintained, probably with Labrador, until 1347.

By the year 1100 there were 50,000 colonists in Iceland and perhaps another 3000 in Greenland. Thereafter the colder climate made the life harder in both countries and the sea connection, which became more necessary, also became more perilous. At a difficult time in the sixteenth century the Danish government considered evacuating the whole population of Iceland. But by this time, for already a century, the Greenland colony had died out. The last storm-driven visitors from Iceland were recorded in 1408. Thereafter for a century or more, according to Velbaek, the colonists had been deprived not only of grain but also of iron; they had been compelled to make their weapons out of bone and antler. Such a small inbred group could not be expected to adapt itself to such drastically changed conditions. The last wave of Eskimos, almost purely paleolithic hunters and equally without metal weapons, advancing eastwards along the northern shores of Canada, reached Greenland in the fifteenth century and overwhelmed the survivors.

d. Conquerors in Normandy

In the tenth century the Vikings, as we may suppose by the capture of women, had advanced to the last stage of their evolution. In this guise we can follow them over several momentous generations which left them no longer merely Vikings but conquerors. The transformation began when they switched their attack from the poorer and more primitive northern coasts of Europe to the richer lands of a Roman or Romanized province of France.

The Saxons, arriving by sea, had settled in the harbours of northern and western Gaul at the same time that the Franks were occupying the interior. Now, four centuries later, the Vikings moved inland and, after fifty years of invasion, established themselves in Rouen, Bayeux and in other towns and villages. Finally in the year 912 Charles the Simple was compelled, as Alfred the Great had been thirty years earlier in England, to recognize the invaders. He met Rollo the Viking leader, now nearly seventy years of age, at St Clair-sur-Epte, near Paris. He accepted him as his vassal, had the elderly heathen quickly baptized, and gave him his daughter, Gisèle, in marriage.

The treaty was a success. Immigration continued but irregular raiding was repulsed by Rollo himself. Soon the Norsemen in Rouen had taken French wives and were speaking French. They had conquered Normandy but in doing so the Norsemen had become Normans.

III. THE NORMAN DEVELOPMENT

a. In France

The transformation of the Normans, unlike that of the Icelanders, was not the result of their conversion to Christianity. On the contrary, it was in spite of this conversion, for nowhere was baptism allowed to interfere with the polygamy of the invaders, that is of the new governing class. In consequence nowhere, save on the advancing frontiers of Islam, was hereditary fertility more strongly favoured by selection. The offices of Archbishop of Rouen and Bishop of Bayeux were usually the perquisites of the bastard sons of the Duke.

The disregard of Christian restrictions on propagation is well expressed in the definition given by the Normans to their own kind of marriage, *more danico*: on this principle the rights of inheritance were explicitly extended to the progeny of all kinds of intercourse forbidden by the Church.[1]

In these circumstances the influence of the Norman race was bound to increase among the mass of the population: a process of Normanization. On the other hand, among the legitimate inheriting governing class, which began by being largely Norse, a reverse change was taking place: a process of—what shall we call it—Francification, Gallification, Romanization, or merely civilization?

It was indeed all these things. Rollo himself had married as his first wife a daughter of the Count of Bayeux with the Frankish or Romance name of Berengar. She gave him his heir who in turn married a Breton girl. The third in the line (Richard I, see Pedigree 15) married a daughter of Hugh, the first Capet King of France, who gave him his heir. But by a more famous lady, the Duchess Gunnor from Denmark, he produced seven sons and daughters who turned the Norman nobility into a family network and also within a few generations scattered his descendants over France, Flanders and Burgundy as well as all the northern countries.

We may therefore understand what was happening in the tenth century in Normandy if we see it as the place where the southward movement of the barbarians and the northward movement of Romanized people were most actively interpenetrating. It was the place where the Viking leaders, themselves a governing class, were hybridizing on a large scale with the newly established governing class of Capetian France. It was this hybridization which produced the race and the phenomenon we know as the Normans.

The plainest effect of this hybridization was that the Normans, without altogether losing their knowledge of the sea, had acquired an understanding of the horse with harness and stirrups, and hence of the armed horseman, the knight equipped for battle. How had they come to possess this new gift? They had evidently derived it from the Franks. Whether the Franks had it from Gaullish ancestors is less certain but probable. For during four centuries the

[1] I.e. to those born *ex adulterino, incestuoso, et damnato sive illicito coitu.* In consequence, within the diocese of Bayeux where the Normans and their progeny were thickest on the ground, still today there are found the highest proportion in France, 14 per cent, of families bearing surnames derived from the mother's personal name (Lechanteur, 1950).

Gauls had provided auxiliary cavalry for the Roman armies. It was the gift that would win the battle of Hastings for the Norman invaders. It was indeed for long a gift of so great a selective advantage that it would be handed down to the present day through thirty generations of aristocratic propagation.[1]

The Norman mastery of the horse needs to be carefully considered.[2] The horse had been selectively increased in size to seat a rider in early Persian history. He had been fitted with iron shoes in pre-Roman Noricum. He had been given a bare-foot stirrup in India at the same time. And the Gauls had provided him with iron harness fittings at the beginning of their long service with the Roman army. Finally, it seems to have been in the heart of the horse country, in the Altai region, that the full iron stirrup and perhaps also the nailed horseshoe appeared. It was these inventions combined with armour which made possible the feudal knight. And it was the skill with which this new hybrid Norman race fitted themselves and their whole feudal society to the service of this weapon that made the Norman knight in the course of the eleventh century into an invincible instrument of war.

A second effect of this hybridization was to produce in the Norman nobility a notable capacity to govern. It was a capacity united (as Poole points out) with the most disagreeable personal qualities, those indeed which we associate with a rising governing class, calculating and single-minded, aggressive and ruthless.

But they show us by contrast with other men just what it was that gave them this capacity to govern. They came entirely fresh to the business of government. And they were completely dedicated to establishing their own power by exploiting the abilities of others. Without any ideas of their own they were prepared to use all races and classes of men who were willing to serve them without any regard for the prejudices which go with either civilized or religious education.

This revelation of governing capacity was, to be sure, wonderfully assisted by time and place. Their position at the very junction of the southern and the northern worlds was crucial for their success. The Frankish language and the Christian religion brought them straight into the Roman world from which they could at once draw the men of law and learning, the craftsmen, the technicians and the artists they needed for the work of a great advance in government.

b. In Italy

In the tenth century, having established themselves by war, the Normans discovered that they could advance their affairs almost as much by marriage. But in the following century they continued under the leadership of particular individuals the most active prosecution of war. In the first place they became masters of the south of Italy. This extraordinary enterprise began in 1015 with the employment of Norman knights as mercenaries by the Greeks and Lombards who were disputing the control of the States of Apulia and

[1] So long indeed as to lose battles for the most recent of their horse-loving descendants.

[2] See De Laet (1957); Derry and Williams (1960), and Lynn White (1962).

Calabria. Four of the twelve sons of Tancred, a small noble of Hauteville in Normandy, were successively able to turn the tables on their enemies and their employers.

At one point in these struggles, in 1042, the Normans met a Viking chieftain, Harald Hardrada, who, having entered the Varangian Guard, was commanding the Byzantine fleet of the Empress Zoë: so the Norsemen together had circumnavigated Europe.[1]

By the time of his death in 1085 after fifty years of fighting, the ablest amongst these Normans, Robert nicknamed Guiscard, had employed his forces with such success, and so manipulated the disputes of the pope with the eastern and western emperors that, although he failed to become emperor in Constantinople, he was able to leave for his successors the Kingdom of the Two Sicilies. This State began as a fief of the pope under the family now renamed Altavilla. It was to remain in some sort a European power for eight hundred years.

During those centuries Sicily underwent a tragic but also an instructive course of evolution. The Normans found their kingdom peopled by many races and as many religions. In addition to the native Siciliot peasantry in the country, there were in the towns Byzantines whom they called Greeks, Italians whom they called Lombards, Arabs and Moors whom they called Saracens; and of course there were also Jews. These people were already resident in Sicily; but others continued to arrive, and more than one Tunisian emir was willing to serve as a Norman admiral.

While the Normans ruled their feudal state for two centuries all these civilized peoples were equally tolerated, and often generously encouraged. They were able therefore to repeat the achievements of Islamic civilization. The cathedral of Monreale and the medical school of Salerno are to be reckoned as monuments of this enlightened co-operation. At the same time the Normans themselves were often operating as servants or allies in the struggles of the pope, maintaining his power against subversion from within or suppression from without.

The Norman kingdom thus remained a multiracial society. But to do so, like the corresponding Islamic states, it had to become a caste society. Not only did the five races continue to live and breed apart but the Norman governing class also remained a sixth race in isolation. Through the men they employed and the women they married they exchanged ideas with other governing classes of Europe and especially with their own kindred on the other side of Europe, in Normandy. The northern countries were eager to welcome the artists, craftsmen and scholars sent to them from what was for the moment the most civilized country in the western world. And that country was most civilized because, at that time, it was the channel through which men of ability and learning were passing from Islam into Christendom.

That was during the two centuries of Norman rule. It was a golden age which vanished when the caste society of Sicily and the south hardened and other more flexible Christian states drew away to the north the enterprise which the Normans had momentarily sheltered.

[1] Oxenstierna (1967).

Thus at the present day Sicilian and all southern Italian society still bears the stamp of its origins in Muslim segregation and Muslim toleration. The remote Norman kings and barons became the absolute monarchs and the absentee landlords of a later age. And their agents became the most effective criminal caste in the world. An almost accidental conquest long ago had established a society which prospered by the fruitful migration and diffusion which it permitted, but was sterilized when, through changes in the world outside, that migration was brought to an end. Nowhere better than in Sicily can we see the interaction between historical processes inside and outside the country, each determined in its course but quite unrelated before they came into collision.

IV. THE NORMAN CLIMAX

a. The People of Britain

Before we study the assault of the Normans on England, and their penetration of the Celtic lands which followed it, we ought to look at the origins and character of the inhabitants at that time. We ought also to estimate the importance of the continuities and the discontinuities in their history. These discontinuities are particularly easy to establish in islands which are themselves geographically discontinuous. But islands such as the British Isles are also the easiest objects in which to demonstrate continuity. We already have some notion of the evidence. Let us summarize it.

The British Isles are remote from the Nuclear Region where agriculture and civilization began. Their original paleolithic population was cut off from Europe about 6000 B.C. They have been colonized by a series of waves of invaders, immigrants and pioneers over the whole period from 3000 B.C. What kind of country did these people find in Britain? They found a country containing sharper differences and wider ranges of soil and rock, minerals and waterways, climate and vegetation than any other similar area in the world. What each new party or tribe of immigrants did, therefore, was to search out the places to live that suited them best: their genetic variation was thus matched by their ecological choice. Britain was indeed an open field for colonization by the most diverse peoples. But these peoples were in remarkably close proximity to one another: there were no large uniform zones and therefore no large homogeneous populations.

In these circumstances it is not surprising that newcomers arrived in Britain from all the adjoining shores as well as from the Mediterranean. The result was, as we have seen, three types of event. First, the establishment of separate communities with different means of livelihood. Secondly, the occurrence of some hybridization; and thirdly, the subjection of one group by another creating social stratification. What now appears, however, is that the separate communities, ecologically adapted to the extremely diverse habitats available, have permitted in Britain, no less than in the Ancient East, a continuity of highly sub-divided races and cultures. This interpretation, which we owe to Beddoe, and later to Peake and Fleure, is confirmed in several ways.

First, we see the continuity which began with neolithic and bronze age invasions continuing to give us Celtic settlements, Roman temples and Saxon cemeteries on the same site.[1] Secondly, we see the traces in boundaries and place names demonstrating that Celts and Saxons lived peacefully side by side in the country for centuries after the Saxon invasions.[2] And the evidence that the great dykes which divided the country, notably Offa's Dyke, were established by peaceful agreement between neighbours and not for purposes of defensive warfare.[3]

The most decisive and sudden discontinuity in British history has always been thought to be that due to the Saxon invasions. But now we know that the only extensive Celtic emigration from England, the colonization of Brittany, was due to an Irish and not to a Saxon invasion. At the end of the sixth century there is no doubt that the Saxon invaders, hybridized at all levels, had established themselves as a governing class in the eastern parts replacing the disintegrated Romano-British government, with Anglo-Saxon as the dominant speech. Thus, when Augustine arrived in 597, he made the connection for the Roman Church exclusively with English-speaking people. But throughout the west and north Roman towns persisted. A couple of hundred modern towns stand on Roman sites and their half-Roman names betray the continuity of their habitation. Some of these, like Carlisle and Exeter, had even kept to a Church organization. Beyond there was a fully continuous Celtic Church now separated by unsettled regions from Rome and hence from all the European immigration. This break therefore contributed to the decline and deposition of the Celtic Church and with it the Celtic language and Celtic customs in Britain. But it did not mean a decline or deposition of the racial participation of the earlier inhabitants in the new mixed Anglo-Celtic people of England.[4]

In the country important boundaries persisted between the lighter uplands and hill-pastures in Celtic hands and the heavier lowland soils now cleared and ploughed by the Saxons. And in the towns too there persisted, as we have seen, the quarters occupied by Saxons, Celts and foreign traders. England, and the Celtic provinces adjoining it, were thus populated by diverse peoples suited to their diverse and largely rural habitats and governed by ruling classes almost as purely northern, barbarian, and unromanized in their racial origins as the peasantry themselves. They had had no substantial immigration of Mediterranean priests or craftsmen. And of what they had had since Augustine they had even lost a part by migration to the Carolingian Empire during the period of Viking devastation of the last two centuries. Their connection with Europe had been broken. It was this connection, this flow of civilized immigrants, which was restored by those hybridized Vikings, the Norman conquerors.

b. The Conquest of England

William who conquered England and Robert who conquered Sicily lived in the same age; they fought with the same weapons and even with and against the same men. From the contrast between their methods, their policies and

[1] E.g. Bradford and Goodchild (1939) and Myres (1954) on Frilford.
[2] See Glanville Jones (1961). [3] See Sir Cyril Fox (1947).
[4] See especially Jackson and Chadwick in Tolkien (1963).

their achievements we can therefore learn something about them and about the societies they helped to create.

When the Conqueror invaded England he claimed to come as the legitimate heir to the throne and he did his utmost to give his Conquest this appearance. He came to terms with the cities of London and Winchester and even, after some mishandling, with Exeter. He had to give them charters. And they had to let him build castles within their walls. He largely accepted the Saxon methods and divisions of local government and the Saxon titles and offices. The peasantry also, as in all conquests, remained where they were. It was by his relations with the governing class that he transformed English society.

The new order was determined by the events of the first five years, from 1066 to 1071. During this time (as Stenton has shown) about half of the male English landed proprietors, the thegns, were killed in battle or rebellion. For the remainder, the life of the new Norman governing class, the French speech, the knightly training, the perpetual horsemanship, were bound to be unbearable. Some went to serve foreign kings whether in Hungary or Sweden, Scotland or Ireland, or in Constantinople. And some slipped down into the lower class of peasantry from which a few probably rose again to give us such names as Audley and Berkeley, Lumley and Worsley. Within Britain, however, the Saxon womenfolk must have had much greater racial influence than the men, and quite a different influence. They had not been killed in battle and they did not so readily fly overseas. Indeed they had good reason to remain.

The first winter in England William brought his wife over to be crowned at Westminster. But his companions he compelled to remain in England without their Norman women. The situation was the one that accompanies every conquest. A land in the custody of widows and orphans was to be divided among male victors deprived of women. Just how much marriage and how much hybridization occurred we do not know. We can see that Robert d'Oilli, who became Earl of Oxford, acquired a Saxon holding by marrying Judith of Wallingford. And we can see that the Percys of Petworth advanced their rank and moved north by marrying the daughter of the Saxon Earl of Northumberland.

It is however at the royal level that we can judge most accurately the mode of interbreeding. The Conqueror's marital fidelity was unique in the Norman annals. But his son Henry by his marriage united the Norman, Saxon and Scottish royal houses. And by his liaisons he attached himself to every race, Norman, Saxon and Welsh and to every social class in his kingdom. His descendants from these unions are remarkable for, while on one side they spread through the Norman baronage, on the other side they influenced the growth of learning and of the learned class (Pedigree 16). To understand how this influence worked we must examine particular families beginning with that of the Conqueror himself.

c. Norman Families

The Conqueror was not only a bastard but, like most bastards, specifically a class hybrid. His mother, Arlette, was not of a working-class family. Her father's profession of *pellarius* or furrier suggests a Mediterranean merchant.

Pedigree 16. The Connections of William the Conqueror

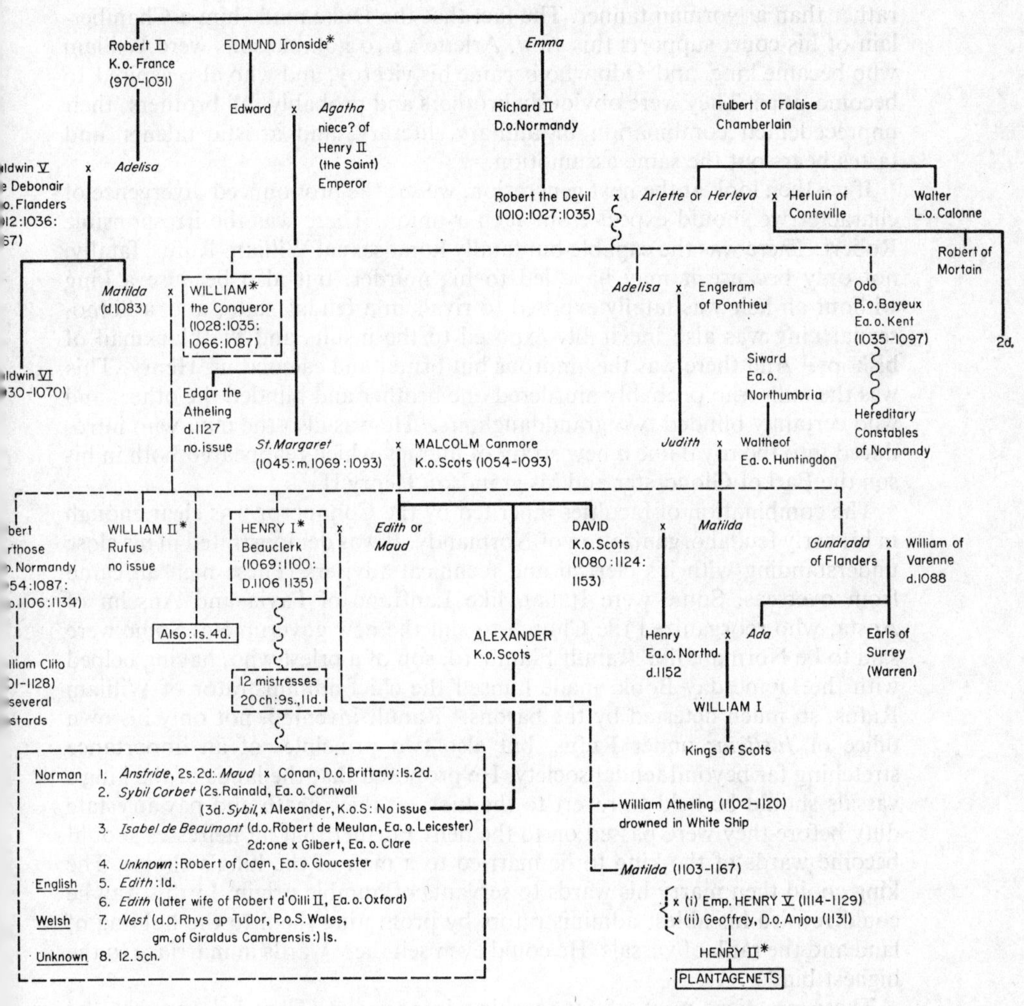

The Connections of the Conqueror (partial), illustrating:

i. interbreeding of Normans, English, Scots and Welsh following the Conquest both legitimately and illegitimately;
ii. genetic influence of Henry I on all levels of society;
iii. consanguinity of William and Matilda (through common descent from Hugh Capet) which led to the prohibition of this marriage by a Council at Rheims in 1049;
iv. descent of the Warrens which prevented one of them marrying a bastard daughter of Henry I who was a second cousin;
v. origin of Robert, Earl of Gloucester, patron of Geoffrey of Monmouth and thus sponsor of the Arthurian legend.

N.B. Odo was born after the marriage of Arlette to Herluin but may have been a son of Duke Robert.

* *Asterisks mark Kings of England.*

From H. B. George 1904, G. H. White 1949, Isenburg 1953.

rather than a Norman tanner. The fact that the Duke made him a Chamberlain of his court supports this view. Arlette's two notable sons were William who became king, and Odo who became his viceroy, and who also aspired to become pope. They were obviously brothers and probably full brothers; their unprecedented combination of military, literary, and artistic talents and tastes bears out the same assumption.

If we then look at the next generation, we see the pronounced divergence of character we should expect from such a union. There was the irresponsible Robert. There was the capable but fatally homosexual William Rufus, fatally, not only because it may have led to his murder, but also because a king without an heir was fatally exposed to rivals in a feudal state; and a homosexual king was also inevitably exposed to the insults and the blackmail of bishops.[1] And there was the amorous but brutal and calculating Henry. This was the man who probably murdered one brother and blinded the other; and who certainly blinded two granddaughters.[2] He was also the man who introduced into the royal line a new strain of literacy which reappeared both in his son the Earl of Gloucester and his grandson Henry II.

The combination of faculties inherited by the Conqueror was clear enough in his early feudal organization of Normandy. It was demonstrated in his close understanding with his clerical and technical advisers. These men all came from overseas. Some were Italian, like Lanfranc of Pavia and Anselm of Aosta, who reorganized the Church to suit the new government. Some were said to be Norman, like Ranulf Flambard, son of a priest who, having helped with the Domesday Book, made himself the chief administrator of William Rufus, so much detested by the barons.[3] Ranulf invented, not only his own office of *Justiciar* under Rufus, but also two principles of an importance stretching far beyond feudal society. He proposed that the lands of the king's vassals should be held to revert to the king on their death and pay an estate duty before they were passed on to the heir. Further that all heiresses should become wards of the king to be married to a man of the king's choice. The king could then marry his wards to servants of humble origin. In this way he could reward his ablest administrators by promoting them to the holding of land and the rank of vassals. He could even sell these wards in marriage to the highest bidder.

These practices were of far-reaching importance. They led to what the barons described as the *disparagement* of heiresses. It was detested by them because it took their breeding programme out of their hands and put it ultimately in the hands of the Crown. If they had submitted to this control as a class they would have been changed; but they would also have been saved. Their purely aggressive quality would have been tempered by an intelligent literacy. Their desperate addiction to inbreeding would have been frustrated. They would have ceased to be a fighting caste strictly adapted to the needs of the twelfth century. Their fertility would have been maintained. And they would therefore not have destroyed themselves by their own unrestrained powers three centuries and nine generations later in the Wars of the Roses.

[1] See Poole (1955).
[2] Christopher Brooke (1963).
[3] See Southern (1933) and also *D.N.B.*

The royal attempt to control wards was however withdrawn by the terms of Magna Carta in 1215.[1] These terms were to be reaffirmed throughout the middle ages. It was only under the new monarchy of the Tudors that a new nobility had to submit once more to royal control and the marriage of wards then once more became a main source of royal revenue and aristocratic recruitment.[2] The work of Ranulf was continued by Roger, a priest met by Henry as a young man near Caen. Roger became Bishop of Salisbury and Justiciar under Henry and Stephen. He undertook to remodel the administrative system.

These Norman achievements do not mean that the Saxons contributed little to the new administration. During the century before the Conquest, despite the Danish invasions, there had been a rapid technical development.[3] What had happened was that the new kings and bishops speaking French welcomed a flow into England of French talent of new and especially literate kinds which itself gave scope for the native talent of the English in new fields. The educated and literate class expanded by immigration and was increasingly and intelligently employed through the effective restoration of England to intercourse with the Roman world.

In the development of this class the breeding of the clergy played a vital part. Anselm and Henry I agreed at the Synod of Westminster to condemn the marriage of clergy (as well as homosexual practices and the slave trade). Henry, or his Justiciar, then taxed or fined those who had married and indeed later, in 1128, threatened to sell their wives as slaves, breaking one law, as Slocombe says, in order to enforce another. But there was no tax on the children of unmarried clergy. Nor was there a lack of employment for the sons of bishops. Ranulf's sons and nephews became clerics and lords. Roger's sons and grandsons continued as bishops, chancellors, treasurers, and also one of them as a notable historian.

d. The New Society

The fact that the Conqueror was able to distribute a large part of the land of England to his followers has often been referred to as a 'spoliation of England by the Normans'. We now see that this is a misleading description of what happened. And as a description of its consequences it confuses a number of social and political problems which need to be seen separately before they are put together.

From the position he had won, and continued to enforce with the help of his ministers, William enjoyed unprecedented authority. This enabled him to tighten the relations of rights and duties all the way down the chain of authority from monarch to serf. Each class enjoyed and tried to maintain its own privileges, still asserted in Magna Carta, which included the right of being tried by their peers. But it was a right which, with the blurring of legal class distinctions, could be maintained only for the great vassals.[4]

[1] Holt (1955). [2] Hurstfield (1958).

[3] For example the number of water-mills in England had increased about tenfold in this period (Lynn White, 1962; Syson, 1965).

[4] *Judicium parium,* Maine (1861); Holdsworth (1942).

Now we have seen how, under Charlemagne's successors, the office given by the sovereign was transformed by his officers into the land inherited by their descendants. And that in this inheritance the undivided land came by custom to pass usually to the eldest son who was the most likely to be strong enough to defend it. Thus, as Maine puts it, the younger son 'sank into the priest, the soldier of fortune, or the hanger-on of the mansion'. This transition was often favoured by family agreements with or without compensation to the disinherited.

The Norman Conquest led to a repetition of this development but with other new factors contributing at different social levels. With small estates, at one extreme, the English system of a divisible estate, inheritance by 'gavelkind' might continue unimpaired up to 1926. With the great vassals, at the other extreme, quite different forces came into play. Barons were summoned to attend the King's Council or Parliament. Who should be summoned? At first it seemed a burden to be borne. The eldest had to bear it. Later the burden became an honour to be asserted, a right to be demanded. The very effectiveness of English administration with its constant reiteration of charters and agreements, the Norse and Saxon interest in representative government, the small, defined and constant size of the country, all these factors tended to standardize procedure in rights, and duties, and their inheritance.

Thus, practice turning into law, the English system became the most exact in the inheritance of lands, titles and duties. Primogeniture in England became more effective than in other feudal countries. Only for the royal line itself did the rule continue to be in doubt. Not till Henry III's accession in 1216 did primogeniture become unmistakable.

The Norman kings were not over-hasty in applying primogeniture to themselves. But, as we saw, they quickly discovered that this rule of inheritance could be used to make themselves guardians of young heirs, as well as heiresses where there was no son. While the Crown was advancing its powers in this way, the barons on their side were discovering that the Crown needed military service less than money. Gradually, as they assumed that they owned the land, they also assumed that they had a responsibility for its good management rather than for military service.

Exact inheritance by primogeniture had the effect of directing the evolution of society along an entirely new course. And it had a more pronounced effect in England than on the continent of Europe. It excluded younger sons not only from the inheritance of estates but also from the social class of their ancestors. They were compelled to make good on their own. If they stayed in the country the social classes were mixed in every generation. If they went abroad the nations themselves were mixed. This was indeed one of the impulses behind the Norman and Frankish wars of expansion which were to occupy the centuries following the Conquest: the Crusades, the invasion of Ireland and later the Hundred Years War.

Parallel with these effects on migration and social diffusion was the conflict between the king and the barons and their varying agreements in regard to his interference in their marriages and their inheritance. These agreements were a second important factor in defining the status and also in establishing the mobility of social classes in England during the middle ages. The king was happy to blur the distinctions between classes so long as his own position was kept apart. The barons, however, succeeded in keeping themselves apart as well. They had their own laws; they continued to be judged by their own equals. They had their own lands, their own marriages, their own liberties which were to include the right to control their own serfs.

But in securing all these liberties, or rather privileges, the English barons had in fact secured too much. Every other class, the monarchs above and the artisans below, was remarkably mixable. But the nobility, isolated from these and also isolated from Europe, became steadily more inbred. The extinction of families in the male line led to the marriage of heiresses to ambitious lords: it led to larger and larger estates held by fewer and fewer lords. The small inbred body of peers, infertile with a few notable exceptions, long selected for no art but war, then fell upon one another and largely destroyed their caste. The country, of course, was then found to be much better off without them.

e. The Celtic Lands

The most immediate effect of the Conquest outside England was the arrival a few months later of Saxon refugees at the court of Malcolm Canmore, king of Scotland. The Saxon princess, Margaret, married the king and was soon in charge of the kingdom. She introduced the English speech to the court and the clergy. She bore six sons three of whom became king. But none of them were allowed Celtic names. And when her son Edgar became king in 1107 he moved his court from Celtic Dumfermline to English Edinburgh. By this time his sister was Queen of England. The process of Anglicization then became also a process of Normanization. What spread in Scotland were in fact the four elements for which England and English immigrants could be the intermediary: the Roman Church, the English language, the Anglo-Norman administration, and the Norman feudal knighthood acting on the principle of military service in return for a holding of land from the king.

Some Anglo-Norman families were in this way able to plant themselves as chieftains on the Scottish clans of the Highlands which even adopted names like Sinclair. Others became embodied in the Lowland nobility and, intermarrying with the royal dynasty, like Bruce, Balliol, and Comyn, were soon able to dispute the Scottish Crown.[1]

While these movements were taking place the Scottish frontier with England was being shifted back and forth with changing power and interest and the changing opportunities given by the marriage of feudal heiresses and internal rebellion. The same shifts affected the frontier with Wales. Here also there was a distinction between remoter Welsh chieftains who kept aloof and others who married into the Saxon, Norman and later English governing classes. A sister of the English Earls, Edwin and Morcar, had married a Prince of North Wales. Conflict was mitigated by migration and hybridization all through the succeeding centuries as the English-speaking gentry pushed into

[1] These processes of penetration and hybridization must be distinguished from the results of their reversal following the union of the Crowns. Then there arose great Scottish landlords who had married back into England and were now effectively English. These were the villains of the Highland clearances (see Ian Prebble, 1963).

Wales by marriage and the Welshmen made their way across by cattle-droving to the pastures (and, much later, the leather tanneries) of Northampton.[1]

It is in the south of Wales that we meet the patroness of all Norman hybridization. Nesta, daughter of Rhys ap Tewdwr (or Theodore or Tudor) was born about 1075. She inherited from her father the lordship of Caeraw or Carew. By a husband, Gerald of Windsor, and half a dozen lovers, including Henry I, and perhaps a cousin who set Pembroke Castle on fire in order to abduct her, she bore nearly twenty children. Fitzgerald, Fitzstephen, Fitz-henry, Le Gros, Barry, and Carew are some of the names they and their descendants bore. Earls of Kildare, Desmond and Barrymore were some of the titles their families acquired in Ireland where one of her grandsons, Gerald the Welshman (Giraldus Cambrensis), described their conquests. But their importance for us is that from this hybrid stock, energetic and fertile, a large part of the mediaeval aristocracy, as well as the modern population, of the British Isles must be descended (Pedigree 16).

A hundred years or three generations after the Conquest of England, this original brood of Nesta, led by a Norman, Richard de Clare, or Strongbow, made the next step in Norman expansion and invaded Ireland.

This was a localized and purely Norman enterprise whose effects stretch forward to the present day. Before we follow it therefore we must look at a work of collaboration, a joint effort whose effects were more immediate and more widespread: the Crusades.

V. THE CRUSADES

a. The New Principle

The intrusion of the Vikings and their descendants into all parts of Europe had, by the end of the eleventh century, done nothing to soften or sweeten the warlike temper of the military governing classes with whom they had inter-bred. They were at this time constantly employed in raids, wars and insurrections. Western Europe was already beginning to bristle with their fortifications. Yet the fringes of their territories were under constant attack from pagan and infidel enemies.

It was in these circumstances that Pope Urban II convened a Council of the Church to meet in the Cathedral of Clermont. At this time, following Hilde-brand, the papacy was approaching the height of its authority in Europe. But when he made his concluding address to the Council (on November 27, 1095) the Pope was thinking beyond the limits of his own time or his own authority. He was also thinking as a Frenchman. He had invited to this gathering in the heart of France not only some 250 bishops but also a large assembly of French nobles. He exhorted his Christian brethren to give up fighting one another. Instead, with cross as their emblem they should vow to take up arms against the threatening enemies of the faith, Arabs and Turks, and should free the Holy Places for the worship of Christian pilgrims. The Pope also made certain

[1] For the marriage situation in the upper classes a neat account is that given by Shakespeare of the union of Glendower's daughter with Mortimer, a grandson of Lionel, Duke of Clarence's Irish marriage (*Henry IV*, Pt. 1).

promises which enlarged upon earlier practice. The soldiers of Christ who might lose their lives in this holy enterprise would receive an everlasting reward. They would by his *indulgence* (the first use of this potent word) be relieved of paying for the cost of their sins whether by penance or by purgatory. And for those who expected to survive he suggested that the promised lands, now in the hands of Muslim princes, were indeed richer than their own.

A variety of movements that we know as the Crusades followed from the Pope's appeal. We shall never be able to measure fully their effects on the people of Europe or of the Ancient East. But what happened certainly provides us with a test of many of the principles at work in the evolution of society.

Large bodies of warriors of all ranks in the feudal hierarchy set forth. There were kings and barons often with their wives. There were knights, squires and men-at-arms, some heroes, some desperadoes; some were penniless but some were rich heirs who had ensured their success by gifts to the Church. But as a body they were picked fighting men, picked for their enterprise and confidence in war. The year 1095 was a climax, not only for the papacy, but also for the whole hybrid class of fighting men now to be called Franks but largely of Norman and Viking descent. They were men whose fighting spirit was all the more eager for the unspoilt enthusiasm of their recent conversion to Christianity, which they were now authorized to regard as a fighting religion. These men were organized in expeditions, or bound by feudal loyalties, or entirely free from duty or discipline. They marched through Constantinople or they sailed from Marseilles, Venice or Palermo. They attacked first the Arabs and the Turks of Palestine, Syria and Egypt. But they also turned aside to assault easier or richer, or healthier objectives which included Christian cities or powers. They set up feudal governments under kings and counts, who allied themselves with the charitable orders of knights. These orders, the Hospitallers and Templars, being vowed to celibacy and service, were endowed by the Pope with obligatory offerings from all the Churches of western Christendom. Hence, by the recruitment of younger sons, they were quickly expanded into the strongest weapon of the Church and one of the mainstays of the whole crusading operation.

Thus, beneath this great movement, the interests of many diverse groups of people were at work. The first of these, we may say, since the Pope set the movement going, were the interests of the Church. These were wars for the extension of the power of the papacy. Every expedition was promoted by the preaching of the most eloquent spell-binders. It was also accompanied by bishops, abbots and priests who, after encouraging and advising the fighting men, expected and usually received their share in the earthly prizes.

The second interest was that of the fighting men. The spearhead of the crusading armies was the knightly governing class of France, Frankish and Norman with its offshoots in Sicily, Spain and elsewhere, men dedicated to fighting for its own sake. In addition many were younger sons, landless men, trouble makers whom their elder brothers, their neighbours and their liege lords were glad to get rid of, men determined to get land or spoil whether they won it by fighting, by robbery, or by marriage with the heiresses of those who had died. And there were a few men, barons or knights, who were civilized, cultured, Romanized to the point where they undoubtedly looked upon their mission as a service to God and to their fellow men. In a word, it was not the motives of the Crusaders that were mixed so much as the men themselves.

The enormous success of the Pope's appeal, the continual flow of men from the west into the east for two centuries, and the great diversity of these men are all evidence of the shortage of land following a growth of the wealth and population of Western Europe, and above all in northern France and Flanders in the three earlier centuries which had followed Charlemagne. They are evidence of the success of the Roman priesthood and of the northern knights who were now profitably mingling their activities in feudal society. And they are particular evidence of the way in which these two racially and culturally opposed elements in society could exploit one another for their common advantage.

As time went on the elements of mutual exploitation or co-operation developed and the elements of devotion were often obscured. Safety and power led to luxury and arrogance. In the fourth Crusade, the Venetian Doge, Enrico Dandolo, blind old man though he was, succeeded in harnessing the warlike spirit of the northerners to the commercial policy of his republic. Behind his religious exhortations however the wealth of the prize, in this case the Christian city Constantinople, united the diverse interests of priest and warrior, ruler and merchant with a zeal that might well have seemed religious.

Frankish or Latin principalities established themselves in 1096 along a coastal strip from Gaza to the Gulf, from Jerusalem to Antioch and beyond. There they continued until the fall of Acre on May 18, 1291. Except that Richard Cœur de Lion added Cyprus, captured from the Greeks in 1190, it was a diminishing territory. Their government was in principle feudal. The suzerain was the King of Jerusalem, the first king being the brother of Godfrey of Bouillon. And his barons demanded the right to elect their king. But, owing to the high death rate among the warrior sons, eight times in eight generations the descent passed through a daughter; one of these married four husbands, three of whom in succession were kings. The man whom in practice they elected was therefore the warrior husband they chose, usually from among themselves, for the daughter and heiress of his predecessor. The elective and hereditary principles, both matrilinear and patrilinear, were thus fused in one Christian and constitutional ceremony.

Not only these men but also the Orders of Hospitallers and Templars, endowed as we have seen, built over their two centuries the great castles of Syria and Palestine which survive today bearing witness to the strength of the warriors and the skill of the engineers, usually Italians, whom they employed.

The documents of the time reveal the character of the Frankish society and hence the conditions which governed its behaviour and evolution during the six generations of its existence.[1] The conquerors were familiar with the problems of taking possession of new territories by dispossessing a former military governing class. But in Syria they were confronted with a situation of unforeseen complexity. The population was largely Arabic-speaking. But a

[1] Admirably summarized by Régine Pernoud (1959).

part were Jews and a part Christian sects, Orthodox and Armenian, Jacobite and Maronite, who were supposed to be their friends. The bulk, however, both urban and peasant, were Muslim.

The conquerors found themselves following the pattern of government of their Muslim predecessors. They had discovered that it was the only pattern that worked.

Like the Arab conquerors they needed food and only the peasants could produce it. The cultivated land, therefore, as had happened a dozen times before, was left in the hands of the peasants, Muslim or Christian. The local government, especially of Muslims, was left in local hands. And every individual or group was treated in accordance with his value to the new governing class; treated therefore without regard to his religion. The Arab interpreter and the Syrian physician were indispensable: they were respected and trusted. The Christian minorities were often of little importance: they were worse treated than the corresponding Muslims. And as for the mosques they were converted into churches. But the Muslims could often share them.

It thus became clear to the conquerors and the conquered, and to the great surprise of later arrivals, that the struggle was one between two military or knightly governing classes which knew one another as Franks and Muslims. The two ruling groups remained separate. Although Richard Cœur de Lion offered his sister to Saladin they never intermarried. But both groups changed with the passage of time. The Franks on their side, although united in religion, were disunited from the beginning in every other respect. In language, they spoke *Langue d'oil* in Jerusalem, *Langue d'oc* in Tripoli, and Italian in those ports where Venetian, Genoese and Pisan merchants struggled in diverse dialects to advance their diverse interests. The disunity of the Franks flourished in proportion to their prosperity and the remoteness of their heroic beginnings. It flourished also in disregard of the rising dangers to their security from Mongols in the east and mamelukes in the south. And when the crisis came, with the Mongol invasions and the triumph of the mamelukes over both the Mongols and themselves, it was too late to unite.

The Muslims remained united by their predominantly Arabic language. But they were often split between the interests of princes in Aleppo, Damascus and Cairo. They were split before Saladin by the Shiah faith of the Fatimid sultans in Cairo. And they were continually hampered by the Shiah Assassins who, emerging from their Persian stronghold during the first Crusade, established themselves in the central mountains of Syria, and murdered even more Muslim than Christian leaders. Latterly, however, the Muslim power was united in the hands of the Mameluke fighting corps. These Turkoman slaves, as we have seen, were employed by Saladin's successors in Cairo. Their strict discipline and racial uniformity enabled them in the end, in 1250, to supplant their employers and forty years later under their leaders, Baibars and his successor, to expel the last Christians from Palestine.

During the two centuries of the Christian rule, however, a new and revolutionary situation had existed. It was a reversal of the genetic relations which had prevailed between Christendom and Islam for the previous five centuries. A fighting element of the Muslim population, having needed employment and

Table 28. *Time Chart of the Crusades* (I–VIII)
After Runciman (1951–1954); Pernoud (1959).

Crusades numbered traditionally

Left:	Ecclesiastical data	Ordinary type:	Christian data
Inset:	Military data	Italics:	Muslim data

Square brackets: Contemporary chroniclers

	1058–1090	Normans take Sicily from the Muslims (after 200 years)
	1072–1109	Spanish kings retake Toledo and Valencia from the Moors
	1073–1085	Hildebrand Pope as GREGORY VII
	1080	Hospital of St John of Jerusalem founded
	1118	Knights enrolled 1128: Templars founded
I	1096–1099	URBAN II (1088–1099) and Peter the Hermit [William of Tyre]
		Godfrey of Bouillon founds the Kingdom and Dynasty of Jerusalem with counties of Tripoli, Antioch and Edessa
	1100–1101	Stephen of Blois and others rebuffed in Anatolia
	1123–1124	Venetians set up in Tyre
	1144	*Zengi, Atabeg of Mosul, recaptures Edessa*
II	1147–1149	EUGENIUS II (1145–1153) and St Bernard
		Conrad III and Louis VII rebuffed at Damascus
		Crusading fleet captures Lisbon
		North German forces attack pagan Wends
	1187	*Saladin of Mosul, Sultan of Egypt* (1169–1193), *destroys Franks at Hattin and takes Jerusalem*
III	1189–1192	Richard Cœur de Lion annexes Cyprus from the Greeks and with Philip Augustus and Frederick I recaptures Acre
		During the siege, Teutonic Knights founded: windmills introduced. Richard proposes Saladin's brother should turn Christian and marry his sister
IV	1202–1204	INNOCENT III (1198–1216) and Fulk of Neuilly
		German-Venetian alliance attacks and takes Constantinople
		Baldwin of Flanders, first Latin Emperor [Villehardouin]
	1212	Crusading children kidnapped by slave-dealers near Marseilles and sold to Egypt
V	1218–1221	King John of Jerusalem with Papal Legate Pelagius capture Damietta in Egypt but lose it again
	1209–1226	Albigensian heretics or Cathars suppressed
	1231–1233	Inquisition set up
	1245	200 Cathars burnt in Montségur
VI	1228–1229	GREGORY IX (1227–1241)
		Frederick II, atheist and excommunicated Emperor, becomes to Q. of Jerusalem by marriage, receives Holy Places by treaty with Saladin's brother
	1244	*Baibars, the Egyptian Mameluke, defeats the Christians at Gaza and takes Jerusalem*

VII	1248–1254	St Louis of France captured while marching on Cairo [Joinville]
	1260–1268	*Baibars destroys the Northern Principalities*
VIII	1270–1272	GREGORY X (1271–1276)
		St Louis and Charles of Anjou attack Tunis
		Edward of England fails to advance from Acre
	1274	Abortive project for east and west joint crusade
	1291	*Khalil, mameluke Sultan, takes Acre, the last Christian stronghold in the east*
	1305	CLEMENT V (1305–1314)
	1309	Order of Hospitallers occupy Rhodes; 1523–1799 withdraw to Malta
	1310	Order of Templars destroyed by Philip the Fair of France
	1348	Black death carried by black ship rat brought from China, taken from Mecca by pilgrims, to Palestine and thence by Italian trading fleet to Europe: it ends an epoch in the Mediterranean
	1492	Expulsion of Moors from Granada

found it under Christian masters, was converted to Christianity. These people were no doubt chiefly derived from the Turkish mercenaries, the forerunners of the Mamelukes, introduced by the Abbassid caliphs. They were known as *Turcoples* and, when Saladin captured them, they were massacred as renegades.

Conversion to Christianity occurred however in all except the governing classes of the Muslim community. Scholars and craftsmen, sailors and peasants, and of course the women who married Christian traders and soldiers, all were able by baptism to cross the belligerent boundary. And having done so, they became part of the Christian world, moving and migrating and hybridizing within the Christian and European society. It was these people who for two centuries brought a new infusion of eastern arts, eastern learning and eastern race into Latin Europe.

When therefore we work out the balance of racial movement during the crusades we have a complicated account to draw up. It has been said that over half a million Christians moved east during the Crusades into the Syrian provinces. Probably a similar number moved back. But those who came back were a different kind of population: a large proportion of them were people of Muslim and hybrid extraction. Some were people who, as we know, had preferred the Frankish to the Muslim methods of government. Others were people who believed that their talents would make them a living more easily in Europe than in Asia. Whatever the causes however, the results were a continuation of the ancient but usually anonymous movement by which for four thousand years the ancient east had been enriching Europe. More especially we can see that this movement was connected with the development in Italy of new industries, such as glass-making in Venice,[1] and new schools with a medical bias beginning in Salerno, Pisa and Bologna. It was through these cities and through Sicily that most of the intellectual traffic flowed.

[1] As Derry and Williams point out.

Christian churches and Christian universities thus soon came to be illuminated by the skill and learning, the technology and the scholarship, of the Muslim east.

One example there seems to have been of an invention moving against the ancient current. That was the introduction of windmills with horizontal axles. They appeared in Acre during the siege in 1190. Later they appeared in Rhodes probably with the Knights Hospitallers. Here was a first sign of the great western growth of engineering which three hundred years later was to appear in Europe and came to flower in the Scientific Revolution. But all those later stages owed something to the westward movement from the countries of Asia to which we ultimately owe a share in the making of all our civilization.

b. The Principle Applied

The European rulers of Church and State, who watched the development of the Crusades for two centuries, learnt several lessons from the experience which they attempted to apply to their own advantage. The first, as we have seen, were the rulers of Venice. They turned the Crusades against the Eastern Empire and made their own Empire out of the pickings.

At the same time the Hohenstaufen, established as emperors, saw that the principle of the Crusade could be used to extend their dominions. During the third Crusade they sponsored the foundation of a new order of Teutonic Knights. They were to be confined to the German language and were thus easily persuaded to return from the Holy Land and to attack the heathen Slavs on their own borders. In the south, where the Germans were slowly advancing as a forest-felling people, the Knights could do nothing. But in the north they could fight their way across the open steppes against the Slavs. So they advanced, inserfing Wendish peasants and dominating Polish towns.[1] They created the military State of Prussia and later colonized the Baltic Provinces beyond it. The ruling class they established, the Junkers and Baltic barons, was entirely military like the Norman ruling class in Ireland.

No less enterprising were the Spanish kings whom the Pope's words encouraged to take the offensive against the Moorish powers in the Peninsula. Their Portuguese satellites were immediately successful. Combining with a fleet of English and Flemish Crusaders on their way to Syria they captured Lisbon from the Moors. In doing so they established the State of Portugal. It was a Christian state with a northern governing class, and also northern maritime and mercantile classes. And it was these together who, 300 years later, assisted by Italian and Majorcan, as well as Muslim and Jewish, cartographers and navigators, were to burst across the oceans and open the New World to Europe.

In the next century a more sinister application of the crusading principle was invented by the Church, in collaboration with Frankish and Norman nobles. Its method was to turn the Crusaders on to the enemies of the Church within Christendom, using them to destroy heretics. This policy, however, belongs to a new chapter in the history of Europe.

[1] Hence the Slav names of towns which, like Leipzig and Potsdam, persist in north Germany, as discussed by Isaac Taylor.

VI. IRELAND

a. Racial Conflict

While certain groups of Norman leaders were entering into the vast enterprise of the Crusades a small body of Normans in Wales were preparing to embark on a more limited operation of a less obviously sacred purpose. It was for the conquest and colonization of Ireland. In the year 1170 the Norman forces assembled in Pembroke for the invasion. They were a small body, perhaps a thousand Flemish men-at-arms, three hundred Welsh bowmen and a hundred knights. But they were heavily armed and were able, after some awkward moments, to defeat both their Viking kinsmen and the linen-shirted Irish.

The invaders quickly occupied Dublin and conquered Leinster. Indeed, their leader Strongbow having married the daughter of a displaced king, they thought they might now rule the country. This time however the enterprise was checked by the power of the Crown of England: the world in which Vikings had moved freely was beginning to be tied up within the great framework of feudal and papal Europe. This generation were no longer free to conquer where they would. The invaders had hoped to be as independent as their Norman kinsmen in Sicily, or for that matter their remote Viking kinsmen in Ireland. They had established genetically the hybrid governing classes of new societies. But the societies as a whole, with their network of literate men and legal and clerical institutions were now taking control. The Plantagenet king in England was at the moment the most powerful ruler in Europe. He had in his hands (according to Giraldus) a Bull from the Pope—now, without precedent, an Englishman, Adrian IV—giving him the task, which he had prudently solicited, of reforming the Church in Ireland. He intended to take the responsibility for himself. He did not intend to see his barons turn the adjoining island into a powerful independent kingdom. Henry went to Ireland in October 1171 and stayed six months. He established the English kings as Lords of Ireland.

Henry would have been surprised to know, however, that what he had established in Ireland was not a government. Rather it was a state of war. It was a state of war lasting for 750 years and unique in the history of human societies. Henry himself knew very well the conflict that was developing in England between the barons who were acquiring the political coherence of an hereditary caste and the royal government. He saw that this conflict had been transferred across the Channel where the Crown being remote was at a disadvantage. But he could certainly not have reckoned that on this conflict would be superimposed another quarrel, more lasting and far more unhappy—that between the English and the Irish peoples.

This quarrel can be understood only in terms of the profound racial difference between the Gaelic-speaking natives and the English-speaking invaders, a difference which even today, after twenty generations of limited hybridization, is still not seriously blurred.

The English were sober, industrious, mechanical, calculating and ruthless; characteristics invaluable in government. The native Irish by contrast were imaginative, unpredictable and even irresponsible. Their pre-Aryan and perhaps paleolithic speech had died out only in the ninth century and they had more left of their paleolithic instincts. For them hunting, fishing and shooting were universal and instinctive recreations. Their hereditary caste of poets and soothsayers, the filid, they respected too much for the Church, even for Columba, to disparage. And although the filid were disappearing their inheritance has always remained in the literary gifts of the people. These then were people who loved their land even if they knew less than the invaders how to cultivate it.[1]

When we add to these genetic differences the associated contrast between the two languages and between the tribal and feudal orders of society, their habits of responsibility and of inheritance, we see that there were the materials of conflict: the two races seemed to agree only in being warlike. There was of course one and only one remedy: intermarriage. And this was the remedy adopted. Slowly the two races fused. But, since the Irish were much more numerous, the result of hybridization was to produce a very small and diminishing number of nearly pure English, all in the towns; a large and not much diminishing number of nearly pure Irish, all in the country; and an increasing number of mixed but predominantly Irish people everywhere, known sometimes as 'degenerate English' and sometimes as the 'Middle Nation'. Into this mass the Welsh followers of the Fitzgeralds, Walshes and Barrets, Merricks and Joyces had long disappeared save for their locally continuing names. Above all the aristocracy, both chieftains and barons, having both Irish and Norman names were after a few generations as Irish as they were Norman in their ancestry: the Irish kings, unlike the Saxon nobles, had not been driven out and were never killed off.

Now, to the indignation of kings and governments in England, these Irish lords proved to be converts to Irish law, language, and loyalty. It has been said that if the kings of England could have spared the time they could have repaired this disloyalty and re-oriented Irish society. The Scottish kings had the same problem and, by their efforts, they succeeded in holding Gaelic-speaking chiefly society together.

Such was the situation of diminishing influence and disappearing revenue which English kings for two hundred years, while remaining usually at a safe distance, had attempted to remedy. For Edward III the position was made worse by his own French wars. France had promised more plunder to him and his nobles than Ireland could offer. Too much occupied himself to visit his dependency, he decided to send his third son, Lionel, to restore English rule. The young man, aged twenty-three, arrived in 1361 as Deputy or Governor.

His father, wishing to put great fiefs in the hands of his six sons, had already arranged for him to marry at the age of fourteen the heiress of William de Burgh (or Burgo or Burke) the Norman-Irish Earl of Ulster and Lord of Connaught whose title and lands were assigned to him. He was now also made Duke of Clarence in acknowledgement of his wife's ancestor, the founding

[1] These generalizations may be tested by contemporary experience, as well as by the history of agriculture in Ireland. But we discredit the myth that with a consignment of the first Irish export, hunting dogs destined for Rome, the enslaved Saxon St Patrick in 411 is said to have escaped from Ireland.

Earl of Clare. And his wife was presented with a most ingratiating young English page, the future poet Geoffrey Chaucer.

This marriage was a striking diplomatic gesture and it might have done something to unite the two peoples. To be sure, genetically Irish ancestry passed through it to all later lines of English sovereigns. Politically however it was not consummated by a union. Rather it was contradicted by a violent assertion of disunion, an attempt to separate for ever the English and Irish races by a decree drawn up for the Duke of Clarence in 1366, and known to history as the Statutes of Kilkenny.

These Statutes were introduced by an unusually straightforward and significant explanation.[1] The English, it states, having conquered the native people governed them well. But these English have now degenerated from their ancient character. They have given up their own habits, apparel, and mode of riding with a Norman saddle; they have forsaken their own laws and their own language in order to follow the ways of their Irish enemies. They have even taken to marrying these enemies (which indeed they had begun to do in 1162). With friendship to the enemy loyalty to the king has decayed.

Now for the remedy.

All these practices, according to the Statutes, must cease. No more intermarriage. No more Irish or 'Brehon' law which is indeed no law. No more entertaining of Irish minstrels, poets, or story-tellers. No more Irish speech or Irish surnames even for Irish servants. No church livings for any Irish-speaker. No more sale of arms, armour or war-horses to the Irish. The English area, the south-easterly third of the country, must be reserved for loyal citizens conforming to English habits and entirely cut off from the disloyal Irish outside this Pale or boundary. Thus war was declared between the two peoples. And, since the young Duke left Ireland for ever in the following year, it was in effect a war declared from London.

For two centuries these Statutes remained in force: that is, until the reign of Elizabeth, a queen who was herself, we may notice, descended from Irish ancestors through both parents, both Boleyns and Tudors. But inevitably they failed to take effect. Irish manners, Irish speech and the Irish community and race spread. Why? Because of what happened in each level of society.

First, the Irish peasantry, who were indispensable for feeding the country within the Pale, remained entirely Irish. They did not even mix to the extent of picking up the valuable and not too recondite English and Norman practice of cheese-making. Secondly, the middle classes in the towns were a population slowly recruited from English towns and Irish countryside. They were themselves therefore already and permanently half Irish and incapable of drawing the line against their own brethren. And thirdly the Norman-Irish aristocracy continued to intermarry both with those chiefs who were almost purely Gaelic and with English nobles like young Clarence. They were, as always, willing to marry where they could get most land or most rank. And they were not willing to make their marriages to suit what had become to them an alien government.

[1] Which has been translated from the Norman French and discussed by Curtis.

b. Religious Conflict

The Tudors warily postponed dealing with Ireland until they had fully exercised their new administration in England. But when in the end, in 1536, Henry VIII attempted to undertake it, he found himself provided with a new weapon of incalculable effect. His decision to make himself Head of the Church might be acceptable to the Irish people. But when, under Elizabeth in 1560, a prayer book in English followed, it was the Irish speech of the people as well as their religion that were challenged. Indeed by this one step the people were bound for ever to their old religion.

How different was the position in Wales! Here the language was in danger of extinction. Here zealous translators reconstructed the language in order to translate the Bible into the native tongue. By this one stroke, also in the reign of Elizabeth, the language was restored and the religion reformed. But no Gaelic translation of the Bible has ever been attempted for the Irish people: the translation two centuries later was made for the Highland Scots.

The English attempt to impose the English language with the reformation ruined the chances of the reformation with the Irish people. At the same time, however, it also ruined the chances of the Gaelic language: without a native Bible the native language could never expand as the Welsh language expanded in Wales. It could, and did, contract.

The failure of the Reformation beyond the Pale in Ireland made the differences between the two peoples doubly irreconcilable. With the Spaniards in Flanders, to avoid a Catholic encirclement, the English government felt itself compelled to undertake some kind of reconquest. The process actually began under Henry VIII. It proceeded, such was the continuity of established interests, under the Catholic Queen Mary. And it went forward for 150 years. It had two sides. One was the conversion of the native Irish governing class, that is the nobility with both Norman and Gaelic patronymics, as an alternative to confiscation and deportation or extirpation. The other was the implantation, not of English as such, but of Protestants who could be relied upon to keep down and keep away from the Catholic Irish.

The conversion of the Irish nobility to Protestantism was attempted in two steps. First, Henry VIII made forty Irish chiefs into peers. This generous gesture made them more amenable to control but it did not guarantee a permanent conversion. Secondly, James I set up a Court of Wards where Irish peers who were minors might be educated. In this way, by 1640, the Earls of Ormonde, Kildare, Barrymore, Thomond and Inchiquin had been taken, whether for breeding or for fighting, into the Protestant community or camp. These were to set the example for the English-marrying absentee landlords of a later day.

The parallel attack on the unconverted and unreliable governing class may be said to have begun with Henry VIII's removal of the Fitzgeralds, the centre of Norman-Irish nationalism. The tenth Earl of Kildare and five of his uncles were brought to London and in 1537 hanged, drawn and quartered at Tyburn. The second step was the intimidation, defeat and flight of the principal Gaelic chiefs, a hundred of them, led by two Earls, the O'Neill of Tyrone and the O'Donnell of Tyrconnell. These men left Ireland for exile in Rome in 1607.

The third step, following the exile of 30,000 Catholic Irish troops to France and Spain, was Cromwell's deportation of the remaining Irish gentry across the Shannon in 1653. And the last step, known as the 'Flight of the Wild Geese', was the acceptance of exile by almost the whole of the remaining Catholic gentry in Ireland under the terms of the surrender of Limerick in 1691. These men established over a period of sixty years the French king's Irish Brigade. Their descendants have never ceased to appear as establishment figures, generals, ambassadors and statesmen, in all Catholic countries, in France, Austria, Italy, Spain and South America.[1]

c. The Decapitated Society

Thus, in the course of 150 years of struggle, English governments had established their power in Ireland. In view of their struggle with two Catholic powers, Spain and France, they were bound to do it. And they could scarcely have done it in any other way. But in doing it they had created a social disaster, unique in Europe, which they neither intended nor understood. They had removed, directly or by conversion, the whole of the Catholic gentry. The Catholic peasantry were thus left in their own country cut off from their national leaders, educators and communicators and even, we may add, hybridizers, for bastardy itself declined. They were thus prevented from acquiring any leaders of their own race or their own religion. More than this: the penal laws against Catholics, who were uneducated, inevitably had a severer effect than had Louis XIV's similar laws against the Huguenots who were largely educated and not racially recognizable. In short the Catholic population was cut off from the whole of civilization, Irish, English or European. In the towns a small mixed Catholic and Protestant society continued. But in the country landowning Protestants and landless Catholics constituted a caste society as rigid as any that has been known.

Into this society were introduced Protestants, English and Scottish colonists and European refugees. There was Richard Boyle (1566–1643) fresh from Elizabethan Cambridge who made his fortune by matrimony and perhaps by embezzlement; and who used it to build new towns and new industries and endow the fifteen children who made his name famous. He was one of the men (would there had been more! Cromwell said) who first took Ireland out of the middle ages. There were also the Huguenots, gay, enterprising and socially stratified who also brightened the life of Irish cities and mixed and married with their Protestant neighbours. And there were the Moravians from the Palatinate, planted on farms near Limerick, who being unsociable have preserved their distinct speech and character, sour, industrious, and cleanly, almost down to the present day.[2]

These people mostly in the towns, supporting the Irish but now Protestant landlords, made the combined Irish government for the century after the Catholic expulsion. It was the period of the Protestant Ascendancy, a period,

[1] For example, two forceful, conservative and devout presidents of the French Republic: Marshall MacMahon (1808–1893), who suppressed the Commune in Paris in 1871 (see ch. 22), and General de Gaulle (b. 1890); see Duffy (1964).

[2] Last described and traced historically by Hayes (1937).

while it lasted, of remarkable advance. During this time Dublin became a great capital whose splendid achievement can still be seen. This city was the product of a union and hybridization of Irish natives and English immigrants in the two social classes: the governors, military and political, and the intellectuals, artistic, literary and technical. The two classes were, in economy and in administration, necessary to one another and successful together.

A new international situation brought this prosperity to an end. The American and French revolutions and the threat of Napoleon made the position of the small Protestant minority, only a tenth of the population, untenable. The government then had to be strengthened from outside if Ireland was to be held down by Protestants. It was therefore removed from Dublin by the Act of Union. Quickly the governing class departed to London and the social and intellectual structure of the capital fell to the ground. The Protestant landlords, whose houses we may still see, withdrew, taking their rents with them, to England. And the Protestant architects, writers and dramatists followed them. Protestant society in Ireland was decapitated in 1800 just as Catholic society had been decapitated in 1691. Ireland had been stripped a second time.

The character of the small Protestant Irish community does not need to be given any borrowed description. It has described itself in legible characters. On the one hand they have bred almost the whole of the notable literary figures coming from Ireland in the last three centuries.[1]

On the other hand, the Irish Protestant governing class, generally illiterate[2] like those other military frontiersmen, the Junkers in Prussia descended from Teutonic knights, have provided an indispensable source of military (not naval) commanders, good and bad, over the period, from Wellington to Montgomery.

The effect of the Reformation in Ireland is a special instance of its effect throughout Europe. It split society into a number of genetically segregated non-intermarrying groups of a specialized professional character. But, whereas between most Protestant groups conversion is possible and not infrequent, the separation of Catholic and Protestant which happened in Ireland is hard and permanent.[3]

A further grave obstacle to change in Ireland was the great famine of 1845–1849. The growth of the potato had in a hundred years doubled the population of Ireland. The Irish cultivator had at last found a crop whose dangerously easy cultivation suited his temperament.[4] But in the space of thirty

[1] Pre-union and pre-famine: Goldsmith, Sheridan and Moore; post-union and post-famine: Wilde, Shaw, Yeats, Joyce, O'Casey, Beckett; first crosses: the three Brontës and Sir Richard Burton; living in Ireland: Swift, Congreve, Sterne, and Borrow (see Douglas Hyde, 1899, himself a Protestant and later President of Eire).

[2] The one notable military-literate combination among the Protestant Irish, T. E. Lawrence, was significantly illegitimate.

[3] In Ulster blood group frequencies demonstrate its permanence; see Mourant (1954).

[4] Woodham-Smith (1962) notes that the Irish peasantry (like root cultivators in India or Africa) were unable or unwilling to grind or to sow grain given them in relief of famine.

years, the potato disease brought the population back to half again by famine and by emigration. The people who were lost by emigration, to England and the United States, were inevitably, and as we can see from what they have done, the most enterprising selection. Once again the immobility and conservatism of Ireland were strengthened. By inbreeding within classes Irish society was thus genetically fixed and stabilized at a pre-industrial stage and this has hindered its evolution in step with its neighbours. Only the disappearance of the barriers between Catholic and Protestant can break this evolutionary stalemate.

The history of Ireland illustrates nearly all the important genetic principles in the development of societies. These are quite ordinary in showing the origins of stratification and the effects of migration, hybridization and assortative mating. They are even paralleled in showing the processes by which societies are mutilated. All empires decapitate their subordinate societies just as all capitals decapitate the societies of their provinces. There are the Turkish, Russian and Austrian examples. That is how societies mature and grow old. The French Catholic population in Canada was decapitated by the desertion of its governing class after the conquest by the Protestant English-speaking invaders of 1759. The Flemish-speaking population of Belgium was decapitated by its separation from Holland in 1830. Where Ireland is unique is in the succession of decapitations. And, of course, in the unique racial character of the Irish people, isolated on the oceanic edge of the western world.

20

THE JEWISH INVOLVEMENT

I. THE PAGAN SUPREMACY

AT THE BEGINNING of the Christian era the Roman Empire had become the dominant force controlling the development of European society. Just at this time, however, the emperors encountered the fatal obstacle to the mode of development that seemed right to them and their governing class. They had hoped to establish a universal religion harmonizing the worship of all the gods of the Empire and thus unifying the peoples under their rule. But they encountered the Jews, a people who would not accept, or even pretend to accept, a multiplicity of gods.[1]

In the year 6 the House of Herod collapsed and the imperial government had to take the Jewish provinces under direct rule. They quickly discovered that the Jews, although their religious and political ideas were in a continual revolutionary turmoil, were united in their devotion to a form of 'atheism', an uncompromising national religion, a faith abstracted from idols yet respecting places, which was both unfamiliar and inconvenient to the new governors.

They did not know that this religion and this people were to remain a challenge to all the governments and peoples of Europe for indefinite ages in the future. Handling the problem maladroitly the Romans found themselves faced in A.D. 66 with a rebellion of unequalled ferocity. It ended, not with the capture of Jerusalem, the enslavement of the Jewish prisoners and the burning of the Temple in A.D. 70, but only three years later with the fall of the Jewish fortress of Masada and the suicide of its defenders. Even this was not enough. Another war under Hadrian sixty years later completed the destruction of the city and its replacement by a new foundation. With the Shrine and its wealth disappeared the office of high priest and the sect of the Sadducees. The whole

[1] See especially Parkes (1962); also Dimont (1962); Teller (1966) and Fishberg (1911).

body of observing Jews were expelled from Judaea. They found themselves scattered from the Euphrates to the Rhine.

These events, as we have seen, made final and irrevocable the schism which had just appeared within the Jewish people. On one side stood the stable traditional or orthodox majority tied to the ritual of the law. And on the other side stood the rapidly evolving and slowly increasing Christians. After the destruction of Jerusalem the next Bishop of Aelia Capitolana (as it was now called) appointed in A.D. 135 was no doubt, like his predecessors, a Jew by descent. But he could no longer be described officially as a Jew. He was a Christian. The line of cleavage between Jews and Christians was now clear. Each side struggled to convert the other and to convert the polytheists around them, and even to spread the word among the heathens beyond the Roman frontiers. Both sides converted scholars and professional men. The Jews converted certain pagan tribes, notably among the Berbers. They even developed their ancient rules to allow easy conversion spread over three generations. But in general they were less adaptable and less successful than the Christians. It was not always a bitter struggle. In Palestine itself Jews and Christians were willing to employ the same artisans to make non-pagan mosaics for synagogues and for churches.[1]

The mode of evolution of the Jews had now decisively changed. The early Jewish nation had been a complete society, gaining its recruits for their gift of filling a niche in a balanced society, a gift, as we may say, of *complementation*. When they became an oppressed minority in a foreign country they were selected for their religious devotion. Those who were not passionately and innately and genetically disposed to follow the precepts and respect the discipline of their spiritual guides, the priestly caste, left the group. Thereby the group became purified and selected, culled and winnowed, as much as any thoroughbred race improved by artificial breeding with a particular purpose, bent or aptitude in view.[2]

Thus the Jewish community slowly lost much of its national class-stratified character. But in doing so it certainly intensified its racial character. No one stayed a member of an alien and distrusted minority unless he felt bound to it by ties of kinship: temperamental or intellectual, professional or cultural, but above all ancestral. At the same time the numbers of Jews increased through their own character and training, their social and religious coherence, their superior fertility, orderly family life and cleanly habits, all of them controlled by the law as interpreted by their learned men.

Conversely Christian doctrines were not designed or developed to encourage either sexual propagation or hygienic survival. Christian numbers therefore, we have to suppose, increased solely by conversion. The Christian conversion meant, at first entirely, and later partly, hybridization between Jews and Gentiles. Thus there was a gradual infiltration of Jewish ancestry or Jewish genes into the Christian community. It is a process which has continued to

[1] Kitzinger (1965).

[2] As Gibbon puts it for his purpose (ch. XV): 'As the protection of Heaven was deservedly withdrawn from the ungrateful race, their faith acquired a proportionable degree of vigour and purity.'

this day. There was however a breeding barrier between those who remained Jews and those who became Christians; hence the two genetic communities diverged rather than converged. In both religious and secular character they stood opposed. In Egypt, and nowhere else so clearly, their opposition was heightened by the contrast of language and social class between the Jews who spoke the more learned Greek and the Christians who adopted the more popular Egyptian, that is Coptic. The Alexandrian Jews, unadulterated by crossing, retained the specialized gifts of craftsmanship, writing and trade, and therefore were able and willing to move about very widely. The Christian Copts, their hybrid cousins, remained strictly settled and have never migrated from Egypt. At least not since they set out, perhaps competing with a less successful Jewish mission, to convert Ethiopia in the second century.

What held the Jews together during these centuries of dispersal? Certainly their own religious writings and the learned men who interpreted them. But it was necessary that the learned men should have some central authority to guide them. This authority partly came from the retreat of Babylon beyond the dangerous reach of Rome. But it partly had to be reconstituted by the Romans themselves. They needed a representative who could speak for the Jews and they gave the office of Patriarch to the House of Hillel, a family of Pharisees. In them it continued hereditary for ten generations and from a centre at Tiberias they established a body of teachers, known as Rabbis, less strictly hereditary than themselves who have continued to mould the doctrines of Judaism to suit the needs of the Jews in a changing world down to this day. During those early years they were concerned above all with matching the development of Christianity and with replacing the ritual of sacrifice by the more intelligent practice of charity; that is with generally modernizing the religion which could now be freed from the control of the old priesthood.

The *Torah*, which is both the Law and the Light of the Jewish religion, had already a double character. It had a written part which was contained in the Pentateuch. The unwritten part consisted of the traditional beliefs of the Jewish people, which had been debated between rival sects of teachers, the Sadducees and Pharisees. Now it came to be written by the Rabbis, and established as orthodox teaching. This last development was parallel with the growth of Christian teaching under the Fathers of the Church and it reached its peak in the writings of Maimonides (A.D. 1135–1204).

II. THE ROMAN CHURCH

The greatest change to which Judaism had to be accommodated was of course the adoption of Christianity as the official religion by Constantine. Jealousy of the Jews, fear of their more ancient doctrines which had largely been embezzled, as it were, by the Christians, required that their religion should be destroyed. In order to do so it was necessary to destroy them as a race, a race inheriting the guilt of having killed the God of the Christians, a race whose guilt might however be compounded by conversion of the individual to Christianity.

To achieve this end it was not enough to insult the Jewish people and all

Jewish institutions formally and officially on all possible occasions, secular and religious. It was also necessary to prohibit all attempts to convert Christians or pagans to Judaism; and equally to prohibit all attempts to prevent the conversion of Jews to Christianity. Both these offences became punishable by death. Intermarriage without conversion was of course also forbidden. For the aggressive Christian majority, the war which had been a cold war for two centuries now became a hot war between two mutually exclusive breeding groups. So it has remained intermittently down to the present day.

In their social relations with the Jews, Christian communities followed the lead of their rulers, the kings and the Church. There were a few wise rulers, such as Theodoric the Goth and King James of Aragon, the Emperor Frederick II, and later the merchant governors of the Netherlands; and a few wise popes such as Gregory the Great. These understood the peculiar benefits which the Jews could confer on the commerce and on the culture of their societies. To Charlemagne they were indispensable as ambassadors, to his officials as traders: for them *mercatores* and *Judaei* meant the same thing. His son, Louis the Pious, seeing that the Jews were unprotected, gave them his passport and assigned them to suitable quarters in his cities.

Protection, however, as we have seen, always carries with it the seeds of subjection. Slowly the Jews found themselves in the position of serfs. As serfs however they were not a rural majority but an urban minority more skilled and, in a bookish sense, more civilized than the majority of Christians who crowded around them. These people were now the chattels of the sovereign, a sovereign usually in need of funds which they alone could supply.

Muslim viziers had already discovered to what good use the Jews could be put in these circumstances. The Jews were, until the thirteenth century, almost the only people in Europe who knew how to count money and generally calculate proportions and rates of interest, and handle precious metals. They were also indeed the only people who could escape the Church's prohibition of usury. They were thus the self-made instruments of public taxation. Later, as we shall see, the Church took over this role.

So it was that, when the climate changed, and the Church found itself embroiled with Muslim infidels and also Christian heretics, a third kind of crusade against the Jews seemed likely to be popular as well as profitable. In the resulting persecution, Church, king and mob co-operated in marking out their victims and in taking their spoils.

The first important step was taken by a very politic pope, Innocent III, whom we shall meet again. In 1215, he ordered that all Jews, men and women, should wear a distinguishing badge, commonly a yellow badge, to set them apart as a public danger or, alternatively, as public victims. This policy took several centuries to reach its climax and its goal. In the cities of Europe, of the middle ages, as in all previous ages, the different races, religions and trades, which as we have seen are always connected, were segregated in different quarters. Gradually the Jewish quarters—later known in Italy as ghettoes (perhaps from *borghetto*) were publicly owned, legally confined in area, and sometimes walled, gated and locked at night. Protection and subjection were thus completely identified.

Ghettoes were characteristic of the cities in the innumerable but variable principalities of Italy and Germany. In Italy, where the Jews had been preceded for over a thousand years by Cretans, Etruscans, Greeks and Hellenized peoples, the economic success of the Jews, and also the public reaction to it, were less marked than elsewhere. For this reason the Roman Jewish community, protected by pope and people, has remained alone in Europe almost undisturbed for two thousand years.[1] Elsewhere the resistance to the Jews has been based on popular suspicion of mysterious Jewish qualities and was naturally proportionate to popular ignorance. Now in Western Europe there were powerful kings who knew how to exploit this situation. They thought they would do better to attack the Jews directly. After having extracted the heaviest possible ransoms, playing cat-and-mouse many times, the kings of England and France expelled the whole unconverted community.[2] The kings of Spain and Portugal welcomed the refugees (Froissart tells us); but they turned them out as soon as they had expelled the Muslim invaders in 1492.

At the end of the twelfth century, before this upheaval had begun, Benjamin of Tudela could leave his native Navarre and travel freely, visiting the chief cities of Europe and Africa, Persia and India. His descendants would find themselves harried from one Christian country to another, uncertain of any protection and liable to insult and blackmail wherever they went. The people responsible for these changed conditions were quite unaware of the causes at work or the consequences that would ensue. What were they?

Both the causes and the consequences concern the conversion of the Jews to Christianity. For forty generations the Jews had now been settled, first in pagan, and then in Christian Europe. For over thirty generations they had been under pressure to be converted to Christianity. Owing to loss by conversion, no doubt, the Jews in Europe probably remained constant in number at about a million from the time of Constantine to the sixteenth century.[3] With each succeeding generation the residue had become more resistant to conversion. Every time the Jews were persecuted, every time they were expelled, individuals had to choose between abandoning their homes and their possessions or their religion and their community. Every time individuals made this choice the ancient Hebrew principle of winnowing came into play. Every time the residue of Jews, faithful to their religion and their community, were those who had survived selectively the alternative appeal of the Christian world with its easier rules and richer opportunities.

On the other hand with each succeeding generation the Christian majority had been leavened by hybridization with the converted Jews. As Jewish society tightened and narrowed, Christian society loosened and broadened. As Jews became more obedient to their Rabbis, Christians became more disobedient to their bishops. The learning and scholarship, the commercial

[1] L. C. Dunn (1959).

[2] From England 16,000 'serfs of the Royal Household', descendants of the Jews who came with the Conqueror to set his financial house in order, were said to have been expelled by Edward I in 1291. It was an overestimate according to Cecil Roth (1964); some were supposed to have remained in Oxford as a secret community.

[3] Parkes (1962).

talent and technical skill of the Jews had passed into what were becoming the professional classes of Christian Europe, even in Italy into the governing classes. The Christian community was now genetically competent to do the work the Jews had done in the past. In London Lombard Street replaced Jewry. And in the matter of taxation the Church had to raise the funds and incur the odium that the Jews had for so long collected and suffered. The Jews, as princes and bishops now believed, had been transformed: from a nefarious sect they had become an expendable race.

Before we follow the Jews out of Western Europe we must consider in a longer perspective what they had done there. The process of squeezing them into Christian society was in genetic effect the same kind of process as the earlier penetration of the western Mediterranean by the Greeks. Both were in an opposite direction and both were opposed in method to the prevailing contemporary processes of eastward military conquest. Both were part of the movement of literate and articulate, skilled and intellectual people out of the Ancient East and their merging with the more primitive peoples of Northern and Western Europe. It was this movement which was responsible for the spread of urban societies. At the end of this movement the Greeks had disappeared: they were messengers. But the Jews had obstinately refused to disappear: they were custodians. However much they were squeezed, a residue remained as effective as ever in treasuring what they held sacred, their culture and the memory of the home where their ancestors had created it. The reason why this is so depends in part on the history of what followed from their expulsion.

III. SPAIN AND THE SEPHARDIM

Spain is, after Ireland, the most isolated country in Europe. It is in part for this reason that its people have a genetically uncompromising character in which they are equalled only by the genetically isolated Jews. And this character has been expressed most violently in the long history of their relations with the Jews. When Reccared, King of the Visigoths, who came to power in Spain in 586, gave up his Arian heresy and made his peace with the Pope he was establishing a desirable union of intermarriage between his own military governing class of illiterate invaders and the earlier literate governing class derived from Celtiberian chieftains and from Roman, Phoenician and Byzantine colonists. It was not necessary for him at the same time to forbid the intermarriage of Christians with Jews. But in 589 he did so. His bishops were afraid of the expansion of Judaism by marriage and breeding. And in doing so he laid down the principle, so often to be reaffirmed, of the complete segregation of the religions and races in Spain.

The relation of Christian rulers with Jewish and Muslim subjects became a serious problem with the reconquest of southern Spain, except Granada, between 1220 and 1251. The crusade which appeared to inspire the reconquest was continued by a policy of conversion. The converted Muslims (or Moors) were known as *Moriscos*, the converted Jews by the more insulting name of *Marranos* (or pigs).

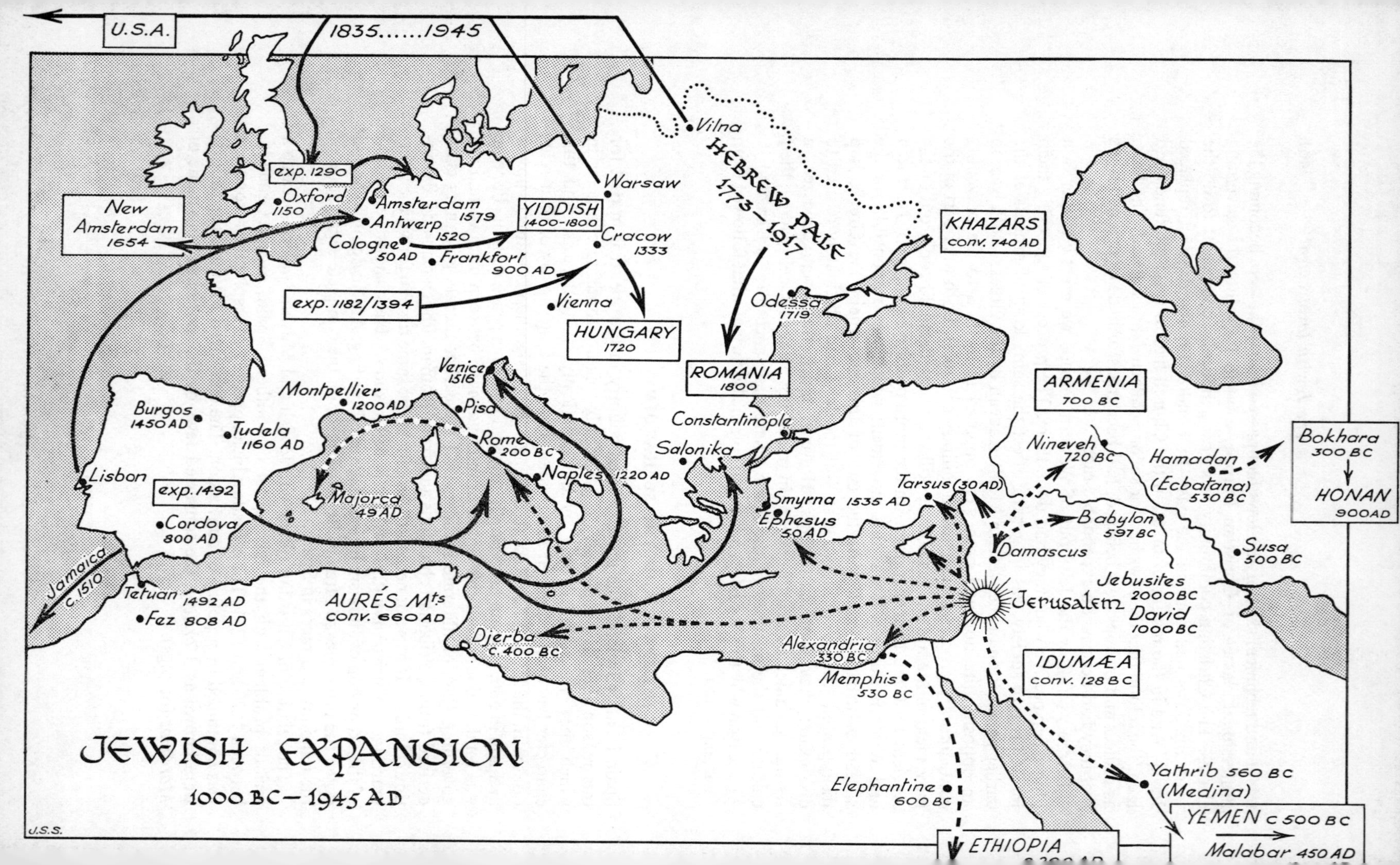
JEWISH EXPANSION
1000 BC – 1945 AD
U.S.A.
1835……1945
exp. 1290
Oxford 1150
New Amsterdam 1654
Amsterdam 1579
Antwerp 1520
Cologne 50 AD
Frankfort 900 AD
YIDDISH 1400-1800
Warsaw
Cracow 1333
Vilna
HEBREW PALE 1773–1917
exp. 1182/1394
Vienna
HUNGARY 1720
Odessa 1719
KHAZARS conv. 740 AD
ROMANIA 1800
ARMENIA 700 BC
Venice 1516
Montpellier 1200 AD
Pisa
Burgos 1450 AD
Tudela 1160 AD
Rome 200 BC
Naples 1220 AD
Constantinople
Salonika
Lisbon
exp. 1492
Majorca 49 AD
Cordova 800 AD
Smyrna 1535 AD
Ephesus 50 AD
Tarsus (30 AD)
Nineveh 720 BC
Hamadan (Ecbatana) 530 BC
Bokhara 300 BC
HONAN 900 AD
Babylon 597 BC
Damascus
Susa 500 BC
Jebusites 2000 BC
David 1000 BC
Jerusalem
Jamaica c. 1510
Tetuan 1492 AD
Fez 808 AD
AURÉS Mts conv. 660 AD
Djerba c. 400 BC
Alexandria 330 BC
Memphis 530 BC
IDUMÆA conv. 128 BC
Elephantine 600 BC
Yathrib 560 BC (Medina)
ETHIOPIA
YEMEN c 500 BC
Malabar 450 AD
J.S.S.

Table 29. *Jewish Migrations*

1. BABYLONIAN CAPTIVITY: 721–530 B.C.	
[721 B.C.	Israel deported to Assyrian Empire]
597	Judah deported to Babylon: Temple destroyed
	Jewish colonies in Elephantine, Yathrib, Djerba
2. PERSIAN and GREEK DISTRIBUTION: 530–70 B.C.	
	Jews move throughout Empires of Cyrus and Alexander and old Greek, Etruscan and Phoenician colonies (e.g. Crimea, Spain, Italy, North Africa and Yemen)
	Jewish quarter in Alexandria 330 B.C.
3. ROMAN DISPERSAL: 70 B.C.–A.D. 320	
[216	Jews probably in Rome]
48	Caesar's charter of religious freedom for Jews
A.D. 6	Jewish provinces (Judaea, Samaria and Idumea) put under direct Roman control
70	Jerusalem sacked by Titus
135	City razed; Temple destroyed by Hadrian
	Jews dispersed throughout Empire and to Babylon: first waves reach Ethiopia *c.* A.D. 200, Malabar *c.* A.D. 450,
313	Edict of Milan: Jews become *secta nefaria*
4. MUSLIM DISTRIBUTION: A.D. 640–1400	
640–808	Jews in new cities of Cairo, Baghdad and Fez
740	Second wave colonizes Spain; A.D. 850: Sicily
5. CATHOLIC DISPERSAL: A.D. 1096–1880	
[589	King Reccared, Arian Visigoth, reconciled with Rome, prohibits marriage with Jews]
[820	Louis the Pious introduces 'protection' of Jews]
1096	Crusade massacres begin
1215	Jewish badge } imposed by Papal Bull
1556–1870	Roman ghetto } imposed by Papal Bull
1182–1394	Expulsions from France (1290 from England)
1133	Jews invited to Poland
1472	Establishment of Spanish Inquisition
1492, 1496	Expulsion from Spain
1492	Jews escape to Italy and Turkey; 1520, invited to Antwerp
1579	To Amsterdam; 1656: to England
1789	Admitted to France with rights
6. ORTHODOX PERSECUTION: 1762–1917	
1762	Hebrew Pale decree in Russia prohibits movement of Jews into old territories from Poland, Bessarabia, Tartary and Caucasus
1825	Quota conscription of Jewish boys at 12
1881	Alexander III: pogroms and expulsions begin in chief Russian cities
7. NAZI PERSECUTION (1933–1945)	
8. COMMUNIST PERSECUTION (see ch. 24)	

Fig. 17. The Jewish Dispersal or Expansion

The principal movements of Jews from 1000 B.C. up to 1945 with dates of arrival or flourishing in different countries.

conv.: dates of conversion of Gentile peoples.

exp.: dates of expulsion of Jews by Christian states.

After Parkes, Teller, Dimont, Graves and Hogarth and others

This policy was enforced with varying degrees of enthusiasm and success and also varying impact on different social classes of the Jews. At the top moderation was necessary. Burgos Cathedral, the climax of Gothic architecture in Spain, was built in the fifteenth century. It was built (as Sitwell supposes) by Jewish architects from Cologne; and it was first governed by a converted Jewish bishop. And it seems certain that Jewish navigators and craftsmen, especially from Majorca, assisted Prince Henry, Columbus and Vasco da Gama in their great enterprises. Two steps in the growth of persecution were however notable. One was the establishment of the Spanish Inquisition in 1478. By Papal Bull the King of Spain was authorized to control the prosecution, conviction and execution of heretics. This institution undertook to organize the *autos-da-fé* or 'acts of faith' which continued for three centuries; that is until the French invasion of 1808 put an end to them. These ceremonies were attended by the king, the court, the clergy and the people. Thus human sacrifice by gladiatorial combat which had been suppressed as a pagan Roman ritual by Christian influence was now restored in its full vigour by the Christian Roman Church.[1]

To this attack Jews were almost immune but the *conversos* were highly vulnerable. For experience soon showed that conversion was no cure for unbelief. The source was believed to be ineradicable or, as we might say, genetic. There was no remedy but expulsion or extinction. The unconverted were expelled by decree in 1492. Naturally the converted could not be expelled: they could only be watched and punished. And when they happened to be men of wealth or worth, or even like certain Majorcans indispensable for enterprises like the great navigations, they were likely to be protected.

In the course of the following twenty years what happened to the Spanish Jews who survived has been roughly estimated, according to Dimont, as follows:

Survived in Spain as Marranos:	*Expelled and Received Abroad:*
50,000	45,000 in Turkey.
	15,000 in North Africa and Egypt.
	10,000 in southern France and Holland.
	10,000 in northern Italy.
	10,000 in South America, Jamaica, and unknown places.

There were others who went to Morocco when the Moriscos, who had been sheltering them, were themselves expelled in 1609.

What happened to the Marranos? Their history was diverse. The poorer Jews, who were mostly the earlier converts, abandoned all Jewish rites and it seems that in the cities they were often successful in losing themselves in the lower classes of Spanish society. In remote and isolated villages however their fate was different. Their scriptures were lost, their Rabbis departed and their prayers became defective and confused. But they clung to their festivals and their secret rites and maintained their separate character, their separate breeding communities. Circumcision with its incriminating evidence was abandoned;

[1] See Unwin (1960); Dimont (1962), and Nada (1962) on Charles II, ch. 23.

Abraham and Esther became saints; but the converted Jews remain to this day as indestructible racial societies concealed in Spain and Portugal.[1]

The literate and well-to-do Jews were expelled after the edict of 1492. They became the *Sephardim*, the 'exiles from afar'. But some were able to remain in Spain by being converted immediately after the edict of expulsion. They were not however allowed to forget their ancestral delinquency. Thirty generations of separate breeding had, as we have seen, strengthened the initial difference. It was therefore natural enough (on his assumptions) for Philip II to demand that the converted Jews and their descendants should not be allowed to exist as a secret and underground movement. Such cryptic Jews should for ever wear a yellow hat, be barred from all offices of profit and honour and all possibilities of intermarriage with authentic long-term non-Jewish Christians.[2]

This reminder of their vulnerable status led to further emigration. Among Marranos there was the mother of Michel de Montaigne. There was also Dr Ruy Lopez, the physician of Queen Elizabeth, falsely charged and executed at Tyburn in 1594.[3] And there was a stream of Marranos who, on leaving Spain, proved to be unconverted. They passed mainly to Antwerp and Amsterdam and largely contributed to the cultural and commercial triumphs of the Netherlands during the coming two centuries.

The main body of exiles however were the unconverted Jews who accepted the hospitality of the Ottoman sultan in Turkey and Egypt. Bajazet II declared that these people would enrich him and at the same time impoverish Spain. He proved to be right. They settled in Constantinople, Salonika and Smyrna; later they followed the Turks to Palestine and Egypt. In these countries they provided the professional classes needed by the young Empire as a substitute for the displaced Christian Greeks.

Among the Jewish colony in Turkey conditions changed in the next century so as once more to expose the disadvantages for a rich minority of the Jewish faith. In the year 1648 a revelation came to a certain Jew living in Smyrna named Shabbetai Zvi. This man declared himself to be the awaited Messiah. He was captured and, renouncing his pretensions, adopted Islam. But his followers, the Dönmeh, constituted a small sect which still survives as a kind of Islamic Marrano. Openly Muslims, privately educated, and racially Jews, the Dönmeh were bound to be a source of political unrest. Their time came after eight generations.

By 1907 the ordinary Jews of Salonika numbered 60,000 or half the population. It was the largest and most coherent colony in Turkey. Until they were nearly destroyed in 1943 they retained, with the characteristic conservatism of inbred communities, both the Jewish dress and the archaic Castilian speech they had used in fifteenth-century Spain. But they included a

[1] See Sitwell (1950); Novinsky and Paulo (1967).

[2] See Judd Teller (1966). The goldsmiths (*Xueta*) survive as a double professional caste in two streets of Palma, Majorca. They are the strictest Catholics and also the purest Jews. Charles III twice revoked (1773, 1782) racial discrimination and the prohibition of intermarriage against Jews. But in Majorca his decrees were, as such decrees usually are, without effect (Graves and Hogarth, 1965).

[3] See Lytton Strachey (1928).

group of Dönmeh and these proved to be the moving spirits behind the Young Turk Revolution of 1908 which heralded the end of the Ottoman Empire.[1]

The Jews who left Spain or stayed in Spain, converted or unconverted, and lost their lives for their race and their religion, were few in number. But, as Parkes and also Galton have put it, Spain lost more with them than she gained with her Empire in the Indies. Her decay proceeded step by step with the suppression of heresy and infidelity and the hunting out of the Jews. Spain never recovered from her victory over the Jews.

IV. POLAND AND THE ASHKENAZIM

The Jews who were forced or squeezed out of England, France and Western Europe in the thirteenth century benefited from the misfortunes of the Christians in Eastern Europe at that time. In the middle of the century Tartar invaders had sacked and burnt the wooden settlements and towns of Poland. The Teutonic knights had restored a Christian and settled government but between the illiterate Slavonic-speaking peasants and their equally illiterate German-speaking rulers and protectors there was no satisfactory means of communication. There was no professional class, literate or technical, to organize, to administer and generally to provide. Western townsmen were invited to come and fill the gap, to build brick towns where the wooden settlements had stood. To Cracow alone there came a stream of Germans and Dutch, Flemings and Walloons, 'Gallics' and Italians, Hungarians and Moravians, and a few Scots. And with them also came Jews. First there were refugees from the Adriatic ports. A century later Casimir the Great (who himself took and loved and perhaps converted a Jewish mistress) gave his royal guarantees to the Jews and they came in larger numbers. They knew themselves as *Ashkenazim* which was the Hebrew name for Germans.

Rarely, since the time of Alexander, had there been seen so clearly the formation of cities peopled by one race embedded in a countryside peopled by another race and governed by a military caste of a third race. Each race spoke a different language. Elsewhere the Jews had spoken the language of the governing class but here the Germanic rulers were outnumbered by the Jews and the Jews were outnumbered by the Slavonic serfs. So they created a new language which they knew and we know as Yiddish. It was Low German from the Rhineland spiced with Aramaic from the Talmud of the Rabbis and occasional Polish where necessary. But it was unwritten: the folk language of an illiterate people whose language of learning was written Hebrew.

Only after 1792 did people think of putting this literature into writing. With the kingdom of Poland divided between Prussia, Austria and Russia, the ancient political structure on which the Yiddish-speaking Jews had built had now disappeared.

The Jews who had provided the bulk of the professional classes in Poland thus found themselves, in place of their Polish patrons or friends, faced with three unfamiliar and hostile governments. The Austrian government could still until 1907 dissolve the marriages of Christians and Jews as illegal.[2] The

[1] Fishberg (1911); Luke (1963).

[2] See Fishberg (1911).

Russian government in varying alliance with the Orthodox Church found almost the only common ground with its people in its method of dealing with the Jews. It confined, harried, expelled and massacred the Jewish population within the territories that it annexed during and after the partition of Poland.[1] The result of these new persecutions was to drive the Jews out of Poland first southwards into Hungary and Rumania and secondly westwards into Germany, England and the United States. The most fruitful of these new migrations was the one which took them into Holland.

Equal civil rights had been given to the Spanish Jews, the Marrano exiles, in Holland during the seventeenth century and the advantages arising were what attracted the less fortunate Jews from Eastern Europe. In Holland therefore the two kinds of Jews, long parted, encountered one another. Both sides were astonished and shocked to discover that if they were indeed still one race they were certainly no longer one tribe or one class. On one side were the well-dressed, well-educated Sephardim, assimilated to the Muslim and Christian upper classes of Spain and Portugal, speaking not only their native *Ladino* but also other literate languages. These were the people who had produced Spinoza. On the other side were the simple old-fashioned Ashkenazim, strict in their traditional discipline, but deviant in their religious rites, following working-class occupations, and speaking nothing but their own uncouth Yiddish dialect. These were people who seemed to have produced nothing. Poverty and isolation, emigration and inbreeding, had brought them so low. Later, however, in easier circumstances and larger communities, they would produce a Heine and a Mendelssohn, a Karl Marx and a family of Rothschilds.

Naturally the Sephardim would have nothing to do with their downtrodden kinsmen. For over a century, behaving like different sects of Christians, they would not pray together, or eat together; still less would they consent to breed together. Between the two branches of Israel there was no intermarriage until 1812, when it had become clear that the junior branch was making good.[2] The two branches geographically isolated for fifty generations had diverged in evolution as we might expect. But why had they diverged so fast and so far?

The reason in general terms is quite clear. The Jews dispersed in the Roman Empire had belonged to different classes of a stratified nation. Within the Empire and its successors they had fitted themselves into different class positions within the developing class structures of different societies, especially Christian and Muslim. The savage selective pressure of success and failure, of conversion and persecution, had compelled the most rapid adaptation. These forces together were potent enough. But in addition they were acting on a community which was at the same time subject to slight hybridization with the Christian or Muslim majority around it.[3]

[1] An account of the persisting social relations of the three races or classes in Russian Poland is given by Isaac Babel for the year 1920.

[2] A Montefiore then married a Cohen (F. M. Wilson, 1959). The Rothschilds (and also the Marxes) met these difficulties later and overcame them (Morton, 1962).

[3] The evidence of this hybridization and flow of genes is that, although Jews in Europe always have different frequencies of blood groups from the Christian

This hybridization so far as it led into the Jewish community was bound to be illegitimate. It was governed by an early and prudent rabbinical pronouncement that any child must be accepted as Jewish if its mother was Jewish.

After the American and French Revolutions outstanding individuals among the Jewish communities of Europe and America were able to take advantage of the rights slowly conferred on Jews. These men were probably the result of the hybridization which had been taking place. Pure Jewish stocks long stabilized in different parts of Europe were in the eighteenth century being mixed very little with non-Jewish people but most thoroughly with one another.[1]

V. BLACK AND WHITE JEWS

At the time of the Roman dispersal, when Jews were scattered over the three continents Jewish Law had failed to forbid polygamy. It had, of course, always been the privilege and the symbol of power and wealth. When the Jews came to be living among Christians it was clear however that if antagonism was to be reduced polygamy had to be abandoned.[2] In Muslim countries however no such question arose and rich Jews like rich Muslims were able to keep a suitable establishment of wives and concubines. The same was true of the Jewish communities that established themselves early in the Christian era in the Yemen, in Abyssinia, and in Malabar. In the absence of Christian persecution such polygamy was bound to mean hybridization, usually by bringing Muslim or pagan women into the Jewish harem. The consequences of this hybridization are to be seen both in the divergence of Asian and African from European populations of Jews and in their convergence on the local non-Jewish populations. These changes express themselves in physical, intellectual and cultural terms which as always are inseparable. They can moreover be put in a graded series. The extremes of this series are found together in the Jews of Cochin.[3]

It seems that groups of Jews had been arriving in India at intervals since the Babylonian Captivity. At Cochin they exist as three colonies, White, Brown and Black all claiming Jewish descent. The White are indeed physically and by blood groups Jewish: they are traders speaking Malayalam and living in Jew Town Street. The Black Jews, who claim long exposure to the sun as the cause of their colour, are obviously Muslim-Hindu hybrids of the local type of Moplahs who acquired Judaism as slaves of the Whites. They have no

populations around them, they depart from the average Jewish frequencies in the direction of these populations: there is a correlation between neighbours, always slight in Europe, larger elsewhere (Mourant, 1954, 1959).

[1] We know for example that the family of Benjamin Disraeli, eminent in architecture, literature and politics, were derived from marriages in England between Italian and Portuguese stocks. Isaac Disraeli, the hybrid product, broke his connection with the Sephardic synagogue. But his son, baptized, asserted his connection with the Jewish race, for example in *Coningsby* and *Sybil* (see *D.N.B.*).

[2] It was condemned by Rabbi Gershom of Mainz (960–1028); see Parkes (1962).

[3] See Macfarlane (1938); Zinkin (1958); Hutton (1961) also refers to the Ben-i-Israel of Bombay.

priests or teachers of their own but strictly observe and follow the rituals of the White Jews. They themselves exist in two sub-castes. Finally the Brown Jews are half-breeds of the Black and White; they are excluded by both parental groups and largely lapse into Christianity.

Intermediate between White and Black Jews of Cochin are the Jews of the Yemen. They are the result of interbreeding, largely we may suppose polygamous, on the part of Jewish missionary immigrants with their converts before the Muslim or even the Christian era. As was to happen later with Islamic conversion, polygamy and conquest are aspects of a single process. The Yemeni Jews are no longer genetically distinguishable from the Yemeni Muslims: they are one race.

VI. FALASHA AND BALEMBA

The Marranos show how Judaism may survive when the teachers and the scriptures are removed but the race continues pure. The Black Jews show how it may survive when the teachers continue in a separate racial caste. And the Yemeni Jews show how it may survive when teachers and taught are transformed by hybridization. These changes are somewhat different from the sectarian divergences such as those of the Mandaeans or Sabians, the Samaritans and Karaites, and the Tartar sects within the Hebrew Pale in Russia. For they are forms of deterioration due to a breakdown in genetic continuity. They reach the extreme in Africa.

The first authentic penetration of Judaism deep into Africa seems to have led to the conversion of Amharic-speaking people who constituted the ruling class in the Axumite kingdom probably before the Christian era. The converting priests or missionaries may have come by way of Egypt or of the Yemen or even by boat along the Red Sea. They took their name of *Falasha* or 'stranger' presumably from this foreign origin. Their priests translated the Hebrew scriptures into Ethiopic and introduced Jewish rituals and feasts and Jewish synagogues. In the long struggles with pagans, Muslims and Christians over two thousand years many principles and practices were exchanged. When they were finally torn apart, the Falashas were left with a goddess Sanbat instead of the Jewish sabbath, the Christian practice of monasticism, and three sects each with its own high priest. The Christians were left with the distinction between clean and unclean animals but, more important, they were left in power. The Falashas were deprived of their kings and reduced in numbers to a fraction and in status to serfdom: but, after all this, still rigorously preserving their genetic and religious exclusiveness.

For us the significance of the Falashas is that they have introduced into the heart of Africa the Hebrew scriptures and observances together with the same skilled crafts for which the Jews were to become famous in Europe. Not only in pottery but in weaving and masonry and above all in metal work the Falashas excel other peoples of Central Africa. They have the appearance of being the vestiges of a nation, diverse in colour and character, a nation which at one time had supported the culture of Axum.[1]

[1] See Seligman and others.

From the progenitors of the modern Falasha we might expect that castes or tribes of skilled craftsmen would have made their way all over Africa but notably into the iron- and gold-bearing regions of Rhodesia. There, between the thirteenth and the sixteenth centuries, they might have taken part in creating the Empire whose traces are seen in the fortresses of Zimbabwe. The evidence that this is what happened is contained most clearly in the existing tribe of Balemba.[1]

The Balemba are a caste associated today with certain Venda and Suto tribes of the Transvaal and Rhodesia. They are distinguished by their Semitic or Hamitic features from their negro neighbours. They have no chiefs of their own but serve the Venda and Suto Chiefs, by whom they are valued owing to their skill in metal work and pottery. They do no cultivation or stockbreeding and speak their own as well as the Venda language. They follow the Jewish rules for the kosher killing and eating of flesh. Their initiation rites include circumcision, a service which they also perform for the Venda. They forbid the homosexual practices customary in the initiation camps of true Bantu. Their legends recall a covenant between God and his chosen people given to a great king with sacred symbols which are still kept by an hereditary guardian. They also recall, like other Bantu peoples but more accurately, their migration from the northern lakes and forests and their life in a Zimbabwe city. The Venda and all the strangers outside their breeding group they describe as pagans or gentiles (*vhasenzi*).

The Balemba are one step further removed from the Jews of the ancient world than the Falasha. That step consists simply in the connected loss of their scriptures and of the teachers who could copy and read them. Almost everything else they have kept: the tribal rites and the manual skills, the physical appearances and the legendary history. All this preservation they owe to their rejection of breeding outside their genetic community, a rejection made possible only by the fact that their neighbours respected and valued them as a genetic community, as a little race of their own. No doubt other traces of Judaism still exist scattered, unrecognized, over Africa.

VII. NEW ISRAEL

To the Romans in the time of Titus, and to the Jews alike, the clash between the imperial and the national ideas seemed inevitable and compromise impossible. Men capable of compromise, like Josephus, were rare. In a sense we may say that a compromise was reached 250 years later in the adoption of Christianity by Constantine. But that compromise could not have been reached at any earlier time; and even then it satisfied only the Christians, and not all of them.

Meanwhile, for the Jews, until the day when they might return to their Shrine, the destruction of Jerusalem was a crime which could not be forgiven. Could not be forgiven by whom? By those whose forefathers had created Judaism; by the race which created the culture of what was to them a Holy Place.

[1] See N. J. van Warmelo and Schapera (ch. 28).

The Zionist leaders of 1800 years later were compelled to pursue the course they took by an historic sense innate and also better nourished than that of any other group of people in the world; more particularly of the Christians and Muslims who might wish to share these Holy Places. They knew what their people had suffered. It was no worse than the sufferings of poor and unprotected people anywhere for they have usually been ignored by the historians who write for governing classes. But these people had a genetic and cultural continuity which stored their wrongs in a collective memory and gave them inevitably a racial character.

When after two generations of Zionist endeavour the State of Israel was born in 1948 it was thus inevitably based on the belief of the founders that the Jews were in some sense one race. How else could they be said to have a homeland? And were they not descended from common ancestors through sixty or seventy generations of dispersal?

But during these generations the Jews had been a people governed by others; a people depending for their survival on their ability to fit into societies from which they were racially excluded; and on their ability to evade persecution, pagan, Christian and Muslim. The Sephardim were too well off where they were to return. But the Ashkenazim, when they arrived in Israel, had an unexpected reunion. Differences, far greater than those that separated them from the Sephardim, now separated them from the mixed and hybrid Jews of Asia and Africa, or from some of their brethren in Europe. The European Jews, interbred and rapidly evolving through this interbreeding, included some of the most advanced as well as some of the most backward people in the world. And in Jerusalem itself a modern society found itself side by side with an orthodox community, *Mea Shearim*, which now continued as a beleaguered ghetto.

Surprising as this discovery was it meant that the people of the new state were genetically differentiated just like the classes of any other modern nation. Their difference from other nations lay in their knowledge of their own past, a past so close to that of civilization itself.

Part VII

Societies in Conflict

The modern European world arose from several connected upheavals of thought and activity. They were the Reformation, the Renaissance and the Scientific and Industrial Revolutions. All of them led to social conflicts and political revolutions which were the work of particular individuals. These individuals were bred by, and worked in, particular social classes which evolved over a period of many generations subject to the different religious beliefs which held them together. Each revolutionary experience taught later revolutionaries how to improve the methods they used first in achieving revolution and then in preventing its recurrence.

21

THE REFORMATION AND THE CHURCH

I. REVOLT IN THE SOUTH

a. Clerical

THE MIDDLE AGES may be seen as the period of nearly a thousand years in which Europe lived under a double government, spiritual and secular. In this government or empire the power and authority of Church and of princes were on the surface in perpetual opposition but under the surface in perpetual collusion.

The longer this state of polarization continued the more complex became both the opposition and the collusion. This we see in their relations to the growth of forces which were opposed to both but to which the small national authorities could adapt themselves more readily than could the unified authority of the Church. These were the forces leading to the Reformation.

The forces that were at work were felt by both the ruling class and the mass of the people. But they had first to be put into words by educated men. These were bound to be mostly men who studied in universities and at first themselves belonged to the priesthood and depended on the Church for their living. One of the earliest of them was Berengarius of Tours (999–1088) who argued publicly for forty years with Church Councils, with Lanfranc and with Pope Gregory VII himself that transubstantiation was against the scriptures, against the Fathers, and even against reason. Another was the Franciscan John of Fidanza (1221–1274) who criticized the sale of indulgences to sinners, but nevertheless became a bishop, a cardinal and a saint. Yet another was Thomas Gascoigne (1403–1458) who used his position as Chancellor of the University of Oxford not only to pursue heretics but to argue hotly (and rightly it would seem) that bishops ought not to live, as they did, on the sale of licences to priests for the keeping of concubines.

These were common sense and popular grounds of complaint against the

Church's misuse of its authority. But quite another ground of criticism appeared when scholars were able to examine the documentary evidence on which the Church based the authority itself. It then appeared that there was nothing in the Bible to show that God approved of popes or even of kings. And as for the later evidence, a large part of it was fabricated: the Church had been sustained historically and legally by a programme of invention accumulating over a period of about seven hundred years.

The opportunities which the growing Church had offered, in the writing of history and the drawing of legal, social and political conclusions from it, had naturally, from the time of the Evangelists, attracted to its employment literate men, of whose talents in western Christendom it ultimately acquired a monopoly. When these faithful scholars noticed the disadvantages to the Faith arising from defects in the records, there was no possibility of criticism which might deter them from making good the defects. It was obvious that a letter must have been written by Pope Clement I in Rome to James, the brother of Christ, in Jerusalem explaining how Peter, on whom the Church was founded (Matthew 16: 18), had bequeathed the Church to him and his successors. The absence of this letter having been discovered, a century later, its loss was repaired by a plausible reconstruction. And on this reconstruction the spiritual authority of the bishops of Rome came to be based wherever its authenticity was accepted, that is to say throughout the western world.

As years passed by, the business of renovating, repairing and expanding the archives of the pope had become an industry in Rome with branches in dioceses such as Rheims and Mainz connected with northern kings. Books of decrees, of which the later were genuine but the earlier false, came into circulation a few centuries after the demise of their supposed authors.

The climax of this practice had been reached during the critical period when King Pippin of the Franks and his son were negotiating with successive popes for the mutual recognition of their secular and spiritual sovereignties, a period which terminated with the coronation of Charlemagne by the pope, in Rome on Christmas Day 800. The critical document in this negotiation had been the so-called *Donation of Constantine*, wherein the converted Roman Emperor was said to have contritely surrendered the whole of his imperial power to the Bishop of Rome.[1]

With the growth of universities in Padua and Paris during the twelfth century new opinions began to find expression about the authenticity of documents. Authors independent of the papal offices were now happy to take sides with kings and emperors against the Church. It was through their connection with these universities that two great contemporary critics, Dante (1265–1321) and Marsiglio (1270–1342), were led first to expose the clerical forgeries and then to dispute the foundations of the Canon Law and the papal power.

The result was to release a stream of revelations, spread over the succeeding centuries. There was pathos and also irony in the historical contrast which

[1] In the crisis of his confession wetting, it was claimed, the imperial garments. Gibbon's ironical account is extended and confirmed by the detailed modern studies of Ullmann. See also Howell Smith (1950).

then appeared. There were those poor, weak, early popes using secret fraud to protect themselves from their powerful enemies. But in doing so, they had exposed their rich and often vicious successors to the attacks of an unforeseen foe, the scholars of a revived learning.[1] Before these academic criticisms had fully developed however attacks from two other quarters had found a vulnerable target.

b. Secular

One of these attacks came from within western society. It was the work of Peter Waldo, a merchant of Lyons, who embraced poverty, preached the Christian virtues and found himself in the year 1170 the leader of an heretical sect. His humble followers, the Waldensians, were hunted out of the cities and took refuge in many remote places but chiefly in the valley of the Durance. Here they remained until they were massacred in 1545, but some again escaped to even remoter valleys in Piedmont.

From time to time during the following four centuries their messengers and missionaries have reminded northern governments (notably on one occasion John Milton, the Latin Secretary in London) that protest against the Church was possible even in Italy. They have also shown us that heretical beliefs and customs were capable of sustaining viable and socially complete communities in several parts of Europe.[2]

The other attack came when a body of strange missionaries penetrated into the cities of Western Europe from the east. These people were derived from the Bogomils (Bougres to the French) whose tombs we may still see in Bosnian Serajevo. They owed their survival first to the conflict in the Balkans between east and west and later to the toleration of the Turkish invaders. From Christianity they took the New Testament but they rejected the divinity of Christ and the authority of bishops together with the saints and all their images. From Thracian Orphism they may have derived a belief in the transmigration of souls or metempsychosis. They were described by the Church as Manichaeans, following Justinian's classification of heresies. From the Manichaeans they seem indeed to have taken the notion of a Kingdom of Satan from which one escaped only by forswearing material pleasures including the eating of flesh, the making of war and the propagation of the species. This extreme of virtue (or perhaps perversion) was usually postponed by their followers, the *Credentes*, until later in life when they were solemnly initiated as Cathari or *Perfecti*.[3]

The sect as a whole were not celibate missionaries. They advanced by conversion and also by breeding. They converted masses of people of all classes.

[1] The business or industry of inventing the relics of saints is analogous with that of faking historical documents since both were necessary supports for the Catholic Church. It began much earlier however and it has continued much later. Moreover, it was only in response to the Reformation that the industry moved west and became localized in Rome.

[2] E.g. Guardia Piemontese near the Albanian colony of Lungro in Calabria (*The Times*, June 7, 1965; see Douglas, 1915).

[3] Heer (1961); see also Coles (1968) and Brereton (1968).

They did so by assimilating the diverse heresies of the Rhineland, Flanders, and Champagne. But they reached their climax in Provence whose people were (and still are) so strongly contrasted in race, culture, speech and politics with their northern neighbours. It is a contrast which derives from their pre-Roman peasantry, their Roman colonization, and their post-Roman Visigothic nobility, and perhaps even from the effects of the Saracen invasion. The Counts of Toulouse, the citizens of Albi and the peasants of Languedoc were in various ways disillusioned with the profit-making devices, the Latin liturgy, and the foreign speech of the Roman clergy. But nobody objected to the sharing of parish churches between local Catholics and local Cathari.[1] The respect which the Cathari, like the Waldenses, paid to women, and to the idea of profane love celebrated by their troubadours was taken as a challenge to the system of the Roman priesthood as well as to the habits of the military governing class, Frankish and Norman. And it is evident that, when cities so rich as those of Languedoc added a doctrine of pacifism to their heresy, predatory attack could not be long delayed. It was intolerable that unarmed people should dare to repudiate the principle of the Crusades.

The attempt to extirpate the Catharic sect, whom we know as Albigensians, quickly followed. It was in three parts. The first part was casual and local: denunciation in Rheims in 1157, burning in Cologne in 1163, flogging in Oxford.[2] The second part began when the Pope, in 1209, denounced the sect as heretical and proclaimed a Crusade. The Norman-Frankish nobles of northern France thereupon assembled under Simon de Montfort and attacked and occupied the southern province, putting down repeated insurrections.

These campaigns taught the Church and the barons how to raise money, seize land, and assert orthodoxy in a single operation. Its success prepared the way for the third stage of suppression. The popes discovered a substitute for irregular lynching. They invented a body of ecclesiastical law and ceremonial directed by the Holy Office, or Inquisition. It began its work in 1231. It was to be administered by that arm of the Church which, being new and poor, enjoyed most public esteem, namely the mendicant orders of friars, especially the Dominicans.

The practice of the Inquisition in dealing with heresy soon came to be based on that of the usual despotic secular powers of civilized societies, when dealing with treason. It was to extract confessions under torture and to threaten all witnesses for the defence with the same charge as the defendant. On conviction being secured, State officials undertook to burn the condemned and to collect their confiscated property. Church and State were therefore in collusion at all stages. They were partners in a joint and profitable enterprise,[3] which was to play a great part in the development of western society.

Meanwhile, the struggle with the Albigensians had been marked by the

[1] Brian Stone (1964); Peter Bradley (1965). This practice was also followed by Puritan sects in England under the Commonwealth, e.g. in Exeter cathedral, (see Chadwick, 1964).

[2] See J. B. Russell (1965).

[3] The Inquisition continued in Spain until 1834 but had its most painful effects there in the sixteenth century. See Rayner Unwin (1965) for individual details of later Spanish procedure; also Nada (1962).

burning of 180 heretics at Minerve on July 12, 1210, and of 200 more on March 15, 1244, at Montségur. By the sieges and battles and burnings over forty years not only the heresy but also the civilization of Provence were stamped out. Or seemed to have been. But, as with the Waldensians, it would be safer to say that the heresy and the civilization were each dispersed. They were separately dispersed and their literate continuity was broken. But within the abundant folds of European society the scattered fragments were saved in both cultural and genetic senses. Disguised as faithful priests and as less faithful scholars, they hid themselves in safer, remoter and poorer places and they were kept alive until better times should come.

II. REVOLT IN THE NORTH

a. Wycliffe

It was inevitable that a better time and place should be found; that the example of individual criticism and collective dissent should be gathered together in socially more highly organized and literately more coherent forms of protest. This happened within fifty years of the appearance of the works of Dante and Marsiglio; it happened in England, in the University of Oxford; and it happened through the personality of a secular priest, John Wycliffe, a notable scholar and a teacher with a wide following.

At this time, at the end of the reign of Edward III, there was no more discontent with the Church than there had been at the beginning, when rioters had attacked the Abbeys of Bury, St Albans and Abingdon.[1] But now the discontent had moved higher in society and acquired a broader character.

The English people now had a language of their own and, through Langland and Chaucer, they were acquiring a voice of their own, a voice which expressed both social protest and national character. Moreover, for forty years they had been at war with France. Abroad it was a war of plunder. But at home it was a war of liberation from the foreign dominance with which the Church was connected.

At the beginning of the century, in 1309, Philip the Fair, King of France, had persuaded a French Pope to desert Rome and to set up house in Avignon. Here, under French control, he had at once been compelled to connive at the king's use of the Inquisition in destroying the Order of the Templars and confiscating their property. The grounds given were plausibly not so much those of heretical belief as of homosexual practice. French popes, surrounded by French cardinals, continued to serve French policy until they finally returned to Rome in 1377. But the return was followed at once by a split between French and Italian factions and the election of two popes, French and Italian, who competed for power over the next forty years.

All this went on while the popes continued to take English dues and fees and to allot to their own kinsmen the revenues of English sees which they never needed to visit.

To Wycliffe in England the split or schism in the papacy must have seemed the chance of a lifetime, the opportunity for humbling, expelling or destroying

[1] Oxonienses, 1966.

the papacy and thus putting Christendom to rights. The fact that it coincided with the accession of a boy king under the tutelage of divided councillors made it no less of an opportunity. Now was the time therefore to collect the evidence for reform in terms of Church doctrines, and to express its advantages in terms of national politics and finance. Wycliffe was already known as the anti-papal adviser of the king's uncle, John of Gaunt, when Parliament invited him to come to London and state the case for them against paying papal taxes. From this point his development was unavoidable.

As his argument got under way it broadened its scope. What Wycliffe and his followers were demanding meant an end, not merely to paying foreign and absentee bishops and popes, but also to indulgences and confessions, to images, to pilgrimages and crusades. It was not for the priest, said Wycliffe, to ask whether the layman, a sinner, was to be forgiven. On the contrary it was for the layman to ask whether the priest, also a sinner, was to be paid his tithes. Or indeed whether the pope, who was equally a sinner, was to receive taxes.[1]

But, if the tables were to be turned on the Church in this way, if the doctrines of a thousand years were to be revoked, an alternative authority, an older and more exalted source of inspiration must be put in its place. That source, as the reformers knew, was the Bible. Here was a grave obstacle. The priests, at least of the higher class, could read the Vulgate in Jerome's Latin. The nobles, or some of them, could, if they wished, read fragments of the Bible that were translated into French. But for the mass of the people there was nothing. They could not read because there was no English writing for them to read. English prose, apart from pious and platitudinous tracts, did not exist.

In this crisis Wycliffe, with two devoted followers, Nicholas Hereford and John Purvey, recognized that the only basis for a movement of the people against the Church, would be an English translation of the Bible. They accordingly set about the translation of the Vulgate; the task was completed twelve years after Wycliffe's death; that is in 1396. It was an heroic work carried out in secrecy and seclusion.

In its immediate purpose of converting society to a new way of life the translated Bible was thwarted. Its authors were pursued and their work was suppressed. Yet without intention it succeeded in two other achievements. For, as the first example of great prose literature in English, it began, with greater effect than our native poets could have achieved, the separation of the educated language of our people from the mass of popular dialects. And by its example, at the end of a little over a century, it opened the way for transplanting, not only religion but also literature and civilization, from their Mediterranean sources to a new field of development in northern Europe. The ground, of course, had been prepared by a thousand years of northward migration of merchants, craftsmen and scholars. And it was due to this preparation that the result was the most successful literary operation in history.

The other line of attack aimed at the ruling class. Wycliffe believed that he had the support he needed there in the two sons of Edward III, the Black

[1] For the Lollard Conclusions, see Bettenson (1940) and McFarlane (1953).

Prince and John of Gaunt. But the Prince died and when it came to the crunch, John slipped away. Clearly they knew all that Chaucer (whose sister-in-law John of Gaunt married) was to put into the *Canterbury Tales*, to the discredit of the Church, its priests, monks and nuns, pardoners and summoners. Clearly also they, like the nobility in general, would have been glad to take over the lands of the monastic orders and the revenues of the bishops. They had seen it done earlier in France and, helped by the king, their successors were later to do it in England. Moreover they had not the past or the future inducement to fidelity of the Italian or French nobles, who might have a cardinal in every family, eligible at the age of twelve, to take the papacy and its patronage in rotation. Nor the present inducement of their French enemies, who had had the Pope, a Frenchman and a prisoner, on their soil. But the ruling class and the royal houses, Plantagenet, Lancaster and York, failed when the crisis came. The legitimate Richard and the usurping Henry stood by the Church. Why?

It was that the interests of Church and State had come to be mingled in every channel of government throughout Christendom. The most general notion in feudal society was that of power and property descending from the highest lord through intermediates to the meanest serf. If secular power descended from the king through his barons, so spiritual power and grace descended from the pope through his bishops and his priests. The Church had skilfully built its social structure and its devotional practices round the feudal society. The two systems were inextricably engaged. If the pope were disturbed where would the king and his nobles stand?

Many particulars reinforced the general argument. All dynasties depended on their recognition by the pope; all kings depended on the authentication of the pope for the legitimacy of their marriages and their offspring; the whole legal profession depended on the Canon Law for its fees; all universities depended on episcopal administrators for their repeated endowments. Thirty generations of custom and convenience supported the established order, now so corrupt.

There was yet another factor affecting the behaviour of the English ruling class at this time: their general level of intelligence and education. Europe, at that time, owing to the growth of the wealth and power of the merchants and craftsmen in the Italian cities, stood on the threshold of the Renaissance. The English nobles were on the threshold of the Wars of the Roses. The reason for this contrast is plain. In the Italian cities, led by Florence and Venice, merchants were able to intermarry with the highest nobility: Medici with Colonna. They governed with the help of a secular educated class. In England the larger merchants could hope to claim the daughters of the smaller gentry. But great English nobles were above marrying merchants' daughters; they were still a narrow inbred military caste. Their methods of government were illiterate. They depended above all on the education of the Church, on the skill and cunning of the priesthood.

They needed clerical administrators, lawyers and tax-collectors. They even needed clerical taxes, for when the pope had extracted his revenue through the priests, the king could take over nine-tenths of it for himself. And if property was a joint interest, so also was authority. They feared excommunication, with all its consequences for their possessions. They feared for their status in Christian society. And if they had any doubts the Peasants' Revolt of 1381 settled them.

Here was a dangerous rebel, Wat Tyler, co-operating with a Wycliffian priest, John Ball, in demanding the abolition of serfdom.[1] The implications of Wycliffe's teaching on *dominion* became fatally clear. The pope had maintained that his blessing alone justified dominion over men and things. Wycliffe maintained that freedom from sin was sufficient. The pope's blessing was sold to the strong and the rich; Wycliffe's blessing might be given to the weak and poor. When the king and the nobles faced Wat Tyler they knew that they must stand shoulder to shoulder with the bishops in suppressing both the rebels and the reformers. The great *possessioners* in the Church and their kinsmen, the great *possessors* in the State, proved to be one establishment.

The Inquisition had been dealing with heretics in Europe very effectively for 150 years. Now in 1397 the bishops asked for the practice to be admitted in England.[2] Parliament passed the Bill *de haeretico comburendo* in March 1401. But the new king, Henry IV, could not wait for it to become law. He had already, in February, ordered the first heretic to be burnt at Smithfield in London.

Unfortunately for the king, no wealthy heretics with large estates to confiscate raised their voices in protest. Only one nobleman, Sir John Oldcastle, Lord Cobham, fell for heresy and for treason. His followers were dispersed and after three years in hiding he was caught and hanged in 1417.

The reforming movement, with its political climax of insurrection, is the first great issue, at once political, social, and religious, in which the English people were deeply engaged. And opinion is still divided on its rights and its wrongs. The liberal and modern view, ever since the Reformation, has looked back only to condemn the persecutors. But looking from within the times another view can be gained and has been stated. If reform and revolution had been allowed to take their course in the England of Wycliffe and Oldcastle, could a new government, rejecting papal authority and clerical administration, have in fact replaced the establishment of the time and created an orderly society? We have to admit that it could not. The nobles and the king had judged right. What was to be possible a century later was not possible at that time. Of the bishops too we may say that as Christians they were weak or wicked; and as men of understanding, they were narrow or stupid; but as politicians, they understood the interests of their class, which happened at that moment to coincide with those of the nation.

When therefore McFarlane says that the bishops were merely fulfilling their professional duty in pursuing heresy, and adds that they persecuted with compassion and burnt with reluctance, he is facing us with one of the paradoxes of social history. Governing classes may be operating in their own selfish interests. They may understand nothing of the more civilized classes

[1] See Froissart for an upper class view of the struggle (Brereton 1968).

[2] The wheel had turned full circle since the days when the Saxon Archbishop Wulfstan had pleaded for preserving men's lives for the sake of Christian charity (Whitelocke, 1952).

whose propagation will replace them in the future. But they may nevertheless be the best safeguard for the future gradual development of those classes and of their civilization.

For over a hundred and fifty years, the Church and State in England combined to burn heretics. But fear of the milder penalties of loss of property and patronage was enough to deprive Wycliffe's movement of its educated leaders. Clergy and gentry conformed. All that were left to believe and to suffer were the illiterate mass of the people, who had been inspired to think for themselves, but could not at that time think clearly enough or far enough ahead. It was these people who continued to mutter their curses on the great possessioners of the Church and who earned thereby the name of Lollards.

These Lollards were almost exclusively craftsmen, that is skilled artisans.[1] This was a class which grew in strength with their own enterprise and with the wealth of the country which their enterprise so largely created. And when printing brought the Bible within the reach of these men, nothing could prevent them from taking their religion into their own hands. Their descendants were to be the mainstay of puritanism in England, the core of Cromwell's army and of Monmouth's rebellion, and the founders of nonconformity and, in large measure, of the industrial, commercial and scientific revolutions that were to follow.

Meanwhile the bishops were busily chasing the followers and destroying the writings of Wycliffe. But they were haunted, secretly haunted, by the new vision which in due course was going to overthrow the old order. For they were obtaining, and evidently studying, copies of the new Bible of the heretics. Reading it in their own tongue can it have failed to impress a few of them, as it may still impress us, with a beauty beyond that of the rituals and doctrines they practised and preached? It was, however, from the scholars and scholarship of Oxford, apparently repressed but actually dispersed, that other more quickly visible effects arose. For the embers quenched at home were carried overseas and soon burst into flame.

b. Jan Hus

Czech scholars accompanying Anne of Bohemia to her wedding with the young King Richard in 1383 found Oxford recovering from the condemnation of Wycliffe the previous November. They were able to obtain copies of his writings and took them back with them to their own country. Here after a few years they found their greatest exponent, Jan Hus (1370–1415).

The sparks of reform now fell on dry tinder. Bohemia, in the heart of Europe, was a country at the meeting of many ways. It was also an ancient country rich in mines and in miners, hard, independent and adventurous. These men harboured not only Cathars but so many heretical sects that the Inquisition had never been able to get the upper hand of them. Moreover Bohemia was at this moment in the throes of social discord. The original

[1] McFarlane enumerates their trades: weavers, fullers and dyers, tailors, glovers and shoemakers, coopers, carpenters, millers and masons, blacksmiths and goldsmiths, thatchers, ploughmen and small freeholders, scriveners and parchment-makers. There were also poor chaplains, unbeneficed clergy.

racial contrast of social classes, which had reached a climax in England three hundred years earlier, had now reached its climax in Bohemia. The country had not acquired—and owing to the religious dispute which followed, never did acquire—the character or illusion of racial unity seen in England. The privileged nobility, clergy and townspeople were German-speaking. The unprivileged gentry, clergy and country people were Czech-speaking. The university of Prague was mixed. Into this dangerous world came the papal schism, the writings of Wycliffe and the preaching of Hus. Little wonder that a storm blew up.

The university was the centre of the storm. It was made of four nations. In 1409 the Bavarians, Saxons and Poles deserted it. The fourth nation, the Czechs, remained to stand by their leader Hus. The Archbishop excommunicated Hus. Two hundred volumes of Wycliffe's writings were seized and burnt. But the teaching continued; the infection spread. Four years later a Council of the Church was convened at Constance to heal its schisms and to allay its disorders. Hus was enticed to it with a safe conduct. After two years of trial he was condemned and burnt.

This act was not the end of the Hussites. On the contrary it was their beginning. A sectarian party not only, like the Lollards, anti-clerical and anti-noble, but also anti-German grew up in Bohemia and Moravia. It was a party which began to attract the dispersed leaders of reform from other countries. Peter Payne (1380–1455), the Wycliffite Principal of an Oxford society, St Edmund Hall, came and stayed for forty years to preach revolt. Educated Waldensian refugees, or missionaries, leaving their illiterate brethren in the mountains, came to Bohemia and, propagating themselves and their faith, became bishops of a new congregation.

To deal with these activities the Inquisition was powerless. A Crusade was needed and the assault, promoted by Pope Martin V in 1420, led to the Hussite wars which continued for thirteen years. In the end the reformers were not destroyed but divided. The majority compromised and accepted a Czech national Church which later returned to Rome. A minority became after many vicissitudes Moravian Brethren.

The light had again been apparently extinguished, but only in the country of its origin. Again its people had been dispersed. The Moravian Brethren, taking Wycliffe's teaching to its logical conclusion, believed that it was conduct that mattered and that the Sermon on the Mount should be taken as a literal guide to conduct. Taking also the Hebrew teaching of the winnowing, they scattered over Europe and later over America, discovering and cherishing the Hidden Seed: a genetic community strictly inbred and selectively successful. Like their kinsmen the Lollards of England, they were earnest and diligent craftsmen. And with them they helped to form the hard core of the coming Reformation.[1]

[1] See (i) *E.B.* (1929) art.: 'Moravian Brethren', and Southey (1820) for their connection with John Wesley whom they largely inspired on the voyage to America in 1735; (ii) Hayes (1937) for their refugee colonies planted by the English in Ireland; (iii) Bertrand Gille (1966) for their place in the development of Renaissance engineering following the Hussite wars.

III. REFORMATION BY GOVERNMENT

a. Luther

In Western Europe at the end of the fifteenth century there were men in all countries and in all the educated classes who were aware of what Wycliffe and Hus had said and silently took their part against the Inquisition which had crushed them. And whenever they had the chance, as with the fanatical Florentine monk Savonarola, they enthusiastically affirmed their revolt. But every time such signs appeared the strength of governments was thrown into the scale on the side of authority. When Savonarola had been burnt in the Piazza della Signoria in Florence in 1497, order seemed to have been restored.

So the Inquisition was able to deter the critics. But in deterring them, like all dictatorships, it had destroyed the evidence of its own disintegrating authority. From the time that Gutenberg in 1456 had printed his Latin Bible at Mainz, the Bible itself had begun to carry through the work of reform without the need for outside agitation. Parts of the Bible soon began to be printed in the vernacular languages: German in 1466, Flemish in 1477, and soon in French, Spanish, Czech and even Italian versions. Notably not in English: the Church in England knew the danger of Wycliffe's translation and England did not see the printed Bible until sixty years after Germany.

Gradually the great debate spread through society and through Europe, everywhere undermining respect for official teaching. The discussion returned from the people to the scholars. Erasmus revised the Greek New Testament and, translating it into Latin, proved that Jerome's Vulgate, used by the Church, was often in error. It was in the following year that Luther in Wittenberg challenged the Church: the dam had broken.

Why did it break at that place and at that time? There was nothing now known that had not been known long before. There was nothing now said that had not been said before. It was the political and social situation that was new. One reason was that the Elector of Saxony, along with a number of his 300 colleagues governing states within the Holy Roman Empire, knew that, with an aged Emperor and a particularly outrageous attempt to sell indulgences for the Pope, the favourable moment had come to resist. Indeed the Elector of Saxony in founding his university in 1502 and in appointing Luther as a professor in 1512 must have foreseen the coming value of a theological adviser in resisting papal demands. But another reason was that the whole pace of events was now faster than had ever been known before, owing to the invention of printing. What had seemed to be a modest whisper was quickly magnified to a world-shaking challenge, one which the pope and the emperor were bound to meet.

During the next thirty years of struggle and war the people of Germany divided themselves into Catholics and Protestants. The peasants, the scholars and the princes in their principalities, the merchants and artisans in their free cities, sorted themselves out into the opposed groups. In this division it has usually been said that while citizens of the free cities were chiefly Protestant, in the principalities subjects followed their rulers, Catholic or Protestant. But to this statement two qualifications must be made. In the first place wise rulers often paid attention to the opinions of their subjects. And in the second place a stubborn minority of subjects always had opinions of their own. In the small states of Germany these minorities were disposed to migrate. But in the larger states of England and France they at first chose to resist or to fight where they stood.

b. Cranmer

When Henry VIII broke with Rome in 1534 and declared himself Supreme Head of the Church in England he really meant it. He intended that he would manage his own and his country's affairs, marital and doctrinal, and keep the Church revenues and monastic wealth of his country in his own hands or distribute them to his servants as the endowments of a new nobility. But what he did, six years later, in putting an English Bible in every parish church, as Rome could have told him, was inevitably to destroy the unity he wanted to create. Bishops were of course required to enforce the authority of the king and maintain the unity of the Church but the clergy themselves began to have opinions of their own and to diverge more and more from the rules they had been given. As Henry himself declared with feeling in his last address to Parliament (of December 24, 1545): 'I see and hear daily that you of the clergy preach one against another. . . . Some be too stiff in their old *Mumpsimus*, other be too busy and curious in their new *Sumpsimus*.'

It was in these circumstances that the government of his son introduced a prayer book, a uniform order of Church service compiled by Henry's archbishop, Thomas Cranmer. This prayer book in effect became the pliable means of keeping the people within one Church. It was assisted perhaps by the violent interruption of Mary. And it was reinforced by Elizabeth's insertion of the Thirty-nine Articles of Religion in 1561. Here was a device which papered over the rents and tears of doctrine. It also fully put the Church of England in the middle of the diverging ways the people were following. It seemed to make possible a gradual release of the tension between authority and enquiry during the dangerous century that followed Henry's declaration of his supremacy. France was engaged in religious wars. Spain was preoccupied with the conquest of the New World and with the suppression of rebellion of her Protestant subjects in the Netherlands. But in England the ferment of thought proceeded without breaking up the framework of society.

IV. GOVERNMENT BY REFORMATION

a. Calvin

By the middle of the sixteenth century the official religions, Catholic and Protestant, were establishing themselves in stable opposition as the systems of belief of the ruling classes in Germany and England. But in France, in the Netherlands and in Scotland, the Catholic Church was struggling to hold down the revolt. This was the position when the French theologian, John Calvin, a refugee from France, gained control in Geneva. Calvin's opinions, like Luther's, were adjusted to the political task that he saw ahead of him. This was to convert Catholic states and peoples to the Protestant Reformation.

And, since he had to design his own instrument for this, to convert all peoples, Protestant as well as Catholic, to belief in his particular instrument of Protestantism.

Calvin's instrument was of two mutually adapted parts, doctrinal and political. His dogma that his own people were the elect of God, alone to be saved, demanded his practice that the Church should be inseparable from their government and that the affairs of the whole State and of every individual in it should conform to the word of God and the judgment of the elect. And these were the same thing, for they were to be interpreted by Calvin.

This view of the world, or this plan of campaign, was (as Elton has pointed out) well aimed at the task of penetrating Catholic countries, or indeed any country with an established religion, and of doing so without the help of the ruling class. Indeed it seemed rather to be aimed at displacing the ruling class. For it moulded itself not to the needs of the old governors but to the aspirations of the artisans, merchants and preachers who had first seized upon it. How had this come about? It was on account of the evolution of the city of Geneva itself.

Calvin had come to settle permanently in Geneva in the year 1541. At that time it was a small city with an undistinguished past. Its population of 13,000 inhabitants were said to be easy-going or loose-living according to the persuasion of the speaker. They were made up of diverse Protestant sects managing to coexist with a large Catholic minority. Now, during the twenty-three years in which Geneva became the seat of Calvin's revolution, all this was changed. All Catholics and all deviant Protestants were converted or expelled. Their place had been taken by Protestant refugees from France. There were thirteen Protestant pastors in the city, all of French origin.[1]

Half way through his revolt (in 1553, at the time when John Knox visited Geneva) Calvin obtained the transfer of the right of excommunication from the City Councils to the Church Consistory. Discipline was now in his hands. During the next years the body of foreign refugees were swelled by the English escaping from Mary's Catholic persecution. All these men had come to seek or even to obey Calvin. When the natives protested at this flood of foreigners their own leaders had to fly in terror. Only four needed to be put to death to establish Calvin's dictatorship—a dictatorship governing everything from the State policy to what had formerly been thought the private life of the individual.

Thus Geneva was a city, like all other great cities, created by immigrants. It differed in this respect from cities like Athens or Venice that its immigrants were a sudden flood of refugees, of a new kind and controlled in a new way. For the Protestant refugees from France were refugees attracted by Calvin himself, attracted by his preaching and his practice, his doctrine and his discipline. And since his discipline was a very strict rule they were likewise a strictly selected population, a unique population. Their presence indeed may still be felt in Geneva today. They were remarkable for their skill, their diligence and their gravity. They brought into the city its cloth manufacture,

[1] Chadwick (1964). Of the university which Calvin founded the same must have been true.

invariably a source of wealth and a concomitant of puritanism. They brought in printing and much scholarship in the person of the great Robert Estienne.[1] And they established the fruitful and significant industry from which the 1500 modern Swiss watchmaking firms are derived.[2] These were only the first examples of the extraordinary talents which the French Protestants were to breed and to disperse over Europe.[3]

Exact professions bring with them exact and therefore dogmatic beliefs but here the order had also been reversed. The beliefs had in turn attracted the professions. By selective migration the whole combination had become self-exaggerating. And it was to this self-exaggeration that the extremism of Calvin and of Geneva was due. From it had come the Catholic principle of excommunication. But it now operated in reverse and was in danger of breaking contact between the Lutheran and Calvinist universities. From it also came the Catholic sanction, the burning for heresy, now to be used by Calvin. The victim was Miguel Serveto, the brightest figure of the Reformation to come from Spain and one of the great precursors of the Scientific Revolution. Almost like Jan Hus, 150 years earlier, he was enticed to Geneva in 1553. He was there tried and convicted of disputing the divinity of Jesus. Calvin would have had him beheaded, but the City Fathers preferred the Roman rite and he was burnt.[4]

b. The Huguenots

In Geneva Calvin's Church was concentrated and paramount. But in his native France, where it was dispersed and persecuted, his ideas had their most far-reaching effect. For the French Protestant community the name of Covenanter or Eidgenosse had become Huguenot. Its first national synod was held in Paris in 1559. Here it was agreed that all Churches should be equal in rank; likewise all their ministers and all their elected governing bodies of elders. Hence there would be no bishops. From this decision, implicit in Calvin's teaching, sprang the Presbyterian rule in Church government.

The enthusiasm for the new rule grew as its converts discovered the scope it gave for individual initiative and capacity not only in theological argument but in practical government. The Huguenot minority in France swiftly expanded and thirteen years later it threatened to dominate the nation and the State. It was at this point that the Catholic retort to Protestantism came to a head.

[1] Steinberg (1955).

[2] The most famous product of the Huguenot exiles in Geneva, Jean Jacques Rousseau (1712–1778), was the son of a watchmaker.

[3] Another impulse to the growth of modern Swiss commerce is said to have come from the French royalist and Catholic refugees following 1789. Their capital developed Swiss banking. But its technique owed more to the Prussian Protestant, Jacques Necker (1732–1804), who, before the Revolution, attempted to reform the finances of France.

[4] The book for which Serveto was burnt was his *Restitutio Christianismi* (1552). Here seventy-six years before Harvey he explained the circulation of the blood. All accessible copies of his book were burnt; only three survived and his discovery therefore remained unknown (Steinberg, 1955).

Table 30. *The Great Reformers:* 1300–1600

A list of scholars and preachers, all ordained Catholic clergy, with their chief writings and places of work. (For maps, see Chadwick, p. 140; Elton, p. 13.)

PRECURSORS			
1. MARSIGLIO	1270–1342	Padua	attacks papacy 1342
2. JOHN WYCLIFFE	1330–1384	Oxford	attacks papacy 1378
3. JAN HUS	1370–1415[1]	Prague	attacks papacy 1402
4. GIROLAMO SAVONAROLA	1452–1497[1]	Florence	reformer of morals 1494
5. DESIDERIUS ERASMUS[2]	1466–1536	Basle *et al.*	revises Greek N.T. 1516
GERMANIC			
6. MARTIN LUTHER[3]	1483–1546	Wittenberg	condemns indulgences 1517
7. PHILIPP MELANCTHON[4]	1497–1560	Wittenberg	author of Augsburg Confession 1530
8. ULRICH ZWINGLI	1484–1531[5]	Zürich	political reformer 1518
9. THOMAS MÜNTZER	1489–1525[6]	Leipzig	Anabaptist: Peasants' War 1524
10. MENNO SIMONS	1496–1561	Holland	founds Mennonites 1537
ENGLISH			
11. THOMAS CRANMER[7]	1489–1556[1]	Cambridge	Ab. of Canterbury 1532
12. WILLIAM TYNDALE	1492–1536[1]	C., Antwerp	English N.T. 1525
ROMANCE			
13. JACQUES LEFEVRE	1455–1537	Etaples	French N.T. 1524
14. JEAN CALVIN[8]	1509–1537	Geneva	new order 1541
15. MIGUEL SERVETO[9]	1511–1553[1]	Avignon *et al.*	} deny divinity of Christ
16. FAUSTO SOZZINI[10]	1525–1604	Basle-Rakow	}

[1] Burnt as heretics.
[2] Bastard born in Rotterdam; doubted whether Revelation was written by John.
[3] Son of miner.
[4] Son of an armourer, Greek name given by his great-uncle, the Hebraist Johann Reuchlin.
[5] Killed in battle.
[6] Executed as a rebel.
[7] Married secretly in 1531.
[8] Son of a notary apostolic of Noyon, Picardy, by an innkeeper's daughter.
[9] Son of a notary of Tudela, Navarre; a distinguished medical teacher in Paris.
[10] Of a noted Sienese family; founder of Socinianism.

The Catholic Church had been arming itself to resist the reformers. The weapon of the Inquisition had effectively broken in the hands of the Pope, the Fathers of the Church had gathered in Council at Trent and had refashioned the face of the Church itself. There they returned at intervals for nearly twenty years (1545–1548, 1551–1552, 1562–1563). Undoubtedly the Church emerged stronger.[1] It now had the Order of Jesuits founded in 1540 and soon well-fitted to lead the counter-attack. They were to recover Poland. They were

[1] The hand was stronger and the face less repulsive but the papacy remained a political caucus of Italian nobles. Its operation in 1581 has been described with an appropriate obscenity by Roger Peyrefitte (1964).

to assault England and the Netherlands. But in France a different instrument was pressed into the hands of a Catholic king, the weapon of massacre. On the night of St Bartholomew, in 1572, some five thousand Huguenots were killed. All their leaders in Paris were dead except those who, like Henry of Navarre, temporarily forswore their faith.

Again, as so often before, the deadly persecution of a sect in one country led to the spread of the sect to others. The disaster of 1572 damaged Calvinism in France. But it led to a dispersion like that of the Jews. The Calvinists were strengthened in England, in Holland, and in Scotland. And from these countries they spread westwards to Ireland and to the English colonies in America, southwards to the Dutch colony in South Africa and eastwards to the province of Brandenburg.

In all these countries except Brandenburg where a dynastic opportunity let it in, Calvinism developed as the core of the great movement of social reform which we know as puritanism. And everywhere it first implied and then expressed a revolt against social authority and a revolt against monarchy itself. It is in this sense that we must understand Henry of Navarre and James I of England giving up their Calvinism and returning to the company of bishops as soon as the convenient moment arrived. James might have foreseen that in England in 1642, seventy years after the night of St Bartholomew, Calvinism would become one of the chief instruments in dethroning first the bishops and then the king.

22

THE REFORMATION AND SOCIETY

I. THE REVOLUTIONARY SECT

a. Experiment in Germany

IN THE GERMANY OF LUTHER, the England of Cranmer and even the France of Calvin, the authority and sympathy of princes had compelled or persuaded the reformers to look upon reformation as a means of throwing out the papacy, the priestly tradition which clung to it, and the financial apparatus which supported it. In doing this they had had to re-establish the alternative authority of the scriptures. They soon discovered that if they were not to destroy the fabric of society along with the papacy the scriptures needed contemporary interpretation, that is interpretation in the interests of property rather than of learning.

For throughout the basin of the Rhine were rich cities independent of great rulers, cities filled with enterprising, often intelligent and partly educated populations. These people, reading the Bible, saw what it meant, not for the comfortable scholar or theologian, but for the needy mechanic, the impoverished artisan and their neighbour, the frequently starving peasant. They had seen the rich liberating themselves with the plunder of the Church. They had seen the scholars liberating themselves by rewriting the laws and the liturgies of the Church. Now the moment of their liberation had come.[1]

For these people two kinds of liberation were at hand. The first arose from the immediate practical task of the self-governing congregation. In the centuries to come the congregation was to be the training ground for a new kind of governing class, people who would govern not principalities and

[1] Chadwick gives an illuminating account both of the Reformation Radicals within Christendom and of contemporary Christian life under the Turks.

political movements but smaller communities, the workers in expanding industrial firms.

The second kind of liberation arose from the Bible itself, from its far-reaching social and political message, written in the primitive terms needed by simple people. Among them a new way of life might be established for those who read the message aright and followed the proper rituals and timings of baptism, marriage and communion. Among them every possible combination of Biblical precept was somewhere adopted. It was a world suddenly opened to experiment. And, although none was found to forswear marriage, polygamy and promiscuity had their exponents on good authority.[1]

Such were the origins of the Peasants' War of 1524 in South Germany; of the Anabaptist Confession of Schleitheim, near Schaffhausen, in 1527; of the New Kingdom of Zion in Münster in 1533; and of an insurrection in Amsterdam in 1535. Successive violent and war-like groups, taking their cue from the Old Testament, aroused enough opposition in one orderly society after another to destroy themselves. But the opposite enthusiasm which took its cue from the New Testament held its ground in the ancient Protestant stronghold of Moravia.

Here Jacob Hutter had been executed in 1536 for advocating his communist principles and here his brethren established their socialist, pacifist and fundamentalist societies. As Hutterites they spread across Germany westward to Holland where one of their leaders, Menno Simons, gave his name to the Mennonite sect. Two remarkable properties then revealed themselves in these groups. The first was their social and economic success. Their industry, skill and devotion to their own group, created from each group a perfect welfare state with a selective advantage for a higher fertility than had ever been favoured in Christian societies before.[2]

The material success of the Anabaptists seemed to support their conviction that they alone were spiritually saved. Naturally, therefore, they were greatly preoccupied with the ritual definition of their several communities. Whether the test of salvation was by immersion, or washing, or singing, or publicly confessing, they always tended to split and always feared to fuse. Excommunication allowed them to elaborate the severity of the code and to diminish the size of the group. Thus the breeding system rapidly evolved. What had been one radical equalitarian minority of the elect picked out from a stratified society became many such groups. All of them were inbred and therefore genetically stable and culturally conservative. Being utterly isolated from the rest of society by their rejection of authority, luxury and war, they were driven to retain a primitive habit of life and it has been only by agriculture that they have been able to prosper. But, in spite of all persecution, like the Jews in Christendom, the Hutterites and Mennonites multiplied not by conversion but by propagation. Driven into Turkey and into Russia and later fragmented by further schisms, by no means could these people be exterminated; nowhere did they fail to multiply. And when, flying from Tsarist conscription in 1872,

[1] Though not apparently celibacy, which was Roman, nor castration, which was Greek, and long survived in the Russian sect of Skoptzi (Sitwell, 1955).

[2] Darlington (1960) on cousin marriage.

they took refuge in North and South America, they brought with them their bushels of hard baking Russian wheat on which future millions in both hemispheres would depend for their bread.[1]

b. Civil War in England

In England the Elizabethan settlement created the semblance of peace. The government hoped, as governments will, that it could damp down the fermentation of ideas for ever. But beneath the surface the leaven continued to work with effects more far-reaching than anywhere else in Christendom. The 37th and 38th of the 39 Articles had condemned the Anabaptists for their abominable idea of rejecting property and war. Two Anabaptists had been burnt. But it was not possible by mere intimidation to suppress ideas of this instinctive depth and scriptural validity.

The original ideas which led to the Reformation in England as elsewhere were the work of few men. But the dissolution of the monastic orders and the redistribution of their property, including that of the universities, the growth of the cities and prosperity of some of the citizens, led to extensive movements of people and changes of ownership between different parts of the country, between different social classes, and between town and country. There was such a turmoil as had not occurred even at the Norman Conquest. In addition there were important movements of Protestant refugees into England from France and the Netherlands whose specific effect we shall consider later.

The sixteenth century in England was thus one of those decisive periods of outbreeding or hybridization and of growing genetic heterogeneity whose importance in history we have learnt to recognize. The disturbance of the breeding system leads to the breaking up of families and their traditions and the intrusion of new people and new practices. And in the second and third generation it leads to the recombination of genes appropriate to the recombination of ideas.

It was inevitably in the churches and through the sermons of preachers that these ideas, indistinguishably religious, social and political, sorted themselves out. In doing so they sorted out the preachers and their congregations and created the great cleavage between the old order which pursued art, leisure and luxury and the new puritan order which rejected all three.

In this matter of sorting out Charles I provided just what was needful in his own person and in that of his unfailing adviser Archbishop Laud. Neither of them could understand that there were new classes of people who were quite capable of managing their affairs without the help of kings or bishops and who had their own ideas of God, man and society, very diverse ideas and held with very great conviction. What the King and the Archbishop did understand however was that if these people were allowed to meet in their congregations and in their parliaments they were bound to hatch out ideas aimed to destroy the old order. And this was what above all they attempted to avoid.

To the puritans there was the agonizing choice between emigration to the New England colonies, following the example of the *Mayflower* in 1620, and staying to fight for independence at home. It was a choice considered by

[1] Buller (1919).

Oliver Cromwell himself.[1] Conflict in the end was inevitable but it was hastened by the king's handling of his problem. It is difficult to think of any English monarch who could have managed matters worse.

Naturally when the break came between Parliament and the king, legal, religious and economic principles were invoked to support the claims of each side. Every possible conflict of interest was involved between the shifting social classes, the fact being that the Protestant Reformation, by allowing each group to form its own beliefs based on its own interpretation, had led to each social class having its own views on religious belief and Church organization. Instead of the harmony of a society which accepted the interpretation of a single Catholic Church there was the conflict between genetic groups which thought for themselves and thought differently. It was these genetic groups which were tentatively assembled in two parties.

The Civil War came in 1642 only when each of these parties confidently, indeed over-confidently, believed that it could win. It believed that it was socially stratified to the extent of being in itself competent to wage war. On the king's side was a society based on agriculture led by a traditional nobility, and a traditional Church with its still largely ancient ritual, both commanding the respect of an illiterate and servile rural population whose beliefs like those of their leaders were derived from feudal society. On the Parliament's side was a society based on the new techniques and trades of the city, the lower levels often rejecting authority, the higher levels intending to establish their own. In the lower levels were the 'Brownists, Anabaptists and Atheists' denounced by the king in his opening address to the troops. In the higher levels were the new gentry, despised by Clarendon, who with fortunes made in the city had bought or married into their rural estates.[2]

The revolution in its victory found itself divided between these two factions. Authority of course won the battle because authority was what Cromwell and his major-generals were able to impose. But they did not need the religious uniformity demanded by the weak king. They could afford to have Presbyterians in the choir, Independents in the nave and Baptists in the crypt. For ten years the strength of the army was the safeguard of the State.

c. *The Evolution of Sects*

In doctrine, though not in morals, the toleration of the Commonwealth repeated and enlarged the toleration of Elizabeth. There was an immense debate from which the old authority and uniformity could never again be fully rescued. Again there was an influx of people from abroad seeking this freedom of debate. A Jewish colony was admitted from Amsterdam, a colony itself, as we have seen, of refugees from the Spanish Inquisition. Other refugees from Catholic persecution had earlier brought intellectual doubts into the northern countries. The repudiation of the doctrine of Trinity and the Athanasian Creed by the Spaniard Servetus and the Italian Sozzini or Socinus had brought back a rejection of the Trinitarian mysteries into the Protestant countries. These ideas now began to take hold in Presbyterian congregations in England.

[1] According to Clarendon, at the time of the Grand Remonstrance in December 1641. See also Bridenbaugh (1968).

[2] See Christopher Hill (1940).

From the conservative and less educable Congregationalists there split off during the eighteenth century the sceptical and more educable Unitarians, people who were to play their part four or five generations later in the Industrial Revolution.

Thus, in the welter of discussion, the social and professional character of the new sects underwent evolutionary change. Not only the Unitarians but another sect, owing to its intellectual character, underwent a social promotion.

It was during the Civil War that George Fox set out on his personal quest for truth by preaching the rejection of war. He transformed his followers into a society, which then preserved itself. It did so both by its books of registration and by its intellectual and temperamental coherence. All these things together with their strict moral discipline underlay the commercial and technical success of his Society of Friends. By the time they were known as Quakers they were becoming a homogeneous inbred group seeking to alleviate poverty but needing to turn outside their own community if they were to find it.

How had the Quakers improved their position? Their repudiation of pretended beliefs and meaningless ceremonies, as well as their respect for women, inevitably led them to drop their least intelligent and also least successful adherents to whom ritual, formality and status meant most. The Quaker practice of logical severity was pre-adapted to commercial success and, by its example, led to a revolution in commercial methods which spread through all Protestant societies.[1]

At the same time the Quakers had repudiated, more emphatically than other puritans, the cult of art and beauty. Their prescription of drab colours for women's as well as men's dress led to another process of social evolution whose understanding we owe to two Quakers. For it was John Dalton (Table 32) who discovered the nature of the genetic colour blindness he had himself inherited. And it was Francis Galton who showed that the gene for colour blindness was more frequent among Quakers than in the population at large.[2]

Taking all social levels together it was generally a rule that the fiercest excommunication and the strictest exclusiveness were found in the sects, mostly of urban artisans, which embraced the strictest religious forms. Trade guilds with their separate churches, still well seen in Norwich, no doubt already in the Catholic middle ages constituted effective breeding groups. But among the dissenting Protestant sects the strictness of breeding communities was obviously enhanced. Thus in England the division between the Church of England and the dissenting sects, which became established during the turmoil and movement of the Civil War, was a difference between one socially stratified body and many independent bodies in each of which religion was itself the means and the marker of stratification. A diversity of breeding groups, some inbred and some outbred, thus came into existence continuing to proliferate and to fragment down to the twentieth century. These were the social and genetic conditions which underlay the evolution of English society in the critical period of the Industrial Revolution.

[1] See Wagner (1960) who also notes that they lost their most successful early family—that of William Penn.

[2] Bloomfield (1955); Darlington (1964).

II. UNIFORMITY AND TOLERATION

a. The Problem

Voltaire, in his study of Louis XIV (ch. 36) asked how it is that while the differences among pagan religions could be peacefully accommodated, Christian and, he might have added, Muslim disputes have always led to bloodshed and war. The reason is that the religions of the Book have claimed to answer, and for the faithful have succeeded in answering, all the problems of the relations of the individual to society in this world and the next. The educated classes multiplying in literate societies had in the course of the Reformation created a picture of the world, its past, present and future, expressed in exact terms based on holy writ. Any dispute about any part of this picture undermined the peace and order of the whole of society. And no compromise was possible on matters which had been made plain for all time in writing. Religion, which had been used by the Jews and in a different sense by the Hindus, to bind people together in groups, had now been reconstructed so as to divide larger societies into smaller groups.

Islam, as we have seen, had quickly compromised on one point. Muslims had agreed, and had been compelled to agree, to tolerate Jews and Christians as inferior members of society. And when fervour decayed, enlightened Muslim sovereigns in Cordoba or Delhi could admit the other religions even to equality. Schism within the faith however for long appeared as a challenge, and heretics were exterminated in peace and war.

For the Christians, once theirs had been admitted as the official faith of the Empire, all infidels and heretics seemed the proper object of enmity. Muslims, being by definition foreigners, they could meet by war. Jews, being the people who had rejected Christ, and being also a defenceless minority, they could and should persecute with a view to their conversion. It was a policy which, as we have seen, yielded a trickle of notable converts century after century. But the growth of schism within the Christian faith was much more serious than the survival of enemies outside it. Hence the attempts of popes and kings to enforce obedience to a uniform religious code. Hence also, when the pope failed in Christendom at large, the attempts of each prince to maintain an established version of the old religion with an established priesthood to support his own authority within his own dominions. It was then seen that, in the absence of a prince, a republican form of government both favoured and was favoured by a diversity of sects, Christian, Jewish, or whatever they might be.

Even princes however found toleration necessary. At Augsburg in 1553, in London in 1561, and at Nantes in 1598, successively the princes of Germany, England and France discovered different formulae by which a religion, which had hitherto bound each country together, could be prevented in its discords from tearing each country asunder. Their formulae were in each case a compromise between the desire for uniformity and the need for toleration.

The German princes agreed to live and let live. Each would require his own people to conform to the Church he chose. But each would allow his dissenters to go elsewhere. And there were 300 states among which the citizen of the

Holy Roman Empire could choose his home. Selective migration thus became for the first time a political principle applied on a national scale.

This compromise broke down after sixty-five years with the opening of the Thirty Years War, the most disastrous conflict that Europe had ever suffered. In appearance this war began as a struggle between Catholic and Protestant States. It ended merely as a struggle between states, neighbouring states, diverging in the political interests, the social structure, and the genetic character of their peoples. At the end of the war the religious differences between the states and peoples remained. The compromise was re-established much in the form in which it survives today. For two hundred years, until religious enthusiasm had ceased to dominate society, it delayed the political unification of Germany.

b. France and the Huguenots

The most dangerous of all divisions in society was that arising from the growth of the Calvinist sect in France. The strength of the Huguenots came from three genetically distinct quarters. First, there were the peasants of the Cevennes. It was these people whose origins were later to be correctly diagnosed by Pope Clement XI as 'the execrable race of the ancient Albigenses', who were to rebel against Louis XIV and for nine years (1702–1711) to hold his armies at bay. Secondly, there were the artisans and merchants of certain cities, especially the northern and western sea-ports. Dieppe and La Rochelle, like Hull and Bristol in the English Civil War, made themselves into the fortresses of a puritan republic which had to be reduced (as they were in the eight years from 1621) if a single royal government was to be maintained. Thirdly, there were the Huguenot nobility led by the families of Henry of Navarre, Condé and Coligny who were engaged with the formidable Catholic families of Lorraine, the Guises, in a feudal struggle for control of the government. It was these men of power whom Catherine of Medici and her son Henry III wanted to destroy or coerce by the massacre of St Bartholomew.

In France, as in Britain, only the most inaccessible and backward regions, Brittany and the Auvergne, stood firm in the Catholic faith. The Civil War which followed showed the Protestants as an integrated society, complete at all social levels, passionately united in their doctrines, and already nearly balanced with the Catholics in wealth. No peace was therefore possible, only an armistice. This armistice was the Edict of Nantes. It was promulgated by Henry IV on April 13, 1598, five years after his conversion to the Roman Church.

This was an act of partial toleration. On the one hand it confirmed the rights of the Huguenots. It allowed them their own churches, cemeteries and law courts; it admitted them to the public schools, universities and hospitals; and it allowed them (sometimes) to serve in public office.[1] But, on the other hand, it was also an attempt at containment. It was intended to prevent the extension of the heresy. At once a cold war began. When they thought it would pay them to do so the Huguenots broke the law; and when they did so

[1] See Chadwick (1964).

the governments of Louis XIII revised the law. So it went on. Was there any solution?

A solution was in fact found in the years following 1661 by Louis XIV's minister Colbert. This great man, who began as a protégé of Mazarin, was the son of a draper of Rheims. He recognized that France needed all the men skilled in the new trades that she could find, all the artisans and men of commerce and finance that the world contained. Family allowances were introduced in 1666 to increase the skilled population; and tariffs to promote industry. But these were not enough. Glass and silk workers were imported from Venice and Milan and weavers from the Protestant Netherlands.[1] At the same time, in his own administration, Colbert freely employed French Protestants, thereby contenting them and establishing, as Voltaire puts it, the best government France had ever had.

The effect of Colbert's policy was to increase the strength of France. But unfortunately the people and the world at large saw this prosperity as the wonderful work of the king. It was a view that Louis himself began to take. The theatrical picture of himself as the source of all power and glory which he had cultivated as a play in his youth became in his maturity an article of belief. It contributed to the disastrous part he himself was to play in the real world. And the first and greatest of his disasters arose from his treatment of the Huguenots.

By 1677 the early fury of Protestant enthusiasm had waned in France as elsewhere. It had waned so far that Louis supposed he might reduce the Protestants to obedience and conformity by bribes and threats. For eight years he tormented them. In the end, desperately asserting his authority, Colbert being now dead, he revoked the Edict of Nantes. That was in October 1685. All Protestant ministers were to be expelled from France. They were to leave the country of their fathers within fifteen days. At once the congregations as well as the ministers began to emigrate. Louis tried to close the frontier, but he failed. And the magnitude of his failure gradually became apparent. It was beyond anything that he or his foolish advisers could have imagined. Here indeed was the one step by which, far beyond the limits of his dominions, the great king had inadvertently altered the course of history.

Having started on the suppression of the Huguenots, Louis could not bear to turn back. There were forced conversions. There were even some voluntary conversions of the elder sons of men of property. There was also the civil war in the Cevennes. And there was a medal struck in 1715 to celebrate the expunging of Protestantism in France. But Protestantism was never expunged. Two years before the Revolution Huguenot marriages were once more recognized. Three years after it Huguenots were sitting in the National Convention which condemned Louis XVI. And in the intervening years Louis had had to rely on the advice of a foreign Protestant, Necker, imported from Geneva, to restore his finances. The persecution of the Protestants had indeed been a step in the downfall of the French monarchy.

But this was only one side of the story. Nearly half a million Huguenots left

[1] Guaranteed their religious freedom, they founded the industry at Abbeville: we may still see the first houses they built (see Rudé, 1964).

France within a few years of the Revocation. The benefit they brought to the Protestant nations who gave them shelter was incalculable, but we must attempt to calculate it. Everywhere the Huguenots strengthened the Protestant enemies of Catholic France. Their contribution was technical, commercial and scientific. It more than counter-balanced the contrary military recruitment of Irish Catholics. Suddenly the secular process of migration from the rich and technically advanced south of Europe to the poorer north was speeded up a hundredfold. Just as they had earlier been developed by Huguenots in Switzerland, so now in Prussia, Holland and England new industries were founded and old ones were revived. By 1830 it was said that a third of the population of Berlin was of Huguenot descent. By today this must be true of all the great cities of Protestant Europe.

In this last wave of expulsion eighty thousand Huguenots came to England.[1] Half went on to Ireland and America. Half remained. At the top of society were the fighting men, the Marquis de Ruvigny whose son became Earl of Galway and three brothers Ligonier.[2]

These were among the men who officered the four Huguenot regiments serving (as Macaulay relates) with William III in his Irish campaign. At the bottom of society were the modest weavers of Spitalfields. They were a community whom Isaac Taylor could recognize two centuries later by their physique, manners and dress, by their cage-birds and window-boxes, their Friendly Societies and their flower-shows. Between these extremes were a more varied throng, the progeny of intermarriage with the English; usually with dissenters (whence the Martineaus) but also with Anglicans to give such unexpected descendants as Sydney Smith, Samuel Romilly, Edward Bouverie Pusey, and Cardinal Newman. The pure Huguenots were never inclined to literature, learning or the arts but this intermarriage yielded in the third generation England's greatest actor David Garrick, in the fourth our most respected archaeologist Henry Austin Layard, and in the sixth, through the American Jeromes (from La Rochelle) Winston Churchill. Similarly in Germany the arts and the sciences have never been more brilliantly combined than in the two half-Huguenot brothers, Alexander and Wilhelm von Humboldt.[3]

The great racial contribution of the Huguenots to the English people, like that of hybrid origins generally in all societies, has been concealed by the practice of a man with an outlandish name taking his native wife's name on intermarriage.[4]

[1] F. M. Wilson (1959).

[2] Who fought in all Marlborough's battles; the eldest surviving to become commander-in-chief of the British army fifty years later and so nominally responsible for the appointment of Wolfe and the conquest of Canada from the French.

[3] See Kellner (1960).

[4] Thus by male descent Oliver Cromwell was Williams and Welsh; and the great-grandfather of Arthur Wellesley, Duke of Wellington (himself a cousin of John Wesley) was Colley and Irish. Yet Wellington denied he was Irish: 'a man is not a horse' he said 'because he was born in a stable'. So also with the Churchills and the Percys. For the Roman custom and Augustus himself see ch. 13.

Nevertheless the Huguenots, from what we know, tell us more than any other racial group except the Jews of the distinction between the inbred and outbred effects of migration. At home the Protestants continued inbred as a useful but not very remarkable section of society.[1] Abroad, so far as they remained inbred, they introduced and developed their manufactures of textiles, glass and metalwork, technical achievements contributing to the new growth of industry. Yet outbred, they yielded over a period of six generations outstanding new individuals in every field of activity and culture. But to see how the propagation of the Huguenots took effect we must return to the social evolution of England itself.

c. The Intrusion of the Sciences

The fifteenth century saw, with the revival of learning in Italy, also the most rapid development of those practices and ideas in Europe generally which were to give rise to the Scientific and Industrial Revolutions. As in all historical interpretation there has been a desire to represent these developments in terms of the paramount effects of particular discoveries, like the invention of printing, or of particular discoverers, like the great Florentine Leonardo da Vinci (1452–1519). Recently more elaborate and more convincing interactions have come to be understood and explained.[2]

The most obvious of these interactions is that between the mechanic and the philosopher. The mechanic is faced with the practical problems of spinning and weaving, mining and smelting, stoneworking and shipbuilding, using the power of wind and water for pumping or milling, and above all of constructing the engines of war. He works with his hands. He turns his mind to the things he handles. His problems were those already faced by his paleolithic ancestors, who devised the first implements for fashioning wood and for killing animals and men. Like them his numbers were great; his rewards were poor; and his position in society was humble.

The philosopher on the other hand is able to generalize events, to imagine rules, to construct hypotheses and to handle numbers. He is not paleolithic. He sprang from roots in Sumeria and Egypt and also later independently in China. In Europe, so far as the future of science was concerned, he was represented in Ionia and in Alexandria. Later his kind had been concentrated in the Mediterranean, but he had risen in society and was obviously among the educated classes.

Now in the fifteenth century the growth of both war and prosperity had brought these opposed types, which have always been selectively separated in society, once again into fruitful contact on a new scale. Superimposed on the secular movement of artists and scholars into the more barbarous north there were now reverse and cross currents. The Hussite wars at the beginning of the century had affected the people of Bohemia and southern Germany, who were already technically most advanced, and their inventions spread into France. The French invasion of Italy at the end of the century had surprised the Italians by its sophisticated artillery. Soon the German printers were to invade

[1] Recently they have given France a President, M. Gaston Doumergue, and an industrialist, M. Peugeot.

[2] Notably by Gille (1964).

Flanders and England, and to set up their presses next to the libraries of Venice. Soon also the building of dykes and canals was to take Dutch engineers and workmen with their advanced methods of drainage to Germany, Poland and Russia as well as England. At the same time Arab and Jewish technicians in Portugal, Genoese navigators in Spain, and Venetian navigators in England provided the practice and theory which gave the control of the sea to these new nations.

All these inventions and improvements opened new roads and stimulated further the movements of people from which they had themselves been originally derived. All of them resulted in contact between the opposed types of the mechanic and the philosopher, the artisan and the mathematician, who were themselves usually derived from different races, nations and social classes. The origin of Leonardo himself is not unrepresentative of an age which has been called, in view of these movements, the century of bastards and adventurers.[1] Like his great contemporary Erasmus of Rotterdam (1466–1536), he was illegitimate and therefore in our present sense that outstandingly important individual, an unusual cross between two opposite or incompatible social types.

It is to this origin that Leonardo owes his versatile and also his ambiguous position in history. For the great artist suffered from an unquenchable curiosity equally about the theory of organic heredity and the practices of mechanical engineering.[2] Inevitably, in Gille's opinion, his curiosity, so highly dispersed, was bookish and erudite rather than effective and original. Yet Leonardo's union of interests makes the first climax in the creativeness of the Scientific Revolution.

The effect of the philosopher and the mechanic on one another was to turn both of them into something of a scientist. Gille sees the change expressed in the replacement of the mechanic's 'recipe' by the scientist's 'reason'. We may also see it in the strivings of Bacon towards experiment, so successful in theory, so unsuccessful—indeed so fatal—in practice. And we may see it in the collaboration of Robert Boyle, the articulate philosopher and his skilful technician Robert Hooke, a collaboration in which we can only guess the proportions of indebtedness.

These were indeed the circumstances in which societies were needed for bringing together the diverse and opposed types of men necessary for the new 'philosophy'. For this reason the new academies of science came into existence. The Accademia dei Lincei came to be established in Rome in 1603. A French Académie des Sciences after thirty years of unofficial life was recognized by Louis XIV in 1666 as an offshoot of Académie Française. An Invisible College of experimenters on Baconian principles began to meet in London in 1645 and later in Oxford. Having convinced the monarch, Charles II, that its purposes were free from politics and religion and might be useful to the State, its members secured a charter as the Royal Society in 1662. It was this society,

[1] At the end of the fifteenth century every princely house in Italy had passed through illegitimate lines (Burckhardt, 1860).

[2] He was the first modern man to give reasons for rejecting the theory of the inheritance of an acquired character (Zirkle, 1951; Darlington, 1964).

independent of the literary and political establishment, which sponsored the great discoveries of Newton and Hooke and the foundation of the Greenwich Observatory, and by its foreign correspondence and publication over the whole field of developing knowledge, chiefly inaugurated the forward leap of science in Europe at the end of the seventeenth century.

But in order to understand how this happened we have to look back at the development of religion in just this critical period.

d. England and the Dissenters

A period of painful toleration or, if we like, of dynamic equilibrium in religious belief was initiated in England by Elizabeth's Act of Uniformity in 1559. It roughly corresponded with the period of relaxation in France, Germany and Italy. And it was accompanied by the greatest explosion of speculative thought and experiment that the world had yet known. The teaching of Bacon, the physical experiments of Galileo and the biological experiments of Harvey went along with the establishment of scientific academies. They also went along with the development of Protestant colleges in France, and in England with a harmonious union of the humanities and natural science in the two universities of Oxford and Cambridge. Examinations were still held for the degree of M.A. and natural science was included as an obligatory part of their curriculum.[1] The culmination of this glorious period of enquiry in England was inevitably a great advance in the sciences. But it was also almost inevitably war.

After the Restoration in 1660 the king with his cavaliers, the Church of England with its bishops, were once more back in the saddle. With the remarkable exception of the king they were not concerned with advancing knowledge. Their problem was how they should re-establish themselves after their defeat and exile.

Clearly they were not strong enough to suppress the sects which had ridden roughshod over them. But clearly also they were bound to do everything in their power to discourage or silence those who were now their hereditary enemies. In doing so they found themselves in a better position than the Catholic monarch and his friends in France. For opposition was itself divided on opposite sides of the central Church of the Establishment. On one side was the small papist minority to which, for bad political reasons but (in view of their Guise and Medici ancestors) on good genetic grounds, the king and his brother were secretly inclined. On the other side was the powerful but divided puritan minority of Presbyterians and Independents whose partisans sitting in the Church's livings throughout England had lost some of their independence but very little of their convictions.

It was in these circumstances that the Chancellor brought in, during four years, the four bills which together came to be known after him as the Clarendon Code. Although during the next two hundred years these laws were frequently relaxed or remitted and in Scotland were totally undone, their effect on the evolution not only of the English but of all related societies,

[1] Curtis (1959).

Scottish, Irish and American, has never ceased to this day. Their terms were as follows:

(i) *Act of Uniformity:* all ministers of the Church of England must accept the Prayer Book, notably the Thirty-nine Articles.
(ii) *Corporation Act:* all municipal office-holders, i.e. in chartered boroughs, must take the Church of England sacraments.
(iii) *Conventicle Act:* no religious assemblies may be held outside the Church of England.
(iv) *Five Mile Act:* no ministers ejected under (i) may teach in schools or live in or near chartered boroughs.

The Clarendon Code and its derivatives in England, like the revocation of the Edict of Nantes, had no alternative except a return to civil war. There is no point therefore in asking how much England lost or gained by the division or polarity or double stratification which it instituted. All we can do is to note its particular effects as they worked through the centuries on individuals, on communities and on the nation as a whole.

The Code represented a step forward from the moral intolerance of Cromwell and even more so from the doctrinal intolerance of Charles I. There were to be no more burnings or even hangings for purely religious and non-political opinions. The crux of coercion was now to be economic: it secured its object without taking life. Two thousand dissenting ministers were deprived, to use the official term, of their livings; and deprived also of the means of spreading their religious, social or political views. Two thousand conforming parsons were given the vacant endowments.

Following the expulsion of the Catholic king and the introduction of his Calvinist successor in 1688 the third prohibition was relaxed. All Protestant dissenters, except the Unitarians, might then build their own chapels. Otherwise the Code stood for two centuries and the revolution it made proved to be permanently irreversible. Why? Because the separation of dissenters and conformers created a situation which, on this scale, was new in the history of human societies. For it put on one side a rich, hierarchical, conforming Establishment. And on the other side it put a poor but independent, nonconforming, tolerated opposition. Both communities were new; both were self-propagating. Either could convert the other; but neither for some time did convert the other. Not, that is, until the great changes worked by the dissenters a century later began to transform the whole system.

Let us look at the contrast between these two societies, first in the most general terms.

On the one side was the Establishment resting on the universities of Oxford and Cambridge. There, in monastic institutions now purged of dissenting elements and reserved as the seminaries of Wycliffe's lay and clerical possessioners, young men were to be instructed by officially celibate tutors. They were to be taught to love God, to honour the king, and to cherish the past, its learning, literary and theological, legal and medical, and sometimes its beauty; and to spend their incomes, which they hoped not to have to earn, with a regard for present ease rather than eternal salvation. These were the people, to be sure, who, distributed through the England of the eighteenth century, sponsored and to some extent created its country houses, and preserved and adorned its cities and villages, laying out the whole land in elegant classical proportions. But they were also the people who explained the immutable order of a deeply stratified society to respectful congregations in their parish churches. Those churches, which they found so conveniently stripped by the puritans of the effigies of saints, they were able to fill with their own monuments, the tombs of the new masters, the squires or landlords of the locality who, when living, had come to church less to worship than to be worshipped, and having departed, were deified like so many smaller Caesars.

On the other side were the dissenters, people of a different, a contrasted, genetic mould. They were mostly poor. They were used to working with their

Table 31. *Scientists at Oxford under the Commonwealth*[1]

JOHN WILKINS	1614–1672	H. Wadham 1648–1659 (dep. as H. Trinity, Camb. 1660) Sec. R.S. 1662. Bishop 1668
JOHN WALLIS	1616–1703	Prof. Geometry 1649–1703; D.D. (M.A. Camb. 1640)
JONATHAN GODDARD	1617–1675	H. Merton 1651–1660. M.D. Physician to Cromwell; made first English telescope
SETH WARD	1617–1689	H. Jesus (dep.). Prof. Astronomy 1649–1661. Bishop 1662 (M.A. Camb. 1640)
RALPH BATHURST	1620–1704	H. Trinity 1664–1670. M.D. 1654. Chaplain to king 1662
THOMAS WILLIS	1621–1675	Prof. Nat. Phil. 1669–1675. Chemist
WILLIAM PETTY	1623–1687	Vice-Pres. Brasenose 1651. Prof. Anatomy, 1641–1645? M.D., Kt. Economist
ROBERT BOYLE	1627–1691	Worked in Oxford 1654–1663. Boyle's Law 1662
THOS. MILLINGTON	1628–1704	F. All Souls. Prof. Nat. Phil. 1675–1704. M.D. Kt. (M.A. Camb. 1657). Botanist
THOMAS SYDENHAM	1629–1689	F. All Souls 1648–1651. M.B. A founder of Clinical Medicine (Cavalry Captain)
CHRISTOPHER WREN	1632–1723	F. All Souls 1653–1661. Prof. Astronomy 1661–1673. Kt. Architect
ROBERT HOOKE	1635–1703	Worked with Willis and Boyle in Oxford 1654–1663. M.A. 1663. *Micrographia* 1663

H. Head of a College; F. Fellow of a College; dep. deprived or expelled.

[1] All were founding Fellows of the Royal Society in 1662–1663 except Sydenham (see *D.N.B.*).

Under the Commonwealth the possibilities of scientific discussion brought the founders of the Scientific Revolution together first in London, then, owing to the greater freedom and quiet and also the accommodation and endowments, to Oxford. Their interests covered the whole range of sciences from mechanics, mathematics and astronomy to chemistry, economics and botany. They were mostly parliamentarian but a few were royalist (Ward, Bathurst) or had royalist connections (Wren) and one (Wilkins), although deprived as Head of Trinity College, Cambridge, later became a bishop.

hands, being largely craftsmen by profession. They were strenuous, inquisitive, energetic, determined to learn useful things, to follow the truth and seek salvation in their own way. They were eager therefore to govern themselves in their own communities. But they were deprived of churches and schools. They were compelled to meet secretly or, later, when they were allowed, to build their own conventicles with their own hands. Some of course escaped to Holland and to America. Some made their way into the remoter parts of the north and the west. Others found a refuge in small new towns without the privileges, or for them the disabilities, of a charter.

As one makes one's way through this country today one can still easily pick out the two Englands that these two groups, these two races, of people have created. The one, ever contracting, with its harmonious streets and buildings is derived from the easy-going Anglican Establishment. The other, still expanding, with its still dark satanic mills is derived from the hard-headed and hard-working, exact and exacting nonconformist pioneers of the Industrial Revolution.

Between the two great and opposed groups there was a third, a group in a social sense embodied in the Establishment, but in a genetic sense outside it. These were the smaller party whom we may label trimmers and time-servers: the Vicars of Bray. They were of many kinds. There was the presbyterian, James Sharpe, who turned his coat to become Archbishop of St Andrews, and cheerfully chased out his former friends to twenty miles from every town; that is, until they cut his throat. There was also the king himself, the Supreme Head of the Church of England who kept his crown by concealing his Romish views and from time to time issuing a Declaration of Indulgence, which he was all too soon required to withdraw.

For us more important than the decisions of kings and bishops were those made by the small band of experimental philosophers or scientists who had gathered in Oxford and Cambridge under the favour of the Commonwealth. These men, for the most part, had exacting standards for all their beliefs. At a time when people devoted so much thought to the problems of religious salvation, the keenest minds were bound to boggle at the mumbo-jumbo of official doctrine. Many of them could not digest the Thirty-nine Articles. They could not believe in one incomprehensible any more than in three incomprehensibles. They could not always even pretend to believe. They and their pupils became dissenters (Table 31).

What happened to these scientists? In Oxford Goddard ceased to be Warden of Merton and Petty did not return. Boyle and Hooke went to London. In Cambridge Wilkins, made Master of Trinity College by Cromwell, was ejected and John Ray followed him out. There was to be sure at this moment a new opportunity in London for two or three scientists. The king was sponsoring his new Royal Society. There they could continue their enquiries. Provided they discussed neither religion nor politics; provided also that they were able to work without revenue, subsidy or endowment. For the king was able to give his portrait to his new academy but he was unable to provide money. The king never wavered in his devotion to science but in his financial priorities it always came second to his ladies. By this skilful operation, this royal and unremunerative rescue, science in England was cut off from the sources of endowment; cut off also from the means of propagating itself in the universities.

Among all these men however there was one exception, the most notable of all, one who, like his sovereign, was prepared to concede in silence what a public office would require. This man was Isaac Newton. Concealing his Unitarian scruples and his Fifth Monarchy doubts, Newton was able to secure dispensation from Holy Orders and allowed to hold the Lucasian Chair of Mathematics in Cambridge.[1]

His university, his country, and the world at large may be grateful to Newton for his prudence or cowardice. Lesser men stood by their principles. They were expelled from Oxford and Cambridge. And with their expulsion the Church secured its hold over all the richer foundations, schools and universities throughout the country. The non-admission of dissenters, as well as Catholics and Jews, destroyed the diversity of race, class and opinion on which all progress, but especially scientific discovery, depends.

At Cambridge the new professor of mathematics (Whiston) engaged in reconciling Newton's science with the Book of Genesis. And the new professor of botany (Martyn) wrote an interesting commentary on Virgil's *Georgics*. The experimental sciences had disappeared from the educational establishment of the nation which came to be filled with a self-generating succession of acceptable place-seekers, pursuing repetitive learning. Everywhere the bishops had the jobs to give and the places to fill; they made the rain and the fine weather, the temper and the fashion of eighteenth-century England.

III. THE INDUSTRIAL REVOLUTION

a. The Inventors

The Industrial Revolution was the movement by which men sought and found the means of making machines do their work for them. It eventually gathered up into itself the whole body of scientific and technical discovery by which man had come to control his environment or, as we say, control nature.

The separate streams from which this revolution sprang may be traced back to antiquity. They may be recognized in the middle ages in the development of mills, of mining and agricultural tools, and of the engineering of warfare. It was from the craftsmen directly engaged on these practical problems that the initial impulses for the revolution came.

Most trades continued for centuries without any serious advance. The miners and smelters, the engineers and navigators, the spinners and weavers, were all moving slowly and separately. But in the great century of fermenta-

[1] Later, when the professor who succeeded him was ejected for expressing the views which Newton had kept to himself, Newton continued to remain silent. Keynes (posthumously, 1947) notes that Newton was however excluded by his nonconformity from his second ambition to become Master of Trinity College, a post filled instead by the classical scholar, Richard Bentley, who had no obvious scruples of any kind.

tion and toleration it seemed that all trades and all learning might be brought together in the universities. At that time Hakluyt lectured on navigation, Hooke invented pumps and microscopes, and Petty taught anatomy and discussed economics, all in the same university at Oxford. But this seventeenth-century university synthesis was never allowed to mature. It was cut short, as we have seen, by the Clarendon Code. The end was reached by another path when the problem of power was met in the mines. The mines not only presented the problem, they also, in England, offered the coal which was part of its solution. And finally they offered the native skill of the community of miners. The steps of the revolution therefore came with the successive improvements made in the steam engine, designed for working in mines. These improvements, first empirical and later scientific, served to draw craftsmen of many kinds into the torrent of confident experiment which began to transform the world in the half-century following James Watt.

The people who worked this transformation grew up among dissenters in England, among Presbyterians in Scotland and among foreign immigrants, refugees from religious persecution of other kinds. The development here followed two main lines with little overlapping, the scientific and the industrial. On the scientific side there was of course a deep cleavage between the different sciences and a wide range and a mixed character in the social origins of the great discoverers (Tables 32, 33).[1] But we notice that after 1662 only two of the sixteen scientists (Halley and Malthus) had been able to gain entrance to an English university. The influence of the Quakers is seen in Dalton, Young and Davy. And the Warrington Academy (for Dissenters) employed Priestley (1761–1767) and taught Malthus (1779–1783).[2] Finally it was to the Royal Institution after 1800, owing to its lack of religious restrictions, that Young, Davy and Faraday owed their support.

On the industrial side we find again a cleavage between practical inventors like Hargreaves and Crompton, organizers like Wilkinson, Wedgwood and Arkwright, and the imaginatively scientific like Watt, who overlapped with the scientists and even, in the solitary case of Cartwright, were acceptable in an English university. Among these the organizers were Quakers, Unitarians and sceptics, while the inventors probably subscribed to a more modest, literal and fundamentalist form of dissent.[3]

The one meeting point of the pioneers in science and industry in the seminal period of the eighteenth century was the Lunar Society. This society met at Birmingham and Lichfield between 1766 and 1791 and it included

[1] Newton was a hybrid between dull farmers and his mother's distinguished family. They were the Ayscoughs or Askews. From her sister were descended the scientists James and Charles Hutton; and from herself the Earls of Portsmouth, and two noted wits, Catherine Barton (Halifax's mistress and Swift's friend) and the Rev. Sydney Smith (see Galton, 1869; De Morgan, 1885; Keynes, 1947).

[2] Malthus owed some of his social philosophy to this experience, notably his contradiction of the official Anglican view of Paley to whom the perfect society is one of 'a laborious and frugal people administering to the demands of a luxurious nation' (see Zirkle, 1959).

[3] Asa Briggs (1952); Bloomfield (1955).

Table 32. *Founders of the Scientific Revolution in Britain, born between* 1620 *and* 1800[1]

See *D.N.B.* and Bloomfield (1955).

Name	*Dates Birthplace*	*Father*	*Education and Religion*	*Appointments*	*Works*
JOHN RAY	1627–1705 Braintree, Essex	blacksmith	Cambridge: excluded as dissenter 1662	supported by patron	founder of systematic biology and natural history in Britain etc.
ROBERT BOYLE	1627–1691 Lismore, Ireland	E. of Cork industrial pioneer	Eton; Geneva, France	none	Boyle's Law[1] *Sceptical Chemist*
ROBERT HOOKE	1635–1703 I.o.Wight	minister	Westminster School C.C. Oxford 1653	R.S. Curator of Expts.	inventor and architect *Micrographia* 1665
ISAAC NEWTON[2]	1642–1727 Woolsthorpe, Lincs.	small farmer	left school at 14; Cambridge 1661 secret Unitarian	P.R.S. Prof. Maths Master of Mint Kt.	mathematical, optical and gravitational principles
JOHN FLAMSTEED[3]	1646–1719 Denby, Derbys.	maltster	self-educated ordained 1675	1st Astronomer Royal (1675–1719)	catalogue of stars: basis of modern astronomy
EDMUND HALLEY[4]	1656–1742 London	soap-boiler	St Paul's School, and Oxford	2nd Astronomer Royal (1721–1742)	terrestrial magnetism Arabic scholar
ABRAHAM DE MOIVRE	1667–1754 Vitry	gentry	Huguenot Academy of Sedan; to England 1688	none	founded actuarial science on probability theory
ADAM SMITH	1723–1790 Kirkcaldy	customs and law	Glasgow Univ.	Prof. at Glasgow	*Wealth of Nations* (1776). Founder of modern economics
JAMES HUTTON[5]	1726–1797 Edinburgh	merchant	Edinburgh, Paris and Leyden	none	Theory of the Earth (1785). Founder of modern geology

JOSEPH PRIESTLEY[6]	1733–1804 Birstall, Yorks.	cloth-dresser	Unitarian	Presbyterian minister	discovered oxygen (1774). Radical critic of Christian doctrine
WILLIAM HERSCHEL[7]	1738–1822 Hanover	musician	Moravian Protestant	King's Astronomer Kt.	astronomer; discovered Uranus (1781)
ROBERT MALTHUS	1766–1834 Guildford	gentry	Anglican, various	schoolmaster (Haileybury)	Theory of Population (1798). Law of Diminishing Returns
JOHN DALTON	1766–1844 Cockermouth, Cumbd.	weaver	Quaker	schoolmaster (Manchester)	Atomic Theory (1808) colour blindness
THOMAS YOUNG	1773–1829 Milverton, Som.	gentry	Quaker, widely travelled	physician, professor R.I. 1801	Egyptologist. Theories of Light and Vision, of Elasticity and Tides
HUMPHRY DAVY	1778–1829 Penzance	gentry	taught by Quaker saddler	P.R.S. Kt. professor R.I. 1805	chemical and electrical discoveries
MICHAEL FARADAY	1791–1867 Newington, Surrey	blacksmith	Sandemanian asst. to Davy	professor R.I. 1833	electro-magnetic induction (1830)

[1] In collaboration with Hooke.
[2] A class cross (see text). Unable to become Master of T.C. owing to not having been ordained.
[3] Unable to become Professor of Astronomy at Oxford owing to not being a graduate of Oxford or Cambridge.
[4] Denied Chair of Astronomy of Oxford on grounds of his religious views 1691, but accepted for Chair of Geometry, 1703.
[5] Cousin of Charles Hutton (For. Sec. R.S.), and both descended from Newton's mother's family (Ayscough).
[6] Married John Wilkinson's sister, 1762. Emigrated to U.S.A., 1794.
[7] Brother of Caroline and father of Sir John Herschel, both notable astronomers.

Note: All these were Fellows of the Royal Society; none after Halley was connected with the Universities of Oxford or Cambridge.

Table 33. *Founders of the Industrial Revolution in Britain, born between* 1650 *and* 1810

Name	*Dates Birthplace*	*Father*	*History*	*Works*
Thomas Savery	1650?–1715 nr. Totnes	Huguenot origin	military engineer	invented the first steam engine, 1698
Thomas Newcomen	1663–1729 Dartmouth	ironmonger	corresponded with R. Hooke	partner of Savery
Abraham Darby I[1]	1677–1717 nr. Dudley	farmer	Quaker; apprentice to malt-mill maker in Birmingham	coke-smelting of iron at Coalbrookdale, 1708
John Dolland (d'Hollande)	1706–1761 Spitalfields	silk-weaver	Huguenot, F.R.S.	optical inventor (also s. Peter and g.s. George)
James Hargreaves	1720–1778 Blackburn	carpenter and weaver	unknown, employed by R. Peel, g.f. of P.M.	spinning jenny, 1764
John Smeaton	1724–1792 nr. Leeds	unknown	descended from Thos. Smeton, convert of Calvin. F.R.S. 1753	Eddystone Lighthouse, 1759
John Wilkinson	1728–1808 Clifton, Cumbd.	iron-trade inventor	atheist and disciple of Tom Paine	castings for the iron bridge at Broseley, 1769
Matthew Boulton	1728–1809 Birmingham	silver-stamper	unknown, F.R.S.	Soho works 1762, partner of Watt

Josiah Wedgwood	1730–1795 Burslem	potter	Unitarian, F.R.S.	a founder of the modern pottery industry
Richard Arkwright	1732–1792 Preston	unknown	barber's apprentice	organized the mechanization of cotton spinning and weaving
James Watt	1736–1819 Greenock	engineer inventor[2] magistrate	grammar school F.R.S.	steam engine, 1769 composition of water, 1783
Edmund Cartwright	1743–1823 Marnham, Notts.	gentry	D.D. Fellow of Magdalen College, Oxford	power-loom (1785) and wool-combing machine; agricultural experimenter; poet
Samuel Crompton	1753–1827 nr. Bolton	spinner and weaver	working spinner	spinning mule, 1779
Thomas Telford	1757–1834 nr. Dumfries	shepherd	working mason	civil engineer and architect; writer
Richard Trevithick	1771–1833 Illogan, Corn.	mine-manager	Methodist, self-educated	first steam locomotive, 1801
George Stephenson	1781–1848 nr. Newcastle	colliery fireman	colliery work	Stockton–Darlington railway (1819–1825)
Isambard K. Brunel	1806–1859 Portsmouth	engineer and inventor[3]	R.C. Paris	railway, steamship and artillery engineer

[1] See Raistrick (1953).

[2] And grandson of a mathematics teacher.

[3] Sir Marc Brunel, F.R.S., French royalist refugee. Mother: Sophia Kingdom.

Boulton, Watt, Wedgwood and Priestley. These people were brought together, not by a great university or academy, but by a great individual. That is by Erasmus Darwin (1731–1802), physician, evolutionist and poet. Notice that it was through its meetings that the marriages took place by which he became the grandfather of Charles Darwin and of Francis Galton.[1]

It took a brash inquisitive Scot, James Boswell, to step across from the old academic world to the new industrial world. But even he could not move Dr Johnson to contemplate the 'mighty machines' of Boulton and Watt. On the contrary Johnson playfully expressed the view that his Lichfield was a city of philosophers: 'we work with our heads, and make the boobies of Birmingham work for us with their hands'. That was one of the historic misunderstandings of the year 1776.

For at this moment we have, on the one hand, Darwin's circle of friends in Birmingham creating our own Industrial Revolution while celebrating the political revolutions in America and France. And, on the other hand, we have Johnson's circle of admirers in London deploring new and uncomfortable ideas. The contrast expresses the cleavage, the enduring cleavage, between the two sides of English society.

The Scots indeed at that moment were the only people who could step across the gulf in English society. For in Scotland the Clarendon Code was revoked when the bishops were in turn ejected by the Revolution of 1688. It was for this main reason that the eighteenth century saw a revival of both learning and science in Scotland. After David Hume and Adam Smith came the founder of modern geology, James Hutton, and the new race of Scottish engineers, James Watt, Thomas Telford, John McAdam and their successors. In consequence the Scottish universities embarked on modern engineering and medicine while these subjects were still smothered in England; a circumstance which served to enhance the flow of Scottish migration into England arising from the Industrial Revolution.[2]

b. The Work of the Dissenters

The Industrial Revolution arose out of the inventions of particular individuals in particular communities, chiefly dissenting communities. As it developed it naturally transformed the life of these communities. They prospered and multiplied. Or, more precisely, some prospered and others multiplied.

The body of dissenters as a whole were recruited by French Huguenots and in Ireland by German Moravians. They were also later recruited by the revolt of John Wesley's Methodists. These were, in the later French phrases, *menu peuple* and *sans culottes*. They were little men who were tired of being trodden on by big men. Whether these were big Churchmen or big Quakers, they all wore fine clothes. The Methodists therefore marked themselves out by re-asserting the modesty of their dress. And, like all serious religious sects, they bound themselves together in a genetic community by Wesley's requirement of no marriage with outsiders.[3]

[1] Pearson (1930); Schofield (1963). [2] See W. J. Reader (1966).
[3] Southey (1820).

All these, together with the Baptists and Congregationalists who accepted the Trinitarian formula, played a modest part in the development of industry. They multiplied but did not prosper greatly. Those who rejected the conventional formulae prospered without multiplying. These were the Unitarians and the Quakers. Their sceptical and rigorous intelligence underlay the greatest developments.

The dissenting section of society had thus become socially, intellectually and genetically diversified in its sects. This diversification was indeed at the root of the separate emigration and separate location of the sects at the beginning of the North American colonies. For it was the Independents or Congregationalists who established themselves in New England, the Baptists in Rhode Island, the Huguenots and Dutch Reformed Church in New York, the Quakers and later the Mennonites in Pennsylvania, the Presbyterians in eastern New Jersey, the Catholics in Lord Baltimore's colony, and so on. Each original community had been a stratified society of masters and servants. Now following the successful example of the Quakers each community in turn discovered the profit that was to be made from tolerating other kinds of dissent; from letting in later comers as servants or indentured convicts, without demanding the religious conformity of the pioneers.

Later immigrations and dispersions have vastly complicated the original picture of social stratification and geographical differentiation in the American colonies and their successor states. When dissenters became rich and strong the Episcopacy began, as in England, to claim their respect or deference. But, as each region separately evolves, the genetic differentiation of regions remains in America after 300 years, as it does in England after 1500 years, of colonization.

In England each city had its own society stratified by dissent. We cannot do better than take the example of Birmingham.[1] This city, like many others, was created, as we may say, by the Act of Uniformity. In ancient Coventry and Nottingham with their charters, the bulk of the population being dissenters were denied a voice in their own affairs. But in Birmingham with no charter, even in 1664, the workers were free men. In Birmingham therefore the smiths and foundrymen congregated; they escaped the supervision of the clergy and magistrates in the older cities.[2]

The first congregation in Birmingham to build itself a chapel called themselves Presbyterians but in fifty years, in 1748, they had split into Congregationalists and Unitarians. Quakers were there already. Baptists appeared in 1738, Methodists (following Wesley) in 1752 and a few years later Jews. A century later the success of Birmingham, created by the dissenters, had brought in an immigrant wave of ordinary churchgoers outnumbering the

[1] See Gill and Briggs; as also Hoskins on Exeter, and Green and Young on Norwich.

[2] Not only in Birmingham but also, as Tom Paine puts it, in a footnote, in Manchester cotton-spinners and in Sheffield steel-founders, who were chiefly dissenters, had withdrawn to an 'asylum' from the persecution of the Established Church in the chartered towns. These men, he adds, are beginning to go abroad to set up their industry and enjoy freedom in new countries.

founding communities. The whole census has been recorded for 1851 by Gill: we may classify them as follows:

FOUNDERS		IMMIGRANTS	
Methodist	6,000	Church of England	20,000
Baptist	4,200	Roman Catholic (Irish)	3,400
Unitarian	1,850	Presbyterian (Scottish)	464
Quakers	544	Jews	185

Yet the driving force remained with the founders and with the higher class of the founders. As Briggs puts it, from 1840 to 1880 the mayors were almost continuously Unitarian: the Nettlefolds were preparing for an industrial empire, the Chamberlains for a political one. But the Member of Parliament (1857–1885) was the Quaker radical, John Bright.

Outside Birmingham and Liverpool the Quaker meeting-house had a more important part to play than the Unitarian chapel in the development of industry and finance. Their solemn probity as well as their intelligence, we cannot doubt, advanced the Barclays, Gurneys and Lloyds as bankers. Their social responsibility must have contributed to the success of the Cadburys, Frys and Rowntrees in the cocoa industry. Similar gifts must have helped the Crosfields, Gossages and Hudsons to build up the soap business. So it was that a new and genetically contrasted governing class grew up, with hardly more scientific enterprise than the Church of England's establishment but corresponding to it in wealth and preparing to challenge it in political power.

The independence and initiative of the dissenting communities had indeed directed them not only towards industrial advance but also towards political self-government. Every congregation was a training ground for responsible opinion and action. And it was the inborn character of the dissenters, individualist and empirical, which created their industries, their religion and their politics. It was the character, together with the religious organization it had given them, and the industrial opportunities it had created for them, that gave them economic success and turned them repeatedly, when the occasion arose, in 1789, in 1838 and again in the twentieth century, towards industrial development, in management and in labour, rather than towards political revolution.

The new industrial and dissenting groups retained their coherence. Digging themselves in, they became an alternative establishment based on their separately intermarried genetic communities. It lasted until the end of the nineteenth century when the religious beliefs underlying it, those beliefs often described as the 'nonconformist conscience', began to crumble. They crumbled at the top where conditions had most changed; for the community was itself stratified on its urban foundations in parallel with the corresponding entrenched establishment stratified on its rural foundations.

It is profitable to study the shifting grounds of conflict between the two opposed societies. For the official establishment, while apparently retreating, have always been protected in their retreat by the ownership of the land, the Church, the universities and the schools, by their fairly direct control of titles and honours and in general of the paraphernalia of monarchy; in short by their control, which they were willing to sell at the price of conversion or matrimony, of the basis of deference in society.[1]

The combining of hybridization, directed migration, civilization and social promotion recurring all over Europe, may be illustrated in many nineteenth-century families in Britain. Thus in one family we have the succession:[2]

1. Thomas Gladstones Merchant of Leith. Presbyterian. 1737–1809.	2. Sir John Gladstone Slave-owner of Liverpool. Evangelical. 1764–1835. (m. Ann Robertson, d. of Provost of Dingwall, Ross-shire.)	3. Rt Hon W. E. Gladstone Prime Minister. High Churchman (Eton and Christ Church, Oxford). 1809–1898. (m. Catherine Glynne of Hawarden Castle, Flintshire.)

This family shows us, not only its own evolution, but the profound effect of a changing environment on a perceptive observer. For Gladstone himself was transformed in his view of society by his changing experience as he moved south from Scottish Liverpool to Oxford and to London.

This advantage of the land-based establishment has been prolonged up to the present day by the fact that every advance of industry enriched the landlords in their resistance to industry. It also strengthened the government in war against rival powers and revolting colonies and in the seizure of new territories, all of them activities repudiated in their time by the leaders of the dissenting communities, men of the kind of Darby, Wilkinson, Nettlefold and Galton. They had unwittingly given an empire to an establishment who thought they had won it themselves.[3]

The sharpness of the contrast between the established and dissenting communities has thus been blurred by selective promotion, migration and intermarriage during the last century. The dissenters, no longer fierce in their dissent, no longer poor or austere in their habit, in their higher levels have been drawn into the establishment and broken down by hybridization. And even at the lower levels their habit of sectarian inbreeding is slowly fading away. All that remains clearly defined of the great cleavage of 1661 are at the two extremes: on the one hand, the citadels of the establishment in our remoter

[1] A basis of deference which, like so much else in England, is reflected in the position of the corresponding Episcopalian sect in the U.S.A. (Vance Packard, 1964; see ch. 25).

[2] See *D.N.B.* and Magnus (1954).

[3] Even, so they said, on the playing-fields of Eton, a school near Windsor endowed by King Henry VI in 1440 for the free education of twenty-five poor boys. There, to be sure, like Robert Boyle, the victor of Waterloo was first introduced to English society (see *D.N.B.*).

landed aristocracy, our old universities, our 'public' schools, and our churches; and, on the other hand, the citadels of dissent and protest among the Exclusive Brethren, the extreme nationalists of Wales and Scotland, and the short-lived fanatical fringes of political organization.

c. The Universities

In England the barriers of the seventeenth century were not broken down by any single revolutionary step. The Reform Bill of 1832 put the puritan creators of the Scientific and Industrial Revolutions, after being thwarted, as Laver has it, for two centuries, on the threshold of political power. They demanded that the universities should be opened to them. And after forty years, in 1871, the universities of Oxford and Cambridge were opened, not only to dissenters, but also to Jews and Catholics. Clerical control was relaxed in 1878 and the vow or appearance of celibacy for teachers and tutors was abandoned.[1]

These reforms did not, however, produce the effects that had been hoped or feared of them. The body of teachers in these two universities make their own rules of life and above all elect their own successors. Colleges established on monastic principles continued to exclude women, to discourage the sciences, to defer to the Church, and to pursue the pupils who would later provide the benefactions and maintain the social status that benefactions bring. A system of scholarships attached the colleges to similarly endowed 'public' schools with a similar interest in social promotion. The universities of Oxford and Cambridge have therefore continued to the present day to maintain the seventeenth-century opposition to the society and culture of the dissenters, with a consequent intellectual impoverishment of both the excluders and the excluded.

Thus it was not possible to reform rich and independent corporations by legislation from a distance. The new kind of pupils were admitted but only to be subjected to the old kind of education given by the old body of self-perpetuating tutors, and competitive games were taken as a satisfactory substitute for intellectual activity.

At this point Bagehot's principle of *deference* is seen to dominate the social situation. All the weaker or lower strata of society are liable to be impressed with the standards of conduct followed by those stronger than themselves. An intelligent deference is, of course, an advantage for the development of any stratified society. It is only when the deference they feel and show appears to be misguided, or preserved beyond its natural term of life, that we describe this reaction as one of *snobbery*.[2] The universities became the main channel of social promotion and of government employment throughout a large empire. So it was that the social prestige and wealth of the two universities, following the older practices of an older governing class, imposed themselves on the rising industrial and commercial classes who were in general happy to kick away the ladder of science and technology, dirt and squalor, by which they,

[1] One Oxford don objecting to the first proposal is reported to have asked 'How many of us, after all, have ever seen a dissenter eat?' For another glimpse of the two castes or societies in action see Disraeli's *Sybil* (1845).

[2] See the Duke of Bedford for a well-informed contemporary view.

and their country, had ascended from poor beginnings. For in England it was the wealth derived from the sweat and the smoke of the north which more and more largely supported the green and pleasant south. And it was on continued scientific and technical invention that the continuation of that wealth would depend.

Thus when Gladstone came from Liverpool and Asquith from Huddersfield to breathe the clean air, imbibe the classical spirit, and enjoy the rich amenities of Oxford, no one could tell them of the forces which were changing the world they were living in and their own country's position in it.[1] Nor, of course, could any such disagreeable ideas be imparted to the civil service which administered the policies of such a confident establishment. It was their senior members who could warn new recruits when preparing (in 1934) for the crisis of a coming war that they should not endanger their judgment or their integrity by sitting on committees together with scientists.[2]

What was true of the nation's statesmen and bureaucrats was and still is true of the men responsible for particular industries. In the universities they were taught to believe that the science and technology which had created their wealth were now beneath their notice. They left it to other nations to build the future on foundations of which they had been unaware.

The Clarendon Code had induced a social cleavage in English life much more durable than anyone had imagined simply because it legally exaggerated a cleavage and an opposition that were genetically already existing. That is why the two sides neither could nor would understand one another. That is also why the old establishment still holds the old endowments in Oxford and Cambridge and still has not surrendered them. In consequence the educational system has remained stunted, not by poverty, but by the wealth of its mediaeval and Catholic foundations, an old inherited wealth from which the Protestant world and younger nations have not yet suffered. The principles of hardened stratification which we suppose to have accounted for decay in other empires now express themselves in processes which are still easily visible.

The contrast with France and Germany is worth noting in this respect. For in France, while it was Napoleon who advanced science most by his patronage, it was to the old régime that Laplace (1749–1827) and Lavoisier (1743–1794), who organized the metric system in 1791, owed their appointments. In Germany the variety of universities sponsored by rival princes of different religious persuasions made for competition and also a freedom and range of development which was to bring its reward and, to be sure, its penalty in the nineteenth century.

The opposition between Anglican and dissenter, having a genetic and class basis, was changed not at all by the French Revolution. It was shifted only by the evolution of the whole society. On the surface this shift seemed to be the effect of deference to outstanding individuals, particularly to John Wesley and William Wilberforce who in dramatic circumstances underwent religious conversion from one standard, one stereotype of belief and behaviour

[1] From this pattern the Chamberlains and the Baldwins (from Birmingham and Broseley) scarcely diverged.

[2] Darlington (1948); Snow (1959); Nicholson (1967).

to another. But in fact it was the balance of influence of the social classes that was undergoing conversion.[1]

This process of conversion in the end effected a switch in the whole outward behaviour or standard of deference of the English people in the first half of the nineteenth century. It was a switch correlated with three basic social events which were themselves connected: the growing dominance of the industrial towns and classes, the passing of the Reform Bill in 1832, and the replacement of the elderly and dissolute Hanoverian monarchs by the puritanical court of a young queen and her consort. What individuals now did was little changed; but what they said they did, and what they demanded that others should do, underwent a complete although temporary revolution.

[1] See Muriel Jaeger (1956).

23

REVOLUTION IN THE WEST

I. GENETIC THEORY AND SOCIAL REFORM (1640–1789)

THE PRINTED BIBLE, as we have seen, quickly raised social problems in the minds of its readers. What was the justification for certain individuals or classes having greater power or wealth than others? The answer had been given by Plato[1] and Aristotle and, one might say also, by Moses, that some men were inherently better than others through being Greeks or Jews as opposed to barbarians or gentiles who alone could be slaves. It was an answer which was no longer easily applied when the whole community were baptized Christians. But it became easier when they were Anglicans, Lutherans or Presbyterians.

The issue was for the first time squarely brought before the world at the climax of the English Civil War between 1646 and 1649. In the course of the struggle those ideas which had been choked ever since the suppression of the Lollard movement now came to the surface. In the army and in the city there were men who began to grumble. They asked what the war had been fought to win and what had indeed been won. Was it just to establish the Grandees, a new governing class of generals? Or could the principles be set out for a new and permanent constitution proclaiming certain natural rights of man, not a charter given by authority but an *Agreement of the People*.

The Grandees had their strong arm in Cromwell and their mouthpiece in Milton. The grumblers, or *Levellers* as their enemies called them, had neither military strength nor learned eloquence. They were fanatical and eccentric and in their social origins and religious views they were seen to be diverse.[2]

[1] Plato's discussion in the *Republic* is the most rational before the last century, for while he recognizes social classes differing in their hereditary gifts he also admits the propriety of social movement following variation (i.e. genetic recombination) in these gifts.

[2] Lilburne (1613–1657) died a Quaker but his father was evidently a fine gentleman for he was the last man in England to demand the feudal trial by battle in a civil lawsuit (Frank, 1955; Hill, 1940).

What united the Levellers was their belief, an optimistic belief derived largely from the Bible, that common men, including the common soldiers who had fought the war, were universally reasonable and educable. They required no authority, lay or clerical, to govern them. They knew how to govern themselves and had a right to do so. Their gospel was inevitably one of equality and rationality. For them 'by natural birth all men are equally and alike born to like property, liberty and freedom'. Hence Wistanley demanded land for all. Rainborowe demanded votes for all. A third, Jubbes, demanded religious freedom for all, even for papists.

In January 1649 the king had been tried and executed and in May a Republic had been proclaimed. For Cromwell the time seemed ripe for the invasion and resettlement of Ireland. But for the Levellers, England ought to be put straight first. Their propaganda led to a mutiny in the army. But within a week Cromwell had rounded up 300 mutineers in Burford church and when he had shot five of them (on May 13th) the revolt was broken.

Their mistake had been the mistake of the Lollards: they had come a few generations too soon in the evolution of society. One generation later John Locke put in written form the principles for which he considered the puritans had fought. His *Treatises on Government and Letters on Toleration* published in 1685 showed the government deriving its authority from the sovereign people, the two being bound to one another by an agreement or contract whose terms might evolve, an agreement demanding co-operation and toleration from all parties. But for the time being the sovereign people were middle-class people and the agreement was an agreement to safeguard their property. These views provided the theoretical argument not only for the settlement of the English Revolution three years later but also for the American Declaration of Independence of 1776 and for the French assertion of the Rights of Man in 1789.

Such views in fact derived from the growth of rich commercial classes in England and Holland whose confidence had been established by the rise of the English and Dutch Republics. They had nothing to do with the Levellers but they produced their own revolutions. They shook off the remains, or most of the remains, of feudalism in Holland, in England and in her American colonies. But in other parts of Europe the mythical power of kings, exercised over still largely feudal societies, was unchallenged. And the new ideas were not enough to destabilize the great established feudal societies of Catholic, Protestant or, of course, Orthodox Europe. That had to be achieved by a more dramatic challenge to the traditional ideas of human society. To understand such traditional ideas at this time we need to look at the royal families themselves.

II. THE CRISIS OF MONARCHY

While the workaday European world was occupied in the ten generations which followed the Reformation with real problems affecting the future of mankind, the royal rulers continued to be occupied, or, we may say, preoccupied, with their own future which seemed to them the most important thing in the world. Their marriages, the offspring of these marriages, arising or failing to arise for reasons we understand but they did not, trivial as they may appear to us now, these things reacted at every step on the lives of the peoples and the development of the nations. Evolution was now proceeding so fast that the inventions of scientists, the ideas of philosophers, the work of artisans and both the wisdom and the madness of monarchs all made rapid and effective connections and therefore have to be considered by us in these connections.

Take first the behaviour of the royal caste as a whole. We have seen how they developed by severe competition into an outbred network continually selected for their professional excellence. They were in fact bred to, for, and in their profession. They were in it, like artisans, soldiers or lawyers, because they liked their jobs. They liked to be kings. They enjoyed governing because they, and usually others, believed they did it well.

They expected, and others expected them, to command armies, to appoint lay, clerical and military officials, to negotiate treaties, to plan cities, to grant charters, to administer and when necessary to reform the law, to conduct and to dominate the grand ceremonies of the State. Above all they had to marry and to breed and to avoid boy favourites or *mignons*. That was where, in England, William II, Edward II and Richard II had come to grief; and in France Henry III and Louis XIII likewise.

As time went on, and notably with the coming of the Renaissance, kings began more and more to specialize and to delegate. They had to face more complex problems. To meet these new duties they had been prepared by intermarriage. In their male lines they were barbarians. On the female side they descended from Byzantine and even Muslim dynasties.[1] Financial acumen and artistic judgment were brought in by Italian families such as the Medici. Naturally from all this recombination there were some failures. Moreover in the basic process of social evolution, that of choice of professions, they had less scope than any of their subjects. Some, like Henry VI, would willingly have stepped down if they had dared or their wives and kinsmen had allowed them to do so.

Now the position of the royal caste was radically changed by the Reformation and changed in a sense which did not trouble the subject peoples at all. The whole body of royal families of Christendom had bred together for twenty generations according to the Mosaic rules elaborated by Justinian and enforced by the popes. Now, in the space of a generation and without being seen, the system, their system, had dissolved. The old body of prohibitions on inbreeding had gone to pieces and a new body of prohibitions, on outbreeding, had come into play. The rise of Luther in 1517 meant that within twenty years western Christendom was divided into two worlds, Protestant and Catholic, within which marriage was easier and between which it was more difficult. The capture of Rome and the pope, Clement VII, by the imperial troops in 1527 meant that the Emperor could make his own rules for marriage to serve his own ends. The bar to incest was set not by the pope but in effect by public

[1] See Pine (1954); Moncreiffe and Pottinger (1956).

opinion. Public opinion among Protestants in the north excluded uncle-niece marriage. But not among Catholics in the south.

The Hapsburg emperors with their power and glory would thus be able, or so they thought, to do as they wanted with the Catholic royal families and through them in the long run with Catholic Europe. Let us see what they made of the job.

It was Maximilian I, son of the first member of his family to be elected Roman Emperor, who established the power of the Hapsburgs in Europe. He did it by marriage and not by war, his own marriage, his son's and his grandsons'.[1] The marriages being deliberately with heiresses did not prove highly fertile. But being equally deliberately outbreeding marriages they kept the family going to produce Charles V, an Emperor who ruled such vast territories that he had to divide them with his brother. From this division, at the Treaty of Brussels in 1522, there followed a process of repeated inbreeding. First it was between the two Hapsburg lines and then between them and three other royal lines with which they now attempted to interbreed for their security especially against France. In this business of posting their daughters back and forth it often happened that where a cousin died an uncle had to take his place or one brother succeeded another. Philip II set the example: His Catholic Majesty, himself the son of a cousin marriage, married three cousins and a niece. Thus the Mosaic restrictions of Catholic Europe were thrown overboard by the Catholic kings. They returned unawares to the pagan habit which had wrecked the Achaemenids, the Pharaohs, the Ptolemies and the Caesars (Pedigree 17).

The succession of repeated heiress-marriages and cousin- or uncle-niece marriages would have destroyed any ordinary family. But a third circumstance prolonged the decline of the network of Catholic dynasties and the misery it brought with it. That was the suspension in their favour of the ordinary processes of natural selection. Their ancestors had had to fight for their thrones; or even for survival. The contemporary Guises and Bourbons fought like devils and that was how they got to the top. The new emperors were protected by the glory of their ancestors and also by the Renaissance development of administration in depth. When Charles V won his greatest victories it was because he did not know where his armies were fighting. And none of his legitimate and inbred descendants even dared to face the terrors of personal combat.

Here there is no doubt of the effect of inbreeding on a largely infertile and thoroughly unwarlike family. For their illegitimate and outbred descendants were numerous, and they were often fertile, capable and warlike. They provide a control to the great Hapsburg experiment.[2] So also does the contrast

[1] As was said later: '*alii bella gerunt*, *tu felix Austria nube*'! The Emperor was however as enterprising in the clerical as in the matrimonial field. At the age of fifty-two and six years before Luther's protest, on the security of the crown jewels, he attempted to borrow from the Fugger banking house of Nuremberg the funds with which to buy the College of Cardinals, secure his election as pope, and solve the problem of Europe. The bankers unfortunately turned him down (Nada, 1962).

[2] Charles V's bastard Don John of Austria (1545–1578) was the victor of Lepanto.

of the Stuarts with the later Bourbons of Hapsburg descent. Both of them lost battles. But, while the Stuarts usually fought, the Bourbons always ran away. The difference later had decisive historical consequences.

The Europe which had been dominated by the two branches of the Hapsburg family was transformed by the coming of the Bourbons. For by their rule within a century France became the richest, strongest and culturally the most advanced state in Europe. During this time France was safeguarded by the marriage of the King, Louis XIII, his sister, and his sons with the Austrian and the Spanish Hapsburgs and with the British Stuarts. Moreover the Spanish marriage of his son, Louis XIV, brought Spain into the Bourbon property only forty years later. Thus the Bourbons, who had damaged themselves genetically, fortified themselves politically by their Hapsburg marriages.

Fortunately for them, in the beginning the Bourbons had neither inbred nor had they married heiresses. They succeeded by their own qualities, by fighting. But their survival was a near thing. Louis XIII was a pederast and left no heir till his last years. His second son, the Duke of Orléans, inherited his father's addiction which reduced his political value as a young man. It did not however prevent him later, through his eleven legitimate children, from becoming the ancestor, for the *best* of them many times, of all the otherwise declining Catholic royal families of Europe. Thus the hereditary fertility of one man, even a pervert, can save a whole race. It was indeed by inbreeding on the Hapsburg pattern, between the two Bourbon lines, that the very fertile but otherwise ineffective Louis XV was begotten.[1]

The effect of the Bourbons on the Stuarts through the marriage of Charles I was felt in quite a different dimension from the Catholic marriages. For by this marriage the Stuarts entered the Catholic network. Charles II and James II were both converts to the Roman Church by their mother's heredity and despite their own environment and their whole dynastic interest. The Stuarts indeed destroyed themselves by trying to breed a Catholic dynasty for a Protestant country.

The non-Catholic royal families were numerous, poor, equally new, and relatively free from intermarriage with the more subtle and civilized Catholics. Naturally therefore they maintained the war-like character of their ancestors. That is why in the seventeenth and eighteenth centuries we still see, leading their troops to victory, Gustavus Adolphus and Charles XII of Sweden, Peter the Great of Russia and George II of England and his son, Butcher Cumberland. It is also why we see the last Catholic pretender Charles Edward Stuart leading his troops to defeat in 1745.

The breeding behaviour of the European royal families arose from political causes which are transparently clear. But its genetical and therefore political consequences were entirely hidden from the operators themselves. The kinship they created gave a kind of unity behind the increasingly ridiculous intrigues and wars which they conducted. This unity consisted in their uniform recognition of the rights of kings, to be jointly maintained against the newer and

Philip IV's thirty bastards included a second Don John of Austria (1629–1679) who left more mark than any of his legitimate descendants (Nada, 1962).

[1] See Nancy Mitford (1966); also Nada (1962) and *E.B.* (1929) art.: 'Bourbon.'

Pedigree 17. Pedigree showing the Role of Hapsburg Inbreeding in the Development of the European Catholic Royal Families

After Nada (1962); Petrie (1963) and E.B. (1929)

Notes:

As with the Caesars and other dynasties two main stages may be separated:

i. *Outbreeding* designed here to enlarge the dominions of the family and secure them against other states, especially France and the Ottoman Empire.

ii. *Inbreeding* designed to secure the alliances of the kindred sovereigns.

Note that:

a. When inbred lines failed, outbreeding, legitimate or illegitimate, gave a fresh start or a more viable progeny (e.g. Don John, victor of Lepanto 1571).

b. Philip II had two other infertile marriages not shown here (see Petrie 1963):

(i) Maria, d. of John III of Portugal (*c*).
(iii) Elizabeth, d. of Henry II of France.

c. Hapsburg inbreeding was shrewdly observed but its consequence falsely predicted in the English ballad of 1623 (Pinto and Rodway 1965)

Shee's ne're like to bee Mother:
For her incestuous house could not
Have children but begott
By Uncle or by Brother.

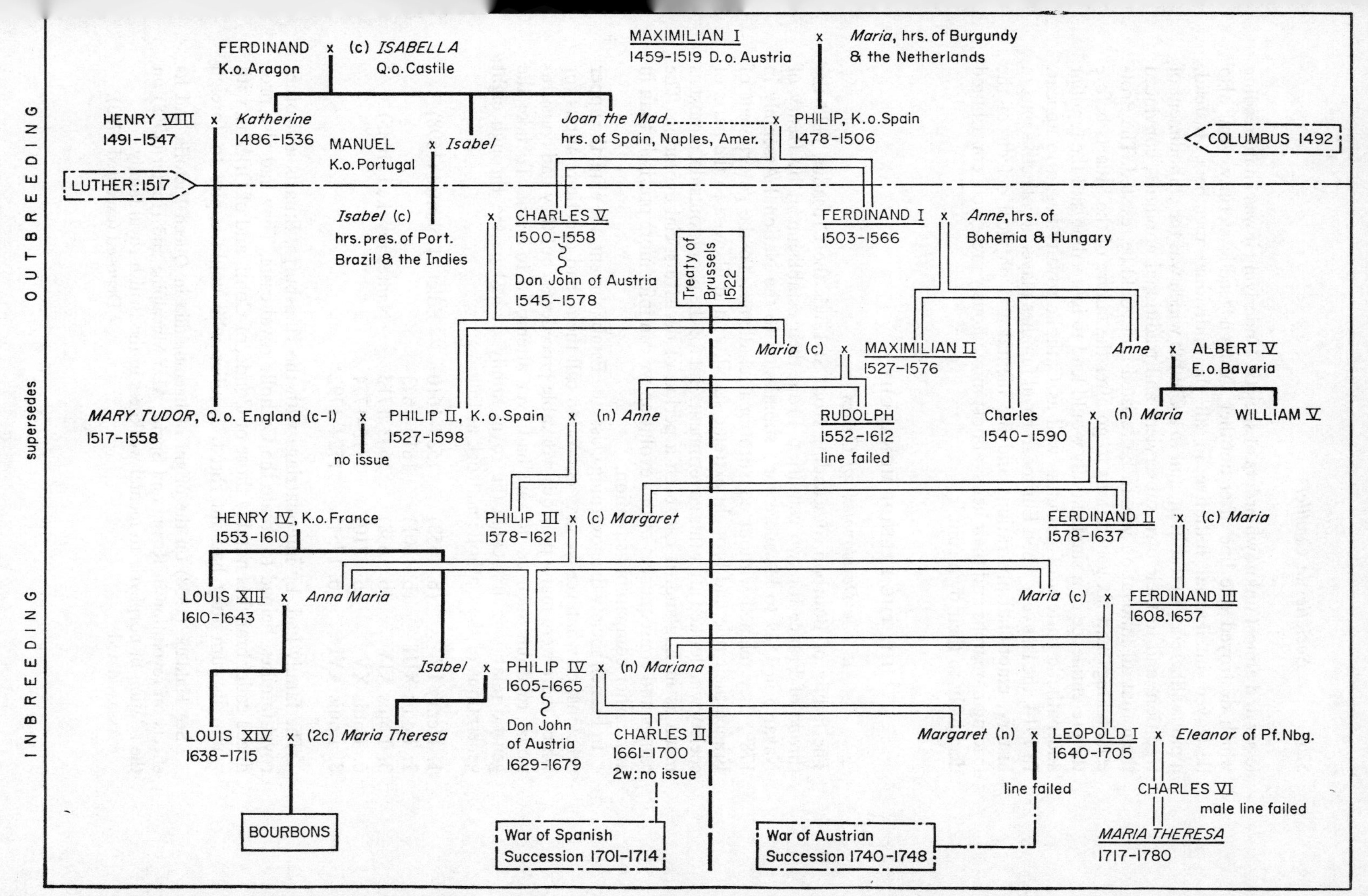

OUTBREEDING
supersedes
INBREEDING
FERDINAND K.o.Aragon
x (c) ISABELLA Q.o.Castile
MAXIMILIAN I 1459-1519 D.o. Austria
x Maria, hrs. of Burgundy & the Netherlands
HENRY VIII 1491-1547
x Katherine 1486-1536
MANUEL K.o.Portugal
x Isabel
Joan the Mad
hrs. of Spain, Naples, Amer.
x PHILIP, K.o.Spain 1478-1506
COLUMBUS 1492
LUTHER:1517
Isabel (c)
hrs. pres. of Port. Brazil & the Indies
x CHARLES V 1500-1558
Don John of Austria 1545-1578
Treaty of Brussels 1522
FERDINAND I 1503-1566
x Anne, hrs. of Bohemia & Hungary
Maria (c) x MAXIMILIAN II 1527-1576
Anne x ALBERT V E.o.Bavaria
MARY TUDOR, Q.o. England (c-l) 1517-1558
x no issue
PHILIP II, K.o.Spain 1527-1598
x (n) Anne
RUDOLPH 1552-1612 line failed
Charles 1540-1590
x (n) Maria
WILLIAM V
HENRY IV, K.o.France 1553-1610
PHILIP III 1578-1621 x (c) Margaret
FERDINAND II 1578-1637 x (c) Maria
LOUIS XIII 1610-1643 x Anna Maria
Maria (c) x FERDINAND III 1608.1657
Isabel x PHILIP IV 1605-1665 x (n) Mariana
Don John of Austria 1629-1679
LOUIS XIV 1638-1715 x (2c) Maria Theresa
CHARLES II 1661-1700 2w: no issue
Margaret (n) x LEOPOLD I 1640-1705 x Eleanor of Pf.Nbg.
line failed
CHARLES VI male line failed
MARIA THERESA 1717-1780
BOURBONS
War of Spanish Succession 1701-1714
War of Austrian Succession 1740-1748

lesser and almost unknown orders of society. Underlying it was an inbreeding which destroyed one line after another through genetic sterility. And also destroyed intellectual initiative in all the individual members. Instead, a pious adherence to tradition, and to a Church which was the embodiment of tradition, and to their own subservient and traditional nobilities, convinced them that all innovation was to be resisted and could be resisted. The Protestant kings had six generations to go after the failure of the Stuarts before the pre-eminence of a single family would lead to inbreeding and the familiar and pathetic pattern of pagan as well as Catholic royalty began to appear. In 1914, the last year when European royal families played a collective part in history, emotional aberrations and the mental and physical defects of the leading monarchs and their heirs, almost miraculously preserved, contributed decisively to their own ruin.[1]

III. THE FRENCH MONARCHY

a. The Development of Castes

The family of Bourbon, descending from St Louis the Crusader, held the throne of France for two centuries. From their establishment by Henry of Navarre in 1589 to his successor's submission to the National Assembly in 1789, they reigned without constitutional challenge. To the government of France their rule had brought extreme stability; and likewise to the parts of society who looked after this government. But for the people outside, almost as much as in England, it had been a period of decisive social evolution. The causes and consequences of this evolution we can infer more precisely than in any earlier comparable situation.

In French society the governing class, the Establishment, the élite, the upper echelons, or whatever we may choose to call them, had genetic relations for which there were many previous workable precedents; but they had constitutional relations such as no one had ever attempted to work. To take the genetic relations: first came the royal family. It had passed through eight generations of the Catholic network as follows:

1. Henry IV	(b. 1553)	1589–1610[2]	Edict of Nantes (1598)
2. Louis XIII	(b. 1601)	1610–1643	
3. Louis XIV	(b. 1638)	1643–1715	Nantes revoked (1685)
6. Louis XV	(b. 1710)	1715–1774	
8. Louis XVI	(b. 1754)	1774–1792[3]	

The family had, by intermarriage with the Hapsburgs, Stuarts and other royal families, helped to create the Catholic royal caste. They had also produced cadet branches notably those of Condé, of Conti, and of Orléans, with whom in turn they had interbred, families who could aspire to foreign

[1] See Haldane (1938) on the origin of haemophilia in Queen Victoria and its effects on revolution in Russia and Spain. Also Macalpine and Hunter (1968) on the relation of porphyria to mental weakness in the British royal family.

[2] Assassinated.

[3] Deposed (executed 1793).

thrones. And there were bastard lines of varying social status. All these helped to make a middle layer between the royal caste and the non-royal nobility.[1]

Second came the hereditary nobility of feudal and fighting origins, the *noblesse d'épée* or *noblesse de race*. Here rank was graded or estimated by length of pedigree and by title from Prince or Duke down to Viscount and Baron, titles carefully copied in England. Into the equation wealth also entered. The poorer could not afford the expenses of the court and had to live obscurely in the distant provinces. Wealth moreover was liable to diminish since primogeniture was not asserted with English rigour and, with their title, all sons inherited some share of the estate. Abortion, infanticide, poisoning and the whole Venetian system had not yet given way to modern forms of family planning. But naturally younger sons were pressed into the Church which was able to provide for the care of celibate aristocrats more amply than was possible in the confined and declining state of Venice.[2]

Within the French Church there thus survived the same layered mediaeval pyramid which had lost its shape along with its clerical celibacy in the Protestant countries of Europe. It was parallel with that of the nobility. The bastard sons of kings and younger sons of dukes became cardinals, bishops and so on down the scale. And since the Church owned nearly half the landed property in the country its endowments were a source of comfort to the whole nobility.

Now, before the time of the Bourbons, in Rome and Byzantium, the principle had been understood that the safety of the Crown depended on keeping the non-royal nobility out of the royal administration. What began as policy assisted by genetic inclination was confirmed by habit and convention: they were confined to the one profession of arms. And having been elbowed into this profession they gradually succeeded in elbowing everybody else out of it. With Louis XV (in 1756) all generals began to be ennobled and conversely with Louis XVI (in 1781) the royal commission began to be the exclusive but less and less glorious privilege of the *noblesse*. Commoners had been given commissions free under Louis XIV. Under his successor they were not even allowed to buy them.

This policy would have ruined the French army in another generation. But up to the Revolution its effect was not clearly disadvantageous. The joint prestige of the army and the nobility was enough to attract recruits from the Catholic nobility of Europe including Jacobite exiles from Scotland and Ireland. This flow kept the army of Louis XVI up to the highest standard and helped to make it the foundation of French revolutionary success.

How then did the King recruit his administrators? As in other countries they bought or bribed rather than earned their way into his civil, just as much as into his military, service. And they came from varied sources, the professional and commercial classes, the lower ranks of the clergy and the provincial

[1] Illustrated by the family tree of Louis XIV and the personal histories given by Miss Mitford.

[2] Thus the proportion of bishops who were of noble parentage increased more steeply in France than in England during the eighteenth century (Ravitch, 1965; also Hampson, 1963).

or foreign nobility. So far as they were clergy the great administrators like Richelieu (1585–1642) or the Italian Mazarin (1602–1661) became cardinals. So far as they were laymen like Colbert (1619–1683) or Turgot (1727–1781) they moved into a *noblesse de robe*. In addition, since Louis XIV had in 1692 replaced elective by nominated municipal government with purchasable offices, there was also a lower order of *noblesse de cloche*. From these new orders administrators began to be exclusively recruited. Thus they in turn hardened into a third stratified order of society. And where the father had been a draper the grandson became a duke. They were designed to check an hereditary nobility but they themselves became one.

The effect of professional caste formation was seen in the increasing need of the régime for foreign professional talent. The scandals of military incompetence in the Seven Years War[1] and importation of commanders like Marshal Saxe and financiers like Necker was a sign, not of genetic decay, but of an increased genetic rigidity. This rigidity allowed, however, for a particular kind of matrimonial latitude. The distinction between castes was patrilinear. Royal, feudal and bureaucratic rank in the son could therefore be exchanged in the marriage market for wealth or beauty in the daughter.[2] But, by contrast with England, hereditary privilege slowed down the mixing. And by contrast also with ancient Rome the system only partly repeated the breeding character of the Roman Republican governing class. There patricians and plebeians made a freer matrimonial bargain. They had also an elasticity of adoption and stood together on a broader basis to protect their united senatorial interests against the mercantile *parvenu*. But when the crisis came, just as the Roman nobles produced Gracchi, so the French nobles produced men who betrayed their class in an attempt to save the nation.

In the first century of its life the vigour of great reformers swept the régime along. The State had been only slightly shorn of its feudal encumbrances by Richelieu, but French prosperity contrasted with the decay of Spain and the devastation of Germany. In the second century however these advantages were no longer enough. The splendour of Louis XIV's youth gave place to the extravagance, the obstinacy and the downright folly of his latter years, mental errors no doubt aggravated by his own physical diseases. It also gave place to the idleness, incompetence and lack of purpose of his successors. But above all the graded ranks of society were now crystallizing out into a hierarchy of inbred layers each of them becoming genetically fixed in their abilities as each of them became conventionally fixed in their restricted powers and their augmented privileges.

What were these privileges? They were of two kinds, economic and constitutional.[3] The economic privileges of the nobility consisted in their immunity to taxation and their rights to tolls and tariffs. They also consisted in the forced labour of their peasants, free or inserfed; forced we must remember with

[1] See Ogg (1965).

[2] The reciprocal cross, noblewoman by commoner, yielded a *noblesse de ventre:* this matrilinear rank was unofficial.

[3] Both of them reviewed by de Tocqueville (1856) and summarized by George Rudé (1964).

the sanction of the seigneurial gibbet in the background. To these we may add their collateral rights to the better part of the revenues of the Church derived from tithes and rents. These parasitic endowments would have slowly strangled a nation at peace. But for a state at war with other states not similarly handicapped they were bound to hasten disaster. At the end of Louis XV's reign France was still rich as a nation. But as a state she was bankrupt. Even the king (and his mistress) could see what they could not avert: *après nous le déluge.*

b. The Constitutional Remedies

Louis XIV had been equipped with despotic power and was completely confident in his use of it. He knew, and everyone knew, who was responsible for the government. He had never done anything except to please himself. However ill-informed he might be, he at least never had any doubts. And, if he had any qualms, his political police, an Italian invention he owed to Mazarin, would set them at rest. For he had in his pocket, and so had hundreds of his officials, a seal which could, and often did with a *lettre de cachet,* consign any of his subjects to oblivion. Now came his successor, Louis XVI, equipped with just the same despotic power and with a little more than the average incapacity of the whole Catholic royal caste; with no idea therefore how to use his power except to take new advice from some friend or relation as each new difficulty arose.

Here the constitution might have offered some remedy. But again the constitution rested on the absolute privileges of its component orders, none of whom had in effect been on speaking terms since before the time of Richelieu. Richelieu and Mazarin had succeeded in creating the machinery of a secret and despotic policy which was invaluable to them and to Louis XIV. But in doing so they had buried the machinery of advice and discussion. It now had to be resurrected.

There had been in time past three traditional means of consultation. The first of these were the *parlements.* These bodies had, as a matter of routine, been used to confirm royal proposals or help royal officials. They were thirteen in number, metropolitan and regional. They consisted of hereditary magistrates and represented fractions, metropolitan or provincial, of the *noblesse de robe* or *noblesse de cloche.* They had been willing to declare Louis XIV's bastards legitimate. They had been able to deal with local famines and hang local rioters. But it was a different matter when they had to rule on national problems, above all on problems of their own taxation.

Naturally they proved interested only in preserving the rights of their order against the claims of the State. So the King tried a second remedy. He attempted to pick an Assembly of Notables that would be more helpful to the state and not too painful to the establishment. The Assembly met and produced a flood of contradictory ideas, few of them helpful and some of them obviously painful. At last the king took the obvious but desperate step of convening the only representative body the nation knew, although it had not known it since 1614. This was the Estates General.

IV. THE FRENCH REVOLUTION

a. The Overthrow

By this step the king, hardly seeing the consequences, had initiated a revolution.

It is true that by their traditional structure the Estates seemed well buffered against change. They consisted of three separate houses, the nobility, the clergy and the Third Estate, the people. But it was not clear how the people were to be represented. A rash improvisation was attempted. The property qualifications of the British and American electorates were removed. Or were they overlooked? The whole of the male householders over the age of twenty-five in France were given the vote. Even Protestants were allowed to vote—and to be elected. To be sure, the voting was through the nomination of electors who by several successive steps nominated the ultimate working representatives. Clearly even without manipulation this process would favour the literate, the prudent, and the well-to-do. It was bound to muffle the voice of violence; how much so would later transpire. But, as it appeared, it was the most democratic system of election that had so far been attempted for any nation in history.

How sudden and dangerous a change this constituted may be seen from the fact that the 600 nobles and clergy of the upper houses mainly represented 3 per cent of the total population of 24 millions (Table 35). It was a proportion not very different from that of the electors for the House of Commons in Britain at that time. But the Third Estate, also with its 600 members, might claim to represent nearly all the remaining and opposing 97 per cent.

Where were the Estates to meet? A great deal depended on the choice of site. The Palace of Versailles had provided for a century the accommodation of the nation's government. There the king lived and hunted, surrounded by his most opulent but not, as it turned out, his most enlightened, nobles. Thither therefore the Estates must repair, the nobles and bishops entering by the front door in splendid array, the Third Estate admitted at the side and by royal command, clad in respectful black.

They met on May 5, 1789. It quickly became clear that the nobles in overwhelming majority would stand by their own interests and at all costs would stand apart from the Third Estate. They illustrated the enduring principle that social groups always act stubbornly in their own interests when placed in homogeneous assemblies. Whether they are an old aristocracy, new industrialists, or the members of an academic faculty, whether they are homogeneous by breeding, by nomination or by selection, they reject discordant voices from inside or from outside. The aristocrats had already seen to it that the likeliest traitor, the Comte de Mirabeau, should not represent them. He sat with the Third Estate.

After weeks of argument the Third Estate were joined by rebels from above: 50 nobles, 44 bishops, and 200 parish priests; they then felt strong enough to ignore the residue and to declare themselves a National Assembly. And strong enough they were, for when the King, a week later, called on his French guards to disperse the Assembly the troops refused. It was then that the people of

Table 34. *Time Chart of the French Revolution*
After Rudé *et al.*

1789	*March*	Beginning of peasant riots
	May 5th	Estates General of 1200 deputies meet at Versailles
	June 17th	Third Estate with 250 sympathizers form National or Constituent Assembly
	July 14th	Citizens of Paris take the Bastille Nobles begin to emigrate
	August 27th	Declaration of the Rights of Man and Citizen
	October 5th–6th	National Guards fetch the king and the Assembly to Paris
1790	*July 12th*	Civil Constitution or nationalization of the clergy
1791	*June 20th*	King's flight to Metz intercepted
	September 14th	Constitution proclaimed by the king
	October 1st	Legislative Assembly meets
1792	*April 20th*	War declared on Austria and Prussia
	April 25th	Guillotine introduced
	August 10th	Populace under Paris *commune* captures Tuileries
	September	Prison massacres in Paris
	September 20th	Prussians defeated at Valmy National Convention meets (782 members, 2 working men)
	September 22nd	King deposed; Republic proclaimed; Year One begins
1793	*January 21st*	King executed
	February 1st	England declares war
	March	Peasant insurrections begin in the west
	June 2nd	Convention purged by populace Jacobin Constitution: economic revolution
	July 28th	Committee of Public Safety, Cabinet of a 'Revolutionary Government'
	August 23rd	*Levée en masse:* general mobilization with purchasable exemption
	September	Beginning of Terror
1794	*June 26th*	All foreign invaders expelled (Fleurus)
	July 21st	Vendéan insurrection checked
	June–July	Great Terror (1300 victims in Paris)
	July 28–29th	Robespierre and 92 Jacobins executed Jacobin Club closed
1795	*August*	Directory of Five set up
	October 4th	Royalist riot in Paris crushed by the army
	October 27th	Convention gives place to a Two-House Legislature.
1796 to	*March* *April* 1797	Bonaparte's Italian campaign
1797	*May 31st*	Republic of Venice dissolved
	May	Socialist conspiracy of Babeuf suppressed
1798 to	*May* *August* 1799	Bonaparte's campaign in Egypt
1799	*November 9th*	*Coup d'état* of 18 Brumaire: beginning of the Napoleonic Empire

Paris set about arming themselves, and stormed the royal prison of the Bastille. It was then that the recalcitrant nobles began to leave the country and to look for armed support from their foreign friends in foreign courts abroad. At once the Assembly set to work to frame a declaration of the Rights of Man which was to be the programme for their work. It was not a programme that they could fulfil at Versailles. For that they had to move to Paris and thither with the help of revolutionary troops they moved, first the king (who had his last hunt on October 5th) and then themselves. The capital which Louis XIV had deserted and disarmed a century before was restored to its central armed authority.

The Assembly occupied the next two years in putting their programme into the practical form of a written constitution. This document established the following revolutionary changes:

(i) sovereignty of the nation *vis-à-vis* the king;
(ii) near-abolition of all feudal privileges of one man over another;
(iii) separation of the legislative, executive and judicial powers;
(iv) male suffrage, not universal but on a property-owning basis;
(v) near-freedom of religious worship to Protestants and Jews with an equal civil status for the clergy.

So far on the English model, but going further to the American model:

(vi) admissibility of all citizens to all civil and military offices and to equality before the law.

The abolition of the nobility and hence of hereditary titles, except those of the king's family, the prohibition of trade unions, the confiscation of most of the Church's property, the establishment of the metric system, under Lavoisier's guidance, and the division of the country into departments, all these further acts showed what the Assembly had in mind.

To the king and his friends the conclusion was only too clear. France was not going to be the kind of country they wanted to live in. However, they could see signs of disunity within the Assembly; they could see that the incomplete confiscation of feudal and of Church property was leading to conflict between town and country, between one region and another, and between the Assembly and the citizens of Paris. The king decided to slip away and join the nobles who had already escaped to Germany. He was caught and brought back and made to proclaim the new constitution. But the confidence between the king and the Assembly was broken. As things stood, and with that king, constitutional monarchy would evidently not work.

b. The English Comparison

We can now make a useful comparison. The social and also the individual situation in France in 1791 was not unlike that in England at the corresponding moment of its Civil War and Revolution 144 years earlier, in 1647.

A thousand years of reciprocal migration of the peoples, of exchange of genes and of ideas between them, had led to a corresponding economic development and social structure in England and France. But the profound genetic difference between the corresponding components of society, both individuals and classes, continually reacting with their historic and geographical differences, has never succeeded in diminishing the contrasts or the barriers between the two countries. At every stage therefore the comparison between these nations illuminates the study of society.

We see at once that the constitutions of the two countries, and especially the modes of election to the legislature, were strikingly contrasted. Nevertheless the principle of deference as well as the inherent technical character of representation had secured in France in 1789, with nearly universal franchise, the same result that had arisen in England in 1642 from a restricted franchise based on property, and was to reappear after reform in 1832. The National Assembly socially corresponded with the House of Commons at its more representative periods. They each represented a prosperous educated class, professional and commercial, which was genetically akin and politically allied to an enlightened section of the aristocracy. It was also supported, but with increasing suspicion, by a less articulate but equally purposeful body of artisans.

These artisans were especially concentrated in the great cities and sea-ports: places of movement, enterprise and hybridization. These were the centres of puritanism in England and Protestantism in France. But here we notice, or rather it is Montesquieu, Mirabeau *père*, and de Tocqueville who notice, a transformation which had taken place in the two centuries since the massacre of St Bartholomew. At that time the backwardness of Paris had turned the balance in France against Protestantism. Since that time Paris had not grown disproportionately; it still housed only half a million or one-fiftieth of the nation's inhabitants; but it had attracted all the nation's talents. From being an ordinary old-fashioned French city, shut off from the sea and the outside world, and therefore rejecting Protestantism, it had become the centre of advanced thought; a centre not only for France but for all Europe; and a centre not of Protestantism, for that was no longer the issue, but of industry, commerce and enlightenment. Indeed the separation of the court from the capital, in freeing the court to develop its pleasures, had freed the capital to develop its ideas. Thus Paris was able to lead the French Revolution as London had led the English Revolution, but to lead it with even more disproportionate effect.

In both France and England the established government was headed by an absolute monarch whose powers far outran his judgment in using them. Each monarch also was virtuously wedded to a foreign wife and deprived of advice from any native mistress. The two differed however, as we have noticed, in that the Stuart, like all his kindred, was prepared to fight while the Bourbon-Hapsburg (twice descended from Charles V) was prepared only to run away.

Supporting the monarch and opposing the commercial and industrial classes of the capital and the great cities were the backward rural provinces of the north-west of France who revolted in support of their run-away monarch. They corresponded to those of the north and west in England who fought for Charles. In England those peasants, gentry and clergy, cut off geographically from both new people and new ideas, were united in their support of the old order in Church and State. In France they had been cut off from interbreeding by sharper class divisions. The new bourgeoisie were known in town and in country. But they stood apart. Despised by the nobility they themselves despised the peasants and the workers. In France therefore there was an opposition between town and country and the struggle in the country took on a different character from that in the towns, the result in the end being that the agricultural proletariat often lost rather than gained from the Revolution.[1]

The great contrast between the French and English Revolutions arose however from the development of ideas during the intervening years. Society was now becoming conscious of its structure and meaning. In both countries there were the devout and traditional peasantry. But in place of the numerous fanatical sects of the English revolutionaries whose conflicting religious beliefs were connected with their conflicting political views, the French now had only a mild anti-clerical infidelity. It was an infidelity connected with the confiscation of Church property on the one hand, and with an understanding of the theories of society and religion expounded by the new French thinkers on the other. It was no longer from a study of the Bible but of the encyclopaedists and the incipient science of the Industrial Revolution that the French revolutionaries derived their principles of reform. This was despite the fact, noted by de Tocqueville, that in 1757 the publication of books 'contrary to religion' had been made punishable by death, a frightful threat that no one dared to fulfil.

To apply these intellectual principles in the stress of the revolution was however bound to lead to continual shifts in the grounds of argument and the alignment of parties.

c. The Fourth Estate

When therefore the rift occurred between Louis and the Assembly, and when the foreign monarchies and the dissident peasantry took arms in support of the old order, a new combination of revolutionary forces soon appeared. Then the municipal government of Paris began to feel its strength. It was a strength derived from its position, from its control of a populace and of a militia which it could arm, and from its policy which was to make a complete constitutional and economic revolution.

The same opposition had arisen in England after the Civil War between Parliament and the city. But in England both Parliament and the army leaders were strengthened by their long experience of government. Families such as the Cromwells had sat in every Parliament for a century and formed by intermarriage a firmly bonded caste capable through their leader of forcing their will on the whole of their party.[2] The French National Assembly and the revolutionary movement had to create its own parties from the policies of ill-assorted, partly inexperienced, and mostly opportunist individuals like Mirabeau and Lafayette, Danton and Robespierre;[3] individuals, moreover,

[1] See Cobban (1955) who quotes the *cahiers de doléances* of the *états généraux.*

[2] See Maurice Ashley (1957).

[3] Men who had earlier wished to be known as d'Anton and de Robespierre (Hampson, 1963).

struggling through the stress of foreign invasion, civil war, famine and economic crisis. It was in these circumstances that the citizens of Paris, on August 10 1792, took a large part of the government into their own hands.

Who were these citizens of Paris who elected their own government, their *commune*? They included the men of property and the intellectuals who were already represented in the Assembly. But they also included a large class of artisans who had in effect been unrepresented. These were men employed in workshops, men of a class who in England were already struggling in powered factories with the problems of the Industrial Revolution. In years to come, delayed in France by the revolutionary wars, the new power would force the bulk of this class down into the new proletariat while allowing a very few to make their way up into management and ownership. But at this time these

Table 35. *Estimated Numbers of Political Executions in France*
After Hampson (1963).

	Date	*Executed*	*Class*
TERROR	Sept. 1793–July 1794 (Population: 24m.)	40,000*	1158 were nobility or 3 per cent of the total†
COMMUNE	May 1871 (Population: 40m.)	16,000	Communists, nearly all in Paris
LIBERATION	June–Dec. 1944 (Population: 40m.)	40,000	Nazi collaborators under auspices of Vichy

* Of these 10,000 died in prison.
† 400,000 nobility were 2 per cent of whole population. 16,000 nobles had fled abroad; their lands, like those of the Church, were confiscated and sold chiefly to wealthier individuals among the bourgeoisie, the peasantry and their own kinsmen.

plebeians, *menu peuple*, included enough active and enterprising but long frustrated men to seize their terrible moment of opportunity. In England they were to remain the *lower orders*. And in France they were abused as *sans culottes*, men wearing workmen's trousers rather than gentlemen's breeches. As a political force they were awakened by the Declaration of the Rights of Man. Soon they were not ashamed of their nickname. But they liked even better to be known as *patriotes*, a term and an idea which together submerged them in the future of France and of Europe.

The power of the artisans was released by the political clubs in Paris. It was in the Club des Cordeliers that the cry was first raised of *Liberté!*, *Egalité!*, *Fraternité!*[1] The cry was later to be absorbed in the heraldry and nullified in the politics of the Republic. But at the time it set in motion tremendous forces.

So it was that the Paris *commune*, in alliance with the clubs set up by groups of radical deputies, drove the Revolution to its climax. It was a multiple climax. First the Tuileries Palace was captured and the excited populace were

[1] On June 30, 1793 (*Oxford Dict. Quot.* French: anonymous). The Club, founded by Danton, Marat and Camille Desmoulins, took its name from the former Franciscan friary in which it met just as the Jacobins took their name from their Dominican monastery.

allowed or encouraged to massacre the men and women awaiting trial in the prisons. Secondly, the king was deposed, tried and executed. Thirdly a new National Convention was elected on a nearly universal manhood suffrage. Fourthly, a central government with a cabinet of twelve, the Committee of Public Safety, was set up. It was a cabinet inspired by the Jacobin Club which, under the leadership of Robespierre, purged the Convention and the whole nation by the terror of summary execution. Thus it was able to set in motion all those radical reforms which had been rejected by the Assembly. It was able to decree in principle free universal education in France and the abolition of slavery in the colonies. And it was able to plan a policy of genuine economic equality, price and wage control in the towns, land and debt annulment for the peasants, freedom of speech for all.[1]

And one last achievement: supported by this government of terror, the revolutionary armies were able to drive its enemies off the soil of the Republic.

The fact that the Fourth Estate had been badly treated by the other Estates, notably by the Third, did not qualify them to govern. But it prepared them for vengeance. And the vengeance which they inflicted in the year of the Terror strengthened the Jacobin government and carried France through the perils of the next year, the Year Two. It was this year which set the course, not only for the rest of the French Revolution, but for a large part of the future development of Europe. The revolution that was established when the Jacobins were deposed, put in power, however, not the Fourth, but the Third, Estate. It was the educated class who were to seize the responsibilities of government and reap its benefits in the coming century. And this applied, not only to France, but to all the other western countries that profited by her Revolution, whether liberated like Italy, conquered like Germany, or untouched like England.

V. THE BEGINNING OF EMPIRE

a. Diversion to Conquest

As soon as the fear of invasion was removed, the government which had removed it was pulled down. The great revolutionary wave began to subside and withdraw. Within a month of the expulsion of the enemy the Jacobin leaders had all been executed and with this last stroke the terror had come to an end. At the same time the Jacobin constitution together with the Jacobin economic and equalitarian reforms disappeared. Mild and weak governments took the place of the terrible Committee of Public Safety.

What had happened? Without any debate or planning at home the victories of the revolutionary armies were enough to divert the nation's interest from internal reform to external conquest. These victories had not been won by zealous religious partisans untrained in war like the English commanders of

[1] Across the Channel the fear of the Jacobins must have reinforced motives of prudence and compassion in suggesting the introduction of minimum wages, made up from the rates, for agricultural workers in 1795. This was the Speenhamland policy, so called from the meeting-place of the Berkshire magistrates (Hammond, 1911).

the Civil War. They had been won by professional officers trained in the schools of the royal army before the Revolution began. These were men willing to apply new military ideas, pre-revolutionary French ideas of mobile warfare. They were willing to apply them because they were young. They were able to apply them because they were in command: all the older generals had been dismissed, frightened into defection by the Jacobin government or actually executed. Now that the Jacobins had gone, the men of the hour, the saviours of the Republic, were therefore the young generals who had dared to stick to their guns.[1]

It need not surprise us that these men, chosen by a fearfully effective elimination for their ability to defeat foreign armies and conquer foreign powers, had come to regard this business as the proper and entire object of war. Nor need it surprise us that the French people and the French armies found it easy to shift their aim in war, or to raise their sights, from the defence of the Revolution to its imposition on their neighbours; from a doctrine of no conquests in 1791 to the enthusiasms of the liberation of Italy in 1796 and the adventure in Egypt of 1799.

The liberation of oppressed nations proved a disappointment to the liberators. For France the Napoleonic episode was disastrous. The twenty-five years of war meant a loss to the French people of over a million able men killed on the battlefields of Europe. It was a loss perhaps as serious as that of the Huguenots a century earlier. It also meant that, at the very beginning of the Industrial Revolution, the lead passed to Britain. It was a lead which held for the coming century. It served to separate Britain still further economically and culturally from the rest of a Europe which had been drawn together by Napoleon and by the legal code and the metric system which he had imposed.

But for Europe the errors of Napoleon proved unintentionally as beneficial as those equally personal errors of Louis XIV. The whole process of European social and national evolution was violently accelerated. Within all countries with an articulate and literate class, that is all except Russia, Spain and Turkey, it created a common interest in the whole field of culture, but above all in the field of social and political reform.

In the middle of the eighteenth century the governing classes of all European countries were still united by their common knowledge of the French language and literature. And they were separated by this knowledge from the social classes beneath them. This unity and this separation, which controlled their breeding systems and their caste character, were both largely swept away by the French Revolution, that is no less by its victories than by its ultimate defeat. In place of them grew a recognition of the value of the separate national languages and cultures, a unity within linguistic groups of people who came to assert their political strength or demand their political unity. The speakers of each language began to think of themselves as distinct races. The assumption was true, although only of particular social classes and local

[1] Pichegru (1761–1804), Jourdan (1762–1833), Hoche (1768–1797), and a little later Augereau, the eldest (1757–1816), Joubert (1769–1799), Moreau (1763–1813), Bernadotte (1764–1844) and Bonaparte (1769–1821).

groups within them. For it is only small groups of people that choose to set themselves apart who can even slowly become races apart.

From these ideas, however, arose national movements of several kinds. On the one hand there was the internal unification of the German and Italian nations which was indispensable for the advancement of their people. And on the other hand there was the external liberation of the several Balkan peoples. This was a process separating them from the important capitals of Vienna and Constantinople which they had themselves contributed to peopling, and thus for some time it was a process delaying their advancement.

In these ways the French Revolution sometimes advanced, sometimes diverted, and sometimes delayed the processes of internal development. These and many similar effects were practical and largely unintended. But there were other effects arising intentionally from the Revolution and related in theory with the ideas of the revolutionaries which have not only continued but have gathered strength down to our own time. For all the great political ideas of the following centuries, although often conceived earlier in Holland and England, had been born during the Revolution. These we must now consider.

b. Nationalism

In every people in Europe initiative was promoted by the shaking up and hybridization of the French revolutionary wars. In the aristocracies, particularly of France, the business of hybridization was personally supervised by Napoleon himself. It had the effect, together with the adroit diplomacy of Talleyrand, of preventing a fatal cleavage in French society and, as much as the emancipation or endowment of the peasantry, it served to consolidate the Revolution. But the strength of the new initiative owed most to the growth of national feeling accompanying the suppression of some nations as in Poland and Ireland and the unification of others as in Germany and Italy. And its direction was naturally peaceful for some, warlike for other, social classes.

Napoleon had opened up the future of Germany by reducing the number of her principalities from four hundred to forty. The beneficiary of this rationalization proved to be Prussia. Her military governing class, the Junkers, were derived from the Teutonic Knights. They corresponded, as we saw, to the Protestant Anglo-Irish landlords. The Junker class was conveniently attached to the absolute monarchs of the Hohenzollern Dynasty.

Now, after Waterloo, Prussia found herself enlarged by the possession of the Rhineland. It was a gift proposed by Talleyrand at the Congress of Vienna, a gift of territory of whose human and industrial potentialities he was largely unaware.[1] The King of Prussia owed it to the strength he acquired in this way that he was able to resist the revolution of 1848 by artfully setting up a parliament of limited powers. Further, he was able to restore his position entirely when he discovered in this parliament a strong and devoted minister. Bismarck held the office of Prime Minister from 1862 to 1890. The part he played in the long-delayed unification of Germany was decisive and enduring. In his first

[1] Cooper (1932); Nicolson (1946).

nine years he was able, by the defeat of Denmark, Austria and France in successive wars to make Prussia dominant in Germany and Germany dominant in Europe. In this way the most active agent in the developing relations of the European states came to be under one sovereign and in one capital. It was the Prussian officer caste from which, on one side, Bismarck sprang.[1]

German unity, so necessary for the German people, could scarcely have been achieved in any other way. But the price to be paid was heavy. With each step in its own national success, military, diplomatic, and cultural, the new German Establishment became stronger, more authoritarian and of course more military. It naturally compared its position with that of all the neighbouring European powers. France, Britain and Holland had in Africa and Asia vast and rich 'possessions'; the name reflects the temper of the period. Russia was similarly governing and civilizing, colonizing and exploiting, great areas and populations from Bessarabia to Turkestan. The opportunity to compete was irresistible. And the competition aggravated the growth of national feeling.

In this evolution German nationalism came last but soon took the lead. Following the Napoleonic wars the aristocratic Prussian-officer caste began to assimilate congenial elements from the rest of Germany by a process in which the universities with their practice of duelling played a part. The German officer, it now appeared, had acquired an immunity to the civil law. He was responsible only to the sovereign. And after 1888 this sovereign was the German Emperor William II, outstanding among European sovereigns for his enterprise, his vanity and his lack of judgment.

It was in these circumstances that the world heard of extraordinary examples of arrogance on the part both of the Emperor and of his officers. The incidents at Köpenick in 1906[2] and at Zabern in 1913 amused or shocked people outside Germany. But people inside Germany were more and more frightened by what was happening to them. It was a process of cumulative intimidation.

The intimidation of the German intellectuals sprang from a disorder of the social system. It was due to a maladjustment like that in England under Charles I or in France under the Old Régime. Being constitutional it could be ended only by war. It had begun with the resistance to Napoleon in 1813 to 1815. It took shape in 1830. It gathered momentum in 1848 and 1870, and later still with the introduction and extension of conscription to the regular army. At each stage it changed the character and relative proportions of the emigration of Germans to Russia and France, Britain and the United States. Military dominance in Germany thus reached its full expression against the background of a German national character which was itself becoming more disciplined and even more submissive than that of the neighbouring peoples.

[1] Bismarck was, characteristically for such a unifier, a class cross: his father was a Junker: his mother was of the professional and intellectual family of Mencken.

[2] On October 16, 1906, a cobbler, in the uniform of a captain, purchased in an old clothes shop, was able to co-opt a squad of soldiers and with them arrest the Burgomaster of Köpenick and remove the town funds. For other features of the Emperor's life and character, see Morré (1909).

Freedom to emigrate was in those days a freedom which despotic governments had lost the habit of curtailing. For over a century there was a steady flow out of Germany of opponents of the new régime and the new way of life. As with the Huguenots leaving France also for a century, it was a highly selective flow. The people who left Germany went under all kinds of pressures from personal distaste, like Heinrich Heine, to direct police action, like Karl Marx. They included a varied assortment of reformers and liberals, pacifists and intellectuals. Such an emigration, it is clear, inherently aggravates the disorder which gives rise to it. These were people whose individual and collective influence, if they had remained, would have been very great in creating a powerful and peaceful Germany. They were also people of the very opposite character to those who were being lost to their colonies by the two other great western powers, Britain and France. It was their loss that freed Germany for the cultivation of a military, anti-intellectual, and therefore in the end anti-Jewish, sentiment.

The development of the European nations in the nineteenth century was thus influenced in all cases in the first place by the French Revolution and the following military aggression. Thereafter it was influenced by the long-familiar circumstances of selective migration, in which the unification of Germany under Prussia, and the direction of Prussia by a small governing class, played ultimately, in both 1914 and 1939, a significant part. But at every stage in development from 1789 to the present day the effects of individuals in decisive positions, some weak, some strong, some far-seeing and some seeing not at all, have also had their decisive effects.

VI. REVOLUTION BY THEORY

a. Babeuf

In achieving their Revolution, the men of 1789, no less than their successors, the Jacobins of 1793, had relied on the principles of Rousseau and Diderot. In doing so, the government of Robespierre were bound to wreak their vengeance on oppressors and traitors. If they had done so with discrimination the Fourth Estate might have permanently established its position in France. Universal suffrage might have been preserved and reaction held at bay. But the panic on both sides was too severe. And discrimination is not the characteristic gift of the Fourth Estate. Moreover, the people as a whole were frightened and even nauseated by what had happened. The new government of the Directory profited by this mood. Since it was a government which inevitably relied on the governing abilities of the professional and commercial classes it also inevitably favoured the economic interests of these classes. It was also a government in which promotion was bought just as it had been bought under the monarchy. But now it was bought by the profits and the profiteers of confiscation. The sale of Church and emigré property was the basis of a new governing class.

The new government was therefore based on property. It was a government willing or even anxious to come to terms with the exiled but respectable monarchy but quite unwilling to come to terms with the working classes.

The Fourth Estate now found themselves therefore deserted by the politicians who had climbed to power on their shoulders.

How different indeed the world now seemed to the Third and the Fourth Estates! To the gay Talleyrand, the noble bishop of Bourbon days and the prince and diplomat of Napoleon's time, returning from two years' exile, Paris was a city of joy freed from terror and bloodshed. To the serious Babeuf, the former Protestant and now the socialist attempting to restore the principles of Rousseau and Diderot, Paris was a city of starvation; its people were deprived of all right to determine their own future; their spokesmen were silenced by a government far better equipped to oppress, and far more determined to exploit, the manual workers than any earlier monarchy.[1]

Babeuf and his friends had prepared a *Manifesto of Equals*. They had taken the theories of Rousseau and the slogans of the clubs as their gospel. They conspired to overthrow the Directory by insurrection. At the time all human hopes seemed on their side but all human expectations were manifestly against them. Babeuf and his friends were caught, tried and executed by the new dictators. Their speeches were suppressed and their writings were lost only to be rediscovered and brought to light in 1884 after a century more of revolutions attempted and destroyed.[2]

b. The Chartists

During this century, owing to conditions which, as we have seen, were at once racial and environmental, contemporary and historic, Britain began to diverge more sharply than ever before from the rest of Europe. In Britain society and government changed by gradual reform assisted often by the effects of foreign war. In Europe they were changed by revolution and civil war. The reason for the difference is best seen from considering the Chartist movement.

The Industrial Revolution in England gave the owners of the new industries, as well as the increasingly parasitic landlords, a wonderful chance of acquiring wealth rapidly from the employment of labour. For the first time in history, in the eighteenth century, the population of Britain nearly doubled: it rose from 8 to 15 million. This increase sprang from three conditions. First, there was the absence of invasion which devastated most other European countries. Secondly, there was the increased productivity of British agriculture. This resulted from the cultivation of turnips for sheep in England, and the potato for man in Ireland, from the breeding of improved cattle; all due to a few able innovators, Coke and Townshend in Norfolk, Bakewell in Leicester and Collings in Durham.[3] Thirdly, there was the development of the new industries which provided employment. And lastly, there was the improved public health. This began in 1762 with local government bills dealing with water supply and sewage; it was maintained by Jenner's invention of small-

[1] These points of view are given us by Duff Cooper (1932) on Talleyrand (1755–1837) and by Edmund Wilson (1940) on Babeuf (1760–1790). So sharply are the classes contrasted in their experience and their judgement of the same events.

[2] See Postgate (1920) for the whole revolutionary documentation.

[3] See Drummond and Wilbraham (1939); Fussell and McGregor (1961); Moller (1964).

pox vaccination in 1796; and it concluded with the agitation of great reformers such as Southwood Smith and Edwin Chadwick. These tremendous reforms brought a new level of cleanliness and public health to Christian countries, a level which Mohammedan laws, a thousand years earlier, had established in the Muslim world. After 1840 there was no serious epidemic of cholera in England and the population began to increase even faster. It was this rapid increase which magnified and multiplied the opportunities for the exploitation of cheap labour in the countries in which industry was concomitantly developing.

The existence of a parliamentary government however presented the means for continual experiments in reform. Reform of parliamentary representation and election, and reform by parliament when elected, both provided endless opportunities for discussion and some opportunities for action.

The gravest crisis in the movement for political reform in Britain followed the disappointment of the working classes with the results of the Reform Bill in 1832. The enlarged electorate included only the middle classes. And the new House of Commons proved to be marvellously like the old House of Commons and not very unlike their elder kinsmen in the House of Lords which had itself been recently enlarged by Pitt. The protest took the form of petitions for a *charter* demanding universal franchise, petitions presented by mass meetings organized at the times of greatest distress between 1837 and 1848.[1] But every return of prosperity broke the force of protest and the Chartists, who were always looking for leaders in the educated classes, for this reason failed to find them.[2]

Meanwhile the successful start of trade unions in 1842, the repeal of the Corn Laws in 1846, and the first Factory Act of 1847 (reducing the working day to ten hours), all of them influenced by the Chartist agitation, were slowly effective in smothering it. They also led to the slow succession of reforms in education which grudgingly opened the possibilities for social advancement to enterprising individuals in many fields. All these changes diverted the efforts of educated reformers away from revolutionary channels. At the same time they sieved out of the working classes the very people who by their genetic character would have been best fitted to lead revolutionary movements. It is a process which continues today with the same effect.

Thus, although discussion had been delayed to the point at which revolution was only just avoided, it had made possible reform by trial and without much error. It had been learnt, during a century of reform, that in a country where property was diverse in character and in which wealth and ownership were being rapidly created and distributed, the propertied classes, although usually united in defence of most property, were not by any means always united in defence of all property. It had further been learnt that the extension of the franchise, even when it eventually became universal, did not in fact lead to a proportional representation of all classes of citizen. Representatives

[1] The Charter of 1837 quoted by Postgate showed that the Commons were almost entirely connected with business and landowning interests, i.e. Third Estate not Fourth. Further, 250 members were elected by constituencies with less than 1000 voters.

[2] See Mather (1965) and also Disraeli in *Sybil* (1848).

were always, implausible as it may seem, more intelligent than those they represented. Bagehot's principle of deference ensured that (contrary to the fears expressed by J. S. Mill in 1861) the less educated and less educable were represented by the more educated and more educable.

c. Marx and Engels

These processes of reform in Britain were paralleled in the United States and Switzerland and other countries. They depended on a freedom of discussion which was only economically restricted. In democratic countries people who are willing to starve have always been free to protest. But in Germany, Russia, and the whole of Catholic Europe, even this freedom was specifically denied by police action. For this reason it was in Britain, and therefore in London, that exiles from Europe sought refuge during the nineteenth century and made their plans for revolutions to be carried out in their own countries.[1]

These men came, for the most part, from the educated classes, propertied or professional. Most came from groups denied their opportunities in society on national, racial or religious grounds: Irish in Britain, Poles in Russia, Jews in Germany and later in Russia, bastards (like Herzen) anywhere.

In the eighteenth century, thinkers had discussed the structure of society without a systematic study of the revolutions which had changed it. And revolutionaries had acted without acknowledging their debt to the thinkers. Perhaps the inspired engagement of Tom Paine, the fiery author of *The Rights of Man*, as foreign secretary for the American Congress, and later his passage to Paris was a sign of the approaching union of theory and practice in revolution. This union was consummated by Karl Marx (1819–1882). Among all the nineteenth-century revolutionaries Marx was significant for us because, having discovered something new about society, he explained how it should be used to change society. What he discovered has therefore been used, as he intended, if not in the way he intended, in order to effect this change.

Karl Marx was the son of a Jewish intellectual and rabbinical family of Trier.[2] His father, like many others and following a familiar pattern, had embraced Christianity in order to escape from the restrictions imposed on Jews when, in 1815, the Prussian government replaced the French. The young Marx bitterly resented the oppressions to which Christians as much as Jews were now subjected. For this was a new police state unchecked by parliament or trial by jury. He therefore fled, first to France then to England. There he stayed for forty years. Throughout that time he was associated with Friedrich Engels, a man probably of Huguenot descent and the son and heir of a well-to-do German cotton manufacturer. Together they prepared the statement, first privately circulated in February 1848, and later known as the *Communist Manifesto*. What did they say?

The statement begins with the startling phrase 'The history of all hitherto existing society is the history of class struggles.' It continues with the predic-

[1] See E. H. Carr (1933); Edmund Wilson (1940); and F. M. Wilson (1959).

[2] But he was a cross: his mother was a Sephardim (Feuer, 1968. Encounter, 31: 15).

tion that the condition of the working classes will for some time get worse. There will be no escape without fighting for it. And it ends, 'Working men of all countries, unite!' It was a call to battle and to revolution and as such it has acted with varying success from that day to this. We recognize the voice of the Hebrew prophet with his vision of Armageddon. We are moved by the moral fervour of the call for justice in society. We are astounded by the courage and the honesty of the challenge to oppressors whom we also loathe. But having felt and said these things we are bound to examine the underlying assumptions of Marx and Engels and their present scientific justification.

The first great assumption Marx was making in this statement was that society had been changing from its beginnings; that the change had in the long run been one of progress or improvement; and this progress was both desirable and inevitable. This view was taken, not so much from history, as from Hegel's interpretation of history. It was an interpretation conforming so well with the temper of the century that it seemed to arise from it. As indeed did the term *evolution* which Herbert Spencer gave to the whole process in 1863. Today we can accept the assumption of change. But the question as to whether we call it progress we can put aside for the time being.

The second great assumption that Marx was making was that since the rulers of feudal society with its developing evils (or contradictions) had been overthrown by a lower or subordinate class to establish capitalist society, so capitalist society with its developing evils could or should now be overthrown to establish a new and better order. What order? The workers should unite to establish a proletarian society. It should begin, to use the phrase of the French revolutionary, Blanqui, with a 'dictatorship of the proletariat'; but it should be a society in which class melted and disappeared and the State itself withered away: in the end there would be a perfect society; the millennium would be attained.

To us it is now clear that the capitalist system and the Scientific and Industrial Revolutions were the work of men of enterprise and invention, individual discoverers and innovators. These men always by hybridization with earlier governing classes took part in forming the new classes which benefited from their innovations. The new classes became the owners of property and dominated the society which their forebears (or some of them) had in part created. What then were the proletariat doing to transform the society which they were going to govern—and govern, it was hoped, so much better than their predecessors?

Unfortunately the proletariat as a whole were doing little to change the society they lived in. Stability, often oppressive, is always maintained in society by the inaction of large numbers. Change, constructive or destructive, always springs from the action of small numbers, indeed from the work of individuals, of men like Marx and Engels. At all stages in its evolution society is transformed by such outstanding individuals. Such men and women arise with different frequencies from all social classes especially from hybridization, legitimate or illegitimate, between classes and races. Only we may except, as Marx and Engels did, the 'social scum': the worthless *lumpenproletariat*, the people of the Fourth Estate, who fail to understand the class struggle. Their existence we all recognize, although our estimate of their bulk varies with time and place.

The proletariat as a whole, however, were not even listening to Marx's explanation of the part they were to play. They were thinking, as they had always thought, of their own problems from day to day or at most from week to week. The people who were listening were a small self-elected body of revolutionaries, exiles derived from the propertied and intellectual classes of those lands where tyrannical autocracies prevented them making themselves heard or felt. Which meant, as the nineteenth century advanced, more and more exclusively the lands of the German, the Austrian and above all the Russian Empires.

It was in this strange society, this rapidly evolving fiercely disputing political underworld, made up of men eager to learn how to seize power from their enemies, the police governments, that the seeds sown by Marx germinated.[1] It was these men who learnt that any revolution they attempted, if it was to succeed, must be carried out in the interests of the proletariat and with the support of the proletariat. Before we consider how this was to be done we have to return to look at the ideas and the evidence underlying Marx's views. What was his view of the relations of individuals and classes, their differentiation, their equality or inequality, and of the part they played in the evolution of society?

d. Equality: Political and Genetic

The question of human equality had first broken into the political scene in the words of the Levellers. But they had no chance of a hearing except in terms of the Bible. And, in the Bible, the Old Testament could be quoted as vehemently against equality as the New Testament could be quoted in favour of it. The matter was otherwise in the eighteenth century. Now reason and nature, and what we may call science, could give their evidence. And their first spokesman had been again a Protestant, re-entering France from the independent city of Geneva: Jean Jacques Rousseau (1712–1778).

Rousseau had opened the subject in 1753 in a discussion of the origins of human inequality. His argument was that men had evolved from a primitive equality to the advanced, or rather degenerate, inequality of civilization. This view precisely expresses our opinion today. But how had this inequality arisen? Apparently, either by an environmental accident or by a genetic indeterminacy, in either case unexplained.[2] Once arisen in this way the inequality aggravated itself on the principle of the inheritance of acquired characters foreshadowed by Buffon, whom Rousseau quotes.

All this happens within societies, within tribes. But the differences *within* tribes of men or animals, as we now know, are of the same genetic character as those *between* tribes. Both equally underlie the changes and the divergences of evolution. Neither Rousseau nor for that matter Buffon could in their

[1] A society delightfully described by E. H. Carr (1933) and by Edmund Wilson (1940).

[2] '*Un homme étoit-il éminent en pouvoir, en vertu, en richesse ou en crédit, il fut seul élu magistrat, et l'État devint monarchique.*'

time know this. Hence we find Rousseau in the same essay on inequality examining the causes of tribal and racial differences on quite a different footing from social differences.

Take the Hottentot, he says, away from his parents. Remove him to a remote country. Bring him up under civilized conditions. He seems transformed. But return him to his own country and he seizes the first opportunity to desert his benefactors and return to his own people. Evidently, exclaims Rousseau, the inequalities and differences between races are inborn and ineradicable: environment or education is in this matter without effect.

Thus Rousseau is adopting the view that, on the one hand, the differences between races are original differences: they were created at the beginning and have persisted ever since Creation. But, on the other hand, within races or tribes or societies evolution is proceeding; changes are occurring owing to the effects of use and disuse arising from external circumstances or from efforts of the will. Such indeed was the universal popular and pre-scientific assumption or superstition.

Since the time of Rousseau the repetitions of philosophic writers, social and historical, have consolidated this superstition into a belief. For such writers it has become an axiomatic and intuitive principle not requiring the support of scientific evidence. Notably Lamarck, emboldened by the French Revolution, applied it to the study of biology. And later Herbert Spencer, Bergson, and a host of others, applied it to the study of society. There it has floated freely and causelessly ever since.[1]

Even Darwin who wished to rest his theory of evolution on purely scientific evidence slipped in this acceptable superstition, or, as he said, tentative hypothesis, alongside his own scientific theory of natural selection. So he left his readers uncertain of where he stood; or where nature stood. Naturally therefore Marx, when he wished in 1867 to dedicate *Das Kapital* to Darwin, did not need to be more exact or more explicit than his master.[2]

It was all too easy to imply or to assume that social classes diverged as a result of their diverging activities. The whole process, as Rousseau imagined, was self-aggravating. Furthermore, Lamarck and Darwin, Hegel and Spencer, now all converged in one grand evolutionary agreement embracing species and races, nations and classes. None had been created. All had diverged. Internal activity and external circumstances, the climate and the soil, the will of man or the purpose of nature, had pressed forward this process, inevitable, irresistible and organic. Nay more: Marx and Engels had also discovered that the process was something above and beyond the ordinary rules of scientific evidence. It had an ultimate inherent validity. It was dialectical.

Thus in 1866 Marx writing to Engels accepts the theory of Trémaux. This man has made 'an important advance over Darwin'. How? Because he shows 'that the prevailing geological formation itself tartarized and mongolized the Slavs' and further 'that the common Negro type is only a degeneration from a

[1] See Darlington (1964).

[2] See Isaiah Berlin (1939); privately, however, Marx considered himself much more exact than Darwin: see Avineri (1967) and below.

much higher one'. Thus, for Marx, there are inferior races; and they have arisen by direct Lamarckian and not by indirect, Darwinian, or selective, evolution.[1]

Thus also the biological laws underlying the evolution of society are for Marx simple and direct. The process of history is inevitable. Those who are *against* it are doomed. Let us therefore be *with* it. All we can hope to do is to hasten or retard its progress. The individual, small or great, can do no more than subscribe to the new morality which holds it to be the great end of being to strive for the millennium.

Before examining the political use that was made of Marx's theory, its Messianic promise and its equalitarian therapy for social ills, with a dictatorship of the proletariat replacing the old sovereignty of the people, we must return to the scientific evidence.

First, we notice that heredity is not something soft which can be squeezed or moulded; nor is it a spirit which can be exorcised. It is a hard structure whose chemical and biological properties and visible shape, as seen in the chromosomes, have been revealed to us during the last hundred years, that is since Marx wrote *Das Kapital* and Galton wrote *Hereditary Genius*. Heredity as much as wealth underlies any materialist interpretation of history.

Secondly, we now see that races and classes, their inbreeding and their outbreeding, all arise from the same kinds of adaptive genetic differences developed under natural selection, selective migration and so on. Indeed class differences ultimately all derive from genetic and, usually, racial differences. For us it is the inequalities which create advances in society rather than advances in society which create the inequalities.

Thirdly, we see that individuals owe their individuality to genetic recombination; and this individuality is continually reacting with changing conditions to produce effects which, though unexpected, are often far-reaching, the more so since they do not diminish with the passage of time. It is impossible to suppose that Alexander's decision to turn east, Columbus' decision to turn west, and Caesar's decision to turn north, all due to the characters of these three men, are not today continuing to have their effects, albeit unintended effects. They did not alter, as in Plekhanov's phrase, the rate of change in history; they altered the course of history. Similarly, the characters of Laud and Clarendon affected the whole colonization of the United States—although that was not their intention. Similarly again for Karl Marx: he altered the course of history but not in the way he expected to alter it.

In these fundamental notions Marx is in error. And unnecessarily so. For economists before him, like Adam Smith, and after him, as we have seen, like Maynard Keynes, have shown an awareness of the causes and consequences of individuality, an awareness conforming entirely to the genetic understanding of today.[2]

[1] We can understand why such passages, as Zirkle remarks (1959), were removed by the censor in Russia after, as well as before, the Revolution.

[2] Thus Adam Smith in *The Wealth of Nations* (1776) Book 1, ch. 10 (i), explains the statistical contrast as follows:
'Put your son apprentice to a shoemaker, and there is little doubt of his learning

But there is one respect in which Marx's judgment, although imperfect, is indispensable for the understanding of society. This is the notion of the class struggle.

All stratified societies, as we have seen, arise and prosper through the mutual dependence of classes which differ genetically and have differed from their beginning. Co-operation is therefore the long-term condition of survival of such societies. To be sure, all social co-operation, even within the family, involves also competition and conflict. But, as we have seen, animal species, as well as paleolithic man, have found various means of compromise as a substitute for life-and-death struggle. These compromises stretch from the control of population to the use of threat and retreat in place of war. We owe it to Kropotkin as well as to Carr Saunders that we now understand, what was not clear to Marx, to Darwin, or to Tennyson, that nature red in tooth and claw told only half the story of the relations of classes and races of men and animals.

All working together of human beings therefore demands a compromise between the largely instinctive urge of self-interest and the largely rational understanding of joint interest.

In the relations between classes in society these considerations are as important as they are between individuals in a family. The important variable is then the breeding relations of the classes. Where classes interbreed they also intergrade in their physical, mental and emotional characteristics. Antagonism is therefore slow to develop and hard to maintain. But, where they do not interbreed, the exclusiveness of the more privileged classes creates homogeneity, aggravates prejudice, and concentrates antagonism. It is then that the privileged class, becoming a caste, commonly agrees to turn from co-operation towards exploitation.

All the great religions, notably those derived from Judaism, have condemned this exploitation, but they have too easily also recommended the exploited classes to bear their lot without complaint: to render to Caesar the things that are Caesar's. The Christian Churches of the last two centuries, the period of the Industrial Revolution, failed to meet the crisis of industrial slavery just as earlier they had failed to meet the crisis of chattel slavery and the slave trade. The professional priesthood had been bought. Religion had become fraudulent. It had become the means of concealing, justifying and implementing oppression by the governing class. It had become, as Marx and Engels put it, the opium of the people. They therefore argued that if their sufferings were to be remedied the people had to treat their exploiters, not as Christian brethren, but as enemies in a class war, implacable enemies in an unrelenting war.

Unfortunately for this argument the working class, urban in Western Europe or peasant in Russia, did not know how to destroy their exploiters; nor what they would do when they had destroyed them. They felt dependent

to make a pair of shoes. But send him to study the law, and it is at least twenty to one if he ever makes such proficiency as will enable him to live. To excel in a profession in which but few arrive at mediocrity is the most decisive mark of what is called genius or superior talent.'

and rightly so. They needed leaders from another class. In Western Europe by gradual selection from inside and from outside the trade unions these leaders have come to them. And they would have done so, much more slowly in Russia. But there another course was followed. Perhaps it had to be followed. It was a course arising out of Marx's own argument and doctrine. And the men who did it were the men inspired by this doctrine.

24

REVOLUTION IN THE EAST

I. THE TSAR'S EMPIRE

a. The People

THE STOCKS from which the Russian people grew were as diverse as those of their western neighbours. Russia was accessible first to nomadic invaders; the hunting and fishing Finns occupied the northern forests and the pastoral Lapps the arctic tundra; cattle-driving Aryans, caravanning craftsmen from Armenia, passed to Sweden, horse-riding Scythians and Mongols swept across her southern plains seeking their appropriate habitats; and finally boat-building colonists and traders settled along her great rivers, first Greeks from the Black Sea and then Norsemen from the Baltic.

It was the Viking, Varangian or Ruotsi slave-owning war-lords who, learning to speak Russian, first gave their foreign name to the language and to the country. They set up fortified trading posts, the Kremlins of a later day on which they based their principalities. First Rurik made himself Prince of Novgorod (862–879) and then his successors moved south to Kiev where they encountered Greek traders, Greek craftsmen and Greek priests.

Vladimir, as we have seen, was the first to fall in love with the power and beauty of Byzantium. He was baptized in 989 in order to marry the Princess Anna; their son and successor, Yaroslav (1019–1054), was able to marry his daughters into the royal houses of Norway and France. Craftsmen and traders then began to make their way into Russia from both western and eastern Christendom, from the Hansa ports of the Baltic and from the Greek ports on the Black Sea. But the Eastern Church with its Hellenic alphabet, being closer at hand, was left in possession of Russia.

This was not the first, but certainly the most splendid, contact and hybridization of Greek and barbarian on the soil of Russia. Connection with Greek Byzantium was however sundered, effectively for ever, after two centuries. In 1236 the Tartar invasions (derived from Genghiz Khan's expansion of the previous generation) spread over the whole river basins of the Volga, the Don and the Dnieper and even penetrated into Poland and Hungary driving out the trade and the traders from the cities. At the same time that the nomads cut off the Russians from the south, that is from Greek immigration, they were converted to Islam and the political barrier was hardened into a religious one.

The next three centuries during which Russian and Polish princes pushed back the Tartars were however a period of hybridization across the fighting frontier. The new governing class which was built up round Moscow interbred with the Tartars and the Grand Duke Ivan I in 1340 was willing to collect the taxes and dues demanded by his overlords. The peasantry, during enslavement by the Khans, were hybridized only with the invaders. But when independence was won in 1472 we find the ruler, Ivan III, marrying Sophia Paleologa the last of the Byzantine Dynasty.[1]

The new Russia that emerged in the sixteenth and seventeenth centuries from the long struggle with the Tartars was thus transformed in racial character and social structure. The principality of Moscow survived and grew by the strength of its princes and by the authority with which they both protected and subjected their nobles, or boyars, and the boyars in turn their peasants. The conditions were those in which serfdom, the attachment of the peasant to the soil, had been strongly developed in the barbarian west, and in Russia the same feudal organization was repeated. But here the attachment relied more on force and less on natural devotion to the soil than in the west. The reasons for this were twofold. The first reason was the prolonged frontier condition. Pastoral nomadism was ingrained through hybridization with the Tartar horsemen, the Kazaks or Cossacks, in all the frontier peasantry. In consequence, from the beginning to the present day, the Russian peasant has been fiercely oppressed and has fiercely rebelled against his oppressors: he demanded a consideration which he never received and opportunities which he has rarely been able to win for himself.

Secondly, the towns of Russia were too few and far between. They could neither provide places of escape for serfs nor a class of mediators who could temper the lords' severity or the serfs' rebellion. Proper mediators appeared in Russia only much later, notably the Jews, whose service in this respect we have seen described by Isaac Babel. The only mediators that the princes knew were of other kinds. There were the *oprichnina* who, under Ivan the Terrible in the sixteenth century, dragooned his boyars; and there was the Secret Chancellery which, under Alexis a century later, intercepted their plots. They were the forerunners of a long line of soldiers and police who, reinforced by spies and informers, were to protect the ruler and to exercise his authority in the Russia of the Tsars.[2]

This Russia had won its new-found strength from its restored connection with western Christendom. It became the meeting-ground of two great streams of migration. The first was an emigration eastwards, the slow colonization of Siberia by hunters and traders which began in the reign of Ivan the Terrible. The greater number of the early colonists, being sparse and remote from their

[1] See T. T. Rice (1963).

[2] Hoetsch (1960); see also Mosca (1938).

own people, hybridized with the paleolithic Yakuts tribes. They repeated the process that had happened in Western Europe 4000 years earlier and created a sub-neolithic people of higher intelligence by civilized standards.[1]

The second movement was the inflowing stream of western artisans, traders and soldiers. Meanwhile, native Muscovites, like their descendants today, were forbidden to go abroad without the ruler's permission; and if they went their wives were kept as hostages against their return. Slowly over a period of three hundred years the Kremlin rose to dominate the city. It was the work of foreign craftsmen and artists.[2] Outside, a foreign quarter, European and Chinese, for long constituted the bulk of the town. Foreign immigration however was, as always and everywhere, resented by the masses, welcomed by their rulers. In the same year, 1690, Catholic Scotsmen and Protestant Frenchmen, refugees from warring states, met in the hospitality of a Moscow that was still innocently neutral. This process was brought to a tremendous climax by the efforts of Peter the Great (1672–1725).[3]

b. The Autocracy

Who was this extraordinary man? The first Romanov, Tsar Michael, had been a great-nephew of Ivan the Terrible. He had been happy to govern with the advice of his father, the wise Patriarch of Moscow. The second Romanov, Tsar Alexis, had been happy to govern in part with the advice of his nobles. He had had several insignificant children, but by a noble Tartar wife (Natalya Naryshkina) he begot this son who, combining in himself the qualities of several ancestors, needed no advice from his own people in showing him how to govern his Empire.

In the event Peter did much more than govern: he transformed. It was not that he Europeanized Russia. That was a process which began slowly long before him and went on slowly long after him. It was the skill and force with which he pursued this single purpose of overwhelming and destroying the environment into which he had been born. Take his devotion to ships and to the sea. There was nothing in his surroundings, his education, or apparently in his ancestry, to suggest that he should make them the key to the future of Russia. Yet clearly this devotion was in his character. It was this that sent him to Holland and England to learn the trade. And it was this that made him attack the Swedes and the Turks rather than the easier victims

[1] Not all the Russian pioneers however were lost by hybridization in this way. One community of 400 pure Russians survives today at Russkoe Ustye at the mouth of the Indigirka river (71°N, 149°E) speaking and singing old Russian and armed with bows and spears. They have lost their class structure and their knowledge of reading, writing and baking bread. But they have preserved everything that an entirely pure-bred race could be expected to preserve in this environment. This survival is decisive evidence that the colonists brought their women with them by boat, by-passing the diverse tribes of horse, dog and cattle-rearing, steppe and forest-living, Tungus (Zenzinov, 1924)

[2] Its walls were built by two Italians, Fioravanti and Marco Ruffo, in 1485–1491; the tower on the Spassky Gate was built by a Scotsman, Christopher Galloway, in 1625 (T. T. Rice, 1963).

[3] See Ian Grey (1962).

the Poles. It was this too that made him found Petersburg in the swamps at the mouth of the Neva and to make his capital a sea-port with a navy manned by the sea-going Finns of his new territory.

The foundation of Petersburg was outwardly a symbol of the cultural and technical westernization of Russia; but it was inwardly the means of creating the tsarist state. For it centred the new Russian society on an autocracy which was now free of the control or even the objections of the landed nobles. It was an autocracy which, unlike its Byzantine forerunners, regularly intermarried with foreigners, with the Protestant royal caste of Europe, and so permanently severed itself from its own people, and even to an unusual degree from its own nobility also. For their social connection and their genetic affinity remained rather with the German barons of the Baltic provinces which Peter absorbed. And their interests were identified with the German officials who in the coming centuries came into the country to make their living in the Tsar's administration.

Everything that this administration did however continued to be done with a barbarian zeal and barbarous severity. It could not otherwise have survived with a turbulent nation of boundless extent. It was this zeal that took Russian colonists to the frontiers of India and China and across the Bering Strait into Alaska and California.[1] In this way the foundations of a multiracial Tsar-centred Empire with a Russian-speaking governing class were laid. But they were laid in the shape prescribed by administrators introduced by Peter and his successors to establish firm government. Even the census that they carried out was bound to fix the social structure of the time. So it must always be with a census whether in Russia or in Norman England or British India.

Here however was a rigid administration resulting from cultural westernization inevitably but unintentionally frustrating the social and political westernization which, without the autocracy, would have followed it.

In his programme of westernization Peter had two weapons which have always, since the bronze age, been used by vigorous autocrats: sending Russians to the west to learn, and importing western craftsmen and scholars to teach, to work and to live. Now the learning and teaching outside Russia were not successful. It was the importation and immigration into Russia which led to a permanent advance in Russian society. English shipwrights, Austrian engineers, Scotch soldiers and scholars, Dutch printers and foundrymen, Italian architects, came to Russia, married Russian wives and created the slowly expanding urban and industrial middle class. Similarly (as Grey notes) of the 100,000 Swedish (or at least non-Russian) prisoners of war who should have returned home after the Treaty of Nystadt in 1721 a majority refused to leave: they had discovered the immense opportunities that the new Russia offered to the skill and literacy that only foreigners at first possessed. This recruitment from foreign prisoners continued after every invasion of Russia; after the retreat of Napoleon from Moscow, of the French and British from the Crimea, and of the Germans from Stalingrad. After each

[1] It took them also into Persia whence after ten years (1723–1732), finding that the diseases of the country were a deterrent no human zeal could overcome, they wisely withdrew (Ian Grey, 1962).

invasion an army of foreigners was incorporated in old Russian society creating by hybridization the new Russian professional and technical classes.

Even so the development of Russia continued to lag behind the west. The reason was the strength of the autocracy, and the rigidity of the social system which it demanded. Thus, at the beginning of the nineteenth century three great threats came which were together to destroy the autocracy and transform the system. These were the ideas of the French political Revolution, the techniques of the English Industrial Revolution, and the armies of Napoleon. The third threat was the most sudden and most violent but Russian armies and commanders assisted by the folly of the invader saved the country. So far as Napoleon was concerned the invasion was defeated. But his defeat gave the autocracy just that last touch of confidence which brought it in the end to its ruin. For Napoleon's invasion had brought Russia for the first time into Europe. Educated Russians, but not their rulers, now saw what Western Europe meant and many of them could never again see their own country or their own government in the same sentimental light. And after ten years' thought they began to take action, fumbling their way towards revolt.

c. Repression and Reform

The result of the new European impact on Russia was the demand for just those rights in Russia which the French Revolution had attempted to win in the west. For this demand the autocracy was prepared. The Tsar Nicholas I (1825–1855) foresaw the new movement and was determined to suppress it. He strengthened the system of repression to meet the new situation.

The political police, now two centuries old, became the main safeguard of authority in Russia. The instrument which had been partly dismantled in Western Europe was now assembled in Russia with growing, uncontrolled and secret power. The reformers were thus compelled to become revolutionaries and the only weapon they seemed to have was conspiracy with assassination. Their weapon failed with Alexander I and Nicholas I. But with their more intelligent and more promising successor, Alexander II (1855–1881), it disastrously succeeded.

The reply to the assassination of Alexander II was, almost inevitably, severer repression. In the next twenty-five years Siberian exile, which had its beginnings in 1825, reached its climax as the treatment for revolutionaries.[1] For peasants the army was the means of control: the peasant armed and in uniform from one region could always be used to massacre the peasant unarmed and without uniform in another region.

Looking for a remedy for the nation's troubles after the defeat of the Crimean war, the new Tsar Alexander II had at once taken the advice of the reformers. The first step in modernizing Russian society and in avoiding revolution must be, he decided, to liberate the serfs. But who was to pay for this magnanimous gesture? Three-quarters of the population were serfs:

[1] See Semyonov (1947); Dostoevsky (1861) in describing his own prison camp at Omsk in the years from 1850 to 1854 illuminates the whole problem of social structure; see also Deutscher (1949); Ulam (1965); Fischer (1965).

private serfs and crown serfs, land serfs, house serfs and, since Peter the Great, industrial serfs.[1]

The Tsar had no money after the war. The gentry were in debt. Obviously the serfs themselves would have to pay their owners. But how much? Four years were spent in arguing the point with the landowners. In the end, which for most of Russia came with a decree on March 3, 1861, serfs were given plots of land of their own. At the same time the owners were paid compensation for this land by the State out of a public loan. This loan the liberated serfs were expected to repay in forty-nine years out of the profits of cultivating their land. But the necessary profit could have been won from this land only if capital had been provided to modernize the equipment. Thus the serfs who were compelled to provide the loan were the people who themselves needed the loan.

A situation which had been known since ancient times thus repeated itself: the bulk of the 70 million serfs found themselves worse off as free men than when they had been bound to the soil. And the step which was to settle the Empire unsettled it once and for all. Now therefore there were more disturbances on the land than ever before. At the same time the condition of the towns was radically altered in a way that had been expected. As free men, the serfs were legally allowed and economically compelled to move into the towns. Hitherto this could happen only by escape or by purchase. Now an inbred society moved into, and itself turned into, an outbred society. And the towns grew as they had done fifty years earlier in England and about equally fast.

The new iron industry began in 1869. The Baku oilfield opened up in 1873. Factories sprang up in Petersburg, Moscow and the Don basin.[2] Railways began to stretch out across the Russian plain and over Siberia. In 1904 they reached the shores of the Pacific. This rapid expansion of industry was made possible, as in the United States forty years earlier, by loans from the older industrial countries. Foreign capital combined with foreign skill had brought the Industrial Revolution to Russia.

[1] The first Russian census of 1897 gave the total population of the Empire as 130 million. In 1861 the figure was probably about 92 million. Of these three-quarters, or 69 million, were serfs: 47 million private property, 22 million crown property: see Moller (1964).

[2] For example near the knee of the Donetz a steel industry grew up whose first blast furnaces were built in 1869 by a body of steel workers from Merthyr and Middlesbrough led by a Welshman, John Hughes, and his four sons. This foundation was justly commemorated by the name Hughesovka or Yusovka shown on the maps. In 1940 the town reached a population of 600,000, and its name was changed by its most distinguished citizen, Nikita Krushchev, to Stalino. It is now known as Donetsk (Bowen, 1960). Similarly, Edward Charnock (1876–1967) and his brothers of Chorley, Lancs., introduced the cotton industry to Moscow about 1903. His elder brother Clem founded the first Russian football team, the Morozovtsi, who were national champions up to 1914: R. B. Lockhart and A. Wavell played in it. After the Revolution the mills were confiscated, the managers shot, and the founder sentenced to death *in absentia* (*The Guardian*, November 4, 1967).

In thirty years a new element had sprung up in Russian society. The industrial proletariat had multiplied tenfold in thirty years and now numbered over two million. They were people of hybrid origin. They were relatively more alert and more literate and more open to communication than the peasantry. But they were treated just as badly and packed much more closely. They were suffering the same horrors that Engels had described in Manchester fifty years earlier. But they were also benefiting from an expansion of education at all levels from the primary school to the university.[1]

Now in 1904, Japan, threatened by the new Russian railway to the east, to the open ice-free sea of the fortified Port Arthur, went to war, defeated the Tsar's armies, captured his fortress and sank his fleet. The weakness of the government was exposed at the same moment that the poverty of the workers was aggravated. It was the men in the great new factories, as well as their kinsmen the sailors in the fleet, who then revolted. And in their revolt they were for the first time on a large scale brought into speaking terms with men in another world, the waiting, planning and plotting intellectual revolutionaries.

II. LENIN AND HIS PARTY

For Karl Marx's dream of revolution to be realized a society was wanted different from any he knew. It had to be a society with a negligible middle class. For although Marx himself belonged to the educated professional class, and although he had lived for forty years in England where beyond all previous experience that class was growing up, he found no place for them in his scheme of things. They had ignored him: he intended to ignore them. Again, it had to have a proletariat reduced to such despair as even Marx and Engels had not seen in their youth in England. Such a society was not to be found during Marx's lifetime; but in the despised Tartarized Russia, after the sufferings of war in 1905 and again in 1917, it did recognizably exist.

Also needed for Marx's plan was a man of a different character, experience and even race from the master, the perfect disciple who, with all Marx's resolution, and with none of his misgivings, could turn the master's social words into political deeds. Such a man in fact appeared at the right moment. His origin was as remarkable as his fate. But, since in this respect he by no means answered to Marx's prescription, it is only now that we can show it in the light of day (Pedigree 18).

Vladimir Ilyitch Ulyanov, known to his fellow plotters, to the Tsarist police, and later to the world, as Lenin, was a man of hybrid origin. On his father's side he came from serfs and Tartars in the mixed Russian-colonized port of Astrakhan on the Caspian. From his father he inherited what Trotsky describes in compliment as a 'plebeian Russian' face. By this he means Mongolian as opposed to the more European features characteristic of the upper and middle classes and also of the western cities of Russia.

His father was Russian-speaking and Orthodox by religion and a science teacher by profession. He had risen by his merits to be a director of schools

[1] George Kennan (1968).

Pedigree 18. The Rise of the Ulyanovs
After Wilson (1940), Ulam (1965), Fischer (1965)

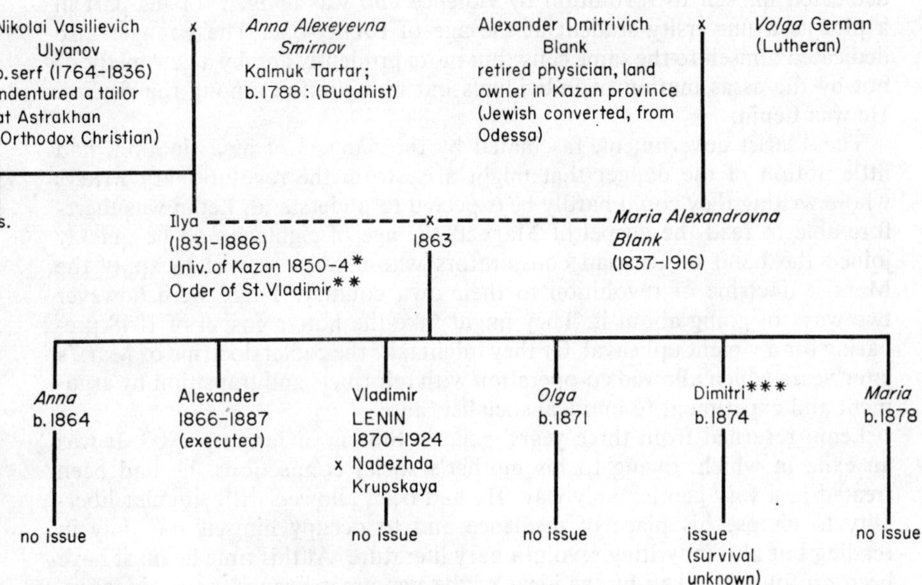

* Rector N. I. Lobachevski (1793–1856), the pioneer of non-Euclidean geometry.
** Carrying the hereditary title of *Excellency*.
*** Imprisoned 1898.

with an hereditary title, evidence of the social mobility possible on the periphery of the expanding Tsarist Empire.

His mother sprang by contrast from an old-established professional class and from two entirely different racial communities. Her people on her mother's side were Germans planted in the basin of the Volga by Catherine the Great three generations earlier as part of her plan to improve the agricultural practices of her adopted country. The community had prospered but the plan had miscarried. The Germans, so far as they were peasants, had built their own Lutheran churches and had therefore kept apart from the Orthodox natives. Inbred and resistant to hybridization, so far from conveying improvements to their neighbours, they had remained as archaic in their German agriculture as in their German speech.[1] But Lenin's grandmother had broken out of this community and married a well-to-do retired Jewish physician, Alexander Blank. Lenin's four grandparents were thus of four different races and religions and both his father and his mother's father were of the professional class from whom, as he himself was to declare, all

[1] Their Republic, established by Stalin, was dissolved by him in 1941 and great numbers of the peasants were then deported in anticipation of treachery. In the 1959 census however the survivors were reported as numbering 1,619,000. The community was 'rehabilitated' by decree in 1964.

revolutionary teachers were derived. The products of this unparalleled hybridization were six children including two remarkable sons. The elder dedicated himself to revolution by violence and was hanged for his part in a plot as a university student at the age of twenty-one. The younger also dedicated himself to the same cause but more prudently and by a new method: not by the assassination of individuals but by agitation among the masses. He was Lenin.

The Tsarist government, fascinated by the dangers of assassination, had little notion of the danger that might arise from the revolutionary writers whose writing they could hardly be expected to understand. Lenin was therefore able to read the gospel of Marx at the age of eighteen and he quickly joined the band of Russian conspirators whose purpose was to apply the Marxist doctrine of revolution to their own country. There were however two ways of going about it. They might take the hotter gospel of 1848 preparing for a violent upheaval. Or they might take the cooler doctrine of Marx's later years which allowed co-operation with reformers and transition by argument and experiment to an ideal socialist State.

Lenin returned from three years' exile in Siberia in January 1900. It was an exile in which, owing to his mother's social connections, he had been treated in a very gentlemanly way. He had been allowed with singular liberality to choose his place of residence and to occupy himself not only in reading but also in writing revolutionary literature. At this time he must have been profoundly taken by the ideas of the two great French revolutionaries, Babeuf and Blanqui. He was bound to notice that their humane character was responsible for their intellectual successes and their practical failures. It was Louis Auguste Blanqui (1805–1881) who had inspired the movement which led to the Paris Commune of 1871. He was responsible for two potent phrases. One was the 'Industrial Revolution' which described something real in the past. The other was the 'Dictatorship of the Proletariat' which described something imaginary in the future. For Lenin it seemed a perfect description, not of the end he had in view, so much as of the necessary means of attaining it.

Lenin realized that the proletariat were incapable of either seizing or exercising power. What was needed was a firmly indoctrinated, firmly disciplined party, firmly led by a single-minded devoted organizer, rather like himself, a party which should act as trustees for the proletariat in overthrowing the old government and in setting up the new. This was (as Ulam points out) the first great revision of Marx's doctrine, the recipe for revolution in Russia.

Lenin, and no doubt many of his later colleagues, were profoundly unconscious of the illusion or the fraud they were practising on themselves and proposing to practise on the workers and peasants of the world. After all they knew very little personally of these workers and peasants or of their work; the hammer and sickle they were to give them as emblems were not tools which the revolutionaries had themselves been accustomed to handle.[1]

[1] Note that Lenin's sole enthusiasm outside revolution was hunting, a paleolithic activity which sets him apart from the peasant and the artisan as well as from the other Bolsheviks.

They were swept forward by a belief in the unknown and the incredible, much as the early Christians had been. But their goal was to be achieved more quickly. Equipped with his illusion Lenin, in 1903, had firmly decided for the hot version of the Marxist programme. Accordingly he attended a conference of Russian Marxist revolutionaries in London. There he was able to persuade a momentary majority, by a quick manœuvre, on a snap vote, to support this plan of action. For the majority *bolsheviki*, as opposed to the minority *mensheviki*, it was to be outright revolution: no compromise with the Tsar; no co-operation with those who would compromise: nothing less than war to the knife; but, of course, at the moment they chose.

The young leader, now thirty-three, at once set to work in London, Geneva and Cracow gathering together and moulding into one piece the fragments of his party. The purpose was single-minded. The arguments were severe but so was the discipline.

Not for nothing had the apostles of Marxism enriched their spiritual life with their master's invective. Now it appeared that Lenin surpassed Marx himself in the terminology of malice and hatred, indignation and contempt. The expressions which were later to erupt into the newspapers of the world took their origin in the letters of Lenin. His denunciations began to establish and classify the forms of treachery, heresy and deviation.[1] In the heroic few who withstood the ferocity of their leader, devotion to him and to the life of plotting and counter-plotting which they all led was naturally consuming. The example and the teachings of Marx as interpreted by the new leader were ineluctable. And the prize for all this effort and suffering was nothing less than the soul and the people and the empire of Russia.

At the time the prospects seemed bleak. But unexpectedly the hopes of the conspirators were raised. In the days of hunger and defeat at the beginning of 1905 modest protests in Petersburg provoked a small massacre. A train of disorders followed throughout the year and were similarly crushed. Lenin's part in the proceedings had been uncertain and unheroic. But he had been learning. It had been, as he said, a rehearsal. And two experiments necessary for revolutionary science had been set in motion.

The first experiment grew out of an unwilling concession of the Tsar: the election of a representative assembly. This was the Duma, something unheard of since the accession of Peter the Great. To be sure it was to be elected with all the devices of indirect nomination and weighted categories known to the Tsar's advisers. And when elected the advice it gave always led to its dissolution and the imprisonment of the more radical members. For the Tsar, following the examples of kings, Stuart and Bourbon, of whose history he was certainly unaware, preferred to take the advice of his foreign wife, misled by her private charlatans. Nevertheless the Duma was a step forward:

[1] An historical glossary of these terms, the ammunition of verbal terrorism, would be worth compiling. Adventurism, careerism and philistinism, chauvinism and economism, revisionism and opportunism of heretics or Mensheviks were added to the capitalism, colonialism and imperialism of the class enemies who are supported by those petty bourgeois riff-raff and hooligans who were later to become hyenas and cannibals. Most of the classical references however are in Ulam (1965).

it opened the way for parliamentary discussion and what might have been representative government.

The second experiment was more novel and in the end provided Lenin with the stronger weapon. It arose, not from his efforts, but from the agitation of the Mensheviks among the strikers and the mutineers. To maintain their resistance they had formed councils or committees. Inevitably these *Soviets* were organized for action and prepared for violence. They were the ready-made link between the revolutionary intellectuals who needed followers and the uneducated masses who needed leaders. At this time and in these connections two young revolutionaries, both twenty-five years old, first came into the public eye: Trotsky in Petersburg, Stalin in Tiflis. Such men forged the link which Lenin was later to use for his purpose.

III. THE CRISIS OF 1917

Both experiments bore fruit in 1917. Three years of war mismanaged by the Tsar's government had led to defeat and famine. In the end the troops were so demoralized that even in the capital, in Petrograd, the guards would no longer obey the Tsar's orders to fire on the crowds demanding bread in the streets. As soon as this happened (on March 11th, N.S.) it was obvious that the crowds for the moment were in command. The successor of Ivan the Terrible suddenly ceased to be terrible. He was dethroned without trouble and the Duma, in consultation with the Soviet of the Petrograd workers, formed a government. Its members were mixed. They were gentry and professional, liberal and socialist, but as a whole—how could it be otherwise?—inexperienced and divided in facing the fearful problems that confronted them. Beginning without authority they failed to acquire it. Nevertheless the government could agree, and the Petrograd Soviet (now seated two thousand strong alongside them in the Tauride Palace) could hardly contradict them, that they should follow the example of the French Revolution and proceed to the election by universal suffrage of a Constituent Assembly.

No sooner was this decided however in the summer of 1917, than the city of Petrograd became the scene of a struggle between the rival forces. On one side was the Provisional Government led by the liberal Kerensky and hurriedly assembled with its diverse members and divergent policies. On the other side was Lenin returned from Switzerland together with his party followers; organizing the political prisoners freed by the government, together with the exiles and émigrés it had welcomed back, haranguing the uncertain workers and soldiers not yet convinced of his doctrine. And all with what purpose? With the purpose simply of overthrowing the government and seizing their power for the Soviets at the moment when the Soviets themselves, at least in Petrograd and Moscow, had fallen under the control of the party.

Here again was repeated the conflict between Cromwell and the Levellers, between the liberals of 1789 and the Jacobins of 1793, between the National Government of 1871 in Versailles and the Blanquist Communards of Paris. To Marx these conflicts had seemed to be conflicts between two classes. But owing to Marx's own teaching this conflict had now become something different: a conflict between two ways of organizing classes for the processes of government. The one depended on public election of representatives and governments. Such people are inherently educated and hence often propertied; and they often favour the privileges of the educated and their opportunities of exploiting the uneducated. The other depended on associations of the unprivileged who being also uneducated favour the authority of individuals, often called demagogues or tyrants, who often exploit the obedience or credulity of their uneducated followers.

Both these methods of government involve their exponents in the use of deceptive jargon, the making of specious promises and in general of political manipulation. Now for one who believed that in the enduring interests of society private property must be speedily and effectively abolished the second alternative was the only course to follow and Lenin was correct in following it. But it meant that he must be the demagogue and the tyrant. And he must organize a party which would convey his instructions with absolute obedience to the uneducated masses. These functions he learnt in the summer of 1917. What he did not understand and hardly liked to learn was that the party, and the mode of instruction, would be prolonged by the permanence of those uneducated masses whose character, on so little evidence, he was so confident of being able to change.

One of his followers, however, knew the people. He also knew what the people had in store for their governors because, unlike Marx and Lenin, he understood what people of different races and classes could and could not do. This man was Stalin. To him we shall return.

Given his policy of immediate socialism and the confiscation of property, so necessary for capturing the government, Lenin knew that the election of a Constituent Assembly was the one step he must forestall. The Constituent Assembly was bound to have the same educated, professional and propertied bias as its French predecessor. On the other hand the Soviets were already beginning to show something of the character of the workers' clubs in the Paris of 1793. They were showing the genuinely anti-professional and anti-propertied bias of the Fourth Estate. For them the demands in the cities for bread to eat and in the country for land to plough were becoming overpowering. Peace was a third gift that Lenin could offer them, a peace that would protect the Revolution in Russia and even allow its contagion to spread to the other war-sick countries of Europe.

Peace however proved to be a doubtful issue. The Revolution had revived the national feeling of the Russian armies, officers and men alike. For eight months after the March upheaval the struggle therefore continued, a struggle centred in the capital. On one side was the open government, uncertainly and unwisely endeavouring to continue the war with the foreign invaders, while attempting to master mutiny and famine and two million deserters at home, and allowing freedom of speech for all its enemies. And on the other side were the Bolshevik conspirators supported by German money and operating through a small committee under Lenin. This committee, publishing its own newspaper, was able to promise all things to soldiers, workers and peasants and thus convert the Soviets to their policies. The question thus was: could the Soviets be brought sufficiently under the influence of Lenin's Bolshevik followers to overthrow the government before the government took steps to suppress them?

The crisis came on November 7 (N.S.) 1917. The second All-Russian Congress of Soviets was to meet in Petrograd, in the Smolny Institute, that day. Now was the chance, Trotsky argued, and he had his way. The workers had been armed by the government through the Soviets for the defence of the Revolution. Their arms they now turned against the government for the Soviets. They seized the vital centres in the capital. They captured the whole personnel of the government in the Winter Palace and marched them off under guard to the fortress of Peter and Paul.

The Congress of the Soviets under a Bolshevik chairman now voted to appoint a Bolshevik government and to implement the Bolshevik policies, land for the peasants and peace with Germany. And, having voted, its members returned to their towns and villages to carry through the Revolution on the spot.

The party of Lenin was in power.

IV. THE COMMUNIST STATE

a. The Apparatus of Dictatorship

It was an almost bloodless *coup d'état* on the lines of Cromwell and Napoleon. A small determined body of men had seized power. These men were diverse in race, class and character. They were trained in poverty and seasoned in conspiracy but inexperienced in government. They knew that their power existed at the centre, but only at the centre. They knew that they could keep their power only if their leader had talents and temper as sound as a Cromwell or Napoleon. The few who knew Lenin, and only those few, could have any confidence in the result.

The first steps needed were to protect and establish the centre of power and from this base to destroy over the widest area, and with the least disturbance, all possible alternative governments. On November 8th Lenin appointed a governing committee, his commissars (the term was Trotsky's), with the purpose of doing these things.[1] Peace was to be negotiated with the central powers. Freedom and friendship were to be offered to all the great racial regions conquered by the Tsarist Empire, the Ukraine, Transcaucasia, Turki-speaking Central Asia and Siberia. Land was to be distributed among the peasants. Industry was to be seized and nationalized. All foreign debts were to be repudiated. And a little department known by the initials Che-Ka was to observe and supervise, to arrest and to liquidate (a term of Lenin's whose meaning only gradually became clear) all enemies of the people, that is of the Bolshevik government.

Of these proposals the only one which encountered no difficulties was the

[1] The Jews, among both Bolsheviks and Mensheviks, had borne half the burden of the long struggle; in deference to Russian proletarian anti-Semitism, however, all but Trotsky were left out of the government. It was the most distinctive proletarian influence on Lenin's Revolution.

last. The business of the Cheka was in the first instance to save the country as much as to save the government. For the Bolshevik propaganda had destroyed the authority of the Provisional Government by undermining authority of all kinds. In every unit in the army and navy and in every office and factory in the country one man was now as good as another. If famine was to be averted and the enemy held at bay authority had to be restored by processes as ruthless as those that had been used to disintegrate it. It was in these circumstances and with this excuse that Lenin could refer to 'our excellent Cheka'. But very quickly the functions of the new organization took on a more specific, and also more traditional, colour.

On November 25th, elections had been promised to the Constituent Assembly. The elections were to be supervised by the Cheka. Thus the Bolsheviks, in spite of their negligible standing in the country at large, managed to secure 175 of the 707 seats.[1] This however was not enough to carry the day. When Lenin convened the Assembly on January 18th they rejected the proposals he put to them. They were at once adjourned by force, that is by the Cheka. Constitutional opposition then no longer existed.

It was now clear that the Bolshevik Party, the party of Lenin, had become the only proper instrument for the dictatorship of the proletariat. All weaker brethren, all Menshevik and other schismatics, could be forgotten. All other political individuals and factions gradually came to realize that they had lost the legal right to exist which they had possessed in that short spell between March and November 1917. Henceforth Lenin's party, renamed on March 8 1918, the Russian Communist Party, was to be the sole organ of discussion, and the sole basis of government, in the country.

Before these processes could be consolidated or developed Lenin and his government, under the threat of the German advance, had to desert Petrograd. On March 10th, evading the Railwaymen's Union which had Menshevik principles, they stole away from their exposed capital and set up their headquarters in a hotel in Moscow.[2]

In Moscow further developments followed a shooting incident. On August 30th the head of the Cheka was assassinated and Lenin was wounded. Thereupon 600 prisoners were executed by the Moscow Cheka and terror became unrestricted. The communist government was beset in all directions. The territories of what had been the Empire were in the hands of twenty-five separate governments. What remained to the Soviets was successively threatened by three Russian 'white' armies, by British, Japanese and Czech forces 'intervening' in the struggle and by a foreign war with a Polish army under French command. And if this was not enough all authority had been destroyed in Soviet territory by the Bolshevik gospel of destruction to all officers, managers, specialists, bourgeois, capitalists and gentry, in short almost everyone who knew how to exercise authority.

To meet these fearful assaults, two daring experiments were tried and they

[1] E. H. Carr (1950) gives the details. See also Jankovsky (1965).

[2] They remained in Moscow until the next German threat in November 1941 (Alleluyeva, 1967). The circumstances are described by Bruce Lockhart (1940) and by Ulam (1965).

proved successful in saving Lenin's Revolution. In the first place the whole surviving Tsarist personnel was embodied in the communist machine. The process began at once with the creation of the Red Army in 1918. It continued with the civil service, the universities and schools. And in the political police the Tsar's *Okhrana* was now naturally operating its apparatus from the offices of the Cheka but without the misgivings of its former masters.[1]

In the course of these processes it was necessary to ensure the loyalty in practice of men who were often bound to be disloyal in principle. On the French revolutionary precedent, communist commissars were therefore attached to the head of every unit to supervise or to spy, to discipline or to denounce. Who then was to control these political controllers? Being members of the party they came under the control of a commissar of the Workers' and Peasants' Inspectorate. This official could move each man where he wanted him; or dispose of him altogether. All public employments thus became political employments, the subject of treasonable prosecution and matters of life and death.

These measures, drastically enforced at great cost of life, gradually restored authority and concentrated it in the hands of a few men in the government in Moscow. Everything therefore depended on their loyalty to Lenin, to the party, and to one another. An appearance of *esprit de corps*, to use a pre-revolutionary and bourgeois phrase, was thus all-important. Nor did it fail. Indeed it became, under these conditions of perpetual suspense, an obsession with terrifying possibilities which were later to be revealed to the world as well as to the participants themselves.

Discipline and fidelity, however, did not alone solve the problems of bread and butter. The whole economy of the country was foundering under the stress of the general confiscation of private property by the State. Faced first with famine and then with a mutiny of the sailors at Kronstadt, the very men who had put him in power, Lenin turned about in March 1921 and, overriding the protests of his own party, restored for a time the right of private trading. It was a move which enabled the communist State to survive and later to recover its ownership and control. At the same time Lenin's government, by combinations of military and political strategy, was able to recover the great provinces which temporarily it had had to surrender. By 1923 the Ukraine, White Russia and Transcaucasia had been brought back under the control of Moscow. They were embodied in what was to become the Soviet Union.

Why, we may ask, were these provinces recovered while no progress was made with any of the western border states, Finland, Estonia, Latvia, Lithuania and Poland? The reason was twofold. The border states had a non-Russian-speaking middle class. These educated and propertied people resisted the imposition equally of the Russian officials and of communist methods. The position of Georgia in this respect was significant. The Georgians maintained their independence for four years; but, being isolated and

[1] The Cheka, like the untouchables in India, had its name changed to conceal its character. It became successively the OGPU, NKVD, MVD, and MGB. It was last heard of as the KGB, a force of 750,000 men.

remote, their resistance could be crushed by force in July 1921. It was force, however, accompanied by a new kind of blackmail. Party officials, political police and the new Red Army, together and apparently without Lenin's knowledge, removed those members of the Georgian government who objected to the suppression of Georgian independence. Peace was restored; integration was complete.

b. The Struggle for the Succession

Lenin was partly incapacitated by a stroke in March 1922 and, after further strokes, died in January 1924. With death approaching he had time to contemplate the vast problems that he seemed to have solved and to turn over in his mind the equally vast problems he had created, problems he was bound to leave for his successors to tackle. He had devised or improvised the theory and the practice of a new kind of government. It was a government of necessity employing the men, individuals and classes available to him in Russia. It had therefore of necessity taken a structure not so unlike that of the society which had preceded it. Names had changed but procedures and institutions had survived. He himself had filled the familiar role of a Russian autocrat for whom power was an end in itself and all means of securing it were theoretically correct. Was it possible that this apparatus and this theory of government might prove permanent? Might it perhaps fall into the hands again of a single man? And, if it did, might not his successor abuse the absolute power he inherited, as all autocrats (save himself) had always done?

The conditions under which Lenin was permitted to meditate were far from reassuring. In the interests of his own health which was of supreme importance to the State, his cabinet, his Politburo, were able to prevent him interfering in the government and especially criticizing their actions, augmenting their numbers and so on. The dictator now found himself under dictation.

Lenin's Marxist mentor, Plekhanov, had shown twenty years earlier that Great Men, try as they might, could do nothing to alter the course of history. But Lenin had devoted his own life to precisely this attempt. And when he looked at his colleagues now he saw men who were, in their own opinion, qualified to pursue the same ends and only too clearly bent on doing so. Two of them were a particular danger: Trotsky and Stalin. They were manifest rivals, born in the same year (1879), old fighters in the cause of revolution, opposed in character and revolutionaries for quite different reasons. Who were these men?

Leon Davidovich Bronstein or Trotsky came from the Ukraine. He was the son of a Jewish farmer employing labour, that is a *Kulak*. He had been the President of the Petersburg Soviet in the fighting year of 1905. But in peacetime he had made his living as a journalist widely travelling in Europe and America. In the days of crisis in 1917 he had hesitated to align himself with Lenin and often later he had held his own opinions. But in the government Lenin had made him Commissar, first for Foreign Affairs, and later for War, in which capacity he had created the Red Army and finished the Civil War.

Stalin, who began life as Joseph Vissarionovich Djugashvili, was a man of a different race and class and origin. He was the son of the first outbred generation of liberated Georgian serfs. His activity as an agitator and revolutionary had kept him busy inside Russia. When out of prison he had worked ceaselessly organizing and teaching the workers politically. He began in Tiflis and then moved to the rapidly growing Baku oilfield. Men of many races and varying character and aptitude were crowded together in the new industries. He had got to know them as no revolutionary had known them before for the reason that he was a good listener who wrote little and spoke less. Lenin made him Commissar for Nationalities in 1917. In this capacity he had suppressed, in the way we saw, the independence of his own country, Georgia. And in 1919 he had taken over the invisible office of the Inspectorate of Workers and Peasants. Finally, one month after Lenin's stroke, the Politburo made this hard-working man General Secretary of the party.

The contrast between these two men could not on the surface have been more emphatic: Trotsky the eloquent talker, literate, quick-witted, somewhat vain, popular hero and man of the world; and Stalin the silent listener, aloof, slow and circumspect and perhaps envious, the inconspicuous and apparently unoriginal administrator. But beneath the surface this contrast had led to differences in method, in purpose, in policy; and also differences in the position acquired in the new governing system, the apparatus of the Russian Communist Party on which the future of these two men and the future of the revolution now depended.

These differences in character were clear enough during Lenin's lifetime. But once he was dead the contrast in power between the two men became gradually evident. Trotsky had been responsible for what were in other governments the great public offices and his achievements were known all over the world. Stalin had acquired the two most secret and apparently most subservient posts to be held by one of the five members of the Politburo. As Commissar for the Workers' and Peasants' Inspectorate he was the man who controlled and employed the supervisory agents in the whole civil administration. As General Secretary of the Central Committee of the Communist Party he was the man who decided what was to be discussed at all the meetings when members of the government were appointed or dismissed. Such posts, to be sure, are of little importance in an ordinary open government. But in a closed communist government they proved to be the positions of final power. The subservient secretary proved to be the master of the apparatus he had laboriously created.

Around the dying dictator a protracted drama was played out. It intensified over the two years of his successive strokes. It is from this long struggle that we have most to learn about the new system of government. What was it that held them together? It was not their love of one another. Each feared what actually happened, namely that one of them, the successor, would kill the rest. Nor was it love of, or from, the Russian people. The Cheka was the witness and the measure of that love. Nor, again, was it love of Lenin. More and more they all, even Trotsky, feared what his rage might do to them.

The Tsars had always feared the people. The communists in addition feared one another. Only one thing held them together and that was the party. It was not so much the power that it gave them. It was the practice of conspiracy which it embodied. Conspiracy exists in all governments with power. But here the power was absolute and was held exclusively by men trained in professional conspiracy. It therefore came to dominate everything. It was the practice for which they had been selected by Lenin and to which they had chosen to give their tormented lives, the practice which they now applied against one another, the practice which most of them were to reveal when they later came to confess their sins in public declaration. Like Hindu society, on a vast scale, this little clique, on a small scale, was obsessed with, and united by, its own appalling divisions.

Did this mean that Stalin could seize the central power in his own hands on the death of Lenin? Not yet. It was this possibility which Lenin had foreseen and in his last testament he had warned the Central Committee of the danger. Thereby no doubt he had delayed the result. But after five years of manœuvres the delayed result nevertheless followed. Stalin had in this time secured the relegation of Trotsky and one by one of the other possible leaders. He had packed with his own followers both the Politburo above him and the police force below him. So in 1929 he became the fully fledged heir of Lenin and absolute head of the communist State.[1]

There had been one of those reversals of power which in the past had so often quietly transformed despotic states. Those appointed to serve and protect the government had become the government itself. The slaves had become masters, the mameluke had become sultan. A police state had come into existence, something unpredicted by Marx and disregarded by Lenin the shrewd politician who showed himself unequal to this supreme test.

What were these manœuvres, the devious steps, by which this long journey had been completed? They were diverse in method and effect and in degree of success. The unoriginal secretary had proved to be, in his chosen field, the most tireless experimenter, the most original virtuoso. To illustrate the technique of the beginner who was to advance so far, take a clumsy example which happens to be of social significance.

It had been the intention of the communist leaders while creating their own machine to dismantle the apparatus of religious worship. Their object was to supersede all religious sects, Christian, Muslim and Jewish alike, by the new totally embracing community of belief in the government. Within St Isaac's Cathedral in the city renamed Leningrad, an Anti-God Museum had been assembled for the public instruction. The drum of the dome was now encircled by the warning words in letters of gold that Religion is the Opium of the People. But the mass of the Russian people had been accustomed to see their Tsar as the representative of God on Earth. For them their dead saints had been the witness of God's love and the ancient music of their Church, reaching a climax at Easter, had been the celebration of the living unity of the whole nation.

[1] Deutscher's description of Stalin's rise to power is also a social history of the Revolution.

The intellectual writings of Marx and Engels, so satisfying to the members of the Politburo (themselves so long intellectually dispossessed), were inadequate to meet these deep emotional needs of the masses. Something else was needed and the death of Lenin might easily suggest to his successors the new means of providing it. Stalin had spent five years of his youth in a theological seminary run by Russian monks in Tiflis; he was expelled in May 1899. It was he who arranged that the death of Lenin should be used to impose the cult of Lenin equally on the intellectual Politburo above and on the innocent people below. He saw that an imperishable body embalmed in a great tomb should be sited at the centre of the annual festival of the Revolution immediately under the walls of the citadel. This was a first step in the creation of a communist religion. A second step he thought might be the compilation of a liturgy for the new faith. He quickly drafted its terms: sonorous, repetitive, sentimental and somewhat remote from the teachings of dialectical materialism. This devotional statement he read to a congress of Soviets five days after Lenin's death.[1]

Unfortunately for Stalin's scheme the repugnance of the old communists (including Lenin's widow, Krupskaya) for religious forms discouraged the pursuit of this too crude initiative. It was dropped. But in place of it another more effective practice appeared. The quotation of Lenin as a basis of policy came most easily to his most exact and devoted disciple. The sacred scripture was a substitute for original speculation. And it answered an even greater purpose. For by everlasting quotation the disciple became the apostle and there emerged not only the cult of Lenin but also the cult of that apostle, the cult of the living ruler, of Stalin himself.

By the time the five years of Stalin's labours had been completed, labours spent in the Politburo, in the Central Committee, in the Inspectorate, in the Cheka (now the O.G.P.U.) and in the party at large, the position of Lenin's successor was unassailable. Any personal act or opinion *deviating* from the *party line*, which was the name given to the policy of the *leader*, was the signal for expulsion from the party, dismissal from employment or relegation to a labour camp where the *criminal* might be *rehabilitated* if he succeeded in surviving. This, for great numbers of Russians, proved to be the means of establishing Lenin's Revolution.

c. The Autocracy Returns

Having settled his personal problem to his own satisfaction, Stalin could now turn to larger, or at least publicly larger, issues. Before the death of Lenin his and Trotsky's original grand programme had begun to seem questionable. Was it in fact certain that the Soviet government must safeguard its position by at once promoting world revolution? Or would it do better first to put its own house in order, achieving the perfect state of socialism at home, and developing its own backward agriculture and industry, before it embarked on a world crusade?

[1] The experimental litany used by Stalin is translated by Deutscher (1949). Each verse consists of two parts: (i) 'Comrade Lenin ordained us to . . .' and (ii) 'We vow to thee Comrade Lenin . . .'.

Trotsky, as indeed Lenin, had grown up with the first programme in mind. And it was one which he was admirably fitted to carry out by his talent and temperament, and by his experience before and since the Revolution. Stalin, on the other hand, was quite unfitted to expound or execute such a programme. He knew nothing of the world outside Russia. Fortunately for him the outside problem, its opportunities and its dangers alike, slowly faded from sight. But the inside problem came continually nearer. Its opportunities beckoned; its dangers threatened. In the end Stalin had no choice in the matter. By 1929 the Revolution's chickens had come home to roost: the country was faced with famine for the peasants or the unthinkable alternative of a request by the government for foreign food or money.

In 1917 the agricultural land of Russia had been handed over to the peasants. In 1928 there were now some 25 million holdings on whose harvests over 100 million people depended directly for their living and the whole state depended for its survival. Among these holdings a top class of less than 10 per cent were reasonably equipped and managed by capable and successful farmers able to buy modern tools and employ labour efficiently: these were the Kulaks. A bottom class of 25 per cent were almost destitute. They were men still working with some five million home-made wooden ploughs, older than the implements of classical antiquity. Between these two classes were a majority of middling men precariously holding their own.

What had happened was that in the two generations since the liberation of the serfs they had split up into classes which coped with varying success with the problems of farming on their own. And in the ten years since the expulsion of the landlords the less successful, now totally unprotected, unassisted and unadvised, were beginning to go to the wall.

The obvious remedy was to provide equipment and advice from above. The Kulaks might have been put in charge of co-operative or collective farms using their own equipment. But the Kulaks were not well disposed to the co-operative experiments of a threatening socialist government. They were not therefore invited to co-operate. Instead their equipment was confiscated for the collective farms. These were put under the management, not of experienced farmers, but of political inspectors. And they themselves, over a period of five years, were deported and massacred. At the same time and for the same purpose the whole farming livestock was ordered to be impounded. The peasants, not only the Kulaks, resisting these measures, slaughtered half their livestock for lack of which the whole country, apart perhaps from the party, suffered hunger and starvation.[1]

Collectivization of Soviet agriculture, at this frightful cost, was almost completed in ten years. Two purposes seemed to have been accomplished. The practice of public ownership and the prohibition of private trading had been established. And the control of the peasants by the government, that is by the central government through the Communist Party, had also been established. But unfortunately the peasant community, the character, the ability and the instincts of the individual peasants, had been changed, not for the better, but for the worse. The men on whom the country could have best

[1] Isaac Deutscher describes the development of this catastrophe.

depended to use the modern methods of extensive agriculture had been destroyed. And the men who were left were those who were capable of the individual labour and unremitting industry of which peasants always have been capable; that is, if they were allowed to work by their ancient methods for themselves—which was precisely what they were not allowed to do.

What was now the remedy? It became necessary to allow the collectivized peasants to cultivate private plots of land and keep private stock of their own. And what was the result? Thirty years later (in 1967) Stalin and the generation of his collectivizers having passed away, private land and private stock are now the source of one-third of the agricultural produce of the Soviet Union. But this produce has barely maintained itself at the level it had in Tsarist Russia. Thus mechanization, co-operation, and collectivization, which have gone hand in hand in raising production in countries with private farming, when enforced and managed by the State, have left the Soviet Union economically no better off than when it began; and humanly worse off than ever before.[1]

In capitalist countries scientific research with its technical applications was at this time rapidly advancing agricultural production. It was doing so through the enterprise of selectively favoured individual farmers. But in communist Russia where such farmers had been selectively eliminated these advances had failed to occur.[2]

In his land policy Stalin was applying to agriculture the principle of organization and planning by the State which Lenin had seen as the necessary corollary of State ownership in industry. The methods which he had taken as a model were those (as Carr points out) which he had seen in action before and during the war in the western capitalist countries. They were now applied by Stalin on a larger and more ambitious scale in order to develop Russian industry and bring it up to the level it had reached in the older industrial countries; but without the help of the stored capital on which they had founded their growth. In other words, by the toil, thrift and hardship of the workers themselves. So far as heavy industry was concerned, so necessary both for agriculture and for war, enormous advances were made between 1928 and the German attack in 1941. But they were advances which had to be paid for, not partly, like those of early English industry, but entirely out of the profits made by industry from the exploitation of cheap labour. The faster the development, the harsher the exploitation, whether it was a private capitalist or Stalin himself as head of the socialist State.

Moreover, into this development of Russian industry and Russian society,

[1] Exact comparisons are not possible with deceptive statistics and changing frontiers but, according to Deutscher, Russian grain production was 86m tons in 1913, 95m tons in 1940, 80m tons in 1950–1953.

[2] A secondary aspect of this policy was the attempt to impose bogus scientific methods in agriculture, particularly in plant and animal breeding, methods conforming with a Marxist and Lamarckian theory of heredity. These were advocated by Trofim Lysenko, who served Stalin for twenty-five years as President of the Lenin Academy of Agricultural Science and became a kind of biological Rasputin for the new autocrat (Darlington, 1948).

Stalin had brought another factor as significant as that of State control and State planning: it was the State exclusiveness which he held to be the necessary corollary of socialism in one country. Already in 1930 his government began to block up the entrances and the exits on the Russian frontiers. The old autocrats had often prevented Russians leaving the country; and information coming into the country. The new autocrat now in addition prevented foreigners entering the country and information going out of it. The whole of Russia was now confined, segregated and imprisoned. The impermeable secrecy which descended on Russia no doubt gave military and political security. The old revolutionary activity could no longer be repeated. This was a short-term advantage to the government. But there was a long-term drawback which has been accumulating over the years.

Recruitment had over a whole millennium, and even in the worst periods of Tsarist oppression, created and expanded the technical and professional classes of Russian society. It was now brought to a sudden end. The great spring from which freely moving peoples had always refreshed themselves was suddenly dried up. It was a drying-up from which both halves of the world suffered but Russia, being the smaller half, indeed about a sixth, was bound to suffer most.

To compensate for this new barrier the Revolution had broken down certain old barriers of race and class so that Jews and Armenians, Poles, Finns and Georgians were now filling high offices in the government and the party. They had become for a time a part of the Russian Establishment, political, professional and academic. It might have seemed an indispensable part. But for the Jews, who were intellectually and culturally the most important of these peoples, this freedom was gradually curtailed. It was not only a recurrence of the Russian proletarian prejudice. The Jews had become dangerous to the government. Some of them had religious beliefs, others had foreign or 'cosmopolitan' connections. At the same time the Communist Party, being a privileged group, had rejected the freedom of social relations which they had cherished before they had their privileges. As Trotsky early, and Djilas later, observed, they had become a new governing class, segregated and once more exclusively Russian-speaking as well as communist-thinking; and endeavouring like all such classes to preserve themselves from the undesirable consequences of that natural selection to which their less fortunate compatriots are inevitably exposed.

The establishment of the new communist governing class has however differed from that of any previous governing class in history. Owing to Marx's and Lenin's ignorance of certain historical details they both believed that the correct course of revolution lay in hatred and struggle followed by extirpation of one governing class by its successor. They did not know that in all previous revolutions conflict had been followed by hybridization and not by extirpation. By this ferocious fallacy they have delayed their recovery from the consequences of their work.

V. THE CONTROL OF SOCIETY

The study of revolutions now enables us to ask how far people who attempt to change society suddenly and radically are capable of changing it in a direction they intend and thereby improving it.

The Russian Revolution has obviously fallen short of the expressed hopes of Lenin. Many of its disappointments may be attributed to its rulers' fears of foreign attacks, fears justified by events. The purges by which Stalin in the years 1935 to 1938 put away a large part of the higher-ranking officials of his State and officers of his army were (according to Deutscher) a side effect of these fears. But they also arose from Marxist belief, a mistaken belief, that, like the Kulaks none of these men were irreplaceable.

The repression of literature, the arts and the sciences by Stalin and of all the activities of the professional classes also arose from similar contempt for the individuals and hatred for their class. These attitudes were equally appropriate for Tsarists and for Marxists. But when the crisis of the second war came in 1941 it was found that a price had to be paid for these policies. Communist generals had to be replaced by good generals who were not usually communists at all.

To be sure Russia was saved from a repetition of the disasters of the Tsarist wars of 1855, 1904 and 1915. Now it was 1812 which set the pattern for defence as well as attack. But in order to survive the crisis of the war, the attack on Stalingrad in the winter of 1942 to 1943, Stalin was compelled to throw overboard most of those principles inculcated by Marx which Lenin and he had not earlier discarded.

Already under Lenin differences of pay had had to be introduced, and differences of status had had to be proclaimed, and with Stalin's industrialization, to stimulate competitive efficiency, they had had to be carried beyond the proportions known in the west. Now in the army, epaulettes were brought in to distinguish the uniforms of officers, and orders named after the generals Suvorov and Kutuzov assimilated the glories of imperial history to the needs of the communist régime. Exclusive guards regiments with imperial antecedents reappeared. The political commissars, first installed by Trotsky in his professional Red Army, now found themselves demoted in the organization of the Soviet army. Finally, with the approaching Soviet invasion of the Orthodox Balkan states, the Russian Orthodox Church, after exactly twenty-five years in the cold, was now embraced by the communist dictator. Its patriotic *raison d'être* was admitted and its Synod was convened in Moscow.

Thus nationalism was not too reluctantly restored to its former place. Racial antagonism, uneasily diverted in 1917, was now admitted and officially approved. Class structure was recognized. Social deference was encouraged. And superstition, so far as it was useful, was rehabilitated. The ideas of communism had been jettisoned in favour of prejudices which might be shared with the proletariat and the bourgeoisie of a philistine capitalist or imperialist society.

In order to preserve the communist fatherland most of the precepts of the communist fathers had been sacrificed. And the communist fathers themselves, who on principle disapproved of assassination, had now all been assassinated. A reversal of principle has always accompanied the adoption of a new religion by a governing class. But it could be accomplished with unexampled speed and completeness when it was the religion of the governing class itself which had changed. Certain words of Gibbon in reference to Justinian may be easily adapted to describe the result. The extremes of democracy and despotism had been confounded in attempting (ostensibly) to attain the perfect equality of man.

If we now look back over fifty years at the history of the communist Revolution in Russia we see that we have more to learn from it about the nature of human societies than from any previous episode in human history. Never before has such an attempt been made to alter the character of a society. It was an attempt planned on the basis of a knowledge of a succession of previous attempts. It was carried out with a great deal of skill and with unexampled conviction and ruthlessness. And at the end of this period of trial the Russian people, their character, their beliefs, their achievements have changed no more, perhaps rather less, and have improved no more, perhaps rather less, than the people of adjoining countries which have been subjected to no such drastic experimental coercion.

Rising in society were new classes favoured by industrialization, administration and education; new classes which were hybridized with the old professional class. At the top of society was a Communist Party highly selected for its ability to work its own apparatus. And the peasants, suffering as they had always done for having talents which are more abundant than those of any other class, stay where they have always been, at the bottom of society. The tremendous power of the environment exercised by the wills of the most powerful rulers ever known has failed to alter the class structure, the basic genetic character or even the behaviour of the people in the direction expected by their rulers.

The great Marxist experiment was an attempt to change or at least hasten the course of history by altering the lives of peoples and the relations of all races, nations and classes. In the first place Lenin believed he could with advantage displace an obsolete governing class by violent means, replacing it by new people united in their understanding of Marxist theory and thereby capable of governing better. Here he was successful; but no more successful than his moderate socialist predecessors would have been.

Secondly, he thought he could do this throughout the world. Here he was right only so far as Russia was concerned. For the ruling class were not universally obsolete, or universally incapable of hybridization and adaptation. Class structure was of widely different efficiency in different countries for genetic reasons of which Marx and Lenin were unaware. And even where their prescription could be followed as in China, again for genetic reasons, the result was unexpected and the interests of communist states quickly conflicted.

Thirdly, Lenin's successor Stalin succeeded in developing out of urban outbred populations an industrial society like that in older countries. By central control derived from his Tsarist predecessors and by copying instead of inventing he was able to do this as quickly but with the same kind of exploitation and suffering as in western capitalist societies.

Fourthly, Stalin failed even more disastrously than his Tsarist predecessors in applying coercion to Russian peasant populations. Peasants were capable of being led within the limits which the course of their biological evolution allowed them; but their inbred populations cannot change as quickly as those of townsmen; and none could be forced to change his inborn character by any power on earth.

Fifthly, under the stress of international conflict, Stalin was free to abandon all the Marxist assumptions on the structure of society on which he had been brought up. Equalitarianism, rationalism as opposed to religion, internationalism as opposed to racialism, all went by the board in order to secure the survival of his own authority and his own new communist governing class. He thus left his successors in a difficult position. They are equipped with a theory of society and government which equals that of the old western Christian and capitalist states in confusion and already far surpasses it in fraudulence.

Finally, with all their enduring efforts and power, both of them without precedent, Lenin and his successors proved that Great Men can alter the course of history. Not only have Great Men had great effects, but little men in great positions have had equally great effects. For without Nicholas II, as small a man as history has recorded, Lenin himself could scarcely have found a place in history. The difference between them is that the Great Men, unlike the little men, have produced in part the effects they hoped or expected to produce. But they could have their expected effects only so far as they were operating in fields where enough was known to allow of confident predictions. Such confident predictions have been made for a long time in the fields of science and technology. And in those slowly expanding fields, predictions have been fulfilled. Marx and Lenin believed they were working in a field, the study of society, that allowed of such predictions.

They believed that ideas reflect material foundations of society such as they themselves could control. But we now see that the ideas developing in different societies which have inherited these opinions (as in Russia and China) are manifestly divergent and contrasted. The material foundations, we now see, include not only economic but also genetic structure. The variable factors now acting are seen to be individual, national, and even racial.

Marx and Lenin were thus premature. They were premature, not in the sense of Wycliffe or Servetus, who had the right ideas a century before society was ready for them, but in the sense that they had ideas a century before the growth of knowledge had provided the necessary basis of inference or application. We continue the study of society with more patience in the hope of providing just this basis.

Part Eight

Separate Worlds

Expansion of peoples brought agriculture from Western Asia not only to Europe, Egypt and India but also to China and later to Indonesia and tropical Africa. It was independently discovered in America. In all these centres, societies developed independently. In all of them the same rules of assortative mating and stratification gave rise to governing and priestly, technical and peasant classes or castes. In all of them the expansion of successful societies and classes was accompanied by limited hybridization and by the institution of slavery. The evolutionary directions of the separated peoples were dictated in part by the different character of the native and immigrant races; in part by the different kinds of crops and stock which they exploited; and in part by the different kinds of diseases to which their different climates exposed them.

25

AMERICA

I. THE COLONIZATION OF AMERICA

THE FIRST MEN (and women) broke through into America from North-Eastern Asia by a land bridge over the Bering Strait during the last ice age. Probably during a warm spell in the twelfth millennium B.C. hunting bands were able to slip between the Rocky Mountain and Laurentian ice caps. In the course of 500 years they seem (following Hayne's account) to have spread over most of unglaciated North America. There the hunters encountered vast herds of herbivorous animals: mammoth, camel, horse and bison. What happened? Both sides to the encounter experienced a crisis unprecedented in their history. The new weapons and skills of the latest paleolithic men achieved much more quickly what had been done in Africa 50,000 years earlier. Within the space of 6000 years thirty-five mammalian genera had been exterminated in North America.[1] The human species multiplied; the great animals vanished. All except the bison, the caribou and the deer were killed off in the quest for food.

We must at once ask why animals were exterminated so fast in the New World which survived in the Old World. Several factors were probably concerned. One is that North America is smaller than the Old World and its communications easier for man. Another is that man had long reached equilibrium with his victims, his enemies and his diseases in the Old World. But in entering the New World the very movement which gave him his victims freed him from his enemies and his diseases; that is until he met the Spaniards. An explosion of the magnitude that occurred in the newly invaded continent was thus out of the question under any other conditions.

Such seems to have been the beginning of man's life in America. In another three thousand years he had probably reached the Fuegian extremity of South America and had begun to occupy the islands of the Caribbean.

[1] P. S. Martin (1966): see ch. 2.

Meanwhile further waves of migrants, colonists or invaders followed one another. They were all from the same Mongolian stock with olive skins, straight black hair and more or less folded eyelids. The last were the sub-neolithic Aleuts and Eskimos who colonized Alaska and the northern coasts of Canada during the first millennium A.D.[1]

This great population of Mongolian peoples was restricted in its variation by its restricted origin from one arctic section of Old World peoples. It has never produced in its five hundred generations any mutations which could give curly hair (or even fair hair apart from the albino mutants of Panama), a heavy beard or a black skin colour. Natives of the Venezuela coast have, like Arabs in the Hadhramaut, to paint their faces to protect themselves from the sun. Nevertheless the American peoples became greatly diversified in other respects. Why? Because as they expanded in numbers the pressure of natural selection was removed. Resistance to the Old World diseases disappeared or failed to develop; even some of the Old World blood groups were lost in the rapid expansion, an easy circumstance for which their posterity would pay dearly. But new adaptations appeared, notably to life in the high Andes, in the tropical forest and in the great deserts of north and south. But the important region for diversification we can hardly doubt was the complex area on either side of the central isthmus through which all populations entering South America had to pass.

II. THE ORIGINS OF AGRICULTURE

The origins of agriculture in the New World are to be traced to the same period of human activity, following the retreat of the ice, as in the Old World. They are also to be located in the regions where human movements were similarly funnelled by the constrictions of the land areas. They were however, by the very shape of these constrictions, separated from one another by high mountains, dense forests and dry deserts, strung in a line at vast distances apart. The 4000 tortuous and chequered miles from Arizona to Bolivia are sharply contrasted with the uninterrupted span of a thousand miles on the edge of the Fertile Crescent.

It was for this reason that the beginnings of settled cultivation appeared in America at isolated places where different peoples made use of different crops; and later, combinations of crops, for no one crop could sustain life as completely and effectively as wheat, or later rice, in the Old World. Thus, as Mangelsdorf has shown, maize, beans and squashes all appeared first as wild plants eaten by man in Mexico in the fifth millennium B.C. The squashes, including gourds and pumpkins, may well have been carried forward in the general southward movement of paleolithic hunting and collecting peoples

[1] These were the people who in the fourteenth century formed a colony in north Greenland, the polar Eskimos who, isolated for fifteen generations, formed one of the pure races in the world. They were also the people who brought the Norse colony in south Greenland to an end at about the same time. A little later, in 1682 and 1684, two of these venturous Eskimos appeared in their kayaks as castaways on the coast of Scotland (Ann Savours, 1963).

so that different species came to be hybridized and selected for diverse uses at an early stage. The same is true of the sweet potato which arose from crossing and doubling the chromosomes of several scattered wild species. Already paleolithic man had presumably learnt to collect all the plants from which spices and beverages, poisons and drugs, could be extracted. These were evidently circulated among peoples as fast as the staple food crops. Thus, in the third and second millennia B.C., the movements of peoples brought together not only a diversity of human beings but also a diversity of crops and of technical inventions, notably pottery, on which village and later city life could be based.

It seems to have been later that manioc and sweet potato, as well as tobacco and cocoa, were eventually able to move against the first current of invasion in the contrary direction from Peru to Mexico. This happened during the great formative period, as it has been suitably named, of the first millennium B.C. when national states were coming into being in both Mexico and Peru. Yet equally significant, as Prescott tells us, was the failure of certain crops to pass the barrier of the isthmus of Panama. Potatoes did not make their way into North America until the Spaniards brought them to Florida and the English to Virginia. And the practice of smoking, which migrants carried from Mexico across the Mississippi and the Appalachians in the first millennium A.D., never made its way back to Peru, the country of origin of tobacco, whose inhabitants were still taking snuff in 1532. Similarly llamas and guinea pigs remained in the south; turkeys stayed in the north.

The evidence suggests that this movement was not due to a regular traffic on land but rather to accidental castaways, that is to fishing folk carried, as is described by Bernal Diaz, along the Pacific coasts. Similarly the pineapple was taken across the Caribbean from Brazil to Mexico. Unconnected with these far-reaching accidents were certain transoceanic contacts of great interest. The improved sweet potato, carried by navigators as a supply of food, enabled them by chance at some time in the first millennium B.C. to reach the Polynesian islands and to transplant their crop, as Heyerdahl has argued, and to create a temporarily stratified society with megalithic rulers, first in the Marquesas and later on Easter Island. Conversely, at an earlier time, Japanese pottery was brought by castaways to Ecuador.[1] Whether like the Polynesian, the American civilizations owed a serious debt, racially or culturally, to such transoceanic crossings must remain in question. Castaways, even without women, could have a marked effect on small and primitive island populations but much less on large stratified continental societies. The Americans were probably independent and effectively isolated until the Spanish discovery.

Independently they discovered the steps in the domestication of plants. These steps inevitably and on the same lines transformed the cultivators from collectors into peasants as they had done in the Old World. Inevitably then the peasant societies were attacked, subjected, protected and governed by hunting peoples with whom they were successively integrated by stratification. To quote a late instance, the Mayas were overwhelmed by invaders in

[1] Meggers and Evans (1966).

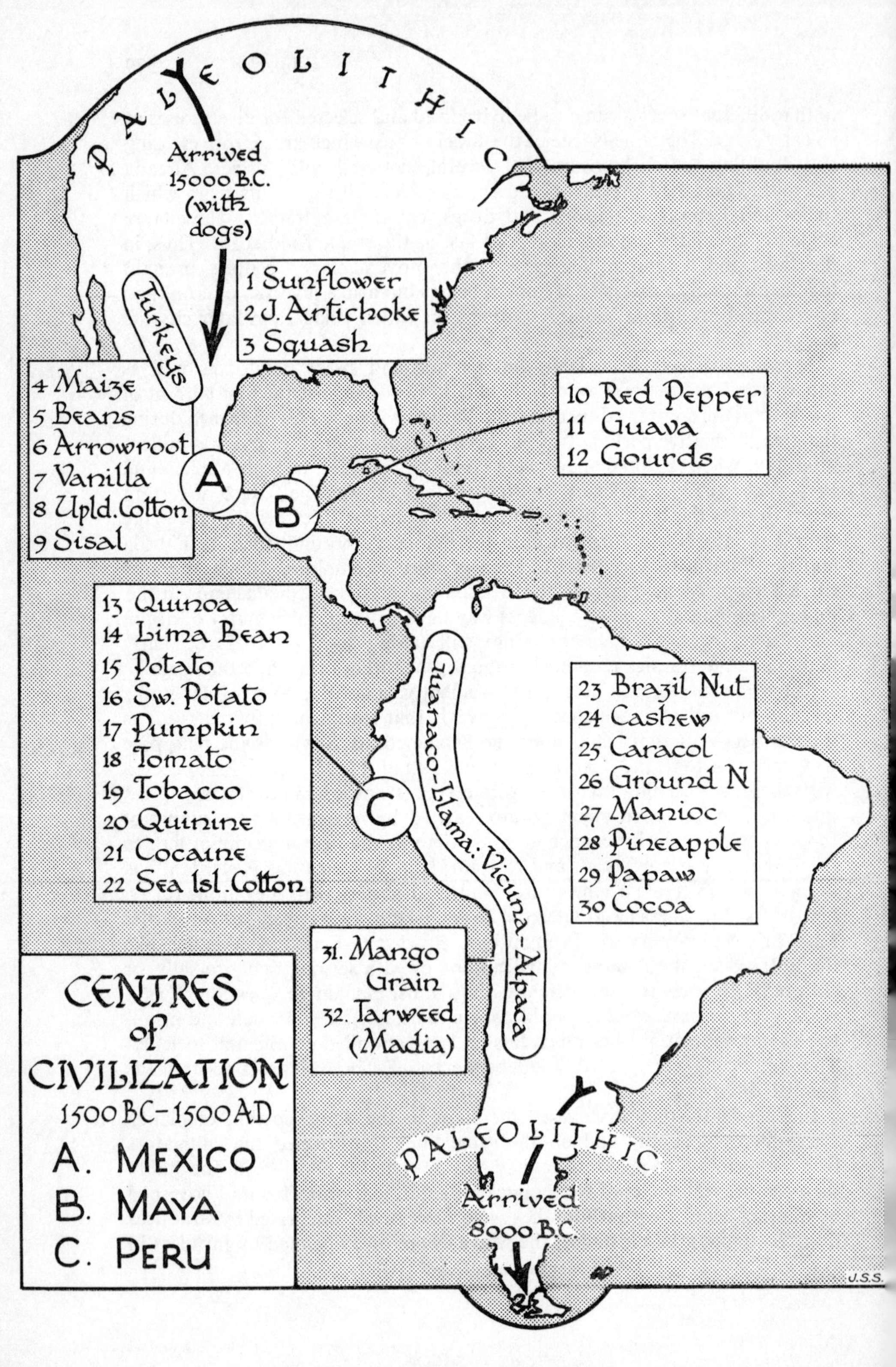
PALEOLITHIC
Arrived 15000 B.C. (with dogs)
Turkeys
1 Sunflower
2 J. Artichoke
3 Squash
4 Maize
5 Beans
6 Arrowroot
7 Vanilla
8 Upld. Cotton
9 Sisal
A
B
10 Red Pepper
11 Guava
12 Gourds
13 Quinoa
14 Lima Bean
15 Potato
16 Sw. Potato
17 Pumpkin
18 Tomato
19 Tobacco
20 Quinine
21 Cocaine
22 Sea Isl. Cotton
C
Guanaco-Llama: Vicuna-Alpaca
23 Brazil Nut
24 Cashew
25 Caracol
26 Ground N
27 Manioc
28 Pineapple
29 Papaw
30 Cocoa
31. Mango Grain
32. Tarweed (Madia)
CENTRES of CIVILIZATION
1500 BC–1500 AD
A. MEXICO
B. MAYA
C. PERU
PALEOLITHIC
Arrived 8000 B.C.
J.S.S.

A.D. 800; they then assimilated the invaders just as the Sumerians had assimilated the Semites in Babylonia 3000 years earlier.

Not merely were the New World peoples independent of the Old World; they remained largely independent of one another in those respects most needed for their civilized survival. On the one hand, they had discovered independently but in parallel the arts of pottery and masonry, the cultivation of crops, the methods of irrigation, the mining of gold and silver. And in the development of society they had discovered the uses of slavery and of religion with a parallel addiction to bloody rituals which culminated with the Aztecs in a morbid addiction to human sacrifice. But the invention of hieroglyphic writing and of numerals (including a figure for zero) and a precise calendar, by the Maya priesthood had entirely failed to reach the Peruvian Empire a thousand years later. Conversely the Peruvian art of smelting bronze had failed to reach the Mayas or the Aztecs.[1]

Here we see the limited effect of communication by fishing folk and castaways. Only popular materials and techniques could be transmitted. Except by conquest and the fusion of whole societies, religious mysteries, writing and mathematics, the use of minerals and metals, could not pass from one

[1] Easby (1966).

Fig. 18. Neolithic America with its centres of civilization

Map showing the places of origin of species of crops and stock domesticated by the original Americans prior to A.D. 1500.

From Willey (1960); Mangelsdorf, et al. *(1964); Darlington (1963); Kupzow (1965)*

The crops may be classified by use as follows:

A. Grains, seeds and nuts: 1, 4, 13, 23, 24, 31, 32.
B. Pulses: 5, 14, 25, 26.
C. Roots: 2, 6, 15, 16, 27.
D. Fruits and vegetables: 3, 10, 11, 12, 17, 18, 28, 29.
E. Essences: 7, 19, 20, 21, 30.
F. Fibres: 8, 9, 22.

Notes:

i. Maize is unique among the great cultivated crops for the transformation it underwent, by selection, in the second and third millennia B.C. (Darlington 1963).

ii. Squash, gourds and pumpkins are (apart from the bottle gourd) cross-fertile cultivated forms of plants no longer existing in the wild but probably distributed from Texas to Peru. They were hybridized and selected by people moving south from Mexico. The same is true of the sweet potato whose improved forms were probably carried in the first millennium A.D. (together with its South American name, *Kumara*) by a Kon-Tiki type of raft to Easter Island, Polynesia and later New Zealand (see Nishiyama *et al.*, 1962, Yen 1963).

iii. The roots of manioc or bitter cassava (*Manihot utilissima*) contain HCN which is extracted to yield the edible tapioca. Peruvian crops of less importance were derived from species of *Oxalis* (oca), *Tropaeolum* (anu) and *Ullucus* (ulluco) (Hawkes 1967).

iv. Sisal (*Agave*) is a source not only of fibre but of sap which is fermentable and detergent. From Mexico also came the grain amaranths, the jack bean (*Canavalia*) and the avocado pear.

v. The wild vicuna and guanaco were hunted for meat by the Incas. They had already been selected in domestication, the smaller *alpaca* to produce wool, the larger *llama* as a beast of burden. The paucity of domesticable animals in America was due to their over-hasty extinction by hunters, 12,000–8000 B.C.

society to another. Their transfer is always prevented by the secrecy and segregation of professional castes.

Another aspect of this problem is seen in the maintenance of separate languages. The New World peoples were speaking an estimated 2000 languages which could be grouped in perhaps thirty families, nearly as many as in the Old World today. This diversity all springing up in 15,000 years from a restricted racial stock in Eastern Asia indicates the very recent development of the etymological, although not of the phonetic, elements of linguistic diversity. But it also reflects an important difference in the development of New World societies, the absence of the great linguistic expansions, Aryan and Semitic, Bantu and Chinese, which must have extinguished many language families in the Old World. These expansions depended partly on the possession of livestock which indeed slightly assisted the expansion of the Inca Empire. They also depended partly on the existence of great plains of cultivable land on which cultivators could rapidly move and multiply.

Both these conditions were largely absent in America. Movement was blocked by mountains, forests and the sea. And by the time of the Inca and Aztec Empires the spread of deserts in Mexico and Chile was obstructing movement in the same way as it would have done in Central Asia if expansion had not carried agriculture across it in the third millennium B.C.[1]

III. THE EXPANSION OF CULTURE

It is in the light of these deteriorating conditions that we must look at the expansion of the Mexican and Peruvian cultures in their last years.

During the last century of the old order, a tribe known as the Incas broke out from the Altiplano by Lake Titicaca, a region some 12,000 feet above sea level. They seized the city of Cuzco, established their leader as the ruler or Inca and themselves as the governing class of a new state, indeed an Empire whose buildings recall the masonry of Egypt and the megalithic voyagers of the Old World. Two successive rulers extended their conquests northwards to Quito in Ecuador and southwards to the River Maule in the fertile centre of Chile. It was a span of 2500 miles, equal to the breadth of Alexander's conquests.

The Empire the Incas won they systematically consolidated. And the methods they used, as all the sources agree in showing, had much in common with those of the Persians, the Hellenes and the Romans.[2] They planted in their colonies Inca governors, metropolitan garrisons, chosen colonial farmers, and in addition the priests of the royal cult of the Sun. The operation was evidently the joint work of a warrior tribe and priestly caste. The subject

[1] Raglan (1962).

[2] Prescott uses all the sources but Cieza de Léon (edited by Driver) makes one important point more explicit than the Victorian scholar. Full brother-sister marriage was the rule. Its object was to ensure that if the queen's sons were not the king's they were at least his nephews: the descent was still royal. Genetic laws were more sacred than marital vows. This principle may well have favoured brother-sister marriage in Egypt.

populations they did not enslave but rather inserfed under imperial control, governing them with the help of the local nobility, the preceding rulers. Always they paid careful regard to the genetic adaptation of their peoples for different altitudes. In this way they ensured peace, stability and continued expansion of the Empire which did not cease in its short existence to be multilingual. Their policy of expansion included the building of roads, terraces and irrigation systems and the introduction of their own advanced crops and industries into unpopulated regions.[1] It was in this way that the area of maize cultivation was extended, probably to the Atlantic Coast, and new crops brought into the Empire from Chile as well as from the Amazon and Plate river basins.

With Mexican culture we can be less certain of its precise mode of expansion. But in general terms it did not arise from the expansion of power from either the Maya or the Aztec capital. The Mayas could never break out of Yucatan. And the Aztecs devoted themselves to subjugating neighbours for two purposes. The first was to extract the tribute which made their lagoon capital as rich and populous as Venice and not altogether unlike it. The second was to take, not slaves or serfs for breeding, but victims for a ritual sacrifice. They had been arrested at a stage of development, emotional and religious development, well known as we have seen in Old World societies, where the spiritual value of blood sacrifice was more highly esteemed than the material value of slave labour. From this arrest bronze and cattle might well have helped them to escape. However this may be, with such a practice, conquest could not be the means of spreading their civilization. The expansion of culture from Mexico in the first millennia (B.C. and A.D.) took the course we infer in the Mediterranean in the third and second millennia B.C.; it depended on adventurers and exiles, individuals, families and tribes, going out, first into the barbarian perimeter, and then into the paleolithic world to the north.

In this way new societies sprang up which were partly agricultural and always hybrid. They were sufficiently changed and disconnected from Mexico to lose the Mexican arts of metal-working and writing. Of these societies the earliest, appearing in the first millennium B.C. on the Arizona plateau, constituted the one almost purely agricultural people known in America. They were the Pueblo tribes. And, since they have maintained their separate character and independence against warlike neighbours for over sixty generations, we may now speak of them as the Pueblo race.

The Pueblo character has been maintained. As in Mexico and Peru the men delve and build and the women spin and weave. But it has been an equalitarian society without even an hereditary priesthood. Crossing the Mississippi, however, and finding their way up the Ohio river and round the south of the Appalachians, Mexican migrants gave their arts to fighting plainsmen. Societies then arose by conquest with stratified hereditary castes ruled by chiefs and kings. They maintained castes of slaves and built great tombs and temples in the first millennium A.D. These societies bore the same genetic and cultural relation to Mexico that the Etruscan societies bore to

[1] Parsons and Denevan (1967).

Babylonia. They were submerged by northern invaders and from them arose others with the characteristic primitive system where women delve and men hunt or fight. The later expansion of these societies northwards proved to be one of the few linguistic expansions in America. By the sixteenth century the Cherokees of the south had established their language among the Iroquois of the north. Among these people blood sacrifice and torture preserve the Mexican cultural and racial character which is so sharply contrasted with that of the Pueblos.[1]

For nearly all the peoples of North America the cultivation of maize was the undiluted expression of their own diluted origin from Mexico. Yet there were certain tribes where civilized infiltration, probably due to the capture of female prisoners from more advanced societies, brought in not agriculture but a new social character. One of these was the Chinooks who seem to have lived, according to La Farge, purely by trading. Others were the Nootka group of tribes of the north-west, and the Iroquois of the north east. All they were prepared to cultivate was tobacco. Among them there grew up within exogamous clans a gradation of lineages by social rank. This gradation led to the appearance of hereditary chiefs who maintained their position by the capture and ceremonial killing of slaves from neighbouring tribes. The wealth of the Nootka, derived from fishing and whaling, seems to have led them to adopt from neolithic societies the practices that suited them and their country best.[2]

The varied history of the North American Indians seems to offer a picture of what had happened four millennia earlier when the neolithic expansion in the Old World carried the first farmers through paleolithic territory. Hybridization with hunters and fishers produced a great variety, an almost endless variety, of newly balanced race relations, social structures and means of subsistence. And many of the barbarian societies so generated long survived the disappearance of the civilized parental Empire.

IV. THE SPANISH CONQUEST

In the year 1492 the Catholic princes of Castile and Aragon completed their crusade in their own country by the conquest of Granada. In the same year their agent and emissary Columbus arrived in the West Indies.

These islands they found thickly populated with tribes whose Arawakan

[1] Conversely it should be noted that these people tolerated transvestist individuals, known in each tribe as *berdache*. These were permanent and genetic homosexuals distinct from the recognized homosexual phase of adolescent life which, in common with most primitive warlike tribes, they generally encourage (see La Farge, 1956).

[2] The system of lineage gradation among the isolated paleolithic Nootka can hardly be derived otherwise than from disruptive selection within each exogamous clan stimulated by the rare situation of great differences in wealth. The same may be true of the Iroquois who however rejected slavery. Among pastoral Nilotic tribes, as described by Lucy Mair, it more probably arises by decay towards an equalitarian society from stratified antecedents with the usual occupational differentiation in Egypt.

language shows us that they had entered the great crescent of islands from the Trinidad end, that is from the South American continent, perhaps a thousand years earlier. They were now in process of being driven out, or eaten up, by a second wave of invaders, the Caribs or original cannibals, entering from the same direction. But neither race had made any regular connection with the adjoining coasts of the North American continent.

The new invaders were adventurers and also crusaders by long habit. They came mostly from the mountain and frontier province of Estremadura. From their island bases in Hispaniola, Cuba and Jamaica (Xaymaca to the Arawak) they began the invasion of the unknown lands and conquest of the unknown civilizations of mainland America.

Within twenty-five years, in 1517, they began to explore the coast of Mexico. In two years the boldest, shrewdest and most versatile of these adventurers, Hernando Cortes, a young man of thirty-four, confronted and overthrew the State and civilization of Mexico. The great Aztec mountain capital was captured by a force whose core was six hundred Spaniards. Twelve years later his apprentice Pizarro, improving on the ruthlessness of Cortes, repeated this revolution in Peru with a nuclear force of 183 men.

The whole series of operations were militarily and politically without precedent. Socially they proved to be the most illuminating encounter in history. Here the civilizations and the races of the Old and the New World were for the first time brought face to face. People who had been separated in ancestry for over 500 generations suddenly were arguing, fighting and, as it quickly appeared, interbreeding with one another. They were profoundly contrasted in temperament and character, in language and equipment. But for social structure they found no difficulty in translating the terms for king or chief, for priest or slave. And even the procedure of the Mexican court and the standards of good manners were quickly as clear to the guests as they were to their hosts.

Cortes and Pizarro destroyed for ever the social and political structure on which the native empires rested. In the space of a few years they had replaced the native warrior-and-priest establishment of the pagan empires by the warrior-and-priest establishment of the Christian and Spanish or hybrid governors. To do this, the forces they had employed were of two kinds. On the one hand there were the soldiers seeking gold, silver and slaves, and ruthlessly slaughtering the native soldiers, especially the nobles, when they stood in the way. On the other hand there were the Catholic priests, friars and monks. These men abetted the slaughter when conversion was the object. But when conversion had been achieved and their rule accepted, they devoted themselves to preserving the people of the conquered or converted races. It was a policy whose wisdom may be traced to the precepts of Deuteronomy.

The equipment and literacy and the resulting confidence of the *conquistadores* as soldiers were the first condition of their success. But we are bound to admire the skill with which their commanders and their priestly advisers gradually converted both their followers and their enemies to the opinion that they were not pursuing merely gold, silver and slaves but were swept forward by a desire to reform the abominable religious practices of the natives.

The methods of population control used by the Aztec ruling class in Mexico were genuinely paleolithic, obviously effective, but none the less deeply resented by their subjects and condemned by the Spaniards. Ritual cannibalism which has usually been disguised by other religions was here flaunted before the visitors.[1] The sodomy of the celibate priests, concealed in Christendom, was here exposed by the appearance of boys dressed in girls' clothing. These experiences nicely prepared the way for a religious and moral crusade. Profiting by this moral advantage, Cortes in his two years of assault on the Aztec rulers had transformed the basis of his reputation in the Aztec dependencies from one of magic to one of intelligence—intelligence in the use of social, political and military power.

In this crusade the first and most influential converts were women who, having been won in battle, were informally but effectively wedded to the invaders. It is difficult to see how Mexico could have been conquered without the courage, charm and wit as an interpreter of one native *Cacique*, of Tabarco. This lady converted as Doña Marina accompanied Cortes to Mexico where she gave birth to Don Martin Cortes. Later a sister of the Inca likewise gave birth to the hybrid historian Garcilasso Inca de la Vega (1540–1616). These events consolidated the conquest. In one process they destroyed an old governing class and created a new subject race.

Religion, equipment and women were all turned to their use by the skill of the *conquistadores*. But two more weapons are to be reckoned almost equal to the other three in contributing to the Indian overthrow. Both of them were derived from the 14,000 years or so of history of the Indians in America.

The first was the horse, itself of recent Moorish descent. Gunpowder and visions of the saints brought magical elements to the aid of the Spaniards. The horse brought another. For over two thousand years the horse had helped his riders to govern Europe: it had maintained government. For the Indians it destroyed government. Its novelty disarmed them. The horse-and-rider appeared to be (as Diaz suggests) a single organism. Sixteen of these supernatural enemies, repeating the work of the Hyksos in Egypt 3000 years earlier, were enough to rout an army.

Already by 1524, as Wyman has pointed out, the demands of the colonists from America had depleted Spain of horses. Now for a century and a half the horse made the Spaniards from Santa Fé to the Pampas masters of the New World: that very animal of which the Indians in their own halcyon days as invading colonists had over-hastily deprived themselves.

The second weapon in the hands of the Spaniards worked more slowly and less openly. It was disease. During the first visit of Columbus, Europeans and Indians had begun to exchange diseases: in fifteen days we had acquired the great pox and in fifteen years they had the smallpox. Measles, tuberculosis,

[1] It seems from Diaz' account of Montezuma's zoo that the captives were now slaughtered to provide food for animals although the animals were first acquired to dispose of the parts of bodies not consumed by the warriors. And a pile of 100,000 skulls remained to commemorate the fulfilment of duty and the appeasement of the gods.

yellow fever and malaria followed. From the point of view of this exchange the Old World and the New World were two separated but unequal units of population. When they met it was the smaller and more homogeneous population which suffered the more. And the only group which could benefit from the exchange were the hybrids which might arise from the encounter. The result was to decide not only the immediate process of conquest but also the enduring racial character of the peoples of America.[1]

V. GENETIC RECONSTRUCTION

What happened in the sixty years following the arrival of the Spaniards has been described by the friar of Seville, Bartolomé de las Casas, who at the age of eighteen accompanied Columbus. He was appalled by the atrocities which his countrymen committed in their pursuit of wealth. In effect he attributed the destruction of the native peoples to systematic slaughter. But since he did not know how to estimate either the numbers of the natives or the effects of disease we can rely very little on his account.[2]

Certainly, however, in these years following the impact of the European invaders on the native Indians there was a tremendous genetic reconstruction. The reconstruction arose from three kinds of assault on the native peoples. First, there was their killing in a series of brutal conflicts. Secondly, there was their extermination in the pure forms in which they had existed by waves of infectious disease. And thirdly, there was their hybridization with the invaders.

So far as the Spaniards and Portuguese were concerned in what we call Latin America, the first of these assaults was concentrated in the sixteenth century. But so far as the English-speaking people were concerned it was concentrated in the nineteenth century. It was part of the expansion of the United States. The character of the assault was therefore quite different. Further, although the hybridization has been continuous over the centuries in all parts of America, it has been on a much larger scale among the Latins, who (apart from governors) brought no women of their own, than among the English who (apart from traders) brought their women with them.[3] The English assault thus struck the Indians after they had hybridized, acquired resistance to European disease, and adopted European weapons and horses.

It is to these varied combinations of circumstance that the varied processes

[1] I have discussed the evidence, the causes and some of the consequences of the exchange of diseases in *Genetics and Man*: see Diaz (1568); Reid (1910); Willey (1960); Brothwell (1967).

[2] He puts the population of the West Indies in 1492 at 8 million and suggests that in America as a whole the Spaniards had massacred 50 million natives in the intervening 60 years. The picture painted by Diaz is more plausible. *cf.* Table 36 and Washburn (1964).

[3] The first examples were Cortes with his Doña Marina and John Rolfe with his Pocahontas; from both unions many Americans claim descent (see Diaz, 1568; Washburn, 1965). Latterly, Gauguin assumed that his talents and his features were derived from the Inca royal family (Charmet, 1966).

of development of the American peoples are due. For example, the immediate impact of disease following isolation and before hybridization led to the destruction of the Caribs in the sixteenth century, of the Fuegians in the nineteenth century, and of the fishermen on Lake Titicaca in the twentieth century.[1] But the Indians of the United States are nearly as numerous as they were before the European invasion. What happened to the great advanced societies? The warriors had been slain; the priests driven out; the temples and palaces destroyed; the myth of the nation and the king had been broken;

Table 36. *Estimated Indian-speaking Populations of America*

After H. E. Driver (1964); La Farge (1956); Lipschutz (1966).

<table>
<tr><th>Region</th><th>c. 1500</th><th>1650</th><th>1900</th><th>1960</th></tr>
<tr><td>Tribal North</td><td>2m</td><td>2m</td><td>0·3m</td><td>0·6m</td></tr>
<tr><td>Caribbean (1492)</td><td>2m</td><td>extinct</td><td>—</td><td>—</td></tr>
<tr><td>MEXICO (1519)</td><td>5·5m*</td><td rowspan="2">1·5m</td><td rowspan="2">—</td><td rowspan="2">2·5m†</td></tr>
<tr><td>YUCATAN</td><td>1m</td></tr>
<tr><td>PERU (1532)</td><td>10m</td><td>2m?</td><td>—</td><td rowspan="2">6m?</td></tr>
<tr><td>Tribal South</td><td>3m</td><td>1·5m?</td><td>—</td></tr>
<tr><td>TOTAL</td><td>30m</td><td></td><td></td><td></td></tr>
</table>

* In Mexico City, the 200-year-old capital of the Aztecs, there were 60,000 dwellings (or, say 200,000 inhabitants) according to Cortes at the time he destroyed it in November 1521. See W. T. Sanders (1966: *Am. Anthr.* 68).

† Of these one-quarter speak Nahua (Aztec), and one-sixth Maya, two of the twenty-odd languages.

Notes

Indian-speakers, those little hybridized with Europeans, are now outnumbered in most parts of Latin America by Spanish- and Portuguese-speaking Indian-African-European hybrids.

Indian-speaking populations are now extinct, not only in the West Indies, but also in Uruguay and nearly so in Argentina.

and a new governing class had been imposed on a socially decapitated community. It was a governing class which had little idea of agriculture, irrigation or stockbreeding even in their own country. They had come for gold and silver and what there was they took. But when this precious stuff was gone they were somewhat at a loss in their new country. The great vegetable gardens of the Aztecs and the vast terraces and aqueducts of the Incas fell into decay never to recover.

In Peru indeed there was also a precise indicator of the change in the government of society. In 1535, within three years of his conquest, Pizarro had founded a new capital. He had removed the seat of government from highland Cuzco to coastal Lima: a city where Spaniards could live and breathe, a port where the spoils of South America could be collected and the spoliation could be controlled by officials despatched for the purpose from Madrid.

In these disastrous circumstances it was hybridization that slowly saved, not the native peoples, but great populations which are derived from them.

[1] Pawson (1967).

To this immense reconstruction all the chief peoples of the Old World have contributed. This alone is a complex but obvious foundation. What is less obvious is the nature of the hybridization.

In distinguishing between Indian and hybrid communities we have to be wary of the inexact and fluctuating popular terminology. In genetics there is a serious difference between first- and second-generation hybrids. But the popular terms never make this Mendelian distinction. Mestizo, mulatto and creole have slowly lost what meaning they had. The crucial test in practice is the linguistic one. For the tribe which preserves its native language does so because it is following the way of life of the tribe. It may have hybridized with people of European origin so that there has been what we may call a flow of European genes into the community. Indian tribes had themselves generally interbred through war. Captured men were commonly tortured and killed. But women were frequently and men occasionally adopted and married into the tribe. The reason they gave was genetically sound: the hybridization would *strengthen* the nation. The same process worked with white traders and white prisoners.[1]

Following this hybridization there will usually have been a selective loss of the hybrid progeny who have deserted the community. The two successive processes leave an adaptive line of separation which is both genetic and ecological and which also follows the linguistic boundary.[2]

Using every kind of evidence we find that all degrees of admixture of one race with another have occurred. And, the mixture having occurred, all degrees of social stability and consequent inbreeding have followed, carrying in their train the formation of new races or classes filling new places in new societies.

Take a few examples. What are regarded as the native Indian tribes of the United States and Canada were mostly subject to hybridization in the eighteenth and the nineteenth centuries. Some of their most notable chiefs were half-breeds.[3] This often and obviously contributed to the ability with which they adopted European weapons and horses and confronted the Europeans in peace and war. The same kind of step was responsible for the development of the Gaucho, the cowboy of the Pampas, a new race which having flourished for a century or two, and left its mark on history and legend, has now nearly disappeared.

Some of these new peoples are almost purely Indian but merely changed in the ease with which they are able to take part in the new employments of civilized life. The most notable of these are the Mohawks.[4] This tribe had

[1] See La Farge; also Doddridge and Benjamin Franklin in Washburn.

[2] The same principle seems to govern the evolution of nomadic peoples who, like gipsies or Vlachs, live among settled populations in Europe; and of paleolithic hunters who become sub-neolithic after living alongside neolithic people and stealing their women in Africa or Brazil.

[3] See Malone (1956); Horan (1959); Philbrick (1965).

[4] Described by La Farge, by Conly, and in detail by Mitchell. The Mohawks are one of the Iroquois Six Nations first studied by Lewis H. Morgan in 1851. Their genetic tenacity and also their breeding and political relations with Europeans have been discussed by Edmund Wilson (1960).

been selected for its skill in canoe and raft-navigation for six generations. In 1886, a bridge was being built through their territory near Montreal, and they discovered that their balancing abilities enabled them to work at heights and hence to earn great respect and large rewards in an industrial society. They had retained their paleolithic restlessness and their tribal character: they would desert one activity for another without prediction or explanation and in a body. But, as a tribe, as a race, they were pre-adapted to high steel construction and the industry fell into their hands. They became a social group based in a district of New York. Slowly no doubt the Mohawks will enter into the anonymous but professionally stratified structure of American society.

Beside this favourable example we must put less happy situations. Whereas native quarters appear in European-founded cities of Africa, Asia and Australia, they do not appear in America. The pure natives as opposed to their hybrid neighbours are always selectively eliminated by the strict alternatives of disease and hybridization.[1]

For hybridization is the origin of the populations, impoverished, illiterate, and exploited, who have collected on the outskirts of most great Latin American cities. They have little prospect of improvement from further hybridization and selection, since their Indian ancestors came for the most part from tribes in which the women cultivated and the men hunted, a mode of life that is now outmoded. What the women cultivated, moreover, through the coastal areas of Brazil was chiefly not grain but roots, the crops which create, as we shall see, the most improvident of peoples and those least capable of regular labour.

In the transformation of the Indians, the most important agent has in fact been the new opportunities of stockbreeding. In this field the tribal Indian groups can succeed even where they are altogether unhybridized and, like gipsies, are stable, unadaptable and (in our arbitrary sense) ineducable. It was their own horses, as we saw, that put the Spaniards in power. In the three centuries after Cortes these horses ran wild and bred wild beyond the reach of their masters. The daring Navaho Indians moving south from Canada met these horses in Arizona about 1660. They soon tamed them. Twenty years later the effects were seen. The mild Pueblo Indians revolted and for a dozen years expelled their conquerors from their capital of Santa Fé.

Later the tables were turned again. By 1770 the wild horses had reached the Mississippi and what we now know as Canada. Soon over five million *mesteños* had become the mustanges of Anglo-Saxons. The Indian tribes of the plains had adopted them and with their help and the use of firearms they were able to block the advance of American colonists moving into the west in the nineteenth century. In parallel, if not in partnership, with American cowboys mounted on descendants of those same mustangs they were also able very nearly to exterminate the last great grazing animal of the plains, the bison. The animal to which the bison and the mustang gave place was the Longhorn breed of cattle, introduced also by the Spaniards, and developed

[1] A fact noted by a pioneer of medical genetics, Archdall Reid (1910).

in the time of the cowboys in Texas.[1] On the other hand the third important animal introduced by the Spaniards, the sheep, has produced flocks which are now tended in the Rocky Mountains by shepherds of European Basque, and also of Indian Navaho, ancestry.

Thus, as happened in the Old World, the new business of pastoralism could be managed in America by hunters; but where the native grain-cultivators had died out or been killed off their place could be taken only by a race of people adapted to the cultivation of the soil. Where could they be found? The answer was, in Africa.

VI. NEGRO SLAVERY

Their isolation always makes it most convenient to follow the evolution of societies on islands and for the history of the African immigration into America Jamaica is a most convenient starting point. It was the Spanish governor of Jamaica who, in the year 1515, twenty-three years after the discovery, was first faced with the problem of how to replace the disappearing native Arawak population. His spiritual adviser, Bartolomé de las Casas, recommended him to import slaves from the Portuguese agencies or 'factories' in West Africa. This business had been authorized by Papal Bull in 1442. Two years later the first Negro slaves arrived.

Jamaica was seized by an English fleet in 1655 under Admirals Venables and Penn and thereafter the importation increased, only to be stopped when it was prohibited by the British government in 1807; that is after 290 years.[2]

Throughout this time the slaves came by capture and purchase from different African tribes whose different character was soon evaluated by their purchasers. They therefore fetched different prices at auction and passed, as slaves had done in classical times (and as recorded by Cave), into different occupations. Each of these constituted a breeding community of its own. Thus, there were the *Mandingoes*, who were later preferred by the French, and therefore went to Haiti. There were the *Popos* and *Whidahs* from Dahomey who were used for heavy work in the sugar plantations. There were the *Angolas*, *Calabars* and *Gambias* among whom the women could be used for heavier work than the men. There were the *Iboes* from Nigeria, some of whom (like Bushmen) would pine away and die from slavery except in the house. And finally there were the warlike Ashanti who became known as *Morenos* or darkies; not being cultivators they were given the suitable task of looking after the pigs.[3]

On the English seizure of Jamaica the equilibrium of the Spanish-Negro society was suddenly upset. The house-slaves were faithful and fled with their Spanish masters to Cuba. The field-slaves stayed with the English who wanted to use them to work their new sugar plantations, those plantations which were to make further fortunes for the English governing class, the

[1] See Bolton (1908); J. D. Horan (1959); Durham and Jones (1965).

[2] The illicit beginning of the English trade by Hawkins is described by Unwin—its equally illicit end by Canot and by O'Callaghan.

[3] See Hugh Cave (1962); Harcourt-Smith (1966).

Beckfords and the Russells, the Grosvenors and the Gladstones. Most were amenable. The Morenos (who were now named Maroons) refused to give up their pigs. Hybridization with the native Arawak as well as with the errant English had not helped to make them more tractable tillers of the soil. After eighty years of revolt the Maroons won. They were left free to live, a distinct isolated ecological race of hybrid origin inbred for eight or nine generations. A few by the colour of their eyes showed their English ancestry; all showed in their habits of tending domesticated pigs and hunting wild ones the character of the Ashanti and the Arawak.

The other groups of field-slaves had quite a different history. They were adapted to field work. And they were not ill-adapted to slavery. No doubt many were like the Damara, described by Galton who seem to invite slavery. But after three or four generations the invitation was less certain. During this time their white employers had taken black or mulatto concubines. Many of their progeny had been freed and had even become slave-owners themselves. But many had remained slaves.

Thus the slaves were now racially changed. They were now more variable in features and in colour, in intelligence and in temperament. They were no longer the same people who had arrived from Africa with Hawkins and his successors and submitted to slavery. The genetic basis of the original relation of master and slave had disintegrated. It is not surprising therefore that rebels began to appear. In 1770 revolt broke out and it continued intermittently for a whole century.

At the end of the eighteenth century the French Revolution called the attention of Europeans to the fact that slavery was becoming socially undesirable as well as practically unworkable. Already to slave-owners like George Washington, property in slaves had seemed to be a diminishing asset. The struggle for emancipation went back and forth in France while Britain with command of the seas was able with some effect to prohibit the trade in slaves from 1806. The abolition was attended with disputes over compensation to owners and with the real problem that the liberated slave having lost his subjection also lost his protection and sometimes his employment. In these circumstances the process of emancipation dragged on all through the nineteenth century (Table 37). And, out of reach of the British Navy, in Abyssinia and Arabia, it was never achieved (O'Callaghan, 1961; Bisch, 1962).

When the slaves were freed in Jamaica (as indeed throughout the British territories), that is in the period from 1833 to 1838, they were thus already a diverse population with an established social and genetical class structure. This structure was now developed and consolidated by economic differences. The white population was also divided into the propertied class and the 'poor whites'. These were largely descended from indentured labourers and transported convicts who still form a mildly criminal class. The two stratified populations thus met under new conditions. What happened? The result has been well described by Henriques.

Both the black and the white populations agreed in preferring the white as partners for breeding. Thus on one side there was assortative mating.

Table 37. *Dates of Abolition of Negro Slavery in Europe and America*

Showing the connection with political revolutions.

	Enacted	*Completed*
Mexico	1829	
Great Britain	1833	1838
France	1848	
Portugal	1858	1878
Holland	1863	
U.S.A.[1]	1863	1865
Cuba[2]	1886	
Brazil[3]	1888	

[1] See Heffner (1952). Note: the Mason and Dixon line between Pennsylvania and Maryland drawn up by these two astronomers in 1763 became the boundary between free and slave states by the Missouri Compromise of 1820. See fig. 19.

[2] Half a million slaves freed; one-third of the population.

[3] 700,000 slaves freed.

This has kept the two groups apart. And on the other side there were a proportion of dark women who preferred white (or later Chinese) concubinage to dark marriage. And since two-thirds of all children in Jamaica are illegitimate this process has been effective in bringing the two groups together.

Conversely there were also a proportion of dark spinsters in every generation as happens in India under the same rule of hypergamy. An increase of white ancestry or white genes or fair skins inevitably followed in the population.

So much for change in the population as a whole. But its stratification retained the traditional colour-marking. The economically more successful dark men always marry lighter-coloured wives than their less successful kinsmen. Thus, apart from the poor whites, the gradations of colour as well as the extremes of colour have remained indicators of social and economic success and of intelligence and ability so far as they can be measured by such success. Further, colour (with which must be included Negro hair curl and features) is taken as the major factor in Jamaica to be set against economic status in the marriage market. Just indeed as birth, name, education, speech, and good looks in general, are taken in countries where the racial contrasts are smaller. For example, even within families, parents will keep their darker children out of society for the benefit of the lighter sibs. The selective differential operates in every social as well as sexual relationship.

In Jamaica as elsewhere the diversified products of race mixture have created a class structure adapted to diverse occupations. There is an upper class, white or nearly white, propertied and professional and entirely Anglican or Roman Catholic in religion. There is a middle class, mainly coloured or nearly black, mainly Baptist in religion, mainly trading and clerical in occupation. And there is a lower class divided into a small class of poor whites and a large class of Negroes of the darkest colour who are largely unskilled wage-earners and peasant farmers. Among these flourish the Revivalist sects and the African cults, symptoms of pre-rational intelligence. Finally, there are the special immigrant groups with their own trades like the Syrians and the Hindus. There are also the Chinese who used to farm but have now, as in South-East Asia, taken over the retail trading in which no other race can compete with them.

Table 38. *The Racial Census of Jamaica as Estimated:* 1611–1791

After Henriques (1953).

Government	*Spain*—(1655)—*England*		
Race	1611	1673	1791
European	696	7700	30,000
Native Arawakan	74	—	—
Free, Negro and Coloured	107	—	10,000
Morenos, Maroons / Foreigners[1]	75	—	1,400
Slaves, Negro and Coloured	558	*c.* 10,000	250,000

[1] Chiefly German Jews invited by Diego Columbus about 1510 and Portuguese Jews perhaps invited by Cromwell: this community today flourishes and multiplies. Judah P. Benjamin was its most notable descendant.

Note:

In 1655 the Spanish colony had 3000 inhabitants. Today the population numbers 1·8 million.

In all this adjustment of race, class and occupation, it is a question of each genetic group finding the niche or the gap in the social structure which it can most profitably fill. We may thus say that, on the one hand, the value to society of the place the individual finds to fill is a measure of his success as an individual. But on the other hand the extent to which the society can find individuals, or indeed groups of individuals, qualified to create a coherent productive structure with usefully interdependent parts is a measure of its success as a society.

The great slave trade from Africa to America has everywhere had similar general consequences. But there has been one broad contrast. In Tropical Latin-America Europeans, failing to take their own women, have always been in a minority. The multiplying hybrid population has been treated with only modest discrimination: economic stratification was effective enough. But in Temperate Anglo-Saxon North America the Europeans have always been in a majority and they have attempted to draw a line between themselves and their hybrids. They have done so all the more fiercely because of the English-American political assumption that all 'whites' are equal. The consequences of this assumption we shall have to examine.

First, however, let us notice one very simple numerical consequence of the introduction of Negro slaves into America.

The demand for labour adapted to cultivation had led to the importation of African slaves over a period of three hundred years to the number of some fifteen million. This transfer had had no long-term effect on the numbers and little on the quality of the population of Africa. But in America today the transferred slaves have left some forty or fifty million hybrid and coloured but predominantly Negro descendants.[1]

Thus the Negro population exported as slaves to Christian America has not only been maintained, by breeding it has been greatly increased. Now a somewhat greater number of slaves have been exported northwards from Africa into Islamic countries over the four times longer period from A.D. 700 to A.D. 1960. But the breeding effect has been trifling. Whether we attempt to consider the number of descendants or the genetic influence we may say that Islamic slavery, by castration, infanticide, and perversion, has almost deleted the progeny of the African slaves in Arab countries. Christian slavery, on the other hand, has been responsible for an increase in the African contribution to the numbers of mankind today, an increase which it seems could have come about in no other way.

VII. THE ENGLISH COLONIES

The first English settlements to succeed in America were the two nuclei formed at Jamestown in Virginia in 1607 and in Massachusetts in 1620. In a sense the colonists were all exiles from England. They were people dissatisfied with the economic opportunities or with the religious beliefs of the moment in their native country. But they arranged themselves subject to their leading men around these two original foci of settlement. The royalists, Anglicans and gentry, had come as feudal tenants to occupy Virginia in the south which promised well for farming. The rebels, dissenters and tradesmen, had come as freeholders to occupy New England in the north which was more closely confined by the mountains and the Indian tribes and offered harsher prospects with furs, fish and forest as the chief means of subsistence.[2]

To the first emigrant parties were soon added refugees from the recurrent disturbances of the most disturbed century in English history. Catholics, fearing the puritans, came under Lord Baltimore's protection to colonize Maryland in 1633. In 1682 Quakers, sponsored by the son of Admiral Penn, established their Utopia in Pennsylvania whose frontier with Maryland was to separate north and south.

Refugees of another kind came to swell the colonies in the persons of kidnapped Irishmen and Africans, indentured servants escaping from poverty, and adventurers and explorers of many nations, paupers and criminals. These men came without any endowment but their own skill and energy and their ability to survive by their own efforts. Development progressed by the growth of servitude or slavery in the south. It also progressed through bursts of intolerance in the north. For the people of Massachusetts, themselves the victims of persecution, proved the most violent of persecutors of dissent. The extreme concentration of extreme beliefs led to extreme policies in

[1] In south Brazil the mean skin colour was found to be half-white (G. A. Harrison *et al.*, 1967).

[2] To be sure, the Pilgrim Fathers had also been making sail for Virginia. They reached their haven in Plymouth because they were blown off their course. But their successors in 1630 aimed for the Bay Colony.

maintaining the purity of the new society. By 1637, having annihilated the heathen natives, the tribe of Pequots, they had set upon their own heretics and named eighty-two deviations as grounds for punishment or purging. Until 1684 belief, not taxation, was the grounds for franchise. The famous climax came seven years later when thirty-two witches were executed in the little settlement of Salem.

Those who were rejected by this stern commonwealth of the godly sought refuge in the adjoining lands. So it was that new colonies were set up in the time of the English Commonwealth in New Hampshire, Rhode Island and Connecticut, all with their own characters and constitutions.

In the following century much more diversity had been added. The partly French colony of Maine marked one end. At the other end the new English colony of Georgia had been colonized on high principles by General Oglethorpe with the help of German Moravians and John Wesley. In the middle were the Dutch Protestants of New Netherlands with Huguenot recruits seated in Manhattan. Close at hand were the Quaker colonies of New Jersey and Pennsylvania. These, as we saw earlier, were the first to learn the lesson of religious and social tolerance. And tolerance spread as the colonies came to be seen, and to see themselves, as a coherent whole, a people having a common origin and history, and common interests in trade, government and war. The passions of a century of religion had cooled and distances between the formerly warring sects allowed co-existence to grow into co-operation.

Yet both the strength and the weakness of the colonies arose from their divergent individualities. Those profound differences of opinion about God reflected differences of opinion about man and society which were based on inborn differences of character. These had decided the people of each colony to collect together in one community. Migrations had always been selective. Never before had beliefs and opinions so actively and explicitly determined them. The unity of interest between the colonies was responsible for the American Revolution. Their disunity of belief and interest was responsible for the Civil War.[1]

VIII. THE AMERICAN REVOLUTION

By the year 1775 the chain of English colonies stretched down the whole eastern coast of North America to the frontier of Florida. The colonists numbered nearly three millions—a third as many as the population of Britain. Their successful growth as an almost purely European society had been due to the freedom of migration of both landowners and peasants in England, a country freed more fully than its neighbours and rivals from feudal attachment to the soil. It had also been due to the alternating persecution of Protestants and Catholics in France and Holland as well as in England, Scotland and Ireland.

In the early years of their growth the colonists had been threatened by French and Spanish forces on all their frontiers. The last colony of Georgia

[1] These problems are discussed from different points of view by Nye and Morpurgo and by Handlin.

based on Savannah had been set up in 1735 in order to defend the southern boundary against Spain. Only in 1759 had the French danger been relieved by the conquest of Canada. The native Indians remained in occupation of a western frontier of over a thousand miles (see Fig. 19). The home government had used them as allies against foreigners and was not averse to using them as a restraint and perhaps as a support against the colonists.

Now the peace of 1763 transformed the situation. The annexation of Canada and part of the Mississippi valley removed the French threat. To the colonists now the fear of Indian disturbance was converted into the opportunity for colonial expansion. An immediate divergence of interest arose between the Home Government and the colonies. The Home Government wanted to settle the Indian problem by pacifying the Indians. To do so, it proclaimed its intention to fix the colonial boundaries along the Appalachian watershed leaving the belt between the mountains and the Mississippi as an Indian reserve. That was in 1763. It also wanted the colonies to pay for their defence of this thousand-mile frontier. The colonies on the contrary were under pressure from their own people on the frontier to abolish the frontier, to expel the hunting Indians into the vast lands to the west and to take over for agriculture the whole vacant territory. The colonists were becoming aware of what would be their manifest destiny.

The strip of land rising from the sea to the Appalachians was narrow. It had never been rich. It was soon to be impoverished by erosion. Beyond the mountains lay freedom and wealth. But the Home Government, which had protected the colonies, was now disloyally confining them and protecting the Indians.[1]

In these circumstances the King's Agent for Indian Affairs, Sir William Johnson, played a decisive part. He was a man with great experience of the Mohawks in the north, experience which included some Indian wives. Observing that there were few or no Indians settled in the valley of the river Ohio, of whose position the people in London were not very certain, he fixed this river as the colonial boundary. That was in 1765. Thereby he opened what were to be the states of Kentucky and Tennessee to the immediate advance of the mountain colonists. And what were to be Alabama and Mississippi, and a great deal beyond, he opened up to the later advance of the southern planters.[2]

These almost accidental concessions have been much disputed in their causes and their consequences. The new lands pleased the poor men in the hills with results which changed the later course of American history. But the rich men in the plains became no more submissive; for their concern was not with territory but with taxes.

The leading men of New England, of Pennsylvania, and of Virginia, diverse in religion, occupation and character as they were, were mostly coming to the same conclusion, a conclusion which was to be confirmed by experience. It was that they could govern their own country to better advantage for their own people than anybody seated in England or sent from England. They

[1] It was a situation which was to recur; first in South Africa sixty years later when slavery had been abolished.

[2] See F. S. Philbrick (1965).

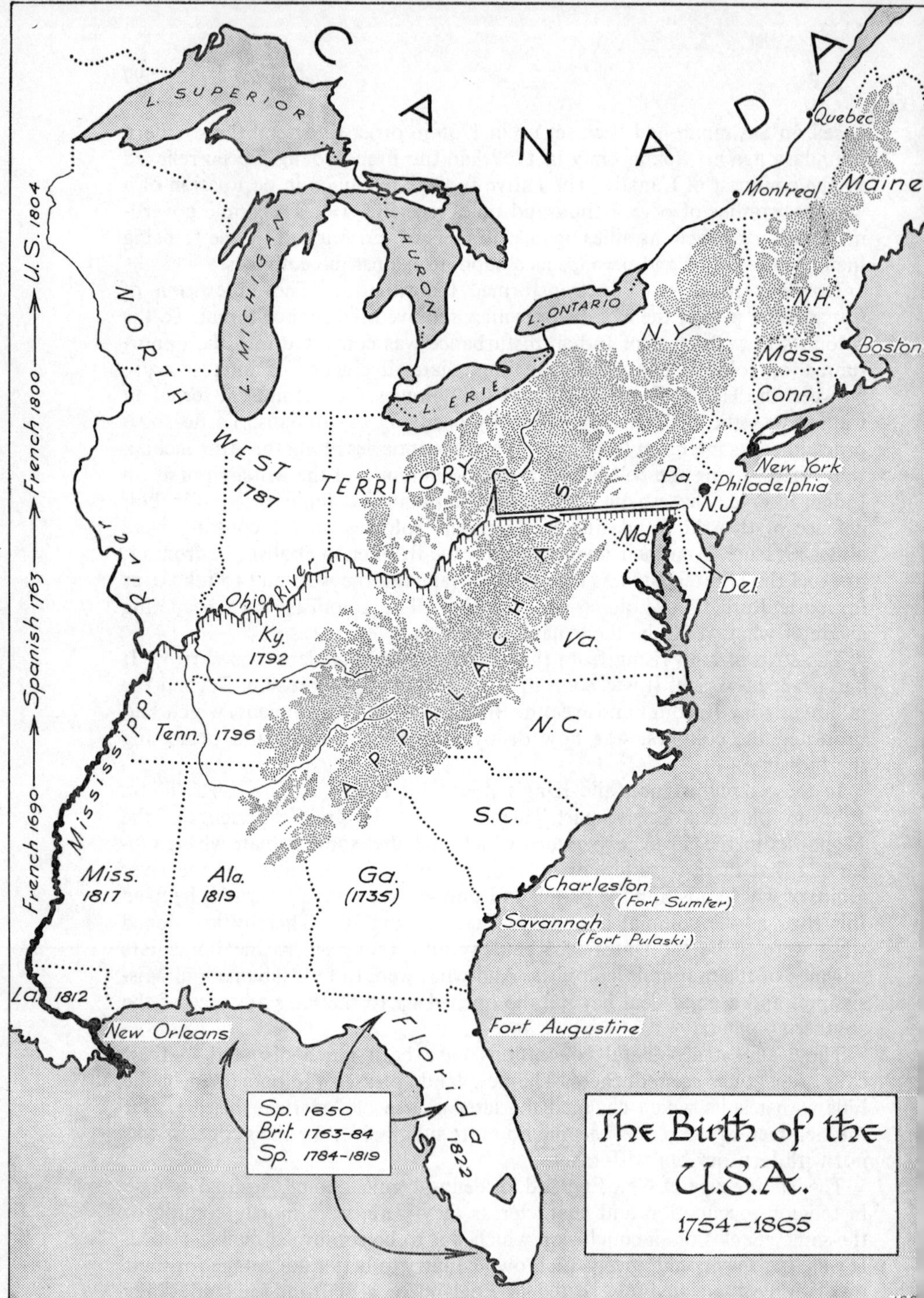

Fig. 19. The Birth of the Union: the Struggle for Territory, the Expansion of the English Colonies and the Civil War Between States (1754–1865)

The Eastern U.S.A. showing State Boundaries and the Appalachian Mountains (contour 1000 feet). Dates are those of annexation of territories and incorporation of states (from Sale and Karn 1962).

Double Line: Mason and Dixon's boundary originally between Pennsylvania and Maryland.

Hatched Boundary: Territory given to the Colonies by Sir William Johnson's allocation of 1765 (see Philbrick 1965). The Missouri Compromise of 1820 fixed the northern limit of slave-owning at this line.

concluded also that they could give it a greater future. And if they did not agree precisely how this was to be done they were content to conceal their differences until the struggle with the Home Government was settled.

To carry through a revolution, however, as in the English Civil War, the support of the masses was needed. Religion was no longer any help. But the words of the Levellers could still be repeated with effect. And to them could be added the telling phrases of the French philosophers. What could be done with such phrases had been shown by the English rebel Tom Paine in his *Common Sense* in January 1776. And they found their echo six months later when Thomas Jefferson drafted the Declaration of Independence.

With this statement the American privileged class, or the great majority of them, had not only challenged the British Establishment. They had become reluctant revolutionaries in their own society. By this propaganda device they were able to command the support of enough of their own people to carry the country with them. It was not, however, enough to enable them to win the war. That happened only after nine years during which the colonial forces, now known as the Continental Army, were helped by France and Spain in Europe and by the expeditionary force of the young Lafayette fighting beside them.

The consequences of their victory were more disturbing to the victorious than to the defeated parties. The British Crown had been toppled in America by force of arms. But the French Crown, as it turned out within twenty years, was to be toppled in France itself by the debts it had contracted and the ideas it had fomented in those remote colonies on the other side of the Atlantic.

Nor was it plain sailing for the revolutionary aristocracy themselves. The same problem arose, when the war was over, as in the England of 1649. All men, they had said, were created equal. To the slave-owners of Maryland and Virginia the Negro was temporarily overlooked. Had they not laws in every state forbidding the marriage of white to Negro? To the mountaineers of Kentucky the native Indian might also be overlooked. Was he not soon to be driven off his lands? And to the men of property a quiet reservation might be made that suffrage could not be given to the illiterate, the pauper and the vagabond. And would not the new state need the authority of a senate and a president to preserve the law?

Authority had to be restored. The American Constitution of 1787 showed that the Revolution had been, like the English Civil War, a struggle between two governing classes: the one old and established, the other new and challenging; the one formally monarchical and hierarchical, the other formally republican; but both resting on hereditary, propertied and social distinctions.

Now however a change had occurred. For Cromwell the hereditary and social distinctions could be admitted. For the Americans such distinctions had to be muted, indeed almost repudiated.

A tension was brought into the national life between theory and practice, a tension which had to be concealed. For the theory of equality held the nation together while the practices of competition and discrimination moved it forward. This was a problem which Alexis de Tocqueville, who looked at

American society while the conflict was developing (between 1835 and 1840), could never understand. For he was concerned with the *ideas* of aristocracy and democracy; the possibility of their having a genetic basis was entirely withheld from him.

The tension, and the frauds or illusions necessary to conceal it, developed until the Civil War which may be described as an attempt to release the tension and free the nation from its burden. But when the war had been fought the tension still remained and remains to this day, as in all western nations, unresolved.

Another issue had however been resolved. The puritans of New England, the Quakers of Pennsylvania, the Catholics of Maryland, the Episcopalians of Virginia, and the Huguenots of north and south were all of one mind: they would not try to force one religion on to the State. The principle that had bound tribes and nations together since before those beginnings in Sumer was no longer to be enforced. In a world of persecution the United States was to be united not by uniformity of belief or ritual but by an educated toleration; and by the common interest which this new principle gave to the people, increasingly diversified people, whom it was to protect. And, as the stratification of society persisted, and as economic privilege grew through the vast expansion and immigration of the coming centuries, the doctrine of equality also persisted to give comfort or hope to those less favoured in the struggle for existence.

At the same time the religious sects increased in number. They reflected even more faithfully than the dialects of speech the increasing diversity of society. Each formed a little community within the whole nation. Each man could choose his own sect and, as in England rising by his own efforts, he could promote himself from Baptist to Presbyterian and on to Episcopalian.[1] Thus a perceptibly tribal sub-division could be maintained in what had become a society so remote and abstract that the individual would otherwise have been socially and therefore morally lost.

Religion thus came to render a service in the United States most resembling that of the local cults of the Roman Empire. The need for unity and the haunting fear of secession from the artificial federation were met by impressing cultural instead of religious uniformity. Only in recent years has it been found that cultural uniformity is itself not indispensable and the separate preservation of Indian, Mexican, Negro and local cultures may be a source of strength to a republic which is also manifestly an empire. These, however, are only beginnings of new and unprecedented steps in social evolution.

IX. THE CIVIL WAR

a. Three Peoples: North, South and Mountain

To understand what happened in 1860 we have to look not at the political division into states which seemed so important but at the social communities into which, partly unknown to themselves, the people of the whole Union were divided.

[1] Packard (1959).

On the one hand, there was southern society, dominated by men of Cavalier ancestry, with feudal traditions, military, rural and anti-urban, conservative and inbred. These were the planter-masters. They had needed and had recruited few skilful artisans and few professional men. What they had needed was a cheap servile labour force for growing cotton, tobacco and rice. They had for this purpose imported enough Negro slaves to maintain and expand their feudal society. Their policy had been an immense financial success. But they had thereby been led to expel the old indentured white labourers who had become, as in Jamaica, and for the same reason, 'poor whites', squatters on the poorer lowlands, woodsmen relying on pigs or, as they say, hogs, and fishing; an inbred community lacking the initiative to migrate, the wretched dregs at the bottom of society.

On the other hand, there was northern society dominated by the power of the new industries created by the endlessly enterprising and technically inventive people descended from dissenting English artisans of the seventeenth and eighteenth centuries. They had recruited and developed their professional class. What they needed was an abundant supply of unskilled labour which the successful slavery of the south and the abolition of the slave trade denied them. Among them moralin dignation could easily be aroused against the whole institution of slavery. For it was outmoded economically in the eyes of the rich. And in the eyes of the poor it offended against the principle of equality expounded in the Constitution.

Apart from these two great opposed societies there was a third society, inarticulate and unregarded, but weighing heavily in the ultimate issue: the people of the mountains.[1]

The Appalachian mountains are covered with forest save for a few crosswise breaks and the lengthwise creases of narrow river valleys. They separated the populous coastal colonies from the wide basin of the Mississippi and the wide territories of the Indians. But into them slowly filtered adventurous farmer-hunters coming from parts of Europe where farmer-hunters were still living. First came Lutheran and Moravian refugees from the Palatinate and Switzerland who moved into western Pennsylvania in 1682. They were followed by 30,000 evicted tenants of Antrim known as 'Scotch-Irish' who acted as a buffer protecting the Germans from the Indians whom they quickly exterminated. To these people English and Huguenots were soon added as the whole people expanded to the south and filled the mountains.

The Mountain Whites, as they were named, had a character of their own. Their first great leader was Daniel Boone who led his people into Tennessee in 1768 and later into Kentucky. That was three years after Sir William Johnson's new frontier agreement. In 1772, rebelling against the Crown, he gave himself a written constitution. He had made the first free republic in America.

The mountain men gave Washington his first Regiment of Foot and, as Alden tells us, they proved to be his favourite troops from Saratoga to King's Mountain. But when the war was over this did not help them; the

[1] Memorably described by Horace Kephart (1913); Malone (1956); and Joseph Hall (1960).

first tax to be levied was on the distilled corn liquor which was the livelihood of the mountain men of Pennsylvania. They fought the government; they were defeated; and they began to move south through Indian country.

By 1830 there were a million permanent settlers in the southern mountains. They were a tall, uncouth but ecologically adapted race and sufficiently varied to produce great men. They had already given birth to David Crockett, Sam Houston (of Texas), John Calhoun (of Georgia), 'Stonewall' Jackson (as he was to be named). And they had also given birth to Abraham Lincoln.[1]

When these Roundheads of the south (as they have been named) were confronted by the crisis of 1860 they cheated all expectations. The state governments supposed they would stand by their own southern states. Nothing of the kind. They had detested bishops and tithes and all authority long ago. Now they detested slaves and slave-owners alike. And for good measure they detested the whole institution of slavery. The strongest group at once seceded from Virginia to form the new state of West Virginia. And the whole mountain people stood for the Union. In doing so they fatally split the Confederacy.

When the war was over, although much was changed, the action of the mountain people made no difference to their position. They had helped to gain the victory a second time. But once more the rights of this strange race were ignored. The boundaries of the states settled a century earlier by royal astronomers in England and ignoring the mountains and the valleys proved to be the unalterable law under the Constitution of the Republic. The mountain people remained partitioned among eight states, seven of which held them to be a treacherous minority.

Forty years later there were still three million native highlanders settled in the southern Appalachians. Only 18,000 foreign immigrants had invaded their fastnesses. But a generation of discouragement had left them as a genetic residue. The great adventurers had departed to the west. Those who stayed were illiterate, inbred, conservative, as poor as the surviving Cherokees in the adjoining valleys. And somewhat worse off than the slaves that they continued to despise but had helped to liberate.

b. Lincoln and Whitney

No one can doubt that Abraham Lincoln in the brief four years of his government greatly altered the character of the United States. He did so, not so much by his own skill in government or even by its successful political issue in the preservation of the union or the abolition of slavery, either of which might well have been accomplished without him. He did it rather by stating the purposes for which he held that society should be maintained and governed. In doing so he made a contribution to our understanding of all societies. And, in doing so, he also revealed to the American people a picture of themselves and a purpose for themselves which they were glad to recognize and to take as a model. His achievement was thus social and personal.

[1] Although Lincoln and his mother were both illegitimate we know that three of his grandparents came from the mountains. The fourth, to whom he ascribed his abilities, was probably a Virginia slave-owning planter (Joseph Hall, 1960).

His invention was intellectual and literate. He introduced certain illusions or deceptions without which, as it begins to appear, a great nation cannot exist.

To some extent these illusions are due to the selective treatment that historians have given to the record of Lincoln's opinions. For they were very much the opinions of the mountain people of his day. They owed their success to the fact that they included none of the illusions of either the north or the south. For example in his speech at Charleston, Illinois, September 18 1858, Lincoln said:

'I am not nor ever have been in favour of making voters or jurors of Negroes, nor of qualifying them to hold office, nor to intermarry with white people; and I will say in addition to this that there is a physical difference between the white and black races which I believe will for ever forbid the two races living together on terms of social and political equality.'

Lincoln did not then know (how could he know?) the diverse products of hybridization that were only beginning to appear among the Negroes with results that would much later falsify his expectations. What he said was merely an honest opinion based on fair observation at the time he said it.

It is paradoxical but also salutary in face of this experience to turn to another American of remarkable character whose inventions were technical and whose impact on society was concerned merely with the sordid problem of making one pair of hands do what a few hundred pairs of hands had done before. This other man was Eli Whitney.[1]

Eli Whitney was born in Massachusetts in 1765 and graduated from Yale University at the age of twenty-seven. He sought employment in Georgia and found a job as a tutor at Savannah. Mexican cotton had been introduced from the West Indies to the Sea Islands of South Carolina six years earlier.[2] He found that it had created a grave economic problem owing to a difficulty in harvesting that had existed for about five thousand years: it took a slave ten hours to separate a pound of lint from three pounds of cotton seed. Within two weeks, by putting together a toothed cylinder, a wire screen and a revolving brush, Whitney had invented the cotton gin, a machine which worked a thousand times as fast as human fingers.

That was in 1792. In the seventy years following this invention the cotton yearly produced in the southern states rose from 4000 bales to four million bales. In the same time the slave population rose from probably less than one million to four million. And the price of slaves rose threefold. Within a much shorter time the cotton exported from Savannah and Charleston was supplying the power looms which employed half a million cotton workers in the north of England.

The new prosperity of the cotton industry led to its westward expansion into the Mississippi basin and the plains of Texas. With it went the practice of slavery and the new confidence of the southern planters. A whole civilization flowered on the product of Eli Whitney's alien ingenuity. For he was not, and could not have been, a southerner. Meanwhile he was cheated of any reward.

[1] See Heffner (1952) and Whitridge (1956). [2] See Darlington (1963).

His invention was pirated and he returned to New England famous but also penniless.

Back at home Whitney learnt in 1798 of the danger of war with the French Republic. He pointed out to the government in Washington that by new methods of mass production in two years he could provide them with 10,000 muskets.

Other men, notably Le Blanc in France and Joseph Bramah and Marc Brunel[1] in England had had the idea before of making tools to make machines whose parts were standard and interchangeable. They had actually tried it out. But special factors now worked in Whitney's favour. There was a President, Thomas Jefferson, who had met Le Blanc, understood the principle and saw its merits. And for a very telling reason its merits were greater than they could have been in Europe. The recruitment of the Southern population had always been lacking in craftsmen. This was where construction was always held up. The country was too poor to tempt the skilled migrant and craftsmen can be bred only from craftsmen. Thus in America machine production would not, as in Europe, displace the craftsman. It would make good his absence. So a vast new channel of development was opened in the northern states. The mechanical ingenuity of the Yankee had now been fed with the invention on which the prosperity and the population of northern society were to be multiplied.

Eli Whitney had thus, in turn, created the strength of both the south and the north. But naturally the people from whom he came were the people who benefited most. The south knew only how to use the product of his invention. The north knew how to use the cause of it, the inventiveness itself. When the crisis came, and the two armies faced one another by the Potomac, Whitney had been dead for thirty-five years. But it was to his work that both the slavery of the south and the industry of the north, which destroyed it, owed their strength.

Since long before the invention of agriculture the interactions of the individual inventor and his invention with his own society and with other societies have followed the principles we see in the case of Eli Whitney. There are suitable communities for breeding great inventors. And there are also suitable communities for applying their inventions. But never before, not even in the English Civil War, have such dramatic and contrasted consequences of these principles ensued so quickly from the work of one man.

c. The Aftermath

The triumphs of successive empires, Athenian and Roman in the iron age, British and American in the industrial age, were based on ruthless competition, on a kind of struggle which those who gained by it, the governing classes of each in turn, held to be the proper mode of activity of a free society. Each in turn believed its success and its power to be due to its own inherent virtues and accordingly saw no need to change its habits to meet the situation created by its own success: by its own methods and with its own talents it could guarantee the future prosperity of the society under its protection.

[1] See Table 33. Wilkinson also played a part.

How misleading these assumptions could be we have seen in the earlier instances. In the United States today the same situation repeats itself. But it is complicated by new genetic factors whose understanding or misunderstanding may for some time dominate the nation's development.

The Negro slaves of the south were kept in a state of subjection which offended the instinctive feelings of the mass of the white population in the north who did not own slaves. At the same time the industrial leaders of the north reckoned that an abundant supply of Negro labour, unskilled and low-priced, would favour the development of mechanized urban industry under their control and for their benefit. The victory of the north in the Civil War enabled them in due course to confirm this expectation.

Negro workers from the fields of the south were now free to move into the cities of the north. There they found greater comfort and greater warmth than any they had known before. At first their migration was a trickle. But in due course (after 1890) the old Confederate states discovered that they could change their constitutions and disfranchise the emancipated Negroes. The trickle then grew into a stream. Twenty years later a new need and a new opportunity arose. With great external wars the manufacturers, serving the nation's needs and their own interests, demanded more labour. The Negro stream grew into a flood. The comfort of the city then became congestion, its centre became a slum, and its free and freely multiplying Negro population found themselves the inhabitants of a new ghetto.

The black people of the north now numbered nearly ten millions. They were the products of migration within a somewhat hybridized and in consequence genetically diverse community. Their movements were therefore selective. The northern Negro was more enterprising and less subservient than those he had left behind. Like his kinsmen who went first into Ontario, or his other kinsmen who later made their university in Alabama, or his most remote kinsmen who were first picked out in Barbados, he was more intelligent than the rest. And he often obviously had more white ancestry.

So, in the north as well as in the south, a new coloured society grew up. It was a socially, economically and educationally stratified society. It was however one such stratified society segregated and *encapsulated* within another stratified society. Such a situation had often existed before. The Hakka or the Manchus in China, the Normans in England, the English in Ireland or India, the Afrikaners in South Africa and a hundred others had been similarly encapsulated racial minorities. But they were encapsulated by their own choice, by their belief in their own superiority. The Negro community in the United States, on the other hand, amounting now to one-eighth of the whole nation was labelled by its colour and by its capacity, in the eyes of the other seven-eighths, as inferior. It was certainly a source of unskilled labour of the kind which has, as we know, suffered selective disadvantage at every crisis throughout human evolution. They had long been at the bottom of society but they were now at the bottom of the deepest society, outside India, that the world had ever seen.

It was the deepest society in the sense of comprising the richest and the poorest of mankind. This depth of contrast was the consequence of that competition to which the white Establishment of this most successful nation believed it owed its success. It was at the same time the cause of fear, mutual fear, between the contrasted communities. The danger and the fear of assassination grew in the north as they had done in the south. And in place of constitutional exclusions by white proprietors in the south the Negroes were now faced by the constitutional exclusions of the trade unions in the north.[1]

Thus the Negro found himself freed from a protection of which he still stood in need while by no means freed from a humiliation of which he might formerly have been unaware. He was thrown into a 'free' society such as none of his ancestors in Africa or America had ever known, a society created by white men for white men. He was thrown also into a struggle in which there was more scope for sentiment than for compassion, a struggle in which all but a few of those who were marked by their colour were bound to be losers.

Violence has been provoked by these disappointments not only in the United States but following Negro immigration in Britain also. Three possible ways may be seen of turning it aside.

The first and, for lawyers, the most obvious solution is to legislate: to abolish discrimination and segregation by law. Advances have been made in this way in regard to voting and jury service. But in more personal relations deeper resistance has been met. Are Negroes to live in the same quarters and to attend the same schools as whites? Common education in universities is accepted because entrance examinations are themselves a means of discrimination. Common education in schools is not willingly accepted. Common residence in streets is resisted. And it cannot be enforced. Throughout history all cities have been based on the assortment of races and classes and we cannot doubt that they always will be.

In short, racial discrimination has a genetic basis with a large instinctive and irrational component. Its action may be modified by education or by economic processes. But it cannot be suppressed by law.

The second solution is a continuation of the first. All states by 1967 had repealed their laws prohibiting white-Negro intermarriage. But intermarriage and social integration can never be separated. Sexual relations are a continuation of social relations; and conversely likewise. This is precisely why white societies resist integration and why Abraham Lincoln considered intermarriage unthinkable. What we have seen of Jamaica and of other countries, however, has shown that social conflict is always softened where slow hybridization has slowly led to a gradation of character and of colour. It is softened because, where sexual barriers are broken, social promotion is no longer excluded. Moreover, on this question of principle, the genetic lesson is unequivocal. The mixing of races, uncontrolled by law, determined only by individual or family choice, has never been free. It has always been restrained. And being restrained it has never been deleterious.

[1] For example in 1916 the national Plumbers' Union, faced by a Negro invasion took defensive measures. It resorted to an hereditary qualification for membership. Thereby it revived the principles which the Theodosian Code had applied to meet an earlier crisis.

The third solution is the social remedy: to protect the less skilled and therefore less fortunate classes, whether white or Negro, from the worst consequences of free competition. Such protection is easier in the racially more homogeneous societies of Northern Europe. But in the United States the price that has to be paid by the rich for sharing the benefits of a multiracial society with the poor is something they have not yet been prepared to reckon.

We may, however, attempt the reckoning with the help of a new, coherent and honest study of the whole problem on the part of Carmichael and Hamilton. Representing the Negro community, these writers argue that the cultural integrity, social interests and self-esteem of the Negro community can be preserved, as they should be, only by the assertion of their independent racial character within the nation. To this political assertion they give the name of *Black Power*.

This policy, leading to segregation of the two races and denying them a common evolutionary future, parallels the South African policy of *apartheid*. It is not to be lightly dismissed. But before we accept it we must look at its underlying assumptions. The Negro writers condemn what they describe as racism. 'By "racism",' they say, 'we mean the predication of decisions and policies on considerations of race for the purpose of *subordinating* a racial group and maintaining control over that group.' When we look back over history, however, what do we see? The application of this principle has governed the evolution of all advancing societies since soon after the beginning of agriculture. And it has been the means of their advancement. The conquering Normans despised the Saxon serfs and based their policies on the need for subordinating this racial group. They were so successful, we may argue, that the English agricultural labourer today still inherits much of the character and many of the disabilities of his subordinated ancestors.

Between these two situations we must of course notice certain significant differences. First, in mental and physical character the contrast between lord and serf in England was bridged by a range of intermediate types. Across this range, hybridization occurred more frequently than between black and white. Discrimination was therefore increasingly based on knowledge. Secondly, the lord and the serf, unlike the black and white, propagated themselves in balanced proportions. This knowledge and this balance are crucial for the harmony of all mixed societies.

The Negro community multiplies more quickly than the white. And it is more liable to unemployment. In times of stress there is less demand for Negro labour than for white. Precisely the same differences appear between the unskilled and the skilled labour in purely white societies. Every new discovery, technical or scientific, exposes the less skilled individual and community to redundancy and discrimination. Thus, as we saw during the Industrial Revolution, differences in skill and multiplication, in unemployment and exploitation, are connected in an inevitable sequence. And this sequence has selectively favoured increasing skill in human societies ever since the first tools were made.

A condition of harmony between social classes, and above all between black and white, is therefore to break this sequence and to balance the multiplication of the two communities. The more the Negro birth rate is reduced the better the Negroes are bound to be treated. Now the white community has created the society whose fruits both are enjoying. It has also discovered the means of controlling the increase of population. It is now for the two communities together to apply this knowledge to solve harmoniously, if they can, the problem they have together unwittingly created.

In considering these various remedies for a social crisis sharp differences of opinion will be found to arise among populations by region and by class. Nor need we expect purely rational arguments to be the most successful in advancing one opinion or another. For, in both white and Negro communities, as we have noticed in the past where great evolutionary processes have been in question, reason and instinct will continue to be in opposition; and reason will not easily secure the advantage.

X. THE GREAT RESETTLEMENT

a. Ecological Types

The establishment of the American Republic was an act of repudiation by men who had escaped from what they felt to be the errors and oppressions of the Old World. But at once it became an invitation to those who should wish to follow their example. The invitation has been accepted in such numbers that the genetic contribution of the later comers to the population now equals or exceeds, for no one can measure the mixture, that of the revolutionary founders (Table 39).

Table 39. *The Growth and Origin of the Population of the U.S.A.*

After *E.B.* (1929), etc.

Total Population		*Total Immigrants*	
1790	3·9m	1783–1820	*c.* 0·25m
1860	31·4m[1]	1820–1840	0·67m
1910	92·0m	1840–1880	9·04m
1920	105·7m	1880–1920	23·49m
1960	179·3m[2]	1920–1960	8·19m

[1] Loss of population 1860–70, due to the effects of the Civil War, computed at 2·5m.

[2] 158·8m White, 18·9m Negro, 1·6m Other Races.

The newcomers arrived from Ireland after the famine of 1846, and from Germany after the revolution, or rather the reaction, of 1848. From Russia there came Jews after the pogroms of 1881 and Gentiles after the Revolution of 1917. From the poor lands of Sweden came farmers in search of land and from the overcrowded cities and villages of Italy and Greece came men in nearly every walk of life.

Where did these different kinds of people go to find a living? Those who went to work on the land looked for the climate and the soil that suited them best. It was a problem of genetic adaptation to diverse ecological conditions.

The original English, as we have seen, divided themselves by sect and party, temperament and wealth, between north and south. The Germans went to the Midwestern plains; the Swedes and the Finns settled round the northern lakes; Italians took wine-growing to California. Mexicans moved across the frontier into California, New Mexico and Texas. Meanwhile specialists and craftsmen went, as they always have done, straight to their necessary places of employment. Cornish miners took up their task forming colonies in Wisconsin, in Colorado and in Nevada. And in the towns the skill of one kind of Greek found an outlet in restaurant-keeping while that of another kind, from Chios, developed merchant banking in Baltimore.

Meanwhile the Jews were able to develop for the first time free of the demands for conversion. Their skill in medicine and mathematics, which had served kings and sultans in the Old World for two millennia, and their skill in music and the law, which they had turned to their own use for three millennia, they could now apply to the use of society as a whole.

The new immigration of the period from 1840 to 1940 came at the same time as the great surge of the native American people which pushed the frontier westward to the Pacific coast. This movement involved yet a second selection for restlessness and rootlessness, favouring energy at the expense of sedentary and bookish meditation.[1] The successive waves of frontiersmen, the fighters and later cowboys from Kentucky, the miners from Pennsylvania, the sod-men or farmers from New England, were perpetually quarrelling.[2] They came together. But they did not easily coalesce. Still less did those who followed coalesce with them or with one another. Not only were Protestant, Catholic and Jew kept apart by their religious barriers to breeding, but every Protestant group was divided by sect in separate breeding communities, which were, as we have seen, economically stratified. In each town they remained in their own quarters as has happened in every race- or class-divided city since the first cities were built. The separation by colour was arbitrary but easy. It could scarcely fail to be applied when in the same towns the top white Episcopalians could not cross the social frontier and the breeding barrier of a street to find a house or a wife.[3] Thus there grew up in the west as in the east a diverse and balanced society with a character of its own, one stage further removed from its European origins.

Thus freedom of movement, freedom of religion, and freedom of occupation seem to have produced in the United States a certain degree of coalescence; a greater coalescence and a more frequent hybridization perhaps than has ever been known before in human history. But that coalescence is utterly remote from the random mixture of a freely interbreeding population. The mixture in settling has everywhere separated and assorted in level and in locality according to the inborn and genetic inclinations of its component individuals and families. It is assorted into communities in such a way as to

[1] With a few notable and temporary exceptions: Mark Twain's energy was itself bookish and he did not settle in the west.

[2] See F. S. Philbrick and J. D. Horan for their earlier and their later battles.

[3] 'Crossing the tracks' as this feat of exogamy has been known in Philadelphia (Baltzell, 1958).

preserve that culture, as well as that genetic character which each would lose by coalescence.

b. A Criminal Class

Not all the communities so preserved are of obvious value to the life of the nation. In all advanced societies crime takes two forms. One is sporadic and unorganized. Of this kind was the momentary blaze of shooting which killed, it is said, some 20,000 men in the western states between 1870 and 1895. The gunmen had been drawn to the lawless frontier. But they did not breed: they killed one another.[1] The second kind is organized, disciplined and professional. And in so far as it succeeds it is self-perpetuating and hereditary. Of this second kind are the Thugs whom we have met in India, the Corsicans in France and many Italian groups, of which the most potent is the Sicilian Mafia.[2]

The Mafia, beginning perhaps as agents for absentee landlords, had already become the underground government of Sicily under the Bourbons. After Garibaldi's liberation in 1860 they continued as a state within a state. They maintained themselves by blackmail and assassination and by enforcing a strict code of honour within their true-breeding society.

The principle of this code or law of behaviour is known in Italian as *omertà* but it depends indeed on a principle universally effective in stratified and probably already existing in unstratified societies. It is that the member of a subordinate social group must not tell tales or 'sneak' about his friends to the agents or officers of a higher group with a higher authority.[3]

This principle the Mafia and similar societies discovered how to apply in an extreme form. It enabled them to treat the authorities, that is the law and all its servants, not as mere enemies, but as vermin. In this way they turned the tables on society; their superb doctrine tested by centuries of use in Sicily enabled the Mafia to grasp the opportunities of the modern world. With it they came to America.

The first *Mafiosi* arrived in New Orleans in 1890. There, eleven of them, imprisoned for murder, were lynched by the kinsmen of their victims. The United States government, not understanding the system on this introductory occasion, innocently agreed to pay $30,000 compensation for this act of justice. So it began. Selecting their recruits exclusively among Sicilian immigrants, they trained them by the discipline of the gun and increased them by regular inbreeding in the stratified ranks of the hierarchy. They made themselves into *cosa nostra*, an unparalleled organization, the compact governing class of the criminal world.

[1] Mark Twain strikes a rich vein in his account of life in the west at an earlier date (1859–66).

[2] The European origin of the Mafia is described by Norman Lewis, their American expansion by Frederick Sondern, their contemporary life in Sicily by Gavin Maxwell.

[3] It was this principle which had worked so well in the Sicilian Vespers, the massacre of all the French, perhaps 300,000, in Sicily on Easter Monday, 1282 (Runciman, 1958).

They established a multiracial syndicate in which the undisciplined and unrelated gangs of their Irish and Jewish predecessors could only hope to play a subordinate part. When the era of liquor-prohibition was reached (1920–33) the syndicate had advanced from a national to an international scope. The death rate was high but the stock was prolific and the community prospered. The most illustrious families of *cosa nostra* were now joined in marital alliances of the same character, although for such a different purpose, as the old Philadelphia Quakers and the European royal dynasties with which we are familiar. These are people for whom there is no possibility of coercion, correction, or conversion. Nothing on earth will make them come to terms with the general body of society. They are a race apart.

c. The Establishment

The ecological assortment of the people in Europe has taken 150 generations. In the United States the corresponding processes have been condensed into ten generations. Or rather condensation has been attempted, for no one has yet been able to speed up genetic processes. Indeed there have been setbacks. Migration was far from creating a perfect balance at each stage of colonization as the criticisms of Mrs Trollope and other visitors have often revealed. The intellectual temper for long lagged behind the European taste.[1]

This attitude, this national climate, was to drive many artists and writers into exile. They returned to Europe. For, while the manual craftsman will often go where his talents are most lacking and most needed, the imaginative craftsman usually demands the company of kindred spirits. Only slowly has new immigration, partly Jewish, further hybridization, and further assortment softened in some places the American resentment against speculative thought. So new recruitment has stopped the reverse flow of civilization. This has been a process of maturing. It is a process whose operation, when it affects the development of the American Establishment, is also bound to affect the rest of mankind.

A social class, it is now clear, is a group of people who breed together because they work together and work together because they breed together. This is true equally of servile and of ruling classes. In the Old World all ruling classes began as military groups who attached to themselves other social classes of loyal helpers. By mixing and breeding with the higher levels of these auxiliaries they changed themselves from a military to a civil professional bias and aptitude. The United States began at an advanced stage of this transformation. But owing to its own rapid economic development and geographical expansion no single group has been able for any length of time to stabilize its position as a governing class. All that can be seen are many strands of family continuity. There is the military planter aristocracy of the south which was continuous in the case of Washington with its English origins. There is the financial and industrial network of the north beginning in the cities of Boston, New York and Philadelphia. And there are now

[1] A fair example is the observation of Lowes Dickinson in 1900 of the academic American as one interested in any fact but in 'no idea except as it can be shown in direct relation to fact' (E. M. Forster, 1962).

newer centres from which men arise who aspire to manage the affairs of the nation, men who need be neither white, nor Anglo-Saxon, nor Protestant.[1]

In the United States, however, as in Europe, it is not merely the pinnacles of fame or notoriety that are of enduring significance. It is also the larger and more diverse breeding group, the people who keep the whole administrative machine going and ensure its stability. This group maintains uniform, predictable and largely conventional, but slowly changing, opinions. It is this group which constitutes an Establishment.

In the United States it is economically powerful and, being connected, as in England, with particular schools and universities, it is in process of becoming genetically related. It is young as Establishments go, being merely some six or seven generations old. Like its centre in the capital it is continually expanding and is therefore still rapidly evolving. On its evolution the future of the nation depends, as the future of the Soviet Union depends on that of the upper levels of the more hastily assembled and more secretly selected Communist Party.

[1] Baltzell has described the history of these families and Packard has noted their behaviour.

26

CHINA

I. THE ORIGINS

AGRICULTURE CAME TO CHINA during the third millennium B.C. It first appeared on the rich wind-blown loess soils of the Yellow river valley some 500 miles from the sea. Not wheat and barley, but millet (*Panicum*) and buckwheat (*Fagopyrum*), were its original mainstay. These were however crops that we should expect to be picked up as weeds of wheat and barley during those intervening millennia of the neolithic expansion when the early farmers moved eastwards across the heart of Asia.

The first cultivators probably brought with them sheep and goats, to which were soon added the native pig. All these immigrants and the men who brought them came, not into the south as in Europe, but into the north. Future immigrants and invaders would come into China by the same route; all of them, that is, except one: in the first millennium B.C. rice and its cultivators began to make their way inland and northwards from the coasts of Indo-China. Their peaceful expansion over another period of a thousand years slowly reached the northern limits of their crop in the basin of the Yangtse river. The first farmers in northern China were already highly adapted peasants irrigating their crops, spinning and weaving wool, learning also to use the hemp and the hemp nettle for the production of rope and cloth. They were men and women who had five thousand years of experience behind them of living in coherent and latterly, perhaps, stratified societies which had carried them across the continent from their distant origins.

How had they travelled? They had come by the only possible route through the oases of the Tarim basin and the long valley of Kansu. In a later age this route was to dry up. The oases were to be smothered in the terrible Taklamakan desert and the steppes beyond were to be infested by no less terrible horsed bowmen. Then it would be the hazardous Silk Road from east to west. But in the third millennium we may suppose it still allowed a peaceful transit through well-watered country populated by sparse unorganized paleolithic tribes. Nevertheless the migrant farmers probably needed a thousand years or more to make their journey of three thousand miles.

The arrival of agriculture in China so long after its origin in the west led to a striking difference in the sequence of its development. The art of firing pots made from clay had been discovered by the oven bakers in the west a thousand or more years after the beginning of agriculture. But potters seem to have arrived in China and Japan prior to the arrival of farmers. There as elsewhere pot-baking had moved into the territory of the hunters and collectors in advance of crop-cultivating.

The explanation is fairly clear. Crops are dependent on climate; they have to be selectively adapted to new climates. Pots are independent of climate; they are dependent only on the skill of the potter in finding clay and fuel. People could make pots, therefore, who had not yet the right grain for settled farming in a new country. But the potters who arrived in China were people who had gifts of technical invention which other races of men had not yet displayed, those same gifts which were later to distinguish their Chinese and Japanese descendants above all other people.[1]

After about a thousand years, a second wave of invaders entered China through the valley of Kansu. They reflected, as we should expect, the racial and the cultural transformations of Western Asia. These people, the Shang, according to Coon, had western heads and also, according to Wissmann, a western or Aryan Sun-God. Moreover, their patrician caste had a form of ancestor-worship recalling the Aryan religions of the classical world in the west. It was a habit destined to favour the growth of their own population, and destined also to make a great impression in China. Probably they brought wheat and barley as their staple grain crops. Certainly they brought with them bronze and also chariots drawn by small horses. Evidently they had made the journey across Asia more quickly than their predecessors for it was only a few centuries earlier that the Hyksos had overwhelmed Egypt with just such chariots. To be more precise, however, these newcomers must have consisted of diverse classes of men who forged bronze swords, bred horses, built chariots and fought with the swords, the horses and the chariots.

This new society with its combination of the horse domesticated in Central Asia and the metal-smelters from Persia now subdued or dominated the peoples of the Yellow river. It enabled the Shang rulers to push their frontier southwards beyond where the steppe meets the forest and the mountains, and nearly to the Yangtse river. Thus the first Chinese Dynasty used their new grain-farming home as a base for attacking and absorbing the paleolithic people in front of them while they kept the nomad kinsmen they had left behind them at bay. This task occupied a whole half-millennium of their history.

It was no doubt the horse that brought bronze-workers so quickly from the west within a few centuries. But the horse could not bring iron-workers with the same speed. Their independent tribes with their secret and magic rituals

[1] Watson (1966); as we saw, some early Japanese pottery was transported to America (ch. 25).

moved less freely. They were dispersed, as we have seen, only on the fall of the Hittite Empire and they arrived in China about 700 B.C.

A remarkable reversal of the steps in handling their metal shows us the development that they had undergone in their long journey or at the end of it. In the west the casting of iron had to wait three thousand years (1500 B.C. to A.D. 1500). But in China casting seems to have been invented almost at once. The method of forging on the other hand was delayed until 300 B.C. Only then could they make swords. And it was with these swords that the Ch'in Emperor established the unity of China. He broke down the hereditary and locally autonomous feudal society which had grown up in the expanding Empire of the previous eight hundred years of the Chou Dynasty. The independent growth and special skill of metal-working in China thus profoundly affected the development of the country.

It was one of the special gifts derived from this skill which gave the Chinese armies the cross-bow with the bronze lock. This invention came at a fortunate moment. A two-thousand-mile Great Wall had been built by the Ch'in Emperor in the third century B.C. Together with the cross-bow it preserved China against the attacks of the Hun horsemen. For the horsemen could climb the wall but their horses could not; then the men who dismounted were shot down.[1]

It was this saving of China from submergence which later turned the nomads against the Roman and Indian Empires. Whether this saving was to China's advantage in the long run is another question.

These technical successes allowed the Ch'in Emperor to unite China and to extend its frontiers to Manchuria and Viet Nam, to abolish hereditary feudal principalities and even to subdue the scholars and to burn the traditional books which he saw as an obstacle to reform. They also led to the strength and prosperity of the Han Dynasty which followed him. It was the Han Emperors who began the Grand Canal from Tien-tsin to Nanking and who founded most of the cities of China on the sites which (in contrast with those of the west and to the sorrow of archaeologists) they still occupy today.

These energetic rulers also employed Scythian mercenaries to extend their frontiers. By their somewhat heroic enterprise they were able to make contact (as Woolley shows in relation to the Tarim basin) with the Scythian kings of the Punjab who sent the first Buddhist missionaries to China, men who were to pass on elements of both Indian and Chinese civilization to the Japanese.

They were also able to make contact with Rome, sending silk and the peach in exchange for gold and the vine. And finally they were able with great effect to compete with India in exporting their art and technology to the peoples of South-East Asia already converted to Indian Buddhism. By this competitive invasion they created the frontier between north and south Viet Nam which persists to this day as one of the great racial boundaries of the world. In all these movements, we may note, the paths that were being followed were those already trodden repeatedly in the movements of paleolithic times and were to be trodden again in modern migrations.

[1] de Camp (1963); Watson (1966).

Table 40. *The Dynasties of China*

After Silcock (1936); Goodrich (1943); Wissmann (1956); Coon (1954); Woolley (1958); Marsh (1961); Cottrell (1962); FitzGerald (1962); Purcell (1962); Needham (1963); Wittfogel (1964); and Watson (1960, 1966).

SHANG 1500–1027 B.C.	Aryan-connected conquerors bring in bronze, horses and chariots. Also perhaps wheat and barley.
CHOU 1027–249	Empire grows and breaks up into separate feudal states. Beginnings of Great Wall in the north (400 B.C.); and of documented and dated history: Confucius: 551–479. Mencius 372–319 *Capital* (after 710): Lo-yang in Honan
CH'IN 247–209	Empire united from Manchuria to Viet Nam by warrior hill chieftains of Kansu with forged iron swords. Feudal hereditary ranks replaced by imperial civil service but the books are burnt. Great Wall continuous *Capital:* Hsien Yang in Shensi
HAN 202 B.C.–A.D. 220	Wall extended to protect road to the west from Hun horsemen. Land and sea connections with India and Rome. Silk goes out. Buddhists come in. Grand Canal begun. Tea cultivated. Paper invented. Numerals appear with decimal places *Capital:* (i) Ch'ang-an, (ii) Lo-yang
Three Kingdoms A.D. 220–489	Tibetans invade from the west; Turks and Mongols from the north; their rulers absorbed in the governing class. Refugees begin to colonize the south. They also take Buddhism, writing and civilization to Japan
T'ANG 618–907	Founder marries a Tartar: unity now permanent. Civil service examination system developed. Zoroastrian and Nestorian refugees and the Buddhists found monasteries, all of which are later dissolved. Muslim and also hill tribe mercenaries *Population:* 60m (FitzGerald) *Capital:* Ch'ang-an
Five Dynasties 907–960	Partition
SUNG 960–1279	Muslims, Mongols and the desert break the link with the west. Growth of isolation and scholastic conservatism. *Capital:* K'ai-fêng in Honan North lost to the Mongols: 1126. *Capitals of South:* (i) Nanking (ii) Hangchow
MONGOL 1279–1368	Mongol military caste government. Mongolia and Tibet under tribute. Lamaism dominant. Attacks on Burma, Java and Japan. Western contacts revived (Marco Polo). Cotton and Sorghum brought into the north *Population:* falls from 100m to 50m *Capital:* Cambaluc (Yu Chou or Pekin)
MING 1368–1644	Founded by a former Buddhist monk. Movable metal type printing in Korea (1402). Maritime expeditions to Arabian coast (1405–1433). Anti-foreign reaction: burning of the ships (1525). Office of Prime Minister abolished: Emperor ruler *Capitals:* K'ai-fêng and Nanking: after 1421: Pekin

MANCHU 1644–1911	Again a dynasty of northern conquerors. Christianity made illegal (1723). Civil service becomes a propertied and graded caste (Marsh). T'ai P'ing Rebellion, 1851–64 *Capital:* Pekin

Revolution of Sun Yat-sen	1912
Revolution of Mao Tse-tung	1949

II. THE PEOPLE

a. Racial Strains

At this creative moment in the development of China we have to look at the different peoples who were between them working out the future of their society.

The first kind of people were those occupying the two rich low-lying agricultural regions which formed the heart of the Empire. Those to the north of the Yangtse river were peasants originally recruited from Central Asia. They were growing the temperate cereals, millet and the wheat and barley which followed it. Those to the south were peasants originally recruited from the deltas of Viet Nam and Cambodia but now hybridized with peasants migrating from the north. They were growing chiefly rice in terraces skilfully constructed and prudently irrigated on the fertile hillsides. They were in addition growing important new crops: cotton, tea, and mulberries for silkworms.

The second kind of people were the herdsmen[1]; people who roamed on horseback over the grasslands of the whole region from Manchuria to the Carpathians. These people when they had Aryan leaders were known as Scythians; when they had Mongol or Hun leaders they were known by the language they spoke or perhaps as Turks or Tartars. These people still survive today in the increasingly arid steppes of Outer Mongolia. They are not greatly changed except that they have lost their most enterprising sons. And the use of the bow is now a sport and not a livelihood. There still they breed their horses, cows, yaks and hybrid yaks, goats, sheep and reindeer, living on their meat and their milk, a diet as restricted as that of the pastoral tribes in East Africa.

These are the people whose more dangerous forebears or kinsmen for three thousand years assaulted the Chinese Empire. Their ancestors probably invented the bow. They domesticated the horse and, two thousand years later, they invented the stirrup. They were connected in turn with the Shang, the Ch'in, the T'ang, the Mongols and the Manchus. And through them they may obviously be connected with the whole of the living population of China. But more directly of course they contributed to the military governing classes, the landowners and gentry of earlier times, none of whom long escaped hybridization with the native Chinese.

The third kind of people were the paleolithic tribes. Among them there were hunters who had earlier domesticated the dog, the ancestor of the modern Chow, and used it for hunting or for meat when hunting failed. There were also fishers, fowlers and collectors, all of whom were gradually

[1] See Woolley, Lattimore, FitzGerald.

brought under the control of the city-centred states, gradually confined to the more hilly or swampy, less fertile and generally peripheral parts of the country; and gradually eroded, hybridized, and assimilated on their edges by the advancing peasants and urban populations; gradually also conscripted or enslaved by the imperial government itself.

The survivors of the paleolithic tribes who did not succumb to the Empire do not of course represent those earlier peoples who did succumb. They are all hillmen. Some of them continue under northern pressure to move south into Burma and Thailand and Laos as they have been doing for thousands of years. Others hold their ground. Such are the Lolo and Miao who resisted the plainsmen and even defeated them. Indeed they turned the tables on the conquerors, for the Lolo hunting and fighting tribes in the head waters of the Yangtse enslaved the Chinese peasants and herdsmen from the valleys and with their hybrids created a three-class society, like that of the Tuareg of the Sahara, which they govern with the same ferocity.[1]

The men of the plains and valleys, hybridized with the advancing peasants, evidently provided the forced labour needed for the great works of building the Great Wall and later the Grand Canal. Their massive deportation and fearful death rate must have helped to wear down, although it could not level out, the great original heterogeneity of the Chinese population. It must have helped also, together with the absence of internal barriers to movement, in replacing a diverse and regional government by a uniform, central and imperial governing class.

b. Social Classes

The struggles, the invasions, the conquests of the three great groups of people have played the main part in creating the stratified structure of Chinese society. At the beginning the craftsmen from the remote west, who came in with the Shang and the Chou, had combined with the native potters and weavers to build the artisan classes which slowly expanded in the cities of China. But there were also the many smaller immigrant groups discussed by Twitchett. In the seventh century A.D. came Buddhist and Nestorian missionaries, not all of whom were celibates, and Jewish and Zoroastrian refugees, very few of whom were celibates. In the seventh century came Muslim traders and seamen to establish colonies in the southern ports. In Canton alone as many as 100,000 Arabs were registered. All of these have long since been assimilated in the urban Chinese population. They have been nuclei around which technical, commercial, and scholarly classes have aggregated to make their diverse contributions to Chinese society although their patronymics have mostly been obliterated in the native speech and orthography.

After all this assimilation has taken place, China, *Chung Kuo*, the heartland, still today consists of the great central mass claiming to be the 'sons of Han', who are surrounded by the peripheral peoples: the Muslims, Chinese- and Turki-speaking, the Manchus, the Mongols and the Tibetans.[2]

[1] Weyer (1959).

[2] Represented by the four other bars in the now unremembered Chinese republican flag of 1911 (Hudson, 1965).

These processes of assimilation have helped to prevent, and have never been retarded by, the development of slavery in China. Already during the Han period all the types of slavery that were known in the west had come into existence in China. Captives, criminals and debtors were bought and sold in slave-markets by private, imperial and monastic owners. But the proportion of the population enslaved, instead of being ten or twenty per cent as in the contemporary western states, in China never exceeded one per cent. Slavery never became the basis of industry or agriculture. It was almost entirely domestic.

The decisive factor in creating Chinese agriculture (as explained by Wilbur) had been the dependence of both lords and peasants on centrally organized processes of irrigation. The communities which survived were those where the peasants had been willing to submit to forced labour which their masters had been capable of organizing for the building of dykes and canals, and later of bridges and walls. It was a relationship of lord and serf favoured by sixty generations of selection under alternating conditions of prosperity and famine; a relationship with which, given the genetic character of both classes, no other system could have competed.

And with regard to genetic character it is not difficult to see where it came from. It came from the pastoral and hill people around the agricultural populations of China. They, like American Indians, the Jews in the Roman Empire, and the pastoral Hamites in Africa, were racially incapable of enslavement and hardly capable of subjection. Of this Chinese independence of character the habit of ancestor-worship and the ensuing respect for propagation are adaptively favoured aspects. The form that slavery took was another.

In China it was evidently found at the beginning that slavery could not be used as the basis of a breeding programme. It could not therefore create a class structure. Male slaves could be kept only by castration. Female slaves were then bound to become the concubines of their owners. The result provided for hybridity and heterogeneity but not directly for social stratification. This was the principle described by Marco Polo as applied by the Mongols to prisoners of war. And it was the established social principle in China.

In every famine in China starving peasants sold their children to slave-dealers who provided the eunuchs and girls needed for the harems and brothels, male and female, of the great cities. It was a trade continuing as in the west for two thousand years. Often, so far as the eunuchs in government service were concerned, it had similarly great political effects.

Thus the mass incidence of racial slavery common to Greece and Rome, perpetuating for some generations the physical differences between social classes, seems to have been replaced in China by an immediate hybridization to be followed by differentiation among the products. So far as there were products, for in China abortion, infanticide and homosexuality have never been curtailed by the Hebrew beliefs in the sanctity of human life and the sinfulness of perversion. The instinctive and explicit desire for descendants, the desire to become an ancestor, was always enough to guarantee the future of the race.

c. Script and Scribes

Writing, wherever it has been invented, has been the agent of civilized development. Yet Plato (in *Phaedrus*) had already seen some of the dangers of writing and Chinese scholars were to see others. Plato suggested that writing favoured forgetfulness. But he was thinking of the individual and not of the race or of society. On a long view we have to think of the whole evolution of speech. Speech passes the need for memory from things to words. It makes one observation serve for many repetitions. Writing takes this transference a stage further. For those who can write, for the literate classes, writing transfers the need for memory-for-things to the need for memory-for-spelling, for arrangement and literary presentation in words; or, as we may say, for scholarship.

All this technical transformation means that a need has been created, and a selective advantage established, in the evolution of society for a new class of man, the scholar, for whom words and books are better understood or more easily understood than things and even people. This transfer of advantage had led to the promotion of scholarship and the segregation of a scholarly or, as is sometimes said, of an educated class. This promotion and segregation were relieved among the Jews and Greeks (and through them among their neighbours and their successors) by the introduction of an alphabetic script. The alphabet proved in the end to be the key to their intellectual advancement and our own. But for the Chinese this invention never came. And writing itself proved in the end to be a stumbling-block, a system inherently incapable of adaptation or reformation.

In China as in the west writing began by the use of picture signs to represent words. It began also a millennium later than in the west, but even so probably not through diffusion. The first of these signs stood for things, then came others for ideas, and finally compounds were made to represent sounds for things-with-ideas. Already under the Shang 2500 such characters are identifiable though not now all decipherable. Today 5000 are academically indispensable and 8000 are effectively used with up to 20 strokes in each character. And the lexicographer could, already in 1719, attain a climax of 40,000 items.

Naturally the replacement of this decorative but monstrous system by alphabetic writing had been proposed by Nestorian and other immigrant scholars in one age after another.[1] But the proposal has met with several obstacles which together were fatal. A poverty of consonants and richness of vowel sounds, which are shared with Polynesian, are carried to an extreme in Chinese and especially and increasingly in the Pekin dialect. This development seems (for reasons we considered earlier) to be connected with the racial character of the Chinese in respect of the vocal apparatus and the musical sense. It is associated with, and even perhaps demands, the use of tonal differences, single or double, for each vowel sound. Chinese speech therefore requires an extra class of symbols to represent it phonetically.

Before this system could be reformed it had been stabilized by the Ch'in

[1] Turkish clerks under Ghengis Khan could maintain their independence of Chinese society by using their Nestorian alphabetic script (Lattimore, 1963).

Emperor. He made his regional Ch'in script standard for the whole of his Empire. By the time block-printing came in with the T'ang Dynasty therefore Chinese writing had been set in its permanent and uniform character. Thus the writing stood still and remained capable of putting on paper in uniform style a language which was itself diversifying. It was even capable of being transferred by Buddhist monks to Japan. The Chinese speech, to be sure, owing to the rapid expansion of the stock of original cultivators within a geographically continuous country, might still seem to be one language at least in the broad sense in which the Romance languages of Europe were formerly one language. But it had diverged at the popular and colloquial level into many dialects which correspond, as dialects always do, with distinct breeding groups of people.[1]

In China the official script became in this way a powerful social as well as administrative agent. On the one hand, it provided a uniform means of communication among diverse people of a vast empire and over a vast period from the T'ang to the present day. And, on the other hand, it became the agent of authority and therefore a symbol of status by which the emperor and his mandarin administrators set themselves apart from the manual workers, the illiterate, the inarticulate peasants and artisans who laboured for them in their separate hardly intercommunicating societies.

The scholars could understand one another throughout the country both in speech and writing with decisive effect in promoting and preserving the unity of the T'ang Empire. With the great merchants, alone in China they had this power. They had devoted as a rule more than half their lives to acquiring it: to learning the use of those thousands of pictograms, ideograms and phonograms. They thus had an advantage over the mass of the population of which any simplified phonetic and alphabetic writing would at once have deprived them. Moreover, those beautiful characters were by their aesthetic quality and perceptual requirements adapted to the class and the race which had created them for their own use, and interlocked them with the beautiful and idiosyncratic literature which they were required to represent.

So it was that the special character of Chinese speech, itself a product of the Chinese race, contributed to the hardening of the class structure of the Chinese people. It contributed also to the parallel hardening of the mechanical basis of its differentiation in the form of writing which had been almost unchanged for two thousand years. With each new dynasty the system of learning, the method of examinations, and the class structure which rested on them, were shaken and a revolution was threatened. The capital was shifted to a new site within the 700-mile triangle: Pekin–Hangchow–Ch'ang-an. But, when society had settled down again, it was seen to have settled once more into the cultural as well as the genetic mould which the learned class themselves eternally constituted. Impatiently, perhaps desperately, the

[1] Such dialects exist today among Chinese at home and abroad especially in the twelve million Chinese now settled in South-East Asia. For example, six mutually unintelligible dialects or languages are said to be spoken by the Chinese communities in the one city of Singapore at the present day (Bloodworth, 1967).

Ch'in Emperor had burnt the books and the Sung critic (quoted by Twitchett) had condemned the examinations. But the structure of society had too long been governed by its own machinery of government. Learning had proved so perfect a means of administration that it had become an end in itself. And each new intruding race of conquerors, after some resistance, became captive to the system of the conquered. Just as Greek learning subdued the Romans, so Chinese learning, combined with the Chinese inventions of writing, paper and printing successively seemed to subdue the Tartars, the Mongols, and the Manchus. But above all they locked up and imprisoned the Chinese themselves who saw no other world that could compare with their own.

The rigid structure of Chinese writing with its complex and irremediable genetic basis has had a decisively limiting effect in three ways. First, it has hindered the growth of the Chinese Empire beyond the frontiers reached by the expansion of the mandarin class itself under the T'ang Dynasty. Tibet, Korea and Sinkiang, Viet Nam and Malaya could be brought under tribute but, having their own writing and their own independent literate class, they could not be directly administered. Even today Chinese writing is a major obstacle to the government of Sinkiang by the Chinese. Only the barbarous and largely paleolithic south-western province of Yunnan could be effectively colonized and absorbed. Of course colonists could penetrate and exist, as they do today in their millions, in all parts of South-East Asia. But these colonists went always as traders and craftsmen without their scholars.

Secondly, the mandarin class had been developed with its examination system by the Han Emperors as a buttress for the central government against feudal usurpers. But it gradually hardened into a propertied and privileged caste. They were increasingly successful in the great triennial examinations for office which they themselves had devised. Thus more and more sharply were they cut off from the subject citizens and merchants as well as from the manually-working artisans. They had recognized at an earlier stage that sages invent new things like paper and printing, clocks and gunpowder; but artisans repetitively propagate them.

A time came (as Needham has pointed out) when the artisans had lost their arts. The scholars then tried to help them. They knew the *signs* for the technical terms used by the sages of earlier days. But (as sometimes happens in the west with philosophers whose help is not however so urgently necessary) the eastern sages no longer knew the *things*. So the culture was lost just as the art of pottery is lost where there is no clay; or no potter. The barrier, a genetic barrier, between the literate and the illiterate cuts off the learning that literacy should have kept alive.

In yet a third and even wider sense Chinese writing shifted the direction of growth of Chinese society. This we must now notice.

d. The Struggle for Isolation

The brief century of Mongol government disturbed Chinese thought for some time after the Mongol Dynasty had been overthrown. It did so because Kublai Khan imported administrators, scholars, and merchants from the west, the Saracen governors and others reported by Marco Polo. These people brought in western ideas and western literature. They let a new light into China and in doing so they aroused a determined opposition among the traditional Chinese administrators, the mandarin class. At first the new Ming Dynasty with its foreign and Buddhist influence favoured the outward-looking enterprise of their predecessors. But a struggle soon began between the Inlanders and the Outlanders. It seems to have been the greatest issue in the history of the Chinese Empire, one comparable with that of the Reformation in Europe. Unfortunately for all of us, in China the Reformers, the Outlanders, lost.

Tradition and the mandarins won. By imperial edict of 1525 the sea-going ships were burnt—those ships with which the Chinese had made contact with the Arab-trading coast of Africa. At the very moment (as Davidson points out) when the Europeans were for the first time entering the Indian Ocean, the Chinese turned their backs on it and on the whole outside barbarian world.

The successful application of the magnetic compass to navigation at sea a century after it had been invented by Flavio of Amalfi was due to its being taken up by Prince Henry the Navigator (assisted by Arab and Jewish scholars, artisans and seamen) in exploring the African coast. In China, on the other hand, the invention had been made about three centuries earlier. It was no doubt applied to the great voyages of the Ming admirals (obviously assisted by Arab immigrants) like Cheng Ho, the Muslim eunuch, to Ceylon, to the Persian Gulf and to the Red Sea.[1] But all these came to nothing when the anti-foreign party triumphed and the ships were burnt.

Pekin remained under the Ming what Hangchow had been under the Sung, the largest city in the world. But it was no longer, as its inhabitants supposed, in every sense the greatest city in the world. For ten generations isolation was to arrest the evolution of the Chinese people. It was a shorter period than the arrest of the dark ages in Europe. But in Europe those ages were ages of fruitful hybridization. They had created in the end more, much more, than they had destroyed. In China the ages of arrest were ages of seclusion and what they created was a little more of the same things that had gone before.

All professions as they establish themselves within an established society become impermeable to ideas from outside them. But when the great Mandarin profession became a caste reinforced by calligraphy and stabilized by heredity, by property, and by seclusion, it became also the most impermeable system in the world.

The bureaucratic and scholarly system which had been a spur to enterprise and invention in the beginning became the means of frustrating them in the end.

A similar course of events affected Japan. In that country the succession of waves of invaders, bringing in the neolithic and bronze ages, introducing Buddhism and writing, had followed a parallel and racially comparable course to that in China. But in addition there had been a continual flow into Japan, first of Koreans and then of Chinese, both preceding and following

[1] Goodrich (1943).

the conversion of the State to Buddhism and the introduction of Chinese writing.[1]

With this long-continued assimilation of Chinese immigrants and their Chinese practices into Japanese society it is not surprising that the Japanese reaction to European contact closely followed the Chinese model. Europeans were effectively excluded by the despotic government of the Shogun in 1647. As in China this decision followed a bitter conflict. It came ten years after the siege and massacre of the Japanese who had been converted to Christianity. Only in 1854 was the exclusion revoked. It followed American pressure and led again to bitter conflict. Again the deep racial barrier between east and west was the primary agent in this enforced exclusion. But the barrier of writing and hence of scholarship and education was a powerful reinforcement.

In the evolution of China and Japan we see evidence of the genetic character of these two peoples who are inherently different from any other peoples: racially but not as a rule adaptively in respect of any earlier difference in conditions. We also see evidence of environmental circumstances notably different from those in which other peoples and their civilizations had developed. In the genetic category we must put, not only the artistic and technical, commercial and social gifts of the Chinese and Japanese peoples, but also the apparently secondary and intellectually negligible properties of their speech and writing. In the environmental category we must put the selectively rigorous conditions under which the Chinese and Japanese peasants learnt the formidable task of cultivating and irrigating their grain, and the immediate advantage, but later disadvantage, of being spared the dark ages of western barbarism and the national separation of the western peoples.

When however we look at this opposition of the innate and the environmental more closely we see that each of the environmental circumstances has in fact a genetic component. The cultivation of grain selected the Chinese race for their skill and ingenuity, their prudence and their discipline. The repulse of the barbarians resulted from the use of these qualities. None of these things happened by chance or good fortune. All of them were traceable to the enduring action of selection on the heredity of the individual and the race. And their effects concern the future of mankind as a whole.

e. Tibet: a Diversion

Tibetan society is the supreme example of isolation. It illustrates the causes and consequences of isolation in all fields of human activity. The tableland consists of hill country at 14,000 to 16,000 feet, and valley land as low as 12,000 feet, above sea level. The whole people are therefore adapted, like the inhabitants of the Andean Altiplano, to living in a rarefied atmosphere under

[1] In A.D. 540 over 7000 Chinese houses were registered in the Japanese census (*E.B.*, 1929). Later, in the thirteenth century, Buddhists were escaping to Japan from the Mongol invasions. One Chinese Abbot then set up at Kiti-Kamakura a monastery whose family of hereditary carpenters, Professor FitzGerald tells me, was still in its service in the twentieth century.

which all strangers are at a disadvantage; they are ecologically isolated from all their neighbours.

Tibet can however be approached from Sikkim and Nepal, from Kashmir, from Mongolia, and from China and from these four directions have come the immigrant waves of population whose sequence can be conjectured during the last three thousand years.[1] The herdsmen occupying the hills probably came from Mongolia in the second millennium B.C. bringing yaks, dzos (yak-ox hybrids) and sheep. They were recruited by later Tartar and Mongol immigrants.

Next came valley cultivators who probably arrived much later in the first millennium B.C. and came chiefly from China. Thirdly came the military conquerors of Tibet. They were probably Tartar or Hun pastoralists who came in the first centuries A.D. Their king in the seventh century took the decisive step, analogous to that of contemporary barbarian kings in Europe, of marrying two foreign wives, one from Nepal and one from China. They converted the king and the people to Buddhism. Thus Tibet was opened for the last time to heavy foreign immigration from which sprang by hybridization both the landowning and the artisan classes. At the same time the Buddhist religion brought in the practice of monasticism and the art of writing with an Indian alphabet.

From this foundation was derived the evolution of Tibet. It was wholly internal. The monks soon corresponded in stratification with the secular society and they were quickly found to be sharing the wealth and responsibilities of the landowning class. Moreover, while a homosexual life was regarded as virtuous, being evidence of heterosexual celibacy, it could be readily abandoned. The original order of 'Red Hat' Lamas could marry and had to be assisted after the fourteenth century by a reformed order of 'Yellow Hats' who at least began their vocation as genuine non-propagating celibates.

This system led, as in Christian countries, to the gradual accumulation of wealth by the monasteries enriched from the bequests made by the pious to ensure their salvation. Every village in Tibet (until 1951) had a monastery attached to it like a great quiescent parasite. The system also led to a concomitant decline in the wealth and the population of the country. It was a decline assisted by the erosion of the soil and the desertion of the land and their serfs by the landlords. For these people were now a closed caste living on their farmed revenues as absentees in the capital.

Whatever we think of scientific, technical and political progress and of the changes that have taken place in the name of progress in the world outside Tibet during the last millennium, what has happened in Tibet shows us that the absence of progress also has disadvantages which are not likely to be foreseen. It also shows us the crucial importance of inbreeding as a means of arresting all processes of innovation.

[1] The recent account of Harrer here reinforces the evidence of documentary history and of our dating of the movements of crops and stock in general. He also reveals the special character of all the tribes and classes he encountered in Tibet: notably the Khampas, a pure race of murderers who deserve to be put in the criminal class next to the Thugs and the Mafiosi.

III. RELIGION, SUPERSTITION AND REFORM

a. Class and Custom

During the Shang and Chou periods China reveals, even more clearly than the contemporary Aryan states of the west, the contrasts of custom and belief between the social classes of contrasted racial origins. These we can now more closely examine.[1]

On the one hand were the patricians betraying their remote pastoral antecedents by their chariot-driving and (after 307 B.C.) horse-riding methods of making war. These people bore the names and pedigrees of their patrilinear clans. They were their own priests and conducted ritual sacrifices to the ancestors and gods of their families. Their marriages moreover were celebrated with formality regulated by clan exogamy.

On the other hand were the peasants who expanded their cultivation under the protection and subjection of the walled cities built by these warrior nobles. Their gods were the symbols of soil and crop and fertility. They mated at their spring festivals; their marriages were consecrated only by their offspring; and their families were nameless.

Before the end of the Chou period, we can see the evidence of the merging of the opposed religions, an assimilation which no doubt followed a limited but inevitable interbreeding. The burials of chiefs slowly ceased to be celebrated by human sacrifices even in their original homeland of the Yellow River valley. The marriages of the peasants began to be regulated and their families named by clans. And the written symbols for the peasants' gods of the soil and the patricians' ancestral spirits began to take the form of the same erect, cylindrical, and manifestly phallic character.

b. The Birth of Empire

When the nobles had absorbed in their several expanding principalities the intervening paleolithic tribes and divided the whole heartland of China between them, they began to make war on one another. The need for local loyalty then became most urgent. It was met by wandering philosophers, men of mixed noble and urban extraction, who devised systems of conduct resting on deference and devotion to the ruler, systems which came to be attributed to one author, Confucius.

These codes of behaviour were later taken as the bible of the scholarly Establishment which supported, and was supported by, the Han Empire. They then became the basis of obedience, not to little local lords, but to the throne of the nascent Empire and they spread, not without the influence of intermarriage, through the whole of Chinese society.

Within 200 miles of one another along the Yellow river valley lay the four successive capitals of this Empire: Lo-yang (of the Chou), Hsien Yang (of the Ch'in), Ch'ang-an (of the Han and T'ang), and K'ai-fêng (of the Sung). The localization of capitals was due to the concentration of agricultural wealth in this region. It meant that peasants, warriors, and later scholars all spread from this single heartland. And this in turn gave a coherence to the

[1] FitzGerald (1935).

whole Empire which repeatedly enabled a single ruler to restore its unity after a partition within, or an irruption without, had broken it up. In the geographically divided west there could, and still can, always be two or more capitals with their empires. The genetic, cultural, linguistic, and religious unity of the west was thus always—and most fortunately—obstructed. But in China in the long run there could be only one capital and the man who occupied it became the ruler of the Empire.[1]

It was this situation which allowed the Han emperors to establish themselves as the ultimate protectors of law and order for the State and thus, for the people, the sole mediators between Heaven and Earth; mediators who later found it convenient to make themselves altogether invisible to their subjects on earth.

c. Foreign Religions

When the great western religions entered China, first Buddhism from India, then from Persia, Nestorian Christianity and Manicheism, and later still Zoroastrianism, Judaism and Islam, enlightened emperors, especially the early T'ang, saw no danger but rather a benefit in the picturesque variety of beliefs they brought into the Empire. For all of them at first timidly submitted to the authority of the Emperor, the Son of Heaven, whose divine status they perhaps failed to recognize.

Soon, however, it was otherwise. The intruders began to convert the native peoples and in doing so they inevitably began to challenge the native Establishments. The emperor, the mandarins, the Confucian code of loyalty, and the whole body of literary wisdom that had filtered through the sieve of codified acceptability, all of these were endangered at the top of society at the same time that the native superstitions were being uprooted at the bottom. Buddhism, by its monasticism, usually homosexual, questioned the Chinese worship of ancestry and belief in propagation. Christianity, by its theory of a divine ruler capable of punishing human rulers, threatened the Chinese theory of the absolute Emperor. When these implications became explicit the Establishment took the necessary action. The intruders were despoiled, humbled or expelled. And China had to do without the men who were to guide the social evolution of the west, and by their conflicts achieve its political transformation.

The evolution of Chinese society was therefore being controlled, we can now see, by the religious and ethical system it had created. Both the society and the system were being arrested in their development by the scholarly hierarchy. They were being arrested at a stage where the hierarchy was everything and the individual nothing. And the whole people in each generation were being selected for their success in submitting to this code of belief and behaviour. The whole society was being held together and also held back by its Confucian literature as was Hellenistic society by its Homeric literature. Chinese society was held together and held back in this way, however, not for a few generations but right down to the present day.

[1] FitzGerald (1933).

d. Native Superstitions

The suppression of the western religions had another kind of effect in what concerned the illiterate classes of Chinese society. In the western world, Judaic, Christian or Muslim, a religious intolerance springing from the Jews, and a scientific intolerance springing from the Greeks, had a profound evolutionary effect on society. By begetting, by teaching, and also, we must admit, by mutual persecution they built up an integrity of thought and behaviour in the professional and intellectual classes which gave its peculiar character to western civilization.

This integrity, this connected understanding, forced underground in the west the disconnected superstitions of all the primitive and pagan societies which the new religions had submerged; all the superstitions, that is to say, save those of each particular religion. For Christianity, although anti-intellectual by the standards of Cicero or Gibbon and anti-scientific by the standards of Galileo or Harvey, was a necessary weapon in destroying the alternative unorganized superstitions inherited from the paleolithic world.

These superstitions were not, to be sure, destroyed. They continued to be held by simple and uneducated people everywhere. But they ceased to be respectable: they had been submerged. In China the superstitious needs of simple people remained unsubmerged. Instead they were diverted into a number of disconnected social channels. The peasant without discouragement continued to worship the gods of his own fields and his own crops. He was also comforted by the native quackery of the Taoists and the naturalized magic of the Buddhists.

With the townsman matters were different. He could take refuge in secret societies in which suppressed religions, especially Buddhism, could disguise themselves. These societies, parallel in their aims and methods with western freemasonry, became an absorbing interest to all dissident elements in the cities. And in later times their underground structure made them the natural channels for revolutionary and also for Mafia-like criminal activities.[1]

A third field of superstitious fancy was organized by the Establishment itself for its own ends. Astrology was as acceptable to emperors and mandarins in China as to Brahmins in India and to pagan (and erring Christian) rulers throughout the west. It first owed its importance to the function of the ruler in calculating the calendar and in deciding accordingly the proper times for ploughing and sowing by the stars. But in the end it came to be the means of timing all the great ceremonial activities of the Son of Heaven.

Thus it happened that when the Jesuits arrived in China under the Ming it was for their knowledge of the physical rather than the spiritual heavens that they slowly gained the favour of the court. It was then that Mattheo Ricci was able to examine the astrolabes and armillary spheres brought to Pekin under the Mongols. They had been shifted under the first Ming Emperor three degrees south, to Nanking. But they had never been adjusted for the difference of latitude. So superstition had undone itself at the very source.[2]

[1] Now open to study only in the overseas Chinese communities within the British settlements of Hong Kong and Singapore (Bloodworth, 1966).

[2] Collis (1941).

By its exploitation at the highest level in an unchallengeable hierarchy superstition undid much more than itself. In the west, social, ethical and religious ideas had been brought, first into opposition, then into connection with experimental science. But in China, as also in India, the only other society where the genetical prerequisites for making this connection were in evidence, the opposition could never be recognized and the connection could never be made. Religion and science, and society itself, were shrunk and shrivelled by their intellectual incoherence and separation. For this reason it might be said at the end of this separate development that the educated classes in China believed in nothing, the uneducated in everything.

e. The Last Dynasty

The differences of religious ideas and social theory between China and the west were deep enough already in the seventeenth century. They were deepened further with the coming of the Manchus in 1644. Under native dynasties attempts at reform had been repeatedly blocked. Economic reform had been squashed by the late Sung Establishment. Exploration and foreign trade had been cut short by the early Ming. But now the capital had been occupied by a foreign power. What line would the new dynasty take?

The Manchus took the line of least resistance. Like the English a century later in India, but with less to offer in compensation, the Manchus decided that the least change was the safest policy. They would stand by the most conservative native interests, social, economic and intellectual. They would keep the old Establishment. Further, for themselves, they would maintain a strict policy of segregation in breeding and in administration. In each great city they would build their own Tartar city. With the Chinese there would be no intermarriage only concubinage. For the emperor even his concubines (from whom his wives were promoted) must all be selected from Manchu families.

Thus the Manchus formed a caste, a closer caste than the Mongols before them. And for this caste they reserved half the administrative posts (for which they were ill-suited). For them too three-quarters of the military guards, the Banners, were also reserved, one-quarter only being open to their bastard hybrid offspring. At the same time, like Roman senators and succeeding western aristocracies, the Manchus denied themselves the despised activities of trade and industry—for which their pure breed, to be sure, naturally unfitted.

So much for the general problem of the Manchus. Their special problem was that of the cleavage, geographical, cultural and genetic, between north and south in their subject Empire. The north had never recovered from the devastations of the Mongols and the ensuing expansion of the desert. The people of the south were now more cultured, more prosperous and more numerous. They had naturally resisted the barbarous invaders most fiercely. Instead of attempting to win their loyalty by generous treatment, the Manchus resolved to squeeze the former rebels out of the public service. The choice of mandarins by examination was to be weighted in favour of the north. And the examinations themselves continued to be weighted in favour of strict Confucian principles.

The political devotion of emperors to high Confucian principles in the Establishment did not prevent them from being equally devoted to the low feelings of the masses. Still in the nineteenth century they were spending their funds on the pious work of repairing Taoist and Buddhist temples and so insuring against popular discontent. In this matter of policy, east and west were entirely at one.

The invariably defensive attitude of the Manchu Establishment, and the inbreeding which underlay it, enfeebled at once the governing race and the native culture. Just when Europe was entering its second stage of advance with social and political, scientific and industrial revolutions, China was being imprisoned in the ideas and methods of an earlier age. The Manchu military and the native mandarins had made themselves into two hardened castes, minorities mutually supporting and mutually selecting one another; depending on one another for the wealth they were able to squeeze out of a nation from whose life they were now equally and utterly divorced.

f. Rebellion and Revolution

The decay of the Manchus was at last exposed to their people and to the world by their collapse in face of the first British aggression in the Opium War of 1840. This evidence was to be confirmed by the success of the western assaults on Pekin in 1860 and 1900. The only reaction to these disasters possible within China was bound to come from regional discontent; that is from the natural genetic cleavage between the old and conservative north and the new and progressive south.

The Tartar and Mongol invasions, which forced the Sung in 1126 to withdraw from K'ai-fêng to Hangchow, and in the end destroyed them, pressed the educated and skilled classes of the northern cities to fly in the same direction and to fly further. They fled to old colonies and to new settlements, to Korea and Japan, to Annam and Java, and to many other countries. But above all they made their new homes in the south. Here, in the Canton basin in the provinces which had been annexed only under the T'ang, they were furthest within China from Pekin, the Mongol and also the Manchu capital. They were also closest to the European traders who were now beginning to enter the southern ports. They soon assimilated the great Arabic-speaking Muslim trading colony of Fukien[1] and in this way must have become well-fitted to engage in friendly commerce with foreigners.

Some of the northerners who had moved into Canton in Sung times became known as 'guest families' or *Hakka*. They survive today as a distinct community, never having intermarried with the Cantonese, and preserving their own archaic northern dialect. They are to be described not as a caste but as a whole encapsulated society. This educated and well-knit community seems to have played a leading part in the forty-year resistance to the Manchu conquest. They suffered, and enjoyed, the consequences of their opposition to

[1] Whose names, Professor FitzGerald tells me, are still to be found in some of the leading families of the province today.

the conquerors. As administrators they became unemployed. But as intellectuals they were freed from the restrictions of the Establishment. It was among them that revolt in the end broke out.

The revolt took an indirect form such as had been known in Europe three centuries earlier. Here was no open economic, political, or military challenge. It began with a rejection, such as we might expect from the Hakka, of the social and religious assumptions of the old Chinese Establishment. And it came to the surface with the announcement in the year 1837 of a new form of Christianity conceived by its founder.

Such was the origin of the T'ai P'ing rebellion. After fourteen years of preaching the leader found himself at the head of an army which proclaimed him as the Heavenly King and seized for him all the central provinces of southern China. After two more years of fighting the T'ai P'ing generals captured Nanking, the greatest walled city in China—or in the world—and made it their capital.

Thus in 1853 the T'ai P'ing leaders set up what proved to be the first modern westernized government known to China. It foreshadowed in many respects that created fifteen years later by the Meiji Emperor in Japan. But it went further. One of their objects was to spread Christianity. It was however Christianity with a difference for the T'ai P'ing leaders had not been baptized.[1] They did not even seem to mind whether it was their own brand of doctrine which was to be adopted, or one of the many more orthodox brands that were being propagated in China at the time by western missionaries.

Another of the T'ai P'ing objects was to emancipate women, beginning by abolishing the atrocious practice of foot-binding. A third object was to open the whole country to foreign trade. The long-standing suspicion and exclusiveness of China, the government and the people, was to give place to such friendship and communication as were familiar in the Christian west.

These policies and purposes expressed the character of the T'ai P'ing leaders. They were, as was said by Europeans in China at the time, a different race from the Manchus and the mandarins, a different race from the people who had been misgoverning China for so long.

Seven years after the T'ai P'ing had set up in Nanking in the centre of China, British and French forces seized Pekin in the north, destroyed the Summer Palaces of the emperors, and brought the Manchu Empire to terms. The terms were that these foreign governments were to control for their own profit the foreign trade of China. Which meant that they at once saw their interest and their duty in helping to its feet the tottering government that had accepted their terms. Willingly they lent their weapons and their commanders to the Manchu Emperor. After another four years of struggle, armies under General Gordon and other Christian officers had defeated the Christian rebels and restored the powers of the least Christian government in the world.

Much may be said for the colonial enterprise of Europeans in Africa, India and elsewhere, but nothing can be said for the exploitation of China

[1] And they failed to translate into Chinese the difficult doctrine of the Trinity. But their policies, we may feel, were founded on a better understanding of Christian principles than those of contemporary European governments (FitzGerald, 1935).

which followed this victory. The T'ai P'ing rebellion was the most fundamental disturbance of Chinese society since the foundation of the Empire. The wars that it engendered are said to have cost the lives of one-third of the 400 million population of China. And with it, in the end, was destroyed one of the great opportunities in the history of mankind. For when revolution came in 1911, the damage that had been done in the preceding fifty years, the long misrule due to the Dowager Empress,[1] the accumulating corruption and humiliation of foreign control, these left no means of recovery except by the coming of a new despotism. That despotism came after another forty years of suffering with the communist victory in 1949 under Mao Tse-tung.

This Communist Revolution, after another twenty years, has confirmed several of the formidable lessons that we had already learnt from the Russian Revolution. Disciplined and unified government has restored strength to the Chinese State, or rather Empire, and self-esteem to the Chinese people. But in doing so it has restored, and more than restored, national isolation. It has exaggerated the Chinese suspicion of foreign governments. It has done so without making any concession to communist governments that are not under its control; it has disregarded communist just as much as Christian ideas of the brotherhood of men and peoples.

From these experiences we may foresee other parallel developments. The Chinese, like the Russian, Communist Party will attempt to establish itself as a governing class. And it will adjust its social policies to this social change. Further evolution, however, can hardly fail to restore some initiative to the Chinese educated class which remains indispensable for government. And with it will come a freer exchange of ideas between nations.

The opportunity of breaking down the barriers of culture and race between east and west has come several times in history. It happened under the T'ang. It happened again with the T'ai P'ing. Each time it was missed. It will be for another generation to see when the chance comes again.

[1] Tzu-Hsi (1838–1908): see Varé (1936).

27

OCEANIA

I. CONTINENTAL ORIGINS

SOUTH-EAST ASIA has a special place in any account of the development of civilization owing at once to its remoteness from the Nuclear Area and its own geographical discontinuity. Split up by high mountains and dense forest and dispersed by the ocean in thousands of islands it was protected from the documentary means of recording its own history. That history has however been revealed to us by other means. The present distribution, development and behaviour of its plants, animals and men tell us a great deal about how they have come to be where they are. And since the whole situation is without parallel it provides us with a cumulative experiment in reconstructing as well as in understanding the processes of history.

South-East Asia was largely occupied as recently as ten thousand years ago by dark peoples conveniently known as Australoid. But ever since that paleolithic time the superior technical skill of the Mongolian peoples in the north has enabled them to expand and to invade the accessible valleys of Burma, Thailand, Viet Nam and finally Malaya and all the islands. They have left the Australoid peoples in possession of only the hills, the forests and the swamps, with their greatest stronghold in still largely unknown New Guinea.[1] It may well be this pressure from the north which pushed the Australoid peoples into colonizing, first Australia and then overseas Melanesia. This great movement created the paleolithic basis of the modern peoples of South-East Asia. But superimposed on it during the first millennium B.C. came the forerunners of the neolithic expansion. Moving along the coasts from the Ganges delta, they brought with them the cultivation of rice and the making of pottery and later, towards the end of the millennium, the forging and use of bronze.

We cannot yet be certain of the order of events following the impact of

[1] See Coon (1962), Map 13, and our endpapers.

these invasions on the paleolithic peoples around the coasts of the islands. We can, however, see what the middle stages of invasion were like if we look at the population of one of the more slowly invaded islands at the present day. The situation in Sarawak as seen by Haddon in 1888 is still much the same today. He found a series of racial strata moving downwards in society and backwards in time as he moved inwards on the island.

The pure Australoid peoples surviving on adjoining islands had disappeared without trace. Farthest inland were the brown nomadic hunters and collectors, the Punan and the Ukit. They had the paleolithic virtues and vices of keen eyesight, alert observation, and incapacity for what neolithic man calls work. Next came the Land Dyaks, neolithic people with primitive agriculture and with headmen having no class character and little power. These people had occupied all the cultivable land during the first millennium A.D. After them had come the warlike agriculturists, the Kayans, forging their own iron weapons and tools and having a class structure with strong chiefs. Next in turn were the Sea Dyaks, originally pirates, aggressive neighbours with shifting agriculture. They were led by Malays, but non-Muslims, for the Dyaks are pig-eating people. Last of all were the three groups of civilized invaders: the Muslim Malays, a highly stratified community led by rajahs; the Chinese immigrants who had made themselves responsible for trade, finance and mining; and in the nineteenth century, the most diverse of all, the Europeans.

This is an historical succession. And it is also an ecologically and socially predictable succession for each newcomer has benefited from his predecessors by trade; or taking advantage of them by war has pushed them back into the mountains and forests. And through hybridization or enslavement he has helped to build a stratified society.

The early stages of this succession depended on two great innovations. The first was the systematic and combined propagation of new crops brought together from Burma, Siam, Malaya and perhaps Java. They were chiefly food crops, as follows:

Great yam (*Dioscorea spp.*) and taro yam (*Colocasia spp.*), sugar-cane, banana and breadfruit; paper mulberry for cloth; and coconut for almost all purposes.

These plants, apart from the coconut, were mostly triploid and sexually sterile. They could therefore be propagated vegetatively without seed. Which means that they could be cultivated with the minimum labour and forethought, a freedom from effort which we know commends itself highly to paleolithic peoples.[1] Thus when stocks of cattle, pigs and domestic fowls arrived from India both these and the immigrant cultivators themselves could multiply their numbers.

The second innovation was that of the outrigger canoe. On the Mekong, Salween and Irrawaddy rivers are still to be seen (according to Hornell) all the steps of development between the dug-out canoe and the outrigger boat with sails. This boat constructed of wood with stone adzes was designed

[1] Problems discussed by Burkill (1951, 1953); see also Merrill (1945); Sharp (1957); Barrau (1960) and Simmonds (1963).

to be propelled by paddles. Later, when sails were added and it proved to be capable of long voyages in the open sea.

Earlier canoes had been intended by their builders for deep-sea fishing but this new vessel they soon used for exploration, expansion and colonization. First, they colonized the accessible shores of the Indonesian islands. But those canoe-builders who learnt the arts of navigation had suddenly opened to themselves wide regions of ocean dotted with uninhabited islands suitable for cultivating the tropical crops which they now had at their disposal. Their base for the next steps was, we suppose, the richest island, Java. From here they set sail across the Indian Ocean. In the first century A.D. (having missed or disregarded Mauritius, Réunion, the Chagos and the Seychelles) they reached and colonized the great uninhabited island of Madagascar. They marked their discovery with their own racial character,[1] their own language, their own canoes and their precious crops. Those Indonesian crops which they had used to sustain them on their voyage of a month or more they soon carried on to the mainland to create a revolution in African life.

II. COLONIZATION BY SEA

In the next two or three centuries, by the co-operation, we must suppose, of designers and artisans, sailors and pilots, the Indonesians developed an improved canoe. They discovered that a single outrigger on either the windward or the leeward side, with half the drag of a double outrigger, was just as good a safeguard in a storm. With it they reached Ceylon and contributed, as we can see, to the racial character of the fisherfolk of Malabar. Then with even greater effect they embarked on their greatest enterprise: they set sail into the Pacific Ocean.

Between 300 and 700 A.D. they ventured out into the great wastes of the central Pacific. They reached Tahiti. At this secondary base in the next five centuries they built great double sailing-canoes which carried up to 250 men and women, larger vessels than any that are known today. With them they made their way to the Marquesas, Hawaii (a new form of Java) and New Zealand. Later still, and perhaps accidentally, they returned north-west and colonized the islands of Micronesia, missing however Bonin and Koto-sho.[2] They also returned south-west and perhaps in the fifteenth century reached and risked a landing on the closer-packed islands of Melanesia already colonized by Australoid peoples from New Guinea whose colour they modified and whose language they sometimes displaced.[3] They had by 1500 colonized every one of the main islands of the Pacific.

The rapidity of these movements and the expansions of population which resulted from them are without parallel in the history of man except perhaps in the colonization of America during the last ice age. It is therefore

[1] The Malagasies, no longer great navigators, still with their ancestral instinct, direct strangers, as men of Norse extraction often will, by the points of the compass rather than by left or right hands (Rogers, 1962).

[2] Leach (1937).

[3] See Firth (1961) on Tikopia.

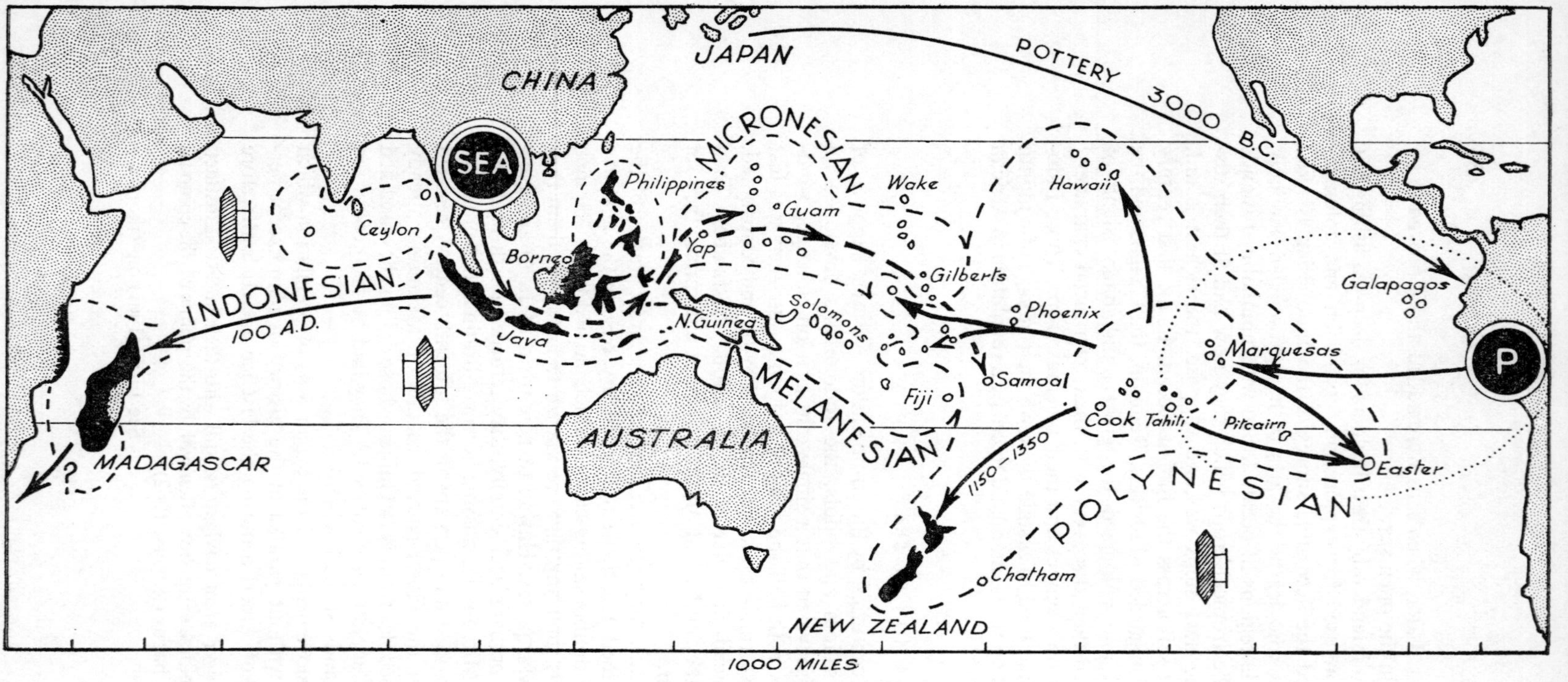

Fig. 20 The Indonesian Expansion 500 B.C – A.D 1500

1. *Canoe Distribution:* (i) Double Outriggers from coasts shown black: Indonesian and Madagascan (after Haddon & Hornell 1936, Hornell 1946)
   (ii) Single Outriggers within three Pacific language areas
2. *Lines of Colonization* (after Sharp, 1956, and others)
3. *Language Areas:* Indonesian, Polynesian, Micronesian and Melanesian (after Coon 1965, Map 14 and Goode's Atlas, 1964, p. 46)

(SEA), (P) & (J) sources of original Pacific Island food plants, thus:
S.E. Asia: Breadfruit,[1] Banana,[1] Yam,[1] Taro,[1] Cocoanut[2].
Peru: Sweet Potato[1] (Kumara[3]).
Java: Sugar Cane.

(1) Seedless triploid varieties (2) same name from Madagascar to Hawaii (3) same name

significant that both expansions entailed, as we might expect, the loss of the B blood group, the least frequent of the ABO alleles.[1] With it may well have been lost, in both America and Oceania, resistance to some of those diseases which proved so disastrous to the isolated peoples when Europeans reintroduced them.

The Indonesian expansion left the people divided into what are linguistically related groups in Madagascar, in Polynesia and in Micronesia, and the less closely related, physically diverse and obviously hybridized Melanesians. Among these the kinship of the Polynesians, apart from the blood groups, is most strikingly shown by their speech. Gibbings has described its phonetic homogeneity, a wide musical register corresponding to an abundance of vowels and a deficiency of consonants. These are indelibly marked racial characters found in association nowhere else in the world except in China.

III. THE NAVIGATORS

The study of the Indonesian colonizations, owing to the vast dispersal and separately identifiable histories of the islands they occupied, is of importance quite disproportionate to the numbers and character of the people concerned. How are we to suppose that it was accomplished? A thousand years was available. Superb skills in boat-building and navigation were also available. Were the canoe voyages guided by premeditated planning? Or were they, as Captain Cook and lately Andrew Sharp have supposed, the work of castaways, the results of accident and disaster? Or had it something of both?

The geographical complexity of the oceans colonized by the Indonesians has given us what we can turn into exceptional evidence of the modes of colonization. In Polynesia alone there are three hundred large habitable islands and innumerable small ones. Some are high and volcanic and rich in Asiatic flora like Hawaii and Tahiti. Others are low atolls of coral with few plants. Some are clustered, others solitary.

In view of the immense distances covered, it is hard to understand the results except in terms of voyages being deliberately planned with known and previously explored destinations. The evidence on the other hand in favour of accident has been assembled by Sharp.

First there are the large number of islands which were still uninhabited in the eighteenth century. Most of these are marked by the fact that they were necessarily given European names by their discoverers, such as the Bonin Islands near Japan, Christmas Island on the equator, Norfolk and Chatham Islands in the south and Pitcairn the refuge of the *Bounty* mutineers. Secondly, some of these islands had evidently been visited by castaways. For in the Phoenix Islands rats had landed and bred; and on Pitcairn breadfruit had established itself; they had been brought by men without women. And thirdly, the boundaries of the three racial divisions of Oceania are themselves erratic. Tikopia and Rennell within Melanesia, and other islands as far as Nikuoru in Micronesia, have a Polynesian character.

These observations suggest, however, not accident so much as interruption.

[1] Mourant (1954); Simmons *et al.* (1965).

Europeans, to be sure, equipped with their sailing ships, mariners' compasses, quadrants and eventually chronometers, discovered uninhabited islands in Polynesia. But they were less important islands than the hitherto undiscovered or deserted islands of other oceans, Madeira, and Azores, Falklands, Juan Fernandez and Galápagos. Some of these had, like those in Polynesia, been visited and deserted earlier: the Azores by Carthaginians, the Galápagos by Peruvians. In all oceans, planned and accidental discovery must have continued side by side.

In Oceania, however, there were special grounds for interruption. As colonization advanced and populations increased, war, slavery, hybridization and finally disease played their apparently accidental part in arresting and diverting the colonists. Malaria and yaws preceded the introduction of the great European killing diseases, smallpox and measles.[1] The climax of enterprise had, it seems, already passed when Magellan sailed his ships through the straits into the Pacific.

In order to assess the relative importance of accident and planning in Oceanic colonization we now need to bring together the evidence of different kinds in relation to particularly significant islands.

IV. EASTER ISLAND

Here is a Polynesian island notable beyond all others ever since its discovery by Europeans in 1722. At that time (according to Heyerdahl) it had been inhabited for a thousand years. But since 1400 miles of ocean separated its inhabitants from their nearest living neighbours, and since they had no wood to replace the canoes with which they had arrived on the island, they had lost their canoes and with them their knowledge of any world outside their own. Indeed they may well, like certain Caroline Islanders in a like case, have come to believe that they were the only people in the world.

The Easter Islanders had brought fowls and rats with them from a more central part of Polynesia. But they had no pigs or dogs, no coconuts or breadfruit. Evidently therefore their colonization had not been planned. But they had acquired one food plant whose presence affected, not only the history of the Pacific islands, but all of our interpretation of that history. They had the sweet potato.

The sweet potato, *Ipomoea batatas*, comes from tropical America where it occurs in many forms both wild and cultivated. Its cultivated forms are mostly sterile but their roots, carried by canoe, serve both for the voyagers' food and their own propagation at the end of the voyage.

The sweet potato had been taken all over the Pacific before the Europeans arrived there, that is probably before 1500. And everywhere from Hawaii to New Zealand it was known by the Amerindian name of *kumara*. It had been brought into the Pacific by men, in boats, and to be precise, from Ecuador.[2]

Since there was never any reverse traffic from Easter Island to the rest of the Pacific, the sweet potato must have been brought to some less remote islands, such as the Marquesas, and distributed from them. The evidence of

[1] See Luke (1962). [2] Barrau (1957, 1960, 1961); Yen (1963).

this course was found by Heyerdahl in the shape of stone statues of the kinds which are characteristic of the Amerindian peoples from Peru and Ecuador to the Maya country of Mexico. The enormous stone heads and stone walls of Easter Island have their counterpart in the Marquesas and there are traces of stone-quarrying and fortification in the intermediate islands, even in Pitcairn. Moreover on Easter Island there occur stone tablets with picture writing arranged in reversed boustrophedon style of a kind which is known nowhere else in the world save among the Cuna Indians of Panama.

These discoveries support the view that voyagers, exiles, explorers or castaways from the American coasts reached the Marquesas and other islands and established themselves there. They probably reached the uninhabited Galápagos Islands without women and consequently died out—leaving only pottery (as found by Heyerdahl) as evidence of their visit. If they arrived, as they probably did, in Polynesia also without women and without sufficient materials for raising crops (for the sweet potato alone is scarcely enough) they must have come after the Polynesian settlement. Having bred with Polynesian women, their offspring would have survived as a new hybrid strain.

According to the traditions collected by Heyerdahl there was in Easter Island a caste division between priestly rulers, the 'long ears' commemorated by the stone statues, and the people who worked with their hands. The vast labour needed for cutting, transporting and erecting the statues seems to demand, just as it did in Egypt, a disciplined social order based on just such a hierarchical class structure. This structure seems to have broken down with the depopulation which followed the two disastrous contacts with Europeans.[1]

Successive colonizations by contrasted races, the first Polynesian, planned, and mixed in sexes, the second Amerindian, accidental and only male, would account for the development in eastern Polynesia of a stratified society having only the Polynesian language. The same combination of accident and planning is shown by the crops. In Easter Island they have the marks of accident. But in the Pacific as a whole they demand planning.

This evidence of the combination of accident and planning allows us to consider the evolution of Polynesian societies in general.

V. THE RISE AND FALL OF ISLAND SOCIETIES

In the course of thirty generations great communities grew up in all the larger islands both central and peripheral. The European intrusion of the nineteenth century partly disintegrated this structure since all stocks that were not changed by hybridization with the newcomers were reduced by their diseases. But we know that before this interference there was in all of them an hereditary class structure.[2]

[1] The social structure of the island was finally broken by a Peruvian slave raid followed by a smallpox epidemic in 1862. But there is still time for blood group studies of eastern Polynesia to answer this and other disputed questions of its history.

[2] Rivers (1914, 1924); Grimble on the Gilbert and Ellice Islands (1952); Sahlins (1958); Marsack (1961); Firth (1961); Luke (1962).

At the head of society stood kings and chieftains tracing their lineage in Samoa or Tonga for the whole thirty generations and worshipping their own gods often with the assistance of a related class of priests. For example the dynasty of Tonga fifteen generations ago split into priestly and secular lines which were only recently reunited in the person of Queen Salote (1918–65). Related to these also was a landowning class. On a lower level stood the technical castes at the head of which spiritually and socially stood the canoe-makers whose finest masterpieces we may still see in museums. Beneath them were the pilots, and the sailors, the builders and the carpenters, the fishermen and the peasants. And in Tonga, according to Rivers, there were sub-castes of masons, net-makers, barbers, cooks, tattooers, morticians, and club and whale-tooth carvers.

The histories of the islands show that the kings and the privileged classes won their status in war. And the slave classes of New Zealand and of Fiji showed what war did to those at the other end of the scale. In New Zealand tradition asserts that the later colonists, arriving in a great fleet, subdued their predecessors. In Fiji the taller, paler Polynesians similarly subdued the darker Melanesians who were enslaved or driven into the hills. And, in the Marquesas as well as in Fiji, the conquered might suffer from the rituals of cannibalism.

No doubt, as we find elsewhere, it was from a general segregation between victor and vanquished, or, as Rivers expressed it, between the 'enterprising stranger' and the obedient native, that the separation of ruler and ruled and the basic class structure originally derived. But from a limited crossing, a restricted hybridization, between them there arose the later extremes of genetic diversification of occupations, and of the castes which pursued and maintained them.

It may be argued that the Hawaiians claimed to be the 'purest' of Polynesians. So they were in respect of colour and in their distance from coloured Melanesia.[1] But they had, within their colours, the steepest of class gradients and the most despotic of kings. Like the English colonists in America, they must therefore have had the genetic basis of these class distinctions when they arrived. The Hawaiians and the Maoris might therefore reflect with pride that their colonies were the reward of the longest, the most highly skilled and most carefully planned of all navigations. And that they reached their destinations, not as chance castaways, but as already differentiated and organized societies.

The processes by which the island societies arose cannot however be fully understood without examining the somewhat better authenticated processes by which they have decayed. So long as they were not exposed to new and widespread infections, but only to the dangers of war and the benefits of migration and hybridization, the oceanic populations seemed to be vigorously developing. But they were decaying in two respects. The first concerned governing classes. Real authority of chieftains, notably in the Gilberts and

[1] The Oceanic people are conscious of colour wherever they see it. Girls who wish to rise in society by a favourable marriage will bleach their skins in Micronesia as diligently as in any other colour-graded population (Grimble, 1952).

Samoa,[1] had often been replaced by merely ceremonial activities, a decay analogous to that among the equalitarian Hamitic tribes in Africa.

Closer at hand however is the analogy with what has happened in certain small island societies to the ordinary professional castes.[2] In islands all the way from Hawaii to New Zealand, from Tonga to Tikopia, the making of the outrigger canoe was the work of a caste. But in certain islands this caste, originally indispensable for the whole colonization of Oceania, had died out. The causes were various, definable and sometimes interlocking. In Easter Island it was simply through lack of wood. In Woodlark, near New Guinea, it was secondary and indirect being due to the extinction of the caste of stone adze-makers. In the New Hebrides it happened directly through the extinction of the canoe-making caste themselves. Whatever these causes the consequences would be various and partly inevitable: unless, as happened in one island, the caste was recovered by immigration from outside, there was an end to migration and an end to sea fishing.

Different kinds of sequence in cause and effect are shown by the gradual failures of pottery-making and bow-and-arrow-making in the islands over several centuries. This was not due, Rivers argues, to lack of clay or of wood. It was due to local extinction of castes which could not readily be recruited by one small island from another. As in advanced societies, the danger of caste extinction is enhanced rather than diminished when a particular caste, whether canoe-making or arrow-making, enhances its status by acquiring, perhaps through intermarriage, a priestly activity and in consequence a parasitic habit.[3]

Such extinction in very small populations might be at random but in general it would be favoured in two ways: either from too much inbreeding which might destroy the stock, or from too much outbreeding which might destroy the skill. An equilibrium which can be easily maintained in large and accessible societies will easily fail in small and inaccessible ones.

All the island communities are assemblies of co-operating and complementary castes. The loss of any one of these castes entailed an irreversible loss to the culture of the community. It was irreversible because the castes were created at an earlier stage of development when movement and hybridization were free owing to the processes of discovery. But for this reason also it is clear that the great discoveries were made by people whose stratified structure was created, partly before and partly during, their movement into the Pacific. In fact just at the time when their kings claim to have established themselves. Further, this structure was not produced by chance castaways but by migrations planned by the founders of these royal lines.

The knowledge of what happens in these island societies, we can now see, is important beyond the islands themselves for the study of all societies. For great continental societies, as we have learnt, are divided by social distinctions and genetic barriers into groups which closely compare with the map of Oceania. In India the islands are visible to the least discerning eye. In Europe their shores and shoals are blurred but they none the less exist. The coming

[1] Marsack (1961). [2] Rivers (1912); Raglan (1939, 1962).

[3] see Thurnwald (1932, p. 127).

of a dark age on the overthrow of the Roman Empire meant the merging and disappearance of many islands which were recovered (in new shapes) after a thousand years of selective movement, selective assortment, and selective breeding. But the map of the Pacific shows us that no such creative reconstruction could ever happen there.

VI. EUROPEAN EPILOGUE

The immense area of the Pacific and the immense number of its populated islands make each of them a separate workshop in which the effects of the European discovery can be separately studied. The island of Tahiti, however, is not only central in the ocean but also in the earlier history of Polynesia and in the documentation of Europeans.

The island was discovered by the Spanish navigator Quiros in 1606. But its real uncovering came 160 years later. Wallis in 1767, Bougainville in 1768, Cook in 1769 and in following years, a Spanish vessel in 1774, Bligh in 1791 (taking away cuttings of the seedless breadfruit in his *Bounty*), the London Missionary Society (settling permanently for conversion) in 1797, the Russian explorer, Bellingshausen (noting the consequences of conversion to Protestant Christianity) in 1820, all these led up to the French annexation in 1843. The population of Tahiti had by then been reduced from an original 40,000 to about 6000 and the character and way of life of the surviving inhabitants had been proportionately diminished by this fatal impact.[1]

What had happened? One factor was the capacity of the leading Europeans for long-range purposeful activities forcing their own equipment and ideas, especially their ideas about religion and sexual reproduction, on populations who were genetically unsuited to use them. Both firearms and Christianity require the slow adaptation which Europeans had had time to allow them. The Polynesians had been evolved as navigators but as cultivators they had never depended for their survival on the labour or the foresight needed to grow grain. They might have (as Melville says in *Typee* and *Omoo*) twenty words to express the stages in growth of a coconut but 'days and years were all the same to them'. The word for *time*, according to Marsack, had to be taken in Samoa from the English.

When Europeans discovered what rich rewards could be gained from growing sugar-cane on Fiji or mining phosphates in the Gilbert Islands they therefore imported Indian and Chinese labourers for these purposes. Thus they created more productive societies, but societies divided between races who had nothing to offer one another but strife.[2] Conversely when Polynesians were mistakenly deported as indentured farm workers to Australia (under the name of *Kanakas*) the experiment was a failure for both sides and it was abandoned.[3]

[1] To use the appropriate phrase of Alan Moorehead (1966). See also Darwin (1845); Melville (1847); and Graves (1949).

[2] Grimble (1952); Luke (1962).

[3] British governments felt able to encourage indentured labour in the Pacific during the nineteenth century while busily suppressing the slavetrade in the Atlantic (see Horton, 1965).

The great disaster for the Polynesians arose, however, from the blind unplanned and unforeseen biological effects of the contact between long-separated races. The islanders were prepared to receive Cook's gifts of horses, cattle, sheep, geese and citrus fruits, the produce of Europe and Asia, and they were rightly grateful. But his sailors and their successors of several nations quickly conveyed to them the diseases of all these continents and of America as well. Yaws and malaria they had brought themselves from Melanesia. But tuberculosis, measles and gonorrhoea they received from Europe; smallpox and typhoid from Asia; syphilis from America. These were gifts for which the Polynesians were unprepared.

Sexual promiscuity had been entirely suitable in the disease-free island whose population had been limited only by perversion, abortion and infanticide. But it now gave rapid circulation to all the new infections but especially to the venereal diseases. Gradually, after three generations of infection, hybridization and selection, the population of Tahiti, as would be expected, began to recover and it has, after six generations, returned to what it was before Bougainville and Cook accepted the hospitality of the islanders. But it is now a different population. The castes which maintained the arts on which the way of life of the Ocean People had rested, castes created in thirty generations, had in six generations fallen to pieces. The mutual need, mutual fostering, and mutual selection had all dissolved together.[1]

[1] Gibbings (1948); Firth (1961).

28

AFRICA

I. BEFORE AGRICULTURE

THE COASTLINE OF AFRICA nowhere greatly encourages sailors or fishermen. It is not surprising therefore that the islands around the continent and out of sight of the shore, in late paleolithic times, still remained uninhabited. But the continent itself was more evenly populated than it is today and more fully populated than Europe at that time. By the evidence they have left in the earth, as well as by our knowledge of their successors, we may divide the scattered tribes of its inhabitants into three kinds.

To speak first of those who have been driven farthest, there are the people known as Capoids to the anthropologist, as Khoisan to the linguist, or as Bushmen to the traveller, since they were so named by the Dutch of the Cape in the seventeenth century. They are hunters and collectors of the dry steppes or *veld*. They are all that remains of the people whose rock paintings record their skill of eye and hand all the way from the Cape through the Sahara to the Atlas mountains. Now they are confined to the Kalahari desert, itself enlarging as they diminish, to small pockets in the Transvaal, and, as the hybrid Sandawe, to a district of Tanzania.

We recognize the Bushmen by their clicked speech, by their Mongoloid skins, eyelids and cheek-bones and by the storage of fat in the buttocks of their women. By their wrinkled skins when meat is scarce, we recognize them also as the children of the African desert with its cycle of plenty and famine. And by their sexual apparatus, and their abilities in finding the animals and plants they need, we know them to be quite unique. They also know themselves to be unique. Confident in their immemorial and racial addiction to hunting they hold their neighbours in contempt both for their habits and their colour; and they avoid although they cannot always reject hybridization. Their hybrids with the expanding Negroes indeed already occupy a large part of South Africa. And with Europeans also they are interfertile.[1]

In the protection of the equatorial rain forest there lived a different kind of people, the pygmies. There are other races of pygmies living on islands, the Andamans, the Philippines, and New Guinea. But the people of the Congo forest lived and still live on an island they have created themselves, an island of smell. All the great races of man differ in smell; they dislike one another's smell and are kept apart by it. But in the nostrils of all other races the pygmies positively stink. It is a property which has arisen from their genetic and ecological isolation. But as with intelligence, having arisen it reinforces the conditions from which it arose. It is a barrier to hybridization. And its effectiveness is conclusively demonstrated by their difference in height and colour from the taller and darker Negro peoples who surround them.

Like the Bushmen these pygmies are a race attached to a retreating habitat. They also therefore survive only as a retreating people, as relics living in racial and linguistic as well as environmental islands. The Negroes who surround them and despise them are again despised by them since, like the Bushmen, the pygmies know how to live where no one else can live. Like the Bushmen therefore they have changed if at all only in the direction of greater specialization and even smaller size.[2]

But there was a third kind of people in Africa, who were more diverse and less specialized than the forest and desert hunters. These were people who, profiting from the bows and harpoons which they had themselves improved, were able to form permanent settlements in the most favoured regions of the Nile, the Niger and the Rift valleys. These were woolly-haired, black-skinned people, ancestors of the Negroes and themselves a new race in process of development and differentiation.

It was these people who received the messages and assimilated the messengers of the new agricultural way of life coming up the Nile valley in the sixth millennium B.C. What they received and assimilated however was not agriculture itself. The art of making pottery moved faster into the tropics and ran ahead of the arts of agriculture and stock-raising. Pottery quickly made its appearance from the Niger to the Rift valley lakes: the crops and stock did not follow for another two or three millennia.[3]

This prolonged and, as we may say, selective arrest of movement was due to the same cause as in China. Clay and even fuel for pottery were everywhere for the taking. But domesticated crops and stocks, like the farmer who brought them, had to be adapted to the new climates. But, unlike him, they had no means of changing themselves to suit these climates by crossing with wild relatives, with their paleolithic precursors, already adapted to the local con-

[1] Schapera (1930); Trevor (1950); Tobias (1954, 1959); Story (1958); Laurens van der Post (1961); and Coon (1965).

[2] Moorehead (1959); Turnbull (1961); Schaller (1960).

[3] Oliver and Fage (1962); Slye (1962). Similarly in the Amazon valley, the Mato Grosso, the art of making pottery is still spreading from pre-Columbian Peru apparently through the capture of neolithic women by the men of hunting tribes (Cowell, 1960).

ditions. There were no wild wheat or barley and no wild cattle or sheep in Africa any more than there were in China. What happened?

II. FARMERS AND HERDSMEN: THE FOUR STREAMS

The Hamitic-speaking people from Palestine or Arabia were versatile or dual-purpose or mixed farmers and herdsmen. Having entered the Nile valley they spread out in four streams flowing in four directions. West they turned along the Mediterranean coast hybridizing with the fair-skinned people of the Atlas mountains. Thus they established the farmers and herdsmen who populated the whole of North-West Africa who constituted the new Berber race and spoke the new western Hamitic languages. We are able to find out how these people fared and who followed them owing to the unique position, at the end of their journey, of the Canary Isles.

The seven Canary Isles lie between 100 and 250 miles off the coast of Africa at latitude 28°. The people who colonized them were isolated from the continent and from one another, owing to their having no metal or hard stone to make boats for the return voyage against the offshore currents. They were successively marooned and developed, like Darwin's finches on the Galápagos Isles, into separate races. This allows us to trace the separation of waves of people crossing the continent and derived from the neolithic and later expansions. Hooton's careful study has led him to suggest that there were seven successive colonizations of the islands. These would cover the period between about 2000 B.C. and A.D. 1000 as follows:

(i) Mediterranean-Negroid people with sheep and goats but no crops or pots, i.e. neolithic pastoralists. Non-warlike. Survive in westernmost *Hierro*.

(ii) Caucasian-Capoid people with barley, pottery and also the dog-worship and dog-eating after which (following Pliny) the islands came to be named. These warlike people brought the whistling language to *Gomera* (1500 B.C.).

(iii) Tall warrior invaders, said to be of Nordic type, became kings in the large central islands of *Gran Canaria* and *Tenerife*; perhaps they brought the Berber dialect of the Guanches.

(iv) A shorter, possibly Semitic people brought in wheat, fine pottery and bronze. Repelled from *Tenerife*, they occupied *Gran Canaria* (*c.* 800 B.C.).

(v) Carthaginian explorers and slave raiders left Numidian (i.e. Berber) inscriptions in the peaceful island of *Hierro* (*c.* 300 B.C.). (A Roman peace followed from 200 B.C. to A.D. 400.)

(vi) Arab invaders (the 'Saracen Kings') mastered the eastern islands of *Lanzarote* and *Fuerteventura* (A.D. 1100).

(vii) Franco-Spanish conquest of the whole group (A.D. 1401–95).

This record preserved by the islands indicates that as in Asia the fast-moving pastoralists left the farmer behind in their expansion. And similarly the light shifting farmers with their barley and dogs left behind the heavy settled farmers with their wheat, pottery and bronze. Something more is shown by the remains of the separate societies. There are great differences in the character of the peoples not only in the different islands successively colonized but also within each of the larger islands.[1] Thus differentiated or racially stratified societies seem to have been established by the later invaders. These societies fiercely maintained their independence against the Spanish conquerors.

So much for the western stream and its diversification on its three-thousand-mile journey across Africa.

Two other streams flowed across the steppes to the east and to the west of the Nile. For the most part these were perforce herdsmen whose herds multiplied to destroy the pasture they excessively grazed. Slowly, in seven thousand years they converted their steppes into the Eastern and the Western Deserts. In the east they survive today little changed as the Beja. In the west they underwent great changes as the fertile prairies they occupied slowly dried out. The great irrigation works they built in later times when they were known as Garamantes and Gaetuli (discussed by Wellard) are now covered with sand. But they bear witness to the long struggle of the cultivators as they retreated into the scattered oases of the Fezzan and the Tibesti.

What mattered for the future of Africa however was the stream, or rather the slow trickle, of Hamitic farmers and herdsmen who made their way up the Nile. These people, as we have seen, settled in Egypt. They then overflowed into Nubia or the land of Cush. Approaching the foothills of Abyssinia they penetrated the region between the upper branches of the Nile which has been called the island of Meroë. At that time it was well-watered forest country. Here they met the Negroes with whom later they were to create first a stratified society and later by hybridization a new race of Nilo-Hamites. Here they had found the door into Africa.

III. THE DOOR INTO AFRICA

During the course of this evolution the Hamites undertook several decisive enterprises the results of which issued in succession from the land of Cush. The first was that in the fifth millennium they domesticated the ass who became the bearer of their caravans until the camel took his place four thousand years later. The second was that they took their agriculture up the valleys and on to the tableland of Abyssinia. The rise of 5000 feet demanded an ecological transformation in the men, in their crops, and in their cattle. But it was accomplished. In the third millennium people of highly Egyptian character were building their megalithic monuments in the highlands.[2]

On this journey the methods as well as the materials of agriculture were transformed. Terraced cultivation was organized although, for reasons we shall consider later, it was not maintained. The decay in Abyssinia seems however to have prepared the way for an advance beyond it.

In their changing habitat the wheat and barley introduced by the advancing farmers were often displaced by introducing weeds from the immensely

[1] Shown by the skulls in the Museum of Santa Cruz (Cuscoy, 1958).

[2] Jésman (1963).

variable wild grains of tropical Africa. From these, by unconscious selection, the women cultivators with their flint hoes and sickles produced two valuable new crops, great millet and sesame. In the second millennium these crops spread north and south of the rain forest and also eastwards to the coast. Thence they passed by the Sabaean Lane, or by coastwise voyage, to the Indus valley. And thence again, later still, all over the tropical world.[1]

The new African grains were one of the foundations of the future African peoples not only in themselves and in Africa but as a preparation for the exchange of crops, stock and people between continents.

What came on the return voyage from the Indus valley were cotton and cattle. The cotton was fairly soon (at least in 400 B.C.) to be spun and woven in Meroë. The Indian cattle, and inevitably the herdsmen who brought them, were hybridized with the native stocks. The Hamitic Longhorns, and the Shorthorns that followed them in Old Kingdom Egypt, had already been taken along all the watered coasts and valleys of North Africa and even into the forests of West Africa. But in Abyssinia they were now crossed with the humped zebu cattle arriving from India. It was therefore from Abyssinia that there issued the new hybrid races, intermediate and recombined in character, conveniently known as Sanga cattle. And it was these Sanga cattle with their still predominantly Hamitic herdsmen who crossed the equator and colonized South Africa. During the first millennium B.C. it seems likely that the herdsmen reached the Cape.[2]

IV. MEROË

Meanwhile the Cushite kingdom was governed by exiles or adventurers, priests or kings, who had left Egypt to make their fortunes in the rich gold-producing land to the south. When Egypt had decayed they used their wealth and strength to return and establish their own dynasty in the land of their forefathers. And when in turn they were driven out of Thebes and Napata by the Assyrians they were able to restore their power in Meroë. For the Assyrians worked with iron, fought with iron and conquered with iron. They needed fuel and the Kingdom of Meroë, too remote to conquer, still had the unfelled forest to provide it. Gold, bronze and now iron were the materials which drew the men who knew how to work them to Meroë. They made of it, for nearly a thousand years, not only the door into Africa but also the workshop and the marshalling-yard of the continent.[3]

During this thousand years when such great things were happening in Europe and China we have to note with equal attention what happened and what failed to happen in the world of Meroë. From Meroë divine kings, mounted on horseback, armed with bronze and iron weapons, and perhaps, as tradition asserts, with some Jewish followers, spread across Africa as far as the Yoruba tribe, the Niger valley and the Kingdom of Ghana. But after these military and spiritual triumphs there followed no writing, no wheel,

[1] Burkill (1953); Doggett (1965).

[2] See Seligman (1957); Clark (1962, 1964); Singer and Lehmann (1963); Payne (1964).

[3] Arkell (1955); Oliver (1961); Oliver and Fage (1962).

no plough, and no smelting of iron. The scholars and craftsmen who were needed to maintain and propagate these arts did not venture forth on the expeditions of warriors and kings. What happened to the kings themselves is therefore concealed from us. And the writing of Meroë itself, a cursive, presumably alphabetic, but also perhaps somewhat secret, script, is still undeciphered.

But after a thousand years a change came. By that time the people of Meroë, like the people of Sumer, had impoverished their land. They had felled the forests to smelt the iron. Now therefore it was the turn of the people on newer land, higher up in the hills. The moment came when the district of Axum was invaded and subdued by a horse-riding, Semitic-speaking, scribe-maintaining warrior people from Arabia who had grown strong by protecting and exploiting the spice merchants of the Yemen. In the year 333 A.D. the Axumites were converted to the Coptic Christianity of Alexandria and a few years later with crusading zeal they fell upon their rich pagan neighbours in Meroë and put an end to their industry and indeed their whole society.

The new Christians were the Amharic governing class which has remained in power in Abyssinia, despite Falasha and Muslim vicissitudes, ever since that time. As their soil and their civilization have in turn slowly decayed they have retreated into the safety of the agricultural highlands shifting their headquarters (one can hardly call it a capital) first to Gondar and then in the nineteenth century to Addis Ababa. The sack of Meroë was their one achievement but its consequences are with us today. For with its priestly government they had dispersed, or, shall we say, released, the iron-workers. Just as had happened earlier in Anatolia the caste still held on to its secrets. But henceforth they were put at the disposal of most of the peoples of the continent. For the first time the smiths were free to come and go, to mine and forge iron for any tribe in Africa.

West Africa, alone at that time, already had its iron-workers. A tribe of pastoral Berbers, the Tuareg, had established horse caravans across the not-so-dry Sahara for the Carthaginian service. They must have been served by the same kinds of attendant castes that they have, as we shall see, today. And, since they were trading in gold and in slaves they required weapons. It seems very likely therefore that they maintained a caste of smiths who no doubt would have reached them from Phoenicia.

Since the fall of Meroë such castes of iron-workers have been wandering all over Africa much as they have done in Arabia or India. They are analogous to the gipsies and other wandering peoples in Europe who specialize in working as tinkers. Sometimes these artisans speak the language of the settled people being known then in England as travellers; and sometimes, despite some hybridization, they have kept their own language which they have derived from India and are then known by many misleading names, such as gipsies, *zigeuner* or Romany; and sometimes they are derived from hybridization between gipsies and the settled folk and have taken the settled language when they are known again by other names such as Didikai.[1]

[1] For their history and behaviour see Clébert (1961) or George Borrow (1841); for their evolution and genetics see Arnold (1959) and Darlington (1959b).

But the iron-working castes of Africa are even more diverse and more important than their analogues in Europe. They have evolved from their several origins in Meroë, among the Berber tribes, and by later immigration from Arabia.

Since they have always remained endogamous castes the smiths have also kept their own physical as well as occupational character. Sometimes also like the Balemba, whom we recognize by their Hebrew mythology and rituals, they have also kept their own religious character. Among the pastoral Hamitic people of the east, such as the Masai and Gallas (as Rivers noted) they have even kept their own language. These last smiths are on a social level with the warriors, being indeed indispensable to them. On the other hand, among the white Tuareg to whom they were equally indispensable, they have the servile status of all the other black castes. Colour and probably temperament, not service, defined their social position.

Among the black tribes of Africa the black castes of craftsmen can be seen to change their status with their value. Thus the status of native miners and metal workers was formerly higher. In the twelfth century they could export iron ore in Arab dhows from Zanzibar to Malabar. But in the last century European ore has ruined the native trade; the native castes have therefore lost their status and merged in the tribes with which they had been associated to form homogeneous societies. No doubt such fusions are responsible for the origin of tribes with more versatile skills. Such fusions could be either vertical, to give such people as the copper-workers of Musina in the Transvaal who mined, smelted and forged their copper, or they could be horizontal, to give tribes like the Gwaris of Nigeria whose men worked with metal, wood and leather, while their women worked with pottery, tiles and, since cultivation is always in their hands, the hoe.[1]

V. THE BANTU

a. Their Origin and Expansion

At about the same time as the spread of iron-working north of the equator in Africa, south of the equator an equally far-reaching change occurred with a complementary effect. This began with the introduction by the Indonesians of their food plants into Madagascar: great yams, taros and bananas proved to be the main providers but with them came breadfruit and coconuts, sugar-cane and rice.[2]

Thus where the new tropical crops met the new iron-workers in the centre of Africa, probably in the Congo basin, the men were provided with new iron spearheads, the women with new iron hoes and both with abundant new sources of food. And it was in this region and about the fifth or sixth century A.D. that the expansion of Bantu-speaking peoples began.

[1] van Warmelo (1940); Davidson (1959); Slye (1963).

[2] The Indonesian theory is Murdock's; the entrance by Madagascar is discussed by Oliver and Fage (1962); confirmatory botanical evidence we owe to Simmonds (1962). The possibility is by no means excluded of an additional Indonesian expansion by sea round the Cape to West Africa (Hutton, 1946; Gray, 1962; Kirk, 1962).

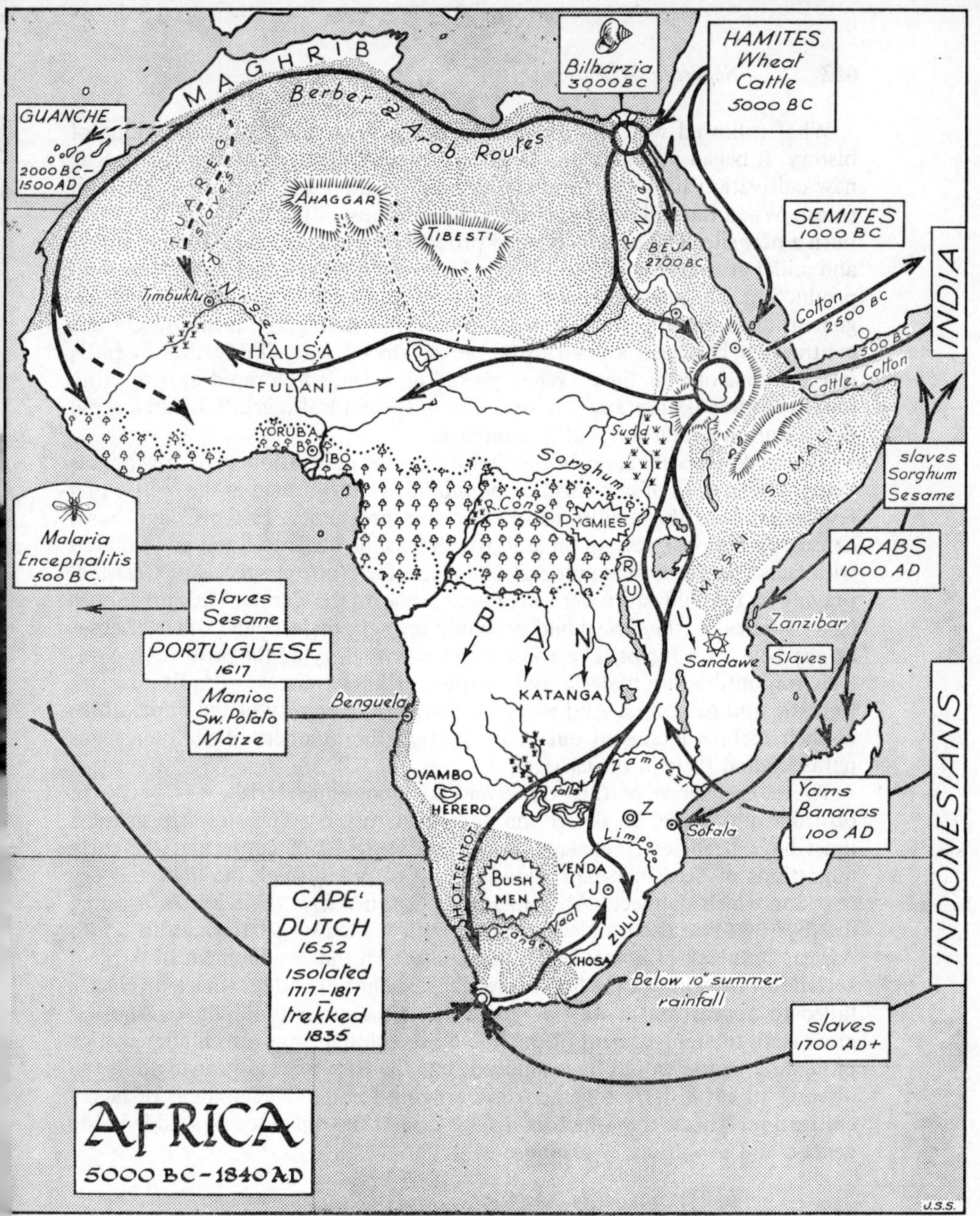

Fig. 21. The Colonization of Africa

Map showing: i. The lakes, rivers, cities, tribes and peoples of Africa mentioned in the text.
ii. The main agricultural and also malarial and often marshy zones of moderate rainfall between the dry steppes and the rain forest.
iii. The great cattleways of all periods free of tsetse flies.
iv. The strongholds of the paleolithic peoples, Bushmen and pygmies.
v. The probable centres of origin of the socially and genetically significant diseases.
vi. The chief colonizing movements into Africa by Hamites, Semites, Indonesians, Arabs, Portuguese and Dutch.
vii. The places of origin or routes of incoming and outgoing of the chief African crops.
viii. The incoming and outgoing slave routes of different periods.
ix. The mining region of Katanga, source of copper, cobalt, manganese, tin, zinc and radium.

Races after Seligman (1957) and Coon (1965); language after Coon and Schapera; historical development after Oliver and Fage (1962); plant and animal migrations after Burkill, et al.; *Bushmen after Trevor; pre-history from Basil Davidson.*

What followed was one of the half-dozen great linguistic expansions of history. It began probably on the eastern edge of the tropical rain forest. The new cultivation took the form of periodic slashing and burning of areas of forest. When the soil of each clearing was exhausted the family moved on to burn a new site. The beginners were probably hybrids between hunters inside and millet growers outside the forest. For them it was an easy method of food production. The propagation of the roots of yams did not require the hundred-generation apprenticeship or selection of the first grain farmers. On the contrary, it has been known to be picked up by paleolithic tribes in India in the course of a lifetime.[1] When picked up it leads to a rapid growth of an unselected population, rapid destruction of the natural vegetation and a rapid deterioration of the soil and its drainage.

All the dangers inherent in the first origins of cultivation were now aggravated. The growth of new farming populations transformed in the course of a few generations the conditions of their own prosperity. In the Congo basin dense populations grew up on land which became liable to flood and infested with tsetse flies and mosquitoes.[2] The tsetse flies (fifteen species of *Glossina*) preying on the wild cattle were already at home on the Congo. The mosquitoes (sixty species of *Anopheles*) had probably brought malaria and other diseases up the Nile from Egypt. These insects were now carrying the protozoan parasites responsible for malaria and sleeping sickness, diseases deadly to man, to cattle and to horses. And every increase in the density of the populations of their victims increased out of proportion the numbers of the dangerous parasites and their insect carriers.

The consequence of this grave and long-continued crisis was partly to obstruct and partly to divert the course of history. The sleeping sickness must have been less prevalent when there were fewer cattle and the early migrations of herdsmen had allowed them to get through the high and dry corridor which connects Abyssinia with South Africa. But horses arriving in Abyssinia two thousand years after cattle, failed to get through to South Africa. This lack of horses had a grave effect on the development of African societies. For, without the horse, the wheeled chariot and all wheeled vehicles failed to appear and a warrior governing class never took shape. Another great step, the replacement of the hoe by the plough, was also hindered. For ploughing, cattle would have sufficed, but the ease of yam-growing and the diseases of cattle were together discouraging for the development of heavy cultivation. To all these factors a final disastrous difficulty was added: the genetic and evolutionary response to malaria.

b. The Impact of Malaria

Malaria probably reached Egypt at the time of her imperial decline. Perhaps, in conjunction with older diseases such as bilharzia and the lack of iron and fuel, it played some part in that decline. The great wars connected with the rise of Persia, Macedon and Rome had no doubt rapidly extended its circulation. Alexander himself may have died of it. To this terrible threat, as we have seen, the endangered populations have responded by selectively

[1] Burkill (1951). [2] Livingstone (1958); see also Mattingly (1960).

favouring genetic mutations. These have created several new blood pigments, haemoglobins, which are resistant to digestion by the malarial parasite. But they have the harmful effect of replacing energy by lethargy in the man or woman who carries them. In some peoples they may have helped to turn the alert and the free into the submissive and the enslavable. Further, as we saw, the price paid for immunity includes the killing in infancy of a quarter of the progeny, the so-called homozygotes.

The haemoglobin mutations have obviously arisen at different times and places in the course of the last two millennia, but they probably appeared first among the Bantu. They have enabled great races to survive at the price of racial damage distributed by breeding through the whole population. Conversely, such pure pastoral people as there were adjoining the expanding Bantu must often have been wiped out by the malaria and the sleeping sickness to which, without hybridization, they had no reply.[1]

c. Their Chiefs

The Bantu and the other Negro cultivating peoples had no means of knowing what was happening to them in the successive interactions of cultivation, disease, and mutation. Their expansion was therefore bound to be blind, violent, and spasmodic. Without ruthless warfare they could hardly have broken out of the destructive cycle with which they began. The means of warfare leading to directed migration seems to have been provided by chiefs who came to them from disease-free Hamitic and Semitic tribes, all of them pastoral, living around the Abyssinian highlands.

What is the evidence of this origin for the Bantu chiefs? It is of two general kinds. First, the chiefs themselves, like the European nobility, trace their patrilinear pedigrees for ten, twenty, or, in an extreme case among the Xhosa, for thirty generations. They all believe that swimming across the Zambesi they came from the region of the lakes in the north.[2] This was indeed the direction from which the Hottentots and also the Bantu cattle had come and from which historically the Bantu people themselves are known to have come.[3]

Secondly, there is the circumstantial evidence of the recent origins of chiefs and of caste generally among the northern Bantu. This evidence is one of the keys to the evolution of the whole race.

[1] A new evolutionary principle of general interest arises from the malaria-haemoglobin chain of reactions in man. At the first impact of malaria this environmental occurrence became the determining factor in the evolution of the peoples affected by the disease. After the occurrence of the counter-strokes, the mutations, these at once became the dominant factors in the evolution of the peoples affected by them. Thus the relative importance of heredity and environment is seen to be reversed by particular events affecting the life and death of individuals; and the importance of heredity itself depends on the size of the breeding group.

[2] João dos Santos (1609) states that the King of Mutapa could not cross the Zambesi for lack of boats (Axelson, 1954).

[3] My own enquiries have been confined to chiefs of the Venda and Suto tribes. But the history of the Balemba metal workers and of the copper miners of Rhodesia worked out by van Warmelo is a detailed corroboration of the same view.

VI. THE EVOLUTION OF CHIEFS

The evolution of African societies in the region of the great lakes can be understood as the result of the coming together of the three basic adaptive groups of African people since the beginning of the Bantu.

(i) Nilotic pastoral people represented by the several tall tribes of the Sudan and also by the Alur and Luo farther south, who have moved up the Nile valley from the north.
(ii) Bantu agricultural people represented in mixed form by the Kikuyu and related tribes.
(iii) The paleolithic pygmies, hunting and collecting people of the Congo forest.

All these peoples until recently were primitive in their social structure. The pastoral and agricultural people had incorporated people who had brought the knowledge, the capacity and the materials for stockbreeding and cultivation into their societies. But they retained the exogamous patrilineages of their paleolithic ancestors.

The people who brought in the new faculties were remembered as the male ancestors of favoured lineage clans. But, since these clans were compelled to outbreed, genetic differences between them and other clans continually tended to fade away and survive only in ritual leadership. Exogamy prevailed over class. Lineage systems in asserting themselves have re-asserted the character of the homogeneous society. Numerous pastoral and agricultural peoples, and some with a mixed type of farming, have thus survived.

But the need for government and authority has grown as the tribes have grown. Not merely the size of the social units but also their density and their frequent conflicts, have called for leadership. But leadership is just what could not be provided so long as the leading ritual or magical lineages have been compelled to interbreed with the others. Great increase of wealth in certain families could arise from skilful management. Great loss of wealth could follow migration, outlawing or capture in war. Neither could establish a genuine aristocracy or a genuine slavery, only their simulacra.

As Lucy Mair has very well shown a grading of clan lineages and their hereditary privileges and titles could develop; but no grading of hereditary authority and responsibility. On the contrary another non-hereditary system—the potentiality for which exists in all human societies—was called into play. This is the system of age-gradation. The male members of society are graded in age-sets. Those who have reached the age of initiation are grouped over a period of four, five, six or more years. They pass through their lives in these groups following a traditional cycle of occupations and responsibilities, child, warrior, elder and so on. This system of grading supplies the need for a hierarchy in authority where, in an equalitarian society, there is no means of maintaining a genetic differentiation of classes. It gives a formal recognition of a principle already informally apprehended in the paleolithic tribe.

These systems hold east of the Nile and Lake Victoria. But west of the

Nile and the great lakes quite a different situation arose. Its origin, growth and decay have probably repeated themselves many times in Bantu history. But it has been only during the last three or four centuries that these processes could be demonstrated. Their consequences provide us with a test of the modes of origin of stratified societies in general.

In the richer agricultural country of Uganda dense agricultural populations came, during this period, to be governed by hereditary chiefs and kings. These peoples all have a mixed pastoral and agricultural economy. They mostly have a clear distinction between two castes, a lower agricultural and a higher pastoral. The royal lineage, and the important chiefly lineages, all come from the pastoral caste which is often physically distinguishable and resembles the type of the Nilotic pastoral peoples.

The best-preserved and indeed diagrammatic example of this type of society is found in the Ruandi and Rundi tribes which live in the country adjoining the Mountains of the Moon. Here there are three castes which are separated in breeding and in function and distinctly marked by their gradation in size. There are the tall pastoral governing group, the Watutsi, numbering one in seven of the tribe. There are in some sections an inferior pastoral group from a later wave of immigrants, the Hima. There are the agricultural serfs, the Hutu, of medium height, forming the mass of the people, of largely Bantu origin. And there are the hunting and collecting people, the Twa of forest pygmy origin little changed from the paleolithic state of society except that they have acquired, as we know paleolithic people did in Africa, the art and business of making pottery.

At a later stage in the evolution of classes are the southern Ha people which include no hunters or pygmies. They have their two castes: the agricultural Ha from which the whole tribe takes its name and the Tusi corresponding to the Nilotic governors of the Ruanda tribes. But interbreeding has occurred and the occupational distinction between the groups is therefore breaking down. The tribe is, or rather was, on the way not to the kind of equalitarian situation of the eastern Bantu but rather to the chief-governed type of society of the south.

Despite their physical distinctions we can see signs in these tribes of the breakdown of caste barriers. Among the Nkole, with their famous cattle, the serfs can have their own small chiefs who are not entitled to inflict blood revenge on their masters. Among the Ha the occupational distinctions have broken down. All such breakdowns of caste arise from, and in turn give rise to, interbreeding. Such interbreeding however is itself the inevitable consequence of the intrusion of the Bantu custom of chiefly polygamy. The chief usually takes a Great Wife from his own caste in another tribe, but he also has a dozen supplementary wives from the lower ranks of his own tribe, and he inherits all but one of his father's dozen wives as well.[1]

[1] Shaka Zulu (1787–1828) was exceptional. He had 1200 wives but succeeded in begetting only one acknowledged child (Ritter, 1955). Exceptional also is the Rain Queen of Mojaji who lives on the wetter side of the Transvaal and from whom I learnt that her official *wives* for the last four generations have owed their offspring to her brothers.

Owing to this practice, as we move south, there is a breakdown of the old noble castes; there is also an enlargement of chiefly ancestry in the tribe. And the chiefly families become a channel for the introduction of foreign ancestry into the mass of the people.

By a fortunate circumstance we may see, not only the end stages of class evolution in the Bantu, but also its beginnings. They are revealed by what has been recently happening to the Alur, the Nilotic tribe most closely situated to the Watutsi. These are a purely pastoral people like the Nuer or the Dinka. They have a chiefly clan with a ritual status in the life of their tribe. But the adjoining equalitarian Bantu, living in their dense agricultural tribes while maintaining their paleolithic breeding system, have been troubled by unmanageable dissensions. In their difficulties they have repeatedly invited the chiefs of the Alur to send their sons, with their followers or clients, to come and rule over them.[1]

The comparison with the Tuareg of the Sahara shows what is significant in these conditions.[2] The Tuareg governing class or nobles are tall, lean and fair-skinned. They are of pastoral origin and live by caravanning and slave-owning and slave-trading. They are nominally Muslim but being of pure Berber race they keep their own Berber language and Punic alphabet, their own priestly caste, and ancient matrilinear dominance and descent. Now this governing class owns personal slaves and also tribal serfs in several castes; they are all of Negro race, the captives of war in the Niger valley. In addition they have a caste which has arisen from noble-serf crossing and which behaves as an intermediate class. The isolated conditions of desert life, conditions of slowly increasing austerity, have given rise to extreme inbreeding and an extremely intractable and unadaptable character in the Tuareg nobles. It has also preserved (as in Ruanda) in diagrammatic form the structure of a society which has been the standard pattern along the whole border of Negro and white peoples between Rabat and Oman for the last four or five millennia. Indeed, since the time when the first Pharaoh announced his edict that no Negro was to pass the frontier of his state on the First Cataract of the Nile.

Such are the two extremes in the mode of origin of governing classes in all peoples: invitation of foreign families and conquest by foreign invaders. In their later history these differences of origin are forgotten. But the genetic difference between the classes is maintained so long as the difference of activity continues between the governors and the governed.

VII. THE COLONIZATION OF SOUTH AFRICA

The expanding Bantu reached the Limpopo perhaps in the seventh century. Here they were on the frontier of the tropics. They had to leave behind their tropical crops, their yams and bananas. They could also leave behind their malaria and sleeping sickness: they could therefore begin to breed cattle like the Hottentots they found in front of them. How were they equipped to face a temperate climate? They had goats and sheep, as well as cattle, but no

[1] Lucy Mair (1962); see also Oliver (1955).

[2] See Rodd (1926); Miner (1953); Oliver and Fage (1962); Boahen (1962).

Table 41. *The Relations of the Native Peoples of South Africa*
After Schapera (1930, 1937–56; with Goodwin, Flourie, Van Warmelo and others). See also Tobias (1955, 1959) and Wrigley (1962).

Division	*Native Name*	*Numbers*	*Life*	*Height*	*Colour*	*Language Group*	*Phonetics Clicks*	*TH*
WESTERN								
1. BUSHMEN	Khoi/San	40,000	H+C	D	Yellow	Khoisan	5	—
2. HOTTENTOT	Nama	30,000	P		Yellow	Hamite	4	—
3. BERG DAMARA	Chou Dama	40,000	P+C	M	Black	Hamite	4	—
4. SANDAWE, *etc.*	—	21,000	P+A	M	Medium	Hamite	3	—
5. CATTLE DAMARA	Herero	40,000	P	T	Variable	Bantu	3	usual
6. OVAMBO	—	270,000	P+A	T	Variable	Bantu	3 ?	rare
EASTERN								
7. ZULU	(royal clan)	—	P+A	T	Nr. Black	Bantu	3	Tonga
8. XHOSA	—	—	P+A	T	'Red Kaffir'	Bantu	3	—
9. SUTO	Basuto	—	P+A	T	Nr. Black	Bantu	1	—
10. VENDA	Bavenda	—	P+A	T	Nr. Black	Bantu	0	—

H, Hunting; C, Collecting; P, Pastoral; A, Agricultural

Notes:

1. Includes the 'Black Heikum', a tribe who speak Bantu and practise settled agriculture; also the Transvaal enclave near Lake Chrissie who have four clicks (Pienaar, 1938).
2. The Hottentot language, which phonetically approaches Khoisan, is classified as Hamitic by grammar rather than by etymology (Meillet and Cohen, Schapera). The extinct *Strandloper* group included metal workers.
3. The Chou Dama or 'Dung Blacks' picked up their Hamitic dialect as slaves of the Hottentots. But 'their tongues are too thick to click well' (Vedder and Hahn, 1928).
4. An enclave in central Tanzania who recall their descent from a hunting people; 500 years ago they were driven by famine to become serfs of a Nilotic P+A people who gave them cattle in exchange for women. Thus also they acquired chiefs (Trevor, 1950). The Turkana people probably had a similar origin (Hillaby, 1964).
5. The tribe's dental fricative is perhaps due to their traditional marker-mutilation of middle top incisor notching or extraction. It is said to be absent in the Kaokoveld populations.
6. Described along with the Nama and Dama peoples by Galton.
7. This tribe was the foundation of the Empire of Shaka based on his inventions of the stabbing spear and the fighting *impi* (Ritter, 1955). The Tonga district has the dental fricative.
8. The Xhosa tribes get their lighter colour and clicks from Hottentot ancestors. The coastal tribes in addition have Arab, Malay and some European ancestry especially in the chiefly caste.
9. The name Suto means Black and is evidently like Dama the denigratory description of neighbours.
10. The Venda and the Suto have the Semitic subcaste, the Balemba.

horses. They could spin wool and cotton but they had no loom. They had millet but no wheat, rice or maize. They had their coppersmiths and iron-smiths to work for them making hoes, picks and spears; but they had no wheel, spoked or solid, no plough and no idea or method of irrigation. They had no seaworthy boats and there were no lakes with fish. And they were cut off by the impassable tropics from any people who knew how to make and use the things they lacked. No wonder that their southward movement was halted for five hundred years.

Their problems were difficult but not insoluble. They solved them by hybridization. And of the precise modes, frequencies and distributions of hybridization we have a number of sources of evidence, documentary, biological and linguistic. Before considering them, however, we must look at the completed movement as it appeared at the critical date of 1834 when the European colonists in their Cape Province met the Bantu advance south of the Drakensberg Mountains.

At this time a number of tribes had distributed themselves in South Africa according to their ecological preferences, the agricultural tribes in the fertile plains, the pastoral tribes on the drier tablelands, leaving the Bushmen in occupation of the growing Kalahari desert.

West of the desert there were two kinds of Bantu tribes: the largely agricultural Ovambo and the lighter-skinned purely pastoral, and as usual proud and warlike, Herero. These two groups rightly claimed common descent: they had diverged by occupational and ecological selection within one of the expanding and hybrid Bantu stocks. A third group, the Chou-Dama or Dung Blacks, despised and rejected by both the others, was evidently the product of hybridization with the Bushmen. Living on the poorest land they supported themselves by keeping goats and collecting wild plants.

East of the Kalahari the Bantu tribes had occupied the Transvaal and Natal. The line of ten-inch summer rainfall had brought them all to a stop. Beyond that line and south of the desert was the shrinking territory of the Hottentots with cattle and sheep, still in 1930 recalling to Schapera those of North Africa. The character of the Hottentots we can no longer describe with certainty since they have largely died out and the explorers of the time have not told us enough.[1] Fortunately, however, the comparison of South African languages provides us with a partial solution of our problem and one which agrees with the trends of our other evidence (Table 41). It agrees in showing, first, that the Bushmen have hybridized with a first wave of advancing Hamitic pastoralists, the Hottentots, during the last two millennia or more. And, secondly, that over the latter half of this time the Hottentots have hybridized with the advancing Bantu. The results of these two invasions and hybridizations, Hottentot and Bantu, are evident. They have carried the Bushman clicks into the speech of the invaders. But they have submerged them in proportion to the distance from the Bushman centre in the Kalahari desert and to the loss of the primitive Bushman hunting character.

[1] See Axelson (1954). What Galton recorded (1853) is, to be sure, of interest beyond merely African studies but he could not compare the whole range of South African peoples that we now know.

The two great invasions, however, failed to carry through to South Africa any organization higher than a tribal one or any technique more advanced than was needed for mining and smelting copper and iron. Today even the fishermen of South Africa are the hybrid people derived from Malay ancestors imported as slaves by the Dutch in the eighteenth century.

VIII. ZIMBABWE AND TIMBUKTU

All great expansions damage or even destroy the peoples and the habitats at whose expense they are made. The Negro expansions were somewhat more destructive for Africa than their predecessors had been for Asia and Europe. Warlike chiefs equipped with iron weapons led their peoples into the struggle or scramble for new territories. Even a new flash in the pan like the Zulu Empire of the nineteenth century made itself felt 2000 miles to the north in Tanzania. Meanwhile the tribes themselves had to be continually reconstructed in their genetic resistance to disease, in their caste distinctions and behaviour and in their management of crops and stock.

In these conditions we must expect from the peoples some achievements. But we must also expect them to be more precarious and less stable than such achievements have been elsewhere in the world. In fact for the Bantu the only element of stability proved to be the grammar of their language: everything else changed.[1]

In this expansion the chiefs and the smiths who made their weapons, came from the north. In the ninth or tenth century they came into the almost empty land to the south. There seeking gold they found also copper and iron. The sand and the ores were both in the healthier highlands between the Congo and the Limpopo, the region we now know as Katanga, one of the great mineral treasure-houses of the world. The traders who wanted these things and would pay for them came in the first place overland from Abyssinia. But later, attracted by ivory and slaves, they came from overseas by easier ways: they were Arabs sailing in dhows. From Mukallah they reached the coast of Zanj, Zanzibar and Sofala in Mozambique. Later still, attracted by the wealth that gives employment and patronage, there came artisans, engineers, scribes and historians. They came first no doubt from Abyssinia and Arabia, but later, in the eleventh and twelfth centuries, from as far afield as India and China.[2]

It was by this immigration that states arose with strong and rich rulers capable of organizing the metal industries and trades, and the construction of the great stone buildings of which we may see the remains at Zimbabwe and elsewhere in Rhodesia. These rulers, to judge from their bones, were of Hamitic race. But they were probably superseded later by hybrid Bantu chiefs. The last of these governed the Bantu Empire of Mutapa which in the seventeenth century became dependent on the Portuguese now controlling the mouth of the Zambesi.

1 Noni Jabavu (1960) has given a moving account of the racial and cultural contrast between the agricultural Baganda of the north and the pastoral Xhosa of the far south, the Transkei.

2 Dart (1939); Davidson (1959, 1964); Oliver (1961); Stokes and Brown (1966).

Table 42. *Supposed Origins and Distributions of the Historic Diseases of Man*

After Folke Henschen (1962).

	Climatically Less Selective		*Climatically More Selective*	
	Air-borne	*Contact, Water, Soil*	*Animal Vectors*	
OLD WORLD	V. Poliomyelitis (O.K.)	B. Cholera (India)	*Temperate*	
	Smallpox (China)	Typhoid (unknown)	B. Typhus (Athens, 430 B.C.)	*lice*
	Measles (Medit.)	Gonorrhoea (O.K.)	Plague (O.T.; Samuel)	*fleas*
	Diphtheria (O.K.)	Tetanus (Greece)	*Tropical*	
	B. **Pneumonia** (O.K.)		V. **Yellow Fever**[1] (W. Africa)	*mosquito*
			B. Leprosy (O.K.)	*fleas*
			P. Encephalitis[2] 1, 2 (Africa)	*tsetse*
			Malaria[2] (Africa, 1000 B.C.)	*mosquito*
		H. Trichinosis (pig: S.W. Asia)	H. Filariasis (tropics)	*mosquito*
		Hookworm spp. (Africa, warm climates)	Bilharzia[2] (O.K.)	*snail*
NEW WORLD	—	B. **Syphilis** (to O.W. 1492)	*Tropical* P. Encephalitis, 3	*lice*
PALEOLITHIC	B. Tuberculosis (cold climates)	B. Yaws (fly-borne)	—	

V. virus. B. bacteria, *Rickettsia* or spirochaete. P. protozoa. H. helminth. O.K. Old Kingdom, Egypt. Black type signifies important transfer O.W./N.W.

[1] Derived probably from African monkeys (Mattingly, 1960; see also Yoeli, 1960).

[2] Deadly diseases of Africa for which no simple genetic resistance can be selected.

The states however fell to pieces. The miners and smiths continued to live and work dispersed among the tribes where we see them being finally displaced today. The kings also continued to be represented by chiefs who are without doubt their hybridized descendants. But the organization, the coherent social structure, had disappeared.

At the same time as Zimbabwe, a greater city, whose history we know better, rose and fell in West Africa. That is Timbuktu.[1] This city, placed significantly where the dry Sahara touches the fertile Niger valley, owed its origin to the meetings of different peoples. The nomadic Tuareg in the tenth century had already long used it as the site of the summer camp where they refreshed their flocks, harvested their crops, and collected their slaves from the Negro kingdoms to the south. But in the following century (in 1076) Berbers from Morocco established Islam in this territory and with it a settled urban society centred in Timbuktu itself. Here was the crossroads for trade in gold and salt, in horses and weapons, as well as slaves. Here therefore came the wealth and the ordered literate government which attracted scholars from Fez and took pilgrims to Mecca.

Timbuktu continued to be the great market and meeting place of West African people and Muslim governors and scholars of Arabian and Jewish extraction for five hundred years. During this period in the flourishing kingdoms to the south the sculptors of Benin and Ife were at work. Then in 1590 another army from Morocco, equipped now with firearms, fell upon the city, looted it, and turned it into a Moorish colony. The new rulers interbred with the Negro population and the city thereupon slowly declined into subservience to its older masters, to the pure-bred Tuareg, utterly inflexible in their nomadic and predatory habits. And this was a state from which it has never recovered.

IX. THE DECLINE OF AFRICA

The most hopeful developments of African life have been eclipsed in the last five hundred years. The manifold reasons are now discernible. They are manifold and in part they are successive and cumulative. They concern each of the special characteristics of human life on the continent.

In the first place disease has obstructed every racial and cultural development in Africa. It has damaged Africans. And it has deterred or destroyed all immigrants and invaders of Africa who did not protect themselves from disease by hybridization. Why should disease have played such a dominant part in the development of man in Africa? The reason can be expressed without serious distortion or misunderstanding in very general terms.

We may now classify the historically important and frequently fatal diseases of man according to the kinds of agents that cause them, the means of transmitting these agents, and the possibilities of resisting or avoiding them (Table 42). We then find that the greater part arose in the Old World where man had his origins. We also find that the greater part are climatically indifferent because they are due to viruses and bacteria that are directly infectious

[1] Described by Horace Miner, see Hodgkin in Oliver (1961).

and contagious. These diseases are probably all of them the object of genetic adaptations favouring resistance which arise in populations that have long been exposed to them: hence the grave effects of taking them to new countries. Beyond these, however, there is a last class of diseases, chiefly due to protozoa and helminth worms, and carried by or directly due to tropical animal parasites. To these, genetic resistance of a harmless kind has never been built up in man. Nor indeed could the hygienic instructions, disseminated by Islam and Hinduisim, and so useful in dealing with directly water-borne diseases, have been of any value with these parasites. It is these tropical diseases which began to cripple the development of African societies just at the moment when African populations reached the numbers and densities necessary for civilization.

If we go further and compare the great regions of human habitation in relation to their continuance of habitation and to their proportion of tropical area, we see that there is a gradient from one extreme to the other, a gradient of expected vulnerability (Table 43).

Table 43. *Relation of Disease Generation and Resistance in Human Populations to their Climate, Size and Duration*

Continent or Land Mass	*Proportion of Hospitable Area within Tropics*	*Duration of Human Habitation*
AFRICA	0·75	2×10^7
EURASIA	0·15	2×10^6
AMERICA	0·45	2×10^4
AUSTRALIA	0·33	
OCEANIA	0·90	2×10^3
NEW ZEALAND	0·00	8×10^2
		in years

On this basis of comparison we see why Africa, the oldest home of man, is the home of the most dangerous of man's diseases, dangerous both to Africans and to other peoples. We also see the special position of India where the confrontation with disease of an invading non-tropical people is associated with, and succeeds only by virtue of, extraordinary precautions of caste and of cleanliness. And we also notice, conversely, the extreme vulnerability of the four newest regions of habitation when Europeans suddenly exposed them to the diseases derived from the older ones.

We may summarize the history of continental contact by saying that outside Europe and Asia it has been necessary for civilization but fatal for people. Africa's diseases destroyed first Africans then the intruders into Africa. But the intruders' diseases destroyed the peoples of America and the Pacific.

After disease the next most important factor in the arrest of African development has been, as in Polynesia, the too-easy progress of agriculture. In Europe and Asia the slow, painfully slow and laborious, spread of grain-growing selected an industrious peasantry and by its slowness protected the soil and the vegetation from, not all, but some of the effects of exploitation. The exploiters, however, were released upon Africa with a much shorter period of probation. The spread of slash-and-burn agriculture was combined with the fatal abundance of the tropical root crops imported from Asia and America. Further, the spread of pastoralism with over-grazing, known just as well in Asia, was more widespread in Africa. Both these ruined the drainage and destroyed the soil. Thus both agriculture and pastoralism encouraged the diseases which in turn damaged or ruined them.

At the same time the growth of the root crops favoured the development of the most easy-going races in the world. They were made more so both by malaria and by its dangerous genetic antidote. The pastoral peoples never have been and never could be enslaved. The agricultural peoples were enslaved by the native pastoralists, such as the Tuareg and the Somalis, and by the foreign invaders, Muslim and Christian, Arab and European.

The damage done to the African peoples was not in loss of manpower, or in the quality of the loss. The slaves were people selected, not for skill or courage or learning but (as Galton observed in the course of his travels in the Sudan and in Damaraland) for genetic docility or the genetic diseases favouring docility. Even more readily than in Europe and Asia, the slaves bought or stolen from Africa could be replaced by their remaining kinsmen without change of character or loss of numbers. The damage done was due to the weapons used by the invaders. After 1500, improved fire-arms began to be a means of breaking down the structure of native society. A simple indicator of the change is the fact that the Portuguese, in 1492, were unwilling to attack the Hottentots and therefore decided to settle in Angola and Mozambique. But in 1652 the Dutch with their new firearms could confidently land and settle at the Cape.

These biological, technical, and social conditions combined to bring about the downfall of Zimbabwe and also of Timbuktu. But not these alone. For the failure of penetration of the technicians and scholars of the old civilizations also contributed. And that arose from the action of disease in obstructing the growth of orderly society. The failure of the literate religions allowed cannibalism to flourish and the bloodiest despots could enjoy unlimited esteem. At the same time a disorderly polygamy in all stratified societies prevented the survival of castes so efficient, even though so unamiable, as those of the Tuareg.

The entry to Africa has never been easy. The recruitment of skilled artisans from the Ancient East was evidently limited in the time of Meroë. The recruitment of scribes, scholars and teachers has always been difficult. The deserts and the forests, the diseases, the parasites and predators, including the termites, are barriers which can all of them be overcome by adventurous individuals or whole migrating peoples. But they cannot, or rather will not, be overcome by the scholars and teachers. For during the last two millennia such men could seek and find a living in the countries of Europe and Asia, a living and also the protection they needed; such a protection as was always to be derived from the great literate religions.

Wise men go where they expect to prosper in peace. They say: *ubi bene ibi patria*. And from the time of Hannibal to the re-entry of the Europeans the flow of great abilities has for this reason been away from Africa.

X. COLONIES AND STATES

The century of relative peace between 1815 and 1914 enabled the industrial states of Europe to seize control of most of Africa, that is of lands and peoples which, lacking most of what Europe possessed, yet possessed a little that Europe lacked. In Africa, as earlier in America, the Europeans wanted to take the wealth and to offer their religion in exchange. But now they could do more. They could abolish the trade in slaves which they had developed. And they could hand over the European achievements in medicine, agriculture and engineering for the immediate use of both parties to the transaction.

This complex and variegated colonial experiment was fraught with hopeful and also hazardous possibilities for Africa. But between the years 1957 and 1964 it was abruptly terminated. Most of Africa was freed from the rule of European states. These changes constitute the largest series of innovations in government ever to be suddenly attempted. They also constitute an experimental series. For each is *controlled* by contemporary as well as historical comparisons among the racially contrasted regions of the continent. Let us therefore take a glance at these regions (Table 44).

Table 44. *Lands and Peoples of Africa Classified by Race and Class Structure*

SEMI-ARABIC MUSLIM RULING CLASSES *Christian Minorities* (1) Social or (2) Racial	Egypt (1): B 1799–1882–1956 Libya (1): 1912–1951 Tunis (1): F (I) 1881–1956 Algeria (1): F 1830–1962 Morocco: F (S) 1912–1956	Sudan (2): B 1899–1955 Somalia: B.F.I. 1887–1960 Zanzibar: G.B. 1880–1964 Mauretania, Mali: F 1842-1958
NON-MUSLIM RULING CLASSES	Abyssinia (Ethiopia) (I: 1936–1941) *Amharic*	Madagascar: F 1895–1950 *Indonesian*
NEGRO EX-COLONIES, EX-CHIEFTAIN-RULED TO 1880–1900		
French (1958–60)	Belgian (1960)	British (1957–60)
Cameroon, Guinea Chad, Ivory Coast Dahomey, Senegal Gabon, F. Congo, etc.	B. Congo Ruwanda Burundi	Nigeria, Kenya Ghana, Tanzania Uganda, Malawi Zambia
NEGRO SLAVE RE-SETTLEMENTS (West Africa)		
Sierra Leone, B: from 1787	Liberia, U.S.A.: from 1822, 1847	
EUROPEAN-DOMINATED REGIONS		
Portuguese Colonies (since 1498) Angola and Mozambique	Dutch and British Colonies (since 1652) South Africa: 1961; Rhodesia: 1966; and dependencies (Botswana: 1965, etc.)	

B, F, I, S: British, French, Italian and Spanish
Dates are those of invasion, liberation, revolution, etc.

First, there is the ancient kingdom of Abyssinia little changed by these events and indeed not greatly changed by the events of the last millennium. For although nominally Christian its religion derives from the Old Testament rather than the New. The governing class is a feudal slave-owning nobility speaking the Amharic language and derived, as we saw, from Semitic conquerors. The subject peoples include the ferocious Danakil and the only less ferocious Galla, and for all parties mutilation is still the means of punishment as well as the purpose of war.[1]

Second, there is Morocco whose traditional Sheriffian monarchy, displaced by French rule, finds itself in conflict with a newly educated urban population that has grown up with the encouragement of the French and under their protection.[2]

Third, there is Algeria ruled since 1962 by those partisans who, in a war of eight years, had succeeded in expelling the French rulers together with their French-speaking dependants, merchants, cultivators, urban workers, skilled and unskilled, of general Mediterranean and Christian origin. The victorious insurgents were divided between Muslim peasants and herdsmen and an urban leadership, partly educated and partly communist. By this war the Berber peoples whose tenacity, military and religious, we first met in the campaigns of Hannibal and Jugurtha once again made their mark in history.

Fourth, there is Tunisia whose government, independent since 1956, depends on a slowly evolving governing class which is derived from ancient, indeed Carthaginian and Roman origins, and has continually developed itself by peaceful relations with its non-Muslim neighbours, the French and Italian administrative, technical and mercantile communities.

Fifth, there are the two Portuguese colonies of Angola and Mozambique, the oldest European settlements in black Africa, dating from Vasco da Gama's voyage of 1498. These colonies, great in area if not in culture, are distinguished from all others by the existence of a strong half-breed population, intermediate in intelligence and education between the colonists and the native peoples and concerned above all to co-operate with both sides in securing a stable stratified society.

Sixth, there is Egypt with an ancient community of *Fellahin* or peasants, now Arabic-speaking, and a variety of linguistic and religious groups: native Coptic, Jewish, Greek, Arab, Turkish, Italian, French and English—in order of antiquity; the whole, as we have seen, governed by a succession of foreign invaders. The last of these have been the French and British who, since Napoleon, by administration, the development of commerce, the building of dams and canals and their memorable excavations, have restored the land and the history, and multiplied the wealth of the population, of the country. A new military class of native birth but mixed origin and uncertain character have by stages expelled one after the other the British army of occupation, the parasitic foreign dynasty, and the Jewish commercial community. They have done so in interests which were ostensibly native, nationalist and 'Arab' but whose future orientation is altogether doubtful.

Seventh, there is the South African Republic whose people consist of four

[1] Buxton (1949); O'Callagham (1961).
[2] Maxwell (1966).

fractions of different racial origins and legal status. They are: African 67 per cent, White 20 per cent, Coloured or Hybrid 10 per cent and Asian 3 per cent. The 'White' population is of Dutch, Huguenot, German and British extraction. The non-British part speaks the Afrikaner language which is often slightingly referred to as Kitchen-Dutch and reflects the hybridization of the original settlers with their Hottentot, Indonesian and Bantu slaves and servants. These Afrikaner speakers are bound together however by their race, their language, and their devout attachment to the fundamentalist Dutch Reformed Church with which they began. But they are still more tightly bound together by the history which has followed these origins. The first part of this history arose from their rejection between 1717 and 1802 of white immigration from Holland in favour of coloured slavery. The second part, its necessary sequel, arose from their tenacious and ultimately successful resistance, both political and military, to the policy instituted by British governments in 1835 of suppressing slavery.

This Afrikaner evolution culminated inevitably in the strict racial segregation and Bantu labour laws which sought to stabilize Afrikaner and white or near-white supremacy in South Africa and led to secession from the British Commonwealth in 1961. A parallel evolution aligned the British colony of Rhodesia with South Africa. It led to a rejection of British interference in the colony and, as with the American colonies in 1776, to a unilateral declaration of independence.

Both these segregationist states are now enjoying a prosperity which they owe to an efficient government and also to a skilful exploitation of great natural resources and of an abundant supply of cheap negro labour. Both are threatened by the rigidity of their principles. They believe in genetics but they reject evolution. It is a mistake which has often been made before, by nobles, by mandarins and by zealots. It is a mistake which they can survive in the short term. But in the long term it has always proved detrimental.

Eighth, there are the two states founded to accommodate, in addition to their native populations, settlements of liberated African slaves from Britain and its American colonies. The first of these, Sierra Leone, was founded by British emancipators in 1787. Since women were lacking in the first expedition, the shortage was made good from British prisons. The result, whether from this hybridization or from colonial rule which continued till 1961, was to produce the more stable and respectable of black African communities. The second state, Liberia, was founded by emancipators in the United States in 1822. It became independent in 1847. Unfortunately, beyond showing its flag at sea, this state has never succeeded in using its independence to any serious purpose.[1]

Last, there are the twenty black republics which became independent of French, British and Belgian rule between 1957 and 1964. These lands and peoples had for sixty or seventy years been suffering or enjoying a vast social transformation. Chiefly governments, tribal organization, language and customs, and pagan religions had been giving place to centralized government, under partly European laws and languages, accompanied by educa-

[1] Greene (1936).

tional, agricultural and medical services. These operations had been carried out with varying effort, diverse or uncertain motives and unequal success. They had a tentative and experimental character. How are we to estimate them in relation to the whole evolutionary and historical process?

These operations, owing to the very recent development of European technology, both in killing and in healing, had been condensed into two generations. In this time they had attempted to do what in Europe, India and China had occupied a hundred generations. During this short time the intruding white administrators and technicians had remained marked as a separate caste. They had hybridized as yet very little with the native population. The native societies had thus not become stratified with professional and governing classes related to the means of government and production that were now being used. How could it be otherwise in two generations? Twelve generations of Roman rule did not civilize and stabilize British society. With a shorter spell of colonial rule today African society would have been enabled to follow the European or Asian pattern. The process was, however, broken off prematurely. In some sense the histories of Meroë, Timbuktu, and Zimbabwe repeated themselves.

In the space of seven years the twenty colonies voted to be independent. Their votes were given with universal suffrage in secret ballot. They adopted written constitutions devised by erudite Europeans to maintain the practices of representative government. These steps constituted something not previously known in social and political history outside certain Latin American republics. Throughout the world successful governments have always been established by governing classes which owed their position to successful struggle. They have won their way by foreign conquest or by native insurrection. Representative government has arisen as a method of subjecting such governing classes to the scrutiny, control and also recruitment of broader classes of increasing literacy. The setting up of representative government in the absence of either a governing class or a literate society was thus an undertaking fraught with the utmost danger for the supposed beneficiaries.

In the newly independent states there followed a variety of changes. In all of them there was some loss of prosperity and some decay of order with the transfer of power. In some a single leader was strong enough for a while to maintain a central authority and to keep devoted European officials in his service. In others a disciplined military junta or communist party could use its hierarchical structure to achieve the same result. Whatever the system, its success depended more on the character and abilities of the men who worked it than on the political assumptions on which they pretended to rest their power.

In the absence of such capable leaders, however, within each colony, or on their removal by assassination, tribal hatreds and personal struggles displaced orderly government. Large wars or small insurrections broke down the administration.[1] The communities, commercial, educational and medical, whose co-operation had built up the prosperity of the colonies were foreign. Whether they were European, Indian or Arab they were exposed to racial

[1] Stacey (1962), Andreski (1968).

resentment. They were often expelled. Irrigation and drainage, transport and sanitation suffered. The endemic diseases of former times, notably malaria and bilharzia, began to encroach. And with the flight of the foreigners Africans themselves often took refuge in the states that were still under European control. For, as has been observed before, people selectively migrating will often fear the appearance of slavery less than the reality of starvation.

From these events we may draw certain general conclusions. Biological evolution without doubt is continuing among the peoples of Africa. Natural selection is still its motive force. But ability to compete rather than to co-operate is once more the measure of success. War, famine and disease are once more the most effective agents of discrimination. In the long run this may be for the best. But in the short run we must lament the loss of individuals, tribes and communities who could have helped in building the richer stratified societies now, as so often before, interrupted in their growth in Africa.

The visible consequence of this regression we must also lament. It is that the economic contrasts of the world which were beginning to diminish are now once more increasing. The colonized and genetically stratified societies are, as always, advancing faster than the uncolonized or de-colonized and unstratified societies. The developed countries are developing faster than the undeveloped countries. Africa is moving no longer towards but once more away from Europe.

From this costly and often cruel experiment Europeans as well as Africans are now in a position to learn useful lessons. But first they have to unlearn certain stereotyped formulae. They have to learn instead those biological and evolutionary rules to which all societies will always be subject.

Conclusion

29

MAN AND SOCIETY

I. THE FORERUNNERS

IN THE PRESENT ACCOUNT we have been trying to discover how man and his societies have come into being. The evidence, assumptions and inferences that we have needed to use are of many kinds. For the most part they have long been foreseen, collected and employed by enquirers in this field and before going any further and attempting to reach certain general and also rigorous conclusions we must acknowledge our debt to certain of the forerunners.[1]

In the first place we must acknowledge Darwin. What we owe to him is that, following Malthus, he showed man as an animal, an organism that could and must be studied as an animal, using all the scientific methods that can be applied to any other animal. This meant that, in his heredity and variation, in his physical, emotional and mental properties, his individual, social and racial character, in his diseases and in his speech, in his behaviour and in his beliefs, he was a proper object of experimental study; and in all these respects his evolution was subject to the principles of natural selection with all its special forms of sexual selection, artificial selection and unconscious selection.

In the second place we must acknowledge those who followed most closely after Darwin; notably Galton who was the first seriously to study human intelligence, its measurement, its inheritance, its evolution and its diversity; and the first to apply this new knowledge to problems of history and of primitive and advanced society. We may, to be sure, admit today that intelligence is a more subjective notion than Galton supposed. We may believe that intelligence concerns those mental faculties which have increased the chances of survival in our own kind of society, the one which arose in a particular part of Asia and now dominates the world. And that this standard has not

[1] Acknowledgments on the biological side will be found in my *Genetics and Man*.

necessarily an eternal validity, that it itself is undergoing evolution. Nevertheless this idea has to be one of the beginnings of our discussion.

In the third place we must state our debt to those who have revealed the unexpected complications of Darwin's theory. Of these the most notable was Carr-Saunders, who showed that human, like animal, societies regulate their reproduction and hence their numbers by instinctive moral controls which reduce competition and avoid conflict. In doing this he showed that the breeding processes were themselves part of a genetic system whose evolution is now understood in animals and plants generally. But in man deference to religious teachers may distort or suppress the innate morality of primitive people.

Entering another field we must acknowledge the inspiration of Fustel de Coulanges who recognized that the stratified societies of cities were derived from the co-operation of different races. The genetic principle implied has underlain the studies of the sociologists, Gumplowicz and Sorokin, and of the historians, Acton and Pirenne. But above all the archaeologist, Flinders Petrie, turned this idea into a working hypothesis which illuminates our enquiry.

Flinders Petrie, reviewing problems of civilization especially from the point of view of artistic creation, wrote: 'The rise of the new civilization is conditioned by an immigration of a different people . . . it arises from a mixture of two different stocks. That effect of mixture cannot take place all at once. There are barriers of antipathy, barriers of creed, barriers of social standing, but every barrier to race fusion gives way in time. . . .' Thus in a few phrases written in 1911, Petrie brings together the principles of the religious breeding group, of assortative mating, of social stratification, of racial differentiation and of genetic recombination: all of them principles with which he was familiar through knowing in person Bateson and Pearson, the rival exponents of genetics and biometry at that time.

When we turn to another field, that of anthropology, we again recognize an immense debt. But we are bound to be surprised that Rivers in understanding the origins of stratified societies among primitive peoples, and Raglan in revealing the stagnation and frequent loss of culture of these peoples, did not see more of the connections with other sciences. Or indeed the relation between two sides of anthropology: their own side being obsessed with the avoidance of outbreeding, while the other, derived from Lewis Morgan, was obsessed with the avoidance of inbreeding. For it is the two together which govern the course of human evolution. We may also be surprised that Gordon Childe in sorting out with superb judgment the origins of civilization in Europe felt obliged by his beliefs to exclude the genetic evidence flowing from his own as well as from all other human studies.

There are other fields of enquiry which can only now be brought into relation with biological ideas, but we ought nevertheless to acknowledge their connection. There is the notion of a social environment, an environment determined by the genetic character of the society in which the individual lives. In this connection two contributions stand out. There is Bagehot's notion of deference. To a certain extent this may be said to be the means by which the reason of one class attempts to impose itself on the instincts of another in what it assumes to be the interests of both. When we disapprove of its object we call it snobbery. When we approve, we call it loyalty. But the principle of deference explains and illuminates the second great contribution, which is Lecky's history of morals. For in this history we see how relatively dominant individuals and classes spread over Europe to create the moral environment of relatively recessive or subservient individuals and classes and so changed the standards of opinion and behaviour of the whole society: the whole body acquired the complexion of a thin skin. In some degree this kind of attitude must govern the behaviour of all stratified societies.

The last of all the great disciplines to be brought into service concerns agriculture. When Vavilov declared his belief that in the domestication of plants lay the secret of man's history it might have seemed a wild figure of speech. But forty years later we notice that it is a truth indispensable for the understanding of the past. At the same time, however, we see the opposite side of the picture, the destruction of man's habitat by agriculture. It was first revealed to us by Alexander von Humboldt and by George Perkins Marsh, but they have been followed by devoted successors, devoted because they were voices crying in the wilderness. The principle they have taught us is that every new source from which man has increased his power on the earth has been used to diminish the prospects of his successors. All his progress has been made at the expense of damage to his environment which he cannot repair and could not foresee. Surely this is the most practical of all the lessons of history. But only if we are able to assess the extent to which this damage has altered the past course of events in order to foretell how such damage may alter the future course of his evolution.

Finally, we must acknowledge our debt to those who have first understood that the history of man, being the most complex of all enquiries, demands the use of all the methods at our disposal, not just one tidy professional package. The idea was clear enough in Acton's words when he asserted, as an historian, that 'an educated man cannot become so on one study alone', and again 'if men of science owe anything to us we may learn much from them.' When he said these things he was obviously thinking of Darwin and it was natural that Wells, a Darwinian, twenty years later should see the point and attempt to do the job.

To be sure, Wells in writing his *Outline of History* used evidence which we dispute in order to reach conclusions which we doubt. But his idea of one history of man is vindicated. It has become the only aim that we can justify today. And we are indebted to his successor, Carleton Coon, for maintaining that aim with the much greater resources at his command.

II. THE ADVANCE OF ARCHAEOLOGY

The possibilities of a unified history of man have been transformed in the last twenty years by the sudden development of two sciences, the complementary sciences as they now appear, of archaeology and genetics. They are not new sciences, being each in the strictest sense over a century old. But a single technical advance has transformed the one and several theoretical advances have reshaped the other.

The method of exact dating by the radioactive isotope of carbon (C^{14}) has shaken out the primary long-standing uncertainties from archaeology. It has established the directions of movement of peoples, of their faculties and of their inventions throughout the prehistoric world. The result has been to show precisely that most earlier archaeological inferences of time and movement were correct but a few were wrong. Hence we have now been able to show the whole of Old World agriculture and civilization as deriving from the Nuclear Zone in the Ancient East. And the whole spread from this centre has been seen as due to the movements of people, of men and women, of populations whose breeding created the nations of mankind.

As a correction to this argument we can however be assured that agriculture did arise independently and in parallel and with different people and different crops in the New World. Thus new ideas were rare enough among primitive peoples (as Raglan maintained), but given enough time and the right people in the right place great ideas could appear more than once and having appeared they did give rise to parallel series of events.

From these rare beginnings however, the founding ideas have marched on foot, ridden on horseback and sailed on the sea, all of them at speeds we can measure. But—and this is what is so easy for civilized man to forget—never until our own times have they spread by word of mouth; never have they flown on wings.

Until our own time culture has been tied to the people who invented it or to their descendants. It was, as Peake and Fleure put it, the Beaker Folk who wandered about Europe living in European societies: it was not disembodied Beaker Culture. So when the archaeologist follows culture he is tracing the movements of people and the changes of society, their growth and their decay; and from this tracing he can understand the causes and the connections between such processes. Above all he can expect to fit them into the framework of documented history which is waiting to receive them. And we can expect to establish those continuities of descent, propagation and transmission, indeed of cause and effect, on which the unity of history is seen to depend.

III. THE ADVANCE OF GENETICS

From the new development of genetics even more far-reaching consequences ensue. For the evolution of man and society arises from what individual men and women do, and from the purposes they have in doing it; in other words from their character, which in the long run is conditioned by genetic processes. What we have now come to understand is that these genetic processes are entirely at the mercy of the system of breeding.

Breeding varies, as we have seen, between the opposite poles of inbreeding and outbreeding. With inbreeding heredity is all-powerful; determination is absolute: the group, the population, the caste or the race are invariable; they can be destroyed or removed but if they remain nothing can change them. With outbreeding heredity disintegrates; recombination produces unpredictable variability, endless innovation. Uncertainty, organized uncertainty, dominates not the organism but the population; determination in controlling evolution is transferred to the selective power of the environment. Between these two extremes, it now appears, every species of animal and plant is adapted to preserve some kind of balance. In man, since the neolithic revolution, the balance has fluctuated between extremes owing to the social vicissitudes we have seen. But where it has failed to be preserved we have also seen the results in the great crises of history.

Not however only in crises. The slow evolutionary advance in human intelligence has been accentuated and also diversified by the stratification of societies. It has varied and complicated the means by which the breeding balance is maintained in them. All governing classes, and all slave classes, evidently arose in the beginning from the coming together of different races to form stratified societies which always competed favourably with unstratified societies. They were more competent because their genetically different classes co-operated to give a more complex, more efficient product than any primitive homogeneous societies. They were also more adaptable because hybridization between classes could, and in the event of social change always did, release new variability in the stratified society (Fig. 22).

Now stratified societies, having established themselves, attracted and assimilated strangers to form the new classes or castes which combined to build cities and nations. But they did so only very slowly. Cities, like agriculture, spread out of the narrow temperate zone into new climates only with difficulty. Northwards towards the arctic or southwards into the tropics they moved by slow re-stratification that, is by selective migration and by hybridization with people living in those climates. Only thus could they adapt themselves to the new conditions. For the more complex the society with its numerous separately inbreeding castes, the slower its re-adaptation.

By contrast with the immensely slow spread of agriculture and of cities, the great expansions of small classes are rapid. Whether they are craftsmen or warriors but especially when they are equipped with horses or ships, they can attach themselves to new societies. If they are governors they may carry a governing class language over the immense areas that are marked by the Aryan and Semitic, the Chinese and Arabic, Indonesian and Bantu languages. All these have depended on a governing class hybridizing with its subjects but at the same time, as a caste, keeping apart from its subjects. In this way repeated expansions with successive waves of dilution have carried these governing classes and their languages across the earth.

No society can however reach a high development without some kind of priesthood, which organizes a religion designed to govern its breeding behaviour. If breeding behaviour is left at the sole discretion of a governing class, that class, and with it the whole society, is liable to disintegrate. To understand this we must look once more at the origins of new classes in general.

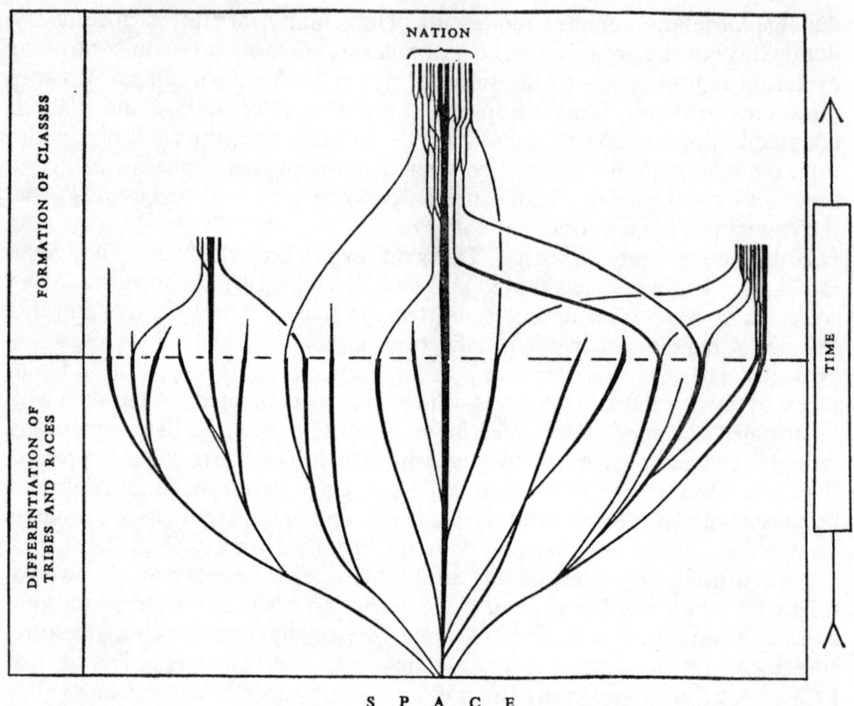

Fig. 22. The Origin of Class Structure

Diagram showing how the differentiation of tribes before agriculture is related in space and time to their later aggregation in social classes to form stratified nations with disruptive selection giving rise to secondary stratification.

From Darlington 1958: Eug. Rev. 50: 169

IV. NEW CLASSES

The founders of a new dynasty, whether Cyrus or the Ch'in Emperor, Augustus or William the Conqueror, have a characteristic origin. When we know where they come from we find that such men arise by outbreeding: often outbreeding so decisive that they are bastards. Having established their conquest they endeavour to keep it within their family. That is why we find the Pharaohs and Achaemenids, Ptolemies and Caesars, early and late, and the Hapsburgs, all turning from outbreeding to inbreeding when they reach the top. All in turn brought down their dynasties in this way. Only the mediaeval European kings were prevented from doing the same. They were prevented by the fact that there was a tribe of kings large enough to form an outbred caste whose intermarriage made for both political coherence and genetic stability.

They were also prevented by the papacy. For, when the papacy lost its strength, the most powerful of the Catholic monarchs, the Hapsburgs and the Bourbons, pursuing their immediate ends of political power, turned to the most extreme inbreeding, and ruined themselves through the defective individuals produced as a result.

Even moderate inbreeding, however, frequently endangers the survival of governing classes, not through specific defects but merely through stabilizing a type which has lost its value. Ogdai, son of Ghengis Khan, was told by his chief minister, 'Your empire was won on horseback, but you can't rule it on horseback'.[1] The aristocracies of Europe through inbreeding have retained an addiction to the horse, a genetic and adaptive habit which enabled their ancestors to win wars. But on more recent battlefields it has carried them, as it carried the Mongols, headlong to disaster. The instincts of the mass are not in these cases to be overcome by the intelligence of the individual.

Consider now the position of the technical discoverer. In ancient times, although he might exceptionally become divine he was almost always anonymous. We therefore know nothing of his parents or his progeny. But we know that if he was a horse-tamer he kept his discovery to his tribe; and if he was an iron-smelter he kept it, with the aid of magic, to his family. In either case, if he was successful he created a new caste; it was bound to inbreed. But if his discovery proved to be a source of wealth or power, his caste was bound to expand. The inventions of the few thus come to provide for the employment of the many. Then their inbreeding soon begins to relax and the new invention produces a new social class.[2]

Thus the breeding system of a social group determines its success or failure. It is also in turn modified in quite different ways by that success or failure, according to the changing function of the group in the society of which it forms a part.

V. UNSTABLE SOCIETIES

The most striking contrast in the modern world is that between the Hindu society with its well-preserved professional castes and the European societies with their flexible classes and increasing though always limited mobility. The contrast, however, is the same as that between agricultural and urban societies throughout the world. It is also the same as that between an early and a later stage of European development. Its origin lies in the city.

In cities people of different castes and professions were originally separated in their different quarters. But it is clear that hybridization between castes was easier in the city than on the land where peasants formed the enduring and overwhelming majority. Moreover the cities with their higher death rate have been continually recruited from the land. It is by hybridization from these sources of recruitment that a large part of social advance has proceeded. And hybridization has accelerated with the growth of cities. The most obvious and recent consequence has been the Industrial Revolution which has multiplied in turn migration, hybridization and innovation.

[1] *cit*. Mosca (1895).

[2] Intermediate between these two extremes is the Rothschild family: among the descendants of the founder out of fifty-eight marriages half were between first cousins and half were between unrelated spouses (Morton, 1962).

Societies which have followed the Industrial Revolution, and have indeed been created by it, have two new characteristics. The means of livelihood, the kinds of profession or trade, are more diverse and more unstable than in any society in the past. And the populations, although graded in broader social classes with different kinds of aptitude, are composed of individuals bred by intermarriage within these broader classes and therefore no longer specifically adapted to a fixed and stable occupation. The two factors in the process of living, the man and the job, are thus both more and more finely divided than they have ever been before in history. And this is both the cause and the consequence of the rapidity of technical invention.

VI. CHOICE OF OCCUPATION: THE HERO AND THE MISFIT

From the parallel subdivision of society and of its occupations arise both social and historical problems and their solutions. The first of these is the problem of choice of occupation. The son who no longer wishes to follow the trade of his father has to make a choice. Inevitably he chooses to do what either he or other people think he does best. At one extreme the resolute character, the man of destiny, follows his own judgment. He seeks out or creates his own environment and even that of his posterity. At the other extreme, the weak man is compelled to heed the opinion of others and take what work they will give him. But between these two extremes lie most of the interactions of individuals with society and with the world as a whole in which they find themselves. All of them arise from the genetic character of individuals and the genetic structures of society. From their changing effects in turn arises the changing pattern of human activity.

It is a pattern which changes most rapidly in the divided society of the large cities and in countries where movement is easiest, least restricted by poverty, or by religious or linguistic distinctions. Then the degree of outbreeding is highest. And with the high degrees of outbreeding comes a higher proportion of individuals at both our extremes: the creative and the defective.

First, consider the defective, the unfit recombination. He lies in the field of sociology and raises its greatest problem. The misfit may be a mental, social or sexual misfit. He may be delinquent or criminal. He is the price that has to be paid for hybridization. He is the burden that has to be carried by society as a whole in return for the most adaptable breeding system. Fortunately he is, as a rule, of reduced viability and fertility. Natural selection has in this way so far prevented the burden from becoming intolerable.

Next, consider the creative recombination. He is the inventor, the artist or the hero. He lies in the field of history and raises its greatest problem. Does he in fact change the course of history? The answer is that in terms of the ultimate destiny of man, which is probably extinction, he does not. But on a shorter view, where the events of a few hundred years or the fate of only a few nations seem to matter, he may alter it. For what we call great men are due to unique genetic recombinations and occur at particular times and places. What they do affects the prospects of every other man who follows them. Sadly of course we must also admit that small men in great positions may have as great effects as great men in those positions. Their characters are equally determined. The difference is, almost by definition, that their effects are never what they intended.

VII. THE LAST UNCERTAINTIES

The coming of the great man is not predictable. In his origin there are two sources of uncertainty, one genetic, the other environmental. The genetic source is that the creative individual is always a unique recombination arising from outbreeding, arising indeed from the organized uncertainty of recombination on whose exploitation organic evolution depends. The environmental source of uncertainty lies almost entirely in the organic world outside mankind, almost entirely indeed in the world of microbes. We cannot foretell the whole future of infectious disease. We can however make an important prediction about its effects on man. It is that man's future prospects are proportionate to the amount of genetic diversity he maintains among the interfertile members of his own species. In this respect, more than in any other, the loss of any primitive and apparently unsuccessful tribe affects the future of mankind as a whole. In this respect mankind is one; and for us men are undoubtedly the most precious of animals.

In order to preserve him it is not enough that we refrain from killing him. We have also to preserve the diverse habitats which diverse peoples need for their survival. To be sure, the restricted and specialized habitats of civilization give the greatest opportunities for what we (in an arrogance we have come to share with Galton) are pleased to call intelligence. But we have now learnt that intelligence is of many kinds. It has to be measured not on one scale but on many. And its diversity, if lost, cannot easily be recovered. We have therefore to preserve these diverse habitats, along with their diverse inhabitants, from damage which civilization has so far so wantonly wrought upon them.

James Burnett Monboddo
1714–1790

Thomas Paine
1737–1809

Thomas Robert Malthus
1766–1834

Alexander von Humboldt
1769–1859

George Perkins Marsh
1801–1882

Charles Robert Darwin
1809–1882

Lewis Henry Morgan
1818–1881

Karl Heinrich Marx
1818–1883

Heinrich Schliemann
1822–1890

Francis Galton
1822–1911

Walter Bagehot
1826–1873

Numa Denis Fustel de Coulanges
1830–1889

Edward Burnett Tylor
1832–1917

John Emerich Edward Dalberg Acton
1834–1902

William Edward Hartpole Lecky
1838–1903

Peter Alexeivich Kropotkin
1842–1921

William Matthew Flinders Petrie
1853–1942

Gaetano Mosca
1858–1940

Jens Otto Harry Jespersen
1860–1943

Henri Pirenne
1862–1935

William Halse Rivers Rivers
1864–1922

Herbert George Wells
1866–1946

Alexander Carr-Saunders
1886–1967

Nikolai Ivanovich Vavilov
1887–1943

Vivian Gordon Childe
1892–1957

BIBLIOGRAPHY

Abbreviations:

1. E.B., Encyclopaedia Britannica. 14th ed. 1929.
2. D.N.B., Dictionary of National Biography. Oxford University Press (1903, 1953).
3. O.C.D., Oxford Classical Dictionary (to A.D. 337) 1949.
4. L.E.M., Larousse Encyclopaedia of Mythology, 1961. (*see* Graves)
5. O.T. and N.T., Old Testament and New Testament in various versions in English.
6. C.A.H., Cambridge Ancient History.
7. I.L.N., Illustrated London News (archaeology section).
8. P.N.A.S.: Proc. Nat. Acad. Sci. (Washington).

GENERAL AND MAPS

AITCHISON, L. 1960. *A History of Metals* (2 vol.). Macdonald, London.

ARMSTRONG, RICHARD. 1967. *The Early Mariners*. Benn, London.

BAGLEY, J. J. 1965. *Historical Interpretation: 1066–1540*. Penguin, London.

BATESON, W. 1928. *Essays and Addresses*. Cambridge U.P.

BIBBY, G. 1957. *The Testimony of the Spade*. Collins, London.

CARY, M., and WARMINGTON, E. H. 1929 (1963). *The Ancient Explorers*. Methuen, Penguin, London.

CHENEY, C. R. 1948. *Handbook of Dates for Students of English History* (Christian Era). London, R. Hist. Soc.

CLARK, GRAHAME. 1961. *World Prehistory*. Cambridge U.P.

COON, CARLETON S. 1954. *The History of Man*. Knopf, N.Y.; Cape, London.

—— 1965. *The Living Races of Man* (Maps). Knopf, N.Y.

DARLINGTON, C. D., and MATHER, K. 1950. *Genes, Plants and People*. Allen and Unwin, London.

DARLINGTON, C. D., 1967. *The Genetics of Society as 'Human Society and Genetics'* in *Race and Modern Science*. Ed. R. E. Kuttner. Soc. Sci. P., N.Y.

DARWIN, C. 1872. *The Descent of Man*. Murray, London.

DEBENHAM, F. 1960. *Discovery and Exploration*. Hamlyn, London.

DEEVEY, E. S. 1960. 'The Human Population'. *Sci. Am. 203:* 195–204.

DERRY, T. K., and WILLIAMS, T. I. 1960. *A Short History of Technology from Earliest Times to A.D. 1900*. Oxford U.P.

DRUMMOND, J., and WILBRAHAM, A. 1947. *The Englishman's Food*. Cape, London.

EAST, W. G. 1935 (1962). *An Historical Geography of Europe*. Methuen, London.

FISHER, R. A. 1930. *The Genetical Theory of Natural Selection*. Oxford U.P.

FORD, E. B. 1965. *Genetic Polymorphism*. Faber, London.

FULLER, J. L., and THOMPSON, W. R. 1960. *Behaviour Genetics*. Wiley, London and N.Y.

GALTON, SIR FRANCIS. 1883 (1951, 1958). *Inquiries into Human Faculty and its Development*. Dent, Cassell, Eug. Soc., London.

GANSHOF, F. L. 1950. 'Nobility.' *Chambers's Enc.*

GARN, STANLEY M. 1960. *Readings on Race*. Thomas: Springfield, Ill.

GEORGE, H. B. 1904. *Genealogical Tables illustrative of Modern History*. 4th ed. Oxford U.P.

GIBBON, EDWARD. 1766–1788. *The History of the Decline and Fall of the Roman Empire*. (Ed. J. B. Bury) (1896–1900). Methuen, London.

GRAVES, ROBERT (*et al.*) 1961. *Larousse Encyclopaedia of Mythology*. (L.E.M.) Hamlyn, London.

GRANT, MICHAEL. 1965. *The Civilisations of Europe*. Weidenfeld, London.

GROLLENBERG, LUC. H. 1959. *A Shorter Atlas of the Bible*. Nelson, Edinburgh.

HADDON, ALFRED CORT, 1934. *History of Anthropology*. Watts, London.

HARRISON, G. A. *et al.* 1964. *Human Biology*. Oxford U.P.

HEYDEN, A. A. M. VAN DER, and SCULLARD, H. H. 1959. *Atlas of the Classical World*. Nelson, London.

HORNELL, J. 1946. *Water Transport: Origins and Early Evolution*. (Indonesian Outriggers) Cambridge U.P.

HUXLEY, J. S. 1942. *Evolution: the Modern Synthesis*. Allen and Unwin, London.

MAINE, SIR HENRY. 1861–1885. *Ancient Law*. Dent, London (1906, 1917).

MEILLET, A., and COHEN, M. *et al.* 1952. *Les Langues du Monde*. C.N.R.S., Paris.

MOURANT, A. E. 1954. *The Distribution of the Human Blood Groups*. Blackwell, Oxford.

—— 1959. 'Blood Groups and Anthropology.' *B. Med. Bull. 15:* 140–2.

PEAKE, H. J. E., and FLEURE, H. J. 1927–36. *The Corridors of Time I–IX*. Oxford U.P.

PIGGOTT, STUART (ed.) 1961. *The Dawn of Civilisation*. Thames and Hudson, London.

PRITCHARD, J. E. (ed.) 1955. *Ancient Near Eastern Texts*. Princeton U.P.

SHOTWELL, JAMES T. 1939. *The History of History*. Columbia U.P.: N.Y.

STEINBERG, S. H. 1955 (1966). *Five Hundred Years of Printing*. Penguin, London.

SUMNER, W. G. 1906. *Folkways*. Ginn, N.Y.

TAYLOR, ISAAC. 1864–1907. *Words and Places* (7 editions). Routledge, London.

TAX, SOL (ed.) 1960. *Evolution after Darwin* (3 vols.). Chicago U.P.

THOMAS, W. L. 1956. (with C. O. Sauer, M. Bates, L. Mumford (ed.)) *Man's Role in Changing the Face of the Earth*. Chicago U.P. (Wenner-Gren Symp.)

TYLOR, EDWARD B. 1881. *Anthropology*. Macmillan, London.

VAN DER MEER, F. 1954. *Atlas of Western Civilisation*. Elsevier, Amsterdam.

WEYER, EDWARD. 1959. *Primitive Peoples Today*. Hamilton, London.

WOOLLEY, LEONARD. 1958. *History Unearthed*. Benn, London.

ZIRKLE, CONWAY. 1951. 'The knowledge of heredity before 1900', in *Genetics in the 20th Century*. Macmillan, N.Y.

1. ORIGIN OF MAN

ARDREY, ROBERT. 1961. *African Genesis*. Collins, London.

CLARK, W. E. LE GROS. 1959. 'Crucial evidence for human evolution'. *P. Am. Phil. Soc. 103:* 159–172.

COON, CARLETON S. 1955. 'Human Variability and Natural Selection in Climate and Culture'. *Am. Nat. 89:* 257–279.

—— 1962. *The Origin of Races*. Knapp. N.Y.

DARLINGTON, C. D. 1959. *Darwin's Place in History*. Blackwell, Oxford.

DART, R. A. 1925. '*Australopithecus africanus*, the Man-Ape of South Africa'. *Nature 115:* 2884, 195–9.

DARWIN, C. 1859. *The Origin of Species*. Murray, London.

HAAG, W. G. 1962. 'The Bering Strait Land Bridge'. *Sci Am. 206:* 112–123.
HOOIJER, D. A. 1962. 'Palaeontology of Hominid Deposits in Asia.' *Adv. Sci. 18:* 485–9.
HULSE, F. S. 1961. *Adaptation, Selection and Plasticity in Human Evolution.* Wayne S.U.P., Detroit.
KOENIGSWALD, G. H. R. VON. 1960. *Die Geschichte des Menschen.* Springer, Berlin.
MANGELSDORF, P. C. 1952. *Plants and Human Affairs.* Notre Dame U.P. (Indiana) Nieuwland Lectures (5).
OAKLEY, K. 1957. 'Tools Makyth Man.' *Antiquity 31:* 199–209.
POST, R. H. 1962. 'Population differences in vision acuity' (selection relaxation). *Eug. Quart. 9:* 189–212.
RENSCH, B. 1959. 'Gerichtete Entwicklung in der Stammesgeschichte.' *Deutsch. Ak. Naturf. Leopoldina 21:* 101–116.
——1960. 'The Laws of Evolution'; in Sol Tax (General).
ROBINSON, J. T. 1962. 'Origin and adaptive radiation of the Australopithecines': in Evolution und Hominisation (Ed. Kurth). Fischer, Stuttgart. (Smithsonian Report for 1961.)
SCHALLER, GEORGE B. 1964 (1965). *The Year of the Gorilla* (and also pygmies). Chicago U.P.
SEMENOV, S. A. 1964. *Prehistoric Technology.* Cory, Adams, London.

2(i). THE EXPANDING SPECIES

BARNICOT, N. A. 1959. 'Climatic Factors in the Evolution of Human Populations.' *C.S.H. Symp. Quant. Biol. 24:* 115–129.
BISCH, JØRGEN. *Behind the Veil of Arabia.* Allen and Unwin, London.
BRAY, R. S. 1965. 'Malaria, monkeys and man.' *Adv. Sci. 21:* 453.
CAMPBELL, BERNARD G. 1966. *Human Evolution, an Introduction to Man's Adaptations.* Aldine, Chicago.
CLARK, JOHN G. D. 1961. *World Prehistory.* Cambridge U.P.
COON, C. S. 1966. 'The taxonomy of human variation.' *An. N.Y. Ac. Sci. 134:* 516–523.
DARWIN, CHARLES. 1839 (1845). *The Voyage of H.M.S. Beagle.* Murray, London.
DODGE, B. S. 1962. *Plants that Changed the World.* Phoenix, London.
GALTON, SIR FRANCIS. 1853. *Narrative of an Explorer in Tropical South Africa.* Murray, London.
—— 1869. *Hereditary Genius.* Collins, Fontana; London, 1962.
GATES, R. R. 1961. 'The Melanesian dwarf tribe of Aiome, New Guinea.' *Riv. Int. Gen. Med. Gem. 10:* 277–311.
GLASS, BENTLEY. 1960. 'The genetic basic of human racial differences'. *B.I.O.S. 31:* 1–20.
GOODHART, C. B. 1960. 'The evolutionary significance of human hair patterns and skin colouring.' *Advance Sci. 17:* 53–59.
HARRISON, G. A. 1961. *Genetic Variation in Human Populations.* (A. E. Mourant, Blood Groups. A. C. Allison, Abnormal Haemoglobins. G. A. Harrison, Pigments.) Pergamon, Oxford.
—— *et al.* 1967. 'Skin colour in southern Brazil populations.' *Hum. Biol. 39:* 21–31.
HITZEROTH, H. W. *et al.* 1964. 'Albinism among the Bantu of South Africa.' *Mankind Qly. 5:* 81–86.
HORNELL, J. 1946. *Water Transport: Origins and Early Evolution.* Cambridge U.P.
HOWELLS, W. W. 1960. 'The Distribution of Man.' *Sci. Am. 203* (3)*:* 113–127.
HUNT, E. D. Jr. 1959. 'The Continuing Evolution of Modern Man.' *Cold Spring Harb. Symp. Quant. Biol. 24:* 245–254.

JENKINS, T. G. 1959. 'The ancient craft of coracle making.' *Country Life 125:* 716–7.

KEITH, SIR ARTHUR. 1948. *A New Theory of Human Evolution.* Watts, London.

LUNDMAN, B. 1961. *Stammeskunde der Völker* (*Ethnogonie*). Lundequistska Bokhandeln, Uppsala.

MALINOWSKI, B. 1926. *Crime and Custom in Savage Society.* Routledge, London.

MARTIN, PAUL S. 1966. 'Africa and Pleistocene overkill.' *Nature 212:* 339–342.

MONCKTON, C. A. W. 1920 (1936). *Some Experiences of a New Guinea Resident Magistrate.* (2: ch. 8.) Penguin, London.

MOUNTFORD, CHARLES P. 1948 (1953). *Brown Men and Red Sand.* Robertson, Melbourne.

PAWSON, I. G. 1967. 'Life on the Altiplano' (Bolivia). *Geog. Mag. 40:* 57–64.

RAGLAN, LORD. 1939. *How came Civilisation?* Methuen, London.

—— 1962. 'Prehistoric men—What can we know of them?' *Rat Annual:* 1962. 31–41.

SCHWIDETZKY, IISE (ed.). 1962. *Die neue Rassenkunde.* Fischer, Stuttgart.

SCOTT, J. P., and FULLER, J. L. 1965. *Genetics and the Social Behaviour of the Dog.* Chicago U.P.

SPUHLER, J. N. (ed.). 1958. 'Natural Selection in Man.' *Amer. Anthrop. 60:* 1–72. Detroit (Wayne U.P.).

TURNBULL, C. M. 1961. *The Forest People* (African Pygmies). Chatto, London.

WASHBURN, S. L. 1960. 'Tools and Human Evolution.' *Sci. Am. 203* (3): 62–75.

2(ii). SPEECH

BALLARD, C. F., and BOND, E. K. 1960. 'Variations of Jaw Form and of Oro-facial Behaviour including those for articulation, etc.' *Speech, Path. & Ther. 3:* 55–63.

BALLARD, C. F. 1961. 'Oro-facial Behaviour.' *Publ. Hlth. Lond. 76:* 10–18.

—— 1963. 'Posture and behaviour of the lips and tongue; the implications in orthodontics, prosthetics and speech.' *Trans. Eur. orthod. Soc.* 1–22.

BROSNAHAN, L. F. 1961. *The Sounds of Language.* Heffer, Cambridge.

—— 1962. 'The influence of Genetics on Language.' *Discovery, 23:* 400–403, London.

DAHLBERG, A. A. 1963. 'Dental evolution and culture.' *Hum. Biol. 35:* 237–249.

DARLINGTON, C. D. 1947. 'The Genetic Component of Language.' *Heredity 1:* 269–286.

DU BRUL, E. L. 1958. *Evolution of the Speech Apparatus.* Thomas, Springfield, Ill.

GABRIEL, A. C. 1948. 'Genetic types in Teeth', in *Essays in Biology*, Austral. Med. Pub. Co., Sydney.

GUPPY, NICHOLAS. 1958. *Wai-Wai: through the forests north of the Amazon.* Murray, London.

HOCKETT, C. D. 1960. 'The Origin of Speech.' *Sci. Am. 203* (3): 88–96.

KROGMAN, W. M. 1967. 'Genetic factors in the human face, jaws and teeth etc.' *Eug. Rev. 59:* 165–192.

LASKER, G. W. and LEE, M. M. C. 1967. 'Racial Traits in the Human Teeth.' *J. Forens. Sci. 2:* 401–419.

LUCHSINGER, R. 1961. 'Die Sprachentwicklung von ein- und zweieiigen Zwillingen und die Vererbung von Sprachstörungen in den ersten drei Lebensjahren.' *Folia phoniat. 13:* 66–76.

PALMER, L. S. 1957. *Man's Journey through Time.* Hutchinson, London.

STEIN, L. 1949. *The Infancy of Speech and the Speech of Infancy.* Methuen, London.

TRATMAN, E. K. 1956. 'Human Teeth and Archaeology.' *Adv. Sci. 12:* 419–423.

TULLEY, W. J. 1962. 'Long-term orthodontic results recorded by cineradiography. *Dent. Practnr., 12:* 253–260, London.

3. BREEDING SYSTEMS

BATES, DAISY. 1938 (1966). *The Passing of the Aborigines.* Murray, London.

BENEDICT, BURTON. 1967. 'Anthropological Aspects of Population Control.' *Pop. Study Group* (2) 49–56, Roy. Soc., London.

CARPENTER, C. R. 1942. 'Sexual Habits of Primates.' *Biol. Symp.8:* 177.

CARR-SAUNDERS, A. M. 1922. *The Population Problem: a study in human evolution.* Oxford U.P.

COON, C. S. *et al.* 1961. 'Symposium on crowding, stress and natural selection.' *P.N.A.S. 47:* 427–464.

CHRISTIAN, J. J. 1961. 'Phenomena associated with population density.' *P.N.A.S. 47:* 428–449.

COWELL, ADRIAN. 1960. *The Heart of the Forest* (Amazon Tribes). Gollancz, London.

DARLINGTON, C. D. 1943. 'Genetics and the Evolution of the Mating System in Man.' (Jolly and Rose) *Ann. Eug. 12:* 44–5.

—— 1943. 'Race, Class and Mating in the Evolution of Man.' *Nature 152:* 315–319.

—— 1960. 'Cousin marriage and the evolution of the breeding system in man.' *Heredity, 14:* 297–332.

—— 1961. 'Instincts and morals.' *Rat. Annual,* 23–34.

DARLINGTON, C. D., and MATHER, K. 1949. *The Elements of Genetics.* Allen and Unwin, London.

—— 1950. *Genes, Plants and People.* Allen and Unwin, London.

EVERSLEY, D. E. C. 1959. *Social Theories of Fertility and the Malthusian Debate.* Oxford U.P.

FINCH, B. E. and GREEN, H. 1964. *Contraception through the Ages.* P. Owen, London.

FORD, C. S. and BEACH, F. 1965. *Patterns of Sexual Behaviour.* Eyre and Spottiswoode, London.

FORD, E. B. 1964. *Ecological Genetics.* Methuen, London.

FORTES, MEYER. 1959. 'Primitive Kinship.' *Sci. American 200:* 146–158.

GAJDUSEK, D. CARLETON. 1964. 'Factors governing the genetics of primitive human populations.' (New Guinea, Polynesia, S. America.) *C. Spring Har. Symp. Q. Biol. 29:* 121–135.

GOODALL, J. 1963. 'My life among wild Chimpanzees.' *N. Geog. Mag. 124:* 272–308.

HALDANE, J. B. S. 1924. *Daedalus or Science and the Future.* Kegan Paul, London.

—— 1957. 'Natural Selection in Man.' *Acta Gen. Stat. Med. 6:* 321–332.

HUTTON, J. H. 1946. *Caste in India.* Cambridge U.P.

HUXLEY, SIR JULIAN (ed.) 1966. 'A discussion on ritualisation of behaviour in animals and man.' *Phil. Trans. Roy. Soc. London,* B. *251:* 247–526.

JOLLY, A. T. H. and ROSE, F. G. 1943. 'The place of the Australian aboriginal in the evolution of society.' *Ann. Eug. 12:* 44–87.

LEVI-STRAUSS, C. 1949. *Les structures élémentaires de la parenté.* P. Univ., France, Paris.

MAJUMDAR, D. N. 1958. *Races and Cultures of India.* Asia Pub. Ho. Bombay *et al.*

MOURANT, A. E. 1961. *The Distribution of the Human Blood Groups.* Blackwell, Oxford.

MURDOCK, G. P. 1949. *Social Structure.* Macmillan, N.Y.

SCHALLER, GEORGE. 1965. *The Year of the Gorilla.* Collins, London.

SCHULTZ, A. H. 1957. 'Past and Present Views of Man's Specialisations.' *Irish J. Medical Sci.* (6) *380:* 341–356.

TURNBULL, C. M. 1961. *The Forest People* (African Pygmies). Chatto, London.

WALLACE, A. F. C. 1961. 'On being just complicated enough.' *P.N.A.S., 47,* 458–464.
WASHBURN, S. L. 1962. *Social Life of Early Man.* Methuen, London.
WASHBURN, S. L., and DE VORE, I. 1961. 'Social Life of Baboons.' *Sci. Am. 204* (6) 62–71.
WESTERMARCK, E. 1926. *Short History of Human Marriage.* Macmillan, London.
WYNNE EDWARDS, V. C. 1962. *Animal Dispersion in relation to Social Behaviour.* Oliver and Boyd, Edinburgh.
ZUCKERMAN, S. 1932. *The Social Life of Monkeys and Apes.* Kegan Paul, London.

4. AGRICULTURE

AITCHISON, L. 1960. *A History of Metals.* Macdonald, London.
BRAIDWOOD, R. J. 1960. 'The Agricultural Revolution.' *Sci. Am. 203* (3): 131–148.
BRAIDWOOD, R. J., COON, C. S., LINTON, R., MANGELSDORF, C., and OPPENHEIM, LEO. 1953. 'Did man once live by beer alone?' *Am. Anthrop. 55:* 515–526.
BRAIDWOOD, R. J., HOWE, B. HELBAEK, H., MASON, F. R., REED, C. A., and WRIGHT, JR. H. E. 1960. *Prehistoric Investigations in Iraqi Kurdistan.* Chicago U.P.
CARRINGTON, RICHARD. 1958. *Elephants.* Chatto, London.
CHILDE, V. G. 1942. *What Happened in History.* Penguin, London.
—— 1958. *The Pre-History of European Society.* Cassell, London.
COCKRILL, W. R. 1967. 'The Water Buffalo.' *Sci. Am. 217:* 118–125.
COLE, S. 1961. *The Neolithic Revolution.* Brit. Mus. (Nat. Hist). 2nd ed., London.
DARLING, F. FRASER. 1956. 'Man's Ecological Dominance through Domesticated Animals on Wild Lands.' *See* W. L. Thomas (General), pp. 778–787.
DARLINGTON, C. D. 1963*a*. *Chromosome Botany and the Origins of Cultivated Plants.* 2nd ed. Allen and Unwin, London.
—— 1963*b*. 'Psychology, Genetics and the Process of History.' *Br. J. Psych. 54:* 293–8.
DIMBLEBY, G. W. 1962. *The Development of British Heathlands and the Soils.* Oxford U.P.
DIMBLEBY, GEOFFREY. 1967. *Plants and Archaeology.* Barker, London.
DODGE, B. S. 1962. *Plants that changed the World.* Phoenix, London.
DIXON, J. E. *et al.* 1968. 'Obsidian and the origins of trade.' *Sci. Am. 218* (*3*)*:* 38–46.
ELTON, C. S. 1958. *The Ecology of Invasion by Animals and Plants.* Methuen, London.
ENGELBRECHT, TH. 1916. 'Über die Entstehung einiger feldmässig angebauter Kulturpflanzen.' *Geog. Zt. 22:* 328–334.
GLACKEN, C. J. 1956. 'Changing Ideas of the Habitable World.' *See* W. L. Thomas (General) pp. 70–92.
GLESINGER, EGON. 1960. 'The Mediterranean Project' (Maps). *Sci. Am. 203* (1)*:* 86–103.
GODWIN, H. *et al.* 1965. *Essays in Crop Plant Evolution.* Cambridge U.P.
GRZIMEK, BERNHARD. 1967. *Four-Legged Australians* (Animals and Men, Papua). Collins, London; Sydney.
HARLAN, J. R., and ZOHARY, D. 1966. 'Distribution of wild wheats and barley.' *Science. 153:* 1074–1080.
HARRIS, DAVID R. 1967. 'New light on plant domestication.' *Geog. Rev. 57:* 90–107.
HELBAEK, H. 1959. 'Domestication of food plants in the Old World.' *Science 130:* 365–372.
HELBAEK, Hans. 1966. 'Commentary on the Phylogenesis of *Triticum* and *Hordeum.*' *Economic Botany 20:* 350–360.
HOLE, F. 1962. 'The origins of agriculture in south-western Asia.' *N. Sci. 13:* 577–9.

HUTCHINSON, J. B. 1962. 'History and relationship of the world's cottons.' *Endeavour, 21:* 5–15.

HUTCHINSON, SIR JOSEPH. 1966. 'Land and human populations.' *Adv. Sci. 23:* 241–254.

JACKS, G. V. and WHYTE, R. O. 1944. *The Rape of the Earth: a World Wide Study of Soil Erosion.* Faber, London.

KENYON, K. 1957. *Digging up Jericho.* Benn, London.

LAMB, H. H. 1960. 'The World's Changing Climate.' *Listener 63:* 613–14.

MANGELSDORF, P. C. 1953. 'Agricultural Origins and Dispersals.' *Am. Antiquity 19:* 87–90.

MELLAART, JAMES. 1964. 'A Neolithic City in Turkey.' *Sci. Am. 210:* 94–104.

—— 1966. 'Chatal Huyuk—the World's Oldest City.' *I.L.N., 248:* 26–27.

—— 1967. *Çatal Huyük.* Thames and Hudson, London.

MOURANT, A. E., and ZEUNER, F. E. 1963. 'Man and Cattle. Symposium on Domestication.' *R. Anthr. Inst. Oc. Paper,* 18.

OPPENHEIM, LEO. 1950. 'On Beer and Brewing Techniques in Ancient Mesopotamia.' *Supp: J. Am. Or. Soc.*

PHILLIPS, E. D. 1961. 'The nomad peoples of the Steppes.' *See* Piggott 1961 (General).

REED, C. A. 1959. 'Animal Domestication in the Prehistoric Near East.' *Science 130:* 1629–39.

RODDEN, R. J. 1965. 'An early neolithic village in Greece.' *Sci. Am. 212:* 83–93.

RYDER, M. L. 1966. 'The exploitation of animals by man.' *Adv. Sci. 23:* 9–18.

SEMENOV, S. A. 1957 (1964). *Prehistoric Technology* (trans. M. W. Thompson). Cory, London.

VAVILOV, N. I. 1926. 'Studies on the Origin of Cultivated Plants.' *B. App. Bot. 16* (2): 139–248.

ZEUNER, F. E. 1959. *The Pleistocene Period: its Climate Chronology and Faunal Successions.* Hutchinson, London.

—— 1963. *A History of Domesticated Animals.* Hutchinson, London.

ZOHARY, M. 1962. *Plant Life in Palestine.* Ronald, N.Y.

5. BABYLONIA

ADAMS, R. M. 1960. 'The Origin of Cities.' *Sci. Am. 203*(3): 153–168.

ALBRIGHT, W. F. 1957. *From the stone age to Christianity.* Doubleday, N.Y.

CHILDE, V. GORDON. 1951. *Social Evolution.* Watts, London.

COULBORN, R. 1959. *Origin of Civilised Societies.* Oxford U.P.

DOUGHTY, C. M. 1888. *Travels in Arabia Deserta.* Cape, London (abridged) Penguin 1956.

EDWARDS, CHILPERIC. 1934. *The World's Earliest Laws* (Hammurabi). Watts, London.

ETKIN, W. 1954. 'Social Behaviour and the Evolution of Man's Mental Faculties.' *Am. Nat. 88:* 129–142.

FRIEDRICH, JOHANNES. 1957 (1962). Entzifferung Verschollener Schriften und Sprachen (trans. as *Extinct Languages*). Phil. Lib., N.Y. and Owen, London.

GUTKIND, E. A. 1956. *Our world from the air: conflct and adaptation* (*land use*). *See* W. L. Thomas (General).

JACOBSON, TH., and ADAMS, R. M. 1958. 'Salt and silt in ancient Mesopotamian agriculture.' *Science 128:* 1251–8.

LLOYD, SETON. 1961. *The Art of the Ancient Near East.* Thames and Hudson, London.

MALLOWAN, M. E. L. 1961. *The Birth of Written History. See* Piggott (General).

MENDELSOHN, I. 1949. *Slavery in the Ancient Near East.* Oxford U.P.

MOSCATI, S. 1960. *The Face of the Ancient Orient*. Routledge, London.
MUMFORD, LEWIS. 1956. 'The Natural History of Urbanization.' *See* W. L. Thomas (General) pp. 328–398.
—— 1961. *The City in History*. Secker, London.
PARROT, ANDRÉ. 1960. *Sumer* (Arts of Mankind). Thames and Hudson, London.
ROUX, G. 1964. *Ancient Iraq*. Allen and Unwin, London.
SAGGS, H. W. F. 1965. *Everyday Life of Babylonia and Assyria*. Batsford, London, Putman, N.Y.
SANDERS, N. K. 1960. *The Epic of Gilgamesh* (trans). Penguin, London.
THESIGER, W. 1959. *Arabian Sands*. Longman, London.
WOOLLEY, LEONARD. 1961. *Art of the World: Mesopotamia and the Middle East*. Methuen, London.

6. EGYPT

ALDRED, C. 1961. *The Egyptians*. Thames and Hudson, London.
BAEDEKER, KARL. 1929. *Egypt and the Sudan* (Map, Egypt). Baedeker, Leipzig.
COTTRELL, LEONARD. 1950. *The Lost Pharaohs*. Evans, London.
—— 1955. *Life under the Pharaohs*. Evans, London.
DESROCHES-NOBLECOURT, C. 1963. *Tutankhamen: Life and Death of a Pharaoh*. Joseph, London.
EMERY, W. B. 1961. *Archaic Egypt*. Longman, London.
GARDINER, A. 1961. *Egypt of the Pharaohs*. Oxford U.P.
KEES, HERMANN. 1961. *Ancient Egypt: a cultural topography* (trans.). Faber, London.
LANE, E. W. 1836 (5th ed. 1860). *The Manners and Customs of the Modern Egyptians* (Islam). Dent (Everyman) London.
MURRAY, MARGARET. 1949. *The Splendour that was Egypt*. Sidgwick, London.
POSENER, G. 1962. *A Dictionary of Egyptian Civilisation*. Methuen, London.
VELIKOVSKY, IMMANUEL. 1960. *Oedipus and Akhnaton*. Sidgwick, London.

7. THE MAKING OF EUROPE

ALBRIGHT, W. F. 1957. *From Stone Age to Christianity*. Doubleday, N.Y.
ATKINSON, R. J. C. 1956. *Stonehenge*. Hamilton, London.
BATH, B. H. S. VAN. 1963. *The Agrarian History of Western Europe*. Arnold, London.
BOSCH-GIMPERA, P. 1951. 'Problèmes de toponymie celtique en Espagne.' *Proc. 3 Int. Congr. Topon.*, Louvain, 497–506.
BOWEN, E. G. 1941. *Wales* (Bronze Age). Cardiff U.P.
BRØGGER, A. W. 1936. 'Bronze Age Exploration.' *Pres. Add. Int. Cong. Archeol.*, Oslo.
BROWN, ELIZABETH S. 1965. 'Distribution of the *ABO* and Rhesus (D) bloodgroups in the North of Scotland.' *Heredity*, *20:* 289–303.
CHILDE, V. GORDON. 1926. *The Aryans*. Kegan Paul, London.
—— 1958 *The Pre-History of European Society*. Penguin, London.
CHIRODI, C. *et al.* 1957. *Conosci l'Italia II: La Flora*. Tour. Club Italiano, Milan.
DANIEL, E. GLYN. 1958. *Megalith Builders of Western Europe*. Hutchinson, London.
DAUZAT, ALBERT, 1963. *Les Noms de Lieux*. Delagrave, Paris.
EVANS, E. ESTYN. 1956. 'The Ecology of Peasant Life in W. Europe'. *See* W. L. Thomas (General).
FUSTEL DE COULANGES, N.D. 1864. *La Cité antique*. Paris and Blackwell P.B. Oxford.
GODWIN, H. 1960. 'Radiocarbon dating and Quaternary History in Britain.' *P.R.S.* (B) *153:* 287–320.

GRAVES, ROBERT. 1947. *The White Goddess.* Faber, London.
GURNEY, O. R. 1961. *The Hittites.* Penguin, London.
HEICHELHEIM, F. M. 1956. 'Effects of Classical Antiquity on the Land.' *see* W. L. Thomas symp. (General).
HOYLE, FRED. 1966. 'Stonehenge—an eclipse predictor.' *Nature, 211:* 454–456.
HUBSCHMID, J. 1951.' Das Baskische und der Vorindo-germanische topographische Wortschatz Europäische Sprachen'. *Proc. 3 Int. Congr. Topon.*, Louvain, 183–191.
JESPERSON, OTTO. 1922 (1946). *Mankind, Nation and Individual.* Allen and Unwin, London.
MONGAIT, A. L. 1961. *Archaeology in the U.S.S.R.* Penguin, London.
MULLER-BECK, H. 1961. 'Prehistoric Swiss Lakes.' *Am. Sci. 205:* 138–147.
OZGUÇ, TAHSU. 1963. 'An Assyrian trading post.' *Sci. Am. 208:* 96–106.
PIGGOTT, STUART. 1965. *Ancient Europe from the Beginnings of Agriculture to Classical Antiquity.* Edinburgh U.P.
PFEIFER, G. 1956. 'The Quality of Peasant Living in Central Europe.' *See* W. L. Thomas (General) pp. 240–277.
ROSS, ANNE. 1967. *Pagan Celtic Britain.* Routledge, London.
THIEME, PAUL. 1958. 'The Indo-European Language.' *Sci. Am. 199:* 63–74.
THOM, ALEXANDER. 1967. *Megalithic Sites in Britain.* Oxford U.P.
TURNER, JUDITH. 1965. 'The history of forest clearance.' (in Britain). *P.R.S.* (B) *161:* 343–353.
WOOD, P. D. 1961. 'Strip lynchets reconsidered.' *Geog. J. 127:* 449–459.

8. GREEKS

ALSOP, JOSEPH. 1965. *From the Silent Earth* (Greek Bronze Age). Secker, London.
ANDREWES, A. 1956. *The Greek Tyrants.* Hutchinson, London.
BOARDMAN, JOHN. 1964. *The Greeks Overseas.* Penguin, London.
BAULIER, FRANCIS, and LANGHAM, G. 1953 (1955). *Greece* (Crete, Delphi, Athens, Sparta). Hachette, Paris.
BOWRA, C. M. 1957. *The Greek Experience.* Weidenfield, London.
BURN, A. R. 1965. *A Traveller's History of Greece.* Hodder, London.
BURNET, J. 1930. *Early Greek Philosophy.* Black, London.
BURTON-BROWN, T. 1959. *Early Mediterranean Migrations.* Manchester U.P.
CARY, M. 1949. *Geographical Background of Greek and Roman History.* Oxford U.P.
COTTRELL, LEONARD. 1953 (1955). *The Bull of Minos.* Evans, London.
EVANS, J. 1961. 'Earliest Settlement at Knossos.' *Ill. London News 239:* 366–7.
FARRINGTON, B. 1961. *Greek Science.* Penguin, London.
FINLEY, M. I. 1963. *Ancient Greeks.* Chatto, London.
GOAD, H. 1958. *Language in History.* Penguin, London.
GORDON, CYRUS H. 1962. *Before the Bible: the Common Background of Greek and Hebrew Civilisation.* Collins, London.
GRAVES, ROBERT. 1947. *The White Goddess.* Faber, London.
HAMMOND, N. G. L. 1959. *History of Greece to 322 B.C.* Oxford U.P.
HELBAEK, HANS. 1963. 'Late Cypriot vegetable diet at Apliki.' *Op. Athen. 8:* 171–186, Lund.
HERODOTUS (484–425 B.C.). *The Histories* (trans. Carter). Oxford U.P.
HUTCHINSON, R. W. 1967. *Prehistoric Crete.* Penguin, London.
HUXLEY, G. L. 1961. *Crete and the Luwians.* Oxford U.P.
—— 1966. *The Early Ionians.* Faber, London.
KITTO, H. D. F. 1955. *The Greeks.* Penguin, London.

LIVINGSTONE, SIR R. 1943. *Thucydides' History of the Peloponnesian War* (trans.) Oxford U.P.

LLOYD, SETON. 1961. *The Art of the Ancient Near East.* Thames and Hudson, London.

MICHELL, H. 1964. *Sparta.* Cambridge U.P.

MENDELSOHN, I. 1949. *Slavery in the Ancient Near East.* Oxford U.P.

MORETTINI, A. 1950. *Olivicoltura.* R.E.D.A., Rome.

NILSSON, M. P. 1932. *The Mycenaean Origin of Greek Mythology.* Cal. U.P.

ROSTOVTZEFF, M. I. 1926–30. *History of the Ancient World* (trans.). Oxford U.P.

SELTMAN, C. 1954. *Women in Antiquity.* Thames and Hudson, London.

9. SEMITES AND JEWS

BATES, E. SUTHERLAND. 1936. *The Bible designed to be read as Literature.* Heinemann, London.

BERTHOLLET, A. 1926. *History of Hebrew Civilisation.* Harrap, London.

CRUDEN, ALEXANDER. 1737 (1876). *Complete Concordance of the Old and New Testament.* Wesleyan Conf. Office, London.

CULICAN, WILLIAM. 1961. 'The first merchant venturers: sea peoples of the Levant.' *See* Piggott (General).

GADD, C. J. 1958. 'Harran inscriptions of Nabonidus.' *Anatol. Stud. 8:* 35–40.

GRAETZ, H. 1891. *History of the Jews.* Jewish Pub. Soc., U.S.A.

GRAVES, R., and PATAI, R. 1963. *Hebrew Myths.* Cassell, London.

HARDEN, DONALD. 1962 (1963). *The Phoenicians.* Thames and Hudson, London.

JACOBS, LOUIS. 1964. *Principles of the Jewish Faith.* Mitchell, London.

KENYON, K. M. 1965. 'Ancient Jerusalem.' *Sci. Am. 213:* 84–91.

LEWY, H. and J. 1943. 'The origin of the week and the oldest West Asiatic calendar.' *Heb. Union Coll. Ann. 17:* 1–152, Cincinnati.

LINDBLOM, J. 1963. *Prophecy in Ancient Israel.* Blackwell, Oxford.

LOWDERMILK, W. C. 1944. *Palestine, Land of Promise.* Gollancz, London.

MOSCATI, S. 1959. *The Semites in Ancient History.* Wales U.P., Cardiff.

—— 1960. *The Face of the Ancient Orient.* Routledge, London.

NILSSON, MARTIN P. 1920 (1960). *Primitive Time-Reckoning.* Lund, Oxford U.P.

ORLINSKY, H. M. 1960. *Ancient Israel.* Cornell U.P.

PFEIFFER, R. H. 1950. *Introduction to the Old Testament.* Black, London.

PRITCHARD, J. B. (Ed.) 1955. *Ancient Near Eastern Texts relating to O.T.* Oxford; Princeton U.P.

SIMOONS, F. J. 1961. *Eat not this Flesh.* Wisconsin U.P.

DE VAUX, R. 1957 (1961). *Ancient Israel.* (Les Institutions de l'Ancien Testament.) Darton, London.

WRIGHT, G. E. (ed.). 1961 (1965). *The Bible and the Ancient Near East.* Doubleday, N.Y.

YADIN, YIGAEL. 1964. *The Art of Warfare in Biblical Lands.* Weidenfeld, London.

10. PERSIA

BICKERMAN, E. 1966. 'The Seleucids and the Achaemenids.' *Acc. Naz. Lincei, Roma, Q. 76:* 87–117.

GHIRSHMAN, R. 1951. *Iran* (before Islam). Payot, Paris (Penguin, London, 1954)

HINZ, WALTHER, 1964. *Das Reich Elam.* Kohlhammer, Stuttgart.

MAZZARINO, S. 1966. 'Le vie di communicazione fra Impero achemenide e il mondo greco.' *Acc. Naz. Lincei, Roma, Q. 76:* 75–83.

OLMSTEAD, A. T. 1948. *History of the Persian Empire* (Achaemenids). Chicago U.P.

STARK, FREYA. 1937. *Baghdad Sketches.* (Devil Worshippers.) Murray, London.

SYKES, PERCY. 1921. *History of Persia.* Macmillan, London.
WULFF, H. E. 1966. 'The qanats of Iran.' *Sci. Am. 218 (4):* 94–105.

11. MACEDON

ARRIAN (A.D. 91–180). *Life of Alexander the Great.* Introd. and trans. A. de Selincourt. Penguin, London, 1958.
BEVAN, EDWYN R. 1927. *A History of Egypt under the Ptolemaic Dynasty.* Methuen, London.
FARRINGTON, B. 1961. *Greek Science.* Penguin, London.
FORSTER, E. M. 1938. *Alexandria.* Whitehead Morris, Alexandria.
HOGARTH, D. G. 1897. *Philip and Alexander of Macedon.* Murray, London.
PARR, P. J. 1962. 'Petra of the Nabataeans.' *Ill. London News 241:* 746–9.
PLUTARCH (A.D. 45–125). *Life of Alexander.* (Loeb Edn., 1919.) Heinemann, London.
ROSTOVTZEFF, M. I. 1925. *A History of the Ancient World: Greece.* (Trans. and Rev. 1962). Oxford U.P.
SCHOFF, W. H. (trans 1912). *Periplus of the Erythraean Sea.* Longman, London.
STARK, FREYA. 1958. *Alexander's Path.* Murray, London.
TARN, W. W. 1933a. 'Alexander the Great and the Unity of Mankind.' *P. B. Ac. 19:* 1–46.
—— 1933b. 'The Lineage of Ptolemy I.' *J. Hell. St. 53:* 57–61.

12. ROME

BAILEY, C. (ed.) 1923. *The Legacy of Rome.* Oxford U.P.
—— 1932. *Phases in the Religion of Ancient Rome.* Oxford U.P.
BLOCH, R. 1962. 'The Etruscans.' *Sci. Am. 206:* 83–94
—— 1960. *The Origins of Rome.* Thames and Hudson, London.
CHARLES-PICARD, G. and C. 1961. *Daily Life in Carthage* (trans.) Allen and Unwin, London.
CHIODI, CESARE. 1957. *L'Italia fisica.* Touring Club It., Milan.
CORRADI, G. 1961. *L'Italia storica.* Touring Club It., Milan.
COTTRELL, LEONARD. 1960. *Enemy of Rome* (Hannibal). Evans, London.
GRANT, MICHAEL. 1960. *The Romans.* Weidenfeld, London.
—— 1960. *Cicero: Introduction to Works.* Penguin, London.
—— 1967. *Gladiators.* Weidenfeld, London.
GRANT, M., and POTTINGER, D. 1960. *Romans.* Nelson, London.
HEITLAND, W. E. 1922. *The Roman Fate.* Cambridge U.P.
HEURGON, JACQUES. 1964. *Daily Life of the Etruscans* (trans.). Weidenfeld, London.
HODGKIN, T. 1880. *Italy and her Invaders.* Oxford U.P.
HUS, ALAIN. 1961. *The Etruscans.* Evergreen, N.Y.
LIDDELL HART, B. H. 1927. *Greater than Napoleon: Scipio Africanus.* Blackwood, London.
LIVY (59 B.C.–A.D. 17). *Early History of Rome* (Books I–V) (trans. introd. Aubrey de Selincourt). Penguin (1960) London.
MCDONALD, A. H. 1966. *Republican Rome* (Monuments). Thames and Hudson, London.
MATTINGLY, H. 1948. *Tacitus on Britain and Germany.* Penguin, London.
MÜNZER, F. 1920. *Römische Adelsparteien und Adelsfamilien.* Stuttgart.
PARKER, H. M. D. 1928 (1958). *The Roman Legions.* Heffer, Cambridge.
PICARD, G. 1963. *Carthage.* (trans.). Elek, London.
PLUTARCH (46–120 A.D.). *Fall of the Roman Republic* (trans. Rex Warner 1958). Penguin, London.
POLYBIUS (205–125 B.C.). *The Histories* (trans. W. R. Paton). Loeb, London.

RADICE, BETTY. 1965. *Introduction to Livy: the War with Hannibal.* (Maps.) Penguin, London.

RICHARDSON, EMELINE. 1966. *Etruscan Sculpture.* Collins (UNESCO) London.

SALLUST (86–34 B.C.). *The Jugurthine War and the Conspiracy of Cataline* (trans., introd. S. A. Handford, 1963). Penguin, London.

SYME, SIR RONALD. 1937. *The Roman Revolution.* Oxford U.P.

TOYNBEE, A. J. 1965. *Hannibal's Legacy.* Oxford U.P.

WARMINGTON, B. H. 1960. *Carthage.* Hale, London.

WESTERMANN, W. L. 1955. 'The Slave Systems of Greek and Roman Antiquity.' *Mem. Amer. Phil. Soc. 40:* (180 pp.) Philadelphia.

13. AUGUSTUS AND THE EMPIRE

BAYNES, N. H. 1943. 'Decline of the Roman Empire in Western Europe.' *J. Roman St. 33:* 29–35.

BOAK, A. E. R. 1955. *Manpower Shortage and the Fall of the Roman Empire.* Ann Arbor: U.M.P.

BUCHAN, JOHN. 1937. *Augustus.* Hodder, London.

BURY, J. B. 1923. *History of the Later Roman Empire* (395–565). Macmillan, London.

COWELL, F. R. 1961. *Everyday Life in Ancient Rome.* Batsford, London.

FINLEY, M. I. (ed.). 1960. *Slavery in Classical Antiquity.* Heffer, Cambridge.

FRANK, TENNEY. 1916. 'Race mixture in the Roman Empire.' *Am. Hist. Rev. 21:* 698–708.

KAGAN, D. 1962. *Decline and Fall of the Roman Empire.* Heath, Boston.

KATZ, SOLOMON. 1955. *The Decline of Rome and the Rise of Mediaeval Europe.* Cornell U.P.

LAST, HUGH. 1934. 'The Social Policy of Augustus.' *Camb. Ancient Hist. 10:* 14, 425–464.

MACMULLEN, RAMSEY, 1967. *Enemies of the Roman Order: Treason, Unrest and Alienation in the Empire.* Oxford and Harvard U.P.

MARRISON, L. W. 1957. *Wines and Spirits* (Maps). Penguin, London.

REINHOLD, M. 1933. *Marcus Agrippa.* Humphrey: Geneva, N.Y.

ROPER, A. G. 1913. *Ancient Eugenics.* Blackwell, Oxford.

ROSTOVTZEFF, M. I. 1957. *Social and Economic History of the Roman Empire.* (2nd ed.) Oxford U.P.

STARK, FREYA. 1966. *Rome on the Euphrates.* Myrray, London.

SUETONIUS (A.D. 69–140). *The Twelve Caesars* (trans. R. Graves). Penguin, London. (1957.)

WALBANK, F. W. 1953. *The Decline of the Roman Empire in the West.* Wishart, London.

14. CHRISTIANITY

BEDE (673–735). *Ecclesiastical History of the English Nation* (introd. V. D. Scudder). Dent, London (1910).

BETTENSON, H. 1943. *Documents of the Christian Church.* Oxford U.P.

CLINTON, H. F. 1845–1850. *Fasti Romani.* Oxford U.P.

DARLINGTON, C. D. 1961. 'Cousin marriage and population structure (Mennonites).' *Eug. Rev. 53:* 139–144.

DEANESLEY, M. 1964. *Augustine of Canterbury.* Nelson, London.

DUDDEN, F. H. 1905. *Gregory the Great.* Longmans, London.

FREND, W. H. C. 1965. 'The Church in the Roman Empire.' *The Listener 74:* 750–752.

JONES, A. H. M. 1948. *Constantine and the Conversion of Europe*. Hodder, London.
—— 1964. *The Later Roman Empire*. Blackwell, Oxford.
JOSEPHUS, FLAVIUS (A.D. 37–95). *The Jewish War* (trans., introd. G. A. Williamson). Penguin, London (1959).
KITZINGER, E., and SENIOR, E. 1941. *Portraits of Christ*. Penguin, London.
LECKY, W. E. H. 1877. *History of European Morals*. Longman, London.
MAY, HERBERT G. *et al*. 1962. *Oxford Bible Atlas*. Oxford U.P.
PARKES, JAMES. 1964. *A History of the Jewish People*. Penguin, London.
PLINY (A.D. 61–113). *Letters* (trans., introd. B. Radice). Penguin, London (1963).
SANDFORD, W. A. C. 1957. 'Mediaeval Clerical celibacy in England.' *General Mag. 12:* 371–5, 401–3.
SISMONDI, J. C. L. S. de. 1821–1844. 31 vol. *Histoire des Français*. T. and Würtz, Paris.
SMITH, A. D. HOWELL. 1950. *Thou art Peter: a history of Roman Catholic doctrine and practice*. Watts, London.
STARK, FREYA. 1966. *Rome on the Euphrates* (and in Anatolia). Murray, London.
TYLER, PHILIP. 1966. 'The pattern of Christian belief in Sekhukuniland.' *Church Rev.*, April, London.
VERMES, G. 1962 (1965). *The Dead Sea Scrolls in English*. Penguin, London.
WIDENGREN, G. 1966. The Mythraic mysteries in the Greco-Roman world (and Christian origins). *Acc. Naz. Lincei, Roma, Q. 76:* 443–455.
WILLIAMS, GLANVILLE. 1958. *The Sanctity of Life and the Criminal Law*. Faber, London.
WILLIAMSON, G. A. 1959. *Josephus: 'The Jewish War'* (introd.) trans. Penguin, London.
—— 1964. *The World of Josephus*. Secker, London.

15. ISLAM

ALPORT, E. A. 1954. 'The Mzab.' *J. R. Anth. Inst. 84:* 34–44.
AYALON, D. 1951. *L'Esclavage du Mamelouk*. Israel Oriental Soc. Pub. 1, Jerusalem.
BISCH, JØRGEN. 1962. *Behind the Veil of Arabia*. Allen and Unwin, London.
BRADFORD, ERNLE. 1964. *The Great Siege: Malta 1565*. Penguin, London.
BRIERLEY, T. 1965. 'Mauritania.' *Geog. Mag. 37:* 754–765
BURTON, RICHARD F. 1886. 'The Thousand Nights and a Night.' (Alf Laylah wa Laylah.) *Terminal Essay 10:* 63–302. Kamashastra Society, Benares.
CASKEL, W. 1954. 'The Beduinisation of Arabia.' *Am. Anthrop. 56:* 36–46.
DOUGHTY, C. M. 1888. *Travels in Arabia Deserta*. London, Cape (1921); Abb. Duckworth (1908); Penguin (1956).
GABRIELI, FRANCESCO. 1968. *Muhammad and the Conquests of Islam*. Weidenfeld, London.
GLUBB, SIR JOHN B. (Pasha). 1963. *The Great Arab Conquests*. Hodder, London.
—— 1964. *The Empire and the Arabs*. Hodder, London.
—— 1965. *The Course of Empire: the Arabs and their Successors*. Hodder, London.
HARDY, M. J. L. 1963. *Blood Feuds and the Payment of Blood Money in the Middle East*. Handy, Beirut.
HOGARTH, D. G. 1922. *Arabia*. Oxford U.P.
KRITZECK, J. 1964. *Anthology of Islamic Literature*. Penguin, London.
LANE, E. W. 1836. See ch. 6.
LANE-POOLE, STANLEY. 1894. *The Mohammedan Dynasties: Chronological and General Tables*. Constable, London.
LEVY, REUBEN. 1957. *The Social Structure of Islam* (2nd edn.). Cambridge U.P.
MARGOLIOUTH, D. S. 1905. *Mohammed and the Rise of Islam*. Putnam, N.Y.

MAXWELL, GAVIN. 1957. *A Reed Shaken by the Wind.* Longman, London.
—— 1966. *Lords of the Atlas* (Morocco 1893–1956). Longman, London.
RODWELL, J. M. 1909. *The Koran; with Introduction.* Dent, London.
STARK, FREYA. 1937. *Baghdad Sketches.* Murray, London.
—— 1941. *A Winter in Arabia.* Murray, London.
THESIGER, W. 1959. *Arabian Sands.* Longman, London.
TORREY, C. C. 1933. *The Jewish Foundations of Islam.* Bloch, N.Y.
VAN BEEK, GUS. 1961. *South Arabian History and Archaeology. See* G. E. Wright 1961.
WATT, W. MONTGOMERY. 1952. *Muhammed at Mecca.* Oxford U.P.
—— 1961. *Islam and the Integration of Society.* Routledge, London.

16. HINDUISM

BAILEY, F. G. 1960. *Tribe, Caste and Nation* (in Orissa). Manchester U.P.
BANKS, M. *Caste in Jaffna* (N. Ceylon). *See* Leach (1960).
BARTH, F. 1960. *See* Leach 1960.
BOSE, N. K. 1965. 'Calcutta: a premature metropolis.' *Sci. Am. 213:* 91–102.
BRUCE, GEORGE. 1968. *The Stranglers: the Cult of Thuggee and its Overthrow in British India.* Longmans, London.
CORPS, E. V. 1965. 'Assam.' *Geog. Mag. 37:* 666–681.
DALES, G. F. 1966. 'The Decline of the Harappans'. *Sci. Amer. 214:* No. 5: 93–100.
DE VOS, G., and WAGATSUMA, H. 1966. *Japan's Invisible Race* (Caste). Calif. U.P., Berkeley.
EDWARDES, MICHAEL. 1961. *A History of India.* Thames and Hudson, London.
GLOB, P. V., and BIBBY, T. G. 1960. 'A forgotten civilisation of the Persian Gulf' (Bahrein and Oman). *Sci. Am. 203:* 62–71.
GOUGH, E. K. 'Caste in a Tanjore Village.' *See* Leach 1960.
HODSON, T. C. 1937. *India: Census Ethnography: 1901–1931.* Gov. India Press, Delhi.
HUTTON, J. 1857. *A popular account of the Thugs and Dacoits, the Hereditary Garrotters and Gang-robbers of India.* (*cit.* J. H. Hutton).
HUTTON, J. H. 1941 (1961). *Caste in India* Cambridge U.P.
JENKINS, A. C. 1960. 'A vanishing people' (Todas) *Cm. 57:* 635–639.
KOSAMBI, D. D. 1950. *The Culture and Civilisation of Ancient India in Historical Outline.* Routledge, London.
—— 1956. *An Introduction to the Study of Indian History.* Luzac, London. Probsthian, London 1957.
—— 1967. 'Living prehistory in India.' *Sc. Am. 216:* 105–114.
KROEBER, A. L. 1931. 'Caste.' *Enc. Soc. Sciences,* London.
LEACH, E. R. (ed.). 1960. *Aspects of Caste in South India, Ceylon and North-West Pakistan.* Cambridge U.P.
LUIZ, A. A. D. 1962. 'Tribes of Kerala', *B.A.J.S.S.,* Delhi.
MAJUMDAR, D. J. 1958. *Races and Cultures of India.* Asia P. Ho., Bombay.
NEWELL, W. H. 1955. 'The Brahman and Caste Isogamy in Northern India.' *J.R. Anthrop. Inst. 85:* 101-110.
OUWERKERK, L. 1945. *The Untouchables of India.* Oxford U.P., London.
PIGGOTT, STUART. 1950 (1952). *Prehistoric India.* Penguin, London.
POCOCK, D. F. 1960. 'Caste and Varna.' *Man. 60:* 183.
RAO, S. R. 1961. 'New Light on Indus Valley Civilisation.' *I.L.N. 238:* 302–4.
RISLEY, H. H. 1908 (1915). *The People of India.* Thacker, Calcutta.
ROUSSELL, A. 1961. 'Stamp Seals of 4000 years ago: Failaka.' *I.L.N. 238:* 142–3.
SPEAR, PERCIVAL. 1965. *A History of India* (vol. 2). Penguin, London.

SRINIVAS, M. N., and BÉTEILLE, A. 1965. 'The "Untouchables" of India.' *Sci. Am. 213:* 13–17.
THAPAR, ROMILA, 1966. *A History of India* (vol. 1). Penguin, London.
THURSTON, E., and RANGACHARI, K. 1909. *Castes and Tribes of Southern India.* Madras Gov. Press.
WALLBANK, T. 1958. *A Short History of India and Pakistan.* New American Library (Mento) N.Y.
WHEELER, SIR MORTIMER. 1966. *Civilisations of the Indus Valley and Beyond.* Thames and Hudson, London.
WILSON, J. 1877. *Indian Caste* (*cit.* J. H. Hutton).
WOODRUFF, PHILIP. 1953. *The Men who Ruled India.* Cape, London.

17(i). BYZANTIUM

BAYNES, N. H., and MOSS, H. ST. L. B. (ed.) 1948. *Byzantium.* Oxford U.P.
RUNCIMAN, STEVEN. 1933. *Byzantine Civilisation.* Arnold, London.
SEWTER, E. R. A. 1953 (1966). *Fourteen Byzantine Rulers: the Chronographia of Michael Psellus.* Routledge, Penguin, London.
TODOROV, N. *et al.* 1965. *Bulgaria: Historical and Geographical Outline.* Gov. Pub., Sofia.
WILLIAMSON, G. N. 1966. *Procopius: the Secret History* (introd.). Penguin, London.
WITTFOGEL, K. A. 1963. *Oriental Despotism.* Blackwell, Oxford.

17(ii). THE TURKS

ALDERSON, A. D. 1956. *The Structure of the Ottoman Dynasty.* Oxford U.P.
BRADFORD, ERNLE. 1961. *The Great Siege: Malta 1565.* Hodder, London.
BURTON, A. N. 1965. 'Calabria.' *Geog. Mag. 38:* 207–221.
COLES, PAUL. 1968. *The Ottoman Impact on Europe.* Thames and Hudson, London.
CREASY, E. S. 1961. *History of the Ottoman Turks.* (Trans. Zeine.) Khayats, Beirut.
DOUGLAS, NORMAN. 1915. *Old Calabria.* Secker, London.
JENKINS, ROMILLY, 1961. *The Dilessi Murders* (Clefts and Armatoles). Longman, London.
LEWIS, GEOFFREY. 1965. *Turkey.* (3rd ed.) Benn, London.
LIAS, GODFREY. 1955. *Kazak Exodus: 1951–54.* Evans, London.
LYBYER, A. H. 1913. *The Government of the Ottoman Empire in the Time of Suleiman the Magnificent.* Camb. Mass. U.P.
MERRIMAN, R. B. 1944. *Suleiman the Magnificent.* Harvard U.P.
MILLER, BARNETTE. 1941. *The Palace School of Muhammad the Conqueror.* Harvard U.P.
NEWALL, V. and J. 1963. 'Crossing into Albania.' *Geog. Mag. 36:* 304–312.
SITWELL, SACHEVERELL. 1955. *Selected Works* (Roumania: Skopzi). Hale, London.
VUCINICH, WAYNE S. 1965. *The Ottoman Empire: its Record and Legacy.* Nostrand, N.Y.

17(iii). VENICE

ARGENTI, P. P. 1955. *Libro d'Oro de la Noblesse de Chio.* Oxford U.P.
BLOCH, MARC. 1940 (1961). *Feudal Society.* Routledge, London.
BROWN, HORATIO R. F. 1902. *The Venetian Republic.* Dent, London.
CIPOLLA, CARLO M. 1965. *Guns and Ships in the Early Phase of European Expansion: 1400–1700.* Collins, London.
DAVIS, J. C. 1963. *The Decline of the Venetian Nobility as a Ruling Class.* J. Hopkins, Baltimore.

DEMOLINS, EDMOND. 1898. *Les Français d'Aujourd'hui; les types sociaux du Midi et du Centre.* Firmin-Didot, Paris.

JUSSERAND, J. J. 1889 (1925). English Wayfaring Life in the Middle Ages. Allen and Unwin, London.

PFEIFER, G. 1956. 'The Quality of Peasant Living in Central Europe.' *See* W. L. Thomas, pp. 240–277.

SHAW, M. R. B. (introd., trans.) 1963. *Chronicles of the Crusades: Joinville and Villehardouin.* Penguin, London.

PIRENNE, HENRI. 1925. *Mediaeval Cities.* (trans.). Princeton U.P.

YOUNG, ARTHUR. 1794. *Travels in France.* Bury St. Edmunds (and London 1890).

18 and 19. REFERENCES TO BRITAIN (Ch. 18 and 19)

BARROW, G. W. S. 1956. *Feudal Britain.* Arnold, London.

BEDDOE, J. 1885. *The Races of Britain.* Trübner, London.

BRADFORD, J. S. P., and GOODCHILD, R. G. 1939. 'Excavations at Frilford, Berks.' *Oxoniensia 4:* 1–70.

BRERETON, GEOFFREY. 1968. *Froissart's Chronicles* (introd.) Penguin, London.

DARBY, H. C. 1956. 'The Clearing of the Woodland in Europe.' *See* W. L. Thomas symp. (General) pp. 183–216.

DARLING, F. FRASER. 1963. 'The unity of ecology.' *Adv. Sci. 20:* 297–306.

EKWALL, B. O. E. 1954. *Street Names of the City of London.* Oxford U.P.

FLEURE, H. J. 1951. *A Natural History of Man in Britain.* Collins, London.

FOX, SIR CYRIL. 1947. *The Personality of Britain.* N. Mus. Wales, Cardiff·

GODWIN, H. 1960. 'Radiocarbon dating and Quaternary History in Britain.' *P.R.S.* (B) *153:* 287–320.

GREEN, B., and YOUNG, R. M. R. 1964. *Norwich—The Growth of a City.* Norwich Museums Committee.

HARDEN, D. B. (Ed.) 1956. *Dark Age Britain.* Methuen, London.

HODGEN, MARGARET. 1952. 'Change and History'. (Technical Immigration.) *Viking Pub. Anthrop. 18:* N.Y.

HOSKINS, W. G. 1960. *Two Thousand Years in Exeter.* Townsend, Exeter.

JOLLIFFE, J. E. A. 1933. *Pre-Feudal England: the Jutes.* Oxford U.P.

JONES, GLANVILLE. 1961. 'Settlement patterns in Anglo-Saxon England.' *Antiquity 35:* 221–232.

KEEN, MAURICE. 1966. *The Outlaws of Mediaeval Legend.* Routledge, London.

LARGE, J. S. P. A. 1967. 'Copper for the Queen.' *Countryman 68:* 101–107.

LEWIS, M. J. T. 1965. *Temples in Roman Britain.* Cambridge U.P.

LEYSER, KARL. 1960. 'England and the Empire in the early Twelfth Century.' *Trans. R. Hist. Soc.* (5) *10:* 61–83.

MERRIFIELD, RALPH. 1965. *The Roman City of London.* Benn, London.

MITCHELL, R. J., and LEYS, M. D. R. 1958. *A History of London Life.* Longman, London.

MYRES, J. N. L. 1954. *The Oxford Region.* Brit. Ass.: Oxford U.P.

ORWIN, C. S. and C. S. 1938. *The Open Field.* Oxford U.P.

PEVSNER, N. 1956. *The Englishness of English Art.* Penguin, London.

PROTHERO, ROWLAND E. (LORD ERNLE). 1912. *English Farming Past and Present.* Heinemann, London.

QUINAULT, R. E. 1967. 'London and the great leap forward'. *The Listener 78:* 115.

RASMUSSEN, STEEN. 1934. *London, the Unique City.* Cape, London.

RUSSELL, J. C. 1948. *British Mediaeval Population.* Albuquerque U.P., N. Mexico.

TOLKIEN, J. R. R. *et al.* 1963. *Angles and Britons.* Wales U.P., Cardiff.

WAGNER, A. R. 1960. *English Genealogy*. Oxford U.P.
—— 1961. *English Ancestry*. Oxford U.P.
WATKIN, I. MORGAN. 1965. 'ABO blood groups, human history and language in Herefordshire. . . .' *Heredity 20:* 83–95.
—— 1967. 'Human genetics in Worcestershire and the Shakespeare Country.' *Heredity*, 22: 349–358.
WHITELOCK, DOROTHY. 1952. *The Beginnings of English Society*. Penguin, Harmondsworth.
—— (ed.) 1961. *Anglo Saxon Chronicle*. Eyre and Spottiswoode, London.

18. NEW NATIONS

BLOCH, MARC. 1961. *Feudal Society*. Routledge, London.
—— 1961. *Development of Class Distinctions from service, dependance and protection.* Routledge, London.
BROOKE, CHRISTOPHER. 1963. *The Saxon and Norman Kings*. Batsford, London.
DARBY, H. C. 1956. 'The Clearing of the Woodland in Europe.' *See* W. L. Thomas symp. (General) pp. 183–216.
ESTYN EVANS, E. 1956. 'The Ecology of Peasant Life in Western Europe.' *See* W. L. Thomas (General) pp. 217–239.
HALPHEN, LOUIS. 1947. *Eginhard: Vie de Charlemagne*. Belles Lettres, Paris.
FLEURE, H. J. 1922. *The Peoples of Europe* (maps). Oxford U.P.
GINI, CORRADO. 1949. 'The physical assimilation of the descendants of immigrants.' *Hereditas* S.V. 234–243.
HOSKINS, W. G. 1960. *Two Thousand Years in Exeter*. Townsend, Exeter.
HIJLKEMA, RIET. 1951. *National Costumes in Holland.* (Staphorst.) Meulenhoff, Amsterdam.
HUTTON, E. 1950. *The Cosmati: the Roman marble workers of the XII and XIII Centuries*. Routledge, London.
ISENBURG, W. K. PRINZ VON. 1956. *Stammtafeln z. Geschichte der Europäische Staaten* (IV B). Marburg.
JACKSON, R. 1966. 'The Village that Time Forgot.' (Staphorst.) *The Humanist 10:* 180–183, London.
JENKINS, A. C. 1967. *The Golden Band: Holland's Fight against the Sea*. Methuen, London.
LAET, S. J. DE. 1957. *Archaeology and its Problems*. Phoenix, London.
LEYSER, K. J. 1960. 'England and the Empire in the early Twelfth Century.' *Trans. R. Hist. Soc.* (V) *10:* 61–83.
MOLLER, H. 1964. *Population Movements in Modern European History*. Macmillan, London and N.Y.
PIRENNE, HENRI. 1939 (1968). *Mohammed and Charlemagne* (trans.). Allen and Unwin, London.
—— 1925. *Mediaeval Cities* (trans.). Princeton U.P.
RUNCIMAN, S. 1958. *The Sicilian Vespers: a History of the Mediterranean World in the later Thirteenth Century*. Cambridge U.P.
SISAM, K. 1953. 'Anglo-Saxon Royal Genealogies.' *Proc. Brit. Academy*, Oxford U.P.
SOUTHERN, R. W. 1953. *The Making of the Middle Ages*. Hutchinson, London.
TAWNEY, R. H. 1938 (1926). *Religion and the Rise of Capitalism*. Penguin, London.
TOURVILLE, HENRI DE. 1907. *The Growth of Modern Nations: A history of the particularist form of society*. (trans.) Arnold, London.
ULLMANN, W. 1961. *Principles of Government and Politics in the Middle Ages*. Methuen, London.
VEEN, J. VAN. 1962. *Dredge, drain, reclaim: the art of a nation*. Nijhoff, Hague.

19. THE INTRUDERS—VIKINGS, BRITAIN, CRUSADES, IRELAND

ATIYA, A. S. 1962. *Crusade, Commerce and Culture.* Oxford U.P.

BRØGGER, A. W. 1929. *Ancient Emigrants: a History of the Norse Settlements in Scotland (A.D. 780–1500).* Oxford U.P.

BRØNDSTED, JOHANNES. 1960. *The Vikings.* Penguin, London.

CURTIS, EDMUND. 1950. *A History of Ireland* (6th ed.) Methuen, London.

DOUGLAS, DAVID C. 1964. *William the Conqueror: the Norman Impact upon England.* Eyre and Spottiswoode, London.

—— 1947. 'The Rise of Normandy.' *Proc. Brit. Acad. 33:* 1–32.

DUFFY, C. 1964. *The Wild Goose and the Eagle: a Life of Marshal von Browne 1705–1757.* Chatto, London.

HASKINS, C. H. 1918. *Norman Institutions.* Ungar, N.Y.

HAYES, RICHARD. 1937. 'The German Colony in County Limerick.' *N. Munster Antiq. Jour. 1:* 42–53.

HOLDSWORTH, SIR WM. 1908–42. 'A History of English Law.' *Primogeniture 3:* 171–3, Methuen, London.

HOLT, J. C. 1965. *Magna Carta.* Cambridge U.P.

HURSTFIELD, JOEL. 1958. *The Queen's Wards: Wardship and Marriage under Elizabeth I.* Longman, London.

HYDE, DOUGLAS. 1899 (1967). *A Literary History of Ireland.* Benn, London.

JONES, GWYN. 1964. *The Norse Atlantic Saga.* Oxford U.P.

LECHANTEUR, F. 1951. 'Matronymie en Basse Normandie'. *Proc. 3 Int. Cong. Toponymie, Louvain.* 756–763.

LEWIS, BERNARD. 1967. *The Assassins: a Radical Sect in Islam.* Weidenfeld, London.

LOYD, L. C. 1961. *The Origins of some Anglo-Norman Families.* Leeds U.P.

LOYN, H. R. 1962. *Anglo-Saxon England and the Norman Conquest.* Longman, London.

LUNDMAN, BERTIL. 1962. 'The Racial History of Scandinavia.' *Mankind Quart. 3* (2) 1–13.

MAGNUSSON, M., and PALSSON, H. 1966. *King Harold's Saga* (Introd., Trans.) Penguin, London.

OMAN, C. W. 1893. *Warwick the Kingmaker.* Macmillan, London and N.Y.

OXENSTIERNA, E. 1967. 'The Vikings.' *Sci. Am. 216:* 67–77.

PÉRIER, PHILIPPE. 1964. 'Recherches d'un "Comité des Fjords". ' *Rev. Int. Soc. II. 2:* 3–27.

PERNOUD, RÉGINE. 1959. *The Crusaders* (trans.) Oliver and Boyd, Edinburgh.

PLUCKNETT, T. F. T. 1945. *The Legislation of Edward I.* Oxford U.P.

POOLE, A. L. 1955. 2nd ed. *From Domesday Book to Magna Carta.* Oxford U.P.

PREBBLE, J. 1963. *The Highland Clearances.* Secker, London.

RUNCIMAN, STEVEN. 1951–4. *A History of the Crusades.* Cambridge U.P.

SCHOENBECK, BENGT. 1966. 'Swedish golden age and Viking art now in London.' *I.L.N. 248:* 25–27.

SLOCOMBE, G. 1960. *Sons of the Conqueror.* Hutchinson, London.

SOUTHERN, R. W. 1933. 'Ranulf Flambard and Early Anglo-Norman Administration.' *Trans. R. Hist. Soc. 16:* 95–128.

STENTON, SIR FRANK M. 1943. *Anglo Saxon England.* Oxford U.P.

—— 1944. 'English Families and the Norman Conqueror.' *Trans. R. Hist. Soc. 26:* 1–12.

SYSON, LESLIE. 1965. *British Water Mills.* Batsford, London.

TURNER, JUDITH. 1965. 'The history of forest clearance' (in Britain). *Proc. R. Soc. (B). 161:* 343–353.

VELBAEK, C. L. 1964. 'Vikings in Greenland.' *I.L.N. 244:* 90–92.

WATKIN, I. MORGAN. 1960. 'A Viking Settlement in Little England.' *Man. 60:* 193.

WHITE, G. H. 1949. 'Henry I's illegitimate children.' *The Complete Peerage 11.* app. D. 105–121.

WHITE, LYNN. 1962. *Mediaeval Technology and Social Change.* Oxford U.P.

WOODHAM-SMITH, C. 1962. *The Great Hunger: Ireland 1845–9.* Hamilton, London.

20. JEWISH INVOLVEMENT

ABRAHAMS, ISRAEL, 1896. *Jewish Life in the Middle Ages.* Macmillan, London and N.Y.

BABEL, ISAAC. 1963. *Lyubka the Cossack* (trans.). Signet, N.Y.

BENTWICH, N. 1960. *The Jews in our Time.* Pelican, London.

DIMONT, MAX I. 1962. *Jews, God and History.* Simon and Schuster, N.Y. (and Signet).

DUNN, L. C. 1959. *Heredity and Evolution in Human Populations.* Harvard U.P. (Oxford U.P.)

FISHBERG, MAURICE. 1911. *The Jews.* Scott, London, N.Y.

—— 1923. 'Intermarriage between Jews and Christians.' *2nd Int. Cong. Eugenics, 2:* 125–133, N.Y.

GRAVES, R., and HOGARTH, P. 1965. *Majorca Observed.* Cassell, London.

HARRISON, G. B. 1965. *The Elizabethan Journals* (Lopez). Doubleday, N.Y.

HUXLEY, ELSPETH. 1964. 'Jews in the United Kingdom.' *Punch,* January 15th, London.

KAMEN, HENRY. 1965. *The Spanish Inquisition.* Weidenfeld, London.

KITZINGER, ERNST. 1965. *Israeli Mosaics of the Byzantine Period.* Collins, London (UNESCO).

LUKE, SIR HARRY. 1963. 'Salonika: 1907–1962.' (Jews, Vlachs.) *Geog. Mag. 36:* 290–296.

MACFARLANE, E. W. E. 1938. 'Racial affinities of the Jews in Cochin.' *Bengal 3:* 1–23.

MORTON, F. 1962. *The Rothschilds.* Secker, London.

MOURANT, A. E. 1959. 'The blood groups of the Jews.' *Jewish J. Sociol. 1:* 155–176.

NOVINSKY, A., and PAULO, A. 1967. 'The last Marranos.' *Commentary* (N.Y. 22) *5:* 76–82.

PEYREFITTE, R. 1965. *Les Juifs* (minimal value). Flammarion, Paris.

ROTH, CECIL. 1932 (1960). *History of the Marranos.* London, Harper (Mayflower, 3rd. Ed.).

ROTH, C. 1960. 'The Perpetual Pattern of Revolution.' *The Listener 64:* 465–466.

—— 1964. *A History of the Jews in England.* Oxford U.P.

SITWELL, SACHEVERELL. 1950. *Spain.* Batsford, London.

STRACHEY, LYTTON. 1928. *Elizabeth and Essex.* Chatto, London.

TELLER, JUDD. 1966. *The Jews.* Bantam, N.Y.

ZINKIN, T. 1958. 'The Jews of Cochin—white, black and brown.' *M. Guardian* (December 18, 1958).

21. REFORMATION AND CHURCH

ATKISON, W. C. 1960. *A History of Spain and Portugal.* Penguin, London.

BASKERVILLE, GEOFFREY. 1937. *English Monks and the Suppression of the Monasteries.* Cape, London.

BRADLEY, PETER. 1965. 'Languedoc: land of the Albigensians today.' *Geog. Mag. 38:* 489–502.

BYRNE, M. ST. CLAIRE. 1936. *The Letters of King Henry VIII.* Cassell, London.

COGHILL, NEVILL. 1951. *Chaucer's Canterbury Tales* (Introduction). Penguin, London.
CROSSLEY, F. H. 1935. *The English Abbey* (revd. 1962, Little). Batsford, London.
CHADWICK, OWEN. 1964. *The Reformation*. Penguin, London.
ELTON, G. R. 1962. *Reformation in Europe 1517–1559*. Collins, London.
GREGOROVIUS, FERDINAND. 1874. *Lucrezia Borgia* (trans. 1948). Phaidon, London.
HEER, FRIEDRICH. 1961 (1962). *The Mediaeval World: 1100–1350* (trans.). Weidenfeld, London.
HOWELL SMITH, A. D. 1950. *Thou Art Peter: a History of Roman Catholic Doctrine and Practice*. Watts, London.
MCFARLANE, K. B. 1953. *John Wycliffe and the Beginnings of English Nonconformity*. English U.P.
PERCY, LORD EUSTACE. 1937. *John Knox*. Hodder, London.
PEYREFITTE, ROGER. 1964. *The Prince's Person* (trans.). Secker, London.
RUSSELL, J. B. 1965. *Dissent and Reform in the Early Middle Ages*. U. Calif. Press.
SOUTHEY, ROBERT. 1820. *Life of John Wesley*. Various edns.
STONE, BRIAN. 1964. *Mediaeval English Verse*. Penguin, London.
ULLMANN, WALTER. 1963. 'The Inquisition: an Explanation.' *The Listener 59:* 671–3.
—— 1965. *A History of Political Thought: the Middle Ages*. Penguin, London.
UNWIN, RAYNER. 1960. *The Defeat of John Hawkins*. Allen and Unwin, London.
VALE, EDMUND, 1956. *A Portrait of English Churches*. Batsford, London.

22. REFORMATION AND SOCIETY

BAREA, ILSA. 1966. *Vienna: Legend and Reality* (Protestant expulsion). Secker, London.
BEDFORD, DUKE OF. 1965. *Book of Snobs*. Owen, London.
BLOOMFIELD, PAUL. 1955. *Uncommon People: a Study of England's Elite*. Hamilton, London.
BONAR, JAMES. 1931. *Theories of Population from Raleigh to Arthur Young*. Allen and Unwin, London.
BOSWELL, JAMES. 1791. *Life of Samuel Johnson*. Various editions.
BRIDENBAUGH, CARL. 1968. *Vexed and Troubled Englishmen, 1590–1642*. Oxford U.P.
BRIGGS, ASA. 1952. *History of Birmingham 1865–1938*. Oxford U.P.
BULLER, A. H. R. 1919. *Essays on Wheat* (Mennonites). Macmillan, N.Y.
BURCKHARDT, JACOB (1818–97). 1860. *The Civilisation of the Renaissance of Italy* (trans. 1878). Phaidon: Allen and Unwin (1940), London.
CARR-SAUNDERS, A. M. and JONES, D. CARADOG. 1927. *Survey of the Social Structure of England and Wales*. Oxford U.P.
CHADWICK, OWEN. 1964. *The Reformation* (maps). Penguin, London.
CLARENDON, EDWARD HYDE, EARL OF. 1702–4. *The Rebellion and the Civil Wars in England.* Oxford U.P. (various).
COLEMAN, Terry. 1965 (1968). *The Railway Navvies*. Hutchinson, Penguin, London.
CURTIS, M. H. 1959. *Oxford and Cambridge in Transition 1558–1642*. Oxford U.P.
DARLINGTON, C. D. 1948. *The Conflict of Science and Society*. Watts, London.
DISRAELI, BENJAMIN. 1845. *Sybil or The Two Nations*. Various editions.
GILL, CONRAD. 1952. *History of Birmingham: Manor and Borough to 1865*. Oxford U.P.
GILLE, BERTRAND. 1966. *The Renaissance Engineers* (trans.). Humphries, London.

GUN, W. T. J. 1928. *Studies in Hereditary Ability.* Allen and Unwin, London.
HARTLEY, SIR HAROLD. 1967. 'John Dalton and the Atomic Theory.' *P.R.S.* (A) *300:* 291–315.
HILL, CHRISTOPHER. 1940. *The English Revolution, 1640.* Wishart, London.
HOSKINS, W. G. 1955. *English Landscape.* Hodder, London.
JAEGER, MURIEL. 1956. *Before Victoria: Changing Standards and Behaviour, 1787–1837.* Chatto, London.
KEYNES, LORD. 1947. 'Newton, the Man.' *Newton Tercentenary Celebrations* (*Roy. Soc.*) Cambridge U.P.
LAVER, JAMES. 1966. *The Age of Optimism: Manners and Morals 1848-1914.* Weidenfeld, London.
LEONARDO DA VINCI. 1952. *Selections from the Notebooks.* Oxford U.P.
MCLACHLAN, H. 1943. *Warrington Academy.* Manchester: Chetham Soc.
MACAULAY, LORD. 1848, 1855. *The History of England* (*1688–1700*). Various editions.
MACDERMOT, E. T. 1911. *The History of the Forest of Exmoor.* Barnicott, Taunton.
MAGNUS, PHILIP. 1954. *Gladstone: a Biography.* Murray, London.
MANUCY, ALBERT. 1949. *Artillery throughout the Ages.* U.S.G.P.O., Washington.
MOLLER, HERBERT. 1964. *Population Movements in Modern European History.* Macmillan, N.Y.
MORGAN, AUGUSTUS DE. 1885. *Newton: his Friend: and his Niece.* Elliott Stock, London.
NICHOLSON, MAX. 1967. *The System* (Jowettocracy). Hodder, London.
ORWIN, C. S. 1929. *The Reclamation of Exmoor Forest.* Oxford U.P.
PAINE, THOMAS. 1791. *Rights of Man: being an Answer to Mr. Burke's Attack on the French Revolution* (7th ed.). Everyman 1941, London.
PLUMB, J. H. 1955. *Sir Robert Walpole.* Oxford U.P.
PEARSON, HESKETH. 1930. *Doctor* (*Erasmus*) *Darwin: The Lunar Society.* Dent, London.
—— 1965. *Extraordinary People* (The non-Establishment). Heinemann, London.
RAISTRICK, ARTHUR. 1953. *Dynasty of Ironfounders.* (Darby, Wilkinson, Knight.) Longman, London.
READER, W. J. 1966. *Professional Men.* (19th-century England.) Weidenfeld, London.
SCHOFIELD, R. E. 1963. *The Lunar Society of Birmingham* (1767). *Roy. Soc. Notes and Rec. 21:* 144–161.
—— 1967. *The Lunar Society of Birmingham: a Social History of Provincial Science and Industry etc.* Oxford U.P.
SITWELL, SACHEVERELL. 1955. *Selected Works* (Roumania: Skoptzi). Hale, London.
SNOW, C. P. 1959. *The Two Cultures and the Scientific Revolution.* Cambridge U.P.
SOUTHEY, ROBERT. 1820. *Life of John Wesley.* Various editions.
TAWNEY, R. H. 1926. *Religion and the Rise of Capitalism.* Murray, London.
TREVELYAN, G. M. 1938. *The English Revolution: 1688–1689.* Oxford U.P.
TREVOR ROPER, H. R. 1957. *Historical Essays* (Quakers). Macmillan, London and N.Y.
TURNER, REV. WM. 1813–1815. *The Warrington Academy.* Warrington Lib. Mus. Com. (1957).
WAGNER, A. R. 1960. *English Genealogy.* Oxford U.P.
WHITE, TERENCE H. 1950. *The Age of Scandal* (*1740–1820*). Cape, London.
YOUNG, ARTHUR. 1794. *Travels in France.* Bury St. Edmunds and London (1890).
ZIRKLE, CONWAY. 1959. *Evolution, Marxian Biology and the Social Scene.* Penna. U.P.

23. REVOLUTION IN THE WEST

ACTON, LORD. 1906. *Lectures on Modern History*. Macmillan, London.
ASHLEY, MAURICE. 1957. *The Greatness of Oliver Cromwell*. Macmillan, N.Y.
AVINERI, SHLOMO. 1967. 'From Hoax to Dogma: a Footnote on Marx and Darwin.' *Encounter 28:* 30–32.
BERLIN, ISAIAH. 1939. *Karl Marx*. Butterworth, London.
CARR, E. H. 1933 (1949). *The Romantic Exiles*. Gollancz, London.
COBBAN, ALFRED. 1965. *The Social Interpretation of the French Revolution*. Cam-. bridge U.P.
COOPER, DUFF. 1932. *Talleyrand*. Cape, London.
CRANKSHAW, EDWARD. 1962. *The Fall of the House of Habsburg* (Franz Josef). Longman, London.
DARLINGTON, C. D. 1964. *Genetics and Man*. Allen and Unwin, London. (Penguin 1966).
DRUMMOND, J. C., and WILBRAHAM, A. 1939. *The Englishman's Food*. Cape, London.
FORD, FRANKLIN L. 1953. *Robe and Sword: the Regrouping of the French Aristocracy after Louis XIV*. Harper, N.Y.
FRANK, JOSEPH. 1955. *The Levellers*. Harvard U.P.
FUSSELL, G. E., and MCGREGOR, O. R. 1961. *Ernle's English Farming: Introduction*. Heinemann, London.
HALDANE, J. B. S. 1938. 'Blood royal.' *Mod. Quart. 1:* 129.
HAMMOND, J. L. and B. 1911 (1927). *The Village Labourer*. Longman, London.
HAMPSON, NORMAN. 1963. *A Social History of the French Revolution*. Routledge, London. (Toronto U.P.)
KROPOTKIN, P. A. 1902. *Mutual Aid, a factor of Evolution*. Heinemann, London.
MACALPINE, IDA *et al.* 1968. *Porphyria—a Royal Malady*. B.M.A. London.
MARX, KARL. 1852. *The Eighteenth Brumaire of Louis Bonaparte*. Allen and Unwin, London (1926).
MARX, K., and ENGELS, F. 1848 (trans. 1888). *Manifesto of the Communist Party*. London: Lawrence (1934) Penguin (1967).
MATHER, F. C. 1965. *Chartism*. Hist. Assn., London.
MITFORD, NANCY. 1966. *The Sun King* (Louis XIV). Hamilton, London.
MONCREIFFE, IAIN, and POTTINGER, DON. 1956. *Blood Royal*. Nelson, Edinburgh.
MORRÉ, HAROLD. 1909. *20 Jahre S.M.: heitere Bilder zu ernsten Ereignissen*. Lust. Blätter, Berlin.
NADA, JOHN. 1962. *Carlos the Bewitched: the last Spanish Hapsburg: 1661–1700*. Cape, London.
NICOLSON, HAROLD. 1946. *The Congress of Vienna*. Constable, London.
OGG, DAVID. 1965. *Europe of the Ancien Régime*. London, Collins.
PETRIE, SIR CHARLES. 1963. *Philip II of Spain*. Eyre and Spottiswoode, London.
PINE, L. G. 1954. *They came with the Norman Conqueror*. Evans, London.
PINTO, V. DE S., and RODWAY, A. E. 1957. *The Common Muse* (Bourbons). Chatto, London.
POSTGATE, R. W. 1920. *Revolution from 1789 to 1906*. Richards, London.
RAVITCH, N. 1965. 'French and English Bishops in the 18th Century.' *Hist. Jour. 8:* 309–325.
ROUSSEAU, JEAN-JACQUES. 1753. *Discours sur l'Origine et les Fondements de l'Inégalité parmi les Hommes*. Cambridge U.P. (1941).
RUDÉ, GEORGE. 1964. *Revolutionary Europe*. Collins (Fontane), London.
STONE, BRIAN. 1964. *Mediaeval English Verse*. Penguin, Harmondsworth.

TOCQUEVILLE, ALEXIS DE. 1858. *The Old Regime and the French Revolution.* Doubleday, N.Y. (4th ed. trans.).
VOLTAIRE. 1751, 1756. *Le Siècle de Louis quatorze.* Various editions.
WILSON, EDMUND. 1940. *To the Finland Station.* W. H. Allen, London.
WILSON, F. M. 1959. *They came as Strangers.* Hamilton, London.

24. REVOLUTION IN THE EAST

ALEXANDROV, VICTOR. 1966. *The End of the Romanovs.* (Rasputin, Nicholas II, Lenin: trans.). Hutchinson, London.
ALLELUYEVA, SVETLANA. 1967. *Twenty Letters to a Friend* (Stalin). Hutchinson, London.
AVINERI, SHLOMO. 1967. 'From Hoax to Dogma: a Footnote on Marx and Darwin.' *Encounter 28:* 30–32.
BERLIN, ISAIAH. 1939. *Karl Marx.* Butterworth, London.
BOWEN, E. J. 1960. 'Welsh Emigration Overseas.' *Adv. Sci. 17:* 260–271.
CARR, E. H. 1950. *The Bolshevik Revolution.* Macmillan, London.
—— 1967. 'The significance of the Russian Revolution.' *The Listener 78:* 598–602.
DARLINGTON, C. D. 1948. 'The retreat from science in Soviet Russia.' *Nineteenth Century, 142:* 157–168 (see Darlington and Mather 1950).
DEUTSCHER, ISAAC. 1949 (1966). *Stalin.* Oxford U.P. and Penguin.
—— 1959. 'The moral dilemmas of Lenin.' *The Listener* February 5th 245–7.
DJILAS, M. 1957. *The New Class: an analysis of the communist system.* Thames and Hudson, London.
DOSTOEVSKY, FYODOR. 1861. *The House of the Dead.* Heinemann, London.
FISCHER, LOUIS. 1965. *The Life of Lenin.* Weidenfeld, London.
GREY, IAN. 1962. *Peter the Great.* Hodder, London.
HOETZSCH, OTTO. 1966. *The Evolution of Russia.* Thames and Hudson, London.
JANKOVSKY, J. 1965. *The Memoirs of Ivanov Razumnik.* Oxford U.P.
KENNAN, GEORGE. 1968. 'Causes of the Russian Revolution' in *Revolutionary Russia* ed. R. Pipes. Harvard U.P.
LENIN, VLADIMIR I. 1933 (1914). *The Teaching of Karl Marx.* Lawrence, London.
LOCKHART, R. H. BRUCE. 1932 (1950). *Memoirs of a British Agent.* Penguin, London.
MARX, KARL. 1852. *The Eighteenth Brumaire of Louis Bonaparte.* Allen and Unwin, London. (1926.)
MARX, K., and ENGELS, F. 1848 (trans. 1888). *Manifesto of the Communist Party.* Lawrence, London (1934).
MOSCA, GAETANO 1895 (3rd ed. 1923, trans. 1938). *The Ruling Class.* McGraw Hill, N.Y.
PAUSTOVSKY, CONSTANTIN. 1964 (trans. 1965). *Slow Approach of Thunder* (*1914–1917*). Panther, N.Y.; Harvill, London.
PLEKHANOV, G. V. 1898. *The Role of the Individual in History* (trans. 1940). Wishart, London.
PRICE, PHILIPS. 1968. 'The October Revolution.' *M. Guardian Reports* (1917).
RICE, T. T. 1963. *A Concise History of Russian Art.* Thames and Hudson, London.
SEMYONOV, YURI. 1937 (1944). *The Conquest of Siberia.* Routledge, London.
SHELYAPINA, N. 1964. 'Early Moscow.' *I. London News 245:* 190–2.
TROTSKY, LEO DAVIDOVICH (BRONSTEIN). 1929. *Lenin: Biography.* Enc. Brit.
—— 1934. *The History of the Russian Revolution* (trans.). Gollancz, London.
ULAM, ADAM B. 1965. *Lenin and the Bolsheviks.* Secker, London.
VERNADSKY, G. 1959. *The Origins of Russia.* Oxford U.P.

ZENZINOV, V. M. 1924. 'With an exile in Arctic Siberia.' *Nat. Geog. Mag. 46:* 695–718.

25. AMERICA

ADAMS, RAMON F. 1944. *Western Words: A Dictionary of the Range, Cow Camp and Trail.* U. Oklahoma P., Norman, Okla.

ALDEN, J. R. 1962. *The American Revolution: 1775–1783.* Harper, N.Y.

BALTZELL, E. D. 1958 (1962). *An American Business Aristocracy.* Macmillan, Collier, N.Y.

BOLTON, H. E. 1908 (1959). *Spanish Exploration in the South West 1542–1706.* Barnes and Noble, N.Y.

BROTHWELL, D. R. 1967. 'The Amerindians of Guyana: a biological review'. *Eug. Rev. 59:* 22–45.

BURTON, SIR RICHARD. 1862. *The City of the Saints and across the Rocky Mountains to California.* Longman, London.

BUSHNELL, G. H. S. 1963. *Peruvian Archaeology.* Cambridge U.P.

CANOT, THÈODORE. 1854. *Memoirs of a Slave Trader.* (ed. A. W. Lawrence, 1929). Cape, London.

CARMICHAEL, STOKELY and HAMILTON, C. V. 1967. *Black Power: the Politics of Liberation in America.* Random (Vintage) N.Y.

CAVE, HUGH B. 1962. *Four Roads to Paradise* (Jamaica and Slavery). Redman, London.

CHARMET, RAYMOND. 1966. *Paul Gauguin.* Blandford, London.

COE, MICHAEL D. 1964. 'The Chinampas of Mexico.' *Sci. Am. 211* (1): 90–98.

COLEMAN, J. S. 1966. *Equality of Educational Opportunity.* U.S.D. Health etc., Washington.

COMER, J. P. 1967. 'The social power of the negro.' *Sci. Am. 216* (4): 21–27.

CONLY, R. L. 1955. 'Mohawks scrape the Sky', in *Indians of the Americas.* N. Geog. Mag., Washington.

DIAZ, B. 1568. *The Conquest of New Spain.* Penguin, London. (trans. J. M. Cohen, 1963).

DRAKE, ST. CLAIR, and CLAYTON, HORACE R. 1945 (1962). *Black Metropolis: A Study of Negro Life in a Northern City.* Harcourt (Harper N.Y.).

DRIVER, H. E. 1964. *The Americas on the Eve of Discovery.* Prentice, N. J.

DURHAM, P., and JONES, E. L. 1965. *The Negro Cowboys.* Dodd, N.Y.

DURRELL, GERALD. 1961. *The Whispering Land* (Argentina). Hart-Davis, London.

EASBY, D. T. 1966. 'Early Metallurgy in the New World.' *Sci. Amer. 214:* 73–81.

FORSTER, E. M. 1962. *Goldsworthy Lowes Dickinson.* Arnold, London.

GUPPY, NICHOLAS. 1958. *Wai-Wai: through the Forests north of the Amazon.* Murray, London.

GUTHEIM, F. 1949. *The Potomac.* Rinehart, N.Y.

HALL, JOSEPH S. 1960. *Smoky Mountain Folks and their Lore.* G.S.M. Nat. Hist. Ass. Asheville (L. Cong. Cat. No. 60.53449).

HANDLIN, O. 1963. *The American People.* Hutchinson, London.

HARCOURT-SMITH, S. 1966. 'The Maroons of Jamaica.' *History Today, 16:* 21–28.

HARRISON, G. A. *et al.* 1967. 'Skin colour in southern Brazilian populations' (white and negro). *Hum. Biol. 39:* 21–31.

HAWKES, J. G. 1967. 'The history of the potato.' *J. R. Hort. Soc. 92:* 207–224.

HAYNES, C. VANCE. 1966. 'Elephant hunting in North America.' *Sci. Amer. 214:* 104–112.

HEFFNER, R. D. 1952 (1956). *A Documentary History of the United States.* Mentor, N.Y.

HENRIQUES, F. 1953. *Family and Colour in Jamaica*. Eyre and Spottiswoode, London.

HORAN, J. D. 1959. *The Great American West*. Crown, N.Y.

KEPHART, HORACE. 1913 (1926). *Our Southern Highlanders*. Macmillan, N.Y.

KUPZOW, A. J. 1965. 'The formation of areas of cultivated plants.' *Zeits. Pfl. zücht. 53:* 53–66.

LA FARGE, OLIVER. 1956. *A Pictorial History of the American Indian*. Spring, London.

LANDSTRÖM, BJÖRN. 1967. *Columbus* (trans.) Allen and Unwin, London.

LANNING, E. P. 1965. 'Early man in Peru.' *Sci. Am. 213:* 68–76.

LEWIS, NORMAN. 1964. *The Honoured Society: the Mafia Conspiracy Observed*. Collins, London.

LINCOLN, ABRAHAM. *Speeches and Letters: 1832–1865*. Dent (Everyman), London.

LIPSCHUTZ ALEJANDRO. 1966. 'Movimentos demograficos en Hispano-america en el siglo XVI.' *Rev. Int. Soc.* (S. II). 2: 219–238.

MALONE, H. T. 1956. *Cherokees of the South*. Georgia U.P., Athens.

MANGELSDORF, P. C. *et al.* 1964. 'Domestication of corn.' *Science 143:* 538–545.

MAXWELL, GAVIN. 1957. *God Protect Me from My Friends*. Longman, London.

MEGGERS, B. J., and EVANS, CLIFFORD. 1966. 'A transpacific contact in 3000 B.C.' *Sci. Am. 214:* 28–35.

MILLON, RENE. 1967. 'Teotihuacan' (100 B.C.–A.D. 750). *Sci. Am. 216:* 38–48.

MITCHELL, JOSEPH. 1960. *The Mohawks in High Steel*. (*See* Edmund Wilson.)

NISHIYAMA, I. *et al.* 1962. 'Mexican wild forms of sweet potato'. *Econ. Bot. 16:* 305–314.

NYE, R. B., and MORPURGO, J. E. 1955, 1964. *A History of the United States I, II*. Penguin, London.

PACKARD, VANCE. 1959. *The Status Seekers*. Longman, London.

PARSONS, J. J., and DENEVAN, W. M. 1967. 'Pre-Columbian Ridged fields.' *Sci. Am. 217:* 93–100.

PAWSON, I. G. 1967. *Life on the Altiplano. Geog. Mag. 40:* 57–64.

PHILBRICK, F. S. 1965. *The Rise of the West*. Harper, N.Y.

POLE, J. R. 1966. *Political Representation in England and the Origins of the American Republic*. Macmillan, London.

PRESCOTT, W. H. 1847 (1882). *History of the Conquest of Peru*. Various editions.

RAGLAN, LORD. 1962. 'Prehistoric men—What can we know of them?' *Rat. An.* (1962) 31–41.

REID, G. ARCHDALL. 1910. *The Laws of Heredity*. Methuen, London.

ROLT, L. T. C. 1965. *A Short History of Machine Tools*. M.I.T.P., Cambridge, Mass.

RUNCIMAN, STEVEN. 1958. *The Sicilian Vespers: a History of the Mediterranean World in the later Thirteenth Century*. Cambridge U.P.

SALAMAN, R. N. 1949. *The History and Social Influence of the Potato*. Cambridge U.P.

SALE, R. D., and KAREN, E. D. 1962. *American Expansion: A Book of Maps*. Dorsey: Homewood, Ill.

SAVOURS, ANN. 1963. 'Early Eskimo Visitors to Britain.' *Geog. Mag. 36:* 336–343.

SIMONS, R. D. G. Ph. 1961. *The Colour of the Skin in Human Relations*. Elsevier, Amsterdam.

SONDERN, FREDERICK. 1958. *The Brotherhood of Evil: the Mafia*. Gollancz, London and N.Y.

TOCQUEVILLE, A. DE. 1835 (1840). *Democracy in America*. Various trans.

TWAIN, MARK. 1871 (1962). *Roughing It*. Harper, Signet, N.Y.

UNWIN, RAYNER. 1960. *The Defeat of John Hawkins*. Allen and Unwin, London.

WASHBURN, W. E. (ed.) 1964. *The Indian and the White Man*. Doubleday, N.Y.

WEATHERWAX, P. 1955. *History and Origin of Corn* (Maize) in 'Corn and Corn Improvement' 1–16. N.Y. Academic Press.
WHITRIDGE, A. 1956. 'Eli Whitney: Nemesis of the South.' *Am. Heritage Reader* 76–86. Dell, N.Y.
WILLEY, G. R. 1960. *Historical patterns and evolution in native new world cultures. See* Tax (General).
WILSON, EDMUND. 1960. *Apologies to the Iroquois*. Farras, Straus, N.Y. and London.
WYMAN, WALKER D. 1945. *The Wild Horse of the West*. Nebraska U.P., Lincoln.
ZIMMERMAN, CARLE C. 1966. 'The people and changing culture of the North American plains.' *Rev. Int. Soc.* (S. II). 2: 153–202.

26. CHINA

BLOODWORTH, DENNIS. 1967. *Chinese Looking Glass*. Secker, London.
BOULNOIS, LUCE. 1963. *La Route de la Soie*. Arthaud, Paris.
CAMP, L. SPRAGUE DE. 1960. *The Ancient Engineers*. Doubleday, N.Y.
COLLIS, MAURICE. 1941. *The Great Within* (*1644–1850*). Faber, London.
—— 1946. *Foreign Mud* (Opium War). Faber, London.
—— 1959. *Marco Polo*. Faber, London.
COON, C. S. 1958. 'An anthropogeographic excursion.' *Am. Anthr. 60:* 29–42.
COTTRELL, LEONARD. 1962. *The Tiger of Ch'in*. Evans, London.
CREEL, H. G. 1937. *The Birth of China*. Ungar, N.Y.
FITZGERALD, C. P. 1933. *Son of Heaven* (T'ang). Cambridge U.P.
—— 1935 (1960). *China: A short cultural history*. Cresset, London.
—— 1962. *China* (3rd ed.) Cresset, London.
—— 1964. *The Chinese View of Their Place in the World*. Oxford U.P.
—— 1966. *A Concise History of South-East Asia*. Heinemann, London.
FOSTER, JOHN. 1939. *The Church of the T'ang Dynasty*. S.P.C.K., London.
GERNET, JACQUES. 1962. *Daily Life in China on the Eve of the Mongol Invasion* (*1250–1276*). (trans. H. M. Wright). Allen and Unwin, London.
GOODRICH, L. C. 1943. *A Short History of the Chinese People*. Harper, N.Y.
GOVINDA (LAMA). 1960. 'This was Tibet.' *The Listener 64:* 730–2.
HARRER, HEINRICH. 1955. *Seven Years in Tibet: 1944–51* (trans. R. Graves). Hart-Davis, London.
HO, PING-TI. 1962. *The Ladder of Success in Imperial China*. Columbia U.P., N.Y.
HOOKHAM, HILDA. 1962. *Tamburlaine the Conqueror*. Hodder, London.
HUDSON, GEOFFREY. 1965. 'Fifteen years after—the Chinese State.' *China Quarterly 21:* 61–73.
HUDSON, G. F. 1931. *Europe and China*. Arnold, London.
LATHAM, R. E. (trans.) 1959. *The Travels of Marco Polo*. Penguin, London.
LATTIMORE, OWEN. 1963. 'Chingis Khan and the Mongol Conquests.' *Sci. Am. 209:* 55–75.
LOEWE, MICHAEL. 1966. *Imperial China*. Paragon, N.Y.
MARSH, ROBERT M. 1961. *The Mandarins: the Circulation of Elites in China, 1600–1900*. Glencoe, N.Y.
NEEDHAM, JOSEPH. 1947. *Science and Society in Ancient China*. Watts, London.
—— 1954–63. *Science and Civilisation in China*. (4 vols.) Cambridge U.P.
—— 1963. 'Science and society in China and the West.' *Scientific Change* (ed. A. C. Crombie). Heinemann, London.
—— 1965. *Science and Civilisation in China*. Cambridge U.P.
—— *et al.* 1964. *The Legacy of China*. Oxford U.P.
PRATT, SIR JOHN T. 1945. *China and Britain*. Collins, London.
PURCELL, VICTOR. 1962. *China* (*Modern*). Benn, London.

REISCHAUER, E. O., and FAIRBANK, J. K. 1961. *East Asia: the Great Tradition.* Allen and Unwin, London.

RICHARDS, H. E. 1962. *Tibet and its History.* Oxford U.P.

SILCOCK, ARNOLD. 1936. *Introduction to Chinese Art and History.* Faber, London.

STEIN, SIR M. AUREL. 1933. *On Ancient Central Asian Tracks.* Macmillan, London.

SWANN, PETER C. 1966. *The Art of Japan.* Crown, N.Y., Thames and Hudson, London.

TWITCHETT, D. C. 1963. 'The ideology of traditional China.' *The Listener 69:* 589–591.

VARÉ, DANIELE. *The Last of the Empresses (1861–1907).* Murray, London.

WALEY, ARTHUR. 1952. *The Real Tripitaka.* Allen and Unwin, London.

WATSON, WILLIAM. 1960. *Archaeology in China.* Parrish, London.

—— 1961. *China: the civilisation of a single people.* (*See* Piggott, General.)

—— 1966. *Early Civilisation in China.* Thames and Hudson, London.

WILBUR, C. MARTIN. 1943. *Slavery in China during the Former Han Dynasty.* (206 B.C.—A.D. 23). Chicago: Field Mus. N.H.

WISSMANN, H. VON. 1956. 'The dry belt of Asia etc.' *See* W. L. Thomas (General).

WITTFOGEL, KARL A. 1956. 'The Hydraulic Civilizations.' *see* W. L. Thomas (General) pp. 152–164.

WITTFOGEL, K. A. 1957. *Oriental Depotism.* Yale U.P.

27. OCEANIA

BARRAU, JACQUES. 1957. *L'énigme de la patate douce en Océanie.* Etudes d'Outre-Mer, Marseille.

—— 1960. 'Plant introduction in the tropical Pacific.' *Pacific Viewpoint 1:* 1–10.

—— 1961. *Subsistence Agriculture in Polynesia and Micronesia.* Honolulu, Bishop Museum: Bull. 223.

BEIGHTON, P. 1966. 'The People of Easter Island'. *Geog. Mag. 39:* 253–262.

BLOFELD, J. 1960. *People of the Sun* (Siam). Hutchinson, London.

BUCK, SIR PETER. 1949. *The Coming of the Maori.* Whitcombe, Wellington, N.Z.

BURKILL, I. H. 1951. 'The rise and decline of the Yam in the service of man.' *Adv. Sci. 7:* 443–448.

—— 1953. 'Habits of man and the origins of the cultivated plants of the Old World.' *Proc. Linn. Soc. 162:* 12–42.

BURNS, SIR ALAN. 1963. *Fiji* (The Cannibals). H.M.S.O., London.

COEDÈS, G. 1966. *The Making of South East Asia.* (trans.) Routledge, London.

COLLINDER, PER. 1954. *A History of Marine Navigation* (trans.) (Polynesia: N.Z. A.D. 950). Batsford, London.

DARWIN, CHARLES. 1842 (1874). *The Structure and Distribution of Coral Reefs.* Smith Elder, London.

—— 1845. *Journal of Researches . . . during the Voyage of H.M.S. Beagle.* Murray, London.

FIRTH, RAYMOND. 1929. *Maori. Enc. Brit.*

FIRTH, R. W. 1936, 1957. *We, the Tikopia.* Allen and Unwin, London.

—— 1961. *The History and Traditions of Tikopia.* Polynesian Soc., Wellington, N.Z.

FREEMAN, J. D. 1955. *Iban Agriculture* (Sarawak). H.M.S.O., London.

GIBBINGS, ROBERT. 1948. *Over the Reefs* (Polynesia). Dent, London.

GRAVES, ROBERT. 1949. *The Isles of Unwisdom.* (Mendaña and Quiros 1595–1606.) Cassell, London.

GRIMBLE, ARTHUR. 1952. *A Pattern of Islands* (Gilbert Isles). Murray, London.

HADDON, A. C. 1901. *Head Hunters, Black, White and Brown* (Borneo). Methuen, London.

HADDON, A. C., and HORNELL, J. 1936. 'Canoes of Oceania.' *Bernice Mus.*, *27* Hawaii.

HEYERDAHL, THOR. 1952. *American Indians in the Pacific*. Allen and Unwin, London.

—— 1958. *Aku-Aku: the Secret of Easter Island*. Allen and Unwin, London.

HEYERDAHL, THOR, and FERDON, E. N. 1965. *Easter Island and the East Pacific*. Allen and Unwin, London.

HORTON, D. C. 1965. *The Happy Isles* (Solomons). Heinemann, London.

JONES, A. M. 1964. *Africa and Indonesia: the evidence of the xylophone etc*. E. J. Brill, Leiden.

JONKER, F. P. 1962. 'Heyerdahl's Kon-Tiki Theory and Ethnobotany.' *Rep. Smithsonian Instn*. 1961: 535–550.

LEACH, E. R. 1937. 'The Yami of Koto-sho' (near Formosa). *Geog. Mag. 5:* 417–434.

LUKE, SIR HARRY. 1962. *Islands of the South Pacific*. Harrap, London.

MARSACK, C. C. 1961. *Samoan Medley*. Hale, London.

MEGGERS, B. J., and EVANS, C. 1966. 'A transpacific contact in 3000 B.C.' *Sci. Am. 214:* 28–35.

MELVILLE, HERMAN. 1846. *Typee* (Polynesia: Marquesas). Oxford U.P.

—— 1847. *Omoo* (Christianisation of Tahiti). Oxford U.P. (1924).

MERRILL, E. D. 1945. *Plant Life of the Pacific World*. Macmillan, N.Y.

—— 1954. 'The botany of Cook's voyages.' *Chron. Bot. 14:* 161–384.

MOOREHEAD, ALAN. 1966. *The Fatal Impact: the invasion of the South Pacific: 1767–1840*. Hamilton, London.

PURCELL, VICTOR. 1965. *South and East Asia since 1800*. Cambridge U.P.

RIESENBERG, S. H. 1965. 'Table of voyages affecting Micronesian Islands.' *Oceania 36:* 155–168.

RIVERS, W. H. R. 1912. *The Disappearance of Useful Arts* (*in Oceania*). Festskr. Ed. Westermark, Helsingfors.

—— 1914. *History of Melanesian Society*. Cambridge U.P.

ROGERS, ALAN. 1962. 'North, South, East, West' (Malagasies). *The Countryman 59:* 625–6.

SAHLINS, M. D. 1958. *Social Stratification in Polynesia*. Washington U.P., Seattle.

SHARP, ANDREW. 1957. *Ancient Voyagers in the Pacific*. Penguin, London.

SIMMONS, R. T. *et al*. 1965. 'Blood Group genetic variations in natives of the Caroline Islands and in other parts of Micronesia.' *Oceania*, *36:* 132–154.

THIERRY, SOLANGE. 1961. *Madagascar*. Petite Planète, Paris.

THURNWALD, R. C. 1932. *Economics in Primitive Communities*. Oxford U.P.

YEN, D. E. 1963. 'The New Zealand Kumara or Sweet Potato.' *Econ. Bot. 17:* 31–43.

28. AFRICA

ALIMEN, H. 1957. *The Prehistory of Africa*. (trans. Brodrick). Hutchinson, London.

ALLAN, WM. 1965. *The African Husbandman*. Oliver and Boyd, Edinburgh.

ALLISON, P. A. 1963. 'Effect of human settlement on the vegetation of Africa.' *J.Afr. Hist. 3:* 241–9.

ANDRESKI, STANISLAV. 1968. *The African Predicament*. Joseph, London.

ARKELL, A. J. 1961. *A History of the Sudan* (to 1821). London U.P.

ARNOLD, HERMANN. 1959. *Vaganten, Komödianten, Fieranten und Briganten*. Thieme, Stuttgart.

—— 1960. 'Bevölkerungsbiologische Beobachtungen an Sippenwanderern'. *Homo 11:* 60–66.

AXELSON, E. 1954. *South African Explorers*. Oxford U.P.

Bartlett, H. H. 1956. 'Fire, Primitive Agriculture, and Grazing in the Tropics.' *See* W. L. Thomas (General) pp. 692–720.

Bates, Marston. 1956. 'Man as an Agent in the Spread of Organisms.' *See* W. L. Thomas (General), pp. 788–806.

Berry, R. J. 1967. 'Genetical Changes in mice and men' (malaria, porphyria). *Eug. Rev. 59:* 78–96.

Boahen, A. Adu. 1962. 'The Sahara caravan trade in the nineteenth century' (and earlier). *J. Afr. Hist. 3:* 349–59.

Borrow, George. 1841. *The Zincali: an account of the Gypsies of Spain.* Murray, London.

Buxton, David R. 1949 (1956). *Travels in Ethiopia.* Benn, London.

Clark, J. Desmond. 1964. *The Pre-History of Southern Africa.* Penguin, London.

—— 1962. 'The Spread of food production in Sub-Saharan Africa.' *J. Afr. Hist. 3:* 211–228.

Clébert, Jean-Paul. 1961 (1967). *Les Tziganes.* Arthaud, Paris. (The Gypsies, trans. C. Duff, Vista, London.)

Crowder, Michael. 1962. *The Story of Nigeria.* Faber, London.

Cuscoy, L. D. 1958. *Catalogo-Guia del Museo.* Santa Cruz de Tenerife.

Darlington, C. D. 1959. 'Gypsies and Didikais.' *Heredity, 13:* 533–537.

Dart, Raymond A. 1939. 'A Chinese Character as a wall motive in Rhodesia.' *S. Afr. J. Sci. 36:* 474–6.

Davidson, Basil. 1959 (1964). *Old Africa Rediscovered* (History and Pre-History). Gollancz, London.

—— 1964. *The African Past* (Chronicles). Longman, London.

Dean, Geoffrey. 1963. *The Porphyrias* (Cape Dutch). Pitman, London.

Denis, Armand. 1963. *On Safari* (Pygmies). Collins, London.

Doggett, H. 1965. *The development of the cultivated Sorghums. See* Hutchinson, 1965.

Doke, C. M. 1937. *Language. See* I. Schapera 1937–56.

Emery, W. B. 1965. *Egypt in Nubia.* Hutchinson, London.

Galton, Francis. 1853. *Narrative of an Explorer in Tropical South Africa.* London. (Ward Lock, 1891).

Gelfand, M. 1965. *Witch Doctor* (Shona). Harvill, London.

Gibbs, J. L. 1964. *Peoples of Africa.* Holt, N.Y.

Gray, R. *et al.* 1962. 'African History and Archaeology' (3rd Confce). *J. Afr. Hist. 3:* 173–374.

Greene, Grahame. 1936. *Journey without Maps* (Sierra Leone and Liberia). Heinemann, London.

Guthrie, Malcolm. 1962. *Prehistory of the Bantu languages. J. Afr. Hist. 3:* 273–282.

Hahn, C. H. L. *et al.* 1928. 'The Native Tribes of South West Africa.' (Ovambo, Berg Damara etc.) *Cape Times*, Cape Town.

Henschen, Folke. 1962 (1966). *The History of Diseases* (trans.). Longman, London.

Heyden, A. M. van der, and Scullard, H. H. 1959. *An Atlas of Africa.* Gollancz, London.

Hillaby, John. 1964. *Journey to the Jade Sea* (L. Rudolf). Constable, London.

Hooton, E. A. 1925. 'Ancient Inhabitants of the Canaries.' *Harvard Afr. St. 7:* 1–401.

Hutchinson, Sir J. B. (ed.) 1965. *Essays in Crop Plant Evolution.* Cambridge U.P.

Hutton, J. H. 1948 (as 1946). 'West Africa and Indonesia: a problem in distribution.' *J. R. Anthrop. Inst. 76:* 155–169.

Jabavu, Noni. 1960. *Drawn in Colour* (Xhosa, Baganda). Murray, London.

JÉSMAN, C. 1963. *The Ethiopian Paradox*. Oxford U.P.

JONES, A. M. 1964. *Africa and Indonesia: the evidence of the xylophone and other musical and cultural factors*. E. J. Brill, Leiden.

KIRK, W. 1962. 'The North East Monsoon and some aspects of African History.' *J. Afr. Hist. 3:* 263–7

KUPER, H. 1960. *An African Aristocracy: Rank among the Swazi*. Oxford U.P.

LIVINGSTONE, F. B. 1958. 'Anthropological implications of Sickle Cell Gene Distribution in West Africa.' *Am. Anthrop. 60:* 533–562.

MAIR, LUCY. 1962. *Primitive Government*. Penguin, London.

MATTINGLY, P. F. 1960. 'Ecological aspects of the evolution of mosquito-borne virus diseases.' *Trans. R. Soc. Trop. Med. and Hyg. 54:* 97–112.

MIDDLETON, J., and TAIT, D. (ed.) 1958. *Tribes without Rulers: Studies in African Segmentary Systems*. Routledge, London.

MINER, HORACE. 1953. *The Primitive City of Timbuctoo*. Princeton U.P.

MOOREHEAD, ALAN. 1959. *No Room in the Ark* (E. Africa). Hamilton, London.

—— 1960. *The White Nile*. Hamilton, London.

MURDOCK, G. P. 1959. *A Cultural History of Africa*. Yale U.P.

—— 1959. *Africa, its People and their Culture History*. McGraw Hill, N.Y.

O'CALLAGHAN, SEAN. 1961 (1965). *The Slave Trade*. Blon (Consul), London.

OLIVER, R. 1955. 'Traditional Histories of Buganda etc.' *P. R. Anthrop. Inst. 85:* 111–117.

OLIVER, ROLAND (Ed.) 1961. *The Dawn of African History*. Oxford U.P.

OLIVER, ROLAND and FAGE, J. D. 1962. *A Short History of Africa*. Penguin, London.

PAYNE, W. J. A. 1964. 'The origin of domestic cattle in Africa.' *Emp. J. Exp. Agric. 32:* 97–113.

PIENAAR, P. DE V. 1938. 'Click Formation and Distribution.' *Proc. 3 Cong. Phonetic Sci., Ghent*. 344–353.

POST, LAURENS VAN DER. 1961. *Heart of a Hunter* (Bushmen). Hogarth, London.

POTGIETER, H. L. 1960. *The Transkei and its Places*. Transkei Pubs. Umtata.

PRITCHARD, E. E. EVANS. 1948. *Divine Kinship of the Shilluk*. Cambridge U.P.

RITTER, E. A. 1955. *Shaka Zulu: Rise of the Zulu Empire*. Longman, London.

RODD, F. R. 1926. *People of the Veil* (Tuareg). Macmillan, London.

SCHAPERA, I. 1930. *The Khoisan Peoples of South Africa*. Routledge, London.

—— 1937–56. with Goodwin, A. J. H., Van Warmelo, N. J. (*et al.*) *Bantu Speaking Tribes of South Africa*. Routledge, London.

SELIGMAN, C. G. 1930 (1957). *Races of Africa*. Oxford U.P.

SIMMONDS, N. W. 1962. *The Evolution of the Bananas*. Longmans, London.

SINGER, R., and LEHMANN, H. 1963. 'The haemoglobins of Africander cattle.' *R. Anthrop. Inst. Occ. Paper 18:* 119–125.

SLYE, JONATHAN. 1962. 'Neolithic Craft in Nigeria: Potters' communities.' *I.L.N. 241:* 251–3.

—— 1963. 'The Gwaris: tribesmen of Nigeria and their art.' *I.L.N. 243:* 856–7.

STACEY, TOM. 1965. *Summons to Ruwenzori* (*1962–3*). Secker, London.

STOKES, E., and BROWN, R. (ed.) 1966. *The Zambesian Past*. Manchester U.P.

STORY, R. 1958. 'Some Plants used by Bushmen in Obtaining Food and Water.' *Survey Mem. 30*, Pretoria.

TOBIAS, P. V. 1954. 'On a Bushman-European Hybrid Family.' *Man. 14:* 178–182.

—— 1955. 'Somatic origins of the Hottentots.' *Afr. Studies 14* (1): 1–22.

—— 1959. 'The Nuffield-Witwatersrand University Expeditions to Kalahari Bushmen, 1958–9.' *Nature, 183:* 1011–1013.

TREVOR, J. C. 1950. 'The physical characters of the Sandawe.' *J. R. Anthrop. Inst. 77:* 61–78.

TURNBULL, C. M. 1961. *The Forest People* (African Pygmies). Chatto, London.
ULLENDORF, E. 1960. *The Ethiopians*. Oxford U.P.
VEDDER, H. H. *et al.* 1928. 'Native Tribes of South West Africa.' *Cape Times*, Cape Town.
WARMELO, N. J. VAN (ed.) 1940. 'The Copper Miners of Musina' (History of the Ba-Lemba). *Dept. Native Aff. Ethn. Pub. 8*, Pretoria.
WELLARD, JAMES. 1964. *The Great Sahara*. Hutchinson, London.
WRIGLEY, CHRISTOPHER. 1962. 'Linguistic clues to African history.' *J. Afr. Hist. 3:* 269–272.
YOELI, MEIR. 1960. 'Animal Infections and Human Diseases' (Yellow Fever). *Sci. Am. 202* (5): 161–170.

29. CONCLUSION

BAGEHOT, WALTER. 1865. *The English Constitution*. Collins, London, 1963.
—— 1873. 'Physics and Politics or Thoughts on the application of the Principles of Natural Selection and Inheritance to Politics.' *Selected Essays*, Nelson, London, 1927.
DARLINGTON, C. D. 1958. The control of evolution in man. *Eug. Rev. 50:* 169–178.
DUNN, L. C. 1951. *Genetics in the Twentieth Century*. Macmillan, London, N.Y.
FRANKLIN, BENJAMIN. 1755. *Observations concerning the Increase of Mankind and the Peopling of Countries* (Boston). *See* Eversley (1959) Oxford U.P.
GINSBURG, B. E. 1958. 'Genetics as a tool in the study of behaviour.' *Persp. Biol. and Med. 1:* 397–424.
GLACKEN, C. J. 1956. *Changing Ideas of the Habitable World. See* W. L. Thomas (General) pp. 70–92.
GOBINEAU, J. A. DE (1816–1882). *The Inequality of Human Races* (trans. 1915). Heinemann, London.
GUMPLOWICZ, LUDWIG. 1899. *Outlines of Sociology* (Grundriss der Soziologie, 1885: Vienna). Philadephia.
HOBBES, THOMAS. 1651. *Leviathan*. Cambridge U.P. (1904).
HUXLEY, J. S. 1951. *Genetics, Evolution and Human Destiny. See* Dunn 1951.
KELLNER, L. 1962. *Alexander von Humboldt*. Oxford U.P.
MARSH, GEORGE PERKINS. 1864. *Man and Nature* (1st edn.). Scribner, N.Y., Sampson Low, London.
—— 1874, 1886. *The Earth as Modified by Human Action*. (2nd and 3rd Edns.) Scribner, N.Y., Sampson Low, London.
MOSCA, GAETANO. 1895. *The Ruling Class*. McGraw Hill, N.Y.
PETRIE, W. M. FLINDERS. 1911. *The Revolutions of Civilization*. Harper, London.
RIVERS, W. H. R. 1924. *Social Organisation*. Routledge, London.
SEARS, PAUL B. 1956. *The process of environmental change by man. See* W. L. Thomas (General) pp. 471–484.
SOROKIN, PITIRIM. 1927. *Social Mobility*. Harper, N.Y.

Index

THE WORLD AFTER
AGRICULTURE